The Gendered Society Reader

The Gendered Society Reader

Fourth Edition

Michael Kimmel
STATE UNIVERSITY OF NEW YORK AT
STONY BROOK

Amy Aronson
FORDHAM UNIVERSITY

New York   Oxford
OXFORD UNIVERSITY PRESS
2011

Oxford University Press, Inc., publishes works that further Oxford University's
objective of excellence in research, scholarship, and education.

Oxford   New York
Auckland   Cape Town   Dar es Salaam   Hong Kong   Karachi
Kuala Lumpur   Madrid   Melbourne   Mexico City   Nairobi
New Delhi   Shanghai   Taipei   Toronto

With offices in
Argentina   Austria   Brazil   Chile   Czech Republic   France   Greece
Guatemala   Hungary   Italy   Japan   Poland   Portugal   Singapore
South Korea   Switzerland   Thailand   Turkey   Ukraine   Vietnam

Published by Oxford University Press, Inc.
198 Madison Avenue, New York, New York 10016
http://www.oup.com

Oxford is a registered trademark of Oxford University Press

Library of Congress Cataloging-in-Publication Data

The gendered society reader / [edited by] Michael Kimmel, Amy Aronson. — 4th ed.
p.   cm.
ISBN 978-0-19-973371-2 (pbk. : acid-free paper)
1. Sex role.   2. Sex differences (Psychology)   3. Gender identity.   4. Sex discrimination.
5. Equality.   I. Kimmel, Michael S.   II. Aronson, Amy.   III. Kimmel, Michael S. Gendered society.
HQ1075.G4672 2011
305.3—dc22

2009050885

Printing number: 9 8 7 6 5 4 3 2

Printed in the United States of America
on acid-free paper

CONTENTS

*Indicates selections new to this edition

Introduction

MICHAEL KIMMEL

Every day there's another story about how women and men are different. They say we come from different planets—women from Venus, men from Mars. They say we have different brain chemistries, different brain organization, different hormones. Different bodies, different selves. They say we have different ways of knowing, listen to different moral voices, have different ways of speaking and hearing each other.

You'd think we were different species. In his best-selling book, the pop psychologist John Gray informs us that not only do women and men communicate differently, "but they think, feel, perceive, react, respond, love, need, and appreciate differently" (Gray 1995, 5). It's a miracle of cosmic proportions that we ever understand one another!

Yet here we all are, together, in the same classes, eating in the same dining halls, walking on the same campus, reading the same books, being subject to the same criteria for grading. We live in the same houses, eat the same meals, read the same newspapers, and watch the same TV shows. What gives?

One thing that seems to be happening is that we are increasingly aware of the centrality of gender in our lives. In the past four decades, the pioneering work of feminist scholars, both in traditional disciplines and in women's studies, has made us increasingly aware of the centrality of gender in shaping social life. We now know that gender is one of the central organizing principles around which social life revolves.

This wasn't always the case. Four decades ago, social scientists would have only listed social class and race as the master statuses that defined and proscribed social life. If you wanted to study gender in the 1960s in social science, for example, you would have found one course to meet your needs—"Marriage and the Family"— which was sort of the "Ladies Auxiliary" of the social sciences. There were no courses on gender. But today, gender has joined race and class in our understanding of the foundations of an individual's identity. Gender, we now know, is one of the axes around which social life is organized, and through which we understand our own experiences.

While much of our cultural preoccupation seems to be about the differences between women and men, there are two near-universal phenomena that define the experiences of women and men in virtually every culture we have ever known. First: *Why is it that virtually every single society differentiates people on the basis of gender?* Why are women and men perceived as different in every known society? What are the differences that are perceived? Why is gender at least one—if not the central—basis for the division of labor? And, second: *Why is it that virtually every known society is also based on male domination?* Why does virtually every society divide social, political, and economic resources unequally between the genders? Why is a gendered division of labor also an unequal division of labor? Why are women's tasks and men's tasks valued differently?

Of course, there are dramatic differences among societies regarding the type of gender differences, the levels of gender inequality, and the amount of violence (implied or real) that is necessary to maintain both systems of difference and domination. But the basic facts remain: *virtually every society known to us is founded upon assumptions of gender difference and the politics of gender inequality.*

Most of the arguments about gender difference begin, as does this book, with biology. Women and men *are* biologically different, after all. Our reproductive anatomies are different, as are our reproductive destinies. Our brain structures differ, our brain chemistries differ. Our musculature is different. We have different levels of different hormones circulating through our different bodies. Surely, these add up to fundamental, intractable, and universal differences, and these differences provide the foundation for male domination, don't they?

In these models, biological "sex"—by which we mean the chromosomal, chemical, anatomical apparatuses that make us either male or female—leads inevitably to "gender," by which we mean the cultural and social meanings, experiences, and institutional structures that are defined as appropriate for those males and females.

"Sex" is male and female; "gender" refers to cultural definitions of masculinity and femininity—the meanings of maleness or femaleness.

Biological models of sex difference occupy the "nature" side of the age-old question about whether it is nature or nurture that determines our personalities. Of course, most sensible people recognize that both nature *and* nurture are necessary for gender development. Our biological sex provides the raw material for our development—and all that evolution, different chromosomes, and hormones have to have some effect on who we are and who we become.

But biological sex varies very little, and yet the cultural definitions of gender vary enormously. And it has been the task of the social and behavioral sciences to explore the variations in definitions of gender. Launched originally as critiques of biological universalism, the social and behavioral sciences—anthropology, history, psychology, sociology—have all had an important role to play in our understanding of gender.

What they suggest is that what it means to be a man or a woman will vary in four significant ways. First, the meanings of gender vary from one society to another. What it means to be a man or a woman among aboriginal peoples in the Australian outback or in the Yukon territories is probably very different from what it means to be a man or a woman in Norway or Ireland. It has been the task of anthropologists to specify some of those differences, to explore the different meanings that gender has in different cultures. Some cultures, like our own, encourage men to be stoic and to prove their masculinity, and men in other cultures seem even more preoccupied with demonstrating sexual prowess than American men seem to be. Other cultures prescribe a more relaxed definition of masculinity, based on civic participation, emotional responsiveness, and the collective provision for the community's needs. Some cultures encourage women to be decisive and competitive; others insist that women are naturally passive, helpless, and dependent.

Second, the meanings of masculinity and femininity vary within any one culture over time. What it meant to be a man or a woman in seventeenth-century France is probably very different from what it might mean today. My own research has suggested that the meanings of manhood have changed dramatically from the founding of America in 1776 to the present (see Kimmel 2006). (Although for reasons of space I do not include any historical material in this volume, inquiries into the changing definitions of gender have become an area of increasing visibility.)

Third, the meaning of masculinity and femininity will change as any individual person grows. Following Freudian ideas that individuals face different developmental tasks as they grow and develop, psychologists have examined the ways in which the meanings of masculinity and femininity change over the course of a person's life. The issues confronting a man about proving himself, feeling successful, and the social institutions in which he will attempt to enact those experiences will change, as will the meanings of femininity for prepubescent women, women in child-bearing years, and post-menopausal women, or for women entering the labor market and those retiring from it.

Finally, the meanings of gender will vary *among* different groups of women and men within any particular culture at any particular time. Simply put, not all American men and women are the same. Our experiences are also structured by class, race, ethnicity, age, sexuality, region of the country. Each of these axes modifies the others. Just because we make gender visible doesn't mean that we make these other organizing principles of social life invisible. Imagine, for example, an older, black, gay man in Chicago and a young, white, heterosexual farm boy in Iowa. Wouldn't they have different definitions of masculinity? Or imagine a twenty-two-year-old heterosexual poor Asian American woman in San Francisco and a wealthy white Irish Catholic lesbian in Boston. Wouldn't their ideas about what it means to be a woman be somewhat different? The interplanetary theory of gender differences collapses all such differences, and focuses *only* on gender. One of the important elements of a sociological approach is to explore the differences *among* men and *among* women, since, as it turns out, these are often more decisive than the differences between women and men.

If gender varies across cultures, over historical time, among men and women within any one culture, and over the life course, that means we really cannot speak of masculinity or femininity as though they were constant, universal essences, common to all women and to all men. Rather, gender is an ever-changing fluid assemblage of meanings and behaviors. In that sense, we must speak of *masculinities* and *femininities,* in recognition of the different definitions of masculinity and femininity that we construct. By pluralizing the terms, we acknowledge that masculinity and femininity mean different things to different groups of people at different times.

At the same time, we can't forget that all masculinities and femininities are not created equal. American men and women must also contend with a dominant definition, a culturally preferred version that is held up as the model against which we are expected to measure ourselves. We thus come to know what it means to be a man or a woman in our culture by setting our definitions in opposition to a set of "others"—racial minorities, sexual minorities. For men, the classic "other" is, of course, women. It often feels imperative that men make it clear—eternally, compulsively, decidedly—that they are not "like" women.

For both women and men, this is the "hegemonic" definition—the one that is held up as the model for all of us. The hegemonic definition of masculinity is "constructed in relation to various subordinated masculinities as well as in relation to women," writes sociologist R. W. Connell (1987, 183). The sociologist Erving Goffman once described this hegemonic definition of masculinity like this:

> In an important sense there is only one complete unblushing male in America: a young, married, white, urban, northern, heterosexual, Protestant, father, of college education, fully employed, of good complexion, weight, and height, and a recent record in sports.... Any male who fails to qualify in any one of these ways is likely to view himself—during moments at least—as unworthy, incomplete, and inferior. (Goffman 1963, 128)

Women also must contend with such an exaggerated ideal of femininity. Connell calls it "emphasized femininity." Emphasized femininity is organized around compliance with gender inequality, and is "oriented to accommodating the interests and desires of men." One sees emphasized femininity in "the display of sociability rather than technical competence, fragility in mating scenes, compliance with men's desire for titillation and ego-stroking in office relationships, acceptance of marriage and child care as a response to labor-market discrimination against women" (Connell 1987, 183, 188, 187). Emphasized femininity exaggerates gender difference as a strategy of "adaptation to men's power" stressing empathy and nurturance; "real" womanhood is described as "fascinating" and women are advised that they can wrap men around their fingers by knowing and playing by "the rules."

The essays in the first four sections of this book recapitulate these disciplinary concerns and also present the development of the sociological argument chronologically. Following Darwin and others, biological evidence was employed in the nineteenth century to assert the primacy of sex differences, and the section on biological differences presents some evidence of distinct and categorical biological differences, and a couple of critiques of that research from a neurobiologist and a psychologist respectively. Cross-cultural research by anthropologists, among them Margaret Mead, perhaps the nation's most historically celebrated cultural anthropologist, offered a way to critique the claims of biological inevitability and universality lodged in those biological arguments. The selections in this section demonstrate how anthropologists have observed those cross-cultural differences and have used such specific cultural rituals as initiation ceremonies or the prevalence of rape in a culture to assess different definitions of gender.

Psychological research also challenged biological inevitability, locating the process of *acquiring* gender within the tasks of the child in his or her family. Achieving successful gender identity was a perilous process, fraught with danger of gender "inversion" (homosexuality) as the early and renowned social psychologist Lewis Terman saw it in his treatise on *Sex and Personality* in 1936. Subsequent psychological research has refined our understanding of how individuals acquire the "sex roles" that society has mapped out for them.

And it falls to the sociologist to explore the variations *among* different groups of women and men, and also to specify the ways in which some versions of masculinity or femininity are held up as the hegemonic models against which all others are arrayed and measured. Sociologists are concerned less with the specification of sex roles, and more with the understanding of *gender relations*—the social and political dynamics that shape our conceptions of "appropriate" sex roles. Thus, sociologists are interested not only in gendered individuals—the ways in which we acquire our gendered identities—but also in gendered institutions—the ways in which those gendered individuals interact with one another in the institutions of our lives that shape, reproduce, and reconstitute gender.

In that sense, sociologists return us to the original framing questions—the near-universality of assumptions about gender difference and the near-universality of male domination over women. Sociologists argue that male domination is reproduced not only by socializing women and men differently, but also by placing them in organizations and institutions in which specifically gendered norms and values predominate and by which both women and men are then evaluated and judged. Gendered individuals do not inhabit gender-neutral social situations; both individuals and institutions bear the mark of gender.

The four central, institutional sections of this book explore how the fundamental institutions of family, education, religion, and the workplace express and normalize gender difference, and, in so doing, reproduce relations of inequality between women and men. In each of these arenas, the debates about gender differences and inequality have been intense, from the questions about the division of household labor, sexual orientation of parents, the effect of religion on gender identity, comparable worth, workplace discrimination, and a variety of other critical policy debates. The essays in these sections will enable the reader to make better sense of these debates and understand the ways in which gender is performed and elaborated within social institutions.

Finally, we turn to our intimate lives, our bodies, and our experiences of friendship, love, and sex. Here differences between women and men do emerge. Men and women have different ways of loving, of caring, and of having sex. And it turns out that this is true whether the women and men are heterosexual or homosexual—that is, gay men and heterosexual men are more similar to each other than they are different; and, equally, lesbians and heterosexual women have more in common than either does with men. On the other hand, the differences between women and men seem to have as much to do with the shifting definitions of love and intimacy, and the social arenas in which we express (or suppress) our emotions, as they do with the differences in our personalities. And there is significant evidence that the gender gap in love and sex and friendship is shrinking as women claim greater degrees of sexual agency and men find their emotional lives (with lovers, children, and friends) impoverished by adherence to hegemonic definitions of masculinity. Men and women do express some differences in our intimate lives, but these differences are hardly of interplanetary cosmic significance. It appears that women and men are not from different planets—not opposite sexes, but neighboring sexes. And we are moving closer and closer to each other.

This may be the most startling finding that runs through many of these essays. What we find consistently is that the differences between women and men do not account for very much of the different experiences that men and women have. Differences *between* women and men are not nearly as great as the differences *among* women or *among* men—differences based on class, race, ethnicity, sexuality, age, and other variables. Women and men enter the workplace for similar reasons, though what they find there often reproduces the differences that "predicted" they would have different motivations. Boys and girls are far more similar to each other in the classroom, from elementary school through college, although everything in the school—from their textbooks, their teachers, their experiences in the playground, the social expectations of their aptitudes and abilities—pushes them to move farther and farther apart.

The most startling conclusion that one reaches from examining the evidence on gender difference is that women and men are not from different planets at all. In the end, we're all Earthlings!

References

Connell, R. W. *Gender and Power.* Stanford: Stanford University Press, 1987.

Goffman, Erving. *Stigma.* Englewood Cliffs, NJ: Prentice-Hall, 1963.

Gray, John. *Men Are from Mars, Women Are from Venus.* New York: Harper Collins, 1995.

Terman, Lewis and Catherine Cox Miles, *Sex and Personality.* New York: McGraw-Hill, 1936.

Changes to the Fourth Edition:

- The addition of a new section on The Gender of Religion (Part VII).
- Twenty-two new essays, including four new pieces on The Gendered Media, and new coverage of:
  - Non-heterosexual families
  - Adolescent masculinities in the classroom
  - The effect of race on the academic performance of boys
  - Muslim women
- A new, separate Instructor's Manual/Test Bank is now available for *The Gendered Society Reader* (contact Oxford University Press).

Acknowledgments

The editors wish to thank the following reviewers for their feedback on the third edition: Rachel Hagewan, University of Nebraska–Lincoln; Kim Korinek, University of Utah; Jamee Kristen, University of Nebraska–Lincoln; Gina Petonito, Miami University; Ashley Pryor, University of Toledo; and Jenny M. Stuber, University of North Florida.

Anatomy and Destiny

BIOLOGICAL ARGUMENTS ABOUT GENDER DIFFERENCE

Anatomy, many of us believe, is destiny; our constitution of our bodies determines our social and psychological disposition. Biological sex decides our gendered experiences. Sex is temperament. Biological explanations offer perhaps the tidiest and most coherent explanations for both gender difference and gender inequality. The observable differences between males and females derive from different anatomical organization, which make us different as men and women, and those anatomical differences are the origin of gender inequality. These differences, as one biologist put it, are "innate, biologically determined, and relatively resistant to change through the influences of culture."

Biologists rely on three different sets of evidence. Evolutionists, such as sociobiologists and evolutionary psychologists, argue that sex differences derive from the differences in our reproductive anatomies—which compel different reproductive "strategies." Because a female must invest much energy and time in ensuring the survival of one baby, her "natural" evolutionary instinct is toward high sexual selectivity and monogamy; females are naturally modest and monogamous. Males, by contrast, are naturally promiscuous, since their reproductive success depends upon fertilizing as many eggs as possible without emotional constraint. Males who are reproductively unsuccessful by seduction, biologists tell us, may resort to rape as a way to ensure that their reproductive material is successfully transmitted to their offspring.

A second source of evidence of biological difference comes from some differences in brain function and brain chemistry. In the late nineteenth century, studies showed definitively that men's brains were heavier or more complex than women's, and thus that women ought not to seek higher education or vote. (Similar studies also "proved" that the brains of white people were heavier and more complex than those of black people.) Today, such studies are largely discredited, but we still may read about how males and females use different halves of their brains, or that they use them differently, or that the two halves are differently connected.

Finally, some biologists rely on the ways in which the hormonal differences that produce secondary sex characteristics determine the dramatically divergent paths that males and females take from puberty onward. Testosterone causes aggression, and since males have far more testosterone than females, male aggression—and social, political, and economic dominance—is explained.

To the social scientist, though, this evidence obscures as much as it reveals, telling us more about our own cultural needs to find these differences than the differences themselves. Biological explanations collapse all other sources of difference—race, ethnicity, age—into one single dichotomous variable that exaggerates the differences between women and men, and also minimizes the similarities between them. "Believing is seeing," notes sociologist Judith Lorber, and seeing these differences as decisive is often used as a justification for gender inequality.

The readings in this section offer critiques of these biological arguments. Martha McCaughey weighs the empirical evidence from evolutionary psychology and finds it somewhat lighter than the extensive media coverage it has received. Mixing a critique of the biology and that media coverage, McCaughey exposes evolutionary psychology as a "useful fiction," answering cultural needs even if it cannot answer scientific questions. Neuroprimatologist Robert Sapolsky suggests that the research on hormonal differences does not make a convincing case. And biologist Anne Fausto-Sterling critiques genetic determinist arguments while celebrating the remarkable diversity that the biological record actually affords. Together, these essays reveal that recourse to biology exclusively may justify existing inequalities by reference to observed differences and ignoring observed similarities. It's more than bad politics: it's also bad science.

Caveman Masculinity: Finding Manhood in Evolutionary Science[1]

MARTHA MCCAUGHEY

The Caveman as Retrosexuality

Most of us can call up some image of prehistoric man and his treatment of women. He's a shaggy, well-muscled caveman, whose name is Thor, and we might picture him, club in hand, approaching a scrawny but curvaceous woman, whom he bangs over the head and drags by the hair into a cave to mate. I'm sure the majority of readers recognize this imagery. Indeed, today an image of modern men as guided by such prehistoric tendencies is even celebrated on T-shirts sold to American men on web sites that allow people to post and sell their own designs. One such image for sale on the cafepress web site features a version of Thor, wearing a fur pelt and holding a club, accompanied by the slogan "ME FIND WOMAN!" Another image available for T-shirts, boxer shorts, baseball caps, and coffee mugs features a man dressed in a one-shoulder fur pelt, with his club, smiling behind a cavewoman who is wearing a fur bikini outfit and cooking a skinned animal on a spit, with the saying "MENS PRIORITYS [sic] : 10,000 YEARS LATER AND STILL ON THE HUNT FOR FOOD AND SEX!" Another image features only the club, with the saying, "caveman: primitive pimpin'."

Everywhere we look we can find applications of an increasingly fashionable academic exercise—the invocation of evolutionary theory to explain human male behaviors, particularly deplorable behaviors such as sexual harassment, rape, and aggression more generally. The familiar portrayals of sex differences based in evolution popularize and legitimize an academic version of evolutionary

thought known increasingly as evolutionary psychology, a field referred to as the "science of the mind."[2] The combination of scholarly and popular attention to evolution and human male sexuality has increasingly lodged American manhood in an evolutionary logic. The discourse of evolutionary science—however watered down or distorted the "science" becomes as it flows through popular culture—has become part of popular consciousness, a sort of cultural consensus about who men are.

The evolutionary theory is that our human male ancestors were in constant competition with one another for sexual access to fertile women, who were picky about their mate choices given the high level of parental investment required of the human female for reproduction—months of gestation, giving birth, and then years of lactation and care for a dependent child. The human male's low level of parental investment required for reproduction, we are told, resulted in the unique boorishness of the hairier sex: He is sexually promiscuous, he places an enormous emphasis on women's youth and beauty, which he ogles every chance he gets, he either cheats on his wife or wants to, and he can be sexually aggressive to the point of criminality.

We find references to man's evolutionary heritage not only on T-shirts but in new science textbooks, pop psychology books on relationships, men's magazines, and Broadway shows. There are caveman fitness plans and caveman diets. *Saturday Night Live's* hilarious "Unfrozen

Based on Martha McCaughey, *The Caveman Mystique: Pop-Darwinism and the Debates over Sex, Violence, and Science* (New York: Routledge, 2008).

Caveman Lawyer" and the affronted caveman of the Geico car insurance ads joke about the ubiquity of caveman narratives. More disturbingly, the Darwinian discourse also crops up when men need an excuse for antisocial behavior. One man, who was caught on amateur video participating in the Central Park group sexual assaults in the summer of 2000, can be heard on video telling his sobbing victim, "Welcome back to the caveman times." How does a man come to think of himself as a caveman when he attacks a woman? What made so many American men decide that it's the DNA, rather than the devil, that makes them do it?

Using the late sociologist Pierre Bourdieu's theory of habitus, or the account of how cultural ideas are taken up in the form of bodily habits and tastes that reinforce behavioral norms and social inequality, I suggest that scientific theories find their way into both popular culture and men's corporeal habits and attitudes. Evolution has become popular culture, where popular culture is more than just media representations but refers to the institutions of everyday life: family, marriage, school, work—all sites where gender and racial knowledges are performed according to images people have available to them in actionable repertoires, scripts, and narratives. As popular culture, evolutionary narratives offer men a way to think of, and embody, male sexuality.

That an evolutionary account of heterosexual male desire has captured the popular imagination is obvious from *Muscle and Fitness* magazine's article on "Man the Visual Animal," which explains why men leer at women. Using a theory of the evolved difference between human male and female sexual psychologies developed by leading evolutionary psychologist Donald Symons, the article offers the following explanation under the subheading "Evolution Happens":

Not much has changed in human sexuality since the Pleistocene. In his landmark book *The Evolution of Human Sexuality* (Oxford University Press, 1979), Symons hypothesizes that the male's sexual response to visual cues has been so rewarded by evolution that it's become innate.[3]

Such stories provide a means by which heterosexual male readers can experience their sexuality as acultural, primal: "The desire to ogle is your biological destiny."[4]

Evolution may happen (or may have happened), but these stories do not just happen. Their appeal seems to lie precisely in the sense of security provided by the imagined inevitability of heterosexual manhood. In a marketplace of masculine identities the caveman ethos is served up as Viagra for the masculine soul. Just as the 1950s women suffering what Betty Friedan famously called the "feminine mystique" were supposed to seek satisfaction in their Tupperware collections and their feminine figures, men today have been offered a way to think of their masculinity as powerful, productive, even aggressive—in a new economic and political climate where real opportunities to be rewarded for such traits have slipped away.[5]

It's hardly that most men today find themselves raising children at home while female partners bring home the bacon. But, like the 1950s housewife, more men must now find satisfaction despite working below their potential (given that their job skills have lost their position to technology or other labor sources) in a postindustrial service economy that is less rewarding both materially and morally. As journalist Susan Faludi puts it in her book *Stiffed*:

The fifties housewife, stripped of her connections to a wider world and invited to fill the void with shopping and the ornamental display of her ultrafemininity, could be said to have morphed into the nineties man, stripped of his connections to a wider world and invited to fill the void with consumption and a gym-bred display of his ultramasculinity.[6]

On top of the economic changes affecting men, during the 1990s a growing anti-rape movement also challenged men, taking them to task for the problem of violence against women. More state and federal dollars supported efforts to stop such violence, and men increasingly feared complaints and repercussions for those complaints. The rape trials of Mike Tyson and William Kennedy

Smith, Jr., the increasingly common school shootings (executed overwhelmingly by boys), the sexual harassment of women by men at the Citadel, the media attention given to the notorious Spurr Posse (a gang of guys who sought sex for "points" at almost all costs), the local sexual assault trials of countless high school and college athletic stars, the sexual harassment allegations against Supreme Court Justice nominee Clarence Thomas, and the White House sex scandals involving Bill Clinton meant more men lost ground. Indeed, the 1990s saw relentless—though not necessarily ill-founded—criticism of men's sexual violence and other forms of aggression.

Right-wing leaders were as upset with men as were feminists and other progressives. Those opposing abortion rights argued that sexual intercourse without procreation was undermining male responsibility, and those opposing women's equal-rights legislation argued that women's liberation would only allow men to relinquish their economic obligations to their families, sending women and children into divorce-induced poverty. Considering that critics of men came from both liberal and conservative camps, and from among men as well as women, it seems fair to say that in turn-of-the-century America moral disdain for men, whatever their age, race, or economic rank, had reached an all-time high.

For some men, the response was to cultivate a rude-dude attitude—popularized by Howard Stern, *The Man Show,* and MTV's endless shows about college spring-break vacations. For some others, the response was to face, with a sense of responsibility and urgency, men's animal natures and either accept or reform their caveman ways. While some men were embracing the role of consumers and becoming creatures of ornamentation—the "metrosexuals"—other men revolted against metrosexuality, embracing a can-do virility that Sara Stewart in *The New York Post* referred to as "retrosexuality," or that "cringe-inducing backlash of beers and leers."[7] Caveman masculinity is a form of retrosexuality that seems to carry the authority of objective science.

The popular understanding of men's sexuality as naturally vigorous and irrepressibly heterosexual helps fuel a culture Michael Kimmel[8] labeled "guyland" in his book by that name. Guyland is a social space in addition to a life stage, in which young single men act rough, gruff, sexually aggressive, and anti-gay, and do lewd, rude-dude things—resenting anything intellectual, politically correct, or smacking of either responsibility or women's authority. According to Kimmel, the five main markers of adulthood—leaving home, completing one's education, starting work, getting married, and becoming a parent—no longer happen all at once and so have left young men without a clear social marker of manhood.[9] In this context, the caveman discourse offers guys a *biological* marker of manhood.

Interestingly, feminist philosopher Sandra Lee Bartky made an argument about women's changing status impacting women's bodily comportment, saying that modern Western women began to restrict and constrict their bodies more as they gained institutional and social freedoms.[10] Bartky writes:

> As modern industrial societies change and as women themselves offer resistance to patriarchy, older forms of domination are eroded. But new forms arise, spread, and become consolidated. Women are no longer required to be chaste or modest, to restrict their sphere of activity to the home, or even to realize their properly feminine destiny in maternity: normative femininity is coming more and more to be centered on a woman's body—not its duties and obligations…[but] its presumed heterosexuality and its appearance.[11]

While women are now expected to restrict themselves in a tightly controlled, carefully managed feminine bodily comportment to compensate for their increased freedoms, I would suggest, appropriating Bartky, that we now see men finding their freedom and power in a bodily comportment just the opposite of Bartky's modern feminine woman: Men are boozing and belching their way to a lack of restrictions—to combat the increased restrictions they find in life and law.

Evolutionary theorists offer their ideas not to promote the caveman identity or fuel men's aggression, but in part because they believe the scientific facts about men's nature could help society address, and remedy, the violence and other problems so many have been blaming on men. What these scholars didn't predict is that so many average Joes would take up their ideas for slightly different reasons, namely as a move to feel powerful and domineering in a world squeezing men's resources and demanding that they be civil. Because of the ways caveman discourse appeals to many guys, it's important to consider the caveman story not simply as it is told by evolutionary scholars but as it is taken up throughout popular culture.

The Caveman as Popular Scientific Story

Popular culture is a political Petri dish for Darwinian ideas about sex. Average American guys don't read academic evolutionary science, but many do read about science in popular magazines and in bestselling books about the significance of the latest scientific ideas. As such, it is worth examining—even when magazine writers and television producers intentionally "dumb down" relatively sophisticated academic claims. In this section, I look at the way some popular texts make sense of evolutionary claims about men. Later I suggest that the caveman ideology, much of which centers on men's aggressive heterosexuality, gets embodied and thereby reproduced.[12]

In September of 1999, *Men's Health* magazine featured a caveman fitness program. Readers are shown an exercise routine that corresponds to the physical movements their ancestors would have engaged in: throwing a spear, hauling an animal carcass, honing a stone. A nice-looking, clean-shaven young man is shown exercising, his physical posture mirrored by a scruffy animal-skin-clad caveman behind him in the photo. Each day of the week-long routine is labeled according to the caveman mystique: building the cave home; the hunt; the chase; the kill; the long trek home; prepare for the feast; and rest. That an exercise plan is modeled after man-as-caveman reveals the common assumption that being a caveman is good for a man, a healthy existence.

Another issue of *Men's Health* magazine explains "the sex science facts" to male readers interested in "the biology of attraction." We follow the steps of a mating dance, but don't quite understand that's what we're doing. Indeed, we must learn the evolutionary history of sex to see why men feel the way they do when they notice a beautiful woman walking down the street:

> Of course, out there in the street, you have no thoughts about genetic compatibility or childbearing. Probably the farthest thing from your mind is having a child with that beautiful woman. But that doesn't matter. What you think counts for almost nothing. In the environment that crafted your brain and body, an environment in which you might be dead within minutes of spotting this beauty, the only thing that counted was that your clever neocortex—your seat of higher reason—be turned off so that you could quickly select a suitable mate, impregnate her, and succeed in passing on your genes to the next generation.[13]

The article proceeds to identify the signals of fertility that attract men: youth, beauty, big breasts, and a small waistline. Focusing on the desire for youth in women, the article tells men that "the reason men of any age continue to like young girls is that we were designed to get them pregnant and dominate their fertile years by keeping them that way.... When your first wife has lost the overt signals of reproductive viability, you desire a younger woman who still has them all.[14] And, of course, male readers are reminded that "your genes don't care about your wife or girlfriend or what the neighbors will say.[15]

Amy Alkon's *Winston-Salem Journal* advice column, "The Advice Goddess," uses an evolutionary theory of men's innate loutishness to comfort poor "Feeling Cheated On," who sent a letter complaining that her boyfriend fantasizes about other women during their lovemaking. The Advice Goddess cited a study by Bruce J. Ellis and Donald Symons (whose work was also mentioned in *Muscle & Fitness*) to conclude that "male sexuality is all about variety. Men are hard-wired to want you, the entire girls' dorm next door, and the entire girls' dorm next to that."[16]

Popular magazines tell men that they have a biological propensity to favor women with the faces of 11½-year-old girls (where the eyes and chin are close together) and a waist-to-hip ratio of .7 (where the waist measures 70% that of the hips). Men are told that their sexist double standard concerning appearance is evolutionary. Some of this research is very speculative—for instance, in some studies, men are simply shown photos of women with specific waist-to-hip ratios and then asked, "Would you like to spend the rest of your life with this woman?"—as though such staged answers reveal something about the individuals' real-life choices (or genes). But the results of this research make great copy.

Men's Health magazine in 1999 offered an article called "The Mysteries of Sex....Explained!" and relied on evolutionary theory, quoting several professors in the field, to explain "why most women won't sleep with you." The article elucidates:

> Stop blaming your wife. The fault lies with Mother Nature, the pit boss of procreation. Neil M. Malamuth, Ph.D., professor of psychology at UCLA, explains. "You're in Las Vegas with 10 grand. Your gambling strategy will depend on which form your money takes. With 10 chips worth $1,000 each, you'd weigh each decision cautiously. With 10,000 $1 chips, you'd throw them around." That's reproductive strategy in a nutshell.[17]

Popular magazine articles like this follow a standard formula. They quote the scientists, reporting on the evolutionary theorists' research, and offer funny anecdotes about male sexuality to illustrate the research findings. This *Men's Health* article continues to account for men's having fetishes: "Men are highly sexed creatures, less interested in relationship but highly hooked on visuals," says David Givens, Ph.D., an anthropologist. "'Because sex carries fewer consequences for men, it's easier for us to use objects as surrogate sexual partners.' Me? I've got my eye on a Zenith, model 39990."[18]

It's not just these popular and often humorous accounts of men that are based in some version of evolutionary theory. Even serious academic arguments rely on evolutionary theories of human behavior. For example, Steven Rhoads, a member of the University of Virginia faculty in public policy, has written *Taking Sex Differences Seriously* (2004), a book telling us why gender equity in the home and the workplace is a feminist pipe dream. Rhoads argues that women are wrong to expect men to take better care of children, do more housework, and make a place for them as equals at work because, he states, "men and women still have different natures and, generally speaking, different preferences, talents and interests."[19] He substantiates much of his argument about the divergent psychological predispositions in men and women with countless references to studies done by evolutionary scholars.

News magazines and television programs have also spent quite a bit of time popularizing evolutionary science and its implications for understanding human sex differences. The ABC news program *Day One* reported in 1995 on evolutionary psychologist David Buss's book, *The Evolution of Desire*.[20] Buss appeared on the show, which elaborated his theory by presenting us with supermodel Cindy Crawford and Barbie (the doll), presumably as representations of what men are wired to find desirable. As Buss explained in the interview, our evolutionary forebrothers who did not prefer women with high cheekbones, big eyes, lustrous hair, and full lips did not reproduce. As Buss put it, those men who happened to like someone who was older, sicker, or infertile "are not our ancestors. We are all the descendants of those men who preferred young healthy women and so as offspring, as descendants of those men, we carry with us their desires."[21] On that same television show, *Penthouse* magazine publisher Bob Guccioni was interviewed and explained that men are simply biologically designed to enjoy looking at sexy women: "This may be very politically incorrect but that's the way it is....It's all part of our ancestral conditioning."[22] Evolutionary narratives clearly work for publishers of pornography marketed to men.

Newsweek's 1996 cover story, "The Biology of Beauty: What Science Has Discovered About Sex Appeal," argues that the beautylust humans exhibit "is often better suited to the Stone Age than to the Information Age; the qualities we find alluring may be powerful emblems of health, fertility and resistance to disease...."[23] Though "beauty isn't all that matters in life," the article asserts, "our weakness for 'biological quality' is the cause of endless pain and injustice."[24]

Sometimes the magazines and TV shows covering the biological basis of sexual desire give a nod to the critics. The aforementioned *Newsweek* article, for instance, quotes feminist writer Katha Pollitt, who insists that "human beings cannot be reduced to DNA packets."[25] And then, as if to affirm Pollitt's claim, homosexuality is invoked as an example of the countless non-adaptive delights we desire: "Homosexuality is hard to explain as a biological adaptation. So is stamp collecting....We pursue countless passions that have no direct bearing on survival."[26] So when there is a nod to ways humans are not hardwired, homosexual desires are framed as oddities having no basis in nature, while heterosexual attraction along the lines of stereotypical heterosexual male fantasy is framed as biological. Heterosexual desire enjoys a *biologically correct* status.

Zoologist Desmond Morris explains how evolutionary theory applies to humans in his 1999 six-part television series, *Desmond Morris' The Human Animal: A Personal View of the Human Species.*[27] The first show in the series draws from his book, *The Naked Ape,* explaining that humans are relatively hairless with little to protect themselves besides their big brains.[28] This is stated as we watch two naked people, one male and one female, walk through a public place where everyone else is dressed in modern-day clothing. Both are white, both are probably 25 to 30 years old, both look like models (the man with well chiseled muscles, a suntan, and no chest hair; the woman thin, yet shapely with larger than average breasts, shaved legs, and a manicured pubic region). This presentation of man and woman in today's aesthetically ideal form as the image of what all of us were once like is *de rigueur* for any popular representation of evolutionary theory applied to human sexuality. No woman is flabby, flat chested, or has body hair; no man has pimples or back hair. These culturally mandated ideal body types are presented as

the image of what our human ancestors naturally looked like and desired. In this way and others, such shows posit modern aesthetic standards as states of nature.

Time magazine's 1994 cover story on "Our Cheating Hearts" reports that "the emerging field known as evolutionary psychology" gives us "fresh detail about the feelings and thoughts that draw us into marriage—or push us out."[29] After explaining the basics about men being less discriminating about their sexual partners than women, the article moves on to discuss why people divorce, anticipating resistance to the evolutionary explanation:

> Objections to this sort of analysis are predictable: "But people leave marriages for emotional reasons. They don't add up their offspring and pull out their calculators." But emotions are just evolution's executioners. Beneath the thoughts and feelings and temperamental differences marriage counselors spend their time sensitively assessing are the stratagems of the genes—cold, hard equations composed of simple variables: social status, age of spouse, number of children, their ages, outside romantic opportunities and so on. Is the wife really duller and more nagging than she was 20 years ago? Maybe, but maybe the husband's tolerance for nagging has dropped now that she is 45 and has no reproductive future.[30]

In case *Time* readers react to the new evolutionary psychology as part of a plot to destroy the cherished nuclear family, they are told that "progress will also depend on people using the explosive insight of evolutionary psychology in a morally responsible way....We are potentially moral animals—which is more than any other animal can say—but we are not naturally moral animals. The first step to being moral is to realize how thoroughly we aren't."[31]

While many accounts of evolution's significance for male sexuality seem simply to rationalize sexist double standards and wallow in men's loutishness, a number of pop-Darwinist claims have the moral purpose of liberating men from being controlled by their caveman natures. Their message: men can become enlightened cavemen. These stories make an attempt to liberate men by getting them to see themselves differently. They tell men that they are cavemen with potential. They either make fun of men's putatively natural shortcomings or encourage them to cage the caveman within through a kind of scientific consciousness-raising.

For example, Jeff Hood's book *The Silverback Gorilla Syndrome* uses the logic of let's-face-that-we're-cavemen to get men to become more compassionate and peaceful.[32] Hood, an organizational consultant and nature lover, recognizes the common problems of contemporary Western masculinity: fierce competition in the workplace; a lack of introspection and authentic relationships; and a reliance on cunning and bluffery to maintain one's self-image or position of power. This form of masculinity is an exhausting, life-threatening charade, which costs men their marriages and their health, and threatens the entire planet due to the destruction men wreak on the environment and on other people.

Hood's introduction explains:

> In the course of emerging from the jungles of our primate ancestors, we have stumbled onto, some would say earned, a thing called awareness. This faculty has spawned a body of knowledge leading to science, industry, technology—and ultimately increased comfort and longer lives. But it has also sparked an illusion of separation from the rest of the animal kingdom. Forging ahead in the quest for control over our destiny and our planet, we act as if the laws of nature do not apply to us. We are blind to the many ways in which the dominant attitudes and competitive behavior we have inherited threaten to push us dangerously out of balance with our world. Our saving grace may be to use our awareness instead for tempering the silverback gorilla syndrome that has brought us success at such great cost. This book is an attempt to increase that awareness.[33]

Hood wants to turn men into responsible, compassionate creatures, insisting that awareness of the caveman within—an inner gorilla whom Hood playfully calls "Big G"—is the only way out.

Even well-meaning applications of evolutionary theory like Hood's book, however, fail to question the idea of men's heterosexual, aggressive

inner core or evolved psychology. As such, they have a limited ability to move beyond the assumptions that lead so many others to use the same basic theory to rationalize being boorish. Men reformed via an evolutionary consciousness are still going to see themselves as different from, and even superior to, women.

The Caveman as Embodied Ethos

In a culture so attached to scientific authority and explication, it is worth examining the popular appeal of evolutionary theory and its impact on masculine embodiment. The popularity of the scientific story of men's evolved desires—however watered down or distorted the science becomes as enthusiasts popularize it—can tell us something about the appeal and influence of that story.

If the evolutionary stories appeal to many men, and it seems they do indeed, it's because they ring true. Many men feel like their bodies are aggressive. They feel urges, at a physical level, in line with evolutionary theoretical predictions. The men who feel like cavemen do not see their identity as a fiction; it is their bodily reality and seems to be backed by the authority of science.

The work of Pierre Bourdieu provides a tool for understanding how power is organized at the level of unconscious embodiment of cultural forces. I suggest that popular manifestations of scientific evolutionary narratives about men's sexuality have a real material effect on many men. Bourdieu's theory of practice develops the concepts of *habitus* and *field* to describe a reciprocally constitutive relationship between bodily dispositions and dominant power structures. Bourdieu concerned himself primarily with the ways in which socioeconomic class is incorporated at the level of the body, including class-based ways of speaking, postures, lifestyles, attitudes, and tastes.

Significant for Bourdieu is that people acquire tastes that mark them as members of particular social groups and particular social levels.[34] Membership in a particular social class produces and reproduces a class sensibility, what Bourdieu (1990) called "practical sense."[35] Habitus is "a somatized social relationship, a social law converted into an embodied law."[36] The process of becoming competent in the everyday life of a society or group constitutes habitus. Bourdieu's notion of embodiment can be extended to suggest that habitus, as embodied field, amounts to "the pleasurable and ultimately erotic constitution of [the individual's] social imaginary."[37]

Concerning the circulation of evolutionary narratives, we can see men taking erotic pleasure in the formation of male identity and the performance of accepted norms of heterosexual masculinity using precisely these tools of popular evolutionary science. Put differently, pop-Darwinism is a discourse that finds its way into men's bones and boners. The caveman story can become a man's practical sense of who he is and what he desires. This is so because masculinity is a dimension of embodied and performative practical sensibility—because men carry themselves with a bodily comportment suggestive of their position as the dominant gender, and they invest themselves in particular lifestyle practices, consumption patterns, attire, and bodily comportment. Evolutionary narratives thus enter the so-called habitus, and an aestheticized discourse and image of the caveman circulates through popular culture becoming part of natural perception, and consequently is reproduced by those embodying it.

In his study of the overwhelmingly white and male workspace of the Options Exchange floor, sociologist Richard Widick uses Bourdieu's theory to explain the traders' physical and psychical engagement with their work. Widick holds that "the traders' inhabitation and practical mastery of the trading floor achieves the bio-physical psycho-social state of a natural identity."[38] Hence the traders describe their manner as a "trading instinct." In a similar way, American men with what we might call a caveman instinct can be said to have acquired a "pre-reflexive practical sense" of themselves as heterosexually driven.[39]

Bourdieu gives the name "symbolic violence" to that process by which we come to accept and embody power relations without ever accepting them in the conscious sense of knowing them and choosing them. We hold beliefs that don't need to be thought—the effects of which can be "durably and deeply embedded in the body in the form of dispositions."[40] From this perspective, the durable dispositions of evolutionary discourse are apparent in our rape culture, for example, when a member of the group sexual assault in New York tells the woman he's attacking, "Welcome back to the caveman times." Embodying the ideology of irrepressible heterosexual desire makes such aggression appear to be natural.

Bourdieu's theory allows us to see that both cultural and material forces reveal themselves in the lived reality of social relations.[41] We can see on men's bodies the effects of their struggle with slipping economic privilege and a sense of entitlement to superiority over women. If men live out power struggles in their everyday experiences, then caveman masculinity can be seen as an imagined compensation for men's growing sense of powerlessness.[42] To be sure, some men have more social and economic capital than others. Those with less might invest even more in their bodies and appearances.[43]

Sociologist R. W. Connell discusses the significance of naturalizing male power. She states:

> The physical sense of maleness is not a simple thing. It involves size and shape, habits of posture and movement, particular physical skills and the lack of others, the image of one's own body, the way it is presented to other people and the ways they respond to it, the way it operates at work and in sexual relations. In no sense is all this a consequence of XY chromosomes, or even of the possession on which discussions of masculinity have so lovingly dwelt, the penis. The physical sense of maleness grows through a personal history of social practice, a life-history-in-society.[44]

We see and believe that men's power over women is the order of nature because "power is translated not only into mental body-images and fantasies, but into muscle tensions, posture, the feel and texture of the body."[45] Scientific discourse constitutes the field for some men in the constructed figure of the caveman, enabling those men to internalize such an identity. The caveman thus becomes an imaginative projection that is experienced and lived as real biological truth.

In his book, *Cultural Boundaries of Science,* Thomas Gieryn comments on the cultural authority of science, suggesting that "if 'science' says so, we are more often than not inclined to believe it or act on it—and to prefer it to claims lacking this epistemic seal of approval."[46] To his observation I would add that we are also more likely to *live* it. Ideas that count as scientific, regardless of their truth value, become lived ideologies. It's how modern American men have become cavemen and how the caveman ethos enjoys reproductive success.

Cultural anthropologist Paul Rabinow gives the name "biosociality" to the formation of new group and individual identities and practices that emerge from the scientific study of human life.[47] Rabinow offers the example of neurofibromatosis groups whose members have formed to discuss their experiences, educate their children, lobby for their disease, and "understand" their fate. And in the future, he points out, "… [i]t is not hard to imagine groups formed around the chromosome 17, locus 16,256, site 654,376 allele variant with a guanine substitution."[48] Rabinow's concept of biosociality is instructive here; for the discourse of the caveman offers this form of biosociality. The caveman constitutes an identity based on new scientific "facts" about one's biology.

Of course, evolutionary psychologists might insist that men's desires are, in some final instance, biological properties of an internal psyche or sexual psychology. I am suggesting, in line with Bourdieu, that men's desires are always performed in relation to the dominant discourses in circulation within their cultural lifeworlds, either for or against the representations that permeate those lifeworlds. We can see that a significant number of men are putting the pop-Darwinian rhetoric to good use in social interactions. The scientific discourse of the caveman (however unscientific we might regard it by the time it gets to everyday guys reading magazines and watching TV) is corporealized, quite literally incorporated into living identities, deeply shaping these men's experiences of being men.

The Caveman as Ethnicity

I recognize the lure of the caveman narrative. After all, it provides an explanation for patterns we do see and for how men do feel in contemporary society, tells men that they are beings who are the way they are for a specific reason, offers them an answer about what motivates them, and carries the authority of scientific investigation about their biological makeup. Evolutionary theory offers an origin story. Plus, it's fun: thinking of the reasons you might feel a certain way because such feelings might have been necessary for your ancestors to survive a hostile environment back in the Pleistocene can be a satisfying intellectual exercise.

In telling men a story about who they are, naturally, pop-Darwinism has the normalizing, disciplinary effect of forging a common, biological identity among men. Embodying ideology allows men to feel morally exonerated while they reproduce that very ideology. The discourse of male biological unity suppresses many significant differences among men, and of course many ways in which men would otherwise identify with women's tastes and behaviors. The evolutionary explanation of men's sexual behavior is an all-encompassing narrative enabling men to frame their own thoughts and experiences through it. As such it's a *grand narrative,* a totalizing theory explaining men's experiences as though all men act and feel the same ways, and as though the ideas of Western science provide a universal truth about those actions and feelings.

I'm skeptical of this kind of totalizing narrative about male sexuality because evolution applied to human beings does not offer that sort of truth. The application of evolutionary theory to human behavior is not as straightforwardly scientific as it might seem, even for those of us who believe in the theory of evolution by natural selection. It is a partial, political discourse that authorizes certain prevalent masculine behaviors and a problematic acceptance of those behaviors. I think there are better—less totalizing, and differently consequential—discourses out there that describe and explain those same behaviors. I'm also skeptical of men's use of the evolutionary narrative because, at its best, it can only create "soft patriarchs"—kinder, gentler cavemen who resist the putative urges of which evolutionary science makes them aware.[49]

Because evolutionary stories ultimately affirm a vision of men as naturally like one another, and naturally unlike women, caveman masculinity lends itself to becoming an "ethnic option," a way of identifying and living one's manhood. Sociologist Mary C. Waters explains that ethnic identity is actually not "the automatic labeling of a primordial characteristic" but instead is a complex, socially created identity.[50] The caveman as an ethnicity reveals an embrace of biology as a reaction to social constructionist understandings of masculinity, feminist demands on men, and the changing roles of men at work and in families. As an ethnicity, caveman masculinity is seen as not only impossible but undesirable to change.[51]

Did scholars in evolutionary psychology intend to present modern men with such an ethnic option? Of course not. To repeat: Darwinian ideas are often spread by enthusiasts—secondary school teachers, science editors of various newspapers and magazines, and educational television show producers—who take up evolutionary theorists' ideas and convey them to mass audiences. Evolutionary thinking has become popular in part because it speaks to a publicly recognized predicament of men. Changing economic patterns have propelled men's flight from marriage and breadwinning, in conjunction with women's increased (albeit significantly less prosperous) independence. If a man today wants multiple partners with as little commitment as possible, evolutionary rhetoric answers why this is so.

Evolutionary discourse doesn't offer a flattering story about men. But, more significantly, many people don't understand that it's *a story*. Evolution has become not only a grand narrative but a lived ideology. Maleness and femaleness, like heterosexuality and homosexuality, are not simply identities but *systems of knowledge*.[52] And those systems of knowledge inform thinking and acting. Bourdieu's concept of habitus explains the ways in which culture and knowledge, including

evolutionary knowledge, implant themselves at the level of the body, becoming a set of attitudes, tastes, perceptions, actions, and reactions. The status of science as objective, neutral knowledge helps make evolution a lived ideology because it feels truthful, natural, real.

Taking the historical and cultural changes affecting men seriously and embracing the diversity among men demand new understandings of masculinity, identity, and science. In gaining such a sociological perspective, men might resist making gender a new ethnicity and instead take a great leap forward to become new kinds of men.

Notes

1. A version of this essay also appears in the new edition of *Men's Lives,* edited by Michael Kimmel and Michael Messner.
2. For defenses of the study of the popularization of scientific discourse, and exemplary studies of the popularization of Darwinian discourse in different eras, see Alfred Kelly, *The Descent of Darwin: The Popularization of Darwinism in Germany, 1860–1914* (Chapel Hill: University of North Carolina Press, 1981) and Alvar Ellegard, *Darwin and the General Reader: The Reception of Darwin's Theory of Evolution in the British Press, 1859–1872* (Chicago: University of Chicago Press, 1990).
3. Mary Ellen Strote, "Man the Visual Animal," *Muscle and Fitness* (February 1994): 166.
4. Ibid., 166.
5. Betty Friedan, *The Feminine Mystique* (New York: Dell Publishing Company, Inc., 1963).
6. Susan Faludi, *Stiffed: The Betrayal of the American Man* (New York: HarperCollins, 1999), 40.
7. Sara Stewart, "Beasty Boys—'Retrosexuals' Call for Return of Manly Men; Retrosexuals Rising," *The New York Post,* July 18, 2006.
8. Michael Kimmel, *Guyland: The Perilous World Where Boys Become Men* (New York: HarperCollins, 2008).
9. Ibid., 24–25.
10. Sandra Lee Bartky, "Foucault, Femininity, and the Modernization of Patriarchal Power," in *The Politics of Women's Bodies*, ed. Rose Weitz (New York: Oxford University Press, 1998), 25–45.
11. Ibid., 41–42.

12. My argument here parallels a study of the pervasive iconography of the gene in popular culture. In *The DNA Mystique: The Gene as a Cultural Icon* (New York: W. H. Freeman, 1995), Dorothy Nelkin and M. Susan Lindee explain that popular culture provides "narratives of meaning" (p. 11). Those narratives filter complex ideas, provide guidance, and influence how people see themselves and evaluate other people, ideas, and policies. In this way, Nelkin and Lindee argue, DNA works as an ideology to justify boundaries of identity and legal rights, as well as to explain criminality, addiction, and personality. Of course, addict genes and criminal genes are misnomers—the definitions of what counts as an addict and what counts as a crime have shifted throughout history. Understanding DNA stories as ideological clarifies why, for example, people made sense of Elvis's talents and shortcomings by referring to his genetic stock (Ibid., 79–80). To call narratives of DNA ideological, then, is *not* to resist the scientific argument that deoxyribonucleic acid is a double-helix structure carrying information forming living cells and tissues, but to look at the way people make sense of DNA and use DNA to make sense of people and events in their daily lives.

13. Laurence Gonzales, "The Biology of Attraction," *Men's Health* 20.7 (2005): 186–93.

14. Ibid., 192.

15. Ibid., 193.

16. Amy Alkon, "Many Men Fantasize During Sex, But It Isn't a Talking Point," *Winston-Salem Journal,* 29 September 2005, p. 34.

17. Greg Gutfeld, "The Mysteries of Sex ... Explained!," *Men's Health* April (1999): 76.

18. Ibid., 76.

19. Steven R. Rhoads, *Taking Sex Differences Seriously* (San Francisco: Encounter Books, 2004), 4.

20. David M. Buss, *The Evolution of Desire: Strategies of Human Mating* (New York: Basic Books, 1994).

21. David M. Buss, interview by *Day One*, ABC News,

22. Ibid.

23. Geoffrey Cowley, "The Biology of Beauty," *Newsweek* 127 (1996): 62.

24. Ibid., 64.

25. Ibid., 66.

26. Ibid.

27. *Desmond Morris' The Human Animal: A Personal View of the Human Species* ["Beyond Survival"] directed by Clive Bromhall (Discovery Communication/TLC Video, 1999).

28. Desmond Morris, *The Naked Ape* (New York: Dell Publishing Company, Inc., 1967).

29. Robert Wright, *The Moral Animal: Evolutionary Psychology and Everyday Life* (New York: Pantheon Books, 1994), 45.

30. Ibid., 50.

31. Ibid., 52.

32. Jeff Hood, *The Silverback Gorilla Syndrome: Transforming Primitive Man* (Santa Fe, NM: Adventures in Spirit Publications, 1999).

33. Ibid., 1.

34. Pierre Bourdieu, *Distinction: A Social Critique of the Judgment of Taste* (Cambridge: Harvard University Press, 1984).

35. Pierre Bourdieu, *The Logic of Practice* (Stanford: Stanford University Press, 1990).

36. Pierre Bourdieu, *Masculine Domination* (Stanford: Stanford University Press, 2001).

37. Richard Widick, "Flesh and the Free Market: (On Taking Bourdieu to the Options Exchange)," *Theory and Society* 32 (2003): 679–723, 716.

38. Ibid., 701.

39. Ibid.

40. Bourdieu, *Masculine*, 39.

41. Lois McNay, "Agency and Experience: Gender as a Lived Relation," in *Feminism After Bourdieu,* ed. Lisa Adkins and Bev Skeggs (Oxford: Blackwell Publishing, 2004), 177.

42. See McNay, 175–90, for a discussion of emotional compensation and lived experience.

43. See Beverley Skeggs, *Formations of Class and Gender: Becoming Respectable* (London: Sage Publications, 1997), for a study pointing this out about working class women.

44. R. W. Connell, *Gender and Power: Society, the Person and Sexual Politics* (Cambridge: Polity Press, 1987), 84.

45. Ibid., 85.

46. Thomas F. Gieryn, *Cultural Boundaries of Science: Credibility on the Line* (Chicago: The University of Chicago Press, 1999), 1.

47. Paul Rabinow, *Making PCR, A Story of Biotechnology* (Chicago: University of Chicago Press, 1996), 101–2.

48. Ibid., 102.

49. I am appropriating W. Bradford Wilcox's term, from his book *Soft Patriarchs, New Men: How Christianity Shapes Fathers and Husbands* (Chicago: University of Chicago Press, 2004). Wilcox argues that the Christian men's movement known as the Promise Keepers encourages men to spend more time with their wives and children without ever challenging the fundamental patriarchal family structure that places men at the top.

50. Mary C. Waters, *Ethnic Options: Choosing Identities in America* (Berkeley: University of California Press, 1990), 16.

51. See Michael S. Kimmel, *Manhood in America: A Cultural History* (New York: Free Press, 1996), 127–37.

52. Steven Seidman, *Difference Troubles: Queering Social Theory and Sexual Politics* (Cambridge, UK: Cambridge University Press, 1997), 93.

Testosterone Rules

ROBERT M. SAPOLSKY

Face it, we all do it—we all believe in stereotypes about minorities. These stereotypes are typically pejorative and false, but every now and then they have a core of truth. I know, because I belong to a minority that lives up to its reputation. I have a genetic abnormality generally considered to be associated with high rates of certain socially abhorrent behaviors: I am male. Thanks to an array of genes that produce some hormone-synthesizing enzymes, my testes churn out a corrosive chemical and dump the stuff into my bloodstream, and this probably has behavioral consequences. We males account for less than 50 percent of the population, yet we generate a huge proportion of the violence. Whether it is something as primal as having an ax fight in a rain forest clearing or as detached as using computer-guided aircraft to strafe a village, something as condemned as assaulting a cripple or as glorified as killing someone wearing the wrong uniform, if it is violent, we males excel at it.

Why should this be? We all think we know the answer: something to do with those genes being expressed down in the testes. A dozen millennia ago or so, an adventurous soul managed to lop off a surly bull's testicles, thus inventing behavioral endocrinology. It is unclear from the historical records whether the experiment resulted in grants and tenure, but it certainly generated an influential finding: that the testes do something or other to make males aggressive pains in the ass.

That something or other is synthesizing the infamous corrosive chemical, testosterone (or rather, a family of related androgen hormones that I'll call testosterone for the sake of simplicity, hoping the androgen specialists won't take it the wrong way). Testosterone bulks up muscle cells—including those in the larynx, giving rise to operatic basses. It makes hair sprout here and there, undermines the health of blood vessels, alters biochemical events in the liver too dizzying to contemplate, and has a profound impact, no doubt, on the workings of cells in big toes. And it seeps into the brain, where it influences behavior in a way highly relevant to understanding aggression.

Robert M. Sapolsky, "Testosterone Rules," *Discover* (March 1997). Reprinted with the permission of the author.

Genes are the hand behind the scene, directing testosterone's actions. They specify whether steroidal building blocks are turned into testosterone or estrogen, how much of each, and how quickly. They regulate how fast the liver breaks down circulating testosterone, thereby determining how long an androgenic signal remains in the bloodstream. They direct the synthesis of testosterone receptors—specialized proteins that catch hold of testosterone and allow it to have its characteristic effects on target cells. And genes specify how many such receptors the body has, and how sensitive they are. Insofar as testosterone alters brain function and produces aggression, and genes regulate how much testosterone is made and how effectively it works, this should be the archetypal case for studying how genes can control our behavior. Instead, however, it's the archetypal case for learning how little genes actually do so.

Some pretty obvious evidence links testosterone with aggression. Males tend to have higher testosterone levels in their circulation than do females, and to be more aggressive. Times of life when males are swimming in testosterone—for example, after reaching puberty—correspond to when aggression peaks. Among many species, testes are mothballed most of the year, kicking into action and pouring out testosterone only during a very circumscribed mating season—precisely the time when male–male aggression soars.

Impressive though they seem, these data are only correlative—testosterone found on the scene repeatedly with no alibi when some aggression has occurred. The proof comes with the knife, the performance of what is euphemistically known as a subtraction experiment. Remove the source of testosterone in species after species, and levels of aggression typically plummet. Reinstate normal testosterone levels afterward with injections of synthetic testosterone, and aggression returns.

The subtraction and replacement paradigm represents pretty damning proof that this hormone, with its synthesis and efficacy under genetic control, is involved in aggression. "Normal testosterone levels appear to be a prerequisite for normative levels of aggressive behavior" is the sort of catchy, hummable phrase the textbooks would

use. That probably explains why you shouldn't mess with a bull moose during rutting season. But it's not why a lot of people want to understand this sliver of science. Does the action of testosterone tell us anything about individual differences in levels of aggression, anything about why some males—some human males—are exceptionally violent? Among an array of males, are the highest testosterone levels found in the most aggressive individuals?

Generate some extreme differences and that is precisely what you see. Castrate some of the well-paid study subjects, inject others with enough testosterone to quadruple the normal human levels, and the high-testosterone males are overwhelmingly likely to be the more aggressive ones. Obviously, extreme conditions don't tell us much about the real world, but studies of the normative variability in testosterone—in other words, seeing what everyone's natural levels are like without manipulating anything—also suggest that high levels of testosterone and high levels of aggression tend to go together. This would seem to seal the case that interindividual differences in levels of aggression among normal individuals are probably driven by differences in levels of testosterone. But that conclusion turns out to be wrong.

Here's why. Suppose you note a correlation between levels of aggression and levels of testosterone among normal males. It could be because (a) testosterone elevates aggression; (b) aggression elevates testosterone secretion; or (c) neither causes the other. There's a huge bias to assume option a, while b is the answer. Study after study has shown that if you examine testosterone levels when males are first placed together in the social group, testosterone levels predict nothing about who is going to be aggressive. The subsequent behavioral differences drive the hormonal changes, rather than the other way around.

Because of a strong bias among certain scientists, it has taken forever to convince them of this point. Suppose you're studying what behavior and hormones have to do with each other. How do you study the behavioral part? You get yourself a notebook, a stopwatch, a pair of binoculars. How do you measure the hormones and analyze the genes that regulate them? You need some gazillion-dollar machines; you muck around with radiation and chemicals, wear a lab coat, maybe even goggles—the whole nine yards. Which toys would you rather get for Christmas? Which facet of science are you going to believe in more? The higher the technology, goes the formula, the more scientific the discipline. Hormones seem to many to be more substantive than behavior, so when a correlation occurs, it must be because hormones regulate behavior, not the other way around.

This is a classic case of what is often called physics envy, a disease that causes behavioral biologists to fear their discipline lacks the rigor of physiology, physiologists to wish for the techniques of biochemists, biochemists to covet the clarity of the answers revealed by molecular geneticists, all the way down until you get to the physicists who confer only with God. Recently, a zoologist friend had obtained blood samples from the carnivores he studies and wanted some hormones in the samples tested in my lab. Although inexperienced with the technique, he offered to help in any way possible. I felt hesitant asking him to do anything tedious, but since he had offered, I tentatively said, "Well, if you don't mind some unspeakable drudgery, you could number about a thousand assay vials." And this scientist, whose superb work has graced the most prestigious science journals in the world, cheerfully answered, "That's okay. How often do I get to do real science, working with test tubes?"

Difficult though scientists with physics envy find it to believe, interindividual differences in testosterone levels don't predict subsequent differences in aggressive behavior among individuals. Similarly, fluctuations in testosterone levels within one individual over time don't predict subsequent changes in the levels of aggression in that one individual—get a hiccup in testosterone secretion one afternoon and that's not when the guy goes postal.

Look at our confusing state: normal levels of testosterone are a prerequisite for normal levels of aggression. Yet if one male's genetic makeup predisposes him to higher levels of testosterone than the next guy, he isn't necessarily going to be more aggressive. Like clockwork, that statement makes the students suddenly start coming to office hours in a panic, asking whether they missed something in their lecture notes.

Yes, it's going to be on the final, and it's one of the more subtle points in endocrinology—what's referred to as a hormone having a "permissive effect." Remove someone's testes and, as noted, the frequency of aggressive behavior is likely to plummet. Reinstate pre-castration levels of testosterone by injecting the hormone, and pre-castration levels of aggression typically return. Fair enough. Now, this time, castrate an individual and restore testosterone levels to only 20 percent of normal. Amazingly, normal pre-castration levels of aggression come back. Castrate and now introduce twice the testosterone levels from before castration, and the same level of aggressive behavior returns. You need some testosterone around for normal aggressive behavior. Zero levels after castration, and down it usually goes; quadruple levels (the sort of range generated in weight lifters abusing anabolic steroids), and aggression typically increases. But anywhere from roughly 20 percent of normal to twice normal and it's all the same. The brain can't distinguish among this wide range of basically normal values.

If you knew a great deal about the genetic makeup of a bunch of males, enough to understand how much testosterone they secreted into their bloodstream, you still couldn't predict levels of aggression among those individuals. Nevertheless, the subtraction and reinstatement data seem to indicate that, in a broad sort of way, testosterone causes aggressive behavior. But that turns out not to be true either, and the implications of this are lost on most people the first thirty times they hear about it. Those implications are important, however—so important that it's worth saying thirty-one times.

Round up some male monkeys. Put them in a group together and give them plenty of time to sort out where they stand with each other—grudges, affiliative friendships. Give them enough time to form a dominance hierarchy, the sort of linear ranking in which number 3, for example, can pass his day throwing around his weight with numbers 4 and 5, ripping off their monkey chow, forcing them to relinquish the best spots to sit in, but numbers 1 and 2 still expect and receive from him the most obsequious brownnosing.

Hierarchy in place, it's time to do your experiment. Take that third-ranking monkey and give him some testosterone. None of this within-the-normal-range stuff. Inject a ton of it, way higher than what you normally see in rhesus monkeys, give him enough testosterone to grow antlers and a beard on every neuron in his brain. And, no surprise, when you check the behavioral data, he will probably be participating in more aggressive interactions than before.

So even though small fluctuations in the levels of the hormone don't seem to matter much, testosterone still causes aggression, right? Wrong. Check out number 3 more closely. Is he raining aggressive terror on everyone in the group, frothing with indiscriminate violence? Not at all. He's still judiciously kowtowing to numbers 1 and 2 but has become a total bastard to numbers 4 and 5. Testosterone isn't causing aggression, it's exaggerating the aggression that's already there.

Another example, just to show we're serious. There's a part of your brain that probably has lots to do with aggression, a region called the amygdala. Sitting near it is the Grand Central Station of emotion-related activity in your brain, the hypothalamus. The amygdala communicates with the hypothalamus by way of a cable of neuronal connections called the stria terminalis. (No more jargon, I promise.) The amygdala influences aggression via that pathway, sending bursts of electrical excitation that ripple down the stria terminalis to the hypothalamus and put it in a pissy mood.

Once again, do your hormonal intervention: flood the area with testosterone. You can inject the hormone into the bloodstream, where it eventually makes its way to the amygdala. You can surgically microinject the stuff directly into the area. In a few years, you may even be able to construct animals with extra copies of the genes that direct testosterone synthesis, producing extra hormone that way. Six of one, half a dozen of the other. The key thing is what doesn't happen

next. Does testosterone make waves of electrical excitation surge down the stria terminalis? Does it turn on that pathway? Not at all. If and only if the amygdala is already sending an excited volley down the stria terminalis, testosterone increases the rate of such activity by shortening the resting time between bouts. It's not turning on the pathway, it's increasing the volume of signaling if it is already turned on. It's not causing aggression, it's exaggerating the preexisting pattern of it, exaggerating the response to environmental triggers of aggression.

In every generation, it is the duty of behavioral biologists to try to teach this critical point, one that seems a maddening cliché once you get it. You take that hoary old dichotomy between nature and nurture, between intrinsic factors and extrinsic ones, between genes and environment, and regardless of which behavior and underlying biology you're studying, the dichotomy is a sham. No genes. No environment. Just the interaction between the two.

Do you want to know how important environment and experience are in understanding testosterone and aggression? Look back at how the effects of castration are discussed earlier. There were statements like "Remove the source of testosterone in species after species and levels of aggression typically plummet." Not "Remove the source...and aggression always goes to zero." On the average it declines, but rarely to zero, and not at all in some individuals. And the more social experience an individual had being aggressive prior to castration, the more likely that behavior persists sans cojones. In the right context, social conditioning can more than make up for the complete absence of the hormone.

A case in point: the spotted hyena. These animals are fast becoming the darlings of endocrinologists, sociobiologists, gynecologists, and tabloid writers because of their wild sex reversal system. Females are more muscular and more aggressive than males, and are socially dominant to them, rare traits in the mammalian world. And get this: females secrete more of certain testosterone-related hormones than the males do, producing muscles, aggression, and masculinized private parts that make it supremely difficult to tell the sex of a hyena. So high androgen levels would seem, again, to cause aggression and social dominance. But that's not the whole answer.

High in the hills above the University of California at Berkeley is the world's largest colony of spotted hyenas, massive bone-crunching beasts who fight each other for the chance to have their ears scratched by Laurence Frank, the zoologist who brought them over as infants from Kenya. Various scientists are studying their sex reversal system. The female hyenas are bigger and more muscular than the males and have the same weirdo genitals and elevated androgen levels as their female cousins back in the savanna. Everything is just as it is in the wild—except the social system. As those hyenas grew up, there was a very significant delay in the time it took for the females to begin socially dominating the males, even though the females were stoked on androgens. They had to grow up without the established social system to learn from.

When people first realize that genes have a great deal to do with behavior—even subtle, complex, human behavior—they are often struck with an initial evangelical enthusiasm, placing a convert's faith in the genetic components of the story. This enthusiasm is typically reductive—because of physics envy, because reductionism is so impressive, because it would be so nice if there were a single gene (or hormone or neurotransmitter or part of the brain) responsible for everything. But even if you completely understood how genes regulate all the important physical factors involved in aggression—testosterone synthesis and secretion, the brain's testosterone receptors, the amygdala neurons and their levels of transmitters, the favorite color of the hypothalamus—you still wouldn't be able to predict levels of aggression accurately in a group of normal individuals.

This is no mere academic subject. We are a fine species with some potential, yet we are racked by sickening amounts of violence. Unless we are hermits, we feel the threat of it, often every day, and should our leaders push the button, we will all be lost in a final global violence. But as we try to understand this feature of our sociality, it is critical to remember the limits of the biology. Knowing the genome, the complete DNA sequence, of some suburban teenager is never going to tell us why that kid, in his after-school chess club, has developed a particularly aggressive style with his bishops. And it certainly isn't going to tell us much about the teenager in some inner city hellhole who has taken to mugging people. "Testosterone equals aggression" is inadequate for those who would offer a simple biological solution to the violent male. And "testosterone equals aggression" is certainly inadequate for those who would offer the simple excuse that boys will be boys. Violence is more complex than a single hormone, and it is supremely rare that any of our behaviors can be reduced to genetic destiny. This is science for the bleeding-heart liberal: the genetics of behavior is usually meaningless outside the context of the social factors and environment in which it occurs.

Of Genes and Gender

ANNE FAUSTO-STERLING

Recent research has established beyond a doubt that males and females are born with a different set of "instructions" built into their genetic code. Science is thus confirming what poets and parents have long taken for granted.

—*Tim Hackler*
Mainliner, 1980

The relation between gene, environment and organism is not one-to-one but many-to-many. Given the genes and the environment one cannot predict the organism. Given the organism, we cannot infer its genotype or the environment in which it developed.

—*Richard Lewontin*
Human Diversity, 1982

LET'S FACE IT: the belief that genes dictate our behavior has enormous appeal. For starters, our daily observations seem to confirm the notion. The other day, for example, I came upon a photograph of myself, aged nine, and realized with astonishment how much I looked like my nine-year-old niece. Not only do we regularly observe physical similarities among family members, we also note behavioral ones. If genes account for the fact that both my mother and I have curly hair, then might they not also explain why my father, brother, and I all gesture energetically when we speak? Family resemblances, be they genetic or learned, offer deep psychological comfort. My amazed recognition of myself physically reincarnated in the person of my niece matched my pleasure at sensing immortality. My body will some day pass from this earth, but part of me will remain, passing itself on, perhaps, to generations yet unborn. And should my children turn out to be brilliant or successful, so much the better. I can claim half the credit, since half their genes came from me.

But genes are double-edged. One invokes them to take praise for the good, but blames them to get emotional respite from the bad. (My weight problem? It's not my fault. I inherited a craving for sweets; besides, the women in my family tend to be overweight.) We can even blame our genes for social ills. Anthropologist Lionel Tiger, for instance, writes that failure to accept women's genetic limitations leads to economic discrimination. Implying that political efforts to obtain male/female equality seem likely to fail, he suggests instead that social scientists should reconsider their nongenetic view of the origins of widespread social patterns but "particularly the effect of genes on the situation of women."[1]

The popular press and scientists alike have apparently fallen in love with the gene. Maya Pines, for example, wrote in the *New York Times* about the rapidly expanding field of behavior genetics. Not only have scientists in this area begun to talk about things such as the genetic basis of shyness, she writes, in addition they "are establishing ties between heredity and stuttering, dyslexia and alcoholism."[2] At the same time, reports continue to appear, even in very recent scientific publications, linking genes to criminal behavior[3] and, as always, to IQ.[4]

Moving from physical similarities among family members to genetic bases for individual behavior such as shyness, alcoholism, or criminality and

Anne Fausto-Sterling "Of Genes and Gender," from *Myths of Gender* (New York: Basic Books, 1992).

then beyond, to consider genetic causes of complex social structures, we jump over enormous intellectual chasms. In the following pages we will look before we leap at what lies below, examining the questions: what are genes and how do they work; how do genes interact with environment to affect behavior; and how do genes participate in the genesis of biological differences between males and females? In considering these topics we must keep in mind the seductive nature of genetic explanations, allowing ourselves to sustain some intellectual discomfort in search of solid and accurate explanation. The strong—albeit erroneous—belief that genetic differences are unchangeable make this neither an easy nor an idle task. More often than not the phrase *genetic basis* encodes the meaning "change is impossible."[5]

What Are Genes and How Do They Work?

In the beginning scientists had no physical account of the gene. Gregor Mendel, for instance, abstracted a set of rules to describe the inheritance of traits in adult pea plants, such as red or white flowers or smooth or wrinkled peas. His rules, which grew out of observations of the final stage of plant development (rather than, for example, from looking at the pea plant embryo), depended upon the frequency of appearance of a particular trait, or *phenotype,* as geneticists label characteristics such as flower color, fruit texture, plant height, and so on, which make up the appearance, behavior, and growth characteristics of the plant. Mendel described something in peas that we all are familiar with in humans. A brown-haired set of parents may have only brown-haired children, but those children will sometimes produce blond offspring. In Mendelian terms we describe this observation by speaking of factors, which the early Mendelians called genes, which lead to the production of different hair colors. These factors exist in alternate states (for example, red rather than white flowers, smooth versus wrinkled fruit, or blond versus brown hair) called *alleles,* which influence the development of a particular phenotype.

Mendel abstracted from his results the rule that some alleles dominate others. A *dominant* allele for brown hair (designated *B*), for example, when paired with a *recessive* allele for blond (designated *b*) results in the appearance of a brown-haired *Bb* child. The pairing of two recessive alleles would result in a blond (*bb*) child. Since two different gene combinations, *BB* and *Bb,* can produce a brunette, geneticists say that two different *genotypes* can produce the same *phenotype. BB* and *bb* individuals are called *homozygous* and *Bb* individuals are *heterozygous.* A shorthand conceptualization of these possibilities as applied to round and wrinkled peas appears in Figure 1.1.

The distance traveled from Mendel's abstract rules of inheritance to our present-day conceptualization of genetic information is great. In the first quarter of this century many geneticists pictured genes as particles linked together on chromosomes, structures found inside the cell's nucleus: the most frequent image was of beads on a string. Continued experimentation, however, chipped away at this picture; great controversies erupted over the definition of a gene. Was it a rule for predicting phenotypic frequencies or a tangible physical entity?[6] Dr. G. Ledyard Stebbins, a well-known evolutionary biologist, points out that the

> ...entire history of Mendelian genetics has consisted of discoveries that have modified...the Mendelian laws of heredity [which] have been so strongly modified by successive discoveries that in their original form they are useful only for elementary teaching.[7]

And herein lies one problem: because of these modifications, the word *gene* has several meanings.[8] Due to the confusion the word imparts to discussions of genetic causation, Stebbins provides a working definition:

> Biological heredity is transmitted by means of molecular templates, consisting of nucleic acids, that replicate with the aid of enzymes. These templates provide the code...for the synthesis of specific proteins, the largest class of working molecules of the body.[9]

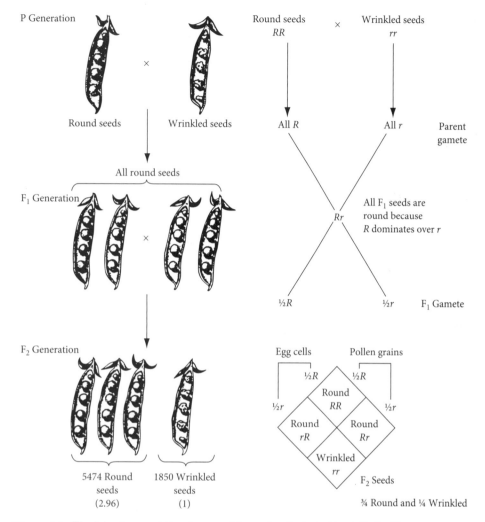

Figure 1.1. The Inheritance of Dominant and Recessive Traits in Mendel's Pea Plants.

Note: Francisco Ayala and John Kiger, Jr., *Modern Genetics*, 2d ed. (Menlo Park, Calif.: Benjamin/Cummings, 1980), 34. Copyright © 1984 and 1980 by The Benjamin Cummings Publishing Company, Inc. Reprinted by permission.

Most frequently, the large molecule called DNA (deoxyribonucleic acid) forms the genetic material. Chromosomes, structures visible inside the cell's nucleus, consist of DNA in combination with other large molecules. The DNA molecule itself is a long chain composed of variously ordered repetitions of four differently shaped links called *bases*. The links, which behave as bases when dissolved singly in water, are chemically connected to molecules of phosphoric acid, which actually form the backbone of the long, spiral nuclei and molecule. The phosphoric acid component gives the DNA molecule as a whole the chemical properties of an acid. The order in which the links hang together forms a code, or as Stebbins calls it, a "molecular template." As part of the process of cell division, the DNA template, with the aid of enzymes, stamps out another copy of itself, so that when one cell divides into two each new cell contains the same DNA code as its parent. Biologists call this process *replication.*

Cells engage not only in replication, however, but also in protein synthesis; like DNA, proteins are also chainlike molecules. But instead of base links, the protein chain consists of connected amino acids. Not all of the more than twenty naturally occurring amino acids show up in every protein molecule, and many are repeated more than once in the same molecules. Thus each protein uniquely combines certain amino acids in a particular order on the protein chain. Two proteins consisting of the same kinds of amino acid may have very different chemical properties if the quantities of each type differ or if the amino acid links are arranged in different orders. The number and type of an amino acids can combine in an almost infinite variety of different linear arrays, each a protein with special chemical properties, playing individual biological roles within an organism.

Triplets of bases linked together in particular orders on the DNA chain contain a code for particular amino acids. Imagine that the four bases found in DNA had the shapes of either a circle, a triangle, a square, or a trapezoid. Suppose that the order Circle-Square-Triangle provided the template for the synthesis of a particular amino acid, say, glutamic acid (O–□–Δ = glutamic acid), while the order Square-Circle-Triangle) coded for a different amino acid, perhaps aspartic acid (□–O–Δ = aspartic acid). A stretch of DNA that ran Circle-Square-Triangle-Square-Circle-Triangle (O–□–Δ–□–O–Δ) would code, then, for two links in the protein chain—glutamic acid followed by aspartic acid. During the past twenty-five years it has become clear that the four different links on the DNA chain arrange themselves in enough different triplet combinations to code for the twenty or so amino acids that combine in different numbers and orders to make up the thousands of different proteins in our bodies. Figures 1.2 and 1.3 provide

illustrations of the DNA template and its role in DNA and protein synthesis. One can see from the drawings that the expression of the genetic code is complex, involving first the *transcription* of the code into an intermediate, "messenger" RNA molecule, followed by the *translation* of the transcribed code into a particular protein. Several different types of RNA (ribonucleic acids) as well as enzymes specialized for involvement in protein synthesis participate in these processes.*

All of this, though, is a far and abstract cry from Tiger's discussion of "the effect of genes on the situation of women," or even from the consideration of wrinkled peas or towheads. In order to connect our understanding of the genetic code and protein synthesis with our original questions about genes and behavior, we must move from the submicroscopic DNA molecules to visible, easily observable traits. To illustrate, I will use an example from medical genetics in which the steps leading from DNA and protein to unmistakable clinical symptoms are well explained.

Consider the following case history. A patient complains of severe physical weakness. Her episodes of extreme pain seem worse when she exerts herself or travels to high altitudes; her anemic blood contains abnormal red cells which appear, under the microscope, to be bent into the shape of a half-moon or sickle. Even with proper care the patient may, over the years, experience increasingly severe attacks of weakness, at times showing impaired mental function, heart and kidney failure, and paralysis.

All of these symptoms characterize a genetically inherited disease called sickle-cell anemia. In adults a normally functioning red blood cell contains large amounts of the protein hemoglobin (called hemoglobin A, for Adult), which binds the oxygen taken into the lungs. This hemoglobin-bound oxygen, carried throughout the body by the circulating blood, keeps our cells breathing. The cells of a person afflicted with sickle-cell disease also produce hemoglobin, but in an abnormal

---

* The drawing in figure 1.3 details the process of protein synthesis. Note that in addition to messenger RNA, *transfer RNA* (tRNA) molecules and *ribosome* structures consisting of *ribosomal* RNA and protein are also involved in the process.

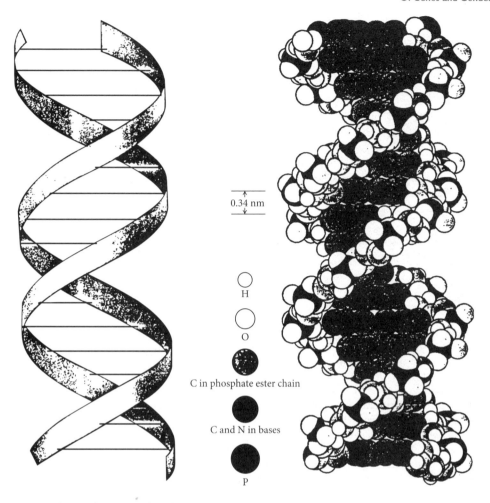

0.34 nm

○ H

○ O

● C in phosphate ester chain

● C and N in bases

● P

Figure 1.2. The Structure of DNA.
The DNA double helix: the ribbons of the model on the left and the strings of dark and shaded atoms in the space-filling model on the right represent the sugar-phosphate "backbones" of the two strands. The bases are stacked in the center of the molecule between the two backbones.

Note: Salvador E. Luria, Stephen Jay Gould, and Sam Singer, *A View of Life* (New York: Benjamin/Cummings, 1981), 43. Copyright © by The Benjamin Cummings Publishing Company, Inc. Reprinted by permission.

form called hemoglobin S, which binds oxygen less efficiently than does the normal molecule. When more than enough oxygen is available, the presence of hemoglobin S may not matter, but under stressful conditions such as physical exertion or high altitude, hemoglobin S literally crystallizes inside the red blood cell. As a result of this change in the physical state and shape of the molecule, the entire red blood cell deforms to take on

its characteristic sickle shape. The sickling itself has a variety of effects: the body's own defenses rapidly destroy the injured cells, causing severe anemia which can lead to physical weakness, impaired mental function, and heart failure. The misshapen cells may also get stuck in the narrow capillary blood vessels, causing severe pain as well as heart problems, brain, lung, and kidney damage, and possible paralysis (see Figure 1.4).

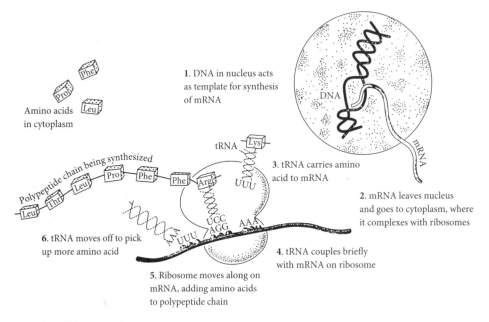

Figure 1.3. Protein Synthesis.
Messenger RNA is synthesized, one chain of the DNA gene serving as the template. This mRNA then goes into the cytoplasm and becomes associated with ribosomes. The various types of tRNA in the cytoplasm pick up the amino acids for which they are specific and bring them to a ribosome as it moves along the mRNA. (The letters A, C, G, and U each stand for a particular base.) Each tRNA bonds to the mRNA at a point where a triplet of bases complementary to an exposed triplet on the tRNA occurs. This ordering of the tRNA molecules automatically orders the amino acids, which are then linked by peptide bonds. Synthesis of the polypeptide chain thus proceeds one amino acid at a time in an orderly sequence as the ribosomes move along the mRNA. As each tRNA donates its amino acid to the growing polypeptide chain, it uncouples from the mRNA and moves away into the cytoplasm, where it can be used again. (Note that the various molecules and organelles shown here are not drawn to scale with respect to one another or to the cell.)

Note: William T. Keeton, *Biological Science*, 3d ed., illus. Paula di Santo Bensadoun (New York: Norton, 1980, 647. Reproduced by permission of W. W. Norton & Company, Inc. Copyright © 1980).

Understanding the differences in physical properties of the normal and abnormal forms of hemoglobin gives us a good basis for comprehending how the disease generates its symptoms. But we understand even more because we know exactly what has happened to the DNA of a person with sickle-cell disease. Each of us carries two similar chromosomes (*homologues*) bearing a stretch of DNA with appropriate base sequences ready for transcription and translation into the sequence of amino acids that make up hemoglobin A. A person with sickle-cell disease, however, carries two homologues in which one of the bases

in the DNA sequences coding for hemoglobin has changed, or *mutated*. As a result, the sixth amino acid from one end of the hemoglobin molecule is transformed from glutamic acid to valine. In sum, this single base change in DNA results in a single amino acid substitution in a large protein molecule. The structure of the new amino acid changes the overall physical properties of the protein, so that it becomes less able to bind oxygen and less soluble inside the cell.

This example contains within it two important points. First, a simple alteration in the base sequence of DNA can have complex results.

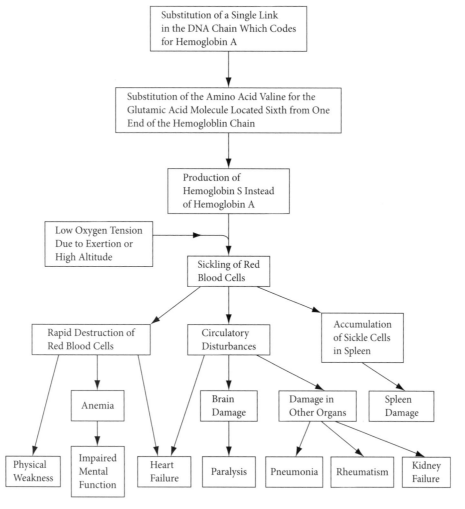

Figure 1.4. Chain of Events in Sickle-Cell Anemia.

Note: The frequency of individual symptoms depends on chance environmental changes, quality of medical care, and individual differences.

Figure 1.4 illustrates the cascade of events stemming from the single base change in question. The second point, which is perhaps the more important for our consideration of genes and behavior, is that even knowing that a person carries a specifically understood genetic defect does not enable us to predict the course of the disease in any particular individual. How much we can say with certainty depends entirely on the level of biological organization we choose to describe. If we describe the disease at the protein level, for example, we can safely state that all people who are homozygous for the genetic information coding for hemoglobin S will carry the hemoglobin S molecule: 100 percent predictability—a scientist's dream. But if we were to try to predict whether a particular sickle-cell patient would have leg ulcers (15 percent of them do), an enlarged heart (68 percent do), pneumonococcal meningitis (2 percent do), and so on, we would be at a loss for an answer.[10] At the level of the full-blown sickle-cell disease, each patient differs. The reasons are many, including differences among individuals in access to quantity and quality of medical care, different physical environments, different patterns of physical activity, different personality patterns, and individual differences in other (nonhemoglobin) genetic information that could directly or indirectly influence the course of the disease.

In short, while it is accurate shorthand to say that the sickle-cell mutation causes the production of an abnormal protein, it is wrong to say that it will cause any particular condition, for example, an enlarged heart, in any particular individual. At the whole, adult level of organization, genes alone do not produce biological phenotypes. Instead an individual's developmental and environmental history in combination with his or her total genetic endowment (all the genetic information encoded in the DNA),* as well as chance, contribute to the final phenotype. By the same token, genes alone do not determine human behavior. They work in the presence and under the influence of a set of environments.

Not By Genes Alone: The Brain and Behavior

Genes are thought to affect everything from our emotions to our legal system.[11] Researchers have asked whether males have a math gene, whether the Y chromosome causes aggressive behavior, and whether women are genetically programmed to have strong maternal feelings, to be verbally expressive, and to be better at relational than analytic skills. Harvard's E. O. Wilson suggests that "the genetic bias is intense enough to cause a substantial division of labor even in the most free and most egalitarian of future societies...even with identical education and equal access to all professions, men are likely to continue to play a disproportionate role in political life, business and science."[12] Genes apparently direct brain development which affects our behavior which determines our social structure. Although the reasoning is simple, little credible evidence actually exists to

sustain such a chain of argument. Its logic, in truth, flies in the face of much of what we know about the biology of development.

If the brain codes for behavior and genes code for the brain, it must be a very complex cryptograph indeed, one for which biologists have yet to identify all of the basic symbols. The intricacy of the problem defies imagination. A human brain contains about 10^{10} (100 billion) cells, most of which have thousands of connections leading to or from other cells. Furthermore, each cell is itself chemically complex. One scientist estimates that during its lifetime every cell in the human brain must contend with the properties or activities of 10^9 giant molecules, including proteins, polysaccharides, and nucleic acids such as DNA.[13]

We do, nevertheless, have a degree of insight into brain development. Figure 1.5 provides an overview of some of its major known events. This picture is quite different from that describing sickle-cell anemia (see Figure 1.4), in which the arrows connect a primary event—a change in base sequence in the DNA—to the appearance of a specific disease. In contrast to the relatively straightforward development of the red blood cell, the development of brain tissue is bewilderingly complex. Few of the biochemical details of the events described in Figure 1.4 are known, and one must keep in mind that each arrow in the drawing in reality runs through hundreds of boxes still unlabeled out of ignorance. Evidently we cannot envision brain development in terms of linear or even branching events. Instead we must think of a fine network, far more intricate than the random overlaying of hundreds of differently shaped spiderwebs.

Chastened by the level of the brain's complexity and the degree of our ignorance, let's look anyway at a few salient bits of knowledge. The human brain develops continuously in utero and continues the process of maturation for quite a number

---

* A staggering amount of information goes into the development of a human being. We all have twenty-three pairs of chromosomes (one set contributed from each parent) and each chromosome contains one enormously long DNA molecule. Estimates suggest that there is enough DNA in each of our cells to contain information for from ten thousand to fifty thousand different proteins.

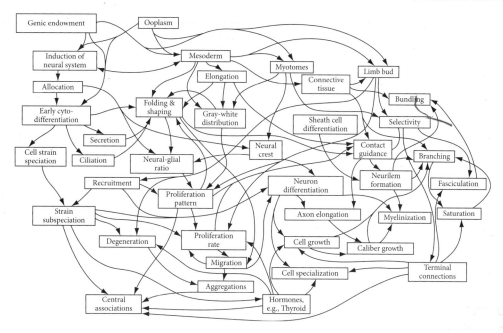

Figure 1.5. Causal Relations in Neurogenesis.

Note: Benjamin H. Willier, Paul A. Weiss, and Victor Hamburger, *Analysis of Development* (Philadelphia: W. B. Saunders, 1955), 392.

of years after birth. The total *number* of nerve cells is established during the first half of pregnancy.* But not so with all their interconnections, which continue to multiply during the first four years of life.[15] Glial cells, which continue to multiply in the brain and spinal cord for several years after birth, play an important role in making the so-called white matter, or myelin, material that provides electrical insulation for the long nerve fibers. In addition to aiding in the transmission of electrical impulses, myelin's presence or absence is probably quite important in the establishment of the myriad cell-to-cell connections built up between the cells of the brain. The increasing complexity of the interneuron network that develops during the first two years after birth provides impressive confirmation of something obvious to any casual observer of child development. Newborn infants have only the simplest physical skills. During their first three years, however, they learn to sit up, walk, run, talk, feed themselves, climb jungle gyms, and so on. The inside-the-brain correlate of all this is that cells of the central nervous system make new physical connections with one another, while simultaneously losing old ones. One theory in fact holds that the brain cells make more connections with one another than they actually end up using, and that employment of a particular neuronal pathway helps to establish its permanency, the less used connections eventually dissolving away.[16]

A central feature of brain development thus emerges. *The physical structure of the adult brain— its size, number of cells, and most importantly its neuronal pathways—establishes itself in intimate interaction with the environment of the developing individual.* Nutrition, exercise, physical contact with other humans, exposure to varying sorts of visual and cognitive stimuli, all these and more influence brain structure. As Dr. T. Wiesel stated in his Nobel Prize lecture, "such sensitivity of the nervous system to the effects of experience may

---

* Recent studies on adult birds suggest that nerve cells in adults may also increase in number.[14]

represent the fundamental mechanism by which the organism adapts to its environment during the period of growth and development."[17]

In addition to Wiesel's extensive work showing the role of postnatal experience in the development of the visual system, numerous other examples (some well defined, others merely suggestive) demonstrate the interdependence of body structure and environment. For instance, studies on the children of women who were pregnant during the Dutch famine of 1945 suggest that maternal starvation during the last third of gestation may slow the development of fat cells. The children born to these mothers were more likely than others to develop into thin adults and had fewer than average fat storage cells in their body. Furthermore, starvation during the first and second trimesters may affect the part of the brain, the hypothalamus, involved in regulating appetite. Children born of mothers starved during the first six months of pregnancy show a higher than average frequency of obesity because of overeating.[18] Hence a casual observation that "obesity runs in families" tells us little about genetic causes, for the caloric intake of the mother—an environmental rather than a genetic factor—could influence both the structure and the number of fat cells as well as the eating behavior of the child.

There are other examples. One-day-old infants show exact, prolonged segments of movement correlating precisely in time with the speech patterns and rhythm of the adults talking to them.[19] This type of observation could go a long way toward explaining the transmission of physical mannerisms characteristic of individual families or even speech patterns of entire cultures.[20] Consider the studies showing that infants in certain West Kenyan farming communities learned to sit, stand, and walk at an earlier age than did American children to whom they were compared; observations revealed that the African mothers deliberately, through the use of play, forms of swaddling and carrying, and directly imposed practice, taught their babies each of these skills, in contrast to their American counterparts. The conclusion: we can properly consider the development of motor skills—often thought of by development psychologists as genetically directed—only in the context of a child's physical and social environment.[21]

A further complexity emerges from these examples, all three of which illustrate the ways in which a particular body structure develops only in a particular context. If the first take-home lesson in thinking about complex human traits is that linear chainlike causal explanations (genes code for the number of fat cells which in turn determine an individual's tendency toward obesity) are simply wrong, then the second is that the alternative idea of "environmental determinism" is also an oversimplification. My examples provide insight into the fact that the word *environment* itself has multiple meanings and numerous levels of complexity. In the example of the mothers in the Dutch famine, I suggested that one needs to look in utero to identify some of the critically relevant components of the environment, in the example of the babies mimicking adult movements, "environment" appears in the form of non-conscious adult behavior patterns critically transmitted during early infancy; while in the third example, the West Kenyan versus American mothers, "environment" turns up as a conscious teaching process. In all three cases the environmental factors described have done far more than establish some part of a psychological predisposition. They have interacted with a growing body to change the numbers and types of cells within it as well as to alter their connections to one another.

Modern psychology books often list four different theories of gender development—biological determinist, psychoanalytic, social learning, and cognitive developmental—writing about them as if they were mutually exclusive.[22] Examples of biological/environmental interactions teach us that the four theories are really like nonparallel lines: at some point, either close by or distant, they must intersect with one another. By trying to simplify and limit the intricacy of thought about human behavioral development, we trap ourselves into thinking at only one level or another, solely at the level of biology or of social learning.

Environment is not only multi-tiered, it is also without time limits. It exerts, rather, a cumulative continuum of effects over an entire lifetime. Studies in the United States and abroad, for example, have shown that severe malnutrition in infancy can cause mental retardation in later life. When one recalls the extensive brain development occurring during early childhood, such a finding makes some sense. It turns out, however, that when a child experiencing severe infant malnutrition subsequently grows up in an enriched social environment, the potential damage to IQ does not appear. Only severely malnourished children who *in addition* remain in economically and socially impoverished situations suffer from mental retardation.[23] In other words, one cannot surmise the effects of a condition encountered at one point in development without knowledge of the situation at other times in an individual's life. Each of us has many histories: the genetic histories of our ancestors; the chance encounter of a particular egg bearing some assortment of genetic information with a particular sperm bearing some other set; the racial/social, economic, and psychological histories of our families; our sex, birth order, and role within the family; our interactions with myriad adults, children, places, and schools as we grow up. In short all the chance events, from an inspiring concert attended at the last minute to a sudden death or severe accident or illness, form part of our individual histories which cumulatively change with each passing year. It is the sum of these events that becomes part of what for convenience's sake we call environment.

It may seem that we have digressed from our discussion of male and female development. The sexes are, after all, genetically different; the environment cannot change the presence of a Y or a pair of X chromosomes. But before returning to the issue, let us sum up. We have seen that genes are a historical concept supplanted in the era of molecular biology by knowledge of genetic information encoded in DNA. In a functioning cell the information may translate into a protein with the help of other molecules and multimolecular structures. If we define a trait or phenotype at the level of the translated protein, and if we consider all those genes involved in regulating the rates of synthesis and breakdown of both the specific protein in question and proteins in general, we can roughly state that the genotype determines the phenotype. If instead we consider more complex traits, occurring at supracellular levels of biological organization, the relatively simple correlation between genotype and phenotype breaks down. Two geneticists most graphically summarized the point when they wrote, "the hopelessness of the task of understanding behavior from single analytic approaches can be compared to the hopelessness of seeking linguistic insights by a chemical analysis of a book!"[24] Finally, a proper understanding of brain development suggests that while genetic information plays a key role in the unfolding of many details of the brain's structure, extensive development of nervous connections occurs after birth, influenced profoundly by individual experience. The brain's final "wiring diagram" as so many writers like to call it, is not a printed circuit, stamped out in accordance with a great genetic blueprint. It resembles more the weaving of an untutored artisan who, starting out with a general plan in mind, modifies it in the course of his or her work, using the available material and dyes, while covering up or making creative use of mistakes in pattern.

Nature Constructs Gender: X's, Y's, and the Hormones of Sexual Development

It is commonly held that sex is determined at the moment of conception. Eggs fertilized by Y-chromosome-bearing sperm develop into boys, those by X-chromosome-bearing sperm into girls. Behind the nursery rhyme's sugar, spice, snails, and puppy-dog tails stand male and female genes. Or so one hears. In truth, the roles in sexual development of the X and Y chromosomes are poorly understood. Even those fetal events about which considerable information exists are described differently depending upon who writes the account; the story of the development in utero of male and female babies, fascinating in its own right, illustrates how deep cultural assumptions can condition the descriptive language used by scientists and in the process set limits on the scope of experimental exploration.

Consider the following real-life incidents:

1. An apparently normal boy baby has convulsions a few weeks after birth. Medical workups show that he has a disease that interferes with the adrenal glands' synthesis of the hormone cortisone. Further examination reveals that this "boy" has two X chromosomes, ovaries, oviducts, and uterus. In fact "he" is really a girl whose vaginal lips have fused to become a scrotum and whose clitoris has developed into a penis. Genital surgery, treatment for the adrenal malfunction, and a name change produce a child who eventually grows up, marries, and has children.[25]

2. A child born in a small village in the West Indies works at her mother's side learning the female roles of washing and cooking, only to find at puberty that her voice deepens, a beard grows, and her clitoris enlarges into a penis. Eventually he takes a wife and fathers children.[26]

Both cases exemplify the unhinging of sexual development, the separation of gonadal, hormonal, and behavioral states from each other and from the X and Y chromosomes. When, where, and how do such changes originate? Studies of these situations furnish insights into the intricacies of sexual development while simultaneously fueling controversy over the biological bases of gender-related behavior.

Until the sixth week of development, XX and XY embryos are anatomically identical. During this early period each develops an embryonic gonad dubbed the "indifferent gonad" because of its sameness in both XX and XY embryos. In similar fashion the other internal structures of both the male and female reproductive systems begin to form, so that by the first month and a half of embryonic development all the embryos, regardless of which sex chromosomes reside inside their cells, have a set of female (Müllerian) ducts as well as a set of male (Wolffian) ducts, see Figure 1.6. In XX embryos, the female ducts normally develop into the oviducts, uterus, cervix, and upper vagina, while in XY embryos the male ducts usually become the vas deferens, epididymis, and ejaculatory ducts. In other words, six weeks after fertilization all embryos are sexually bipotential, containing those parts needed to become either a male or a female. Although we have no idea which genes are involved in the process of reaching this early stage of sexual development, logically they must be present in both sexes.

So far, so good; now enter the Y chromosome. During the sixth week genetic information present on the Y becomes actively involved in promoting the synthesis of a protein called the H-Y antigen. Although the exact function of the antigen remains the subject of active research, it appears in humans to play some role in helping the tissues of the indifferent gonad to organize themselves into an embryonic testis.[27] The fetal testis contains recognizable sperm-producing tubules as well as the ability to synthesize hormones, two of which—testosterone and Müllerian Inhibiting Substance (MIS)—promote further events in the process of what has at this point clearly become male development.

Fetally synthesized testosterone, one of a group of chemically interrelated hormones called *androgens,* influences the male duct system to enter a period of active growth, while MIS, as its name suggests, ensures the degeneration of the still-present female duct system. Androgens and the chemically similar *estrogens* are not proteins but complex derivatives of the molecule cholesterol. The cell synthesizes them from a cholesterol base in an ordered series of steps, each governed by a different protein. Thus one or more sets of genes, coding for the proteins that catalyze each synthetic step, must be involved in the synthesis of one steroid hormone. These genetic messages are not located on the Y chromosome, being scattered instead on the X and one or more of the twenty-three pairs of non-sex chromosomes. In fact, as many as nineteen different genetic loci, not only on the X but on many different chromosomes, are known to be involved in the process of human sexual differentiation.[28] Although in males the Y must somehow involve itself with

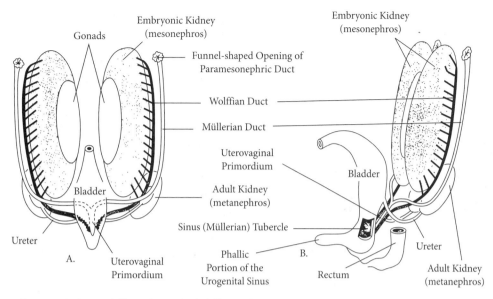

Figure 1.6. Internal Genitalia at the Indifferent Stage.

Note: Keith L. Moore, *The Developing Human: Clinically Oriented Embryology* (Philadelphia: W. B. Saunders, 1973), 209. *A.* is a sketch of a frontal view of the posterior abdominal wall of a seven-week embryo showing the two pairs of genital ducts present during the indifferent stage. *B.* is a lateral view of a nine-week fetus showing the sinus (Müllerian) tubercle on the posterior wall of the urogenital sinus.

the selective translation of some of this information, individuals of both sexes remain genetically bipotential with regard to their ability to make androgens and estrogens. Stated in other terms, males and females have identical road maps for sexual development, but the Y chromosome helps the six-week-old male embryo choose the first of many branches taken in pursuing the destination of male development.

By comparison with all we know about male development, the genetic basis of female differentiation remains obscure. The most commonly told tale is that the fetal ovary produces no special sex hormones but that any embryo lacking testosterone develops in a female direction. Under usual conditions an XX gonad begins by the twelfth week following fertilization to develop into an ovary. The male duct system degenerates while the female system differentiates into the internal organs of the reproductive system. The view that females develop from mammalian embryos deficient in male hormone seems, oddly enough, to have satisfied the scientific curiosity of embryologists for

some time, for it is the only account one finds in even the most up-to-date texts (see Figure 1.7). Yet cracks have started to appear in this unanimous facade.[29] A recent review article, for instance, points out that the XX gonad begins synthesizing large quantities of estrogen at about the same time that the XY gonad begins to make testosterone. Just what does all that estrogen do? The authors report:

> Embryogenesis normally takes place in a sea of hormones…derived from the placenta, the maternal circulation, the fetal adrenal glands, the fetal testis, and possibly from the fetal ovary itself.…*It is possible that ovarian hormones are involved in the growth and maturation of the internal genitalia of the female.*[30] [Emphasis added]

Clearly, in contrast to the body of work done on male development, the final word on the genetic control of female development has yet to be written. That it has not yet been fully researched is due both to technical difficulties[31] and to the willingness of researchers to accept at face value the idea

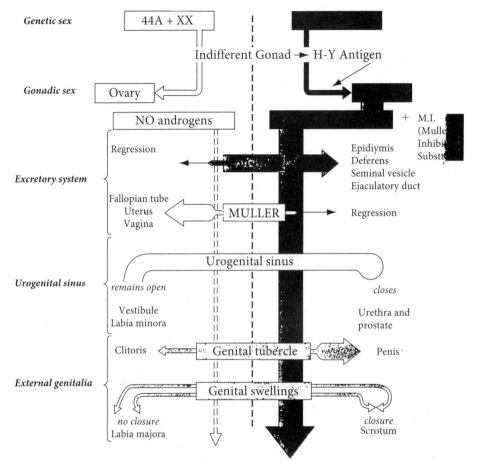

Figure 1.7. Textbook Accounts of Male and Female Embryonic Development.

Note: H. Tuchmann-Duplessis et al., *Illustrated Human Embryology*, vol. 2, trans. L. S. Hurley (New York: Springer-Verlag, 1972), 100.

of passive female development. Because it is in the nature of research in developmental biology to always look for underlying causes, failure to probe beyond the "testosterone equals male"—"absence of testosterone equals female" hypothesis is a lapse which is at first difficult to understand. If, however, one notes the pervasiveness throughout all layers of our culture of the notion of "female as lack,"[32] then one learns from this account that such rock-bottom cultural ideas can intrude unnoticed even into the scientist's laboratory.

So far I've offered an account of the embryonic growth of the internal parts of the reproductive system. During an overlapping time period,

however, the external genitalia also begin development. Until the eighth week of fetal life the external genitalia of the human embryo remain identical in both sexes. Figure 1.8 describes the process by which the bipotential structure called the genital tubercle develops into either a penis or a clitoris, while the mounds of tissue called labioscrotal swellings develop into either a scrotum or the large lips of the vagina. The hormone dihydrotestosterone, secreted during the eighth week of development by the fetal testis, influences the external genitalia to develop in a male direction. In XX fetuses the female structures become evident by twelve weeks. As in the case of the

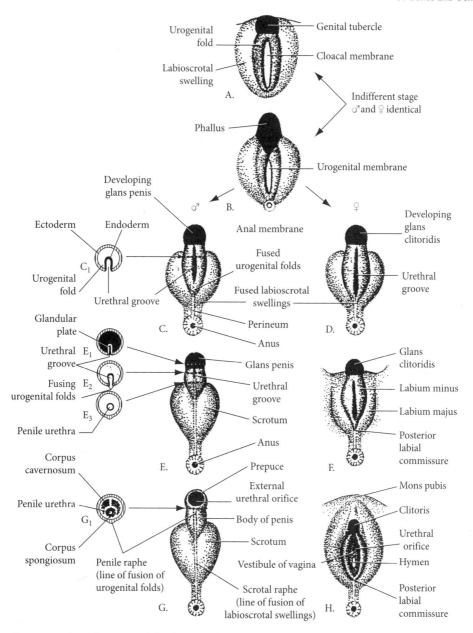

Figure 1.8. Development of the External Genitalia from the Indifferent Stage.

Note: Keith L. Moore, *The Developing Human*, 2d ed. (Philadelphia: W. B. Saunders, 1977), 219. Diagrams *A* and *B* illustrate the development of the external genitalia during the indifferent stage (four to seven weeks). *C, E,* and *G* show the stages in the development of male external genitalia at about nine, eleven, and twelve weeks, respectively. To the left are schematic transverse sections (C_1, E_1 to E_3, and G_1) through the developing penis illustrating the formation of the penile urethra. *D, F,* and *H* show stages in the development of female external genitalia at nine, eleven, and twelve weeks, respectively.

internal reproductive system, the possible role of estrogen, progesterone, or other hormones in the development of external genitalia remains largely unexplored.

Most of the time, sexual development comes off without a hitch. Yet we began this discussion with two examples in which some of the different processes became unglued. In the first, a child identified as a boy on the basis of its external genitalia turned out to have two X chromosomes, ovaries, and oviducts. The cause of the confusion: a genetically inherited disease called adrenogenital syndrome (AGS). Individuals suffering from this illness lack an enzyme (protein) that normally converts precursor molecules (called 17-hydroxy-progesterone) into cortisone.[33] As a result large quantities of this precursor, not normally present in an XX embryo because of its immediate change into cortisone, become converted instead into androgens. This happens *after* the degeneration of the internal system of male ducts, but *before* the final formation of the external sex organs. The resulting baby bears two X chromosomes, internal female organs, a clitoris so enlarged that it may be mistaken for a penis *(is a penis?)*, and labial folds that have fused to form an empty scrotum.

The converse example involves XY individuals unable to make dihydrotestosterone (DHT) during fetal development. This results in the birth of a child with female or ambiguous external genitalia, due to the missing DHT, but with male internal genitalia, because the synthesis of testosterone itself and of Müllerian Inhibiting Substance occurs normally (see Figure 1.7). At puberty, however, testosterone rather than DHT serves as the masculinizing agent, and induces in these children the belated development of the penis and scrotum. These individuals have male genes and gonads, a somewhat abnormal fetal hormonal sex, a female infant anatomical sex, and a male adult hormonal and anatomical sex!

Clearly our binary, either/or categories of male and female do not work when we look at these genetic defects. Not even the sex organs are categorical. At what point in its growth do we stop calling the genital tubercle a clitoris and start calling it a penis? How small does a penis have to be before we call it a clitoris? And how many more experiments must we undertake before people stop writing that "the Adam Principle…governs the differentiation of the genital anatomy, namely that to differentiate a male something must be added"?[34] In summarizing an account of male and female development one might just as easily highlight their similarities, their identical starting points and minor divergences, and even sing the praises of some imagined underlying Female Principle that governs all development unless interfered with by some external agent such as testosterone. As with so many of the issues discussed herein, the facts are there for all to see. Which ones are emphasized and how the tale is told, however, seems to depend not on some objective truth but on the attitudes, be they conscious or subconscious, of the raconteur.

The Biology of Gender Revisited

In 1981 "The Sexes" made the cover of *Newsweek*. The definitive-sounding subtitle, "How They Differ and Why," heralded what turned out to be a far from conclusive article. Following an opening quotation (from playwright August Strindberg) alleging different biological natures for men and women, the authors wrote:

> Research on the structure of the brain, on the effects of hormones, and in animal behavior, child psychology and anthropology is providing new scientific underpinnings for what August Strindberg and his ilk viscerally guessed: men and women *are* different.

The article, though, concluded with the following:

> Perhaps the most arresting implication of the research up to now is not that there are undeniable differences between males and females but that their differences are so small relative to the possibilities open to them.[35]

The take-home message is hard to fathom. Are males and females different or aren't they? The authors of the *Newsweek* article hedged their bets, and well they might, for reasons that lie deep in the nature of research on the biology of gender. Nothing could illustrate this more clearly than the current debate about the hormonal basis of gender identity.

At its heart the controversy centers on that hardy perennial, the nature-versus-nurture debate. On one side stand psychologist Dr. John Money and his associates, proponents of the idea that gender identity becomes fixed during the first three years of a child's life, depending primarily on the sex of rearing rather than on such details as the presence or absence of a Y chromosome, ovaries, or the like. On the opposite side, one finds physician and researcher Dr. Julianne Imperato-McGuinley and her co-workers. They assert that gender identity can remain flexible throughout childhood, but that the hormones of puberty fix it irrevocably. To them the sex of rearing may be less important than the sex hormones that appear during adolescence. To top it all off, each group has apparently compelling evidence to support its position.

Money has devoted a considerable portion of his career to examining and following up on children, such as those affected by adrenogenital syndrome, whose correct chromosomal sex was identified only months or years into childhood. He found that sex reassignment was easily effected if it occurred during the first three years of life, but that later changes were psychologically difficult if not impossible. A child raised as a boy until age twelve, for example, experienced deep distress when he developed breasts. Although the physical evidence of puberty suggested that he might be a girl, he was not swayed and opted to have a double mastectomy in order to clear up the confusion.[36] In general Money found that pairs of children matched for identity of physical development accepted opposite gender identities if they were raised as members of the opposite sex.

Imperato-McGuinley also studied sexually incongruous individuals, most of whom came from three rural villages in Santo Domingo. The people in her study had the above-mentioned genetically inherited deficiency for the androgen dihydrotestosterone. While all thirty-eight of those identified as DHT-deficient had ambiguous genitalia, eighteen were raised as females. At puberty, as their voices deepened, these "girls"

grew adult-sized penises and scrotums. The phenomenon, which would certainly surprise most North Americans, is common enough in these little towns that the villagers have coined a word, literally translated as "penis-at-twelve," to describe such children. Of the eighteen raised as girls, sixteen seem to have successfully assumed a male gender role, marrying and fathering children.

The Dominican research team also paid attention to the social aspects of being male or female in a small Santo-Domingan village. The roles set aside for each sex are strict, with males permitted a great deal more freedom and social life outside the home. "The girls are encouraged to stay with their mothers or play near the house....After 11 or 12 years of age the boys seek entertainment at the bars...the girls...stay home and help with the household chores....Fidelity is demanded from the women but not from the men."[37] Thus one could imagine that having the option of becoming a male might have its attractions to a young teenager raised as a female. This would especially be true if that female had abnormal genitalia and knew of the penis-at-twelve syndrome. The degree of conscious articulation of difference—the awareness of belonging to a third sex—among the DHT-deficient children raised as girls or among their parents is unclear. Imperato-McGuinley simply says they were unambiguously raised as girls. Unless one does not believe in subconsciously motivated behavior, however, it is a bit difficult to accept the claim that these children were raised just like any genitally normal girl.

Imperato-McGuinley and her co-workers drew two conclusions, both apparently at variance with Money's. First, "gender identity is not unalterably fixed in childhood but is continually evolving," and second, "when the sex of rearing is contrary to the testosterone-mediated biologic sex, the biologic sex prevails."[38] Their first conclusion is accurate only if one assumes that neither the parents nor the children raised as girls realized that they had the penis-at-twelve syndrome. If they did know, it is possible that the children were raised with the option of future maleness built into their psychological development. If this were the case, then these children do not necessarily provide data in conflict with Money's. On the other hand, Money's notion of irrevocable psychological fixation may itself be too rigidly stated. Humans, especially children, are full of surprises. And so it may be with the development of gender identity.

Ferreting out the meaning of the second conclusion is a bit more difficult. Imperato-McGuinley seems to believe that hormones can override extensive early psychological programming. Examination of the data and a literal reading of her words, however, reveals a second meaning. She writes that when the option is to choose the *testosterone-mediated* sex—that is, when a child raised as a girl has a chance to become a boy—then it makes this choice. The reasons for that choice *could,* of course, be entirely hormonal, but given that in these villages boys are freer and that these children look like boys, one can easily imagine a nonbiological mediation of choice. Both meanings appear, inseparably, in the data. The preferred interpretation is up to us, but we have only our sociopolitical instincts on which to lean in exercising our option. The hard facts permit no final judgment, for a key bit of information is missing: Are there biologically mediated situations under which children raised as *boys* would choose to become *girls,* even though the social setting permits males greater freedom? Without such a natural control one cannot unscramble the implications of Imperato-McGuinley's data.

Sex, then, is no simple matter. Most often all the components of biologic sex concur and an infant, identified at birth as either male or female, is raised accordingly. Cases in which biologic and assigned sexes differ reveal enormous psychological flexibility. Some children, perhaps even to the age of puberty, can cope with changing their sex, provided at least that the change agrees with their anatomy. But it is difficult for young people to handle a disagreement between their external anatomical sex and their assigned sex—not a particularly surprising observation. In all of the cases studied both by Money's and by Imperato-McGuinley's groups, either the assigned sex changed spontaneously to agree with the visible anatomy or doctors surgically altered the anatomy to bring it more into line with the assigned sex.

Whichever the direction of change, though, the human hallmark of enormous biological complexity and psychological flexibility shines through.

Conclusion: From Gene to Gender

We began this chapter by trying to figure out whether it makes any sense to talk about genes that control behavior. Let us conclude by stating that a "pure" biological explanation of anything as complex and unpredictable as human behavior would by its very nature be unequal to the task. Genetic information specifically encodes for the amino acid sequences of particular proteins. Complex traits, however, arise not simply by the accretion of a set of macromolecules; they form part of yet larger and more complex physical forms such as cells, tissues, and organs. To do so they must be present in the right amounts at the right time and be organized in the correct spatial configurations. All of this is subject to three influences: genetic regulatory information, intrusion from the external environment, and chance variations in development. In other words, referring to a genetic ability to perform math or music, or to a biological tendency toward aggressive behaviour obscures rather than informs. To understand human development we need to know a great deal more about how the environment affects physical growth and patterns, and how individual variation including genetic variation plays into each different life history to produce adults with different competencies and potentials.

The discussion of sexual development illustrates two points: the first, is that a scientist's cultural vision can limit his or her scientific vision. What research has offered us to date under the rubic of "sexual development" is an analytical account of *male* development. The absence of the second sex seems to have gone unnoticed in theories of sexual differentiation. The second point is that children show a great deal of (albeit not total) flexibility in the development of a gender self-concept. Studies of fetal development, however, as well as analyses of the differing reproductive physiologies of adult males and females raise a series of related but as yet unresolved questions. Some scientists hold, for instance, that male/female differences in behavior stem from different hormonal environments encountered in utero. Indeed, in other animals embryonic exposure to testosterone sometimes changes the physical structure of the brain. But even if human behavior were *unaffected* by fetal androgens, surely the vast differences in hormone levels circulating in the bloodstreams of male and female adults could influence our behavior. Or so it is said.

Notes

1. Lionel Tiger, "The Possible Biological Origins of Sexual Discrimination," *Impact of Science* on Society 20(1970): 37.
2. Maya Pines, "Behavior and Heredity: Links for Specific Traits Are Growing Stronger," New *York Times,* 29 June 1982, section C.
3. S. Mednick, W. F. Gabrielli, and B. Hutchings, "Genetic Influences in Criminal Convictions," *Science* 224(1984): 891–93.
4. John Maddox, "Genetics and Heritable I.Q.," *Nature* 309(1984): 579, T. W. Teasdale and D. R. Owen, "Heredity and Familial Environment in Intelligence and Educational Level—A Sibling Study," *Nature* 309(1984): 620–22.
5. Richard C. Lewontin, Steven Rose, and Leon Kamin, *Not in Our Genes* (New York: Random House, 1984).
6. Philip Kitcher, "Genes," *British Journal of the Philosophy of Science* 33(1982): 337–59.
7. G. Ledyard Stebbins, "Modal Themes: A New Framework for Evolutionary Syntheses," in *Perspectives on Evolution,* ed. R. Milkman (Sunderland, Mass.: Sinauer, 1982).
8. Kitcher, "Genes."
9. Stebbins, "Modal Themes," 4.
10. Stanley Robbins and R. S. Cotran, *Pathologic Basis of Disease* (Philadelpia: W.B. Saunders, 1979).
11. R. D. Alexander, *Darwinism and Human Affairs* [Seattle: University of Washington Press, 1980).
12. E. O. Wilson, "Human Decency is Animal," *New York Times Magazine,* 12 Oct. 1975.
13. Paul Weiss, "The Living System: Determinism Stratified," in *Beyond Reductionism: The Altbach Symposium,* ed. A. Koestler and J. R. Smithies (Boston: 1969).
14. J. A. Paton and F. N. Nottebohm, "Neurons Generated in the Adult Brain are Recruited into Functional Circuits," *Science* 225(1984): 1046–48.
15. Roger Lewin, "Nutrition and Brain Growth," in *Child Alive,* ed. R. Lewin (New York: Anchor Books, 1975).
16. Dale Purves and J. W. Lichtman, "Elimination of Synapses in the Developing Nervous System," *Science* 210(1980): 153–57.
17. T. N. Wiesel, "Postnatal Development of the Visual Cortex and the Influence of Environment," *Nature* 299(1982): 592.
18. G. Ravelli, Z. Stein, and M. Susser, "Obesity in Young Men after Famine Exposure in Utero and Early Infancy," *New England Journal of Medicine* 295(1976): 349–53. See also J. C. Somogyi and H. Haenel, eds., *Nutrition in Early Childhood and its Effects in Later Life* (Basel: S. Karger, 1982).
19. W. S. Condon and L. W. Sander, "Neonate Movement is Synchronized with Adult Speech: Interactional Participation and Language Acquisition," *Science* 183(1974): 99–101.
20. W. S. Condon and L. W. Sander, "Synchrony Demonstrated between Movements of the Neonate and Adult Speech," *Child Development* 45(1974): 456–62.
21. C. M. Super, "Environmental Effects on Motor Development: The Case of 'African Infant Precocity,'" *Developmental and Medical Child Neurology* 18(1976): 561–67.
22. I. Frieze et al., Women *and Sex Roles: A Social Psychological Perspective* (New York: Norton, 1978).
23. S. A. Richardson, "The Relation of Severe Malnutrition in Infancy to the Intelligence of School Children with Differing Life Histories," *Pediatric Research* 10(1976): 57–61.
24. G. S. Omenn and A. G. Motulsky, "Biochemical Genetics and the Evolution of Human Behavior," in *Genetics, Environment and Behavior: Implications for Educational Policy,* ed. L. Ehrmann, G. S. Omenn, and E. Caspari (New York: Academic, 1972), 131.
25. A. Ehrhardt and H. Meyer-Bahlburg, "Effects of Prenatal Sex Hormones on Gender-Related Behavior," *Science* 211(1981): 1312–18.
26. R. Rubin, J. Reinsich, and R. Haskett, "Postnatal Gonadal Steroid Effects on Human Behavior," *Science* 211(1981): 1318–24.
27. U. Muller and E. Urban, "Reaggregation of Rat Gonadal Cells in *vitro:* Experiments on the Function of H-Y Antigen," *Cytogenetics and*

Cellular Genetics 31(1981):104–7; and U. Muller et al., "Ovarian Cells Participate in the Formation of Tubular Structures in Mouse/Rat Heterosexual Gonadal Co-Cultures," *Differentiation* 22(1982): 136–38.

28. J. D. Wilson et al., "Recent Studies on the Endocrine Control of Male Phenotypic Development," in *Sexual Differentiation: Basic and Clinical Aspects,* ed. M. Serio et al. (New York: Raven, 1984).

29. B. H. Shapiro et al., "Neonatal Progesterone and Feminine Sexual Development," *Nature* 264(1976): 795–96.

30. Wilson, George, and Griffin, "The Hormonal Control of Sexual Development," 1283.

31. Ibid.

32. Simone de Beauvoir, *The Second Sex* (New York: Knopf, 1952).

33. Figure 1.9 shows the relationship of cortisone to testosterone/cholesterol and estrogen.

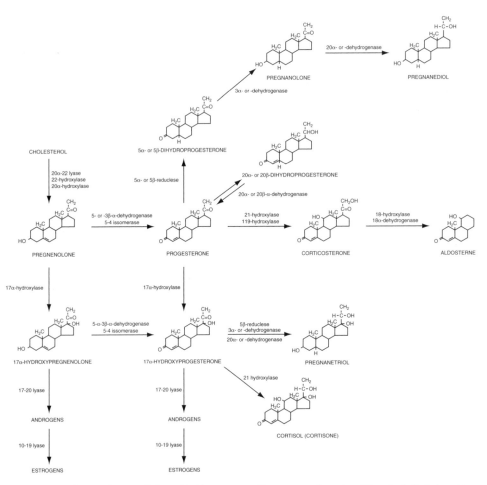

Figure 1.9. Biosynthesis of Steroid Hormones: Demonstrating the Chemical Relationship between Cholesterol, Progesterone, Cortisone, and the Estrogens and Androgens.

Note: Harvey Leder, "Essentials of Steroid Structure, Nomenclature Reactions, Biosynthesis and Measurements," in *Neuroendocrinology of Reproduction*, ed. Norman T. Adler (New York: Plenum, 1981), 54–55. Reprinted by permission.

34. John Money, *Love and Lovesickness* (Baltimore: Johns Hopkins University Press, 1970), 5.

35. David Gelman et al., "Just How the Sexes Differ," *Newsweek*, 18 May 1981.

36. John Money and Anke A. Ehrhardt, *Man and Woman, Boy and Girl: Differentiation and Dimorphism of Gender Identity from Conception to Maturity* (Baltimore: Johns Hopkins University Press, 1972).

37. Julianne Imperato-McGuinley et al., "Steroid 5-Alpha-Reductase Deficiency in Man: An Inherited Form of Male Pseudohermaphroditism," *Science* 186(1974): 1213–15. See also Julianne Imperato-McGuinley et al., "Androgens and the Evolution of Male-Gender Identity among Male Pseudohermaphrodites with a 5-Alpha-Reductase Deficiency," *New England Journal of Medicine* 300 (1979): 1236–37, and Letters in answer to Imperato-McGuinley et al., *New England Journal of Medicine* 301(1979): 839–40.

38. Imperato-McGuinley et al., "Androgens and the Evolution of Male-Gender Identity," 1235–36.

PART

2

Cultural Constructions of Gender

Biological evidence helps explain the ubiquity of gender difference and gender inequality, but social scientific evidence modifies both the universality and the inevitability implicit in biological claims. Cross-cultural research suggests that gender and sexuality are far more fluid, far more variable, than biological models would have predicted. If biological sex alone produced observed sex differences, Margaret Mead asked in the 1920s and 1930s, why did it produce such *different* definitions of masculinity and femininity in different cultures? In her path-breaking study, *Sex and Temperament in Three Primitive Societies*, Mead began an anthropological tradition of exploring and often celebrating the dramatically rich and varied cultural constructions of gender.

Anthropologists are more likely to locate the origins of gender difference and gender inequality in a sex-based division of labor, the near-universality of and the variations in the ways in which societies organize the basic provision and distribution of material goods. They've found that when women's and men's spheres are most distinctly divided—where women and men do different things in different places—women's status tends to be lower than when men and women share both work and workplaces.

Some researchers have explored the function of various cultural rituals and representations in creating the symbolic justification for gender differences and inequality based on this sex-based division of labor. For example, Gilbert Herdt describes a variety of "coming out" processes in a variety of cultures, thus demonstrating (1) the connections between sexual identity and gender identity and (2) the dramatic variation among those identities. And Karen Paige and Jeffrey Paige discuss several reproductive rituals and find that elaborate rituals often signal shifts in the micropolitical arrangements between women and men in that culture. Such rituals not only construct identity but also difference—and thus inequality.

Men as Women and Women as Men: Disrupting Gender

JUDITH LORBER

This thing here, you call this a person? There is no such thing as a person who is half male half female.

Meira Weiss forthcoming

The French writer Colette felt that she was a "mental hermaphrodite" but had "a sturdy and perfectly female body" (Lydon 1991, 28). When she offered to travel with a noted womanizer, he said that he traveled only with women: "Thus when Damien declares that he travels only with women, implying that a woman is what Colette is not, the only linguistically possible conclusion is that she must be a man. But she and we know this not to be the case, despite her willingness to admit to a certain 'virility.' What then, can Colette legitimately call herself?" (29).[1] Cool and rational androgynous women are social men, one step removed from the "mannish lesbian" (Newton 1984). Men who use a highly emotionally charged vocabulary may be judged romantic geniuses, but their masculinity may be somewhat suspect, as was Byron's (Battersby 1989).

The history of a nineteenth-century French hermaphrodite illustrates the impossibility of living socially as both a woman and a man even if it is physiologically possible (Butler 1990, 93–106). Herculine Barbin, who was raised in convents as a girl, after puberty, fell in love with a young woman and had sexual relations with her. At the age of twenty-two, Herculine (usually called Alexina) confessed the homosexuality to a bishop, and after examination by two doctors, was legally recategorized as a man and given a man's name. But Herculine's genitals, as described in two doctors'

reports, were ambiguous: a one-and-a half-inch long penis, partly descended testicles, and a urethral opening (Foucault 1980, 125–28). One doctor reasoned as follows:

> Is Alexina a woman? She has a vulva, labia majora, and a feminine urethra, independent of a sort of imperforate penis, which might be a monstrously developed clitoris. She has a vagina…. These are completely feminine attributes. Yet, but Alexina has never menstruated; the whole outer part of her body is that of a man, and my explorations do not enable me to find a womb. Her tastes, her inclinations, draw her toward women. At night she has voluptuous sensations that are followed by a discharge of sperm; her linen is stained and starched with it. Finally, to sum up the matter, ovoid bodies and spermatic cords are found by touch in a divided scrotum. These are the real proofs of sex…. Alexina is a man, hermaphroditic, no doubt, but with an obvious predominance of masculine sexual characteristics. (127–28)

But Barbin, now called Abel, did not feel he was fully a man socially because he did not think any woman would marry him, and at the age of thirty he ended a "double and bizarre existence" via suicide. The doctor who performed the autopsy felt that the external genitalia could just as well have been classified as female, and that, with a penis-clitoris capable of erection and a vagina, Barbin was physiologically capable of bisexuality (128–44). But there was no social status of man-woman.

What would have become of Herculine Barbin one hundred years later? Surgery to remove the

---

Barbin, Herculine (1980). *Herculine Barbin: Being the Recently Discovered Memoirs of a Nineteenth-century French Hermaphrodite.* introd. Michel Foucault, trans. Richard McDougall. New York: Pantheon Books.

testicles, enlarge the vagina, and make the penis smaller? Then hormones to produce breasts and reduce body hair? Or closure of the vaginal opening, release of the testes, cosmetic surgery to enlarge the penis, and administration of testosterone? Having been brought up as a girl, but loving a woman, would Barbin have identified as a "man," a "lesbian," or a "bisexual"? Would the woman who loved him as a woman accept him as a husband? Without surgery or gender reassignment, would Herculine and Sara have been accepted as a lesbian couple today? Without surgery, but with gender reassignment, would Abel and Sara have been accepted as a heterosexual couple? Would Barbin have used a gender-neutral name, dressed in a gender-neutral way? What sex would be on her or his official documents? What kind of work would he or she have done?[2]

One possibility was documented in 1937. A hermaphrodite named Emma, who had a penis-like clitoris as well as a vagina, was raised as a girl. Emma had sexual relationships with a number of girls (heterosexual sex), married a man with whom she also had heterosexual sex, but continued to have women lovers (Fausto-Sterling 1993). She refused to have vaginal closure and live as a man because it would have meant a divorce and having to go to work. Emma was quite content to be a physiological bisexual, possibly because her gender identity was clearly that of a woman.

Anne Fausto-Sterling says that "no classification scheme could more than suggest the variety of sexual anatomy encountered in clinical practice" (1993). In 1992, a thirty-year-old Ethiopian Israeli whose social identity was a man was discovered at his Army physical to have a very small penis and a very small vagina. Exploratory surgery revealed vestigial ovaries and vestigial testicles, a uterus, and fallopian tubes. He was XY, but when he was classified a male at birth it was on the basis of how the external genitalia looked, and the penis took precedence. Because he had been brought up as a man and wanted to have this identity supported physiologically, his penis was enlarged and reconstructed, and the vagina was closed and made into a scrotum.

Testosterone was administered to increase his sexual desire for women.[3]

"Penis and Eggs"

When physiological anomalies occur today in places with sophisticated medical technology, the diagnosis, sex assignment, and surgical reconstruction of the genitalia are done as quickly as possible in order to minimize the intense uncertainty that a genderless child produces in our society (Kessler 1990). Other cultures, however, are more accepting of sex and gender ambiguity.

In the Dominican Republic, there has been a genetic phenomenon in which children who looked female at birth and were brought up as girls produced male hormones at puberty and virilized. Their genitalia masculinized, their voices deepened, and they developed a male physical appearance (Imperato-McGinley et al. 1974, 1979). They are called *guevedoces*. (penis at 12) or *machihembra* (first woman, then man) or *guevotes* (penis and eggs). According to one set of reports, sixteen of nineteen who were raised as girls gradually changed to men's social roles—working outside the home, marrying, and becoming heads of households (Imperato-McGinley et al. 1979). One, now elderly, who emigrated to the United States, felt like a man, but under family pressure lived as a woman. One, still in the Dominican Republic, had married as a woman at sixteen, had been deserted after a year, continued to live as a woman, and wanted surgery to be a "normal" woman. Not all those who lived as men had fully functioning genitalia, and all were sterile.

The physicians who studied thirty three of these male pseudohermaphrodites (biologically male with ambiguous-appearing genitalia at birth) claim that the nineteen who decided without medical intervention that they would adopt men's identities and social roles despite having been raised as girls "appear to challenge both the theory of the immutability of gender identity after three or four years of age and the sex of rearing as the major factor in determining male-gender identity" (Imperato-McGinley et al. 1979, 1236). Their report stresses the effects of the hormonal input and secondary male sex characteristics at puberty, despite the mixture of reactions and gradualness of the gender changeover.

Another physician (Baker 1980) questions whether the pseudohermaphrodites were reared unambiguously as girls, given their somewhat abnormal genitalia at birth, and an anthropologist (Herdt 1990) claims that culturally, the community recognized a third sex category, since they had names for it. Although the medical researchers described the parents' reactions during the course of the virilization as "amazement, confusion, and finally, acceptance rather than hostility" (Imperato-McGinley et al. 1979, 1235–36), their interviews with the pseudohermaphrodites revealed that as children, they had always suffered embarrassment because of their genitalia, and they worried about future harassment whether they chose to live as women or as men. That is, they were never unambiguously girls socially, and their appearance and sterility undercut their claims to be men. Nonetheless, most chose to live as men. Virilization was not total, but it provided the opportunity for the choice of the more attractive social role.[4] According to the medical researchers: "In a domestic setting, the women take care of the household activities, while the affected subjects work as farmers, miners or woodsmen, as do the normal males in the town. They enjoy their role as head of the household" (Imperato-McGinley et al. 1979, 1234).

In Papua New Guinea, where the same recessive genetic condition and marriage to close relatives produces similar male pseudohermaphrodites, the culture does have an intergender category (*kwolu-aatmwol*). Many of these children were identified by experienced midwives at birth and reared anticipatorily as boys (Herdt 1990; Herdt and Davidson 1988). Although the *kwolu-aatmwols* went through boys' rituals as they grew up, their adult status as men was incomplete ritually, and therefore socially, because they were sterile and also because they were embarrassed by the small size of their penises. They rarely allowed themselves to be fellated by adolescent boys, a mark of honor for adult men, although some, as teenagers, in an effort to become more masculine, frequently fellated older men. In their behavior and attitudes, they were masculine. Their identity as adult men was stigmatized, however, because

they did not participate in what in Western societies would be homosexual (and stigmatized) sex practices, but in that culture made them fully men (Herdt 1981).

The pseudohermaphrodites who were reared as girls, either because they were not identified or their genital anomalies were hidden, did not switch to living as men when they virilized. Rather, they tried very hard to live as women, but were rejected by the men they married. Only at that point did they switch to men's dress, but they were even more ostracized socially, since they did not undergo any men's rituals. According to Gilbert Herdt and Julian Davidson: "Once exposed, they had 'no place to hide and no public in which to continue to pose as 'female.' It was only this that precipitated gender role change. Yet this is not change to the male role, because the natives know the subjects are not male; rather they changed from sex-assigned female to turnim-men, male-identified kwolu-aatmwol" (1988, 53).

Thus, neither childhood socialization nor pubescent virilization nor individual preferences was definitive in the adult gender placement of these male pseudohermaphrodites. Their assigned status was problematic men; away from their home villages, they could pass as more or less normal men. One was married, but to a prostitute; he had been "ostentatiously masculine" as an adolescent, was a good provider, and was known as "a fearless womanizer" (Herdt and Davidson 1988).

Switching Genders

Transsexuals have normal genitalia, but identify with the members of the opposite gender. Since there is no mixed or intermediate gender for people with male genitalia who want to live as women or people with female genitalia who want to live as men, transsexuals end up surgically altering their genitalia to fit their gender identity. They also undergo hormone treatment to alter their body shape and hair distribution and to develop secondary sex characteristics, such as breasts or beards. Transsexuals do not change their sex completely (Stoller 1985, 163). Their chromosomes remain the same, and no man-to-woman transsexual has a uterus implant, nor do any women-to-men transsexuals produce sperm. They change gender; thus, the accurate terms are *man-to-woman* and *woman-to-man*, not *male-to-female* and *female-to-male*.

Discussing only men-to-women transsexuals, Richard Docter sees the process as one in which more and more frequent cross-dressing reinforces the desire to completely switch genders:

> The cross-gender identity seems to grow stronger with practice and with social reinforcements of the pseudowoman. In unusual cases, the end result is a kind of revolution within the self system. The balance of power shifts in favor of the cross-gender identity with consequent disorganization and conflict within the self system. One result can be a quest to resolve the tension through sexual reassignment procedures or hormonal feminization. (1988, 3)

Transsexuals, however, have also indicated a sense from an early age of being in the wrong body (Morris 1975). Sexologists and psychiatrists have debated whether this anomalous gender identity is the result of biology, parenting, or retrospective reconstruction.[5]

The social task for transsexuals is to construct a gender identity without an appropriately gendered biography.[6] To create a feminized self, men-to-women transsexuals use the male transvestite's "strategies and rituals" of passing as a woman—clothing, makeup, hair styling, manicures, gestures, ways of walking, voice pitch, and "the more subtle gestures such as the difference in ways men and women smoke cigarettes" and the vocabulary women use (Bolin 1988, 131–41). Creating a new gender identity means creating a paper trail of bank, social security, educational, and job history records; drivers' licenses, passports, and credit cards all have to be changed once the new name becomes legal (pp. 145–46). Then significant others have to be persuaded to act their parts, too. Discussing men-to-women transsexuals, Anne Bolin notes:

> The family is the source of transsexuals' birth and nurturance as males and symbolically can be a source of their birth and nurturance as females. Thus, when their families accept them as females,

refer to them by their female names, and use feminine gender references, it is a profound event in the transsexuals' lives, one in which their gender identity as females is given a retroactive credence.... The family is a significant battleground on which a symbolic identity war is waged.... Because an individual can only be a son or daughter [in Western societies], conferral of daughterhood by a mother is a statement of the death of a son. (1988, 94)

The final rite of passage is not only passing as a visibly and legally identifiable gendered person with a bona fide kinship status but passing as a *sexual* person. For Bolin's men-to-women transsexuals, "the most desirable condition for the first passing adventure is at night with a 'genetic girlfriend' in a heterosexual bar" (p. 140).

Some transsexuals become gay or lesbian. In Anne Bolin's study population of seventeen men-to-women transsexuals, only one was exclusively heterosexual in orientation (1988, Fig. 1, 62). Nine were bisexual, and six were exclusively lesbian, including two transsexuals who held a wedding ceremony in a gay church.[7] Justifying the identification as lesbian by a preoperative man-to-woman transsexual who had extensive hormone therapy and had developed female secondary sexual characteristics, Deborah Heller Feinbloom and her co-authors argue that someone "living full-time in a female role must be called a woman, albeit a woman with male genitalia (and without female genitalia)," although potential lovers might not agree (1976, 69).[8] If genitalia, sexuality, and gender identity are seen as a package, then it is paradoxical for someone to change their anatomy in order to make love with someone they could easily have had a sexual relationship with "normally." But gender identity (being a member of a group, women or men) and gender status (living the life of a woman or a man) are quite distinct from sexual desire for a woman or man. It is Western culture's preoccupation with genitalia as the markers of both sexuality and gender and the concept of these social statuses as fixed for life that produces the problem and the surgical solution for those who cannot tolerate the personal ambiguities Western cultures deny.[9]

Gender Masquerades

Transvestites change genders by cross-dressing, masquerading as a person of a different gender for erotic, pragmatic, or rebellious reasons. Since they can put on and take off gender by changing clothes, they disrupt the conventional conflation of sex, sexuality, and gender in Western cultures much more than transsexuals do.

François Timoléon de Choisy was a seventeenth-century courtier, historian, ambassador, and priest who was "indefatigably heterosexual" but a constant cross-dresser. The Abbé de Choisy married women twice, once as a woman, once as a man, and both spouses had children by him. He survived the turmoil of gender ambiguity by going to live in another community or country when the censure got too vociferous (Garber 1992, 255–59). The Chevalier (sometimes Chevalière) d'Eon de Beaumont, a famous cross-dresser who lived in the eighteenth century, seems to have been celibate. Because D'Eon did not have any sexual relationships, English and French bookmakers took serious bets on whether d'Eon was a man or a woman. Physically, he was a male, according to his birth and death certificates, and he lived forty-nine years as a man (259–66). He also lived thirty-four years as a woman, many of them with a woman companion who "was astounded to learn that she was a man" (265). Garber asks: "Does the fact that he was born a male infant and died 'with the male organs perfectly formed' mean that he was, in the years between, a man? A 'very man'" (255)? A man in what sense—physical, sexual, or gendered?

Some men who pass as women and women who pass as men by cross-dressing say they do so because they want privileges or opportunities the other gender has, but they may also be fighting to alter their society's expectations for their own gender. One of her biographers says of George Sand:

> While still a child she lost her father, tried to fill his place with a mother whom she adored, and, consequently, developed a masculine attitude strengthened by the boyish upbringing which she received at the hands of a somewhat eccentric tutor who encouraged her to wear a man's clothes.... For the rest of her life she strove, unconsciously, to recreate the free paradise of her childhood, with the result that she could never submit to a master.... Impatient of all masculine authority, she fought a battle for the emancipation of women, and sought to win for them the right to dispose freely of their bodies and their hearts. (Maurois 1955, 13)[10]

Natalie Davis calls these defiers of the social order disorderly women. Their outrage and ridicule produce a double message; they ask for a restoration of the social order purified of excesses of gender disadvantage, and their own gender inversion also suggests possibilities for change (1975, 124–51).[11]

During the English Renaissance, open cross-dressing on the street and in the theater defied accepted gender categories.[12] In early modern England, the state enforced class and gender boundaries through sumptuary laws that dictated who could wear certain colors, fabrics, and furs. Cross-dressing and wearing clothes "above one's station" (servants and masters trading places, also a theatrical convention) thus were important symbolic subverters of social hierarchies at a time of changing modes of production and a rising middle class (Howard 1988). Since seventeenth-century cross-dressing up-ended concepts of appropriate sexuality, the fashion was accused of feminizing men and masculinizing women: "When women took men's clothes, they symbolically left their subordinate positions. They became masterless women, and this threatened overthrow of hierarchy was discursively read as the eruption of uncontrolled sexuality" (Howard 1988, 424).

The way the gender order got critiqued and then restored can be seen in a famous Renaissance play about a cross-dressing character called the "roaring girl." The Roaring Girl, by Thomas Middleton and Thomas Dekker, written in 1608–1611, was based on a real-life woman, Mary Frith, who dressed in men's clothes and was "notorious as a bully, whore, bawd, pickpurse, fortune-teller, receiver [of stolen goods], and forger" (Bullen 1935, 4). She also smoked and drank like a man and was in prison for a time. She lived to the age of seventy four. In Middleton and Dekker's play, this roaring girl, called Moll Cutpurse, becomes a model of morality. She remains chaste, and thus free of men sexually and economically, unlike most poor women, as she herself points out:

> Distressed needlewomen and trade-fallen wives,
>   Fish that must needs bite or themselves be bitten,
>   Such hungry things as these may soon be took
>   With a worm fastened on a golden hook. (III, i, 96–97)

Her cross-dressing allows her to observe and question the ways of thieves and pickpockets not to learn to be a criminal but to protect herself. She can protect any man who marries her:

> You may pass where you list, through crowd most thick,
>   And come off bravely with your purse unpick'd.
>   You do not know the benefits I bring with me;
>   No cheat dares work upon you with thumb or knife,
>   While you've a roaring girl to your son's wife. (V, ii, 159–63)

But she feels she is too independent to be a traditional wife:

> I have no humour to marry; I love to lie a' both sides a' the bed myself: and again, a' th' other side, a wife, you know, ought to be obedient, but I fear me I am too headstrong to obey; therefore I'll ne'er go about it. (II, ii, 37–41)

Her other reason for not marrying is that men cheat, lie, and treat women badly. If they changed, "next day following I'll be married," to which another character in the play responds: "This sounds like doomsday" (V, ii, 226–27), not likely to happen soon.

Despite her gloomy views on men and marriage, Moll helps a young couple marry by pretending to be wooed by the man. His father, who has withheld his consent for his son's original choice, is so outraged that the son is thinking of marrying Moll Cutpurse that he willingly consents to his son's marriage to the woman he had loved all along. Thus, rather poignantly, Moll's independence and street smarts are invidious traits when compared to those of a "good woman." Her cross-dressing is not a defiance of the gender order, but rather places her outside it:

> 'tis woman more than man,
>   Man more than woman; and, which to none can hap
>   The sun gives her two shadows to one shape;
>   Nay, more, let this strange thing walk, stand, or sit,
>   No blazing star draws more eyes after it. (I, i, 251–55)

Moll Cutpurse's social isolation means that the gender order does not have to change to incorporate her independence as a woman: "a politics of despair…affirms a seemingly inevitable exclusion of marginal genders from the territory of the natural and the real" (Butler 1990, 146).

Affirming Gender

In most societies with only two gender statuses—"women" and "men"—those who live in the status not meant for them usually do not challenge the social institution of gender. In many ways, they reinforce it. Joan of Arc, says Marina Warner (1982) in discussing her transvestism, "needed a framework of virtue, and so she borrowed the apparel of men, who held a monopoly on virtue, on reason and courage, while eschewing the weakness of women, who were allotted to the negative pole, where virtue meant meekness and humility, and nature meant carnality" (147). A masculine woman may be an abomination to tradition, but from a feminist point of view, she is not a successful rebel, for she reinforces dominant men's standards of the good: "The male trappings were used as armor—defensive and aggressive. It…attacked men by aping their appearance in order to usurp their functions. On the personal level, it defied men and declared them useless; on the social level, it affirmed male supremacy, by needing to borrow the appurtenances to assert personal needs and desires...; men remain the touchstone and equality a process of imitation" (Warner 1982, 155).[13]

Joan of Arc said she donned armor not to pass as a man, but to be beyond sexuality, beyond gender. She called herself *pucelle*, a maid, but socially, she was neither woman nor man. She was an "ideal androgyne": "She could thereby transcend her sex; she could set herself apart and usurp the privileges of the male and his claims to superiority. At the same time, by never pretending to be other than a woman and a maid, she was usurping a man's function but shaking off the trammels of his sex altogether to occupy a different, third order, neither male nor female, but unearthly, like the angels" (Warner 1982, 145–46).

When Joan was on trial, she was denuded of her knightly armor and accused of female carnality, and then she was burned at the stake—as a woman and a witch. Twenty-five years later, at her rehabilitation trial, and in 1920, when she was declared a saint, she was presented as a sexless virgin, amenorrheic and possibly anorectic.

As a heroine today, Joan of Arc is more likely to be a symbolic Amazon, a woman warrior, than an ideal androgyne, sexless and saintly. The ambiguity of her gender representation was corroborated by one of the first women to enter West Point to be trained with men as an army officer. On her first day in the dining hall, Carol Barkalow "was startled to find among the depictions of history's greatest warriors the muralist's interpretation of Joan of Arc. There she stood in silver armor, alongside Richard the Lion Hearted and William the Conqueror, sword uplifted in one hand, helmet clasped in the other, red hair falling to her shoulders, with six knights kneeling in homage at her feet" (1990, 27). As Barkalow found later, the warrior maid had set little precedent for the acceptance of women as military leaders. The mixed-gender message of the portrait was prescient, for the main problem at West Point seemed to be one of categorization—women army officers were suspect as women when they looked and acted too much like men, but they were a puzzlement as soldiers when they looked and acted like women.

Other Genders

There are non-Western societies that have third and fourth genders that link genitalia, sexual orientation, and gender status in ways quite different from Western cultures. These statuses demonstrate how physical sex, sexuality, and gender interweave, but are separate elements conferring different levels of prestige and stigma.

The Native America berdache is an institutionalized cross-gendered role that legitimates males doing women's work. The berdache can also be a sacred role, and if a boy's dreaming indicates a pull toward the berdache status, parents would not think of dissenting. Although it would seem logical that societies that put a high emphasis on aggressive masculinity, like the Plains Indians, would offer the berdache status as a legitimate way out for boys reluctant to engage in violent play and warfare, berdaches do not occur in all warlike tribes and do occur in some that are not warlike (Williams 1986, pp. 47–49).[14]

Berdaches educate children, sing and dance at tribal events, tend the ill, carry provisions for war parties, and have special ritual functions (Whitehead 1981, 89; Williams 1986, 54–61). Among the Navahos, berdaches not only do women's craft work, but also farm and raise sheep, which are ordinarily men's work: "Beyond this, because they are believed to be lucky in amassing wealth they usually act as the head of their family and have control of the disposal of all the family's property" (Williams 1986, 61).

Berdaches are legitimately homosexual:

Homosexual behavior may occur between non-berdache males, but the cultures emphasize the berdache as the usual person a man would go to for male sex. With the role thus institutionalized, the berdache serves the sexual needs of many men without competing against the institution of heterosexual marriage. Men are not required to make a choice between being heterosexual or being homosexual, since they can accommodate both desires. Nevertheless, for that minority of men who do wish to make such a choice, a number of cultures allow them the option of becoming the husband to a berdache. (Williams 1986, 108–9)

Since homosexual relationships do not make a man into a berdache, Walter Williams makes a distinction between homosexuality, as sexual relations between two men, and heterogendered sexual relations, between a man and a berdache: "The berdache and his male partner do not occupy the same recognized gender status" (96). Two berdaches do not have sexual relations with each other, nor do they marry. In some cultures, the berdache's husband loses no prestige; in others, he does, coming in for kidding for having an unusual sexual relationship, like a young man married to an older woman (Williams 1986, 113). Sometimes the joking is because the berdache is a particularly good provider. The berdache's husband is not labeled a homosexual, and if a divorce occurs, he can easily make a heterosexual marriage.

The berdache is not the equivalent of the Western male homosexual (Callender and Kochems 1985). The berdache's social status is defined by work and dress and sometimes a sacred calling; the social status of modern western homosexual men is defined by sexual orientation and preference for men as sexual partners (Whitehead 1981, 97–98). The berdache's gender status is not that of a man but of a woman, so their homosexual relationships are heterogendered; homosexual couples in Western society are homogendered.

The Plains Indians had a tradition of *warrior women*, but a cross-gender status for younger women was not institutionalized in most Native American tribes (Blackwood 1984, 37). Harriet Whitehead argues that because men were considered superior in these cultures, it was harder for women to breach the gender boundaries upward than it was for men to breach them downward (1981, 86). Walter Williams speculates that every woman was needed to have children (1986, 244). The tribes that did allow women to cross gender boundaries restricted the privilege to women who claimed they never menstruated Whitehead 1981, 92). Young women could become men in societies that were egalitarian and tolerant of cross-gendered work activities (Blackwood 1984). Among the Mohave, a girl's refusal to learn women's tasks could lead to her being taught the same skills boys learned and to ritual renaming,

nose piercing, and hair styling as a man. At that point, her status as a man allowed her to marry a woman and to do men's work of hunting, trapping, growing crops, and fighting. She was also expected to perform a man's ritual obligations. Because divorce was frequent and children went with the mother, cross-gendered women could rear children. Adoptions were also common. Sexually, cross-gendered women were homosexual, but, like berdaches, their marriages were always heterogendered—they did not marry or have sexual relationships with each other.[15] Among less egalitarian Native American societies, a legitimate cross-gender status, *manly hearted woman*, was available for post-menopausal women who acquired wealth (Whitehead 1981, 90–93). In some African cultures today, a wealthy woman can marry a woman and adopt her children as a father (Amadiume 1987).

Lesbians in Western societies differ from cross-gendered women in Native American and African societies in that they do not form heterogendered couples. Both women in a lesbian couple continue to be identified socially as women; neither becomes a "husband." If they have children, neither becomes a "father," both are mothers to the children (Weston 1991).

Hijras are a group in northern India who consider themselves intersexed men who have become women; many, but not all, undergo ritualistic castration (Nanda 1990). They serve both a legitimate cultural function as ritual performers, and an illegitimate sexual function, as homosexual prostitutes. Sometimes they are considered women, sometimes men, but they are deviant in either status not because of their sexuality but because they don't have children. Hijras are required to dress as women, but they do not imitate or try to pass as ordinary women; rather, they are as deviant as women as they are as men:

> Their female dress and mannerisms are exaggerated to the point of caricature, expressing sexual overtones that would be considered inappropriate for ordinary women in their roles as daughters, wives, and mothers. Hijra performances are burlesques of female behavior. Much of the comedy

of their behavior derives from the incongruities between their behavior and that of traditional women. They use coarse and abusive speech and gestures in opposition to the Hindu ideal of demure and restrained femininity. Further, it is not at all uncommon to see hijras in female clothing sporting several days growth of beard, or exposing hairy, muscular arms. The ultimate sanction of hijras to an abusive or unresponsive public is to lift their skirts and expose the mutilated genitals. The implicit threat of this shameless, and thoroughly unfeminine, behavior is enough to make most people give them a few cents so they will go away. (Nanda 1986, 38)

Hijras live separately in their own communal households, relating to each other as fictive mothers, daughters, sisters, grandmothers, and aunts. Occupationally, they sing and dance at weddings and births, run bathhouses, work as cooks and servants, and engage in prostitution with men; or they are set up in households by men in long-term sexual relationships. The hijras who Serena Nanda interviewed came from lower class, middle-caste families in small cities and said they had wanted to dress and act as women from early childhood. They left home because of parental disapproval and to protect their siblings' chances for marriage (65).

Hijras worship Bahuchara Mata, a mother-goddess. Shiva is also sometimes worshiped by hijras, for his manifestation in half-man, half-woman form. In the great Indian legend, the *Mahabharata,* one of the heroes, Arjuna, lives for a year in exile as a woman, doing menial work and teaching singing and dancing. Those who were not men and not women were blessed by Ram in the Hindu epic, *Ramayana.* In addition to these Hindu religious connections, Islam is also involved in hijra culture. The founders of the original seven hijra communal "houses," or subgroups, were said to be Muslim, and in keeping with this tradition, modern houses also have Muslim gurus. This religious legitimation and their performance of cultural rituals integrate hijras into Indian society, as does the Indian tradition of creative asceticism. Young, sexually active hijras, however, are seen by

the elders as compromising the ascetic sources of their legitimacy.

Hijras seem to resemble transvestite performers (female impersonators or "drag queens") in modern Western society. But transvestite performers do not have roots in Western religious tradition, nor are they castrated. Castrated hijras do not have the same social status as men-to-women transsexuals in Western societies, since transsexuals act as normal women, and hijras do not. In some respects, hijras resemble the castrati of European operatic tradition.

In the seventeenth century, because the Roman Catholic church forbade women to sing in public, women's parts were sung by castrati, boys whose testicles were removed in adolescence so their voices would remain soprano. Throughout the eighteenth century, castrati and women singers both appeared on the operatic stage, often in competition, although the castrati had the advantages of far superior training, respectability, church support, and fame. There was constant gender reversal in casting and plot. Women contraltos sang men's roles in men's clothes (now called "trouser roles"); soprano castrati sang the "leading ladies" in women's costumes (*en travesti*); and both masqueraded in plots of mistaken or hidden identity in the clothes of the role's opposite but their actual gender.

Casanova, in his memoirs, tells of being sexually attracted to a supposed castrato, Bellino, in the early 1740s. This attraction totally confounded his notorious ability to "smell" a woman in his presence, so he was much relieved, when he seduced Bellino (in anticipation of homosexual sex), to find out that Bellino was a woman soprano posing as a eunuch in order to sing in Rome. Of course, she sang women's roles. She had heterosexual sex with Casanova, although this womanizer was just as ready to make love with a man (Ellison 1992).[16]

A third type of institutionalized intermediate gender role are the xaniths of Oman, a strictly gender-segregated Islamic society in which women's sexual purity is guarded by their wearing long, black robes and black face masks when in public and by not mingling with men other than close relatives at home (Wikan 1982, 168–86). Xaniths are homosexual prostitutes who dress in men's clothes but in pastel colors rather than white, wear their hair in neither a masculine nor a feminine style, and have feminine mannerisms. They sing and eat with the women at weddings, mingle freely with women, but they maintain men's legal status. (Women are lifelong minors; they must have a male guardian.) They are not considered full-fledged women because they are prostitutes, and women, in Oman ideology, may engage in sexual acts only with their husbands. The xaniths' social role is to serve as sexual outlets for unmarried or separated men, and thus they protect the sexual purity of women. The men who use them as sexual outlets are not considered homosexual, because supposedly they always take the active role.

Xaniths live alone and take care of their own households, doing both men's work—the marketing—and women's work—food preparation. Being a xanith seems to be a family tradition, in that several brothers will become xaniths. They move in and out of the gender status fairly easily, reverting to manhood when they marry and successfully deflower their brides. To be considered a man, a groom must show bloody evidence of defloration or accuse his bride of not having been a virgin. A xanith, therefore, who shows he has successfully deflowered a virgin bride becomes a man. Just as a female in Oman culture is not a woman until she has intercourse, a male is not a man until he successfully consummates his marriage. A woman, though, can never revert to the virgin state of girlhood, but a man can revert to xanithhood by singing with the women at the next wedding.

In the sense that passive homosexual sex rather than heterogendered behavior is the defining criteria of status, the xanith is closest to the feminized homosexual prostitute in Western culture, but not, according to Wikan, to homosexual men in other Middle Eastern cultures:

Homosexual practice is a common and recognized phenomenon in many Middle Eastern cultures, often in the form of an institutionalized practice whereby older men seek sexual satisfaction with younger boys. But this homosexual relationship generally has two qualities that make it fundamentally different from that practiced in Oman. First, it is part of a deep friendship or love relationship between two men, which has qualities, it is often claimed, of being purer and more beautiful than love between man and woman.... Second, both parties play both the active and the passive sexual role—either simultaneously or through time. (1982, 177)

One Or The Other, Never Both

Michel Foucault, in the introduction to Barbin's memoirs, says of the concept of "one true sex": Biological theories of sexuality, juridical conceptions of the individual, forms of administrative control in modern nations, led little by little to rejecting the idea of a mixture of the two sexes in a single body, and consequently to limiting the free choice of indeterminate individuals. Henceforth, everybody was to have one and only one sex. Everybody was to have his or her primary, profound, determined and determining sexual identity; as for the elements of the other sex that might appear, they could only be accidental, superficial, or even quite simply illusory. (1980, viii)

Yet, in Western societies, despite our firm belief that each person has one sex, one sexuality, and one gender, congruent with each other and fixed for life, and that these categories are one of only two sexes, two sexualities, and two genders, hermaphrodites, pseudohermaphrodites, transsexuals, transvestites, and bisexuals exhibit a dizzying fluidity of bodies, desires, and social statuses. According to Annie Woodhouse, "punters" are men "who don't want to go to bed with a man, but don't want to go to bed with a real woman either." So they go to bed with men dressed as women (1989, 31). The ambiguous appearance of the women Holly Devor (1989) interviewed was typed as "mannish," and so they had difficulty being considered "opposite" enough for heterosexual relationships. As lesbians, their appearance was not only acceptable, but they could, and did, sexually excite other women when passing as men, as did Deborah Sampson, the woman who fought in the American Revolution in a man's uniform, and Nadezhda Durova, the Russian "cavalry maiden" in the Napoleonic Wars (Durova 1989; Freeman and Bond 1992). Marjorie Garber writes of Yvonne Cook, a man who dresses as a woman, considers herself a lesbian and has a woman lover who dresses as a man (1992, 4).

All these components can change and shift back and forth over days, weeks, months, and years. With unisex clothing, gender can change in minutes, depending on the context and the response of others to gender cues. Bisexuals have long-term serial relationships with women and men, but may define themselves as either heterosexual or homosexual. Transvestites consciously play with sexual and gender categories. Gay men, lesbians, and bisexuals cross Western culture's sexual boundaries but do not always challenge gender norms. Transsexuals, in their quest for "normality," often reaffirm them. Through their "subversive bodily acts," all demonstrate the social constructedness of sex, sexuality, and gender (Butler 1990, 79–141). But they have not disrupted the deep genderedness of the modem Western world. And to maintain genderedness, to uphold gender boundaries, the "impulses toward, or fear of, turning into someone of the opposite sex" that many ordinary, normal people feel, have to be suppressed (Stoller 1985, 152).

The norms, expectations, and evaluation of women and men may be converging, but we have no social place for a person who is neither woman nor man. A man who passes as a woman or a woman as a man still violates strong social boundaries, and when transsexuals change gender, they still cross a great divide. In this sense, Western culture resembles the intensely gendered world of Islam, where all the rules of marriage, kinship, inheritance, purity, modesty, ritual, and even burial are challenged by people of ambiguous sex (Sanders 1991). Rather than allowing the resultant social ambiguity to continue, medieval Islamic jurists developed a set of rules for gendering hermaphrodites: "A person

with ambiguous genitalia or with no apparent sex might have been a biological reality, but it had no gender and, therefore, no point of entry into the social world: it was unsocialized" (Sanders 1991, 88). As in modern Western society, a person who was neither woman nor man had no social place and could have no social relationships without disturbing the social order: "What was at stake for medieval Muslims in gendering one ungendered body was, by implication, gendering the most important body: the social body" (89). The social body in modern Western society, both for the individual and the group, is, above all, gendered.

Notes

1. The passage as Colette wrote it is: "At a time when I was, when at least I believed I was insensitive to Damien, I suggested to him that he and I would make a pair of ideal traveling companions, both courteously selfish, easy to please, and fond of long silences. . . .

   'I like to travel only with women,' he answered.

   The sweet tone of his voice scarcely softened the brutality of his words . . . He was afraid he had hurt my feelings and tried to make up, with something even worse.

   'A woman? You? I know you would like to be one . . . '" (1933, 75; ellipses in the original).
2. After reclassification, Barbin, who had been a certified and competent schoolteacher, had to look for men's work. Bolin (1988, 156–57) notes a similar problem for men-to-women transsexuals who worked in fields dominated by men.
3. Richard Sadove M.D., personal communication. Dr. Sadove did the reconstructive surgery.
4. Fausto-Sterling 1985, 87–88, Herdt 1990, 437–38.
5. Most of the research is on men-to-women transsexuals. For reviews, see Bolin 1987; Docter 1988. For a scathing critique of transsexual research and practice, see Stoller 1985, 152–70. For a critique of the medical construction of transsexualism as a fixed core identity, see Billings and Urban 1982.
6. See Garfinkel 1967, 116–85, for a detailed account of how Bill-Agnes managed the practical details of passing while constructing a new gendered

identity. Raymond (1979) is critical of men-to-women's gender identity because they have not had the previous experience of women's oppression.

7. Bolin's data on five transsexuals' postoperative sexual relationships indicated that three were bisexual and one was lesbian (181).

8. There have also been relationships between women-to-men and men-to-women transsexuals; these, however, are heterosexual and heterogendered (Money 1988, 93).

9. Actually, the mark of gender identity in Western culture is the penis—the person who has one of adequate size is male and a man; the person who does not, is not-male, not a man. Femaleness and womanhood seem to be more problematic and need more "work" to construct. For an opposite view about masculinity, see Gilmore 1990.

10. Also see Heilbrun 1988, 32–36; L. J. Kaplan 1991, 492–500.

11. Also see Smith-Rosenberg 1985.

12. Dollimore 1986; Greenblatt 1987, 66–93; Howard 1988; Lavine 1986. On the fluidity of representations of bodily sex during the Renaissance, see Laqueur 1990a, 114–34. On the "semiotics of dress" in modern life, see E. Wilson 1985.

13. Also see Wheelwright 1989, 9–15.

14. Bolin lists seventy North and South American Indian tribes that have berdaches (1987, 61n).

15. By the end of the nineteenth century, the adoption of Western sexual and gender mores led to the delegitimation of the female cross-gender status (Blackwood 1984, 39–40), but not the male, according to W. L. Williams (1986).

16. The last known castrato, Alessandro Moreschi (1858–1922), made a series of recordings in 1902. and 1903, the year Pope Pius X formally banned castrati from the papal chapel, but he sang in the Sistine Chapel choir until 1913 (Ellison 1992, 37).

The Politics of Birth Practices: A Strategic Analysis

KAREN E. PAIGE AND JEFFERY M. PAIGE

The customary practices and beliefs associated with childbearing have been the subject of much detailed ethnographic description and speculative analysis (cf. Sumner, 1934; Crawley, 1902; Frazier, 1922; Webster, 1942; Ford, 1964). Description and theory have both focused on two widespread birth customs—the restriction and segregation of women during pregnancy and childbirth and the observance of couvade by men during their wife's post-delivery confinement. Some customary restrictions on women such as sexual abstinence for specified periods during the pregnancy or the avoidance or prohibition of particular foods or articles of clothing are almost universally observed. However, some societies restrict a woman's normal social contacts by instituting special rules of avoidance, particularly the avoidance of men, ostensibly to protect the society against the

Karen E. Paige and Jeffery M. Paige, "The Politics of Birth Practices: A Strategic Analysis," from *American Sociological Review* 38 (December 1973):663–76. Reprinted with permission.

contamination and uncleanness associated with feminine reproductive activities. In some cases women are strictly segregated during the birth process and may be confined in special huts, restricted to their own residence, or removed to another community. The most widely discussed birth custom involving men is the couvade which usually includes customary dietary and occupational observances and post-partum seclusion of the husband. In some societies the husband observes all the restrictions observed by his pregnant wife; and when she goes into delivery, he may seclude himself in his residence and fast for a week or more. While in some cases the restrictions for the husband are even more extensive than the wife's, in most societies he performs such minimal cermonial duties as cutting the umbilical cord after delivery, preparing a birth feast for relatives, performing sacrifices, or helping his wife with her daily chores. While these minor practices are generally not classified as couvade, they are similar in form if not in intensity.

Birth practices have been examined from several theoretical perspectives including sociological functionalism (Norbeck, 1961; Van Gennep, 1961), psychoanalytic personality theory (Bettelheim, 1954; Deveraux, 1950), and the social psychological theory of ritual (Radcliffe-Brown, 1952a). While these theories have been the focus of much cross-cultural study and theoretical debate (Homans, 1941; Ayres, 1954; Burton and Whiting, 1961; Young, 1963), relatively less attention has been paid to the earliest theory of birth practices first proposed by Tylor in 1889. Tylor claimed that couvade was most often practiced in societies in which paternity rights were customarily held by the mother's kinsmen rather than by her husband and concluded that the couvade represented a pre-legal method by which husbands attempted to establish paternity rights over their biological offspring. Tylor's theory has been handicapped by his inadequate sample of societies and by its association with discredited 19th century theories of the evolution of descent systems. Malinowski (1931), however, suggested a similar explanation of couvade in a discussion of social paternity. He

argued that paternity rights must be socially legitimated and that performance of rituals during the birth process served that purpose. "The function of couvade," he argued, "is the establishment of social paternity by the symbolic assimilation of the father to the mother...and is an integral part of the institution of the family" (Malinowski, 1931:631). Neither of these theories is described in sufficient detail to permit prediction of cross-cultural variation in birth practices; and neither, of course, is concerned with the birth practices of women. Nevertheless the idea of social paternity is central to understanding the determinants of birth practices. This paper extends the argument of Tylor and Malinowski to account for both cross-cultural variation in birth practices and for the practices of women as well as men.

Theory

Were social paternity an automatic consequence of biological parenthood, there would be no need to engage in birth practices to assert claims to offspring. But as Malinowski (1927) demonstrated, paternity rights are established through social concensus or contractual agreement and not through the biological process of conception, pregnancy, and childbirth. The birth of a child not only affirms biological parenthood but also allows an opportunity for interested parties to lay claim to the child's allegiance. These claimants are not limited to the biological parents. In fact the individual with the greatest biological involvement in the birth—the mother—is rarely given authority over her own children. Jural rights to control a child's political allegiance, economic activities, property, or inheritance usually rest with males, though not necessarily with the child's biological father. These rights define the role of sociological father, or *pater*, who is customarily distinguished from the biological father or *genitor*. It is not uncommon for the two roles to be played by different individuals. Paternity rights may be claimed by an individual or group of individuals who provided property used as brideprice regardless of their gender or kinship relation to the genitor. The role of sociological father may be played by the maternal brother, a lineage head, ceremonial kinsmen, state agencies, women, or even decedents. In most societies, of course, the biological father has jural as well as personal authority over his offspring. Even in this case, however, paternity rights are established by the marriage contract; and the competing claims of the wife's kinsmen may be relinquished only in exchange for property or personal service on the part of the husband.

Since paternity rights depend on social consensus or contractual agreements, individuals or groups can attempt to influence the consensus or renegotiate the agreement to their advantage. Paternity rights are subject to dispute in all societies, but the problem is acute in simpler societies where kinship is the major determinant of social position, economic resources, and political power. The greater the importance of such ties in determining social structure, the greater the significance of paternity rights in controlling the political and economic activities of others. Gaining paternity rights means gaining a contributor to the communal economy, a new supporter of a political faction, and an additional ally in a feud. With such important issues at stake, it is not surprising that the birth of a child is the focus of paternity conflict in many societies.

While legitimate rights to offspring may have been theoretically established at marriage, the birth of a child gives them practical significance. It requires that nominal rights be recognized, that ambiguities in customary rights be clarified and that conflicting claims be resolved. Childbirth represents an opportunity for all potential claimants to reopen negotiations, accuse other claimants of bad faith, to demand compensation for real or imagined malfeasance. No matter who is recognized as the sociological father or how his rights have been established, claims can always be challenged and rights ignored.

In societies in which the wife's kinsmen hold jural authority over her children, the husband may try to use his personal authority to claim his children's allegiance for his own kin group. In societies where the husband's and wife's kinsmen share jural authority or where authority is shared by members of a corporate lineage, there may be continual competition for children's primary allegiance. Even in societies where the wife's kinsmen relinquish paternity rights at marriage, they may try to reclaim these rights after a child is born.

Competition over paternity is most apparent in divorce proceedings when the husband may have to relinquish his paternity rights or choose between yielding parental authority or forfeiting wealth or property transferred to the wife's family at marriage. In some cases, the husband may retain authority over male children but yield it over the female children. Whatever the social arrangements concerning paternity, a claimant can always find some grounds for questioning the rights of the sociological father.

In complex societies paternity disputes are the subject of litigation, and a formal judicial apparatus is available to settle them and enforce claims. But those societies in which kinship is most important in determining social structure are the least likely to have such formal mechanisms. This does not mean, of course, that agreements cannot be reached or claims successfully defended; but it does suggest that the tactics of paternity disputes should take a different form in simple societies. Paternity rights are often the subject of bargains negotiated between groups of kinsmen. These bargains may involve substantial amounts of property and can be enforced by the organized military power of the respective kin groups. While such agreements are not legally enforceable, their terms cannot be violated without serious financial or political consequences. In such a situation the main interest of both parties is to insure that nothing upsets their agreement. Ceremonial attempts by males of either faction to assert additional paternity rights would only threaten the agreement. Where explicit, enforceable bargains exist, male birth rituals are neither necessary nor desirable. Both parties to the bargain have an interest in making sure that the contract is fulfilled by the birth of a healthy offspring with unambiguous paternity. Their main focus during pregnancy and birth should be to insure that nothing happens to the biological mother that could threaten either the health of the child or their claims to its allegiance. Given the biological uncertainties of childbearing and the benefits of claiming paternity rights, this may be a formidable task. The restriction or segregation of women during pregnancy and birth can be interpreted as a method of protecting the established rights of claimants against these dangers.

This interpretation suggests that maternal restrictions during pregnancy and birth and the couvade are alternate strategies to establish or defend paternity rights. The birth practices of both men and women depend on the nature of the bargains over paternity rights in a given society. Since the nature of the bargains which lead to restrictions on women should differ from those which lead to ritual involvement by men, each will be considered separately.

Maternal Restrictions

If the restriction of women during the birth process represents an attempt to insure the fulfillment of a previously negotiated contract, then a potential claimant's interest in the proceedings should vary with the importance of the bargain. When breach of contract leads to great financial loss or to the threat of violent retaliation from other interested factions, concern with a successful birth and efforts to monitor the birth process should increase. The importance of the bargain and the subsequent interest in the birth process should depend on two major factors: (1) the amount of property involved in the negotiations and (2) the claimants' power to enforce the agreement. These considerations, of course, are not limited to disputes over paternity and stated more generally simply indicate that the significance of a bargain depends on the size of the payoff and the finality of the terms.

Payoffs

The payoffs in a paternity bargain always involve the relative wealth and power of individuals and kin groups, but the payoffs may be increased by direct property exchanges either at marriage or after a successful birth. While paternity rights do not always depend on the exchange of wealth and may be established by the marriage itself, substantial payments usually confer rights to the woman's offspring. The institution of brideprice in particular is usually interpreted as a direct payment for the reproductive capacity of the wife (cf. Mair 1971; Fortes 1962; Radcliffe-Brown 1952b, 1950). The close association between brideprice and paternity rights is indicated by the fact that payments may be made only after the birth of an offspring or may be made in installments contingent on the wife's continued fertility. The brideprice represents compensation to the wife's kinsmen for the loss of potential offspring to their lineage. As Mair has observed the sum paid in brideprice may be equivalent to the sum paid in compensation for homicide, an indication of the close association between the loss of living and potential kinsmen.

The payment of brideprice or any other exchange of wealth does not assure that paternity rights will be realized. Accidents of reproduction may make the contract meaningless. Given the high rate of fetal and infant mortality in most pre-industrial societies, the possibility is strong that the terms of the paternity agreement will not be fulfilled. Failure to produce an offspring may result from such purely medical problems as barrenness, fetal death or infant disease; but it may also result from infanticide or abortion. Whatever the cause, the potential claimant may demand compensation from the wife's kinsmen. If the wife is barren, her husband may demand that her father give him an additional wife, a child of his own, or some of his property or animals. If a wife is guilty of abortion, her kinsmen may be compelled to pay for the fetus. Any irregularity in the birth process may also occasion additional demands for compensation. The potential claimant can use a breach birth, a birth mark, or even suspected witchcraft to reopen negotiations. However the wife's kinsmen may be in a poor position to meet demands for compensation. Property received for paternity rights is not saved but dispersed among kinsmen, used to buy wives, or pay blood debts and other outstanding obligations. Failure to produce offspring may therefore disrupt an elaborate pattern of financial and kinship obligations. It will certainly lead to renewed haggling and mutual recrimination and may prompt sorcery or outright violence. Clearly, both sets of kinsmen have a vested interest in fulfilling the original contract. The husband's kinsmen must assure that offspring are born in return for wealth already expended and the wife's kinsmen are interested in avoiding the return of wealth they have already spent. The main interest of both parties during pregnancy and birth should be in insuring that nothing happens to upset the contract.

There are a number of ways maternal birth practices might function to protect a bargain. Rules requiring social isolation, avoidance of men, confinement in birth huts or removal to another community all facilitate the surveillance and control of both the mother and potential claimants. Restricting and confining the mother limits the possibility of disrupting the birth through abortion, infanticide, or kidnapping. Segregation from men limits the possibility that other male claimants, such as an unsuccessful suitor or an adulterer, can present their claims. Confinement and isolation also mean that contact with the mother can be limited to the agents of the kin groups with a legitimate interest in the birth. Often, agents of both interested parties will be present at delivery which enables them not only to monitor the mother but also one another. Often it is only after some indication that delivery is successful and the infant's sex determined that additional negotiations and transfer of brideprice occur. If some biological accident disrupts the birth, the limited contacts of the mother and the presence of kin group agents insure that conflict over compensation can be limited and that blame will not be unjustly assigned. In a society with no recourse to police or judiciary, kin groups must monitor other claimants and their own members to insure that contracts will be respected.

Enforcement Power

The importance of a paternity bargain depends not only on the amount of property exchanged but also on the enforcement power of the interested parties. There would be little point in carefully monitoring the birth process were there no way to apply sanctions to those who disrupted it. Similarly there would be little point in investing substantial amounts of property in rights to future offspring were there no way to defend these rights or demand compensation for default. In simple societies, enforcement power depends on the organized military and political power of groups of kinsmen. A man without kin backing has only his own strength and personality to defend his rights. Enforcing paternity bargains requires that the males of a kin group act together and use force if necessary to defend their interests. Such groups have been termed *fraternal interest groups* by Van Velzen and Van Wettering (1960). They demonstrate that fraternal interest groups are indeed associated with the use of force to defend kin group interests. Societies with such groups were significantly more likely to engage in violent retaliation over adultery, personal injury, and murder. Otterbein (1968), Otterbein and Otterbein (1965), and Ember and Ember (1971) have similarly demonstrated that internal warfare and blood feuds are more likely in societies containing fraternal interest groups. Paige (in press) has demonstrated that factional conflicts between fraternal interest groups are reflected in the form of the sovereign decision making structure in the society. The political power of a fraternal interest group gives kinsmen the ability to enforce the restrictions on maternal behavior and maintain the mother's isolation from other claimants.

The existence of fraternal interest groups depends on a society's dominant residence pattern. Their formation is facilitated by patrilocal and avunculocal residence and inhibited by matrilocal, bilocal and neolocal residence. In both patrilocal and avunculocal residence consanguinally related males live together in the same community. In patrilocal residence sons live with their fathers after marriage, and in avunculocal residence nephews live with their maternal uncles. In matrilocal, bilocal and neolocal residence kin are dispersed rather than localized. In matrilocal residence sons live with their wives' families, in neolocal residence sons live separately, and when residence is bilocal sons may or may not live with their father. Patrilocal or avunculocal residence has therefore been generally used to indicate the presence of fraternal interest groups. While patrilocal or avunculocal residence produces communities in which residence and kinship reinforce one another, other forms of residence produce conflicting patterns of allegiance. An individual owes allegiance both to his own kinsmen, many of whom live elsewhere, and to the members of his local community. In patrilocal and avunculocal societies, groups of related males with similar interest in a paternity dispute will be able to act as a unit. In societies with other residence patterns, communities will likely contain individuals whose loyalties lie with competing claimants, and concerted action will be difficult.

Residence patterns which facilitate the formation of fraternal interest groups should make both contractual agreements over paternity and restrictions on women more likely. Clearly, however, the effects of fraternal interest groups on maternal restrictions are not independent of the effects of wealth exchange and demands for compensation. Compensation cannot be successfully demanded if sanctions are not available to enforce the demand, and wealth will not be risked when no agreement can be enforced. Wealth exchange and demands for compensation should, therefore, both be associated with the presence of fraternal interest groups. Since wealth exchange, demands for compensation, and the presence of fraternal interest groups can each be considered a measure of the presence of explicit paternity bargains, each should be positively associated with the presence of maternal restrictions. While these zero-order relationships are clearly implied by the argument associating maternal restrictions with paternity bargains, the effect of each variable controlling for the others is less clear. Specifying the complete causal model associating the characteristics of paternity bargains with maternal restrictions requires empirically investigating the indicators' interrelationships. If our theory is incorrect, however, even the zero-order relationships will not

hold, so that it seems advisable to examine these predictions empirically before examining the entire causal model in more detail.

Husband Ritual Involvement

The ritual involvement of husbands in the birth process through dietary observances or post-delivery seclusion can be viewed as an attempt to assert paternity rights in the absence of more potent sources of influence. While such observances can be used to influence public opinion in any society they are most effective in societies where enforceable paternity agreements do not exist. No amount of ritual activity is likely to alter paternity agreements based on the expenditure of several years earnings or the power of an important lineage. In fact when paternity agreements are carefully monitored unwarranted ritual claims could be viewed as a threat to the agreement and lead to attempts at retaliation. When the backing of courts or organized kinsmen is available, ritual is a poor substitute for legal or political action. A potential claimant would be ill advised to spend two weeks in a hammock or avoid turtle meat if he could claim his child by hiring a lawyer or organizing a war party. If such enforcement power is unavailable, however, a husband loses little by making ritual claims since none of the other claimants are in any position to stop him except by engaging in ritual themselves. In particular, the husband's ritual involvement helps offset the implicit claims of his wife's kinsmen dramatized by the wife's undeniable role in the birth. The husband's involvement in the birth can then be viewed as a form of psychological warfare useful when opportunities for more direct forms of conflict are restricted.

Ritual conflict is not limited to paternity disputes and, as Service (1966) and Gluckman (1965) have pointed out, is a common method of adjudicating quarrels in societies which lack organized enforcement power. Such ritual conflicts as the Eskimo song duel or the Tiwi spear throwing contest provide alternatives to litigation or private vengeance. As Service suggests, these contests allow each party to state his grievances publicly and attempt to influence community opinion in his favor. They also allow other community members to decide which side they favor. Eventually the contests make clear where the majority opinion lies, and the losing party will usually not press his claims further. Ritual conflict is particularly likely when disputes involve kinsmen or members of the same community or when societies lack the organization necessary for military activity. Gluckman suggests that ritual may also be used if individual and group interests are in conflict or if cross-cutting allegiance patterns inhibit more direct forms of conflict.

If the husband's ritual involvement in the birth occurs in the absence of enforcement power, then husband involvement and maternal restriction represent alternate strategies in paternity disputes. Maternal restrictions depend on the presence of enforceable bargains, while husband involvement depends on their absence. This inverse relationship between husband involvement and maternal restrictions depends fundamentally on the unequal role of men and women in the birth process. While women bear children, paternity rights are almost invariably controlled by men. Thus women are objects not actors in most paternity negotiations. Both the ritual involvement of husbands in the birth and the restriction of women are primarily tactics used by male claimants to protect rights over offspring being produced by women. When males are effectively organized they can use this power to control the birth process to their own advantage. When they lack such power, they must find alternative strategies to assert their claims.

The interrelationships between fraternal interest groups, wealth exchange, compensation, and birth practices suggested by the above analysis can be summarized in the following set of hypotheses:

1. The presence of fraternal interest groups should be positively associated with the presence of maternal restrictions and negatively associated with the presence of husband involvement.

2. The presence of wealth exchange should be positively associated with the presence of maternal restrictions and negatively associated with the presence of husband ritual involvement.

3. The presence of demands for compensation should be positively associated with the presence of maternal restrictions and negatively associated with the presence of husband involvement.

4. Fraternal interest groups, wealth exchange, and demands for compensation should all be positively associated with one another.

5. Maternal restrictions should be negatively associated with husband ritual involvement during the birth process.

Method

The Sample

The hypotheses stated above were tested in a sub-sample of 114 societies selected from the Standard Cross-Cultural Sample (SCCS) recently developed by Murdock and White (1969). The SCCS is a stratified sample of world societies designed to minimize the effects of historical diffusion by including only one society from each of 186 distinct sampling provinces (Murdock, 1968). Each province consists of a cluster of societies with similar culture, language, and location. Subsamples from the SCCS are not limited to 186 societies listed by Murdock and White, and other societies from the same sampling province may be substituted for those on the original list. The present sub-sample was selected by first taking every second society on the SCCS list. In cases where ethnographic materials were more readily available on an adjacent society than on the society selected by this rule, the better described society was substituted. Societies with matrilineal descent were over-sampled by adding any metrilineal society which was adjacent to a non-matrilineal society selected by the every other case rule. Thirteen societies on which data had already been collected for a pilot study were added to the initial sample. In no case, however, was more than one society included from the same sampling province. The complete sub-sample of societies and the sampling provinces they represent are listed in Appendix 1.

Table 1 compares the distribution of societies by world region for the SCCS and the current sub-sample. The sub-sample is reasonably representative of the SCCS except for the underrepresentation of societies in the Circum-Mediterranean. This is a result of oversampling matrilineal societies which are rare in this region. Matrilineal societies make up 21 percent of the sub-sample but only 14 percent of the SCCS. Of the twenty-four matrilineal societies appearing on the SCCS list, twenty-three were included in the present sub-sample. Matrilineal descent was over-sampled because of its association with avunculocal and matrilocal residence and the significance of these residence patterns in the argument concerning fraternal interest groups. A single random sample would contain too few of these residence patterns to examine the effects of fraternal interest groups in different residence configurations.

Measures of Birth Practices

The customary birth practices of both men and women were coded from ethnographic sources on each society. All sources were coded independently by three graduate students each of whom had training in coding ethnographic materials and was fluent in at least one foreign language. All sources cited by Murdock and White in the SCCS were coded in the original ethnographic language when that language was English, French, Spanish, or German. Supplementary sources in Russian, Danish, and Arabic were not consulted. All additional ethnographic materials available as of 1972 in the University of California library and the Human Relations Area File microfilm collection were also consulted. Thus the coded data should be more representative of the true distribution of world cultures than is the usual cross-cultural analysis based on HRAF or English language sources only.

The presence or absence of each custom was determined by using the score obtained by two out of three coders when the coding decision was not unanimous. Customs were coded for the time period and locale specified in Murdock's Ethnographic Atlas (1967) and Murdock and

Table 1. Regional Distribution of Societies

World Region	Subsample (N = 114)	SCCS (N = 186)
Africa	16%	15%
Circum-Mediterranean	11	15
East Eurasia	17	18
Insular Pacific	19	17
North America	19	18
South America	18	17

White's SCCS (1969). The original codes for birth practices in this study therefore refer to the same period and place as the codes in Murdock's Atlas. This makes it possible to include Murdock's codes for wealth exchange and residence in the analysis of birth practices. Only observable changes in behavior during the birth process were coded. Beliefs and myths about childbearing were not used as indicators of actual practice. The customary behavior of both men and women could be ordered into Guttman-type scales. The ordering of each set of customs and their cumulative frequencies are presented in Table 2.

The Maternal Restrictions Scale measures the degree of constraint on women's behavior during the birth process. The practices making up this scale range from minor restrictions on work or apparel to confinement in specially built dwellings or removal from the community. The five-item scale in Table 2 has a coefficient of reproducibility of .93 (see White and Saltz, 1967, for computation procedures). While all the items in the scale represent some restriction of women, not all are necessary to monitor the birth and protect previously negotiated contracts. Only the two highest categories, social avoidance and structural seclusion, permit close monitoring and control of the birth process. For purposes of analysis, therefore, these two categories were collapsed into a single category indicating the presence of significant maternal restrictions. The remaining three categories were correspondingly collapsed into a low restriction category.

The Husband Involvement Scale measures the degree to which husbands change their behavior

Table 2. Measures of Birth Practices

Custom Category	Item	Cumulative Frequency	Custom Category Description
Maternal Restrictions Scale[a]			
Social (High):			
Structural Seclusion	5	24.3%	Confined to dwelling during pregnancy at least 2 weeks prior to delivery; secluded in special hut; moved to other community during birth process.
Social Avoidance	4	48.6	Contact with people, especially men, is restricted during pregnancy. Pregnant women avoided and believed to be unclean and dangerous, evil.
Personal (Low):			
Sex Taboo	3	63.1	Sexual relations with husband restricted for at least two months before delivery.
Food Taboo	2	82.9	Eating certain foods during either pregnancy or post-partum is restricted.
Minor	1	100.0	Restrictions on looking at ugly objects, wearing certain clothing, working too hard, etc.
Husband Involvement Scale[b]			
Couvade (High):			
Seclusion	5	16.2%	Secluded in dwelling during pregnancy or post-partum with or without mother and child. May also be considered unclean. Avoids others.
Post-partum Work Taboo	4	29.7	Refrains from performing normal tasks during post-partum period. Must remain close to home; contact with others minimized.
Food Taboo	3	44.1	Refrains from eating certain foods during pregnancy or post-partum.
Minor (Low):			
Minor Observances	2	64.0	Minor ritual observances, such as seeking a vision, performs birth-related sacrifices. May help wife with daily chores.
Informal	1	100.0	Residual category: no changes in normal behavior. No ritual observances.

[a] Coef. of reproducibility = .93. (Missing cases: Basque, Rhade, Amahauca)
[b] Coef. of reproducibility = .96. (Missing cases: Suku, Rhade, Aweikoma)

in ways which indicate an active ritual involvement in the birth process. The lowest scale category indicates the absence of any changes in husband behavior and the highest indicates confinement and seclusion. The coefficient of reproducibility for the five-item scale is .96. Only the three highest categories—seclusion, post-partum work and food taboos—include behaviors which could be called couvade, and for purposes of analysis these three categories were collapsed into one.

Minor behavioral changes such as helping wives with chores were grouped with the absence of any behavioral change in a low involvement category. The scale as it appears in the analysis, therefore, indicates simply the presence or absence of couvade in a particular society.

Measures of Bargaining

The index of the presence or absence of fraternal interest groups was simply the dominant residence pattern as coded by Murdock and Wilson (1972: 261, Col. 9) and Murdock (1967: 156, Col. 16). Fraternal interest groups were considered present if residence was patrilocal or avunculocal and absent if residence was matrilocal, bilocal, or neolocal.

The index of wealth exchange was based on Murdock's (1967: 155, Col. 12) code for mode of marriage which included various types of marital transactions. Wealth exchange was considered present if property was transferred either in the form of brideprice, substantial gifts, or sister exchange as part of the marital bargain. Wealth exchange was considered absent when no substantial amount of property was exchanged. Bride service, therefore, was combined with the code indicating the absence of any substantial consideration at marriage. Dowries were also excluded from the wealth exchange category since property five-item scale is .96. Only the three highest

categories—seclusion, post-partum work and food taboos—include behaviors which could be called couvade, and for purposes of analysis these three categories were collapsed into one is not exchanged but settled on a daughter and remains her property regardless of the outcome of the marriage.

The index of compensation demands was developed from the original ethnographic sources. Compensation demands were coded present when the husband or his kinsmen demanded payment of gifts or return of some or all of the bride wealth in cases of infanticide, abortion, or barrenness. They were also coded present when barrenness, infanticide, or abortion were grounds for divorce and divorce led to compensation demands.

Results

The zero-order relationships between each of the three measures of paternity bargains and each of

Table 3. Birth Practices and Fraternal Interest Groups

Extensiveness of Birth Customs	Dominant Residence Pattern			
	Fraternal Interest Groups Present		Fraternal Interest Groups Absent	
	Patrilocal	Avunculocal	Neolocal & Bilocal	Matrilocal
Maternal Restrictions[a]				
High	60.0	71.4	35.7	24.0
(Social)	(39)	(5)	(5)	(6)
Low	40.0	28.6	64.3	76.0
(Personal)	(26)	(2)	(9)	(19)
Total	100.0	100.0	100.0	100.0
	(65)	(7)	(14)	(25)
Husband Involvement[b]				
High	33.3	14.3	76.9	64.0
(Couvade)	(22)	(1)	(10)	(16)
Low	66.7	85.7	23.1	36.0
(Minor)	(44)	(6)	(3)	(9)
Total	100.0	100.0	100.0	100.0
	(66)	(7)	(13)	(25)

[a] x^2 (FIG present vs. absent) = 10.958, p <.001, Φ^2= .099
[b] x^2 (FIG present vs. absent) = 14.255, p <.001, Φ^2= .127

the two measures of birth practices are presented in percentage form in Tables 3, 4, and 5. The same set of relationships also appears in the correlation matrix of Table 6. Tables 3, 4, and 5 present the data necessary to test Hypotheses 1, 2, and 3 respectively. The data in Table 3 present the associations between fraternal interest groups and birth practices specified by Hypothesis 1. The data support the predictions for both maternal restrictions and husband ritual involvement in the birth process. The presence of fraternal interest groups is positively associated with the presence of maternal restrictions (r = .31) and negatively associated with husband involvement (r = -.36). The distribution of birth practices by residence type in Table 3 indicated that the effect of fraternal interest groups is not a consequence of a particular form of residence.

Residence rules that localize groups of kinsmen facilitate maternal restrictions but inhibit husband involvement. Rules that disperse kinsmen have the opposite effect. Thus both avunculocal and patrilocal residence have the same effect on birth customs even though avunculocality concentrates maternal uncles and nephews and patrilocality concentrates fathers and sons. Similarly, the effects of matrilocal, bilocal, and neolocal residence are the opposite of avunculocal and patrilocal residence even though males are dispersed among their wives' kinsmen in one case and scattered throughout the society in the other two cases. Residence rules, therefore, exert their effect on birth practices by determining the ability of kinsmen to organize fraternal interest groups to defend paternity rights.

The effects of wealth exchange and demands for compensation are similar to those of fraternal interest groups. Hypotheses 2 and 3 suggested that both indicators should be positively associated with maternal restrictions and negatively associated with husband involvement. The data in Table 4 confirm the predictions for the effect of wealth exchange on both sets of birth practices. The correlation between the presence of wealth exchange and the presence of maternal restrictions is .29, while the corresponding correlation

Table 4. Birth Practices and Wealth Exchange

Extensiveness of Birth Customs	Wealth Exchange	
	Present	Absent
Maternal Restrictions[a]		
High	64.7	35.6
(Social)	(33)	(21)
Low	35.3	64.4
(Personal)	(18)	(38)
Total	100.0	100.0
	(51)	(59)
Husband Involvement[b]		
High	31.4	55.9
(Couvade)	(16)	(33)
Low	68.6	44.1
(Minor)	(35)	(26)
Total	100.0	100.0
	(51)	(59)

[a] $x^2 = 9.277$, $p < .005$, $\Phi^2 = .084$
[b] $x^2 = 6.679$, $p < .01$, $\Phi^2 = .061$

Table 5. Birth Practices and Compensation Demands

Extensiveness of Birth Customs	Compensation Demands	
	Present	Absent
Maternal Restrictions[a]		
High	71.4	29.5
(Social)	(30)	(13)
Low	28.6	70.5
(Personal)	(12)	(31)
Total	100.0	100.0
	(42)	(44)
Husband Involvement[b]		
High	38.1	53.5
(Couvade)	(16)	(23)
Low	61.9	46.5
(Minor)	(26)	(20)
Total	100.0	100.0
	(42)	(43)

[a] $x^2 = 15.078$, $p < .0005$, $\Phi^2 = .175$
[b] $x^2 = 2.028$, $p = ns$, $\Phi^2 = .024$

for husband involvement is –.25. The predictions for the effects of demands for compensation were, however, supported only for the case of maternal restrictions (Table 5). Demands for compensation for barrenness, infanticide, or abortion are significantly associated with maternal restrictions ($r = .42$); but the relationship with husband involvement, while in the expected direction, is not statistically significant ($r = -.15$).

The remaining correlations in Table 6 present data necessary for testing Hypotheses 4 and 5. Hypothesis 4 suggested that since fraternal interest groups, wealth exchange, and demands for compensation all indicated the presence of binding agreements over paternity, all three indices should be correlated with one another. As might be expected the strongest relationship is between wealth exchange and demands for compensation ($r = .67$). Clearly, claimants are in a much better position to demand their money back if they have paid something in the first place. Wealth exchange is also positively associated with the presence of fraternal interest groups ($r = .38$) suggesting that explicit payments for paternity are more likely when contracts can be enforced by organized groups of kinsmen. Similarly demands for compensation are more likely in the presence of fraternal interest groups ($r = -.37$) suggesting that fraternal interest groups may provide the power necessary to extract compensation. As the theoretical analysis implied, the various factors of a paternity bargain are interdependent.

Hypothesis 5 suggested that maternal restrictions and husband involvement should be alternate strategies for asserting paternity claims. This hypothesis is only weakly supported by the data ($r = -.24$). It is clear that a number of societies combine both practices and a number of societies lack both.

While the pattern of zero-order relationships generally supports the theoretical analysis, the various effects are obviously not independent of one another. The path diagrams in Figure 2.1 represent the effects of each variable controlling for the others, and permit a more detailed examination of the causal sequence linking paternity bargains and birth practices. The notation in Figure 2.1 is based on Duncan's (1966) description of path analysis. Both models in Figure 2.1 assume that fraternal interest groups and wealth exchange are predetermined variables and that compensation demands depend on both. Both models also assume that birth practices in turn depend on compensation demands, wealth exchange and fraternal interest groups. The model accounts for 47 per cent of the variance of compensation demands, but it is clear that most of this effect is contributed by the direct path from wealth exchange to compensation demands. In fact the direct path from fraternal interest groups to compensation demands is not significantly different from zero. The indirect effects of fraternal interest groups through its correlation with wealth exchange is greater than its direct effects. In this case the path diagrams

Table 6. Zero-Order Correlations of Indicators of Bargaining and Birth Practices

	Wealth Exchange	Compensation Demands	Husband Involvement	Maternal Restrictions
Fraternal Interest Groups	.38***	.37***	-.36***	.31***
Wealth Exchange		-67***	-.25***	.29**
Compensation Demands			-.15	.42***
Husband Involvement				-.24*

* p < .01
** p. < .005
*** p. < .001

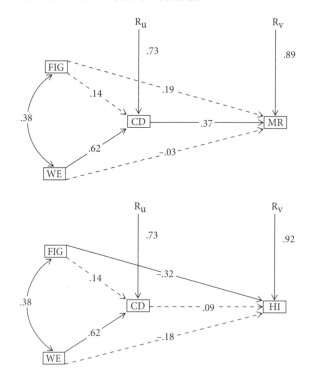

Figure 2.1. Path Diagrams for Maternal Restrictions (MR) and Husband Involvement (HI).

simply emphasize the importance of wealth exchange as the principal determinant of compensation demands.

The complete causal model accounts for 20 per cent of the variance in maternal restrictions and 15 per cent of the variance in husband involvement. The relative contributions of the three bargaining variables, however, distinctly differ in the two cases. Only compensation demands have a statistically significant direct effect on maternal restrictions. In fact almost the entire correlation between wealth exchange and maternal restrictions is a result of the intervening effect of compensation demands. Wealth exchange alone has almost no direct effect on maternal restrictions. The effect of fraternal interest groups is slightly larger, but still insignificant. The path diagram suggests a revision of the orginal theoretical analysis. The strong effect of compensation demands and the relative absence of any direct effects of

wealth exchange or fraternal interest groups indicates that attempts to monitor the birth will occur only when payoffs are directly contingent on a successful delivery. If payments for paternity rights are not refundable, there would be less point in monitoring the birth process. In such a situation the property is lost in any event and no amount of surveillance will protect the investment. Similarly, when no property is involved the threat of retaliation represented by a fraternal interest group is not sufficient to induce claimants to protect their agreement. This result could suggest that fraternal interest groups represent potential enforcement power. The decision to use the organized power of kinsmen may rest on the importance of the paternity bargain, and only those bargains which involve refundable property may be important enough to lead to actual retaliation. If this were the case, fraternal interest groups would exert their effect only because of their association with demands for compensation. This in fact seems to be the conclusion suggested by the path diagram for maternal restrictions.

While demands for compensation are the only significant direct determinant of maternal restrictions, they have almost no direct effect on husband involvement. Only the absence of fraternal interest groups has any statistically significant direct effect on husband involvement. Neither the amount of property involved nor the possibility that it may be demanded back seem to inhibit ritual claims. Husbands who cannot count on the support of organized groups of kinsmen apparently assert ritual claims even if disruption of the birth can sometimes lead to compensation demands. Ritual conflict over paternity therefore seems to depend on residence rules which establish cross-cutting patterns of allegiance and inhibit direct conflict.

Conclusions

The pattern of results in the two path diagrams indicates that of the variables examined, compensation demands are the most important determinant of maternal restrictions, while fraternal interest groups are the most important determinant of husband involvement. Paternity agreements are monitored only when their disruption has immediate economic consequences. Paternity rights may be claimed through ritual involvement even when they are established by explicit bargains, as long as direct conflict is inhibited by the absence of fraternal interest groups. Both these findings support the general hypothesis that birth practices represent tactics in negotiations over paternity.

While this hypothesis is concerned with customary behavior at birth, the theory itself is not limited to conflicts over paternity. Birth can be seen as one of a number of critical social transitions involving the transfer or exchange of important rights and privileges. The consequences of the size of payoffs and the effects of enforcement power in such situations should be similar whatever the issue. If ritual conflict over paternity is more likely because cross-cutting allegiance patterns inhibit direct conflict, then the absence of fraternal interest groups should lead to increased ritual conflict over other issues. Similarly male interests in restricting the behavior of mothers during pregnancy and childbirth is part of a larger pattern of male control over women's activities. The analysis of paternity bargains should provide concepts useful in understanding other conflicts over the control and subordination of women by men. The politics of birth practices therefore represent a special case of bargaining tactics in the absence of centralized authority.

Acknowledgments

This study was supported by funds granted to Karen Paige by the Dept. of Psychology, University of California, Davis. We are particularly indebted to Linda Fuller, who supervised data collection, and to the coders—Kathy Barchak, Christi Bengard, Hart Guenther, and Setha Low. We also wish to thank the Survey Research Center, University of California, Berkeley, for providing services and facilities.

References

Ayres, Barbara. 1954. *A cross-cultural study of factors relating to pregnancy taboos.* Unpublished Ph.D. Dissertation, Harvard University.

Bettelheim, Bruno. 1954. *Symbolic wounds.* Glencoe, Ill: Free Press.

Burton, R. and J. Whiting. 1961. The absent father and cross-sex indentity. *Merrill-Palmer Quarterly 7* (Winter): 85–95.

Crawley, Ernest. 1902. *The mystic rose.* London: Macmillan.

Duncan, Otis. 1966. Path analysis: Sociological examples. *American Journal of Sociology 72* (July): 1–16.

Deveraux, George. 1950. The psychology of feminine genital bleeding. *International Journal of Psychoanalysis 31* (Winter): 237–57.

Ember, Melvin, and Carol Ember. 1971. The conditions favoring matrilocal versus patrilocal residence. *American Anthropologist 73* (June): 571–94.

Ford, Clellan. 1964. A comparative study of human reproduction. *Yale University Publication in Anthropology Number 32.* New Haven: Human Relations Area File Press.

Fortes, Meyer. 1962. Introduction. In Meyer Fortes (ed.) *Marriage in tribal societies*, Cambridge: Cambridge University Press.

Frazier, J. G. 1922. *The golden bough*. London: Macmillan.

Gluckman, Max. 1965. *Politics, law, and ritual in tribal society*. Chicago: Aldine.

Homans, George. 1941. Anxiety and ritual: the theories of Malinowski and Radcliffe-Brown. *American Anthropologist* 43 (April): 164–72.

Mair, Lucy. 1971. *Marriage*, London: Penguin

Malinowski, Bronislaw. 1927. *Sex and regression in savage society*. New York: Harcourt, Brace.

Malinowski, Bronislaw. 1931. Culture. In Seligman, E. (ed.) *Encyclopedia of the social sciences*. London: Macmillan.

Murdock, George. 1967. Ethnographic atlas: As summary. *Ethnology* 6 (April): 109–236.

Murdock, George. 1969. World sampling provinces. *Ethnology* 7 (July): 305–26.

Murdock, George, and Douglas White. 1969. Standard cross-cultural sample. *Ethnology* 8 (October): 329–69.

Murdock, George, and Suzanne Wilson. 1972. Settlement patterns and community organization: cross-cultural codes 3. *Ethnology* 11 (July): 254–95.

Norbeck, Edward. 1961. *Religion in primitive society*. New York: Harper Brothers.

Otterbein, Keith. 1968. Internal war: A cross-cultural study. *American Anthropologist* 70 (April): 277–89.

Paige, Jeffery. Forthcoming. Kinship and polity in stateless societies. *American Journal of Sociology*.

Radcliffe-Brown, A. 1950. Introduction. Pp. 1–85 in A. Radcliffe-Brown and D. Forde (eds.) *African systems of kinship and marriage*. London: Oxford University Press.

Radcliffe-Brown, A. 1952a. Taboo, Pp. 133–52 in A. Radcliffe-Brown, *Structure and function in primitive society*. London: Oxford University Press.

Radcliffe-Brown, A. 1952b. Patrilineal and matrilineal succession. Pp. 32–48 in A. Radcliffe-Brown, *Structure and function in primitive society*. London: Oxford University Press.

Service, Elman. 1966. *The hunters*. Englewood Cliffs, N.J.: Prentice-Hall.

Sumner, William. 1934. *Folkways*. Boston: Ginn.

Tylor, Edward. 1889. On the method of investigating the development of institutions; applied to laws of marriage and descent. *Journal of the Royal Anthropological Institute* 18: 245–69.

Van Gennep, Arnold. 1961. *The rites of passage*. Chicago: University of Chicago Press.

Van Velzen, H. and W. Van Wettering. 1960. Residence, power groups and intrasocietal aggression.... *International Archives of Ethnography* 49: 169–200.

Webster, H. 1942. *Taboo: A sociological study*. Stanford: Stanford University Press.

White, B. and E. Saltz. 1967. The measurement of reproducability. Pp. 241–57 in D. Jackson and S. Messick, *Problems in human assessment*. New York: McGraw Hill.

Young, Frank. 1965. *Initiation rites*. New York: Bobbs-Merrill.

Appendix 1. Sample Societies and Sampling Provinces (SP), Husband Involvement Scores (H), and Maternal Restrictions Scores (M).

SP	Society	H	M	SP	Society	H	M	SP	Society	H	M
AFRICA				**EAST EURASIA** (cont'd)				**NORTH AMERICA** (cont'd)			
1	Nama	2	5	78	Ainu	5	3	140	Twana	4	4
2	Kung	1	4	80	Korea	1	5	141	Hupa	4	2
3	Thonga	3	4	81	Tungus	1	4	142	Klamath	2	5
6	Suku	1	1	85	Lepcha	4	2	144	Yokut	4	2
7	Lamba	1	1	87	Garo	4	1	146	Paiute	3	2
9	Nyakyusa	3	4	88	Lakher	2	1	149	Sanpoil	3	5
11	Luguru	1	2	90	Lamet	4	2	150	Gros Ventre	2	4
13	Ganda	3	5	91	Thai	1	1	152	Micmac	2	4
14	Mongo	1	5	92	Andaman	3	2	153	Ojibwa	2	4
15	Mbuti	3	2	96	Rhade	.	.	154	Hidatsa	1	3
19	Dahomey	2	4	8	Thanala	1	3	157	Creek	4	3
20	Ashanti	2	5					159	Pawnee	4	1
24	Bambara	2	5	**INSULAR PACIFIC**				161	Apache	1	3
26	Tallensi	3	4	101	Iban	4	2	162	Navaho	3	2
29	Tiv	2	5	104	Bali	2	4	163	Papago	4	5
33	Azande	3	2	107	Alor	4	3	165	Tarasco	2	3
37	Shilluk	1	5	108	Murngin	2	3	166	Zapotec	1	1
38	Masai	2	5	109	Arunta	1	5				
				112	Kiwai	5	4	**SOUTH AMERICA**			
CIRCUM-MEDITERRANEAN				113	Wogeo	5	5	168	Miskito	4	5
28	Hausa	1	5	114	Kapauku	2	2	169	Bribri	3	4
32	Fur	5	5	115	Palauan	1	5	170	Cuna	5	2
41	Somali	1	4	116	Yap	3	5	172	Goajiro	2	4
42	Amhara	1	5	117	Ifaluk	3	3	173	Callinago	5	3
46	Tuareg	1	5	118	Marshall	2	4	175	Warrau	5	1
47	Rif	1	2	120	Manu	1	5	178	Carib	5	3
51	Hebrew	1	4	121	Lesu	1	4	179	Saramacca	1	2
52	Rwala	1	4	122	Trobriand	2	5	180	Mundurucu	5	1
55	Gheg	1	2	123	Kurtatchi	5	2	182	Witoto	5	3
56	Basque	1	.	124	Ontonge Java	1	1	183	Jivaro	5	3
58	Lapp	1	4	125	Tikopia	2	4	184	Amahuaca	1	.
62	Kurd	1	1	128	Fiji	3	5	186	Aymara	1	1
				129	Samoa	1	2	187	Siriono	5	2
EAST EURASIA				130	Maori	2	4	188	Nambicuara	5	2
63	Basseri	1	1	131	Marquesa	5	5	190	Timbira	5	1
66	Vedda	1	1					191	Tupinamba	5	1
67	Chenchu	2	1	**NORTH AMERICA**				194	Aweikoma	.	1
68	Baiga	1	3	132	Aleut	1	4	196	Lengua	3	2
70	Burusho	2	5	133	Copper Eskimo	4	2	198	Mapuche	1	5
72	Kazak	1	1	136	Eyak	4	5	200	Yahgan	5	4
73	Yurak Samoved	1	4	138	Kaska	3	3				
76	Chukchee	1	4	139	Kwakiutl	3	4				

Coming of Age and Coming Out Ceremonies Across Cultures

GILBERT HERDT

Coming of age and being socialized into the sexual lifeways of the culture through ceremonies and initiation rites are common in many cultures of the world. These traditions help to incorporate the individual—previously a child, possibly outside of the moral rules and sexual roles of the adult group—into the public institutions and practices that bring full citizenship. We have seen in prior chapters many examples of these transitions and ceremonial practices, and we are certainly justified in thinking of them as basic elements in the human condition. Coming of age or "puberty" ceremonies around the world are commonly assumed to introduce the young person to sexual life as a heterosexual. In both traditional and modern societies, ritual plays a role in the emergence of sexuality and the support of desires and relationships expected in later life.

Yet not all of this is seamless continuity, and in the study of homosexuality across cultures we must be aware of the gaps and barriers that exist between what is experienced in childhood or adolescence and the roles and customs in adulthood that may negate or oppose these experiences. Ruth Benedict (1938) stresses how development in a society may create cultural discontinuities in this sexual and gender cycle of identities and roles, necessitating rituals. She hints that homosexuality in particular may cause discontinuity of this kind, and the life stories of many gays and lesbians in western society reveal this problem. But in all societies, there is an issue of connecting childhood with adulthood, with the transition

from sexual or biological immaturity to sexual maturity. In short, these transitions may create a "life crisis" that requires a social solution—and this is the aim of initiation ceremonies and rites of transition. Rituals may provide for the individual the necessary means to achieve difficult changes in sexual and gender status. Particularly in deeply emotional rituals, the energy of the person can be fully invested or bonded to the newfound group. This may create incredible attachments of the kind we have observed among the ancient Greeks, the feudal Japanese, and the Sambia of New Guinea, wherein the younger boy is erotically involved or partnered with an older male. In the conditions of a warrior society, homoerotic partnerships are particularly powerful when they are geared to the survival of the group.

The transition out of presumptive heterosexuality and secrecy and into the active process of self-identifying as gay or lesbian in the western tradition bears close comparison with these rites of passage. In the process of "coming out"—the current western concept of ritual passage—as gay or lesbian, a person undergoes emotional changes and a transformation in sexuality and gender that are remarkable and perhaps equal in their social drama to the initiation rites of small societies in New Guinea and Africa. Thus, the collective aspirations and desires of the adolescent or child going through the ritual to belong, participate in, and make commitments to communities of his or her own kind take on a new and broader scope.

Coming out is an implicit rite of passage for people who are in a crisis of identity that finds them "betwixt and between" being presumed to be heterosexual and living a totally secret and hidden life as a homosexual. Not until they enter into the gay or lesbian lifeway or the sexual culture of the gay and lesbian community will they begin to learn and be socialized into the rules, knowledge, and social roles and relationships of the new cultures. For many people, this experience is liberating; it is a highly charged, emotional, and dramatic process that changes them into adult gays or lesbians in all areas of their lives—with biological families, with coworkers, with friends or schoolmates, and with a sexual and romantic partner of the same gender, possibly for the rest of their lives.

This transformation in the self and in social relations brings much that is new and sometimes frightening. An alternative moral system is opened up by the rituals. Why people who desire the same gender require a ritual when others in our society do not is painfully clear, Ritual is necessary because of the negative images, stigma, and intense social contamination that continue to exist in the stereotypes and antihomosexual laws of our society. To be homosexual is to be discredited as a full person in society; it is to have a spoiled identity—as a homosexual in society or as a frightened closet homosexual who may be disliked by openly gay and lesbian friends. But perhaps of greatest importance are the repression and social censorship involved: to have one's desires suppressed, to even experience the inner or "true" self as a secret.

It is hard to break through this taboo alone or without the support of a community because doing so exposes the person to all sorts of risk, requires considerable personal resources, and precipitates an emotional vulnerability that for many is very difficult to bear. But that is not all. For some people in our society, homosexuality is a danger and a source of pollution. Once the person's homosexuality is revealed, the stigma can also spread to the family, bringing the pollution of shame and dishonor to father and mother, clan and community. This is the old mask of the evil of homosexuality.... And this is what we have found

in a study of these matters in Chicago (Herdt and Boxer 1996).

It is very typical to see an intense and negative reaction of family members to the declaration of same-sex desires by adolescents, even this late in the twentieth century. Society changes slowly and its myths even more slowly. For many people, homosexuality is an evil as frightening to the imagination as the monsters of bad Hollywood movies. Many people find it extremely difficult to deal with homosexuality and may exert strong pressures on their young to hide and suppress their feelings. Consequently, young people may feel that by declaring their same-sex desires, they will betray their families or the traditions of their sexual culture and its lifeways, which privilege marriage and the carrying on of the family name. And the younger person who desires the same gender may be afraid to come out for fear of dishonoring his or her ethnic community in the same way. To prevent these reactions, many people—closet homosexuals in the last century and many who fear the effects today—hide their basic feelings and all of their desires from their friends and families.

Here is where we may learn a lesson from other cultures. The mechanism of ritual helps to teach about the trials and ordeals of passages in other times and places, which in itself is a comfort, for it signals something basic in the human condition. To come out is to openly challenge sexual chauvinism, homophobia, and bias—refusing to continue the stigma and pollution of the past and opening new support and positive role models where before there were none. Through examples from New Guinea, the Mojave, and the Chicago gay and lesbian group, I examine these ideas in the following pages.

Many cultures around the world celebrate coming of age with a variety of events and rituals that introduce the person to sexual life. Indeed, initiation can be an introduction to sexual development and erotic life (Hart 1963). In Aboriginal Australia and New Guinea wherever the precolonial secret societies of the region flourished, the nature of all sexual interaction was generally withheld from prepubertal boys and girls until initiation. It often began their sense of sexual being, even if they had not achieved sexual puberty, since maturation often occurred late in these societies. Many of the Pacific societies actually disapproved of childhood sexual play, for this was felt to disrupt marriage and social regulation of premarital social relations. The Sambia are no different, having delayed sexual education until the initiation of boys and girls in different secret contexts for each. The stories of Sambia boys are clear in associating the awakening of their sexuality in late childhood with their initiation rites and fellatio debut with adolescent bachelor partners. The definition of social reality was thus opened up to same-gender sexuality.

Sambia Boys' Ritual Initiation

The Sambia are a tribe numbering more than two thousand people in the Eastern Highlands of Papua New Guinea. Most elements of culture and social organization are constructed around the nagging destructive presence of warfare in the area. Descent is patrilineal and residence is patrilocal to maximize the cohesion of the local group as a warriorhood. Hamlets are composed of tiny exogamous patriclans that facilitate marriage within the group and exchange with other hamlets, again based on the local politics of warfare. Traditionally, all marriage was arranged; courtship is unknown, and social relationships between the sexes are not only ritually polarized but also often hostile. Like other Highlands societies of New Guinea, these groups are associated with a men's secret society that ideologically disparages women as dangerous creatures who can pollute men and deplete them of their masculine substance. The means of creating and maintaining the village-based secret society is primarily through the ritual initiation of boys beginning at ages seven through ten and continuing until their arranged and consummated marriages, many years later. The warriorhood is guaranteed by collective ritual initiations connecting neighboring hamlets. Within a hamlet, this warriorhood is locally identified with the men's clubhouse, wherein all initiated bachelors reside. Married men frequent the clubhouse constantly; and on occasion (during fight times, rituals, or their wives' menstrual periods) they sleep there. An account of Sambia culture and society has been published elsewhere and need not be repeated here (Herdt 1981).

Sambia sexual culture, which operates on the basis of a strongly essentializing model of sexual development, also incorporates many ideas of social support and cultural creation of the sexual; these ideas derive from the role of ritual and supporting structures of gendered ontologies throughout the life course of men and women. Sexual development, according to the cultural ideals of the Sambia life plan, is fundamentally distinct for men and women. Biological femaleness is considered "naturally" competent and innately complete; maleness, in contrast, is considered more problematic since males are believed incapable of achieving adult reproductive manliness without ritual treatment. Girls are born with female genitalia, a birth canal, a womb, and, behind that, a functional menstrual-blood organ, or *tingu*. Feminine behaviors such as gardening and mothering are thought to be by-products of women's natural *tingu* functioning. As the *tingu* and womb become engorged with blood, puberty and menarche occur; the menses regularly follow, and they are linked with women's child-bearing capacities. According to the canonical male view, all women then need is a penis (i.e., semen) in facilitating adult procreation by bestowing breast milk (transformed from semen), which prepares a woman for nursing her newborn. According to the women's point of view, however, women are biologically competent and can produce their own breast milk—a point of conflict between the two gendered ontologies. This gives rise to a notion that women have a greater internal resilience and health than males and an almost inexhaustible sexual appetite. By comparison, males are not competent biologically until they achieve manhood, and thus they require constant interventions of ritual to facilitate maturation.

The Sambia believe that boys will not "naturally" achieve adult competence without the interventions of ritual, an idea that may seem strange but is actually common throughout New Guinea, even in societies that do not practice boy-inseminating rites (Herdt 1993). Among the Sambia, the practice of age-structured homoerotic relations is a transition into adulthood. The insemination of boys ideally ends when a man marries and fathers a child. In fact, the vast majority of males—more than 90 percent—terminate their sexual relations with boys at that time. Almost all the men do so because of the taboos and, to a lesser degree, because they have "matured" to a new level of having exclusive sexual access to one or more wives, with genital sexual pleasure being conceived of as a greater privilege.

The sexual culture of the Sambia men instills definite and customary lifeways that involves a formula for the life course. Once initiated (before age ten), the boys undergo ordeals to have their "female" traces (left over from birth and from living with their mothers) removed; these ordeals involve painful rites, such as nose-bleedings, that are intended to promote masculinity and aggression. The boys are then in a ritually "clean" state that enables the treatment of their bodies and minds in new ways. These boys are regarded as "pure" sexual virgins, which is important for their insemination. The men believe that the boys are unspoiled because they have not been exposed to the sexual pollution of women, which the men greatly fear. It is thus through oral intercourse that the men receive a special kind of pleasure, unfettered by pollution, and the boys are thought to acquire semen for growth, becoming strong and fertile. All the younger males are thus inseminated by older bachelors, who were once themselves semen recipients.

The younger initiates are semen recipients until their third-stage "puberty" ceremony, around age fifteen. Afterward, they become semen donors to the younger boys. According to the men's sacred lore and the dogmas of their secret society, the bachelors are "married" to the younger recipient males—as symbolized by secret ritual flutes, made of bamboo and believed to be empowered by female spirits that are said to be hostile to women. During this time, the older adolescents are "bisexuals" who may inseminate their wives orally, in addition to the secret insemination of the boys. Eventually these youths have marriages arranged

for them. After they become new fathers, they in turn stop sexual relations with boys. The men's family duties would be compromised by boy relations, the Sambia men say.

The growth of males is believed to be slower and more difficult than that of females. Men say that boys lack an endogenous means for creating manliness. Males do possess a *tingu* (menstrual blood) organ, but it is believed to be "dry" and nonfunctional. They reiterate that a mother's womb, menstrual blood, and vaginal fluids—all containing pollution—impede masculine growth for the boy until he is separated by initiation from mother and the women's world. Males also possess a semen organ (*keriku-keriku*), but unlike the female menstrual blood organ, it is intrinsically small, hard, and empty, containing no semen of its own. Although semen is believed to be the spark of human life and, moreover, the sole precipitant of biological maleness (strong bones and muscles and, later, male secondary-sex traits: a flat abdomen, a hairy body, a mature glans penis), the Sambia hold that the human body cannot naturally produce semen; it must be externally introduced. The purpose of ritual insemination through fellatio is to fill up the *keriku-keriku* (which then stores semen for adult use) and thereby masculinize the boy's body as well as his phallus. Biological maleness is therefore distinct from the mere possession of male genitalia, and only repeated inseminations begun at an early age and regularly continued for years confer the reproductive competence that culminates in sexual development and manliness.

There are four functions of semen exchange: (1) the cultural purpose of "growing" boys through insemination, which is thought to substitute for mother's milk; (2) the "masculinizing" of boys' bodies, again through insemination, but also through ritual ordeals meant to prepare them for warrior life; (3) the provision of "sexual play" or pleasure for the older youths, who have no other sexual outlet prior to marriage; and (4) the transmission of semen and soul substance from one generation of clansmen to the next, which is vital for spiritual and ritual power to achieve its rightful ends (Herdt 1984b). These elements of institutionalized boy-inseminating practices are the object of the most vital and secret ritual teachings in first-stage initiation, which occurs before puberty. The novices are expected to be orally inseminated during the rituals and to continue the practice on a regular basis for years to come. The semen transactions are, however, rigidly structured homoerotically: Novices may act only as fellators in private sexual interactions with older bachelors, who are typically seen as dominant and in control of the same-sex contacts. The adolescent youth is the erotically active party during fellatio, for his erection and ejaculation are necessary for intercourse, and a boy's oral insemination is the socially prescribed outcome of the encounter. Boys must never reverse roles with the older partners or take younger partners before the proper ritual initiations. The violation of such rules is a moral wrong that is sanctioned by a variety of punishments. Boy-inseminating, then, is a matter of sexual relations between unrelated kin and must be seen in the same light as the semen exchanges of delayed sister exchange marriage: Hamlets of potential enemies exchange women and participate in semen exchange of boys, which is necessary for the production of children and the maturation of new warriors.

Ritual initiation for boys is conducted every three or four years for a whole group of boys as an age-set from neighboring villages. This event lasts several months and consists of many ordeals and transitions, some of them frightening and unpleasant, but overall welcomed as the entry into honorable masculinity and access to social power. It culminates in the boys' entry into the men's clubhouse, which is forbidden to women and children. The boys change their identities and roles and live on their own away from their parents until they are grown up and married. The men's house thus becomes their permanent dormitory and secret place of gender segregation.

Sambia girls do not experience initiation until many years later, when they undergo a formal marriage ceremony. Based on what is known, it seems doubtful that the girls undergo a sexual period of same-gender relations like those of the boys, but

I cannot be sure because I was not permitted to enter the menstrual hut, where the initiations of girls were conducted. Males begin their ritual careers and the change in their sexual lives early because the transformation expected of the boys is so great. Girls live on with their parents until they are married and achieve their first menstruation, which occurs very late, age nineteen on average for the Sambia and their neighbors. A secret initiation is performed for the girls in the menstrual hut. Only then can they begin to have sexual relations with their husbands and live with them in a new house built by husband and wife.

The first-stage initiation ceremonies begin the events of life crisis and change in identities for the boys. They are young. After a period of time they are removed to the forest, where the most critical rituals begin to introduce them to the secrets of the men's house and the secret society of the men's warriorhood. The key events involve blood-letting rituals and penis-and-flute rites, which we study here from observations of the initiation conducted in 1975 (Herdt 1982). Here the boys experience the revelation of sexuality and the basic elements of their transition into age-structured homoerotic relations.

On the first morning of the secret rituals in the forest, the boys have fierce and painful nose-bleeding rituals performed on them. This is believed to remove the pollution of their mothers and the women's world that is identified with the boys' bodies. But it is also a testing ground to see how brave they are and the degree to which their fathers, older brothers, and the war leaders of the village can rely on the boys not to run and hide in times of war. Afterward, the boys are prepared by their ritual guardian, who is referred to as their "mother's brother," a kind of "male mother," for the main secret teaching that is to follow. They are dressed in the finest warrior decorations, which they have earned the right to wear through the initiation ordeals. And this begins their preparation for the rites of insemination that will follow. Now that their insides have been "cleansed" to receive the magical gift of manhood—semen—they are taken into the sacred chamber of a forest setting, and there they see for the first time the magical flutes, believed to be animated by the female spirit of the flute, which protects the men and the secrecy of the clubhouse and is thought to be hostile to women.

The key ceremony here is the penis-and-flutes ritual. It focuses on a secret teaching about boy insemination and is regarded by the men and boys alike as the most dramatic and awesome of all Sambia rituals. It begins with the older bachelors, the youths with whom the boys will engage in sexual relations later, who enter the chamber dressed up as the "female spirits of the flutes." The flute players appear, and in their presence, to the accompaniment of the wailing flutes, some powerful secrets of the men's cult are revealed. The setting is awesome: a great crowd waiting in silence as the mysterious sounds are first revealed; boys obediently lining up for threatening review by elders; and boys being told that secret fellatio exists and being taught how to engage in it. Throughout the ritual boys hear at close range the flute sounds associated since childhood with collective masculine power and mystery and pride. The flutes are unequivocally treated as phallic—as symbols of the penis and the power of men to openly flaunt their sexuality. The intent of the flutes' revelation is threatening to the boys as they begin to guess its meaning.

I have observed this flute ceremony during two different initiations, and although my western experience differs greatly from that of Sambia, one thing was intuitively striking to me: The men were revealing the *homoerotic meanings* of the sexual culture. This includes a great preoccupation with the penis and with semen but also with the mouth of the boy and penile erection, sexual impulses, homoerotic activities in particular, and the commencement of sexuality in its broadest sense for the boys. If there is a homoerotic core to the secret society of the Sambia, then this is surely where it begins. These revelations come as boys are enjoined to become fellators, made the sharers of ritual secrets, and threatened with death if they tell women or children what they have learned. They have to keep the secret forever.

Over the course of many years I collected the stories of the boys' experiences as they went through these rituals. The boys' comments indicated that they perceived several different social values bound up with the expression of homoerotic instruction in the flute ceremony. A good place to begin is with childhood training regarding shame about one's genitals. Here is Kambo, a boy who was initiated, talking about his own experience: "I thought—not good that they [elders] are lying or just playing a trick. That's [the penis] not for eating.... When I was a child our fathers said, 'This [penis] is not for handling; if you hold it you'll become lazy.' And because of that [at first in the cult house] I felt—it's not for sucking." Childhood experience is a contributing source of shame about fellatio: Children are taught to avoid handling their own genitals. In a wider sense Kambo's remark pertains to the taboo on masturbation, the sexual naïveté of children, and the boys' prior lack of knowledge about their fathers' homosexual activities.

Another key ritual story concerns the nutritive and "growth" values of semen. A primary source of this idea is men's ritual equation of semen with mother's breast milk, as noted before. The initiates take up this idea quickly in their own subjective orientations toward fellatio. (Pandanus nuts, like coconut, are regarded as another equivalent of semen.) The following remark by Moondi is a typical example of such semen identifications in the teachings of the flute ceremony: "The 'juice' of the pandanus nuts,... it's the same as the 'water' of a man, the same as a man's 'juice' [semen]. And I like to eat a lot of it [because it can give me more water],... for the milk of women is also the same as the milk of men. Milk [breast milk] is for when she carries a child—it belongs to the infant who drinks it." The association between semen and the infant's breast food is also explicit in this observation by Gaimbako, a second-stage initiate: "Semen is the same kind as that [breast milk] of women.... It's the very same kind as theirs,... the same as pandanus nuts too.... But when milk [semen] falls into my mouth [during fellatio], I think it's the milk of women." So the boys are taught beliefs that are highly motivating in support of same-gender sexual relations.

But the ritual also creates in boys a new awareness about their subordination to the older men.

Kambo related this thought as his immediate response to the penis teaching of the flute ceremony: "I was afraid of penis. It's the same as mine—why should I eat it? It's the same kind; [our penises are] only one kind. We're men, not *different* kinds." This supposition is fundamental and implied in many boys' understandings. Kambo felt that males are of one kind, that is, "one sex," as distinct from females. This implies tacit recognition of the sameness of men, which ironically suggests that they should be not sexually involved but in competition for the other gender. Remember, too, the coercive character of the setting: The men's attempt to have boys suck the flutes is laden with overt hostility, much stronger than the latent hostility expressed in lewd homosexual jokes made during the preceding body decoration. The boys are placed in a sexually subordinate position, a fact that is symbolically communicated in the idiom that the novices are "married" to the flutes. (Novices suck the small flute, which resembles the mature glans penis, the men say.) The men thus place the boys in an invidious state of subordination during which the boys may sense that they are being treated too much like women. Sometimes this makes them panic and creates fear and shame. In time, however, a different feeling about the practice sets in.

Nearly all the novices perform their first act of fellatio during the days of initiation, and their story helps us to understand what happens later in their masculine development. Let me cite several responses of Moondi to this highly emotional act:

I was wondering what they [elders] were going to do to us. And...I felt afraid. What will they do to us next? But they put the bamboo in and out of the mouth; and I wondered, what are they doing? Then, when they tried out our mouths, I began to understand...that they were talking about the penis. Oh, that little bamboo is the penis of the men....My whole body was afraid, completely afraid,...and I was heavy, I wanted to cry.

At that point my thoughts went back to how I used to think it was the *aatmwogwambu* [flute spirit], but then I knew that the men did it [made the sounds]. And...I felt a little better, for before

[I thought that] the aatmwogwambu would get me. But now I saw that they [the men] did it.

They told us the penis story....Then I thought a lot, as my thoughts raced quickly. I was afraid—not good that the men "shoot" me [penetrate my mouth] and break my neck. Aye! Why should they put that [penis] inside our mouths! It's not a good thing. They all hide it [the penis] inside their grass skirts, and it's got lots of hair too!

"You must listen well," the elders said. "You all won't grow by yourselves; if you sleep with the men you'll become a *strong* man." They said that; I was afraid....And then they told us clearly: semen is inside—and when you hold a man's penis, you must put it inside your mouth—he can give you semen....It's the same as your mother's breast milk.

"This is no lie!" the men said. "You can't go tell the children, your sisters."...And then later I tried it [fellatio], and I thought: Oh, they told us about *aamoonaalyi* [breast milk; Moondi means semen]—it [semen] is in there.

Despite great social pressures, some boys evince a low interest in the practice from the start, and they seldom participate in fellatio. Some novices feverishly join in. Those are the extremes. The great majority of Sambia boys regularly engage in fellatio for years as constrained by taboo. Homoerotic activities are a touchy subject among males for many reasons. These activities begin with ceremony, it is true, but their occurrence and meaning fan out to embrace a whole secret way of life. What matters is that the boys become sharers of this hidden tradition; and we should expect them to acquire powerful feelings about bachelors, fellatio, semen, and the whole male sexual culture.

One story must stand for many in the way that the Sambia boys grow into this sexual lifeway. One day, while I was talking idly with Kambo, he mentioned singing to himself as he walked in the forest. I asked him what he sang about; and from this innocuous departure point, he said this: "When I think of men's name songs then I sing them: that of a bachelor who is sweet on me; a man of another line or my own line. When I sing the song of a creek in the forest I am happy about that place....Or some man who sleeps with me—when he goes elsewhere, I sing his song. I think of that man who gave me a lot of semen; later, I must sleep with him. I feel like this: he gave me a lot of water [semen]....Later, I will have a lot of water like him."

Here we see established in Kambo's thought the male emphasis on "accumulating semen" and the powerful homoerotic relationships that accompany it. Even a simple activity like singing can create a mood of subjective association with past fellatio and same-gender relationships with the older males. Kambo's last sentence contains a wish: that he will acquire abundant manliness, like that of the friend of whom he sings.

No issue in recent reviews has inspired more debate than the basic question of whether—or to what extent—sexual feelings and erotic desires are motives or consequences of these cultural practices. Does the Sambia boy desire sexual intercourse with the older male? Is the older male sexually attracted to the boy? Indeed, what does "erotic" or "sexual" mean in this context, and is "desire" the proper concept with which to gauge the ontology? Or do other factors, such as power or kinship, produce the sexual attraction and excitement (conscious or unconscious) necessary to produce arousal and uphold the tradition (Herdt 1991)?

Although Sambia culture requires that men eventually change their focus to marriage and give up boy-inseminating, some of the men continue to practice age-structured relations because they find them so pleasurable. A small number of individual men enjoy inseminating boys too much to give up the practice. They develop favorites among the boys and even resort to payment of meat when they find it difficult to obtain a boy who will service them. In our culture these men would probably be called homosexuals because of their preference for the boys, their desires, and their need to mask their activities within the secret domain of ritual. But such an identity of homosexual or gay does not exist for the Sambia, and we must be careful not to project these meanings onto them, for that would be ethnocentric. We can, however, see how they live and what it means to have such an experience—in the absence of the sexual identity system of western culture.

One of these men, Kalutwo, has been interviewed by me over a long period of time, and his sexual and social history reveals a pattern of broken, childless marriages and an exclusive attraction to boys. As he got older, he would have to "pay" the boys with gifts to engage in sex, but when he was younger, some of the boys were known to be fond of him as well (Herdt and Stoller 1990). Several other males are different from Kalutwo in liking boys but also liking women and being successfully married with children. They would be called bisexual in our society. They seem to enjoy sexual pleasure with women and take pride in making babies through their wives, yet they continue illicitly to enjoy oral sex with boys. But Kalutwo disliked women sexually and generally preferred the closeness, sexual intimacy, and emotional security of young men and boys. As he got older, it was increasingly difficult for him to obtain boys as sexual partners, and this seemed to make him feel depressed. Moreover, as he got older, he was increasingly at odds with his male peers socially and stood out from the crowd, having no wife or children, as expected of customary adult manhood. Some people made fun of him behind his back; so did some of the boys. In a society that had a homosexual role, Kalutwo might have found more social support or comfort and perhaps might have been able to make a different transition into middle age. But his village still accepts him, and he has not been turned away or destroyed—as might have occurred in another time had he lived in a western country.

Perhaps in these cases we begin to understand the culture of male camaraderie and emotional intimacy that created such deeply felt desire for same-gender relations in ancient Greece and Japan, in which sexual pleasures and social intimacies with the same gender were as prized as those of intercourse and family life with women. No difficulty was posed to society or to self-esteem so long as these men met their social and sexual obligations and were honorable in their relations with younger males. We know from the anthropological reports from New Guinea that such individuals existed elsewhere as well, and among the Malekula and Marind-anim tribes, for example, adult married men would continue such relations with boys even after reaching the age of being grandfathers in the group, for this was expected.

Mojave Two-Spirit Initiation

My reading of the gender-transformed role among American Indians has shown the importance of two spirits in Native American society for the broader understanding of alternative sexualities. What I have not established thus far is the development of the role in the life of the individual. Among the Mojave Indians, a special ceremony in late childhood marked a transition into the third-gender role that allowed for homoerotic relations so long as they were between people in different gender roles. The two spirit was the product of a long cultural history that involved myth and ceremonial initiation. The ceremonies were sacred and of such importance that their official charter was established in the origin myths of the tribe, known from time immemorial. The meanings of this transition deserve to be highlighted as another variation on coming of age ceremonies in nonwestern cultures.

The Mojave child was only about ten years old when he participated in the ceremony for determining whether a change to two spirit would occur. Perhaps this seems young for a coming of age ceremony; but it might be that the very degree of change and the special nature of the desires to become a man-woman required a childhood transition. In the Mojave case, it was said that a Mojave boy could act "strangely" at the time, turning away from male tasks and refusing the toys of his own sex. The parents would view this as a sign of personal and gender change. Recall that mothers had dreams that their sons would grow up to become two spirits. No doubt this spiritual sign helped to lend religious support for the ceremony. At any rate these signs of gender change were said by the Mojave to express the "true" intentions of the child to change into a man-woman. Nahwera, a Mojave

elder, stated: "When there is a desire in a child's heart to become a transvestite that child will act different. It will let people become aware of that desire" (Devereux 1937, 503). Clearly, the child was beginning to act on desires that transgressed his role and required an adjustment, through ritual, to a new kind of being and social status in the culture.

Arrangements for the ceremony were made by the parents. The boy was reported to have been "surprised" by being offered "female apparel," whereon the relatives waited nervously to see his response. Devereux reported that this was considered both an initiation and an ultimate test of the child's true desires. "If he submitted to it, he was considered a genuine homosexual....If the boy acted in the expected fashion during the ceremony he was considered an initiated homosexual, if not, the gathering scattered, much to the relief of the boy's family" (Devereux 1937, 508). The story suggests that the parents in general may have been ambivalent about this change and may not have wanted it. Nevertheless, true to Mojave culture, they accepted the actions of the boy and supported his decision to become a two-spirit person. The Mojave thus allowed a special combination of a child's ontological being and the support of the family to find its symbolic expression in a ready-made institutionalized cultural practice. It only awaited the right individual and circumstances for the two-spirit person to emerge in each community in each generation.

Both the Sambia example of age-structured relations and the Mojave illustration of gender-transformed homosexuality reveal transitions in late childhood up to age ten. What is magical about age ten? It may be that certain critical developmental changes begin to occur around this time—desires and attractions that indicate the first real sexuality and growing sense of becoming a sexual person. In fact, our study in Chicago revealed that nine and one-half years for boys and ten years for girls were the average age when they were first attracted to the same gender (Herdt and Boxer 1996).

Coming Out—Gay and Lesbian Teens in America

Ours is a culture that defines male and female as absolutely different and then goes to great lengths to deny having done so; American culture reckons "heterosexual" and "homosexual" as fundamentally distinctive kinds of "human nature" but then struggles to find a place for both. Although such gender dimorphism is common in the thinking of nonwestern peoples, the latter idea is rare in, even absent from, many cultures—including our own cultural ancestors, the ancient Greeks. The Greeks described people's sexual behaviors but not their being as homosexual or heterosexual. As we have seen, the Greeks did not place people in categories of sexuality or create sexual classifications that erased all other cultural and personality traits. In our society today this kind of thinking is common and permeates the great symbolic types that define personal being and social action in most spheres of our lives. For many heterosexuals, their worldview and life course goals remain focused on the greatest ritual of reproduction: the church-ordained marriage. And this leads to parenting and family formation. Many think of this ritual process as "good" in all of its aspects. Others see same-gender desire as an attack on that reproductive and moral order, a kind of crisis of gender and sexuality that requires the assertion of a mythical "family values," descended from nineteenth-century ideals, that are seldom relevant to heterosexuals today, let alone to gays and lesbians.

Coming out is another form of ritual that intensifies change in a young person's sexual identity development and social being. It gives public expression to desires long felt to be basic to the person's sexual nature but formerly hidden because of social taboos and homophobia. The process leads to many events that reach a peak in the person's young adult years, especially in the development of gay or lesbian selves, roles, and social relations. Coming out continues to unfold across the entire course of life: There is never really an end to the process for the simple reason that as gay or lesbian people age and their social situations change, they continue to express in new, relevant ways

what it means to be gay or lesbian. Such a social and existential crisis of identity—acted out on the stage of the lesbian and gay community—links the social drama of American youths' experiences with those of tribal initiations, such as those of the Sambia and Mojave, played out in the traditional communities. Of course, these two kinds of drama are different and should not be confused, but they share the issues of handling same-gender desires in cultural context.

Two different processes are involved. First is the secretive act of "passing" as heterosexual, involving the lone individual in largely hidden social networks and secret social spaces....In many towns and cities, especially unsophisticated and traditionally conservative areas of the country, the possibilities are only now emerging for gay/lesbian identification and social action. Second is the coming out in adolescence or young adulthood.

Initially the gay or lesbian grows up with the assumption of being heterosexual. As an awareness of same-gender desires emerges, a feeling of having to hide these desires and pretend otherwise, of acting straight, leads to many moments of secrecy. Later, however, sexual and social experiences may yield a divergent awareness and a desire to be open. What follows is a process of coming out—typically begun in urban centers, sometimes in high school, sometimes later, after the young person has left home for college, work, or the service—that leads to self-identification as gay or lesbian. Through these ritual steps of disclosure all kinds of new socialization and opportunities emerge, including entrance into the gay and lesbian community.

Being and doing gay life are provisioned by the rituals of coming out, and they open significant questions for thinking about youths in search of positive same-gender roles. American teenagers may seem less exotic to the gay or lesbian reader; but they are more of an oddity to the heterosexual adult community as they come out. To many in our own society, these youths look "queer" and "strange" and "diseased," attitudes that reflect historical stereotypes and cultural homophobia.

The growing visibility of the lesbian and gay movement in the United States has made it increasingly possible for people to disclose their desires and "come out" at younger ages. Over the past quarter century, the evidence suggests that the average age of the declaration of same-gender desires has gotten earlier—a lot earlier, as much as ten years earlier than it was in the 1970s—and is for the first time in history a matter of adolescent development. It is not a matter for everyone, of course, but increasingly for those who become aware and are lucky to have the opportunities to begin a new life. In our study of gay and lesbian self-identified youths in Chicago, we found that the average age for boys and girls' "coming out" was sixteen. But we also found that the earliest awareness of same-gender attraction begins at about age ten, which suggests that the desires are a part of the deeper being of the gay or lesbian person.

Gay and lesbian teenagers are growing up with all of the usual problems of our society, including the political, economic, and social troubles of our country, as well as the sexual and social awakening that typifies the adolescent experience. I have already noted how American society and western cultures in general have changed in the direction of more positive regard for gays. This does not mean, however, that the hatred and homophobia of the past are gone or that the secrecy and fear of passing have faded away. People still fear, and rightly so, the effects of coming out on their lives and safety, their well-being and jobs, their social standing and community prestige. These youths are opting to come out as openly lesbian or gay earlier in the life course than ever before in our society. Yet they experience the troubles of feeling themselves attracted to the same gender, with its taboos and sorrows of stigma and shame, not knowing what to do about it. Fortunately, the gay and lesbian culture provides new contexts of support; these youths have institutions and media that talk about it; they learn from adult role models that they can live relatively happy and rewarding lives with their desires.

We can study how one group of adolescents in Chicago has struggled with these issues while preparing for socialization and coming out in the context of the lesbian and gay community. The study of gay, lesbian, and bisexual youths in Chicago was located in the largest gay social services agency of the city, Horizons Community Services. Horizons was created in the early 1970s out of the gay liberation movement, and by 1979 it had founded a gay and lesbian youth group, one of the first in the United States. The agency is based in the gay neighborhood of the city, and it depends on volunteers and the goodwill and interest of friends of the agency. In recent years the youths have led the Gay and Lesbian Pride Day Parade in Chicago and have become a symbol of social and political progress in gay culture in the city.

The Horizons study was organized around the youth group, for ages thirteen to twenty, but the average age of the youths interviewed in depth was about eighteen. We interviewed a total of 202 male and female youths of all backgrounds from the suburbs and inner city, white and black and brown. Many people of color and of diverse ethnic subcultures in Chicago have experienced racism and many forms of homophobia, and these have effectively barred their coming out. The group tries to find a place for all of these diverse adolescents; no one is turned away. Group meetings are coordinated by lesbian and gay adults, esteemed role models of the teens. They facilitate a discussion of a variety of topics, particularly in matters of the coming out process, such as fears and homophobic problems at school or home, and issues of special interest to the teens. The youth group has an active social life as well, hosting parties and organizing social events, such as the annual alternative gay and lesbian prom, held on the weekend of high school proms in Chicago, for the youth members.

Protecting teens from the risk of infection from AIDS is another key goal of Horizons' sponsorship of the youth group. AIDS has become an increasingly important element of the youth group discussions. "Safe sex" is promoted through educational material and special public speakers. In general, the socialization rituals of the group prepare the youths for their new status in the gay and lesbian community, and the rituals culminate in marching in the Gay and Lesbian Pride Day Parade every June.

The lesbian or gay youth is in the throes of moving through the symbolic "death" of the heterosexual identity and role and into the "rebirth" of their social being as gay. As a life crisis and a passage between the past and future, the person is betwixt and between normal social states, that is, between the heterosexual worlds of parents and the cultural system of gay and lesbian adults. To the anthropologist, the youths are symbolically exiting what was once called "homosexuality" and entering what is now called "gay and lesbian." To the psychologist, their transition is from dependence and internalized homophobia to a more open and mature competence and pride in the sexual/gender domains of their lives. The transformative power contained in the rituals of coming out as facilitated by Horizons helps in the newfound development of the person. But it also helps in the lives of everyone touched by a youth who is coming out. As long as this process is blocked or resisted, the pull back into passing as heterosexual is very tempting.

Back in the 1960s,... coming out was a secret incorporation into the closet "homosexual" community. Studies at the time showed that the more visible contexts of engaging in same-sex contacts might lead to de facto coming out, but these were generally marginal and dangerous places, such as public toilets, where victimization and violence could occur. To come out in secret bars, the military, toilets, or bus depots did not create a positive identification with the category of gay/lesbian. There was generally no identity that positively accorded with gay or lesbian self-esteem as we think of it today. Thus, we can understand how many people found it revolutionary to fight back against homophobia and begin to march openly in parades in the 1970s. Nevertheless, the change was uneven and difficult.

People who continue to pass as straight when they desire people of the same gender and may in fact have sexual relations with them present a perplexing issue—not only for lesbians and gay men but also for society as a whole. This kind of person, through secrecy and passing, serves as a negative role model of what not to be. Alas, there are many movie stars, celebrities, and sports heroes who live closeted lives of this kind—until they are discovered or "outed" by someone. Many youths are frightened or intimidated when they discover adults they know and love, such as teachers, uncles, family friends, or pastors, who pass as heterosexual but have been discovered to desire the same gender. Adolescents can be angered to discover that a media person they admire has two lives, one publicly heterosexual and one privately homosexual. This is a cultural survival of the nineteenth-century system of closet homosexuality, with its hide-and-seek games to escape the very real dangers of homophobia. In contrast, positive role models provided by the largely white middle-class adult advisers at Horizons are the crucial source for learning how to enter the gay and lesbian community.

Cultural homophobia in high school is a powerful force against coming out. Learning to hide one's desires is crucial for the survival of some youths, especially at home and at school, the two greatest institutions that perpetuate homophobia in the United States. Our informants tell us that standard slurs to put people down in the schools remain intact. To be slurred as a "dyke" or a "faggot" is a real blow to social esteem. But "queer" is the most troubling epithet of all. To be targeted as a "queer" in high school is enormously troubling for the youths, somehow more alienating and isolating, an accusation not just of doing something "different" but of being something "unnatural." One seventeen-year-old eleventh grade boy remarked to us that he was secretive at school. "I'm hidden mostly—cause of the ways they'll treat you. Okay, there are lots of gangs.... They find out you're [what they call] a faggot and they beat on you and stuff. If they ask me I say it's none of their business." The role of secrecy, passing, and hiding continues the homophobia. Ironically, as Michelle Fine (1988, 36) notes in her study of black adolescent girls in New York City high schools, it was the gay and lesbian organization in the school that was the most open and safe environment in which young African-American girls could access their own feelings. They could, with the support of the lesbian and gay teenage group, start to become the agents of their *own* desires. Our study has shown that in Chicago most lesbian or gay youths have experienced harassment in school; and when this is combined with harassment and problems at home, it signals a serious mental health risk, especially for suicide. And the risk of suicide before lesbian or gay youths come to find the support of the Horizons group is very great.

The ritual of coming out means giving up the secrecy of the closet. This is a positive step toward mental health, for life in the closet involves not only a lot of hiding but also a good deal of magical thinking, which may be detrimental to the person's well-being. By magical thinking, I mean mainly contagious beliefs about homosexuality such as the common folk ideas of our culture that stereotype homosexuality as a disease that spreads, as well as the historical images of homosexuality as a mental illness or a crime against nature. These magical beliefs support homophobia and warn about the dangers of going to a gay community organization, whispering how the adolescent might turn into a monster or sex fiend or be raped or murdered or sold into slavery.

Another common contagious fear is the belief that by merely contacting other gays, the adolescent's "sin or disease" will spread to the self and will then unwittingly spread to others, such as friends and siblings. One of the common magical beliefs of many adults and parents is that the youth has merely to avoid other gays and lesbians in order to "go straight." This is surely another cultural "leftover" from the dark myth of homosexuality as evil. . . . If the adolescent will only associate with straights, the parent feels, this strange period of "confusion" will pass, and he or she will become heterosexual like everyone else. Such silly stereotypes are strongly associated with the false notion that all gay or lesbian teens are simply "confused," which was promoted by psychologists in the prior generation. This belief is based on the cultural myth that same-sex desires are "adolescent" desires of a transient nature that may be acquired or learned but can go away; and if the self ignores them, the desire for the opposite sex will grow in their place. Magical fears of contracting AIDS is a

new and most powerful deterrent to coming out among some youths. Many youths fear their initial social contact with anyone gay because they think they might contagiously contract AIDS by being gay or lesbian or by interacting socially with gays.

The gender difference in the experience of coming out as a male or a female highlights the cultural pressures that are still exerted on teens to conform to the norm of heterosexuality in our society. Girls typically have more heterosexual experience in their histories, with two-thirds of the girls having had significant heterosexual contact before they came to Horizons. Since the age of our sample was about eighteen, it is easy to see that relatively early on, between the ages of thirteen and seventeen, girls were being inducted into sexual relations with boys. We face here the problem of what is socially necessary and what is preferred. Only one-third of the boys had had heterosexual experience, and fully two-fifths of them had had no sexual experience with girls. Note also that for many of the boys, their sexual contacts with girls were their lesbian-identified friends at the Horizons youth group. The boys tended to achieve sexual experiences earlier than the girls, by age sixteen, at which point the differences in development had evened out. Both genders were beginning to live openly lesbian or gay lives.

Clearly, powerful gender role pressures are exerted on girls to conform to the wishes of parents, siblings, peers, and boyfriends. Some of this, to use a phrase by Nancy Chodorow (1992) about heterosexuality as a compromise formation, results in a compromise of their desires, even of their personal integrity, in the development of their sexual and self-concept. But as we know from the work of Michele Fine (1992), who studied adolescent sexuality among African-American girls in the New York City schools, females were not able to explore and express their desires until they located a safe space that enabled them to think out loud. In fact, they could not become the agents of their own desires until they had located the gay and lesbian youth group in the high school! There, some of them had to admit, contrary to their stereotypes, they found the gay youths more accepting and open of variations than any of their peers or the adults. The lesson here is that when a cultural space is created, people can explore their own desires and better achieve their own identities and sociosexual goals in life.

We have found that four powerful magical beliefs exist in the implicit learning of homophobia and self-hatred among gay and lesbian youths. First is the idea that homosexuals are crazy and heterosexuals are sane. Unlearning this idea involves giving up the assumption of heterosexual normalcy in favor of positive attitudes and role models. Second is the idea that the problem with same-gender desires is in the self, not in society. Unlearning this belief means recognizing cultural homophobia and discovering that the problem with hatred lies not in the self but in society. Third is the magical belief that to have same-gender desires means giving up gendered roles as they were previously known and acting as a gender-transformed person, a boy acting or dressing as a girl, a girl living as a boy, or either living as an androgyne. There is nothing wrong with these transformations. What we have seen in the cross-cultural study, however, is that there are a variety of ways to organize same-gender desires. The old ways of gender inversion from the nineteenth century are only one of these. Unlearning gender reversal means accepting one's own gendered desires and enactments of roles, whatever these are, rather than living up to social standards—either in the gay or straight community.

Fourth is the belief that if one is going to be gay, there are necessary goals, rules, roles, and political and social beliefs that must be performed or expressed. This idea goes against the grain of American expressive individualism, in which we feel that each one of us is unique and entitled to "know thyself" as the means of social fulfillment. The key is that there is not one perfect way to be gay; there are many divergent ways. Nor is there any single event, or magic pill, that will enable the process of coming out. It is a lifelong process, as long as it takes to live and find a fulfilling social and spiritual lifeway in our culture.

Lesbian and gay youths have shown that coming out is a powerful means of confronting the unjust, false, wrongful social faces and values of prejudice in our culture. Before being out, youths are asking, "What can we be?" or "How can we fit into this society?" Emerging from the secrecy, these youths are making new claims on society to live up to its own standards of justice. The rituals of coming out are a way of unlearning and creating new learning about living with same-gender desires and creating a positive set of relationships around them. Surely the lesson of the gay movement is that hiding desires and passing as something other than what one is are no less injurious to the normal heart and the healthy mind of gay youths than was, say, passing as a Christian if one was a Jew in Nazi Germany or passing as white in the old South or in South Africa under apartheid.

Lesbian and gay youths are challenging society in ways that are no less revolutionary than discriminations based on skin color, gender, or religion. A new of kind of social and political activism has arisen; it goes beyond AIDS/HIV, but builds on the grief and anger that the entire generation feels about the impact of the pandemic on gay and lesbian culture. Some call this new generation queer. But others prefer lesbian or gay or bisexual or transgendered. Perhaps the word is less important than the commitment to building a rich and meaningful social world in which all people, including lesbians and gays, have a place to live and plan for the future.

We have seen in this chapter how a new generation of lesbian- and gay-identified youths has utilized transition rituals to find a place in the gay and lesbian community. It was the activism and social progress of the lesbian and gay culture that made this huge transformation possible. The emergence of a community enabled the support of youth groups and other institutions for the creation of a new positive role model and self-concept. Youths are beginning to take up new status rights and duties, having a new set of cultural ideas to create the moral voice of being gay, bisexual, lesbian, or queer. The rituals, such as the annual Gay and Lesbian Pride Day Parade, make these newly created traditions a lived reality; they codify and socialize gay and lesbian ideals, knowledge, and social roles, bonding past and future in a timeless present that will enable these youths to find a place in a better society.

References

Benedict, Ruth. 1938. "Continuities and discontinuities in cultural conditioning." *Psychiatry* 1:161–167.

Chodorow, Nancy J. 1992. "Heterosexuality as a Compromise Formation: Reflections on the Psychoanalytic Theory of Sexual Development." *Psychoanalysis and Contemporary Thought* 15:267–304.

Devereux, George. 1937. "Institutionalized Homosexuality Among the Mohave Indians." *Human Biology* 9:498–527.

Fine, Michelle. 1988. "Sexuality, Schooling, and Adolescent Females: The Missing Discourse of Desire." *Harvard Education Review* 58:29–53.

Hart, C. W. M. 1963. "Contrasts Between Prepubertal and Postpubertal Education." In *Education and Culture,* ed. G. Spindler, pp. 400–425. New York: Holt, Rinehart and Winston.

Herdt, Gilbert. 1981. *Guardians of the Flutes: Idioms of Masculinity.* New York: McGraw-Hill.

———. 1982. "Fetish and Fantasy in Sambia Initiation." In *Rituals of Manhood,* ed. G. Herdt., pp. 44–98. Berkeley and Los Angeles: University of California Press.

———. 1984b. "Semen Transactions in Sambia Culture." In *Ritualized Homosexuality in Melanesia,* ed. G. Herdt, pp. 167–210. Berkeley and Los Angeles: University of California Press.

———. 1991. "Representations of Homosexuality in Traditional Societies: An Essay on Cultural Ontology and Historical Comparison, Part II." *Journal of the History of Sexuality* 2:603–632.

———. 1993. "Introduction." In *Ritualized Homosexuality in Melanesia,* ed. G. Herdt, pp. vii–xliv. Berkeley and Los Angeles: University of California Press.

———, and Andrew Boxer. 1996. *Children of Horizons: How Gay and Lesbian Youth Are Forging a New Way Out of the Closet.* Boston: Beacon Press.

———, and Robert J. Stoller. 1990. *Intimate Communications: Erotics and the Study of Culture.* New York: Columbia University Press.

PART 3

Psychology of Sex Roles

Even if biology were destiny, the founder of psychoanalysis Sigmund Freud argued, the process by which biological males and females become gendered men and women does not happen naturally nor inevitably. Gender identity, he argued, is an achievement—the outcome of a struggle for boys to separate from their mothers and identify with their fathers, and of a parallel and complementary struggle for girls to reconcile themselves to their sexual inadequacy and therefore maintain their identification with their mothers.

Subsequent generations of psychologists have attempted to specify the content of that achievement of gender identity, and how it might be measured. In the early 1930s, Lewis Terman, one of the country's most eminent social psychologists, codified gender identity into a set of attitudes, traits, and behaviors that enabled researchers to pinpoint exactly where any young person was on a continuum between masculinity and femininity. If one had successfully acquired the "appropriate" collection of traits and attitudes, one (and one's parents') could rest assured that one would continue to develop "normally." Gender nonconformity—boys who scored high on the femininity side of the continuum or girls who scored high on the masculine side—was a predictor, Terman argued, for sexual nonconformity.

Homosexuality was the sexual behavioral outcome of a gender problem, of men who had not successfully mastered masculinity or women who had not successfully mastered femininity.

In this section Janet Shibley Hyde reviews all the studies of gender difference in psychology—traits, attitudes, and behaviors—and finds few, if any, really big differences. It turns out that the empirical research reveals that we're all from planet Earth.

Despite these similarities, an enormous cultural and psychological edifice is concerned with creating, sustaining, and reproducing gender difference, and then convincing us that it's natural, inevitable, and biologically based. C. J. Pascoe, for example, shows how homophobic teasing and bullying serve as a sort of policing device to make sure that boys (and to a lesser extent girls) remain conformists to gender norms. Joan Letendre examines the ways in which girls resist those norms and express their "normal, biological" emotions of anger and aggression.

Peggy Giordano and her colleagues expose a curious phenomenon: that adolescent boys seem to be more romantic—despite all the cultural prescriptions against it—than girls. What they reveal, though, is that such romantic longings are also based on fantasy ideals of romance and love, rather than the more pragmatic approaches of girls. More boys subcribe to romantic fantasies of "love at first sight" than do girls. Love is something you have, boys think, not something you necessarily have to do.

The Gender Similarities Hypothesis

JANET SHIBLEY HYDE

The mass media and the general public are captivated by findings of gender differences. John Gray's (1992) *Men Are from Mars, Women Are from Venus*, which argued for enormous psychological differences between women and men, has sold over 30 million copies and been translated into forty languages (Gray, 2005). Deborah Tannen's (1991) *You Just Don't Understand: Women and Men in Conversation* argued for the *different cultures hypothesis:* that men's and women's patterns of speaking are so fundamentally different that men and women essentially belong to different linguistic communities or cultures. That book was on the *New York Times* bestseller list for nearly four years and has been translated into twenty-four languages (AnnOnline, 2005). Both of these works, and dozens of others like them, have argued for the *differences hypothesis:* that males and females are, psychologically, vastly different. Here, I advance a very different view—the *gender similarities hypothesis* (for related statements, see Epstein, 1988; Hyde, 1985; Hyde & Plant, 1995; Kimball, 1995).

The Hypothesis

The gender similarities hypothesis holds that males and females are similar on most, but not all, psychological variables. That is, men and women, as well as boys and girls, are more alike than they are different. In terms of effect sizes, the gender similarities hypothesis states that most psychological gender differences are in the close-to-zero ($d \leq 0.10$) or small ($0.11 < d < 0.35$) range, a few are in the moderate range ($0.36 < d < 0.65$), and very few are large ($d = 0.66$–1.00) or very large ($d > 1.00$).

Although the fascination with psychological gender differences has been present from the dawn of formalized psychology around 1879 (Shields, 1975), a few early researchers highlighted gender similarities. Thorndike (1914), for example, believed that psychological gender differences were too small, compared with within-gender variation, to be important. Leta Stetter Hollingworth (1918) reviewed available research on gender differences in mental traits and found little evidence of gender differences. Another important reviewer of gender research in the early 1900s, Helen Thompson Woolley (1914), lamented the gap between the data and scientists' views on the question:

> The general discussions of the psychology of sex, whether by psychologists or by sociologists show such a wide diversity of points of view that one feels that the truest thing to be said at present is that scientific evidence plays very little part in producing convictions. (p. 372)

The Role of Meta-Analysis in Assessing Psychological Gender Differences

Reviews of research on psychological gender differences began with Woolley's (1914) and Hollingworth's (1918) and extended through Maccoby and Jacklin's (1974) watershed book *The Psychology of Sex Differences*, in which they reviewed more than 2,000 studies of gender differences in a wide variety of domains, including abilities, personality, social behavior, and memory. Maccoby and Jacklin dismissed as unfounded many popular beliefs in psychological gender differences, including beliefs that girls are more "social" than boys; that girls are more suggestible; that girls have lower self-esteem; that girls are better at rote learning and simple tasks, whereas boys are better at higher level cognitive processing; and that girls lack achievement motivation. Maccoby and Jacklin concluded that gender differences were well established in only four areas: verbal ability, visual-spatial ability, mathematical ability, and aggression. Overall, then, they found much evidence for gender similarities. Secondary reports of their findings in textbooks and other sources, however, focused almost exclusively on their conclusions about gender differences (e.g., Gleitman, 1981; Lefrançois, 1990).

Shortly after this important work appeared, the statistical method of meta-analysis was developed (e.g., Glass, McGaw, & Smith, 1981; Hedges & Olkin, 1985; Rosenthal, 1991). This method revolutionized the study of psychological gender differences. Meta-analyses quickly appeared on issues such as gender differences in influenceability (Eagly & Carli, 1981), abilities (Hyde, 1981; Hyde & Linn, 1988; Linn & Petersen, 1985), and aggression (Eagly & Steffen, 1986; Hyde, 1984, 1986).

Meta-analysis is a statistical method for aggregating research findings across many studies of the same question (Hedges & Becker, 1986). It is ideal for synthesizing research on gender differences, an area in which often dozens or even hundreds of studies of a particular question have been conducted.

Crucial to meta-analysis is the concept of effect size, which measures the magnitude of an effect—in this case, the magnitude of gender difference. In gender meta-analyses, the measure of effect size typically is d (Cohen, 1988):

$$d = \frac{M_M - M_F}{s_W},$$

where M_M is the mean score for males, M_F is the mean score for females, and s_W is the average within-sex standard deviation. That is, d measures how far apart the male and female means are in standardized units. In gender meta-analysis, the effect sizes computed from all individual studies are averaged to obtain an overall effect size reflecting the magnitude of gender differences across all studies. In the present article, I follow the convention that negative values of d mean that females scored higher on a dimension, and positive values of d indicate that males scored higher.

Gender meta-analyses generally proceed in four steps: (a) The researcher locates all studies on the topic being reviewed, typically using databases such as PsycINFO and carefully chosen search terms. (b) Statistics are extracted from each report, and an effect size is computed for each study. (c) A weighted average of the effect sizes is computed (weighting by sample size) to obtain an overall assessment of the direction and magnitude of the gender difference when all studies are combined. (d) Homogeneity analyses are conducted to determine whether the group of effect sizes is relatively homogeneous. If it is not, then the studies can be partitioned into theoretically meaningful groups to determine whether the effect size is larger for some types of studies and smaller for other types. The researcher could ask, for example, whether gender differences are larger for measures of physical aggression compared with measures of verbal aggression.

The Evidence

To evaluate the gender similarities hypothesis, I collected the major meta-analyses that have been conducted on psychological gender differences. They are listed in Table 1, grouped roughly into six categories: those that assessed cognitive variables, such as abilities; those that assessed verbal or nonverbal communication; those that assessed social or personality variables, such as aggression or leadership; those that assessed measures of psychological well-being, such as self-esteem; those that assessed motor behaviors, such as throwing distance; and those that assessed miscellaneous constructs, such as moral reasoning. I began with meta-analyses reviewed previously by Hyde and Plant (1995), Hyde and Frost (1993), and Ashmore

(1990). I updated these lists with more recent meta-analyses and, where possible, replaced older meta-analyses with more up-to-date meta-analyses that used larger samples and better statistical methods.

Hedges and Nowell (1995; see also Feingold, 1988) have argued that the canonical method of meta-analysis—which often aggregates data from many small convenience samples—should be augmented or replaced by data from large probability samples, at least when that is possible (e.g., in areas such as ability testing). Test-norming data as well as data from major national surveys such as the National Longitudinal Study of Youth provide important information. Findings from samples such as these are included in the summary shown in Table 1, where the number of reports is marked with an asterisk.

Inspection of the effect sizes shown in the rightmost column of Table 1 reveals strong evidence for the gender similarities hypothesis. These effect sizes are summarized in Table 2. Of the 128 effect sizes shown in Table 1, 4 were unclassifiable because the meta-analysis provided such a wide

Table 1. Major Meta-Analyses of Research on Psychological Gender Differences

Study and Variable	Age	No. of Reports	d
Cognitive Variables			
Hyde, Fennema, & Lamon (1990)			
Mathematics computation	All	45	−0.14
Mathematics concepts	All	41	−0.03
Mathematics problem solving	All	48	+0.08
Hedges & Nowell (1995)			
Reading comprehension	Adolescents	5*	−0.09
Vocabulary	Adolescents	4*	+0.06
Mathematics	Adolescents	6*	+0.16
Perceptual speed	Adolescents	4*	−0.28
Science	Adolescents	4*	+0.32
Spatial ability	Adolescents	2*	+0.19
Hyde, Fennema, Ryan, et al. (1990)			
Mathematics self-confidence	All	56	+0.16
Mathematics anxiety	All	53	−0.15
Feingold (1988)			
DAT spelling	Adolescents	5*	−0.45
DAT language	Adolescents	5*	−0.40
DAT verbal reasoning	Adolescents	5*	−0.02
DAT abstract reasoning	Adolescents	5*	−0.04
DAT numerical ability	Adolescents	5*	−0.10
DAT perceptual speed	Adolescents	5*	−0.34
DAT mechanical reasoning	Adolescents	5*	+0.76
DAT space relations	Adolescents	5*	+0.15
Hyde & Linn (1988)			
Vocabulary	All	40	−0.02
Reading comprehension	All	18	−0.03
Speech production	All	12	−0.33

(continued)

Table 1. (*continued*)

Study and Variable	Age	No. of Reports	d
Cognitive Variables			
Linn & Petersen (1985)			
Spatial perception	All	62	+0.44
Mental rotation	All	29	+0.73
Spatial visualization	All	81	+0.13
Voyer et al. (1995)			
Spatial perception	All	92	+0.44
Mental rotation	All	78	+0.56
Spatial visualization	All	116	+0.19
Lynn & Irwing (2004)			
Progressive matrices	6–14 years	15	+0.02
Progressive matrices	15–19 years	23	+0.16
Progressive matrices	Adults	10	+0.30
Whitley et al. (1986)			
Attribution of success to ability	All	29	+0.13
Attribution of success to effort	All	29	−0.04
Attribution of success to task	All	29	−0.01
Attribution of success to luck	All	29	−0.07
Attribution of failure to ability	All	29	+0.16
Attribution of failure to effort	All	29	+0.15
Attribution of failure to task	All	29	−0.08
Attribution of failure luck	All	29	−0.15
Communication			
Anderson & Leaper (1998)			
Interruptions in conversation	Adults	53	+0.15
Intrusive interruptions	Adults	17	+0.33
Leaper & Smith (2004)			
Talkativeness	Children	73	−0.11
Affiliative speech	Children	46	−0.26
Assertive speech	Children	75	+0.11
Dindia & Allen (1992)			
Self-disclosure (all studies)	—	205	−0.18
Self-disclosure to stranger	—	99	−0.07
Self-disclosure to friend	—	50	−0.28
LaFrance et al. (2003)			
Smiling	Adolescents and adults	418	−0.40
Smiling: Aware of being observed	Adolescents and adults	295	−0.46
Smiling: Not aware of being observed	Adolescents and adults	31	−0.19

Table 1. (*continued*)

Study and Variable	Age	No. of Reports	d
Communication (*continued*)			
McClure (2000)			
Facial expression processing	Infants	29	−0.18 to −0.92
Facial expression processing	Children and adolescents	89	−0.13 to −0.18
Social and Personality Variables			
Hyde (1984, 1986)			
Aggression (all types)	All	69	+0.50
Physical aggression	All	26	+0.60
Verbal aggression	All	6	+0.43
Eagly & Steffen (1986)			
Aggression	Adults	50	+0.29
Physical aggression	Adults	30	+0.40
Psychological aggression	Adults	20	+0.18
Knight et al. (2002)			
Physical aggression	All	41	+0.59
Verbal aggression	All	22	+0.28
Aggression in low emotional arousal context	All	40	+0.30
Aggression in emotional arousal context	All	83	+0.56
Bettencourt & Miller (1996)			
Aggression under provocation	Adults	57	+0.17
Aggression under neutral conditions	Adults	50	+0.33
Archer (2004)			
Aggression in real-world settings	All	75	+0.30 to +0.63
Physical aggression	All	111	+0.33 to +0.84
Verbal aggression	All	68	+0.09 to +0.55
Indirect aggression	All	40	−0.74 to +0.05
Stuhlmacher & Walters (1999)			
Negotiation outcomes	Adults	53	+0.09
Walters et al. (1998)			
Negotiator competitiveness	Adults	79	10.07
Eagly & Crowley (1986)			
Helping behavior	Adults	99	+0.13
Helping: Surveillance context	Adults	16	+0.74
Helping: No surveillance	Adults	41	−0.02
Oliver & Hyde (1993)			
Sexuality: Masturbation	All	26	+0.96

(*continued*)

Table 1. (*continued*)

Study and Variable	Age	No. of Reports	d
Social and Personality Variables (*continued*)			
Sexuality: Attitudes about casual sex	All	10	+0.81
Sexual satisfaction	All	15	−0.06
Attitudes about extramarital sex	All	17	+0.29
Murnen & Stockton (1997)			
Arousal to sexual stimuli	Adults	62	+0.31
Eagly & Johnson (1990)			
Leadership: Interpersonal style	Adults	153	−0.04 to −0.07
Leadership: Task style	Adults	154	0.00 to −0.09
Leadership: Democratic vs. autocratic	Adults	28	+0.22 to +0.34
Eagly et al. (1992)			
Leadership: Evaluation	Adults	114	+0.05
Eagly et al. (1995)			
Leadership effectiveness	Adults	76	−0.02
Eagly et al. (2003)			
Leadership: Transformational	Adults	44	−0.10
Leadership: Transactional	Adults	51	−0.13 to +0.27
Leadership: Laissez-faire	Adults	16	+0.16
Feingold (1994)			
Neuroticism: Anxiety	Adolescents and adults	13*	−0.32
Neuroticism: Impulsiveness	Adolescents and adults	6*	−0.01
Extraversion: Gregariousness	Adolescents and adults	10*	−0.07
Extraversion: Assertiveness	Adolescents and adults	10*	+0.51
Extraversion: Activity	Adolescents and adults	5	+0.08
Openness	Adolescents and adults	4*	+0.19
Agreeableness: Trust	Adolescents and adults	4*	−0.35
Agreeableness: Tendermindedness	Adolescents and adults	10*	−0.91
Conscientiousness	Adolescents and adults	4	−0.18
Psychological Well-being			
Kling et al. (1999, Analysis I)			
Self-esteem	All	216	+0.21
Kling et al. (1999, Analysis II)			
Self-esteem	Adolescents	15*	+0.04 to +0.16
Major et al. (1999)			
Self-esteem	All	226	+0.14
Feingold & Mazzella (1998)			
Body esteem	All	—	+0.58
Twenge & Nolen-Hoeksema (2002)			
Depression symptoms	8–16 years	310	+0.02

Table 1. (*continued*)

Study and Variable	Age	No. of Reports	d
Psychological Well-being (*continued*)			
Wood et al. (1989)	Adults	17	−0.03
Life satisfaction	Adults	22	−0.07
Happiness			
Pinquart & Sörensen (2001)			
Life satisfaction	Elderly	176	+0.08
Self-esteem	Elderly	59	+0.08
Happiness	Elderly	56	−0.06
Tamres et al. (2002)			
Coping: Problem-focused	All	22	−0.13
Coping: Rumination	All	10	−0.19
Motor Behaviors			
Thomas & French (1985)			
Balance	3–20 years	67	+0.09
Grip strength	3–20 years	37	+0.66
Throw velocity	3–20 years	12	+2.18
Throw distance	3–20 years	47	+1.98
Vertical jump	3–20 years	20	+0.18
Sprinting	3–20 years	66	+0.63
Flexibility	5–10 years	13	−0.29
Eaton & Enns (1986)			
Activity level	All	127	+0.49
Miscellaneous			
Thoma (1986)			
Moral reasoning: Stage	Adolescents and adults	56	−0.21
Jaffee & Hyde (2000)			
Moral reasoning: Justice orientation	All	95	+0.19
Moral reasoning: Care orientation	All	160	−0.28
Silverman (2003)			
Delay of gratification	All	38	−0.12
Whitley et al. (1999)			
Cheating behavior	All	36	+0.17
Cheating attitudes	All	14	+0.35
Whitley (1997)			
Computer use: Current	All	18	+0.33
Computer self-efficacy	All	29	+0.41
Konrad et al. (2000)			
Job attribute preference: Earnings	Adults	207	+0.12
Job attribute preference: Security	Adults	182	−0.02
Job attribute preference: Challenge		63	+0.05

(*continued*)

Table 1. (*continued*)

Study and Variable	Age	No. of Reports	d
Miscellaneous			
Job attribute preference: Physical work environment	Adults	96	−0.13
Job attribute preference: Power	Adults	68	+0.04

Note: Positive values of *d* represent higher scores for men and/or boys; negative values of *d* represent higher scores for women and/or girls. Asterisks indicate that data were from major, large national samples. Dashes indicate that data were not available (i.e., the study in question did not provide this information clearly). No. = number; DAT = Differential Aptitude Test.

Table 2. Effect Sizes (n = 124) for Psychological Gender Differences, Based on Meta-Analyses, Categorized by Range of Magnitude

Effect sizes	Effect Size Range				
	0–0.10	0.11–0.35	0.36–0.65	0.66–1.00	>1.00
Number	37	59	19	7	2
% of total	30	48	15	6	2

range for the estimate. The remaining 124 effect sizes were classified into the categories noted earlier: close-to-zero ($d \leq 0.10$), small ($0.11 < d < 0.35$), moderate ($0.36 < d < 0.65$), large ($d = 0.66–1.00$), or very large ($> .1.00$). The striking result is that 30% of the effect sizes are in the close-to-zero range, and an additional 48% are in the small range. That is, 78% of gender differences are small or close to zero. This result is similar to that of Hyde and Plant (1995), who found that 60% of effect sizes for gender differences were in the small or close-to-zero range.

The small magnitude of these effects is even more striking given that most of the meta-analyses addressed the classic gender differences questions—that is, areas in which gender differences were reputed to be reliable, such as mathematics performance, verbal ability, and aggressive behavior. For example, despite Tannen's (1991) assertions, gender differences in most aspects of communication are small. Gilligan (1982) has argued that males and females speak in a different moral "voice," yet meta-analyses show that gender differences in moral reasoning and moral orientation are small (Jaffee & Hyde, 2000).

The Exceptions

As noted earlier, the gender similarities hypothesis does not assert that males and females are similar in absolutely every domain. The exceptions—areas in which gender differences are moderate or large in magnitude—should be recognized.

The largest gender differences in Table 1 are in the domain of motor performance, particularly for measures such as throwing velocity ($d = 2.18$) and throwing distance ($d = 1.98$) (Thomas & French, 1985). These differences are particularly large after puberty, when the gender gap in muscle mass and bone size widens.

A second area in which large gender differences are found is some—but not all—measures of sexuality (Oliver & Hyde, 1993). Gender differences are strikingly large for incidences of masturbation and for attitudes about sex in a casual, uncommitted relationship. In contrast, the gender difference in reported sexual satisfaction is close to zero.

Across several meta-analyses, aggression has repeatedly shown gender differences that are moderate in magnitude (Archer, 2004; Eagly & Steffen, 1986; Hyde, 1984, 1986). The gender difference in physical aggression is particularly reliable

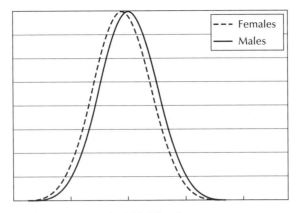

Figure 3.1. Graphic Representation of a 0.21 Effect Size

Note: Two normal distributions that are 0.21 standard deviations apart (i.e., $d = 0.21$). This is the approximate magnitude of the gender difference in self-esteem, averaged over all samples, found by Kling et al. (1999). From "Gender Differences in Self-Esteem: A Meta-Analysis," by K. C. Kling, J. S. Hyde, C. J. Showers, and B. N. Buswell, 1999, *Psychological Bulletin*, 125, p. 484. Copyright © 1999 by the American Psychological Association.

and is larger than the gender difference in verbal aggression. Much publicity has been given to gender differences in relational aggression, with girls scoring higher (e.g., Crick & Grotpeter, 1995). According to the Archer (2004) meta-analysis, indirect or relational aggression showed an effect size for gender differences of −0.45 when measured by direct observation, but it was only −0.19 for peer ratings, −0.02 for self-reports, and −0.13 for teacher reports. Therefore, the evidence is ambiguous regarding the magnitude of the gender difference in relational aggression.

The Interpretation of Effect Sizes

The interpretation of effect sizes is contested. On one side of the argument, the classic source is the statistician Cohen (1969, 1988), who recommended that 0.20 be considered a small effect, 0.50 be considered medium, and 0.80 be considered large. It is important to note that he set these guidelines before the advent of meta-analysis, and they have been the standards used in statistical power analysis for decades.

In support of these guidelines are indicators of overlap between two distributions. For example, Kling, Hyde, Showers, and Buswell (1999) graphed two distributions differing on average by an effect size of 0.21, the effect size they found for gender differences in self-esteem. This graph is shown in Figure 3.1. Clearly, this small effect size reflects distributions that overlap greatly—that is, that show more similarity than difference. Cohen (1988) developed a U statistic that quantifies the percentage of nonoverlap of distributions. For $d = 0.20$, $U = 15\%$; that is, 85% of the areas of the distributions overlap. According to another Cohen measure of overlap, for $d = 0.20$, 54% of individuals in Group A exceed the 50th percentile for Group B.

For another way to consider the interpretation of effect sizes, d can also be expressed as an equivalent value of the Pearson correlation, r (Cohen, 1988). For the small effect size of 0.20, $r = .10$, certainly a small correlation. A d of 0.50 is equivalent to an r of .24, and for $d = 0.80$, $r = .37$.

Rosenthal (1991; Rosenthal & Rubin, 1982) has argued the other side of the case—namely, that seemingly small effect sizes can be important and make for impressive applied effects. As an example, he took a two-group experimental design in which one group is treated for cancer and the other group receives a placebo. He used the method of binomial effect size display (BESD) to illustrate the consequences. Using this method, for example, an r of .32 between treatment and outcome, accounting for only 10% of the variance, translates into a survival rate of 34% in the placebo group and 66% in the treated group. Certainly, the effect is impressive.

How does this apply to the study of gender differences? First, in terms of costs of errors in scientific decision making, psychological gender differences are quite a different matter from curing cancer. So, interpretation of the magnitude of effects must be heavily conditioned by the costs of making Type I and Type II errors for the particular question under consideration. I look forward to statisticians developing indicators that take these factors into account. Second, Rosenthal used the r metric, and when this is translated into d, the effects look much less impressive. For example, a d of 0.20 is equivalent to an r of 0.10, and Rosenthal's BESD indicates that that effect is equivalent to cancer survival increasing from 45% to 55%—once again, a small effect. A close-to-zero effect size of 0.10 is equivalent to an r of .05, which translates to cancer survival rates increasing only from 47.5% to 52.5% in the treatment group compared with the control group. In short, I believe that Cohen's guidelines provide a reasonable standard for the interpretation of gender differences effect sizes.

One caveat should be noted, however. The foregoing discussion is implicitly based on the assumption that the variabilities in the male and female distributions are equal. Yet the greater male variability hypothesis was originally proposed more than a century ago, and it survives today (Feingold, 1992; Hedges & Friedman, 1993). In the 1800s, this hypothesis was proposed to explain why there were more male than female geniuses and, at the same time, more males among the mentally retarded. Statistically, the combination of a small average difference favoring males and a larger standard deviation for males, for some trait such as mathematics performance, could lead to a lopsided gender ratio favoring males in the upper tail of the distribution reflecting exceptional talent. The statistic used to investigate this question is the variance ratio (VR), the ratio of the male variance to the female variance. Empirical investigations of the VR have found values of 1.00–1.08 for vocabulary (Hedges & Nowell, 1995),

1.05–1.25 for mathematics performance (Hedges & Nowell), and 0.87–1.04 for self-esteem (Kling et al., 1999). Therefore, it appears that whether males or females are more variable depends on the domain under consideration. Moreover, most VR estimates are close to 1.00, indicating similar variances for males and females. Nonetheless, this issue of possible gender differences in variability merits continued investigation.

Developmental Trends

Not all meta-analyses have examined developmental trends and, given the preponderance of psychological research on college students, developmental analysis is not always possible. However, meta-analysis can be powerful for identifying age trends in the magnitude of gender differences. Here, I consider a few key examples of meta-analyses that have taken this developmental approach (see Table 3).

At the time of the meta-analysis by Hyde, Fennema, and Lamon (1990), it was believed that gender differences in mathematics performance were small or nonexistent in childhood and that the male advantage appeared beginning around the time of puberty (Maccoby & Jacklin, 1974). It was also believed that males were better at high-level mathematical problems that required complex processing, whereas females were better at low-level mathematics that required only simple computation. Hyde and colleagues addressed both hypotheses in their meta-analysis. They found a small gender difference favoring girls in computation in elementary school and middle school and no gender difference in computation in the high school years. There was no gender difference in complex problem solving in elementary school or middle school, but a small gender difference favoring males emerged in the high school years (d = 0.29). Age differences in the magnitude of the gender effect were significant for both computation and problem solving.

Kling et al. (1999) used a developmental approach in their meta-analysis of studies of gender differences in self-esteem, on the basis of the assertion of prominent authors such as Mary Pipher (1994) that girls' self-esteem takes a

Table 3. Selected Meta-Analyses Showing Developmental Trends in the Magnitude of Gender Differences

Study and Variable	Age (years)	No. of Reports	d
Hyde, Fennema, & Lamon (1990)			
Mathematics: Complex problem solving	5–10	11	0.00
	11–14	21	−0.02
	15–18	10	+0.29
	19–25	15	+0.32
Kling et al. (1999)			
Self-esteem	7–10	22	+0.16
	11–14	53	+0.23
	15–18	44	+0.33
	19–22	72	+0.18
	23–59	16	+0.10
	>60	6	−0.03
Major et al. (1999)			
Self-esteem	5–10	24	+0.01
	11–13	34	+0.12
	14–18	65	+0.16
	19 or older	97	+0.13
Twenge & Nolen-Hoeksema (2002)			
Depressive symptoms	8–12	86	−0.04
	13–16	49	+0.16
Thomas & French (1985)			
Throwing distance	3–8	—	+1.50 to +2.00
	16–18	—	+3.50

Note: Positive values of d represent higher scores for men and/or boys; negative values of d represent higher scores for women and/or girls. Dashes indicate that data were not available (i.e., the study in question did not provide this information clearly). No. = number.

nosedive at the beginning of adolescence. They found that the magnitude of the gender difference did grow larger from childhood to adolescence: In childhood (ages 7–10), $d = 0.16$; for early adolescence (ages 11–14), $d = 0.23$; and for the high school years (ages 15–18), $d = 0.33$. However, the gender difference did not suddenly become large in early adolescence, and even in high school, the difference was still not large. Moreover, the gender difference was smaller in older samples; for example, for ages 23–59, $d = 0.10$.

Whitley's (1997) analysis of age trends in computer self-efficacy is revealing. In grammar school samples, $d = 0.09$, whereas in high school samples,

$d = 0.66$. This dramatic trend leads to questions about what forces are at work transforming girls from feeling as effective with computers as boys do to showing a large difference in self-efficacy by high school.

These examples illustrate the extent to which the magnitude of gender differences can fluctuate with age. Gender differences grow larger or smaller at different times in the life span, and meta-analysis is a powerful tool for detecting these trends. Moreover, the fluctuating magnitude of gender differences at different ages argues against the differences model and notions that gender differences are large and stable.

The Importance of Context

Gender researchers have emphasized the importance of context in creating, erasing, or even reversing psychological gender differences (Bussey & Bandura, 1999; Deaux & Major, 1987; Eagly & Wood, 1999). Context may exert influence at numerous levels, including the written instructions given for an exam, dyadic interactions between participants or between a participant and an experimenter, or the sociocultural level.

In an important experiment, Lightdale and Prentice (1994) demonstrated the importance of gender roles and social context in creating or erasing the purportedly robust gender difference in aggression. Lightdale and Prentice used the technique of deindividuation to produce a situation that removed the influence of gender roles. *Deindividuation* refers to a state in which the person has lost his or her individual identity; that is, the person has become anonymous. Under such conditions, people should feel no obligation to conform to social norms such as gender roles. Half of the participants, who were college students, were assigned to an individuated condition by having them sit close to the experimenter, identify themselves by name, wear large name tags, and answer personal questions. Participants in the deindividuation condition sat far from the experimenter, wore no name tags, and were simply told to wait. All participants were also told that the experiment required information from only half of the participants, whose behavior would be monitored, and that the other half would remain anonymous. Participants then played an interactive video game in which they first defended and then attacked by dropping bombs. The number of bombs dropped was the measure of aggressive behavior.

The results indicated that in the individuated condition, men dropped significantly more bombs ($M = 31.1$) than women did ($M = 26.8$). In the deindividuated condition, however, there were no significant gender differences and, in fact, women dropped somewhat more bombs ($M = 41.1$) than men ($M = 36.8$). In short, the significant gender difference in aggression disappeared when gender norms were removed.

Steele's (1997; Steele & Aronson, 1995) work on stereotype threat has produced similar evidence in the cognitive domain. Although the original experiments concerned African Americans and the stereotype that they are intellectually inferior, the theory was quickly applied to gender and stereotypes that girls and women are bad at math (Brown & Josephs, 1999; Quinn & Spencer, 2001; Spencer, Steele, & Quinn, 1999; Walsh, Hickey, & Duffy, 1999). In one experiment, male and female college students with equivalent math backgrounds were tested (Spencer et al., 1999). In one condition, participants were told that the math test had shown gender difference in the past, and in the other condition, they were told that the test had been shown to be gender fair—that men and women had performed equally on it. In the condition in which participants had been told that the math test was gender fair, there were no gender differences in performance on the test. In the condition in which participants expected gender differences, women underperformed compared with men. This simple manipulation of context was capable of creating or erasing gender differences in math performance.

Meta-analysts have addressed the importance of context for gender differences. In one of the earliest demonstrations of context effects, Eagly and Crowley (1986) meta-analyzed studies of gender differences in helping behavior, basing the analysis in social-role theory. They argued that certain kinds of helping are part of the male role: helping that is heroic or chivalrous. Other kinds of helping are part of the female role: helping that is nurturant and caring, such as caring for children. Heroic helping involves danger to the self, and both heroic and chivalrous helping are facilitated when onlookers are present. Women's nurturant helping more often occurs in private, with no onlookers. Averaged over all studies, men helped more ($d = 0.34$). However, when studies were separated into those in which onlookers were present and participants were aware of it, $d = 0.74$. When no onlookers were present, $d = 20.02$. Moreover, the magnitude of the gender difference was highly correlated with the degree of danger in the helping situation; gender differences were largest favoring males in situations with the most danger. In short, the gender difference in helping behavior can be large, favoring males, or close to zero, depending on the social context in which the behavior is measured. Moreover, the pattern of gender differences is consistent with social-role theory.

Anderson and Leaper (1998) obtained similar context effects in their meta-analysis of gender differences in conversational interruption. At the time of their meta-analysis, it was widely believed that men interrupted women considerably more than the reverse. Averaged over all studies, however, Anderson and Leaper found a d of 0.15, a small effect. The effect size for intrusive interruptions (excluding back-channel interruptions) was larger: 0.33. It is important to note that the magnitude of the gender difference varied greatly depending on the social context in which interruptions were studied. When dyads were observed, $d = 0.06$, but with larger groups of three or more, $d = 0.26$. When participants were strangers, $d = 0.17$, but when they were friends, $d = -0.14$. Here, again, it is clear that gender differences can be created, erased, or reversed, depending on the context.

In their meta-analysis, LaFrance, Hecht, and Paluck (2003) found a moderate gender difference in smiling ($d = -0.41$), with girls and women smiling more. Again, the magnitude of the gender difference was highly dependent on the context. If participants had a clear awareness that they were being observed, the gender difference was larger ($d = -0.46$) than it was if they were not aware of being observed ($d = -0.19$). The magnitude of the gender difference also depended on culture and age.

Dindia and Allen (1992) and Bettencourt and Miller (1996) also found marked context effects in their gender meta-analyses. The conclusion is clear: The magnitude and even the direction of gender differences depend on the context. These findings provide strong evidence against the differences model and its notions that psychological gender differences are large and stable.

Costs of Inflated Claims of Gender Differences

The question of the magnitude of psychological gender differences is more than just an academic concern. There are serious costs of overinflated claims of gender differences (for an extended discussion of this point, see Barnett & Rivers, 2004; see also White & Kowalski, 1994). These costs occur in many areas, including work, parenting, and relationships.

Gilligan's (1982) argument that women speak in a different moral "voice" than men is a well-known example of the differences model. Women, according to Gilligan, speak in a moral voice of caring, whereas men speak in a voice of justice. Despite the fact that meta-analyses disconfirm her arguments for large gender differences (Jaffee & Hyde, 2000; Thoma, 1986; Walker, 1984), Gilligan's ideas have permeated American culture. One consequence of this overinflated claim of gender differences is that it reifies the stereotype of women as caring and nurturant and men as lacking in nurturance. One cost to men is that they may believe that they cannot be nurturant, even in their role as father. For women, the cost in the workplace can be enormous. Women who violate the stereotype of being nurturant and nice can be penalized in hiring and evaluations. Rudman and Glick (1999), for example, found that female job applicants who displayed agentic qualities received considerably lower hireability ratings than agentic male applicants ($d = 0.92$) for a managerial job that had been "feminized" to require not only technical skills and the ability to work under pressure but also the ability to be helpful and sensitive to the needs of others. The researchers concluded that women must present themselves as competent and agentic to be hired, but they may then be viewed as interpersonally deficient and uncaring and receive biased work evaluations because of their violation of the female nurturance stereotype.

A second example of the costs of unwarranted validation of the stereotype of women as caring nurturers comes from Eagly, Makhijani, and Klonsky's (1992) meta-analysis of studies of gender and the evaluation of leaders. Overall, women leaders were evaluated as positively as men leaders ($d = 0.05$). However, women leaders portrayed as uncaring autocrats were at a more substantial disadvantage than were men leaders portrayed similarly ($d = 0.30$). Women who violated the caring stereotype paid for it in their evaluations. The persistence of the stereotype of women as nurturers leads to serious costs for women who violate this stereotype in the workplace.

The costs of overinflated claims of gender differences hit children as well. According to stereotypes, boys are better at math than girls are (Hyde, Fennema, Ryan, Frost, & Hopp, 1990). This stereotype is proclaimed in mass media headlines (Barnett & Rivers, 2004). Meta-analyses, however, indicate a pattern of gender similarities for math performance. Hedges and Nowell (1995) found a *d* of 0.16 for large national samples of adolescents, and Hyde, Fennema, and Lamon (1990) found a *d* of −0.05 for samples of the general population (see also Leahey & Guo, 2000). One cost to children is that mathematically talented girls may be overlooked by parents and teachers because these adults do not expect to find mathematical talent among girls. Parents have lower expectations for their daughters' math success than for their sons' (Lummis & Stevenson, 1990), despite the fact that girls earn better grades in math than boys do (Kimball, 1989). Research has shown repeatedly that parents' expectations for their children's mathematics success relate strongly to outcomes such as the child's mathematics self-confidence and performance, with support for a model in which parents' expectations influence children (e.g., Frome & Eccles, 1998). In short, girls may find their confidence in their ability to succeed in challenging math courses or in a mathematically oriented career undermined by parents' and teachers' beliefs that girls are weak in math ability.

In the realm of intimate heterosexual relationships, women and men are told that they are as different as if they came from different planets and that they communicate in dramatically different ways (Gray, 1992; Tannen, 1991). When relationship conflicts occur, good communication is essential to resolving the conflict (Gottman, 1994). If, however, women and men believe what they have been told—that it is almost impossible for them to communicate with each other—they may simply give up on trying to resolve the conflict through better communication. Therapists will need to dispel erroneous beliefs in massive, unbridgeable gender differences.

Inflated claims about psychological gender differences can hurt boys as well. A large gender gap in self-esteem beginning in adolescence has been touted in popular sources (American Association of University Women, 1991; Orenstein, 1994; Pipher, 1994). Girls' self-esteem is purported to take a nosedive at the beginning of adolescence, with the implication that boys' self-esteem does not. Yet meta-analytic estimates of the magnitude of the gender difference have all been small or close to zero: *d* = 0.21 (Kling et al., 1999, Analysis I), *d* = 0.04–0.16 (Kling et al., 1999, Analysis II), and *d* = 0.14 (Major, Barr, Zubek, & Babey, 1999). In short, self-esteem is roughly as much a problem for adolescent boys as it is for adolescent girls. The popular media's focus on girls as the ones with self-esteem problems may carry a huge cost in leading parents, teachers, and other professionals to overlook boys' self-esteem problems, so that boys do not receive the interventions they need.

As several of these examples indicate, the gender similarities hypothesis carries strong implications for practitioners. The scientific evidence does not support the belief that men and women have inherent difficulties in communicating across gender. Neither does the evidence support the belief that adolescent girls are the only ones with self-esteem problems. Therapists who base their practice in the differences model should reconsider their approach on the basis of the best scientific evidence.

Conclusion

The gender similarities hypothesis stands in stark contrast to the differences model, which holds that men and women, and boys and girls, are vastly different psychologically. The gender similarities hypothesis states, instead, that males and females are alike on most—but not all—psychological variables. Extensive evidence from meta-analyses of research on gender differences supports the gender similarities hypothesis. A few notable exceptions are some motor behaviors (e.g., throwing distance) and some aspects of sexuality, which show large gender differences. Aggression shows a gender difference that is moderate in magnitude.

It is time to consider the costs of overinflated claims of gender differences. Arguably, they cause harm in numerous realms, including women's opportunities in the workplace, couple conflict and communication, and analyses of self-esteem problems among adolescents. Most important, these claims are not consistent with the scientific data.

References

American Association of University Women. (1991). *Shortchanging girls, shortchanging America: Full data report*. Washington, DC: Author.

Anderson, K. J., & Leaper, C. (1998). Meta-analyses of gender effects on conversational interruption: Who, what, when, where, and how. *Sex Roles, 39*, 225–252.

AnnOnline. (2005). *Biography: Deborah Tannen*. Retrieved January 10, 2005, from http://www.annonline.com.

Archer, J. (2004). Sex differences in aggression in real-world setting: A meta-analytic review. *Review of General Psychology, 8*, 291–322.

Ashmore, R. D. (1990). Sex, gender, and the individual. In L. A. Pervin (Ed.), *Handbook of personality: Theory and research* (pp. 486–526). New York: Guilford Press.

Barnett, R., & Rivers, C. (2004). *Same difference: How gender myths are hurting our relationships, our children, and our jobs*. New York: Basic Books.

Bettencourt, B. A., & Miller, N. (1996). Gender differences in aggression as a function of provocation: A meta-analysis. *Psychological Bulletin, 119*, 422–447.

Brown, R. P., & Josephs, R. A. (1999). A burden of proof: Stereotype relevance and gender differences in math performance. *Journal of Personality and Social Psychology, 76*, 246–257.

Bussey, K., & Bandura, A. (1999). Social cognitive theory of gender development and differentiation. *Psychological Review, 106*, 676–713.

Cohen, J. (1969). *Statistical power analysis for the behavioral sciences*. New York: Academic Press.

———. (1988). *Statistical power analysis for the behavioral sciences* (2nd ed.). Hillsdale, NJ: Erlbaum.

Crick, N. R., & Grotpeter, J. K. (1995). Relational aggression, gender, and social–psychological adjustment. *Child Development, 66*, 710–722.

Deaux, K., & Major, B. (1987). Putting gender into context: An interactive model of gender-related behavior. *Psychological Review, 94*, 369–389.

Dindia, K., & Allen, M. (1992). Sex differences in self-disclosure: A meta-analysis. *Psychological Bulletin, 112*, 106–124.

Eagly, A. H., & Carli, L. L. (1981). Sex of researchers and sex-typed communications as determinants of sex differences in influenceability: A meta-analysis of social influence studies. *Psychological Bulletin, 90*, 1–20.

Eagly, A. H., & Crowley, M. (1986). Gender and helping behavior: A meta-analytic review of the social psychological literature. *Psychological Bulletin, 100*, 283–308.

Eagly, A. H., Johannesen-Schmidt, M. C., & van Engen, M. L. (2003). Transformational, transactional, and laissez-faire leadership styles: A meta-analysis comparing women and men. *Psychological Bulletin, 129*, 569–591.

Eagly, A. H., & Johnson, B. T. (1990). Gender and leadership style: A meta-analysis. *Psychological Bulletin, 108*, 233–256.

Eagly, A. H., Karau, S. J., & Makhijani, M. G. (1995). Gender and the effectiveness of leaders: A meta-analysis. *Psychological Bulletin, 117*, 125–145.

Eagly, A. H., Makhijani, M. G., & Klonsky, B. G. (1992). Gender and the evaluation of leaders: A meta-analysis. *Psychological Bulletin, 111*, 3–22.

Eagly, A. H., & Steffen, V. (1986). Gender and aggressive behavior: A meta-analytic review of the social psychological literature. *Psychological Bulletin, 100*, 309–330.

Eagly, A. H., & Wood, W. (1999). The origins of sex differences in human behavior: Evolved dispositions versus social roles. *American Psychologist, 54*, 408–423.

Eaton, W. O., & Enns, L. R. (1986). Sex differences in human motor activity level. *Psychological Bulletin, 100*, 19–28.

Epstein, C. F. (1988). *Deceptive distinctions: Sex, gender, and the social order*. New Haven, CT: Yale University Press.

Feingold, A. (1988). Cognitive gender differences are disappearing. *American Psychologist, 43*, 95–103.

———. (1992). Sex differences in variability in intellectual abilities: A new look at an old controversy. *Review of Educational Research, 62*, 61–84.

———. (1994). Gender differences in personality: A meta-analysis. *Psychological Bulletin, 116*, 429–456.

Feingold, A., & Mazzella, R. (1998). Gender differences in body image are increasing. *Psychological Science, 9*, 190–195.

Frome, P. M., & Eccles, J. S. (1998). Parents' influence on children's achievement-related perceptions. *Journal of Personality and Social Psychology, 74*, 435–452.

Gilligan, C. (1982). *In a different voice: Psychological theory and women's development.* Cambridge, MA: Harvard University Press.

Glass, G. V., McGaw, B., & Smith, M. L. (1981). *Meta-analysis in social research.* Beverly Hills, CA: Sage.

Gleitman, H. (1981). *Psychology.* New York: Norton.

Gottman, J. (1994). *Why marriages succeed or fail.* New York: Simon & Schuster.

Gray, J. (1992). *Men are from Mars, women are from Venus: A practical guide for improving communication and getting what you want in your relationships.* New York: HarperCollins.

———. (2005). *John Gray, Ph.D. is the best-selling relationship author of all time.* Retrieved January 10, 2005, from http://www.marsvenus.com.

Hedges, L. V., & Becker, B. J. (1986). Statistical methods in the meta-analysis of research on gender differences. In J. S. Hyde & M. C. Linn (Eds.), *The psychology of gender: Advances through meta-analysis* (pp. 14–50). Baltimore: Johns Hopkins University Press.

Hedges, L. V., & Friedman, L. (1993). Sex differences in variability in intellectual abilities: A reanalysis of Feingold's results. *Review of Educational Research, 63*, 95–105.

Hedges, L. V., & Nowell, A. (1995, July 7). Sex differences in mental test scores, variability, and numbers of high-scoring individuals. *Science, 269*, 41–45.

Hedges, L. V., & Olkin, I. (1985). *Statistical methods for meta-analysis.* San Diego, CA: Academic Press.

Hollingworth, L. S. (1918). Comparison of the sexes in mental traits. *Psychological Bulletin, 15*, 427–432.

Hyde, J. S. (1981). How large are cognitive gender differences? A meta-analysis using w^2 and d. *American Psychologist, 36*, 892–901.

———. (1984). How large are gender differences in aggression? A developmental meta-analysis. *Developmental Psychology, 20*, 722–736.

———. (1985). *Half the human experience: The psychology of women* (3rd ed.). Lexington, MA: Heath.

———. (1986). Gender differences in aggression. In J. S. Hyde & M. C. Linn (Eds.), *The psychology of gender: Advances through meta-analysis* (pp. 51–66). Baltimore: Johns Hopkins University Press.

Hyde, J. S., Fennema, E., & Lamon, S. (1990). Gender differences in mathematics performance: A meta-analysis. *Psychological Bulletin, 107*, 139–155.

Hyde, J. S., Fennema, E., Ryan, M., Frost, L. A., & Hopp, C. (1990). Gender comparisons of mathematics attitudes and affect: A meta-analysis. *Psychology of Women Quarterly, 14*, 299–324.

Hyde, J. S., & Frost, L. A. (1993). Meta-analysis in the psychology of women. In F. L. Denmark & M. A. Paludi (Eds.), *Psychology of women: A handbook of issues and theories* (pp. 67–103). Westport, CT: Greenwood Press.

Hyde, J. S., & Linn, M. C. (1988). Gender differences in verbal ability: A meta-analysis. *Psychological Bulletin, 104*, 53–69.

Hyde, J. S., & Plant, E. A. (1995). Magnitude of psychological gender differences: Another side to the story. *American Psychologist, 50*, 159–161.

Jaffee, S., & Hyde, J. S. (2000). Gender differences in moral orientation: A meta-analysis. *Psychological Bulletin, 126*, 703–726.

Kimball, M. M. (1989). A new perspective on women's math achievement. *Psychological Bulletin, 105*, 198–214.

———. (1995). *Feminist visions of gender similarities and differences.* Binghamton, NY: Haworth Press.

Kling, K. C., Hyde, J. S., Showers, C. J., & Buswell, B. N. (1999). Gender differences in self-esteem: A meta-analysis. *Psychological Bulletin, 125*, 470–500.

Knight, G. P., Guthrie, I. K.. Page, M. C., & Fabes, R. A. (2002). Emotional arousal and gender differences in aggression: A meta-analysis. *Aggressive Behavior, 28*, 366–393.

Konrad, A. M., Ritchie, J. E., Lieb, P., & Corrigall, E. (2000). Sex differences and similarities in job attribute preferences: A meta-analysis. *Psychological Bulletin, 126*, 593–641.

LaFrance, M., Hecht, M. A., & Paluck, E. L. (2003). The contingent smile: A meta-analysis of sex differences in smiling. *Psychological Bulletin, 129*, 305–334.

Leahey, E., & Guo, G. (2000). Gender differences in mathematical trajectories. *Social Forces, 80*, 713–732.

Leaper, C., & Smith, T. E. (2004). A meta-analytic review of gender variations in children's language use: Talkativeness, affiliative speech, and assertive speech. *Developmental Psychology, 40*, 993–1027.

Lefrançois, G. R. (1990). *The lifespan* (3rd ed.). Belmont, CA: Wadsworth.

Lightdale, J. R., & Prentice, D. A. (1994). Rethinking sex differences in aggression: Aggressive behavior in the absence of social roles. *Personality and Social Psychology Bulletin, 20*, 34–44.

Linn, M. C., & Petersen, A. C. (1985). Emergence and characterization of sex differences in spatial ability: A meta-analysis. *Child Development, 56*, 1479–1498.

Lummis, M., & Stevenson, H. W. (1990). Gender differences in beliefs and achievement: A cross-cultural study. *Developmental Psychology, 26*, 254–263.

Lynn, R., & Irwing, P. (2004). Sex differences on the progressive matrices: A meta-analysis. *Intelligence, 32*, 481–498.

Maccoby, E. E., & Jacklin, C. N. (1974). *The psychology of sex differences*. Stanford, CA: Stanford University Press.

Major, B., Barr, L., Zubek, J., & Babey, S. H. (1999). Gender and self-esteem: A meta-analysis . In W. B. Swann, J. H. Langlois, & L. A. Gilbert (Eds.), *Sexism and stereotypes in modern society: The gender science of Janet Taylor Spence* (pp. 223–253). Washington, DC: American Psychological Association.

McClure, E. B. (2000). A meta-analytic review of sex differences in facial expression processing and their development in infants, children, and adolescents. *Psychological Bulletin, 126*, 424–453.

Murnen, S. K., & Stockton, M. (1997). Gender and self-reported sexual arousal in response to sexual stimuli: A meta-analytic review. *Sex Roles, 37*, 135–154.

Oliver, M. B., & Hyde, J. S. (1993). Gender differences in sexuality: A meta-analysis. *Psychological Bulletin, 114*, 29–51.

Orenstein, P. (1994). *Schoolgirls: Young women, self-esteem, and the confidence gap*. New York: Anchor Books.

Pinquart, M., & Sörensen (2001). Gender differences in self-concept and psychological well-being in old age: A meta-analysis. *Journal of Gerontology: Psychological Sciences. 56B*, P195–P213.

Pipher, M. (1994). *Reviving Ophelia: Saving the selves of adolescent girls*. New York: Ballantine Books.

Quinn, D. M., & Spencer, S. J. (2001). The interference of stereotype threat with women's generation of mathematical problem-solving strategies. *Journal of Social Issues, 57*, 55–72.

Rosenthal, R. (1991). *Meta-analytic procedures for social research* (Rev. ed.). Newbury Park, CA: Sage.

Rosenthal, R., & Rubin, D. B. (1982). A simple, general purpose display of magnitude of experimental effect. *Journal of Educational Psychology, 74*, 166–169.

Rudman, L. A., & Glick, P. (1999). Feminized management and backlash toward agentic women: The hidden costs to women of a kinder, gentler image of middle managers. *Journal of Personality and Social Psychology, 77*, 1004–1010.

Shields, S. A. (1975). Functionalism, Darwinism, and the psychology of women: A study in social myth. *American Psychologist, 30*, 739–754.

Silverman, I. W. (2003). Gender differences in delay of gratification: A meta-analysis. *Sex Roles, 49*, 451–463.

Spencer, S. J., Steele, C. M., & Quinn, D. M. (1999). Stereotype threat and women's math performance. *Journal of Experimental Social Psychology, 35*, 4–28.

Steele, C. M. (1997). A threat in the air: How stereotypes shape intellectual identity and performance. *American Psychologist, 52*, 613–629.

Steele, C. M., & Aronson, J. (1995). Stereotype threat and the intellectual test performance of African Americans. *Journal of Personality and Social Psychology, 69*, 797–811.

Stuhlmacher, A. C., & Walters, A. E. (1999). Gender differences in negotiation outcome: A meta-analysis. *Personnel Psychology, 52*, 653–677.

Tamres, L. K., Janicki, D., & Helgeson, V. S. (2002). Sex differences in coping behavior: A meta-analytic review and an examination of relative coping. *Personality and Social Psychology Review, 6,* 2–30.

Tannen, D. (1991). *You just don't understand: Women and men in conversation.* New York: Ballantine Books.

Thoma, S. J. (1986). Estimating gender differences in the comprehension and preference of moral issues. *Developmental Review, 6,* 165–180.

Thomas, J. R., & French, K. E. (1985). Gender differences across age in motor performance: A meta-analysis. *Psychological Bulletin, 98,* 260–282.

Thorndike, E. L. (1914). *Educational psychology* (Vol. 3). New York: Teachers College, Columbia University.

Twenge, J. M., & Nolen-Hoeksema. S. (2002). Age, gender, race, socioeconomic status, and birth cohort differences on the Children's Depression Inventory: A meta-analysis. *Journal of Abnormal Psychology, 111,* 578–588.

Voyer, D., Voyer, S., & Bryden, M. P. (1995). Magnitude of sex differences in spatial abilities: A meta-analysis and consideration of critical variables. *Psychological Bulletin, 117,* 250–270.

Walker, L. J. (1984). Sex differences in the development of moral reasoning: A critical review. *Child Development, 55,* 677–691.

Walsh, M., Hickey, C., & Duffy, J. (1999). Influence of item content and stereotype situation on gender differences in mathematical problem solving. *Sex Roles, 41,* 219–240.

Walters, A. E., Stuhlmacher, A. F., & Meyer, L. L. (1998). Gender and negotiator competitiveness: A meta-analysis. *Organizational Behavior and Human Decision Processes, 76,* 1–29.

White, J. W., & Kowalski, R. M. (1994). Deconstructing the myth of the nonaggressive woman: A feminist analysis. *Psychology of Women Quarterly, 18,* 487–508.

Whitley, B. E. (1997). Gender differences in computer-related attitudes and behavior: A meta-analysis. *Computers in Human Behavior, 13,* 1–22.

Whitley, B. E., McHugh, M. C., & Frieze, I. H. (1986). Assessing the theoretical models for sex differences in causal attributions of success and failure. In J. S. Hyde & M. C. Linn (Eds.), *The psychology of gender: Advances through meta-analysis* (pp. 102–135). Baltimore: Johns Hopkins University Press.

"Dude, You're a Fag": Adolescent Masculinity and the Fag Discourse

C. J. PASCOE

"There's a faggot over there! There's a faggot over there! Come look!" yelled Brian, a senior at River High School, to a group of 10-year-old boys. Following Brian, the 10-year-olds dashed down a hallway. At the end of the hallway Brian's friend, Dan, pursed his lips and began sashaying towards the 10-year-olds. He minced towards them, swinging his hips exaggeratedly and wildly waving his arms. To the boys Brian yelled, "Look at the faggot! Watch out! He'll get you!" In response the 10-year-olds raced back down the hallway screaming in terror.

(From author's fieldnotes)

The relationship between adolescent masculinity and sexuality is embedded in the specter of the faggot. Faggots represent a penetrated masculinity in which "to be penetrated is to abdicate power" (Bersani, 1987: 212). Penetrated men symbolize a masculinity devoid of power, which, in its contradiction, threatens both psychic and social chaos. It is precisely this specter of penetrated masculinity that functions as a regulatory mechanism of gender for contemporary American adolescent boys.

Feminist scholars of masculinity have documented the centrality of homophobic insults to masculinity (Lehne, 1998; Kimmel, 2001) especially in school settings (Wood, 1984; Smith, 1998; Burn, 2000; Plummer, 2001; Kimmel, 2003). They argue that homophobic teasing often characterizes masculinity in adolescence and early adulthood, and that anti-gay slurs tend to primarily be directed at other gay boys.

This article both expands on and challenges these accounts of relationships between homophobia and masculinity. Homophobia is indeed a central mechanism in the making of contemporary American adolescent masculinity. This article both critiques and builds on this finding by (1) pointing to the limits of an argument that focuses centrally on homophobia, (2) demonstrating that the fag is not only an identity linked to homosexual boys[1] but an identity that can temporarily adhere to heterosexual boys as well and (3) highlighting the racialized nature of the fag as a disciplinary mechanism.

"Homophobia" is too facile a term with which to describe the deployment of "fag" as an epithet. By calling the use of the word "fag" homophobia—and letting the argument stop with that point—previous research obscures the gendered nature of sexualized insults (Plummer, 2001). Invoking homophobia to describe the ways in which boys aggressively tease each other overlooks the powerful relationship between masculinity and this sort of insult. Instead, it seems incidental in this conventional line of argument that girls do not harass each other and are not harassed in this same manner.[2] This framing naturalizes the relationship between masculinity and homophobia, thus obscuring the centrality of such harassment in the formation of a gendered identity for boys in a way that it is not for girls.

"Fag" is not necessarily a static identity attached to a particular (homosexual) boy. Fag

C. J. Pascoe, "'Dude, You're a Fag': Adolescent Masculinity and the Fag Discourse" from *Sexualities* 8, no. 3 (2005): 329–346. Copyright © 2005. Reprinted with the permission of Sage Publications, Inc.

talk and fag imitations serve as a discourse with which boys discipline themselves and each other through joking relationships.[3] Any boy can temporarily become a fag in a given social space or interaction. This does not mean that those boys who identify as or are perceived to be homosexual are not subject to intense harassment. But becoming a fag has as much to do with failing at the masculine tasks of competence, heterosexual prowess and strength or in anyway revealing weakness or femininity, as it does with a sexual identity. This fluidity of the fag identity is what makes the specter of the fag such a powerful disciplinary mechanism. It is fluid enough that boys police most of their behaviors out of fear of having the fag identity permanently adhere and definitive enough so that boys recognize a fag behavior and strive to avoid it.

The fag discourse is racialized. It is invoked differently by and in relation to white boys' bodies than it is by and in relation to African-American boys' bodies. While certain behaviors put all boys at risk for becoming temporarily a fag, some behaviors can be enacted by African-American boys without putting them at risk of receiving the label. The racialized meanings of the fag discourse suggest that something more than simple homophobia is involved in these sorts of interactions. An analysis of boys' deployments of the specter of the fag should also extend to the ways in which gendered power works through racialized selves. It is not that this gendered homophobia does not exist in African-American communities. Indeed, making fun of "Negro faggotry seems to be a rite of passage among contemporary black male rappers and filmmakers" (Riggs, 1991: 253). However, the fact that "white women and men, gay and straight, have more or less colonized cultural debates about sexual representation" (Julien and Mercer, 1991: 167) obscures varied systems of sexualized meanings among different racialized ethnic groups (Almaguer, 1991; King, 2004).

Theoretical Framing

The sociology of masculinity entails a "critical study of men, their behaviors, practices, values and perspectives" (Whitehead and Barrett, 2001:

14). Recent studies of men emphasize the multiplicity of masculinity (Connell, 1995) detailing the ways in which different configurations of gender practice are promoted, challenged or reinforced in given social situations. This research on how men do masculinities has explored gendered practices in a wide range of social institutions, such as families (Coltrane, 2001), schools (Skelton, 1996; Parker, 1996; Mac and Ghaill, 1996; Francis and Skelton, 2001), workplaces (Cooper, 2000), media (Craig, 1992), and sports (Messner, 1989; Edly and Wetherel, 1997; Curry, 2004). Many of these studies have developed specific typologies of masculinities: gay, Black, Chicano, working class, middle class, Asian, gay Black, gay Chicano, white working class, militarized, transnational business, New Man, negotiated, versatile, healthy, toxic, counter, and cool masculinities, to name a few (Messner, 2004). In this sort of model the fag could be (and often has been) framed as a type of subordinated masculinity attached to homosexual adolescent boys' bodies.

Heeding Timothy Carrigan's admonition that an "analysis of masculinity needs to be related as well to other currents in feminism" (Carrigan et al., 1987: 64), in this article I integrate queer theory's insights about the relationships between gender, sexuality, identities and power with the attention to men found in the literature on masculinities. Like the sociology of gender, queer theory destabilizes the assumed naturalness of the social order (Lemert, 1996). Queer theory is a "conceptualization which sees sexual power as embedded in different levels of social life" and interrogates areas of the social world not usually seen as sexuality (Stein and Plummer, 1994). In this sense queer theory calls for sexuality to be looked at not only as a discrete arena of sexual practices and identities, but also as a constitutive element of social life (Warner, 1993; Epstein, 1996).

While the masculinities' literature rightly highlights very real inequalities between gay and straight men (see for instance Connell, 1995), this emphasis on sexuality as inhered in static identities attached to male bodies, rather than major organizing principles of social life (Sedgwick, 1990), limits scholars' ability to analyze the myriad ways in which sexuality, in part, constitutes gender. This article does not seek to establish that there are homosexual boys and heterosexual boys and the homosexual ones are marginalized. Rather this article explores what happens to theories of gender if we look at a *discourse* of sexualized identities in addition to focusing on seemingly static identity categories inhabited by men. This is not to say that gender is reduced only to sexuality, indeed feminist scholars have demonstrated that gender is embedded in and constitutive of a multitude of social structures—the economy, places of work, families and schools. In the tradition of post-structural feminist theorists of race and gender who look at "border cases" that explode taken-for-granted binaries of race and gender (Smith, 1994), queer theory is another tool which enables an integrated analysis of sexuality, gender and race.

As scholars of gender have demonstrated, gender is accomplished through day-to-day interactions (Fine, 1987; Hochschild, 1989; West and Zimmerman, 1991; Thorne, 1993). In this sense gender is the "activity of managing situated conduct in light of normative conceptions of attitudes and activities appropriate for one's sex category" (West and Zimmerman, 1991: 127). Similarly, queer theorist Judith Butler argues that gender is accomplished interactionally through "a set of repeated acts within a highly rigid regulatory frame that congeal over time to produce the appearance of substance, of a natural sort of being" (Butler, 1999: 43). Specifically she argues that gendered beings are created through processes of citation and repudiation of a "constitutive outside" (Butler, 1993: 3) in which is contained all that is cast out of a socially recognizable gender category. The "constitutive outside" is inhabited by abject identities, unrecognizably and unacceptably gendered selves. The interactional accomplishment of gender in a Butlerian model consists, in part, of the continual iteration and repudiation of this abject identity. Gender, in this sense, is "constituted through the force of exclusion and abjection, on which produces a constitutive outside to the subject, an abjected outside, which is, after all, 'inside' the subject as its own founding repudiation" (Butler,

1993: 3). This repudiation creates and reaffirms a "threatening specter" (Butler, 1993: 3) of failed, unrecognizable gender, the existence of which must be continually repudiated through interactional processes.

I argue that the "fag" position is an "abject" position and, as such, is a "threatening specter" constituting contemporary American adolescent masculinity. The fag discourse is the interactional process through which boys name and repudiate this abjected identity. Rather than analyzing the fag as an identity for homosexual boys, I examine uses of the discourse that imply that any boy can become a fag, regardless of his actual desire or self-perceived sexual orientation. The threat of the abject position infuses the faggot with regulatory power. This article provides empirical data to illustrate Butler's approach to gender and indicates that it might be a useful addition to the sociological literature on masculinities through highlighting one of the ways in which a masculine gender identity is accomplished through interaction.

Method

Research Site

I conducted fieldwork at a suburban high school in north-central California which I call River High.[4] River High is a working class, suburban 50-year-old high school located in a town called Riverton. With the exception of the median household income and racial diversity (both of which are elevated due to Riverton's location in California), the town mirrors national averages in the percentages of white-collar workers, rates of college attendance, and marriages, and age composition (according to the 2000 census). It is a politically moderate to conservative, religious community. Most of the students' parents commute to surrounding cities for work.

On average Riverton is a middle-class community. However, students at River are likely to refer to the town as two communities: "Old Riverton" and "New Riverton." A busy highway and railroad tracks bisect the town into these two sections. River High is literally on the "wrong side of the tracks," in Old Riverton. Exiting the freeway, heading north to Old Riverton, one sees a mix of 1950s-era ranch-style homes, some with neatly trimmed lawns and tidy gardens, others with yards strewn with various car parts, lawn chairs and appliances. Old Riverton is visually bounded by smoke-puffing factories. On the other side of the freeway New Riverton is characterized by wide sidewalk-lined streets and new walled-in home developments. Instead of smokestacks, a forested mountain, home to a state park, rises majestically in the background. The teens from these homes attend Hillside High, River's rival.

River High is attended by 2,000 students. River High's racial/ethnic breakdown roughly represents California at large: 50 percent white, 9 percent African-American, 28 percent Latino and 6 percent Asian (as compared to California's 46, 6, 32, and 11 percent respectively, according to census data and school records). The students at River High are primarily working class.

Research

I gathered data using the qualitative method of ethnographic research. I spent a year and a half conducting observations, formally interviewing 49 students at River High (36 boys and 13 girls), one male student from Hillside High, and conducting countless informal interviews with students, faculty and administrators. I concentrated on one school because I explore the richness rather than the breadth of data (for other examples of this method see Willis, 1981; MacLeod, 1987; Eder et al., 1995; Ferguson, 2000).

I recruited students for interviews by conducting presentations in a range of classes and hanging around at lunch, before school, after school and at various events talking to different groups of students about my research, which I presented as "writing a book about guys." The interviews usually took place at school, unless the student had a car, in which case he or she met me at one of the local fast food restaurants where I treated them to a meal. Interviews lasted anywhere from half an hour to two hours.

The initial interviews I conducted helped me to map a gendered and sexualized geography of the school, from which I chose my observation sites.

I observed a "neutral" site—a senior government classroom, where sexualized meanings were subdued. I observed three sites that students marked as "fag" sites—two drama classes and the Gay/Straight Alliance. I also observed two normatively "masculine" sites—auto-shop and weightlifting.[5] I took daily fieldnotes focusing on how students, faculty and administrators negotiated, regulated and resisted particular meanings of gender and sexuality. I attended major school rituals such as Winter Ball, school rallies, plays, dances and lunches. I would also occasionally "ride along" with Mr. Johnson (Mr. J.), the school's security guard, on his battery-powered golf cart to watch which, how and when students were disciplined. Observational data provided me with more insight to the interactional processes of masculinity than simple interviews yielded. If I had relied only on interview data I would have missed the interactional processes of masculinity which are central to the fag discourse.

Given the importance of appearance in high school, I gave some thought as to how I would present myself, deciding to both blend in and set myself apart from the students. In order to blend in I wore my standard graduate student gear—comfortable, baggy cargo pants, a black t-shirt or sweater and tennis shoes. To set myself apart I carried a messenger bag instead of a back-pack, didn't wear makeup, and spoke slightly differently than the students by using some slang, but refraining from uttering the ubiquitous "hecka" and "hella."

The boys were fascinated by the fact that a 30-something white "girl" (their words) was interested in studying them. While at first many would make sexualized comments asking me about my dating life or saying that they were going to "hit on" me, it seemed eventually they began to forget about me as a potential sexual/romantic partner. Part of this, I think, was related to my knowledge about "guy" things. For instance, I lift weights on a regular basis and as a result the weightlifting coach introduced me as a "weight-lifter from U.C. Berkeley" telling the students they should ask me for weight-lifting advice. Additionally, my taste in movies and television shows often coincided with theirs. I am an avid fan of the movies "Jackass" and "Fight Club," both of which contain high levels of violence and "bathroom" humor. Finally, I garnered a lot of points among boys because I live off a dangerous street in a nearby city famous for drug deals, gang fights and frequent gun shots.

What Is a Fag?

"Since you were little boys you've been told, 'hey, don't be a little faggot,'" explained Darnell, an African-American football player, as we sat on a bench next to the athletic field. Indeed, both the boys and girls I interviewed told me that "fag" was the worst epithet one guy could direct at another. Jeff, a slight white sophomore, explained to me that boys call each other fag because "gay people aren't really liked over here and stuff." Jeremy, a Latino Junior, told me that this insult literally reduced a boy to nothing, "To call someone gay or fag is like the lowest thing you can call someone. Because that's like saying that you're nothing."

Most guys explained their or others' dislike of fags by claiming that homophobia is just part of what it means to be a guy. For instance Keith, a white soccer-playing senior, explained, "I think guys are just homophobic." However, it is not just homophobia, it is a *gendered* homophobia. Several students told me that these homophobic insults only applied to boys and not girls. For example, while Jake, a handsome white senior, told me that he didn't like gay people, he quickly added, "Lesbians, okay that's *good*." Similarly Cathy, a popular white cheerleader, told me "Being a lesbian is accepted because guys think 'oh that's cool.'" Darnell, after telling me that boys were told not to be faggots, said of lesbians, "They're [guys are] fine with girls. I think it's the guy part that they're like ewwww!" In this sense it is not strictly homophobia, but a gendered homophobia that constitutes adolescent masculinity in the culture of this school. However, it is clear, according to these comments, that lesbians are "good" because of their place in heterosexual male fantasy not necessarily because of some enlightened approach to same-sex relationships. It does however, indicate that using only the term homophobia to describe boys' repeated use of the word "fag" might be a bit simplistic and misleading.

Additionally, girls at River High rarely deployed the word "fag" and were never called "fags." I recorded girls uttering "fag" only three times during my research. In one instance, Angela, a Latina cheerleader, teased Jeremy, a well-liked white senior involved in student government, for not ditching school with her, "You wouldn't 'cause you're a faggot." However, girls did not use this word as part of their regular lexicon. The sort of gendered homophobia that constitutes adolescent masculinity does not constitute adolescent femininity. Girls were not called dykes or lesbians in any sort of regular or systematic way. Students did tell me that "slut" was the worst thing a girl could be called. However, my fieldnotes indicate that the word "slut" (or its synonym "ho") appears one time for every eight times the word "fag" appears. Even when it does occur, "slut" is rarely deployed as a direct insult against another girl.

Highlighting the difference between the deployment of "gay" and "fag" as insults brings the gendered nature of this homophobia into focus. For boys and girls at River High "gay" is a fairly common synonym for "stupid." While this word shares the sexual origins of "fag," it does not *consistently* have the skew of gender-loaded meaning. Girls and boys often used "gay" as an adjective referring to inanimate objects and male or female people, whereas they used "fag" as a noun that denotes only un-masculine males. Students used "gay" to describe anything from someone's clothes to a new school rule that the students did not like, as in the following encounter:

> In auto-shop Arnie pulled out a large older version black laptop computer and placed it on his desk. Behind him Nick said "That's a gay laptop! It's five inches thick!"

A laptop can be gay, a movie can be gay or a group of people can be gay. Boys used "gay" and "fag" interchangeably when they refer to other boys, but "fag" does not have the non-gendered attributes that "gay" sometimes invokes.

While its meanings are not the same as "gay," "fag" does have multiple meanings which do not necessarily replace its connotations as a homophobic slur, but rather exist alongside. Some boys took pains to say that "fag" is not about sexuality. Darnell told me "It doesn't even have anything to do with being gay." J. L., a white sophomore at Hillside High (River High's cross-town rival), asserted "Fag, seriously, it has nothing to do with sexual preference at all. You could just be calling somebody an idiot you know?" I asked Ben, a quiet, white sophomore who wore heavy metal t-shirts to auto-shop each day, "What kind of things do guys get called a fag for?" Ben answered "Anything…literally, anything. Like you were trying to turn a wrench the wrong way, 'dude, you're a fag.' Even if a piece of meat drops out of your sandwich, 'you fag!'" Each time Ben said "you fag" his voice deepened as if he were imitating a more masculine boy. While Ben might rightly *feel* like a guy could be called a fag for "anything…literally, anything," there are actually specific behaviors which, when enacted by most boys, can render him more vulnerable to a fag epithet. In this instance Ben's comment highlights the use of "fag" as a generic insult for incompetence, which in the world of River High, is central to a masculine identity. A boy could get called a fag for exhibiting any sort of behavior defined as non-masculine (although not necessarily behaviors aligned with femininity) in the world of River High: being stupid, incompetent, dancing, caring too much about clothing, being too emotional or expressing interest (sexual or platonic) in other guys. However, given the extent of its deployment and the laundry list of behaviors that could get a boy in trouble it is no wonder that Ben felt like a boy could be called "fag" for "anything."

One-third (13) of the boys I interviewed told me that, while they may liberally insult each other with the term, they would not actually direct it at a homosexual peer. Jabes, a Filipino senior, told me

I actually say it [fag] quite a lot, except for when I'm in the company of an actual homosexual person. Then I try not to say it at all. But when I'm just hanging out with my friends I'll be like, "shut up, I don't want to hear you any more, you stupid fag."

Similarly J. L. compared homosexuality to a disability, saying there is "no way" he'd call an actually gay guy a fag because

There's people who are the retarded people who nobody wants to associate with. I'll be so nice to those guys and I hate it when people make fun of them. It's like, "bro do you realize that they can't help that?" And then there's gay people. They were born that way.

According to this group of boys, gay is a legitimate, if marginalized, social identity. If a man is gay, there may be a chance he could be considered masculine by other men (Connell, 1995). David, a handsome white senior dressed smartly in khaki pants and a white button-down shirt, said, "Being gay is just a lifestyle. It's someone you choose to sleep with. You can still throw around a football and be gay." In other words there is a possibility, however slight, that a boy can be gay and masculine. To be a fag is, by definition, the opposite of masculine, whether or not the word is deployed with sexualized or non-sexualized meanings. In explaining this to me, Jamaal, an African-American junior, cited the explanation of popular rap artist, Eminem,

Although I don't like Eminem, he had a good definition of it. It's like taking away your title. In an interview they were like, "you're always capping on gays, but then you sing with Elton John." He was like "I don't mean gay as in gay."

This is what Riki Wilchins calls the "Eminem Exception. Eminem explains that he doesn't call people 'faggot' because of their sexual orientation but because they're weak and unmanly" (Wilchins, 2003). This is precisely the way in which this group of boys at River High uses the term "faggot." While it is not necessarily acceptable to be gay, at least a man who is gay can do other things that render him acceptably masculine. A fag, by the very definition of the word, indicated by students' usages at River High, cannot be masculine. This distinction between "fag" as an unmasculine and problematic identity and "gay" as a possibly masculine, although marginalized, sexual identity is not limited to a teenage lexicon, but is reflected in both psychological discourses (Sedgwick, 1995) and gay and lesbian activism.

Becoming a Fag

"The ubiquity of the word faggot speaks to the reach of its discrediting capacity" (Corbett, 2001: 4). It is almost as if boys cannot help but shout it out on a regular basis—in the hallway, in class, across campus as a greeting, or as a joke. In my fieldwork I was amazed by the way in which the word seemed to pop uncontrollably out of boys' mouths in all kinds of situations. To quote just one of many instances from my fieldnotes:

> Two boys walked out of the P.E. locker room and one yelled "fucking faggot!" at no one in particular.

This spontaneous yelling out of a variation of fag seemingly apropos of nothing happened repeatedly among boys throughout the school.

The fag discourse is central to boys' joking relationships. Joking cements relationships between boys (Kehily and Nayak, 1997; Lyman, 1998) and helps to manage anxiety and discomfort (Freud, 1905). Boys invoked the specter of the fag in two ways: through humorous imitation and through lobbing the epithet at one another. Boys at River High imitated the fag by acting out an exaggerated "femininity," and/or by pretending to sexually desire other boys. As indicated by the introductory vignette in which a predatory "fag" threatens the little boys, boys at River High link these performative scenarios with a fag identity. They lobbed the fag epithet at each other in a verbal game of hot potato, each careful to deflect the insult quickly by hurling it toward someone else. These games and imitations make up a fag discourse which highlights the fag not as a static but rather as a fluid identity which boys constantly struggle to avoid.

In imitative performances the fag discourse functions as a constant reiteration of the fag's existence, affirming that the fag is out there; at any moment a boy can become a fag. At the same time these performances demonstrate that the boy who is invoking the fag is *not* a fag. By invoking it so often, boys remind themselves and each other that

at any point they can become fags if they are not sufficiently masculine.

> Mr. McNally, disturbed by the noise outside of the classroom, turned to the open door saying "We'll shut this unless anyone really wants to watch sweaty boys playing basketball." Emir, a tall skinny boy, lisped "I wanna watch the boys play!" The rest of the class cracked up at his imitation.

Through imitating a fag, boys assure others that they are not a fag by immediately becoming masculine again after the performance. They mock their own performed femininity and/or same-sex desire, assuring themselves and others that such an identity is one deserving of derisive laughter. The fag identity in this instance is fluid, detached from Emir's body. He can move in and out of this "abject domain" while simultaneously affirming his position as a subject.

Boys also consistently tried to put another in the fag position by lobbing the fag epithet at one another.

> Going through the junk-filled car in the auto-shop parking lot, Jay poked his head out and asked "Where are Craig and Brian?" Neil, responded with "I think they're over there," pointing, then thrusting his hips and pulling his arms back and forth to indicate that Craig and Brian might be having sex. The boys in auto-shop laughed.

This sort of joke temporarily labels both Craig and Brian as faggots. Because the fag discourse is so familiar, the other boys immediately understand that Neil is indicating that Craig and Brian are having sex. However these are not necessarily identities that stick. Nobody actually thinks Craig and Brian are homosexuals. Rather the fag identity is a fluid one, certainly an identity that no boy wants, but one that a boy can escape, usually by engaging in some sort of discursive contest to turn another boy into a fag. However, fag becomes a hot potato that no boy wants to be left holding. In the following example, which occurred soon after the "sex" joke, Brian lobs the fag epithet at someone else, deflecting it from himself:

> Brian initiated a round of a favorite game in auto-shop, the "cock game." Brian quietly, looking at

Josh, said, "Josh loves the cock," then slightly louder, "Josh loves the cock." He continued saying this until he was yelling "JOSH LOVES THE COCK!" The rest of the boys laughed hysterically as Josh slinked away saying "I have a bigger dick than all you mother fuckers!"

These two instances show how the fag can be mapped, momentarily, on to one boy's body and how he, in turn, can attach it to another boy, thus deflecting it from himself. In the first instance Neil makes fun of Craig and Brian for simply hanging out together. In the second instance Brian goes from being a fag to making Josh into a fag, through the "cock game." The "fag" is transferable. Boys move in and out of it by discursively creating another as a fag through joking interactions. They, somewhat ironically, can move in and out of the fag position by transforming themselves, temporarily, into a fag, but this has the effect of reaffirming their masculinity when they return to a heterosexual position after imitating the fag.

These examples demonstrate boys invoking the trope of the fag in a discursive struggle in which the boys indicate that they know what a fag is- and that they are not fags. This joking cements bonds between boys as they assure themselves and each other of their masculinity through repeated repudiations of a non-masculine position of the abject.

Racing the Fag

The fag trope is not deployed consistently or identically across social groups at River High. Differences between white boys' and African-American boys' meaning making around clothes and dancing reveal ways in which the fag as the abject position is racialized.

Clean, oversized, carefully put together clothing is central to a hip-hop identity for African-American boys who identify with hip-hop culture.[6] Richard Majors calls this presentation of self a "cool pose" consisting of "unique, expressive and conspicuous styles of demeanor, speech, gesture, clothing, hairstyle, walk, stance and handshake," developed by African-American men

as a symbolic response to institutionalized racism (Majors, 2001: 211). Pants are usually several sizes too big, hanging low on a boy's waist, usually revealing a pair of boxers beneath. Shirts and sweaters are similarly oversized, often hanging down to a boy's knees. Tags are frequently left on baseball hats worn slightly askew and sit perched high on the head. Meticulously clean, unlaced athletic shoes with rolled up socks under the tongue complete a typical hip-hop outfit.

This amount of attention and care given to clothing for white boys not identified with hip-hop culture (that is, most of the white boys at River High) would certainly cast them into an abject, fag position. White boys are not supposed to appear to care about their clothes or appearance, because only fags care about how they look. Ben illustrates this:

> Ben walked in to the auto-shop classroom from the parking lot where he had been working on a particularly oily engine. Grease stains covered his jeans. He looked down at them, made a face and walked toward me with limp wrists, laughing and lisping in a high pitch sing-song voice "I got my good panths all dirty!"

Ben draws on indicators of a fag identity, such as limp wrists, as do the boys in the introductory vignette to illustrate that a masculine person certainly would not care about having dirty clothes. In this sense, masculinity, for white boys, becomes the carefully crafted appearance of not caring about appearance, especially in terms of cleanliness.

However, African-American boys involved in hip-hop culture talk frequently about whether or not their clothes, specifically their shoes, are dirty:

> In drama class both Darnell and Marc compared their white Adidas basketball shoes. Darnell mocked Marc because black scuff marks covered his shoes, asking incredulously "Yours are a week old and they're dirty—I've had mine for a month and they're not dirty!" Both laughed.

Monte, River High's star football player, echoed this concern about dirty shoes when looking at the fancy red shoes he had lent to his cousin the week before, told me he was frustrated because after his cousin used them, the "shoes are hella scuffed up." Clothing, for these boys, does not indicate a fag position, but rather defines membership in a certain cultural and racial group (Perry, 2002).

Dancing is another arena that carries distinctly fag associated meanings for white boys and masculine meanings for African-American boys who participate in hip-hop culture. White boys often associate dancing with "fag." J. L. told me that guys think "'nSync's gay" because they can dance. 'nSync is an all white male singing group known for their dance moves. At dances white boys frequently held their female dates tightly, locking their hips together. The boys never danced with one another, unless engaged in a round of "hot potato." White boys often jokingly danced together in order to embarrass each other by making someone else into a fag:

> Lindy danced behind her date, Chris. Chris's friend, Matt, walked up and nudged Lindy aside, imitating her dance moves behind Chris. As Matt rubbed his hands up and down Chris's back, Chris turned around and jumped back startled to see Matt there instead of Lindy. Matt cracked up as Chris turned red.

However dancing does not carry this sort of sexualized gender meaning for all boys at River High. For African-American boys dancing demonstrates membership in a cultural community (Best, 2000). African-American boys frequently danced together in single sex groups, teaching each other the latest dance moves, showing off a particularly difficult move or making each other laugh with humorous dance moves. Students recognized K. J. as the most talented dancer at the school. K. J. is a sophomore of African-American and Filipino descent who participated in the hip-hop culture of River High. He continually wore the latest hip-hop fashions. K. J. was extremely popular. Girls hollered his name as they walked down the hall and thrust urgently written love notes folded in complicated designs into his hands as he sauntered to class. For the past two years K. J. won first place in the talent show for dancing. When he danced at assemblies the room

reverberated with screamed chants of "Go K.J.! Go K.J.! Go K.J.!" Because dancing for African-American boys places them within a tradition of masculinity, they are not at risk of becoming a fag for this particular gendered practice. Nobody called K. J. a fag. In fact in several of my interviews boys of multiple racial/ethnic backgrounds spoke admiringly of K. J.'s dancing abilities.

Implications

These findings confirm previous studies of masculinity and sexuality that position homophobia as central to contemporary definitions of adolescent masculinity. These data extend previous research by unpacking multilayered meanings that boys deploy through their uses of homophobic language and joking rituals. By attending to these meanings I reframe the discussion as one of a fag discourse, rather than simply labeling this sort of behavior as homophobia. The fag is an "abject" position, a position outside of masculinity that actually constitutes masculinity. Thus, masculinity, in part becomes the daily interactional work of repudiating the "threatening specter" of the fag.

The fag extends beyond a static sexual identity attached to a gay boy. Few boys are permanently, identified as fags; most move in and out of fag positions. Looking at "fag" as a discourse rather than a static identity reveals that the term can be invested with different meanings in different social spaces. "Fag" may be used as a weapon with which to temporarily assert one's masculinity by denying it to others. Thus "fag" becomes a symbol around which contests of masculinity take place.

The fag epithet, when hurled at other boys, may or may not have explicit sexual meanings, but it always has gendered meanings. When a boy calls another boy a fag, it means he is not a man, not necessarily that he is a homosexual. The boys in this study know that they are not supposed to call homosexual boys "fags" because that is mean. This, then has been the limited success of the mainstream gay rights movement. The message absorbed by some of these teenage boys is that "gay men can be masculine, just like you." Instead of challenging gender inequality, this particular discourse of gay rights has reinscribed it. Thus we need to begin to think about how gay men may be in a unique position to challenge gendered as well as sexual norms.

This study indicates that researchers who look at the intersection of sexuality and masculinity need to attend to the ways in which racialized identities may affect how "fag" is deployed and what it means in various social situations. While researchers have addressed the ways in which masculine identities are racialized (Connell, 1995; Ross, 1998; Bucholtz, 1999; Davis, 1999; Price, 1999; Ferguson, 2000; Majors, 2001) they have not paid equal attention to the ways in which "fag" might be a racialized epithet. It is important to look at when, where and with what meaning "the fag" is deployed in order to get at how masculinity is defined, contested, and invested in among adolescent boys.

Research shows that sexualized teasing often leads to deadly results, as evidenced by the spate of school shootings in the 1990s (Kimmel, 2003). Clearly the fag discourse affects not just homosexual teens, but all boys, gay and straight. Further research could investigate these processes in a variety of contexts: varied geographic locations, sexualized groups, classed groups, religious groups and age groups.

Acknowledgments

The author would like to thank Natalie Boero, Leslie Bell, Meg Jay and Barrie Thorne for their comments on this article. This work was supported by the Center for the Study of Sexual Culture at University of California, Berkeley.

Notes

1. While the term "homosexual" is laden with medicalized and normalizing meanings, I use it instead of "gay" because "gay" in the world of River High has multiple meanings apart from sexual practices or identities.
2. Girls do insult one another based on sexualized meanings. But in my own research I found that girls and boys did not harass girls in this manner with the same frequency that boys harassed each other through engaging in joking about the fag.

3. I use discourse in the Foucauldian sense, to describe truth producing practices, not just text or speech (Foucault, 1978).
4. The names of places and respondents have been changed.
5. Auto-shop was a class in which students learned how to build and repair cars. Many of the students in this course were looking into careers as mechanics.
6. While there are several white and Latino boys at River High who identify with hip-hop culture, hip-hop is identified by the majority of students as an African-American cultural style.

References

Almaguer, Tomas (1991) "Chicano Men: A Cartography of Homosexual Identity and Behavior," *Differences* 3: 75–100.

Bersani, Leo (1987) "Is the Rectum a Grave?" *October* 43: 197–222.

Best, Amy (2000) *Prom Night: Youth, Schools and Popular Culture*. New York: Routledge.

Bucholtz, Mary (1999) "'You Da Man': Narrating the Racial Other in the Production of White Masculinity," *Journal of Sociolinguistics* 3/4: 443–60.

Burn, Shawn M. (2000) "Heterosexuals' Use of 'Fag' and 'Queer' to Deride One Another: A Contributor to Heterosexism and Stigma," *Journal of Homosexuality* 40: 1–11.

Butler, Judith (1993) *Bodies that Matter*. Routledge: New York.

———. (1999) *Gender Trouble*. New York: Routledge.

Carrigan, Tim, Connell, Bob and Lee, John (1987) "Toward a New Sociology of Masculinity," in Harry Brod (ed.) *The Making of Masculinities: The New Men's Studies*, pp. 188–202. Boston, MA: Allen & Unwin.

Coltrane, Scott (2001) "Selling the Indispensable Father," paper presented at *Pushing the Boundaries Conference: New Conceptualizations of Childhood and Motherhood*, Philadelphia.

Connell, R. W. (1995) *Masculinities*. Berkeley: University of California Press.

Cooper, Marianne (2000) "Being the 'Go-To Guy': Fatherhood, Masculinity and the Organization of Work in Silicon Valley," *Qualitative Sociology* 23: 379–405.

Corbett, Ken (2001) "Faggot = Loser," *Studies in Gender and Sexuality* 2: 3–28.

Craig, Steve (1992) *Men, Masculinity and the Media.* Newbury Park: Sage.

Curry, Timothy J. (2004) "Fraternal Bonding in the Locker Room: A Profeminist Analysis of Talk About Competition and Women," in Michael Messner and Michael Kimmel (eds.) *Men's Lives.* Boston, MA: Pearson.

Davis, James E. (1999) "Forbidden Fruit, Black Males' Constructions of Transgressive Sexualities in Middle School," in William J. Letts IV and James T. Sears (eds.) *Queering Elementary Education: Advancing the Dialogue About Sexualities and Schooling*, pp. 49 ff. Lanham, MD: Rowan & Littlefield.

Eder, Donna, Evans, Catherine and Parker, Stephen (1995) *School Talk: Gender and Adolescent Culture.* New Brunswick, NJ: Rutgers University Press.

Edly, Nigel and Wetherell, Margaret (1997) "Jockeying for Position: The Construction of Masculine Identities," *Discourse and Society* 8: 203–17.

Epstein, Steven (1996) "A Queer Encounter," in Steven Seidman (ed.) *Queer Theory/Sociology*, pp. 188–202. Cambridge, MA: Blackwell.

Ferguson, Ann (2000) *Bad Boys: Public Schools in the Making of Black Masculinity.* Ann Arbor: University of Michigan Press.

Fine, Gary (1987) *With the Boys: Little League Baseball and Preadolescent Culture.* Chicago, IL: University of Chicago Press.

Foucault, Michel (1978) *The History of Sexuality, Volume I.* New York: Vintage Books.

Francis, Becky and Skelton, Christine (2001) "Men Teachers and the Construction of Heterosexual Masculinity in the Classroom," *Sex Education* 1: 9–21.

Freud, Sigmund (1905) *The Basic Writings of Sigmund Freud* (translated and edited by A. A. Brill). New York: The Modern Library.

Hochschild, Arlie (1989) *The Second Shift.* New York: Avon.

Julien, Isaac and Mercer, Kobena (1991) "True Confessions: A Discourse on Images of Black Male Sexuality," in Essex Hemphill (ed.) *Brother to Brother: New Writings by Black Gay Men*, pp. 167–73. Boston, MA: Alyson Publications.

Kehily, Mary Jane and Nayak, Anoop (1997) "Lads and Laughter: Humour and the Production of Heterosexual Masculinities," *Gender and Education* 9: 69–87.

Kimmel, Michael (2001) "Masculinity as Homophobia: Fear, Shame, and Silence in the Construction of Gender Identity," in Stephen Whitehead and Frank Barrett (eds.) *The Masculinities Reader*, pp. 266–87. Cambridge: Polity.

———. (2003) "Adolescent Masculinity, Homophobia, and Violence: Random School Shootings, 1982–2001," *American Behavioral Scientist* 46: 1439–58.

King, D. L. (2004) *Double Lives on the Down Low.* New York: Broadway Books.

Lehne, Gregory (1998) "Homophobia Among Men: Supporting and Defining the Male Role," in Michael Kimmel and Michael Messner (eds.) *Men's Lives*, pp. 237–149. Boston, MA: Allyn and Bacon.

Lemert, Charles (1996) "Series Editor's Preface," in Steven Seidman (ed.) *Queer Theory/Sociology.* Cambridge, MA: Blackwell.

Lyman, Peter (1998) "The Fraternal Bond as a Joking Relationship: A Case Study of the Role of Sexist Jokes in Male Group Bonding," in Michael Kimmel and Michael Messner (eds.) *Men's Lives*, pp. 171–93. Boston, MA: Allyn and Bacon.

Mac and Ghaill, Martain (1996) "What about the Boys—School, Class and Crisis Masculinity," *Sociological Review* 44: 381–97.

MacLeod, Jay (1987) *Ain't No Makin It: Aspirations and Attainment in a Low Income Neighborhood.* Boulder, CO: Westview Press.

Majors, Richard (2001) "Cool Pose: Black Masculinity and Sports," in Stephen Whitehead and Frank Barrett (eds.) *The Masculinities Reader*, pp. 208–17. Cambridge: Polity.

Messner, Michael (1989) "Sports and the Politics of Inequality," in Michael Kimmel and Michael Messner (eds.) *Men's Lives.* Boston, MA: Allyn and Bacon.

———. (2004) "On Patriarchs and Losers: Rethinking Men's Interests," paper presented at Berkeley *Journal of Sociology* Conference, Berkeley.

Parker, Andrew (1996) "The Construction of Masculinity Within Boys' Physical Education," *Gender and Education* 8: 141–57.

Perry, Pamela (2002) *Shades of White: White Kids and Racial Identities in High School.* Durham, NC: Duke University Press.

Plummer, David C. (2001) "The Quest for Modern Manhood: Masculine Stereotypes, Peer Culture and the Social Significance of Homophobia," *Journal of Adolescence* 24: 15–23.

Price, Jeremy (1999) "Schooling and Racialized Masculinities: The Diploma, Teachers and Peers in the Lives of Young, African-American Men," *Youth and Society* 31: 224–63.

Riggs, Marlon (1991) "Black Macho Revisited: Reflections of a SNAP! Queen," in Essex Hemphill (ed.) *Brother to Brother: New Writings by Black Gay Men,* pp. 153–260. Boston, MA: Alyson Publications.

Ross, Marlon B. (1998) "In Search of Black Men's Masculinities," *Feminist Studies* 24: 599–626.

Sedgwick, Eve K. (1990) *Epistemology of the Closet.* Berkeley: University of California Press.

———. (1995) "Gosh, Boy George, You Must Be Awfully Secure in Your Masculinity!" in Maurice Berger, Brian Wallis and Simon Watson (eds.) *Constructing Masculinity,* pp. 11–20. New York: Routledge.

Skelton, Christine (1996) "Learning to Be Tough: The Fostering of Maleness in One Primary School," *Gender and Education* 8: 185–97.

Smith, George W. (1998) "The Ideology of 'Fag': The School Experience of Gay Students," *The Sociological Quarterly* 39: 309–35.

Smith, Valerie (1994) "Split Affinities: The Case of Interracial Rape," in Anne Herrmann and Abigail Stewart (eds.) *Theorizing Feminism,* pp. 155–70. Boulder, CO: Westview Press.

Stein, Arlene and Plummer, Ken (1994) "'I Can't Even Think Straight': 'Queer' Theory and the Missing Sexual Revolution in Sociology," *Sociological Theory* 12: 178 ff.

Thorne, Barrie (1993) *Gender Play: Boys and Girls in School.* New Brunswick, NJ: Rutgers University Press.

Warner, Michael (1993) "Introduction," in Michael Warner (ed.) *Fear of a Queer Planet: Queer Politics and Social Theory,* pp. vii–xxxi. Minneapolis: University of Minnesota Press.

West, Candace and Zimmerman, Don (1991) "Doing Gender," in Judith Lorber (ed.) *The Social Construction of Gender,* pp. 102–21. Newbury Park: Sage.

Whitehead, Stephen and Barrett, Frank (2001) "The Sociology of Masculinity," in Stephen Whitehead and Frank Barrett (eds.) *The Masculinities Reader,* pp. 472–6. Cambridge: Polity.

Wilchins, Riki (2003) "Do You Believe in Fairies?" *The Advocate,* 4 February.

Willis, Paul (1981) *Learning to Labor: How Working Class Kids Get Working Class Jobs.* New York: Columbia University Press.

Wood, Julian (1984) "Groping Toward Sexism: Boy's Sex Talk," in Angela McRobbie and Mica Nava (eds.) *Gender and Generation.* London: Macmillan Publishers.

Gender and the Meanings of Adolescent Romantic Relationships: A Focus on Boys

PEGGY C. GIORDANO, MONICA A. LONGMORE, AND WENDY D. MANNING

Increased interest in heterosexual relationships has long been considered a hallmark of adolescence (Waller 1937; Sullivan 1953). Yet sociological attention to adolescent love and romance is dwarfed by the level of cultural interest, ranging from television and film portrayals to parental concerns about teenage sexuality and pregnancy. Recently, media accounts have declared the end of dating and romance among teens in favor of casual hookups that lack feelings of intimacy or commitment (see, e.g., Denizet-Lewis 2004). A large-scale investigation based on a national probability sample of adolescents contradicts this depiction, however: by age 18 over 80 percent of adolescents have some dating experience, and a majority of these liaisons are defined by adolescent respondents as "special romantic relationships" (Carver, Joyner, and Udry 2003). Even relatively young adolescents indicate some romantic relationship experience, and those who do not nevertheless express a strong interest in dating (Giordano, Longmore, and Manning 2001). In spite of the ubiquitous nature of dating relationships during the period, we know little about how adolescents themselves experience the transition from a social life based on same-gender friendships to one that includes romantic involvement (Brown, Feiring, and Furman 1999).

We know much more about the character, meaning, and impact of adolescent peer relations. This research not only underscores that peers and friends are critically important to children and adolescents (see, e.g., Call and Mortimer 2001; Crosnoe 2000; Youniss and Smollar 1985), but it also provides a basis for expecting gender differences in the ways in which adolescents navigate and experience romantic relationships. Maccoby (1990) emphasizes that girls more often forge intimate dyadic friendships and rely on supportive styles of communication, while boys tend to play in larger groups, use a "restrictive" interaction style, and develop a greater emphasis on issues of dominance. In light of these differences, she poses a key developmental question: "What happens, then, when individuals from these two distinctive 'cultures' attempt to interact with one another? People of both sexes are faced with a relatively unfamiliar situation to which they must adapt" (Maccoby 1990:517).

Maccoby argues that the transition to dating is easier for boys, who tend to transport their dominant interaction style into the new relationship. This is consistent with other research on peer socialization that also adapts a spillover argument. While girls are socialized to center attention on personal relationships (Gilligan 1982) and romance, boys' interactions within male peer groups often lead them to define the heterosexual world as another arena in which they can compete and score (Eder, Evans, and Parker 1995). Studies from this peer-based research tradition thus provide a theoretical basis for expecting that as adolescents begin to date, boys will do so with greater

Peggy C. Giordano, Monica A. Longmore, and Wendy D. Manning, "Gender and the Meanings of Adolescent Romantic Relationships: A Focus on Boys," *American Sociological Review* 71 (April 2006): 260–287. Reprinted with permission.

confidence and less emotional engagement (i.e., the notion that boys want sex, girls want romance), ultimately emerging as the more powerful actors within these relationships.

Research on peer relationships has been critical to an understanding of the adolescent period, and is important in that it foreshadows some of the origins of problematic features of male-female relationships, including intimate violence and gender mistrust. Yet perspectives about dating are too heavily grounded in studies of peer interactions and concerns, rather than in research on romantic encounters themselves. In addition, prior research has focused almost exclusively on issues of sexuality, while the relational and emotional dimensions of early heterosexual experiences have often been ignored. The symbolic interactionist perspective that we develop highlights unique features of adolescent romantic relationships that provide a rich climate for additional socialization. Our view is that meanings may emerge from interaction and communication within the romantic context that significantly alter or supplant those developed through peer interactions. This perspective fosters a different view of the ways in which gender influences the crossing-over process, and suggests fundamental limitations of the focus on spillover effects. Further, depictions of girls' experiences, especially concerning issues of sexuality, have become increasingly nuanced, but in prior work boys have often been cast as especially flat or one-dimensional characters (Forster [1927] 1974). Thus, it is important to explore both girls' and boys' perspectives on romance, but our central objective here is to address consequential gaps in knowledge about boys' relationship experiences.[1] The theoretical perspective and findings presented nevertheless have implications for understanding the character and range of girls' experiences, and provide a basic foundation for additional research focused specifically on girls' perspectives.

Background

Prior Research on Adolescent Girls

Most studies of adolescent life emphasize girls' strong relational orientation (e.g., Gilligan 1982;

Martin 1996), as well as fundamental gender inequalities that tend to be reproduced as girls learn to center much time and energy on their romantic attachments (Holland and Eisenhart 1990; Pipher 1994). In a study based on social life within a Midwestern middle school, Eder et al. (1995) conclude that emphases within girls' peer groups (e.g., the notion that one must always be in love, the focus on personal appearance, and concerns over reputation) foster these inequalities and serve to distance young women from their sexual feelings (see also Simon, Eder, and Evans 1992). Within their own peer networks, boys emphasize competition on many levels, and ridicule those who express caring and other positive emotions for girls. Consistent with Maccoby's (1990) spillover hypothesis, then, Eder et al. (1995) argue that these peer emphases influence the character of cross-gender relations: "[M]ost male adolescents and many adults continue to associate excitement with a sense of domination and competition... [while] most girls fail to develop a sense of the depth of their inner resources and power and thus remain dominated and controlled" (Eder et al. 1995:148).

Studies that explore girls' early sexual experiences draw similar conclusions about asymmetries of power within romantic relationships. Holland, Ramazanoglu, and Thomson (1996) initially theorize that there is a sense in which female and male adolescents can be considered "in the same boat" due to their relative inexperience. They subsequently discard this notion, however, based on their analysis of girls' and boys' narrative accounts of their first sexual experiences. The authors argue that girls quickly learn that sex is in large part directed to "supporting and satisfying masculine values and needs" (Holland et al. 1996:159). Thompson's (1995) study of girls' sexual narratives develops a more nuanced portrait, by highlighting significant variations in girls' sexual experiences. Focusing on the highly melodramatic character of many girls' narratives, however, Thompson (1995) concludes that within the contemporary context, the gender gap in orientations toward relationships and sexuality may even have widened. She suggests, for example, that it is no longer as necessary as in earlier eras for boys to engage in preliminary steps of relationship-building to achieve their goal of sexual access, a dynamic that could accentuate rather than diminish traditional differences in perspectives. Interestingly, Risman and Schwartz (2002) have recently developed an alternative hypothesis. Examining aggregate trends that show declining rates of sexual intercourse during the adolescent period, the authors link such changes to "the increasing power of girls in their sexual encounters" (Risman and Schwartz 2002:21), particularly to negotiate the timing and the context within which sexual behavior occurs. Thus, while interpretations of the nature and effects of these dynamic processes differ, prior research points to power as a key relationship dynamic that warrants more direct, systematic scrutiny.

In summary, the emphases of prior studies have been appropriate, as the dynamics highlighted connect in intimate ways to processes that have been limiting or injurious to young women. Areas of concern range from leveled career aspirations (Holland and Eisenhart 1990) to sexual coercion and partner violence (Eder et al. 1995). Nevertheless, this research is itself limited by the focus on the relatively public face of cross-gender relations, such as joking and teasing that occurs within school lunchrooms or during after-school activities. Here the emphasis remains upon the dynamics of the same-gender peer group, providing only glimpses into the more private world of the romantic dyad. Many studies in this tradition also rely on small non-diverse samples, or concentrate on very young adolescents. The heavy focus on issues of sexuality also provides a restricted view of the broader relationship context within which sexual behaviors unfold; that is, of the more basic emotional and other relational dynamics that characterize these relationships. More fundamentally, this portrait of spillover effects does not sufficiently highlight the communicative strengths and relationship competencies that girls bring to these relationships, nor does this literature confront inherent limits to the idea of carry-over effects. These criticisms apply equally to prior research on boys, where similar themes emerge, even though the research base is even more sketchy and incomplete.

Studies of Boys' Romantic and Sexual Lives

Boys have certainly not been ignored in prior research on adolescence. Yet within the many studies that concentrate on boys, romantic relationships have not been a frequent subject. Classic investigations of boys' lives often concentrate on group processes within boys' friendship and peer circles, either as ends in themselves (e.g., Fine 1987), or as peers influence specific outcomes such as delinquency (e.g., Cohen 1955; Sullivan 1989; Thrasher 1927) or the reproduction of the class system (e.g., MacLeod 1987; Willis 1977). These studies do, however, sometimes offer characterizations of boys' romantic attachments. For example, MacLeod (1987) in a classic study of boys' delinquency involvement suggests that "women were reduced to the level of commodities and the discussions sometimes consisted of consumers exchanging information" (MacLeod 1987:280). The relative lack of research on boys' romantic experiences, then, likely stems from scholars' interests in other areas, as well as from their views that male-female relationships are of a limited, or at least a delimited (primarily sexual), interest to adolescent boys themselves. This is consistent with the research reviewed on girls' lives, and again highlights the reach of male peer culture. A consequence, however, is that boys' views about romance are gleaned primarily from analyses of girls' narratives and/or studies based on boys' discourse within the relatively public areas of the male peer group.

A few studies have examined boys' perspectives on romance directly, again often in connection with discussions of sexuality. Wight (1994), for example, observed significant differences in boys' talk about their girlfriends and sex among their peers compared with interviews conducted in more private settings. In the latter context, the working-class Scottish youth whom he studied were much more likely to express insecurities and vulnerabilities regarding the adequacy of their own sexual performances. Nevertheless, Wight

(1994:721) also concludes that only a minority of the boys were engaged emotionally in the relationship aspects of these heterosexual liaisons. He suggests that generally the boys preferred male company and "particularly dislike girls' displays of feminine emotion which make them feel extremely awkward." Despite his more layered view of boys' perspectives, then, Wight's (1994) depiction of boys' attitudes toward romance does not differ greatly from a number of other accounts: "the main excitement of girlfriends is the challenge of chatting them up and getting off with them; once this has been achieved, going out with the girl becomes tedious…only a few came close to expressing trust in, or loyalty to, girls in the way they sometimes did for boys" (p. 714). In contrast, Moffatt (1989), relying on older students' written accounts of their sexual lives, found that a significant number (about one third) of the young men's narratives stressed the importance of romance and love in connection with their sexual experiences. It is unclear whether these differences in findings stem from significant age differences across samples, or variations in the methods employed. Thus, it is important to examine specific aspects of the existing portrait of adolescent males' romantic relationship experiences using a larger, more heterogeneous sample of adolescents.

The present study, then, focuses on basic but foundational research question. Do adolescent boys, as Maccoby (1990) hypothesized, more often than girls express confidence as they cross over to the heterosexual realm? Are adolescent girls more likely to be engaged emotionally, relative to their male counterparts? And, perhaps most central to existing portraits, do boys typically evidence greater power and influence within their early heterosexual liaisons? These questions are interrelated and central to the development of an age-graded, life-course perspective on how gender influences relationship processes.

A Neo-Meadian Perspective on Adolescent Romantic Relationships

In our view, prior work in this area offers an incomplete portrait of the ways in which gender influences the crossing-over process. Further, existing treatments undertheorize the extent to which the romantic relationship itself becomes a potentially important arena of socialization and site for the emergence of meanings. These relationships may occasion new perspectives that coexist with, contradict, and even negate previous peer-based messages. Mead's (1934) symbolic interaction theory and recent extensions in the sociology of emotions tradition (e.g., Collins 2004; Engdahl 2004) provide a useful framework for exploring this general idea.[2]

Two central tenets of symbolic interaction theories are that meanings emerge from the process of social interaction and that the self is continuously shaped by dynamic social processes (Mead 1934). These basic insights foster a highly unfinished, continually emerging view of development, and a caution to the notion that meanings derived from peer interactions are likely to be transported wholesale into the romantic context. As Sandstrom, Martin, and Fine (2002:10) point out, Mead (1934) and later Blumer (1969) emphasized that "social definitions guide action," but also recognized that this involves much more than a "reflex-like application of these definitions."

> We have to determine which objects or actions we need to give meaning and which we can neglect. Moreover, we must figure out which of the many meanings that can be attributed to a thing are the appropriate ones in this context…. [W]hen we find ourselves in some situations, particularly new and ambiguous ones, we discover that no established meanings apply. As a result, we must be flexible enough to learn or devise new meanings. We have this flexibility because we handle the things we encounter through a dynamic and creative process of interpretation. This process allows us to generate new or different meanings and to adjust our actions accordingly.

Scholars such as Corsaro (1985) highlight these dynamics as a way to understand the character of the parents-to-peers transition that reliably occurs during childhood and adolescence (see also Corsaro and Eder 1990). Researchers point out that parental socialization efforts are never fully successful, in that young people inevitably produce novel cultural practices through interaction with their peers. These meanings fit the peer context well, as they are a product of this context. Social forces are thus deeply implicated in the production of meanings; and, as these meanings are shared, they become a further source of social solidarity and self-definition (Fine 1987). This meaning-construction process is never fully stabilized, however, because new "hooks for change" continually present themselves within the environment (Giordano, Cernkovich, and Rudolph 2002). Individuals also possess the unique capacity to develop new plans, including the capacity to carve out new social networks. Yet as Emirbayer and Goodwin (1994) note, these new affiliations will nevertheless in turn have a shaping influence.

These basic insights are integral to many discussions of child and adolescent peer networks, but researchers have not systematically applied the symbolic interactionist or interpretive framework to an understanding of the peers-to-romance transition. It is intuitive to do so for several reasons: First, adolescent romantic relationships definitely qualify as a new situation, one in which interaction and communication hold a central place. Second, the relatively private world of romantic interactions makes it likely that meanings will emerge on site, rather than simply being imported from earlier peer experiences or from the broader culture (see also Simon and Gagnon 1986). The fundamentally reciprocal qualities of dyadic communication enhance these possibilities. Mead ([1909] 1964:101) theorized that the "probable beginning of human communication was in cooperation, not in imitation, where conduct *differed* [emphasis added] and yet where the act of the one answered to and called out the act of the other." Third, scholars point out that contemporary romantic relationships in Western nations lack the heavily scripted qualities that characterized earlier eras or courtship practices within more traditional cultural contexts (Giddens 1992). This too leads us to favor a symbolic interactionist perspective on the meaning construction process. In the following discussion, we explore three basic relationship domains—communication, emotion,

and influence—that allow us to develop further this symbolic interactionist perspective on adolescent romantic relationships.

Communication

We agree with Maccoby's (1990) key assertion that "both sexes face a relatively unfamiliar situation to which they must adapt" (p. 517), but we offer a different perspective on the ways in which gender-related experiences may influence the crossing-over process. Recall Maccoby's suggestion that the transition is easier for boys, who are seen as frequently transporting their dominant interaction style into the new relationship. A competing hypothesis is that because girls have more experience with intimate dyadic communications by virtue of their own earlier friendship experiences, boys must make what amounts to a bigger developmental leap as they begin to develop this more intimate way of relating to another.

Mead (1913:378) pointed out that when engaged in familiar, habitual actions, "the self is not self-conscious." In contrast, on those occasions when the individual's previous repertoire proves inadequate to the task at hand (what Mead termed the "problematic situation"), cognitive processes, including feelings of self-consciousness, are fully engaged. While both girls and boys are likely to experience their initial forays into heterosexual territory as instances of Mead's "problematic situation," this may be even more descriptive of boys' experience, by virtue of the especially strong contrast for boys with the form and content of their earlier peer interactions. Thus, our expectation is that boys, at least initially, will experience a greater level *of communication awkwardness* in connection with their romantic liaisons. Following Mead, this also implies that cues within the new situation will be especially important. Mead noted that while the past (here, youths' understandings derived from peer interactions) is never completely discarded, the current perspective will nevertheless be transformed in light of present circumstances and future plans (Mead 1934; see also Joas 1997:167–98).

Movement into romantic relationships involves more than developing a level of comfort while communicating with the opposite gender. It also requires a full complement of relationship skills, most of them communication based as well. Adolescents must become familiar with the process of making initial overtures, learn how to communicate their needs to partners, manage conflict, and successfully terminate unwanted relationships. Here, too, young women may be more competent and confident in what we will call relationship navigational skills, as they have experienced generally related social dynamics in prior relationships (e.g., friendship troubles and their repair). In addition, norms about dating behavior have become more ambiguous within the contemporary context, but boys are still often expected to make the initial advances. This provides a further reason for them to be more anxious and less certain about how to proceed.

Adolescents' perceived *confidence navigating relationships* requires systematic investigation, however, as prior research has shown that boys frequently score higher on scales measuring general self-esteem and self-efficacy (Gecas and Longmore 2003). Thus focusing only on the self-esteem literature, and the notion that males occupy a position of greater societal privilege, we might expect boys simply to forge ahead with confidence into this new terrain, with little uncertainty about a lack of expertise or preparation. This is also consistent with the idea that girls may lack confidence in their abilities to make their own needs known in relationships, particularly given socialization practices that heighten girls' sensitivities to and concern for the needs of others (Gilligan 1982).

Emotion

Researchers have recently accorded greater significance to the role of emotions in human behavior (e.g., Katz 1999; Massey 2002; Turner 2000). Theorists in the sociology of emotions tradition in particular stress the strongly social basis of emotional processes (e.g., Collins 2004; Thoits 1989). Departing from highly individualistic conceptions of emotions, many sociological treatments focus on the ways in which cultural expectations influence emotion-management as well as emotional expression (e.g., Hochschild

1983). This sociological viewpoint resonates with the peer-based literature reviewed earlier, as it stresses that boys are socialized to avoid or deny softer emotions, and are teased and ridiculed by peers if they reveal signs of weakness or emotionality. In turn, this literature suggests that boys learn to devalue relationships that might engender positive emotions, and to objectify and denigrate the young women who are their partners in romantic interactions. Overall, much previous research provides support for the idea of an emotional closing-off process, as boys are observed making crude comments in the school lunchroom (Eder et al. 1995), describing their romantic relationships as tedious (Wight 1994), or constructing relationships as a game perpetrated on young women for the purpose of sexual conquest (Anderson 1989).

The symbolic, interactionist approach, in contrast, suggests that the new dyadic context opens up additional opportunities for role-taking, defined as "putting oneself in another's position and taking that person's perspective" (Short 1979:1323). Such reciprocal interactions may promote new definitions of the situation, as well as the experience of new emotions. Scholars have recently noted that emotions have clarifying and motivational significance (Frijda 2002), in effect providing valence or energy to new lines of action (Collins 2004). Our central argument, then, is that adolescent romantic relationships become a potentially important arena of socialization and reference, one that fosters new definitions and interrelated emotions. Suggesting that girls typically experience heightened emotionality in connection with their romantic endeavors is hardly a novel assertion. In contrast, however, to the emphases within much of the existing adolescence literature, we argue that boys often develop positive emotional feelings toward partners and accord significance and positive meanings to their romantic relationships. The notion that new attitudes and feelings can emerge from these recurrent sequences of interaction is generally consistent with Thorne's (1993:133) key observation that "incidents of crossing (gender boundaries) may chip away at traditional ideologies and hold out new possibilities."

This educational process and boys' emerging interest, we believe, frequently extends beyond the sexual to include the relationship itself. To the degree that boys engage in a distinctive form of intimate self-disclosure lacking within their peer discourse, and receive both positive identity and social support from a caring female partner, boys in some respects may be seen as more dependent on these relationships than girls, who have a range of other opportunities for intimate talk and social support. Feelings of heightened emotionality or *love* for the partner can be assessed directly, as adolescents are well placed to comment on their own subjective emotional experiences. Here the private interview provides a useful supplement to observational studies of boys' interactions in public settings, as recent work on gender and emotions underscores that the public face of emotions appears more highly gendered than the personal experience of these same emotions (Fischer 2000). It is also important to obtain systematic assessments across a large, heterogeneous sample of adolescents, as most of the research reviewed earlier indicates that some boys develop caring attitudes toward a partner and positive feelings about their romantic relationships. These researchers frequently assert, however, that this adaptation is characteristic of a small subgroup of male adolescents who represent a departure from the more common and traditionally gendered pattern (Anderson 1989; Eder et al. 1995; Wight 1994).

Influence

Social interactions are not only implicated in the production of specific emotional feelings, but as some theorists argue, these emotional processes are capable of transforming the self in more fundamental ways (MacKinnon 1994; Engdahl 2004). The social influence literature emphasizes that the more highly valued the relationship, the more individuals are willing to accede to influence attempts in order to maintain or enhance their standing with valued others (Blau 1964). Viewed from a neo-Meadian perspective, however, positive interactions with significant others influence self-feelings (emotions) and attitudes

that become catalysts in the truest sense. This neo-Meadian viewpoint encompasses but also extends the notion that change is accomplished primarily as a strategic move to preserve the relationship.

If, on the other hand, positive meanings are largely constructed outside the romantic relationship (e.g., as a source of competition and basis for camaraderie with one's male peers), we may expect the romantic partner's influence to be (and to be viewed as) rather minimal (see Collins 2004:238). This is likely to be the case whether the focus is on change in relationship attitudes/behaviors, influence on other aspects of the adolescent's life, or effects on the young person's emerging identity. Thus the character of communication and levels of emotional engagement in these relationships during adolescence are critical dynamics likely to be implicated in the nature and extent of partner influence. Our expectation, following the arguments developed in the previous sections, is that adolescent girls, owing to their greater familiarity with issues of intimacy and skill in communication, will likely make influence attempts, and boys (highly interested/engaged in this new relationship form) will often be receptive to them. Consequently, we do not expect to find significant gender differences in reports of partner influence, as contrasted with the hypothesis of a highly gendered (i.e., boys have more influence) pattern.

Consistent with prior sociological treatments, it is also useful to distinguish *influence* processes, which may be quite subtle, from *power*, often defined as the ability to overcome some resistance or to exercise one's will over others (Weber 1947). Youniss and Smollar (1985) note that much of the time within same-gender friendship relations, reality is "cooperatively co-constructed." This description reflects that the initial similarity of friends favors the development of a relatively egalitarian style of mutual influence. As a close relationship, romantic relations should also entail many instances of cooperative co-construction— but these relationships to a greater extent than friendships also bridge considerable difference. Thus it is not only likely that differences in perspective and conflict will occur, but also that partners will attempt to control or change the other in some way.

It is conventional to argue that structurally based gender inequalities tend to be reproduced at the couple level. On average the male partner acquires more power and control in the relationship (Komter 1989). While these ideas originally were applied to adult marital relations, as suggested earlier, the notion of gendered inequalities of power is also a recurrent theme within the adolescence literature. These power and influence processes require more systematic study, however, because during adolescence, social forces that are generally understood as fostering gender inequalities are still somewhat at a distance (e.g., childbearing, gendered access to the labor force and to other bases of power); thus the reproduction process itself may be markedly less than complete. The symbolic interactionist framework also suggests a more situated, constantly negotiated view of power dynamics, in contrast to a straightforward male privilege argument (see, e.g., Sprey 1999). The assumption of boys' greater power and control also connects to the largely untested assumptions that: (a) boys, on average, effect a dominant interaction style in these fledgling relationships (our communication hypothesis), and (b) girls are systematically disadvantaged by their greater commitment and emotional investment in their romantic endeavors (our emotion hypothesis). Asymmetries of various kinds (demographic, relational, status) are common within adolescent romantic relationships (see Carver and Udry 1997; Giordano, Longmore, and Manning 2001). Our view, however, is that these imbalances in the contours of the relationship need not—during this phase of life—necessarily and systematically privilege male adolescents. In the current analysis, then, our goal with respect to influence and power is to assess and compare adolescent male and female reports about their romantic partner's *influence attempts*, *actual influence* (as perceived by the respondent), and perceptions of the *power balance* within the relationship (defined as getting one's way, given some level of disagreement).

Data and Methods

Data

The Toledo Adolescent Relationships Study (TARS) sample was drawn from the year 2000 enrollment records of all youths registered for the 7th, 9th, and 11th grades in Lucas County, Ohio, a largely urban metropolitan environment that includes Toledo (n = 1, 316).[3] The sample universe encompassed records elicited from 62 schools across seven school districts. The stratified, random sample was devised by the National Opinion Research Center, and includes over-samples of African American and Hispanic adolescents. School attendance was not a requirement for inclusion in the sample, and most interviews were conducted in the respondent's home using preloaded laptops to administer the interview.

From the total sample of 1,316, we focus the present analysis on 957 respondents who reported either currently dating or having recently dated (the previous year).[4] As shown in Table 1, 49 percent of the dating sample is male, and the average age is approximately fifteen years. The race/ethnic distribution is: 69 percent white, 24 percent African American, and 7 percent Hispanic. In-depth interviews were also conducted with a subset (n = 100) of the respondents who had participated in the structured interview. These youths were selected based on their race/gender characteristics, and having indicated some dating experience during the structured interview. This subsample is on average older than the sample as a whole, and includes 51 girls and 49 boys. Of these 40 were white, 33 African American, 26 Hispanic, and one was "other" (Filipino).[5]

Measures

Definition of a Romantic Relationship

We developed a simple definition that precedes the romantic relationships section of the interview schedule: "Now we are interested in your own experiences with dating and the opposite sex. When we ask about 'dating' we mean when you like a guy, and he likes you back. This does not have to mean going on a formal date."[6] The interview schedule elicits information about a number

Table 1. Means/Percentages and Standard Deviations for the Total Sample and Separately for Boys and Girls

	Total		Boys		Girls	
	Mean / %	SD	Mean / %	SD	Mean / %	SD
Dependent Variables (range)						
Communication processes Awkwardness (4–20)	9.87*	3.3	10.10	3.2	9.64	3.4
Confidence (3–15)	10.40*	2.8	9.92	2.8	11.03	2.7
Heightened emotionality Love (4–20)	14.13	3.6	13.91	3.5	14.34	3.6
Influence and power						
Influence attempts (2–10)	3.80*	1.7	4.09	1.7	3.51	1.7
Actual influence (3–15)	6.41*	2.5	6.94	2.5	5.89	2.4
Perceived power balance (4–12)	8.23	1.8	7.63	1.8	8.80	1.7
Independent Variables						
Gender						
Boys	.49	—	—	—	—	—
Girls	.51	—	—	—	—	—
Race						
White	.69	—	.64	—	.66	—
African American	.24	—	.24	—	.23	—
Hispanic	.07	—	.12	—	.11	—
Age (12–19)	15.49	1.7	15.44	1.7	15.54	1.7
Family structure						
Married biological	.46	—	.46	—	.43	—
Single	.26	—	.25	—	.28	—
Step	.16*	—	.19	—	.14	—
Other	.12*	—	.09	—	.15	—
Mother's monitoring (6–24)	20.55*	2.8	20.17	3.0	20.92	2.4
Peer orientation (1–4)	3.16*	.9	3.25	.9	3.08	.9
Mother's education						
<12 years	.11	—	.13	—	.12	—
(12 years)	.32	—	.31	—	.31	—
>12 years	.57	—	.56	—	.57	—
Self-esteem (10–30)	23.80	3.6	23.92	3.4	23.60	3.8
Currently dating						
Yes	.60*	—	.52	—	.67	—
No	.40	—	.48	—	.33	—
Duration of relationship (1–8 months)	4.79*	2.1	4.62*	2.1	4.95	2.1
Sex with romantic partner						
Yes	.28	—	.30	—	.27	—
No	.72	—	.70	—	.73	—
N	957	—	469	—	488	—

Note: Mean/% = mean or percent; N = number; SD = standard deviation.

*$p < .05$ difference between boys and girls (two-tailed tests).

of different types of relationships, but the items and scales that we later describe and the accompanying analyses focus on the adolescent's relationship with a current or most recent partner.

Relationship Qualities/Dynamics

Communication Awkwardness

To measure feelings of communication awkwardness or apprehension we rely on four items: "Sometimes I don't know quite what to say with X," "I would be uncomfortable having intimate conversations with X," "Sometimes I find it hard to talk about my feelings with X," and "Sometimes I feel I need to watch what I say to X" (Powers and Hutchinson 1979) (alpha = .71).

Confidence in Navigating Romantic Relationships

This scale was designed for the TARS study, and it includes three items that tap dating-specific dilemmas and respondents' perceptions of confidence that they would be able to communicate their wishes: "How confident are you that you could…refuse a date?" "tell your girlfriend/boyfriend how to treat you?" and "break up with someone you no longer like?" (alpha = .72).

Heightened Emotionality

To measure the adolescent's level of emotional engagement we use items drawn from Hatfield and Sprecher's (1986) passionate *love* scale, including "I would rather be with X than anyone else," "I am very attracted to X," "the sight of X turns me on," and "X always seems to be on my mind" (alpha = .85).

Influence

We distinguish between the partner's influence attempts and perceptions of "actual" partner influence. *Influence attempts* are indexed by these items: "X sometimes wants to control what I do" and "X always tries to change me" (alpha = .77). *"Actual" influence* reflects the level of agreement that respondents have been influenced by or actually changed things about themselves due to their relationship with the partner. Items include "X often influences what I do," "I sometimes do things because X is doing them," and "I sometimes

do things because I don't want to lose X's respect" (alpha = .71). We note that the influence scales do not require respondents to select who has the most influence in their relationship, but instead to provide an assessment of their perception that partners have made influence attempts and that they have actually made changes or adjustments that they trace to the partner's influence. We then compare girls' and boys' average scores on these indices to gauge perceptions of partner influence.

Power

The measure of power includes a more direct comparative element, as questions focus on the likelihood of getting one's way given some disagreement. This index is modeled on Blood and Wolfe's (1960) *decision power index* revised for use with this younger sample. The scale includes an overall assessment ("If the two of you disagree, who usually gets their way?") and also includes items that reference specific situations: "what you want to do together," "how much time you spend together," and "how far to go sexually." Responses include "X more than me," "X and me about the same," and "me more than X." Higher scores reflect the adolescent's perception of a relatively more favorable power balance, relative to the partner (alpha = .77).

Control Variables

Although our primary objective is to examine similarities and differences in the experience of romantic relationships as influenced by the respondent's gender, we also include control variables in our models. This allows us to account for possible differences between the gender subgroups on other basic characteristics and features of adolescents' lives, and to assess whether these variables operate as mediators of any observed gender differences. In addition to the influence of other sociodemographic characteristics, gender differences in reports about relationships might be influenced by girls' generally higher levels of parental monitoring (Longmore, Manning, and Giordano 2001), or males' greater levels of involvement with peers (as suggested in the foregoing literature review). It is particularly important to control for self-esteem, as responses to items about relationship confidence or perceived power may be influenced by the adolescent's generally efficacious or confident self-views. This would be consistent with Maccoby's (1990) argument that boys move ahead with confidence into the heterosexual context. Thus we not only assess whether, on average, boys tend to report greater relationship confidence, but also whether high self-esteem accounts for any observed gender difference. During adolescence, romantic relationships themselves vary significantly—both in terms of duration and level of seriousness (Carver, Joyner, and Udry 2003). Thus, our models also include controls for *duration* and whether or not the relationship has become sexually intimate. Teens with romantic relationship experience who were not dating at the time of the interview reported about a "most recent" partner; thus we also add a control for whether the referent is a current or most recent relationship.

In addition to *gender* (female = 1), controls are added for *race/ethnicity* (African American, Hispanic, and white were created), and *age*. We also include dummy variables reflecting variations in *mother's education* as a proxy for socioeconomic status (less than 12, greater than 12, where 12th grade completion is the reference category), a strategy that allows for the observation of nonlinear effects. This measure is derived from a questionnaire completed by parents, rather than from youth reports. *Family structure* is represented in the models as a set of dummy variables (single parent, stepparent, other, with married biological as the reference category). *Parental monitoring* is measured by a six-item scale completed by the parent, which includes items such as "When my child is away from home, she is supposed to let me know where s/he is," "I call to check if my child is where s/he said," "My child has to be home at a specific time on the weekends" (alpha = .73). A measure *of peer orientation* is included, which asks respondents, "During the past week, how many times did you just hang out with your friends?" *Self-esteem* is measured with a six-item version of Rosenberg's (1979) self-esteem scale (alpha = .71). Relationship controls include a measure of *duration* of the focal

relationship in months, whether *sexual intercourse* has occurred within the relationship (1 = yes), and whether the relationship is *current* (1 = yes) or most recent.

Analytic Strategy

We estimate zero-order models with gender and then add the remaining covariates to the model. This includes the social and demographic factors (e.g., race/ethnicity, age, mother's education), other network and individual characteristics (parental monitoring, peer orientation, self-esteem), and features of the relationship described (duration, whether the relationship includes sex, whether the referent is a current relationship). Given the nature of our dependent variables, we use ordinary least squares (OLS) to estimate our models. Although we do not develop specific hypotheses in this regard, due to the general importance of the adolescent's other social addresses, and the utility of the concept of intersectionalities as developed in prior theorizing about gender, we also test for differential effects of gender based on race/ethnicity, mother's education, and age by sequentially estimating each model introducing a series of interaction terms (gender by race, gender by mother's education, and gender by age). This allows us to document whether observed patterns of gender similarity and difference generalize across various race/ethnic, SES, and age categories. We also examine interactions between gender and other features of the focal relationship, including duration and whether intercourse has occurred, in order to determine whether the findings with regard to gender reflect a consistent pattern across relationships that vary in longevity and level of sexual intimacy. We use a Chow test to evaluate whether the influence of the total set of covariates on relationship qualities is sufficiently different for boys and girls to warrant analysis of separate models.

Qualitative Data

The in-depth relationship history narratives that we elicited from a subset of the respondents are useful as they serve to validate the quantitative findings, give depth to our conceptual arguments, and provide a starting point for reconciling our results with themes about gender and relationships that have predominated in prior research. Qualitative methods preserve respondents' own language and narrative emphasis, and thus provide an additional vantage point from which to explore the meaning and importance of these relationships from each respondent's point of view (Morse 1994).

The in-depth interviews were generally scheduled separately from the structured interview, and were conducted by a full-time interviewer with extensive experience eliciting in-depth, unstructured narratives. Areas covered in general parallel the structured protocol, but allow a more detailed consideration of respondents' complete romantic and sexual histories. The interview began by exploring the dating scene at the respondent's high school, and subsequently moved to a more personal discussion of the respondent's own dating career. The prompt stated, "Maybe it would be a good idea if you could just kind of walk me through some of your dating experiences—when did you first start liking someone?" Probes were designed to elicit detail about the overall character and any changes in a focal relationship, and about the nature of different relationships across the adolescent's romantic and sexual career. The resulting relationship narratives were tape-recorded and subsequently transcribed verbatim. We relied on Atlas.ti software to assist with the coding and analysis of the qualitative data. This program was useful in the organization of text segments into conceptual categories and refinement of the categories, while retaining the ability to move quickly to the location of the text within the more complete narrative. We also relied on shorter two-to-three-page summaries for some aspects of our analysis.

Because the current study is based on a combined analytic approach, we do not attempt an overview of the qualitative data, as the systematically collected structured data and related quantitative analyses adequately depict aggregate trends. Here we generally limit our discussion of the qualitative material to narrative segments that

(a) illustrate the direction of specific quantitative findings, but that further illuminate them, particularly with reference to the conceptual areas outlined above, and (b) serve to reconcile our results with the perspectives and emphases of prior research. Consistent with our focus in this article, we draw on boys' narratives, recognizing that a comprehensive account of adolescents' heterosexual experiences requires a corollary analysis of girls' perspectives. Other analyses using the TARS data focus specifically on issues of sexuality, both within romantic relationships (Giordano, Manning, and Longmore 2005a) and outside the traditional dating context (Manning, Longmore, and Giordano 2005).

Results

Table 1 presents descriptive statistics for all variables included in the analyses. In addition to the focal relationship variables to be discussed presently, results indicate that, consistent with prior research, female respondents score higher on parental monitoring, relative to their male counterparts. Young women also report relationships of significantly longer duration, and they are more likely to reference a current (rather than "most recent") partner. Male respondents score higher on the measure of time spent with peers, but self-esteem scores did not differ significantly by gender. Table 2 presents results of analyses of boys' and girls' reports of communication awkwardness, confidence navigating relationships, and feelings of love. Table 3 shows results of similar analyses focusing on partner influence attempts and "actual" influence, as well as the perceived power balance within the current/most recent relationship. Results of analyses focused on gender interactions are reported in the text.

Communication

Awkwardness

The first column in Table 2 indicates that, consistent with our hypothesis, boys report significantly higher levels of communication awkwardness in connection to their relationship with a current/most recent partner. Within the context of the

Table 2. Communication and Emotion within Adolescent Romantic Relationships

Gender	Communication Awkwardness		Confidence Navigating Relationships		"Love"	
	1	2	1	2	1	2
(Male)						
Female	−.462*	−.195	1.118***	1.208***	.435	−.020
Race						
(White)	—	—	—	—	—	—
African American	—	.300	—	.167	—	−.553*
Hispanic	—	−.098	—	−.053	—	.104
Age	—	−.094	—	.159**	—	.165*
Family structure (Married biological)	—	—	—	—	—	—
Single	—	.002	—	−.129	—	−.465
Step	—	−.061	—	.030	—	−.743*
Other	—	.410	—	−.253	—	−.788*
Parental monitoring	—	−.042	—	.033	—	.042
Peer orientation	—	−.160	—	−.022	—	.017
Mother's education						
<12 years	—	.060	—	.258	—	−.055
(12 years)	—	—	—	—	—	—
>12 years	—	−.230	—	.095	—	−.023
Self-esteem	—	−.116	—	.180***	—	.032
Duration of relationship	—	−.249***	—	.026	—	.486***
Sex with romantic partner						
(No)	—	—	—	—	—	—
Yes	—	−.635***		.442*		.185
Currently dating						
(No)	—	—	—	—	—	—
Yes	—	−1.583***	—	−.311	—	1.786***
F	4.68	11.74	40.89	8.95	3.58	16.42
R^2	.049	.158	.041	.125	.004	.208

Note: Reference category in parentheses. N = 957.
*$p < .05$; **$p < .01$; ***$p < .001$ (two-tailed tests).

more complete relationship-history narratives elicited from a subset of the respondents (recall that these youths are, on average, slightly older), these communication difficulties are especially likely to surface in boys' references to the early days of their dating careers or in discussions of how a given relationship had changed over time. Jake, for example, mentioned such communication difficulties in connection to his very first romantic relationship:

> Then I like talked to her on the phone, I don't know it was kind of awkward, like long silences when you're talking and stuff like that, and I don't know, then she like broke up with me a week later…[during their conversations] I couldn't like think of anything more to say you know…I really

Table 3. Influence and Power within Adolescent Romantic Relationships

Gender	Influence Attempts		'Actual' Influence		Perceived Power Balance	
	1	2	1	2	1	2
(Male)						
Female	−.583***	−.547***	−1.045***	−1.107***	1.173***	1.215***
Race						
(White)	—	—	—	—	—	—
African American	—	.043	—	−.273	—	.375*
Hispanic	—	−.083	—	−.620	—	.287
Age		−.047		−.039		−.021
Family structure (Married biological)						
Single	—	.067	—	−.206	—	.126
Step	—	−.149	—	−.293	—	.078
Other	—	.260	—	−.060	—	−.005
Parental monitoring	—	−.015	—	−.023	—	.019
Peer orientation	—	.038	—	−.010	—	.066
Mother's education						
<12 years	—	.283	—	.349	—	.433*
(12 years)	—	—	—	—	—	—
12 years	—	−.093	—	.023	—	.043
Self-esteem	—	−.086***	—	−.112***	—	.024
Duration of relationship	—	.077***	—	.137***	—	−.052
Sex with romantic partner						
(No)	—	—	—	—	—	—
Yes	—	.592***	—	−.092	—	.037
Currently daring						
(No)	—	—	—	—	—	—
Yes	—	−.460***	—	−.084	—	−.023
F	28.0	8.06	44.6	6.38	111.4	9.49
R^2	.029	.114	.045	.092	.105	.132

Note: Reference category in parentheses. N = 957.
*$p < .05$; ** $p < .01$; ***$p < .001$ (two-tailed tests).

didn't know [her]; I really wasn't friends before I asked her out, so it was kind of like talking to somebody I really didn't know.... [Jake, 17]

Table 2 presents multivariate results, in which other covariates have been taken into account. Gender differences remain significant in a model that controls for race/ethnicity, age, mother's education, family structure, parental monitoring, peer orientation, self-esteem, and whether the relationship had become sexually intimate (results not shown). The gender gap is explained by the other relationship controls (specifically duration and current dating status), as shown in model 2. This indicates that girls' tendency to be involved in relationships of longer duration and their greater likelihood of referencing a current partner influence the observed gender difference in level of communication awkwardness. The addition of the relationship controls also reduces the effect of age—in the reduced model without relationship controls, age is, as expected, inversely related to perceived awkwardness, but the relationship controls reduce this to non-significance. This suggests intuitive connections between age, relationship seriousness, and perceived awkwardness in communication. Having had sex with the romantic partner is also inversely related to perceived communication awkwardness, but this does not influence the findings with regard to gender and age (not shown). Turning to gender interactions, additional analyses indicate a significant gender by race interaction—white and Hispanic male respondents score significantly higher on communication awkwardness than their female counterparts, but African American male and female respondents do not show this pattern.[7] Interactions of age, mother's education and the various relationship controls (duration, having sex, current dating status) with gender are not significant, however, indicating that, for example, duration has a similar effect on boys' and girls' reports about communication awkwardness.

The findings reported provide general support for the hypothesis outlined, but the relationship between gender and communication awkwardness is relatively modest and not significant in the full model. Aside from the gender differences in duration that we noted, several other factors may have influenced these results, and suggest the need to qualify the hypothesis. First, perceived communication awkwardness is a general feature of early romantic relationships, and undoubtedly characterizes girls' as well as boys' feelings about the crossing-over process. In addition, results point to some variations in the gender pattern by race/ethnicity. Finally, youths completing this section of the interview focused on a specific, and most often, ongoing relationship. While adolescent romantic relationships do contain elements of uncertainty and awkwardness, the narratives also show that the perceived ability to "really communicate" with a particular other often develops as an important basis for both boys' and girls' feelings of positive regard. Although we explore

these ideas further in the sections on emotion and influence, quotes such as the following illustrate this countervailing tendency:

> A lot of the other girls I met in high school, I felt like I had to hold back from them, you know you just couldn't talk about everything with them. With Tiffany you could. Like she wants to know what is on your mind. And if there is something bothering me, you don't have to dress it up or you know, you can just be straight with her all the time. [Tim, 17]

Confidence Navigating Relationships

Table 2 also presents the results of analyses examining effects of gender on perceptions of confidence in navigating romantic relationships. This index provides a more general assessment of confidence in navigating various stages of romantic relationships, and is thus not only focused on the current/most recent partner. When we consider this more general scale, male adolescents, consistent with our hypothesis, report significantly lower levels of relationship confidence. Recall that the scale refers to confidence through such items as "to refuse a date," "tell your partner how to treat you," and "break up with someone you no longer like." Gender differences are significant for responses to each of these items examined separately, as well as for the total scale, and gender remains significant in the model that incorporates the control and other relationship variables, as well as self-esteem. As these confidence items were also completed by non-dating youths, we also assessed the perceptions of confidence of youth who had not yet entered the dating world. The gender difference is significant whether we focus on non-daters, daters as shown in Table 2, or consider the total sample of over 1,300 male and female respondents. These findings thus reflect a gendered portrait, but one that contrasts with Maccoby's (1990) hypothesis about boys' relatively more confident transition into the heterosexual arena.

With regard to other covariates, race/ethnicity and socioeconomic status are not significant predictors in this model, but age is positively related to perceived confidence. Self-esteem is also positively related to these assessments of relationship confidence, and focusing on the other relationship controls, having had sex with the romantic partner is related to greater overall feelings of confidence. None of the gender interactions assessed is significant. This indicates a consistent pattern of gender differences across the various race/ethnic groups, and the lack of a significant interaction of gender and mother's education suggests that this gendered confidence gap is found across various levels of socioeconomic status. Further, while age is positively related to perceived confidence, the age by gender interaction is not statistically significant—the observed gender disparity is evident in reports of older as well as younger respondents. Similarly, while teens who had sex with their boy/girlfriend report greater feelings of confidence navigating their relationships, a gender and sexual intercourse interaction term is not significant, reflecting a consistent pattern of gender differences in "confidence navigating relationships," whether or not the respondents reported that the relationship had become sexually intimate. Duration by gender and self-esteem by gender interactions are also not significant.

As suggested previously, the relationship-history narratives give respondents the opportunity to elaborate on ways in which they have experienced different stages of a number of different relationships (e.g., as they discuss the initial phase of starting a relationship or how they experience a particular breakup). These more wide-ranging discussions align well with the gender differences described earlier. Boys frequently reflect on their lack of confidence when talking about the beginning stages of a relationship, or a desired relationship that never materialized:

> I don't know why I'm so scared to let girls know I like them…like I said I was always nervous at asking them out but that one experience where I crashed and burned that just killed my confidence completely and I have been scared ever since to ask girls out and stuff…[Michael, 17]

This excerpt is useful as it clearly depicts feelings of concern and even inadequacy, feelings that Michael connects to one unfortunate early experience. Michael makes reference earlier within his narrative to what appears to be a generally positive self-image (*know that I'm like a good-looking guy and everything, but I just get so nervous*), even as he offers a candid description of these relationship insecurities. While Michael's discussion includes the notion that such feelings may abate with time and additional experience (e.g., *I don't know how I'm going to be later but hopefully I'll just loosen up*), this awareness does not serve to lessen current feelings of discomfort. Undoubtedly, some of these feelings connect to boys' more often being cast in the role of initiators, but the feelings that some boys describe nevertheless provide a sharp contrast to depictions of boys' confident, privileged positions within these dating situations. Young men who do not appear to possess characteristics viewed as desirable within the context of what Waller (1937) termed "the rating and dating complex" were even more likely to include references to a lack of confidence. James, a slightly built sixteen year old, originally from Latin America, stressed that "girls still think of me as a little shy guy and short…with an accent…young…well it's hard for me because I'm not too experienced." These quantitative and qualitative data thus add to Wight's (1994) observation that adolescent boys frequently experience feelings of anxiety about the adequacy of their sexual performances, as here we document considerable insecurity extending to the broader relationship realm.

The quantitative findings and open-ended narratives also suggest that these feelings of insecurity are not limited to the early stages of the relationship-navigation process. For example, within the context of the structured interview, boys express less confidence about "telling your partner how to treat you," an interview question that was specifically developed with girls in mind. Further, the narratives provide evidence that corresponds with the item that asks about confidence to "break up with someone you no longer like." For example, Bobby indicated that he had experienced considerable trepidation about how to go about breaking up with his girlfriend Sara:

> It really took me like a while I guess to [break up] because I didn't want to like hurt her so I kinda

like waited too long to do it, which was stupid by me. I just kept on like, I couldn't do it. I felt really bad…I just put myself in her shoes and I felt like awful like you know.…Just like she saw a girl with my sweatshirt on and she just felt like what the heck's going on and everything just probably went down for her.…I couldn't do it, I just kept waiting too long to do it.…I didn't want to like hurt her really bad which I knew it would that's why I just kept on waiting so. [Bobby, 16]

Bobby felt sufficiently uncomfortable about the prospect of breaking up that he continued to let things slide rather than speaking directly with Sara about his desire to end the relationship (for example, he repeats some version of "I just couldn't do it" eight times within the longer narrative). From an outsider's perspective, Bobby had rather callously started up a relationship with a new partner, without properly ending things with his current girlfriend. Bobby's own narrative, however, reveals feelings of insecurity and discomfort, concern for Sara's reaction, and intimate connections between these two sets of feelings. This suggests at least the rudiments of a role-taking experience, and the possibility that Bobby has learned important lessons that could be carried forward into the next relationship. When asked about what he had taken from this relationship, Bobby replied, "If I'm feeling a certain way I should just tell them and not just sit there and wait and wait and not tell her." This is consistent with our argument that for adolescent males schooled in the peer dynamics described at the outset, the romantic context itself represents an especially important arena of socialization. Bobby's own narrative does not suggest a complete aversion to such lessons, but at least a general receptivity to learning from them.

Emotion

An examination of reports of feelings of love across the total sample does not reveal a significant gender difference in these feelings of heightened emotionality in connection with the current or most recent relationship. Recall that the scale contains items such as "I would rather be with X than anyone else," "X always seems to be on my

mind," and 'the sight of X turns me on." The multivariate model shown in Table 2 mirrors the bivariate findings: boys and girls report similar levels of feelings of love in connection with the focal relationship. Race/ethnicity (African American or Hispanic, relative to white youth) is not related to reports of heightened emotionality at the bivariate level, but being African American emerges as a significant predictor in the multivariate analysis.[8] The multivariate results also reveal a developmental trend—age is positively related to reports of feelings of love for the partner. Youths living with both parents relative to those residing in single or stepparent families also scored higher on the love scale, but mother's education is not related to reports of love. Longer-duration relationships are also characterized by higher scores on this scale, and, perhaps not surprisingly, when the current partner is the referent, scores are also significantly higher. Sexual intercourse within the relationship is not, however, related to variations in adolescents' reports of feelings of love. Race/ethnicity and gender interactions are not significant, indicating that the pattern of responses by gender is similar across race/ethnic groups. Analyses indicate no significant gender interaction by mother's education. Duration has a similar effect for boys and girls, and the gender by intercourse interaction is not statistically significant. This indicates that having sex does not exert a differential impact on reports of feelings of love provided by male and female respondents.

It could be argued that the items within the love scale capture feelings of sexual attraction as much or more than a strong emotional connection to the partner, or positive feelings about the relationship. The narratives are thus an important adjunct to the quantitative findings, as they allow us further to explore questions of meaning from respondents' own subjectively experienced and uniquely articulated points of view. Many quotes from the narratives are congruent with the quantitative results, and inconsistent with Wight's (1994) conclusion that boys have little interest in the relationship aspects of these liaisons. One index that adolescent relationships can be said to "matter" to many adolescent boys is the sheer length of the relationship-history narratives that they often produced.[9] Here we refer to total length, as well as to lengthy sections discussing particular girlfriends. Will's 74-page narrative contains a very long section about his history with his current girlfriend Jenny, including a detailed story of how they met and a discussion of the various phases within their relationship's development. Will commented directly on the relationship's importance:

I: How important is your relationship to Jenny in your life?
R: About as important as you get. You know, well, you think of it as this way, you give up your whole life, you know, know, to save Jenny's life, right? That's how I feel. I'd give up my whole life, to save any of my friends' life too. But it's a different way. Like, if I could save Jon's life, and give up my own, I would, because that is something you should, have in a friend, but I wouldn't want to live without Jenny, does that make some sense? [Will, 17]

It is important to note that such expressions of positive regard and heightened emotionality are not contained only within the narratives of white middle-class youth, since prior research on African American youth in particular often includes the notion that romance is constructed largely as a kind of disingenuous game or con (e.g., Anderson 1989). Ron and Steve, two African American respondents who participated in the in-depth interview, express intense emotional feelings about their girlfriends:

Yeah, I ain't never, I ain't never like, felt that way about somebody....I tell her that [he loves her] everyday too! Everyday, I see her. [Ron, 17]

I: So, you remember all the dates and stuff?
R: Yeah, I'm like a little girl in a relationship.... [at first] just seemed like every time I was around her I couldn't talk, I was getting butterflies in my stomach, I just was like, discombobulated or something. [Steve, 17]

When asked to be more specific about features of the relationship that make it special or

important, many adolescent boys reference themes that have long been emphasized in the literature on intimacy and social support (e.g., Duck 1997; Prager 2000), including opportunities for self-disclosure (see e.g., Tim's quote on page 274), and the importance of having a partner who is always there for them:

Because she was always there for me. Like with everything. Like when my parents separated, she was there for me to comfort me then. And she helped me pull up my grades up to good grades and she was just always there for me. She always comforted me when I needed a hug. [Nick, 17]

We do not believe that such statements were produced primarily to please the interviewer, since the detailed answers frequently reference concrete instances where emotional support was provided. The narrative histories also frequently include descriptions of the endings of relationships. Breakups often involve disillusionment and other negative feelings, but such discussions also telegraph feelings of loss, providing a further indication of boys' own constructions of the meanings of these relationships:

I: I mean a year and three months is a long...
R: I'm not doing that good but my friends and my mother, they're helping me.
I: In what ways aren't you doing so well?
R: Ah emotionally. I, I can't sleep. I really can't eat that much.
I: I'm sorry.
R: That's okay.
I: How long and this just happened?
R: About a week.
I: Oh wow. So this is very fresh...
I: Do you believe them [friends and mom] that you'll get over it?
R: Yes. Some, someday I'll get over this but hopefully soon. [Eric, 17]
R: She just broke it down to me like, "Yeah, we're at different schools, we're young, we need to see other people."
I: So, why were you upset that you broke up?
R: I don't know. 'Cause I loved her so much. [Derrick, 17]

She kept insisting I wasn't going to work out and I kept insisting I wanted to try it and one night, and like I said I couldn't sleep, and I wrote her a letter, front and back, crying the whole time and then I handed the letter to her the next morning....It was really emotional, like how she hurt me and how it wasn't right. [Cody, 17]

These narratives often specifically mention the emotional realm (e.g., "It was really emotional"; "I'm not doing that good"; "my feelings was hurt"), or referenced behavioral indicators of psychological distress (e.g., "can't sleep," "really can't eat"). It is, however, also important to highlight that while Derrick's narrative communicated that the breakup did have a significant effect on him, he did not possess the social knowledge that other boys may also experience similar emotions (as he attempted to explain his bad mood to his mother, "I'm on my weekly [sic] cycle.").

Influence

Table 3 presents results of analyses examining reports of influence attempts, actual influence, and the perceived power balance within the current or most recent romantic relationship, as constructed by these adolescent respondents. Although most of the arguments developed in the existing literature focus specifically on issues of power, it is useful to consider the power results alongside the broader and perhaps ultimately more useful dynamic of interpersonal influence. Power assumes competing interests and only one victor, while influence focuses on whether the individual has taken the partner into account and actually made some adjustments. This need not involve a strong contrary view that needs to be overcome by the assertion of a power privilege. In line with this, recall that the questions about influence do not require the respondent to make a choice about who has the most influence in the relationship, but only to indicate whether and to what degree respondents believe that they have been influenced by their partner. The power items, in contrast, require a specific comparison of the respondent's own, relative to the partner's ability to get his or her way in a disagreement.

Attempted and actual influence

Results regarding influence attempts indicate a consistent pattern of gender differences: in both the zero-order and multivariate models, male respondents score higher on partner influence attempts. In the multivariate model, lower self-esteem youth report higher levels of partner influence attempts, and all of the relationship controls are significant: youths involved in more serious relationships (as measured by duration and sexual intimacy) report higher levels of partner influence attempts. Youths also describe former partners as making more attempts to influence, relative to reports about current partners. These relationship covariates have similar effects for boys and girls (results not shown).

More surprising than this pattern, however, is the finding that boys also report higher levels of "actual" influence from the romantic partner. The second set of models in Table 3 show a significant gender gap in reports of "actual" partner influence. In addition to a significant effect of gender, Hispanic youth scored lower on partner influence relative to their white counterparts. Lower self-esteem is associated with greater partner influence, and youths involved in longer-duration relationships also scored higher on "actual" influence. Sexual intercourse was not related to perceptions of partner influence. The interactions of gender with other sociodemographic variables as well as other relationship measures were not significant in this model. Thus, these results indicate that the gender gap is consistent across youths who vary in developmental stage, race/ethnicity, mother's education, and seriousness of the relationship.

The scales measuring partner influence (attempts and actual) are rather general (e.g., "X influences what I do"), and thus do not provide a full picture of (a) specific mechanisms of influence, (b) the areas or domains in which boys believe they have been influenced, or (c) the nature of their reactions to various influence attempts. Although a comprehensive examination of these issues is beyond the scope of this analysis, the narrative data do provide a more in-depth portrait of these processes.[10] The specific domains referenced within the narrative accounts are of particular interest, because they indicate influence on many potentially important relationship dynamics and behavioral outcomes—ranging from boys' behavior within the romantic context to academic performance and delinquency involvement. Given boys' initial lack of familiarity and confidence with intimate ways of relating, it is perhaps not surprising to find that some boys indicate that girlfriends had influenced their ability to relate in a more intimate fashion:

Yeah, well it was a while…like about three months. Her mom was having problems…and so like she just kept talking to me a lot you know what I'm saying, and I listened and I tried to help and I had problems and you know we just, that was somebody we could open up to each other, so it was like I could talk to her and she could talk to me. [Todd, 17]

Todd described a gradual process that began with Caroline's willingness to open up to him about some of her own family problems. Eventually Todd found that he could not only be helpful to her, but that he also increasingly began to talk with Caroline about some of his own problems. Although he does not state this directly, Caroline may have influenced not only his willingness to engage in intimate self-disclosure, but the way in which he chose to handle problems that the two had discussed in this more intimate fashion.

In addition to modifications in their relationship-based selves, a number of the narratives reference specific changes that the youths indicate they had made in other important areas of their lives, shifts in perspective and behavior that respondents specifically connect to the influence of their romantic partners. Consider the following narrative excerpts:

[Julie] makes me want to do better in school and stuff. I want to do well because of her because she is really smart and she's got a real good grade point average. Mine isn't as high as hers so I try to be up there and I don't want to look stupid. I don't think she would want me to be dumb. [Rob, 18]

For like um the past two years, you know that I've been with her it has been, you know, about school. We both are carrying 3.8 averages and stuff. You know we're both kind of you know, kind of pushing each other along like, "you should really go do this." So academically, we help each other like a lot. [Dan, 17]

I don't know it's weird but certain things make me want to go out and do better. I don't know why…You know Melanie, Melanie makes me want to do a hell of a lot better you know…[11] [Chad, 18]

As the first quote makes clear, Julie is not simply one more friend who has been added to Rob's total mix of definitions favorable to academic achievement, and this hints at potentially distinctive influence mechanisms across types of reference others (notably peers versus romantic partners). Reciprocal role-taking experiences that elicit positive emotions provide an enriched social terrain for further development, as cognitive, emotional, and behavioral changes reciprocally influence self-views, including views of self in relation to these valued others. Here the positive emotions elicited within the romantic context can be seen as providing energy and valence to compatible or even new lines of action (e.g., Collins 2004). The last quote from Chad nicely evokes this notion of an energizing component.

Theorists have often noted that similar others (e.g., close same-gender friends) are very important as a source of reference. This is a sound assertion, based on basic principles of identification. Nevertheless, relationships based in elements of difference are also potentially important, as contrasts offer more in the way of a developmental challenge (see, e.g., Cooley [1902] 1970:380), and at times a blueprint for how to make specific changes and adjustments (Giordano 1995; Giordano et al. 2002). For example, Todd learns about self-disclosure through his partner's own tendency to self-disclose, as well as her encouragement of his own efforts to do so. Yet describing romantic relationships only in terms of contrasts provides an incomplete portrait of these relationships. If difference were the only dynamic involved, individuals might not be inclined to enter into the type of sustained interaction that results in a social influence process. In short, some level of identification or social coordination necessarily precedes role-taking and in effect makes it possible (see, e.g., Engdahl 2004; Miller 1973).[12] This neo-Meadian view, along with other sociology of emotions theorizing, tends to position emotions at the center of change processes, as individuals draw inspiration from their points of connection and a new direction via the element of contrast.[13]

Perceived Power Balance

The findings and discussion focus on influence processes that may be subtle and incremental. In the examples relating to school performance, Rob wants Julie to think well of him, and Dan and his romantic partner are even more in tune, both having a strong commitment to keeping up their high grade point averages. Yet not all influence attempts lead individuals in a direction they wish to go. As stated at the outset, many of the significant differences that male and female adolescents bring to romantic relationships are not entirely overcome by a developing mutuality of perspectives that we described in the previous section. When interests clearly diverge, considerations of power become especially important.

Table 3 presents results of analyses focused on the perceived power balance in the current or most recent relationship (who has the most say in a disagreement—overall and in relation to specific domains). In the zero-order model, the gender coefficient is statistically significant; boys' scores are lower, indicating on average a relatively less favorable (to self) view of the power balance within their relationship. It is important to point out that the modal response to each question is egalitarian (having equal say); thus these findings reflect a significant gender difference where respondents have diverged from this more common response across the four items that make up this scale. We note also, however, that gender differences are significant for each of the items making up the scale (regarding overall say in relation to decisions about what the couple does and how much time they spend together, as well as about how far to go sexually) and for the total scale score.

Turning to the multivariate results, additional statistical analyses reveal that the best fitting model is a separate model for boys and girls (results not shown).[14] Most of the covariates are similar in their effects on reports of power (youths whose mothers have less than a high school degree saw themselves as having a relatively more favorable power position, and African American youth are also likely to describe a relatively more favorable level of power in their relationships). Some gendered effects of covariates, however, are masked when a combined model is estimated. We find that relationship duration does not influence girls' reports, but longer duration of the relationship is related to *less* perceived power in the case of male respondents. In contrast, while sexual intercourse experience was again not related to girls' reports about power, boys who reported that the relationship had become sexually intimate reported a *more* favorable (to self) power balance, compared with the reports of male adolescents whose relationships had not become sexually intimate. It is important to highlight that within models focused only on the subsample of sexually active male and female youths, the overall gender difference remains significant, with boys reporting a less favorable power balance relative to similarly situated girls. Nevertheless, these intriguing interaction results warrant additional scrutiny and exploration, as we did not have a theoretical basis for expecting these patterns. In addition, it is of interest that the two findings operate in an apparently distinct fashion—the association between duration and lower perceived power on the part of boys is somewhat unexpected from a traditional inequality point of view, while the findings regarding intercourse are more consistent with the idea that sexual involvement is a more pivotal event or marker for male adolescents (Holland et al. 1996).

The quantitative findings provide indications that, in contrast to the direction of much theorizing within the adolescence literature, when male and female respondents departed from an egalitarian description of the power dynamics within their relationships, males were more likely to describe a tilt favoring the partner's greater decision-making power. A number of narratives also highlight distinct interests on the part of partners, and a perceived power balance that corresponds with the statistical results:

> I guess she was more mature than I was and I guess I wasn't on her level you know because she wanted to do it [have sex] more than I did...she said that I wasn't mature enough and you know all that stuff...I was too young, I was scared, I didn't know what I was doing I wasn't ready for it. I think I felt like I was too young...she was my girlfriend and that's what she wanted. [David, 18]

> She's like okay we're going out now, and I tried making plans with my friends, but Amy's like "No we're going out here and we're doing this." I just wasn't going to live with that anymore...there was something about her she always wanted to change me. She wanted me to do this and wear this and do that. I was like okay. Whatever. I'd do it but I don't see it [as] right. [Josh, 17]

David's longer narrative confirms that this adolescent did have sex with his girlfriend, even though he felt that he was not "ready for it." Josh also admitted that he often went along with his former girlfriend's preferences, even though his narrative clearly telegraphed that he experienced this power balance in a negative way ("I don't see it as right," "I just wasn't going to live with that anymore"). The latter quote, then, provides support for the direction of the quantitative results, while reflecting the continuing impact of traditional gender scripts.

Variations

Further support for characterizations emphasized in the peer-based literature can be found when we confront the variability in boys' orientations and relationship styles evident within the narrative histories. This heterogeneity is necessarily somewhat obscured by our focus here on aggregate trends. A symbolic interactionist framework can accommodate explorations of subtypes and variations, as theorists have emphasized that while interactions influence identities, as identities begin to solidify, they become a kind of cognitive filter for decision-making (Matsueda and Heimer 1997). Over time, these differentiated

identities increasingly structure social interaction in line with these self-conceptions. For example, Donny, a 17 year old, had apparently developed a strong identity as a player within his high school. Donny's first sexual experience occurred at an early age, and this respondent estimated about 35 sexual partners. Donny was also unable to recall the names of all of the young women with whom he had become sexually intimate ("I don't know I would have to go through some letters"). While he considered some of these young women girlfriends, he nevertheless often cheated on them, and indicated that he had control within his relationships. Consistent with this portrait, Donny admitted physically abusing at least one young woman he had dated and reacted aversively to the idea of expressing his feelings ("I really don't like talking about my feelings...I don't know I just don't like talking about it").

Donny's narrative thus departs significantly from the aggregate portrait that emerges from the quantitative analysis; yet these types of cases and corresponding identities are important, as they are vivid representations of traditional masculinity that virtually demand attention. Thorne (1993) noted the heavy societal and even research focus on what she termed the "Big Man" social type. It has been important to highlight that the aggregate findings and many narratives do not accord with Donny's perspective; indeed a number of boys specifically position away from this social type in discussions of their own self-views. Yet the number of references to players and other traditional gender attitudes itself affirms the continuing impact of such gender scripts:

> I rather focus on one girl than a whole bunch because I don't think that I'm like some player or something and I really don't like those people that go out and have a bunch of girlfriends and stuff and they think that they're some big pimp or whatever. [Michael, 16]

Additional research on masculine styles such as the player are needed, because (a) a host of negative social dynamics are directly and indirectly associated with this orientation, and (b) adolescents apparently believe that this is a more prevalent and highly valued social role than appears to be the case. Such shared misunderstandings are consequential, and are undoubtedly heavily influenced by the character of peer interactions that have been so effectively captured in prior research. For example, Eric explained why he does not engage in intimate self-disclosure with his male friends: "most of them don't, they don't probably think the way I think or have the feelings that I, feelings that I have for girls." We also saw evidence of this in earlier quotes (e.g., Steve's admission that he is "like the little girl in the relationship," or Derrick's reference to negative emotions after his girlfriend broke up with him, "I'm on my weekly cycle."). Undoubtedly differences between discussions within peer settings and the more private experience of these relationships serves to perpetuate boys' beliefs about the uniqueness of their feelings and emotional reactions.

Conclusions

In this article, we developed a symbolic interactionist perspective on adolescent romantic relationships that draws on Mead's basic insights, as well as recent treatments of the role of emotions in social interaction and self-development processes. Relying on structured interview data collected from a large stratified random sample of adolescents, we found support for hypotheses that differ significantly from traditional accounts of the role of gender as an influence on the relationship dynamics within these romantic liaisons. Results suggest a portrait of adolescent boys as relatively less confident and yet more emotionally engaged in romantic relationships than previous characterizations would lead us to expect. The findings regarding power and influence are also unexpected from a straightforward gender inequality point of view. Although we did not specifically predict systematic gender differences in reports of power and partner influence, these results do follow logically from our conceptual discussion and fit well with the findings concerning communication and emotion.

As boys make the transition from peers to romance, they lack experience with intimate ways of relating (as evidenced by lower perceived

confidence in navigating relationships and at the bivariate level, among white and Hispanic respondents, by greater perceived communication awkwardness), even as they are beginning to develop a high interest and at times strong emotional attachment to certain romantic partners (as evidenced by the absence of strong gender differences on reports of feelings of love for the current/ most recent partner). In line with our symbolic interactionist framework, we argued that these relationships set up conditions favorable to new definitions, to the emergence of new emotions, and, at least within these relationship contexts, to glimpses of a different and more connected view of self. The argument that boys move in a straight line toward autonomy, or the declaration that "heterosexuality is masculinity" (Holland et al. 1996) are global assertions that do not take into account the adjustments that boys as well as girls continually make as they begin to forge this new type of intimate social relationship.

Although additional research is needed on these and other relationship processes, we do not believe that the results derive from unique peculiarities of our measurement approach. First, the findings across various indices are themselves quite consistent. For example, differences on the power and influence scales are all significant and vary in the same direction. In addition, findings fit well with observations based on a range of methods employed during preliminary phases of the TARS study (see, e.g., Giordano et al. 2001), and are further validated by the content of in-depth relationship-history narratives that we also collected and drew upon in the present analysis. We also estimated a series of interactions that in most instances support the idea that documented similarities (feelings of love) and differences (boys' lower confidence levels, perceptions of greater partner power and influence) generalize across respondents who vary significantly in race/ethnic backgrounds, socioeconomic status levels, and age. We also estimated models that contained gender by sexual intercourse and duration interactions, and the lack of significance of these interactions in most models suggests that the observed gender patterns are not strongly influenced by length of the relationship or whether it had become sexually intimate. Exceptions were associations between sexual intercourse experience and duration of the relationship and boys' reports of power, findings that warrant additional research scrutiny. Finally, controls for variations in family and peer dynamics, other basic features of the relationship, and self-esteem, although sometimes significant, did not strongly influence or attenuate these results.

The symbolic interactionist theoretical perspective described at the outset provides a generally useful framework for interpreting our results. As we have suggested throughout this analysis, it is important to avoid an adult vantage point when focusing on early heterosexual relationships. It is quite possible that as boys gain in social maturity and confidence, and links to traditional sources of inequality become more salient, dynamic features within these romantic relationships will more often and more directly correspond to traditional gender scripts. In line with this idea, prior research has shown that certain transition events such as the move from cohabitation to marriage more often depend on male rather than female preferences (see, e.g.; Brown 2000). Another possibility is that the nature of reports of relationship qualities and dynamics we documented in this study reflect cohort changes associated with broader societal level transformations. This interpretation would be consistent with Risman and Schwartz's (2002) recent discussion of apparent temporal shifts in adolescent sexual behavior patterns.

More research is also needed on the heterogeneity within this and other sample groups, as briefly described earlier. Our observations of variation are similar to those described by Moffatt (1989), who found that some university men emphasized love and romance in their personal narratives, while those whom he labeled the "Neanderthals" and "Neoconservatives" held more traditionally gendered views that appeared to influence their relationship styles and sexual behaviors significantly. Since few studies had directly assessed relationship processes during adolescence (and the results provide a strong contrast with key assertions about them contained within the existing literature), our findings should provide a useful

background for exploring such variations in more detail in subsequent analyses.

It would also be useful to examine factors linked to within-individual shifts and variations in the ascendance or movement away from more traditionally gendered patterns and relationship styles (Thorne 1993). This suggests a more situated (again resonant with the symbolic interactionist framework) rather than a fixed or overarching gender inequalities approach to relationship processes. Aside from connections to major life-course transitions, for example, researchers could explore how certain relationship experiences connect to such shifts in perspective. Even within a focal relationship or time period, situations that link to boys' enactment of traditional/nontraditional repertoires need to be further highlighted. As an example, some of the same boys who expressed caring sentiments about their girlfriends undoubtedly make denigrating comments about girls when in the company of their circle of friends. Some boys also described tensions between their wish to spend time with friends and also to be responsive to their girlfriends. The fear of being seen as controlled by their girlfriends and subsequently ridiculed by friends reflects well that boys care very much what their friends think of them (a primary emphasis of prior research), but also what their girlfriends think of them (a conclusion of the present study). In line with this notion, we found that male respondents scored higher on a scale measuring perceived influence from friends as well as on the index of influence from romantic partners (results available on request). The idea of crosscurrents of social influence should in the long run prove more useful than the theme of autonomy so often highlighted as the central dynamic associated with boys' development.

The current analysis focused primarily on boys' perspectives on romance, as this was a particularly noticeable gap in the existing adolescence literature. Nevertheless, a comprehensive understanding of these social relationships obviously awaits more systematic investigations of girls' experiences. Where research has delved into the role of romantic involvement on girls' development, the focus of sociological investigations has, as suggested in the literature review, remained almost exclusively on sexuality or alternatively, negative outcomes—for example, establishing links to depression (Joyner and Udry 2000) and to relationship violence (Hagan and Foster 2001; Halpern et al. 2001), or pointing out how dating derails young women's academic pursuits (Holland and Eisenhart 1990). The conceptual framework and data presented here provide a starting point for a more multifaceted approach to girls' relationship experiences. Future research linking dating and particular outcomes needs not only to assess whether adolescents have entered the dating world, but also to capture variations in partners' attitude and behavioral profiles, as well as the qualitative features of these romantic relationships. It is important to note that girls' narratives provide support for the direction of the results reported here, while also highlighting significant variations. Some young women described what they viewed as egalitarian relationships or a favorable power balance (e.g., "he wears what I want him to wear"), but others stressed that boyfriends had engaged in a range of controlling, intrusive behaviors. The aggregate findings are an important backdrop for further exploring the impact of these variations, as the subset of girls who describe themselves as having low power may experience this power balance in an especially detrimental way (for reasons highlighted in prior work, and because such girls may compare their own situations to those of other teens whose relationships are characterized by less traditionally gendered dynamics). A full exploration from girls' points of view also requires moving beyond the immediate confines of the dating context to consider some of the indirect ways in which involvement in the heterosexual world influences girls' well-being, including concerns about weight and appearance (Pipher 1994), and connections to relationships with parents (e.g., Joyner and Udry [2000] found that some of the gender difference in the dating-depression link was associated with increases in girls' conflicts with their parents).

Finally, the symbolic interactionist perspective highlights the importance of adolescents' own constructions of the nature and meanings of their relationships. This framework recognizes that many important relationship features are inherently subjective (e.g., adolescents are better positioned than others to comment upon their own confidence levels or feelings of love). It is, however, important to supplement the perceptual accounts described here with findings based on other methodological strategies. For example, teens may report a relatively egalitarian power balance, or even greater power on the part of the female partner, but laboratory-based studies or other methods may well uncover more traditionally gendered communication and relationship dynamics that are not well appreciated by adolescents themselves. Yet we hope that researchers will continue to explore the subjectively experienced aspects of adolescent romantic relationships, as these provide an important supplement to peer-focused ethnographies and the behavioral emphasis of large-scale surveys such as the National Longitudinal Study of Adolescent Health (Add Health).

Notes

1. This analysis is also limited to a consideration of heterosexual relationships, as we are particularly interested in the process of "crossing over" from a social life based primarily on same-gender friendships to involvement with heterosexual partners. In addition, the number of respondents who self-identify as homosexual or bisexual at wave one is too small to support a separate analysis. Nevertheless, our conceptual framework and associated measurement emphasis could potentially be useful in connection with future investigations that explore the broader relationship contexts within which gay, lesbian, and bisexual youths' romantic and sexual experiences unfold.

2. The focus on emotions as an important dynamic within social interactions represents a shift from Mead's original cognitive emphasis, but it can be considered neo-Meadian since his more general ideas (e.g., the concept of role-taking and focus on self-processes) are applicable to understanding the emotional as well as cognitive realms of experience (see Engdahl 2004; MacKinnon 1994).

3. All of the schools eventually complied with our requests for these data, as this information is

legally available under Ohio's Freedom of Information Act.

4. Furman and Hand (2004) found similarities in dating involvement in TARS and in their own study. Both studies document higher rates of dating involvement by age than are evident within the National Longitudinal Study of Adolescent Health (Add Health). We note that our reports of (for example) sexual intercourse by age parallel those in Add Health, but a higher percentage of respondents at each age report current romantic involvement: 32 percent of 7th, 41 percent of 9th graders, and 59 percent of 11th grade TARS respondents, compared with 17 percent, 32 percent, and 44 percent of Add Health respondents.

5. This respondent was excluded from the quantitative analysis, but included in our study of the relationship history narratives.

6. This introduction and definition were selected after extensive pre-testing and reflects contemporary trends in dating that are less focused than in earlier eras on formal activities. In addition, the latter type of definition is strongly class-linked, and would tend to exclude lower socioeconomic-status (SES) youth. Our definition also differs from that used in Add Health, where respondents are asked whether they currently have a "special romantic relationship." We wished to avoid selecting on a relationship that the respondent specifically defines as special, since understanding the patterning of relationship qualities is a primary objective of the study.

7. Further examination of the means for all groups indicates that African American male respondents perceive significantly less communication awkwardness than African American girls. In general, this fits with Staple's (1981) hypothesis about the greater social and communication ease of African American youths, but we document a significant gender difference in this regard. These distinct patterns highlight the importance of examining the nature of relationship dynamics among diverse groups of teens, since the bulk of prior research on adolescent relationships focuses on samples of white adolescents or largely white samples of college students (see also Carver et al. 2003).

8. We note that no racial/ethnic differences are observed in multivariate models that include demographic, family, and peer controls. African American youth report relationships of longer duration, and relationships are more likely to include sexual intercourse; when these variables are introduced, the African American coefficient becomes significant. These findings suggest that African American youth may accord differential meanings and emotional significance to different types of relationships. The role of race/ethnicity warrants more systematic investigation than we give it in the current analysis (see Giordano, Manning, and Longmore 2005b for an analysis of race/ethnicity effects on romantic relationships using Add Health data).

9. Martin (1996) makes a similar point in her discussion of the length of girls' romance narratives, but she concludes from her own study that boys "rarely express the feelings of romantic love that girls do" (Martin 1996:68). Our results are not in accord with this conclusion.

10. For a more detailed discussion of specific mechanisms of influence and reactions to influence attempts, see Trella (2005).

11. These narratives provide a strong contrast with Frost's (2001) description of boys' singular concern with what peers think of them, citing Kimmel (1994:128–29): "this kind of policing of identity construction, reflects a profound need to be accepted and approved by men: "There is no strong concern for women's approval as they are in too low a place on the social ladder."

12. Our own interpretation of this dynamic differs slightly from Engdahl (2004) and Miller's (1973) emphases, as we posit a level of recognition of these points of connection on the part of the actors involved.

13. Research is needed on specific domains (e.g., achievement, delinquency, sexuality), where complex portraits of partner influence and gender effects will undoubtedly emerge. TARS data document effects of romantic partners' grades on respondents' grades, net of peer and parent influences, but we find a stronger effect for boys (Phelps et al. 2006). Using Add Health data, we found an effect of partners' minor deviance on respondents' deviance for male and female respondents, but a stronger effect for girls. Effects of the romantic partner's involvement in serious delinquency were comparable for boys and girls (Haynie et al. 2005).

14. Based on statistical tests, we do not find support for separate gender models for any of the other relationship qualities (communication awkwardness, confidence navigating relationships, love, and influence attempts or 'actual' influence).

References

Anderson, Elijah. 1989. "Sex Codes and Family Life among Poor Inner-City Youths." *Annals of the American Academy of Political Social Science* 501:59–79.

Blau, Peter M. 1964. *Exchange and Power in Social Life*. New York: Wiley.

Blood, Robert O. and Donald M. Wolfe. 1960. *Husbands and Wives: The Dynamics of Married Living*. Glencoe, IL: Free Press.

Blumer, Herbert. 1969. *Symbolic Interactionism: Perspective and Method*. Berkeley, CA: University of California Press.

Brown, B. Bradford, Candice Feiring, and Wyndol Furman. 1999. "Missing the Love Boat: Why Researchers Have Shied away from Adolescent Romance." Pp. 1–18 in *The Development of Romantic Relationships in Adolescence*, edited by W. Furman, B. B. Brown, and C. Feiring. New York: Cambridge University Press.

Brown, Susan L. 2000. "Union Transitions among Cohabitors: The Significance of Relationship Assessments and Expectations." *Journal of Marriage and the Family* 62:833–46.

Call, Kathleen T. and Jeylan T. Mortimer. 2001. *Arenas of Comfort in Adolescence: A Study of Adjustment in Context*. Mahwah, NJ: Lawrence Erlbaum Associates.

Carver, Karen P., Kara Joyner, and J. Richard Udry. 2003. "National Estimates of Adolescent Romantic Relationships." Pp. 23–56 in *Adolescent Romantic Relations and Sexual Behavior*, edited by Paul Florsheim. Mahwah, NJ: Lawrence Erlbaum Associates.

Carver, Karen P. and J. Richard Udry. 1997. *Reciprocity in the Identification of Adolescent Romantic Partners*. Presented at the annual meeting of the Population Association of America, March 28, Washington, DC.

Cohen, Albert K. 1955. *Delinquent Boys: The Culture of the Gang*. New York: Free Press.

Collins, Randall. 2004. *Interaction Ritual Chains*. Princeton, NJ: Princeton University Press.

Cooley, Charles H. [1902] 1970. *Human Nature and the Social Order*. New York: Scribner.

Corsaro, William A. 1985. *Friendship and Peer Culture in the Early Years*. Norwood, NJ: Ablex.

Corsaro, William A. and Donna Eder. 1990. "Children's Peer Cultures." *Annual Review of Sociology* 16:197–220.

Crosnoe, Robert. 2000. "Friendships in Childhood and Adolescence: The Life Course and New Directions." *Social Psychology Quarterly* 63: 377–91.

Denizet-Lewis, Benoit. 2004. "Whatever Happened to Teen Romance? (And What Is a Friend with Benefits Anyway?): Friends, Friends with Benefits and the Benefits of the Local Mall" *New York Times*. May 30, p. 30.

Duck, Steve, ed. 1997. *Handbook of Personal Relationships: Theory, Research, and Interventions*. New York: Wiley.

Eder, Donna, Catherine Evans, and Stephen Parker. 1995. *School Talk: Gender and Adolescent Culture*. New Brunswick, NJ: Rutgers University Press.

Emirbayer, Mustafa and Jeff Goodwin. 1994. "Network Analysis, Culture, and the Problem of Agency." *American Journal of Sociology* 99:1411–54.

Engdahl, Emma. 2004. "A Theory of the Emotional Self: From the Standpoint of a Neo-Meadian." Ph.D. dissertation, Department of Sociology, Örebro University, Örebro, Sweden.

Fine, Gary A. 1987. *With the Boys: Little League Baseball and Preadolescent Culture*. Chicago, IL: University of Chicago Press.

Fischer, Agneta H. 2000. *Gender and Emotion: Social Psychological Perspectives*. Cambridge, England: Cambridge University Press.

Forster, Edward M. [1927] 1974. *Aspects of the Novel, and Related Writings*. New York: Holmes and Meier.

Frijda, Nico H. 2002. "Emotions as Motivational States." Pp. 11–32 in *European Review of Philosophy: Emotion and Action*, vol. 5, edited by E. Pacherie. Stanford, CA: CSLI Publications.

Frost, Liz. 2001. *Young Women and the Body: A Feminist Sociology*. New York: Palgrave Macmillan.

Furman, Wyndol and Laura S. Hand. 2004. "The Slippery Nature of Romantic Relationships: Issues in Definition and Differentiation." Presented at the Pennsylvania State Family Symposium, October, Philadelphia, PA.

Gecas, Viktor and Monica A. Longmore. 2003. "Self-Esteem." Pp. 1419–24 in *International Encyclopedia of Marriage and Family Relationships*, 2d ed., edited by James J. Ponzetti, Jr. New York: Macmillan Reference.

Giddens, Anthony. 1992. *The Transformation of Intimacy: Sexuality, Love, and Eroticism in Modern Societies*. Stanford, CA: Stanford University Press.

Gilligan, Carol. 1982. *In a Different Voice: Psychological Theory and Women's Development*. Cambridge, MA: Harvard University Press.

Giordano, Peggy C. 1995. "The Wider Circle of Friends in Adolescence." *American Journal of Sociology* 101:661–97.

Giordano, Peggy C., Stephen A. Cernkovich, and Jennifer L. Rudolph. 2002. "Gender, Crime, and Desistance: Toward a Theory of Cognitive Transformation." *American Journal of Sociology* 107:990–1064.

Giordano, Peggy C., Monica A. Longmore, and Wendy D. Manning. 2001. "A Conceptual Portrait of Adolescent Romantic Relationships." Pp. 111–39 in *Sociological Studies of Children and Youth*, edited by D. A. Kinney. London, England: Elsevier Science.

Giordano, Peggy C., Wendy D. Manning, and Monica A. Longmore. 2005a. "The Qualities of Adolescent Relationships and Sexual Behavior." Presented at the annual meeting of the Population Association of America, April 1, Philadelphia, PA.

———. 2005b. "The Romantic Relationships of African American and White Adolescents." *The Sociological Quarterly* 46:545–68.

Hagan, John and Holly Foster. 2001. "Youth Violence and the End of Adolescence." *American Sociological Review* 66:874–99.

Halpern, Carolyn T., Selene G. Oslak, Mary L. Young, Sandra L. Martin, and Lawrence L. Kupper. 2001. "Partner Violence among Adolescents in Opposite-Sex Romantic Relationships: Findings from the National Longitudinal Study of Adolescent Health." *American Journal of Public Health* 91:1679–85.

Hatfield, Elaine and Susan Sprecher. 1986. "Measuring Passionate Love in Intimate Relations." *Journal of Adolescence* 9:383–410.

Haynie, Dana L., Peggy C. Giordano, Wendy D. Manning, and Monica A. Longmore. 2005. "Adolescent Romantic Relationships and Delinquency Involvement." *Criminology* 43:177–210.

Hochschild, Arlie R. 1983. *The Managed Heart: Commercialization of Human Feeling*. Berkeley, CA: University of California Press.

Holland, Dorothy C. and Margaret A. Eisenhart. 1990. *Educated in Romance: Women, Achievement, and College Culture*. Chicago, IL: University of Chicago Press.

Holland, Janet, Caroline Ramazanoglu, and Rachel Thomson. 1996. "In the Same Boat? The Gendered (In)experience of First Heterosex." Pp. 143–60 in *Theorizing Heterosexuality: Telling it Straight*, edited by D. Richardson. Philadelphia, PA: Open University Press.

Joas, Hans. 1997. *G. H. Mead: A Contemporary Reexamination of His Thought*. Cambridge, MA: MIT Press.

Joyner, Kara and J. Richard Udry. 2000. "You Don't Bring Me Anything but Down: Adolescent Romance and Depression." *Journal of Health and Social Behavior* 41: 369–91.

Katz, Jack. 1999. *How Emotions Work*. Chicago, IL: University of Chicago Press.

Kimmel, Michael S. 1994. "Masculinity as Homophobia: Fear, Shame, and Silence in the Construction of Gender Identity." Pp. 119–41 in *Theorizing Masculinities*, edited by H. Brod and M. Kaufman. London, England: Sage.

Komter, Aafke. 1989. "Hidden Power in a Marriage." *Gender and Society* 3:187–216.

Longmore, Monica A., Wendy D. Manning, and Peggy C. Giordano. 2001. "Preadolescent Parenting Strategies and Teens' Dating and Sexual Initiation." *Journal of Marriage and the Family* 63:322–35.

Maccoby, Eleanor. 1990. "Gender and Relationships: A Developmental Account." *American Psychologist* 45:513–20.

MacKinnon, Neil J. 1994. *Symbolic Interactionism as Affect Control*. Albany, NY: State University of New York Press.

MacLeod, Jay. 1987. *Ain't No Makin' It: Leveled Aspirations in a Low-Income Neighborhood*. Boulder, CO: Westview Press.

Manning, Wendy D., Monica A. Longmore, and Peggy C. Giordano. 2005. "Adolescents' Involvement in Non-Romantic Sexual Activity." *Social Science Research* 34:384–407.

Martin, Karin A. 1996. *Puberty, Sexuality, and the Self: Boys and Girls at Adolescence.* New York: Routledge.

Massey, David S. 2002. "A Brief History of Human Society: The Origin and Role of Emotion in Social Life." *American Sociological Review* 67:1–29.

Matsueda, Ross L. and Karen Heimer. 1997. "A Symbolic Interactionist Theory of Role-Transitions, Role-Commitments, and Delinquency." Pp. 163–213 in *Developmental Theories of Crime and Delinquency*, edited by T. P. Thornberry. New Brunswick, NJ: Transaction.

Mead, George H. [1909] 1964. "Social Psychology as Counterpart to Physiological Psychology." Pp. 94–104 in *Selected Writings: George Herbert Mead*, edited by A. J. Reck. Chicago, IL: University of Chicago Press.

———. 1913. "The Social Self." *Journal of Philosophy, Psychology, and Scientific Methods* 10:374–80.

———. 1934. *Mind, Self, and Society from the Standpoint of a Social Behaviorist.* Chicago, IL: University of Chicago Press.

Miller, David L. 1973. *George Herbert Mead: Self, Language, and the World.* Austin, TX: University of Texas Press.

Moffatt, Michael. 1989. *Coming of Age in New Jersey: College and American Culture.* New Brunswick, NJ: Rutgers University Press.

Morse, Janice M. 1994. "Designing Funded Qualitative Research." Pp. 220–35 in *Handbook of Qualitative Research*, edited by N. Denzin and Y. Lincoln. Thousand Oaks, CA: Sage.

Phelps, Kenyatta D., Peggy C. Giordano, Wendy D. Manning, and Monica A. Longmore. 2006. "The Influence of Dating Partners on Adolescents' Academic Achievement." To be presented at the annual meeting of the North Central Sociological Association, March 23–25, Indianapolis, IN.

Pipher, Mary. 1994. *Reviving Ophelia: Saving the Lives of Adolescent Girls.* New York: Ballantine.

Powers, William G. and Kevin Hutchinson. 1979. "The Measurement of Communication Apprehension in the Marriage Relationship." *Journal of Marriage and the Family* 41:89–95.

Prager, Karen J. 2000. "Intimacy in Personal Relations." Pp. 229–42 in *Close Relationships: A Sourcebook*, edited by C. Hendrick and S. S. Hendrick. Thousand Oaks, CA: Sage.

Risman, Barbara and Pepper Schwartz. 2002. "After the Sexual Revolution: Gender Politics in Teen Dating." *Contexts* 1:16–24.

Rosenberg, Morris. 1979. *Conceiving the Self.* New York: Basic Books.

Sandstrom, Kent L., Daniel D. Martin, and Gary A. Fine. 2002. *Symbols, Selves, and Social Reality: A Symbolic Interactionist Approach to Social Psychology and Sociology.* Los Angeles, CA: Roxbury.

Short, Susan. 1979. "Emotion and Social Life: A Symbolic Interactionist Analysis." *American Journal of Sociology* 84:1317–34.

Simon, Robin W., Donna Eder, and Cathy Evans. 1992. "The Development of Feeling Norms Underlying Romantic Love among Adolescent Females." *Social Psychology Quarterly* 55:29–46.

Simon, William and John H. Gagnon. 1986. "Sexual Scripts: Permanence and Change." *Archives of Sexual Behavior* 15:97–120.

Sprey, Jetse. 1999. "Family Dynamics: An Essay on Conflict and Power." Pp. 667–85 in *Handbook of Marriage and the Family*, 2d ed., edited by M. R. Sussman, S. K. Steinmetz, and G. W. Peterson. New York: Plenum.

Staples, Robert. 1981. *The World of Black Singles: Changing Patterns of Male-Female Relationships.* Westport, CT: Greenwood.

Sullivan, Harry S. 1953. *The Interpersonal Theory of Psychiatry.* New York: Norton.

Sullivan, Mercer L. 1989. *"Getting Paid": Youth Crime and Work in the Inner City.* Ithaca, NY: Cornell University Press.

Thompson, Sharon. 1995. *Going All The Way: Teenage Girls' Tales of Sex, Romance, and Pregnancy.* New York: Hill and Wang.

Thoits, Peggy A. 1989. "The Sociology of Emotions." *Annual Review of Sociology* 15:317–42.

Thorne, Barrie. 1993. *Gender Play: Girls and Boys in School.* New Brunswick, NJ: Rutgers University Press.

Thrasher, Frederic M. 1927. *The Gang: A Study of 1,313 Gangs.* Chicago, IL: University of Chicago Press.

Trella, Deanna L. 2005. "Control and Power Dynamics in Adolescent Romantic Relationships." Masters thesis, Department of Sociology, Bowling Green State University, Bowling Green, OH.

Turner, Jonathan H. 2000. *On the Origin of Human Emotion: A Sociological Inquiry into the Evolution of Human Affect.* Stanford, CA: Stanford University Press.

Waller, Walter. 1937. "The Rating and Dating Complex." *American Sociological Review* 2:727–34.

Weber, Max. 1947. *The Theory of Social and Economic Organization.* Translated by A. M. Henderson and T. Parsons. Edited by T. Parsons. Glencoe, IL: Free Press.

Wight, Daniel. 1994. "Boys' Thoughts and Talk about Sex in a Working-Class Locality of Glasgow." *Sociological Review* 42:703–38.

Willis, Paul E. 1977. *Learning to Labor.* Aldershot, England: Gower.

Youniss, James and Jacqueline Smollar. 1985. *Adolescent Relations with Mothers, Fathers and Friends.* Chicago, IL: University of Chicago Press.

"Sugar and Spice But Not Always Nice": Gender Socialization and Its Impact on Development and Maintenance of Aggression in Adolescent Girls

JOAN LETENDRE

Youth violence is a problem in American society and female adolescent violence is an important and increasing part of the overall dynamic. Although physical aggression is less commonly used by girls than by their male peers, rates of aggression between boys and girls even out when verbal (yelling, teasing, insulting) and indirect forms of aggression (secrets, gossip, telling stories, influencing friends) are included in the comparisons based on gender (Chesney-Lind, 2001; Crick & Grotpeter, 1995). Boys still commit the majority of violent crimes, but there is growing concern that the rates of aggression and delinquency with adolescent girls, particularly those living in urban environments, are increasing more than with males (Chesney-Lind & Brown, 1999; Franke, 2002). In 2002, rates of arrest for aggravated assault increased by 7% for females compared to a 29% decrease for males (Snyder, 2002). It is unclear whether the increase in reported violent female crimes is related to an actual increase in aggression amongst girls or to differences in arrests for incidents of relational aggression (i.e., aggression toward a family member) that might previously have been ignored and to the societal focus on zero tolerance for acts of aggression in schools.

The increased attention to girls and aggression has invoked a surge in popular magazines and films depicting adolescent girls' use of both overt and covert methods of aggression to maintain power and control in relationships. Movies and virtual reality television shows model aggressive behaviors where women are shown exhibiting power over others as they fight back in many

Joan Letendre, "'Sugar and Spice But Not Always Nice': Gender Socialization and Its Impact on Development and Maintenance of Aggression in Adolescent Girls" from *Child and Adolescent Social Work Journal*, 24, No. 4 (August 2007): 353–368.

of the same ways as their male counterparts. The taunting and social ostracism that have historically been a common part of girls' social groupings is increasing in intensity and physical aggressiveness and school officials report that the institution of zero tolerance policies requiring suspension for in-school fighting now affect girls as well as boys. Educators express concern about the increasing tendency for female students to use physical forms of aggression to solve interpersonal problems (Simons, 1997).

Aggressive behavior unchecked puts girls at significant risk for development of more serious social and emotional problems. Aggressive girls have higher rates of loneliness, depression and social isolation than their non-relationally aggressive peers (Crick & Grotpeter, 1995). School failure and dropout, violent relationships with romantic partners, teen pregnancy, repetitive harsh punishment toward their children, and accelerating participation in criminal behaviors have been associated with aggressive behavior in girls (Crick & Grotpeter, 1995; Gorman-Smith, 2003; Smith & Thomas, 2000). Although there is ample literature on the development of aggression in both boys and girls (Atkins, McKay, Talbott, & Arvenitis, 1996; Attar, Guerra, & Tolan, 1994; Fraser, 1996; Patterson, DeBarshe, & Ramsey, 1989) only recently have researchers and practitioners begun to explore the specific gender factors that contribute to its development and expression in girls (Chamberlain, 2003; Chesney-Lind & Brown, 1999; Talbott, Celinska, Simpson, & Coe, 2002).

Female aggression is often expressive rather than instrumental and girls are more likely to fight with those with whom they have close relationships (family members and friends) than with strangers (Chesney-Lind, 2001). Girls have historically used verbal rather than physical means of expressing their anger and asserting power and control over others (Bjorkvist, 1994; Crick & Grotpeter, 1995). Research now suggests, however, that the highly personal, hostile verbal expression of aggression, so characteristic of girls, may additionally lead to increased provocation and ultimately physical altercations (Baines & Adler, 1996; Talbott et al., 2002).

Until recently, the majority of programs for prevention and intervention with aggression in children and adolescents have ignored the gender-specific contributions to its development and expression in girls (Chamberlain, 2003; Chesney-Lind, 2001; Walsh, Peplar, & Levene, 2002). And yet, an understanding of the interplay between the developmental and contextual factors that contribute to the unique ways that girls are socialized to assert themselves, express their feelings and protect themselves from harm can inform program development that truly responds to the unique talents and needs of girls. This article examines the socialization of girls to determine how sociocultural, familial and peer factors impact female development and contribute to the learning of aggressive behaviors that may manifest in different forms depending on environmental context. The continuum of aggressive behaviors, all focused on the commonality of the importance of relationships to girls' will be described. Implications program development that social workers can implement on multiple systems level will be discussed.

Gender Specific Developmental and Relationship Tasks of Girls

The social-psychological development of girls places a high value on relationship and a consideration of the needs of others guides their moral development (Gilligan, 1982; Jordan, Kaplan, Miller, Stiver, & Surrey, 1991). Girls learn from modeling the behaviors of female caretakers to develop an interest in and attention to the other person, focusing on empathic sharing of experiences and an expectation that interactions will be based on mutual sensitivity and responsibility (Surrey, 1991). In contrast, the socialization of boys emphasizes autonomy and goal-directed behavior, which is often divorced from concern for the well being of others. Research suggests that the empathic connectedness that girls learn promotes a positive sense of self and a focus on relationships that mediates aggressive behavior in adolescence (Carlo, Raffaelli, Laible, & Meyer, 1999; Kaukiainen et al., 1999; Moretti, Holland, & McKay, 2001).

Unlike their male peers, who maintain autonomy in relationships with others, girls' sense of themselves is deeply intertwined with connection to others and thus threatened when faced with situations where there is conflict or disagreement. Fear of losing valuable relationships combined with weaker physical strength and less societal power than their male counterparts often contribute to a choice to forgo physical confrontations in lieu of fighting strategies that emphasize verbal interactions (gossiping, taunting) and manipulation of relationships (Bjorkvist, 1994; Pawlby, Mills, Taylor, & Quinton, 1997). Additionally, socio-cultural restrictions on direct expression of feelings and needs also teach girls that they must assert power and manage the anger, hurt, and disappointments that are typical components of any relationship by using covert methods of aggression to inflict psychological pain in the very areas that are considered important to girls: relationships with others. Subsequently, many girls go underground with their emotions at least in situations where social sanctions for this behavior are strong. Nowhere is this situation more pronounced than in junior high/middle school environment where young adolescent girls are bombarded with images of "ideal" physical attractiveness, minimally recognized and supported for academic achievement, and pressured for involvement in heterosexual romantic relationships, often long before they are psychologically ready for the demands of this involvement (Baer, 1999; Simmons & Blyth, 1987).

For adolescent girls living in urban environments, gender, minority status, and socioeconomic class compound the risks to optimal development (Chesney-Lind, 2001). Limited opportunities for achievement in overburdened urban schools, few well-paying jobs, and a high risk for male physical and sexual aggression (Hird, 2000) are strong predictors of delinquent and aggressive behavior in girls (Chesney-Lind, 2001). Additionally, many urban classrooms are training grounds for learning aggression, especially when teachers and peers do not restrict these behaviors (Henry, Guerra, Huesmann, Tolan, & Eron, 2000).

Such social factors, unique to the development of girls' combined with the tendency to ruminate about interpersonal problems, put even the most talented and confident girls at risk for losing confidence and developing psycho-social problems (Reimer, 2002). As a result girls adapt ways of interacting that use their superior social intelligence to promote a sense of power and control over an otherwise threatening and non-reinforcing environment (Chesney-Lind, 2001; Hird, 2000). Much of this control is manifested in covert ways but more recently girls are evidencing increased verbal and physical altercations in their interactions with peers (Talbott et al., 2002).

Parental Contributions to the Learning of Aggression in Girls

Pro-social Relationship Development

Families provide nurturing environments through which their children learn effective ways of interacting with others or inadvertently train them in the use of aggressive and anti-social behaviors. Parental use of warmth and attentiveness, consistent setting of clear limits, rewarding of compliance and careful monitoring of activities teaches both boys and girls that they are valued and cared about, reinforces a belief that adults can be trusted to provide consistent support and guidance, provides a feeling of safety from harm and promotes the development of skills for the many challenges of growing up. These parental practices are consistently associated with the development of pro-social skills and the mediation of aggression in both boys and girls (Chamberlain, 2003; Fraser, 1996).

Girls and boys, however, are socialized within families to develop relationships and manage conflict differently. Modeling by maternal caretakers encourages girls to develop caring, empathic relationships that impact the ways that they learn to assert themselves, manage anger, and protect themselves from harm. As a result of the strong emphasis on the importance of relationships, girls follow stringent gendered codes of behavior and go underground with their needs and emotions as a way of not threatening such important inter-personal connections (Crick & Nelson, 2002). Unsupported in learning more direct methods of expression, girls develop covert ways of get-ting their needs met and asserting their power in relationships with others. In contrast, boys expe-rience far greater freedom and recognition for the development of autonomy and the achievement of goals with a minimum of focus on nurturing relationships. Not dependent on the connection in relationship that is such a prominent part of girls' identity formation, boys historically experience less guilt for direct expression of aggression, par-ticularly when provoked by another boy (Perry, Perry, & Weiss, 1989).

Learning of Aggressive Skills

Families also inadvertently train their daughters to fight in direct and indirect ways. Girls who are socialized in families that fail to provide the safety and modeling that nurture the development of pro-social skills are at particular risk of the devel-opment of aggressive and anti-social behaviors. Specific parental practices, including failure to model and reward non-aggressive interactions, the consistent use of harsh and coercive punish-ment to sanction negative behaviors, and the lack of supervision have been associated with the devel-opment of aggressive and anti-social behaviors in all children and adolescents (Chamberlain, 2003; Fraser, 1996; Patterson et al., 1989). There is some evidence to suggest that such parenting and the overt family conflict that accompany these prac-tices put a particular strain on girls, with their fine tuned attention to interpersonal interactions (Gorman-Smith, 2003) and their learned sense of responsibility for care taking of family members. Molidar (1996) found that girls who were engaged in aggressive and anti-social behaviors reported unhappiness with the lack of emotional support and the degrees of problems in their families. Girls are twice as likely to fight with family mem-bers as their male peers, who experience more distance and independence from and less sense of responsibility for relationships within the family (Chesney-Lind, 2001). Reliance on daughters rather than sons for added responsibilities for childcare and household tasks, limits access to job and age-appropriate extra-curricular activities and may contribute to additional resentment and conflict between girls, their mothers and siblings. As girls struggle for the independence and autonomy that is a normal part of adolescent development, there may be increasingly problematic encounters and escalating aggression between mother and daugh-ter (Chesney-Lind & Brown, 1999). The conflict creates estrangement between the mother and daughter at the time when support and guidance that are needed to safely negotiate the many chal-lenges of coming of age are needed.

Girls are also at greater risk of victimization within their own families. Twice as many violent girls reported abuse at home compared to non-violent peers and one in four reported a history of sexual abuse (Chesney-Lind, 2001). Girls are more frequent victims of sexual abuse than their male peers with the abuse starting earlier and lasting longer (Chesney-Lind & Brown, 1999). "Fighting back," "acting out" or running away are com-mon responses to sexual abuse in delinquent girls (Chesney-Lind, 2001). Leaving home to escape abusive situations puts girls at additional risk of victimization from older males as they attempt to survive in communities that are ill equipped to provide adolescent girls with safe spaces to nur-ture development and insure protection from harm.

Environmental Challenges to Parenting Daughters

In communities where there are multiple stressors to optimal parenting and enormous opportunities for engagement in activities that increase a young adolescent girl's risk of exposure to violence and victimization, parents, primarily mothers, must engage in specific practices that will protect their daughters from harm (Bowen & Chapman, 1996). Mothers must actively think of the situations their daughters will encounter and provide the neces-sary skills to succeed in a society that discrimi-nates against them because of socio-economic status, gender, race and ethnicity. One practice, "truth telling," allows mothers to bolster their daughters' confidence about who she is in relation to her racial and ethnic identity while instructing in behavioral skills that the daughter might use in the challenging situations that she may encounter (Chesney-Lind, 2001; Ward, 1996). Mothers also protect their daughters from harm by placing strong limits on places that their daughters can go and activities that they can engage in (Brodsky, 1996). Finally, an urban study reports that some mothers are as likely to teach their daughters to fight as their sons, and slightly more likely to teach their daughters to strike first in a conflict (Metropolitan Area Child Study Research Group, 2002).

The Peer Group's Role in the Promotion of Aggression

Same Sex Friendships

Peer groups continue the complicated relational socialization of girls that begins in the family. As early as elementary school, children accept strict gender roles and reject peers who exhibit behaviors that are not in keeping with the desired traits of passivity in females and aggression in males (Hess & Atkins, 1998). Both boys and girls suffer rejection for physically aggressive behavior, but girls experience greater social ostracism unless they are involved in a peer group that approves of physically aggressive behaviors (Henry et al., 2000; Smith & Thomas, 2000). The majority of girls then must learn how to ask for what they need, express anger and resolve differences in ways that do not provoke rejection from their peers.

Belonging to a peer group is particularly important to girls during the adolescent years because it bolsters confidence, and reinforces identity, and protects against isolation and victimization from female peers. Securing and maintaining status in the peer group then becomes an all-important task for the adolescent girl and acquiescence to the norms of the group insure her place where she can develop close friendships with same sex peers while waging complicated battles against other girls who threaten her social position (Bjorkqvist, 1994;

Pelligrini & Long, 2002). Girls' superior social intelligence combined with the extreme importance placed on maintaining their status in the group promote sensitivity to perceived slights and insults from other girls. Fights frequently arise from these perceptions and from competition for male attention (Artz, 1999). The response of girls to these hurts will depend on the multiple ways that they have learned to deal with anger and manage differences with others.

Female peer groups have primarily aggressed against other girls by harassing, name-calling, gossiping, spreading rumors, and threatening, and less often by resorting to physical violence. Such covert but destructive social manipulation hides the actions of the aggressor from the victim and oftentimes from the adults who might sanction this social cruelty (Bjorkvist, 1994). Having no or limited access to monitoring from adults the incidents go unreported because the female victims fear retaliation. When girls do report the situations to adults, they often find that the incidents are minimized as a "normal" part of the growing up process. Such responses fail to sanction female relational aggression, provide little protection for less powerful girls to defend themselves from hurtful interactions with peers and do not promote healthy resolution of conflicts and differences amongst girls.

The verbal altercations that have long been a part of girls' fighting can accelerate into physical incidents of aggression (Baines & Adler, 1996; Talbott et al., 2002). When reactions to slights and rejections are extreme, feelings of shame may accompany the incident and result in physical forms of fighting in an effort to save face amongst peers (Hardy, 1998; Purdie & Downey, 2000). Girls who have been reinforced for aggressive behaviors in the home and have had few opportunities to learn alternative ways of interacting around conflict automatically respond with aggression to interpersonal conflicts (Cairns, Cairns Neckerman, Gest, & Gariepy, 1988). Some peer groups actually approve of and encourage physical fighting, bestowing social status and popularity on those who engage in such behaviors (Henry et al., 2000). In other situations, aggressive girls may be rejected by pro-social peers, and subsequently develop friendships with like-minded girls who believe that fighting is a way of solving problems and maintaining their "tough girl" identity.

Romantic Relationships

The pressure for involvement in romantic heterosexual relationships puts many young adolescent girls, particularly those who develop early, at risk of physical and sexual victimization because they lack the social skills to negotiate the increased dependency or intimacy that are characteristics of these relationships, particularly those involving older males (Chesney-Lind, 2001; Hird, 2000; Pawlby et al., 1997). When same-sex relationships are fraught with problems, girls often turn to romantic relationships to meet their social-emotional needs but lack the necessary skills to negotiate these complicated interactions. Research indicates that girls who have less positive relationships with same-sex peers report more stress or relationship violence in their later heterosexual romantic relationships (Feiring, Deblinger, Hoch-Espada, & Haworth, 2002). Perceived fears of rejection from a partner may result in rage and aggression directed toward the male partner and subsequent escalation in verbal and physical aggression between the couple resulting in physical injury (Capaldi & Gorman-Smith, 2003). The risk of harm and the need for protective skills is even greater when adolescent girls are romantically involved with older males (Hird, 2000). Although literature is lacking on same sex romantic relationships, one can posit that some of the same issues that lead to violence in same sex relationships might also be present in intimate relationships between girls.

Implications for Practice: Teaching Girls Assertive Protection Skills

In order to be able to develop fully their own unique contribution to society rather than be involved with courts and juvenile protection systems, girls must learn to protect themselves from harm, ask for what they need, express feelings and understand and resolve differences with family members, girls friends and romantic partners. As social workers, we must intervene with the multiple systems that fail to support optimal development in girls and result in the development of aggressive behavior. Programs that focus on preventing or intervening with female aggression, whether verbal attacks or physical altercations, must promote change in girls' ability to assert themselves and protect themselves from harm. First, we must provide parents with the necessary social support to provide the caretaking, guidance, modeling and protection that is so essential to the normal developmental process of their daughters. Secondly, it is important to refrain from perpetuating the stereotype that exhibiting aggression and anger are inappropriate. In fact aggression and anger are normal and expected responses to negative life events. Thirdly, social workers in schools must evaluate and identify at-risk girls earlier through learning about signal behaviors and demoralizing environments rather than waiting for the same severe symptoms to emerge that might identify a boy for trouble. As has been shown, aggression in girls often manifests in different ways from aggression in boys. Finally, programs that teach girls ways of meeting their needs in socially positive ways need to be funded and developed in all schools. Girls will not outgrow their aggressive behavior, but change can come about through intervention and positive attention in the family, school system and out-of-school groups. Suggested methods that may be included in these programs such as skill-building, all-girl classroom discussions, creating new empowering environments, focusing on peer dynamics, and making older female and male role models available, are discussed in more detail below.

Interventions must begin with the acknowledgment that girls have a high degree of social intelligence that can be used in both constructive and destructive ways. If girls are to change their methods of aggressing against each other, alternative ways of expressing their needs and solving conflict must be modeled and reinforced by both adults and peers. Effective zero-tolerance policies in schools can prohibit all forms of aggression but rather than suspend girls for infractions or ignore such incidents of girl bullying as "normal" parts of growing up, consequences can include teaching alternative methods of resolving differences, asserting their needs and communicating when angry or hurt. Social workers and peer mediators can facilitate conjoint sessions with girls when one or several girls have socially ostracized another girl to increase empathy and facilitate open communication. Support for the victims of such interactions can include the participation of friends or peer mentors to provide an actual physical presence of support for the victim, role playing of assertive ways that the victim can confront her aggressors, and follow-up monitoring to insure that the destructive interactions have ceased.

Clinical interventions for highly aggressive girls must be developed that honor the feminine socialization process and the focus it places on self in relationship to others. Recognition must be given to the value that girls place on relationship and the anxiety that is generated when relationships, whether with friendship or romance, are threatened. Recognizing the importance of the peer group to adolescent girls, psycho-educational, skill building groups can focus on helping girls to think critically about situations where they experience oppression and lack of support for the goals that they want to achieve. Girls can offer mutual aid as they discuss the situations that provoke anxiety, fear, rage and desire to aggress against other girls as a way of maintaining some power and control over feelings and situations that are threatening. Girls can be taught relaxation techniques and positive self-talk that calms their anxiety and rage and helps them to develop empowering, non-aggressive ways of dealing with relationship conflicts. The skill building groups may have an action component that will allow girls to advocate for changes that will make the school environment more supportive and protective i.e. campaign against sexual harassment in the hallways (Gutierrez, 1990).

The high rates of sexual abuse associated with aggression in girls alerts us to the importance of universal programs that educate girls and their parents on ways that girls can be taught to protect themselves from harm. Community wide programs that are instituted in schools, after school programs and churches can put an emphasis on teaching girls that their bodies are their own and that no one has a right to violate this personal space, no matter how close or valuable the relationship. Since girls are sexually abused earlier and for longer periods of time than their male peers, educational programs can be implemented in the early grades to insure that all girls learn to assert themselves and have access to adults who will protect them from this abuse should it occur.

Schools can develop programs that empower adolescent girls. All-girl classroom discussions that focus on building healthy relationships and developing assertiveness skills can be taught as part of the health curriculum. Discussions can address the issues that are important to young adolescent girls in a safe environment where all girls, irrespective of social status, can express their opinions about common concerns. Didactic discussions on issues that concern girls and may lead to aggression such as standards of physical attractiveness, popularity, conflict with friends, and romantic partners, and concerns about sexuality can be balanced with specific activities and role plays that will promote practice of skills that can be used outside of the group. Social workers can facilitate the sessions with the assistance of older adolescents, who can share their experiences and serve as mentors.

Creating an environment where all girls, despite their social status, can share their concerns is important. Careful attention to the peer dynamics in the group and structuring of the activities can ensure that every girl has an opportunity to be recognized and affirmed in the discussion. Cultural differences in gender expectations, communication styles, coming of age expectations and rituals, rules for friendship, and ways of expressing conflict can be explored and skills developed that are sensitive to the norms of the community. By modeling acceptance of diverse opinions, understanding and empathy for difference can be encouraged. Modeling of direct forms of communication can provide girls with alternative methods of getting their needs met and managing conflict.

Providing opportunities for girls to work together in heterogeneous social groupings on specific tasks, such as painting a mural, mentoring younger girls, hosting and performing at a musical event, teaming for athletics, can encourage collaborative work on an activity. Working together on a project encourages positive group interaction and development of leadership qualities (Letendre, 1999). Developing advanced social skills under supervision allows girls the recognition that they crave while creating collaborative win-win working environments. Girls can learn that goal oriented activity as well as relationship building are both important to their sense of competence and well-being.

Interventions that focus on girls must include the input of older female and adult role models who can guide them through the challenges of adolescence. Girls need their mothers and other females to model ways of interacting in the world and yet, many times during adolescence, girls turn away from their mother's guidance in efforts to assert their independence. Mothers must be given the skills and power that are necessary to safely guide their daughters through adolescence. They may have had similar difficult experiences and can thus discuss and learn to model healthy responses that can guide young girls and serve to establish trust and open communication. Mothers can also learn the importance of teaching their sons to develop similar kinds of socially positive, tender, cooperative, nurturant and sensitive qualities that are antithetical to aggressive behavior (Eron, 1980). By so doing, the burden of caretaking experiences in the family may be shared amongst boys and girls so that girls may be freed up to develop other skills. Use of multi-family support groups can decrease the stigma that parents feel when they are singled out for guidance in parenting. The group support offers opportunities for parents to develop collective strategies for protecting their daughters and teaching assertiveness. For parents who live in communities with high rates of violence, strategies can focus on developing neighborhood support for protecting girls from harm.

Groups can be facilitated in places and at times that are accessible to the parents such as community centers, schools, and churches.

Although mothers are the primary role models for their daughters, the importance of the father or male role model in providing a safe male relationship and a buffer to the intensity of the role of the mother is equally important. Fathers provide a supportive, protective relationship, where girls can comfortably interact with a caring male and receive honest feedback on their behaviors. Fathers may also be a resource in helping girls with concerns about relationships. For girls who are living in single-parent families, interaction with male mentors or relatives may increase the support so needed during the stresses of adolescence and lessen the tendency to turn exclusively to peers or romantic relationships for unmet familial needs.

Conclusion

Girls' aggression, whether manifested by covert relational attacks on other girls or by physical confrontation, has long been minimized or not addressed. With the recent increase in reported violent crimes committed by females, girls' aggression is now being re-evaluated to understand the specific gender factors that influence its development, continuance, and effects on others. Interventions developed to prevent and treat aggression in girls must focus on the ways that girls can learn to use their highly developed social skills to assertively express their needs. Interventions at the school, peer group, and family level must emphasize the importance of protecting girls from physical and sexual abuse that are strongly correlated with the development and progression of aggression in girls.

References

Artz, S. (1999). Girl bullies strike dubious blows for gender equity. In C. Enman (Ed.), *Ottawa Citizen*, October 19, 1999.

Atkins, M. S., McKay, M., Talbott, E., & Arvenitis, P. (1996). Conduct and oppositional defiant disorders in children: Implications for school mental health teams. *School Psychology Review, 25,* 274–283.

Attar, B. K., Guerra, N. G., & Tolan, P. H. (1994). Neighborhood disadvantage, stressful life events, and adjustment in urban elementary-school children. *Journal of Clinical Psychology, 23,* 391–400.

Baer, J. (1999). Adolescent development and the junior high environment. *Social Work in Education, 21,* 238–248.

Baines, M., & Adler, C. (1996). Are girls more difficult to work with? Youth workers' perspectives in juvenile justice and related areas. *Crime and Delinquency, 42,* 467–485.

Bjorkqvist, K. (1994). Sex differences, in physical, verbal, and indirect aggression: A review of recent research. *Sex Roles: A Journal of Research, 30,* 177–189.

Bowen, G. L., & Chapman, M. V. (1996). Poverty, neighborhood danger, social support, and the individual adaptation among at-risk youth in urban areas. *Journal of Family Issues, 17,* 641–666.

Brodsky, A. E. (1996). Resilient single mothers in risky neighborhoods: Negative psychological sense of community. *Journal of Community Psychology, 24,* 347–363.

Cairns, R. B., Cairns, B. D., Neckerman, H. G., Gest, S. D., & Gariepy, J. L. (1988). Social networks and aggressive behavior: Peer support or peer rejection. *Developmental Psychology, 24,* 815–823.

Capaldi, D. M., & Gorman-Smith, D. (2003). Physical and psychological aggression in young adult couples. In P. Florsheim (Ed.), *Adolescent romance and sexual behavior: Theory, research and practical implications* (pp. 243–278). New York: LEA Associates.

Carlo, G., Raffaelli, M., Laible, D. J., & Meyer, K. A. (1999). Why are girls less physically aggressive than boys? Personality and parenting mediators of physical aggression. *Sex Roles: A Journal of Research, 40,* 711–729.

Chamberlain, P. (2003). *Treating chronic juvenile offenders; Advances made through the Oregon Multidimensional Treatment Foster Care Model.* Washington, DC: American Psychological Association.

Chesney-Lind, M. (2001). What about girls? Delinquency programming as if gender mattered. *Corrections Today, 63,* 38–45.

Chesney-Lind, M., & Brown, M. (1999). Girls and violence: An overview. In D. Flannery & C. R. Huff (Eds.), *Youth violence: Prevention, intervention and social policy* (pp. 171–199). Washington, DC: American Psychiatric Press.

Crick, N. R., & Grotpeter, J. K. (1995). Relational aggression, gender, and social-psychological adjustment. *Child Development, 66,* 710–722.

Crick, N. R., & Nelson, D. A. (2002). Relational and physical victimization within friendships: Nobody told me there'd be friends like these. *Journal of Abnormal Psychology, 30*(6), 599–608.

Eron, L. D. (1980). Prescription for reduction in violence. *American Psychologist, 35,* 244–252.

Feiring, C, Deblinger, E., Hoch-Espada, A., & Haworth, T. (2002). Romantic relationship aggression and attitudes in high school students: The role of gender, grade, and attachment and emotional styles. *Journal of Youth and Adolescence, 31,* 373–385.

Franke, T. M. (2002). Girls and violence: A cause for concern. *Presentation, Sixth Annual Conference of the Society for Social Work Research,* San Diego, CA., January 18, 2002.

Fraser, M. W. (1996). Aggressive behavior in childhood and early adolescence: An ecological-developmental perspective on youth violence. *Social Work, 41,* 347–361.

Gilligan, C. (1982). *In a different voice: Psychological theory and women's development.* Cambridge, MA: Harvard University Press.

Gorman-Smith, D. (2003). Prevention of anti-social behavior in females. In D. Farrington & J. Coid (Eds.), *Primary prevention of antisocial behavior* (pp. 292–317). Cambridge: Cambridge University Press.

Gutierrez, L. M. (1990). Working with women of color: An empowerment perspective. *Social Work, 35,* 149–154.

Hardy, F. (1998). School bullying: Girl bullies can be just as violent as boys. *The Independent,* June, 27, 7.

Henry, D., Guerra, N. G., Huesmann, L. R., Tolan, P. H., & Eron, L. D. (2000). Normative influences on aggression in urban elementary school classrooms. *American Journal of Community Psychology, 28,* 59–81.

Hess, L. E., & Atkins, M. C. (1998). Victims and aggressors at school. Teacher, self, and peer perceptions of psychosocial functioning. *Applied Developmental Science, 2,* 75–89.

Hird, J. J. (2000). An empirical study of adolescent aggression in the U.K *Journal of Adolescence, 2*, 69–78.

Jordan, J. V., Kaplan, A. G., Miller, J. B., Stiver, I. P., & Surrey, J. L. (1991). *Women's growth in connection.* New York: The Guilford Press.

Kaukiainen, A., Bjorkqvist, K., Lagerspetz, K. L., Osterman, K., Salmivalli, C., Rothberg, S., & Ahlbom, A. (1999). The relationships between social intelligence, empathy, and three types of aggression. *Aggressive-Behavior, 25*, 81–89.

Letendre, J. (1999). Work with alienated middle school boys. Use of an empowerment model. *Journal of Child and Adolescent Group Therapy, 9*, 113–127.

Metropolitan Area Child Study Research Group (2002). Responses of parents to deviant beliefs items. Unpublished raw data.

Molidar, C. E. (1996). Female gang members: A profile of aggression and victimization. *Social Work, 41*, 251–257.

Moretti, M. M, Holland, R., & McKay, S. (2001). Self-other representations and overt aggression in adolescent girls and boys. *Behavioral Sciences and the Law, 19*, 109–126.

Patterson, G. R., DeBarshe, B. D., & Ramsey, E. (1989). A developmental perspective on antisocial behavior. *American Psychologist, 44*, 329–335.

Pawlby, S. J., Mills, A., Taylor, A., & Quinton, D. (1997). Adolescent friendships mediating childhood adversity and adult outcomes. *Journal of Adolescence, 20*, 633–644.

Pellegrini, A. D., & Long, J. D. (2002). A longitudinal study of bullying, dominance, and victimization during the transition from primary school through secondary school. *British Journal of Developmental Psychology, 20*, 259–280.

Perry, D. G., Perry, L. C., & Weiss, R. J. (1989). Sex differences that children anticipate for aggression. *Developmental Psychology, 25*, 312–319.

Purdie, V., & Downey, G. (2000). Rejection sensitivity and adolescent girls' vulnerability to relationship-centered difficulties. *Child Maltreatment, 5*, 338–349.

Reimer, M. S. (2002). Gender, risk, and resilience in the middle school context. *Children and Schools, 24*, 35–47.

Simons, J. (1997). Sugar and spice, and not at all nice; boys don't have the corner on bullying—schoolgirls are becoming increasingly aggressive. *The Denver Rocky Mountain News*, November 23, 1997, Home Front; Ed. F; p. 12F.

Simmons, R. G., & Blyth, D. A. (1987). *Moving into adolescence: The impact of pubertal change and school context.* New York: Aldine De Gruyter.

Smith, H., & Thomas, S. P. (2000). Violent and nonviolent girls: Contrasting perceptions of anger experiences, school, and relationships. *Issues in Mental Health in Nursing, 21*, 547–575.

Snyder, H. N. (2002). Juvenile arrests 2002. Juvenile justice bulletin. Office of juvenile justice and delinquency prevention, September, 2004.

Surrey, J. L. (1991). The "Self in Relation": A theory of women's development. In *Women's growth in connection* (pp. 51–66). New York: The Guilford Press.

Talbott, E., Celinska, D., Simpson, J., & Coe, M. G. (2002). "Somebody else making somebody else fight". Aggression and the social context among urban adolescent girls. *Exceptionality, 10*, 203–220.

Walsh, M. M., Peplar, D. J., & Levene, K. S. (2002). A model of intervention for girls with disruptive behavior problems: The Earlscourt girls connection. *Canadian Journal of Counseling, 36*, 297–311.

Ward, J. V. (1996). Raising resisters: The role of truth telling in the psychological development of African-American girls. In B. J. R. Leadbeater & N. Way *Urban girls: Resisting stereotypes, creating identities* (pp. 85–99). New York: New York University Press.

The Social Construction of Gender Relations

To sociologists, the psychological discussion of sex roles—that collection of attitudes, traits, and behaviors that are normative for either boys or girls—exposes the biological sleight of hand that suggests that what is normative—enforced, socially prescribed—is actually normal. But psychological models themselves do not go far enough, unable to fully explain the variations *among* men or women based on class, race, ethnicity, sexuality, age, or to explain the ways in which one gender consistently enjoys power over the other. And, most importantly to sociologists, psychological models describe how individuals acquire sex role identity, but then assume that these gendered individuals enact their gendered identities in institutions that are gender-neutral.

Sociologists have taken up each of these themes in exploring (1) how the institutions in which we find ourselves are also gendered, (2) the ways in which those psychological prescriptions for gender identity reproduce *both* gender difference and male domination, and (3) the ways in which gender is accomplished and expressed in everyday interaction.

Cynthia Fuchs Epstein took the occasion of her presidential address to the American Sociological Association to survey the various interpersonal and institutional mechanisms of women's near-universal subordination. In her essay, Cecilia Ridgeway fuses both structural and interactionist explanations as she explains how gender both frames all other interactions and provides a structure through which to understand interaction.

Taking a different approach toward similar ends, Candace West and her two collaborators, in two separate essays, make clear that gender is not a property of the individual, something that one *has*, but rather is a process that one *does* in everyday interaction with others. And that what one is doing is not simply doing gender, but also doing difference, which in our society also means doing inequality.

Great Divides: The Cultural, Cognitive, and Social Bases of the Global Subordination of Women

CYNTHIA FUCHS EPSTEIN

The world is made up of great divides—divides of nations, wealth, race, religion, education, class, gender, and sexuality—all constructs created by human agency. The conceptual boundaries that define these categories are always symbolic and may create physical and social boundaries as well (Gerson and Peiss 1985; Lamont and Molnar 2002). Today, as in the past, these constructs not only order social existence, but they also hold the capacity to create serious inequalities, generate conflicts, and promote human suffering. In this address, I argue that the boundary based on sex creates the most fundamental social divide—a divide that should be a root issue in all sociological analysis if scholars are to adequately understand the social dynamics of society and the influential role of stratification. The work of many sociologists contributes to this claim, although I can only refer to some of them in the context of a single article.

The conceptual boundaries that determine social categories are facing deconstruction throughout our profession. Once thought stable and real in the sense that they are descriptive of biological or inherited traits, social categories such as race and ethnicity are contested today by a number of scholars (Barth 1969; Brubaker 2004; Duster 2006; Telles 2004). Indeed, sociologists are questioning the underlying reasoning behind categorical distinctions, noting their arbitrariness, and further, the ways in which they tend to be "essentializing and naturalizing" (Brubaker 2004:9).[1] Yet, not many of these critical theorists have included

gender in this kind of analysis.[2] Where they have, such work tends to be relegated to, if not ghettoized within, the field of "gender studies."[3]

Of course, the categories of race, ethnicity, and gender are real in the sense that—as W. I. Thomas put it in his oft-quoted observation—"if men *[sic]* define situations as real, they are real in their consequences (cited in Merton [1949] 1963:421). Categorization on the basis of observable characteristics often serves as a mobilizing strategy for action against (or for) people assigned to the category and may even force them into a grouplike state (Bourdieu 1991; Brubaker 2004). Alternatively, categorization may create conformity to a stereotype—in the process known as "the self-fulfilling prophecy" (Merton [1949] 1963). But it is one thing for individuals to engage in categorical thinking, and another for social scientists to accept a category with its baggage of assumptions. Today, many social scientists use popular understandings of race, ethnicity, and gender as if they were descriptive of inherent or acquired stable traits, and they treat them as established variables that describe clusters of individuals who share common traits. In this manner, social scientists are no different from the lay public, who, in their everyday activities and thinking, act as if categories are reliable indicators of commonalities in a population.

The consequences of such categorization may be positive or negative for those in a given category. For example, people of color face far more suspicion from the police than do whites, and favored male professors benefit from the evaluation that

---

Cynthia Fuchs Epstein, " Great Divides: The Cultural, Cognitive, and Social Bases of the Global Subordination of Women" from *American Sociological Review*, 72 (February 2007): 1–22.

they are smart and knowledgeable while comparatively, favored female professors tend to be evaluated as nice (Basow 1995). Yet, unlike the basis on which social *groups* may be defined, categories include individuals who may never know one another or have any interaction with each other. However, they may all share selected physical traits or relationships. Skin color, hair texture, genitals, place of birth, and genealogy are among the determinants of categories.

I consider *gender* to be the most basic and prevalent category in social life throughout the world, and in this address, I explore the life consequences that follow from this designation for the female half of humanity. Gender is, of course, based on biological sex, as determined by the identification of an individual at birth as female or male by a look at their genitals. This first glance sets up the most basic divide in all societies—it determines an individual's quality of life, position on the social hierarchy, and chance at survival. The glance marks individuals for life and is privileged over their unique intelligence, aptitudes, or desires. Of course, persons who are transgendered, transsexual, or hermaphrodites[4] do not fit this dichotomous separation, but there is little recognition of categories based on sex other than male and female in almost every society (Butler 1990; Lorber 1994, 1996).

Sex Division and Subordination

The sexual divide is the most persistent and arguably the deepest divide in the world today. Of course, it is only one of many great divides. Boundaries mark the territories of human relations. They are created by "cultural entrepreneurs"[5] who translate the concepts into practice—rulers behind the closed doors of palaces and executive offices; judges in courtrooms; priests, rabbis, and mullahs; leaders and members of unions and clubs; and teachers, parents, and the people in the street. The great divides of society are enforced by persuasion, barter, custom, force, and the threat of force (Epstein 1985). The extent to which boundaries are permeable and individuals can escape categorization, and thus, their assignment to particular social roles and statuses, is a function of a society's or an institution's stability and capacity to change. The ways in which boundaries may be transgressed make up the story of social change and its limits. They are the basis for human freedom.

Of all the socially created divides, the gender divide is the most basic and the one most resistant to social change. As I have suggested before (Epstein 1985, 1988, 1991b, 1992), dichotomous categories, such as those that distinguish between blacks and whites; free persons and slaves; and men and women, are always invidious. This dichotomous categorization is also particularly powerful in maintaining the advantage of the privileged category. With regard to the sex divide, the male sex is everywhere privileged—sometimes the gap is wide, sometimes narrow. Some individuals and small clusters of women may succeed in bypassing the negative consequences of categorization, and in some cases they may even do better educationally or financially than the men in their group. Among women, those from a privileged class, race, or nationality may do better than others. But worldwide, in every society, women as a category are subordinated to men.

I further suggest that the divide of biological sex constitutes a marker around which all major institutions of society are organized. All societal institutions assign roles based on the biological sex of their members. The divisions of labor in the family, local and global labor forces, political entities, most religious systems, and nation-states are all organized according to the sexual divide.

Cultural meanings are also attached to the categories of female and male, which include attributions of character and competence (Epstein 1988, see Ridgeway 2006 for a review). These situate individuals assigned to each category in particular social and symbolic roles. There is some overlap in the roles to which females and males are assigned, but in all societies sex status is the major determinant—it is the master status that determines the acquisition of most other statuses.

Of course, biological sex does prescribe humans' reproductive roles (e.g., child bearer, inseminator). But there is no biological necessity for a woman to become a mother, even though only women can become biological mothers, and a man may or may not choose to become a biological father. Therefore, we can conclude that *all* social statuses and the roles attached to them are *socially* prescribed. Further, norms prescribe (or proscribe) detailed behavior fixed to all social roles. And, because statuses are universally ranked, the statuses women are permitted to acquire usually are subordinate to men's statuses. Furthermore, women's roles are universally paired with roles assigned to men, to the family, in the workplace, and in the polity. Virtually no statuses are stand-alone positions in society; all are dependent on reciprocal activities of those who hold complementary statuses. These too are socially ranked and usually follow the invidious distinctions that "male" and "female" evoke. Almost no statuses are free from gender-typing.

These observations lead me to proposals that I believe are essential for comprehensive sociological analysis today, and to call for the elimination of the boundary that has separated so-called gender studies from mainstream sociology.[6]

Given the ubiquitous nature of sex-typing of social statuses, and social and symbolic behavior, I propose that the dynamics of gender segregation be recognized as a primary issue for sociological analysis and attention be paid to the mechanisms and processes of sex differentiation and their roles in group formation, group maintenance, and stratification.[7] I further suggest that

- Females' and males' actual and symbolic roles in the social structure are a seedbed for group formation and group boundary-maintenance.
- All societies and large institutions are rooted in the differentiation and subordination of females.
- The more group solidarities are in question in a society, the stronger the differentiation between males and females and the more severe is women's subjugation.

The enforcement of the distinction is achieved through cultural and ideological means that justify the differentiation. This is despite the fact that, unlike every other dichotomous category of people, females and males are necessarily bound together, sharing the same domiciles and most often the same racial and social class statuses. Analyses of these relationships are difficult given the ways in which they are integrated with each other and the extent to which they are basic in all institutions.

There is, of course, variation in societies and the subgroups within them, and a continuum exists in the severity of female subordination. Indeed, subordination is not a static process and it varies from almost complete to very little. The process is dynamic in shape and degree. Women gain or lose equality depending on many elements—the state of an economy, the identity politics of groups or nations, the election of conservative or liberal governments, the need for women's labor in the public and private sectors, the extent of their education, the color of their skin,[8] the power of fundamentalist religious leaders in their societies, and their ability to collaborate in social movements. But even in the most egalitarian of societies, the invidious divide is always a lurking presence and it can easily become salient.

It is important to note that women's inequality is not simply another case of social inequality, a view I have held in the past (Epstein 1970). I am convinced that societies and strategic subgroups within them, such as political and work institutions, *maintain their boundaries*—their very social organization—through the use of invidious distinctions made between males and females.[9] Everywhere, women's subordination is basic to maintaining the social cohesion and stratification systems of ruling and governing groups—male groups—on national and local levels, in the family, and in all other major institutions. Most dramatically, this process is at work today in the parts of the world where control of females' behavior, dress, and use of public space have been made representations of orthodoxies in confrontation with modernism, urbanism, and secular society. But even in the most egalitarian societies, such as the United States, women's autonomy over their bodies,[10] their time, and their ability to decide their destinies is constantly at risk when it intrudes on male power.

The gender divide is not determined by biological forces. *No society or subgroup leaves social sorting to natural processes.* It is through social and cultural mechanisms and their impact on cognitive processes that social sorting by sex occurs and is kept in place—by the exercise of force and the threat of force, by law, by persuasion, and by embedded cultural schemas that are internalized by individuals in all societies. Everywhere, local cultures support invidious distinctions by sex. As Jerome Bruner (1990) points out in his thoughtful book, *Acts of Meaning,* normatively oriented institutions—the law, educational institutions, and family structures—serve to enforce folk psychology, and folk psychology in turn serves to justify such enforcement. In this address, I shall explore some spheres in which the process of sex differentiation and the invidious comparisons between the sexes are especially salient.

The Position of Women in the United States and in the Profession of Sociology

It is fitting that my presidential address to the 101st meeting of the American Sociological Association should begin with an analytic eye on our profession. I became the ninth woman president in the ASA's 101 years of existence. The first woman president, Dorothy Swaine Thomas, was elected in 1952, the second, Mirra Komarovsky, almost 20 years later—two women presidents in the first seven decades of the existence of the association. Seven others have been chosen in the 23 years since.[11]

We nine women are symbolic of the positive changes in the position of women in the United States. Our case is situated at the high end of the continuum of women's access to equality. Similarly, our profession has devoted much research attention to women's position in society, though the findings of scholars on the subject are often not integrated with the profession's major theoretical and empirical foci. Many radical voices in the discipline refer to "gender issues" only ritualistically. This is so even though sociological research on gender is one of the major examples of "public sociology" of the past 40 years.

When I was a sociology graduate student at Columbia University in the 1960s, there were no women on the sociology faculty, as was the case at most major universities. The entire bibliography on women in the workplace, assembled for my thesis (1968) on women's exclusion from the legal profession, was exhausted in a few pages. However, it included Betty Friedan's ([1963] 1983) *The Feminine Mystique,* with its attack on Talcott Parsons's (1954) perspective on the functions of the nuclear family and his observation that women's role assignment in the home had exceedingly positive functional significance in that it prevented competition with their husbands (p. 191).[12] She also attacked Freud's ([1905] 1975) theories that women's biology is their destiny, that their feelings of inferiority are due to "penis envy," and his contention "that the woman has no penis often produces in the male a lasting depreciation of the other sex" (Freud 1938:595, footnote 1).

Friedan contributed to both the knowledge base of the social sciences and to the status of women. I believe she did more than any other person in modern times to change popular perceptions of women and their place in the world. While not the first to identify the dimensions of women's inequality,[13] Friedan put theory into practice, building on the attention she received when *The Feminine Mystique* was published. At a moment made ripe by the sensibilities of the civil rights movement and the growing participation of women in the labor force, she took up a challenge posed to her by Pauli Murray, the African American lawyer and civil rights activist, to create "an NAACP for women."[14] With the encouragement and participation of a small but highly motivated group of women in government, union offices, and professional life—white women, African American women, and women from Latin-American backgrounds (a fact that has gone unnoticed far too long)—and with the participation of the third woman ASA president, Alice Rossi, Friedan founded the National Organization for Women in 1966. Working through NOW, Friedan set out to provide political support for implementation of Title VII of the Civil Rights Act of 1964, which prohibited discrimination on the basis of sex as well as race, color, religion, and national origin. The changes accomplished by the organizational work of Friedan, and a number of other activists[15] and scholars,[16] were nothing short of a social revolution. It is a revolution of interest to sociologists not only for its creation of women's rights in employment and education but because *it became a natural field experiment establishing that there was no natural order of things relegating women to "women's work" and men to "men's work."* Yet, like most revolutions it was limited in its accomplishment of its stated goals and its principles are constantly under attack.

But the revolution did motivate research. There has been an explosion of scholarship on the extent of sex divides on macro and micro levels. Social scientists have documented in hundreds of thousands of pages of research the existence and consequences of subtle and overt discrimination against women of all strata and nationalities and the institutionalization of sexism.

The number of studies of the differentiation of women's and girls' situations in social life has grown exponentially in the 40 years since the beginning of the second wave of the women's movement. This work has pointed to women's and girls' vulnerabilities in the home and the workplace; their lower pay and lesser ability to accumulate wealth; their exploitation in times of war and other group conflicts; and the conditions under which an ethos of hyper-masculinity[17] in nations and subgroups controls women's lives. Some of the work of sociologists and of our colleagues in related disciplines has persuaded legislators and judges in many countries to acknowledge the inequalities and harsh treatment girls and women face. Pierre Sané, the Assistant Secretary General of UNESCO, has noted the synergy between social research and human rights activities, and he stresses in international meetings[18] that women's rights must be regarded as human rights and enforced by law.

Let us remember that the "woman question" as a serious point of inquiry for the social sciences is relatively new. In the past, wisdom on this subject came primarily from armchair ideologists, philosophers, legislators, judges, and religious leaders. With few exceptions,[19] these theorists asserted that women's subordinate position was for good reason—divine design, or for those not religiously inclined, *nature* mandated it. Today, a new species of theorists hold to this ideology—fundamentalist leaders in many nations, churches and religious sects in particular—but also scholars, some in the United States, in fields such as sociobiology and evolutionary psychology (e.g., Alexander 1979; Barash 1977; Trivers 1972; Wilson 1975). This was perhaps predictable, if my thesis is correct, because women had started to intrude into male ideological and physical turf in the academy and elsewhere in society, upsetting the practices of male affiliation. The prejudices that pass as everyday common sense also support this ideology, often with backing from sophisticated individuals responsible for making policies that affect girls and women.[20] They have been joined by some well-meaning women social scientists—a few possessing iconic status[21]—who have affirmed stereotypes about females' nature on the basis of poor or no data.[22]

Female Subordination in Global Context

The "woman question" is not just one among many raised by injustice, subordination, and differentiation. It is basic. The denigration and segregation of women is a major mechanism in reinforcing male bonds, protecting the institutions that favor them, and providing the basic work required for societies to function. To ignore this great social divide is to ignore a missing link in social analysis.

I will not illustrate my thesis about the persistence of the worldwide subordination of the female sex with pictures, graphs, or charts. Instead I call on readers' imaginations to picture some of the phenomena that illustrate my thesis. Imagine most women's lifetimes of everyday drudgery in households and factories; of struggles for survival without access to decent jobs. Imagine the horror of mass rapes by armed men in ethnic conflicts, and of rapes that occur inside the home by men who regard sexual access as their right.[23] Imagine also women's isolation and confinement behind walls and veils in many societies. Some examples are harder to imagine—for example, the 100 million women missing in the world, first brought to our attention by the economist Amartya Sen (1990), who alerted us to the bizarre sex ratios in South Asia, West Asia, and China. He pointed to the abandonment and systematic undernourishment of girls and women and to the poor medical care they receive in comparison to males. International human rights groups have alerted us to the selective destruction of female fetuses. It is estimated that in China and India alone, 10,000,000 females were aborted between 1978 and 1998 (Rao 2006). Also hidden are the child brides who live as servants in alien environments and who, should their husbands die, are abandoned to live in poverty and isolation. And there are the millions of girls and women lured or forced into sex work. In the Western world, only the occasional newspaper article brings to view the fact that African women face a 1 in 20 chance of dying during pregnancy (half a million die each year).[24] The persistent segregation of the workplace, in even the most sophisticated societies, in which girls and women labor in sex-labeled jobs that are tedious, mind-numbing, and highly supervised, is out of view. Unseen too are the countless beatings, slights, and defamations women and girls endure from men, including intimates, every day all over the world.

Insistence and Persistence on "Natural Differences"

These patterns are largely explained in the world as consequences stemming from natural causes or God's will. Here, I limit analysis mainly to the view of *natural causation* as the *master narrative*—the narrative that attributes role division of the sexes to biology. Some believe that early socialization cements the distinction. It is clear that strong religious beliefs in the natural subordination of women determine the role women must play in societies.

Biological explanation is the master narrative holding that men and women are naturally different and have different intelligences, physical abilities, and emotional traits. This view asserts that men are naturally suited to dominance and women are naturally submissive. The narrative holds that women's different intellect or emotional makeup is inconsistent with the capacity to work at prestigious jobs, be effective scholars, and lead others. Popularized accounts of gender difference have generated large followings.[25]

But the set of assumptions about basic differences are discredited by a body of reliable research. Although there seems to be an industry of scholarship identifying sex differences, it is important to note that scholarship showing only tiny or fluctuating differences, or none at all, is rarely picked up by the popular press. Most media reports (e.g., Brooks 2006, Tierney 2006) invariably focus on sex differences, following the lead of many journals that report tiny differences in distributions of males and females as significant findings (Epstein 1991a, 1999b). Further, the media rarely report the fact that a good proportion of the studies showing any differences are based on small numbers of college students persuaded to engage in experiments conducted in college laboratories and not in real world situations. Or, in the case of studies indicating the hormonal relationship between men's aggression and women's presumed lack of it, a number of studies are based on the behavior of laboratory animals. Other studies compare test scores of students in college, rarely reporting variables such as the class, race, and ethnicity of the population being studied. Even in these settings, the systematic research of social scientists has proved that males and females show almost no difference or shifting minor differences in measures of cognitive abilities (Hyde 2005) and emotions.[26] And there may be more evidence for similarity than even the scholarly public has access to, because when studies find no differences, the results might not be published in scholarly publications. The Stanford University cognitive psychologist Barbara Tversky (personal communication) notes that when she has sought to publish the results of experiments on a variety of spatial tasks that show no gender differences, journal editors have demanded that she and her collaborators take them out because they are null findings. Even so, we can conclude that under conditions of equality, girls and women perform and achieve at test levels that are the same as or similar to males—and, in many cases, they perform better.[27]

The American Psychological Association has reported officially that males and females are more alike than different when tested on most psychological variables. The APA's finding is based on Janet Hyde's 2005 analysis of 46 meta-analyses conducted recently in the United States. They conclude that gender roles and social context lead to the few differences. Further, they report that sex differences, though believed to be immutable, fluctuate with age and location.[28] Women manifest similar aggressive feelings although their expression of them is obliged to take different forms (Frodi, Macaulay, and Thome 1977). A 2006 report from the National Academy of Sciences found that after an exhaustive review of the scientific literature, including studies of brain structure and function, it could find no evidence of any significant biological factors causing the underrepresentation of women in science and mathematics.[29] Sociologists too have found women's aspirations are linked to their opportunities (Kaufman and Richardson 1982). I observe that like men, women want love, work, and recognition.

So, given similar traits, do women prefer dead-end and limited opportunity jobs; do they wish to work without pay in the home or to be always subject to the authority of men? In the past, some economists thought so. The Nobel Laureate Gary Becker (1981) proposed that women make rational choices to work in the home to free their husbands for paid labor. A number of other scholars follow the rational-choice model to explain women's poorer position in the labor force. Not only has the model proven faulty (England 1989, 1994), but history has proven such ideas wrong. The truth is that men have prevented the incursions of women into their spheres except when they needed women's labor power, such as in wartime, proving that women were indeed a reserve army of labor. As I found in my own research, when windows of opportunity presented themselves, women fought to joint the paid labor force at every level, from manual craft work to the elite professions. Men resisted, seeking to preserve the boundaries of their work domains—from craft unionists to the top strata of medical, legal, and legislative practice (Chafe 1972; Epstein 1970, [1981] 1993; Frank 1980;

Honey 1984; Kessler-Harris 1982; Lorber 1975, 1984; Milkman 1987; O'Farrell 1999; Rupp 1978).

Social and economic changes in other parts of the West, and in other parts of the world, provide natural field experiments to confirm this data from the United States. In the West, where women have always been employed in the unpaid, family workforce, a revolution in women's interest and participation in the paid workplace spiraled after the First World War. In the United States, from 1930 to 1970 the participation of married women ages 35 to 44 in the labor force moved from 10 percent to 46 percent and today it is 77 percent (Goldin 2006). The opening of elite colleges and universities to women students after the 1960s led progressively to their increased participation in employment in the professions and other top jobs. This was the direct result of a concerted effort to use the Civil Rights Act of 1964 to force the opening of these sectors. Ruth Bader Ginsburg and her associates in the Women's Rights Project of the ACLU fought and won important battles in the Supreme Court and Judge Constance Baker Motley, the first African American woman to become a federal judge, ruled that large law firms had to recruit women on the same basis as men to comply with the equal treatment promised by the Civil Rights Act.

Yet even as the ideology of equality became widespread and brought significant changes, the worldwide status of women remained subordinate to that of men. Stable governments and a new prosperity led to something of a revolution in women's statuses in the United States and other countries in the West, notably in Canada with its new charter prohibiting discrimination. There was also an increase in women's employment in the paid labor force in the 15 countries of the European Union, including those countries that traditionally were least likely to provide jobs for women, although the statistics do not reveal the quality of the jobs (Norris 2006). And, of course, women's movements have been instrumental in making poor conditions visible. In countries of the Middle East, the East, and the Global South, women are beginning to have representation in political spheres, the professions, and commerce, although their percentage remains quite small. Women's lot rises or falls as a result of regime changes and economic changes and is always at severe risk.[30] But nowhere are substantial numbers of women in political control; nowhere do women have the opportunity to carry out national agendas giving women truly equal rights.[31]

Structural gains, accompanied by cultural gains, have been considerable in many places. Most governments have signed on to commitments to women's rights, although they are almost meaningless in many regimes that egregiously defy them in practice. And, of course, in many societies women have fewer rights than do men and find themselves worse off than they were a generation ago.[32]

In no society have women had clear access to the best jobs in the workplace, nor have they anywhere achieved economic parity with men. As Charles and Grusky (2004) document in their recent book, *Occupational Ghettos: The Worldwide Segregation of Women and Men,* sex segregation in employment persists all over the world, including in the United States and Canada. Women workers earn less than men even in the most gender-egalitarian societies. Charles and Grusky suggest that the disadvantage in employment is partly because women are clustered in "women's jobs"—jobs in the low-paid service economy or white-collar jobs that do not offer autonomy. These are typically occupational ghettos worldwide. While Charles and Grusky observe that women are crowded into the nonmanual sector, women increasingly do work in the globlized manufacturing economy— for example, in assembly line production that supplies the world with components for computers or in the clothing sweatshops in Chinatowns in the United States and around the world (Bose and Acosta-Belen 1995; Zimmerman, Litt, and Bose 2006; see also Bao 2001; Lee 1998; Salzinger 2003).

Many women in newly industrializing countries experienced a benefit from employment created by transnational corporations in the 1980s and '90s. They received income and independence from their families, but they remained in sex-segregated, low-wage work, subject to cutbacks when corporations sought cheaper labor

markets. As to their suitability for heavy labor, it is common to see (as I have personally witnessed) women hauling rocks and stones in building sites in India and other places. Throughout the world, where water is a scarce commodity it is women who carry heavy buckets and vessels of water, usually on foot and over long distances, because this has been designated as a woman's job and men regard it as a disgrace to help them. Apparently, in much of the world, the guiding principle of essentialism labels as women's jobs those that are not physically easier, necessarily, but rather those that are avoided by men, pay little, and are under the supervision of men.

Of course, women have moved into some male-labeled jobs. As I noted in my book on the consequences of sex boundaries, *Deceptive Distinctions* (1988), the amazing decades of the 1970s and '80s showed that women could do work—men's work— that no one, including themselves, thought they could and they developed interests no one thought they had, and numbers of men welcomed them, or at least tolerated them.

My research shows that women may cross gender barriers into the elite professions that retain their male definition, such as medicine and law (Epstein [1981] 1993), when there is legal support giving them access to training and equal recruitment in combination with a shortage of personnel. Women made their most dramatic gains during a time of rapid economic growth in the Western world.

I first started research on women in the legal profession in the 1960s, when women constituted only 3 percent of practitioners (Epstein [1981] 1993). When I last assessed their achievements (Epstein 2001), women composed about 30 percent of practicing lawyers and about half of all law students. The same striking changes were happening in medicine (they are now almost half of all medical students [Magrane, Lang, and Alexander 2005]), and women were moving into legal and medical specialties once thought to be beyond their interests or aptitudes, such as corporate law and surgery. Yet, even with such advances they face multiple glass ceilings (Epstein et al. 1995). Only small percentages have attained high rank.[33]

And it should come as no surprise that men of high rank,[34] the popular media (Belkin 2003), and right-wing commentators (Brooks 2006; Tierney, 2006) insist that it is women's own choice to limit their aspirations and even to drop out of the labor force. But this has not been women's pattern. Most educated women have continuous work histories. It is true, however, that many women's ambitions to reach the very top of their professions are undermined. For one thing, they generally face male hostility when they cross conventional boundaries and perform "men's work."[35] For another, they face inhospitable environments in male-dominated work settings in which coworkers not only are wary of women's ability but visibly disapprove of their presumed neglect of their families. Women generally face unrelieved burdens of care work in the United States, with few social supports (Coser 1974; Gornick 2003; Williams 2000). And they face norms that this work demands their *personal* attention—a *female's attention.*

Even in the most egalitarian societies, a myriad of subtle prejudices and practices are used by men in gatekeeping positions to limit women's access to the better, male-labeled jobs and ladders of success, for example, partnership tracks in large law firms (Epstein et al. 1995) Alternative routes for women, "Mommy tracks" have been institutionalized—touted as a benefit—but usually result in stalled careers (Bergmann and Helburn 2002). Husbands who wish to limit their own work hours to assist working wives usually encounter severe discrimination as well. Individual men who are seen as undermining the system of male advantage find themselves disciplined and face discrimination (Epstein et al. 1999, Williams 2000). In the United States this may lead to the loss of a promotion or a job. In other places in the world, the consequences are even more dire.[36]

In the current "best of all worlds," ideologies of difference and, to use Charles Tilly's (1998) concept, "exploitation and opportunity hoarding" by men in control keep the top stratum of law and other professions virtually sex segregated. Gatekeepers today don't necessarily limit entry, as that would place them in violation of sex discrimination laws in the United States or put them in an uncomfortable position, given modern Western ideologies of equality. But powerful men move only a small percentage of the able women they hire (often hired in equal numbers with men) upward on the path toward leadership and decision making, especially in professions and occupations experiencing slow growth. Most rationalize, with the approval of conventional wisdom, that women's own decisions determine their poor potential for achieving power.

Inequality in the workplace is created and reinforced by inequality in education. Newspaper headlines reported that more women than men get B.A.s in the United States today (Lewin 2006a) "leaving men in the dust." But a report a few days later noted that the increase is due to older women going back to school, and that women's degrees are in traditional women's fields (Lewin 2006b).

But women's performance and acceptance in the world of higher education in the United States is the good news! Consider the rest of the world. In many countries girls are denied *any* education. Consider, for example, the case of Afghanistan, where the Taliban still are attempting to resume power. In July 2006, they issued warnings to parents that girls going to school may get acid thrown in their faces or be murdered (Coghlan 2006).

Consider that in Southern Asia 23.5 million girls do not attend school and in Central and West Africa virtually half of all girls are also excluded (Villalobos 2006). While poverty contributes to poor educational opportunities for boys as well as girls in many parts of the world, girls' restrictions are far greater. Some fundamentalist societies permit women to get a higher education, but this is to prepare them for work in segregated conditions where they serve other women.

The sex segregation of labor as measured by sophisticated sociologists and economists does not even acknowledge women's labor *outside* the wage-earning structure. Women and girls labor behind the walls of their homes, producing goods that provide income for their families, income they have no control over. Thus, millions of girls and women are not even counted in the labor force, although they perform essential work in the economy (Bose, Feldberg, and Sokoloff 1987).[37]

In addition, females can be regarded as a commodity themselves. They are computed as a means of barter in tribal families that give their girls (often before puberty) to men outside their tribe or clan who want wives to produce children and goods. Men also trade their daughters to men of other tribes as a form of compensation for the killing of a member of another tribe or other reasons.[38] Harmony is re-equilibrated through the bodies of females.

There is much more to report about the roles and position of women in the labor force worldwide—my life's work—but there are other spheres in which females everywhere are mired in subordinate roles. Chief among them are the family and the social and cultural structures that keep women both segregated and in a state of symbolic and actual "otherness," undermining their autonomy and dignity. Nearly everywhere, women are regarded as "others."[39]

Mechanisms Creating "Otherness"

To some extent, women are subject to the process of social speciation—a term that Kai Erikson (1996) introduced (modifying the concept of pseudospeciation offered by Erik Erikson) to refer to the fact that humans divide into various groups who regard themselves as "the foremost species" and then feel that others ought to be kept in their place by "conquest or the force of harsh custom" (Erikson 1996:52). Harsh customs and conquest certainly ensure the subordination of girls and women. I shall consider some of these below.

Kin Structures

In many societies brides are required to leave their birth homes and enter as virtual strangers into the homes of their husbands and their husbands' kin. Because of the practice of patrilocality they usually have few or no resources—human or monetary. Marrying very young, they enter these families with the lowest rank and no social supports. About one in seven girls in the developing world gets married before her 15th birthday according to the Population Council, an international research group (Bearak 2006). Local and international attempts to prevent this practice have been largely unsuccessful.[40]

In exploring the actual and symbolic segregation of women I have been inspired by the work of Mounira Charrad in her 2001 prize-winning book *States and Women's Rights: The Making of Postcolonial Tunisia, Algeria, and Morocco*. The work of Val Moghadam (2003) and Roger Friedland (2002) also informs this analysis. Writing of the relative status of women, Charrad points to the iron grip of patrilineal kin groups in North African societies. She notes how Islamic family law has legitimized the extended male-centered patrilineage that serves as the foundation of kin-based solidarities within tribal groups so that state politics and tribal politics converge. This supports the patriarchal power not only of husbands, but also of all male kin over women so that the clan defines its boundaries through a family law that rests on the exploitation of women. Her study shows how Islamic family law (Sharia) provides a meaningful symbol of national unity in the countries of the Maghreb. This has changed in Tunisia, but it remains the case for other societies—Iraq, Saudi Arabia, Jordan, Kuwait, Afghanistan, southeastern Turkey, parts of Iran, and southern Egypt. As Moghadam (2003) points out, the gender dimension of the Afghan conflict is prototypical of other conflicts today. During periods of strife, segregation and subordination of women becomes a sign of cultural identity. We see it clearly in the ideologies of Hamas and Hezbollah, Iran, Chechnya, and other Islamic groups and societies, and in the ideologies of fundamentalist Christian and Jewish groups. Representations of women are deployed during processes of revolution and state building to preserve group boundaries within larger societies with competing ideologies, and when power is being reconstituted, linking women either to modernization and progress or to cultural rejuvenation and religious orthodoxy.

Few social scientists have paid attention to the role of kin structures and their accompanying conceptual structures in the minds of players in national and international politics, but I believe this negligence persists at our peril as we experience conflicts between kin-based collectivities in the world.

Of course, human sexuality has much to do with the cultural sex divide. The fact that men desire women sexually, and that women also desire men, means that they are destined to live together no matter what the culture and family structures in which they live. And sexuality could, and can, create equality through bonds of connection and affection. As William Goode (1959) points out in an important but perhaps forgotten paper, "The Theoretical Importance of Love," love is a universal emotion. As such it threatens social structures because the ties between men and women could be stronger than the bonds between men. Thus, everywhere the affiliations made possible by love are contained in various ways.

In societies in which marriage is embedded in a larger kin structure beyond the nuclear family, the practices and rules of domicile and the conventions around it have the potential to undermine the possibility of a truly affective marital tie, one that could integrate women in the society. A couple may face a wall of separation—apartheid in the home in separate parts of the compound or house. Or, they may be community-bound or home-bound in fundamentalist religious groups within larger secular societies such as the United States (e.g., the Jewish Satmar community in New York [where women are not permitted to drive] [Winston 2005] or some Christian fundamentalist communities where women are required to home-school their children).

I shall now focus on some other symbolic uses of sex distinctions that facilitate the subordination of women.

Honor

Females are designated as carriers of honor in many societies. Their "virtue" is a symbolic marker of men's group boundaries. As we know from Mary Douglas (1966) and others, we can think about any social practice in terms of purity and danger. In many societies, females are the designated carriers of boundary distinctions. Their conformity to norms is regarded as the representation of the dignity of the group, while males typically have much greater latitude to engage in deviant behavior. To achieve and maintain female

purity, women's behavior is closely monitored and restricted. As Friedland (2002) writes, religious nationalists direct "their attention to the bodies of women—covering, separating and regulating" (p. 396) them, in order "to masculinize the public sphere, to contain the erotic energies of heterosexuality within the family seeking to masculinize collective representations, to make the state male, a virile collective subject, the public status of women's bodies is a critical site and source for religious nationalist political mobilization" (p. 401).

The idea that girls must remain virgins until they marry or their entire family will suffer dishonor is used as a mechanism for women's segregation and subordination all over the world. It is also used as justification for the murder of many young women by male family members claiming to cleanse the girls' supposed dishonor from the family.[41] In particular, we see this at play in parts of the Middle East and among some Muslim communities in the diaspora.

When a woman strays from her prescribed roles, seeks autonomy, or is believed to have had sex with a man outside of marriage, killing her is regarded as a reasonable response by her very own relatives, often a father or brother. In Iraq, at last count, since the beginning of the present war, there have been 2,000 honor killings (Tarabay 2006), and United Nations officials estimate 5,000 worldwide (BBC 2003). In the summer of 2006, the *New York Times* reported that in Turkey, a society becoming more religiously conservative, girls regarded as errant because they moved out of the control of their parents or chose a boyfriend, thus casting dishonor on the family, are put in situations in which they are expected and pressured to commit suicide. Suicide spares a family the obligation to murder her and face prosecution (Bilefsky 2006). Elsewhere, such murders are barely noted by the police.

Female circumcision is also intended to preserve women's honor. In many areas of the African continent, girls are subjected to genital cutting as a prelude to marriage and as a technique to keep them from having pleasure during sex, which, it is reasoned, may lead them to an independent choice of mate.

Conferring on women the symbolism of sexual purity as a basis of honor contributes to their vulnerability. In today's genocidal warfare, the mass rape of women by marauding forces is not just due to the sexual availability of conquered women. Rape is used as a mechanism of degradation. If the men involved in the Bosnian and Darfur massacres regarded rape as an atrocity and a *dishonor* to their cause, it could not have been used so successfully as a tool of war. Further, we know that the Bosnian and Sudanese rape victims, like women who have been raped in Pakistan, India, and other places, are regarded as defiled and are shunned, as are the babies born of such rapes.

Clothing as a Symbolic Tool for Differentiation

The chador and veil are tools men use to symbolize and maintain women's honor. Although men, with some exceptions,[42] wear Western dress in much of the world, women's clothing is used to symbolize their cultures' confrontations with modernity, in addition to clothing's symbolic roles. Presumably worn to assure modesty and to protect women's honor, the clothing prescribed, even cultural relativists must admit, serves to restrict women's mobility. Hot and uncomfortable, women cannot perform tasks that require speed and mobility, and it prevents women from using motorbikes and bicycles, the basic means of transportation in poor societies. Distinctive clothing is not restricted to the Third World. Fundamentalist groups in Europe and the United States also mandate clothing restrictions for women.[43]

Of course, clothing is used to differentiate women and men in all societies. In the past, Western women's clothing was also restrictive (e.g., long skirts and corsets) and today, as women have moved toward greater equality, women and men are permitted to wear similar garb (such as jeans and t-shirts). Of course, fashion prescribes more sexually evocative (thus distinctive) clothing for women than it does for men.

Time and Space

How can we speak of the otherness and subordination of women without noting the power of the variables of time and space in the analysis? In every society the norms governing the use of time and space are gendered (Epstein and Kalleberg 2004). People internalize feelings about the proper use of time and space as a result of the normative structure. Worldwide, the boundaries of time and space are constructed to offer men freedom and to restrict women's choices. In most of the world, women rise earlier than do men and start food preparation; they eat at times men don't. Further, sex segregation of work in and outside the home means a couple's primary contact may be in the bedroom. If women intrude on men's space they may violate a taboo and be punished for it. Similarly, men who enter into women's spaces do so only at designated times and places. The taboo elements undermine the possibility of easy interaction, the opportunity to forge friendships, to connect, and to create similar competencies. In the Western world, working different shifts is common (Presser 2003), which also results in segregation of men and women.

There are rules in every society, some by law and others by custom, that specify when and where women may go, and whether they can make these journeys alone or must appear with a male relative. Some segregation is to protect men from women's temptations (e.g., Saudi Arabia, Iran, the Satmar sect in Monsey, NY) and some to protect women from men's sexual advances (e.g., Mexico, Tokyo, Mumbai). But the consequence is that men overwhelmingly are allotted more space and territorialize public space.

A common variable in the time prescription for women is surveillance; women are constrained to operate within what I am calling *role zones*. In these, their time is accounted for and prescribed. They have less *free* time. In our own Western society, women note that the first thing to go when they attempt to work and have children is "free time." Free time is typically enjoyed by the powerful, and it gives them the opportunity to engage in the politics of social life. Most people who work at a subsistence level, refugees, and those who labor in jobs not protected by the authority of the dominant group, don't have free time either. Slave owners own the time of their slaves.

A Theory of Female Subordination

All of this leads me to ask a basic sociological question. Why does the subordination of women and girls persist no matter how societies change in other ways? How does half the world's population manage to hold and retain power over the other half? And what are we to make of the women who comply?

The answers lie in many of the practices I have described and they remain persuasive with a global perspective. I propose an even more basic explanation for the persistence of inequality, and often a reversion to inequality, when equality seems to be possible or near attainment. In *Deceptive Distinctions* (1988) I proposed the theory that the division of labor in society assigns women the most important survival tasks—reproduction and gathering and preparation of food. All over the world, women do much of the reproductive work, ensuring the continuity of society. They do this both in physical terms and in symbolic terms. Physically, they do so through childbirth and child care. They do much of the daily work any social group needs for survival. For example, half of the world's food, and up to 80 percent in developing countries, is produced by women (Food and Agriculture Organization of the United Nations n.d.; Women's World Summit Foundation 2006). They also prepare the food at home, work in the supermarkets, behind the counters, and on the conveyor belts that package it. In their homes and in schools, they produce most preschool and primary school education. They take care of the elderly and infirm. They socialize their children in the social skills that make interpersonal communication possible. They are the support staffs for men. This is a good deal—no, a great deal—for the men.

Controlling women's labor and behavior is a mechanism for male governance and territoriality. Men's authority is held jealously. Men legitimate their behavior through ideological and theological constructs that justify their domination. Further, social institutions reinforce this.[44]

I shall review the mechanisms:

We know about the use and threat of force (Goode 1972).[45] We know as well about the role of law and justice systems that do not accord women the same rights to protection, property, wealth, or even education enjoyed by men. We know that men control and own guns and the means of transport, and they often lock women out of membership and leadership of trade unions, political parties, religious institutions, and other powerful organizations. We know too that huge numbers of men feel justified in threatening and punishing females who deviate from male-mandated rules in public and private spaces. That's the strong-arm stuff.

But everywhere, in the West as well as in the rest of the world, women's segregation and subjugation is also done *culturally* and through *cognitive* mechanisms that reinforce existing divisions of rights and labor and award men authority over women. Internalized cultural schemas reinforce men's views that their behavior is legitimate and persuade women that their lot is just. The media highlight the idea that women and men think differently and naturally gravitate to their social roles.[46] This is more than just "pluralistic ignorance" (Merton [1948] 1963). Bourdieu ([1979] 1984) reminds us that dominated groups often contribute to their own subordination because of perceptions shaped by the conditions of their existence—the dominant system made of binary oppositions! Using Eviatar Zerubavel's (1997) term, "mindscapes" set the stage for household authorities and heads of clans, tribes, and communities to separate and segregate women in the belief that the practice is inevitable and right. Such mindscapes also persuade the females in their midst to accept the legitimacy and inevitability of their subjection, and even to defend it, as we have seen lately in some academic discourses.

The mindscapes that legitimate women's segregation are the cognitive translations of ideologies that range the spectrum from radical fundamentalism to difference feminism; all are grounded in cultural-religious or pseudoscientific views that women have different emotions, brains, aptitudes, ways of thinking, conversing, and imagining. Such mindsets are legitimated every day in conventional understandings expressed from the media, pulpits, boardrooms, and in departments of universities. Psychologists call them schemas (Brewer and Nakamura 1984)—culturally set definitions that people internalize. Gender operates as a cultural "superschema" (Roos and Gatta 2006) that shapes interaction and cues stereotypes (Ridgeway 1997). Schemas that define femaleness and maleness are basic to all societies. Schemas also define insiders and outsiders and provide definitions of justice and equality.

In popular speech, philosophical musings, cultural expressions, and the banter of everyday conversation, people tend to accept the notion of difference. They accept its inevitability and are persuaded of the legitimacy of segregation, actual or symbolic. Thus, acceptance of difference perspectives—the idea that women often have little to offer to the group, may result in rules that forbid women from speaking in the company of men (in a society governed by the Taliban) or may result in senior academics' selective deafness to the contributions of a female colleague in a university committee room.

Conclusion

In conclusion I want to reiterate certain observations:

Intrinsic qualities are attributed to women that have little or nothing to do with their actual characteristics or behavior. Because those attributions are linked to assigned roles their legitimation is an ongoing project. Changing these ideas would create possibilities for changing the status quo and threaten the social institutions in which men have the greatest stake and in which some women believe they benefit.

Is women's situation different from that of men who, by fortune, color of skin, or accident of birth also suffer from exploitation by the powerful? I am claiming *yes,* because they carry not only the hardships—sometimes relative hardships—but the ideological and cognitive overlay that defines their subordination as legitimate and normal. Sex and gender are the organizing markers in all societies. In no country, political group, or community are men defined as lesser human beings than their *female* counterparts. But almost everywhere women are so defined.

Why is this acceptable? And why does it persist?

So many resources are directed to legitimating females' lower place in society. So few men inside the power structure are interested in inviting them in. And so many women and girls accept the Orwellian notion that restriction is freedom, that suffering is pleasure, that silence is power.[47]

Of course this is not a static condition, nor, I hope, an inevitable one. Women in the Western world, and in various sectors of the rest of the world, have certainly moved upward in the continuum toward equality. Thirty-five years ago I noted how women in the legal profession in the United States were excluded from the informal networks that made inclusion and mobility possible. Now, noticeable numbers have ventured over the barriers. Similarly, there has been a large increase in the numbers of women who have entered the sciences,[48] business, medicine, and veterinary medicine (Cox and Alm 2005). This has changed relatively swiftly. Women didn't develop larger brains—nor did their reasoning jump from left brain to right brain or the reverse. Nor did they leave Venus for Mars. Rather, they learned that they could not be barred from higher education and they could get appropriate jobs when they graduated. The problem is no longer one of qualifications or entry but of promotion and inclusion into the informal networks leading to the top. But the obstacles are great.

In his review of cognitive sociological dynamics, DiMaggio (1997) reminds us of Merton's notion of "pluralistic ignorance," which is at work when people act with reference to shared collective opinions that are empirically incorrect. There would not be a firm basis for the subordinate condition of females were there not a widespread belief, rooted in folk culture, in their essential difference from males in ability and emotion. This has been proven time and time again in research in the "real" world of work and family institutions (e.g., Epstein et al. 1995) and laboratory observations (Berger, Cohen, and Zelditch 1966; Frodi et al. 1977; Ridgeway and Smith-Lovin 1999).

We know full well that there are stories and master social narratives accepted by untold millions of people that have no basis in what social scientists would regard as evidence. The best examples are the basic texts of the world's great religions. But there are also societywide beliefs of other kinds. Belief systems are powerful. And beliefs that are unprovable or proven untrue often capture the greatest number of believers. Sometimes, they are simply the best stories.

We in the social sciences have opened the gates to a better understanding of the processes by which subordinated groups suffer because the use of *categories* such as race and ethnicity rank human beings so as to subordinate, exclude, and exploit them (Tilly 1998). However, relatively few extend this insight to the category of gender or sex. The sexual divide so defines social life, and so many people in the world have a stake in upholding it, that it is the most resistant of all categories to change. Today, Hall and Lamont (forthcoming; Lamont 2005) are proposing that the most productive societies are those with porous boundaries between categories of people. Perhaps there is an important incentive in a wider understanding of this idea. Small groups of men may prosper by stifling women's potential, but prosperous nations benefit from women's full participation and productivity in societies. Societies might achieve still more if the gates were truly open.

Sociologists historically have been committed to social change to achieve greater equality in the world, in both public and private lives. But in this address I challenge our profession to take this responsibility in our scholarship and our professional lives; to observe, to reveal, and to strike down the conceptual and cultural walls that justify inequality on the basis of sex in all of society's institutions—to transgress this ever-present boundary—for the sake of knowledge and justice.

Acknowlegdments

Direct correspondence to Cynthia Fuchs Epstein, Department of Sociology, Graduate Center, City University of New York, 365 Fifth Avenue, New York, NY 10016 (cepstein@gc.cuny.edu). I thank Mitra Rastegar for superb research assistance. I am grateful also to Howard Epstein for dedicated editorial help over many incarnations of this paper and to Kathleen Gerson, Jerry Jacobs, Brigid O'Farrell, Valentine Moghadam, Carol Sanger, and Hella Winston for helpful comments on versions of the address to the ASA.

Notes

1. Brubaker also cites the contributions of Rothbart and Taylor 1992; Hirshfield 1996; and Gil-White 1999 to this perspective.
2. Duster (2006) does include gender.
3. For example, see Epstein 1988; Lorber 1994; Connell 1987; Ridgeway 2006; Bussey and Bandura 1999; Tavris 1992.
4. I have used these commonly used terms, but alternative words such as "trans" and "intersex" are deemed more appropriate by some scholars and advocates.
5. I offer this concept following Becker (1963) who writes of "moral entrepreneurs;" Brubacker (2004) who writes of "ethnopolitical entrepreneurs;" and Fine (1996) who writes of "reputational entrepreneurs."
6. A number of sociologists have specifically called for a greater integration of feminist theory and studies within the mainstream of American sociology (e.g., Chafetz 1984, 1997; Laslett 1996; Stacey and Thome 1985).
7. I am not the first to make this plea (e.g., see Acker 1973; Blumberg 1978; Chafetz 1997).
8. There is, of course, a growing body of scholarship on women of color. See for example, Baca Zinn and Dill (1996); Collins (1998); and Hondagneu-Sotelo (2003).
9. Martin (2004) and Lorber (1994) both consider gender to be a social institution.
10. The most obvious example is the right to have an abortion, which through *Roe v. Wade* (1973) withdrew from the states the power to prohibit abortions during the first six months of pregnancy. In 1989, *Webster* v. *Reproductive Health Services* gave some of that power back. Since that time, President Bush and other legislators proposed a constitutional amendment banning abortions, giving fetuses more legal rights than women. This remains a deeply contested issue in American politics (Kaminer 1990). The National Women's Law Center has expressed concern that the current

Supreme Court cannot be counted on to preserve women's "hard-won legal gains, especially in the areas of constitutional rights to privacy and equal protection" (2006). In many other places in the world women are not protected by their governments. In 2005, the World Health Organization found that domestic and sexual violence is widespread. Amnesty International reports tens of thousands of women are subjected to domestic violence, giving as examples Republic of Georgia and Bangladesh where, when women go to the authorities after being strangled, beaten, or stabbed, they are told to reconcile with their husbands (Lew and Moawad 2006).

11. Information from ASA: http://www.asanet.org/governance/pastpres.html. The current president, Frances Fox Piven, brings the number of women presidents to 10 in 102 years.

12. It is curious that his further observation that the relationship was also "an important source of strain" (p. 191) has rarely been acknowledged, although Friedan did note this in *The Feminine Mystique.*

13. These include (but of course, the list is incomplete) John Stuart Mill and Harriet Taylor, Mary Wollstonecraft, Elizabeth Cady Stanton, Lucretia Mott, Sojourner Truth, Charlotte Perkins Gilman, Emmeline Pankhurst, W.E.B. DuBois, Emma Goldman, and in the years just preceding Friedan's book, Simone de Beauvoir (1949), to whom she dedicated *The Feminine Mystique,* and Mirra Komarovsky (1946; [1953] 2004).

14. I interviewed Friedan in 1999 about the origins of NOW for an article I was writing for *Dissent* (Epstein 1999a).

15. One was Gloria Steinem, who worked with Friedan to establish the National Women's Political Caucus. Steinem became a notable public speaker on behalf of women's rights and established the national magazine *MS.,* which reports on serious women's issues.

16. Friedan recruited me as well in the formation of the New York City Chapter of NOW in 1966. Through her auspices I presented a paper on the negative social consequences for women of segregated help-wanted ads in newspapers at hearings of the EEOC in 1967 on Guidelines for Title VII of the Civil Rights Act and to establish guidelines for the Office of Federal Contract Compliance in 1968.

17. For work on men see especially the work of Kimmel (1996); Connell (1987); Collinson, Knights, and Collinson (1990); and Collinson and Hearn (1994).

18. The most recent was The International Forum on the Social Science-Policy Nexus in Buenos Aires February 20 to 24, 2006.

19. For example, John Stuart Mill (1869) *The Subjection of Women.*

20. A pinpointed policy was enacted recently. Seeking to override a 1972 federal law barring sex discrimination in education (Title IX of the Civil Rights Act of 1964), the Bush administration is giving public school districts new latitude to expand the number of single-sex classes and single-sex schools (Schemo 2006). My own review of studies on the impact of segregated education shows no benefits (Epstein 1997; Epstein and Gambs 2001).

21. Here I refer to a number of "standpoint" theorists such as Belenky et al. (1986), Smith (1990), Hartstock (1998), and of course Carol Gilligan (1982) whose initial study showing a difference in boys' and girls' moral values and moral development was based on eight girls and eight boys in a local school and 27 women considering whether to have an abortion. See also Helen Fisher (1982), an evolutionary anthropologist. These views typically assert that women are naturally more caring, more accommodating, and averse to conflict.

22. See my analysis of this literature in Epstein (1988).

23. For more horrors see Parrot and Cummings (2006).

24. Perhaps the best known eye into this world is that of Nicholas Kristof, the *New York Times* writer, whose Op Ed articles chronicle the horrors faced by women in Africa and the inaction of Western societies to redress them (for example, the United States cut off funding to the United Nations Population Fund, an agency that has led the effort to reduce maternal deaths, because of false allegations it supports abortion) (Kristof 2006).

25. The works of John Gray (1992), the author of *Men Are from Mars, Women Are from Venus* and spin-off titles have sold over 30 million copies in the United States. See also Deborah Tannen's (1990) *You Just Don't Understand* on the presumed inability of men and women to understand each other

on various dimensions, repudiated by the work of the linguistic scholar Elizabeth Aries (1996).

26. There has been a recent flurry over reported differences in male and female brains (cf. Brizendine 2006; Bell et al. 2006) and reports of a 3 to 4 percentage difference in IQ. The brain studies are usually based on very small samples and the IQ studies on standardized tests in which the differences reported are at the very end of large distributions that essentially confirm male/female similarities (see Epstein 1988 for a further analysis).

27. A 2006 *New York Times* report shows that women are getting more B.A.s than are men in the United States. However, in the highest income families, men age 24 and below attend college as much as, or slightly more than their sisters, according to the American Council on Education. The article also reports that women are obtaining a disproportionate number of honors at elite institutions such as Harvard, the University of Wisconsin, UCLA, and some smaller schools such as Florida Atlanta University (Lewin 2006a). A comparison of female and male math scores varies with the test given. Females score somewhat lower on the SAT-M but differences do not exist on the American College Test (ACT) or on untimed versions of the SAT-M (Bailey n.d.).

28. Girls even perform identically in math until high school when they are channeled on different tracks. In Great Britain, they do better than males, as noted in the ASA statement contesting the remarks of then Harvard President Lawrence Summers questioning the ability of females to engage in mathematics and scientific research (American Sociological Association 2005; see also Boaler and Sengupta-Irving 2006).

29. The panel blamed environments that favor men, continuous questioning of women's abilities and commitment to an academic career, and a system that claims to reward based on merit but instead rewards traits that are socially less acceptable for women to possess (Fogg 2006).

30. Hartmann, Lovell, and Werschkul (2004) show how, in the recession of March to November 2001, there was sustained job loss for women for the first time in 40 years. The economic downturn affected women's employment, labor force participation, and wages 43 months after the start of the recession.

31. In Scandinavian countries, women have achieved the most political representation: Finland (37.5 percent of parliament seats), Norway (36.4 percent of parliament seats), Sweden (45.3 percent of parliament seats), and Denmark (38 percent of parliament seats) (U.N. Common Database 2004; Dahlerup n.d.). Of course, women in some societies still do not have the right to vote, and in a few, like Kuwait, where they have just gotten the vote, it is unclear whether they have been able to exercise it independently.

32. This is the case in Egypt, Iran, Iraq, Gaza, and Lebanon as fundamentalist groups have gained power, even in those regimes that are formally secular.

33. The current figure for women partners in large law firms (those with more than 250 lawyers) in the United States is 17 percent, although women are one-half of the recruits in these firms (National Association for Law Placement cited in O'Brien 2006; Nicholson 2006).

34. A national survey of 1,500 professors (as yet unpublished) at all kinds of institutions in the United States conducted by Neil Gross of Harvard and Solon Simmons of George Mason University shows that most professors don't agree that discrimination—intentional or otherwise—is the main reason that men hold so many more positions than do women in the sciences (Jaschik 2006).

35. In studies of jobs dominated by men that are seen as requiring traits that distinguish men as superior to women in intellect or strength, it is reported that men's pride is punctured if women perform them (see Chetkovich 1997 on firefighters; Collinson, Knights, and Collinson 1990 on managers).

36. For example, when the magazine publisher Ali Mohaqeq returned to Afghanistan in 2004 after a long exile he was imprisoned for raising questions about women's rights in the new "democracy." Afghan courts claimed his offense was to contravene the teachings of Islam by printing essays that questioned legal discrimination against women (Witte 2005).

37. Women have been unpaid workers on family farms or in small businesses, taking in boarders, and doing factory outwork (see Bose et al. 1987 for the United States; Bose and Acosta-Belén 1995 for Latin America; and Hsiung 1996 for Taiwan).

38. There are numerous references on the Web to the use of women given in marriage to another tribe or group in the reports of Amnesty International, for example in Papua New Guinea, Afghanistan, Pakistan, and Fiji.

39. The characterization of women as "other" was most notably made by Simone de Beauvoir ([1949] 1993) in her book, *The Second Sex.*

40. Struggles between human rights activists in and out of government and fundamentalist regimes have shifted upward and downward on such matters as raising the age of marriage of girls. For example, attempts by Afghanistan's King Abanullah in the 1920s to raise the age of marriage and institute education for girls enraged the patriarchal tribes who thwarted his regime. Fifty years later a socialist government enacted legislation to change family law to encourage women's employment, education, and choice of spouse. The regime failed in the early 1990s due to internal rivalries and a hostile international climate (Moghadam 2003:270) and the Taliban took power. In the early 1990s they exiled women to their homes, denied them access to education and opportunities to work for pay, and even denied them the right to look out of their windows.

41. A United Nations (2002) report found that there were legislative provisions "allowing for partial or complete defense" in the case of an honor killing in: Argentina, Bangladesh, Ecuador, Egypt, Guatemala, Iran, Israel, Jordan, Lebanon, Peru, Syria, Turkey, Venezuela, and the Palestinian National Authority (of course law does not equal practice). For example, in Pakistan and Jordan honor killings are outlawed but they occur nevertheless.

42. In demonstrations in societies led by religious leaders, men typically wear Western style shirts and trousers although their leaders typically choose clerics' robes and turbans. Leaders of countries outside the "Western" orbit often choose distinctive dress—robes, beards, open neck shirts, and other costumes for ceremonial occasions or to make political statements.

43. Hella Winston (personal communication, September 30, 2006) told me that in the orthodox Jewish community of New Square in New York State, a recent edict by the Rabbi reminded women they were to wear modest dress, specifying that "sleeves must be to the end of the bone, and [to] not wear narrow clothing or short clothing." They were not to ride bikes or speak loudly.

44. Where religious laws govern such areas of civic life as family relations, inheritance, and punishment for crimes, for example, they invariably institutionalize women's subordinate status.

45. As one of many possible examples: when hundreds of women gathered in downtown Tehran on July 31, 2006 to protest institutionalized sex discrimination in Iran (in areas such as divorce, child custody, employment rights, age of adulthood, and court proceedings where a woman's testimony is viewed as half of a man's), 100 male and female police beat them. Reports also noted a tightening of the dress code and segregation on buses and in some public areas such as parks, sidewalks, and elevators. Another demonstration on March 8, 2006 was dispersed as police dumped garbage on the heads of participants (Stevens 2006).

46. The recent book by Louann Brizendine (2006), which asserts that the female and male brains are completely different, offering such breezy accounts as "woman is weather, constantly changing and hard to predict" and "man is mountain," has been on the top 10 on the Amazon.com book list and led to her prominent placement on ABC's 20/20 and morning talk shows. Thanks to Troy Duster for passing this on.

47. For example, a recent poll cited in the *New York Times* (June 8, 2006) indicates that a majority of women in Muslim countries do not regard themselves as unequal (Andrews 2006). Of course, this attitude is widespread throughout the world, including Western societies.

48. Comparing percentages of women attaining doctorates in the sciences from 1970–71 to 2001–2002 the increases were: Engineering .2–17.3; Physics 2.9–15.5; Computer Science 2.3–22.8; Mathematics 7.6–29.

References

Acker, Joan. 1973. "Women and Social Stratification: A Case of Institutional Sexism." Pp. 174–82 in *Changing Women in a Changing Society,* edited by Joan Huber. Chicago, IL: University of Chicago Press.

Alexander, Richard D. 1979. *Darwinism and Human Affairs.* Seattle, WA: University of Washington Press.

American Sociological Association. 2005. "ASA Council Statement on the Causes of Gender Differences in Science and Math Career Achievement" (February 28). Retrieved September 21, 2006 (http://www2.asanet.org/footnotes/mar05/indexthree.html).

Andrews, Helena. 2006. "Muslim Women Don't See Themselves as Oppressed, Survey Finds." *New York Times,* June 7, p. A9.

Aries, Elizabeth. 1996. *Men and Women in Interaction: Reconsidering the Differences.* New York: Oxford University Press.

Baca Zinn, Maxine and Bonnie Thornton Dill. 1996. "Theorizing Difference from Multiracial Feminism." *Feminist Studies* 22:321–31.

Bailey, Justin P. N. d. "Men are from Earth, Women are from Earth: Rethinking the Utility of the Mars/Venus Analogy." Retrieved September 28, 2006 (www.framingham.edu/joct/pdf/J.Bailey.1.pdf).

Bao, Xiaolan. 2001. *Holding Up More Than Half the Sky: Chinese Women Garment Workers in New York City, 1948–92.* Urbana, IL and Chicago, IL: University of Illinois Press.

Barash, David P. 1977. *Sociobiology and Behavior.* New York: Elsevier.

Barth, Frederik, 1969. "Introduction." Pp. 9–38 in *Ethnic Groups and Boundaries: The Social Organization of Cultural Difference,* edited by Frederik Barth. London, England: Allen & Unwin.

Basow, Susan A. 1995. "Student Evaluation of College Professors: When Gender Matters." *Journal of Educational Psychology* 87:656–65.

BBC. 2003. "Speaking Out Over Jordan 'Honour Killings.'" Retrieved September 21, 2006 (http://news.bbc.co.uk/2/hi/middle_east/2802305.stm).

Bearak, Barry. 2006. "The Bride Price." *New York Times Magazine,* July 9, p. 45.

Beauvoir.Simone de. [1949] 1993. *The Second Sex.* New York: Alfred A. Knopf.

Becker, Gary. 1981. *A Treatise on the Family.* Cambridge, MA: Harvard University Press.

Becker, Howard. 1963. *Outsiders: Studies in the Sociology of Deviance.* New York: The Free Press.

Belenky, Mary Field, Blythe Clinchy, Nancy Goldberger, and Jill Tarule. 1986. *Women's Ways of Knowing: The Development of Self, Voice, and Mind.* New York: Basic Books.

Belkin, Lisa. 2003. "The Opt-Out Revolution." *New York Times Magazine,* October 26, p. 42.

Bell, Emily C., Morgan C. Willson, Alan H. Wilman, Sanjay Dave, and Peter H. Silverstone. 2006. "Males and Females Differ in Brain Activation During Cognitive Tasks." *NeuroImage* 30:529–38.

Berger, Joseph, Bernard P. Cohen, and Morris Zelditch Jr. 1966. "Status Characteristics and Expectation States." Pp. 29–46 in *Sociological Theories in Progress,* vol. I, edited by Joseph Berger, Morris Zelditch Jr., and Bo Anderson. Boston, MA: Houghton Mifflin.

Bergmann, Barbara R. and Suzanne Helburn. 2002. *America's Child Care Problem: The Way Out.* New York: Palgrave, St. Martin's Press.

Bilefsky, Dan. 2006. "How to Avoid Honor Killing in Turkey? Honor Suicide." *New York Times,* July 16 section 1, p. 3.

Blumberg, Rae Lesser. 1978. *Stratification: Socioeconomic and Sexual Inequality.* Dubuque, IA: Brown.

Boaler, Jo and Tesha Sengupta-Irving. 2006. "Nature, Neglect & Nuance: Changing Accounts of Sex, Gender and Mathematics." Pp. 207–20 in *Gender and Education, International Handbook,* edited by C. Skelton and L. Smulyan. London, England: Sage.

Bose, Christine E. and Edna Acosta-Belén. 1995. *Women in the Latin American Development Process.* Philadelphia, PA: Temple University Press.

Bose, Christine E., Roslyn Feldberg, and Natalie Sokolof. 1987. *Hidden Aspects of Women's Work.* New York: Praeger.

Bourdieu, Pierre. [1979] 1984. *Distinctions: A Social Critique of the Judgment of Taste.* Cambridge, MA: Harvard University Press.

———. 1991. "Identity and Representation: Elements for a Critical Reflection on the Idea of Region." Pp. 220–28 in *The Logic of Practice,* edited by P. Bourdieu. Stanford, CA: Stanford University Press.

Brewer, William F. and Glenn Nakamura. 1984. "The Nature and Functions of Schemas." Pp. 119–60 in *Handbook of Social Cognition,* vol. 1, edited by R. S. Wyer and T. K. Srull. Hillsdale, NJ: Erlbaum.

Brizendine, Louann. 2006. *The Female Brain.* New York: Morgan Road Books.

Brooks, David. 2006. "The Gender Gap at School." *New York Times,* June 11, section 4, p. 12.

Brubaker, Rogers. 2004. *Ethnicity Without Groups.* Cambridge, MA: Harvard University Press.

Bruner, Jerome. 1990. *Acts of Meaning: Four Lectures on Mind and Culture.* Cambridge, MA: Harvard University Press.

Bussey, Kay and Albert Bandura. 1999. "Social Cognitive Theory of Gender Development and Differentiation." *Psychological Review* 106:676–713.

Butler, Judith. 1990. *Gender Trouble.* New York: Routledge.

Chafe, William H. 1972. *The American Woman: Her Changing Social, Economic and Political Roles: 1920–1970.* Oxford, England: Oxford University Press.

Chafetz, Janet Saltzman. 1984. *Sex and Advantage: A Comparative Macro-Structural Theory of Sex Stratification.* Totowa, NJ: Roman & Allanhyeld.

———. 1997. "Feminist Theory and Sociology: Underutilized Contribution for Mainstream Theory." *Annual Review of Sociology* 23:97–120.

Charles, Maria and David Grusky. 2004. *Occupational Ghettos: The Worldwide Segregation of Women and Men.* Stanford, CA: Stanford University Press.

Charred, Mounira. 2001. *States and Women's Rights: The Making of Postcolonial Tunisia, Algeria and Morocco.* Berkeley, CA: The University of California Press.

Chetkovich, Carol. 1997. *Real Heat: Gender and Race in the Urban Fire Service.* New York: Routledge.

Coghlan, Tom. 2006. "Taliban Use Beheadings and Beatings to Keep Afghanistan's Schools Closed." *The Independent,* July 11. Retrieved July 11, 2006 (http://news.independent.co.uk/world/asia/article1171369.ece).

Collins, Patricia Hill. 1998. *Fighting Words: Black Women and the Search for Justice.* Minneapolis, MN: University of Minnesota Press.

Collinson, David L. and Jeff Hearn. 1994. "Naming Men as Men: Implications for Work, Organization and Management" *Gender, Work and Organization* 1:2–22.

Collinson, David L., David Knights, and Margaret Collinson. 1990. *Managing to Discriminate.* London, England: Routledge.

Connell, R. W. 1987. *Gender and Power: Society, the Person and Sexual Politics.* Stanford, CA: Stanford University Press.

Coser, Rose Laub. 1974. "Stay Home Little Sheba: On Placement, Displacement and Social Change." *Social Problems* 22:470–80.

Cox, W. Michael and Richard Alm. 2005. "Scientists are Made, Not Born." *New York Times,* February 25, p. A25.

Dahlerup, Drude. N.d. "The World of Quotas." *Women in Politics: Beyond Numbers.* International Institute for Democracy and Electoral Assistance. Retrieved September 21, 2006 (http://archive.idea.int/women/parl/ch4c.htm).

DiMaggio, Paul. 1997. "Culture and Cognition." *Annual Review of Sociology* 23:263–87.

Douglas, Mary. 1966. *Purity and Danger: An Analysis of Concepts of Pollution and Taboo.* London, England: Routledge & Keegan Paul.

Duster, Troy. 2006. "Comparative Perspectives and Competing Explanations: Taking on the Newly Configured Reductionist Challenge to Sociology." *American Sociological Review* 71:1–15.

England, Paula. 1989. "A Feminist Critique of Rational-Choice Theories: Implications for Sociology." *The American Sociologist* 20:14–28.

———. 1994. "Neoclassical Economists' Theories of Discrimination." Pp. 59–70 in *Equal Employment Opportunity,* edited by P. Burstein. New York: Aldine De Gruyter.

Epstein, Cynthia Fuchs. 1968. "Women and Professional Careers: The Case of Women Lawyers." Ph.D. Dissertation, Department of Sociology, Columbia University, New York.

———. 1970. *Woman's Place: Options and Limits in Professional Careers.* Berkeley, CA: University of California Press.

———. [1981] 1993. *Women in Law.* Urbana, IL: University of Illinois Press.

———. 1985. "Ideal Roles and Real Roles or the Fallacy of the Misplaced Dichotomy." Pp. 29–51 in *Research in Social Stratification and Mobility,* edited by Robert V. Robinson. Greenwich, CT: JAI Press Inc.

———. 1988. *Deceptive Distinctions.* New Haven, CT and New York: Yale University Press and Russell Sage Foundation.

———. 1991a. "What's Wrong and What's Right With the Research on Gender." *Sociological Viewpoints* 5:1–14.

———. 1991b. "The Difference Model: Enforcement and Reinforcement in the Law." Pp. 53–71 in *Social Roles and Social Institutions: Essays in Honor of Rose Laub Coser,* edited by J. Blau and N. Goodman. Boulder, CO: Westview.

———. 1992. "Tinkerbells and Pinups: The Construction and Reconstruction of Gender Boundaries at Work." Pp. 232–56 in *Cultivating Differences: Symbolic Boundaries and the Making of Inequality,* edited by M. Lamont and M. Founder. Chicago, IL: University of Chicago Press.

———. 1997. "Multiple Myths and Outcomes of Sex Segregation." *New York Law School Journal of Human Rights* XIV: Part One, 185–210, Symposium.

———. 1999a. "The Major Myth of the Women's Movement." *Dissent* 46(4):83–86.

———. 1999b. "Similarity and Difference: The Sociology of Gender Distinctions." Pp. 45–61 in *Handbook of the Sociology of Gender,* edited by J. S. Chafetz. New York: Kluwer Academic/Plenum Publishers.

———. 2001. "Women in the Legal Profession at the Turn of the Twenty-First Century: Assessing Glass Ceilings and Open Doors." *Kansas Law Review* 49:733–60.

Epstein, Cynthia Fuchs and Deborah Gambs. 2001. "Sex Segregation in Education." Pp. 983–90 in *Encyclopedia of Gender,* vol. 2, edited by Judith Worell. Philadelphia, PA: Elsevier.

Epstein, Cynthia Fuchs and Arne Kalleberg, eds. 2004. *Fighting for Time: Shifting Boundaries of Work and Social Life.* New York: Russell Sage Foundation.

Epstein, Cynthia Fuchs, Robert Sauté, Bonnie Oglensky, and Martha Gever. 1995. "Glass Ceilings and Open Doors: The Mobility of Women in Large Corporate Law Firms." *Fordham Law Review* LXTV:291–449.

Epstein, Cynthia Fuchs, Carroll Seron, Bonnie Oglensky, and Robert Sauté. 1999. *The Part Time Paradox: Time Norms, Professional Life, Family and Gender.* New York and London: Routledge.

Erikson, Kai. 1996. "On Pseudospeciation and Social Speciation." Pp. 51–58 in *Genocide: War and Human Survival,* edited by C. Strozier and M. Flynn. Lanham, MD: Rowman & Littlefield.

Fine, Gary Alan. 1996. "Reputational Entrepreneurs and the Memory of Incompetence: Melting Supporters, Partisan Warriors, and Images of President Harding." *The American Journal of Sociology* 101:1159–93.

Fisher, Helen. 1982. *The Sex Contract: The Evolution of Human Behavior.* New York: William Morrow.

Fogg, Piper. 2006. "Panel Blames Bias for Gender Gap." *The Chronicle,* September 29. Retrieved October 24, 2006 (http://chronicle.com/weekly/v53/i06/06a01301.htm.)

Food and Agriculture Organization of the United Nations. N.d. "Gender and Food Security: Agriculture." Retrieved August 5, 2006 (http://www.fao.org/gender/en/agri-e.htm).

Frank, Marian. 1980. *The Life and Times of "Rosie the Riveter."* A study guide for the video *Rosie the Riveter,* Connie Field, director. Los Angeles, CA: Direct Cinema.

Freud, Sigmund. 1938. *The Basic Writings of Sigmund Freud.* Translated by A. A. Brill. New York: Modern Library.

———. [1905] 1975. *Three Essays on the Theory of Sexuality.* New York: Basic Books.

Friedan, Betty. [1963] 1983. *The Feminine Mystique.* New York: W.W. Norton.

Friedland, Roger. 2002. "Money, Sex and God: The Erotic Logic of Religious Nationalism." *Sociological Theory* 20:381–425.

Frodi, Ann, Jacqueline Macaulay, and Pauline Robert Thorne. 1977. "Are Women Always Less Aggressive than Men? A Review of the Experimental Literature." *Psychological Bulletin* 84:634–60.

Gerson, Judith and Kathy Peiss. 1985. "Boundaries, Negotiation and Consciousness: Reconceptualizing Gender Relations." *Social Problems* 32:317–31.

Gilligan, Carol. 1982. *In a Different Voice: Psychological Theory and Women's Development.* Cambridge, MA: Harvard University Press.

Gil-White, Francisco. 1999. "How Thick is Blood? The Plot Thickens…: If Ethnic Actors Are Primordialists, What Remains of the Circumstantialist/Primordialist Controversy?" *Ethnic and Racial Studies* 22:789–820.

Goldin, Claudia. 2006. "The Quiet Revolution That Transformed Women's Employment, Education and Family." *American Economic Association Papers and Proceedings* 96:7–19.

Goode, William J. 1959. "The Theoretical Importance of Love" *American Sociological Review* 24:38–47.

———. 1972. "The Place of Force in Human Society." *American Sociological Review* 37:507–19.

Gornick, Janet 2003. *Families that Work: Policies for Reconciling Parenthood and Employment.* New York: Russell Sage Foundation.

Gray, John. 1992. *Men are from Mars, Women are from Venus.* New York: HarperCollins.

Hall, Peter and Michele Lamont. Forthcoming. *Successful Societies* (working title).

Hartmann, Heidi, Vicky Lovell, and Misha Werschkul. 2004. "Women and the Economy: Recent Trends in Job Loss, Labor Force Participation and Wages." Briefing Paper, Institute for Women's Policy Research. IWPR Publication B235.

Hartstock, Nancy. 1988. *The Feminist Standpoint Revisited, and Other Essays.* Boulder, CO: Westview Press.

Hirschfeld, Lawrence A. 1996. *Race in the Making: Cognition, Culture and the Child's Construction of Human Kinds.* Cambridge, MA: MIT Press.

Hondagneu-Sotelo, Pierrette, ed. 2003. *Gender and U.S. Immigration: Contemporary Trends.* Berkeley, CA: University of California Press.

Honey, Maureen. 1984. *Creating Rosie the Riveter: Class, Gender and Propaganda during World War 2.* Boston, MA: University of Massachusetts Press.

Hsiung, Ping-Chun. 1996. *Living Rooms as Factories: Class, Gender and the Satellite Factory System in Taiwan.* Philadelphia, PA: Temple University Press

Hyde, Janet Shibley. 2005. "The Gender Similarities Hypothesis." *American Psychologist* 60:581–92.

Jaschik, Scott 2006. "Bias or Interest?" *Inside Higher Ed,* September 20. Retrieved September 28 (http://insidehighered.com/layout/set/print/news/2006/09/20/women).

Kaminer, Wendy. 1990. *A Fearful Freedom: Women's Flight from Equality.* Reading, MA: Addison-Wesley.

Kaufman, Debra R. and Barbara Richardson. 1982. *Achievement and Women: Challenging the Assumptions.* New York: The Free Press.

Kessler-Harris, Alice. 1982. *Women Have Always Worked: A Historical Overview.* Old Westbury, CT: Feminist Press.

Kimmel, Michael. 1996. *Manhood in America.* New York: The Free Press.

Komarovsky, Mirra. 1946. "Cultural Contradictions and Sex Roles." *The American Journal of Sociology* 52:184–89.

———. [1953] 2004. *Women in the Modern World: Their Education and Their Dilemmas.* Walnut Creek, CA: AltaMira Press.

Kristof, Nicholas. 2006. "Save My Wife." *New York Times,* September 17, opinion section, p. 15.

Lamont, Michele. 2005. "Bridging Boundaries: Inclusion as a Condition for Successful Societies." Presented at the Successful Societies Program of the Canadian Institute for Advanced Research, October, Montebello, Quebec, Canada.

Lamont, Michele and Virag Molnar. 2002. "The Study of Boundaries in the Social Sciences." *Annual Review of Sociology* 28:167–95.

Laslett, Barbara. 1996. *Gender and Scientific Authority.* Chicago, IL: University of Chicago Press.

Lee, Ching Kwan. 1998. *Gender and the South China Miracle: Two Worlds of Factory Women.* Berkeley, CA: University of California Press.

Lew, Irene and Nouhad Moawad. 2006. "Cheers & Jeers of the Week: Breast Cancer Strategies; Domestic Abuse Unnoticed." *Women's eNews,* September 30. Retrieved October 2, 2006 (http://www.womensenews.org/article.cfm/dyn/aid/2907/context/archive).

Lewin, Tamar. 2006a. "At College's, Women are Leaving Men in the Dust." *New York Times,* July 9, p. A1.

———. 2006b. "A More Nuanced Look at Men, Women and College." *New York Times,* July 12, p. B8.

Lorber, Judith. 1975. "Women and Medical Sociology: Invisible Professionals and Ubiquitous Patients." Pp. 75–105 in *Another Voice,* edited by Marcia Millman and Rosabeth Moss Kanter. Garden City, NY: Doubleday/Anchor.

———. 1984. *Women Physicians: Careers, Status, and Power.* New York: Tavistock Publications.

———. 1994. *Paradoxes of Gender.* New Haven, CT: Yale University Press.

———. 1996. "Beyond the Binaries: Depolarizing the Categories of Sex, Sexuality and Gender." *Sociological Inquiry* 66:143–59.

Magrane, Diane, Jonathan Lang, and Hershel Alexander. 2005. *Women in U.S. Academic Medicine: Statistics and Medical School Benchmarking.* Washington, DC: Association of American Medical Colleges.

Martin, Patricia Yancey. 2004. "Gender as Social Institution." *Social Forces* 82:1249–73.

Merton, Robert K. [1949] 1963. *Social Theory and Social Structure.* Glencoe, IL: The Free Press.

Milkman, Ruth. 1987. *Gender at Work: The Dynamics of Job Segregation by Sex During World War II.* Urbana, IL: University of Illinois Press.

Moghadam, Valentine. 2003. *Modernizing Women: Gender and Social Change in the Middle East.* 2d ed. London, England: Lynne Rienner.

O'Brien, Timothy. 2006. "Why Do So Few Women Reach the Top of Big Law Firms?" *New York Times,* March 19, p. B27.

O'Farrell, Brigid. 1999. "Women in Blue Collar and Related Occupations at the End of the Millenium." *Quarterly Review of Economics and Finance* 39:699–722.

National Women's Law Center. 2006. "New Report Analyzes What's at Stake for Women During Upcoming Supreme Court Term." Press Release. September 27. Retrieved October 2, 2006 (http://www.nwlc.org/details.cfm?id=2857& section=newsroom).

Nicholson, Lisa H. 2006. "Women and the 'New' Corporate Governance: Making In-Roads to Corporate General Counsel Positions: It's Only a Matter of Time?" *Maryland Law Review* 65:625–65.

Norris, Floyd. 2006. "A Statistic That Shortens the Distance to Europe." *New York Times,* September 30, p. C3.

Parsons, Talcott. 1954. "The Kinship System of the Contemporary United States." Pp. 189–94 in *Essays in Sociological Theory.* Glencoe, IL: The Free Press.

Parrot, Andrew and Nina Cummings. 2006. *Forsaken Females: The Global Brutalization of Women.* Lanham, MD: Roman and Littlefield.

Presser Harriet. 2003. *Working in a 24/7 Economy: Challenges for American Families.* New York: Russell Sage Foundation.

Rao, Kavitha. 2006. "Missing Daughters on an Indian Mother's Mind." *Women's eNews,* March 16. Retrieved October 23, 2006 (http://www. womensnews.org/article.cfm?aid=2672).

Ridgeway, Cecilia L. 1997. "Interaction and the Conservation of Gender Inequality: Considering Employment." *American Sociological Review* 62:218–35.

———. 2006. "Gender as an Organizing Force in Social Relations: Implications for the Future of Inequality." Pp. 245–87 in *The Declining Significance of Gender?* edited by Francine D. Blau and Mary C. Brinton. New York: The Russell Sage Foundation.

Ridgeway, Cecilia L. and Lynn Smith-Lovin. 1999. "The Gender System and Interaction." *Annual Review of Sociology* 25:19–216.

Roos, Patricia and Mary L. Gatta. 2006. "Gender Inquiry in the Academy." Presented at the Annual Meeting of the American Sociological Association, August 14, Montreal, Canada.

Rothbart, Myron and Marjorie Taylor. 1992. "Category Labels and Social Reality: Do We View Social Categories as Natural Kinds?" Pp. 11–36 in *Language, Interaction and Social Cognition,* edited by Gun R. Semin and Klaus Fiedler. London, England: Sage.

Rupp, Leila. 1978. *Mobilizing Women for War: German and American Propaganda, 1939–1945.* Princeton, NJ: Princeton University Press.

Salzinger, Leslie. 2003. *Genders in Production: Making Workers in Mexico's Global Factories.* Berkeley, CA: University of California Press.

Schemo, Diana Jean. 2006. "Change in Federal Rules Backs Single-Sex Public Education." *New York Times,* October 25, p. A16.

Sen, Amartya. 1990. "More than 100 Million Women are Missing." *New York Review of Books,* 37(20). Retrieved January 25, 2006 (http://ucatlas.ucsc. edu/gender/Sen100M.html).

Smith, Dorothy. 1990. *The Conceptual Practices of Power: A Feminist Sociology of Knowledge.* Boston, MA: Northeastern University Press.

Stacey, Judith and Barrie Thorne. 1985. 'The Missing Feminist Revolution in Sociology." *Social Problems* 32:301–16.

Stevens, Alison. 2006. "Iranian Women Protest in Shadow of Nuclear Face-off." *Women's eNews,* June 16. Retrieved September 28, 2006 (http://www. womensenews.org/article.cfm/dyn/aid/2780).

Tannen, Deborah. 1990. *You Just Don't Understand: Women and Men in Conversation.* New York: Morrow.

Tarabay, Jamie. 2006. "Activists Seek to Protect Iraqi Women from Honor Killings." *NPR Morning Edition,* May 18. Retrieved June 6, 2006 (http://www.npr.org/templates/story/story. php?storyId=5414315).

Tavris, Carol. 1992. *The Mismeasure of Woman: Why Women are not the Better Sex, the Inferior Sex or the Opposite Sex.* New York: Touchstone.

Telles, Edward. 2004. *Race in Another America: The Significance of Skin Color in Brazil.* Princeton, NJ: Princeton University Press.

Tierney, John. 2006. "Academy of P.C. Sciences." New *York Times,* September 26, p. A23.

Tilly, Charles. 1998. *Durable Inequality.* Berkeley, CA: University of California Press.

Trivers, Robert L. 1972. "Parental Investment and Sexual Selection." Pp. 136–79 in *Sexual Selection and the Descent of Man, 1871–1971,* edited by B. Campbell. Chicago, IL: Aldine.

United Nations. 2002. *Working Towards the Elimination of Crimes against Women Committed in the Name of Honor, Report of the Secretary General.* United Nations General Assembly, July 2. Retrieved October 23, 2006 (http://www.unhchr.ch/huridocda/huridoca.nsf/AllSymbols/985168F508EE799FC1256C52002AE5A9/%24File/N0246790.pdf).

U.N. Common Database. 2004. "Gender Equality: Indicator: Seats in Parliament Held by Women–2004." Retrieved September 21, 2006 (http://globalis.gvu.unu.edu/indicator.cfm?IndicatorID=63&country=IS#rowIS).

Villalobos, V. Munos. 2006. "Economic, Social and Cultural Rights: Girls' right to education." Report submitted by the Special Rapporteur on the right to education. United Nations Commission on Human Rights, Economic and Social Council. Retrieved September 28, 2006 (http://www.crin.org/docs/SR_Education_report.pdf).

Williams, Joan. 2000. *Unbending Gender: Why Family and Work Conflict and What to Do About It.* New York: Oxford University Press.

Wilson, Edward O. 1975. *Sociobiology: The New Synthesis.* Cambridge, MA: Belknap Press of Harvard University Press.

Winston, Hella. 2005. *Unchosen: The Hidden Lives of Hasidic Rebels.* Boston, MA: Beacon Press.

Witte, Griff. 2005. "Post-Taliban Free Speech Blocked by Courts, Clerics: Jailed Afghan Publisher Faces Possible Execution." *Washington Post,* December 11, p. A24.

Women's World Summit Foundation. 2006. "World Rural Women's Day: 15 October: Introduction." Retrieved September 28, 2006 (http://www.woman.ch/women/2-introduction.asp).

Zerubavel, Eviatar. 1997. *Social Mindscapes: An Invitation to Cognitive Sociology.* Cambridge, MA: Harvard University Press.

Zimmerman Mary K., Jacquelyn S. Litt, and Christine E. Bose. 2006. *Global Dimensions of Gender and Care Work.* Stanford, CA: Stanford University Press.

Framed Before We Know It: How Gender Shapes Social Relations

CECILIA L. RIDGEWAY

During the past decade, I have made the case that gender is one of our culture's two or three primary frames for organizing social relations (Ridgeway 1997, 2007). I have also argued that unless we take into account how gender frames social relations, we cannot understand how the gendered structure of contemporary society both changes and resists changing. My purpose here is to spell out this argument in more specific detail. I first explain what I mean by gender as a "primary frame" and describe some of the implications of this approach. Second, and just as important, I explain

Cecilia L. Ridgeway, "Framed Before We Know It: How Gender Shapes Social Relations" from *Gender & Society* 23, no. 2, (April 2009): 145–160. Copyright © 2009 by Sociologists for Women in Society. Reprinted with the permission of Sage Publications, Inc.

why I believe we must incorporate the effects of gender as a primary frame into our analyses of the gendered structure of society. To do this, I offer two empirical illustrations that demonstrate that we cannot understand the shape the gender structure takes in particular situations without taking into account the background effects of the gender frame on behavior. In the first illustration, I show how the gender frame causes the same organizational logic to have rather different implications for gender inequality in two different types of innovative high-tech firms. In the second illustration, I draw on research that shows how the background effects of the gender frame help us understand why some of the societies that have gone farthest in reducing gender inequality nevertheless have some of the most gender-segregated occupational structures in the advanced industrial world (Charles and Bradley 2009).

In discussing the question of "why it matters" whether we incorporate the effects of the gender frame into our analyses, I also wish to address an unresolved tension among feminist scholars in how best to approach the gendered structure of society. In 1987, West and Zimmerman shook up the world of gender theorizing in sociology with their groundbreaking analysis of gender as a social interactional accomplishment, a performance of difference that one "does" rather than "is" (Fenstermaker and West 2002; West and Zimmerman 1987). This "doing gender, doing difference" perspective continues to wield persuasive power, as attested by the rate at which it is cited. Yet, this micro-interactional account of gender has, in some ways, remained an undigested nugget.

As sociologists, most of us are structuralists who see gender and race inequality as rooted in broad organizational and institutional structures with strong material bases. Many feel a theoretical tension between micro-interactional approaches, evocative as they may be, and more structuralist explanatory leanings. There are lingering questions about how to fit the micro-interactional account into institutional structure and how much weight to give the micro account. Micro accounts are appealing and add richness to our understanding, but do they really matter?

Another major innovation in gender theorizing in sociology has partially assuaged this theoretical tension. This is the recognition that gender is a multilevel structure, system, or institution of social practices that involves mutually reinforcing processes at the macro-structural/institutional level, the interactional level, and the individual level (Acker 1990; Lorber 1994; Ridgeway and Smith-Lovin 1999; Risman 1998, 2004). The remaining difficulty, however, is to explicate how these multilevel processes affect one another, beyond simply saying that they generally but not always reinforce one another.

My argument that gender is a primary frame for social relations is at root a micro-interactional approach that owes much to the "doing gender" account, even though my argument is a bit different in emphasis. To make the case that the gender frame matters, I will focus on the interface of the micro-interactional and the institutional and structural levels of analysis. My intent is to shed more light on how these multilevel processes work together to shape the gender structures that emerge. In doing so, I hope to contribute toward resolution of the tension between micro-interactional and structural-level explanations.

Gender as a Primary Frame

What does it mean to say that gender is a primary cultural frame for organizing social relations (Ridgeway 1997, 2006, 2007)? As we know, people depend on social relations with others to attain most of what they want and need in life. Social relations pose a well-known problem, however. To relate to another to accomplish a valued goal, we have to find some way to coordinate our behavior with that other. Classic sociologists such as Goffman (1967) and contemporary game theorists (Chwe 2001) have arrived at the same conclusion about what it takes to solve this coordination problem. For you and me to coordinate effectively, we need shared, "common" knowledge to use as a basis for our joint actions. Common knowledge is cultural knowledge that we all assume we all know. I have argued that actually, we need a particular type of common, cultural knowledge (Ridgeway 2007). We need a shared way of categorizing and defining "who" self and other are in the situation so that we can anticipate how each of us is likely to act and coordinate our actions accordingly.

Coordination and Difference

Systems for categorizing and defining things are based on contrast, and therefore, difference. Something is this because it is different from that. Defining *self* and *other* to relate focuses us on finding shared principles of social difference that we can use to categorize and make sense of one another. The coordination problem inherent to organizing social relations drives populations of people who must regularly relate to one another to develop shared social-category systems based on culturally defined standards of difference.

To manage social relations in real time, some of these cultural-category systems must be so simplified that they can be quickly applied as framing devices to virtually anyone to start the process of defining *self* and *other* in the situation. In fact, studies of social cognition suggest that a very small number of such cultural-difference systems, about three or so, serve as the primary categories of person perception in a society (Brewer and Lui 1989; Fiske 1998). These primary categories define the things a person in that society must know about someone to render that someone sufficiently meaningful to relate to him or her.

Sex/gender, of course, is a form of human variation that is highly susceptible to cultural generalization as a primary category for framing social relations (Ridgeway 2006, 2007). It yields a cultural-difference system that is relevant to sexuality and reproduction and that delineates a line of difference among people who must regularly cooperate with one another. Thus, the male–female distinction is virtually always one of a society's primary cultural-category systems (Glick and Fiske 1999). In the United States, race and age are also primary categories (see Schneider 2004, 96).

Social-cognition studies show that in fact, we automatically and nearly instantly sex categorize any specific person to whom we attempt to relate (Ito and Urland 2003; Stangor et al. 1992). We do this not just in person but also over the Internet and even imaginatively, as we examine a person's resume or think about the kind of person we would like to hire. Studies show that Americans categorize others they encounter on Black or white race almost instantly as well (Ito and Urland 2003). When we categorize another, we by comparison implicitly make salient our own sex and race categorization as well.

We so instantly sex-categorize others that our subsequent categorizations of them as, say, bosses or coworkers are nested in our prior understandings of them as male or female and take on slightly different meanings as a result (Brewer and Lui 1989; Fiske 1998). This initial framing by sex never quite disappears from our understanding of them or ourselves in relation to them. Thus, we frame and are framed by gender literally before we know it. Importantly, however, the extent to which this preframing by gender shapes what happens in a specific situation depends greatly on what else is going on in that situation. As we will see, this is a point at which the gender frame interacts with institutional context. But first, I need to say more about how the gender frame coordinates behavior.

Cultural Beliefs about Gender

Primary categories of person perception, including sex category, work as cultural frames for coordinating behavior by associating category membership with widely shared cultural beliefs about how people in one category are likely to behave compared to those in a contrasting category. These cultural beliefs are shared stereotypes, as in "men are from Mars and women are from Venus." Gender stereotypes are our beliefs about how "most people" view the typical man or woman (Eagly and Karau 2002; Fiske 1998; Fiske et al. 2002). We all know these stereotypes as cultural knowledge, whether or not we personally endorse them. But the point is, because we think "most people" hold these beliefs, we expect others to judge us according to them. As a result, we must take these beliefs into account in our own behavior even if we do not endorse them. In this way, these shared cultural beliefs act as the "rules" for coordinating public behavior on the basis of gender (Ridgeway and Correll 2004).

The use of sex or gender as a primary cultural frame for defining *self* and *other* drives the content of gender stereotypes to focus on presumed gender differences. *Difference* need not logically imply inequality. Yet, among groups of people who must regularly deal with one another, difference is easily transformed into inequality through any of a variety of social processes (Ridgeway 2006). Once inequality is established between groups of people, however, it will reshape the nature of the differences that are culturally perceived as characteristic of the higher and lower status groups (Fiske et al. 2002; Jackman 1994). The content of our gender stereotypes shows the characteristic pattern of status inequality in which the higher status group is perceived as more proactive and agentically competent ("from Mars") and the lower status group is seen as more reactive and emotionally expressive ("from Venus"; Conway, Pizzamiglio, and Mount 1996; Glick and Fiske 1999; Wagner and Berger 1997). Thus, difference and inequality codetermine each other in our shared gender beliefs, and coordination on the basis of them produces social relations of inequality as well as difference (Wagner and Berger 1997).

The social importance of gender as a primary frame for making sense of *self* and *other* and the cultural definition of this frame as a difference that implies inequality create two distinct sets of interests for individuals. These interests affect the extent to which individuals actively gender their behavior. As a belief system that privileges men over women, it gives most men and some women who benefit from male dominance an interest in enacting and maintaining that system. In addition, as a fundamental category for understanding the self, it gives almost all women and men a sometimes powerful interest in enacting essentialist expressions of gender difference. Both types of interests can have consequences for the actions individuals take when the constraining social structures around them give them the space to act on their own.

Hegemonic and Alternative Gender Beliefs

The familiar, widely known gender stereotypes that I have called the rules of gender are not just individual beliefs. They are culturally *hegemonic* beliefs for two reasons. First, these beliefs are institutionalized in media representations, in the images of men and women implied by laws and government policies, and in a wide variety of taken-for-granted organizational practices. Second, the content of these gender beliefs, while they purport to be universal depictions of the sexes, in fact represent most closely the experiences and understandings of gender by dominant groups in society—those who most powerfully shape our institutions. The men and women we see in gender stereotypes look most like white, middle-class heterosexuals. Yet, as Shelley Correll and I have argued, in public places and with strangers, these hegemonic cultural beliefs about gender act as the default rules of gender (Ridgeway and Correll 2004). This makes the public enactment of gender that much more complicated for those who are not white, middle-class heterosexuals.

Although we all know hegemonic gender beliefs, many of us also hold alternative beliefs about gender that we share with a subgroup of similarly minded others—fellow feminists, a racial or ethnic group, or an immigrant group. Some evidence suggests that these alternative cultural beliefs about gender, rather than the hegemonic ones, shape our behavior and judgments most clearly when we are relating to others we believe share those beliefs (Filardo 1996; Milkie 1999). This makes sense if we are using these beliefs to coordinate our behavior with those others. It remains for future research to investigate the contexts in which we systematically rely on alternative gender beliefs, rather than hegemonic beliefs, to guide our behavior.

How Does the Gender Frame Shape Behavior?

Thus far, I have spoken in general terms about the gender frame and cultural beliefs that shape behavior. Exactly how does this shaping process work, however? Also, what about the fact that in any given context in which we relate to others, much more is going on than just gender? In particular, we typically act in the context of some institutional or organizational framework that suggests specific role identities and role relations. What happens to the gender frame in that context? To address these questions, I first describe how the gender frame itself shapes behavior and judgments and then turn to how it interfaces with the organizational frame within which individuals act.

Effects of the Gender Frame

Research shows that sex categorization unconsciously primes gender stereotypes in our minds and makes them cognitively available to shape behavior and judgments (Blair and Banaji 1996; Kunda and Spencer 2003). The extent to which they actually do shape our behavior, however, can vary from negligible to substantial depending on the nature of the particular situation and our own motives or interests. What matters is the extent to which the information in gender beliefs is diagnostic for us in that it helps us figure out how to act in the situation. Research shows that some basic principles guide how this works.

When people in the situation differ in sex category, cultural beliefs about gender become effectively salient and measurably affect behaviors and judgments unless something else overrides them (see Ridgeway and Smith-Lovin 1999). Also, in either mixed or same-sex contexts, gender stereotypes implicitly shape behavior and judgments to the extent that gender is culturally defined as relevant to the situation, as, for instance, with a gender-typed task such as math (Ridgeway and Correll 2004; Ridgeway and Smith-Lovin 1999). The effects of gender beliefs on an actor's behavior will also be greater to the extent the actor consciously or unconsciously perceives the game of gender to be relevant to his or her own motives or interests in the situation (Fiske 1998).

Pulling these arguments together, we can see that the way the gender frame brings cultural beliefs about gender to bear on our expectations for self and other, on our behavior, and on our judgments produces a distinctive pattern of effects. In mixed-sex settings in which the task or context is relatively gender neutral, cultural beliefs that men are more agentically competent and more worthy of status will advantage them over otherwise similar women, but only modestly so. In settings that are culturally typed as masculine, gender beliefs will bias judgments and behaviors more strongly in favor of men. In contexts culturally linked with women, biases will weakly favor women except for positions of authority. A wide variety of research supports this general pattern of effects (see Ridgeway and Correll 2004; Ridgeway and Smith-Lovin 1999).

These effects largely describe the way the gender frame introduces implicit biases into expectations and behaviors that affect gender inequality in the setting. The enactment of inequality, however, is accomplished through the enactment of gender difference (e.g., agentic competence vs. reactive warmth) that implies and creates the inequality. The enactment of gender difference or inequality is fed by the interests the gender frame gives people in understanding themselves as appropriately gendered as well as by the way the gender frame causes them to react to and judge the behaviors of others. As institutionalized cultural "rules," gender beliefs about difference and inequality have a prescriptive edge that people enforce by sanctioning explicit violations. Women are typically sanctioned for acting too domineering and men for being too yielding or emotionally weak (Eagly and Karau 2002; Rudman and Fairchild 2004).

Gender as a Background Identity

How, then, do these contextually varying effects of the gender frame interface with the specific organizational or institutional contexts in which our relations with others occur? People typically confront the problem of coordinating their behavior with another in the context of both a primary person frame (gender, race, and age) and an institutional frame (a family, a university, a place of work). As part of the primary person frame, the instructions for behavior encoded in gender stereotypes are exceedingly abstract and diffuse. For this very reason, they can be applied to virtually any situation, but by the same token, they do not take an actor very far in figuring out exactly how to behave.

In contrast, institutional frameworks, even vague ones such as "the family," are much more specific. They contain defined roles and the expected relations among them. The roles that are embedded in institutional and organizational frameworks are often themselves infused with gendered cultural meanings. Indeed, one of the most powerful ways that the gender frame affects the gendered structure of society is through infusing gendered meanings into the institutional practices, procedures, and role identities by which various organizations operate. For now, however, the point is that these institutional roles, even the gendered ones, provide clearer instructions for behavior in a given context than do the diffuse cultural meanings of the primary gender frame. For individuals, it is these institutional identities and rules that are in the foreground of their sense of who they are in a given context and how they should behave there.

Gender, in contrast, is almost always a background identity for individuals. I have made this point elsewhere, but I wish to emphasize it here because it is essential to understanding how gender shapes social structure (Ridgeway and Correll 2004; Ridgeway and Smith-Lovin 1999). As a background identity, gender typically acts to bias in gendered directions the performance of behaviors undertaken in the name of more concrete, foregrounded organizational roles or identities. Thus, gender becomes a way of acting like a doctor or of driving a car. This, of course, is what West and Zimmerman (1987) meant by "doing gender."

The Interaction of the Gender Frame and Institutional Structure

The extent to which the gender frame flavors or biases the performance of institutional role identities depends on two general factors. The first is the salience and relevance of the gender frame in the situation. As we can infer from above, this depends on the gender composition of the institutional context and the extent to which the activities and roles in the context are themselves culturally gendered. When organizational activities are gendered, the background gender frame becomes more powerfully relevant for actors, and the biases it introduces shape how people carry out those activities and how they fill in the details not

clearly specified by institutional rules. The gendering of institutional tasks or roles, then, empowers the background gender frame in the situation to become a significant part of the process by which people enact their institutional roles. Scholars such as Patricia Martin have given us powerful illustrations of this process (Martin 2003).

A second factor that affects the impact of the gender frame is the extent to which organizational rules and procedures constrain individual discretion in judgments and behavior. The more constrained individuals' actions are, the less scope the gender frame has to implicitly shape their behavior on its own. For this reason, many scholars have recommended formal rules and procedures as devices to suppress stereotype bias and discrimination in employment (Bielby 2000; Reskin and McBrier 2000). On the other hand, feminist scholars have also long pointed out that apparently neutral formal rules and procedures can embody bias in their application or effect (e.g., Acker 1990; Nelson and Bridges 1999; Steinberg 1995).

The gender-framing perspective suggests that whether formal personnel procedures do more good than bad depends not only on the extent to which bias is built into the procedures but also on how powerfully disadvantaging the gender frame would be for women if actors were not constrained by formal procedures. Thus, there is no simple answer to the "are formal rules best" question. But a consideration of the joint effects of the gender frame and the organizational frame allows us to specify how the answer to this question varies systematically with the nature of the context. One of my empirical examples will illustrate this point.

To the extent that cultural beliefs about gender do shape behavior and social relations in an institutional context, either directly through the gender frame acting on individuals or indirectly through biased procedures, these gender beliefs will be reinscribed into new organizational procedures and rules that actors develop through their social relations in that setting (Ridgeway 1997; Ridgeway and England 2007). In this way, the gendered structure of society can be projected into the future through new organizational procedures and forms that reinvent it for a new era.

My argument suggests that the background gender frame is the primary mechanism by which material, organizational structures become organized by gender. By the same token, these organizational structures sustain widely shared cultural beliefs about gender. To the extent that economic, technological, and political factors change these structures and the material arrangements that they create between men and women, these material changes create gradual, iterative pressure for change in cultural beliefs about gender as well.

The Explanatory Importance of the Gender Frame

I will illustrate my abstract arguments about how the gender frame interacts with institutional structures with two empirical examples. My purpose in offering these examples is to demonstrate how we have to take into account the background effects of the gender frame to understand the gender structure that emerges in a given context from particular organizational or institutional structures.

Gender in Innovative, High-tech Firms

My first example comes from studies of the small, science-focused start-up firms that have become a leading edge of the biotechnology and information technology (IT) industries. As Kjersten Whittington and Laurel Smith-Doerr (2008; Whittington 2007) describe, many of these high-tech firms have adopted a new organizational logic called the network form. Work in these firms is organized in terms of project teams that are often jointly constructed with a network of other firms. Scientists in a firm move flexibly among these project teams, and the hierarchies of control over their activities are relatively flat.

Is this informal, flexible structure advantageous or disadvantageous for women scientists who work in these high-tech firms? Whittington and Smith-Doerr's (2008; Whittington 2007) research suggests that the answer is quite different for biotech firms based in the life sciences than it is for firms based in engineering and the physical sciences, such as IT firms. To understand why the same organizational logic plays out so differently for women scientists in one context compared to the other, we need to take into account how the background frame of gender acts in each context.

The life sciences are not strongly gender-typed in contemporary culture. Women now constitute about a third of the PhDs in the area (Smith-Doerr 2004). Applying our framing account to this situation leads us to expect that because of the mixed gender composition of the workforce in this field, cultural beliefs about gender will be salient in biotech firms, but only diffusely so. Because the field is not strongly gender-typed, we expect these background gender beliefs to create only modest advantages for men in expected competence. Facing only modest biases, women scientists in biotech should have the basic credibility with their coworkers that they need to take effective advantage of the opportunities offered by the flexible structure of innovative firms. They should be able to press forward with their interests, work around "bad actors" if necessary, find projects that match their skills, and excel (Smith-Doerr 2004). As a result, in the biotech context, an informal, flexible organizational form could be more advantageous for women than would a more hierarchical structure.

In fact, Whittington and Smith-Doerr (2008) find women life scientists do better in these innovative biotech firms than they do in more traditionally hierarchical research organizations such as pharmaceutical firms. In comparison to more hierarchical firms, women in these flexible firms achieve more supervisory positions (Smith-Doerr 2004) and attain parity with men in the likelihood of having at least one patent to their name (Whittington and Smith-Doerr 2008). Even in these innovative firms, however, the total number of patents women acquire is less than that of comparable men, as it also is in traditional hierarchical firms. This remaining disadvantage is not surprising if we remember that background gender biases still modestly favor men, even in this innovative biotech context.

In contrast to the life sciences, engineering and the physical sciences are still strongly gender-typed in favor of men in our society. Thus, the back-ground gender frame in the IT context is more powerfully relevant and creates stronger implicit biases against women's competence than in biotech settings. In this situation, the informality and flexibility of the innovative firm is unlikely to be an advantage for women scientists and may even be a disadvantage. Facing strong challenges to their credibility, it will be harder for women to take effective advantage of the flexible structure. Also, in the context of a masculine-typed gender frame, the informal work structure may lead to a "boys club" atmosphere in these innovative IT firms.

Consistent with the above analysis, Whittington (2007), in her study of patenting, found that women physical scientists and engineers were no better off in small, flexible, less hierarchical firms than they were in traditional, industrial research and development firms. In both contexts, they were less likely to patent at all and had fewer patents overall than did comparable men. In another study, McIllwee and Robinson (1992) found that women engineers actually did better in a traditional, rule-structured aerospace firm than in a more informal, flexible IT start-up because in the context of a disadvantaging background gender frame, formal rules leveled the playing field to some extent. This example suggests that we cannot understand the full implications of a particular organizational logic for the gender structure it will produce without considering how that organizational logic interacts with the background effects of the gender frame.

Sex Segregation of Field of Study in Affluent Societies

My second example comes from Maria Charles' and Karen Bradley's (2009) provocative study of how the sex-typing of fields of higher education varies across societies. The sex-segregation of fields of study such as the humanities or engineering feeds one of the most durable and consequential gender structures of industrial societies, the sex-segregation of occupations (Charles and Grusky 2004). Gender scholars often puzzle over the fact that some of the societies that have achieved the lowest levels of material inequality between men and women, such as the Scandinavian countries, nevertheless have some of the most sex-segregated occupational structures of advanced industrial societies (Charles and Grusky 2004). How does such sex-segregation persist and even flourish in the face of institutional, political, and economic processes that undermine gender inequality?

Charles and Bradley's analysis shows that we cannot answer this question from a purely economic and structural perspective. Structural factors such as the growth of the service and health sectors in postindustrial economies do contribute to the sex-segregation of jobs and fields of study (Charles and Bradley 2009; Charles and Grusky 2004). But to really explain segregation, we have to take into account how the background frame of gender interacts with cultural developments in highly affluent societies.

As Charles and Bradley (2009) note, contemporary affluent societies tend to embrace a "postmaterialist" ethic of self-expression and self-realization. In the context of wealthy societies that free most of their citizens from the fear of dire material want and that value self-expression, Charles and Bradley argue that the background gender frame powerfully influences the fields of study people pursue. If our fundamental understanding of who we are is rooted in our primary identities, including gender, then many of us will implicitly fall back on cultural beliefs about gender to frame what it means to make life choices that "express" ourselves. There will be a tendency on the part of many us to, in Charles and Bradley's (2009) phrase, "indulge our gendered selves." In support of their argument, they find that affluent postindustrial societies have larger gaps between boys and girls in expressed affinity for math ("I like math"), controlling for boys' and girls' relative mathematical achievement. Furthermore, these culturally gendered affinities more strongly predict the sex-segregation of higher education fields in these societies than in less-developed ones.

An irony of the structural freedoms of advanced affluent societies is that they give their citizens greater space to fall back on an old, deeply ingrained cultural frame as they try to make sense of themselves and others and organize their choices and behaviors accordingly. In the context of economic, legal, and political processes that push against gender inequality in such societies, this reanchoring in the gender frame takes the form of reinvestments in cultural ideas of gender difference. But gender difference is culturally defined in terms that imply gender hierarchy. Thus, although the degree of inequality may decline, we are unlikely to fully eliminate the ordinal hierarchy between men and women in a society that intensifies its organization on the basis of gender difference.

Conclusion

With these examples, I hope I have been convincing that we cannot understand the shape that the gendered structure of society takes without taking into account the background effects of gender as a primary cultural frame for organizing social relations. I hope I have also been convincing that the theoretical tension some feel between micro-interactional and institutional approaches to gender is unnecessary. When it comes to gender, the effects of processes at one level cannot be understood without reference to those at the other level. Although the gender frame acts through the sense-making of individuals as they try to coordinate their behaviors, it does more than add texture and detail to a structural account of gender and society. When considered jointly with an institutional or structural analysis, the effects of the gender frame help us see how gender becomes embedded in new organizational forms and material arrangements. This analysis also suggests that change in the gendered system of a society will be iterative and may not always proceed smoothly. The forces for change come from political, economic, and technological factors that alter the everyday material arrangements between men and women in ways that undercut traditional views of status differences between men and women. The initial impact of such material changes is often blunted because people reinterpret the meaning of these changes through the lens of their existing, more conservative gender beliefs. Yet, even as people do this, the material changes make those more conservative gender beliefs harder and harder to sustain as

meaningful representations of men and women in everyday life. If, over time, changes in the material arrangements between men and women continue to accumulate, the traditional content of cultural beliefs about gender will gradually change as well. A single wave does not move a sandbar, but wave after wave does.

References

Acker, Joan. 1990. Hierarchies, jobs, and bodies: A theory of gendered organizations. *Gender & Society* 4:139–58.

Bielby, William T. 2000. Minimizing workplace gender and racial bias. *Contemporary Sociology* 29:120–28.

Blair, Irene V., and Mahzarin R. Banaji. 1996. Automatic and controlled processes in stereotype priming. *Journal of Personality and Social Psychology* 70:1142–63.

Brewer, Marilynn, and Layton Lui. 1989. The primacy of age and sex in the structure of person categories. *Social Cognition* 7:262–74.

Charles, Maria, and Karen Bradley. 2009. Indulging our gendered selves: Sex segregation by field of study in 44 countries. *American Journal of Sociology* 114, forthcoming.

Charles, Maria, and David B. Grusky 2004. *Occupational ghettos: The worldwide segregation of women and men.* Stanford, CA: Stanford University Press.

Chwe, Michael Suk-Young. 2001. *Rational ritual: Culture, coordination, and common knowledge.* Princeton, NJ: Princeton University Press.

Conway, Michael, M. Teresa Pizzamiglio, and Lauren Mount. 1996. Status, communality, and agency: Implications for stereotypes of gender and other groups. *Journal of Personality and Social Psychology* 71:25–38.

Eagly, Alice H., and Stephen J. Karau. 2002. Role congruity theory of prejudice towards female leaders. *Psychological Review* 109:573–79.

Fenstermaker, Sarah, and Candace West, eds. 2002. *Doing gender, doing difference: Inequality, power, and institutional change.* New York: Routledge.

Filardo, Emily K. 1996. Gender patterns in African American and white adolescents' social interactions in same-race, mixed-sex groups. *Journal of Personality and Social Psychology* 71:71–82.

Fiske, Susan T. 1998. Stereotyping, prejudice, and discrimination. In *The handbook of social psychology, vol.* 2, edited by D. T. Gilbert, S. T. Fiske, and G. Lindzey. 4th ed. Boston: McGraw-Hill.

Fiske, Susan T., Amy J. Cuddy, Peter Glick, and Jun Xu. 2002. A model of (often mixed) stereotype content: Competence and warmth respectively follow from perceived status and competence. *Journal of Personality and Social Psychology* 82:878–902.

Glick, Peter, and Susan T. Fiske. 1999. Gender, power dynamics, and social interaction. In *Revisioning gender,* edited by M. M. Ferree, J. Lorber, and B. B. Hess. Thousand Oaks, CA: Sage.

Goffman, Erving. 1967. *Interaction ritual.* Garden City, NY: Doubleday.

Ito, Tiffany A., and Geoffrey R. Urland. 2003. Race and gender on the brain: Electrocortical measures of attention to the race and gender of multiply categorizable individuals. *Journal of Personality and Social Psychology* 85:616–26.

Jackman, Mary. R. 1994. *The velvet glove: Paternalism and conflict in gender, class, and race relations.* Berkeley: University of California Press.

Kunda, Ziva, and Steven J. Spencer. 2003. When do stereotypes come to mind and when do they color judgment? A goal-based theoretical framework for stereotype activation and application. *Psychological Bulletin* 129:522–44.

Lorber, Judith. 1994. *Paradoxes of gender.* New Haven, CT: Yale University Press.

Martin, Patricia Y. 2003. "Said and done" versus "saying and doing": Gendering practices, practicing gender at work. *Gender & Society* 17:342–66.

McIllwee, Judith S., and J. Gregg Robinson. 1992. *Women in engineering: Gender power, and workplace culture.* Albany: State University of New York Press.

Milkie, Melissa A. 1999. Social comparison, reflected appraisals, and mass media: The impact of pervasive beauty images on Black and white girls' self-concepts. *Social Psychology Quarterly* 62:190–210.

Nelson, Robert, and William Bridges. 1999. *Legalizing gender inequality: Courts, markets, and unequal pay for women in America.* New York: Cambridge University Press.

Reskin, Barbara, and Debra Branch McBrier. 2000. Why not ascription? Organizations' employment of male and female managers. *American Sociological Review* 65:210–33.

Ridgeway, Cecilia L. 1997. Interaction and the conservation of gender inequality: Considering employment. *American Sociological Review* 62:218–35.

———. 2006. Gender as an organizing force in social relations: Implications for the future of inequality. In *The declining significance of gender?* edited by F. D. Blau, M. C. Brinton, and D. B. Grusky. New York: Russell Sage Foundation.

———. 2007. Gender as a group process: Implications for the persistence of inequality. In *The social psychology of gender,* edited by S. J. Cornell. New York: Elsevier.

Ridgeway, Cecilia L., and Shelley J. Correll. 2004. Unpacking the gender system: A theoretical perspective on gender beliefs and social relations. *Gender & Society* 18 (4): 510–31.

Ridgeway, Cecilia L., and Paula England. 2007. Sociological approaches to sex discrimination in employment. In *Sex discrimination in the workplace: Multidisciplinary perspectives,* edited by F. J. Crosby, M. S. Stockdale, and A. S. Ropp. Oxford, UK: Blackwell.

Ridgeway, Cecilia L., and Lynn Smith-Lovin. 1999. The gender system and interaction. *Annual Review of Sociology* 25:1991–216.

Risman, Barbara J. 1998. *Gender vertigo: American families in transition.* New Haven, CT: Yale University Press.

———. 2004. Gender as a social structure: Theory wrestling with activism. *Gender & Society* 18:429–50.

Rudman, Laurie. A., and Kimberly Fairchild. 2004. Reactions to counterstereotypic behavior: The role of backlash in cultural stereotype maintenance. *Journal of Personality and Social Psychology* 87:157–76.

Schneider, David J. 2004. *The psychology of stereotyping.* New York: Guilford.

Smith-Doerr, Laurel. 2004. *Women's work: Gender equality vs. hierarchy in the life sciences.* Boulder, CO: Lynne Rienner.

Stangor, Charles, Laure Lynch, Changming Duan, and Beth Glass. 1992. Categorization of individuals on the basis of multiple social features. *Journal of Personality and Social Psychology* 62:207–18.

Steinberg, Ronnie J. 1995. Gendered instructions: Cultural lag and gender bias in the hay system of job evaluation. In *Gender inequality at work,* edited by J. A. Jacobs. Thousand Oaks, CA: Sage.

Wagner, David G., and Joseph Berger. 1997. Gender and interpersonal task behaviors: Status expectation accounts. *Sociological Perspectives* 40:1–32.

West, Candace, and Don Zimmerman. 1987. Doing gender. *Gender & Society* 1:125–51.

Whittington, Kjersten Bunker. 2007. *Employment structures as opportunity structures: The effects of location on male and female scientific dissemination.* Stanford, CA: Department of Sociology, Stanford University.

Whittington, Kjersten Bunker, and Laurel Smith-Doerr. 2008. Women inventors in context: Disparities in patenting across academia and industry. *Gender & Society* 22:194–218.

Doing Gender

CANDACE WEST AND DON H. ZIMMERMAN

In the beginning, there was sex and there was gender. Those of us who taught courses in the area in the late 1960s and early 1970s were careful to distinguish one from the other. Sex, we told students, was what was ascribed by biology: anatomy, hormones, and physiology. Gender, we said, was an achieved status: that which is constructed through psychological, cultural, and social means. To introduce the difference between the two, we drew on singular case studies of hermaphrodites and anthropological investigations of "strange and exotic tribes."

Inevitably (and understandably), in the ensuing weeks of each term, our students became confused. Sex hardly seemed a "given" in the context of research that illustrated the sometimes ambiguous and often conflicting criteria for its ascription. And gender seemed much less an "achievement" in the context of the anthropological, psychological, and social imperatives we studied—the division of labor, the formation of gender identities, and the social subordination of women by men. Moreover, the received doctrine of gender socialization theories conveyed the strong message that while gender may be "achieved," by about age five it was certainly fixed, unvarying, and static—much like sex.

Since about 1975, the confusion has intensified and spread far beyond our individual classrooms. For one thing, we learned that the relationship between biological and cultural processes was far more complex—and reflexive—than we previously had supposed. For another, we discovered that certain structural arrangements, for example, between work and family, actually produce or enable some capacities, such as to mother, that we formerly associated with biology. In the midst of all this, the notion of gender as a recurring achievement somehow fell by the wayside.

Our purpose in this article is to propose an ethnomethodologically informed, and therefore distinctively sociological, understanding of gender as a routine, methodical, and recurring accomplishment. We contend that the "doing" of gender is undertaken by women and men whose competence as members of society is hostage to its production. Doing gender involves a complex of socially guided perceptual, interactional, and micropolitical activities that cast particular pursuits as expressions of masculine and feminine "natures."

When we view gender as an accomplishment, an achieved property of situated conduct, our attention shifts from matters internal to the individual and focuses on interactional and, ultimately, institutional arenas. In one sense, of course, it is individuals who "do" gender. But it is a situated doing, carried out in the virtual or real presence of others who are presumed to be oriented to its production. Rather than as a property of individuals, we conceive of gender as an emergent feature of social situations: both as an outcome of and a rationale for various social arrangements and as a means of legitimating one of the most fundamental divisions of society.

To advance our argument, we undertake a critical examination of what sociologists have meant by *gender,* including its treatment as a role enactment in the conventional sense and as a "display" in Goffman's (1976) terminology. Both *gender role* and *gender display* focus on behavioral aspects of being a woman or a man (as opposed, for example, to biological differences between the two). However, we contend that the notion of gender as a role obscures the work that is involved in producing gender in everyday activities, while the notion of gender as a display relegates it to the periphery of interaction. We argue instead that participants in interaction organize their various and manifold activities to reflect or express gender, and they are disposed to perceive the behavior of others in a similar light.

To elaborate our proposal, we suggest at the outset that important but often overlooked distinctions be observed among *sex, sex category,* and *gender. Sex* is a determination made through the application of socially agreed upon biological criteria for classifying persons as females or males. The criteria for classification can be genitalia at birth or chromosomal typing before birth, and they do not necessarily agree with one another. Placement in a *sex category* is achieved through application of the sex criteria, but in everyday life, categorization is established and sustained by the socially required identificatory displays that

proclaim one's membership in one or the other category. In this sense, one's sex category presumes one's sex and stands as proxy for it in many situations, but sex and sex category can vary independently; that is, it is possible to claim membership in a sex category even when the sex criteria are lacking. *Gender,* in contrast, is the activity of managing situated conduct in light of normative conceptions of attitudes and activities appropriate for one's sex category. Gender activities emerge from and bolster claims to membership in a sex category.

We contend that recognition of the analytical independence of sex, sex category, and gender is essential for understanding the relationships among these elements and the interactional work involved in "being" a gendered person in society. While our primary aim is theoretical, there will be occasion to discuss fruitful directions for empirical research following from the formulation of gender that we propose.

We begin with an assessment of the received meaning of gender, particularly in relation to the roots of this notion in presumed biological differences between women and men.

Perspectives on Sex and Gender

In Western societies, the accepted cultural perspective on gender views women and men as naturally and unequivocally defined categories of being with distinctive psychological and behavioral propensities that can be predicted from their reproductive functions. Competent adult members of these societies see differences between the two as fundamental and enduring—differences seemingly supported by the division of labor into women's and men's work and an often elaborate differentiation of feminine and masculine attitudes and behaviors that are prominent features of social organization. Things are the way they are by virtue of the fact that men are men and women are women—a division perceived to be natural and rooted in biology, producing in turn profound psychological, behavioral, and social consequences. The structural arrangements of a society are presumed to be responsive to these differences.

Analyses of sex and gender in the social sciences, though less likely to accept uncritically the naive biological determinism of the view just presented, often retain a conception of sex-linked behaviors and traits as essential properties of individuals. The "sex differences approach" is more commonly attributed to psychologists than to sociologists, but the survey researcher who determines the "gender" of respondents on the basis of the sound of their voices over the telephone is also making trait-oriented assumptions. Reducing gender to a fixed set of psychological traits or to a unitary "variable" precludes serious consideration of the ways it is used to structure distinct domains of social experience.

Taking a different tack, role theory has attended to the social construction of gender categories, called "sex roles" or, more recently, "gender roles" and has analyzed how these are learned and enacted. Beginning with Linton (1936) and continuing through the works of Parsons (Parsons 1951; Parsons and Bales 1955) and Komarovsky (1946, 1950), role theory has emphasized the social and dynamic aspect of role construction and enactment. But at the level of face-to-face interaction, the application of role theory to gender poses problems of its own. Roles are *situated* identities—assumed and relinquished as the situation demands—rather than *master identities,* such as sex category, that cut across situations. Unlike most roles, such as "nurse," "doctor," and "patient" or "professor" and "student," gender has no specific site or organizational context.

Moreover, many roles are already gender marked, so that special qualifiers—such as "female doctor" or "male nurse"—must be added to exceptions to the rule. Thorne (1980) observes that conceptualizing gender as a role makes it difficult to assess its influence on other roles and reduces its explanatory usefulness in discussions of power and inequality. Drawing on Rubin (1975), Thorne calls for a reconceptualization of women and men as distinct social groups, constituted in "concrete, historically changing—and generally unequal—social relationships" (Thorne 1980, p. 11).

We argue that gender is not a set of traits, nor a variable, nor a role, but the product of social doings of some sort. What then is the social doing of gender? It is more than the continuous creation of the meaning of gender through human actions. We claim that gender itself is constituted through interaction. To develop the implications of our claim, we turn to Goffman's (1976) account of "gender display." Our object here is to explore how gender might be exhibited or portrayed through interaction, and thus be seen as "natural," while it is being produced as a socially organized achievement.

Gender Display

Goffman contends that when human beings interact with others in their environment, they assume that each possesses an "essential nature"—a nature that can be discerned through the "natural signs given off or expressed by them" (1976, p. 75). Femininity and masculinity are regarded as "prototypes of essential expression—something that can be conveyed fleetingly in any social situation and yet something that strikes at the most basic characterization of the individual" (1976, p. 75). The means through which we provide such expressions are "perfunctory, conventionalized acts" (1976, p. 69), which convey to others our regard for them, indicate our alignment in an encounter, and tentatively establish the terms of contact for that social situation. But they are also regarded as expressive behavior, testimony to our "essential natures."

Goffman (1976, pp. 69–70) sees *displays* as highly conventionalized behaviors structured as two-part exchanges of the statement-reply type, in which the presence or absence of symmetry can establish deference or dominance. These rituals are viewed as distinct from but articulated with more consequential activities, such as performing tasks or engaging in discourse. Hence, we have what he terms the "scheduling" of displays at junctures in activities, such as the beginning or end, to avoid interfering with the activities themselves. Goffman (1976, p. 69) formulates *gender display* as follows:

> If gender be defined as the culturally established correlates of sex (whether in consequence of biology or learning), then gender display refers to conventionalized portrayals of these correlates.

These gendered expressions might reveal clues to the underlying, fundamental dimensions of the female and male, but they are, in Goffman's view, optional performances. Masculine courtesies may or may not be offered and, if offered, may or may not be declined (1976, p. 71). Moreover, human beings "themselves employ the term 'expression,' and conduct themselves to fit their own notions of expressivity" (1976, p. 75). Gender depictions are less a consequence of our "essential sexual natures" than interactional portrayals of what we would like to convey about sexual natures, using conventionalized gestures. Our human nature gives us the ability to learn to produce and recognize masculine and feminine gender displays—"a capacity [we] have by virtue of being persons, not males and females" (1976, p. 76).

Upon first inspection, it would appear that Goffman's formulation offers an engaging sociological corrective to existing formulations of gender. In his view, gender is a socially scripted dramatization of the culture's *idealization* of feminine and masculine natures, played for an audience that is well schooled in the presentational idiom. To continue the metaphor, there are scheduled performances presented in special locations, and like plays, they constitute introductions to or time out from more serious activities.

There are fundamental equivocations in this perspective. By segregating gender display from the serious business of interaction, Goffman obscures the effects of gender on a wide range of human activities. Gender is not merely something that happens in the nooks and crannies of interaction, fitted in here and there and not interfering with the serious business of life. While it is plausible to contend that gender displays—construed as conventionalized expressions—are optional, it does not seem plausible to say that we have the option of being seen by others as female or male.

It is necessary to move beyond the notion of gender display to consider what is involved in doing gender as an ongoing activity embedded in everyday interaction. Toward this end, we return to the distinctions among sex, sex category, and gender introduced earlier.

Sex, Sex Category, and Gender

Garfinkel's (1967, pp. 118–40) case study of Agnes, a transsexual raised as a boy who adopted a female identity at age 17 and underwent a sex reassignment operation several years later, demonstrates how gender is created through interaction and at the same time structures interaction. Agnes, whom Garfinkel characterized as a "practical methodologist," developed a number of procedures for passing as a "normal, natural female" both prior to and after her surgery. She had the practical task of managing the fact that she possessed male genitalia and that she lacked the social resources a girl's biography would presumably provide in everyday interaction. In short, she needed to display herself as a woman, simultaneously learning what it was to be a woman. Of necessity, this full-time pursuit took place at a time when most people's gender would be well-accredited and routinized. Agnes had to consciously contrive what the vast majority of women do without thinking. She was not "faking" what "real" women do naturally. She was obliged to analyze and figure out how to act within socially structured circumstances and conceptions of femininity that women born with appropriate biological credentials come to take for granted early on. As in the case of others who must "pass," such as transvestites, Kabuki actors, or Dustin Hoffman's "Tootsie," Agnes's case makes visible what culture has made invisible—the accomplishment of gender.

Garfinkel's (1967) discussion of Agnes does not explicitly separate three analytically distinct, although empirically overlapping, concepts—sex, sex category, and gender.

Sex

Agnes did not possess the socially agreed upon biological criteria for classification as a member of the female sex. Still, Agnes regarded herself as a female, albeit a female with a penis, which a woman ought not to possess. The penis, she insisted, was a "mistake" in need of remedy (Garfinkel 1967, pp. 126–27, 131–32). Like other competent members of our culture, Agnes honored the notion that there are "essential" biological criteria that unequivocally distinguish females from males. However, if we move away from the commonsense viewpoint, we discover that the reliability of these criteria is not beyond question. Moreover, other cultures have acknowledged the existence of "cross-genders" and the possibility of more than two sexes.

More central to our argument is Kessler and McKenna's (1978, pp. 1–6) point that genitalia are conventionally hidden from public inspection in everyday life; yet we continue through our social rounds to "observe" a world of two naturally, normally sexed persons. It is the *presumption* that essential criteria exist and would or should be there if looked for that provides the basis for sex categorization. Drawing on Garfinkel, Kessler and McKenna argue that "female" and "male" are cultural events—products of what they term the "gender attribution process"—rather than some collection of traits, behaviors, or even physical attributes. Illustratively they cite the child who, viewing a picture of someone clad in a suit and a tie, contends, "It's a man, because he has a pee-pee" (Kessler and McKenna 1978, p. 154). Translation: "He must have a pee-pee [an essential characteristic] because I see the *insignia* of a suit and tie." Neither initial sex assignment (pronouncement at birth as a female or male) nor the actual existence of essential criteria for that assignment (possession of a clitoris and vagina or penis and testicles) has much—if anything—to do with the identification of sex category in everyday life. There, Kessler and McKenna note, we operate with a moral certainty of a world of two sexes. We do not think, "Most persons with penises are men, but some may not be" or "Most persons who dress as men have penises." Rather, we take it for granted that sex and sex category are congruent—that knowing the latter, we can deduce the rest.

Sex Categorization

Agnes's claim to the categorical status of female, which she sustained by appropriate identificatory displays and other characteristics, could be *discredited* before her transsexual operation if her possession of a penis became known and after by her surgically constructed genitalia. In this regard, Agnes had to be continually alert to actual or potential threats to the security of her sex category. Her problem was not so much living up to some prototype of essential femininity but preserving her categorization as female. This task was made easy for her by a very powerful resource, namely, the process of commonsense categorization in everyday life.

The categorization of members of society into indigenous categories such as "girl" or "boy," or "woman" or "man," operates in a distinctively social way. The act of categorization does not involve a positive test, in the sense of a well-defined set of criteria that must be explicitly satisfied prior to making an identification. Rather, the application of membership categories relies on an "if-can" test in everyday interaction. This test stipulates that if people *can be seen* as members of relevant categories, *then categorize them that way*. That is, use the category that seems appropriate, except in the presence of discrepant information or obvious features that would rule out its use. This procedure is quite in keeping with the attitude of everyday life, which has us take appearances at face value unless we have special reason to doubt. It should be added that it is precisely when we have special reason to doubt that the issue of applying rigorous criteria arises, but it is rare, outside legal or bureaucratic contexts, to encounter insistence on positive tests.

Agnes's initial resource was the predisposition of those she encountered to take her appearance (her figure, clothing, hair style, and so on) as the undoubted appearance of a normal female. Her further resource was our cultural perspective on the properties of "natural, normally sexed persons." Garfinkel (1967, pp. 122–28) notes that in everyday life, we live in a world of two—and only two—sexes. This arrangement has a moral status, in that we include ourselves and others in it as "essentially, originally, in the first place, always have been, always will be, once and for all, in the final analysis, either 'male' or 'female'" (Garfinkel 1967, p. 122).

Consider the following case:

This issue reminds me of a visit I made to a computer store a couple of years ago. The person who answered my questions was truly a *salesperson*. I could not categorize him/her as a woman or a man. What did I look for? (1) Facial hair: She/he was smooth skinned, but some men have little or no facial hair. (This varies by race, Native Americans and Blacks often have none.) (2) Breasts: She/he was wearing a loose shirt that hung from his/her shoulders. And, as many women who suffered through a 1950s' adolescence know to their shame, women are often flat-chested. (3) Shoulders: His/hers were small and round for a man, broad for a woman. (4) Hands: Long and slender fingers, knuckles a bit large for a woman, small for a man. (5) Voice: Middle range, unexpressive for a woman, not at all the exaggerated tones some gay males affect. (6) His/her treatment of me: Gave off no signs that would let me know if I were of the same or different sex as this person. There were not even any signs that he/she knew his/her sex would be difficult to categorize and I wondered about that even as I did my best to hide these questions so I would not embarrass him/her while we talked of computer paper. I left still not knowing the sex of my salesperson, and was disturbed by that unanswered question (child of my culture that I am). (Diane Margolis, personal communication)

What can this case tell us about situations such as Agnes's or the process of sex categorization in general? First, we infer from this description that the computer salesclerk's identificatory display was ambiguous, since she or he was not dressed or adorned in an unequivocally female or male fashion. It is when such a display *fails* to provide grounds for categorization that factors such as facial hair or tone of voice are assessed to determine membership in a sex category. Second, beyond the fact that this incident could be recalled after "a couple of years," the customer was not only "disturbed" by the ambiguity of the salesclerk's category but also assumed that to acknowledge this ambiguity would be embarrassing to the salesclerk. Not only do we want to know the sex category of those around us (to see it at a glance, perhaps), but we presume that others are displaying it for us, in as decisive a fashion as they can.

Gender

Agnes attempted to be "120 percent female" (Garfinkel 1967, p. 129), that is, unquestionably in all ways and at all times feminine. She thought she could protect herself from disclosure before and after surgical intervention by comporting herself in a feminine manner, but she also could have given herself away by overdoing her performance. Sex categorization and the accomplishment of gender are not the same. Agnes's categorization could be secure or suspect, but did not depend on whether or not she lived up to some ideal conception of femininity. Women can be seen as unfeminine, but that does not make them "unfemale." Agnes faced an ongoing task of being a woman—something beyond style of dress (an identificatory display) or allowing men to light her cigarette (a gender display). Her problem was to produce configurations of behavior that would be seen by others as normative gender behavior.

Agnes's strategy of "secret apprenticeship," through which she learned expected feminine decorum by carefully attending to her fiancé's criticisms of other women, was one means of masking incompetencies and simultaneously acquiring the needed skills (Garfinkel 1967, pp. 146–47). It was through her fiancé that Agnes learned that sunbathing on the lawn in front of her apartment was "offensive" (because it put her on display to other men). She also learned from his critiques of other women that she should not insist on having things her way and that she should not offer her opinions or claim equality with men (Garfinkel 1967, pp. 147–48). (Like other women in our society, Agnes learned something about power in the course of her "education.")

Popular culture abounds with books and magazines that compile idealized depictions of relations between women and men. Those focused on the etiquette of dating or prevailing standards of feminine comportment are meant to be of practical help in these matters. However, the use of any such source *as a manual of procedure* requires the assumption that doing gender merely involves making use of discrete, well-defined bundles of behavior that can simply be plugged into interactional situations to produce recognizable enactments of masculinity and femininity. The man "does" being masculine by, for example, taking the woman's arm to guide her across a street, and she "does" being feminine by consenting to be guided and not initiating such behavior with a man.

Agnes could perhaps have used such sources as manuals, but, we contend, doing gender is not so easily regimented. Such sources may list and describe the sorts of behaviors that mark or display gender, but they are necessarily incomplete. And to be successful, marking or displaying gender must be finely fitted to situations and modified or transformed as the occasion demands. Doing gender consists of managing such occasions so that, whatever the particulars, the outcome is seen and seeable in context as gender-appropriate or, as the case may be, gender-*in*appropriate, that is, *accountable*.

Gender and Accountability

As Heritage (1984, pp. 136–37) notes, members of society regularly engage in "descriptive accountings of states of affairs to one another," and such accounts are both serious and consequential. These descriptions name, characterize, formulate, explain, excuse, excoriate, or merely take notice of some circumstance or activity and thus place it within some social framework (locating it relative to other activities, like and unlike).

Such descriptions are themselves accountable, and societal members orient to the fact that their activities are subject to comment. Actions are often designed with an eye to their accountability, that is, how they might look and how they might be characterized. The notion of accountability also encompasses those actions undertaken so that they are specifically unremarkable and thus not worthy of more than a passing remark, because they are seen to be in accord with culturally approved standards.

Heritage (1984, p. 179) observes that the process of rendering something accountable is interactional in character:

> [This] permits actors to design their actions in relation to their circumstances so as to permit others, by methodically taking account of circumstances, to recognize the action for what it is.

The key word here is *circumstances*. One circumstance that attends virtually all actions is the sex category of the actor. As Garfinkel (1967, p. 118) comments:

> [T]he work and socially structured occasions of sexual passing were obstinately unyielding to [Agnes's] attempts to routinize the grounds of daily activities. This obstinacy points to the *omnirelevance* of sexual status to affairs of daily life as an invariant but unnoticed background in the texture of relevances that compose the changing actual scenes of everyday life. (italics added)

If sex category is omnirelevant (or even approaches being so), then a person engaged in virtually any activity may be held accountable for performance of that activity as a *woman* or a *man,* and their incumbency in one or the other sex category can be used to legitimate or discredit their other activities. Accordingly, virtually any activity can be assessed as to its womanly or manly nature. And note, to "do" gender is not always to live up to normative conceptions of femininity or masculinity; it is to engage in behavior *at the risk of gender assessment.* While it is individuals who do gender, the enterprise is fundamentally interactional and institutional in character, for accountability is a feature of social relationships and its idiom is drawn from the institutional arena in which those relationships are enacted. If this be the case, can we ever *not* do gender? Insofar as a society is partitioned by "essential" differences between women and men and placement in a sex category is both relevant and enforced, doing gender is unavoidable.

Resources for Doing Gender

Doing gender means creating differences between girls and boys and women and men, differences that are not natural, essential, or biological. Once the differences have been constructed, they are used to reinforce the "essentialness" of gender. In a delightful account of the "arrangement between the sexes," Goffman (1977) observes the creation of a variety of institutionalized frameworks through which our "natural, normal sexedness" can be enacted. The physical features of social setting provide one obvious resource for the expression of our "essential" differences. For example, the sex segregation of North American public bathrooms distinguishes "ladies" from "gentlemen" in matters held to be fundamentally biological, even though both "are somewhat similar in the question of waste products and their elimination" (Goffman 1977, p. 315). These settings are furnished with dimorphic equipment (such as urinals for men or elaborate grooming facilities for women), even though both sexes may achieve the same ends through the same means (and apparently do so in the privacy of their own homes). To be stressed here is the fact that:

> The *functioning* of sex-differentiated organs is involved, but there is nothing in this functioning that biologically recommends segregation; that arrangement is a totally cultural matter…toilet segregation is presented as a natural consequence of the difference between the sex-classes when in fact it is a means of honoring, if not producing, this difference. (Goffman 1977, p. 316)

Standardized social occasions also provide stages for evocations of the "essential female and male natures." Goffman cites organized sports as one such institutionalized framework for the expression of manliness. There, those qualities that ought "properly" to be associated with masculinity, such as endurance, strength, and competitive spirit, are celebrated by all parties concerned—participants, who may be seen to demonstrate such traits, and spectators, who applaud their demonstrations from the safety of the sidelines (1977, p. 322).

Assortative mating practices among heterosexual couples afford still further means to create and maintain differences between women and men. For example, even though size, strength, and age tend to be normally distributed among females and males (with considerable overlap between them), selective pairing ensures couples in which boys and men are visibly bigger, stronger, and older (if not "wiser") than the girls and women with whom they are paired. So, should situations emerge in which greater size, strength, or experience is called for, boys and men will be ever ready to display it and girls and women, to appreciate its display.

Gender may be routinely fashioned in a variety of situations that seem conventionally expressive to begin with, such as those that present "helpless" women next to heavy objects or flat tires. But, as Goffman notes, heavy, messy, and precarious concerns can be constructed from *any* social situation, "even though by standards set in other settings, this may involve something that is light, clean, and safe" (Goffman 1977, p. 324). Given these resources, it is clear that any interactional situation sets the stage for depictions of "essential" sexual natures. In sum, these situations "do not so much allow for the expression of natural differences as for the production of that difference itself" (Goffman 1977, p. 324).

Many situations are not clearly sex categorized to begin with, nor is what transpires within them obviously gender relevant. Yet any social encounter can be pressed into service in the interests of doing gender. Thus, Fishman's (1978) research on casual conversations found an asymmetrical "division of labor" in talk between hetero-sexual intimates. Women had to ask more questions, fill more silences, and use more attention-getting beginnings in order to be heard. Her conclusions are particularly pertinent here:

> Since interactional work is related to what constitutes being a woman, with what a woman is, the idea that it is work is obscured. The work is not seen as what women do, but as part of what they are. (Fishman 1978, p. 405)

We would argue that it is precisely such labor that helps to constitute the essential nature of women as women in interactional contexts.

Individuals have many social identities that may be donned or shed, muted or made more salient, depending on the situation. One may be a friend, spouse, professional, citizen, and many other things to many different people—or, to the same person at different times. But we are always women or men—unless we shift into another sex category. What this means is that our identificatory displays will provide an ever-available resource for doing gender under an infinitely diverse set of circumstances.

Some occasions are organized to routinely display and celebrate behaviors that are conventionally linked to one or the other sex category. On such occasions, everyone knows his or her place in the interactional scheme of things. If an individual identified as a member of one sex category engages in behavior usually associated with the other category, this routinization is challenged. Hughes (1945, p. 356) provides an illustration of such a dilemma:

> [A] young woman...became part of that virile profession, engineering. The designer of an airplane is expected to go up on the maiden flight of the first plane built according to the design. He [sic] then gives a dinner to the engineers and workmen who worked on the new plane. The dinner is naturally a stag party. The young woman in question designed a plane. Her co-workers urged her not to take the risk—for which, presumably, men only are fit—of the maiden voyage. They were, in effect, asking her to be a lady instead of an engineer. She chose to be an engineer. She then gave the party and paid for it like a man. After food and the first round of toasts, she left like a lady.

On this occasion, parties reached an accommodation that allowed a woman to engage in presumptively masculine behaviors. However, we note that in the end, this compromise permitted demonstration of her "essential" femininity, through accountably "ladylike" behavior.

Hughes (1945, p. 357) suggests that such contradictions may be countered by managing interactions on a very narrow basis, for example, "keeping the relationship formal and specific." But the heart of the matter is that even—perhaps, especially—if the relationship is a formal one, gender is still something one is accountable for. Thus a woman physician (notice the special qualifier in her case) may be accorded respect for her skill and even addressed by an appropriate title. Nonetheless, she is subject to evaluation in terms of normative conceptions of appropriate attitudes and activities for her sex category and under pressure to prove that she is an "essentially" feminine being, despite appearances to the contrary. Her sex category is used to discredit her participation in important clinical activities, while her involvement in medicine is used to discredit her commitment to her responsibilities as a wife and mother. Simultaneously, her exclusion from the physician colleague community is maintained and her accountability *as a woman* is ensured.

In this context, "role conflict" can be viewed as a dynamic aspect of our current "arrangement between the sexes" (Goffman 1977), an arrangement that provides for occasions on which persons of a particular sex category can "see" quite clearly that they are out of place and that if they were not there, their current troubles would not exist. What is at stake is, from the standpoint of interaction, the management of our "essential" natures, and from the standpoint of the individual, the continuing accomplishment of gender. If, as we have argued, sex category is omnirelevant, then any occasion, conflicted or not, offers the resources for doing gender.

We have sought to show that sex category and gender are managed properties of conduct that are contrived with respect to the fact that others will judge and respond to us in particular ways. We have claimed that a person's gender is not simply an aspect of what one is, but, more fundamentally, it is something that one does, and *does* recurrently, in interaction with others.

What are the consequences of this theoretical formulation? If, for example, individuals strive to achieve gender in encounters with others, how does a culture instill the need to achieve it? What is the relationship between the production of gender at the level of interaction and such institutional arrangements as the division of labor in society? And, perhaps most important, how does doing gender contribute to the subordination of women by men?

Research Agendas

To bring the social production of gender under empirical scrutiny, we might begin at the beginning, with a reconsideration of the process through which societal members acquire the requisite categorical apparatus and other skills to become gendered human beings.

Recruitment to Gender Identities

The conventional approach to the process of becoming girls and boys has been sex-role socialization. In recent years, recurring problems arising from this approach have been linked to inadequacies inherent in role theory *per se*—its emphasis on "consensus, stability and continuity" (Stacey and Thorne 1985, p. 307), its historical and depoliticizing focus (Thorne 1980, p. 9; Stacey and Thorne 1985, p. 307), and the fact that its "social" dimension relies on "a general assumption that people choose to maintain existing customs" (Connell 1985, p. 263).

In contrast, Cahill (1982, 1986a, 1986b) analyzes the experiences of preschool children using a social model of recruitment into normally gendered identities. Cahill argues that categorization practices are fundamental to learning and displaying feminine and masculine behavior. Initially, he observes, children are primarily concerned with distinguishing between themselves and others on the basis of social competence. Categorically, their concern resolves itself into the opposition of "girl/boy" classification versus "baby" classification (the latter designating children whose social behavior is problematic and who must be closely supervised). It is children's concern with being seen as socially competent that evokes their initial claims to gender identities:

> During the exploratory stage of children's socialization...they learn that only two social identities are routinely available to them, the identity of "baby," or, depending on the configuration of their external genitalia, either "big boy" or "big girl." Moreover, others subtly inform them that the identity of "baby" is a discrediting one. When, for example, children engage in disapproved behavior, they are often told "You're a baby" or "Be a big boy." In effect, these typical verbal responses to young children's behavior convey to them that they must behaviorally choose between the discrediting identity of "baby" and their anatomically determined sex identity. (Cahill 1986a, p. 175)

Subsequently, little boys appropriate the gender ideal of "efficaciousness," that is, being able to affect the physical and social environment through the exercise of physical strength or appropriate skills. In contrast, little girls learn to value "appearance," that is, managing themselves as ornamental objects. Both classes of children learn that the recognition and use of sex categorization in interaction are not optional, but mandatory.

Being a "girl" or a "boy" then, is not only being more competent than a "baby," but also being competently female or male, that is, learning to produce behavioral displays of one's "essential" female or male identity. In this respect, the task of four- to five-year-old children is very similar to Agnes's:

> For example, the following interaction occurred on a preschool playground. A 55-month-old boy (D) was attempting to unfasten the clasp of a necklace when a preschool aide walked over to him.
>
> A: Do you want to put that on?
> D: No. It's for girls.
> A: You don't have to be a girl to wear things around your neck. Kings wear things around their necks. You could pretend you're a king.
> D: I'm not a king. I'm a boy. (Cahill 1986a, p. 176)

As Cahill notes of this example, although D may have been unclear as to the sex status of a king's identity, he was obviously aware that necklaces are used to announce the identity "girl." Having claimed the identity "boy" and having developed a behavioral commitment to it, he was leery of any display that might furnish grounds for questioning his claim.

In this way, new members of society come to be involved in a *self-regulating process* as they begin to monitor their own and others' conduct with regard to its gender implications. The "recruitment" process involves not only the appropriation of gender ideals (by the valuation of those ideals as proper ways of being and behaving) but also *gender identities* that are important to individuals and that they strive to maintain. Thus gender differences, or the sociocultural shaping of "essential female and male natures," achieve the status of objective facts. They are rendered normal, natural features of persons and provide the tacit rationale for differing fates of women and men within the social order.

Additional studies of children's play activities as routine occasions for the expression of gender-appropriate behavior can yield new insights into how our "essential natures" are constructed. In particular, the transition from what Cahill (1986a) terms "apprentice participation" in the sex-segregated worlds that are common among elementary school children to "bona fide participation" in the heterosocial world so frightening to adolescents is likely to be a keystone in our understanding of the recruitment process.

Gender and the Division of Labor

Whenever people face issues of *allocation*—who is to do what, get what, plan or execute action, direct or be directed, incumbency in significant social categories such as "female" and "male" seems to become pointedly relevant. How such issues are resolved conditions the exhibition, dramatization, or celebration of one's "essential nature" as a woman or man.

Berk (1985) offers elegant demonstration of this point in her investigation of the allocation of household labor and the attitudes of married couples toward the division of household tasks. Berk found little variation in either the actual distribution of tasks or perceptions of equity in regard to that distribution. Wives, even when employed outside the home, do the vast majority of household and child-care tasks. Moreover, both wives and husbands tend to perceive this as a "fair" arrangement. Noting the failure of conventional sociological and economic theories to explain this seeming contradiction, Berk contends that something more complex is involved than rational arrangements for the production of household goods and services:

> Hardly a question simply of who has more time, or whose time is worth more, who has more skill or more power, it is clear that a complicated relationship between the structure of work imperatives and the structure of normative expectations attached to work as *gendered* determines the ultimate allocation of members' time to work and home. (Berk 1985, pp. 195–96)

She notes, for example, that the most important factor influencing wives' contribution of labor is the total amount of work demanded or expected by the household; such demands had no bearing on husbands' contributions. Wives reported various rationales (their own and their husbands') that justified their level of contribution and, as a general matter, underscored the presumption that wives are essentially responsible for household production.

Berk (1985, p. 201) contends that it is difficult to see how people "could rationally establish the arrangements that they do solely for the production of household goods and services"—much less, how people could consider them "fair." She argues that our current arrangements for the domestic division of labor support *two* production processes: household goods and services (meals, clean children, and so on) and, at the same time, gender. As she puts it:

> Simultaneously, members "do" gender, as they "do" housework and child care, and what [has] been called the division of labor provides for the joint production of household labor and gender; it is the mechanism by which both the material and symbolic products of the household are realized. (1985, p. 201)

It is not simply that household labor is designated as "women's work," but that for a woman to engage in it and a man not to engage in it is to draw on and exhibit the "essential nature" of each. What is produced and reproduced is not merely the activity and artifact of domestic life, but the material embodiment of wifely and husbandly roles, and derivatively, of womanly and manly conduct. What are also frequently produced and reproduced are the dominant and subordinate statuses of the sex categories.

How does gender get done in work settings outside the home, where dominance and subordination are themes of overarching importance? Hochschild's (1983) analysis of the work of flight attendants offers some promising insights. She found that the occupation of flight attendant consisted of something altogether different for women than for men:

As the company's main shock absorbers against "mishandled" passengers, their own feelings are more frequently subjected to rough treatment. In addition, a day's exposure to people who resist authority in a woman is a different experience than it is for a man.... In this respect, it is a disadvantage to be a woman. And in this case, they are not simply women in the biological sense. They are also a highly visible distillation of middle-class American notions of femininity. They symbolize Woman. Insofar as the category "female" is mentally associated with having less status and authority, female flight attendants are more readily classified as "really" females than other females are. (Hochschild 1983, p. 175)

In performing what Hochschild terms the "emotional labor" necessary to maintain airline profits, women flight attendants simultaneously produce enactments of their "essential" femininity.

Sex and Sexuality

What is the relationship between doing gender and a culture's prescription of "obligatory heterosexuality"? As Frye (1983, p. 22) observes, the monitoring of sexual feelings in relation to other appropriately sexed persons requires the ready recognition of such persons "before one can allow one's heart to beat or one's blood to flow in erotic enjoyment of that person." The appearance of heterosexuality is produced through emphatic and unambiguous indicators of one's sex, layered on in ever more conclusive fashion (Frye 1983, p. 24). Thus, lesbians and gay men concerned with passing as heterosexuals can rely on these indicators for camouflage; in contrast, those who would avoid the assumption of heterosexuality may foster ambiguous indicators of their categorical status through their dress, behaviors, and style. But "ambiguous" sex indicators are sex indicators nonetheless. If one wishes to be recognized as a lesbian (or heterosexual woman), one must first establish a categorical status as female. Even as popular images portray lesbians as "females who are not feminine" (Frye 1983, p. 129), the accountability of persons for their "normal, natural sexedness" is preserved.

Nor is accountability threatened by the existence of "sex-change operations"—presumably, the most radical challenge to our cultural perspective on sex and gender. Although no one coerces transsexuals into hormone therapy, electrolysis, or surgery, the alternatives available to them are undeniably constrained:

> When the transsexual experts maintain that they use transsexual procedures only with people who ask for them, and who prove that they can "pass," they obscure the social reality. Given patriarchy's prescription that one must be *either* masculine or feminine, free choice is conditioned. (Raymond 1979, p. 135, italics added)

The physical reconstruction of sex criteria pays ultimate tribute to the "essentialness" of our sexual natures—as women *or* as men.

Gender, Power, and Social Change

Let us return to the question: Can we avoid doing gender? Earlier, we proposed that insofar as sex category is used as a fundamental criterion for differentiation, doing gender is unavoidable. It is unavoidable because of the social consequences of sex-category membership: the allocation of power and resources not only in the domestic, economic, and political domains but also in the broad arena of interpersonal relations. In virtually any situation, one's sex category can be relevant, and one's performance as an incumbent of that category (i.e., gender) can be subjected to evaluation. Maintaining such pervasive and faithful assignment of lifetime status requires legitimation.

But doing gender also renders the social arrangements based on sex category accountable as normal and natural, that is, legitimate ways of organizing social life. Differences between women and men that are created by this process can then be portrayed as fundamental and enduring dispositions. In this light, the institutional arrangements of a society can be seen as responsive to the differences—the social order being merely an accommodation to the natural order. Thus if, in doing gender, men are also doing dominance and women are doing deference, the resultant social order, which supposedly reflects "natural differences," is a powerful reinforcer and legitimator of hierarchical arrangements. Frye observes:

> For efficient subordination, what's wanted is that the structure not appear to be a cultural artifact kept in place by human decision or custom, but that it appear *natural*—that it appear to be quite a direct consequence of facts about the beast which are beyond the scope of human manipulation.... That we are trained to behave so differently as women and men, and to behave so differently toward women and men, itself contributes mightily to the appearance of extreme dimorphism, but also, the *ways* we act as women and men, and the *ways* we act toward women and men, mold our bodies and our minds to the shape of subordination and dominance. We do become what we practice being. (Frye 1983, p. 34)

If we do gender appropriately, we simultaneously sustain, reproduce, and render legitimate the institutional arrangements that are based on sex category. If we fail to do gender appropriately, we as individuals—not the institutional arrangements—may be called to account (for our character, motives, and predispositions).

Social movements such as feminism can provide the ideology and impetus to question existing arrangements, and the social support for individuals to explore alternatives to them. Legislative changes, such as that proposed by the Equal Rights Amendment, can also weaken the accountability of conduct to sex category, thereby affording the possibility of more widespread loosening of accountability in general. To be sure, equality under the law does not guarantee equality in other arenas. As Lorber (1986, p. 577) points out, assurance of "scrupulous equality of categories of people considered essentially different needs constant monitoring." What such proposed changes can do is provide the warrant for asking why, if we wish to treat women and men as equals, there needs to be two sex categories at all.

The sex category/gender relationship links the institutional and interactional levels, a coupling that legitimates social arrangements based on sex category and reproduces their asymmetry in face-to-face interaction. Doing gender furnishes the interactional scaffolding of social structure, along with a built-in mechanism of social control. In appreciating the institutional forces that maintain distinctions between women and men, we must not lose sight of the interactional validation of those distinctions that confers upon them their sense of "naturalness" and "rightness."

Social change, then, must be pursued both at the institutional and cultural level of sex category and at the interactional level of gender. Such a conclusion is hardly novel. Nevertheless, we suggest that it is important to recognize that the analytical distinction between institutional and interactional spheres does not pose an either/or choice when it comes to the question of effecting social change. Reconceptualizing gender not as a simple property of individuals but as an integral dynamic of social orders implies a new perspective on the entire network of gender relations:

> [T]he social subordination of women, and the cultural practices which help sustain it; the politics of sexual object-choice, and particularly the oppression of homosexual people; the sexual division of labor, the formation of character and motive, so far as they are organized as femininity and masculinity; the role of the body in social relations, especially the politics of childbirth; and the nature of strategies of sexual liberation movements. (Connell 1985, p. 261)

Gender is a powerful ideological device, which produces, reproduces, and legitimates the choices and limits that are predicated on sex category. An understanding of how gender is produced in social situations will afford clarification of the interactional scaffolding of social structure and the social control processes that sustain it.

References

Berk, Sarah F. 1985. *The Gender Factory: The Apportionment of Work in American Households.* New York: Plenum.

Cahill, Spencer E. 1982. "Becoming Boys and Girls." Ph.D. dissertation, Department of Sociology, University of California, Santa Barbara.

———. 1986a. "Childhood Socialization as Recruitment Process: Some Lessons from the Study of Gender Development." Pp. 163–86 in *Sociological Studies of Child Development,* edited by P. Adler and P. Adler. Greenwich, CT: JAI Press.

———. 1986b. "Language Practices and Self-Definition: The Case of Gender Identity Acquisition." *The Sociological Quarterly* 27:295–311.

Connell, R.W. 1985. "Theorizing Gender." *Sociology* 19:260–72.

Fishman, Pamela. 1978. "Interaction: The Work Women Do." *Social Problems* 25:397–406.

Frye, Marilyn. 1983. *The Politics of Reality: Essays in Feminist Theory.* Trumansburg, NY: The Crossing Press.

Garfinkel, Harold. 1967. *Studies in Ethnomethodology.* Englewood Cliffs, NJ: Prentice-Hall.

Goffman, Erving. 1976. "Gender Display." *Studies in the Anthropology of Visual Communication* 3:69–77.

———. 1977. "The Arrangement Between the Sexes." *Theory and Society* 4:301–31.

Heritage, John. 1984. *Garfinkel and Ethnomethodology.* Cambridge, England: Polity Press.

Hochschild, Arlie R. 1983. *The Managed Heart. Commercialization of Human Feeling.* Berkeley: University of California Press.

Hughes, Everett C. 1945. "Dilemmas and Contradictions of Status." *American Journal of Sociology* 50:353–59.

Kessler, Suzanne J., and Wendy McKenna. 1978. *Gender: An Ethnomethodological Approach.* New York: Wiley.

Komarovsky, Mirra. 1946. "Cultural Contradictions and Sex Roles." *American Journal of Sociology* 52:184–89.

———. 1950. "Functional Analysis of Sex Roles." *American Sociological Review* 15:508–16.

Linton, Ralph. 1936. *The Study of Man.* New York: Appleton-Century.

Lorber, Judith. 1986. "Dismantling Noah's Ark." *Sex Roles* 14:567–80.

Parsons, Talcott. 1951. *The Social System.* New York: Free Press.

———, and Robert F. Bales. 1955. *Family, Socialization and Interaction Process.* New York: Free Press.

Raymond, Janice G. 1979. *The Transsexual Empire.* Boston: Beacon.

Rossi, Alice. 1984. "Gender and Parenthood." *American Sociological Review* 49:1–19.

Rubin, Gayle. 1975. "The Traffic in Women: Notes on the 'Political Economy' of Sex." Pp. 157–210 in *Toward an Anthropology of Women,* edited by R. Reiter. New York: Monthly Review Press.

Stacey, Judith, and Barrie Thorne. 1985. "The Missing Feminist Revolution in Sociology." *Social Problems* 32:301–16.

Thorne, Barrie. 1980. "Gender…How Is It Best Conceptualized?" Unpublished manuscript.

Doing Difference

CANDACE WEST AND SARAH FENSTERMAKER

Few persons think of math as a particularly feminine pursuit. Girls are not supposed to be good at it and women are not supposed to enjoy it. It is interesting, then, that we who do feminist scholarship have relied so heavily on mathematical metaphors to describe the relationships among gender, race, and class.[1] For example, some of us have drawn on basic arithmetic, adding, subtracting, and dividing what we know about race and class to what we already know about gender. Some have relied on multiplication, seeming to calculate the effects of the whole from the combination of different parts. And others have employed geometry, drawing on images of interlocking or intersecting planes and axes.

To be sure, the sophistication of our mathematical metaphors often varies with the apparent complexity of our own experiences. Those of us who, at one point, were able to "forget" race and class in our analyses of gender relations may be more likely to "add" these at a later point. By contrast, those of us who could never forget these dimensions of social life may be more likely to draw on complex geometrical imagery all along; nonetheless, the existence of so many different approaches to the topic seems indicative of the difficulties all of us have experienced in coming to terms with it.

Not surprisingly, proliferation of these approaches has caused considerable confusion in the existing literature. In the same book or article, we may find references to gender, race, and class as "intersecting systems," as "interlocking categories," and as "multiple bases" for oppression. In the same anthology, we may find some chapters that conceive of gender, race, and class as distinct axes and others that conceive of them as concentric ones. The problem is that these alternative formulations have very distinctive, yet unarticulated, theoretical implications. For instance, if we think about gender, race, and class as additive categories, the whole will never be greater (or lesser) than the sum of its parts. By contrast, if we conceive of these as multiples, the result could be larger or smaller than their added sum, depending on where we place the signs.[2] Geometric metaphors further complicate things, since we still need to know where those planes and axes go after they cross the point of intersection (if they are parallel planes and axes, they will never intersect at all).

Our purpose in this article is not to advance yet another new math but to propose a new way of thinking about the workings of these relations. Elsewhere (Berk 1985; Fenstermaker, West, and Zimmerman 1991; West and Fenstermaker 1993; West and Zimmerman 1987), we offered an ethnomethodologically informed, and, hence, distinctively sociological, conceptualization of gender as a routine, methodical, and ongoing accomplishment. We argued that doing gender involves a complex of perceptual, interactional, and micropolitical activities that cast particular pursuits as expressions of manly and womanly "natures." Rather than conceiving of gender as an individual characteristic, we conceived of it as an emergent property of social situations: both an outcome of and a rationale for various social arrangements and a means of justifying one of the most fundamental divisions of society. We suggested that examining how gender is accomplished could reveal the mechanisms by which power is exercised and inequality is produced.

Our earlier formulation neglected race and class; thus, it is an incomplete framework for understanding social inequality. In this article, we extend our analysis to consider explicitly the relationships among gender, race, and class, and to reconceptualize "difference" as an ongoing interactional accomplishment. We start by summarizing the prevailing critique of much feminist thought as severely constrained by its white middle-class character and preoccupation. Here, we consider how feminist scholarship ends up borrowing from mathematics in the first place. Next, we consider how existing conceptualizations of gender have contributed to the problem, rendering mathematical metaphors the only alternatives. Then, calling on our earlier ethnomethodological conceptualization of gender, we develop the further implications of this perspective for our understanding of race and class. We assert that, while gender, race, and class—what people come to experience as organizing categories of social difference—exhibit vastly different descriptive characteristics and outcomes, they are, nonetheless, comparable as mechanisms for producing social inequality.

White Middle-Class Bias in Feminist Thought

What is it about feminist thinking that makes race and class such difficult concepts to articulate within its own parameters? The most widely agreed upon and disturbing answer to this question is that feminist thought suffers from a white middle-class bias. The privileging of white and middle-class sensibilities in feminist thought results from both who did the theorizing and how they did it. White middle-class women's advantaged viewpoint in a racist and class-bound culture, coupled with the Western tendency to construct the self as distinct from "other," distorts their depictions of reality in predictable directions (Young 1990). The

consequences of these distortions have been identified in a variety of places, and analyses of them have enlivened every aspect of feminist scholarship (see, for example, Aptheker 1989; Collins 1990; Davis 1981; Hurtado 1989; Zinn 1990).

For example, bell hooks points out that feminism within the United States has never originated among the women who are most oppressed by sexism, "women who are daily beaten down, mentally, physically, and spiritually—women who are powerless to change their condition in life" (1984, 1). The fact that those most victimized are least likely to question or protest is, according to hooks (1984), a consequence of their victimization. From this perspective, the white middle-class character of most feminist thought stems directly from the identities of those who produce it.

Aída Hurtado notes further the requisite time and resources that are involved in the production of feminist writing: "without financial assistance, few low-income and racial/ethnic students can attend universities; without higher education, few working-class and ethnic/racial intellectuals can become professors" (1989, 838). Given that academics dominate the production of published feminist scholarship, it is not surprising that feminist theory is dominated by white, highly educated women (see also hooks 1981; Joseph and Lewis 1981).

Still others (Collins 1990; Davis 1981; Lorde 1984; Moraga and Anzaldúa 1981; Zinn, Cannon, Higginbotham, and Dill 1986) point to the racism and classism of feminist scholars themselves. Maxine Baca Zinn and her colleagues observe that, "despite white, middle-class feminists' frequent expressions of interest and concern over the plight of minority and working-class women, those holding the gatekeeping positions at important feminist journals are as white as are those at any mainstream social science or humanities publication" (1986, 293).

Racism and classism can take a variety of forms. Adrienne Rich contends that, although white (middle-class) feminists may not consciously believe that their race is superior to any other, they are often plagued by a form of "white solipsism"—thinking, imagining, and speaking "as if whiteness described the world," resulting in "a tunnel-vision which simply does not see nonwhite experience or existence as precious or significant, unless in spasmodic, impotent guilt reflexes, which have little or no long-term, continuing usefulness" (1979, 306). White middle-class feminists, therefore, may offer conscientious expressions of concern over "racism-and-classism," believing that they have thereby taken into consideration profound differences in women's experience; simultaneously, they can fail to see those differences at all (Bhavani in press).

There is nothing that prevents any of these dynamics from coexisting and working together. For example, Patricia Hill Collins (1990) argues that the suppression of Black feminist thought stems both from white feminists' racist and classist concerns and from Black women intellectuals' consequent lack of participation in white feminist organizations. Similarly, Cherríe Moraga (1981) argues that the "denial of difference" in feminist organizations derives not only from white middle-class women's failure to "see" it but also from women of color's and working-class women's reluctance to challenge such blindness. Alone and in combination with one another, these sources of bias do much to explain why there has been a general failure to articulate race and class within the parameters of feminist scholarship; however, they do not explain the attraction of mathematical metaphors to right the balance. To understand this development, we must look further at the logic of feminist thought itself.

Mathematical Metaphors and Feminist Thought

Following the earlier suggestion of bell hooks (1981; see also Hull, Scott, and Smith 1982), Elizabeth Spelman contends that, in practice, the term "women" actually functions as a powerful false generic in white feminists' thinking:

> The "problem of difference" for feminist theory has never been a general one about how to weigh the importance of what we have in common against the importance of our differences. To put it that way hides two crucial facts: First, the description of

what we have in common "as women" has almost always been a description of white middle-class women. Second, the "difference" of this group of women—that is, their being white and middle-class—has never had to be "brought into" feminist theory. To bring in "difference" is to bring in women who aren't white and middle class. (1988, 4)

She warns that thinking about privilege merely as a characteristic of individuals—rather than as a characteristic of modes of thought—may afford us an understanding of "what privilege feeds but not what sustains it" (1988, 4).

What are the implications of a feminist mode of thought that is so severely limited? The most important one, says Spelman, is the presumption that we can effectively and usefully isolate gender from race and class. To illustrate this point, she draws on many white feminists who develop their analyses of sexism by comparing and contrasting it with "other" forms of oppression. Herein she finds the basis for additive models of gender, race, and class, and "the ampersand problem":

> de Beauvoir tends to talk about comparisons between sex and race, or between sex and class, or between sex and culture...comparisons between sexism and racism, between sexism and classism, between sexism and anti-Semitism. In the work of Chodorow and others influenced by her, we observe a readiness to look for links between sexism and other forms of oppression as distinct from sexism. (1988, 115)

Spelman notes that in both cases, attempts to add "other" elements of identity to gender, or "other" forms of oppression to sexism, disguise the race (white) and class (middle) identities of those seen as "women" in the first place. Rich's "white solipsism" comes into play again, and it is impossible to envision how women who are not white and middle class fit into the picture.

Although Spelman (1988) herself does not address mathematical metaphors based on multiplication, we believe that her argument is relevant to understanding how they develop. For example, take Cynthia Fuchs Epstein's (1973) notion of the "positive effect of the multiple negative" on the success of Black professional women. According to Epstein, when the "negative status" of being a woman is combined with the "negative status" of being Black, the result is the "positive status" of Black professional women in the job market. Baca Zinn and her colleagues contend that the very idea of this "multiple negative" having a positive effect "could not have survived the scrutiny of professional Black women or Black women students" (1986, 293). They suggest that only someone who was substantially isolated from Black women and their life experiences could have developed such a theory (and, presumably, only someone similarly situated could have promoted its publication in an established mainstream sociology journal).

Spelman's (1988) analysis highlights the following problem: if we conceive of gender as coherently isolatable from race and class, then there is every reason to assume that the effects of the three variables can be multiplied, with results dependent on the valence (positive or negative) of those multiplied variables; yet, if we grant that gender cannot be coherently isolated from race and class in the way we conceptualize it, then multiplicative metaphors make little sense.

If the effects of "multiple oppression" are not merely additive nor simply multiplicative, what are they? Some scholars have described them as the products of "simultaneous and intersecting systems of relationship and meaning" (Andersen and Collins 1992, xiii; see also Almquist 1989; Collins 1990; Glenn 1985). This description is useful insofar as it offers an accurate characterization of persons who are simultaneously oppressed on the basis of gender, race, and class, in other words, those "at the intersection" of all three systems of domination; however, if we conceive of the basis of oppression as more than membership in a category, then the theoretical implications of this formulation are troubling. For instance, what conclusions shall we draw from potential comparisons between persons who experience oppression on the basis of their race and class (e.g., working-class men of color) and those who are oppressed on the basis of their gender and class (e.g., white working-class women)? Would the "intersection of two systems of meaning in each case be sufficient to predict common bonds among them"? Clearly not, says June Jordan: "When these factors of race, class and gender absolutely collapse is whenever you try to use them as automatic concepts of connection." She goes on to say that, while these concepts may work very well as indexes of "commonly felt conflict," their predictive value when they are used as "elements of connection" is "about as reliable as precipitation probability for the day after the night before the day" (1985, 46).

What conclusions shall we draw from comparisons between persons who are said to suffer oppression "at the intersection" of all three systems and those who suffer in the nexus of only two? Presumably, we will conclude that the latter are "less oppressed" than the former (assuming that each categorical identity set amasses a specific quantity of oppression). Moraga warns, however, that "the danger lies in ranking the oppressions. *The danger lies in failing to acknowledge the specificity of the oppression*" (1981, 29).

Spelman (1988, 123–25) attempts to resolve this difficulty by characterizing sexism, racism, and classism as "interlocking" with one another. Along similar lines, Margaret Andersen and Patricia Hill Collins (1992, xii) describe gender, race, and class as "interlocking categories of experience." The image of interlocking rings comes to mind, linked in such a way that the motion of any one of them is constrained by the others. Certainly, this image is more dynamic than those conveyed by additive, multiplicative, or geometric models: we can see where the rings are joined (and where they are not), as well as how the movement of any one of them would be restricted by the others, but note that this image still depicts the rings as separate parts.

If we try to situate particular persons within this array, the problem with it becomes clear. We can, of course, conceive of the whole as "oppressed people" and of the rings as "those oppressed by gender," "those oppressed by race," and "those oppressed by class" (see Figure 4.1). This allows us to situate women and men of all races and classes within the areas covered by the circles, save for white middle- and upper-class men, who fall outside them. However, what if we conceive of the whole as

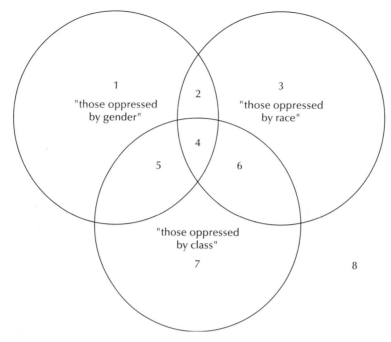

Figure 4.1. Oppressed People.

Note: 1 = White upper- and middle-class women; 2 = Upper- and middle-class women of color; 3 = Upper-and middle-class men of color; 4 = Working-class women of color; 5 = White working-class women; 6 = Working-class men of color; 7 = White working-class men; 8 = White upper- and middle-class men. This figure is necessarily oversimplified. For example, upper- and middle-class people are lumped together, neglecting the possibility of significant differences between them.

"experience"[3] and of the rings as gender, race, and class (see Figure 4.2)?

Here, we face an illuminating possibility and leave arithmetic behind: no person can experience gender without simultaneously experiencing race and class. As Andersen and Collins put it, "While race, class and gender can be seen as different axes of social structure, individual persons experience them simultaneously" (1992, xxi).[4] It is this simultaneity that has eluded our theoretical treatments and is so difficult to build into our empirical descriptions (for an admirable effort, see Segura 1992). Capturing it compels us to focus on the actual mechanisms that produce social inequality. How do forms of inequality, which we now see are more than the periodic collision of categories, operate together? How do we see that all social exchanges, regardless of the participants or the outcome, are simultaneously "gendered," "raced," and "classed"?

To address these questions, we first present some earlier attempts to conceptualize gender. Appreciation for the limitations of these efforts, we believe, affords us a way to the second task: reconceptualizing the dynamics of gender, race, and class as they figure simultaneously in human institutions and interaction.

Traditional Conceptualizations of Gender

To begin, we turn to Arlie Russell Hochschild's "A Review of Sex Roles Research," published in 1973. At that time, there were at least four distinct ways of conceptualizing gender within the burgeoning literature on the topic: (1) as sex differences, (2) as sex roles, (3) in relation to the minority status of

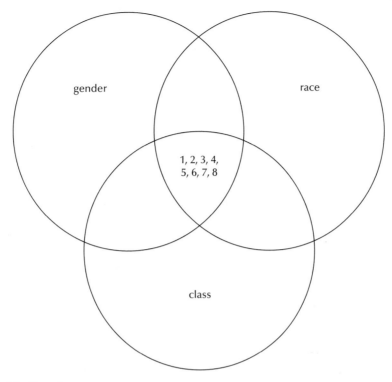

gender

race

1, 2, 3, 4,
5, 6, 7, 8

class

Figure 4.2. Experience.

Note: 1 = White upper- and middle-class women; 2 = Upper- and middle-class women of color; 3 = Upper- and middle-class men of color; 4 = Working-class women of color; 5 = White working-class women; 6 = Working-class men of color; 7 = White working-class men; 8 = White upper- and middle-class men. This fig- ure is necessarily oversimplified. For example, upper- and middle-class people are lumped together, neglect- ing the possibility of significant differences between them.

women, and (4) in relation to the caste/class status of women. Hochschild observes that each of these conceptualizations led to a different perspective on the behaviors of women and men:

> What is to type 1 a feminine trait such as passivity is to type 2 a role element, to type 3 is a minority characteristic, and to type 4 is a response to pow- erlessness. Social change might also look some- what different to each perspective; differences disappear, deviance becomes normal, the minor- ity group assimilates, or power is equalized. (1973, 1013)

Nona Glazer observes a further important dif- ference between the types Hochschild identified, namely, where they located the primary source of inequality between women and men:

The *sex difference* and [*sex*] *roles* approaches share an emphasis on understanding factors that charac- terize individuals. These factors may be inherent to each sex or acquired by individuals in the course of socialization. The *minority group* and *caste/class* approaches share an emphasis on factors that are external to individuals, a concern with the struc- ture of social institutions, and with the impact of historical events. (1977, 103)

In retrospect, it is profoundly disturbing to con- template what the minority group approach and the class/caste approach implied about feminist thinking at the time. For example, Juliet Mitchell launched "Women: The Longest Revolution" with the claim that "[t]he situation of women is differ- ent from that of any other social group...within the world of men, their position is comparable to that of an oppressed minority" (1966, 11). Obviously, if "women" could be compared to "an oppressed minority," they had to consist of someone other than "oppressed minorities" themselves (cf. Hacker 1951).

Perhaps because of such theoretical problems, feminist scholars have largely abandoned the effort to describe women as a caste, as a class, or as a minority group as a project in its own right (see, for example, Aptheker 1989; Hull, Scott, and Smith 1982). What we have been left with, however, are two prevailing conceptualizations: (1) the sex differences approach and (2) the sex roles approach. And note, while the minority group and caste/class approaches were concerned with factors external to the individual (e.g., the structure of social institutions and the impact of historical events), the approaches that remain emphasize factors that characterize the individual (Glazer 1977).

Arguably, some might call this picture oversimplified. Given the exciting new scholarship that focuses on gender as something that is socially constructed, and something that converges with other inequalities to produce difference among women, have we not moved well beyond "sex differences" and "sex roles"? A close examination of this literature suggests that we have not. For example, Collins contends that

> [w]hile race and gender are both socially constructed categories, constructions of gender *rest on clearer biological criteria* than do constructions of race. Classifying African-Americans into specious racial categories is considerably more difficult than noting the *clear biological differences* distinguishing females from males...Women do share common experiences, but the experiences are not generally the same type as those affecting racial and ethnic groups. (1990, 27, emphasis added)

Of course, Collins is correct in her claim that women differ considerably from one another with respect to the distinctive histories, geographic origins, and cultures they share with men of their same race and class. The problem, however, is that what unites them as women are the "clear biological criteria distinguishing females from males."

Here, Collins reverts to treating gender as a matter of sex differences (i.e., as ultimately traceable to factors inherent to each sex), in spite of her contention that it is socially constructed. Gender becomes conflated with sex, as race might speciously be made equivalent to color.

Consider a further example. Spelman launches her analysis with a discussion of the theoretical necessity of distinguishing sex from gender. She praises de Beauvoir (1953) for her early recognition of the difference between the two and goes on to argue,

> It is one thing to be biologically female, and quite another to be shaped by one's culture into a "woman"—a female with feminine qualities, someone who does the kinds of things "women" not "men" do, someone who has the kinds of thoughts and feelings that make doing these things seem an easy expression of one's feminine nature. (1988, 124)

How, then, does Spelman conceive of the social construction of woman? She not only invokes "sexual roles" to explain this process (1988, 121–23) but also speaks of "racial roles" (1988, 106) that affect the course that the process will take. Despite Spelman's elegant demonstration of how "woman" constitutes a false generic in feminist thought, her analysis takes us back to "sex roles" once again.

Our point here is not to take issue with Collins (1990) or Spelman (1988) in particular; it would be a misreading of our purpose to do so. We cite these works to highlight a more fundamental difficulty facing feminist theory in general: new conceptualizations of the bases of gender inequality still rest on old conceptualizations of gender (West and Fenstermaker 1993, 151). For example, those who rely on a sex differences approach conceive of gender as inhering in the individual, in other words, as the masculinity or femininity of a person. Elsewhere (Fenstermaker, West, and Zimmerman, 1991; West and Fenstermaker 1993; West and Zimmerman 1987), we note that this conceptualization obscures our understanding of how gender can structure distinctive domains of social experience (see also Stacey and Thorne

1985). "Sex differences" are treated as the explanation instead of the analytic point of departure.

Although many scholars who take this approach draw on socialization to account for the internalization of femininity and masculinity, they imply that by about five years of age these differences have become stable characteristics of individuals—much like sex (West and Zimmerman 1987, 126). The careful distinction between sex and gender, therefore, is obliterated, as gender is reduced effectively to sex (Gerson 1985).[5] When the social meanings of sex are rerooted in biology, it becomes virtually impossible to explain variation in gender relations in the context of race and class. We must assume, for example, that the effects of inherent sex differences are either added to or subtracted from those of race and class. We are led to assume, moreover, that sex differences are more fundamental than any other differences that might interest us (see Spelman 1988, 116–19, for a critical examination of this assumption)—unless we also assume that race differences and class differences are biologically based (for refutations of this assumption, see Gossett 1965; Montagu 1975; Omi and Winant 1986; and Stephans 1982).

Those who take a sex roles approach are confounded by similar difficulties, although these may be less apparent at the outset. What is deceptive is role theory's emphasis on the specific social locations that result in particular expectations and actions (Komarovsky 1946, 1992; Linton 1936; Parsons 1951; Parsons and Bales 1955). In this view, the actual enactment of an individual's "sex role" (or, more recently, "gender role") is contingent on the individual's social structural position and the expectations associated with that position. The focus is on gender as a role or status, as it is learned and enacted. In earlier work (Fenstermaker, West, and Zimmerman 1991; West and Fenstermaker 1993; West and Zimmerman 1987), we have noted several problems with this approach, including its inability to specify actions appropriate to particular "sex roles" in advance of their occurrence, and the fact that sex roles are not situated in any particular setting or organizational context (Lopata and Thorne 1978; Thorne 1980). The fact that "sex roles" often serve as "master statuses"

(Hughes 1945) makes it hard to account for how variations in situations produce variations in their enactment. Given that gender is potentially omnirelevant to how we organize social life, almost any action could count as an instance of sex role enactment.

The most serious problem with this approach, however, is its inability to address issues of power and inequality (Connell 1985; Lopata and Thorne 1987; Thorne 1980). Conceiving of gender as composed of the "male role" and the "female role" implies a separate-but-equal relationship between the two, one characterized by complementary relations rather than conflict. Elsewhere (Fenstermaker, West, and Zimmerman 1991; West and Fenstermaker 1993; West and Zimmerman 1987), we illustrate this problem with Barrie Thorne and her colleagues' observation that social scientists have not made much use of role theory in their analyses of race and class relations. Concepts such as "race roles" and "class roles" have seemed patently inadequate to account for the dynamics of power and inequality operating in those contexts.

As many scholars have observed, empirical studies of the "female role" and "male role" have generally treated the experiences of white middle-class persons as prototypes, dismissing departures from the prototypical as instances of deviance. This is in large part what has contributed to the charges of white middle-class bias we discussed earlier. It is also what has rendered the sex role approach nearly useless in accounting for the diversity of gender relations across different groups.

Seeking a solution to these difficulties, Joan Acker has advanced the view that gender consists of something else altogether, namely, "patterned, socially produced distinctions between female and male, feminine and masculine...[that occur] in the course of participation in work organizations as well as in many other locations and relations" (1992b, 250). The object here is to document the "gendered processes" that sustain "the pervasive ordering of human activities, practices and social structures in terms of differentiations between women and men" (1992a, 567).

We agree fully with the object of this view and note its usefulness in capturing the persistence and ubiquity of gender inequality. Its emphasis on organizational practices restores the concern with "the structure of social institutions and with the impact of historical events" that characterized earlier class/caste approaches, and facilitates the simultaneous documentation of gender, race, and class as basic principles of social organization. We suggest, however, that the popular distinction between "macro" and "micro" levels of analysis reflected in this view makes it possible to empirically describe and explain inequality without fully apprehending the common elements of its daily unfolding. For example, "processes of interaction" are conceptualized apart from the "production of gender divisions," that is, "the overt decisions and procedures that control, segregate, exclude, and construct hierarchies based on gender, and often race" (Acker 1992a, 568). The production of "images, symbols and ideologies that justify, explain, and give legitimacy to institutions" constitutes yet another "process," as do "the [mental] internal processes in which individuals engage as they construct personas that are appropriately gendered for the institutional setting" (Acker 1992a, 568). The analytic "missing link," as we see it, is the mechanism that ties these seemingly diverse processes together, one that could "take into account the constraining impact of entrenched ideas and practices on human agency, but [could] also acknowledge that the system is continually construed in everyday life and that, under certain conditions, individuals resist pressures to conform to the needs of the system" (Essed 1991, 38).

In sum, if we conceive of gender as a matter of biological differences or differential roles, we are forced to think of it as standing apart from and outside other socially relevant, organizing experiences. This prevents us from understanding how gender, race, and class operate simultaneously with one another. It prevents us from seeing how the particular salience of these experiences might vary across interactions. Most important, it gives us virtually no way of adequately addressing the mechanisms that produce power and inequality in social life. Instead, we propose a conceptual mechanism for perceiving the relations between individual and institutional practice, and among forms of domination.

An Ethnomethodological Perspective

Don Zimmerman concisely describes ethnomethodological inquiry as proposing "that the properties of social life which seem objective, factual, and transsituational, are actually managed accomplishments or achievements of local processes" (1978, 11). In brief, the "objective" and "factual" properties of social life attain such status through the situated conduct of societal members. The aim of ethnomethodology is to analyze situated conduct to understand how "objective" properties of social life achieve their status as such.

The goal of this article is not to analyze situated conduct per se but to understand the workings of inequality. We should note that our interest here is not to separate gender, race, and class as social categories but to build a coherent argument for understanding how they work simultaneously. How might an ethnomethodological perspective help with this task? As Marilyn Frye observes,

> For efficient subordination, what's wanted is that the structure not appear to be a cultural artifact kept in place by human decision or custom, but that it appear natural—that it appear to be quite a direct consequence of facts about the beast which are beyond the scope of human manipulation. (1983, 34)

Gender

Within Western societies, we take for granted in everyday life that there are two and only two sexes (Garfinkel 1967, 122). We see this state of affairs as "only natural" insofar as we see persons as "essentially, originally and in the final analysis either 'male' or 'female'" (Garfinkel 1967, 122). When we interact with others, we take for granted that each of us has an "essential" manly or womanly nature—one that derives from our sex and one that can be detected from the "natural signs" we give off (Goffman 1976, 75).

These beliefs constitute the normative conceptions of our culture regarding the properties of normally sexed persons. Such beliefs support the seemingly "objective," "factual," and "transsituational" character of gender in social affairs, and in this sense, we experience them as exogenous (i.e., as outside of us and the particular situation we find ourselves in). Simultaneously, however, the meaning of these beliefs is dependent on the context in which they are invoked—rather than transsituational, as implied by the popular concept of "cognitive consensus" (Zimmerman 1978, 8–9). What is more, because these properties of normally sexed persons are regarded as "only natural," questioning them is tantamount to calling ourselves into question as competent members of society.

Consider how these beliefs operate in the process of sex assignment—the initial classification of persons as either females or males (West and Zimmerman 1987, 131–32). We generally regard this process as a biological determination requiring only a straightforward examination of the "facts of the matter" (cf. the description of sex as an "ascribed status" in many introductory sociology texts). The criteria for sex assignment, however, can vary across cases (e.g., chromosome type before birth or genitalia after birth). They sometimes do and sometimes do not agree with one another (e.g., hermaphrodites), and they show considerable variation across cultures (Kessler and McKenna 1978). Our *moral conviction* that there are two and only two sexes (Garfinkel 1967, 116–18) is what explains the comparative ease of achieving initial sex assignment. This conviction accords females and males the status of unequivocal and "natural" entities, whose social and psychological tendencies can be predicted from their reproductive functions (West and Zimmerman 1987, 127–28). From an ethnomethodological viewpoint, sex is socially and culturally constructed rather than a straightforward statement of the biological "facts."

Now, consider the process of sex categorization—the ongoing identification of persons as girls or boys and women or men in everyday life (West and Zimmerman 1987, 132–34). Sex categorization involves no well-defined set of criteria that must be satisfied to identify someone; rather, it involves treating appearances (e.g., deportment, dress, and bearing) as if they were indicative of underlying states of affairs (e.g., anatomical, hormonal, and chromosomal arrangements). The point worth stressing here is that, while sex category serves as an "indicator" of sex, it does not depend on it. Societal members will "see" a world populated by two and only two sexes, even in public situations that preclude inspection of the physiological "facts." From this perspective, it is important to distinguish sex category from sex assignment and to distinguish both from the "doing" of gender.

Gender, we argue, is a situated accomplishment of societal members, the local management of conduct in relation to normative conceptions of appropriate attitudes and activities for particular sex categories (West and Zimmerman 1987, 134–35). From this perspective, gender is not merely an individual attribute but something that is accomplished in interaction with others. Here, as in our earlier work, we rely on John Heritage's (1984, 136–37) formulation of accountability: the possibility of describing actions, circumstances, and even descriptions of themselves in both serious and consequential ways (e.g., as "unwomanly" or "unmanly"). Heritage points out that members of society routinely characterize activities in ways that take notice of those activities (e.g., naming, describing, blaming, excusing, or merely acknowledging them) and place them in a social framework (i.e., situating them in the context of other activities that are similar or different).

The fact that activities can be described in such ways is what leads to the possibility of conducting them with an eye to how they might be assessed (e.g., as "womanly" or "manly" behaviors). Three important but subtle points are worth emphasizing here. One is that the notion of accountability is relevant not only to activities that conform to prevailing normative conceptions (i.e., activities that are conducted "unremarkably," and, thus, do not warrant more than a passing glance) but also to those activities that deviate. The issue is not deviance or conformity; rather, it is the possible evaluation of action in relation to normative conceptions and the likely consequence of that evaluation for subsequent interaction. The second point worth emphasizing is that the process of rendering some action accountable is an interactional accomplishment. As Heritage explains, accountability permits persons to conduct their activities in relation to their circumstances—in ways that permit others to take those circumstances into account and see those activities for what they are. "[T]he intersubjectivity of actions," therefore, "ultimately rests on a symmetry between the *production* of those actions on the one hand and their *recognition* on the other" (1984, 179)—both in the context of their circumstances.[6] And the third point we must stress is that, while individuals are the ones who do gender, the process of rendering something accountable is both interactional and institutional in character: it is a feature of social relationships, and its idiom derives from the institutional arena in which those relationships come to life. In the United States, for example, when the behaviors of children or teenagers have become the focus of public concern, the Family and Motherhood (as well as individual mothers) have been held accountable to normative conceptions of "essential" femininity (including qualities like nurturance and caring). Gender is obviously much more than a role or an individual characteristic: it is a mechanism whereby situated social action contributes to the reproduction of social structure (West and Fenstermaker 1993, 158).

Womanly and manly natures thusly achieve the status of objective properties of social life (West and Zimmerman 1987). They are rendered natural, normal characteristics of individuals and, at the same time, furnish the tacit legitimation of the distinctive and unequal fates of women and men within the social order. If sex categories are potentially omnirelevant to social life, then persons engaged in virtually any activity may be held accountable for their performance of that activity as women or as men, and their category membership can be used to validate or discredit their other activities. This arrangement provides for countless situations in which persons in a particular sex category can "see" that they are out of place, and if they were not there, their current problems would not exist. It also allows for seeing various features of the existing social order—for example, the

division of labor (Berk 1985), the development of gender identities (Cahill 1986), and the subordination of women by men (Fenstermaker, West, and Zimmerman 1991)—as "natural" responses. These things "are the way they are" by virtue of the fact that men are men and women are women—a distinction seen as "natural," as rooted in biology, and as producing fundamental psychological, behavioral, and social consequences.

Through this formulation, we resituate gender, an attribute without clear social origin or referent, in social interaction. This makes it possible to study how gender takes on social import, how it varies in its salience and consequence, and how it operates to produce and maintain power and inequality in social life. Below, we extend this reformulation to race, and then, to class. Through this extension, we are not proposing an equivalence of oppressions. Race is not class, and neither is gender; nevertheless, while race, class, and gender will likely take on different import and will often carry vastly different social consequences in any given social situation, we suggest that how they operate may be productively compared. Here, our focus is on the social mechanics of gender, race, and class, for that is the way we may perceive their simultaneous workings in human affairs.

Race

Within the United States, virtually any social activity presents the possibility of categorizing the participants on the basis of race. Attempts to establish race as a scientific concept have met with little success (Gosset 1965; Montagu 1975; Omi and Winant 1986; Stephans 1982). There are, for example, no biological criteria (e.g., hormonal, chromosomal, or anatomical) that allow physicians to pronounce race assignment at birth, thereby sorting human beings into distinctive races.[7] Since racial categories and their meanings change over time and place, they are, moreover, arbitrary.[8] In everyday life, nevertheless, people can and do sort out themselves and others on the basis of membership in racial categories.

Michael Omi and Howard Winant argue that the "seemingly obvious, 'natural' and 'common sense' qualities" of the existing racial order "themselves testify to the effectiveness of the racial formation process in constructing racial meanings and identities" (1986, 62). Take, for instance, the relatively recent emergence of the category "Asian American." Any scientific theory of race would be hard pressed to explain this in the absence of a well-defined set of criteria for assigning individuals to the category. In relation to ethnicity, furthermore, it makes no sense to aggregate in a single category the distinctive histories, geographic origins, and cultures of Cambodian, Chinese, Filipino, Japanese, Korean, Laotian, Thai, and Vietnamese Americans. Despite important distinctions among these groups, Omi and Winant contend, "the majority of Americans cannot tell the difference" between their members (1986, 24). "Asian American," therefore, affords a means of achieving racial categorization in everyday life.

Of course, competent members of U.S. society share preconceived ideas of what members of particular categories "look like" (Omi and Winant 1986, 62). Remarks such as "Odd, you don't look Asian" testify to underlying notions of what "Asians" ought to look like. The point we wish to stress, however, is that these notions are not supported by any scientific criteria for reliably distinguishing members of different "racial" groups. What is more, even state-mandated criteria (e.g., the proportion of "mixed blood" necessary to legally classify someone as Black)[9] are distinctly different in other Western cultures and have little relevance to the way racial categorization occurs in everyday life. As in the case of sex categorization, appearances are treated as if they were indicative of some underlying state.

Beyond preconceived notions of what members of particular groups look like, Omi and Winant suggest that Americans share preconceived notions of what members of these groups are like. They note, for example, that we are likely to become disoriented "when people do not act 'Black,' 'Latino.' or indeed 'white'" (1986, 62). From our ethnomethodological perspective, what Omi and Winant are describing is the accountability of persons to race category. If we accept their contention that there are prevailing normative conceptions of appropriate attitudes and activities for particular race categories and if we grant Heritage's (1984, 179) claim that accountability allows persons to conduct their activities in relation to their circumstances (in ways that allow others to take those circumstances into account and see those activities for what they are), we can also see race as a situated accomplishment of societal members. From this perspective, race is not simply an individual characteristic or trait but something that is accomplished in interaction with others.

To the extent that race category is omnirelevant (or even verges on this), it follows that persons involved in virtually any action may be held accountable for their performance of that action as members of their race category. As in the case of sex category, race category can be used to justify or discredit other actions; accordingly, virtually any action can be assessed in relation to its race categorical nature. The accomplishment of race (like gender) does not necessarily mean "living up" to normative conceptions of attitudes and activities appropriate to a particular race category; rather, it means engaging in action at the risk of race assessment. Thus, even though individuals are the ones who accomplish race, "the enterprise is fundamentally interactional and institutional in character, for accountability is a feature of social relationships and its idiom is drawn from the institutional arena in which those relationships are enacted" (West and Zimmerman 1987, 137).

The accomplishment of race renders the social arrangements based on race as normal and natural, that is, legitimate ways of organizing social life. In the United States, it can seem "only natural" for counselors charged with guiding high school students in their preparation for college admission to advise Black students against advanced courses in math, chemistry, or physics "because Blacks do not do well" in those areas (Essed 1991, 242). The students may well forgo such courses, given that they "do not need them" and "can get into college without them." However Philomena Essed observes, this ensures that students so advised will enter college at a disadvantage in comparison to classmates and creates the very situation that is believed to exist, namely, that Blacks do not do well in those areas. Small wonder, then, that the proportion of U.S. Black students receiving college degrees remains stuck at 13 percent, despite two decades of affirmative action programs (Essed 1991, 26). Those Black students who are (for whatever reason) adequately prepared for college are held to account for themselves as "deviant" representatives of their race category and, typically, exceptionalized (Essed 1991, 232). With that accomplishment, institutional practice and social order are reaffirmed.

Although the distinction between "macro" and "micro" levels of analysis is popular in the race relations literature too (e.g., in distinguishing "institutional" from "individual" racism or "macro-level" analyses of racialized social structures from "micro-level" analyses of identity formation), we contend that it is ultimately a false distinction. Not only do these "levels" operate continually and reciprocally in "our lived experience, in politics, in culture [and] in economic life" (Omi and Winant 1986, 67), but distinguishing between them "places the individual outside the institutional, thereby severing rules, regulations and procedures from the people who make and enact them" (Essed 1991, 36). We contend that the accountability of persons to race categories is the key to understanding the maintenance of the existing racial order.

Note that there is nothing in this formulation to suggest that race is necessarily accomplished in isolation from gender. To the contrary, if we conceive of both race and gender as situated accomplishments, we can see how individual persons may experience them simultaneously. For instance, Spelman observes that,

[i]nsofar as she is oppressed by racism in a sexist context and sexism in a racist context, the Black woman's struggle cannot be compartmentalized into two struggles—one as a Black and one as a woman. Indeed, it is difficult to imagine why a Black woman would think of her struggles this way except in the face of demands by white women or by Black men that she do so. (1988, 124)

To the extent that an individual Black woman is held accountable in one situation to her race category, and in another, to her sex category, we can

see these as "oppositional" demands for accountability. But note, it is a *Black woman* who is held accountable in both situations.

Contrary to Omi and Winant's (1986, 62) use of hypothetical cases, on any particular occasion of interaction, we are unlikely to become uncomfortable when "people" do not act "Black," "people" do not act "Latino," or when "people" do not act "white." Rather, we are likely to become disconcerted when particular Black *women* do not act like Black *women*, particular Latino *men* do not act like Latino *men*, or particular white *women* do not act like white *women*—in the context that we observe them. Conceiving of race and gender as ongoing accomplishments means we must locate their emergence in social situations, rather than within the individual or some vaguely defined set of role expectations.[10]

Despite many important differences in the histories, traditions, and varying impacts of racial and sexual oppression across particular situations, the mechanism underlying them is the same. To the extent that members of society know their actions are accountable, they will design their actions in relation to how they might be seen and described by others. And to the extent that race category (like sex category) is omnirelevant to social life, it provides others with an ever-available resource for interpreting those actions. In short, inasmuch as our society is divided by "essential" differences between members of different race categories and categorization by race is both relevant and mandated, the accomplishment of race is unavoidable (cf. West and Zimmerman 1987, 137).

For example, many (if not most) Black men in the United States have, at some point in their lives, been stopped on the street or pulled over by police for no apparent reason. Many (if not most) know very well that the ultimate grounds for their being detained is their race and sex category membership. Extreme deference may yield a release with the command to "move on," but at the same time, it legitimates the categorical grounds on which the police (be they Black or white) detained them in the first place. Indignation or outrage (as might befit a white man in similar circumstances) is likely to generate hostility, if not brutality, from the officers on the scene (who may share sharply honed normative conceptions regarding "inherent" violent tendencies among Black men). Their very survival may be contingent on how they conduct themselves in relation to normative conceptions of appropriate attitudes and activities for Black men in these circumstances. Here, we see both the limited rights of citizenship accorded to Black men in U.S. society and the institutional context (in this case, the criminal justice system) in which accountability is called into play.

In sum, the accomplishment of race consists of creating differences among members of different race categories—differences that are neither natural nor biological (cf. West and Zimmerman 1987, 137). Once created, these differences are used to maintain the "essential" distinctiveness of "racial identities" and the institutional arrangements that they support. From this perspective, racial identities are not invariant idealizations of our human natures that are uniformly distributed in society. Nor are normative conceptions of attitudes and activities for one's race category templates for "racial" behaviors. Rather, what is invariant is the notion that members of different "races" *have* essentially different natures, which explain their very unequal positions in our society.[11]

Class

This, too, we propose, is the case with class. Here, we know that even sympathetic readers are apt to balk: gender, yes, is "done," and race, too, is "accomplished," but class? How can we reduce a system that "differentially structures group access to material resources, including economic, political and social resources" (Andersen and Collins 1992, 50) to "a situated accomplishment"? Do we mean to deny the material realities of poverty and privilege? We do not. There is no denying the very different material realities imposed by differing relations under capital; however, we suggest that these realities have little to do with class categorization—and ultimately, with the accountability of persons to class categories—in everyday life.

For example, consider Shellee Colen's description of the significance of maids' uniforms to white middle-class women who employ West Indian immigrant women as child care workers and domestics in New York City. In the words of Judith Thomas, one of the West Indian women Colen interviewed,

> She [the employer] wanted me to wear the uniform. She was really prejudiced. She just wanted that the maid must be identified...She used to go to the beach every day with the children. So going to the beach in the sand and the sun and she would have the kids eat ice cream and all that sort of thing...I tell you one day when I look at myself, I was so dirty...just like I came out from a garbage can. (1986, 57)

At the end of that day, says Colen, Thomas asked her employer's permission to wear jeans to the beach the next time they went, and the employer gave her permission to do so. When she did wear jeans, and the employer's brother came to the beach for a visit, Thomas noted,

> I really believe they had a talk about it, because in the evening, driving back from the beach, she said "Well, Judith, I said you could wear something else to the beach other than the uniform [but] I think you will have to wear the uniform because they're very informal on this beach and they don't know who is guests from who isn't guests." (1986, 57)

Of the women Colen interviewed (in 1985), not one was making more than $225 a week, and Thomas was the only one whose employer was paying for medical insurance. All (including Thomas) were supporting at least two households: their own in New York, and that of their kin back in the West Indies. By any objective social scientific criteria, then, all would be regarded as members of the working-class poor; yet, in the eyes of Thomas's employer (and, apparently, the eyes of others at the beach), Thomas's low wages, long hours, and miserable conditions of employment were insufficient to establish her class category. Without a uniform, she could be mistaken for one of the guests and, hence, not be held accountable as a maid.

There is more to this example, of course, than meets the eye. The employer's claim notwithstanding, it is unlikely that Thomas, tending to white middle-class children who were clearly not her own, would be mistaken for one of the guests at the beach. The blue jeans, however, might be seen as indicating her failure to comply with normative expectations of attitudes and behaviors appropriate to a maid and, worse yet, as belying the competence of her employer (whose authority is confirmed by Thomas displaying herself as a maid). As Evelyn Nakano Glenn notes in another context, "the higher standard of living of one woman is made possible by, and also helps to perpetuate, the other's lower standard of living" (1992, 34).

Admittedly, the normative conceptions that sustain the accountability of persons to class category are somewhat different from those that sustain accountability to sex category and race category. For example, despite earlier attempts to link pauperism with heredity and thereby justify the forced sterilization of poor women in the United States (Rafter 1992), scientists today do not conceive of class in relation to the biological characteristics of a person. There is, moreover, no scientific basis for popular notions of what persons in particular class categories "look like" or "act like." But although the dominant ideology within the United States is no longer based explicitly on Social Darwinism (see, for example, Gossett 1965, 144–75) and although we believe, in theory, that anyone can make it, we as a society still hold certain truths to be self-evident. As Donna Langston observes:

> If hard work were the sole determinant of your ability to support yourself and your family, surely we'd have a different outcome for many in our society. We also, however, believe in luck and on closer examination, it certainly is quite a coincidence that the "unlucky" come from certain race, gender and class backgrounds. In order to perpetuate racist, sexist and classist outcomes, we also have to believe that the current economic distribution is unchangeable, has always existed, and probably exists in this form throughout the known universe, i.e., it's "natural." (1991, 146)

Langston pinpoints the underlying assumptions that sustain our notions about persons in relation to poverty and privilege—assumptions that

compete with our contradictory declarations of a meritocratic society, with its readily invoked exemplar, Horatio Alger. For example, if someone is poor, we assume it is because of something *they* did or did not do: they lacked initiative, they were not industrious, they had no ambition, and so forth. If someone is rich, or merely well-off, it must be by virtue of *their own* efforts, talents, and initiative. While these beliefs certainly *look* more mutable than our views of women's and men's "essential" natures or our deep-seated convictions regarding the characteristics of persons in particular race categories, they still rest on the assumption that a person's economic fortunes derive from qualities of the person. Initiative is thus treated as inherent among the haves, and laziness is seen as inherent among the have-nots.[12] Given that initiative is a prerequisite for employment in jobs leading to upward mobility in this society, it is hardly surprising that "the rich get richer and the poor get poorer." As in the case of gender and race, profound historical effects of entrenched institutional practice result, but they unfold one accomplishment at a time.

To be sure, there are "objective" indicators of one's position within the system of distribution that differentially structure our access to resources. It is possible to sort members of society in relation to these indicators, and it is the job of many public agencies (e.g., those administering aid to families with dependent children, health benefits, food stamps, legal aid, and disability benefits) to do such sorting. In the process, public agencies allocate further unequal opportunities with respect to health, welfare, and life chances; however, whatever the criteria employed by these agencies (and these clearly change over time and place), they can be clearly distinguished from the accountability of persons to class categories in everyday life.

As Benjamin DeMott (1990) observes, Americans operate on the basis of a most unusual assumption, namely, that we live in a classless society. On the one hand, our everyday discourse is replete with categorizations of persons by class. DeMott (1990, 1–27) offers numerous examples of television shows, newspaper articles, cartoons, and movies that illustrate how class "will tell" in the most mundane of social doings. On the other hand, we believe that we in the United States are truly unique "in escaping the hierarchies that burden the rest of the developed world" (DeMott 1990, 29). We cannot see the system of distribution that structures our unequal access to resources. Because we cannot see this, the accomplishment of class in everyday life rests on the presumption that everyone is endowed with equal opportunity and, therefore, that real differences in the outcomes we observe must result from individual differences in attributes like intelligence and character.

For example, consider the media's coverage of the trial of Mary Beth Whitehead, the wife of a sanitation worker and surrogate mother of Baby M. As DeMott (1990, 96–101) points out, much of this trial revolved around the question of the kind of woman who would agree to bear and sell her child to someone else. One answer to this question might be "the kind of woman" who learned early in life that poverty engenders obligations of reciprocal sacrifice among people—even sacrifice for those who are not their kin (cf. Stack 1974). Whitehead was one of eight children, raised by a single mother who worked on and off as a beautician. Living in poverty, members of her family had often relied on "poor but generous neighbors" for help and had provided reciprocal assistance when they could. When William and Betsy Stern (a biochemist and a pediatrician) came to her for help, therefore, Whitehead saw them as "seemingly desperate in their childlessness, threatened by a ruinous disease (Mrs. Stern's self-diagnosed multiple sclerosis), [and] as people in trouble, unable to cope without her" (DeMott 1990, 99). Although she would be paid for carrying the pregnancy and although she knew that they were better off financially than she was, Whitehead saw the Sterns as "in need of help" and, hence, could not do otherwise than to provide it. DeMott explains:

> She had seen people turn to others helplessly in distress, had herself been turned to previously; in her world failure to respond was unnatural. Her class experience, together with her own individual nature, made it natural to perceive the helping side

of surrogacy as primary and the commercial side as important yet secondary. (1990, 98)

Another answer to the "what kind of woman" question might be Whitehead's lack of education about the technical aspects of artificial insemination (DeMott 1990, 100). A high school dropout, she thought that this procedure allowed clinicians to implant both a man's sperm and a woman's egg in another woman's uterus, thereby making it possible for infertile couples to have their own genetic children. It was not until just before the birth that Whitehead learned she would be the one contributing the egg and, subsequently, would not be bearing their child but her own. Under these circumstances, it would certainly seem "natural" for her to break her contract with the Sterns at the point of learning that it required her to give them her baby.

The media coverage of Whitehead's trial focused neither on class-based understandings of altruism nor on class-associated knowledge of sexual reproduction; rather, it focused on the question of Whitehead's character:

> The answers from a team of expert psychologists were reported in detail. Mrs. Whitehead was described as "impulsive, egocentric, self-dramatic, manipulative and exploitative." One member of the team averred that she suffered from a "schizotypal personality disorder." [Another] gave it as his opinion that the defendant's ailment was a "mixed personality disorder," and that she was "immature, exhibitionistic, and histrionic."...[U]nder the circumstances, he did not see that "there were any 'parental rights';" Mrs. Whitehead was "a surrogate uterus"..."and not a surrogate mother." (DeMott 1990, 96)

Through these means, "the experts" reduced Whitehead from a woman to a womb, and, therefore, someone with no legitimate claim to the child she had helped to conceive. Simultaneously, they affirmed the right of Betsy Stern to be the mother—even of a child she did not bear. As Whitehead's attorney put it in his summation, "What we are witnessing, and what we can predict will happen, is that one class of Americans will exploit another class. And it will always be the wife of the sanitation worker who must bear the children for the pediatrician" (Whitehead and Schwartz-Nobel 1989, 160, cited in DeMott 1990, 97). The punch line, of course, is that our very practices of invoking "essential differences" between classes support the rigid system of social relations that disparately distributes opportunities and life chances. Without these practices, the "natural" relations under capital might well seem far more malleable.

The accomplishment of class renders the unequal institutional arrangements based on class category accountable as normal and natural, that is, as legitimate ways of organizing social life (cf. West and Zimmerman 1987). Differences between members of particular class categories that are created by this process can then be depicted as fundamental and enduring dispositions.[13] In this light, the institutional arrangements of our society can be seen as responsive to the differences—the social order being merely an accommodation to the natural order.

In any given situation (whether or not that situation can be characterized as face-to-face interaction or as the more "macro" workings of institutions), the simultaneous accomplishments of class, gender, and race will differ in content and outcome. From situation to situation, the salience of the observables relevant to categorization (e.g., dress, interpersonal style, skin color) may seem to eclipse the interactional impact of the simultaneous accomplishment of all three. We maintain, nevertheless, that, just as the mechanism for accomplishment is shared, so, too, is their simultaneous accomplishment ensured.

Conclusion: The Problem of Difference

As we have indicated, mathematical metaphors describing the relations among gender, race, and class have led to considerable confusion in feminist scholarship. As we have also indicated, the conceptualizations of gender that support mathematical metaphors (e.g., "sex differences" and "sex roles") have forced scholars to think of gender as

something that stands apart from and outside of race and class in people's lives.

In putting forth this perspective, we hope to advance a new way of thinking about gender, race, and class, namely, as ongoing, methodical, and situated accomplishments. We have tried to demonstrate the usefulness of this perspective for understanding how people experience gender, race, and class simultaneously. We have also tried to illustrate the implications of this perspective for reconceptualizing "the problem of difference" in feminist theory.

What are the implications of our ethnomethodological perspective for an understanding of relations among gender, race, and class? First, and perhaps most important, conceiving of these as ongoing accomplishments means that we cannot determine their relevance to social action apart from the context in which they are accomplished (Fenstermaker, West, and Zimmerman 1991; West and Fenstermaker 1993). While sex category, race category, and class category are potentially omnirelevant to social life, individuals inhabit many different identities, and these may be stressed or muted, depending on the situation. For example, consider the following incident described in detail by Patricia Williams, a law professor who, by her own admission, "loves to shop" and is known among her students for her "neat clothes":[14]

Buzzers are big in New York City. Favored particularly by smaller stores and boutiques, merchants throughout the city have installed them as screening devices to reduce the incidence of robbery: if the face at the door looks desirable, the buzzer is pressed and the door is unlocked. If the face is that of an undesirable, the door stays pressed and the door is locked. I discovered [these buzzers] and their meaning one Saturday in 1986. I was shopping in Soho and saw in a store window a sweater that I wanted to buy for my mother. I pressed my round brown face to the window and my finger to the buzzer, seeking admittance. A narrow-eyed white teenager, wearing running shoes and feasting on bubble gum glared out, evaluating me for signs that would pit me against the limits of his social understanding. After about five minutes, he mouthed "we're closed," and blew pink rubber at me. It was two Saturdays before Christmas, at one o'clock in the afternoon; there were several white people in the store who appeared to be shopping for things for *their* mothers. (1991, 44)

In this incident, says Williams, the issue of undesirability revealed itself as a racial determination. This is true in a comparative sense; for example, it is unlikely that a white woman law professor would have been treated this way by this salesperson and likely that a Latino gang member would have. This is also true in a legal sense; for example, in cases involving discrimination, the law requires potential plaintiffs to specify whether or not they were discriminated against on the basis of sex *or* race or some other criterion. We suggest, however, that sex category and class category, although muted, are hardly irrelevant to Williams's story. Indeed, we contend that one reason readers are apt to find this incident so disturbing is that it did not happen to a Latino gang member but to a Black woman law professor. Our point is not to imply that anyone should be treated this way but to show that one cannot isolate Williams's race category from her sex category or class category and fully understand this situation. We would argue, furthermore, that how class and gender are accomplished in concert with race must be understood through that specific interaction.

A second implication of our perspective is that the accomplishment of race, class, and gender does not require categorical diversity among the participants. To paraphrase Erving Goffman, social situations "do not so much allow for the expression of natural differences as for the production of [those] difference[s themselves]" (1977, 72). Some of the most extreme displays of "essential" womanly and manly natures may occur in settings that are usually reserved for members of a single sex category, such as locker rooms or beauty salons (Gerson 1985). Some of the most dramatic expressions of "definitive" class characteristics may emerge in class-specific contexts (e.g., debutante balls). Situations that involve more than one sex category, race category, and class category may highlight categorical membership and make the accomplishment of gender, race, and class more

salient, but they are not necessary to produce these accomplishments in the first place. This point is worth stressing, since existing formulations of relations among gender, race, and class might lead one to conclude that "difference" must be present for categorical membership and, thus, dominance to matter.

A third implication is that, depending on how race, gender, and class are accomplished, what looks to be the same activity may have different meanings for those engaged in it. Consider the long-standing debates among feminists (e.g., Collins 1990; Davis 1971; Dill 1988; Firestone 1970; Friedan 1963; hooks 1984; Hurtado 1989; Zavella 1987) over the significance of mothering and child care in women's lives. For white middle-class women, these activities have often been seen as constitutive of oppression in that they are taken as expressions of their "essential" womanly natures and used to discredit their participation in other activities (e.g., Friedan 1963). For many women of color (and white working-class women), mothering and child care have had (and continue to have) very different meanings. Angela Davis (1971, 7) points out that, in the context of slavery, African American women's efforts to tend to the needs of African American children (not necessarily their own) represented the only labor they performed that could not be directly appropriated by white slave owners. Throughout U.S. history, bell hooks observes,

> Black women have identified work in the context of the family as humanizing labor, work that affirms their identity as women, as human beings showing love and care, the very gestures of humanity white supremacist ideology claimed black people were incapable of expressing. (1984, 133–34)

Looking specifically at American family life in the nineteenth century, Bonnie Thornton Dill (1988) suggests that being a poor or working-class African American woman, a Chinese American woman, or a Mexican American woman meant something very different from being a Euro-American woman. Normative, class-bound conceptions of "woman's nature" at that time included tenderness, piety, and nurturance—qualities that legitimated the confinement of middle-class Euro-American women to the domestic sphere and that promoted such confinement as the goal of working-class and poor immigrant Euro-American families' efforts.

> For racial-ethnic women, however, the notion of separate spheres served to reinforce their subordinate status and became, in effect, another assault. As they increased their work outside the home, they were forced into a productive sphere that was organized for men and "desperate" women who were so unfortunate or immoral that they could not confine their work to the domestic sphere. In the productive sphere, however, they were denied the opportunity to embrace the dominant ideological definition of "good" wife and mother. (Dill 1988, 429)

Fourth and finally, our perspective affords an understanding of the accomplishment of race, gender, or class as constituted in the context of the differential "doings" of the others. Consider, for example, the very dramatic case of the U.S. Senate hearings on Clarence Thomas's nomination to the Supreme Court. Wherever we turned, whether to visual images on a television screen or to the justificatory discourse of print media, we were overwhelmed by the dynamics of gender, race, and class operating in concert with one another. It made a difference to us as viewers (and certainly to his testimony) that Clarence Thomas was a Black *man* and that he was a *Black* man. It also made a difference, particularly to the African American community, that he was a Black man who had been raised in poverty. Each categorical dimension played off the others and off the comparable but quite different categorizations of Anita Hill (a "self-made" Black woman law professor, who had grown up as one of 13 children). Most white women who watched the hearings identified gender and men's dominance as the most salient aspects of them, whether in making sense of the Judiciary Committee's handling of witnesses or understanding the relationship between Hill and Thomas. By contrast, most African American viewers saw racism as the most salient aspect of the hearings, including white men's prurient interest in Black

sexuality and the exposure of troubling divisions between Black women and men (Morrison 1992). The point is that how we label such dynamics does not necessarily capture their complex quality. Foreground and background, context, salience, and center shift from interaction to interaction, but all operate interdependently.

Of course, this is only the beginning. Gender, race, and class are only three means (although certainly very powerful ones) of generating difference and dominance in social life.[15] Much more must be done to distinguish other forms of inequality and their workings. Empirical evidence must be brought to bear on the question of variation in the salience of categorical memberships, while still allowing for the simultaneous influence of these memberships on interaction. We suggest that the analysis of situated conduct affords the best prospect for understanding how these "objective" properties of social life achieve their ongoing status as such and, hence, how the most fundamental divisions of our society are legitimated and maintained.

Notes

1. In this article, we use "race" rather than "ethnicity" to capture the commonsensical beliefs of members of our society. As we will show, these beliefs are predicated on the assumption that different "races" can be reliably distinguished from one another.

2. Compare, for example, the very different implications of "Double Jeopardy: To Be Black and Female" (Beale 1970) and "Positive Effects of the Multiple Negative: Explaining the Success of Black Professional Women" (Epstein 1973).

3. In this context, we define "experience" as participation in social systems in which gender, race, and class affect, determine, or otherwise influence behavior.

4. Here, it is important to distinguish an individual's experience of the dynamics of gender, race, and class as they order the daily course of social interaction from that individual's sense of identity as a member of gendered, raced, and classed categories. For example, in any given interaction, a woman who is Latina and a shopkeeper may experience the simultaneous effects of gender, race, and class,

yet identify her experience as only "about" race, only "about" gender, or only "about" class.

5. The ambivalence that dogs the logic of social constructionist positions should now be all too familiar to feminist sociologists. If we are true to our pronouncements that social inequalities and the categories they reference (e.g., gender, race, and class) are not rooted in biology, then we may at some point seem to flirt with the notion that they are, therefore, rooted in nothing. For us, biology is not only not destiny but also not the only reality. Gender, race, and class inequalities are firmly rooted in the ever-present realities of individual practice, cultural conventions, and social institutions. That's reality enough, when we ponder the pernicious and pervasive character of racism, sexism, and economic oppression.

6. That persons may be held accountable does not mean that they necessarily will be held accountable in every interaction. Particular interactional outcomes are not the point here; rather, it is the possibility of accountability in any interaction.

7. To maintain vital statistics on race, California, for instance, relies on mothers' and fathers' self-identifications on birth certificates.

8. Omi and Winant (1986, 64–75) provide numerous empirical illustrations, including the first appearance of "white" as a term of self-identification (circa 1680), California's decision to categorize Chinese people as "Indian" (in 1854), and the U.S. Census's creation of the category "Hispanic" (in 1980).

9. Consider Susie Guillory Phipps's unsuccessful suit against the Louisiana Bureau of Vital Records (Omi and Winant 1986, 57). Phipps was classified as "Black" on her birth certificate, in accord with a 1970 Louisiana law stipulating that anyone with at least one-thirty-second "Negro blood" was "Black." Her attorney contended that designating a race category on a person's birth certificate was unconstitutional and that, in any case, the one-thirty-second criterion was inaccurate. Ultimately, the court upheld Louisiana's state law quantifying "racial identity" and thereby affirmed the legal principle of assigning persons to specific "racial" groups.

10. This would be true if only because outcomes bearing on power and inequality are so different in different situations. Ours is a formulation that is sensitive to variability, that can accommodate, for example, interactions where class privilege and racism seem equally salient, as well as those in which racism interactionally "eclipses" accountability to sex category.

11. As Spelman observes, "The existence of racism does not require that there are races; it requires the belief that there are races" (1988, 208, n. 24).

12. A devil's advocate might argue that gender, race, and class are fundamentally different because they show different degrees of "mutability" or latitude in the violation of expectations in interaction. Although class mobility is possible, one might argue, race mobility is not; or, while sex change operations can be performed, race change operations cannot. In response, we would point out that the very notion that one cannot change one's race—but can change one's sex and manipulate displays of one's class—only throws us back to biology and its reassuring, but only apparent, immutability.

13. Although we as a society believe that some people may "pull themselves up by their bootstraps" and others may "fall from grace," we still cherish the notion that class will reveal itself in a person's fundamental social and psychological character. We commonly regard the self-made man, the welfare mother, and the middle-class housewife as distinct categories of persons, whose attitudes and activities can be predicted on categorical grounds.

14. We include these prefatory comments about shopping and clothes for those readers who, on encountering this description, asked, "What does she look like?" and "What was she wearing?" Those who seek further information will find Williams featured in a recent fashion layout for *Mirabella* magazine (As Smart as They Look 1993).

15. We cannot stress this strongly enough. Gender, race, and class are obviously very salient social accomplishments in social life, because so many features of our cultural institutions and daily discourse are organized to perpetuate the categorical distinctions on which they are based. As Spelman observes, "the more a society has invested in its members' getting the categories right, the more occasions there will be for reinforcing them, and the fewer occasions there will be for questioning them" (1988, 152). On any given occasion of interaction, however, we may also be held accountable

to other categorical memberships (e.g., ethnicity, nationality, sexual orientation, place of birth), and, thus, "difference" may then be differentially constituted.

References

Acker, Joan. 1992a. Gendered institutions: From sex roles to gendered institutions. *Contemporary Sociology* 21:565–69.

———. 1992b. Gendering organizational theory. In *Gendering Organizational Theory*, edited by Albert J. Mills and Peta Tancred. London: Sage.

Almquist, Elizabeth. 1989. The experiences of minority women in the United States: Intersections of race, gender, and class. In *Women: A feminist perspective*, edited by Jo Freeman. Mountain View, CA: Mayfield.

Andersen, Margaret L., and Patricia Hill Collins. 1992. Preface to *Race, class and gender*, edited by Margaret L. Andersen and Patricia Hill Collins. Belmont, CA: Wadsworth.

Aptheker, Bettina. 1989. *Tapestries of life: Women's work, women's consciousness, and the meaning of daily experience*. Amherst: University of Massachusetts Press.

As smart as they look. *Mirabella*, June 1993, 100–111.

Beale, Frances. 1970. Double jeopardy: To be Black and female. In *The Black woman: An anthology*, edited by Toni Cade (Bambara). New York: Signet.

Berk, Sarah Fenstermaker. 1985. *The gender factory: The apportionment of work in American households*. New York: Plenum.

Bhavani, Kum-Kum. In press. Talking racism and the editing of women's studies. In *Introducing women's studies*, edited by Diane Richardson and Vicki Robinson. New York: Macmillan.

Cahill, Spencer E. 1986. Childhood socialization as recruitment process: Some lessons from the study of gender development. In *Sociological studies of child development*, edited by Patricia Adler and Peter Adler. Greenwich, CT: JAI.

Colen, Shellee. 1986. "With respect and feelings": Voices of West Indian child care and domestic workers in New York City. In *All American women*, edited by Johnetta B. Cole. New York: Free Press.

Collins, Patricia Hill. 1990. *Black feminist thought*. New York: Routledge.

Connell, R. W. 1985. Theorizing gender. *Sociology* 19:260–72.

Davis, Angela. 1971. The Black woman's role in the community of slaves. *Black Scholar* 3:3–15.

———. 1981. *Women, race and class*. New York: Random House.

de Beauvoir, Simone. 1953. *The second sex*. New York: Knopf.

DeMott, Benjamin. 1990. *The imperial middle: Why Americans can't think straight about class*. New Haven, CT: Yale University Press.

Dill, Bonnie Thornton. 1988. Our mothers' grief: Racial ethnic women and the maintenance of families. *Journal of Family History* 13:415–31.

Epstein, Cynthia Fuchs. 1973. Positive effects of the double negative: Explaining the success of Black professional women. In *Changing women in a changing society*, edited by Joan Huber. Chicago: University of Chicago Press.

Essed, Philomena. 1991. *Understanding everyday racism: An interdisciplinary theory*. Newbury Park, CA: Sage.

Fenstermaker, Sarah, Candace West, and Don H. Zimmerman. 1991. Gender inequality: New conceptual terrain. In *Gender, family and economy: The triple overlap*, edited by Rae Lesser Blumberg. Newbury Park, CA: Sage.

Firestone, Shulamith. 1970. *The dialectic of sex*. New York: Morrow.

Friedan, Betty. 1963. *The feminine mystique*. New York: Dell.

Frye, Marilyn. 1983. *The politics of reality: Essays in feminist theory*. Trumansburg, NY: Crossing Press.

Garfinkel, Harold. 1967. *Studies in ethnomethodology*. Englewood Cliffs, NJ: Prentice-Hall.

Gerson, Judith. 1985. *The variability and salience of gender: Issues of conceptualization and measurement*. Paper presented at the annual meeting of the American Sociological Association, Washington, DC, August.

Glazer, Nona. 1977. A sociological perspective: Introduction. In *Woman in a man-made world*, edited by Nona Glazer and Helen Youngelson Waehrer. Chicago: Rand McNally.

Glenn, Evelyn Nakano. 1985. Racial ethnic women's labor: The intersection of race, gender and class oppression. *Review of Radical Political Economics* 17:86–108.

———. 1992. From servitude to service work: Historical continuities in the racial division of paid reproductive labor. *Signs: Journal of Women in Culture and Society* 18:1–43.

Goffman, Erving. 1976. Gender display. *Studies in the Anthropology of Visual Communication* 3:69–77.

———. 1977. The arrangement between the sexes. *Theory and Society* 4:301–31.

Gossett, Thomas. 1965. *Race: The history of an idea in America.* New York: Schocken Books.

Hacker, Helen Mayer. 1951. Women as a minority group. *Social Forces* 30:60–69.

Heritage, John. 1984. *Garfinkel and ethnomethodology.* Cambridge, England: Polity.

Hochschild, Arlie Russell. 1973. A review of sex role research. *American Journal of Sociology* 78:1011–29.

hooks, bell. 1981. *Ain't I a woman: Black women and feminism.* Boston: South End.

———. 1984. *From margin to center.* Boston: South End.

Hughes, Everett C. 1945. Dilemmas and contradictions of status. *American Journal of Sociology* 50:353–59.

Hull, Gloria T., Patricia Bell Scott, and Barbara Smith, eds. 1982. *All the women are white, all the Blacks are men, but some of us are brave.* Old Westbury, NY: Feminist Press.

Hurtado, Aída. 1989. Relating to privilege: Seduction and rejection in the subordination of white women and women of color. *Signs: Journal of Women in Culture and Society* 14:833–55.

Jordan, June. 1985. Report from the Bahamas. In *On call: Political essays.* Boston: South End.

Joseph, Gloria, and Jill Lewis, eds. 1981. *Common differences.* Garden City, NY: Anchor.

Kessler, Suzanne J., and Wendy McKenna. 1978. *Gender: An ethnomethodological approach.* New York: Wiley.

Komarovsky, Mirra. 1946. Cultural contradictions and sex roles. *American Journal of Sociology* 52:184–89.

———. 1992. The concept of social role revisited. *Gender & Society* 6:301–12.

Langston, Donna. 1991. Tired of playing monopoly? In *Changing our power: An Introduction to women's studies,* 2d ed., edited by Jo Whitehorse Cochran, Donna Langston, and Carolyn Woodward. Dubuque, IA: Kendall-Hunt.

Linton, Ralph. 1936. *The study of man.* New York: Appleton-Century.

Lopata, Helena Z., and Barrie Thorne. 1987. On the term "sex roles." *Signs: Journal of Women in Culture and Society* 3:718–21.

Lorde, Audre. 1984. *Sister outsider.* Trumansburg, NY: Crossing.

Montagu, Ashley, ed. 1975. *Race & IQ.* London: Oxford University Press.

Mitchell, Juliet. 1966. Women: The longest revolution. *New Left Review* 40:11–37.

Moraga, Cherríe. 1981. La güera. In *This bridge called my back: Radical writing by women of color,* edited by Cherríe Moraga and Gloria Anzaldúa. New York: Kitchen Table Press.

Moraga, Cherríe, and Gloria Anzaiduá, eds. 1981. *This bridge called my back: Writings by radical women of color.* Watertown, MA: Persephone.

Morrison, Toni, ed. 1992. *Race-ing justice, engendering power: Essays on Anita Hill, Clarence Thomas, and the construction of social reality.* New York: Pantheon.

Omi, Michael, and Howard Winant. 1986. *Racial formation in the United States from the 1960s to the 1980s.* New York: Routledge & Kegan Paul.

Parsons, Talcott. 1951. *The social system.* New York: Free Press.

Parsons, Talcott, and Robert F. Bales. 1955. *Family, socialization and interaction process.* New York: Free Press.

Rafter, Nichole H. 1992. Claims-making and sociocultural context in the first U.S. eugenics campaign. *Social Problems* 39:17–34.

Rich, Adrienne. 1979. Disloyal to civilization: Feminism, racism, gynephobia. In *On lies, secrets, and silence.* New York: Norton.

Segura, Denise A. 1992. Chicanas in white collar jobs: "You have to prove yourself more." *Sociological Perspectives* 35:163–82.

Spelman, Elizabeth V. 1988. *Inessential woman: Problems of exclusion in feminist thought.* Boston: Beacon Press.

Stacey, Judith, and Barrie Thorne. 1985. The missing feminist revolution in sociology. *Social Problems* 32:301–16.

Stack, Carol B. 1974. *All our kin: Strategies for survival in a Black community.* New York: Harper & Row.

Stephans, Nancy. 1982. *The idea of race in science.* Hamden, CT: Archon.

Thorne, Barrie. 1980. Gender…How is it best conceptualized? Unpublished manuscript, Department of Sociology, Michigan State University, East Lansing.

West, Candace, and Sarah Fenstermaker. 1993. Power, inequality and the accomplishment of gender: An ethnomethodological view. In *Theory on gender/feminism on theory*, edited by Paula England. New York: Aldine.

West, Candace, and Don H. Zimmerman. 1987. Doing gender. *Gender & Society* 1:125–51.

Williams, Patricia. 1991. *The alchemy of race and rights*. Cambridge, MA: Harvard University Press.

Young, Iris Marion. 1990. Impartiality and the civic public. In *Throwing like a girl and other essays in feminist philosophy*. Bloomington: Indiana University Press.

Zavella, Patricia. 1987. *Women's work and Chicano families: Cannery workers of the Santa Clara Valley*. Ithaca, NY: Cornell University Press.

Zimmerman, Don H. 1978. Ethnomethodology. *American Sociologist* 13:6–15.

Zinn, Maxine Baca. 1990. Family, feminism and race in America. *Gender & Society* 4:68–82.

Zinn, Maxine Baca, Lynn Weber Cannon, Elizabeth Higginbotham, and Bonnie Thornton Dill. 1986. The costs of exclusionary practices in women's studies. *Signs: Journal of Women in Culture and Society* 11:290–303.

The Gendered Family

The current debates about the "crisis" of the family—a traditional arrangement that some fear is collapsing under the weight of contemporary trends ranging from relaxed sexual attitudes, increased divorce, and women's entry into the labor force, to rap music and violence in the media—actually underscore how central the family is to the reproduction of social life—and to gender identity. If gender identity were biologically "natural," we probably wouldn't need such strong family structures to make sure that everything turned out all right.

Though the "typical" family of the 1950s television sitcom—breadwinner father, housewife/mother, and 2.5 happy and well-adjusted children—is the empirical reality for less than 10 percent of all households, it remains the cultural ideal against which contemporary family styles are measured. Andrew Cherlin surveys the new American family and finds an exciting, not threatening diversity.

Scott Coltrane notices a relationship between the housework and child care and the status of women in society. The more housework and child care women do, the lower their status. Thus he suggests that sharing housework and child care is not only a way for husbands and wives to enact more egalitarian relationships, but also a way to ensure that the next generation will have more egalitarian attitudes.

Some who seek to preserve the family suggest that the form of the family—one mother, one father, of different, genetically based sexes—is more important than its content. Judith Stacey and Timothy Biblarz address this issue by asking the question empirically: how does sexual orientation of parents matter? Surprisingly, it does matter, but not in the way that many conservatives might like to hear. It turns out that lesbians and gay men have very stable families, and their children are resilient, stable, and happy.

American Marriage in the Early Twenty-First Century

ANDREW J. CHERLIN

The decline of American marriage has been a favorite theme of social commentators, politicians, and academics over the past few decades. Clearly the nation has seen vast changes in its family system—in marriage and divorce rates, cohabitation, childbearing, sexual behavior, and women's work outside the home. Marriage is less dominant as a social institution in the United States than at any time in history. Alternative path-ways through adulthood—childbearing outside of marriage, living with a partner without ever marrying, living apart but having intimate relationships—are more acceptable and feasible than ever before. But as the new century begins, it is also clear that despite the jeremiads, marriage has not faded away. In fact, given the many alternatives to marriage now available, what may be more remarkable is not the decline in marriage but its persistence. What is surprising is not that fewer people marry, but rather that so *many* still marry and that the desire to marry remains widespread. Although marriage has been transformed, it is still meaningful. In this article I review the changes in American marriage, discuss their causes, compare marriage in the United States with marriage in the rest of the developed world, and comment on how the transformation of marriage is likely to affect American children in the early twenty-first century.

Changes in the Life Course

To illuminate what has happened to American marriage, I begin by reviewing the great demographic changes of the past century including changes in age at marriage, the share of Americans ever marrying, cohabitation, nonmarital births, and divorce.

Recent Trends

Figure 5.1 shows the median age at marriage—the age by which half of all marriages occur—for men and women from 1890 to 2002. In 1890 the median age was relatively high, about twenty-six for men and twenty two for women. During the first half of the twentieth century the typical age at marriage dropped—gradually at first, and then precipitously after World War II. By the 1950s it had reached historic lows: roughly twenty-three for men and twenty for women. Many people still think of the 1950s as the standard by which to compare today's families, but as Figure 5.1 shows, the 1950s were the anomaly: during that decade young adults married earlier than ever before or since. Moreover, nearly all young adults—about 95 percent of whites and 88 percent of African Americans—eventually married.[1] During the 1960s, however, the median age at marriage began to climb, returning to and then exceeding that prevalent at the start of the twentieth century. Women, in particular, are marrying substantially later today than they have at any time for which data are available.

What is more, unmarried young adults are leading very different lives today than their earlier counterparts once did. The late-marrying young women and men of the early 1900s typically lived at home before marriage or paid for room

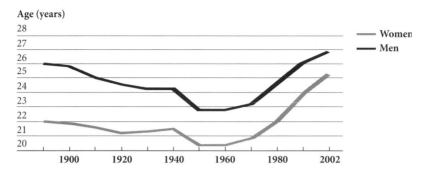

Figure 5.1. Median Age at Marriage, 1890–2002.

Source: U.S. Bureau of the Census, "Estimated Median Age at First Marriage, by Sex: 1890 to Present," 2003, www.census.gov/population/socdemo/hh-fam/tabMS-2.pdf (accessed July 23, 2004).

and board in someone else's home. Even when they were courting, they lived apart from their romantic interests and, at least among women, the majority abstained from sexual intercourse until they were engaged or married. They were usually employed, and they often turned over much of their paycheck to their parents to help rear younger siblings. Few went to college; most had not even graduated from high school. As recently as 1940, only about one-third of adults in their late twenties had graduated from high school and just one in sixteen had graduated from college.[2]

Today's unmarried young adults are much more likely to be living independently, in their own apartments. Five out of six young adults graduate from high school, and about one-third complete college.[3] They are more likely than their predecessors to spend their wages on themselves. Their sexual and intimate lives are also very different from those of earlier generations. The vast majority of unmarried young adults have had sexual intercourse. In fact, most women who married during the 1990s first had intercourse five years or more before marrying.[4]

About half of young adults live with a partner before marrying. Cohabitation is far more common today than it was at any time in the early- or mid-twentieth century (although it was not unknown among the poor and has been a part of the European family system in past centuries). Cohabitation today is a diverse, evolving phenomenon. For some people, it is a prelude to marriage or a trial marriage. For others, a series of cohabiting relationships may be a long-term substitute for marriage. (Thirty nine percent of cohabiters in 1995 lived with children of one of the partners.) It is still rare in the United States for cohabiting relationships to last long—about half end, through marriage or a breakup, within a year.[5]

Despite the drop in marriage and the rise in cohabitation, there has been no explosion of non-marital births in the United States. Birth rates have fallen for unmarried women of all reproductive ages and types of marital status, including adolescents. But because birth rates have fallen faster for married women than for unmarried women, a larger share of women who give birth are unmarried. In 1950, only 4 percent of all births took place outside of marriage. By 1970, the figure was 11 percent; by 1990, 28 percent; and by 2003, 35 percent. In recent years, then, about one-third of all births have been to unmarried women—and that is the statistic that has generated the most debate.[6] Of further concern to many observers is that about half of all unmarried first-time mothers are adolescents. Academics, policymakers, and private citizens alike express unease about the negative consequences of adolescent childbearing, both for the parents and for the children, although whether those consequences are due more to poverty or to teen childbearing per se remains controversial.

When people think of nonmarital or "out-of wedlock" childbearing, they picture a single parent. Increasingly, however, nonmarital births are occurring to cohabiting couples—about 40 percent according to the latest estimate.[7] One study of unmarried women giving birth in urban hospitals found that about half were living with the fathers of their children.

Couples in these "fragile families," however, rarely marry. One year after the birth of the child, only 15 percent had married, while 26 percent had broken up.[8]

Marriage was not an option for lesbians and gay men in any U.S. jurisdiction until Massachusetts legalized same-sex marriage in 2004. Cohabitation, however, is common in this group. In a 1992 national survey of sexual behavior, 44 percent of women and 28 percent of men who said they had engaged in homosexual sex in the previous year reported that they were cohabiting.[9] The Census Bureau, which began collecting statistics on same-sex partnerships in 1990, does not directly ask whether a person is in a romantic same-sex relationship; rather, it gives people the option of saying that a housemate is an "unmarried partner" without specifying the nature of the partnership. Because some people may not wish to openly report a same-sex relationship to the Census Bureau, it is hard to determine how reliable these figures are. The bureau reports, however, that in 2000, 600,000 households were maintained by same-sex partners. A substantial share—33 percent of female partnerships and 22 percent of male partnerships—reported the presence of children of one or both of the partners.[10]

As rates of entry into marriage were declining in the last half of the twentieth century, rates of exit via divorce were increasing—as they have been at least since the Civil War era. At the beginning of the twentieth century, about 10 percent of all marriages ended in divorce, and the figure rose to about one-third for marriages begun in 1950.[11] But the rise was particularly sharp during the 1960s and 1970s, when the likelihood that a married couple would divorce increased substantially. Since the 1980s the divorce rate has remained the same or declined slightly. According to the best

estimate, 48 percent of American marriages, at current rates, would be expected to end in divorce within twenty years.[12] A few percent more would undoubtedly end in divorce after that. So it is accurate to say that unless divorce risks change, about half of all marriages today would end in divorce. (There are important class and racial-ethnic differences, which I will discuss below.)

The combination of more divorce and a greater share of births to unmarried women has increased the proportion of children who are not living with two parents. Figure 5.2 tracks the share of children living, respectively, with two parents, with one parent, and with neither parent between 1968 and 2002. It shows a steady decline in the two-parent share and a corresponding increase in the one-parent share. In 2002, 69 percent of children were living with two parents, including families where one biological (or adoptive) parent had remarried. Not counting step- or adoptive families, 62 percent, according to the most recent estimate in 1996, were living with two biological parents.[13] Twenty-seven percent of American children were living with one parent; another 4 percent, with neither parent.[14] Most in the latter group were living with relatives, such as grandparents.

Where do all these changes leave U.S. marriage patterns and children's living arrangements in the early twenty-first century? As demographers have noted, many of the above trends have slowed over the past decade, suggesting a "quieting" of family change.[15] Marriage remains the most common living arrangement for raising children. At any one time, most American children are being raised by two parents. Marriage, however, is less dominant in parents' and children's lives than it once was. Children are more likely to experience life in a single-parent family, either because they are born to unmarried mothers or because their parents divorce. And children are more likely to experience instability in their living arrangements as parents form and dissolve marriages and partnerships. Although children are less likely to lose a parent through death today than they once were, the rise in nonmarital births and in divorce has more than compensated for the decline in parental death.[16] From the adult perspective, the

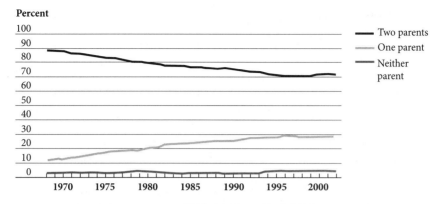

Figure 5.2. Living Arrangements of U.S. Children, 1968–2002.

Source: U.S. Bureau of the Census, "Living Arrangements of Children under 18 Years Old: 1960 to Present," 2003, www.census.gov/population/socdemo/hh-fam/tabCH-1.pdf (accessed July 23, 2004).

overall drop in birth rates and the increases in nonmarital childbearing and divorce mean that, at any one time, fewer adults are raising children than in the past.

Class and Racial-Ethnic Divergence

To complete this portrait of American marriage one must take note of class and racial-ethnic variations, for the overall statistics mask contrasting trends in the lives of children from different racial-ethnic groups and different social classes. In fact, over the past few decades, the family lives of children have been diverging across class and racial-ethnic lines.[17] A half-century ago, the family structures of poor and non-poor children were similar: most children lived in two-parent families. In the intervening years, the increase in single-parent families has been greater among the poor and near-poor.[18] Women at all levels of education have been postponing marriage, but less-educated women have postponed childbearing less than better-educated women have. The divorce rate in recent decades appears to have held steady or risen for women without a college education but fallen for college-educated women.[19] As a result, differences in family structure according to social class are much more pronounced than they were fifty years ago.

Consider the share of mothers who are unmarried. Throughout the past half-century,

single motherhood has been more common among women with less education than among well-educated women. But the gap has grown over time. In 1960, 14 percent of mothers in the bottom quarter of the educational distribution were unmarried, as against 4.5 percent of mothers in the top quarter—a difference of 9.5 percentage points. By 2000, the corresponding figures were 43 percent for the less-educated mothers and 7 percent for the more educated—a gap of 36 percentage points.[20] Sara McLanahan argues that societal changes such as greater opportunities for women in the labor market, a resurgence of feminist ideology, and the advent of effective birth control have encouraged women to invest in education and careers. Those who make these investments tend to delay childbearing and marriage, and they are more attractive in the marriage market.[21] Put another way, women at the top and bottom of the educational distribution may be evolving different reproductive strategies. Among the less educated, early childbearing outside of marriage has become more common, as the ideal of finding a stable marriage and then having children has weakened, whereas among the better educated, the strategy is to delay childbearing and marriage until after investing in schooling and careers.

One result of these developments has been growth in better-educated, dual-earner married-couple families. Since the 1970s these families have enjoyed much greater income growth than have breadwinner-homemaker families or single-parent families. What we see today, then, is a growing group of more fortunate children who tend to live with two parents whose incomes are adequate or ample and a growing group of less fortunate children who live with financially pressed single parents. Indeed, both groups at the extremes—the most and the least fortunate children—have been expanding over the past few decades, while the group of children in the middle has been shrinking.[22]

The family lives of African American children have also been diverging from those of white non-Hispanic children and, to a lesser extent, Hispanic children. African American family patterns were influenced by the institution of slavery, in which marriage was not legal, and perhaps by African cultural traditions, in which extended families had more influence and power compared with married couples. As a result, the proportion of African American children living with single parents has been greater than that of white children for a century or more.[23] Nevertheless, African American women married at an earlier age than did white women through the first half of the twentieth century.[24]

But since the 1960s, the decline of marriage as a social institution has been more pronounced among African Americans than among whites. The best recent estimates suggest that at current rates only about two-thirds of African American women would be expected ever to marry.[25] Correspondingly, the share of African American children born outside of marriage has risen to 69 percent.[26] In fact, about three-fifths of African American children may never live in a married-couple family while growing up, as against one-fifth of white children.[27] The greater role of extended kin in African American families may compensate for some of this difference, but the figures do suggest a strikingly reduced role of marriage among African Americans.

The family patterns of the Hispanic population are quite diverse. Mexican Americans have higher birth rates than all other major ethnic groups, and a greater share of Mexican American births than

of African American births is to married women.[28] Moreover, Mexican American families are more likely to include extended kin.[29] Consequently, Mexican Americans have more marriage-based, multigenerational households than do African Americans. Puerto Ricans, the second largest Hispanic ethnic group and the most economically disadvantaged, have rates of nonmarital child-bearing second only to African Americans.[30] But Puerto Ricans, like many Latin Americans, have a tradition of consensual unions, in which a man and woman live together as married but without approval of the church or a license from the state. So it is likely that more Puerto Rican "single" mothers than African American single mothers are living with partners.

Explaining the Trends

Most analysts would agree that both economic and cultural forces have been driving the changes in American family life over the past half-century. Analysts disagree about the relative weight of the two, but I will assume that both have been important.

Economic Influences

Two changes in the U.S. labor market have had major implications for families.[31] First, demand for workers increased in the service sector, where women had gained a foothold earlier in the century while they were shut out of manufacturing jobs. The rising demand encouraged women to get more education and drew married women into the workforce—initially, those whose children were school-aged, and later, those with younger children. Single mothers had long worked, but in 1996 major welfare reform legislation further encouraged work by setting limits on how long a parent could receive public assistance. The increase in women's paid work, in turn, increased demand for child care services and greatly increased the number of children cared for outside their homes.

The second work-related development was the decline, starting in the 1970s, in job opportunities for men without a college education. The flip side of the growth of the service sector was the decline in manufacturing. As factory jobs moved overseas and industrial productivity increased through automated equipment and computer-based controls, demand fell for blue-collar jobs that high school–educated men once took in hopes of supporting their families. As a result, average wages in these jobs fell. Even during the prosperous 1990s, the wages of men without a college degree hardly rose.[32] The decline in job opportunities had two effects. It decreased the attractiveness of non-college educated men on the marriage market—made them less "marriageable" in William Julius Wilson's terms—and thus helped drive marriage rates down among the less well educated.[33] It also undermined the single-earner "family wage system" that had been the ideal in the first half of the twentieth century and increased the incentive for wives to take paying jobs.

Cultural Developments

But economic forces, important as they were, could not have caused all the changes in family life noted above. Declines in the availability of marriageable men, for example, were not large enough to account, alone, for falling marriage rates among African Americans.[34] Accompanying the economic changes was a broad cultural shift among Americans that eroded the norms both of marriage before childbearing and of stable, life-long bonds after marriage.

Culturally, American marriage went through two broad transitions during the twentieth century. The first was described famously by sociologist Ernest Burgess as a change "from institution to companionship."[35] In institutional marriage, the family was held together by the forces of law, tradition, and religious belief. The husband was the unquestioned head of the household. Until the late nineteenth century, husband and wife became one legal person when they married—and that person was the husband. A wife could not sue in her own name, and her husband could dispose of her property as he wished. Until 1920 women could not vote; rather, it was assumed that almost all women would marry and that their husbands' votes would represent their views. But as the forces

of law and tradition weakened in the early decades of the twentieth century, the newer, companionate marriage arose. It was founded on the importance of the emotional ties between wife and husband—their companionship, friendship, and romantic love. Spouses drew satisfaction from performing the social roles of breadwinner, homemaker, and parent. After World War II, the spouses in companionate marriages, much to everyone's surprise, produced the baby boom: they had more children per family than any other generation in the twentieth century. The typical age at marriage fell to its lowest point since at least the late nineteenth century, and the share of all people who ever married rose. The decade of the 1950s was the high point of the breadwinner-homemaker, two-, three-, or even four-child family.

Starting around 1960, marriage went through a second transition. The typical age at marriage returned to, and then exceeded, the high levels of the early 1900s. Many young adults stayed single into their mid- to late twenties or even their thirties, some completing college educations and starting careers. Most women continued working for pay after they married. Cohabitation outside marriage became much more acceptable. Childbearing outside marriage became less stigmatized. The birth rate resumed its long decline and sank to an all-time low. Divorce rates rose to unprecedented levels. Same-sex partnerships found greater acceptance as well.

During this transition, companionate marriage waned as a cultural ideal. On the rise were forms of family life that Burgess had not foreseen, particularly marriages in which both husband and wife worked outside the home and single-parent families that came into being through divorce or through childbearing outside marriage. The roles of wives and husbands became more flexible and open to negotiation. And a more individualistic perspective on the rewards of marriage took root. When people evaluated how satisfied they were with their marriages, they began to think more in terms of developing their own sense of self and less in terms of gaining satisfaction through building a family and playing the roles of spouse and parent. The result was a transition from the companionate marriage to what we might call the individualized marriage.[36]

The Current Context of Marriage

To be sure, the "companionate marriage" and the "individualized marriage" are what sociologists refer to as ideal types. In reality, the distinctions between the two are less sharp than I have drawn them. Many marriages, for example, still follow the companionate ideal. Nevertheless, as a result of the economic and cultural trends noted above, marriage now exists in a very different context than it did in the past. Today it is but one among many options available to adults choosing how to shape their personal lives. More forms of marriage and more alternatives to it are socially acceptable. One may fit marriage into life in many ways: by first living with a partner, or sequentially with several partners, without explicitly considering whether to marry; by having children with one's eventual spouse or with someone else before marrying; by (in some jurisdictions) marrying someone of the same gender and building a shared marital world with few guidelines to rely on. Within marriage, roles are more flexible and negotiable, although women still do more of the household work and childrearing.

The rewards that people seek through marriage and other close relationships have also shifted. Individuals aim for personal growth and deeper intimacy through more open communication and mutually shared disclosures about feelings with their partners. They may insist on changes in a relationship that no longer provides them with individualized rewards. They are less likely than in the past to focus on the rewards gained by fulfilling socially valued roles such as the good parent or the loyal and supportive spouse. As a result of this changing context, social norms about family and personal life count for less than they did during the heyday of companionate marriage and far less than during the era of institutional marriage. Instead, personal choice and self-development loom large in people's construction of their marital careers.

But if marriage is now optional, it remains highly valued. As the practical importance of marriage has declined, its symbolic importance has remained high and may even have increased.[37] At its height as an institution in the mid-twentieth century, marriage was almost required of anyone wishing to be considered a respectable adult. Having children outside marriage was stigmatized, and a person who remained single through adulthood was suspect. But as other lifestyle options became more feasible and acceptable, the need to be married diminished. Nevertheless, marriage remains the preferred option for most people. Now, however, it is not a step taken lightly or early in young adulthood. Being "ready" to marry may mean that a couple has lived together to test their compatibility, saved for a down payment on a house, or possibly had children to judge how well they parent together. Once the foundation of adult family life, marriage is now often the capstone.

Although some observers believe that a "culture of poverty" has diminished the value of marriage among poor Americans, research suggests that the poor, the near-poor, and the middle class conceive of marriage in similar terms. Although marriage rates are lower among the poor than among the middle class, marriage as an ideal remains strong for both groups. Ethnographic studies show that many low-income individuals subscribe to the capstone view of marriage. In a study of low-income families that I carried out with several collaborators, a twenty-seven-year-old mother told an ethnographer:[38]

> I was poor all my life and so was Reginald. When I got pregnant, we agreed we would marry some day in the future because we loved each other and wanted to raise our child together. But we would not get married until we could afford to get a house and pay all the utility bills on time. I have this thing about utility bills. Our gas and electric got turned off all the time when we were growing up and we wanted to make sure that would not happen when we got married. That was our biggest worry.... We worked together and built up savings and then we got married. It's forever for us.

The poor, the near-poor, and the middle class also seem to view the emotional rewards of marriage in similar terms. Women of all classes value companionship in marriage: shared lives, joint childrearing, friendship, romantic love, respect, and fair treatment. For example, in a survey conducted in twenty-one cities, African Americans were as likely as non-Hispanic whites to rate highly the emotional benefits of marriage, such as friendship, sex life, leisure time, and a sense of security; and Hispanics rated these benefits somewhat higher than either group.[39] Moreover, in the "fragile families" study of unmarried low- and moderate-income couples who had just had a child together, Marcia Carlson, Sara McLanahan, and Paula England found that mothers and fathers who scored higher on a scale of relationship supportiveness were substantially more likely to be married one year later.[40] Among the items in the scale were whether the partner "is fair and willing to compromise" during a disagreement, "expresses affection or love," "encourages or helps," and does not insult or criticize. In a 2001 national survey of young adults aged twenty to twenty-nine conducted by the Gallup Organization for the National Marriage Project, 94 percent of never-married respondents agreed that "when you marry, you want your spouse to be your soul mate, first and foremost." Only 16 percent agreed that "the main purpose of marriage these days is to have children."[41]

As debates over same-sex marriage illustrate, marriage is also highly valued by lesbians and gay men. In 2003 the Massachusetts Supreme Court struck down a state law limiting marriage to opposite-sex couples, and same-sex marriage became legal in May 2004 (although opponents may eventually succeed in prohibiting it through a state constitutional amendment). Advocates for same-sex marriage argued that gay and lesbian couples should be entitled to marry so that they can benefit from the legal rights and protections that marriage brings. But the Massachusetts debate also showed the symbolic value of marriage. In response to the court's decision, the state legislature crafted a plan to enact civil unions for same-sex couples. These legally recognized

unions would have given same-sex couples most of the legal benefits of marriage but would have withheld the status of being married. The court rejected this remedy, arguing that allowing civil unions but not marriage would create a "stigma of exclusion," because it would deny to same-sex couples "a status that is specially recognized in society and has significant social and other advantages." That the legislature was willing to provide legal benefits was not sufficient for the judges, nor for gay and lesbian activists, who rejected civil unions as second-class citizenship. Nor would it be enough for mainstream Americans, most of whom are still attached to marriage as a specially recognized status.

Putting U.S. Marriage in International Perspective

How does the place of marriage in the family system in the United States compare with its place in the family systems of other developed nations? It turns out that marriage in the United States is quite distinctive.

A Greater Attachment to Marriage

Marriage is more prevalent in the United States than in nearly all other developed Western nations. Figure 5.3 shows the total first marriage rate for women in the United States and in six other developed nations in 1990. (Shortly after 1990, the U.S. government stopped collecting all the information necessary to calculate this rate.) The total first marriage rate provides an estimate of the proportion of women who will ever marry.[42] It must be interpreted carefully because it yields estimates that are too low if calculated at a time when women are postponing marriage until older ages, as they were in 1990 in most countries. Thus, all the estimates in Figure 5.3 are probably too low. Nevertheless, the total first marriage rate is useful in comparing countries at a given time point, and I have selected the nations in Figure 5.3 to illustrate the variation in this rate in the developed world. The value of 715 for the United States—the highest of any country—implies that 715 out of 1,000 women were expected to marry. Italy had

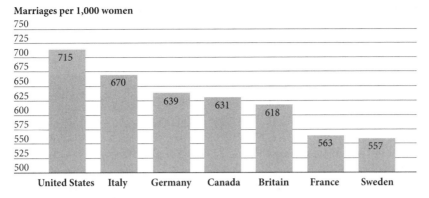

Figure 5.3. Total First Marriage Rates of Women, Selected European and English-Speaking Countries, 1990.

Sources: Alain Monnier and Catherine de Guibert-Lantoine, "The Demographic Situation of Europe and Developed Countries Overseas: An Annual Report," *Population; An English Selection* 8 (1996): 235–50; U.S. National Center for Health Statistics, "Advance Report of Final Marriage Statistics, 1989 and 1990," *Monthly Vital Statistics Report* 43, no. 12, supp. (Government Printing Office, 1995).

a relatively high value, while France and Sweden had the lowest. In between were Britain, Canada, and Germany.

Not only is marriage stronger demographically in the United States than in other developed countries, it also seems stronger as an ideal. In the World Values Surveys conducted between 1999 and 2001, one question asked of adults was whether they agreed with the statement, "Marriage is an outdated institution." Only 10 percent of Americans agreed—a lower share than in any developed nation except Iceland. Twenty-two percent of Canadians agreed, as did 26 percent of the British, and 36 percent of the French.[43] Americans seem more attached to marriage as a norm than do citizens in other developed countries.

This greater attachment to marriage has a long history. As Alexis de Tocqueville wrote in the 1830s, "There is certainly no country in the world where the tie of marriage is more respected than in America or where conjugal happiness is more highly or worthily appreciated."[44] Historian Nancy Cott has argued that the nation's founders viewed Christian marriage as one of the building blocks of American democracy. The marriage-based family was seen as a mini-republic in which the husband governed with the consent of the wife.[45] The U.S.

government has long justified laws and policies that support marriage. In 1888, Supreme Court Justice Stephen Field wrote, "marriage, as creating the most important relation in life, as having more to do with the morals and civilization of a people than any other institution, has always been subject to the control of the legislature."[46]

The conspicuous historical exception to government support for marriage was the institution of slavery, under which legal marriage was prohibited. Many slaves nevertheless married informally, often using public rituals such as jumping over a broomstick.[47] Some scholars also think that slaves may have retained the kinship patterns of West Africa, where marriage was more a process that unfolded over time in front of the community than a single event.[48] The prospective husband's family, for example, might wait until the prospective wife bore a child to finalize the marriage.

The distinctiveness of marriage in the United States is also probably related to greater religious participation. Tocqueville observed, "there is no country in the world where the Christian religion retains a greater influence over the souls of men than in America."[49] That statement is still true with respect to the developed nations today: religious vitality is greatest in the United States.[50]

For instance, in the World Values Surveys, 60 percent of Americans reported attending religious services at least monthly, as against 36 percent of Canadians, 19 percent of the British, and 12 percent of the French.[51] Americans look to religious institutions for guidance on marriage and family life more than do the citizens of most Western countries. Sixty-one percent of Americans agreed with the statement, "Generally speaking, do you think that the churches in your country are giving adequate answers to the problems of family life?" Only 48 percent of Canadians, 30 percent of the British, and 28 percent of the French agreed.[52]

Moreover, family policies in many European nations have long promoted births, whereas American policies generally have not. This emphasis on pronatalism has been especially prominent in France, where the birth rate began to decline in the 1830s, decades before it did in most other European nations.[53] Since then, the French government has been concerned about losing ground in population size to potential adversaries such as Germany.[54] (The Germans felt a similar concern, which peaked in the Nazis' pronatalist policies of the 1930s and early 1940s.)[55] As a result, argues one historian, French family policy has followed a "parental logic" that places a high priority on supporting parents with young children—even working wives and single parents.[56] These policies have included family allowances prorated by the number of children, maternity insurance, and maternity leave with partial wage replacement. In contrast, policies in Britain and the United States followed a "male breadwinner logic" of supporting married couples in which the husband worked outside the home and the wife did not.[57] Pronatalist pressure has never been strong in the United States, even though the decline in the U.S. birth rate started in the early 1800s, because of the nation's openness to increasing its population through immigration.

More Transitions Into and Out of Marriage

In addition to its high rate of marriage, the United States has one of the highest rates of divorce of any developed nation. Figure 5.4 displays the total divorce rate in 1990 for me countries shown in Figure 5.3. The total divorce rate, which provides an estimate of the number of marriages that would end in divorce, has limits similar to those of the total marriage rate but is likewise useful in international comparisons.[58] Figure 5.4 shows that the United States had a total divorce rate of 517 divorces per 1,000 marriages, with just over half of all marriages ending in divorce. Sweden had the second highest total divorce rate, and other Scandinavian countries had similar levels. The English-speaking countries of Britain and Canada were next, followed by France and Germany. Italy had a very low level of predicted divorce.

Both entry into and exit from marriage are indicators of what Robert Schoen has called a country's "marriage metabolism": the number of marriage- and divorce-related transitions that adults and their children undergo.[59] Figure 5.5, which presents the sum of the total first marriage rate and the total divorce rate, shows that the United States has by far the highest marriage metabolism of any of the developed countries in question.[60] Italy, despite its high marriage rate, has the lowest metabolism because of its very low divorce rate. Sweden, despite its high divorce rate, has a lower metabolism than the United States because of its lower marriage rate. In other words, what makes the United States most distinctive is the combination of high marriage and high divorce rates—which implies that Americans typically experience more transitions into and out of marriages than do people in other countries.

A similar trend is evident in movement into and out of cohabiting unions. Whether in marriage or cohabitation, Americans appear to have far more transitions in their live-in relationships. According to surveys from the mid-1990s, 5 percent of women in Sweden had experienced three or more unions (marriages or cohabiting relationships) by age thirty-five. In the rest of Europe, the comparable figure was 1 to 3 percent.[61] But in the United States, according to a 1995 survey, 9 percent of women aged thirty-five had experienced three or more unions, nearly double the Swedish figure and far higher than that of other European nations.[62] By 2002, the U.S. figure had climbed to 12 percent.[63] No other comparable nation has

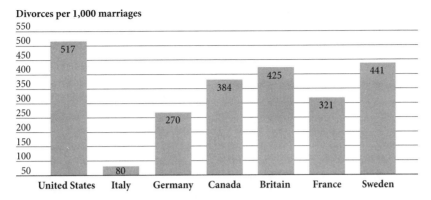

Figure 5.4. Total Divorce Rates, Selected European and English-Speaking Countries, 1990.

Sources: Monnier and de Guibert-Lantoine, "The Demographic Situation of Europe and the Developed Countries Overseas" (see Figure 5.3); U.S. National Center for Health Statistics, "Advance Report of Final Divorce Statistics, 1989 and 1990," *Monthly Vital Statistics Report* 43, no. 9, supp. (Government Printing Office, 1995).

such a high level of multiple marital and cohabiting unions.

American children are thus more likely to experience multiple transitions in living arrangements than are children in Europe. Another study using the same comparative data from the mid-1990s reported that 12 percent of American children had lived in three or more parental partnerships by age fifteen, as against 3 percent of children in Sweden, which has the next highest figure.[64] As transitions out of partnerships occur, children experience a period of living in a single-parent family. And although American children, in general, are more likely to live in a single-parent family while growing up than are children elsewhere, the trend differs by social class. As Sara McLanahan shows in a comparison of children whose mothers have low or moderate levels of education, American children are much more likely than those in several European nations to have lived with a single mother by age fifteen. The cross-national difference is less pronounced among children whose mothers are highly educated.[65]

Also contributing to the prevalence of single-parent families in the United States is the relatively large share of births to unmarried, non-cohabiting women—about one in five.[66] In most other developed nations with numerous nonmarital births, a greater share of unmarried mothers lives with the fathers of their children. In fact, the increases in nonmarital births in Europe in recent decades largely reflect births to cohabiting couples rather than births to single parents.[67] As noted, the United States is seeing a similar trend toward births to cohabiting couples, but the practice is still less prevalent in the United States than in many European nations.

Greater Economic Inequality

Children in the United States experience greater inequality of economic well-being than children in most other developed nations. One recent study reported that the gap between the cash incomes of children's families in the lowest and highest 10 percent was larger in the United States than in twelve other developed countries.[68] The low ranking of the United States is attributable both to the higher share of births to single parents and to the higher share of divorce. But even when the comparison is restricted to children living in single-parent families, children in the United States have the lowest relative standard of living. For example, one comparative study reported that 60 percent of single-mother households in the United States were poor, as against 45 percent in Canada, 40 percent in the United Kingdom, 25 percent in France, 20 percent in Italy, and 5 percent in Sweden.[69] The differences are caused by variations both in the income

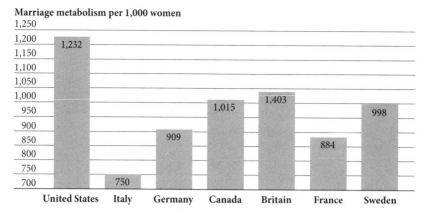

Figure 5.5. Marriage Metabolism, Selected European and English-Speaking Countries, 1990.
Sources: See Figures 5.3 and 5.4.

earned by single parents and in the generosity of government cash transfers. In other words, having a high share of single-parent families predisposes the United States to have a higher poverty rate, but other countries compensate better for single parenthood through a combination of social welfare spending and supports for employed parents, such as child care.

More Controversy over Gay and Lesbian Partnerships

Other developed countries tend to be more open to gay and lesbian partnerships than is the United States. Two European nations, Belgium and the Netherlands, have legalized same-sex marriage. By 2005, courts in seven Canadian provinces had ruled that laws restricting marriage to opposite-sex couples were discriminatory, and the Canadian federal government had introduced a bill to legalize gay marriage nationwide. Many other developed nations, including all the Scandinavian countries and Germany, have amended their family laws to include legal recognition of same-sex partnerships.[70]

France enacted its somewhat different form of domestic partnership, the *pacte civil de solidarité* (PACS), in 1999. Originally conceived in response to the burden placed on gay couples by the AIDS epidemic, the 1999 legislation was not restricted

to same-sex partnerships.[71] In fact, it is likely that more opposite-sex partners than same-sex partners have chosen this option.[72] The PACS does not provide all the legal benefits of marriage. It is a privately negotiated contract between two persons who are treated legally as individuals unless they have children. Even when they have children, the contract does not require one partner to support the other after a dissolution, and judges are reluctant to award joint custody. Moreover, individuals in a same-sex PACS do not have the right to adopt children or to use reproductive technology such as in vitro fertilization.

For the most part, the issue of marriage has been less prominent in European than in North American debates about same-sex partnerships. To this point, no serious movement for same-sex marriage has appeared in Britain.[73] The French debate, consistent with the nation's child-oriented social policies, has focused more on the kinship rights and relationships of the children of the partners than on whether the legal form of partnership should include marriage.[74] In 2004, the mayor of Bègles, France, created a furor—similar to that seen in the United States following the granting of marriage licenses in San Francisco—by marrying a gay couple. But marriage remains less central to the politics of same-sex partnerships in France and elsewhere in Europe than it is in North America.

Marriage Transformed

Marriage remains an important part of the American family system, even if its dominance has diminished. Sentiment in favor of marriage appears to be stronger in the United States than elsewhere in the developed world, and the share of adults who are likely to marry is higher—as is, however, their propensity to get divorced. Increasingly, gay and lesbian activists are arguing, with some success, that they, too, should be allowed to marry. Even poor and near-poor Americans, who are statistically less likely to marry, hold to marriage as an ideal. But the contemporary ideal differs from that of the past in two important ways.

The Contemporary Ideal

First, marriage is now more optional in the United States than it has ever been. Until recently, family formation rarely occurred outside of marriage. Now, to a greater extent than ever before, one can choose whether to have children on one's own, in a cohabiting relationship, or in a marriage. Poor and working-class Americans have radically separated the timing of childbearing and marriage, with many young adults having children many years before marrying. At current rates, perhaps one-third of African Americans will never marry. To be sure, some of the increase in seemingly single-parent families reflects a rise in the number of cohabiting couples who are having children, but these cohabiting relationships often prove unstable. How frequently the option of marriage becomes a reality depends heavily on one's race, ethnicity, or social class. African Americans and less well-educated Americans, for example, still value marriage highly but attain it less frequently than whites and better-educated Americans.

Second, the rewards of marriage today are more individualized. Being married is less a required adult role and more an individual achievement—a symbol of successful self-development. And couples are more prone to dissolve a marriage if their individualized rewards seem inadequate. Conversely, marriage is less centered on children.

Today, married couples in the United States are having fewer children than couples have had at any time in the nation's history except during the Great Depression.

The changes in marriage, however, have not been solely cultural in origin. It is still the norm that a man must be able to provide a steady income to be seen as a good prospect for marriage. He no longer need earn all the family's income, but he must make a substantial, stable contribution. As the labor market position of young men without a college education has eroded, their attractiveness in the marriage market has declined. Many of their potential partners have chosen to have children outside marriage early in adulthood rather than to wait for the elusive promise of finding a spouse. Moreover, the introduction of the birth control pill and the legalization of abortion have allowed young women and men to become sexually active long before they think about marriage.

When the American family system is viewed in international perspective, it is most distinctive for the many transitions into and out of marital and cohabiting unions. Americans are more likely to experience multiple unions over the course of their lives than are Europeans. Moreover, cohabiting relationships in the United States still tend to be rather short, with a median duration (until either marriage or dissolution) of about one year. The median duration of cohabiting unions is about four years in Sweden and France and two or more years in most other European nations.[75] All this means that American children probably face greater instability in their living arrangements than children anywhere else in the developed world. Recent research has suggested that changes in family structure, regardless of the beginning and ending configurations, may cause problems for children.[76] Some of these apparent problems may reflect preexisting family difficulties, but some cause-and-effect association between instability and children's difficulties probably exists. If so, the increase in instability over the past decades is a worrisome trend that may not be receiving the attention it deserves.

Positive Developments

This is not to suggest that all the trends in marriage in America have been harmful to children. Those who live with two parents or with one well-educated parent may be doing better than comparable children a few decades ago. As noted, income growth has been greater in dual-career families, and divorce rates may have fallen among the college educated. In addition, the time spent with their parents by children in two-parent families has gone up, not down, and the comparable time spent by children with single parents has not changed, even though mothers' work outside the home has increased.[77] Working mothers appear to compensate for time spent outside the home by cutting back on housework and leisure—and, for those who are married, relying on modest but noticeable increases in husbands' housework—to preserve time with children.[78]

Meanwhile, the decline in fertility means that there are fewer children in the home to compete for their parents' attention. Middle-class parents engage in an intensive childrearing style that sociologist Annette Lareau calls "concerted cultivation": days filled with organized activities and parent-child discussions designed to enhance their children's talents, opinions, and skills.[79] While some social critics decry this parenting style, middle-class children gain skills that will be valuable to them in higher education and in the labor market. They learn how to communicate with professionals and other adults in positions of authority. They develop a confident style of interaction that Lareau calls "an emerging sense of entitlement," compared with "an emerging sense of constraint" among working-class and lower-class youth.

Marriage and Public Policy

Because marriage has been, and continues to be, stronger in the United States than in much of Europe, American social welfare policies have focused more on marriage than have those of many European countries. That emphasis continues. George W. Bush's administration advocates marriage-promotion programs as the most promising way to assist families. No European country has pursued a comparable policy initiative. Moreover, the issue of gay marriage has received more attention in the United States than in most of Europe. This greater emphasis on marriage in public policy reflects the history and culture of the United States. Policies that build on and support marriage are likely to be popular with American voters because they resonate with American values. Europe's more generous public spending on children, regardless of their parents' marital status, is rooted in concerns about low population growth that have never been strong in the United States. Such public spending on single-parent families also reflects the lesser influence of religion in Europe. So it is understandable that American policymakers wishing to generate support for new family policy initiatives might turn to marriage-based programs.

Yet the relatively high value placed on marriage in the United States coexists with an unmatched level of family instability and large numbers of single-parent families. This, too, is part of the American cultural heritage. The divorce rate appears to have been higher in the United States than in most of Europe since the mid-nineteenth century.[80]

This emblematic American pattern of high marriage and divorce rates, cohabiting unions of short duration, and childbearing among unpartnered women and men makes it unrealistic to think that policymakers will be able to reduce rates of multiple unions and of single parenthood in the United States to typical European levels. Consequently, a family policy that relies too heavily on marriage will not help the many children destined to live in single-parent and cohabiting-parent families—many of them economically disadvantaged—for some or all of their formative years. Only assistance directed to needy families, regardless of their household structure, will reach them. Such policies are less popular in the United States, as the widespread disdain for cash welfare and the popularity of the 1996 welfare reform legislation demonstrate. Moreover, some American policymakers worry that programs that support all parents without regard to partnership status may decrease people's incentive to marry.[81] The dilemma for policymakers is how to make the trade-off between marriage-based and marriage-neutral programs. A careful balance of both is needed to provide adequate support to American children.

Notes

1. W. C. Rodgers and A. Thornton, "Changing Patterns of First Marriage in the United States," *Demography* 22 (1985): 265–79; Joshua R. Goldstein and Catherine T. Kenney, "Marriage Delayed or Marriage Forgone? New Cohort Forecasts of First Marriage for U.S. Women," *American Sociological Review* 66 (2001): 506–19.

2. U.S. Bureau of the Census, "Percent of People 25 Years Old and Over Who Have Completed High School or College, by Race, Hispanic Origin and Sex: Selected Years 1940 to 2002," 2003, table A-2, www.census.gov/population/socdemo/education/tabA-2.pdf (accessed June 24, 2004).

3. Ibid.

4. U.S. National Center for Health Statistics, "Fertility, Family Planning, and Women's Health: New Data from the 1995 National Survey of Family Growth," *Vital and Health Statistics* 23, no. 19 (1997), available at www.cdc.gov/nchs/data/series/sr_23/sr23_019.pdf (accessed July 13, 2004).

5. Larry L. Bumpass and Hsien-Hen Lu, "Trends in Cohabitation and Implications for Children's Family Contexts in the United States," *Population Studies* 54 (2000): 29–41. They note that 49 percent of women aged thirty to thirty-four years old in the 1995 National Survey of Family Growth reported ever cohabiting.

6. U.S. National Center for Health Statistics, "Number and Percent of Births to Unmarried Women, by Race and Hispanic Origin: United States, 1940–99," *Vital Statistics of the United States, 1999*, vol. 1, *Natality*, table 1-17 (available at www.cdc.gov/nchs/data/statab/t991x17.pdf [accessed January 12, 2005]); and U.S. National Center for Health Statistics, "Births: Preliminary Data for 2002," *National Vital Statistics Report* 53, no. 9, www.cdc.gov/nchs/data/nvsr/nvsr53/nvsr53_09.pdf (accessed January 12, 2005). For 2003, the figures were 34.6 percent overall, 23.5 percent for non-Hispanic whites, 68.5 percent for non-Hispanic blacks, and 45 percent for Hispanics.

7. Ibid.

8. Marcia Carlson, Sara McLanahan, and Paula England, "Union Formation in Fragile Families," *Demography* 41 (2004): 237–61.

9. Dan Black and others, "Demographics of the Gay and Lesbian Population in the United States: Evidence from Available Systematic Data," *Demography* 37 (2000): 139–54.

10. U.S. Bureau of the Census, "Married-Couple and Unmarried-Partner Households: 2000" (Government Printing Office, 2003).

11. Andrew Cherlin, *Marriage, Divorce, Remarriage* (Harvard University Press, 1992).

12. Matthew Bramlett and William D. Mosher, *Cohabitation, Marriage, Divorce and Remarriage in the United. States,* series 22, no. 2 (U.S. National Center for Health Statistics, Vital and Health Statistics, 2002), available at www.cdc.gov/nchs/data/series/sr_23/sr23_022.pdf (accessed June 2003).

13. U.S. Bureau of the Census. "Detailed Living Arrangements of Children by Race and Hispanic Origin, 1996," 2001, www.census.gov/population/socdemo/child/p70–74/tab01.pdf (accessed June 28, 2004). The data are from the 1996 Survey of Income and Program Participation, wave 2.

14. Some of the one-parent families contain an unmarried cohabiting partner, whom the Census Bureau normally does not count as a "parent." According to the 1996 estimates cited in the previous note, about 2.5 percent of children live with a biological or adoptive parent who is cohabiting.

15. Lynne Casper and Suzanne M. Bianchi, *Continuity and Change in the American Family* (Thousand Oaks, Calif.: Sage, 2002).

16. David Ellwood and Christopher Jencks, "The Uneven Spread of Single-Parent Families: What Do We Know? Where Do We Look for Answers?" in *Social Inequality,* edited by Kathryn M. Neckerman (New York: Russell Sage Foundation, 2004), pp. 3–118.

17. Sara McLanahan, "Diverging Destinies: How Children Are Faring under the Second Demographic Transition," *Demography* 41 (2004): 607–27.

18. Ellwood and Jencks, "The Uneven Spread of Single-Parent Families" (see note 16).

19. Steven P. Martin, "Growing Evidence for a 'Divorce Divide'? Education and Marital Dissolution Rates in the U.S. since the 1970s," Working

Paper on Social Dimensions of Inequality (New York: Russell Sage Foundation, 2004).

20. McLanahan, "Diverging Destinies" (see note 17).

21. Ibid.

22. Isabel Sawhill and Laura Chadwick, *Children in Cities: Uncertain Futures* (Brookings, 1999); and Donald J. Hernandez, *America's Children: Resources from Family, Government, and Economy* (New York: Russell Sage Foundation, 1993).

23. S. Philip Morgan and others, "Racial Differences in Household and Family Structure at the Turn of the Century," *American Journal of Sociology* 98 (1993): 798–828.

24. Cherlin, *Marriage, Divorce, Remarriage* (see note 11).

25. Goldstein and Kenney, "Marriage Delayed or Marriage Forgone?" (see note 1).

26. U.S. National Center for Health Statistics, "Births: Preliminary Data" (see note 6).

27. Bumpass and Lu, "Trends in Cohabitation" (see note 5).

28. U.S. National Center for Health Statistics, "Revised Birth and Fertility Rates for the 1990s and New Rates for the Hispanic Populations, 2000 and 2001: United States," *National Vital Statistics Reports* 51, no. 12 (Government Printing Office, 2003); and U.S. National Center for Health Statistics, "Births: Final Data for 2000," *National Vital Statistics Report* 50, no. 5 (Government Printing Office, 2002).

29. Frank D. Bean and Marta Tienda, *The Hispanic Population of the United States* (New York: Russell Sage Foundation, 1987).

30. U.S. National Center for Health Statistics, "Births: Final Data for 2000" (see note 28).

31. McLanahan, "Diverging Destinies" (see note 17).

32. Elise Richer and others, *Boom Times a Bust: Declining Employment among Less-Educated Young Men* (Washington: Center for Law and Social Policy, 2003); available at www.clasp.org/DMS/Documents/1058362464.08/Boom_Times.pdf (accessed July 13, 2004).

33. William J. Wilson, *The Truly Disadvantaged: The Inner City, the Underclass, and Public Policy* (University of Chicago Press, 1987).

34. Robert D. Mare and Christopher Winship, "Socioeconomic Change and the Decline in Marriage for Blacks and Whites," in *The Urban Underclass*, edited by Christopher Jencks and Paul Peterson (Brook-

ings, 1991), pp. 175–202; and Daniel T. Lichter, Diane K. McLaughlin, and David C. Ribar, "Economic Restructuring and the Retreat from Marriage," *Social Science Research* 31 (2002): 230–56.

35. Ernest W. Burgess and Harvey J. Locke, *The Family: From Institution to Companionship* (New York: American Book Company, 1945).

36. Andrew J. Cherlin, "The Deinstitutionalization of American Marriage," *Journal of Marriage and the Family* 66 (2004): 848–61.

37. Ibid.

38. Linda Burton of Pennsylvania State University directed the ethnographic component of the study. For a general description, see Pamela Winston and others, "Welfare, Children, and Families: A Three-City Study Overview and Design," 1999, www.jhu.edu\-welfare\overviewanddesign.pdf (accessed July 10, 2004).

39. M. Belinda Tucker, "Marital Values and Expectations in Context: Results from a 21-City Survey," in *The Ties That Bind: Perspectives on Marriage and Cohabitation,* edited by Linda J. Waite (New York: Aldine de Gruyter, 2000), pp. 166–87.

40. Carlson, McLanahan, and England, "Union Formation" (see note 8).

41. Barbara Dafoe Whitehead and David Popenoe, "Who Wants to Marry a Soul Mate?" in *The State of Our Unions, 2001,* The National Marriage Project, Rutgers University, pp. 6–16, 2001, available at marriage.rutgers.edu/Publications/SOOU/NMPAR2001.pdf (accessed February 12, 2004).

42. The estimate assumes that the age-specific marriage rates in the year of calculation (in this case, 1990) will remain unchanged in future years. Since this assumption is unrealistic, the total marriage rate is unlikely to predict the future accurately. But it does demonstrate the rate of marriage implied by current trends.

43. Ronald Inglehart and others, *Human Beliefs and Values: A Cross-Cultural Sourcebook Based on the 1999–2002 Values Surveys* (Mexico City: Siglo Veinciuno Editores, 2004).

44. Alexis de Tocqueville, *Democracy in America,* vol. 1 (New York: Knopf, Everyman's Library, 1994), p. 304.

45. Nancy Cott, *Public Vows: A History of Marriage and the Nation* (Harvard University Press, 2000).

46. Quoted in ibid., pp. 102–03.

47. Herbert G. Gutman, *The Black Family in Slavery and Freedom, 1750–1925* (New York: Pantheon, 1976).

48. Jacqueline Jones, *Labor of Love, Labor of Sorrow: Black Women and the Family from Slavery to the Present* (New York: Basic Books, 1985).

49. Tocqueville, *Democracy in America* (see note 44), p. 303.

50. Grace Davie, "Patterns of Religion in Western Europe: An Exceptional Case," in *The Blackwell Companion to the Sociology of Religion,* edited by Richard K. Fenn (Oxford: Blackwell, 2001), pp. 264–78; and Seymour Martin Lipset, "American Exceptionalism Reaffirmed," *Tocqueville Review* 10 (1990): 3–35.

51. Inglehart and others, *Human Beliefs and Values* (see note 43).

52. Ibid.

53. See the discussion in Ron J. Lesthaeghe, *The Decline of Belgian Fertility, 1800–1970* (Princeton University Press, 1977), p. 304.

54. Alisa Klaus, "Depopulation and Race Suicide: Maternalism and Pronatalist Ideologies in France and the United States," in *Mothers of a New World: Maternalist Politics and the Origins of the Welfare State,* edited by Seth Koven and Sonya Michel (New York: Routledge, 1993), pp. 188–212.

55. Paul Ginsborg, "The Family Politics of the Great Dictators," in *Family Life in the Twentieth Century,* edited by David I. Kertzer and Marzio Barbagli (Yale University Press, 2003), pp. 188–97.

56. Susan Pedersen, *Family, Dependence, and the Origins of the Welfare State: Britain and. France, 1914–1945* (Cambridge University Press, 1993).

57. Ibid.

58. The total divorce rate is formed by summing duration-specific divorce rates prevalent in the year of observation—in this case, 1990. It therefore assumes that the duration-specific rates of 1990 will remain the same in future years. It shares the limits of the total marriage rate (see note 42).

59. Robert Schoen and Robin M. Weinick, "The Slowing Metabolism of Marriage: Figures from 1988 U.S. Marital Status Life Tables," *Demography* 39 (1993): 737–46. Schoen and Weinick used life table calculations to establish the marriage and divorce probabilities for American men and women. Unfortunately, only total marriage rates and total divorce rates are available for other countries. Consequently, I calculated a total divorce rate for the United States from published duration-specific divorce rates for 1990. I then summed the total first marriage rate and total divorce rate for the United States and the other countries displayed in figure 4. Although this procedure is not as accurate as using rates generated by life tables, the difference is unlikely to alter the relative positions of the countries in the figure.

60. Strictly speaking, I should use the total divorce rate for people in first marriages (as opposed to including people in remarriages), but the available data do not allow for that level of precision.

61. Alexia Fürnkranz-Prskawetz and others, "Pathways to Stepfamily Formation in Europe: Results from the FFS," *Demographic Research* 8 (2003): 107–9.

62. Author's calculation from the 1995 National Survey of Family Growth microdata file.

63. Author's calculation from the 2002 National Survey of Family Growth microdata file.

64. Patrick Heuveline, Jeffrey M. Timberlake, and Frank F. Furstenberg Jr., "Shifting Childrearing to Single Mothers: Results from 17 Western Countries," *Population and Development Review* 29 (2003): 47–71. The figures quoted appear in note 6.

65. McLanahan, "Diverging Destinies" (see note 17).

66. About one-third of all births are to unmarried mothers, and Bumpass and Lu report that about 60 percent of unmarried mothers in 1995 were not cohabiting (0.33 × 0.60 = 0.198). Bumpas and Lu, "Trends in Cohabitation" (see note 5).

67. Kathleen Kiernan, "European Perspectives on Nonmarital Childbearing," in *Out of Wedlock: Causes and Consequences of Nonmarital Fertility,* edited by Lawrence L. Wu and Barbara Wolfe (New York: Russell Sage Foundation, 2001), pp. 77–108.

68. Lars Osberg, Timothy M. Smeeding, and Jonathan Schwabish, "Income Distribution and Public Social Expenditure: Theories, Effects, and Evidence," in *Social Inequality,* edited by Kathryn M. Neckerman (New York: Russell Sage Foundation, 2004), pp. 821–59.

69. Poverty was defined as having a family income of less than half of the median income for all families. Bruce Bradbury and Markus Jäntti,

"Child-Poverty across the Industrialized World: Evidence from the Luxembourg Income Study," in *Child Well-Being, Child Poverty and Child Policy in Modern Nations: What Do We Know?* edited by Koen Vleminckx and Timothy M. Smeeding (Bristol, England: Policy Press, 2000), pp. 11–32.

70. Marzio Barbagli and David I. Kertzer, "Introduction," and Paulo Ronfani, "Family Law in Europe," in *Family Life in the Twentieth Century,* edited by David I. Kertzer and Marzio Barbagli (Yale University Press, 2003), respectively, pp. xi–xliv and 114–51.

71. Claude Martin and Irene Théry, "The Pacs and Marriage and Cohabitation in France," *International Journal of Law, Policy and the Family* 15 (2001): 135–58.

72. Patrick Festy, "The 'Civil Solidarity Pact' (PACS) in France: An Impossible Evaluation," *Population et Sociétés*, no. 369 (2001): 1–4.

73. John Eekelaar, "The End of an Era?" *Journal of Family History* 28 (2003): 108–22.

74. Eric Fassin, "Same Sex, Different Politics: 'Gay Marriage' Debates in France and the United States," *Popular Culture* 13 (2001): 215–32.

75. Kathleen Kiernan, "Cohabitation in Western Europe," *Population Trends* 96 (Summer 1999): 25–32.

76. See, for example, Lawrence L. Wu and Brian C. Martinson, "Family Structure and the Risk of Premarital Birth," *American Sociological Review* 59 (1993): 210–32; Jake M. Najman and others, "Impact of Family Type and Family Quality on Child Behavior Problems: A Longitudinal Study," *Journal of the American Academy of Child and Adolescent Psychiatry* 36 (1997): 1357–65.

77. John F. Sandberg and Sandra D. Hofferth, "Changes in Children's Time with Parents, U.S. 1981–1997," *Demography* 38 (2001): 423–36.

78. Suzanne M. Bianchi, "Maternal Employment and Time with Children: Dramatic Change or Surprising Continuity?" *Demography* 37 (2000): 401–14.

79. Annette Lareau, *Unequal Childhoods: Class, Race, and Family Life* (University of California Press, 2003).

80. Goren Therborn, *Between Sex and Power: Family in the World, 1900–2000* (London: Routledge, 2004).

81. This proposition is similar to what David Ellwood has called the "assistance-family structure conundrum." David T. Ellwood, *Poor Support: Poverty and the American Family* (New York: Basic Books, 1988).

Household Labor and the Routine Production of Gender

SCOTT COLTRANE

Motherhood is often perceived as the quintessence of womanhood. The everyday tasks of mothering are taken to be "natural" expressions of femininity, and the routine care of home and children is seen to provide opportunities for women to express and reaffirm their gendered relation to men and to the world. The traditional tasks of fatherhood, in contrast, are limited to begetting, protecting, and providing for children. While fathers typically derive a gendered sense of self from these activities, their masculinity is even more dependent on *not* doing the things that mothers do. What happens, then, when fathers share with mothers those tasks that we define as expressing the true nature of womanhood?

This chapter describes how a sample of twenty dual-earner couples talk about sharing housework and child care. Since marriage is one of the least scripted or most undefined interaction situations, the marital conversation is particularly important to a couple's shared sense of reality. I investigate these parents' construction of gender by examining their talk about negotiations over who does what around the house; how these divisions of labor influence their perceptions of self and other; how they conceive of gender-appropriate behavior; and how they handle inconsistencies between their own views and those of the people around them. Drawing on the parents' accounts of the planning, allocation, and performance of child care and housework, I illustrate how gender is produced through everyday practices and how adults are socialized by routine activity.

Gender as an Accomplishment

Candace West and Don Zimmerman (1987) suggest that gender is a routine, methodical, and recurring accomplishment. "Doing gender" involves a complex of socially guided perceptual, interactional, and micropolitical activities that cast particular pursuits as expressions of masculine and feminine "natures." Rather than viewing gender as a property of individuals, West and Zimmerman conceive of it as an emergent feature of social situations that results from and legitimates gender inequality. Similarly, Sarah Fenstermaker Berk (1985, 204, emphasis in original) suggests that housework and child care

> can become the occasion for producing commodities (e.g., clean children, clean laundry, and new light switches) and a reaffirmation of one's *gendered* relation to the work and to the world. In short, the "shoulds" of gender ideals are fused with the "musts" of efficient household production. The result may be something resembling a "gendered" household-production function.

If appropriately doing gender serves to sustain and legitimate existing gender relations, would inappropriate gender activity challenge that legitimacy? Or, as West and Zimmerman (1987, 146) suggest, when people fail to do gender appropriately, are their individual characters, motives, and predispositions called into question? If doing gender is unavoidable and people are held accountable for its production, how might people initiate and sustain atypical gender behaviors?

By investigating how couples share child care and housework, I explore (1) the sorts of dyadic and group interactions that facilitate the sharing of household labor; (2) how couples describe the requirements of parenting and how they evaluate men's developing capacities for nurturing; and (3) the impact of sharing domestic labor on conceptions of gender.

The Sample

To find couples who shared child care, I initially contacted schools and day care centers in several suburban California communities. Using snowball sampling techniques, I selected twenty moderate- to middle-income dual-earner couples with children. To compensate for gaps in the existing literature and to enhance comparisons between sample families, I included couples if they were the biological parents of at least two school-aged children, they were both employed at least half time, and both identified the father as assuming significant responsibility for routine child care. I observed families in their homes and interviewed fathers and mothers separately at least once and as many as five times. I recorded the interviews and transcribed them for coding and constant comparative analysis.

The parents were primarily in their late thirties and had been living together for an average of ten years. All wives and 17 of 20 husbands attended some college and most couples married later and had children later than others in their birth cohort. The median age at marriage for the mothers was 23; for fathers, 26. Median age at first birth for mothers was 27; for fathers, 30. Fifteen of 20 fathers were at least one year older than their wives. Median gross annual income was $40,000, with three families under $25,000 and three over $65,000. Sixteen of the couples had two children and four had three children. Over two-thirds of the families had both sons and daughters, but four families had two sons and no daughters, and two families had two daughters and no sons. The children's ages ranged from four to fourteen, with 80 percent between the ages of five and eleven and with a median age of seven.

Mothers were more likely than fathers to hold professional or technical jobs, although most were employed in female-dominated occupations with relatively limited upward mobility and moderate pay. Over three-quarters held jobs in the "helping" professions: seven mothers were nurses, five were teachers, and four were social workers or counselors. Other occupations for the mothers were administrator, laboratory technician, filmmaker, and bookbinder. Sample fathers held both blue-collar and white collar jobs, with concentrations in construction (3), maintenance (2), sales (3), business (3), teaching (3), delivery (4), and computers (2). Like most dual-earner wives, sample mothers earned, on average, less than half of what their husband's did, and worked an average of eight fewer hours per week. Eleven mothers (55 percent), but only five fathers (25 percent) were employed less than 40 hours per week. In nine of twenty families, mothers were employed at least as many hours as fathers, but in only four families did the mother's earnings approach or exceed those of her husband.

Developing Shared Parenting

Two-thirds of the parents indicated that current divisions of labor were accomplished by making minor practical adjustments to what they perceived as an already fairly equal division of labor. A common sentiment was expressed by one father who commented.

> Since we've both always been working since we've been married, we've typically shared everything as far as all the working—I mean all the housework responsibilities as well as child care responsibilities. So it's a pattern that was set up before the kids were even thought of.

Women just do more

Nevertheless, a full three-quarters of the couples reported that the mother performed much more of the early infant care. All of the mothers and only about half of the fathers reported that they initially reduced their hours of employment after having children. About a third of the fathers said they increased their employment hours to compensate for the loss of income that resulted from their wives taking time off work before or after the births of their children.

In talking about becoming parents, most of the fathers stressed the importance of their involvement in conception decisions, the birth process, and early infant care to later assumption of child care duties. Most couples planned the births of their children jointly and intentionally. Eighty percent reported that they mutually decided to have children, with two couples reporting that the wife desired children more than the husband and two reporting that the husband was more eager than the wife to become a parent. For many families, the husband's commitment to participate fully in childrearing was a precondition of the birth decision. One mother described how she and her husband decided to have children.

> Shared parenting was sort of part of the decision. When we decided to have children, we realized that we were both going to be involved with our work, so it was part of the plan from the very beginning. As a matter of fact, I thought that we only could have the one and he convinced me that we could handle two and promised to really help (laughs), which he really has, but two children is a lot more work than you realize (laughs).

By promising to assume partial responsibility for childrearing, most husbands influenced their wives' initial decision to have children, the subsequent decision to have another child, and the decision of whether and when to return to work. Almost all of the mothers indicated that they had always assumed that they would have children, and most also assumed that they would return to paid employment before the children were in school. Half of the mothers did return to work within six months of the birth of their first child.

All but one of the fathers were present at the births of their children and most talked about the importance of the birth experience, using terms like "incredible," "magical," "moving," "wonderful," and "exciting." While most claimed that they played an important part in the birth process by providing emotional support to their wives or acting as labor coaches, a few considered their involvement to be inconsequential. Comments included,

"I felt a little bit necessary and a lot unnecessary," and "I didn't bug her too much and I might have helped a little." Three quarters of the fathers reported that they were "very involved" with their newborns, even though the mother provided most of the daily care for the first few months. Over two-thirds of the mothers breastfed their infants. Half of the fathers reported that they got up in the night to soothe their babies, and many described their early infant care experience in terms that mothers typically use to describe "bonding" with newborns. The intensity of father-infant interaction was discussed by fathers as enabling them to experience a new and different level of intimacy and was depicted as "deep emotional trust," "very interior," "drawing me in," and "making it difficult to deal with the outside world."

About half of the fathers referred to the experience of being involved in the delivery and in early infant care as a necessary part of their assuming responsibility for later child care. Many described a process in which the actual performance of caretaking duties provided them with the self-confidence and skills to feel that they knew what they were doing. They described their time alone with the baby as especially helpful in building their sense of competence as a shared primary caretaker. One man said,

> I felt I needed to start from the beginning. Then I learned how to walk them at night and not be totally p.o'ed at them and not feel that it was an infringement. It was something I *got* to do in some sense, along with changing diapers and all these things. It was certainly not repulsive and in some ways I really liked it a lot. It was not something innate, it was something to be learned. I managed to start at the beginning. If you *don't* start at the beginning then you're sort of left behind.

This father, like almost all of the others, talked about having to learn how to nurture and care for his children. He also stressed how important it was to "start at the beginning." While all fathers intentionally shared routine child care as the children approached school age, only half of the fathers attempted to assume a major share of daily infant care, and only five couples described the father as an equal caregiver for children under one year old. These early caregiving fathers described their involvement in infant care as explicitly planned:

> She nursed both of them completely, for at least five or six months. So, my role was—we agreed on this—my role was the other direct intervention, like changing, and getting them up and walking them, and putting them back to sleep. For instance, she would nurse them but I would bring them to the bed afterward and change them if necessary, and get them back to sleep.... I really initiated those other kinds of care aspects so that I could be involved. I continued that on through infant and toddler and preschool classes that we would go to, even though I would usually be the only father there.

This man's wife offered a similar account, commenting that "except for breastfeeding, he always provided the same things that I did—the emotional closeness and the attention."

Another early caregiving father described how he and his wife "very consciously" attempted to equalize the amount of time they spent with their children when they were infants: "In both cases we very consciously made the decision that we wanted it to be a mutual process, so that from the start we shared, and all I didn't do was breastfeed. And I really would say that was the only distinction." His wife also described their infant care arrangements as "equal," and commented that other people did not comprehend the extent of his participation:

> I think that nobody really understood that Jennifer had two mothers. The burden of proof was always on me that he was literally being a mother. He wasn't nursing, but he was getting up in the night to bring her to me, to change her poop, which is a lot more energy than nursing in the middle of the night. You have to get up and do all that, I mean get awake. So his sleep was interrupted, and yet within a week or two, at his work situation, it was expected that he was back to normal, and he never went back to normal. He was part of the same family that I was.

This was the only couple who talked about instituting, for a limited time, an explicit record-keeping system to ensure that they shared child care equally.

> [Father]: We were committed to the principle of sharing and we would have schedules, keep hours, so that we had a pretty good sense that we were even, both in terms of the commitment to the principle as well as we wanted to in fact be equal. We would keep records in a log—one might say in a real compulsive way—so that we knew what had happened when the other person was on.

> [Mother]: When the second one came we tried to keep to the log of hours and very quickly we threw it out completely. It was too complex.

Practicality and Flexibility

Both early- and later-sharing families identified practical considerations and flexibility as keys to equitable divisions of household labor. Most did not have explicit records or schedules for child care or housework. For example, one early involved father reported that practical divisions of labor evolved "naturally":

> Whoever cooks doesn't have to do the dishes. If for some reason she cooks and I don't do the dishes, she'll say something about it, certainly. Even though we never explicitly agreed that's how we do it, that's how we do it. The person who doesn't cook does the dishes. We don't even know who's going to cook a lot of the time. We just get it that we can do it. We act in good faith.

Couples who did not begin sharing routine child care until after infancy were even more likely to describe their division of labor as practical solutions to shortages of time. For example, one mother described sharing household tasks as "the only logical thing to do," and her husband said, "It's the only practical way we could do it." Other fathers describe practical and flexible arrangements based on the constraints of employment scheduling:

> Her work schedule is more demanding and takes up a lot of evening time, so I think I do a lot of the every day routines, and she does a lot of the less frequent things. Like I might do more of the cooking and meal preparation, but she is the one that does the grocery shopping. An awful lot of what

gets done gets done because the person is home first. That's been our standing rule for who fixes dinner. Typically, I get home before she does so I fix dinner, but that isn't a fixed rule. She gets home first, then she fixes dinner. Making the beds and doing the laundry just falls on me because I've got more time during the day to do it. And the yard-work and cuttin' all the wood, I do that. And so I'm endin' up doin' more around here than her just because I think I've got more time.

While mothers were more likely than fathers to report that talk was an important part of sharing household labor, most couples reported that they spent little time planning or arguing about who was going to do what around the house. Typical procedures for allocating domestic chores were described as "ad hoc," illustrated by one mother's discussion of cooking:

Things with us have happened pretty easily as far as what gets done by who. It happened with-out having to have a schedule or deciding—you know—like cooking. We never decided that he would do all the cooking; it just kind of ended up that way. Every once in a while when he doesn't feel like cooking he'll say, "Would you cook tonight?" "Sure, fine." But normally I don't offer to cook. I say, "What are we having for dinner?"

In general, divisions of labor in sample families were described as flexible and changing. One mother talked about how routine adjustments in task allocation were satisfying to her: "Once you're comfortable in your roles and division of tasks for a few months then it seems like the needs change a little bit and you have to change a little bit and you have to regroup. That's what keeps it interesting. I think that's why it's satisfying."

Underlying Ideology

While ad hoc divisions of labor were described as being practical solutions to time shortages, there were two major ideological underpinnings to the sharing of housework and child care: child-centeredness and equity ideals. While those who attempted to share infant care tended to have more elaborate vocabularies for talking about

these issues, later sharing couples also referred to them. For instance, all couples provided accounts that focused on the sanctity of childhood and most stressed the impossibility of mothers "doing it all."

Couples were child-centered in that they placed a high value on their children's well-being, defined parenting as an important and serious undertaking, and organized most of their nonem-ployed hours around their children. For instance, one father described how his social life revolved around his children:

Basically if the other people don't have kids and if they aren't involved with the kids, then we aren't involved with them. It's as simple as that. The guys I know at work that are single or don't have chil-dren my age don't come over because then we have nothing in common. They're kind of the central driving force in my life.

While about half of the couples (11 of 20) had paid for ongoing out-of-home child care, and three-quarters had regularly used some form of paid child care, most of the parents said that they spent more time with their children than the other dual-earner parents in their neighborhoods. One father commented that he and his wife had structured their lives around personally taking care of their children:

An awful lot of the way we've structured our lives has been based around our reluctance to have someone else raise our children. We just really didn't want the kids to be raised from 7:30 in the morning 'till 4:30 or 5:00 in the afternoon by somebody else. So we've structured the last ten years around that issue.

Many parents also advocated treating children as inexperienced equals or "little people," rather than as inferior beings in need of authoritar-ian training. For example, an ex-military father employed in computer research stated, "We don't discipline much. Generally the way it works is kind of like bargaining. They know that there are consequences to whatever actions they take, and we try and make sure they know what the con-sequences are before they have a chance to take the action." Another father described his moral stance concerning children's rights:

> I'm not assuming—when I'm talking about parent-child stuff—that there's an inequality. Yes, there are a lot of differences in terms of time spent in this world, but our assumption has been, with both children, that we're peers. And so that's how we are with them. So, if they say something and they're holding fast to some position, we do not say, "You do this because we're the parent and you're the child."

About half of the parents talked directly about such equity ideals as applied to children.

Concerning women's rights, 80 percent of fathers and 90 percent of mothers agreed that women were disadvantaged in our society, but only two mothers and one father mentioned equal rights or the women's movement as motivators for sharing household labor. Most did not identify themselves as feminists, and a few offered derogatory comments about "those women's libbers." Nevertheless, almost all parents indicated that no one should be forced to perform a specific task because they were a man or a woman. This implicit equity ideal was evidenced by mothers and fathers using time availability, rather than gender, to assign most household tasks.

Divisions of Household Labor

Contributions to 64 household tasks were assessed by having fathers and mothers each sort cards on a five-point scale to indicate who most often performed them (see Table 1). Frequently performed tasks, such as meal preparation, laundry, sweeping, or putting children to bed, were judged for the two weeks preceding the interviews. Less frequently performed tasks, such as window washing, tax preparation, or car repair, were judged as to who typically performed them.

Some differences occurred between mothers' and fathers' accounts of household task allocation, but there was general agreement on who did what.

Table 1 shows that in the majority of families, most household tasks were seen as shared. Thirty-seven of 64 tasks (58 percent), including

all direct child care, most household business, meal preparation, kitchen clean-up, and about half of other housecleaning tasks were reported to be shared about equally by fathers and mothers. Nevertheless, almost a quarter (15) of the tasks were performed principally by the mothers, including most clothes care, meal planning, kinkeeping, and some of the more onerous repetitive housecleaning. Just under one-fifth (12) of the tasks were performed principally by the fathers. These included the majority of the occasional outside chores such as home repair, car maintenance, lawn care, and taking out the trash. As a group, sample couples can thus be characterized as sharing an unusually high proportion of housework and child care, but still partially conforming to a traditional division of household labor. The fathers and mothers in this study are pioneers in that they divided household tasks differently than their parents did, differently from most others in their age cohort, and from most families studied in time-use research.

Managing Versus Helping

Household divisions of labor in these families also can be described in terms of who takes responsibility for planning and initiating various tasks. In every family there were at least six frequently performed household chores over which the mother retained almost exclusive managerial control. That is, mothers noticed when the chore needed doing and made sure that someone adequately performed it. In general, mothers were more likely than fathers to act as managers for cooking, cleaning, and child care, but over half of the couples shared responsibility in these areas. In all households the father was responsible for initiating and managing at least a few chores traditionally performed by mothers.

Based on participants' accounts of strategies for allocating household labor, I classified twelve couples as sharing responsibility for household labor and eight couples as reflecting manager-helper dynamics. Helper husbands often waited to be told what to do, when to do it, and how it should be done. While they invariably expressed a desire to perform their "fair share" of housekeeping and

Table I. Household Tasks by Person Most Often Performing Them

Mother More	Fathers and Mother Equally	Father More
Cleaning		
Mopping	Vacuuming	Taking out trash
Sweeping	Cleaning tub/shower	Cleaning porch
Dusting	Making beds	
Cleaning bathroom sink	Picking up toys	
Cleaning toilet	Tidying living room	
	Hanging up clothes	
	Washing windows	
	Spring cleaning	
Cooking		
Planning menus	Preparing lunch	Preparing breakfast
Grocery shopping	Cooking dinner	
Baking	Making snacks	
	Washing dishes	
	Putting dishes away	
	Wiping kitchen counters	
	Putting food away	
Clothes		
Laundry	Shoe care	
Hand laundry		
Ironing		
Sewing		
Buying clothes		
Household		
	Running errands	Household repairs
	Decorating	Exterior painting
	Interior painting	Car maintenance
	General yardwork	Car repair
	Gardening	Washing car
		Watering lawn
		Mowing lawn
		Cleaning rain gutters
Finance, Social		
Writing or phoning	Deciding major purchases	Investments
Relatives/friends	Paying bills	
	Preparing taxes	
	Handling insurance	
	Planning couple dates	

(continued)

Table I. (*continued*)

Mother More	Fathers and Mother Equally	Father More
Children		
Arranging baby-sitters	Walking children	
	Helping children dress	
	Helping children bathe	
	Putting children to bed	
	Supervising children	
	Disciplining children	
	Driving children	
	Taking children to doctor	
	Caring for sick children	
	Playing with children	
	Planning outings	

Note: Tasks were sorted separately by fathers and mothers according to relative frequency of performance: (1) Mothers mostly or always, (2) Mother more than father, (3) Father and mother about equal, (4) Father more than mother, (5) Father mostly or always. For each task a mean ranking by couple was computed with 1.00–2.49 = Mother, 2.50–3.50 = Shared, 3.51–5.0 = Father. If over 50 percent of families ranked a task as performed by one spouse more than the other, the task is listed under that spouse, otherwise tasks are listed as shared. N = 20 couples.

childrearing, they were less likely than the other fathers to assume responsibility for anticipating and planning these activities. Manager-helper couples sometimes referred to the fathers' contributions as "helping" the mother.

When asked what they liked most about their husband's housework, about half of the mothers focused on their husband's selfresponsibility: voluntarily doing work without being prodded. They commented, "He does the everyday stuff" and "I don't have to ask him." The other mothers praised their husbands for particular skills with comments such as "I love his spaghetti" or "He's great at cleaning the bathroom." In spite of such praise, three-fourths of the mothers said that what bothered them most about their husband's housework was the need to remind him to perform certain tasks, and some complained of having to "train him" to correctly perform the chores. About a third of the fathers complained that their wives either didn't notice when things should be done or that *their* standards were too low. Although the extent of domestic task sharing varied considerably among couples, 90 percent of both mothers

and fathers independently reported that their divisions of labor were "fair."

Some mothers found it difficult to share authority for household management. For instance, one mother said, "There's a certain control you have when you do the shopping and the cooking and I don't know if I'm ready to relinquish that control." Another mother who shares most child care and housework with her husband admitted that "in general, household organization is something that I think I take over." In discussing how they divide housework, she commented on how she notices more than her husband does:

> He does what he sees needs to be done. That would include basic cleaning kinds of things. However, there are some detailed kinds of things that he doesn't see that I feel need to be done, and in those cases I have to ask him to do things. He thinks some of the details are less important and I'm not sure, that might be a difference between men and women.

Like many of the mothers who maintained a managerial position in the household, this mother attributed an observed difference in domestic perceptiveness to an essential difference between women and men. By contrast, mothers who did not act as household managers were unlikely to link housecleaning styles to essential gender differences.

Many mothers talked about adjusting their housecleaning standards over the course of their marriage and trying to feel less responsible for being "the perfect homemaker." By partially relinquishing managerial duties and accepting their husband's housecleaning standards, some mothers reported that they were able to do less daily housework and focus more on occasional thorough cleaning or adding "finishing touches." A mother with two nursing jobs whose husband delivered newspapers commented:

> He'll handle the surface things no problem, and I get down and do the nitty gritty. And I do it when it bugs me or when I have the time. It's not anything that we talk about usually. Sometimes if I feel like things are piling up, he'll say "Well, make me a list," and I will. And he'll do it. There are some things that he just doesn't notice and that's fine: he handles the day-to-day stuff. He'll do things, like for me cleaning off the table—for him it's getting everything off it; for me it's putting the tablecloth on, putting the flowers on, putting the candles on. That's the kind of stuff I do and I like that; it's not that I want him to start.

This list-making mother illustrates that responsibility for managing housework sometimes remained in the mother's domain, even if the father performed more of the actual tasks.

Responsibility for managing child care, on the other hand, was more likely to be shared. Planning and initiating "direct" child care, including supervision, discipline and play, was typically an equal enterprise. Sharing responsibility for "indirect" child care, including clothing, cleaning, and feeding, was less common, but was still shared in over half of the families. When they cooked, cleaned, or tended to the children, fathers in these families did not talk of "helping" the mother; they spoke of fulfilling their responsibilities as equal partners and parents. For example, one father described

how he and his wife divided both direct and indirect child care:

> My philosophy is that they are my children and everything is my responsibility, and I think she approaches it the same way too. So when something needs to be done, it's whoever is close does it…whoever it is convenient for. And we do keep a sense of what the other's recent efforts are, and try to provide some balance, but without actually counting how many times you've done this and I've done that.

In spite of reported efforts to relinquish total control over managing home and children, mothers were more likely than fathers to report that they would be embarrassed if unexpected company came over and the house was a mess (80 percent vs. 60 percent). When asked to compare themselves directly to their spouse, almost two-thirds of both mothers and fathers reported that the mother would be more embarrassed than the father. Some mothers reported emotional reactions to the house being a mess that were similar to those they experienced when their husbands "dressed the kids funny." The women were more likely to focus on the children "looking nice," particularly when they were going to be seen in public. Mothers' greater embarrassment over the kemptness of home or children might reflect their sense of mothering as part of women's essential nature.

Adult Socialization Through Childrearing

Parents shared in creating and sustaining a worldview through the performance and evaluation of childrearing. Most reported that parenting was their primary topic of conversation, exemplified by one father's comment: "That's what we mostly discuss when we're not with our kids—either when we're going to sleep or when we have time alone—is how we feel about how we're taking care of them." Others commented that their spouse helped them to recognize unwanted patterns of interaction by focusing on parenting practices. For instance, one father remarked,

> I'm not sure I could do it as a one-parent family, cause I wouldn't have the person, the other person

saying, "Hey, look at that, that's so much like what you do with your own family." In a one-parent family, you don't have that, you don't have the other person putting out that stuff, you have to find it all out on your own and I'm not sure you can.

Usually the father was described as being transformed by the parenting experience and developing increased sensitivity. This was especially true of discourse between parents who were trying to convert a more traditional division of family labor into a more egalitarian one. A self-employed construction worker said his level of concern for child safety was heightened after he rearranged his work to do half of the parenting:

> There's a difference in being at the park with the kids since we went on the schedule. Before it was, like, "Sure, jump off the jungle bars." But when you're totally responsible for them, and you know that if they sprained an ankle or something you have to pick up the slack, it's like you have more investment in the kid and you don't want to see them hurt and you don't want to see them crying. I find myself being a lot more cautious.

Mothers also reported that their husbands began to notice subtle cues from the children as a result of being with them on a regular basis. The wife of the construction worker quoted above commented that she had not anticipated many of the changes that emerged from sharing routine child care.

> I used to worry about the kids a lot more. I would say in the last year it's evened itself out quite a bit. That was an interesting kind of thing in sharing that started to happen that I hadn't anticipated. I suppose when you go into this your expectations about what will happen—that you won't take your kids to day care, that they'll be with their dad, and they'll get certain things from their dad and won't that be nice, and he won't have to worry about his hours—but then it starts creeping into other areas that you didn't have any way of knowing it was going to have an impact. When he began to raise issues about the kids or check in on them at school when they were sick, I thought, "Well, that's my job, what are you talking about that for?" or, "Oh my god. I didn't notice that!" Where did he get the

intuitive sense to know what needed to be done? It wasn't there before. A whole lot of visible things happened.

Increased sensitivity on the part of the fathers, and their enhanced competence as parents, was typically evaluated by adopting a vocabulary of motives and feelings similar to the mothers', created and sustained through an ongoing dialogue about the children: a dialogue that grew out of the routine child care practices. Another mother described how her husband had "the right temperament" for parenting, but had to learn how to notice the little things that she felt her daughters needed:

> When it comes to the two of us as parents, I feel that my husband's parenting skills are probably superior to mine, just because of his calm rationale. But maybe that's not what little girls need all the time. He doesn't tend to be the one that tells them how gorgeous they look when they dress up, which they really like, and I see these things, I see when they're putting in a little extra effort. He's getting better as we grow in our relationship, as the kids grow in their relationship with him.

Like many fathers in this study, this one was characterized as developing sensitivity to the children by relying on interactions with his wife. She "see things" which he has to learn to recognize. Thus, while he may have "superior" parenting skills, he must learn something subtle from her. His reliance on her expertise suggests that his "calm rationale" is insufficient to make him "maternal" in the way that she is. Her ability to notice things, and his inattention to them, serves to render them both accountable: parenting remains an essential part of her nature, but is a learned capacity for him. Couples talked about fathers being socialized, as adults, to become nurturing parents. This talking with their wives about child care helped husbands construct and sustain images of themselves as competent fathers.

Greater paternal competence was also reported to enhance marital interaction. Fathers were often characterized as paying increased attention to emotional cues from their wives and engaging in more reciprocal communication. Taking responsibility for routine household labor offered some men the opportunity to better understand their mother's lives as well. For instance, one involved father who did most of the housework suggested that he could sometimes derive pleasure from cleaning the bathroom or picking up a sock if he looked at it as an act of caring for his family:

> It makes it a different job, to place it in a context of being an expression of caring about a collective life together. It's at that moment that I'm maybe closest to understanding what my mother and other women of my mother's generation, and other women now, have felt about being housewives and being at home, being themselves. I think I emotionally understand the satisfaction and the gratification of being a homemaker.

More frequently, however, sharing child care and housework helped fathers understand its drudgery. One father who is employed as a carpenter explained how assuming more responsibility for housework motivated him to encourage his wife to buy whatever she needs to make housework easier.

> It was real interesting when I started doing more housework. Being in construction, when I needed a tool, I bought the tool. And when I vacuum floors, I look at this piece of shit, I mean I can't vacuum the floor with this and feel good about it, it's not doing a good job. So I get a good vacuum system. So I have more appreciation for housecleaning. When I clean the tubs, I want something that is going to clean the tubs; I don't want to work extra hard. You know I have a kind of sponge to use for cleaning the tubs. So I have more of an appreciation for what she had to do. I tell her "If you know of something that's going to make it easier, let's get it."

Most sample fathers reported that performance of child care, in and of itself, increased their commitment to both parenting and housework. All of the fathers had been involved in some housework before the birth of their children, but many indicated that their awareness and performance of housework increased in conjunction with their involvement in parenting. They reported that as they spent more time in the house alone with

their children, they assumed more responsibility for cooking and cleaning. Fathers also noted that as they became more involved in the daily aspects of parenting, and in the face of their wives' absence and relinquishment of total responsibility for housekeeping, they became more aware that certain tasks needed doing and they were more likely to perform them. This was conditioned by the amount of time fathers spent on the job, but more than half reported that they increased their contributions to household labor when their children were under ten years old. This did not always mean that fathers' relative proportion of household tasks increased, because mothers were also doing more in response to an expanding total household workload.

Gender Attributions

Approximately half of both mothers and fathers volunteered that men and women brought something unique to child care, and many stressed that they did not consider their own parenting skills to be identical to those of their spouse. One mother whose husband had recently increased the amount of time he spent with their school-aged children commented: "Anybody can slap together a cream cheese and cucumber sandwich and a glass of milk and a few chips and call it lunch, but the ability to see that your child is troubled about something, or to be able to help them work through a conflict with a friend, that is really much different." A list-making mother who provided less child care and did less housework than her husband described herself as "more intimate and gentle," and her husband as "rough and out there." Like many others she emphasized that mothers and fathers provide "a balance" for their children. She described how she had to come to terms with her expectations that her husband would "mother" the way that she did:

> One of the things that I found I was expecting from him when he started doing so much here and I was gone so much, I was expecting him to mother the kids. And you know, I had to get over that one pretty quick and really accept him doing the things the way he did them as his way, and that

being just fine with me. He wasn't mothering the kids, he was fathering the kids. It was just that he was the role of the mother as far as the chores and all that stuff.

A mother who managed and performed most of the housework and child care used different reasoning to make similar claims about essential differences between women and men. In contrast to the mothers quoted above, this mother suggested that men could nurture, but not perform daily child care:

> Nurturance is one thing, actual care is another thing. I think if a father had to—like all of a sudden the wife was gone, he could nurture it with the love that it needed. But he might not change the diapers often enough, or he might not give 'em a bath often enough and he might not think of the perfect food to feed. But as far as nurturing, I think he's capable of caring . . . If the situation is the mother is there and he didn't have to, then he would trust the woman to.

This mother concluded, "The woman has it more in her genes to be more equipped for nurturing." Thus many of the manager-helper couples legitimated their divisions of labor and reaffirmed the "naturalness" of essential gender differences.

Parents who equally shared the responsibility for direct and indirect child care, on the other hand, were more likely to see similarities in their relationships with their children. They all reported that their children were emotionally "close" to both parents. When asked who his children went to when they were hurt or upset, one early- and equal-sharing father commented: "They'll go to either of us, that is pretty indistinguishable." Mothers and fathers who equally shared most direct child care reported that their children typically called for the parent with whom they had most recently spent time, and frequently called her mother "daddy" or the father "mommy," using the gendered form to signify "parent." Most often, parents indicated that their children would turn to "whoever's closest" or "whoever they've been with," thus linking physical closeness with emotional closeness. In-home observations of family interactions confirmed such reports.

The central feature of these and other parental accounts is that shared activities formed an emotional connection between parent and child. Shared activities were also instrumental in constructing images of fathers as competent, nurturing care givers. Two-thirds of both mothers and fathers expressed the belief that men could care for children's emotional needs as well as women. When asked whether men, in general, could nurture like women, mothers used their husbands as examples. One said, "I don't necessarily think that that skill comes with a sex type. Some women nurture better than others, some men nurture better than other men. I think that those skills can come when either person is willing to have the confidence and commitment to prioritize them."

However, the parents who were the most successful at sharing child care were the most likely to claim that men could nurture like women. Those who sustained manager-helper dynamics in child care tended to invoke the images of "maternal instincts" and alluded to natural differences between men and women. In contrast, more equal divisions of household labor were typically accompanied by an ideology of gender *similarity* rather than gender difference. The direction of causality is twofold: (1) those who believed that men could nurture like women seriously attempted to share all aspects of child care, and (2) the successful practice of sharing child care facilitated the development of beliefs that men could nurture like women.

Normalizing Atypical Behavior

Mothers and fathers reported that women friends, most of whom were in more traditional marriages or were single, idealized their shared-parenting arrangements. About two-thirds of sample mothers reported that their women friends told them that they were extremely fortunate, and labeled their husbands "wonderful," "fantastic," "incredible," or otherwise out of the ordinary. Some mothers said that women friends were "jealous," "envious," or "amazed," and that they "admired" and "supported" their efforts at sharing domestic chores.

Both mothers and fathers said that the father received more credit for his family involvement than the mother did, because it was expected that she would perform child care and housework. Since parenting is assumed to be "only natural" for women, fathers were frequently praised for performing a task that would go unnoticed if a mother had performed it:

I think I get less praise because people automatically assume that, you know, the mother's *supposed* to do the child care. And he gets a lot of praise because he's the visible one. Oh, I think that he gets far more praise. I can bust my butt at that school and all he has to do is show up in the parking lot and everybody's all *gah gah* over him. I don't get resentful about that—think it's funny and I think it's sad.

While the fathers admitted that they enjoyed such praise, many indicated that they did not take these direct or implied compliments very seriously.

I get more credit than she does, because it's so unusual that the father's at home and involved in the family. I realize what it is: it's prejudice. The strokes feel real nice, but I don't take them too seriously. I'm sort of proud of it in a way that I don't really like. It's nothing to be proud of, except that I'm glad to be doing it and I think it's kind of neat because it hasn't been the style traditionally. I kind of like that, but I know that it means nothing.

These comments reveal that fathers appreciated praise, but actively discounted compliments received from those in dissimilar situations. The fathers' everyday parenting experiences led them to view parenthood as drudgery as well as fulfillment. They described their sense of parental responsibility as taken-for-granted and did not consider it to be out of the ordinary or something worthy of special praise. Fathers sometimes reported being puzzled by compliments from their wives' acquaintances and judged them to be inappropriate. When I asked one what kinds of reactions he received when his children were infants, he said,

They all thought it was really wonderful. They thought she'd really appreciate how wonderful it was and how different that was from her father. They'd say, "You ought to know how lucky you are, he's doing so much." I just felt like I'm doing what any person should do. Just like shouldn't anybody be this interested in their child? No big deal.

Another father said he resented all the special attention he received when he was out with his infant son:

Constant going shopping and having women stop me and say "Oh it's so good to see you fathers." I was no longer an individual: I was this generic father who was now a liberated father who could take care of his child. I actually didn't like it. I felt after a while that I wanted the time and the quality of my relationship with my child at that point, what was visible in public, to simply be accepted as what you do. It didn't strike me as worthy of recognition, and it pissed me off a lot that women in particular would show this sort of appreciation, which I think is well-intentioned, but which also tended to put a frame around the whole thing as though somehow this was an experience that could be extracted from one's regular life. It wasn't. It was going shopping with my son in a snuggly or on the backpack was what I was doing. It wasn't somehow this event that always had to be called attention to.

Thus fathers discounted and normalized extreme reactions to their divisions of labor and interpreted them in a way that supported the "natural" character of what they were doing.

One mother commented on a pattern that was typically mentioned by both parents: domestic divisions of labor were "normal" to those who were attempting something similar, and "amazing" to those who were not: "All the local friends here think it's amazing. They call him 'Mr. Mom' and tell me how lucky I am. I'm waiting for someone to tell him how lucky *he* is. I have several friends at work who have very similar arrangements and they just feel that it's normal."

Because fathers assumed traditional mothering functions, they often had more social contact with mothers than with other fathers. They talked about being the only fathers at children's lessons, parent classes and meetings, at the laundromat, or in the market. One father said it took mothers there a while before they believed he really shared a range of household tasks.

> At first they ask me, "Is this your day off?" And I say, "If it's the day off for me, why isn't it the day off for you?" "Well, I work 24 hours a day!" And I say, "Yeah, right. I got my wash done and hung out and the beds made." It takes the mother a couple of times to realize that I really do that stuff.

In general, fathers resisted attempts by other people to compare them to traditional fathers, and often compared themselves directly to their wives, or to other mothers.

Fathers tended to be employed in occupations predominantly composed of men, and in those settings were often discouraged from talking about family or children. Several fathers reported that people at their place of employment could not understand why they did "women's work," and a few mentioned that co-workers would be disappointed when they would repeatedly turn down invitations to go out "with the boys" for a drink. One of three self-employed carpenters in the study said that he would sometimes conceal that he was leaving work to do something with his children because he worried about negative reactions from employers or coworkers:

> I would say reactions that we've got—in business, like if I leave a job somewhere that I'm on and mention that I'm going to coach soccer, my son's soccer game, yeah. I have felt people kind of stiffen, like, I was more shirking my job, you know, such a small thing to leave work for, getting home, racing home for. I got to the point with some people where I didn't necessarily mention what I was leaving for, just because I didn't need for them to think that I was being irresponsible about their work, I mean, I just decided it wasn't their business. If I didn't know them well enough to feel that they were supportive. I would just say, "I have to leave early today"—never lie, if they asked me a question. I'd tell them the answer—but not volunteer it. And, maybe in some cases, I feel like, you know, you really have to be a little careful about being too *groovy* too, that what it is that you're doing is just so wonderful. "I'm a father, I'm going

to go be with my children." It isn't like that, you know. I don't do it for what people think of me; I do it because I enjoy it.

Some fathers said their talk of spending time with their children was perceived by coworkers as indicating they were not "serious" about their work. They reported receiving indirect messages that *providing* for the family was primary and *being with* the family was secondary. Fathers avoided negative workplace sanctions by selectively revealing the extent of their family involvement.

Many fathers selected their current jobs because the work schedule was flexible, or so they could take time off to care for their children. For instance, even though most fathers worked full-time, two-thirds had some daytime hours off, as exemplified by teachers, mail carriers, and self-employed carpenters. Similarly, most fathers avoided extra, work-related tasks or overtime hours in order to maximize time spent with their children. One computer technician said that he was prepared to accept possible imputations of nonseriousness:

> I kind of tend to choose my jobs. When I go to a job interview, I explain to people that I have a family and the family's very important to me. Some companies expect you to work a lot of overtime or work weekends, and I told them that I don't have to accept that sort of thing. I may not have gotten all the jobs I ever might have had because of it, but it's something that I bring up at the job interview and let them know that my family comes first.

The same father admitted that it is sometimes a "blessing" that his wife works evenings at a local hospital, because it allows him to justify leaving his job on time:

> At five o'clock or five thirty at night, when there are a lot of people that are still going to be at work for an hour or two more. I go "Adios!" [laughs]. I mean, I *can't* stay. I've gotta pick up the kids. And there are times when I feel real guilty about leaving my fellow workers behind when I know they're gonna be there for another hour or so. About a block from work I go "God, this is great!" [laughs].

Over half of the study participants also indicated that their own mothers or fathers reacted negatively to their divisions of labor. Parents were described as "confused," "bemused," and "befuddled," and it was said that they "lack understanding" or "think it's a little strange." One mother reported that her parents and in-laws wouldn't "dare to criticize" their situation because "times have changed," but she sensed their underlying worry and concern:

> I think both sides of the family think it's fine because it's popular now. They don't dare—I mean if we were doing this thirty years ago, they would dare to criticize. In a way, now they don't. I think both sides feel it's a little strange. I thought my mom was totally sympathetic and no problem, but when I was going to go away for a week and my husband was going to take care of the kids, she said something to my sister about how she didn't think I should do it. There's a little underlying tension about it, I think.

Other study participants reported that disagreements with parents were common, particularly if they revolved around trying to change childrearing practices their own parents had used.

Many couples reported that initial negative reactions from parents turned more positive over time as they saw that the children were "turning out all right," that the couple was still together after an average of ten years, and that the men were still employed. This last point, that parents were primarily concerned with their son's or son-in-law's provider responsibilities, highlights how observers typically evaluated the couple's task sharing. A number of study participants mentioned that they thought their parents wanted the wife to quit work and stay home with the children and that the husband should "make up the difference." Most mentioned, however, that parents were more concerned that the husband continue to be the provider than they were that the wife made "extra money" or that the husband "helped out" at home.

> In the beginning there was a real strong sense that I was in the space of my husband's duty. That came from his parents pretty strongly. The only way that they have been able to come to grips with this in

any fashion is because he has also been financially successful. If he had decided, you know, "Outside work is not for me, I'm going to stay home with the kids and she's going to work," I think there would have been a whole lot more talk than there was. I think it's because he did both and was successful that it was okay.

Another mother noted that parental acceptance of shared parenting did not necessarily entail acceptance of the woman as provider:

> There is a funny dynamic that happens. It's not really about child care, where I don't think in our families—with our parents—I don't get enough credit for being the breadwinner. Well they're still critical of him for not earning as much money as I do. In a way they've accepted him as being an active parenting father more than they've accepted me being a breadwinner.

Here again, the "essential nature" of men is taken to be that of provider. If the men remain providers, they are still accountable as men, even if they take an active part in child care.

Discussion

This brief exploration into the social construction of shared parenting in twenty dual-earner families illustrates how more equal domestic gender relations arise and under what conditions they flourish. All couples described flexible and practical task-allocation procedures that were responses to shortages of time. All families were child-centered in that they placed a high value on their children's well-being, defined parenting as an important and serious undertaking, and organized most of their nonemployed time around their children. Besides being well-educated and delaying childbearing until their late twenties or early thirties, couples who shared most of the responsibility for household labor tended to involve the father in routine child care from the children's early infancy. As Sara Ruddick (1982) has noted, the everyday aspects of child care and housework help share ways of thinking, feeling, and acting that become associated with what it means to be a mother. My findings suggest that when domestic activities are equally shared, "maternal thinking" develops in fathers, too, and the social meaning of gender begins to change. This deemphasizes notions of gender as personality and locates it in social interaction.

To treat gender as the "cause" of household division of labor overlooks its emergent character and fails to acknowledge how it is in fact implicated in precisely such routine practices.

References

Berk, Sarah Fenstermaker. 1985. *The Gender Factory.* New York: Plenum.

Ruddick, Sara. 1982. "Maternal thinking." In *Rethinking the Family*, ed. Barrie Thorne and Marilyn Yalom, 76–94. New York: Longman.

West, Candace, and Don H. Zimmerman. 1987. "Doing gender." *Gender & Society* 1:125–51.

(How) Does the Sexual Orientation of Parents Matter?

JUDITH STACEY AND TIMOTHY J. BIBLARZ

"Today, gay marriage is taking on an air of inevitability" *(Detroit News,* "Middle Ground Emerges for Gay Couples," October 4, 1999, p. A9). So observed a U.S. newspaper from the heartland in September 1999, reporting that one-third of those surveyed in an *NBC News/Wall Street Journal* poll endorsed the legalization of same-sex marriage, while 65 percent predicted such legislation would take place in the new century (Price 1999). During the waning months of the last millennium, France enacted national registered partnerships, Denmark extended child custody rights to same-sex couples, and the state supreme courts in Vermont and in Ontario, Canada, ruled that same-sex couples were entitled to full and equal family rights. Most dramatically, in September 2000 the Netherlands became the first nation to realize the inevitable when the Dutch parliament voted overwhelmingly to grant same-sex couples full and equal rights to marriage. As the new millennium begins, struggles by nonheterosexuals to secure equal recognition and rights for the new family relationships they are now creating represent some of the most dramatic and fiercely contested developments in Western family patterns.

It is not surprising, therefore, that social science research on lesbigay family issues has become a rapid growth industry that incites passionate divisions. For the consequences of such research are by no means "academic," but bear on marriage and family policies that encode Western culture's most profoundly held convictions about gender, sexuality, and parenthood. As advocates and opponents square off in state and federal courts and legislatures, in the electoral arena, and in culture wars over efforts to extend to nonheterosexuals equal rights to marriage, child custody, adoption, foster care, and fertility services, they heatedly debate the implications of a youthful body of research, conducted primarily by psychologists, that investigates if and how the sexual orientation of parents affects children.

This body of research, almost uniformly, reports findings of no notable differences between children reared by heterosexual parents and those reared by lesbian and gay parents, and that it finds

Judith Stacey and Timothy J. Biblarz, "(How) Does the Sexual Orientation of Parents Matter?" from *American Sociological Review*, 66 (April 2001: 159–183). Reprinted with permission.

lesbigay parents to be as competent and effective as heterosexual parents. Lawyers and activists struggling to defend child custody, and adoption petitions by lesbians and gay men, or to attain same-gender marriage rights and to defeat pre-emptive referenda against such rights (e.g., the victorious Knight Initiative on the 2000 ballot in California) have drawn on this research with considerable success (cf. Wald 2000). Although progress is uneven, this strategy has promoted a gradual liberalizing trend in judicial and policy decisions. However, backlash campaigns against gay family rights have begun to challenge the validity of the research.

In 1997, the *University of Illinois Law Review Journal* published an article by Wardle (1997), a Brigham Young University law professor, that impugned the motives, methods, and merits of social science research on lesbian and gay parenting. Wardle charged the legal profession and social scientists with an ideological bias favoring gay rights that has compromised most research in this field and the liberal judicial and policy decisions it has informed. He presented a harshly critical assessment of the research and argued for a presumptive judicial standard in favor of award-ing child custody to heterosexual married cou-ples. The following year, Wardle drafted new state regulations in Utah that restrict adoption and foster care placements to households in which all adults are related by blood or marriage. Florida, Arkansas, and Mississippi also have imposed restrictions on adoption and/or foster care, and such bills have been introduced in the legislatures of 10 additional states (Leslie Cooper, ACLU gay family rights staff attorney, personal communica-tion, September 27, 2000). In March 2000, a paper presented at a "Revitalizing Marriage" conference at Brigham Young University assailed the quality of studies that had been cited to support the effi-cacy of lesbigay parenting (Lerner and Nagai 2000). Characterizing the research methods as "dismal," Lerner and Nagai claimed that "the methods used in these studies were sufficiently flawed so that these studies could not and should not be used in legislative forums or legal cases to buttress any arguments on the nature of homosexual vs.

heterosexual parenting" (p. 3). Shortly afterward, Gallagher (2000), of the Institute for American Values, broadcast Lerner and Nagai's argument in her nationally syndicated *New York Post* col-umn in order to undermine the use of "the sci-ence card" by advocates of gay marriage and gay "normalization."

We depart sharply from the views of Wardle and Gallagher on the merits and morals of les-bigay parenthood as well as on their analysis of the child development research. We agree, how-ever, that ideological pressures constrain intel-lectual development in this field. In our view, it is the pervasiveness of social prejudice and institu-tionalized discrimination against lesbians and gay men that exerts a powerful policing effect on the basic terms of psychological research and public discourse on the significance of parental sexual orientation. The field suffers less from the overt ideological convictions of scholars than from the unfortunate intellectual consequences that follow from the implicit hetero-normative presumption governing the terms of the discourse—that healthy child development depends upon parenting by a married heterosexual couple. While few contribu-tors to this literature personally subscribe to this view, most of the research asks whether lesbigay parents subject their children to greater risks or harm than are confronted by children reared by heterosexual parents. Because anti-gay scholars seek evidence of harm, sympathetic researchers defensively stress its absence.

We take stock of this body of psychologi-cal research from a sociological perspective. We analyze the impact that this hetero-normative presumption exacts on predominant research strategies, analyses, and representations of find-ings. After assessing the basic premises and argu-ments in the debate, we discuss how the social fact of heterosexism has operated to constrain the research populations, concepts, and designs employed in the studies to date.

We wish to acknowledge that the political stakes of this body of research are so high that the ideological "family values" of scholars play a greater part than usual in how they design, con-duct, and interpret their studies. Of course, we recognize that this is equally true for those who criticize such studies (including Wardle [1997], Lerner and Nagai [2000], and ourselves). The inescapably ideological and emotional nature of this subject makes it incumbent on scholars to acknowledge the personal convictions they bring to the discussion. Because we personally oppose discrimination on the basis of sexual orientation or gender, we subject research claims by those sympathetic to our stance to a heightened degree of critical scrutiny and afford the fullest possible consideration to work by scholars opposed to parenting by lesbians and gay men.

The Case Against Lesbian and Gay Parenthood

Wardle (1997) is correct that contemporary scholarship on the effects of parental sexual orientation on children's development is rarely critical of lesbigay parenthood. Few respectable scholars today oppose such parenting. However, a few psychologists subscribe to the view that homosexuality represents either a sin or a mental illness and continue to publish alarmist works on the putative ill effects of gay parenting (e.g., Cameron and Cameron 1996; Cameron, Cameron, and Landess 1996). Even though the American Psychological Association expelled Paul Cameron, and the American Sociological Association denounced him for willfully misrepresenting research (Cantor 1994; Herek 1998, 2000), his publications continue to be cited in amicus briefs, court decisions, and policy hearings. For example, the chair of the Arkansas Child Welfare Agency Review Board repeatedly cited publications by Cameron's group in her testimony at policy hearings, which, incidentally, led to restricting foster child placements to heterosexual parents (Woodruff 1998).

Likewise, Wardle (1997) draws explicitly on Cameron's work to build his case against gay parent rights. Research demonstrates, Wardle maintains, that gay parents subject children to disproportionate risks; that children of gay parents are more apt to suffer confusion over their gender and sexual identities and are more likely to become homosexuals themselves; that homosexual parents are more sexually promiscuous than are heterosexual parents and are more likely to molest their own children; that children are at greater risk of losing a homosexual parent to AIDS, substance abuse, or suicide, and to suffer greater risks of depression and other emotional difficulties; that homosexual couples are more unstable and likely to separate; and that the social stigma and embarrassment of having a homosexual parent unfairly ostracizes children and hinders their relationships with peers. Judges have cited Wardle's article to justify transferring child custody from lesbian to heterosexual parents.[1]

Wardle (1997), like other opponents of homosexual parenthood, also relies on a controversial literature that decries the putative risks of "fatherlessness" in general. Thus, Wardle cites books by Popenoe (1993, 1996), Blankenhorn (1995), and Whitehead (1993) when he argues:

> [C]hildren generally develop best, and develop most completely, when raised by both a mother and a father and experience regular family interaction with both genders' parenting skills during their years of childhood. It is now undeniable that, just as a mother's influence is crucial to the secure, healthy, and full development of a child, [a] paternal presence in the life of a child is essential to the child emotionally and physically. (p. 860)

Wardle, like Blankenhorn, extrapolates (inappropriately) from research on single-mother families to portray children of lesbians as more vulnerable to everything from delinquency, substance abuse, violence, and crime, to teen pregnancy, school dropout, suicide, and even poverty.[2] In short, the few scholars who are opposed to parenting by lesbians and gay men provide academic support for the convictions of many judges, journalists, politicians, and citizens that the sexual orientation of parents matters greatly to children, and that lesbigay parents represent a danger to their children and to society. Generally, these scholars offer only limited, and often implicit, theoretical explanations for the disadvantages of same-sex parenting—typically combining elements of bio-evolutionary theory with social and cognitive learning theories (e.g., Blankenhorn 1995). Cameron et al. (1996) crudely propose that homosexuality is a "learned pathology" that parents pass on to children through processes of modeling, seduction, and "contagion." The deeply rooted hetero-normative convictions about what constitutes healthy and moral gender identity, sexual orientation, and family composition held by contributors to this literature hinders their ability to conduct or interpret research with reason, nuance, or care.

The Case for Lesbian and Gay Parenthood

Perhaps the most consequential impact that heterosexism exerts on the research on lesbigay parenting lies where it is least apparent—in the far more responsible literature that is largely sympathetic to its subject. It is easy to expose the ways in which the prejudicial views of those directly hostile to lesbigay parenting distort their research (Herek 1998). Moreover, because antigay scholars regard homosexuality itself as a form of pathology, they tautologically interpret any evidence that children may be more likely to engage in homoerotic behavior as evidence of harm. Less obvious, however, are the ways in which heterosexism also hampers research and analysis among those who explicitly support lesbigay parenthood. With rare exceptions, even the most sympathetic proceed from a highly defensive posture that accepts heterosexual parenting as the gold standard and investigates whether lesbigay parents and their children are inferior.

This sort of hierarchical model implies that *differences* indicate *deficits* (Baumrind 1995). Instead of investigating whether (and how) differences in adult sexual orientation might lead to meaningful differences in how individuals parent and how their children develop, the predominant research designs place the burden of proof on lesbigay parents to demonstrate that they are not less successful or less worthy than heterosexual parents. Too often scholars seem to presume that this approach precludes acknowledging almost any differences in parenting or in child outcomes. A characteristic

review of research on lesbian-mother families concludes:

> [A] rapidly growing and highly consistent body of empirical work has failed to identify significant differences between lesbian mothers and their heterosexual counterparts or the children raised by these groups. Researchers have been unable to establish empirically that detriment results to children from being raised by lesbian mothers. (Falk 1994:151)

Given the weighty political implications of this body of research, it is easy to understand the social sources of such a defensive stance. As long as sexual orientation can deprive a gay parent of child custody, fertility services, and adoption rights, sensitive scholars are apt to tread gingerly around the terrain of differences. Unfortunately, however, this reticence compromises the development of knowledge not only in child development and psychology, but also within the sociology of sexuality, gender, and family more broadly. For if homophobic theories seem crude, too many psychologists who are sympathetic to lesbigay parenting seem hesitant to theorize at all. When researchers downplay the significance of any findings of differences, they forfeit a unique opportunity to take full advantage of the "natural laboratory" that the advent of lesbigay-parent families provides for exploring the effects and acquisition of gender and sexual identity, ideology, and behavior.

This reticence is most evident in analyses of sexual behavior and identity—the most politically sensitive issue in the debate. Virtually all of the published research claims to find no differences in the sexuality of children reared by lesbigay parents and those raised by nongay parents—but none of the studies that report this finding attempts to theorize about such an implausible outcome. Yet it is difficult to conceive of a credible theory of sexual development that would not expect the adult children of lesbigay parents to display a somewhat higher incidence of homoerotic desire, behavior, and identity than children of heterosexual parents. For example, biological determinist theory should predict at least some difference in an inherited predisposition to same-sex desire; a social constructionist theory would expect lesbigay parents to provide an environment in which children would feel freer to explore and affirm such desires; psychoanalytic theory might hypothesize that the absence of a male parent would weaken a daughter's need to relinquish her pre-oedipal desire for her mother or that the absence of a female parent would foster a son's pre-oedipal love for his father that no fear of castration or oedipal crisis would interrupt. Moreover, because parents determine where their children reside, even one who subscribed to J. Harris's (1998) maverick theory—that parents are virtually powerless when compared with peers to influence their children's development—should anticipate that lesbigay parents would probably rear their children among less homophobic peers.

Bem's (1996) "exotic becomes erotic" theory of sexual orientation argues that in a gender-polarized society, children eroticize the gender of peers whose interests and temperaments differ most from their own. Most children thereby become heterosexual, but boys attracted to "feminine" activities and girls who are "tomboys" are apt to develop homoerotic desires. The impact of parental genes and child-rearing practices remains implicit because parents contribute genetically to the temperamental factors Bem identifies as precursors to a child's native activity preferences, and parental attitudes toward gender polarization should affect the way those innate preferences translate into children's cognition and play. In fact, the only "theory" of child development we can imagine in which a child's sexual development would bear no relationship to parental genes, practices, environment, or beliefs would be an arbitrary one.[3] Yet this is precisely the outcome that most scholars report, although the limited empirical record does not justify it.

Over the past decade, prominent psychologists in the field began to call for less defensive research on lesbian and gay family issues (G. Green and Bozett 1991; Kitzinger and Coyle 1995; Patterson 1992). Rethinking the "no differences" doctrine, some scholars urge social scientists to look for potentially beneficial effects children might derive from such distinctive aspects of lesbigay parenting as the more egalitarian relationships these parents appear to practice (Patterson 1995; also see Dunne 2000). More radically, a few scholars (Kitzinger 1987, 1989; Kitzinger and Coyle 1995) propose abandoning comparative research on lesbian and heterosexual parenting altogether and supplanting it with research that asks "why and how are lesbian parents oppressed and how can we change that?" (Clarke 2000:28, paraphrasing Kitzinger 1994:501). While we perceive potential advantages from these agendas, we advocate an alternative strategy that moves beyond hetero-normativity without forfeiting the fruitful potential of comparative research. Although we agree with Kitzinger and Coyle (1995) and Clarke (2000) that the social obstacles to lesbian (and gay) parenthood deserve rigorous attention, we believe that this should supplement, not supplant, the rich opportunity planned lesbigay parenthood provides for the exploration of the interactions of gender, sexual orientation, and biosocial family structures on parenting and child development. Moreover, while we welcome research attuned to potential strengths as well as vulnerabilities of lesbigay parenting, we believe that knowledge and policy will be best served when scholars feel free to replace a hierarchical model, which assigns "grades" to parents and children according to their sexual identities, with a more genuinely pluralist approach to family diversity. Sometimes, to bowdlerize Freud's famous dictum, a difference *really is* just a difference!

Problems with Concepts, Categories, and Samples

The social effects of heterosexism constrain the character of research conducted on lesbigay parenting in ways more profound than those deriving from the ideological stakes of researchers. First, as most researchers recognize, because so many individuals legitimately fear the social consequences of adopting a gay identity, and because few national surveys have included questions about sexual orientation, it is impossible to gather reliable data on such basic demographic questions as how many lesbians and gay men there are in the general population, how many have children, or how many children reside (or have substantial contact) with lesbian or gay parents. Curiously, those who are hostile to gay parenting tend to minimize the incidence of same-sex orientation, while sympathetic scholars typically report improbably high numerical estimates. Both camps thus implicitly presume that the rarer the incidence, the less legitimate would be lesbigay claims to rights. One could imagine an alternative political logic, however, in which a low figure might undermine grounds for viewing lesbigay parenting as a meaningful social threat. Nonetheless, political anxieties have complicated the difficulty of answering basic demographic questions.

Since 1984, most researchers have statically reproduced numbers, of uncertain origin, depicting a range of from 1 to 5 million lesbian mothers, from 1 to 3 million gay fathers, and from 6 to 14 million children of gay or lesbian parents in the United States (e.g., Patterson 1992, 1996).[4] More recent estimates by Patterson and Freil (2000) extrapolate from distributions observed in the National Health and Social Life Survey (Laumann et al. 1995). Depending upon the definition of parental sexual orientation employed, Patterson and Freil suggest a current lower limit of 800,000 lesbigay parents ages 18 to 59 with 1.6 million children and an upper limit of 7 million lesbigay parents with 14 million children. However, these estimates include many "children" who are actually adults. To estimate the number who are dependent children (age 18 or younger), we multiplied the child-counts by .66, which is the proportion of dependent children among all offspring of 18- to 59-year-old parents in the representative National Survey of Families and Households (Sweet and Bumpass 1996).[5] This adjustment reduces the estimates of current dependent children with lesbigay parents to a range of 1 to 9 million, which implies that somewhere between 1 percent and 12 percent of all (78 million) children ages 19 and under in the United States (U.S. Census Bureau 1999) have a lesbigay parent. The 12-percent figure depends upon classifying as a lesbigay parent anyone who reports that even the idea of homoerotic sex is

appealing, while the low (1 percent) figure derives from the narrower, and in our view more politically salient, definition of a lesbigay parent as one who self-identifies as such (also see Badgett 1998; Black, Maker, et al. 1998).

Across the ideological spectrum, scholars, journalists and activists appear to presume that the normalization of lesbigay sexuality should steadily increase the ranks of children with lesbian and gay parents. In contrast, we believe that normalization is more likely to reduce the proportion of such children. Most contemporary lesbian and gay parents procreated within heterosexual marriages that many had entered hoping to escape the social and emotional consequences of homophobia. As homosexuality becomes more legitimate, far fewer people with homoerotic desires should feel compelled to enter heterosexual marriages, and thus fewer should become parents in this manner.

On the other hand, with normalization, intentional parenting by self-identified lesbians and gay men should continue to increase, but it is unlikely to do so sufficiently to compensate for the decline in the current ranks of formerly married lesbian and gay parents. Thus, the proportion of lesbian parents may not change much. Many women with homoerotic desires who once might have married men and succumbed to social pressures to parent will no longer do so; others who remained single and childless because of their homoerotic desires will feel freer to choose lesbian maternity. It is difficult to predict the net effect of these contradictory trends. However, as fewer closeted gay men participate in heterosexual marriages, the ranks of gay fathers should thin. Even if gay men were as eager as lesbians are to become parents, biology alone sharply constrains their ability to do so. Moreover, there is evidence that fewer men of any sexual orientation actually desire children as strongly as do comparable women (cf. Groze 1991; Shireman 1996), and most demographic studies of sexual orientation find a higher incidence of homosexuality among men than women (Kinsey et al. 1948; Kinsey et al. 1953; Laumann et al. 1994; Michael et al. 1994). Thus, although the ranks of intentional paternity among gay men should increase, we do not believe this will compensate for the declining numbers of closeted gay men who will become fathers through heterosexual marriages. Hence the estimate of 1 to 12 percent of children with a lesbigay parent may represent a peak interval that may decline somewhat with normalization.

A second fundamental problem in sampling involves the ambiguity, fluidity, and complexity of definitions of sexual orientation. "The traditional type of surveys on the prevalence of 'homosexuality,'" remarks a prominent Danish sociologist, "are already in danger of becoming antiquated even before they are carried out; the questions asked are partially irrelevant; sexuality is not what it used to be" (Bech 1997:211). What defines a parent (or adult child) as lesbian, gay, bisexual, or heterosexual? Are these behavioral, social, emotional, or political categories? Historical scholarship has established that sexual identities are modern categories whose definitions vary greatly not only across cultures, spaces, and time, but even among and within individuals (Katz 1995; Seidman 1997). Some gay men, for example, practice celibacy; some heterosexual men engage in "situational" homosexual activity. Some lesbians relinquish lesbian identities to marry; some relinquish marriage for a lesbian identity. What about bisexual, transsexual, or transgendered parents, not to mention those who repartner with individuals of the same or different genders? Sexual desires, acts, meanings, and identities are not expressed in fixed or predictable packages.

Third, visible lesbigay parenthood is such a recent phenomenon that most studies are necessarily of the children of a transitional generation of self-identified lesbians and gay men who became parents in the context of heterosexual marriages or relationships that dissolved before or after they assumed a gay identity. These unique historical conditions make it impossible to fully distinguish the impact of a parent's sexual orientation on a child from the impact of such factors as divorce, re-mating, the secrecy of the closet, the process of coming out, or the social consequences of stigma. Only a few studies have attempted to control for

the number and gender of a child's parents before and after a parent decided to identify as lesbian or gay. Because many more formerly married lesbian mothers than gay fathers retain custody of their children, most research is actually on post-divorce lesbian motherhood. A few studies compare heterosexual and gay fathers after divorce (Bigner and Jacobsen 1989, 1992). If fewer self-identified lesbians and gay men will become parents through heterosexual marriages, the published research on this form of gay parenthood will become less relevant to issues in scholarly and public debates.

Fourth, because researchers lack reliable data on the number and location of lesbigay parents with children in the general population, there are no studies of child development based on random, representative samples of such families. Most studies rely on small-scale, snowball and convenience samples drawn primarily from personal and community networks or agencies. Most research to date has been conducted on white lesbian mothers who are comparatively educated, mature, and reside in relatively progressive urban centers, most often in California or the Northeastern states.[6]

Although scholars often acknowledge some of these difficulties (Bozett 1989; Patterson and Friel 2000; Rothblum 1994), few studies explicitly grapple with these definitional questions. Most studies simply rely on a parent's sexual self-identity at the time of the study, which contributes unwittingly to the racial, ethnic, and class imbalance of the populations studied. Ethnographic studies suggest that "lesbian," "gay," and "bisexual" identity among socially subordinate and nonurban populations is generally less visible or less affirmed than it is among more privileged white, educated, and urban populations (Boykin 1996; Cantu 2000; Carrier 1992; Greene and Boyd-Franklin 1996; Hawkeswood 1997; Lynch 1992; Peterson 1992).

Increasingly, uncloseted lesbians and gay men actively choose to become parents through diverse and innovative means (Benkov 1994). In addition to adoption and foster care, lesbians are choosing motherhood using known and unknown sperm donors (as single mothers, in intentional co-mother couples, and in complex variations of biosocial parenting). Both members of a lesbian couple may choose to become pregnant sequentially or simultaneously. Pioneering lesbian couples have exchanged ova to enable both women to claim biological, and thereby legal, maternal status to the same infant (Bourne 1999). It is much more difficult (and costly) for gay men to choose to become fathers, particularly fathers of infants. Some (who reside in states that permit this) become adoptive or foster parents; others serve as sperm donors in joint parenting arrangements with lesbian or other mothers. An affluent minority hire women as "surrogates" to bear children for them.

The means and contexts for planned parenthood are so diverse and complex that they compound the difficulties of isolating the significance of parental sexual orientation. To even approximate this goal, researchers would need to control not only for the gender, number, and sexual orientation of parents, but for their diverse biosocial and legal statuses. The handful of studies that have attempted to do this focus on lesbian motherhood. The most rigorous research designs compare donor-insemination (DI) parenthood among lesbian and heterosexual couples or single mothers (e.g., Chan, Brooks, et al. 1998; Flaks et al. 1995). To our knowledge, no studies have been conducted exclusively on lesbian or gay adoptive parents or compare the children of intentional gay fathers with children in other family forms. Researchers do not know the extent to which the comparatively high socioeconomic status of the DI parents studied accurately reflects the demographics of lesbian and gay parenthood generally, but given the degree of effort, cultural and legal support, and, frequently, the expense involved, members of relatively privileged social groups would be the ones most able to make use of reproductive technology and/or independent adoption.

In short, the indirect effects of heterosexism have placed inordinate constraints on most research on the effects of gay parenthood. We believe, however, that the time may now be propitious to begin to reformulate the basic terms of the enterprise.

Reconsidering the Psychological Findings

Toward this end, we examined the findings of 21 psychological studies (listed at the bottom of Table 1) published between 1981 and 1998 that we considered best equipped to address sociological questions about how parental sexual orientation matters to children. One meta-analysis of 18 such studies (11 of which are included among our 21) characteristically concludes that "the results demonstrate no differences on any measures between the heterosexual and homosexual parents regarding parenting styles, emotional adjustment, and sexual orientation of the child(ren)" (Allen and Burrell 1996:19). To evaluate this claim, we selected for examination only studies that: (1) include a sample of gay or lesbian parents and children and a comparison group of heterosexual parents and children; (2) assess differences between groups in terms of statistical significance; and (3) include findings directly relevant to children's development. The studies we discuss compare relatively advantaged lesbian parents (18 studies) and gay male parents (3 studies) with a roughly matched sample of heterosexual parents. Echoing the conclusion of meta-analysts Allen and Burrell (1996), the authors of all 21 studies almost uniformly claim to find no differences in measures of parenting or child outcomes. In contrast, our careful scrutiny of the findings they report suggests that on some dimensions—particularly those related to gender and sexuality—the sexual orientations of these parents matter somewhat more for their children than the researchers claimed.[7]

The empirical findings from these studies are presented in Tables 1 and 2. Table 1 summarizes findings on the relationship between parental sexual orientation and three sets of child "outcome" variables: (1) gender behavior/gender preferences, (2) sexual behavior/sexual preferences, and (3) psychological well-being. Table 2 summarizes findings on the relationship between parental sexual orientation and other attributes of parents, including: (1) behavior toward children's gender and sexual development, (2) parenting skills, (3) relationships with children, and (4) psychological well-being.

Table 1. Findings on the Associations between Parents' Sexual Orientations and Selected Child Outcomes: 21 Studies, 1981 to 1998

Variable Measured	Direction of Effect
Gender Behavior/Preferences	
Girls' departure from traditional gender role expectations and behaviors—in dress, play, physicality, school activities, occupational aspirations (Hoeffer 1981; Golombok et al. 1983; R. Green et al. 1986; Steckel 1987; Hotvedt and Mandel 1982).	0/+
Boys' departure from traditional gender role expectations and behaviors—in dress, play, physicality, school activities, occupational aspirations (Hoeffer 1981; Golombok et al. 1983; R. Green et al. 1986; Steckel 1987; Hotvedt and Mandel 1982).	0/+
Boys' level of aggressiveness and domineering disposition (Steckel 1987).	-
Child wishes she/he were the other sex. (Green et al. 1986).	0
Sexual Behavior/Sexual Preferences	
Young adult child has considered same-sex sexual relationship(s); has had same-sex sexual relationship(s) (Tasker and Golombok 1997).	+
Young adult child firmly self-identifies as bisexual, gay, or lesbian (Tasker and Golombok 1997).	0
Boys' likelihood of having a gay sexual orientation in adulthood, by sexual orientation of father (Bailey et al. 1995).	(+)
Girls' number of sexual partners from puberty to young adulthood (Tasker and Golombok 1997).	+
Boys' number of sexual partners from puberty to young adulthood (Tasker and Golombok 1997).	(-)
Quality of intimate relationships in young adulthood (Tasker and Golombok 1997).	0
Have friend(s) who are gay or lesbian (Tasker and Golombok 1997).	+
Self-Esteem and Psychological Well-Being	
Children's self-esteem, anxiety, depression, internalizing behavioral problems, externalizing behavioral problems, total behavioral problems, performance in social arenas (sports, friendships, school), use of psychological counseling, mothers' and teachers' reports of children's hyperactivity, unsociability, emotional difficulty, conduct difficulty, other behavioral problems (Golombok, Spencer, and Rutter 1983; Huggins 1989; Patterson 1994; Flaks et al. 1995; Tasker and Golombok 1997; Chan, Raboy, and Patterson 1998; Chan, Brooks, et al. 1998).	0
Daughters' self-reported level of popularity at school and in the neighborhood (Hotvedt and Mandel 1982).	+
Mothers' and teachers' reports of child's level of affection, responsiveness, and concern for younger children (Steckel 1987).	+
Experience of peer stigma concerning own sexuality (Tasker and Golombok 1997).	+
Cognitive functioning (IQ, verbal, performance, and so on) (Flaks et al. 1995; R. Green et al. 1986).	0
Experienced problems gaining employment in young adulthood (Tasker and Golombok 1997).	0

Sources: The 21 studies considered in Tables 1 and 2 are, in date order: Hoeffer (1981); Kweskin and Cook (1982); Miller, Jacobsen, and Bigner (1982); Rand, Graham, and Rawlings (1982); Golombok, Spencer, and Rutter (1983); R. Green et al. (1986); M. Harris and Turner (1986); Bigner and Jacobsen (1989); Hotvedt and Mandel (1982); Huggins (1989); Steckel (1987); Bigner and Jacobsen (1992); Jenny, Roesler. and Poyer (1994); Patterson (1994); Bailey et al. (1995); Flaks et al. (1995); Brewaeys et al. (1997); Tasker and Golombok (1997); Chan, Raboy, and Patterson (1998); Chan, Brooks, et al. (1998); and McNeill, Rienzi, and Kposowa (1998).

+ = significantly higher in lesbigay than in heterosexual parent context.
0 = no significant difference between lesbigay and heterosexual parent context.
- = significantly lower in lesbigay than heterosexual parent context.
( ) = borders on statistical significance.
0/+ = evidence is mixed.

Positive signs (+) indicate a statistically significant higher level of the variable for lesbigay parents or their children, while negative signs (–) indicate a higher level for heterosexual parents or their children. Zero (0) indicates no significant difference.

While Table 1 reports the results of all 21 studies, our discussion here emphasizes findings from six studies we consider to be best designed to isolate whatever unique effects parents' sexual orientations might have on children. Four of these—Flaks et al. (1995), Brewaeys et al. (1997); Chan, Raboy, and Patterson (1998); and Chan, Brooks, et al. (1998)—focus on planned parenting and compare children of lesbian mothers and heterosexual mothers who conceived through DI. This focus reduces the potential for variables like parental divorce, re-partnering, coming out, and so on to confound whatever effects of maternal sexual orientation may be observed. The other two studies—R. Green et al. (1986) and Tasker and Golombok (1997)—focus on children born within heterosexual marriages who experienced the divorce of their biological parents before being raised by a lesbian mother with or without a new partner or spouse. Although this research design heightens the risk that in statistical analyses the effect of maternal sexual orientation may include the effects of other factors, distinctive strengths of each study counterbalance this limitation. R. Green et al. (1986) rigorously attempt to match lesbian mothers and heterosexual mothers on a variety of characteristics, and they compare the two groups of mothers as well as both groups of children on a wide variety of dimensions.[8] Tasker and Golombok (1997) offer a unique long-term, longitudinal design. Their data collection began in 1976 on 27 heterosexual single mothers and 39 of their children (average age 10) and 27 lesbian mothers and 39 of their children (also average age 10) in England. Follow-up interviews with 46 of the original children were conducted 14 years later, allowing for a rare glimpse at how children with lesbian mothers and those with heterosexual mothers fared over their early life courses into young adulthood.

Children's Gender Preferences and Behavior

The first panel of Table 1 displays findings about the relationship between the sexual orientation of parents and the gender preferences and behaviors of their children. The findings demonstrate that, as we would expect, on some measures meaningful differences have been observed in predictable directions. For example, lesbian mothers in R. Green et al. (1986) reported that their children, especially daughters, more frequently dress, play, and behave in ways that do not conform to sex-typed cultural norms. Likewise, daughters of lesbian mothers reported greater interest in activities associated with both "masculine" and "feminine" qualities and that involve the participation of both sexes, whereas daughters of heterosexual mothers report significantly greater interest in traditionally feminine, same-sex activities (also see Hotvedt and Mandel 1982). Similarly, daughters with lesbian mothers reported higher aspirations to nontraditional-gender occupations (Steckel 1987). For example, in R. Green et al. (1986), 53 percent (16 out of 30) of the daughters of lesbians aspired to careers such as doctor, lawyer, engineer, and astronaut, compared with only 21 percent (6 of 28) of the daughters of heterosexual mothers.

Sons appear to respond in more complex ways to parental sexual orientations. On some measures, like aggressiveness and play preferences, the sons of lesbian mothers behave in less traditionally masculine ways than those raised by heterosexual single mothers. However, on other measures, such as occupational goals and sartorial styles, they also exhibit greater gender conformity than do daughters with lesbian mothers (but they are not more conforming than sons with heterosexual mothers) (R. Green et al. 1986; Steckel 1987).[9] Such evidence, albeit limited, implies that lesbian parenting may free daughters and sons from a broad but uneven range of traditional gender prescriptions. It also suggests that the sexual orientation of mothers interacts with the gender of children in complex ways to influence gender preferences and behavior. Such findings raise provocative questions about how children assimilate gender culture and interests—questions that the propensity to downplay differences deters scholars from exploring.[10]

Consider, for example, the study by R. Green et al. (1986) that, by our count, finds at least 15 intriguing, statistically significant differences in gender behavior and preferences among children (4 among boys and 11 among girls) in lesbian and heterosexual single-mother homes. Yet the study's abstract summarizes: "Two types of single-parent households [lesbian and heterosexual mothers] and their effects on children ages 3–11 years were compared.…No significant differences were found between the two types of households for boys and few significant differences for girls" (p. 167).[11]

Similarly, we note an arresting continuum of data reported, but ignored, by Brewaeys et al. (1997, table 4). Young boys (ages 4 to 8) conceived through DI in lesbian co-mother families scored the lowest on a measure of sex-typed masculine behaviors (the PSAI-preschool activities inventory, rated by parents), DI boys in heterosexual two-parent families were somewhat more sex-typed, while "naturally" conceived boys in heterosexual two-parent families received the highest sex-typed masculine scores. By our calculation, the difference in the magnitude of scores between DI boys with lesbian co-mothers and conventionally conceived sons with heterosexual parents is sufficient to reach statistical significance, even though the matched groups contained only 15 and 11 boys, respectively. Rather than exploring the implications of these provocative data, the authors conclude: "No significant difference was found between groups for the mean PSAI scores for either boys or girls" (Brewaeys et al. 1997:1356).

Children's Sexual Preferences and Behavior

The second panel of Table 1 shifts the focus from children's gender behavior and preferences to their sexual behavior and preferences, with particular attention to thought-provoking findings from the Tasker and Golombok (1997) study, the only comparative study we know of that follows children raised in lesbian-headed families into young adulthood and hence that can explore the children's sexuality in meaningful ways. A significantly greater proportion of young adult children raised by lesbian mothers than those raised by heterosexual mothers in the Tasker and Golombok sample reported having had a homoerotic relationship (6 of the 25 young adults raised by lesbian mothers— 24 percent—compared with 0 of the 20 raised by heterosexual mothers). The young adults reared by lesbian mothers were also significantly more likely to report having thought they might experience homoerotic attraction or relationships. The difference in their openness to this possibility is striking: 64 percent (14 of 22) of the young adults raised by lesbian mothers report having considered same-sex relationships (in the past, now, or in the future), compared with only 17 percent (3 of 18) of those raised by heterosexual mothers. Of course, the fact that 17 percent of those raised by heterosexual mothers also report some openness to same-sex relationships, while 36 percent of those raised by lesbians do not, underscores the important reality that parental influence on children's sexual desires is neither direct nor easily predictable.

If these young adults raised by lesbian mothers were more open to a broad range of sexual possibilities, they were not statistically more likely to self-identify as bisexual, lesbian, or gay. To be coded as such, the respondent not only had to currently self-identify as bisexual/lesbian/gay, but also to express a commitment to that identity in the future. Tasker and Golombok (1997) employ a measure of sexual identity with no "in-between" categories for those whose identity may not yet be fully fixed or embraced. Thus, although a more nuanced measure or a longer period of observation could yield different results, Golombok and Tasker (1996) choose to situate their findings within the "overall no difference" interpretation:

> The commonly held assumption that children brought up by lesbian mothers will themselves grow up to be lesbian or gay is not supported by the findings of the study: the majority of children who grew up in lesbian families identified

as heterosexual in adulthood, and there was no statistically significant difference between young adults from lesbian and heterosexual family backgrounds with respect to sexual orientation. (P. 8)

This reading, while technically accurate, deflects analytic attention from the rather sizable differences in sexual attitudes and behaviors that the study actually reports. The only other comparative study we found that explores intergenerational resemblance in sexual orientation is Bailey et al. (1995) on gay fathers and their adult sons. This study also provides evidence of a moderate degree of parent-to-child transmission of sexual orientation.

Tasker and Golombok (1997) also report some fascinating findings on the number of sexual partners children report having had between puberty and young adulthood. Relative to their counterparts with heterosexual parents, the adolescent and young adult girls raised by lesbian mothers appear to have been more sexually adventurous and less chaste, whereas the sons of lesbians evince the opposite pattern—somewhat less sexually adventurous and more chaste (the finding was statistically significant for the 25-girl sample but not for the 18-boy sample). In other words, once again, children (especially girls) raised by lesbians appear to depart from traditional gender-based norms, while children raised by heterosexual mothers appear to conform to them. Yet this provocative finding of differences in sexual behavior and agency has not been analyzed or investigated further.

Both the findings and nonfindings discussed above may be influenced by the measures of sexual orientation employed. All of the studies measure sexual orientations as a dichotomy rather than as a continuum. We have no data on children whose parents do not identify their sexuality neatly as one of two dichotomous choices, and we can only speculate about how a more nuanced conceptualization might alter the findings reported. Having parents less committed to a specific sexual identity may free children to construct sexualities altogether different from those of their parents, or it may give whatever biological predispositions exist freer reign to determine eventual sexual orientations, or parents with greater ambiguity or fluidity of sexual orientation might transmit some of this to their children, leading to greater odds of sexual flexibility.

Children's Mental Health

Given historic social prejudices against homosexuality, the major issue deliberated by judges and policy makers has been whether children of lesbian and gay parents suffer higher levels of emotional and psychological harm. Unsurprisingly, therefore, children's "self-esteem and psychological well-being" is a heavily researched domain. The third panel of Table 1 shows that these studies find no significant differences between children of lesbian mothers and children of heterosexual mothers in anxiety, depression, self-esteem, and numerous other measures of social and psychological adjustment. The roughly equivalent level of psychological well-being between the two groups holds true in studies that test children directly, rely on parents' reports, and solicit evaluations from teachers. The few significant differences found actually tend to favor children with lesbian mothers (see Table 1).[12] Given some credible evidence that children with gay and lesbian parents, especially adolescent children, face homophobic teasing and ridicule that many find difficult to manage (Tasker and Golombok 1997; also see Bozett 1989:148; Mitchell 1998), the children in these studies seem to exhibit impressive psychological strength.

Similarly, across studies, no relationship has been found between parental sexual orientation and measures of children's cognitive ability. Moreover, to our knowledge no theories predict such a link. Thus far, no work has compared children's *long-term* achievements in education, occupation, income, and other domains of life.[13]

Links between parental sexual orientation, parenting practices, and parent/child relationships may indicate processes underlying some of the links between parents' sexual orientation and the child outcomes in Table 1. Table 2 presents empirical findings about the parents themselves and the quality of parent-child relationships.

Table 2. Findings on the Associations between Parents' Sexual Orientations, Other Attributes of Parents, and Parent-Child Relationships: 21 Studies, 1981 to 1998

Variable Measured	Direction of Effect
Parental Behavior toward Children's Gender and Sexual Development	
Mother prefers child engages in gender-appropriate play activities (Hoeffer 1981; R. Green et al. 1986; M. Harris and Turner 1986).	0/-
Mother classifies the ideal child as masculine (if boy) and feminine (if girl) (Kweskin and Cook 1982).	0
Mother prefers that child be gay or lesbian when grown up (Golombok et al. 1983; Tasker and Golombok 1997).	0
Child believes that mother would prefer that she/he has lesbigay sexual orientation (Tasker and Golombok 1997).	+
Parenting Practices: Developmental Orientations and Parenting Skills	
Mother's developmental orientation in child rearing and parenting skill (Miller et al. 1982; McNeill et al. 1998; Flaks et al. 1995).	0/+
Spouse/partner's developmental orientation in child rearing and parenting skill (Flaks et al. 1995; Brewaeys et al. 1997).	+
Spouse/partner's desire for equal/shared distribution of childcare (Chan, Brooks, et al. 1998).	+
Degree to which mother and spouse/partner share child-care work (Brewaeys et al. 1997; Chan, Brooks, et al. 1998).	+
Similarity between mother's and spouse/partner's parenting skills (Flaks et al. 1995).	+
Similarity between mother's and spouse/partner's assessment of child's behavior and well-being (Chan, Raboy, and Patterson 1998; Chan, Brooks, et al. 1998).	+
Mother allowed adolescent child's boyfriend/girlfriend to spend the night (Tasker and Golombok 1997).	0
Residential Parent/Child Relationships	
Mother's rating of quality of relationship with child (Golombok et al. 1983; M. Harris and Turner 1986; Brewaeys et al. 1997; McNeill et al. 1998).	0
Mother's likelihood of having a live-in partner post-divorce (Kweskin and Cook 1982; R. Green et al. 1986).	+
Spouse/partner's rating of quality of relationship with child (Brewaeys et al. 1997).	+
Child's report of closeness with biological mother growing up (Tasker and Golombok 1997; Brewaeys et al. 1997).	0
Child's report of closeness with biological mother's partner/spouse growing up (Tasker and Golombok 1997; Brewaeys et al. 1997).	0/+
Child felt able to discuss own sexual development with parent(s) while growing up (Tasker and Golombok 1997).	+
Nonresidential Parent/Child Relationships	
(Non-custodial) father's level of involvement with children, limit setting, and developmental orientation in child rearing (Bigner and Jacobsen 1989, 1992).	0/+
Mother's encouragement of child's contact with nonresidential father (Hotvedt and Mandel 1982).	0
Divorced mother's contact with children's father in the past year (Golombok et al. 1983).	+
Child's frequency of contact with nonresidential father (Golombok et al. 1983).	+
Child's positive feelings toward nonresidential father (Hotvedt and Mandel 1982; Tasker and Golombok 1997).	0/(+)

Table 2. (*continued*)

Variable Measured	Direction of Effect
Parent's Self-Esteem and Psychological Well-Being	
Mother's level of depression, self-esteem (Rand et al. 1982; R. Green et al. 1986; Chan, Raboy and Patterson 1998; Golombok et al. 1983).	0/+
Mother's level of leadership, independence, achievement orientation (R. Green et al. 1986; Rand et al. 1982).	0/+
Mother's use of sedatives, stimulants, in- or out-patient psychiatric care in past year (Golombok et al. 1983).	0
Mother ever received psychiatric care in adult life? (Golombok et al. 1983).	+
Mother's level of self-reported stress associated with single-parenthood (R. Green et al. 1986).	0

Sources: See Table 1.

  + = significantly higher in lesbigay than in heterosexual parent context.
  0 = no significant difference between lesbigay and heterosexual parent context.
  - = significantly lower in lesbigay than heterosexual parent context.
  ( ) = borders on statistical significance.
  0/+ = evidence is mixed.

Parental Behavior toward Children's Gender and Sexual Development

The scattered pieces of evidence cited above imply that lesbigay parenting may be associated with a broadening of children's gender and sexual repertoires. Is this because lesbigay parents actively attempt to achieve these outcomes in their children? Data in the first panel of Table 2 provide little evidence that parents' own sexual orientations correlate strongly with their preferences concerning their children's gender or sexual orientations. For example, the lesbian mothers in Kweskin and Cook (1982) were no more likely than heterosexual mothers to assign masculine and feminine qualities to an "ideal" boy or girl, respectively, on the well-known Bern Sex Role Inventory. However, mothers did tend to desire gender-traits in children that resembled those they saw in themselves, and the lesbians saw themselves as less feminine-typed than did the heterosexual mothers. This suggests that a mother's own gender identity may mediate the connection between maternal sexual orientation and maternal gender preferences for her children.

Also, in some studies lesbian mothers were less concerned than heterosexual mothers that their children engage in gender "appropriate" activities and play, a plausible difference most researchers curiously downplay. For example, Hoeffer's (1981) summary reads:

> Children's play and activity interests as indices of sex-role behavior were compared for a sample of lesbian and heterosexual single mothers and their children. More striking than any differences were the similarities between the two groups of children on acquisition of sex-role behavior and between the two groups of mothers on the encouragement of sex-role behavior. (p. 536)

Yet from our perspective, the most interesting (and statistically significant) finding in Hoeffer (1981, table 4) is one of difference. While the heterosexual single mothers in the sample were significantly more likely to prefer that their boys engage in masculine activities and their girls in feminine ones, lesbian mothers had no such interests. Their preferences for their children's play were gender-neutral.

Differences in parental concern with children's acquisition of gender and in parenting practices that do or do not emphasize conformity to sex-typed gender norms are understudied and underanalyzed. The sparse evidence to date based on self-reports does not suggest strong differences between lesbigay and heterosexual parents in this domain.

Parenting Practices: Developmental Orientations and Parenting Skills

The second panel of Table 2 displays findings about parenting skills and child-rearing practices—developmental orientations, parental control and support, parent/child communication, parental affection, time spent with children—that have been shown to be central for many aspects of children's development (introversion/extroversion, success in school, and so on) (Baumrind 1978, 1980). The many findings of differences here coalesce around two patterns. First, studies find the nonbiological lesbian co-mothers (referred to as lesbian "social mothers" in Brewaeys et al. [1997]) to be more skilled at parenting and more involved with the children than are stepfathers. Second, lesbian partners in the two-parent families studied enjoy a greater level of synchronicity in parenting than do heterosexual partners.

For example, the lesbian birth mothers and heterosexual birth mothers who conceived through DI studied by Flaks et al. (1995) and Brewaeys et al. (1997) scored about the same on all measures of parenting. However, the DI lesbian social mothers scored significantly higher than the DI heterosexual fathers on measures of parenting skills, practices, and quality of interactions with children. DI lesbian social mothers also spent significantly more time than did DI heterosexual fathers in child-care activities including disciplinary, control, and limit-setting activities. In fact, in the Brewaeys et al. (1997) study, lesbian social mothers even scored significantly higher on these measures than did biological fathers in heterosexual couples who conceived conventionally. Similarly, in Chan, Raboy, and Patterson (1998), whereas the lesbian birth mothers and co-mother partners evaluated their children's emotional states and social behaviors in almost exactly the same way, heterosexual mothers and fathers evaluated their children differently: Fathers identified fewer problems in the children than did mothers (a similar pattern is observed in Chan, Brooks, et al. 1998, table 4).

These findings imply that lesbian co-parents may enjoy greater parental compatibility and achieve particularly high quality parenting skills, which may help explain the striking findings on parent/child relationships in the third panel of Table 2. DI lesbian social mothers report feeling closer to the children than do their heterosexual male counterparts. The children studied report feeling closer to DI lesbian social mothers as well as to lesbian stepmothers than to either DI fathers or stepfathers (measures of emotional closeness between birth mothers and children did not vary by mother's sexual orientation). Children of lesbian mothers also report feeling more able than children of heterosexual parents to discuss their sexual development with their mothers and their mothers' partners (Tasker and Golombok 1997; also see Mitchell 1998:407). If lesbian social mothers and stepmothers have more parenting awareness and skill, on average, than heterosexual DI fathers or stepfathers, and if they spend more time taking care of children, they may be more likely to earn the children's affection and trust.

We believe (as do Brewaeys et al. 1997; Chan et al. 1998; Flaks et al. 1995) that the comparative strengths these lesbian co-parents seem to exhibit have more to do with gender than with sexual orientation. Female gender is probably the source of the positive signs for parenting skill, participation in child rearing, and synchronicity in child evaluations shown in the comparisons in Table 2. Research suggests that, on average, mothers tend to be more invested in and skilled at child care than fathers, and that mothers are more apt than fathers to engage in the kinds of child-care activities that appear to be particularly crucial to children's cognitive, emotional, and social development (Furstenberg and Cherlin 1991; Simons and Associates 1996). Analogously, in these studies of matched lesbian and heterosexual couples, women in every category—heterosexual birth mother, lesbian birth mother, nonbiological lesbian social mother—all score about the same as one another but score significantly higher than the men on measures having to do with the care of children.[14]

In our view, these patterns reflect something more than a simple "gender effect," however, because sexual orientation is the key "exogenous variable" that brings together parents of same or different genders. Thus, sexual orientation and gender should be viewed as *interacting* to create new kinds of family structures and processes— such as an egalitarian division of child care—that have fascinating consequences for all of the relationships in the triad and for child development (also see Dunne 1999, 2000; Patterson 1995). Some of the evidence suggests that two women co-parenting may create a synergistic pattern that brings more egalitarian, compatible, shared parenting and time spent with children, greater understanding of children, and closeness and communication between parents and children. The genesis of this pattern cannot be understood on the basis of either sexual orientation or gender alone. Such findings raise fruitful comparative questions for future research about family dynamics among two parents of the same or different gender who do or do not share similar attitudes, values, and behaviors.

We know little thus far about how the sexual orientation of nonresidential fathers may be related to their relationships with their children (the fourth panel of Table 2) (and even less about that for custodial fathers). The Bigner and Jacobsen studies (1989, 1992) find similarity in parenting and in father/child relations among heterosexual nonresidential fathers and gay nonresidential fathers. Bozett (1987a, 1987b, 1989) found that in a small sample of children with gay fathers, most children had very positive feelings toward their fathers, but they also worried that peers and others might presume that they, too, had a gay sexual orientation (Bozett did not include a control group of children with heterosexual fathers).

Parental Fitness

The bottom panel of Table 2 demonstrates that evidence to date provides no support for those, like Wardle (1997), who claim that lesbian mothers suffer greater levels of psychological difficulties (depression, low self-esteem) than do heterosexual mothers. On the contrary, the few differences observed in the studies suggest that these lesbian mothers actually display somewhat higher levels of positive psychological resources.

Research on a more diverse population, however, might alter the findings of difference and similarity shown in Table 2. For example, the ethnographic evidence suggests that people of color with homoerotic practices of ten value racial solidarity over sexual solidarity. Boykin, Director of the National Black Gay and Lesbian Leadership Forum, cites a 1994 University of Chicago study which found that among people who engage in homoerotic activity, whites, urbanites, and those with higher education were more likely to consider themselves gay or lesbian (Boykin 1996:36). If, as it appears, racial/ethnic solidarities deter disproportionate numbers of people of color from coming out, they might suffer greater psychological and social costs from living in the closet or, conversely, might benefit from less concern over their sexual identities than do white gay parents. We also do not know whether lesbian couples of different racial/ethnic and social class contexts would display the same patterns of egalitarian, compatible co-parenting reported among the white lesbian couples.

No Differences of Social Concern

The findings summarized in Tables 1 and 2 show that the "no differences" claim does receive strong empirical support in crucial domains. Lesbigay parents and their children in these studies display no differences from heterosexual counterparts in psychological well-being or cognitive functioning. Scores for lesbigay parenting styles and levels of investment in children are at least as "high" as those for heterosexual parents. Levels of closeness and quality of parent/child relationships do not seem to differentiate directly by parental sexual orientation, but indirectly, by way of parental gender. Because every relevant study to date shows that parental sexual orientation per se has no measurable effect on the quality of parent-child relationships or on children's mental health or social adjustment, there is no evidentiary basis for considering parental sexual orientation in decisions about children's "best interest." In fact, given that children with lesbigay parents probably contend with a degree of social stigma, these similarities in child outcomes suggest the presence of compensatory processes in lesbigay-parent families. Exploring how these families help children cope with stigma might prove helpful to all kinds of families.

Most of the research to date focuses on social-psychological dimensions of well-being and adjustment and on the quality of parent/child relationships. Perhaps these variables reflect the disciplinary preferences of psychologists who have conducted most of the studies, as well as a desire to produce evidence directly relevant to the questions of "harm" that dominate judicial and legislative deliberations over child custody. Less research has explored questions for which there are stronger theoretical grounds for expecting differences—children's gender and sexual behavior and preferences. In fact, only two studies (R. Green et al. 1986; Tasker and Golombok 1997) generate much of the baseline evidence on potential connections between parents' and child's sexual and gender identities. Evidence in these and the few other studies that focus on these variables does not support the "no differences" claim. Children with lesbigay parents appear less traditionally gender-typed and more likely to be open to homoerotic relationships. In addition, evidence suggests that parental gender and sexual identities interact to create distinctive family processes whose consequences for children have yet to be studied.

How the Sexual Orientation of Parents Matters

We have identified conceptual, methodological, and theoretical limitations in the psychological research on the effects of parental sexual orientation and have challenged the predominant claim that the sexual orientation of parents does not matter at all. We argued instead that despite the limitations, there is suggestive evidence and good reason to believe that contemporary children and young adults with lesbian or gay parents do differ in modest and interesting ways from children with heterosexual parents. Most of these differences, however, are not causal, but are indirect effects

of parental gender or selection effects associated with heterosexist social conditions under which lesbigay-parent families currently live.

First, our analysis of the psychological research indicates that the effects of parental gender trump those of sexual orientation (Brewaeys et al. 1997; Chan, Brooks, et al. 1998; Chan, Raboy, and Patterson 1998; Flaks et al. 1995). A diverse array of gender theories (social learning theory, psychoanalytic theory, materialist, symbolic interactionist) would predict that children with two same-gender parents, and particularly with co-mother parents, should develop in less gender-stereotypical ways than would children with two heterosexual parents. There is reason to credit the perception of lesbian co-mothers in a qualitative study (Dunne, 2000) that they "were redefining the meaning and content of motherhood, extending its boundaries to incorporate the activities that are usually dichotomized as mother and father" (p. 25). Children who derive their principal source of love, discipline, protection, and identification from women living independent of male domestic authority or influence should develop less stereotypical symbolic, emotional, practical, and behavioral gender repertoires. Indeed, it is the claim that the gender mix of parents has no effect on their children's gender behavior, interests, or development that cries out for sociological explanation. Only a crude theory of cultural indoctrination that posited the absolute impotence of parents might predict such an outcome, and the remarkable variability of gender configurations documented in the anthropological record readily undermines such a theory (Bonvillain 1998; Brettell and Sargent 1997; Ortner and Whitehead 1981). The burden of proof in the domain of gender and sexuality should rest with those who embrace the null hypothesis.

Second, because homosexuality is stigmatized, selection effects may yield correlations between parental sexual orientation and child development that do not derive from sexual orientation itself. For example, social constraints on access to marriage and parenting make lesbian parents likely to be older, urban, educated, and self-aware—factors that foster several positive developmental consequences for their children. On the other hand, denied access to marriage, lesbian co-parent relationships are likely to experience dissolution rates somewhat higher than those among heterosexual co-parents (Bell and Weinberg 1978; Weeks, Heaphy, and Donovan forthcoming, chap. 5). Not only do same-sex couples lack the institutional pressures and support for commitment that marriage provides, but qualitative studies suggest that they tend to embrace comparatively high standards of emotional intimacy and satisfaction (Dunne 2000; Sullivan 1996; Weeks et al. forthcoming). The decision to pursue a socially ostracized domain of intimacy implies an investment in the emotional regime that Giddens (1992) terms "the pure relationship" and "confluent love." Such relationships confront the inherent instabilities of modern or postmodern intimacy, what Beck and Beck-Gersheim (1995) term "the normal chaos of love." Thus, a higher dissolution rate would be correlated with but not causally related to sexual orientation, a difference that should erode were homophobia to disappear and legal marriage be made available to lesbians and gay men.

Most of the differences in the findings discussed above cannot be considered deficits from any legitimate public policy perspective. They either favor the children with lesbigay parents, are secondary effects of social prejudice, or represent "just a difference" of the sort democratic societies should respect and protect. Apart from differences associated with parental gender, most of the presently observable differences in child "outcomes" should wither away under conditions of full equality and respect for sexual diversity. Indeed, it is time to recognize that the categories "lesbian mother" and "gay father" are historically transitional and conceptually flawed, because they erroneously imply that a parent's sexual orientation is the decisive characteristic of her or his parenting. On the contrary, we propose that homophobia and discrimination are the chief reasons why parental sexual orientation matters at all. Because lesbigay parents do not enjoy the same rights, respect, and recognition as heterosexual parents, their children contend with the burdens of vicarious social stigma. Likewise, some of the particular strengths and sensitivities such children appear to display,

such as a greater capacity to express feelings or more empathy for social diversity (Mitchell 1998; O'Connell 1994), are probably artifacts of marginality and may be destined for the historical dustbin of a democratic, sexually pluralist society.

Even in a utopian society, however, one difference seems less likely to disappear: The sexual orientation of parents appears to have a unique (although not large) effect on children in the politically sensitive domain of sexuality. The evidence, while scanty and underanalyzed, hints that parental sexual orientation is positively associated with the possibility that children will be more likely to attain a similar orientation—and theory and common sense also support such a view. Children raised by lesbian co-parents should and do seem to grow up more open to homoerotic relationships. This may be partly due to genetic and family socialization processes, but what sociologists refer to as "contextual effects" not yet investigated by psychologists may also be important. Because lesbigay parents are disproportionately more likely to inhabit diverse, cosmopolitan cities—Los Angeles, New York and San Francisco—and progressive university communities—such as Santa Cruz, Santa Rosa, Madison, and Ann Arbor (Black, Gates, et al. 2000)—their children grow up in comparatively tolerant school, neighborhood, and social contexts, which foster less hostility to homoeroticism. Sociology could make a valuable contribution to this field by researching processes that interact at the individual, family, and community level to undergird parent-child links between gender and sexuality.

Under homophobic conditions, lesbigay parents are apt to be more sensitive to issues surrounding their children's sexual development and to injuries that children with nonconforming desires may experience, more open to discussing sexuality with their children, and more affirming of their questions about sexuality (Mitchell 1998; Tasker and Golombok 1997). It therefore seems likely, although this has yet to be studied, that their children will grow up better informed about and more comfortable with sexual desires and practices. However, the tantalizing gender contrast in the level of sexual activity reported for sons versus daughters of lesbians raises more complicated questions about the relationship between gender and sexuality.

Even were heterosexism to disappear, however, parental sexual orientation would probably continue to have some impact on the eventual sexuality of children. Research and theory on sexual development remain so rudimentary that it is impossible to predict how much difference might remain were homosexuality not subject to social stigma. Indeed, we believe that if one suspends the hetero-normative presumption, one fascinating riddle to explain in this field is why, even though children of lesbigay parents appear to express a significant increase in homoeroticism, the majority of all children nonetheless identify as heterosexual, as most theories across the "essentialist" to "social constructionist" spectrum seem (perhaps too hastily) to expect. A nondefensive look at the anomalous data on this question could pose fruitful challenges to social constructionist, genetic, and bio-evolutionary theories.

We recognize the political dangers of pointing out that recent studies indicate that a higher proportion of children with lesbigay parents are themselves apt to engage in homosexual activity. In a homophobic world, anti-gay forces deploy such results to deny parents custody of their own children and to fuel backlash movements opposed to gay rights. Nonetheless, we believe that denying this probability capitulates to heterosexist ideology and is apt to prove counterproductive in the long run. It is neither intellectually honest nor politically wise to base a claim for justice on grounds that may prove falsifiable empirically. Moreover, the case for granting equal rights to nonheterosexual parents should not require finding their children to be identical to those reared by heterosexuals. Nor should it require finding that such children do not encounter distinctive challenges or risks, especially when these derive from social prejudice. The U.S. Supreme Court rejected this rationale for denying custody when it repudiated discrimination against interracially married parents in *Palmore* v. *Sidoti* in 1984: "[P]rivate biases may be outside the reach of the law, but the law cannot, directly or indirectly, give them effect"

(quoted in Polikoff 1990:569–70). Inevitably, children share most of the social privileges and injuries associated with their parents' social status. If social prejudice were grounds for restricting rights to parent, a limited pool of adults would qualify.

One can readily turn the tables on a logic that seeks to protect children from the harmful effects of heterosexist stigma directed against their parents. Granting legal rights and respect to gay parents and their children should lessen the stigma that they now suffer and might reduce the high rates of depression and suicide reported among closeted gay youth living with heterosexual parents. Thus, while we disagree with those who claim that there are no differences between the children of heterosexual parents and children of lesbigay parents, we unequivocally endorse their conclusion that social science research provides no grounds for taking sexual orientation into account in the political distribution of family rights and responsibilities.

It is quite a different thing, however, to consider this issue a legitimate matter for social science research. Planned lesbigay parenthood offers a veritable "social laboratory" of family diversity in which scholars could fruitfully examine not only the acquisition of sexual and gender identity, but the relative effects on children of the gender and number of their parents as well as of the implications of diverse biosocial routes to parenthood. Such studies could give us purchase on some of the most vexing and intriguing topics in our field, including divorce, adoption, step-parenthood, and domestic violence, to name a few. To exploit this opportunity, however, researchers must overcome the hetero-normative presumption that interprets sexual differences as deficits, thereby inflicting some of the very disadvantages it claims to discover. Paradoxically, if the sexual orientation of parents were to matter less for political rights, it could matter more for social theory.

Acknowledgments

Direct all correspondence to Judith Stacey, Department of Sociology, University of Southern California, Los Angeles, CA, 90089–2539 (jstacey@usc.edu). We are grateful for the constructive criticisms on early versions of this article from: Celeste Atkins, Amy Binder, Phil Cowan, Gary Gates, Adam Green, David Greenberg, Oystein Holter, Celia Kitzinger, Joan Laird, Jane Mauldon, Dan McPherson, Shannon Minter, Valory Mitchell, Charlotte Patterson, Anne Peplau, Vernon Rosario, Seth Sanders, Alisa Steckel, Michael Wald, and the reviewers and editors of *ASR*. We presented portions of this work at: UCLA Neuropsychiatric Institute Symposium on Sexuality; the Feminist Interdisciplinary Seminar of the University of California, Davis; and the Taft Lecture Program at the University of Cincinnati.

Notes

1. In *J.B.F.* v. *JM.F.* (Ex parte J.M.F. 1970224, So. 2d 1190, 1988 Ala. LEXIS 161 [1998]), for example, Alabama's Supreme Court quoted Wardle's (1997) essay to justify transferring custody of a child from her lesbian mother to her heterosexual father.

2. The extrapolation is "inappropriate" because lesbigay-parent families have never been a comparison group in the family structure literature on which these authors rely (cf. Downey and Powell 1993; McLanahan 1985).

3. In March 2000, Norwegian sociologist Oystein Holter (personal communication) described Helmut Stierlin's "delegation" theory (published in German)—that children take over their parents' unconscious wishes. Holter suggests this theory could predict that a child who grows up with gay parents under homophobic conditions might develop "contrary responses." We are unfamiliar with this theory but find it likely that under such conditions unconscious wishes of heterosexual and nonheterosexual parents could foster some different "contrary responses."

4. These estimates derive from an extrapolation of Kinsey data claiming a roughly 10 percent prevalence of homosexuality in the adult male population. Interestingly, Michael et al.'s (1994) revisiting of Kinsey (Kinsey, Pomeroy, and Martin 1948; Kinsey, Pomeroy, Martin, and Gebhard 1953) suggests that Kinsey himself emphasized that different measures of sexual orientation yield different estimates of individuals with same-sex sexual orientations in the population. Had scholars read Kinsey differently, they might have selected his figure of 4 percent of the men in his sample who practiced exclusive homosexual behavior from adolescence onward, rather than the widely embraced 10 percent figure. In fact, the 10 percent number is fundamentally flawed: Kinsey found that of the 37 percent of the white men in his sample who had at least one sexual experience with another man in their lifetime, only 10 percent of them (i.e., 3.7 percent of the entire white male sample) had exclusively same-sex sexual experiences for any three-year period between ages 16 and 55.

5. This assumes that the ratio of number of dependent children to total offspring among current lesbigay parents will be roughly the same as that for all parents and children.

6. The field is now in a position to take advantage of new data sources. For example, the 1990 U.S. census allows (albeit imperfectly) for the first time the identification of gay and lesbian couples, as will the 2000 census (Black, Gates, et al. 2000). From 1989 to the present, the U.S. General Social Surveys (http://www.icpsr.umich.edu/GSS/index.html) have also allowed for the identification of the sexual orientation of respondents, as does the National Health and Social Life Survey (Laumann et al. 1995).

7. We chose to display the specific findings in each of the quantitative studies, rather than to conduct a meta-analysis, because at this stage of knowledge not enough studies are targeted to the same general "outcome" to enable a meta-analysis to reveal systematic patterns. The single meta-analysis that has been done (Allen and Burrell 1996) reached the typical "no difference" conclusion, but its conclusions were hampered by this very problem. The small number of studies available led Allen and Burrell to pool studies focused on quite different parent and child "outcomes," heightening the risk that findings in one direction effectively offset findings in another.

8. Belcastro et al. (1993) point out that R. Green et al. (1986) did not successfully match heterosexual and lesbian single-mother families on the dimension of household composition. While 39 of R. Green et al.'s 50 lesbian single-mother households had a second adult residing in them by one-plus years post-divorce, only 4 of the 40 heterosexual single mothers did so. R. Green et al. (1986) note this difference, but do not discuss its implications for findings; nor do Belcastro et al. (1993).

9. Many of these studies use conventional levels of significance (e.g., $|t| > 1.96$, $p < .05$, two-tailed tests) on minuscule samples, substantially increasing their likelihood of failing to reject the null hypothesis. For example, Hoeffer's (1981) descriptive numbers suggest a greater preference for masculine toys among boys with heterosexual mothers than those with lesbian mothers, but sampling only 10 boys in each group makes reaching statistical significance exceedingly difficult. Golombok, Spencer, and Rutter's (1983, table 8) evidence of a greater average tendency toward "femininity" among daughters raised by heterosexual mothers than those raised by lesbian single mothers does not reach statistical significance in part because their tabular crosscutting leads to very small cell counts (to meet conventional criteria the differences between groups would have to be huge in such cases). Single difference-tests that maximize cell counts (e.g., the percentage of children—male or female—in each group who report gender-role behavior that goes against type) might well yield significant results. Recent research on model selection shows that to find the best model in large samples, conventional levels of significance need to be substantially tightened, but that for very small samples conventional levels can actually be too restrictive (Raftery 1995).

10. Much qualitative work, particularly by lesbian feminist scholars, has been exploring these issues. For example Wells (1997) argues that, unlike what she refers to as "patriarchal families," lesbian co-mother families rear sons to experience rather than repress emotions and instill in daughters a sense of their potential rather than of limits imposed by gender. From a quantitative perspective, this is a "testable" hypothesis that has sizable theoretical implications but which researchers in the field do not seem to be pursuing.

11. The R. Green et al. (1986) research was conducted in a context in which custody cases often claimed that lesbian motherhood would create gender identity disorder in children and that lesbian mothers themselves were unfit. It is understandable that their summary reassures readers that the findings point to more similarities than differences in both the mothers and their children.

12. Patterson (1994) found that children ages 4 to 9 with lesbian mothers expressed more stress than did those with heterosexual mothers, but at the same time they also reported a greater sense of overall well-being. Patterson speculates that children from lesbian-mother families may be more willing to express their feelings—positive and negative—but also that the children may actually experience more social stress at the same time that they gain confidence from their ability to cope with it.

13. The only empirical evidence reported is Tasker and Golombok's (1997) finding of no differences in unemployment rates among young adults that are associated with their parents' sexual orientations. However, some of the children studied were still in school, and the authors provide no information on occupations attained to assess differences in long-term occupational achievements.

14. Chan, Brooks, et al. (1998:415) make interesting connections between these kinds of findings and the theoretical perspectives developed in Chodorow (1978) and Gilligan (1982).

References

Allen, Mike and Nancy Burrell. 1996. "Comparing the Impact of Homosexual and Heterosexual Parents on Children: Meta-Analysis of Existing Research." *Journal of Homosexuality* 32:19–35.

Badgett, M. V. Lee. 1998. "The Economic Well-Being of Lesbian, Gay, and Bisexual Adults' Families." Pp. 231–48 in *Lesbian, Gay and Bisexual Identities in Families: Psychological Perspectives*, edited by C.J. Patterson and A.R. D'Augelli. New York: Oxford University Press.

Bailey, J. Michael, David Bobrow, Marilyn Wolfe, and Sarah Mikach. 1995. "Sexual Orientation of Adult Sons of Gay Fathers." *Developmental Psychology* 31:124–29.

Baumrind, Diana. 1978. "Parental Disciplinary Patterns and Social Competence in Children." *Youth and Society* 9:239–75.

———. 1980. "New Directions in Socialization Research." *American Psychologist* 35:639–52.

———. 1995. "Commentary on Sexual Orientation: Research and Social Policy Implications." *Developmental Psychology* 31:130–36.

Bech, Henning. 1997. *When Men Meet: Homosexuality and Modernity*. Chicago, IL: University of Chicago Press.

Beck, Ulrich and Elisabeth Beck-Gersheim. 1995. *The Normal Chaos of Love.* London, England: Polity.

Belcastro, Philip A., Theresa Gramlich, Thomas Nicholson, Jimmie Price, and Richard Wilson. 1993. "A Review of Data Based Studies Addressing the Affects [*sic*] of Homosexual Parenting on Children's Sexual and Social Functioning." *Journal of Divorce and Remarriage* 20:105–22.

Bell, Alan P. and Martin S. Weinberg. 1978. *Homosexualities: A Study of Diversity among Men and Women.* New York: Simon and Schuster.

Benkov, Laura. 1994. *Reinventing the Family: Lesbian and Gay Parents.* New York: Crown.

Bem, Daryl J. 1996. "Exotic Becomes Erotic: A Developmental Theory of Sexual Orientation." *Pychological Review* 103:320–35.

Bigner, Jerry J. and R. Brooke Jacobsen. 1989. "Parenting Behaviors of Homosexual and Heterosexual Fathers." *Journal of Homosexuality* 18:73–86.

———. 1992. "Adult Responses to Child Behavior and Attitudes toward Fathering: Gay and Nongay Fathers." *Journal of Homosexuality* 23:99–112.

Black, Dan A., Gary Gates, Seth Sanders, and Lowell Taylor. 2000. "Demographics of the Gay and Lesbian Population in the United States: Evidence from Available Systematic Data Sources." *Demography* 37:139–54.

Black, Dan A., Hoda R. Maker, Seth G. Sanders, and Lowell Taylor. 1998. "The Effects of Sexual Orientation on Earnings." Working paper, Department of Economics, Gatton College of Business and Economics, University of Kentucky, Lexington, KY.

Blankenhorn, David. 1995. *Fatherless America: Confronting Our Most Urgent Social Problem.* New York: Basic.

Bonvillain, Nancy. 1998. *Women and Men: Cultural Constructs of Gender.* 2d ed. Upper Saddle River, NJ: Prentice Hall.

Bourne, Amy E. 1999. "Mothers of Invention." *San Francisco Daily Journal,* May 21, pp. 1, 9.

Boykin, Keith. 1996. *One More River to Cross: Black and Gay in America.* New York: Anchor.

Bozett, Frederick W. 1987a. "Children of Gay Fathers." Pp. 39–57 in *Gay and Lesbian Parents,* edited by F. W. Bozett. New York: Praeger.

———. 1987b. "Gay Fathers." Pp. 3–22 in *Gay and Lesbian Parents,* edited by F. W. Bozett. New York: Praeger.

———. 1989. "Gay Fathers: A Review of the Literature." Pp. 137–62 in *Homosexuality and the Family,* edited by F. W. Bozett. New York: Haworth Press.

Brettell, Caroline B. and Carolyn F. Sargent, eds. 1997. *Gender in Cross-Cultural Perspective.* 2d ed. Upper Saddle River, NJ: Prentice Hall.

Brewaeys, A., I. Ponjaert, E. V. Van Hall, and S. Golombok. 1997. "Donor Insemination: Child Development and Family Functioning in Lesbian Mother Families." *Human Reproduction* 12:1349–59.

Cameron, Paul and Kirk Cameron. 1996. "Homosexual Parents." *Adolescence* 31:757–76.

Cameron, Paul, Kirk Cameron, and Thomas Landess. 1996. "Errors by the American Psychiatric Association, the American Psychological Association, and the National Educational Association in Representing Homosexuality in Amicus Briefs about Amendment 2 to the U.S. Supreme Court." *Psychological Reports* 79:383–404.

Cantor, David. 1994. *The Religious Right: The Assault on Tolerance and Pluralism in America.* New York: Anti-Defamation League.

Cantu, Lionel. 2000. "Entre Hombres/Between Men: Latino Masculinities and Homosexualities." Pp. 224–46 in *Gay Masculinities,* edited by P. Nardi. Thousand Oaks, CA: Sage.

Carrier, Joseph. 1992. "Miguel: Sexual Life History of a Gay Mexican American." Pp. 202–24 in *Gay Culture in America: Essays from the Field,* edited by G. Herdt. Boston, MA: Beacon.

Chan, Raymond W., Risa C. Brooks, Barbara Raboy, and Charlotte J. Patterson. 1998. "Division of Labor among Lesbian and Heterosexual Parents: Associations with Children's Adjustment." *Journal of Family Psychology* 12:402–19.

Chan, Raymond W., Barbara Raboy, and Charlotte J. Patterson. 1998. "Psychosocial Adjustment among Children Conceived Via Donor Insemination by Lesbian and Heterosexual Mothers." *Child Development* 69:443–57.

Chodorow, Nancy. 1978. *The Reproduction of Mothering: Psychoanalysis and the Sociology of Gender.* Berkeley, CA: University of California Press.

Clarke, Victoria. 2000. "Sameness and Difference in Research on Lesbian Parenting." Working paper, Women's Studies Research Group, Department of Social Sciences, Loughborough University, Leicestershire, UK.

Downey, Douglas B. and Brian Powell. 1993. "Do Children in Single-Parent Households Fare Better Living with Same-Sex Parents?" *Journal of Marriage and the Family* 55:55–72.

Dunne, Gillian A. 1999. "What Difference Does 'Difference' Make? Lesbian Experience of Work and Family Life." Pp. 189–221 in *Relating Intimacies,* edited by J. Seymour and P. Bagguley. New York: St. Martin's.

————. 2000. "Opting into Motherhood: Lesbians Blurring the Boundaries and Transforming the Meaning of Parenthood and Kinship." *Gender and Society* 14:11–35.

Falk, Patrick J. 1994. "The Gap Between Psychosocial Assumptions and Empirical Research in Lesbian-Mother Child Custody Cases." Pp. 131–56 in *Redefining Families: Implications for Children's Development,* edited by A. E. Gottfried and A. W. Gottfried. New York: Plenum.

Flaks, David K., Ilda Ficher, Frank Masterpasqua, and Gregory Joseph. 1995. "Lesbians Choosing Motherhood: A Comparative Study of Lesbian and Heterosexual Parents and Their Children." *Developmental Psychology* 31:105–14.

Furstenberg, Frank F., Jr. and Andrew J. Cherlin. 1991. *Divided Families.* Cambridge, MA: Harvard University Press.

Gallagher, Maggie. "The Gay-Parenting Science." *New York Post,* March 30, p. 3.

Giddens, Anthony. 1992. *The Transformation of Intimacy: Sexuality, Love and Eroticism in Modern Societies.* Stanford, CA: Stanford University Press.

Gilligan, Carol. 1982. *In a Different Voice: Psychological Theory and Women's Development.* Cambridge, MA: Harvard University Press.

Golombok, Susan, Ann Spencer, and Michael Rutter. 1983. "Children in Lesbian and Single-Parent Households: Psychosexual and Psychiatric Appraisal." *Journal of Child Psychology and Psychiatry* 24:551–72.

Golombok, Susan and Fiona Tasker. 1996. "Do Parents Influence the Sexual Orientation of Their Children? Findings From a Longitudinal Study of Lesbian Families." *Developmental Psychology* 32:3–11.

Green, Richard, Jane Barclay Mandel, Mary E. Hotvedt, James Gray and Laurel Smith. 1986. "Lesbian Mothers and Their Children: A Comparison with Solo Parent Heterosexual Mothers and Their Children." *Archives of Sexual Behavior* 15:167–84.

Green, G. Dorsey and Frederick W. Bozett. 1991. "Lesbian Mothers and Gay Fathers." Pp. 197–214 in *Homosexuality: Research Implications for Public Policy,* edited by J. C. Gonsiorek and J. D. Weinrich. Newbury Park, CA: Sage.

Greene, Beverly and Nancy Boyd-Franklin. 1996. "African-American Lesbians: Issues in Couple Therapy." Pp. 251–71 in *Lesbians and Gays in Couples and Families: A Handbook for Therapists,* edited by J. Laird and R. J. Green. San Francisco, CA: Jossey-Bass.

Groze, Vic. 1991. "Adoption and Single Parents: A Review." *Child Welfare* 70:321–32.

Harris, Judith Rich. 1998. *The Nurture Assumption: Why Children Turn Out the Way They Do.* New York: Free Press.

Harris, Mary B. and Pauline H. Turner. 1986. "Gay and Lesbian Parents." *Journal of Homosexuality* 12:101–13.

Hawkeswood, William. 1997. *One of the Children: Gay Black Men in Harlem.* Berkeley, CA: University of California Press.

Herek, Gregory M. 1998. "Bad Science in the Service of Stigma: A Critique of the Cameron Group's Survey Studies." Pp. 223–55 in *Stigma and Sexual Orientation: Understanding Prejudice against Lesbians, Gay Men, and Bisexuals,* edited by G. M. Herek. Thousand Oaks, CA: Sage.

————. 2000. "Paul Cameron Fact Sheet" (Copyright 1997–2000 by G. M. Herek). Retrieved (http://psychology.ucdavis.edu/rainbow/html/facts_cameron_sheet.html).

Hoeffer, Beverly. 1981. "Children's Acquisition of Sex-Role Behavior in Lesbian-Mother Families." *American Journal of Orthopsychiatry* 51:536–44.

Hotvedt, Mary E. and Jane Barclay Mandel. 1982. "Children of Lesbian Mothers." Pp. 275–91 in *Homosexuality, Social, Psychological, and Biological Issues,* edited by W. Paul. Beverly Hills, CA: Sage.

Huggins, Sharon L. 1989. "A Comparative Study of Self-Esteem of Adolescent Children of Divorced Lesbian Mothers and Divorced Heterosexual Mothers." Pp. 123–35 in *Homosexuality and the Family,* edited by F. W. Bozett. New York: Haworth.

Jenny, Carole, Thomas A. Roesler, and Kimberly L. Poyer. 1994. "Are Children at Risk for Sexual Abuse by Homosexuals?" *Pediatrics* 94:41–44.

Katz, Jonathan Ned. 1995. *The Invention of Heterosexuality*. New York: Dutton.

Kinsey, Alfred C., Wardell B. Pomeroy, and Clyde E. Martin. 1948. *Sexual Behavior in the Human Male*. Philadelphia, PA: W. B. Saunders.

Kinsey, Alfred C., Wardell B. Pomeroy, Clyde E. Martin, and Paul H. Gebhard. 1953. *Sexual Behavior in the Human Female*. Philadelphia, PA: W. B. Saunders.

Kitzinger, Celia. 1987. *The Social Construction of Lesbianism*. London, England: Sage.

———. 1989. "Liberal Humanism as an Ideology of Social Control: The Regulation of Lesbian Identities." Pp. 82–98 in *Texts of Identity*, edited by J. Shorter and K. Gergen. London, England: Sage.

———. 1994. "Should Psychologists Study Sex Differences? Editor's Introduction: Sex Differences Research: Feminist Perspectives." *Feminism and Psychology* 4:501–506.

Kitzinger, Celia and Adrian Coyle. 1995. "Lesbian and Gay Couples: Speaking of Difference." *The Psychologist* 8:64–69.

Kweskin, Sally L. and Alicia S. Cook. 1982. "Heterosexual and Homosexual Mothers' Self-Described Sex-Role Behavior and Ideal Sex-Role Behavior in Children." *Sex Roles* 8:967–75.

Laumann, Edward O., John H. Gagnon, Robert T. Michael, and Stuart Michaels. 1994. *The Social Organization of Sexuality: Sexual Practices in the United States*. Chicago, IL: University of Chicago Press.

———. 1995. *National Health and Social Life Survey, 1992* [MRDF]. Chicago IL: University of Chicago and National Opinion Research Center [producer]. Ann Arbor, MI: Inter-university Consortium for Political and Social Research [distributor].

Lerner, Robert and Althea K. Nagai. 2000. "Out of Nothing Comes Nothing: Homosexual and Heterosexual Marriage Not Shown to be Equivalent for Raising Children." Paper presented at the Revitalizing the Institution of Marriage for the 21st Century conference, Brigham Young University, March, Provo, UT.

Lynch, F. R. 1992. "Nonghetto Gays: An Ethnography of Suburban Homosexuals." Pp. 165–201 in *Gay Culture in America: Essays from the Field*, edited by G. Herdt. Boston, MA: Beacon.

McLanahan, Sara S. 1985. "Family Structure and the Reproduction of Poverty." *American Journal of Sociology* 90:873–901.

McNeill, Kevin P., Beth M. Rienzi, and Augustine Kposowa. 1998. "Families and Parenting: A Comparison of Lesbian and Heterosexual Mothers." *Psychological Reports* 82:59–62.

Michael, Robert T., John H. Gagnon, Edward O. Laumann, and Gina Bari Kolata. 1994. *Sex in America: A Definitive Survey*. Boston, MA: Little Brown.

Miller, Judith Ann, R. Brooke Jacobsen, and Jerry J. Bigner. 1982. "The Child's Home Environment for Lesbian vs. Heterosexual Mothers: A Neglected Area of Research." *Journal of Homosexuality* 7:49–56.

Mitchell, Valory. 1998. "The Birds, the Bees…and the Sperm Banks: How Lesbian Mothers Talk with Their Children about Sex and Reproduction." *American Journal of Orthopsychiatry* 68:400–409.

O'Connell, Ann. 1994. "Voices from the Heart: The Developmental Impact of a Mother's Lesbianism on Her Adolescent Children." *Smith College Studies in Social Work* 63:281–99.

Ortner, Sherry and Harriet Whitehead. 1981. *Sexual Meanings: The Cultural Construction of Gender and Sexuality*. Cambridge, England: Cambridge University Press.

Patterson, Charlotte J. 1992. "Children of Lesbian and Gay Parents." *Child Development* 63:1025–42.

———. 1994. "Children of the Lesbian Baby Boom: Behavioral Adjustment, Self-Concepts and Sex Role Identity." Pp, 156–75 in *Lesbian and Gay Psychology: Theory, Research, and Clinical Applications*, edited by B. Green and G. M. Herek. Thousand Oaks, CA: Sage.

———. 1995. "Families of the Lesbian Baby Boom: Parents' Division of Labor and Children's Adjustment." *Developmental Psychology* 31:115–23.

———. 1996. "Lesbian and Gay Parents and Their Children." Pp. 274–304 in *The Lives of Lesbians, Gays, and Bisexuals: Children to Adults*, edited by R. C. Savin-Williams and K, M. Cohen. Fort Worth, TX: Harcourt Brace College Publishers.

Patterson, Charlotte J. and Lisa V. Freil. 2000. "Sexual Orientation and Fertility." In *Infertility in the*

Modern World: Biosocial Perspectives, edited by G. Bentley and N. Mascie-Taylor. Cambridge, England: Cambridge University Press.

Peterson, John. 1992. "Black Men and Their Same-Sex Desires and Behaviors." Pp. 147–64 in *Gay Culture in America: Essays From the Field,* edited by G. Herdt. Boston, MA: Beacon.

Polikoff, Nancy D. 1990. "This Child Does Have Two Mothers: Redefining Parenthood to Meet the Needs of Children in Lesbian-Mother and Other Nontraditional Families." *Georgetown Law Journal* 78:459–575.

Popenoe, David. 1993. "American Family Decline, 1960–1990: A Review and Appraisal." *Journal of Marriage and the Family* 55:527–41.

———. 1996. *Life without Father.* New York: Free Press.

Price, Deb. 1999. "Middle Ground Emerges for Gay Couples." *Detroit News,* October 4.

Raftery, Adrian E. 1995. "Bayesian Model Selection in Social Research (with Discussion)." *Sociological Methodology* 25:111–95.

Rand, Catherine, Dee L. R. Graham and Edna I. Rawlings. 1982. "Psychological Health and Factors the Court Seeks to Control in Lesbian Mother Custody Trials." *Journal of Homosexuality* 8:27–39.

Rothblum, Ester D. 1994. "'I Only Read About Myself on Bathroom Walls': The Need for Research on the Mental Health of Lesbians and Gay Men.'" *Journal of Consulting and Clinical Psychology* 62:213–20.

Seidman, Steven. 1997. *Difference Troubles: Queering Social Theory and Sexual Politics.* New York: Cambridge University Press.

Shireman, Joan F. 1996. "Single Parent Adoptive Homes." *Children and Youth Services Review* 18:23–36.

Simons, Ronald L. and Associates. 1996. *Understanding Differences between Divorced and Intact Families: Stress, Interactions, and Child Outcome.* Thousand Oaks, CA: Sage.

Steckel, Alisa. 1987. "Psychosocial Development of Children of Lesbian Mothers." Pp. 75–85 in *Gay and Lesbian Parents,* edited by F. W. Bozett. New York: Praeger.

Sullivan, Maureen. 1996. "Rozzie and Harriet?: Gender and Family Patterns of Lesbian Coparents." *Gender and Society* 10:747–67.

Sweet, James and Larry Bumpass. 1996. *The National Survey of Families and Households—Waves 1 and 2: Data Description and Documentation.* Center for Demography and Ecology, Univeristy of Wisconsin–Madison, Madison, WI (http://www/ssc.wisc.edu/nsfh/home. htm).

Tasker, Fiona L. and Susan Golombok. 1997. *Growing Up in a Lesbian Family.* New York: Guilford.

U.S. Census Bureau. 1999. "Population Estimates Program." Population Division, Washington, DC. Retrieved January 5, 2000 (http://www.census.gov/population/estimates/nation/intfile2–1.txt, and natdoc.txt).

Wald, Michael S. 1999. "Same-Sex Couples: Marriage, Families, and Children, An Analysis of Proposition 22, The Knight Initiative." Stanford Institute for Research on Women and Gender, Stanford University, Stanford, CA.

Wardle, Lynn D. 1997. "The Potential Impact of Homosexual Parenting on Children." *University of Illinois Law Review* 1997:833–919.

Weeks, Jeffrey, Brian Heaphy, and Catherine Donovan. Forthcoming. *Families of Choice and Other Life Experiments: The Intimate Lives of Non-Heterosexuals.* Cambridge, England: Cambridge University Press.

Wells, Jess. 1997. *Lesbians Raising Sons.* Los Angeles, CA: Alyson Books.

Whitehead, Barbara Dafoe. 1993. "Dan Quayle Was Right." *Atlantic Monthly,* April, vol. 271, pp. 47–50.

Woodruff, Robin. 1998. Testimony re: "Subcommittee Meeting to Accept Empirical Data and Expert Testimony Concerning Homosexual Foster Parents." Hearing at the Office of the Attorney General, September 9, 1998. Little Rock, AK. Available from the authors on request.

PART 6

The Gendered Classroom

Along with the family, educational institutions—from primary schools to secondary schools, colleges, universities, and professional schools—are central arenas in which gender is reproduced. Students learn more than the formal curriculum—they learn what the society considers appropriate behavior for men and women. And for adults, educational institutions are gendered workplaces, where the inequalities found in other institutions are also found.

From the earliest grades, students' experiences in the classroom differ by gender. Boys are more likely to interrupt, to be called upon by teachers, and to have any misbehavior overlooked. Girls are more likely to remain obedient and quiet and to be steered away from math and science.

All three of the contributions to this section are based on field research. The researchers sat down and talked with boys and girls about what they thought, how they understood both gender difference and gender inequality. Wayne Martino's portraits of middle schoolers are surprising in their gender conformity, especially for the boys. He finds that these discourses are what lie behind boy's difficulties in school, not some putative feminist agenda to keep boys down. Redro Noguera suggests some of the ways those pressures to contorm work themselves out somewhat differently for different groups of boys, and how the current "boy crisis" is really a crisis of race and ethnicity. And Diane Reay takes on the new research on girls' aggression and finds that while both boys and girls can be mean and aggressive, there is a wider range of acceptable identities for girls than there may be for boys. Perhaps thanks to feminism, which did, after all, open up a wider array of possible futures for women, young girls have a wider range of identities from which to choose.

"Spice Girls," "Nice Girls," "Girlies," and "Tomboys": Gender Discourses, Girls' Cultures, and Femininities in the Primary Classroom

DIANE REAY

This article attempts to demonstrate that contemporary gendered power relations are more complicated and contradictory than any simplistic binary discourse of "the girls versus the boys" suggests (Heath, 1999). Although prevailing dominant discourses identify girls as "the success story of the 1990s" (Wilkinson, 1994), this small-scale study of a group of 7-year-old girls attending an inner London primary school suggests that, particularly when the focus is on the construction of heterosexual femininities, it is perhaps premature always to assume that "girls are doing better than boys." While girls may be doing better than boys in examinations, this article indicates that their learning in the classroom is much broader than the National Curriculum and includes aspects that are less favourable in relation to gender equity. Although masculinities are touched on in this article, this is only in as far as they relate to girls. This deliberate bias is an attempt to refocus on femininities at a time when masculinities appear to be an ever-growing preoccupation within education.

However, although the subjects of this research are 14 girls, the position the article takes is that femininities can only be understood relationally. There is a co-dependence between femininities and masculinities which means that neither can be fully understood in isolation from the other. The article therefore explores how a particular group of primary-aged girls is positioned, primarily in relation to dominant discourses of femininity but also in relation to those of masculinity. There is also an attempt to map out their relationships to transgressive but less prevalent discourses of femininity, which in a variety of ways construct girls as powerful. The findings from such a small-scale study are necessarily tentative and no generalised assertions are made about girls as a group. Rather, the aim is to use the girls' narratives and their experiences in school and, to a lesser extent, those of the boys, to indicate some ways in which the new orthodoxy, namely that girls are doing better than boys, does not tell us the whole story about gender relations in primary classrooms.

The last decade has seen a growing popular and academic obsession with boys' underachievement both in the UK and abroad (Katz, 1999; Smithers, 1999). However, as Lyn Yates points out, much of the "underachieving boys' discourse fails either to deal adequately with power or to see femininity and masculinity as relational phenomena" (Yates, 1997). For instance, within the explosion of concern with masculinities in academia, there has been little focus on the consequences for girls of "boys behaving badly." As Gaby Weiner and her colleagues argue:

new educational discourses have silenced demands for increased social justice for girls and women characterised by increasing resistance to policies and practices focusing specifically on them. (Weiner et al., 1997, p. 15)

Jill Blackmore describes attempts by some male academics in Australia to develop programmes for boys which seek to depict boys as powerless in the face of the progress and success of feminism and girls, and, indeed, as victims of their own male psychology (Blackmore, 1999). Jane Kenway writes more broadly of "the lads' movement" in Australia; a general resurgence of concern that boys and men are getting an unfair deal (Kenway, 1995). In Britain, there has been a growing alarm about "boys doing badly" that preoccupies both mainstream and feminist academics alike (Epstein et al., 1998). What gets missed out in these current concerns is the specificity of the "failing boy" and the ways in which other groups of males continue to maintain their social advantage and hold on to their social power (Arnot et al., 1999; Lucey & Walkerdine, 1999). It is within this context of contemporary preoccupation with boys that this article attempts to problematise issues surrounding gender equity and, in particular, to challenge the view that in millennial Britain it is boys rather than girls who are relatively disadvantaged.

The Research Study

The article is based on data from a 1-year study, conducted over the academic year 1997/98, of children in a Year 3 class in an inner-city primary school. 3R comprised 26 children, 14 girls and 12 boys. There were five middle-class children, three girls and two boys, all white apart from Amrit who was Indian. The 21 working-class children were more ethnically mixed. As well as one Somalian and two boys of mixed parentage, there were four Bengali children, three boys and one girl. The social class attribution of the children was based on parental occupations but was also confirmed by information provided by the class teacher. Fifteen of the children were entitled to free school meals. The school is surrounded by 1960s and 1970s public housing estates from which most of its intake is drawn, and indeed, 14 of the children in 3R lived on one of these five estates.

I spent one day a week over the course of the year engaged in participant observation in both the classroom and the playground, amassing over 200 pages of field notes. Additionally, I interviewed all the children, both individually and in focus groups. I also carried out group work activities in which children both wrote and drew on a range of topics from playground games to best friends. As James et al. point out:

> Talking with children about the meanings they themselves attribute to their paintings or asking them to write a story allows children to engage more productively with our research questions using the talents which they possess. (James et al., 1998, p. 189)

The unequal relationship between researcher and researched is compounded when the researcher is an adult and the researched a child. In order to mitigate at least some of the power differentials I organised workshops for the children in which I taught simple questionnaire design and interviewing techniques. The children then compiled their own questionnaires so that they could interview each other. These interviews, as well as those I conducted, 84 overall, were tape-recorded and transcribed. The class teacher and I also collected sociogram data, which enabled us to map out the children's friendship networks and work relationships.

Gender Discourses

Many writers on education have attempted to provide a variety of conceptual tools in order to understand educational contexts and processes (Ball, 1994; Maclure, 1994). A key debate amongst educational researchers has been between structuralist and post-structuralist approaches. Although often these two conceptual approaches are seen as opposing perspectives, in this article, I use and combine what I perceive to be the strengths of both positions to illuminate the ways in which girls both construct themselves, and are constructed, as feminine (see also, Walkerdine, 1991, 1997; Williams, 1997; Walkerdine et al., 2000 for similar approaches). As Davies et al. (1997) assert, power is both located in the structural advantage of individuals and also exercised partly through the construction of discourses.

Multiple discourses contribute not only to how researchers appreciate the conditions of childhood but also to how children come to view themselves (James et al., 1998). Post-structuralist feminists have explored extensively the ways in which different discourses can position girls (Davies, 1993; Hey, 1997; Walkerdine, 1997). It is important to recognise that there are many competing gender discourses, some of which have more power and potency than others for particular groups of girls (Francis, 1998). Such processes of discursive recognition, of feeling a better fit within one discourse than another (Francis, 1999), are influenced by social class. Similarly, gender discourses are taken up differentially by different ethnic groupings. It is also important to stress that girls can position themselves differently in relation to gender discourses according to the peer group context they find themselves in. For example, it soon became evident in my research that girls assume different positions depending on whether they are in single- or mixed-sex contexts. As Gee and his colleagues assert:

> There are innumerable discourses in modern societies: different sorts of street gangs, elementary schools and classrooms, academic disciplines and their sub-specialities, police, birdwatchers, ethnic groups, genders, executives, feminists, social classes and sub-classes, and so on and so-forth. Each is composed of some set of related social practices and social identities (or positions). Each discourse contracts complex relations of complicity, tension and opposition with other discourses. (Gee et al., 1996, p. 10)

I found similar "complex relations of complicity, tension and opposition" in relation to the nexus of gender discourses that these girls draw on. Yet, any local discursive nexus is framed by a wider social context within which, as Valerie Hey (1997) points out, there is a lack of powerful public discourses for girls, leaving them caught between schooling which denies difference and compulsory heterosexuality which is fundamentally invested in producing it. If this gives the impression of a fluid situation in relation to how contemporary girls position themselves as female, there is also substantial evidence of continuities in which, at least for the girls in this research, conformist discourses continue to exert more power than transgressive or transformative ones.

Masculinities in the Classroom: Setting the Context

Although the main focus of this article is how gender discourses position girls at school, in order to understand femininities in this primary classroom, the ways in which masculinities are being played out cannot be ignored. I want to start with two short excerpts from boys. Josh and David, two white, middle-class, 7-year-old boys, interviewed each other about what they like most and least about being a boy:

> J: David, what do you like most about being a boy?
> D: Well, it must be that it's much easier to do things than being a girl, that's what I think. You get to do much better things.
> J: So you think you find being a boy more interesting than being a girl? Is that what you're saying?
> D: Yes because it's boring being a girl.
> J: OK, and what do you like least about being a boy?
> D: Well, I don't know, I can't think of anything.
> J: Well, can't you think really—there must be something.
> D: I'll think [long pause]. Well, it's easier to hurt yourself.
> D: OK What do you like most about being a boy?
> J: I'd probably say that it's better being a boy because they have more interesting things to do and it's more exciting for them in life I find.
> D: Yes, I see. What do you like least about being a boy?
> J: Ohh I'd probably say not being so attractive as girls probably I'd say they're much more attractive than boys.

Josh and David were the only middle-class boys in a Year 3 class of predominantly working-class children. Existing research has found that the culturally exalted form of masculinity varies from school to school and is informed by the local community

(Skelton, 1997; Connolly, 1998). These two boys were adjusting to a predominantly working-class, inner-city peer group in which dominant local forms of masculinity were sometimes difficult for both to negotiate, but in particular, for David (for one thing, he did not like football). They both also found the low priority given to academic work among the other boys problematic. Even so, they were clear that it was still better being a boy.

Both boys, despite their social class positioning, were popular among the peer group. In particular, Josh commanded a position of power and status in the peer group which was virtually unchallenged (see also Reay, 1990). Sociogram data collected from all the children in the class positioned him as the most popular child, not only with the working-class boys in the class but also with the girls. David's positioning is more difficult to understand. His particular variant of middle-class masculinity was far less acceptable to his working-class peers than Josh's. He was studious and hated games. In the exercise where children drew and described their favourite playground activity, David sketched a single figure with a bubble coming out of his head with "thoughts" inside. He annotated it with "I usually like walking about by myself and I'm thinking." However, within the confines of the classroom, for much of the time, he retained both status and power, paradoxically through a combination of being male and clever. When the girls were asked to nominate two boys and two girls they would most like to work with, David was the second most popular male choice after Josh. However, he was the most popular choice with the other boys. The complex issues as to why these two boys were popular when their masculinities did not fit the dominant one within the male peer group are beyond the brief of this article. Rather, what is salient is the relevance of their positioning within the peer group for the group of girls who are the article's main protagonists.

Although the focus has been on "the others" within masculinity, black and white working-class boys (Willis, 1977; Sewell, 1997), it is the association of normativity with white, middle-class masculinity that seems most difficult for girls

to challenge effectively. Disruptive, failing boys' behaviour has given girls an unexpected window of opportunity through which some variants of femininities can be valorised over specific pathologised masculinities, particularly within the arena of educational attainment. Both girls and boys were aware of discourses which position girls as more mature and educationally focused than boys and regularly drew on them to make sense of gender differences in the classroom (see also Pattman & Phoenix, 1999). What seems not to have changed is the almost unspoken acceptance of white, middle-class masculinity as the ideal that all those "others"—girls as well as black and white working-class boys—are expected to measure themselves against. Popular discourses position both masculinity and the middle classes as under siege, suggesting an erosion of both male and class power bases (Bennett, 1996; Coward, 1999). While there have been significant improvements in the direction of increasing equity, particularly in the area of gender, the popularity of Josh and David, combined with the uniform recognition among the rest of the peer group that they were the cleverest children in the class, suggests that popular discourses may mask the extent to which white, middle-class male advantages in both the sphere of education and beyond continue to be sustained.

However, 10 of the 12 boys in 3R were working class. The "failing boys" compensatory culture of aggressive "laddism" (Jackson, 1998) had already started to be played out at the micro-level of this primary classroom. The working-class, white and mixed race boys were more preoccupied with football than the academic curriculum (see also Skelton, 1999). When they were not playing football in the playground, they would often be surreptitiously exchanging football cards in the classroom. Alongside regular jockeying for position within the male peer group, which occasionally escalated into full-blown fights, there was routine, casual labelling of specific girls as stupid and dumb. The three Bengali boys at the bottom of this particular male peer group hierarchy compensated by demonising, in particular, the three middle-class girls. Their strategy echoes that of the subordinated youth in Wight's (1996) study, where in order to gain the approval and acceptance of their dominant male peers, they endeavoured to become active subjects in a sexist discourse which objectified girls.

Sugar and Spice and All Things Nice?

3R had four identifiable groups of girls—the "nice girls," the "girlies," the "spice girls" and the "tomboys" (see Figure 6.1).

The latter two groups had decided on both their own naming as well as those of the "girlies" and the "nice girls," descriptions which were generally seen as derogatory by both girls and boys. "Girlies" and "nice girls" encapsulate "the limited and limiting discourse of conventional femininity" (Brown, 1998), and in this Year 3 class, although there was no simple class divide, the "nice girls" were composed of Donna, Emma and Amrit, the only three middle-class girls in 3R, plus a fluctuating group of one to two working-class girls. The "nice girls," seen by everyone, including themselves, as hard-working and well behaved, exemplify the constraints of a gendered and classed discourse which afforded them the benefits of culture, taste and cleverness but little freedom.

Prevalent discourses which work with binaries of mature girls and immature boys and achieving girls and underachieving boys appear on the surface to be liberating for girls. However, the constraints were evident in the "nice girls'" self-surveillant, hypercritical attitudes to both their behaviour and their schoolwork; attitudes which were less apparent amongst other girls in the class. It would appear that this group of 7-year-old, predominantly middle-class girls had already begun to develop the intense preoccupation with academic success that other researchers describe in relation to middle-class, female, secondary school pupils (Walkerdine et al., 2000).

Contemporary work on how masculinities and femininities are enacted in educational contexts stresses the interactions of gender with class, race and sexuality (Mac an Ghaill, 1988; Hey, 1997; Connolly, 1998). Sexual harassment in 3R (a whole gamut of behaviour which included uninvited touching of girls and sexualised name-calling) was primarily directed at the "girlies" and was invariably perpetuated by boys who were subordinated within the prevailing masculine hegemony either because of their race or social class. However, while sexual harassment was an

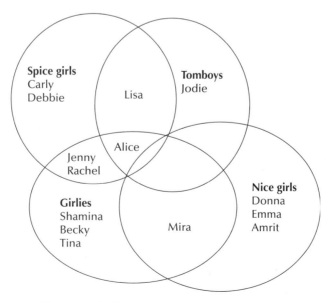

Figure 6.1. Girl groups in 3R.

infrequent occurrence, identifying the "nice girls" as a contaminating presence was not. In the playground, the three working-class Bengali boys were positioned as subordinate to the white and Afro-Caribbean boys; for example, they were often excluded from the football games on the basis that they were not skilful enough. These three boys constructed the "nice girls" as a polluting, contagious "other." They would regularly hold up crossed fingers whenever one of these girls came near them. As a direct result, the "nice girls" began to use the classroom space differently, taking circuitous routes in order to keep as far away from these boys as possible. Barrie Thorne (1993) found similar gender practices in which girls were seen as "the ultimate source of contamination." Like the girls in Thorne's research, the "nice girls" did not challenge the boys but rather developed avoidance strategies which further circumscribed their practices.

Being one of the "nice girls" had derogatory connotations for working-class girls as well as working-class boys. Alice, in particular, was adamant that she could not contemplate them as friends because they were "too boring," while in one of the focus group discussions, Jodie, Debbie and Carly all agreed that "no one wants to be a nice girl." Their views reflect the findings of feminist research which position "being nice" as specific to the formulation of white, middle-class femininity (Jones, 1993; Griffin, 1995; Kenway et al., 1999). For a majority of the working-class girls in the class, being a "nice girl" signified an absence of the toughness and attitude that they were aspiring to.

This is not to construct the "nice girls" as passive in relation to other groups in the class. They often collaborated with Josh and David on classwork and were vocal about the merits of their approach to schoolwork over those of other girls in the class:

> EMMA: The other girls often mess around and be silly, that's why Alice and Lisa never get their work finished.
> DONNA: Yes we're more sensible than they are.
> EMMA: And cleverer.

However, the dominant peer group culture in the classroom was working class and, while this had little impact on the popularity of Josh and David, it did have repercussions for the status and social standing of the "nice girls" within the peer group.

"The limited and limiting discourse of conventional femininity" also had a powerful impact on the "girlies," a group of three working-class girls (two white and one Bengali). Kenway et al., (1999) write about "the sorts of femininities which unwittingly underwrite hegemonic masculinity" (p. 120). Certainly, the "girlies," with their "emphasised femininity" (Connell, 1987, p. 187), were heavily involved in gender work which even at the age of 7 inscribed traditional heterosexual relations. Paul Connolly (1998) describes the ways in which sexual orientation and relations defined through boyfriends and girlfriends seems to provide an important source of identity for young children. This was certainly the case for the "girlies." These girls were intensely active in the work of maintaining conventional heterosexual relationships through the writing of love letters, flirting and engaging in regular discussions of who was going out with who. They were far more active in such maintenance work than the boys.

Both the "girlies" and the "nice girls" were subject to "discourses of denigration" circulating among the wider peer group (Blackmore, 1999, p. 136). In individual interviews, many of the boys and a number of the other girls accounted for the "nice girls'" unpopularity by describing them as "boring" and "not fun to be with," while the "girlies" were variously described by boys as "stupid" and "dumb." While the boys were drawing on a male peer group discourse which positioned the "girlies" as less intelligent than they were, the "girlies" were far from "stupid" or "dumb." Although not as scholarly as the "nice girls," they were educationally productive and generally achieved more highly than their working-class male counterparts. Rather, the working-class discourse of conventional femininity within which they were enmeshed operated to elide their academic achievement within the peer group.

Discourses of conventional femininity also seemed to have consequences for the two Asian girls in the class. Amrit, who was Indian, was from a middle-class background while Shamina was Bengali and working class. Yet, both girls, despite their class differences, shared a high degree of circumscription in relation to the range of femininities available to them in the school context. As Shamina explained, "the spice girls and the tomboys are naughty. I am a good girl." In contrast to the other girls in the girls' focus group discussion, who all claimed to enjoy playing football, both Shamina and Amrit asserted that "football was a boys' game," and Amrit said, "It's not worth bothering with football. It's too boring. Me and my friends just sit on the benches and talk."

Heidi Mirza (1992) argues that the cultural construction of femininity among African-Caribbean girls fundamentally differs from the forms of femininity found among their white peers. In the case of Amrit and Shamina, there were substantial areas of overlap rather than fundamental differences. However, neither managed to carve out spaces in which to escape gender subordination from the boys in the ways that the "spice girls" and the "tomboys," both all-white groups, did. Racism and its impact on subjectivities may well be an issue here. Although it is impossible to make generalisations on the basis of two children, ethnicity, as well as class, appears to be an important consideration in the possibilities and performance of different femininities.

Membership of the "spice girls" revolved around two white, working-class girls, Carly and Debbie. Jenny, Rachel, Alice and Lisa were less consistently members of the group. Lisa and Alice would sometimes claim to be "tomboys" while Jenny and Rachel, when playing and spending time with the "girlies," and especially when Carly and Debbie were in trouble with adults in the school, would realign themselves as "girlies." Very occasionally, when she had quarrelled both with Carly and Debbie, and with Jodie, the one consistent tomboy among the girls, Alice too would reinvent herself as a "girlie."

Although there were many overlaps between both the practices and the membership of the "girlies" and the "spice girls," aspects of the "spice girls" interaction with the boys appeared to transgress prevailing gender regimes, while the "girlies'" behaviour followed a far more conformist pattern. Yet, the "spice girls" were, for much of the time, also active in constructing and maintaining traditional variants of heterosexuality. Their espousal of "girl power" did not exclude enthusiastic partaking of the boyfriend/girlfriend games. There was much flirting, letter writing, falling in and out of love and talk of broken hearts. However, they also operated beyond the boundaries of the "girlies'" more conformist behaviour when it came to interaction with the boys. Debbie and Carly, the most stalwart members of the "spice girls," both described the same activity—rating the boys—as their favourite playground game. As Carly explained, "you follow the boys around and give them a mark out of ten for how attractive they are."

The "spice girls" adherence to so-called girl power also allowed them to make bids for social power never contemplated by the "girlies" or the "nice girls." During a science lesson which involved experiments with different foodstuffs, including a bowl of treacle, Carly and Debbie jointly forced David's hand into the bowl because, as Carly asserted, "he is always showing off, making out he knows all the answers." This incident, which reduced David to tears and shocked the other children, served to confirm the class teacher in her view that the two girls "were a bad lot." The "girls with attitude" stance that Carly and Debbie so valued and their philosophy of "giving as good as they got" were reinterpreted by adults in the school as both inappropriate and counterproductive to learning. Paul Connolly (1998) points out that girls' assertive or disruptive behaviour tends to be interpreted more negatively than similar behaviour in boys, while Robin Lakoff (1975) has described how, when little girls "talk rough" like the boys do, they will normally be ostracised, scolded or made fun of. For the "spice girls," "doing it for themselves" in ways which ran counter to traditional forms of femininity resulted in them being labelled at various times by teachers in the staffroom as "real bitches," "a bad influence" and "little cows." The tendency Clarricoates found in 1978 for girls' misbehaviour to be "looked upon as a character defect, whilst boys' misbehaviour is viewed as a desire to assert themselves" was just as evident in teachers' discourses more than 20 years later.

Debbie and Carly were doubly invidiously positioned in relation to the "girls as mature discourse." They were perceived to be "too mature," as "far too knowing sexually" within adult discourses circulating in the school but they were also seen, unlike the boys and the majority of the girls in 3R, as "spiteful" and "scheming little madams" for indulging in behaviour typical of many of the boys. There were several incidents in the playground of sexual harassment of girls by a small group of boys. Most of the adults dismissed these as "boys mucking about." However, Carly and Debbie's attempts to invert regular processes of gender objectification, in which girls are routinely the objects of a male gaze, were interpreted by teachers as signs of "an unhealthy preoccupation with sex." Their predicament exemplifies the dilemma for girls of "seeking out empowering places within regimes alternatively committed to denying subordination or celebrating it" (Hey, 1997, p. 132). In this classroom, girls like Carly and Debbie seemed to tread a fine line between acceptable and unacceptable "girl power" behaviour. Overt heterosexuality was just about on the acceptable side of the line but retaliatory behaviour towards the boys was not.

Valerie Walkerdine (1997) describes how playful and assertive girls come to be understood as overmature and too precocious. Girls like Debbie and Carly, no less than the girls in Walkerdine's advertisements, occupy a space where girls have moved beyond being "nice" or "girlie." Rather, as sexual little women, they occupy a space where they can be bad. As Walkerdine points out, while it is certainly a space in which they can be exploited, it provides a space of power for little girls, although one which is also subject to discourses of denigration. The forms that denigration take are very different to those experienced by the "nice girls" or the "girlies" but become apparent in teachers' judgments of the two girls' behaviour.

"It's Better Being a Boy"— The Tomboys

The most intriguing case in my research was that of the "tomboys." The "tomboys" in Becky Francis's research study were depicted by another girl in the class as traitors to girlhood:

> Rather than rejecting the aspiration to maleness because it is "wrong" or "unnatural," Zoe argues that "girls are good enough," implying that her girlfriends want to be boys because they see males as superior, and that she is defending girlhood against this sexist suggestion. (Francis, 1998, p. 36)

As I have touched on earlier in the article, in 3R, there was a general assumption among the boys that maleness, if not a superior subject positioning, was a more desirable one. While, in particular the "spice girls," but also at various times both the "girlies" and "nice girls" defended girlhood against such claims, their stance was routinely undermined by the position adopted by the tomboys.

Jodie was the only girl in the class who was unwavering in her certainty that she was not a girl but a "tomboy," although a couple of the other girls in the class for periods of time decided that they were also "tomboys":

> JODIE: Girls are crap, all the girls in this class act all stupid and girlie.
> DIANE: So does that include you?
> JODIE: No, cos I'm not a girl, I'm a tomboy.

On the one hand, Jodie could be viewed as a budding "masculinised new woman at ease with male attributes" (Wilkinson, 1999, p. 37). Yet, her rejection of all things feminine could also be seen to suggest a degree of shame and fear of femininity. Jodie even managed to persuade Wayne and Darren, two of the boys in the class, to confirm her male status. Both, at different times, sought me out to tell me Jodie was "really a boy." It is difficult to know how to theorise such disruptions of normative gender positionings. Jodie's stance combines elements of resistance with recognition. She clearly recognised and responded to prevailing gender hierarchies which situate being male with having more power and status. Jodie appears to operate at the boundaries where femininity meets masculinity. She is what Barrie Thorne (1993) calls "active at the edges."

However, while Thorne reports that it was rarely used among her fourth and fifth graders, the term "tomboy" is frequently used in 3M as a marker of respect by both boys and girls. Being a "tomboy" seems to guarantee male friendship and male respect. Several of the working-class girls in the class, like Alice, appeared to move easily from taking up a position as a "tomboy" through to assuming a "girls with attitude" stance alongside Debbie and Carly to becoming a "girlie" and back again. One week Alice would come to school in army fatigues with her hair scraped back, the next, in Lycra with elaborately painted nails and carefully coiffured hair. However, Alice was unusual among the girls in ranging across a number of subject positions. For most of the girls, although they had choices, those choices seemed heavily circumscribed and provided little space for manoeuvre.

The regulatory aspects of the "girlies" and the "nice girls'" self-production as feminine were very apparent, yet the conformity of the "tomboys" to prevailing gender regimes was far more hidden. While it is important to recognise the transgressive qualities of identifying and rejecting traditional notions of femininity in Jodie's behaviour, the empowering aspects of being a "tomboy" also masked deeply reactionary features embedded in assuming such a gender position. Implicit in the concept of "tomboy" is a devaluing of traditional notions of femininity, a railing against the perceived limitations of being female. This is particularly apparent in Jodie's comments:

> JODIE: I don't really have any friends who are girls cos they don't like doing the things I like doing. I like football and stuff like that.
> DIANE: Don't girls like football?
> JODIE: Yeah, some of them, but they're no good at it.

Perhaps, in part, it is Jodie's obsession with football that contributes to her contradictory gender positionings. As Christine Skelton (1999) points out, there is a close association between football and hegemonic masculinities and, therefore, if Jodie is to be seen as "a football star," she needs to assume a male rather than a female subject positioning.

But there is another possible reading in which Jodie's preoccupation with football facilitates, rather than is the cause of, her flight from femininity. Michelle Fine and Pat Macpherson define girls' identification with football as "both a flight from femininity…and an association of masculinity with fairness, honesty, integrity and strength" (Fine & Macpherson, 1992, p. 197). The girls in their study would call each other boys as a compliment: "Girls can be good, bad or—best of all—they can be boys" (p. 200) and this was definitely a viewpoint Jodie adhered to. Jodie's individualised resistance can be set alongside Carly and Debbie's joint efforts to disrupt prevailing gender orders among the peer group. Yet, paradoxically, Jodie, no less than the "girlies," seemed engaged in a process of accommodating the boys. The means of accommodation may differ but the compliance with existing gender regimes remains. Madeline Arnot (1982) writes of the ways in which boys maintain the hierarchy of social superiority of masculinity by devaluing the female world. In 3R, Jodie was also involved in this maintenance work. Although her practices are not rooted in subordination to the boys, she is still acquiescent in prevailing gender hierarchies. Her practices, no less than those of the "girlies" and the "nice girls," are confirmatory of male superiority.

Connell writes that "it is perfectly logical to talk about masculine women or masculinity in women's lives, as well as men's" (Connell, 1995, p. 163). However, so-called "masculine" girls do not seem to disrupt but rather appear to endorse existing gender hierarchies. All the girls at various times were acting in ways which bolstered the boys' power at the expense of their own. Even Jodie's performance of a surrogate masculinity works to cement rather than transform the gender divide. As a consequence, the radical aspects of transgressive femininities like those of Jodie's are undermined by their implicit compliance with gender hierarchies. Being one of the boys seems to result in greater social power but it conscripts Jodie into processes Sharon Thompson (1994) identifies as "raging misogyny." In my field notes, there are 16 examples of Jodie asserting that "boys are better than girls." Jodie's case is an extreme example of the ways in which girls' ventriloquising of the dominant culture's denigration of femininity and female relations can serve to disconnect them from other girls (Brown, 1998).

Conclusion

Performing gender is not straightforward; rather, it is confusing. The seduction of binaries such as male:female, boy:girl often prevents us from seeing the full range of diversity and differentiation existing within one gender as well as between categories of male and female. Both the girls and boys in 3R were actively involved in the production of gendered identities, constructing gender through a variety and range of social processes (Kerfoot & Knight, 1994). Yet, within this "gender work," social and cultural differences generate the particular toolkit of cultural resources individual children have available to them. There is a multiplicity of femininities and masculinities available in this primary classroom. But this is not to suggest that these children have myriad choices of which variant of femininity and masculinity to assume. They do not. Class, ethnicity and emergent sexualities all play their part, and constrain as well as create options.

Pyke argues that:

Hierarchies of social class, race and sexuality provide additional layers of complication. They form the structural and cultural contexts in which gender is enacted in everyday life, thereby fragmenting gender into multiple masculinities and femininities. (Pyke, 1996, p. 531)

Yet, despite the multiple masculinities and femininities manifested in 3R, there is evidence of hegemonic masculinity in this classroom no less than outside in the wider social world. Within such a context, it makes sense for girls to seek to resist traditional discourses of subordinate femininity. Yet, attempting to take up powerful positions through articulation with, and investment in, dominant masculinities serves to reinforce rather than transform the gender divide. As a consequence, the prevailing gender order is only occasionally disrupted, in particular by the spice girls through their sex play and objectification of a number of the boys and also, paradoxically,

through their working-class status. Unlike the "nice girls" whose activities are circumscribed through being positioned by the boys as a contagious, polluting other, the "spice girls'" positioning as "rough" in relation to sensitive middle-class boys allows them to take up a "polluting" assignment (Douglas, 1966) and use it as a weapon to intimidate the boys.

The girls' struggle to make meaning of themselves as female constitutes a struggle in which gendered peer group hierarchies such as those in 3R position boys as "better" despite a mass of evidence to show they are neither as academically successful nor as well behaved as girls in the classroom. Peer group discourses constructed girls as harder working, more mature and more socially skilled. Yet, all the boys and a significant number of the girls, if not subscribing to the view that boys are better, adhered to the view that it is better being a boy. There are clearly confusions within the gender work in this classroom. To talk of dominant femininity is to generate a contradiction in terms because it is dominant versions of femininity which subordinate the girls to the boys. Rather, transgressive discourses and the deviant femininities they generate like Jodie's "tomboy" and Debbie and Carly's espousal of "girl power" accrue power in both the male and female peer group, and provide spaces for girls to escape gender subordination by the boys.

On the surface, gender relations in this classroom are continually churned up and realigned in a constant process of recomposition. But beneath, at a more subterranean level of knowing and making sense, both boys and girls seem to operate with entrenched dispositions in which being a boy is still perceived to be the more preferable subject positioning. Despite the contemporary focus, both within and without the classroom, on "girl power" (Arlidge, 1999), as Jean Anyon (1983) found almost 20 years ago, it appears that girls' subversions and transgressions are nearly always contained within, and rarely challenge, the existing structures. For much of the time, girls are "trapped in the very contradictions they would transcend." Girls' contestation may muddy the surface water of gender relations, but the evidence of this classroom indicates that the ripples only occasionally reach the murky depths of the prevailing gender order. Within both the localised and dominant discourses that these children draw on, being a boy is still seen as best by all the boys and a significant number of the girls.

Children may both create and challenge gender structures and meanings. However, for much of the time for a majority of the girls and boys in 3R, gender either operates as opposition or hierarchy or most commonly both at the same time. As Janet Holland and her colleagues found in relation to the adolescents in their study, the girls just as much as the boys in this class were "drawn into making masculinity powerful" (Holland et al., 1998, p. 30). The contemporary orthodoxy that girls are doing better than boys masks the complex messiness of gender relations in which, despite girls' better educational attainment, within this peer group, the prevalent view is still that it's better being a boy.

Despite the all-pervading focus on narrow, easily measured, learning outcomes in British state schooling, learning in classrooms is much wider than test results suggest. While test results indicate that girls are more successful educationally than boys, it appears that in this primary classroom girls and boys still learn many of the old lessons of gender relations which work against gender equity. Sue Heath (1999, p. 293) argues that there is a need for school-based work that sensitively addresses issues of gender identity and masculinities within a pro-feminist framework. There is also an urgent need for work that addresses the construction and performance of femininities.

References

Anyon, J. (1983) Intersections of gender and class: accommodation and resistance by working-class and affluent females to contradictory sex-role ideologies, in: S. Walker & L. Barton (Eds.) *Gender, Class and Education* (Lewes, Falmer Press).

Arlidge, J. (1999) Girl power gives boys a crisis of confidence, *Sunday Times*, 14 March.

Arnot, M. (1982) Male hegemony, social class and women's education, *Journal of Education*, 16, pp. 64–89.

Arnot, M., David, M. & Weiner, G. (1999) *Closing the Gender Gap: postwar education and social change* (Cambridge, Polity Press).

Ball, S. J. (1994) *Educational Reform* (Buckingham, Open University Press).

Bennett, C. (1996) The boys with the wrong stuff, *Guardian*, 6 November.

Blackmore, J. (1999) *Troubling Women: feminism, leadership and educational change* (Buckingham, Open University Press).

Brown, L. M. (1998) *Raising Their Voices: the politics of girls' anger* (Cambridge, MA, Harvard University Press).

Clarricoates, K. (1978) Dinosaurs in the classroom: a re-examination of some aspects of the "hidden" curriculum in primary schools, *Women's Studies International Forum*, 1, pp. 353–364.

Connell, R. W. (1987) *Gender and Power* (Sydney, Allen & Unwin).

——. (1995) *Masculinities* (Cambridge, Polity Press).

Connolly, P. (1998) *Racism, Gender Identities and Young Children* (London, Routledge).

Coward, R. (1999) The feminist who fights for the boys, *Sunday Times*, 20 June.

Davies, B. (1993) *Shards of Glass* (Sydney, Allen & Unwin).

Davies, P., Williams, J. & Webb, S. (1997) Access to higher education in the late twentieth century: policy, power and discourse, in: J. Williams (Ed.) *Negotiating Access to Higher Education* (Buckingham, Open University Press).

Douglas, M. (1966) *Purity and Danger: an analysis of concepts of pollution and taboo* (London, Routledge & Kegan Paul).

Epstein, D., Elwood, J., Hey, V. & Maw, J. (1998) *Failing Boys? Issues in Gender and Achievement* (Buckingham, Open University Press).

Fine, M. & Macpherson, P. (1992) Over dinner: feminism and adolescent female bodies, in: M. Fine (Ed.) *Disruptive Voices: the possibilities of feminist research* (Ann Arbor, MI, University of Michigan Press).

Francis, B. (1998) *Power Plays: primary school children's construction of gender, power and adult work* (Stoke-on-Trent, Trentham Books).

——. (1999) Modernist reductionism or poststructuralist relativism: can we move on? An evaluation of the arguments in relation to feminist educational research, *Gender and Education*, 11, pp. 381–394.

Heath, S. (1999) Watching the backlash: the problematisation of young women's academic success in 1990's Britain, *Discourse*, 20, pp. 249–266.

Hey, V. (1997) *The Company She Keeps: an ethnography of girls' friendship* (Buckingham, Open University Press).

Holland, J., Ramazanoglu, C., Sharpe, S. & Thomson, R. (1998) *The Male in the Head: young people, heterosexuality and power* (London, Tufnell Press).

Gee, J. P., Hull, G. & Lankshear, C. (1996) *The New Work Order* (London, Allen & Unwin).

Griffin, C. (1995) Absences that matter: constructions of sexuality in studies of young women friendship groups, paper presented at the *Celebrating Women's Friendship Conference*, Alcuin College, University of York, 8 April.

Jackson, D. (1998) Breaking out of the binary trap: boys' underachievement, schooling and gender relations, in: D. Epstein, J. Elwood, V. Hey & J. Maw (Eds.) *Failing Boys? Issues in Gender and Achievement* (Buckingham, Open University Press).

James, A., Jenks, C. & Prout, A. (1998) *Theorising Childhood* (Cambridge, Polity Press).

Jones, A. (1993) Becoming a "girl": post-structuralist suggestions for educational research, *Gender and Education*, 5, pp. 157–166.

Katz, A. (1999) Crisis of the "low can-do" boys, *Sunday Times*, 21 March.

Kenway, J. (1995) Masculinities in schools: under siege, on the defensive and under reconstruction, *Discourse*, 16, pp. 59–79.

Kenway, J. & Willis, S. with Blackmore, J. & Rennie, L. (1999) *Answering Back: girls, boys and feminism in schools* (London, Routledge).

Kerfoot, D. & Knight, D. (1994) Into the realm of the fearful: identity and the gender problematic, in: H. L. Radtke & H. J. Stam (Eds.) *Power/Gender: social relations in theory and practice* (London, Sage).

Lakoff, R. T. (1975) *Language and Woman's Place* (New York, Harper & Row).

Lucey, H. & Walkerdine, V. (1999) Boys' underachievement: social class and changing masculinities, in: T. Cox (Ed.) *Combating Educational Disadvantage* (London, Falmer Press).

Mac an Ghaill, M. (1988) *Young, Gifted and Black: student–teacher relations in the schooling of black youth* (Buckingham, Open University Press).

Maclure, M. (1994) Language and discourse: the embrace of uncertainty, *British Journal of Sociology of Education*, 15, pp. 283–300.

Mirza, S. H. (1992) *Young, Female and Black* (London, Routledge).

Pattman, R. & Phoenix, A. (1999) Constructing self by constructing the "other": 11–14 year old boys' narratives of girls and women, paper presented at the Gender and Education Conference, University of Warwick, 29–31 March.

Pyke, K. D. (1996) Class-based masculinities: the interdependence of gender, class and interpersonal power, *Gender & Society*, 10, pp. 527–549.

Reay, D. (1990) Working with boys, *Gender and Education*, 2, pp. 269–282.

Sewell, T. (1997) *Black Masculinities and Schooling: how black boys survive modern schooling* (Stoke-on-Trent, Trentham Books).

Skelton, C. (1997) Primary boys and hegemonic masculinities, *British Journal of Sociology of Education*, 18, pp. 349–369.

———. (1999) "A passion for football": dominant masculinities and primary schooling, paper presented to the British Educational Research Association Conference, University of Sussex, 2–5 September.

Smithers, R. (1999) Self-esteem the key for macho boys who scorn "uncool" school, *Guardian*, 16 March.

Thompson, S. (1994) What friends are for: on girls' misogyny and romantic fusion, in: J. Irvine (Ed.) *Sexual Cultures and the Construction of Adolescent Identities* (Philadelphia, PA, Temple University Press).

Thorne, B. (1993) *Gender Play: girls and boys in school* (Buckingham, Open University Press).

Walkerdine, V. (1991) *Schoolgirl Fictions* (London, Verso).

———. (1997) *Daddy's Girl: young girls and popular culture* (London, Macmillan).

Walkerdine, V., Lucey, H. & Melody, J. (2000) Class, attainment and sexuality in late twentieth-century Britain, in: C. Zmroczer & P. Mahony (Eds.) *Women and Social Class: international feminist perspectives* (London: UCL Press).

Weiner, G., Arnot, M. & David, M. (1997) Is the future female? Female success, male disadvantage and changing gender patterns in education, in: A. H. Halsey, P. Brown, H. Lauder & A. Stuart-Wells (Eds.) *Education: culture, economy and society* (Oxford, Oxford University Press).

Wight, D. (1996) Beyond the predatory male: the diversity of young Glaswegian men's discourses to describe heterosexual relationships, in: L. Adkins & V. Merchant (Eds.) *Sexualising the Social: power and the organisation of sexuality* (London, Macmillan).

Wilkinson, H. (1994) *No Turning Back: generations and the genderquake* (London, Demos).

———. (1999) The Thatcher legacy: power feminism and the birth of girl power, in: N. Walters (Ed.) *On the Move: feminism for a new generation* (London, Virago).

Williams, J. (Ed.) (1997) *Negotiating Access to Higher Education* (Buckingham, Open University Press).

Willis, P. (1977) *Learning to Labour: how working class kids get working class jobs* (Farnborough, Saxon House).

Yates, L. (1997) Gender equity and the boys debate: what sort of challenge is it? *British Journal of Sociology of Education*, 18, pp. 337–348.

"Cool Boys," "Party Animals," "Squid," and "Poofters": Interrogating the Dynamics and Politics of Adolescent Masculinities in School

WAYNE MARTINO

In this paper, the focus is on a group of boys attending a co-educational high school in Perth, Western Australia. These boys were interviewed as part of my doctoral research into the formation of masculinities in one particular localised site (see Skelton, 1996). A microanalytic focus is provided, with attention being drawn to how certain boys enact their masculinites within a regime of normalising practices in which sexuality functions as an index of subjectivity (see Butler 1996; Nayak & Kehily, 1996; Epstein, 1997). Thus, specific norms informing the conduct of a group of boys interviewed at one high school are investigated in the light of Foucault's claims abut the production of subjectivity (see Foucault, 1978, 1988a, 1988b).

The work of Foucault provides a useful analytic frame for interpreting how heterosexual masculinities are policed in terms of the category boundary maintenance work (Davies, 1993) that is carried out by certain boys within a heteronormative regime of practices (see Willis, 1977; Kessler et al., 1985; Connell, 1987, 1989, 1994, 1995; Askew & Ross, 1988; Walker, 1988; Frank, 1990, 1993; Frank, 1993; Haywood, 1993; Mac an Ghaill, 1994; Butler, 1995; Davies, 1995, 1996, 1997; Jordan, 1995a, 1995b; Ward, 1995; Nayak & Kehily, 1996; Redman, 1996; Epstein, 1997; Kehily & Nayak, 1997). This is documented here through identification of certain types or categories of boys such as "cool boys," "squids," "party animals" and "poofs." The "cool boys" were actively involved in football and had a high profile at the particular school in question. They were also known as "party animals" because they had a reputation for smoking marijuana and getting drunk

Wayne Martino, "'Cool Boys,' 'Party Animals,' 'Squids,' and 'Poofters': Interrogating the Dynamics and Politics of Adolescent Masculinities in School" from *British Journal of Sociology of Education* 20, No. 2 (1999): 239–263.

at parties. These boys defined themselves against the "squids," the "high achievers," who invested in mental labour (Willis, 1977). Those boys who chose not to play football or who displayed characteristics and traits attributable to gay people became visible targets for the "cool boys" and were derided. In this sense, the research documented here adds to the knowledge about the pivotal role that homophobia plays in the formation of certain abusive forms of heterosexual masculinity, while at the same time highlighting the need to attend to the situationally specific dynamics involved in boys enacting particular masculinities and the occasions on which they feel compelled to do so, at one particular school, in an Australian context.

A Foucauldian Approach to Analysing Masculinities

What is particularly useful about Foucault's work (1982, 1985b, 1987, 1993) with regard to analysing masculinities is the way in which he theorises subjectivity in terms of the subject's insertion into a "certain game of truth." However, it is his refusal to analyse subjectivity using the categories of ideology or the unconscious—which presuppose the operation of a repressive mechanism—that requires examination. This has implications for analysing masculinities because such an interpretive analytic enables one to think about the various ways in which adolescent boys are inserted into a "game of truth" in which they learn about what it means to be a "man." Within a complex field of social practices, it can be argued that boys are incited to adopt certain practices of "masculinity" and, hence, to display themselves as incumbents of certain categories of masculinity on particular occasions (Coleman, 1990). Thus, the conditions operating in one particular school, which enable boys to enter into a particular normalising relation with themselves and others, become the interpretative focus. In this sense, an *a priori* theory of the subject, which presupposes that there is a knowledge about masculinity waiting to be freed from the ideological mechanisms of power at play within the social field, is refused:

> What I wanted to know was *how the subject constituted himself*, in such and such a determined form, as a mad subject or as a normal subject, through

a certain number of practices which were games of truth, applications of power, etc. I had to reject a certain *a priori* theory of the subject in order to make this analysis of the relationships which can exist between the constitution of the subject or different forms of the subject and games of truth, practices of power and so forth. (Foucault, 1987, p. 121: my emphasis).

Foucault is careful to situate this focus on "how the subject constitute[s] himself" within a field or game of truth/power relations. Hence, different forms of the subject cannot be separated from a regime of practices through which power is channelled and particular truths established. In short, the formation of subjectivity is not understood in terms which rely on the explanatory category of ideology. Rather, it is argued, particular cultural techniques for working on and fashioning the gendered self, which are made available through existing regimes of practice, are the focus of investigation. That is, in this paper, attention is drawn to the cultural techniques used by boys to enact particular stylised forms of masculinity in the disciplinary space of the school.

This leads to an investigation of what Foucault (1978) terms "polymorphous techniques of power" in relation to examining the formation of adolescent masculinities. That is, the way in which modalities of power are channelled through normalising regimes of practice to permeate individual modes of behaviour become the focus. Foucault emphasises that such forms of power are organised around particular historically contingent norms for governing such relations to the self and to others:

> …my main concern will be to locate the forms of power, the channels, and the discourses it permeates in order to reach the most tenuous and individual modes of behaviour, the paths that give it access to the rare or scarcely perceivable forms of desire, how it penetrates and controls everyday pleasure—all this entailing effects that may be those of refusal, blockage, invalidation, but also incitement and intensification: in short the 'polymorphous techniques of power'. (Foucault, 1978, p. 11).

It is the intensification and incitement of particular forms of desire within specific regimes of practice which shape the way adolescent boys relate, not only to themselves as gendered subjects, but to one another. However, Foucault (1987) is careful to avoid reducing the constitution of the subject to a general theory of power or culture:

> You do not have towards yourself the same kind of relationships when you constitute yourself as a political subject who goes and votes or speaks up in meeting, and when you try to fulfil your desires in a sexual relationship. There are no doubt some relationships and some interferences between these different kinds of subject but we are not in the presence of the same kind of subject. In each case, we play, we establish with one's self different form of relationship. And it is precisely *the historical constitution of these different forms of subject relating to games of truth that interest me. (ibid.,* (p. 121; my emphasis).

Here, Foucault emphasises the *occasions* for conducting ourselves as particular kinds of subjects. In other words, the way subjects conduct and relate to themselves is tied both to the situationally specific constraints in which they find themselves and to the historical specificity of particular technologies of the self in which the imperatives to relate to oneself as a particular kind of person are formed. In this sense, Foucault is careful to emphasise that, even though one may take an active role in engaging in self-fashioning practices, the individual is not free to invent a form of subjectivity on his/her own accord:

> In would say that if now I am interested, in fact, in the way in which the subject constitutes himself in an active fashion, by the practices of the self, these practices are nevertheless not something that the individual invents by himself. They are patterns that he finds in this culture and which are proposed, suggested and imposed on him by his culture, his society and his social (1987, p. 122).

These discussions concerning the production of subjectivity are an attempt to establish a basis in this paper for drawing attention to how boys engage in certain practices of self-decipherment to monitor and police their *sexuality*. In this way, the limits of proscribing a desirable masculinity are marked out. Foucault, in this sense, highlights the historically contingent role of such confessional practices of self-disclosure and surveillance. These techniques for regulating and fashioning

ourselves, he suggests, are operative within a regime of truth in which sexuality functions as an index of subjectivity in the mobilisation of a productive and individualising form of power.

In his lectures delivered at Dartmouth and in his later works, Foucault (1985a, 1986, 1993) presents such a genealogy of the self, in which he traces a particular "policing of ourselves" to a hermeneutic principle developed within Christianising regimes of practice. The ways in which sexuality functioned within such a regime, Foucault argues, inaugurated a new ethical code of conduct which shifted the way people related to themselves. Through the development of confessional techniques, individuals were incited to discover the truth about their sexuality as an index of their subjectivity and then to verbalise this truth to others. Thus, the focus for Foucault is on the effects of the necessity to declare who we really are. This, he emphasises, becomes caught in a normalising regime in which the imperative to avow a particular identity is invoked.

The interpretive analytic frame outlined is used in this paper to:

(i) highlight the determining factors influencing the various statuses of masculinity in a particular school culture;

(ii) enable a focus on the ways in which the desires of adolescent boys are channelled via the deployment of "polymorphous techniques of power";

(iii) illustrate that a hierarchy of valorised and subordinated masculinities in the lives of a group of adolescent boys is tied to a heteronormative system or "economy of desire" which is formed within a regime of practices in which sexuality functions as an index of subjectivity;

(iv) gesture towards elaborating a political practice for interrogating masculinities in schools.

Interviewing Adolescent Boys

The boys interviewed as part of this study attended a private co-educational school in Perth, Western Australia, and were from a predominantly white middle-class background. This paper draws on a selection of interviews with adolescent boys aged 15–17 attending this school. The researcher spoke to four English classes at this school about his research and invited boys to participate in the project. They were told that the study was attempting to document their thoughts and opinions about school and their relations with their peers. The 25 boys who returned the consent forms were interviewed, with each interview lasting for about 40 minutes (see Martino, 1998a).

Due to the researcher having worked at the school and having taught many (although not all) of the students involved in the study, very little resistance was met from the boys who expressed a willingness to participate in the interviews. The implications of the researcher being acquainted with boys in this study, however, might also have some negative effects. While students might feel more comfortable with and trust a researcher they know with more intimate responses, there could also be a tendency for them to produce specific answers because they know what the researcher expects and wants them to talk about. Furthermore, having taught some of the boys might mean that they had already acquired a vocabulary and an understanding with which to articulate specific issues. For example, gender issues had been discussed in class with specific reference being made to how certain expectations influence gender-specific behaviour. Consequently, the boys might be more aware of the researcher's language use, tone, inflection so that they can "read" the many meanings and intentions behind the questions posed to them. Despite these limitations, however, there appeared to be certain benefits involved in the researcher being acquainted with the interviewees in terms of the latter feeling comfortable and open to expressing their thoughts and opinions without the fear that their masculinity would be brought into question.

However, it is important to emphasise that the selection of interview data is always going to be governed by particular norms. In this case, a focus on the "cool boys" was considered to be important due to the references that many of the interviewees made to this peer group and its impact on their lives at the school in question. This is not to deny that there are potential power relations involved in this research situation. However, the risk of selecting particular interviews to function merely as a means of reinforcing the researcher's own world view was minimised in the doctoral research by, first, the latter documenting his own categories of social analysis through providing observational data of the localised context in which the research was conducted and, second, by ensuring that boys from all identified friendship groups were interviewed.

What was interesting was that even those boys who had not been taught by the researcher also made similar comments about the dynamics and politics between various friendship groups and highlighted the particular role that the "cool boys" had to play in policing the heteronormative limits of acceptable masculinity. The "cool boys," therefore, become the focus for this paper because all of the participants interviewed in the research identified the former as having a significant influence at this particular school. Moreover, boys from different friendship groups also made reference to the "footballers" on the playing field who were considered to be very powerful, both physically and in terms of the "cool" status they had acquired (see interview data for Scott, Brian and Paul). Over 30 boys had gained membership to this group, which contributed significantly to their physical presence and visibility at the school.

Certain questions were used to prompt the boys to talk about their friends and friendship groups at school, which tended to elicit responses about the dynamics and politics of the interplay of masculinities at this particular local site:

- Tell me about your group of friends at school. What are they like? What do you do together? What do you talk about? What do you do at lunch time and recess?
- Can you talk to me about other friendship groups at school and what they are like, how you see them? How would you describe the way they behave? Give specific examples, if you can.
- Are certain groups or boys considered to be more popular than others? Can you explain?

The collected data are used to examine some of the ways in which the boys learn to establish their masculinities at this local site with its constantly shifting parameters of social practices, routines and human interaction. Since as Skeleton (1996) argues, not all schools "operate within identical constraints," such studies are useful in drawing attention to specific practices and strategies that are deployed in maintaining particular forms of masculinity in the daily lives of boys (see Willis, 1977; Kessler et al; 1985; Walker, 1988; Connell, 1989; Frank, 1990; Mac an Ghaill, 1994; Parker, 1996).

About the School

In light of Skelton's claims about differences related to specific institutional sites, it is important to draw attention to some of the characteristics of the particular school in which the study was conducted. It was known as the "football school" and had a reputation in the wider community for producing outstanding football players. The school had won a state competition in Australian Rules Football for 5 years consecutively and assemblies were frequently held to acknowledge the success of the football team. Many of the students had, in fact, expressed irritation about the emphasis placed on football at the official level. Several boys from this school played for one of the local state football teams and had been drafted to the Australian Football League. In this school a definite culture of football was established and supported strongly by school structures and many of the parents. This emphasis on football needs to be acknowledged in light of many of the boys' comments about its role and status in their lives at this particular school.

Enacting Masculinities at School

On the basis of this research, it appears that many boys learn to establish their masculinity in opposition to femininity (see Connell, 1994). In other words, they define their masculinity within a set of cultural and social practices which involve a rejection and denigration of what they consider to be feminine attributes or behaviors that often

serve as markers of homosexuality in the policing of ascendant forms of masculinity (see Ward, 1995; Butler, 1996; Laskey & Beavis, 1996). This is also reflected in the tendency of many boys to avoid expressing their emotions, which appears to be predicated on the basis that showing emotions is considered to be feminine. And as one boy stated in an interview, learning to be masculine involves "staying away as much as possible from being a female."

When this student, who shall be called Jason (aged 16 years), was asked whether he thought it was easy for boys to express what they really think and feel with one another, he stated that it was "a hell of a lot easier for females to do it" and proceeds to explain why he considers this to be the case.

> 74 WAYNE: Why is that?
>
> 75 JASON: Because they're more in to that kind of thing, um, they don't, um, it all comes back to masculinity and stuff like that. Like females sort of, they can talk to each other about personal stuff on a more personal level I think than guys. Guys are sort of like, you can talk to them about personal things but not really like inside feelings that you might really think, you have to sort of go along with the flow a bit. Like you can definitely be your own person but you sort of have to um, like follow on some kind of line. Like you can't really talk about your innermost feelings like if you're quieter or not as rough and stuff as some of the other ones, people might get crap for that.
>
> 76 WAYNE: How? What do you mean, "they'd get crap"?
>
> 77 JASON: Oh, just like in terms of people might call them "wusses" and you know, "poofs" and stuff like that.

In this interview, Jason draws attention to the role of a particular heteronormative form of masculinity that influences the way boys relate to one another in peer group situations. In fact, he points to how specific behaviours are regulated within a regime of practices in which sexuality functions as a mechanism for policing the masculinity of boys within a peer group context. He claims that boys are cautious about expressing their "innermost feelings" out of fear that they risk having their masculinity or sexuality questioned by other boys who might label them a "wuss" or a "poof." These labels are used in a derogatory way by many of the boys, who mark out those students who deviate from displaying an acceptable heterosexual masculinity. To be gay or to be associated with anything that smacks of femininity is to have your masculinity brought into question. "Wuss," in fact, is a sexualised term which is a derivative of "weak pussy" and refers to female genitals. Thus, through using these kinds of cultural techniques, the boundaries of a particular form of masculinity are marked out with those boys failing to meet the *standard* being ostracised. Jason, later in his interview, in fact, makes the point that "if you don't conform, you're sort of cast out almost."

What is important to emphasise here is that gender and sexuality are operationalised through a set of discursive practices involving the process of learning to be a heterosexual male which is based on an avoidance of the "feminine" and homosexuality. Those boys who do not measure up to what is considered to be appropriate *manly* behaviour are positioned as the "other" and are situated outside of the normative frames of reference for attributing desirable masculinity by certain boys, who acquire a particular status which is attributed to the bodily enactment and assertion of heterosexuality (see Nayak & Kehily, 1996; Epstein, 1997). That is, boys are incited to adopt certain modes of relating which are governed by specific norms that require them to enter into a particular normalising relation with themselves and their peers. A particular truth about masculinity becomes established for these boys in accordance with the deployment of sexuality as a means of policing the boundaries of acceptable masculinity. In a Foucauldian sense, sexuality becomes a mechanism by which the limits of a desirable masculinity can be proscribed (see Redman, 1996; Epstein, 1997). What emerges here, in Jason's account of the way he has learned to relate to his peers, is an instance of the intensification and incitement of particular forms

of desire which are governed by regimes of compulsory heterosexuality.

This practice of feminising and sexualising those boys who do not measure up as "other" is also brought out by another boy, Scott (aged 15 years), who draws attention to the pecking order of masculinities that exists within this particular school:

51 WAYNE: I want to ask you what you do at recess and lunchtime at school?

52 SCOTT: It depends really. I mean if there's something on, someone I want to speak to particularly I'll go and speak to them but um average lunchtime would be Joel, Aaron and there's a few other kids who sort of, you know the sort of kids who just want a little group to come to? Other guys don't accept them and we have about three guys like that—we don't really have much in common with them. Everyone else has sort of kicked them out and we can't be bothered doing that cause we don't mind having them around, we're not threatened by them sort of. It doesn't bother me. I've never thought of myself as one of those kids even though I have been—those kids who've sort of bounced around and not been liked by groups. But I've always felt sorry for the kids who have been, whereas I don't think anyone has ever really felt sorry for me about it…I'm sort of the outsider kid. I'd get pushed around by all the different groups and end up with a few friends who sort of tag along 'cause you have to have these friends and if you don't everyone is going to call you names. You've got to have somewhere to go. It's the same at this school. If you sit with one person no one says anything but if you sit and read a book and someone sees you they start making fun of you and it's really strange and they want to hassle you and stuff.

So Scott reiterates how those boys who are placed on the "outside" are treated by the dominant group of boys. Those boys who do not fit the dominant heterosexual model are harassed. In this instance, Scott draws attention to how a boy who chooses to read a book at school can be targeted by other boys. This boy is located on the "outside" through a set of normalising practices which work to reinforce a binary oppositional structuring of gender relations. Within such a hetero/sexist regime, certain practices or behaviours, such as reading or expressing emotions, appear to conflict with what boys consider to be appropriate masculine behaviour (see Martino, 1994a, 1994b, 1996). Accepting and rejecting certain kinds of boys becomes implicated in an ensemble of self-fashioning practices for regulating desirable forms of masculinity. Those boys who "bounce around" from group to group are identified as failing to measure up to particular norms for enacting a stylised form of "cool" masculinity. It is a masculinity that is differentiated through a set of practices or techniques for fashioning a particular demeanour and mode of relating (which involve recourse to bullying).

Scott proceeds to elaborate on the dynamics involved in the way that boys relate to one another, which are structured around an imperative to target those boys who are considered to be on the "outside":

> 64 SCOTT:... To be in the *in* group you have to be hassling someone else and they're all hassling each other. There are quite a few groups like that at this school...there's...that large group, the football playing surfie sort of guys, and they're one big group. But what I've found I haven't *really* hung around their group since early last year, but when I did I mean it was always someone's the brunt of all the crap for one day and then it's someone else the next day...And you know they have their kids that tag along and they're not liked that much and it varies—I was probably one of those kids, I used to get it every now and then.

Scott continues to talk about the power wielded by this group of boys which comprises "probably more than half of all the males in Year 10":

> 72 SCOTT:...It's pretty big group. I think a lot of people hang around there sort of trying not to be noticed by the sort of more bullying people. But there are sub-groups and when I was trying to fit into them their fun part of it would be trying to hassle other people and sort of, yeah, dehumanise them and just keep hassling them
>
> 73 WAYNE: So is that the way they relate to one another?
>
> 74 SCOTT: Yeah. What I'm saying, the reason I was probably picked on was I couldn't do it at that level, so maybe they could see that weakness...I don't know, I never felt like I fitted into those groups. I don't feel like I want to go back there or anything. It's just sort of pointless. But at the same time I feel sorry for them a bit. I mean their relationship with other people is a bit of a mess really...I don't know they just sort of get by hassling everybody and just having a few people they turn to and get them to laugh at the other people and it's all a bit of a mess really.

This interview with Scott emphasises the role of a particular form of masculinity in structuring the way that boys have learned to relate to one another. Such ways of relating are based on a system of verbal abuse and put downs in which a hierarchy of masculinities is established (see also Kessler et al., 1985; Connell, 1989; Jordan 1995a, 1995b). It would appear that a public hegemonic form of masculinity is enacted through a regime of abusive practices in which certain boys, who are placed on the "outside," become a target for harassment. For example, in section 74, Scott indicates that the peer group dynamic revolves around being able "to get a laugh" at the expense of those boys who are designated as the "other" and who are clearly unable or who refuse to engage in such practices (see Kehily & Nayak, 1997; Martino, 1997a). Scott even suggests, in section 72, that some boys choose to be a part of this group to avoid being bullied! In this way, he reiterates the cost involved of not being a part of this group. Moreover, the boys who wield power, according to Scott, are those who belong to the *footballer–surfie* group. In fact, many of the students interviewed mentioned this large group of boys who occupied a space on the playing field.

This is also highlighted by Brian, a member of another distinctive peer group at this particular school, who also comments on the behaviours and practices of the "footballers":

> 120 WAYNE: Can you tell me a bit about what other friendship groups are like at school? How you see them?
>
> 121 BRIAN: Which group though?
>
> 122 WAYNE: Any group that you tend to notice more than the others.
>
> 123 BRIAN: You mean like Miles and Ashley and all those guys on the oval and that?
>
> 124 WAYNE: Well, is that one group that you really notice?
>
> 125 BRIAN: Yeah.
>
> 126 WAYNE: How do you see them in relation to your group?
>
> 127 BRIAN: I don't know…um…they're kind of more like *rebels*…They're more, I don't know, more responsive to violence. They enjoy violence more, I suppose.
>
> 128 WAYNE: What makes you think that about them?
>
> 129 BRIAN: I don't know, just the way they behave and so on, like you know what they do in class, they're loud, they talk up, they kind of stuff around and mess about in class.

Brian differentiates members of his group from the "footballer" group in terms of the latter's responsiveness to violence. He also draws attention to the "cool" stylised demeanour which such boys enact as an instance of asserting their masculinity… they are loud and disruptive in class (see Willis, 1997; Walker, 1988; Mac an Ghaill, 1994; Dixon, 1997; Kehily & Nayak, 1997). It could be assumed that these are the working-class academic "losers" in a British context. However, although loud and disruptive in class, these white middle-class boys are not usually academic failures. Many are successful students but this must be achieved apparently without effort and without any visible signs of excessive mental labour or studiousness.

In the course of this discussion about peer groups at school, he mentions a boy, Ryan, who chooses to associate with a small group of girls only:

> 201 BRIAN: Like, there's Ryan's and Sharon's group, they're a much smaller group.
>
> 202 WAYNE: So how do you see them?
>
> 203 BRIAN: I don't know. They don't like violence.
>
> 204 WAYNE: And other groups do?
>
> 205 BRIAN: Yeah.
>
> 206 WAYNE: What do you mean they don't like violence?
>
> 297 BRIAN: Well, they're more into like the type that watch soapies and so on.
>
> 208 WAYNE: What makes you think that?
>
> 209 BRIAN: I don't know, just the way they behave and so on. They behave like girls. They talk more about girls' stuff like soapies and so on.

Here, Brian differentiates Ryan in terms of his association with girls and, hence, what he talks about (see Connell, 1987, 1994; Segal, 1990; Jordan, 1995a, 1995b). He sees Ryan, in aligning himself with this group of girls, as engaging in discussions about soaps, which are targeted at a sex-differentiated audience. Brian also distinguishes his own practices and interests from those of girls and this is significant in counting as an instance of masculinity. While the "footballers" appear to be enacting a "cool" masculinity through differentiating themselves from other types of boys, such as those who like handball or those who are quiet and work visibly hard, like Brian, it would appear that the latter is tending to enact his masculinity against boys like Ryan who associate with girls (see Clark, 1993). Once again, what emerges is a regime of normalising practices through which boys are incited to adopt certain practices of masculinity and to display themselves as particular kinds of boys. While Brian clearly differentiates himself from "the footballers" in terms of their violent and anti-social behaviour, his masculinity is still self-regulated in accordance with specific norms, which are organised around a devaluing of any association with girls or the "feminine." Thus, Brian's interview represents another instance of how desire to be a "proper boy" within the context of a subordinated peer group is incited through a set of normalising practices and relations, in which a particular status masculinity is invoked on the basis of denigrating the feminised other. Thus, techniques for fashioning a desirable heterosexual masculinity are also used by subordinated boys who are caught within a normalising regime of fashioning particular forms of gendered subjectivity which is tied to a 'heteronormative economy of desire.' In this sense, Brian's interview provides an interesting insight into how other boys, who are not a part of the "footballer group," are also in the business of deploying certain techniques of power in the interests of investing in a particular form of masculinity.

However, what needs to be emphasised is that the "cool boys," unlike Brian who is not a "footballer," are able to establish their position at the top of a hierarchy of social relations and practices at this school because of their active involvement in football. According to many of those interviewed, these boys achieved a particular status and popularity through their involvement and profile in sporting practices such as football, which became another arena for fashioning a particular "cool" masculinity.

Sporting Masculinities

Paul, another boy from a different friendship group at this particular school, also highlights the role of sporting practices such as football. He draws attention to the importance of demonstrating the capacity and skill to engage in this sport, which is tied to establishing a valorised form of "cool" masculinity, a masculinity which many boys work hard at fashioning for themselves.

> 97 WAYNE: What about the popular group? Why do you call them popular? Why are they popular do you think?

> 98 PAUL: Just because that's just what they always were from Year 8. They're always teasing everybody. Gary (he is a member of the *football–surfie* group), I sort of like him, I don't hang around him or anything, but he's not evil or a teasing sort of person, so he's alright to talk to. The other ones are just too good for you. They think they're too good for you but they're just basically stupid. Popular because they play football, that's why. I was never really accepted there because I didn't play football until last year, and so I started playing in a team with all the guys I went to primary school with, the people I actually like. That's why I think they got popular, because they all liked the ones that did good at football, because I couldn't really kick the football. That's how they get popular...I remember in the start of Year 9 David came and Joel came. I'd met Joel a couple of weeks before school started so I just sort of knew him because we went to a party because our families knew each other, so I talked to him for a while. On the first couple of days of Year 9 I was still with them, and then everyone started playing football. I talked to Joel and David and David looked like he'd never played football in his life, and Joel he was really, really good. So instantly, Joel was popular and David wasn't...So a person who was good at football, he became popular. It doesn't make sense but that's what happens.

This interview with Paul illustrates that a high-status masculinity is conferred upon those boys who are skilled at playing football and/or who surf. Through engaging in such practices, certain boys establish a particular profile or "cool" image which enables them to acquire a particular status and popularity. Both this interview and the one with Scott point to the effects of particular form of "cool" masculinity and its impact on the lives of two boys who just do not measure up or who refuse to fashion such a masculinity. And it is such a form of masculinity which appears to be at the basis of boys' rejection and denigration of other practices and behaviours which are considered to be feminine and which involve demonstrating capacities for being sensitive and expressing emotion (see Martino, 1995a). Playing football, therefore, becomes an occasion for boys to enter into a particular normalising relation with themselves and others involving the bodily enactment of one stylised form of hegemonic masculinity.

Nathan, a member of the "cool" group who was not taught by the researcher, like Scott, also draws attention to how those boys who read or who perform are often feminised or labelled in pejorative ways. He indicates in his interview that "a lot of guys don't like reading" and proceeds to discuss the impact of certain stereotypes:

> 31 WAYNE: Why do you think they don't like reading?
>
> 32 NATHAN: Maybe they don't think it's masculine or whatever to read books . . . 'Cause you know when you're brought up as a kid girls always read more books and that—it's just the way you're brought up really . . . it's like a stereotype, you know, girls read more and they don't go out and play sport and, well they do, but it's just like the way most of them have been brought up, like they do a lot of work, do a lot of reading, so they're normally the ones who do better at school and get to the top classes.
>
> 33 WAYNE: And guys don't?
>
> 34 NATHAN: Oh guys do, but you know like they're afraid to um . . . I know a lot of friends who are really smart but they don't want to try because they think they'll get called names and stuff for trying hard, doing extra work and that . . . you know like "squares" and "squids" and "suckers" and that but most of the time you just ignore it. You just say you're going to go somewhere and they're not, so then they shut up.

> 35 WAYNE: So you think that stereotype influences attitudes—is that what you're saying?
>
> 36 NATHAN: Yeah, there's a lot of stereotyping. You know guys are supposed to be big, strong; girls are supposed to be really smart, weak and that. Well, in some cases it is, but not all the time.
>
> 37 WAYNE: Is the stereotyping strong do you think at school?
>
> 38 NATHAN: I think it would be because a guy that does well, they always get called names and that. Girls do it as well, but they're more accepted to be smart than guys are, so it's, I mean, of course they wouldn't want to be called "squids" and that but they still, they don't really mind it.

Thus, a particular cool masculinity involves rejecting school work and high achievement. In this cultural context, the practice of fashioning masculinity as a form of protest against the values and priorities of the educational system is apparently not confined to a particular working-class dynamics (see Willis, 1977). It emerges here within the contours of a much broader phenomenon of enacting a particular form of hegemonic masculinity that is organised around "being cool," which is defined in terms of rejecting the demeanour of the hard-working, high-achieving and compliant student. It is interesting that Nathan perceives being smart as more acceptable for girls because this highlights the gendered dimension of "acting cool" and perhaps accounts for many boys' rejection of schooling. If schools are in the business of producing and regulating certain forms of subjectivity which are perceived to be antagonistic to the performance of a particular kind of "cool" masculinity, this may account for many boys' rejection of schooling, which in this particular instance and within the localised cultural context of an Australian co-educational high school, appears to cut across class boundaries. However, it is important to highlight that these middle-class boys, because of their privileged status—because of their parents' socio-economic standing—are advantaged in ways which working-class boys are not. Thus, there is a particular register of middle-class protest masculinity which appears to be organised for some boys around "acting cool."

This gendered dimension of "acting cool" is further highlighted by Nathan when he starts to talk about the whole idea of studying as a passive practice and hence a devalued, and by implication, feminised activity. For example, he claims that girls have a more positive attitude to school because "they are smart [and] they think about what's going to happen to them when school finishes they're the ones who are going to have a better life so they don't really worry about it as much." Nathan adds, however, that while boys tend to think about study, most of them:

> don't want to sit around a desk and do work for their lives and that. They'd rather be out playing sport, watching TV so they'd rather not think about their education and how smart they want to be 'cause they don't think that when they're older they'll have to work. They just don't want to work, you know, they sit at home and don't want to be stuck behind a desk or, from 6 till 7 or whatever. They'd rather be out doing something else. A lot of girls have the same attitudes but I just think the majority of them are smarter in what they want to do in their future careers or their lives and that ... They think about the consequences in life, you know, like what they do now is going to reflect and lead to what they're going to do when they're older, so if they do well now they're going to do well in the upper school, get a good job and then have a good life, get a lot of money and have a family and that. I suppose a lot of guys don't really see it the same way. They think they can just get through school like on the borderline or whatever, just get a job as a brickie or something that they don't need a lot of education for but they will get paid for it so they think they can get by just doing that.

What Nathan draws attention to is a particular culture of masculinity in which high achievement and reading are rejected by the "cool" guys who would rather play sport or watch TV than "sit around at a desk" and study. And it is through a practice of labelling those boys who do achieve or who are avid readers in derogatory ways as the *other,* that the footballs and the "surfies" are able to establish a particular form of hegemonic masculinity. What is particularly interesting about this interview is that Nathan points to a dimension of counterschool culture in which a group of middle-class boys enact a particular form of protest masculinity. In other words, as Nathan points out in section 34, the "cool" boys "act dumb" in order to establish a hegemonic form of masculinity through which they can demonstrate their opposition to the values embodied in the aims of formal education. This form of protest masculinity is asserted by targeting those boys who achieve such educational aims in derogatory ways as "squares," "squids" and "suckers." What emerges here is yet another type of cultural context in which particular rules and techniques of subjectification for enacting a "cool masculinity" are played out. The criteria for male membership in the cool group are implicated in cultural practices which have much in common, at a general level, with those identified by Willis in a different class and cultural context.

Willis (1977) has also documented how such a form of protest masculinity is enacted by a group of working-class "lads" in a working-class school, which involved defying the values and aims of formal education as well as support of the school institution. Moreover, those boys who conformed to the aims of the institution were targeted by the "lads" as "ear 'oles." The fact that Nathan appears to be documenting a similar dynamic in a middle-class school is interesting and might be related to culturally specific practices within the Australian context. It also relates to the status that is attributed to football at this particular school. The role of such sporting practices in enacting a public form of heterosexual masculinity takes on a particular significance in this local site with its shifting parameters of social practices, routines and patterns of human relations (Skelton, 1996). This also taps into wider cultural practices of "mate-ship" and modes of relating that are imbricated in enacting a public form of heterosexual masculinity which emphasizes a ruggedness and a sense of being an "ordinary bloke" with no pretensions. In short, it would appear that the various registers of a protest form of masculinity are not confined to a particular working-class dynamics. While the broader contours of gendered masculinity appear to emerge in this study as trans-historical and trans-cultural, the details of this phenomenon, it seems, are historically and culturally specific.

Later in the interview, Nathan emphasises the role of sporting practices and its linkage to other attributes in establishing a desirable form of heg-emonic masculinity:

> 88 WAYNE: So um what would lead someone to be rejected then?
>
> 89 NATHAN: Well it could be like you know, say there was a school of like a group of guys that played a lot of sport and that or hang around together and the person comes from overseas or whatever, a new school and is like, you know sits at lunch time and reads on his own, doesn't play much sport, he's gonna get hassled by the guys that play sport and that. They'll want him to come out at the start maybe, come and play sport, but he'd rather read or like be on his own or whatever and then so they think oh we don't need him and he can sit there and have his book the whole time and it'll just, people will... you know how people talk about others and people will get influenced by that and that person is just rejected.

Nathan's reference to the person from overseas who becomes designated as the "other" perhaps points to a form of racism in the maintenance of this style of "cool" masculinity (see also Back, 1994). Furthermore, he highlights the social dif-ferentiation among peer groups at school, in terms of their involvement in different kinds of sports:

> 91 NATHAN: ... everyone's really friends but are mainly friends together in certain groups.

> 92 WAYNE: Tell me a bit more about those groups, so there's the popular group...
>
> 93 NATHAN: Yeah you've got the popular group, you've got the groups that play foot-ball, you've got the basketball groups, the groups you know that hang around, play kingpin. And like there's either groups that go to the library and then there's just groups that just sit around and talk in dif-ferent areas around the school and then they all hang around together and they do stuff on the weekend. Like they're still all friends but they're more friendly with the groups they hang around with.
>
> 94 WAYNE: Tell me about kingpin. What's kingpin?
>
> 97 NATHAN: It's game that they play with a tennis ball. You would hang around with groups like people who are the high achievers and that, they often hang around together, 'cause normally you get some-one who's really smart being in classes with others who are really smart and they start to get together and talk about simi-lar things, so they can relate to each other and sit down and talk whatever. And then other people join other groups—it's just who your friends are really. Like some people might just think of them as a *loser* group if they're not very good achievers or if they're not socially accepted for any reasons then they're thought of as the *loser* group whatever.

Nathan highlights the differentiation among cer-tain groups of boys. Certain practices such as football and handball are imbricated in enact-ing particular versions of masculinity or rather form the basis upon which certain attributions of masculinity are made. For instance, Nathan indi-cates that the "handballers" are high achievers who are also differentiated, in his eyes, through engaging in "kingpin" as a particular stigmatised practice which is set against the *tougher* sport of football. Many of the boys, however engaged in practices of differentiation which were opera-tionalised both within certain peer groups, in terms of how boys related to one another, and in terms of the way they related to other friendship groups. This draws attention to how playing certain kinds of sport is implicated in a wider set of cultural practices for fashioning a hegemonic form of masculinity in which certain norms are operationalised.

Negotiating "Cool" Masculinities

What is interesting is that Nathan, as a high achiever, has been able to successfully negotiate a position of acceptance within the dominant group since he is an esteemed football player and he enjoys surfing. Moreover, he has also developed a highly sophisticated capacity for analysing the peer-group dynamics of adolescent boys in this school, which has enabled him to align himself with the dominant group without compromising his willingness to perform well at school.

126 WAYNE: So how do you fit into this picture then, like 'cause I'd see you as being accepted and quite popular and yet quite a high achiever…?

127 NATHAN: Yeah well 'cause I play a lot of sport I fit into the real sporting group and I surf so, surfing is like, if you surf you're quite cool which a lot of people think that so they try and take it up and then you get more friends by people trying to do what you do. But I've got another friend who plays football, surfs and they're really smart—we get on really well—and I also hang around with people who have similar interests even though they don't care anything about education. So we're still linked—it's mainly by sport that we've all hung around together. We're all linked by that as our basis but a couple of them are *bogans*, a couple are *surfs*, a couple are just…all they do is play sport…and then a couple of us actually commit ourselves to schoolwork—we can find time for both so we balance out as being in the accepted group by the way we are and the sport we

play even though we do spend more time than others doing work.

128 WAYNE: But sport's the key thing then?

129 NATHAN: Yeah I think sport's the main thing that brings people together 'cause like when you go to someone's house you don't really just sit there and talk, you want to go out and do something. So you might not invite somebody over to your house because you know they can't play basketball so you invite people that can play basketball and you get friends like that, so you're not in a team with your friends. I think sport is the main reason why people are friends. 'Cause in our group we've got, say there's like ten guys, there's like three of us who are in at least one extended class and there's four of them that are in modified classes because they spend more time playing sport than they do with their education so they miss out on the education side but some are top athletes or football players and that.

Nathan's point about the function of sport in the context of boys' social relations with one another at this particular school is important. In section 129, he mentions that boys do not "just sit there and talk" when they visit their friends at home, which is significant in highlighting the role of sport as a masculinising practice in the lives of these boys, where being communicative and expressive is associated with femininity. Moreover, to sit down and to talk is framed in opposition to sport which draws attention to the binary frames of reference that are implicated in specific regimes of practice, in which adolescent boys learn to enact their masculinities. Such a normalising regime involves the deployment of public and private gendered categories of the self which are structured in dualistic terms. It is at such a nexus that a hegemonic form of heterosexual masculinity emerges in oppositional relation to femininity and homosexuality (see Martino, 1994a; Butler, 1996; Ward, 1995; Denborough, 1996; McLean, 1996).

Later on in the interview, Nathan outlines what he thinks are some of the problems that boys his age experience in feeling compelled to live up to a particular standard, in which sport functions as an indicator of desirable masculinity:

> 124 WAYNE: What would you say then are some of the problems that boys your age experience?
>
> 125 NATHAN: Well because they have to live up to a certain standard they have to try and sometimes the things that—like education and that—they'll put it off then…they [feel they] should be out doing sport rather than doing education. So then they'll put education off even though they think that it's important to them. So they take a step down in life 'cause you're missing out on your education because…instead of being you know like smart and having heaps of friends and that—they'd rather have heaps of friends and not worry about their education because they think they might lose friends by studying more time in the library and things. They don't want to get stereotyped out of being important and having heaps of friends and that. They don't think it's like cool and macho to do homework and to go to the library when you've got an assignment, going in at lunchtime to do extra work. They think it's really uncool to do that. But then you have to live up to a standard and if you don't make it you get put down.

Thus, "being cool" is a priority for these boys and is established within the context of a hierarchical set of social relations with their peers in which there is a constant jostling of hegemonic and subordinate masculinities (see Kessler et al., 1985; Connell, 1987). Within this regime, doing homework or going to the library become markers of a subordinate form of masculinity. Moreover, rejecting such practices which lead to academic achievement is also a means by which the "cool boys" can establish themselves as *rebels* in their rejection of the institution's values. It is in this sense, as Nathan emphasises, that learning to relate to other boys within the peer-group

context involves the deployment of specific techniques of the self, which are operationalised through a regime of practices involving specific modalities of power (Foucault, 1978). So for Nathan, living up to a particular ideal or version of masculinity is very much a part of his everyday life at school. However, through the ways in which he is able to negotiate his position within the dominant popular group at school, it is possible for him to achieve a particular valorised status as a male, despite his active involvement and achievement in the academic side of school life. In this way, he is able to escape the position of the *other*, which is conferred upon those boys who refuse to or who are unable to measure up to the demands of this form of hegemonic masculinity.

Adam, another member of the "footballer" group, also mentions the need to negotiate his position in the dominant group in order to be accepted. He describes this in terms of balancing the academic and social sides of his life, which is integral to enacting a desirable masculinity that is invested in sport and establishing a particular demeanour:

> 108 ADAM: So I don't know, I think I'm sort of a mixture of both, you know what I mean, it works out alright though, like I think that I can sort of balance that you know, quite well the social side of the school and the education side, 'cause I think there is two sides to school you know, the socialising and the parties, and the parties and all that sort of stuff but also the education and you know you're, it always seems that you have the two groups at school like all the people you know, who are worried about education or the guys that just think that socialising is the way to go and I think that I'm sort of a mixture of both…it works out pretty well but it can often be a bit of a drag sort of, you know trying to balance both um, both the social and the education sort of sides of school.

Thus, meeting the requirements associated with what appears to be two disparate departments of social existence can be "a bit of a drag," in that it creates certain pressures for Adam:

> 112 ADAM:...I think you sort of have to work out whether you're going to be the one who's going to be the social person and sort of school takes a back seat or, you know, school's the number one thing and um social life sort of comes second. So, I don't know, there is a pressure there to either, to be one or the other and whichever one you choose also I think determines what friendship group you're in...So, you know, there is certainly once again a point there, whether you're the "squids" or whatever you want to call them or whether you're the person who's going to be sociable and you know, a "party animal" sort of thing you know, you go out all the time and that sort of stuff, so...

Thus, Adam is caught between two positions—a "squid" and "party animal"—which involves a balancing act to ensure that his masculinity is kept intact in maintaining a "cool" demeanour:

> 115 WAYNE: So guys wouldn't see being smart then and being a high achiever necessarily as being "cool"?
>
> 116 ADAM: Oh no, not at all, not at all. It can, it sort of, it can be on various scales like um, not you know, being the high achiever um a lot of the time isn't "cool," it really I think depends on how you act and how you take it, you know because if you're like the person who is the high achiever and that then that's your life sort of thing, achieving you know is the higher thing. That's your life and you can't get past that or whether you're the person who does that and at the same time is sort of humble about it but also um, you know it's not their "be all and end all." You know, there's also the social side of school and that too that you've got to worry about...it really depends on how you take that on, whether that makes you, if you achieve higher, a person who is really stuck-up and big-headed and that sort

of stuff or whether that makes you a person who sort of builds your character and builds your personality and makes you go out and say hello to people and meet people and that sort of stuff, so it can sort of work both ways in that sense.

What is significant here is Adam's emphasis on acting and "taking on" a particular demeanour, which becomes recognisable as an instance of a stylised "cool" masculinity that must be carefully orchestrated to risk slipping into the category of a "squid."

On the basis of this data, it would appear that these boys invest a lot of energy in maintaining their position within the dominant group. This is understandable in light of the ensuing consequences if they fail to measure up to heterosexist norms for enacting a desirable form of hegemonic masculinity. In negotiating their position within the dominant group, both Adam and Nathan are able to escape the violence of the homophobic and other forms of abuse that are directed at those boys who are not a part of this group and whom Scott talks about. What is highlighted by this research is that negotiating masculinities is imbricated in certain practices of self-regulation which are governed by particular norms for proscribing the limits of a publicly validated form of hegemonic heterosexual masculinity (Frank, 1987). It is within such normalising regimes of practices that particular forms of desire are incited and intensified as boys like Adam and Nathan go about the business of fashioning their masculinities, in the interests of maintaining a cool demeanour which is essential to establishing their status as *proper* boys.

Policing Masculinities

Scott, in one part of the interview, mentions how the "cool boys" make homophobic comments about other boys who are "outside" their group:

> 86 SCOTT:...they walk past and hassle all these other groups and make comments about them.
>
> 87 WAYNE: What comments? Like?

88 SCOTT: "Oh I hate him, he's really gay" or "Gee, those guys are real whatever." I mean it always gets back to gay with all these guys. It's sort of like the big insult…we've had one guy right through from Year 8 and he got stuck with it and everyone decided, oh, you know, oh he's definitely, he's a poofter, we hate him. You can tell the way he talks, he's friends with a lot of girls more than guys. I mean, it's his choice really, but everyone's sort of stuck him with that tag and what surprises me when you talk to him, he's actually really homophobic himself. So it's odd that he's sort of been hassled so much with it and he's like that as well. It's funny that. He doesn't say it as such, but he wouldn't call people gay all the time, but yeah he's definitely homophobic. Strange, 'cause I would have thought that if you got hassled with it…that's like with me I got switched off to it all sort of.

Scott highlights the normalising practices in which sexuality is deployed as a specific category for defining acceptable masculinity. He refers to one boy who has been marked as a "poofter." The criteria for labelling him in this way relate to (i) his manner of speaking, and (ii) the fact that he tends to associate with girls as friends. This boy, therefore, is targeted on two counts, both which have associations with the "feminine" and a rejection of a hegemonic form of masculinity. The way this boy talks, presumably, is considered to be outside the range of what constitutes acceptable modes of speaking for males, and his preference for having girls as friends also confirms that he is engaging in a non-normative practice. Boys are expected to talk in a particular way and to "do masculinity" with other boys. If a boy at school chooses to spend time with girls as friends, he may risk having his masculinity brought into question. Perhaps this is related to the importance of sharing specific gendered practices and interests for boys and girls in the formation of acceptable masculinities and femininities. What is also highlighted by Scott is the role that certain techniques of the self have to play in fashioning different kinds of masculinity which are governed by certain norms. Sexuality

for the "cool boys" is linked to a particular policing of themselves and other boys as means of marking out the boundaries of a desirable form of hegemonic masculinity.

Researchers such as Hite (1981, 1994), for example, have highlighted the role of fathers and other males in instructing boys not to be "sissies" and not to associate with girls as they are growing up. Such practices or ways of relating immediately become more visible within the institutional context of the school, with its regimen of routinised practices and regimes. For instance, the practices of schools and the social relations between people within them are organised around the public spaces of the "playground" and classroom, which are structurally built sites for the deployment of sophisticated apparatuses of surveillance and moral supervision (see Hunter, 1988). Within such spaces, students are not only monitored by school personnel, but learn to monitor themselves within a regime of normalising practices involving the deployment of sexuality. This is reflected in the comment that Scott makes about the boy who is targeted as gay actually being homophobic himself. This points to the extent to which this boy has learned to monitor and to relate to himself within a normalising regime of heterosexist practices. Moreover, it draws attention to the cycle of abuse which is often implicated in a regime of bullying practices, with the victim perpetuating the very practices of which he has been the target.

Thus, through the interviews with adolescent boys that have been included in this paper, it is possible to draw attention to the role of a particular forms of hegemonic heterosexual masculinity in the lives of these boys in terms of how they have learnt to relate to one another. The emphasis and status accorded to football at this particular school also helps to establish the role that sporting practices play in enacting a desirable masculinity for many of the boys. In fact, there was definitely a pecking order of masculinities at this school, with the "footballers" wielding the most power. Those boys who could not play or were not interested in football or who simply did not "measure up," were relegated to an inferior status and harassed as a consequence (see also Lehne, 1976; Arnot, 1984, p. 48; Dunning, 1986; Whitson, 1990;

Messner & Sabo, 1990; Frank, 1993; Butler, 1996; Hinson, 1995; McLean, 1995b; Nickson, 1995; Ward, 1995; Boulden, 1996). What was also highlighted in this study was the role of homophobia in the construction and maintenance of dominant versions of masculinity. It appeared that homophobia was a mechanism or strategy in a particular *gender system* (Connell, 1994) for policing and regulating masculinity for these boys (see Holland et al., 1993; Mac an Ghaill, 1994; Nayak & Kehily, 1996; Epstein, 1997). Moreover, what is also highlighted within the interpretive analytic frames deployed in this paper are the kinds of techniques of subjectification for fashioning a particular form of hegemonic masculinity, which are governed by quite specific norms for fashioning a cool demeanour. An attempt to invoke explanatory categories which resort to invoking conceptualisations of power as a purely repressive mechanism has also been avoided in undertaking an analysis of the data. Interview data with adolescent boys have been used to offer a descriptive analysis of specific norms which appear to govern the social practices through which they are *incited* to adopt certain practices of masculinity.

Placing Masculinities and Homophobia on the Agenda in Schools

The research documented in this paper has implications for addressing issues of masculinity in schools. If particular norms appear to govern the occasions on which boys at this particular school are incited to enact a particular form of masculinity, which has detrimental effects, it would appear that setting targets for teaching boys to develop capacities for interrogating such self-fashioning practices is essential. In an attempt to map the possibility of implementing such a practice, during the interviews, the boys were asked explicitly about masculinity and what it meant to be male. Interestingly, many of them made the point that they had never really been encouraged to think about such issues. Eric, a Year 12 student, aged 17, who had not been taught by the researcher, for instance, talked at length about homophobia and about particular versions of masculinity that are considered to be acceptable in society:

ERIC: ... There seems to be a real thing about homophobia around males which I don't think I understand that well. The only explanation I could come up with is that they are insecure about their own feelings, so that's why they're afraid of other people, other people who are different to themselves.

WAYNE: How do you think that could change? Could it change?

ERIC: It would be hard, it's not going to be easy. It would have to begin with schools, your parents, society, TV, newspapers ... everything is seen as the one type of male stereotype, but it's a particular version of masculinity. You have to be at least sort of interested in sports, you have to like girls and all the rest of it and it is always fed to you from day one ... and you've never actually seen the other version of masculinity which is perfectly normal in the sense that it is just a different way that guys feel about other people, but it's not seen as you are growing up. So, when people see that other people are different to what they've been made to believe all their lives then obviously they will want to reject that sort of behaviour or that sort of person because it's something different and everyone hates change, everyone wants to stick with the things that they know best and all of a sudden you just see this other version of masculinity and you've never like, you know, through your education, you've never been told about it, you never know about that sort of person until you hit high school and that's when people really start calling you names and labelling.

Eric's point about never being told about other versions of masculinity is significant because it highlights that this particular issue has not been addressed in his experience of schooling. When questioned about his use of language, he indicated that his English teacher had discussed issues of masculinity in relation to studying feature articles and short stories in class from a textbook written by the researcher (see Martino & Mellor,

1995). This points to the potentiality of using texts both to introduce students to a particular critical discourse about masculinities and to help them to develop capacities for interrogating gender regimes in which the production of subjectivity is imbricated.

Shaun, another student, also makes a similar point when he claims that in schools "there's no opportunity for guys to get down and think about what they're doing and why they're doing it and stuff like that." When asked why he thinks this is so, he replies:

> I'm not sure. I think one thing is that…it's almost as if, it's like a mismanagement of what they teach in schools. They teach algebra and maths and stuff like this that we will never use later on in life but they won't teach us stuff that is important to us and that we should know and learn. We have to find it out for ourselves and if we don't then we're stuck. Instead of learning how to divide this and do that and stuff that isn't that useful to us in life, maybe they should start teaching us stuff that is related to us and that we need to know about, so like if a situation docs occur and people are expected to do something, they can handle it more instead of just sitting there and going I have to do what these guys say. There has been stuff about don't fall to peer pressure and stuff like that but that's nothing as deep as going into stuff about how you feel about being masculine or what is masculinity. I'm not sure why we don't have the opportunity. It could be an error on our part but I think it's mostly the people that have to teach stuff that maybe they should turn around and look at what they're teaching us. Right now they are teaching us pretty much crap that we will never need to know later on in life but this [masculinity] is something that is pretty important to a whole lot of people.

It would appear that Shaun is advocating an approach which assists boys in developing capacities for critical thinking about the impact of masculinity in their lives. In fact, both Shaun and Eric reiterate the need for issues of masculinity to be explicitly addressed in school. More significantly, both these boys appear to be stressing that they would like to have the opportunity to discuss such gender matters. This is significant in light of the regime of normalising practices, in which a particular form of hegemonic masculinity is implicated as highlighted through the interview data analysed in this paper. These comments also need to be situated within a wider socio-cultural and historical context in which masculinity has become a target of problematisation in governing populations. This is particularly the case with regards to educational attainment, involvement in criminal activity and health-related issues, etc. (see Fletcher, 1993; Newburn & Stanko, 1994; Alloway & Gilbert, 1997; Huggins, 1997). In this the sense, the call for masculinity to become an object of study and critical interrogation in schools is a response to a complex range of socio-cultural and historical factors which have led to "masculinity" being designated a problem and in need of adjustment.

Further Implications of the Research

It would appear, in the light of this research into masculinities and given the concern over boys' educational attainment and behavioural problems in schools, that it is imperative for educators to create spaces for discussing the impact and effects of hegemonic masculinities in school. This is particularly pertinent in light of the research documented in this paper with regards to investigating middle-class boys enacting cool masculinity. In this sense, the focus is not merely on raising awareness, but actively using texts to help students to develop capacities for interrogating masculinities. However, as Davies (1995) has pointed out, it is important to ensure that such practices are not merely recuperated into an alternative binary oppositional gendered framework in which asymmetrical power relations between men and women remain intact. Davies comments on the ways in which apparently non-hegemonic forms of masculinity are "written into and over the more powerful hegemonic masculinities," with new discourses of masculinity being reworked to become the old. For instance, many attempts to address educational reform for boys are grounded in what Cox (1995) terms the competing victim syndrome. The effects of such approaches, which set boys' interests against those of girls, is to reinforce oppositional differences between the former and the latter (see Kenway, 1995, 1997; Yates, 1997). Moreover, these approaches are not based on an adequate theorisation of power and disadvantage (Gilbert & Gilbert, 1995).

In light of the research provided in this paper, it is argued that it is necessary to find ways of interrupting the association between being labelled a "poof" and specific practices and behaviours which are considered to be feminine. Such practices of differentiation become integral to establishing a particular form of hegemonic masculinity. But the question of how students might be encouraged to reflect on the nexus between sexuality and masculinity in this capacity still remains unanswered. The activities and texts used in the textbook *Gendered Fictions* (Martino & Mellor, 1995), which deals with issues around masculinity, have been useful in this respect. Through using the kinds of texts that are included in this book, sociological and political knowledges about the social construction of masculinities can be made available to students along the lines mentioned, in a non-threatening way. Moreover, through the activities that are set up around these texts, students are encouraged to reflect critically on masculinity. For example, students are asked to consider the cultural construction of a hegemonic masculinity which is based on a denigration of the feminised "other" through reading a story about a boy who plays with dolls and who is called "a lily-livered poofter" by his father as a consequence (see Martino, 1995b). In this way, they are encouraged to consider the effects of a hegemonic form of masculinity and to develop an understanding of the role of homophobia in policing specific sex-appropriate practices for boys. The text, therefore, can be used in the literacy classroom as a vehicle for targeting specific issues around the impact of hegemonic masculinities and for exploring the ways in which those boys who do not measure up are treated (see Martino, 1995b, 1997b).

Conclusion

Overall, the research referred to in this paper highlights the role that certain norms play in establishing particular forms of masculinity for a group of adolescent boys at one particular middle-class school in Australia. The complexities and nuances involved in how individual boys negotiate and establish their masculinities are related to wider technologies of normalisation and regulation, in which sexuality is often deployed to police gender boundaries (see Epstein, 1997; Steinberg et al; 1997). Furthermore, the research documented provides some interesting insights into registers of a particular form of "protest masculinity," which is enacted against a regime of institutionalised mental labour by "cool boys" in a middle-class schooling context. In this sense, a Foucauldian analytic focus has enabled attention to be drawn to a regime of normalising practices in which self-fashioning techniques for enacting a particular form of "cool" masculinity, which cut across class boundaries, are established.

In light of this research, it would appear that it is important for those working in schools to help boys to develop specific capacities for understanding the effects of certain currencies of masculinity in their lives. To do so is to engage them in a critical practice which is in the business of adjusting certain norms, informing the enactment of homophobic and heterosexist versions of masculinity in schools. This can be achieved, it has been argued, through deploying texts within a regime of self-problematising practices which are organised around adjusting certain behaviours and modes of thinking that have become recognisable instances of enacting particular forms of masculinity (see Martino, 1998b). This project is in line with McLean's (1995a) call to encourage boys to reflect on and to recognise the injustices in their own lives as a basis for enabling them to develop and value capacities for empathising with other people's experiences of injustice (see also Martino, 1996, 1997b). In this way, a critical practice that helps students to interrogate heterosexist and homophobic versions of masculinity can be developed. Within such a pedagogical context of self-problematisation and adjustment, certain practices and modes of thinking, acting and behaving are linked to the enactment of particular problematic forms of masculinity and this is made explicit for students. That is, the links made between modes of behaviour and the enactment of forms of masculinity selected for analysis and adjustment become the target of a critical practice. Such gender equity initiatives, designed to encourage boys to engage productively with issues related to the politics of masculinity, are presented as complementing attempts to improve and enhance the achievement and social situation of girls in schools.

It would appear that targeting certain modalities of power as an object of critical analysis in relation to boys enacting hegemonic heterosexual masculinities will have pay-offs for both girls and boys. However, based on what some boys said in their interviews, it appears that such critical practices which target "masculinity" and its effects have not yet been developed in schools. The task for educators and administrators in schools is to find ways of broaching these issues of masculinity with students. Until matters related to homophobia and the role it plays in establishing hegemonic heterosexual masculinities are addressed on a whole school level, existing gender regimes will remain intact.

Acknowledgements

I would like to thank Bronwyn Mellor and the reviewers for their comments on earlier drafts of this paper. This paper was presented as part of a symposium entitled, *Addressing Boys' Education: Framing Debates, Implementing Strategies and Formulating Policies*, at the Australian Association for Research in Education (AARE) Annual Conference, Brisbane, 30 November–4 December, 1997.

References

Alloway, N. &. Gilbert, P. (1997) *Boys and Literacy* (Carlton, Curriculum Corporation).

Arnot, M. (1984) How shall we educate our sons?, in: R. Deem (Ed.) *Co-Education Reconsidered* (Milton Keynes & Philadelphia, Open University Press).

Askew, S. & Ross, C. (1988) *Boys Don't Cry: Boys and Sexism in Education* (Milton Keynes, Open University Press).

Back, L. (1994) The 'White Negro' revisited: race and masculinities in South London, in: A. Cornwall, & N. Lindisfarne (Eds) *Dislocating Masculinity: comparative ethnographies* (London and New York, Routledge).

Boulden, K. (1996) Keeping a straight face: schools, students and homosexuality—Part 2, in: L. Laskey & C. Beavis (Eds) *Schooling and Sexualities: teaching for a positive sexuality* (Geelong, Deakin University for Education and Change).

Butler, J. (1996) The Poof paradox: homogeneity and silencing in three Hobart high schools, in: L. Laskey & C. Beavis (Eds) *Schooling and Sexualities: teaching for a positive sexuality* (Geelong, Deakin University, Centre for Education and Change).

Clark (1993) *The Great Divide* (Melbourne, Curriculum Corporation).

Coleman (1990) Doing Masculinity/Doing Theory, in: J. Hearn & D. Morgan (Eds) *Men, Masculinities & Social Theory* (London, Unwin Hyman).

Connell, R. (1987) *Gender and Power* (Cambridge, Polity Press).

Connell, R. (1989) Cool guys, swots and wimps: the interplay of masculinity and education, *Oxford Review of Education*, 15(3), pp. 291–301.

Conneli, R. (1994) Knowing about masculinity, teaching boys and men. Paper presented at the Pacific Sociological Association Conference, San Diego, April.

Cox, E. (1995) Boys and girls and the costs of gendered behaviour. *Proceedings of the Promoting Gender Equity Conference*, 22–24 February (Canberra, ACT Department of Education and Training).

Davies (1993) *Shards of Glass* (Sydney, Allen & Unwin).

Davies, B. (1995) What about the boys? The parable of the bear and the rabbit, *Interpretations*, 28(2), pp. 1–17.

Davies, B. (1996) *Power, Knowledge, Desire: changing school organisation and management practices* (Canberra, Department of Employment, Education, Training and Youth Affairs).

Davies, B. (1997) Constructing and deconstructing masculinities through critical literacy, *Gender and Education*, 9(1) pp. 9–39.

Denborough, D. (1996) Power and Partnership? Challenging the Sexual Construction of Schooling, in: L. Laskey & C. Beavis (Eds) *Schooling & Sexualities* (Geelong, Deakin University Press).

Dixon, C. (1997) Pete's Tool: identity and sex play in the design and technology classroom, *Gender & Education*, 9(1), pp. 89–104.

Dunning, E. (1986) Sport as a male preserve: notes on the social sources of masculine identity and its transformation, *Theory, Culture and Society*, 3(1), pp. 75–90.

Epstein, D. (1997) Boyz' own stories: masculinities and sexualities in schools, *Gender and Education*, 9(1), pp. 105–115.

Fletcher, R. (1993) *Australian Men and Boys…A Picture of Health? Graphs of health indicators for Australian males* (Newcastle, University of Newcastle).

Foucault, M. (1978) in: R. Hurley (Trans.) *The History of Sexuality: Volume I* (New York, Vintage).

Foucault, M. (1982) The subject and power, Afterward, in: H. Dreyfus & P. Rabinow (Eds) *Michel Foucault: beyond structuralism and hermeneutics* (Sussex, The Harvester Press).

Foucault, M. (1985a) in: R. Hurley (Trans.) *The History of Sexuality: Volume 2* (New York, Vintage).

Foucault, M. (1985b) Final interview; Michel Foucault, *Raritan*, 1, pp. 1–13.

Foucault, M. (1986) in: R. Hurley (Trans.) *The History of Sexuality: Volume 3* (New York, Vintage).

Foucault, M. (1987) The ethic of care for the self as a practice of freedom, *Philosophy and Social Criticism*, 12, pp. 113–131.

Foucault, M. (1988a) Technologies of the Self, in: L. Martin, H. Cutman & P. Hutton (Eds) *Technologies of the Self* (Massachusetts, University of Massachusetts Press).

Foucalt, M. (1988b) The Political Technologies of Individuals, in: L. Martin, H. Gutman & P. Hutton (Eds) *Technologies of the Self* (Massachusetts, University of Massachusetts Press).

Foucault, M. (1993) About the beginning of the hermeneuties of the Self, *Political Theory*, 21, pp. 198–227.

Frank, B. (1987) Hegemonic Heterosexual Masculinity, *Studies in Political Economy*, 24, pp. 159–170.

Frank, B. (1990) Everyday masculinities, Thesis submitted in partial fulfilment of the requirements for the degree of Doctor of Philosophy, Dalhousie University, Halifax, Nova Scotia.

Frank, B. (1993) Straight/strait jackets for masculinity: educating for real men, *Atlantis*, 18 (1–2), pp. 47–59.

Gilbert, P. & Gilbert, R. (1995) *What's Going On?: girls' experiences of educational disadvantage* (Canberra, Department of Employment, Education and Training).

Haywood, C. (1993) Using sexuality: an exploration into the fixing of sexuality to make male identities in a mixed sexed sixth form, M.A. Sociology of Education Dissertation, University of Warwick.

Hinson, S. (1995) A practice focussed approach to addressing heterosexist violence in Australian schools, in: L. Laskey. & C. Beavis (Eds) *Schooling and Sexualities: teaching for a positive sexuality* (Geelong, Deakin University, Centre for Education and Change).

Hite, S. (1981) *The Hite Report on Male Sexuality* (New York, Alfred A. Knopf).

Hite, S. (1994) *The Hite Report on the Family* (London, Bloomsbury).

Holland, J., Ramazanoglu, C. & Share., S. (1993) *Wimp or Gladiator: contradictions in acquiring masculine sexuality* (London, Tufnell Press).

Huggins, A. (1997) The Australian male illness, injury and death by socialisation. Unpublished paper, Men's Health Teaching and Research Unit: School of Public Health, Curtin University, Perth, Western Australia.

Hunter, I. (1988) *Culture and Government: the emergence of literary education* (London, Macmillan Press).

Jordan, E. (1995a) Fighting boys and fantasy play: the construction of masculinity in the early years of School, *Gender and Education*, 7(1), pp. 69–86.

Jordan, E. (1995b) Warrior narratives in the kindergarten classroom: renegotiating the social contract, *Gender and Society*, 9(6), pp. 727–743.

Kehily, M. & Nayar, A. (1997) 'Lads and laughter': humour and the production of heterosexual hierarchies, *Gender and Education*, 9(1), pp. 69–87.

Kenway, J. (1995) Masculinities in schools: under siege, on the defensive and under reconstruction?

Discourse: studies in the cultural politics of education, 16(1), pp. 59–79.

Kenway, J. (1997) Boys' education, masculinity and gender reform: some introductory remarks, *Curriculum Perspectives*, 17(1), pp. 57–60.

Kessler, S., Ashenden, D.J., Connell., R. W. & Dowsett, G.W. (1985) Gender relations in secondary schooling, *Sociology of Education*, 58, pp. 34–48.

Laskey, L. Beavis, C. (1996) *Schooling and Sexualities* (Geelong, Deakin University).

Lehne, G. (1976) Homophobia among men, in; S. Deborah & R. Brannon (Eds) *The Forty-Nine Percent Majority* (New York, Random House).

Mac an Ghaill, M. (1994) *The Making of Men* (Buckingham, Open University Press).

Martino, W. (1994a) Masculinity and learning: exploring boys' underachievement and under-representation in subject English, *Interpretations*, 27(2), pp. 22–57.

Martino, W. (1994b) The gender bind and subject english: exploring questions of masculinity in developing interventionist strategies in the English classroom, *English in Australia*, 107, pp. 29–44.

Martino, W. (1995a) Gendered learning practices: exploring the costs of hegemonic masculinity for girls and boys in schools. Paper presented at the Gender Equity Task Force Conference, 22–24 February.

Martino, W. (1995b) Deconstructing masculinity in the English classroom: a site for reconstituting gendered subjectivity, *Gender and Education*, 7(2), pp. 205–220.

Martino, W. (1996). Boys and literacy: addressing the links between masculinity and learning. Paper presented at the Gender Networking Conference for the Department of School Education, Sydney, 28–29 May [forthcoming in: B. Comber & A. Simpson (Eds), *Negotiating Critical Literacies in Local Sites* (London, The Falmer Press)].

Martino, W. (1997a) 'A bunch of arseholes': exploring the politics of masculinity for adolescent boys in schools, *Social Alternatives*, 16(3), pp. 39–43.

Martino, W. (1997b) 'Dick heads, pooftas, try hards and losers': addressing masculinities and homophobia in the literacy classroom. Paper presented at the Gender & Literacy Forum, Primary English Teachers' Association (PETA), Sydney, 27 September.

Martino, W. (1998a) interrogating masculinities: regimes of practice, Doctoral thesis, School of Education, Murdoch University.

Martino, W. (1998b) 'Dickheads', 'poofs', 'try hards' and 'losers': critical literacy for boys in the English classroom, *English in Aotearoa*, 35, pp. 31–57.

Martino, W. &. Mellor, B. (1995) *Gendered Fictions* (Cottesloe, WA, Chalkface Press).

McLean, C. (1995a) What about 'what about the boys', *South Australian Education of Girls and Female Students' Association Inc. Journal*, 4 (3), pp. 15–25.

McLean, C. (1995b) Men, masculinity and heterosexuality, in: L. Laskey & C. Beavis (Eds.) *Schooling and Sexualities: teaching for a positive sexuality* (Geelong, Deakin University, Centre for Education and Change).

McLean, C. (1996) Masculinity and early childhood. Paper presented at the *Gender Equity Conference*, organised by the Catholic Education Office, South Australia, 21 August.

Messner, M. &. Sabo, D. (1990) *Sport, Men and the Gender Order* (Champaign, IL, Human Kinetics Books).

Nayak, A. & Kehily, M. (1996) Playing it straight: masculinities, homophobias and schooling, *Journal of Gender Studies*, 5(2), pp. 211–230.

Newburn, T. & Stanko, E. (1994) *Just Boys Doing Business* (London & New York, Routledge).

Nickson, A. (1996) Keeping a Straight Face: Schools, Students and Homosexuality, Part 1, in: L. Laskey & C. Beavis (Eds) *Schooling & Sexualities: Teaching for a Positive Sexuality* (Geelong, Deakin University Press).

Parker, A. (1996) The construction of masculinity within boys' physical education, *Gender and Education*, 8(2), pp. 114–157.

Redman, P. (1996) Curtis loves Ranjit: heterosexual masculinities, schooling and pupils' sexual cultures, *Educational Review*, 48(2), pp. 175–182.

Segal, L. (1990) *Slow Motion: Changing Masculinities: Changing Men* (London, Virago).

Skelton, C. (1996) Learning to be tough: the fostering of maleness in one primary school, *Gender and Education*, 8(2), pp. 185–197.

Steinberg, D.L., Epstein. D. & Johnson, R. (1997) *Border Patrols: policing the boundaries of heterosexuality* (London, Cassell).

Walker, J.C. (1988) *Louts and Legends* (Sydney, Allen & Unwin).

Ward, N. (1995) 'Pooftah', 'wanker', 'girl': homophobic harassment and violence in schools, in: *Girls & Boys: challenging perspective, building partnerships: Proceedings of the Third Conference of the Ministerial Advisory Committee on Gender Equity*

(Brisbane, Ministerial Advisory Committee on Gender Equity).

Whitson, D. (1990) Sport in the social construction of masculinity, in: M. Messner & D. Sabo (Eds) *Sport, Men and the Gender Order* (Champaign, IL, Human Kinetics Books).

Willis, P. (1977) *Learning to Labour* (Westmead, Saxon House).

Yates, L. (1997) Gender equity and the boys debate: what sort or challenge is it?, *British Journal of Sociology of Education*, 18(3), pp. 337–347.

The Trouble with Black Boys: The Role and Influence of Environmental and Cultural Factors on the Academic Performance of African American Males

PEDRO A. NOGUERA

All of the most important quality-of-life indicators suggest that African American males are in deep trouble. They lead the nation in homicides, both as victims and perpetrators (Skolnick & Currie, 1994), and in what observers regard as an alarming trend, they now have the fastest growing rate for suicide (National Research Council, 1989; Poussaint & Alexander, 2000). For the past several years, Black males have been contracting HIV and AIDS at a faster rate than any other segment of the population (Auerbach, Krimgold, & Lefkowitz, 2000; Centers for Disease Control, 1988; Kaplan, Johnson, Bailey, & Simon, 1987), and their incarceration, conviction, and arrest rates have been at the top of the charts in most states for some time (Roper, 1991; Skolnick & Currie, 1994). Even as babies, Black males have the highest probability of dying in the first year of life (Auerbach et al., 2000; National Research Council, 1989), and as they grow older they face the unfortunate reality of being the only group in the United States experiencing a decline in life expectancy (Spivak,

Prothrow-Stith, & Hausman, 1988). In the labor market, they are the least likely to be hired and in many cities, the most likely to be unemployed (Feagin & Sikes, 1994; Hacker, 1992; Massey & Denton, 1993; Moss & Tilly, 1995; Wilson, 1987).

Beset with such an ominous array of social and economic hardships, it is hardly surprising that the experience of Black males in education, with respect to attainment and most indicators of academic performance, also shows signs of trouble and distress. In many school districts throughout the United States, Black males are more likely than any other group to be suspended and expelled from school (Meier, Stewart, & England, 1989). From 1973 to 1977 there was a steady increase in African American enrollment in college. However, since 1977 there has been a sharp and continuous decline, especially among males (Carnoy, 1994; National Research Council, 1989). Black males are more likely to be classified as mentally retarded or suffering from a learning disability, more likely to be placed in special education (Milofsky, 1974), and

Pedor A. Noguera, "The Trouble with Black Boys: The Role and Influence of Environmental and Cultural Factors on the Academic Performance of African American Males" from *Urban Education* 38, No. 4 (July 2003): 431–459. Copyright © 2003 Corwin Press, Inc. Reprinted by permission.

more likely to be absent from advanced-placement and honors courses (Oakes, 1985; Pollard, 1993). In contrast to most other groups where males commonly perform at higher levels, such as in math- and science-related courses, the reverse is true for Black males (Pollard, 1993). Even class privilege and the material benefits that accompany it fail to inoculate Black males from low academic performance. When compared to their White peers, middle-class African American males lag significantly behind in both grade point average and on standardized tests (Jencks & Phillips, 1998).

It is not surprising that there is a connection between the educational performance of African American males and the hardships they endure within the larger society (Coleman et al., 1966). In fact, it would be more surprising if Black males were doing well academically in spite of the broad array of difficulties that confront them. Scholars and researchers commonly understand that environmental and cultural factors have a profound influence on human behaviors, including academic performance (Brookover & Erickson, 1969; Morrow & Torres, 1995). What is less understood is how environmental and cultural forces influence the way in which Black males come to perceive schooling and how those perceptions influence their behavior and performance in school. There is considerable evidence that the ethnic and socioeconomic backgrounds of students have bearing on how students are perceived and treated by the adults who work with them within schools (Brookover & Erickson, 1969; Morrow & Torres, 1995). However, we know less about the specific nature of the perceptions and expectations that are held toward Black males and how these may in turn affect their performance within schools. More to the point, there is considerable confusion regarding why being Black and male causes this segment of the population to stand out in the most negative and alarming ways, both in school and in the larger society.

This article is rooted in the notion that it is possible to educate all children, including Black males, at high levels. This idea is not an articulation of faith but rather a conclusion drawn from a vast body of research on human development and from research on the learning styles of Black children (Lee, 2000). Therefore, it is possible for schools to take actions that can reverse the patterns of low achievement among African American males. The fact that some schools and programs manage to do so already is further evidence that there exists a possibility of altering these trends (Edmonds, 1979). To the degree that we accept the idea that human beings have the capacity to resist submission to cultural patterns, demographic trends, environmental pressures and constraints, bringing greater clarity to the actions that can be taken by schools and community organizations to support the academic achievement of African American males could be the key to changing academic outcomes and altering the direction of negative trends for this segment of the population (Freire, 1972).

This article explores the possibility that the academic performance of African American males can be improved by devising strategies that counter the effects of harmful environmental and cultural forces. Drawing on research from a variety of disciplines, the article begins with an analysis of the factors that place certain individuals (i.e., African American males) at greater risk than others. This is followed by an analysis of the ways in which environmental and cultural forces interact and influence academic outcomes and how these factors shape the relationship between identity, particularly related to race and gender, and school performance. Finally, strategies for countering harmful environmental and cultural influences, both the diffuse and the direct, are explored with particular attention paid to recommendations for educators, parents, and youth service providers who seek to support young African American males.

The Nature of the "Risk"

The good news is that not all Black males are at risk. I was reminded of this fact on my way to work one morning. Before driving to San Francisco with a colleague, another Black male academic, we stopped to pick up a commuter so that we could make the trip across the Bay Bridge in the faster carpool lane during the middle of the rush hour. As it turned out, the first carpooler to approach our car was another Black male. As we drove across the bridge, we made small talk, going from basketball to the merits of living in the Bay Area, until finally we approached the subject of our careers. The rider informed us that he managed a highly profitable telecommunications firm, and if his plans progressed as he hoped, he would be retiring on a very lucrative pension in Hawaii before the age of 50. Contemplating his financial good fortune and that of my colleague and myself (although the two of us had no plans for early retirement), I posed the question, "What explains why we are doing so well and so many brothers like us are not?"

The answer was not obvious. All three of us were raised in working-class families, had grown up in tough neighborhoods, had close friends and family members who had been killed while they were young, and knew others who were serving time in prison. What made our lives, with our promising careers and growing families, so fortunate and so different? All three of us were raised by both of our parents, but further exploration revealed that none of us had regular contact with our fathers. We all attended public schools, but each of us felt that we had succeeded in spite of, and not because of, the schools we attended. With time running out as we approached our rider's stop, we threw out the possibility that the only thing that spared us the fate of so many of our brethren was luck, not getting caught for past indiscretions and not being in the wrong place at the wrong time.

Viewed in the context of the negative social patterns cited previously, the explanation for our apparent good luck does not seem mysterious. Although it is true that many Black males are confronted with a vast array of risks, obstacles, and social pressures, the majority manages to navigate these with some degree of success. The good news is that most Black males are not in prison, do not commit suicide, and have not contracted HIV/AIDS. These facts do not negate the significance of the problems that confront Black males, but they do help to keep the problems in perspective.

Understanding how and why many Black males avoid the pitfalls and hardships that beset others may help us to devise ways to protect and provide support for more of them.

The effects of growing up in poverty, particularly for children raised in socially isolated, economically depressed urban areas, warrants greater concern, especially given that one out of every three Black children is raised in a poor household (Carnoy, 1994). Here the evidence is clear that the risks faced by children, particularly African American males, in terms of health, welfare, and education, are substantially greater (Gibbs, 1988). A recent longitudinal study on the development of children whose mothers used drugs (particularly crack cocaine) during pregnancy found that when compared to children residing in similar neighborhoods from similar socioeconomic backgrounds, the children in the sample showed no greater evidence of long-term negative effects. This is not because the incidence of physical and cognitive problems among the sample was not high, but because it was equally high for the control group. The stunned researchers, who fully expected to observe noticeable differences between the two groups, were compelled to conclude that the harmful effects of living within an impoverished inner-city environment outweighed the damage inflicted by early exposure to drugs (Jackson, 1998).

A vast body of research on children in poverty shows that impoverished conditions greatly increase the multiplier effect on risk variables (i.e., single-parent household, low birth weight, low educational attainment of parents, etc.) (Gabarino, 1999). Poor children generally receive inferior services from schools and agencies that are located in the inner city, and poor children often have many unmet basic needs. This combination of risk factors means it is nearly impossible to establish cause and effect relationships among them. For example, research has shown that a disproportionate number of poor children suffer from a variety of sight disorders (Harry, Klingner, & Moore, 2000). However, the disabilities experienced by children are often related to poverty rather than a biological disorder. For example, because poor children often lack access to preventive health care, their untreated vision problems are inaccurately diagnosed as reading problems, and as a consequence, large numbers are placed in remedial and special education programs (Harry et al., 2000). Throughout the country, Black children are overrepresented in special education programs. Those most likely to be placed in such programs are overwhelmingly Black, male, and poor (Harry et al., 2000).

The situation in special education mirrors a larger trend in education for African Americans generally and males in particular. Rather than serving as a source of hope and opportunity, some schools are sites where Black males are marginalized and stigmatized (Meier et al., 1989). In school, Black males are more likely to be labeled with behavior problems and as less intelligent even while they are still very young (Hilliard, 1991). Black males are also more likely to be punished with severity, even for minor offenses, for violating school rules (Sandler, Wilcox, & Everson, 1985, p. 16) and often without regard for their welfare. They are more likely to be excluded from rigorous classes and prevented from accessing educational opportunities that might otherwise support and encourage them (Oakes, 1985, p. 53). Consistently, schools that serve Black males fail to nurture, support, or protect them.

However, changing academic outcomes and countering the risks experienced by Black males is not simply a matter of developing programs to provide support or bringing an end to unfair educational policies and practices. Black males often adopt behaviors that make them complicit in their own failure. It is not just that they are more likely to be punished or placed in remedial classes, it is also that they are more likely to act out in the classroom and to avoid challenging themselves academically. Recognizing that Black males are not merely passive victims but may also be active agents in their own failure, means that interventions designed to help them must take this into account. Changing policies, creating new programs, and opening new opportunities will accomplish little if such efforts are not accompanied by strategies to actively engage Black males

and their families in taking responsibility to improve their circumstances. Institutionally, this may require programmatic interventions aimed at buffering and offsetting the various risks to which Black males are particularly vulnerable. However, to be effective such initiatives must also involve efforts to counter and transform cultural patterns and what Ogbu (1987) has called the "oppositional identities" adopted by Black males that undermine the importance they attach to education.

As I will illustrate, one of the best ways to learn how this can be done is to study those schools and programs that have proven successful in accomplishing this goal. Additionally, it is important for such work to be anchored in a theoretical understanding of how the pressures exerted on Black males in American society can be contested. Without such an intellectual underpinning, it is unlikely that new interventions and initiatives will succeed at countering the hazardous direction of trends for African American males.

Structural Versus Cultural Explanations

Epidemiologists and psychologists have identified a number of risk factors within the social environment that when combined, are thought to have a multiplier effect on risk behavior. Lack of access to health care, adequate nutrition, and decent housing, growing up poor and in a single-parent household, being exposed to substance abuse at a young age, and living in a crime-ridden neighborhood are some of the variables most commonly cited (Earls, 1991, p. 14). Similarly, anthropologists and sociologists have documented ways in which certain cultural influences can lower the aspirations of Black males and contribute to the adoption of self-destructive behavior. Ogbu (1987) argued that community-based "folk theories" that suggest that because of the history of discrimination against Black people, even those who work hard will never reap rewards equivalent to Whites, could contribute to self-defeating behaviors (p. 23). There is also evidence that many Black males view sports or music as more promising routes to upward mobility than academic pursuits (Hoberman, 1997, pp. 48–49). Finally, some researchers have found that for some African American students, doing well in school is perceived as a sign that one has "sold out" or opted to "act White" for the sake of individual gain (Fordham, 1996, p. 12; Ogbu, 1990, p. 29).

Despite their importance and relevance to academic performance, risk variables and cultural pressures cannot explain individual behavior. Confronted with a variety of obstacles and challenges, some Black males still find ways to survive and in some cases, to excel. Interestingly, we know much less about resilience, perseverance, and the coping strategies employed by individuals whose lives are surrounded by hardships than we know about those who succumb and become victims of their environment. Deepening our understanding of how individuals cope with, and respond to, their social and cultural environments is an important part of finding ways to assist Black males with living healthy and productive lives.

In the social sciences, explanations of human behavior, especially that of the poor, have been the subject of considerable debate. Most often, the debate centers on those who favor structural explanations of behavior and those who prefer cultural explanations of behavior. Structuralists generally focus on political economy, the availability of jobs and economic opportunities, class structure, and social geography (Massey & Denton, 1993, pp. 7–24; Tabb, 1970, pp. 11–36; Wilson, 1978, pp. 22–46; Wilson, 1987, pp. 12–35). From this perspective, individuals are viewed as products of their environment, and changes in individual behavior are made possible by changes in the structure of opportunity. From this theoretical perspective, holding an individual responsible for their behavior makes little sense because behavior is shaped by forces beyond the control of any particular individual. Drug abuse, crime, and dropping out of school are largely seen as social consequences of inequality. According to this view, the most effective way to reduce objectionable behavior is to reduce the degree and extent of inequality in society.

In contrast, culturalists downplay the significance of environmental factors and treat human behavior as a product of beliefs, values, norms, and socialization. Cultural explanations of behavior focus on the moral codes that operate within particular families, communities, or groups (Anderson, 1990, p. 34). For example, the idea that poor people are trapped within a "culture of poverty," which has the effect of legitimizing criminal and immoral behavior, has dominated the culturalists' perspective of poverty (Glazer & Moynihan, 1963, pp. 221–267; Lewis, 1966, pp. 74–88). For the culturalists, change in behavior can only be brought about through cultural change. Hence, providing more money to inner-city schools or busing inner-city children to affluent suburban schools will do little to improve their academic performance because their attitudes toward school are shaped by the culture they brought from home and the neighborhood in which they live (Murray, 1984, pp. 147–254). According to this view, culture provides the rationale and motivation for behavior, and cultural change cannot be brought about through changes in governmental policy or by expanding opportunities.

A growing number of researchers are trying to find ways to work between the two sides of the debate. Dissatisfied with the determinism of the structuralists, which renders individuals as passive objects of larger forces, and with the "blame the victim" perspective of the culturalists, which views individuals as hopelessly trapped within a particular social/cultural milieu (Ryan, 1976, pp. 32–46), some researchers have sought to synthesize important elements from both perspectives while simultaneously paying greater attention to the importance of individual choice and agency (McLeod, 1987). From this perspective, the importance of both structure and culture is acknowledged, but so too is the understanding that individuals have the capacity to act and make choices that cannot be explained through the reductionism inherent in either framework (Morrow & Torres, 1995, pp. 112–134). The choices made by an individual may be shaped by both the available opportunities and the norms present within the cultural milieu in which they are situated. However, culture is not static and individual responses to their environment cannot be easily predicted. Both structural and cultural forces influence choices and actions, but neither has the power to act as the sole determinant of behavior because human beings also have the ability to produce cultural forms that can counter these pressures (Levinson, Foley, & Holland, 1996, pp. 21–26; Willis, 1977, pp. 62–81).

This is not to suggest that because individuals have the capacity to counter these forces, many will choose or be able to do so. The effects of poverty can be so debilitating that a child's life chances can literally be determined by a number of environmental and cultural factors such as the quality of prenatal care, housing, and food available to their mothers that are simply beyond the control of an individual or even of concerted community action. It would be naive and erroneous to conclude that strength of character and the possibility of individual agency can enable one to avoid the perils present within the environment or that it is easy for individuals to choose to act outside the cultural milieu in which they were raised. Even as we recognize that individuals make choices that influence the character of their lives, we must also recognize that the range of choices available are profoundly constrained and shaped by external forces. For this reason, efforts to counter behaviors that are viewed as injurious—whether dropping out of school, selling drugs, or engaging in violent behavior—must include efforts to comprehend the logic and motivations behind the behavior. Given the importance of agency and choice, the only way to change behavioral outcomes is to understand the cognitive processes that influence how individuals adapt, cope, and respond.

In a comprehensive study of teen pregnancy, Kristen Luker (1996) demonstrated the possibility for synthesizing the two perspectives—structural and cultural explanations of human behaviors that traditionally have been seen as irreconcilable. Teen pregnancy, which for years has been much more prevalent among low-income females than middle-class White females, has traditionally been explained as either the product of welfare dependency and permissive sexual mores (the culturalists) or the unfortunate result of inadequate access to birth control and economic opportunities (the structuralists). Through detailed interviews with a diverse sample of teen mothers, Luker put forward a different explanation that draws from both the cultural and the structural perspectives and acknowledges the role and importance of individual choice. She pointed out that although both middle-class and lower-class girls engage in premarital sex and sometimes become pregnant, middle-class girls are less likely to have babies during adolescence because they have a clear sense that it will harm their chance for future success. In contrast, when confronted with an unexpected pregnancy, poor girls are more likely to have babies; they do not perceive it as negatively affecting their future because college and a good job are already perceived as being out of reach. In fact, many girls in this situation actually believe that having a baby during adolescence will help them to settle down because they will now be responsible for another life (Luker, 1996, pp. 223–236).

Given the importance of individual "choice" to this particular behavior, any effort to reduce teen pregnancy that does not take into account the reasoning that guides decision making is unlikely to succeed. Similarly, efforts to improve the academic performance of African American males must begin by understanding the attitudes that influence how they perceive schooling and academic pursuits. To the extent that this does not happen, attempts to help Black males based primarily on the sensibilities of those who initiate them are unlikely to be effective and may be no more successful than campaigns that attempt to reduce drug use or violence by urging kids to "just say no" (Skolnick & Currie, 1994, p. 429).

Investigations into the academic orientation of Black male students must focus on the ways in which the subjective and objective dimensions of identity related to race and gender are constructed within schools and how these influence academic performance. Although psychologists have generally conceived of identity construction as a natural feature of human development (Cross, Parnham, & Helms, 1991, pp. 13–19; Erickson, 1968, p. 32), sociologists have long recognized that identities, like social roles, are imposed on individuals through various socialization processes

(Goffman, 1959, pp. 23–34). The processes and influences involved in the construction of Black male identity should be at the center of analyses of school performance because it is on the basis of their identities that Black males are presumed to be at risk, marginal, and endangered in school and throughout American society (Anderson, 1990, pp. 23–36; Gibbs, 1988, pp. 113–124; Kunjufu, 1985, p. 23).

Structural and cultural forces combine in complex ways to influence the formation of individual and collective identities, even as individuals may resist, actively or passively, the various processes involved in the molding of the "self." The fact that individuals can resist, subvert, and react against the cultural and structural forces which shape social identities compels us to recognize that individual choice, or what many scholars refer to as agency, also plays a major role in the way identities are constructed and formed (Giroux, 1983, pp. 23–36). For this reason, research on identity must pay careful attention to the attitudes and styles of behavior that African American males adopt and produce in reaction to the social environment and how these influence how they are seen and how they see themselves within the context of school. Writing on the general importance of identity to studies of schooling, Levinson et al. (1996) argued that "student identity formation within school is a kind of social practice and cultural production which both responds to, and simultaneously constitutes, movements, structures, and discourses beyond school" (p. 12).

Students can be unfairly victimized by the labeling and sorting processes that occur within school in addition to being harmed by the attitudes and behavior they adopt in reaction to these processes. For this reason, it is important to understand the factors that may enable them to resist these pressures and respond positively to various forms of assistance that may be provided within school or in the communities where they reside. By linking a focus on identity construction to an analysis of cultural production, it is the goal of this article to gain greater insight into how schools can be changed and how support programs can be designed to positively alter academic outcomes for African American males.

Identity and Academic Performance

It has long been recognized that schools are important sites of socialization. Schools are places where children learn how to follow instructions and obey rules, how to interact with others, and how to deal with authority (Apple, 1982, p. 47; Spring, 1994, p. 34). Schools are important sites for gender role socialization (Thorne, 1993, p. 22), and in most societies, they are primary sites for instruction about the values and norms associated with citizenship (Loewen, 1995, pp. 43–51; Spring, 1994, p. 16).

For many children, schools are also places where they learn about the meaning of race. Although this may occur through lesson plans adopted by teachers, it is even more likely that children learn about race through the hidden or informal curriculum (Apple, 1982, p. 64) and through nonstructured school activities such as recess (Dyson, 1994, p. 21). Even when teachers do not speak explicitly about race and racial issues with children, children become aware of physical differences related to race quite early (Tronyna & Carington, 1990, p. 18). However, children do not become aware of the significance attached to these physical differences until they start to understand the ideological dimensions of race and become cognizant of differential treatment that appears to be based on race (Miles, 1989, pp. 32–47). Name-calling, including the use of racial epithets, serves as one way of establishing racial boundaries even when children do not fully understand the meaning of the words that are used (Tronyna & Carington, 1990, p. 73). Similarly, school practices that isolate and separate children on the basis of race and gender also send children important messages about the significance of race and racial differences (Dyson, 1994, p. 34; Thorne, 1993, p. 45). Schools certainly are not the only places where children formulate views about race, but because schools are often sites where children are more likely to encounter persons of another race or ethnic group, they play a central role in influencing the character of race relations in communities and the larger society (Peshkin, 1991, p. 65).

As young people enter into adolescence and develop a stronger sense of their individual identities (Erickson, 1968, p. 18), the meaning and significance of race also change. Where it was once an ambiguous concept based largely on differences in physical appearance, language, and styles of behavior, race becomes a more rigid identity construct as children learn the historical, ideological, and cultural dimensions associated with racial group membership (Cross et al., 1991, pp. 34–49; Tatum, 1992, p. 39). Even children who once played and interacted freely across racial lines when they were younger often experience a tightening of racial boundaries and racial identities as they get older and begin following patterns of interaction modeled by adults (Metz, 1978, p. 221; Peshkin, 1991, p. 46). Peer groups play a powerful role in shaping identity because the desire to be accepted by one's peers and "fit in" with one's peers often becomes a paramount concern for most adolescents. Research has shown that in secondary school, peer groups assume a great influence over the orientation young people adopt toward achievement (Phelan, Davidson, & Ya, 1998, pp. 10–18), and they profoundly shape the way identities are constituted in school settings (Steinberg, 1996). As adolescents become clearer about the nature of their racial and gender identities, they begin to play a more active role in maintaining and policing these identities. Peer groups are also likely to impose negative sanctions on those who violate what are perceived as established norms of behavior and who attempt to construct identities that deviate significantly from prevailing conceptions of racial and gender identity (Peshkin, 1991).

Despite the importance that several researchers have placed on the role of peer groups in the socialization process, peer groups are by no means the only forces that shape the social construction of identity within schools (Fordham, 1996, p. 47; Ogbu, 1987, p. 87; Solomon, 1992, p. 22; Steinberg, 1996, p. 185). The structure and culture of school plays a major role in reinforcing and maintaining racial categories and the stereotypes associated with them. As schools sort children by perceived measures of their ability and as they single out certain children for discipline, implicit and explicit messages about racial and gender identities are conveyed. To the degree that White or Asian children are disproportionately placed in gifted and honors classes, the idea that such children are inherently smarter may be inadvertently reinforced. Similarly, when African American and Latino children are overrepresented in remedial classes, special education programs, or on the lists for suspension or expulsion, the idea that these children are not as smart or as well behaved is also reinforced (Ferguson, 2000, p. 134). Such messages are conveyed even when responsible adults attempt to be as fair as possible in their handling of sorting and disciplinary activities. Because the outcomes of such practices often closely resemble larger patterns of success and failure that correspond with racial differences in American society, they invariably have the effect of reinforcing existing attitudes and beliefs about the nature and significance of race.

For African American males, who are more likely than any other group to be subjected to negative forms of treatment in school, the message is clear: Individuals of their race and gender may excel in sports, but not in math or history. The location of Black males within school, in remedial classes or waiting for punishment outside the principal's office, and the roles they perform within school suggest that they are good at playing basketball or rapping, but debating, writing for the school newspaper, or participating in the science club are strictly out of bounds. Such activities are out of bounds not just because Black males may perceive them as being inconsistent with who they think they are but also because there simply are not enough examples of individuals who manage to participate in such activities without compromising their sense of self. Even when there are small numbers of Black males who do engage in activities that violate established norms, their deviation from established patterns often places them under considerable scrutiny from their peers who are likely to regard their transgression of group norms as a sign of "selling out."

Researchers such as Ogbu and Fordham have attributed the marginality of Black students to oppositional behavior (Fordham, 1996, p. 46; Ogbu, 1987, p. 34). They argue that Black students hold themselves back out of fear that they will be ostracized by their peers. Yet, what these researchers do not acknowledge is the dynamic that occurs between Black students, males in particular, and the culture that is operative within schools. Black males may engage in behaviors that contribute to their underachievement and marginality, but they are also more likely to be channeled into marginal roles and to be discouraged from challenging themselves by adults who are supposed to help them. Finally, and most important, Ogbu and Fordham fail to take into account the fact that some Black students, including males, find ways to overcome the pressures exerted on them and manage to avoid choosing between their racial and gender identity and academic success. Even if few in number, there are students who manage to maintain their identities and achieve academically without being ostracized by their peers. Understanding how such students navigate this difficult terrain may be the key to figuring out how to support the achievement of larger numbers of Black students.

A recent experience at a high school in the Bay Area illustrates how the interplay of these two socializing forces, peer groups and school sorting practices, can play out for individual students. I was approached by a Black male student who needed assistance with a paper on *Huckleberry Finn* that he was writing for his 11th-grade English class. After reading what he had written, I asked why he had not discussed the plight of Jim, the runaway slave who is one of the central characters of the novel. The student informed me that his teacher had instructed the class to focus on the plot and not to get into issues about race because according to the teacher, that was not the main point of the story. He explained that two students in the class, both Black males, had objected to the use of the word "nigger" throughout the novel and had been told by the teacher that if they insisted

on making it an issue they would have to leave the course. Both of these students opted to leave the course even though it meant that they would have to take another course that did not meet the college preparatory requirements. The student I was helping explained that because he needed the class he would just "tell the teacher what she wanted to hear." After our meeting, I looked into the issue further and discovered that one student, a Black female, had chosen a third option: She stayed in the class but wrote a paper focused on race and racial injustice, even though she knew it might result in her being penalized by the teacher.

This example reveals a number of important lessons about the intersection of identity, school practices, and academic performance. Confronted by organizational practices, which disproportionately place Black students in marginal roles and groupings, and pressure from peers, which may undermine the importance attached to academic achievement, it will take considerable confidence and courage for Black students to succeed. The four Black students in this English class were already removed from their Black peers by their placement in this honors course. In such a context, one seemed to adopt what Fordham (1996) described as a "raceless" persona (the student I was assisting) to satisfy the demands of the teacher, but this is only one of many available options. Two others responded by choosing to leave for a lower level class where they would be reunited with their peers with their identities intact but with diminished academic prospects. The option exercised by the female student in the class is perhaps the most enlightening yet difficult to enact. She challenged her teacher's instructions, choosing to write about race and racism, even though she knew she would be penalized for doing so. Yet she also had no intention of leaving the class, despite the isolation she experienced, to seek out the support of her peers.

This case reveals just some of the ways Black students may respond to the social pressures that are inherent in school experiences. Some actively resist succumbing to stereotypes or the pressure of peers, whereas others give in to these pressures in search of affirmation of their social identity. For those who seek to help Black students and males in particular, the challenge is to find ways to support their resistance to negative stereotypes and school sorting practices and to make choosing failure a less likely option for them. The teacher mentioned in the case just described may or may not have even realized how her actions in relation to the curriculum led her Black students to make choices that would profoundly influence their education. As the following section will illustrate, when educators are aware of the social and cultural pressures exerted on students, the need to choose between one's identity and academic success can be eliminated.

Learning from Students and the Schools that Serve them Well

Fortunately, there is considerable evidence that the vast majority of Black students, including males, would like to do well in school (Anderson, 1990, p. 249; Kao & Tienda, 1998, p. 36). Additionally, there are schools where academic success for Black students is the norm and not the exception (Edmonds, 1979, p. 11; Sizemore, 1988, p. 45). Both of these facts provide a basis for hope that achievement patterns can be reversed if there is a willingness to provide the resources and support to create the conditions that nurture academic success.

In my own research at high schools in northern California, I have obtained consistent evidence that most Black students value education and would like to succeed in school. In response to a survey about their experiences in school, nearly 90% of the Black male respondents ($N = 147$) responded "agree" or "strongly agree" to the questions "I think education is important" and "I want to go to college." However, in response to the questions "I work hard to achieve good grades" and "My teachers treat me fairly," less than a quarter of the respondents, 22% and 18% respectively, responded affirmatively. An analysis of just these responses to the survey suggests a disturbing discrepancy between what students claim they feel about the importance of education, the effort they expend, and the support they receive from teachers (Noguera, 2001). Similar results were obtained from a survey of 537 seniors at an academic magnet high school. African American males were least likely to indicate that they agreed or strongly agreed with the statement "My teachers support me and care about my success in their class" (see Table 1).

Rosalind Mickelson (1990) found similar discrepancies between expressed support for education and a commitment to hard work. Her research findings led her to conclude that some Black students experience what she referred to as an "attitude-achievement paradox." For Mickelson, the reason for the discrepancy is that although many Black students say they value education, such an expression is little more than an "abstract" articulation of belief. However, when pressed to state whether they believe that education will actually lead to a better life for them, the Black students in Mickelson's study expressed the "concrete" belief that it would not. Mickelson concluded that the contradiction between abstract and concrete beliefs toward education explains why there is a discrepancy between the attitudes expressed by Black students and their academic outcomes (pp. 42–49).

Although Mickelson's (1990) findings seem plausible, I think it is also important to consider how the experiences of Black students in schools, especially males, may result in a leveling of aspirations. If students do not believe that their teachers

Table 1. "My Teachers Support Me and Care About My Success in Their Class" (in Percentages) (N = 537)

	Black Male	Black Female	Asian Male	Asian Female	White Male	White Female
Strongly agree	8	12	24	36	33	44
Agree	12	16	42	33	21	27
Disagree	38	45	16	15	18	11
Strongly disagree	42	27	18	16	28	18

care about them and are actively concerned about their academic performance, the likelihood that they will succeed is greatly reduced. In MetLife's annual survey on teaching, 39% of students surveyed ($N = 3,961$) indicated that they trust their teachers "only a little or not at all"; when the data from the survey were disaggregated by race and class, minority and poor students indicated significantly higher levels of distrust (47% of minorities and 53% of poor students stated that they trusted their teachers only a little or not at all) (MetLife, 2000, p. 184). Though it is still possible that some students will succeed even if they do not trust or feel supported by their teachers, research on teacher expectations suggests that these feelings have a powerful effect on student performance (Weinstein, Madison, & Kuklinski, 1995, pp. 124–125). Moreover, there is research that suggests that the performance of African Americans, more so than other students, is influenced to a large degree by the social support and encouragement that they receive from teachers (Foster, 1997, p. 122; Ladson-Billings, 1994, p. 36; Lee, 2000, p. 57). To the extent that this is true, and if the nature of interactions between many Black male students and their teachers tends to be negative, it is unlikely that it will be possible to elevate their achievement without changing the ways in which they are treated by teachers and the ways in which they respond to those who try to help them.

However, there are schools where African American male students do well and where high levels of achievement are common. For example, a recent analysis of the academic performance indicators of public schools in California revealed that there are 22 schools in the state where Black students compose 50% or more of the student population and have aggregate test scores of 750 or greater (1,000 is the highest possible score) (Foster, 2001). Most significantly, when the test-score data for these schools were disaggregated on the basis of race and gender, there was no evidence of an achievement gap. Though schools such as these are few in number, given the fact that there are more than 2,000 public schools in California, the fact that they exist suggests that similar results should be possible elsewhere.

Researchers who have studied effective schools have found that such schools possess the following characteristics: (a) a clear sense of purpose, (b) core standards within a rigorous curriculum, (c) high expectations, (d) a commitment to educate all students, (e) a safe and orderly learning environment, (f) strong partnerships with parents, and (g) a problem-solving attitude (Murphy & Hallinger, 1985; Sizemore, 1988). Though the criteria used to determine effectiveness rely almost exclusively on data from standardized tests and ignore other criteria, there is no disagreement that such schools consistently produce high levels of academic achievement among minority students. Researchers on effective schools for low-income African American students also cite the supportive relations that exist between teachers and students and the ethos of caring and accountability that pervade such schools as other essential ingredients of their success (Sizemore, 1988). Educational reformers and researchers must do more to investigate ways to adopt strategies that have proven successful at schools where achievement is less likely. As Ron Edmonds (1979), formerly one of the leading researchers on effective schools, stated, "We already know more than enough to successfully educate all students" (p. 26). The challenge before educators and policy makers is to find ways to build on existing models of success.

Unfortunately, most African American children are not enrolled in effective schools that nurture and support them while simultaneously providing high quality instruction. Even as pressure is exerted to improve the quality of public education so that the supply of good schools is increased, other strategies must be devised at the community level to provide Black children with support. For example, there are long-standing traditions within Jewish and many Asian communities to provide children with religious and cultural instruction outside of school. In several communities throughout the United States, Black parents are turning to churches and community organizations as one possible source of such support (McPartland & Nettles, 1991). In northern California, organizations such as Simba and the

Omega Boys Club (both community-based mentoring programs) provide African American males with academic support and adult mentors outside of school (Watson & Smitherman, 1996). Organizations such as these affirm the identities of Black males by providing them with knowledge and information about African and African American history and culture and by instilling a sense of social responsibility toward their families and communities (Ampim, 1993; Myers, 1988). Unfortunately, these organizations are small and are largely unable to serve the vast numbers of young people in need. Moreover, it is unlikely that such organizations can completely counter the harmful effects of attendance in unsupportive and even hostile schools because they are designed to complement learning that is supposed to take place in school. Still, the model they provide demonstrates that it is possible to work outside of schools to have a positive influence on the academic performance of African American youth. Given their relative success but small size, it would be advisable to find ways to replicate them elsewhere.

Drawing from the research on mentoring and student resilience that has identified strategies that are effective in supporting the academic achievement of African American students, community organizations and churches can attempt to compensate for the failings of schools. Through after-school and summer school programs, these groups can provide young people with access to positive role models and social support that can help buffer young people from the pressures within their schools and communities (Boykin, 1983). Although such activities should not be seen as a substitute for making public schools more responsive to the communities that they serve, they do represent a tangible action that can be taken immediately to respond to the needs of Black youth, particularly males who often face the greatest perils.

Conclusion: The Need for Further Research

Although this article made reference to the cultural norms, attitudes, and styles of behavior

African American males may adopt and produce that can diminish the importance they attach to academic achievement, the emphasis of this paper has been on the ways in which schools disserve and underserve this population of students. Such an emphasis is necessary because research on effective schools has shown that when optimal conditions for teaching and learning are provided, high levels of academic success for students, including African American males, can be achieved. Put differently, if we can find ways to increase the supply of effective schools, it may be possible to mitigate against some of the risks confronting Black males. This does not mean the question of how to influence the attitudes, behaviors, and stances of Black males toward school and education generally does not need to be addressed or that it does not require further investigation. To the extent that we recognize that all students are active participants in their own education and not passive objects whose behavior can be manipulated by adults and reform measures, then the importance of understanding how to influence behavior cannot be understated. Learning how to influence the attitudes and behaviors of African American males must begin with an understanding of the ways in which structural and cultural forces shape their experiences in school and influence the construction of their identities. In this regard, it is especially important that future research be directed toward a greater understanding of youth culture and the processes related to cultural production.

Like popular culture, youth culture—and all of the styles and symbols associated with it—is dynamic and constantly changing. This is particularly true for inner-city African American youth whose speech, dress, music, and tastes often establish trends for young people across America. For many adults, this culture is also impenetrable and often incomprehensible. Yet, despite the difficulty of understanding and interpreting youth culture, it is imperative that efforts to help Black youth be guided by ongoing attempts at understanding the cultural forms they produce and the ways in which they respond and adapt to their social and cultural environment. Without such an understanding, efforts to influence the attitudes and behaviors of

African American males will most likely fail to capture their imaginations and be ignored.

The importance of understanding youth culture became clear when embarking on research on how the popular media influences the attitudes of young people toward violence. Part of this research attempted to study how young people react to violent imagery in films by watching segments of popular movies with groups of middle school students and discussing their interpretations and responses to the ways violence was depicted. Following a series of discussions of their moral and ethical judgments of the violence conveyed in the films, the students asked to watch the film *Menace to Society* as part of the research exercise. Surprisingly, several of the students owned copies of the film and many had seen the film so many times that they had memorized parts of the dialogue. The film, which tells the story of a young man growing up in south central Los Angeles, is filled with graphic images of violence. After viewing, it became apparent that there might be some truth to the idea that violent films do condition young people to rationalize violent behavior as a legitimate and appropriate way for resolving conflicts and getting what they want. However, when discussing the film, it became clear that most were repulsed by the violence even though they were entertained by it, and rather than identifying with perpetrators of violence in the film, they identified most strongly with those characters who sought to avoid it (Noguera, 1995).

This experience and others like it made me realize how easy it is for adults to misinterpret and misunderstand the attitudes and behavior of young people. Generational differences, especially when compounded by differences in race and class, often make it difficult for adults to communicate effectively with youth. Many adults are aware of the chasm that separates them from young people, yet adults typically take actions intended to benefit young people without ever investigating whether the interventions meet the needs or concerns of youth. There is a need to consult with young people on how the structure and culture of schools contribute to low academic achievement and to enlist their input when interventions to improve student performance are being designed and implemented.

In addition to research on youth culture, there is a pressing need for further research on how identities—especially related to the intersection of race, class, and gender—are constructed within schools and how these identities affect students' attitudes and dispositions toward school, learning, and life in general. Presently such an analysis is largely absent from the policies and measures that are pursued to reform schools and improve classroom practice. Consistently, the focus of reform is on what adults and schools should do to improve student achievement, with students treated as passive subjects who can easily be molded to conform to our expectations. To devise a policy that will enable successes achieved in a particular program, classroom, or school to be replicated elsewhere, we must be equipped with an understanding of the process through which identities are shaped and formed within schools. There is also a need for further research on peer groups and their role in influencing the academic orientation of students.

Much of what I know about the plight of African American males comes from my personal experience growing up as a Black male and raising two sons. I have an intuitive sense that the way we are socialized to enact our masculinity, especially during adolescence, is a major piece of the problem. Researchers such as Geneva Smitherman (1977) and others have argued that Black children, and males in particular, often behave in ways that are perceived as hostile and insubordinate by adults (p. 234). Others suggest that males generally, and Black males especially, have particularly fragile egos and are susceptible to treating even minor slights and transgressions as an affront to their dignity and sense of self-respect (Kunjufu, 1985, p. 16; Madhubuti, 1990, p. 88; Majors & Billson, 1992, p. 92; West, 1993, p. 47). Such interpretations resonate with my own experience, but it is still not clear how such knowledge can be used to intervene effectively on behalf of African American males.

I recall that as a young man, I often felt a form of anger and hostility that I could not attribute to a particular incident or cause. As a teacher, I have observed similar forms of hostility among Black male students, and for the past 3 years, I have witnessed my eldest son exhibit the same kinds of attitudes and behavior. Undoubtedly, some of this can be explained as a coping strategy: Black males learn at an early age that by presenting a tough exterior it is easier to avoid threats or attacks (Anderson, 1990, p. 38). It may also be true, and this is clearly speculation, that the various ways in which Black males are targeted and singled out for harsh treatment (at school or on the streets by hostile peers or by the police) elicit postures of aggression and ferocity toward the world.

Given the range and extent of the hardships that beset this segment of the population, there is no doubt that there are some legitimate reasons for young Black males to be angry. Yet, it is also clear that this thinly veiled rage and readiness for conflict can be self-defeating and harmful to their well-being. One of the consequences of this hostility and anger may be that such attitudes and behaviors have a negative effect on their academic performance. Adults, especially women, may be less willing to assist a young male who appears angry or aggressive. A colleague of mine has argued that what some refer to as the "fourth grade syndrome" the tendency for the academic performance of Black males to take a decisive downward turn at the age of 9 or 10, may be explained by the fact that this is the age when Black boys start to look like young men (Hilliard, 1991, p. 113; Kunjufu, 1985, p. 18). Ferguson (2000) found in his research in Shaker Heights, Ohio, that Black students were more likely than White students to cite "toughness" as a trait they admired in others (p. 23). If these researchers are correct, and if the toughness admired by Black males evokes feelings of fear among some of their teachers, it is not surprising that trouble in school would be common. Gaining a clearer understanding of this phenomenon may be one important part of the process needed for altering academic trends among Black males.

Still, it would be a mistake to conclude that until we find ways to change the attitudes and behaviors of Black males, nothing can be done to improve their academic performance. There is no doubt that if schools were to become more nurturing and supportive, students would be more likely to perceive schools as a source of help and opportunity rather than an inhospitable place that one should seek to escape and actively avoid. Changing the culture and structure of schools such that African American male students come to regard them as sources of support for their aspirations and identities will undoubtedly be the most important step that can be taken to make high levels of academic achievement the norm rather than the exception.

References

Ampim, M. (1993). *Towards an understanding of Black community development.* Oakland, CA: Advancing the Research.

Anderson, E. (1990). *Streetwise: Race, class, and change in an urban community.* Chicago: University of Chicago Press.

Apple, M. (1982). *Education and power.* Boston: ARK.

Aucrbach, J. A., Krimgold, B. K., & Lefkowitz, B. (2000). *Improving health: It doesn't take a revolution. Health and social inequality.* Washington, DC: Kellogg Foundation.

Boykin, W. (1983). On the academic task performance and African American children. In J. Spencer (Ed.), *Achievement and achievement motives* (pp. 16–36). Boston: Freeman.

Brookover, W. B., & Erickson, E. L. (1969). *Society, schools, and learning.* Boston: Allyn and Bacon.

Carnoy, M. (1994). *Faded dreams: The politics and economics of race in America.* New York: Cambridge University Press.

Centers for Disease Control. (1988). Distribution of AIDS cases by racial/ethnic group and exposure category: United States (June 1,1981 to July 4,1988). *Morbidity and Mortality Weekly Report, 55.* 1–10.

Coleman, J., Campbell, E., Hobson, C., McPartland, J., Mood, A., Weinfeld, F., et al. (1966). *Equality of educational opportunity.* Washington, DC: Government Printing Office.

Cross, W., Parnham, T., & Helms, J. (1991). *Shades of Black: Diversity in African American Identity.* Philadelphia: Temple University Press.

Dyson, A. H. (1994). The Ninjas, the X-Men, and the Ladies: Playing with power and identity in an urban primary school. *Teachers College Record, 96*(2), 219–239.

Earls, F. (1991). Not fear, nor quarantine, but science: Preparation for a decade of research to advance knowledge about causes and control of violence in youths. *Journal of Adolescent Health, 12,* 619–629.

Edmonds, R. (1979). Effective schools for the urban poor. *Educational Leadership, 37*(1), 15–27.

Erickson, E. (1968). *Identity: Youth and crisis.* New York: Norton.

Feagin, J. R., & Sikes, M. P. (1994). *Living with racism: The Black middle class experience.* Boston: Beacon.

Ferguson, R. (2000). A *diagnostic analysis of Black-White GPA disparities in Shaker Heights, Ohio.* Washington, DC: Brookings Institution.

Fordham, S. (1996). *Blacked out: Dilemmas of race, identity, and success at Capital High.* Chicago: University of Chicago Press.

Foster, M. (1997). *Black teachers on teaching.* New York: New Press.

Foster, M. (2001). *University of California report of Black student achievement.* Unpublished manuscript. University of California, Santa Barbara.

Freire, P. (1972). *Pedagogy of the oppressed.* New York: Continuum Publishing.

Gabarino, J. (1999). *Lost boys: Why our sons turn to violence and how to save them.* New York: Free Press.

Gibbs, J. T. (1988). *Young, Black, and male in America: An endangered species.* New York: Auburn House.

Giroux, H. (1983). *Theory and resistance in education.* New York: Bergin and Harvey.

Glazer, N., & Moynihan, D. (1963). *Beyond the melting pot.* Cambridge, MA: MIT Press.

Goffman, E. (1959). *The presentation of self in everyday life.* Garden City, NY: Doubleday.

Hacker, A. (1992). *Two nations: Black, White, separate, hostile, unequal.* New York: Scribner.

Harry, B., Klingner, J., & Moore, R. (2000, November). *Of rocks and soft places: Using qualitative methods to investigate the processes that result in disproportionality.* Paper presented at the Minority Issues in Special Education Symposium, Harvard University, Cambridge, MA.

Hilliard, A. (1991). Do we have the will to educate all children? *Educational Leadership, 49*(1), 31–36.

Hoberman, J. (1997). *Darwin's athletes.* New York: Houghton Mifflin.

Jackson, J. (1998). The myth of the crack baby. *Family Watch Library, September/October,* 4–12.

Jencks, C., & Phillips, M. (Eds.). (1998). *The Black-White test score gap.* Washington, DC: Brookings Institution.

Kao, G., & Tienda, M. (1998). Educational aspirations among minority youth. *American Journal of Education, 106,* 349–384.

Kaplan, H., Johnson, R., Bailey, C., & Simon. W. (1987). The sociological study of AIDS: A critical review of the literature and suggested research agenda. *Journal of Health and Social Science Behavior, 28,* 140–157.

Kunjufu, J. (1985). *Countering the conspiracy to destroy Black boys.* Chicago: African American Images.

Ladson-Billings, G. (1994). *The dreamkeepers: Successful teachers of African American children.* San Francisco: Jossey-Bass.

Lee, C. (2000). *The state of knowledge about the education of African Americans.* Washington, DC: American Educational Research Association, Commission on Black Education.

Levinson, B., Foley, D., & Holland, D. (1996). *The cultural production of the educated person.* Albany: SUNY Press.

Lewis, O. (1966). *La vida: A Puerto Rican family in the culture of poverty—San Juan and New York.* New York: Random House.

Loewen, J. (1995). *Lies my teacher told me.* New York: New Press.

Luker, K. (1996). *Dubious conceptions: The politics of teenage pregnancy.* Cambridge, MA: Harvard University Press.

Madhubuti, H. R. (1990). *Black men, obsolete, single, dangerous? The African American family in transition: Essays in discovery, solution, and hope.* Chicago: Third World Press.

Majors, R., & Billson, M. (1992). *Cool pose: Dilemmas of Black manhood in America.* New York: Simon & Schuster.

Massey, D., & Denton, N. (1993). *American apartheid.* Cambridge, MA: Harvard University Press.

McLeod, J. (1987). *Ain't no makin' it.* Boulder, CO: Westview.

McPartland, J., & Nettles, S. (1991). Using community adults as advocates or mentors for at-risk middle school students: A two-year evaluation of Project RAISE. *American Journal of Education, August,* 28–47.

Meier, K., Stewart, J., & England, R. (1989). *Race, class and education: The politics of second generation discrimination.* Madison: University of Wisconsin Press.

Metz, M. (1978). *Classrooms and corridors.* Berkeley: University of California Press.

MetLife. (2000). *The MetLife survey of the American teacher; 2000: Are we preparing students for the 21st century?* New York: Author.

Mickelson, R. (1990). The attitude achievement paradox among Black adolescents. *Sociology of Education, 63*(1), 37–62.

Miles, R. (1989). *Racism.* London: Routledge Kegan Paul.

Milofsky, C. (1974). Why special education isn't special. *Harvard Educational Review, 44*(4), 437–158.

Morrow, R. A., & Torres, C. A. (1995). *Social theory and education: A critique of theories of social and cultural reproduction.* Albany: SUNY Press.

Moss, P., & Tilly, C. (1995). *Raised hurdles for Black men: Evidence from interviews with employers* (Working Paper). New York: Russell Sage.

Murphy, J., & Hallinger, P. (1985). Effective high schools: What are the common characteristics? *NASSP Bulletin, 69*(477), 18–22.

Murray, C. A. (1984). *Losing ground: American social policy, 1950–1980.* New York: Basic Books.

Myers, L. J. (1988). *Understanding an Afrocentric worldview: Introduction to an optimal psychology.* Dubuque, IA: Kendall/Hunt.

National Research Council. (1989). *A common destiny: Blacks and American society.* Washington, DC: National Academy Press.

Noguera, P. (1995). Reducing and preventing youth violence: An analysis of causes and an assessment of successful programs. In California Wellness Foundation (Ed.), *1995 Wellness Lectures* (pp. 25–43). Oakland: California Wellness Foundation and the University of California, Berkeley.

Noguera, P. (2001). Racial politics and the elusive quest for equity and excellence in education. *Education and Urban Society, 34*(1), 27–42.

Oakes, J. (1985). *Keeping track: How schools structure inequality.* New Haven, CT: Yale University Press.

Ogbu, J. (1987). Opportunity structure, cultural boundaries, and literacy. In J. Langer (Ed.), *In language, literacy and culture: Issues of society and schooling* (pp. 42–57). Norwood, NJ: Ablex.

Ogbu, J. (1990). Literacy and schooling in subordinate cultures: The case of Black Americans. In K. Lomotey (Ed.), *Going to school* (pp. 3–21). Albany: SUNY Press.

Peshkin, A. (1991). *The color of strangers, the color of friends.* Chicago: University of Chicago Press.

Phelan, P. A., Davidson, H., & Ya, C. (1998). *Adolescent worlds.* Albany: SUNY Press.

Pollard, D. S. (1993). Gender, achievement and African American students' perceptions of their school experience. *Educational Psychologist, 28*(4), 294–303.

Poussaint, A., & Alexander, A. (2000). *Lay my burden down: Unraveling suicide and the mental health crisis among African Americans.* Boston: Beacon.

Roper, W. L. (1991). The prevention of minority youth violence must begin despite risks and imperfect understanding. *Public Health Reports, 106*(3), 229–231.

Ryan, W. (1976). *Blaming the victim.* New York: Vintage.

Sandler, D. P., Wilcox, A. J., & Everson, R. B. (1985). Cumulative effects of lifetime passive smoking on cancer risks. *Lancet, 1*(24), 312–315.

Sizemore, B. (1988). The Madison School: A turnaround case. *Journal of Negro Education, 57*(3), 243–266.

Skolnick, J. H., & Currie, E. (Eds.). (1994). *Crisis in American institutions* (9th ed.). New York: HarperCollins.

Smitherman, G. (1977). *Talkin' and testifyin': The language of Black America.* Boston: Houghton Mifflin.

Solomon, P. (1992). *Black resistance in high school.* Albany: SUNY press.

Spivak, H., Prothrow-Stith, D., & Hausman, A. (1988). Dying is no accident: Adolescents, violence, and intentional injury. *Pediatric Clinics of North America, 35*(6), 1339–1347.

Spring, J. (1994). *American Education.* New York: McGraw-Hill.

Steinberg, L. (1996). *Beyond the classroom.* New York: Simon & Schuster.

Tabb, W. (1970). *The political economy of the Black ghetto.* New York: Norton.

Tatum, B. D. (1992). Talking about race, learning about racism: The application of racial identity development theory in the classroom. *Harvard Educational Review, 62*(1), 1–24.

Thorne, B. (1993). *Gender play.* New Brunswick, NJ: Rutgers University Press.

Tronyna, B., &. Carington, B. (1990). *Education, racism and reform.* London: Routledge Kegan Paul.

Watson, C., & Smitherman, G. (1996). *Educating African American males: Detroit's Malcom X Academy*. Chicago: Third World Press.

Weinstein, R. S., Madison, S., & Kuklinski, M. (1995). Raising expectations in schooling: Obstacles and opportunities for change. *American Educational Research Journal, 32*(1), 121–159.

West, C. (1993). *Race matters*. Boston: Beacon.

Willis, P. (1977). *Learning to labor*. New York: Columbia University Press.

Wilson, W. (1978). *The declining significance of race*. Chicago: University of Chicago Press.

Wilson, W. (1987). *The truly disadvantaged*. Chicago: University of Chicago Press.

The Gender of Religion

The first time people put in an appearance in the Bible, it's gendered. "Male and female created He them" is the ungrammatical but somehow authoritative way the King James Bible puts it in Genesis (1:27). And this has always been a justification for a divinely ordained binary division between males and females.

But how can we be so sure? After all, it doesn't say "male or female"—as if one had to be only one and not the other. In fact, it might even mean that "He" created each of us as "male and female"—a divinely inspired androgyny.

We needn't necessarily subscribe to these positions to recognize two important things about religion and its relation to gender. First, religion, itself, at least in the Western world, is preoccupied with gender (Eastern religions are far less obsessed with gender). Indeed, prescribing the proper relationships between women and men is one of the Bible's chief preoccupations. And, second, that all such prescriptive elements are subject to multiple interpretations.

The institutional articulation of proper interpretations of doctrine—the fact that religious "experts" tell us what these rather vague prescriptive notions actually mean in everyday life—makes these timeless Biblical truths quite responsive to immediate, concrete, historical needs. For centuries, as Anthony Layng points out, the institution of the church used certain Biblical passages to justify the utter subordination of women. Whether articulated by Dan Brown or feminist theologians, the Biblically inspired but utterly political persecution of independent women is an indelible stain on the history of religious institutions.

Whether in doctrine or in institutional practices, women's second-class status has generated significant resistance from women. And yet, ironically, women are far more religious than men, far more likely to go to church, and far more likely to say that God has a place in daily conversations. David de Vaus and Ian McAllister explain this.

Each generation finds the texts it needs to justify the world as that generation finds it. Today, as the formerly fixed prescriptions of the proper relationships between women and men are being challenged everywhere in the world, new generations of the observant are pointing to different, if equally canonical, texts to justify their position. Jen'Nan Ghazal Read and John Bartkowski show how a new generation of American-born, second-generation Muslim students are re-embracing the veil (much to their parents' shock!) as a way to connect to a global Islamic community that they have actually never known.

To Veil or Not to Veil?: A Case Study of Identity Negotiation Among Muslim Women in Austin, Texas

JEN'NAN GHAZAL READ AND JOHN P. BARTKOWSKI

In light of expanded social opportunities for women in Western industrialized countries, scholars have turned their attention to the status of women in other parts of the world. This burgeoning research literature has given rise to a debate concerning the social standing of Muslim women in the Middle East. On one hand, some scholars contend that Muslim women occupy a subordinate status within many Middle Eastern countries. Some empirical evidence lends support to this view, as many researchers have highlighted the traditional and gendered customs prescribed by Islam—most notably, the veiling and shrouding of Muslim women (Afshar 1985; Fox 1977; Odeh 1993; Papanek 1973; see Dragadze 1994 for review).

On the other hand, a growing number of scholars now argue that claims about the oppression and subjugation of veiled Muslim women may, in many regards, be overstated (Brenner 1996; El-Guindi 1981, 1983; El-Solh and Mabro 1994; Fernea 1993, 1998; Gocek and Balaghi 1994; Hessini 1994; Kadioglu 1994; Kandiyoti 1991, 1992; Webster 1984). Scholars who have generated insider portraits[1] of Islamic gender relations have revealed that Muslim women's motivations for veiling can vary dramatically. Some Muslim women veil to express their strongly held convictions about gender difference, others are motivated to do so more as a means of critiquing Western colonialism in the Middle East. It is this complexity surrounding the veil that leads Elizabeth Fernea (1993, 122) to conclude that the veil (or *hijab*[2]) "means different

things to different people within [Muslim] society, and it means different things to Westerners than it does to Middle Easterners" (see also Abu-Lughod 1986; Walbridge 1997).

Our study takes as its point of departure the conflicting meanings of the veil among both Muslim religious elites and rank-and-file Islamic women currently living in the United States. In undertaking this investigation, we supplement the lone study (published in Arabic) that compares the gender attitudes of veiled and unveiled women (see L. Ahmed 1992 for review). That study, based largely on survey data collected from university women living in the Middle East, demonstrates that while veiled women evince somewhat conservative gender attitudes, the vast majority of them support women's rights in public life and a substantial proportion subscribe to marital equality. We seek to extend these suggestive findings by using in-depth, personal interviews, because data from such interviews are more able to capture the negotiation of cultural meanings by veiled and unveiled respondents, as well as the nuances of these women's gender identities (Mishler 1986).

The importance of our study is further underscored by the influx of Muslims into the United States during recent decades and the increasing prominence of Muslim Americans and Islamic women on the domestic scene (G. Ahmed 1991; Ghanea Bassiri 1997; Haddad 1991a, 1991b; Hermansen 1991). Although population estimates of Muslim Americans vary (ranging from 5 to 8 million), many observers consider Islam to be one of the fastest growing religions in the United States (Johnson 1991; Stone 1991). Moreover, recent research indicates that a majority of Muslims in the United States are university graduates firmly situated within the American middle class (Haddad 1991b). Yet, even as this religious subculture has enjoyed such rapid growth and economic privilege throughout much of the West, Muslims in the United States and abroad have become the target of pejorative stereotypes (Bozorgmehr, Der-Martirosian, and Sabagh 1996; Haddad 1991a, 1991b). Caricatures that portray Islamic women as submissive and backward have become more pervasive within recent years (L. Ahmed 1992; Esposito 1998), but recent research on Muslim women living in the United States has called such unflattering depictions into question (Hermansen 1991). Such research has revealed that Muslim American women creatively negotiate their gender, religious, and ethnic identities in light of dominant U.S. social norms and modernist discourses that often define these women as "other."

Our investigation therefore aims to enrich this growing research literature, while critically evaluating negative stereotypes about Muslim women. After outlining our theoretical perspective, we review the debates that currently characterize Muslim elite discourse concerning the veil. Then, to discern the impact of these broad cultural disputes on the gender identities of women of Islam located in the United States, we analyze interview data collected from a sample of religiously active Muslim women—both veiled and unveiled—currently living in Austin, Texas. Our analysis highlights salient points of ideological divergence, as well as unanticipated points of congruence, between these veiled and unveiled Muslim women concerning this controversial cultural practice.

Theory and Context: Discourse, Identity, and the Landscape of Islam

How can scholars effectively explore the interconnections between broad-based cultural constructions of gender on one hand and the more circumscribed (inter)subjective negotiation of gender relations on the other? In an effort to address these issues, a large number of contemporary feminist theorists and gender scholars have begun to examine discourse as one important medium through which gender is constructed (e.g., Bartkowski 1997a, 1997b, 1998, 2000; Currie 1997; Todd and Fisher 1988; Wodak 1997). Our study is informed by these theoretical insights and by feminist standpoint theories and notions of subjectivity that take seriously women's agency, as well as their bodily practices and everyday experiences, in the negotiation of their gender identities (e.g., Currie 1997; Davis 1997; Hollway 1995; Mahoney and Yngvesson 1992; Smith 1987; West and Fenstermaker 1995; see Mann and Kelley 1997 for review).

Theories of discourse suggest that cultural forms (e.g., gender, religion, ethnicity) are best understood as *constructed*, *contested*, and *intersecting* social phenomena. First, the meanings attributed to the Muslim veil are not endemic to the veil itself; rather, they are produced through cultural discourse and vast networks of social relationships. Social practices that imbue the veil with cultural significance include the rhetoric of religious elites who equate veiling with religious devotion, as well as the actual ostracism of unveiled Muslim women from some Islamic institutions. Second, theories of discourse call attention to the contested character of cultural forms. Cultural symbols are capable of being interpreted in a variety of different ways and often become a site of struggle and contestation. Divergent interpretations of the same cultural practice may be advanced by groups who share a common religious heritage. As evidenced in our analysis below, various factions of Muslim elites offer strikingly different interpretations of the veil and the Qur'anic passages pertaining to this cultural practice. Finally, theories of discourse attune researchers to the multidimensional and overlapping character of cultural forms. Discourses are not discrete ideologies; rather, they are culturally specific modes of understanding the world that intersect with competing viewpoints. As we reveal below, religiously active Muslim women living in the United States are exposed not only to the internecine gender debates waged within Islamic circles mentioned above. These women also construct their gender identities in light of non-Muslim discourses of gender and ethnicity prevalent in late-twentieth-century America.

As noted, we complement these insights with feminist notions of standpoint, subjectivity, and bodily practice. Taken together, these theoretical perspectives suggest that discursive regimes provide social actors with important symbolic resources for identity negotiation and for the legitimation of everyday social and bodily practices (see, e.g., Dellinger and Williams 1997; Stombler and Padavic 1997 for recent empirical treatments). Current gender scholarship construes identity negotiation as a *process* and everyday *practice* that is fraught with ambiguity, contradiction, and struggle. These perspectives stand in bold contrast to more static psychological conceptualizations *of personality* as divorced from lived experience and bodily practice. Therefore, we are careful to recognize how competing discourses of the veil enable veiled Muslim women to legitimate their decision to veil on a variety of grounds—from explicitly antifeminist rationales to feminist justifications for veiling. Yet, at the same time, we reveal how the respondents use their everyday experiences to lend a practical edge to their understanding of the veil and their perceptions of themselves as Muslim women.

The most germane aspects of Muslim theology for this study concern two sets of Islamic sacred texts, the Qur'an and the hadiths (e.g., Munson 1988). The Qur'an is held in high esteem by virtually all Muslims. Not unlike the "high view" of the Bible embraced by various conservative Christian groups, many contemporary Muslims believe that the Qur'an is the actual Word of God that was ably recorded by Muhammed during the early portion of the seventh century. In addition to the Qur'an, many Muslims also look to the hadiths for moral and spiritual guidance in their daily lives. The hadiths, second-hand reports of Muhammed's personal traditions and lifestyle, began to be collected shortly after his death because of the difficulty associated with applying the dictates of the Qur'an to changing historical circumstances. The full collection of these hadiths has come to be known as the *sunna*. Along with the Qur'an, the hadiths constitute the source of law that has shaped the ethics and values of many Muslims.

Within Islam, the all-male Islamic clergy (variously called *faghihs*, *imams*, *muftis*, *mullahs*, or *ulumas*) often act as interpretive authorities who are formally charged with distilling insights from the Qur'an or hadiths and with disseminating these scriptural interpretations to the Muslim laity (Munson 1988). Given that such positions of structural privilege are set aside for Muslim men, Islam is a patriarchal religious institution. Yet, patriarchal institutions do not necessarily produce homogeneous gender ideologies, a fact underscored by the discursive fissures that divide Muslim religious authorities and elite commentators concerning the veil.

Competing Discourses of the Veil in Contemporary Islam

Many Muslim clergy and Islamic elites currently prescribe veiling as a custom in which "good" Muslim women should engage (Afshar 1985; Al-Swailem 1995; Philips and Jones 1985; Siddiqi 1983). Proponents of veiling often begin their defense of this cultural practice by arguing that men are particularly vulnerable to corruption through unregulated sexual contact with women (Al-Swailem 1995, 27–29; Philips and Jones 1985, 39–46; Siddiqi 1983). These experts contend that the purpose of the hijab or veil is the regulation of such contact:

> The society that Islam wants to establish is not a sensate, sex-ridden society....The Islamic system of *Hijab* is a wide-ranging system which protects the family and closes those avenues that lead toward illicit sex relations or even indiscriminate contact between the sexes in society....To protect her virtue and to safeguard her chastity from lustful eyes and covetous hands, Islam has provided for purdah which sets norms of dress, social get-together...and going out of the four walls of one's house in hours of need. (Siddiqi 1983, vii–viii)

Many expositors of the pro-veiling discourse call attention to the uniquely masculine penchant for untamed sexual activity and construe the veil as a God-ordained solution to the apparent disparities in men's and women's sexual appetites. Women are therefore deemed responsible for the management of men's sexuality (Al-Swailem 1995, 29). Some contend that the Muslim woman who veils should be sure that the hijab covers her whole body (including the palms of her hands), should be monotone in color ("so as not to be attractive to draw the attentions to"), and should be opaque and loose so as not to reveal "the woman's shape or what she is wearing underneath" (Al-Swailem 1995, 24–25).

Pro-veiling Muslim luminaries also defend veiling on a number of nonsexual grounds. The veil, according to these commentators, serves as (1) a demonstration of the Muslim woman's unwavering obedience to the tenets of Islam; (2) a clear indication of the essential differences distinguishing men from women; (3) a reminder to women that their proper place is in the home rather than in pursuing public-sphere activities; and (4) a sign of the devout Muslim woman's disdain for the profane, immodest, and consumerist cultural customs of the West (e.g., Al-Swailem 1995, 27–29; Siddiqi 1983, 140, 156). In this last regard, veiling is legitimated as an anti-imperialist statement of ethnic and cultural distinctiveness.

Nevertheless, the most prominent justifications for veiling entail, quite simply, the idea that veiling is prescribed in the Qur'an (see Arat 1994; Dragadze 1994; Hessini 1994; Sherif 1987; Shirazi-Mahajan 1995 for reviews). Several Muslim clergy place a strong interpretive emphasis on a Qur'anic passage (S. 24:31) that urges women "not [to] display their beauty and adornments" but rather to "draw their head cover over their bosoms and not display their ornament." Many of these same defenders of the veil marshal other Qur'anic passages that bolster their pro-veiling stance: "And when you ask them [the Prophet's wives] for anything you want ask them from before a screen (hijab); that makes for greater purity for your hearts and for them" (S. 33:53); "O Prophet! Tell your wives and daughters and the believing women that they should cast their outer garments over themselves, that is more convenient that they should be known and not molested" (S. 33:59).

In addition to these Qur'anic references, pro-veiling Muslim clergy highlight hadiths intended to support the practice of veiling (see Sherif 1987 for review). Many pro-veiling Muslim clergy maintain that the veil verse was revealed to Muhammad at a wedding five years before the Prophet's death. As the story goes, three tactless guests overstayed their welcome after the wedding and continued to chat despite the Prophet's desire to be alone with his new wife. To encourage their departure, Muhammad drew a curtain between the nuptial chamber and one of his inconsiderate companions while ostensibly uttering "the verse of the hijab" (S. 33:53, cited above). A second set of hadiths claim that the verse of hijab was prompted when one of the Prophet's companions accidentally touched the hand of one of Muhammad's wives while eating dinner. Yet a third set of hadiths suggests that the verse's objective was to stop the visits of an unidentified man who tarried with the wives of the Prophet, promising them marriage after Muhammad's death.

In stark contrast to the pro-veiling apologias discussed above, an oppositional discourse against veiling has emerged within Islamic circles in recent years. Most prominent among these opponents of veiling are Islamic feminists (Al-Marayati 1995; Mernissi 1991; Shaheed 1994, 1995; see contributions in Al-Hibri 1982; Gocek and Balaghi 1994; see AbuKhalil 1993; An-Na'im 1987; Anees 1989; Arat 1994; Badran 1991; Fernea 1998 for treatments of Islamic feminism and related issues). Although Islamic feminists are marginalized from many of the institutional apparatuses available to the all-male Muslim clergy, they nevertheless exercise considerable influence via the dissemination of dissident publications targeted at Islamic women and through grassroots social movements (Fernea 1998; Shaheed 1994). Fatima Mernissi (1987, 1991), arguably the most prominent Muslim feminist, is highly critical of dominant gender conceptualizations that construe veiling as the ultimate standard by which the spiritual welfare and religious devoutness of Muslim women should be judged. In *The Veil and the Male Elite: A Feminist Interpretation of Women's Rights in Islam*, Mernissi (1991, 194) queries her readers:

> What a strange fate for Muslim memory, to be called upon in order to censure and punish [Islamic women]! What a strange memory, where even dead men and women do not escape attempts at assassination, if by chance they threaten to raise the *hijab* [veil] that covers the mediocrity and servility that is presented to us [Muslim women] as tradition. How did the tradition succeed in transforming the Muslim woman into that submissive, marginal creature who buries herself and only goes out into the world timidly and huddled in her veils? Why does the Muslim man need such a mutilated companion?

Mernissi and other Muslim commentators who oppose veiling do so on a number of grounds. First, Mernissi seeks to reverse the sacralization of the veil by linking the hijab with oppressive social hierarchies and male domination. She argues that the veil represents a tradition of "mediocrity and servility" rather than a sacred standard against which to judge Muslim women's devotion to Allah. Second, antiveiling Muslim commentators are quick to highlight the historical fact that veiling is a cultural practice that originated from outside of Islamic circles (see Schmidt 1989). Although commonly assumed to be of Muslim origin, historical evidence reveals that veiling was actually practiced in the ancient Near East and Arabia long before the rise of Islam (Esposito 1995; Sherif 1987; Webster 1984). Using this historical evidence to bolster their antiveiling stance, some Muslim feminists conclude that because the veil is not a Muslim invention, it cannot be held up as the standard against which Muslim women's religiosity is to be gauged.

Finally, Islamic feminists such as Mernissi (1991, chap. 5) point to the highly questionable scriptural interpretations on which Muslim clergy often base their pro-veiling edicts (see Hessini 1994; Shirazi-Mahajan 1995). Dissident Islamic commentators call attention to the fact that the Qur'an refers cryptically to a "curtain" and never directly instructs women to wear a veil. Although proponents of veiling interpret Qur'anic edicts as Allah's directive to all Muslim women for all time, Islamic critics of veiling counter this interpretive strategy by placing relatively greater weight on the "occasions of revelation" (*asbab nuzul al Qur'an*)—that is, the specific social circumstances under which key Qur'anic passages were revealed (Mernissi 1991, 87–88, 92–93; see Sherif 1987). It is with this interpretive posture that many Islamic feminists believe the veil verse (S. 33:53) to be intended solely for the wives of Muhammad (Mernissi 1991, 92; see Sherif 1987). Muslim critics of veiling further counter many of the pro-veiling hadith citations by arguing that they are interpretations of extrascriptural texts whose authenticity is highly questionable (Mernissi 1991, 42–48; see Sherif 1987; Shirazi-Mahajan 1995). Finally, critics of hijab point to select verses in the Qur'an that invoke images of gender egalitarianism, including one passage that refers to the "vast reward" Allah has prepared for both "men who guard their modesty and women who guard their modesty" (S. 33:35).

The Veil and Gender Identity Negotiation Among Muslim Women in Austin

To this point, we have drawn comparisons between pro-veiling edicts that link devout, desexualized Muslim womanhood to the practice of veiling and antiveiling discourses that reject this conflation of hijab and women's religious devotion. We now attempt to gauge the impact of these debates on the gender identities of a sample of 24 Muslim women—12 of whom veil, 12 of whom do not. All women in our sample define themselves as devout Muslims (i.e., devoted followers of Muhammad who actively practice their faith). These women were recruited through a combination of snowball and purposive sampling. Taken together, the respondents identify with a range of different nationalities (e.g., Iranian, Pakistani, Kuwaiti) and Muslim sects (e.g., Sunni, Shi'i, Ahmadia). Nineteen women have lived 10 or more years in the United States, while five women in our sample have immigrated in the past 5 years. Their ages range from 21 to 55 years old, and they occupy a range of social roles (e.g., college students, professional women, homemakers). Consistent with the demographic characteristics of U.S. Muslim immigrants at large (Haddad 1991b), our sample is composed of middle-class women with some postsecondary education (either a college degree or currently attending college). Class homogeneity among the respondents is also partly a product of the locale from which the sample was drawn, namely, a university town. Consequently, this study extends cross-cultural scholarship on the intersection of veiling, ethnicity, and nationality for middle-class Muslim women living in Western and largely modernized societies (e.g., Bloul 1997; Brenner 1996; Hatem 1994).

In-depth interviews with these Muslim women were conducted by the first author during 1996 and 1997. The interview questionnaire covered a range of topics, including the women's practical experiences with veiling, the meaning of the veil to them, their reasons for wearing or not wearing the veil and the impact of this decision on their social relationships, their perceptions about the significance of the veil in their country of origin, and the importance of Islamic beliefs and devotional activities (e.g., prayer, scriptural study) to these women. In light of our topic's sensitivity, as well as cultural differences between our respondents and the first author (a non-Muslim unveiled woman), the interviews were not audiotaped. Because many of the women were forthright about their opposition to participating in a study based on tape-recorded interviews, the tenor, depth, and candor of these interviews would have been seriously inhibited if conversations were tape-recorded. Consequently, with the women's consent, handwritten notes were recorded during the course of each interview. Immediately after the interview, these notes were then elaborated into a more detailed set of transcripts. Each transcript was initially evaluated as an independent conversation concerning the significance of the veil and its relationship to the respondent's religious and gender identity. Emergent themes from each interview were flagged and coded during this stage of the analysis. Then, during a second stage

of analysis, we compared the themes that emerged from interviews conducted with each of the two different subgroups of Muslim women (veiled and unveiled).

Interview data collected from these women, identified below by pseudonyms, are designed to address several interrelated issues: What does the veil itself and the practice of veiling mean to these women? Among the women who veil, why do they do so? Among the women who do not veil, how have they arrived at the decision to remain unveiled? Finally, how does each group of our respondents feel about women who engage in the "opposite" cultural practice?

Veiled Contradictions: Perceptions of Hijab and Gender Practices Among Veiled Muslim Women

Religious Edicts and Social Bonds

In several respects, the veiled respondents' accounts of wearing hijab conform to the pro-veiling gender discourse explicated above. Many of the veiled women invoke various sorts of religious imagery and theological edicts when asked about their motivations for veiling. One respondent in her early twenties, Huneeya, states flatly: "I wear the hijab because the Qur'an says it's better [for women to be veiled]." Yet another veiled woman, Najette, indicates that hijab "makes [her] more special" because it symbolizes her commitment to Islam. Mona says outright: "The veil represents submission to God," and Masouda construes the veil as a "symbol of worship" on the part of devout Muslim women to Allah and the teachings of the Prophet Muhammad. Not surprisingly, many veiled women contend that veiling is commanded in the Qur'an.

Of course, this abundance of theological rationales is not the only set of motivations that the veiled women use to justify this cultural practice. For many of the veiled respondents, the scriptural edicts and the religious symbolism surrounding the veil are given palpable force through their everyday gender practices and the close-knit social networks that grow out of this distinctive cultural practice. Indeed, narratives about some women's deliberate choice to begin veiling at a particular point in their lives underscore how religious edicts stand in tension with the women's strategic motivations. Several women recount that they began to veil because they had friends who did so or because they felt more closely connected to significant others through this cultural practice. Aisha, for example, longed to wear the veil while she attended high school in the Middle East approximately three decades ago. Reminiscent of issues faced by her teen counterparts in the United States, Aisha's account suggests that high school was a crucial time for identity formation and the cultivation of peer group relationships. The veil served Aisha as a valuable resource in resolving many of the dilemmas she faced 30 years ago as a maturing high school student. She decided to begin veiling at that time after hearing several prominent Muslim speakers at her school "talk[ing] about how good veiling is." The veil helped Aisha not only to form meaningful peer relationships at that pivotal time in her life (i.e., adolescence) but also continues to facilitate for her a feeling of connectedness with a broader religious community of other veiled Muslim women. During her recent trip to Egypt during the summer, Aisha says that the veil helped her "to fit in" there in a way that she would not have if she were unveiled.

Several other respondents also underscore the significance of Islamic women's friendship networks that form around the veil, which are particularly indispensable because they live in a non-Muslim country (i.e., the United States). In recounting these friendship circles that are cultivated around hijab in a "foreign" land, our veiled respondents point to an important overlay between their gender identities (i.e., good Muslim women veil) and their ethnic identities (i.e., as Middle Easterners). The common foundation on which these twin identities are negotiated is distinctively religious in nature. Hannan touts the personal benefits of veiling both as a *woman*—"the veil serves as an identity for [Islamic] women"—and as a *Muslim:* "[Because I veil,] Muslim people know I am Muslim, and they greet me in Arabic." This interface between gender and ethnicity is also given voice by Aisha, whose initial experiences with the veil were noted above. Aisha maintains, "The veil differentiates Muslim women from other women. When you see a woman in hijab, you know she's a Muslim." Much like the leading Muslim commentators who encourage Islamic women to "wear" their religious convictions (literally, via the veil) for all to see, these veiled respondents find comfort in the cultural and ethnic distinctiveness that the veil affords them. In this way, hijab is closely connected with their overlapping religious-gender-ethnic identities and links them to the broader community (*ummah*) of Islamic believers and Muslim women.

Gender Difference and Women's "Emancipation"

In addition to providing religious rationales for wearing the veil, many of the women who wear hijab also invoke the discourse of masculine-feminine difference to defend the merits of veiling. For several women, the idea of masculine hypersexuality and feminine vulnerability to the male sex drive is crucial to this essentialist rationale for veiling. Despite the fact that veiled women were rather guarded in their references to sex, their nods in that direction are difficult to interpret in any other fashion. In describing the veil's role in Islam and in the lives of Muslim men and women (such as herself), Sharadda states, "Islam is natural and men need some things naturally. If we abide by these needs [and veil accordingly], we will all be happy." She continues, "If the veil did not exist, many evil things would happen. Boys would mix with girls, which will result in evil things."

Similarly, Hannan describes what she perceives to be women's distinctive attributes and their connection to the veil: "Women are like diamonds; they are so precious. They should not be revealed to everyone—just to their husbands and close kin." Like Qur'anic references to women's "ornaments," Hannan is contrasting the "precious" diamond-like feminine character to the ostensibly less refined, less distinctive masculine persona. Interestingly, it is by likening women to diamonds that Hannan rhetorically inverts traditional gender hierarchies that privilege "masculine" traits over their "feminine" counterparts. In the face of those who would denigrate feminine qualities, Hannan reinterprets the distinctiveness of womanhood as more "precious" (i.e., more rare and valuable) than masculine qualities. Women's inherent difference from men, then, is perceived to be a source of esteem rather than denigration.

It is important to recognize, however, that the respondents who invoke this rhetoric of gender difference are not simply reproducing the pro-veiling discourse advanced by Muslim elites. Despite their essentialist convictions, many of the veiled respondents argue that the practice of wearing hijab actually liberates them from men's untamed, potentially explosive sexuality and makes possible for them various sorts of public-sphere pursuits. So, whereas pro-veiling Islamic elites often reason that women's sexual vulnerability (and, literally, their fragile bodily "ornaments") should restrict them to the domestic sphere, many of the veiled women in this study simply do not support this view of domesticized femininity. To the contrary, these women—many of whom are themselves involved in occupational or educational pursuits—argue that the veil is a great equalizer that enables women to work alongside of men. In the eyes of Hannan, women's "preciousness" should not be used to cajole them to remain in the home: "Women who wear the hijab are not excluded from society. They are freer to move around in society because of it."

Rabbab, who attends to various public-sphere pursuits, offers a similar appraisal. She argues that the face veil (hijab) is an invaluable aid for Muslim women who engage in extradomestic pursuits. In advancing this claim, Rabbab uses women who veil their whole bodies (such body garments are called *abaya*) as a counterpoint of excessive traditionalism. When asked what the veil means to her personally, as well as to Muslim women and Islamic culture at large, she says,

> It depends on the extent of the hijab [that is worn].... Women who wear face veils and cover their whole bodies [with abaya] are limited to the home. They are too dependent on their husbands. How can they interact when they are so secluded?... [However,] taking away the hijab

[i.e., face veil] would make women have to fight to be taken seriously [in public settings].... With hijab, men take us more seriously.

This hijab-as-liberator rationale for veiling was repeated by many of the veiled women who pursued educational degrees in schools and on college campuses where young predatorial men ostensibly rove in abundance. Aisha, a 41-year-old former student, recounts how the veil emancipated her from the male gaze during her school years:

> There was a boy who attended my university. He was very rude to all of the girls, always whistling and staring at them. One day, I found myself alone in the hallway with him. I was very nervous because I had to walk by him. But because I was wearing the hijab, he looked down when I walked past. He did not show that respect to the unveiled girls.

Drawing on experiences such as these, Aisha concludes succinctly: "The veil gives women advantages.... They can go to coeducational schools and feel safe." A current student, Najette, says that the veil helps her to "feel secure" in going about her daily activities. Finally, the account of a young female student who is 22 years of age sheds further light on the hijab's perceived benefits in the face of men's apparent propensity to objectify women: "If you're in hijab, then someone sees you and treats you accordingly. I feel more free. Especially men, they don't look at your appearance—they appreciate your intellectual abilities. They respect you." For many of the veiled women in this study, the respect and protection afforded them by the hijab enables them to engage in extradomestic pursuits that would ironically generate sharp criticism from many pro-veiling Muslim elites.

The Discontents of Hijab and Tolerance for the Unveiled

While the foregoing statements provide clear evidence of these women's favorable feelings about hijab, many of the veiled women also express mixed feelings about this controversial cultural symbol. It was not uncommon for the veiled respondents to recount personal difficulties that they have faced because of their decision to wear hijab. Some dilemmas associated with the veil emanate from the fact that these women live in a secular society inhabited predominantly by Christians rather than Muslims. Najette, the same respondent who argued that veiling makes her feel "special," was quick to recognize that this esteem is purchased at the price of being considered "weird" by some Americans who do not understand her motivations for veiling. For women like her, engaging in a dissident cultural practice underscores Najette's cultural distinctiveness in a way that some people find refreshing and others find threatening.

Such points of tension surrounding the veil are evident not only in cross-cultural encounters such as that mentioned above. Even within Muslim circles, the practice of veiling has generated enough controversy to produce rifts among relatives and friends when some of the veiled respondents appear publicly in hijab. Huneeya, a student who veils because she wishes to follow Qur'anic edicts and enjoys being treated as an intellectual equal by her male peers, highlighted just this point of friction with her family members, all of whom except her are "against hijab. [My family members] think it is against modernity."

For some women, the tensions produced within intimate relationships by the veil move beyond the realm of intermittent family squabbles. One veiled respondent, Asma, revealed that extended family difficulties surrounding the veil have caused her to alter the practice of veiling itself, if only temporarily. Her recent experiences underscore the complex machinations of power involved in the contested arenas of family relations and friendships where veiling is concerned. Asma moved to the United States with her husband only two years ago. Asma was quite conscientious about veiling. She relished the sense of uniqueness and cultural distinctiveness afforded to her by the hijab while living in a non-Muslim country. Yet, recent summer-long visits from her mother-in-law presented her with a dilemma. Asma's mother-in-law had arranged the marriage between her son and daughter-in-law. At the time, the mother-in-law greatly appreciated

the conservative religious values embraced by her future daughter-in-law, evidenced in Asma's attentiveness to wearing the veil. Yet, since that time, Asma's mother-in-law had undergone a conversion of sorts concerning the practice of veiling. Quite recently, Asma's mother-in-law stopped wearing the veil and wanted her daughter-in-law to follow suit by discarding the veil as well. Indeed, this mother-in-law felt that Asma was trying to upstage her by using the veil to appear more religiously devout than her elder. Asma's short-term solution to this dilemma is to submit to the wishes of her mother-in-law during her summer visits to the United States. Consequently, for two months each summer, Asma discards her veil. Yet, this solution is hardly satisfactory to her and does not placate Asma's veiled friends who think less of her for unveiling:

> I feel very uncomfortable without the veil. The veil keeps us [Muslim women] from getting mixed up in American culture. But I don't want to make my mother-in-law feel inferior, so I take it off while she is here. I know my friends think I am a hypocrite.

Although Asma is sanctioned by her friends for unveiling temporarily during her mother-in-law's visit, our interview data suggest that the preponderance of veiled women in this study harbor no ill will toward their Muslim sisters who choose not to veil. Despite these veiled women's enthusiastic defenses of hijab, they are willing to define what it means to be a good Muslim broadly enough to include Islamic women who do not veil. When asked, for instance, what she thought being a good Muslim entails, one of our veiled respondents (Najette) states simply: "You must be a good person and always be honest." Echoing these sentiments, Masouda suggests, "Your attitude towards God is most important for being a good Muslim—your personality. You must be patient, honest, giving." Even when asked point-blank if veiling makes a woman a good Muslim, another veiled respondent answers, "Hijab is not so important for being a good Muslim. Other things are more important, like having a good character and being honest." One respondent even took on a decidedly ecumenical tone in detaching veiling from Islamic devotion: "Being a good Muslim is the same as being a good Christian or a good Jew—treat others with respect and dignity. Be considerate and open-minded." In the end, then, these women in hijab are able to distinguish between what veiling means to them at a personal level (i.e., a sign of religious devotion) versus what the veil says about Muslim women in general (i.e., a voluntary cultural practice bereft of devotional significance). These veiled women's heterogeneous lived experiences with the hijab—both comforting and uncomfortable, affirming and tension producing, positive and negative—seem to provide them with a sensitivity to cultural differences that often seems lacking in the vitriolic debates about veiling currently waged by leading Muslims.

Islamic Feminism Modified: Perceptions of Hijab and Gender Practices Among the Unveiled

Patriarchal Oppression and Religious Fanaticism

Just as veiled women draw on the pro-veiling discourse to defend the wearing of hijab, the unveiled women in this study often justify their abstention from this cultural practice by invoking themes from the antiveiling discourse. Several of these unveiled women argue quite straightforwardly that the veil reinforces gender distinctions that work to Muslim women's collective disadvantage. According to many of the unveiled women, the veil was imposed on Muslim women because of Middle Eastern men's unwillingness to tame their sexual caprice and because of their desire to dominate women. Rabeeya, for example, contends that Muslim women are expected to veil because "Middle Eastern men get caught up in beauty. The veil helps men control themselves." Offering a strikingly similar response, Najwa argues that "men can't control themselves, so they make women veil." Using the same critical terminology—that is, *control*—to make her point, Fozia has an even less sanguine view of the veil's role in Islam. When asked about the significance of the veil in Muslim societies, she states flatly: "The veil

is used to control women." In short, many of the unveiled respondents view hijab in much the same way as elite Islamic feminists; that is, as a mechanism of patriarchal control.

Comments such as these suggest points of congruence between the veiled and unveiled respondents' understandings of hijab. Both groups of women seem to agree that hijab is closely related to men's sexuality. Recall that some of the veiled women contrast masculine hypersexuality to a desexualized view of femininity. Such women conclude that the veil is the God-ordained corrective for men's inability to control their own sexual impulses. Likewise, as evidenced in several statements from unveiled women, they link the veil to men's apparent inability (or, better, unwillingness) to contain their sexual desires. However, whereas several of the veiled women see masculine hypersexuality as natural and view the veil as a divine remedy for such sexual differences, many of the unveiled women reject these views. The unveiled respondents seem less willing to accept the notion that categorical gender differences should translate into a cultural practice that (literally and figuratively) falls on the shoulders of women. In a key point of departure from their sisters who wear hijab, the unveiled women in this study trace the origin of the veil not to God but rather to men's difficulties in managing their sexuality (again, "men can't control themselves, so they make women veil"). In men's attempt to manage their sexual impulses, so the account goes, they have foisted the veil on women. Very much in keeping with feminist discourses that take issue with such gendered double standards, the unveiled women conclude that it is unfair to charge women with taming men's sexuality.

Apart from these issues of social control and sexuality, several of the unveiled respondents also invoke themes of religious devotion and ethnic identity when discussing the significance of the veil for Muslims in general and for themselves (as unveiled Islamic women) in particular. Recall that leading Muslims who support veiling often highlight the religious and ethnic distinctiveness of hijab; however, prominent Muslim feminists counter that veiling did not originate with

Islam and should not be understood as central to women's religious devoutness or ethnic identities (as non-Westerners). Echoing these Muslim feminist themes, several of the unveiled respondents seek to sever the veil from its religious and ethnic moorings. Fozia says that Muslim "women are made to believe that the veil is religious. In reality, it's all political," while Fatima asserts, "The veil is definitely political. It is used by men as a weapon to differentiate us from Westerners." Yet another respondent, Mah'ha, argues that it is only "fanatical" and "strict" Muslims who use the veil to draw sharp distinctions between Middle Easterners and Westerners. These remarks and others like them are designed to problematize the conflation of religious devotion, ethnic distinctiveness, and hijab evidenced in the pro-veiling discourse. Whereas the dominant discourse of veiling measures women's devotion to Islamic culture against hijab, many of the unveiled respondents imply—again, via strategic terms such as *political*, *fanatical*, and *strict*—that religious devotion and ethnic identification are good only in proper measure.

This rhetorical strategy allows these unveiled women to claim more moderate (and modern) convictions over and against those whose devotion to Allah has in their view been transmogrified into political dogmatism, religious extremism, and racial separatism. The unveiled women in our study do not eschew religious commitment altogether, nor are they in any way ashamed of their ethnic heritage. To the contrary, the unveiled respondents champion religious commitment (again, in good measure) and are proud to count themselves among the followers of Muhammad. Yet, they are quick to illustrate that their devotion to Allah and their appreciation of their cultural heritage are manifested through means that do not include the practice of veiling. Amna, for example, says, "Religious education makes me feel like a more pious Muslim. I read the Qur'an weekly and attend Friday prayer sermons," while Rabeeya states, "Being a good Muslim means believing in one God; no idolatry; following the five pillars of Islam; and believing in Muhammad." Concerning the issue of ethnoreligious identity, the basic message articulated by many of the unveiled women

can be stated quite succinctly: A Muslim woman can be true to her cultural and religious heritage without the veil. Samiya, a 38-year-old unveiled woman, says as much: "Muslim society doesn't exist on the veil. Without the veil, you would still be Muslim." Therefore, many of the unveiled women believe that the veil is of human (actually, male) origin rather than of divine making. And it is this very belief about the veil's this-worldly origins that enables many of the unveiled women to characterize themselves as devout followers of Muhammad who honor their cultural heritage even though they have opted not to veil.

Standing on Common Ground: Tolerance for the Other Among Unveiled Women

Finally, we turn our attention to the subjective contradictions that belie the prima facie critical reactions of our unveiled respondents toward the veil. Interestingly, just as the veiled women are reluctant to judge harshly their unveiled counterparts, these unveiled women who eschew hijab at a personal level nevertheless express understanding and empathy toward their Middle Eastern sisters who veil. At several points during interview encounters, the unveiled respondents escape the polemical hold of the antiveiling discourse by building bridges to their sisters who engage in a cultural practice that they themselves eschew.

First, several respondents imply that it would be wrong to criticize veiled women for wearing hijab when it is men—specifically, male Muslim elites—who are to blame for the existence and pervasiveness of the veil in Islamic culture. Amna, who does not veil, takes on a conciliatory tone toward women who do so by conceding that "the veil helps women in societies where they want to be judged solely on their character and not on their appearances." How is it that such statements, which sound so similar to the justifications for wearing hijab invoked by veiled women, emanate from the unveiled respondents? The strongly antipatriarchal sentiments of the unveiled women (described in the preceding section) seem to exonerate veiled women from charges of gender traitorism. Recall that many of the unveiled respondents, in fact, locate the origin of the veil in *men's* sexual indiscretion and in *men's* desire to control women: "Middle Eastern *men* get caught up in beauty. The veil helps *men* control *themselves*" (Rabeeya); "*Men* can't control *themselves*, so *they* make women veil" (Najwa); "The veil is *used to control women.* The women are *made to believe* that the veil is religious" (Fozia) (emphasis added). Ironically, it is the very antipatriarchal character of these statements that simultaneously enables the unveiled women to express their stinging criticism of the veil itself while proclaiming tolerance and respect for Islamic women who wear the veil. Indeed, since many of the unveiled respondents construe hijab to be a product of *patriarchal* oppression and assorted *masculine* hang-ups (e.g., struggles with sexuality, a preoccupation with domination and control), veiled women cannot legitimately be impugned for wearing hijab.

Second, many of the unveiled respondents are willing to concede that despite their own critical views of the veil, hijab serves an important cultural marker for Islamic women other than themselves. When asked about the role of the veil among Muslim women she knows in the United States, Rabeeya recognizes that many of her veiled Islamic sisters who currently live in America remain "very, very tied to their culture. Or they are trying to be. They [veil because they] want to feel tied to their culture even when they are far away from home." Because she herself is a devout Islamic woman living in a religiously pluralistic and publicly secularized society, Rabeeya is able to empathize with other Muslim women residing in the United States who veil in order to shore up their cultural identity. Similarly, Sonya draws noteworthy distinctions between her personal antipathy toward veiling and veiled women's attraction to hijab: "Some Muslim women need the veil to identify themselves with the Muslim culture. I don't feel that way."

Finally, several of the unveiled women in our study seem to express tolerance and empathy for their sisters in hijab because, at one time or another in the past, they themselves have donned the veil. Two of the unveiled respondents, for example, are native Iranians who are currently living in the United States. When these women return to Iran, they temporarily don the veil. Najwa, one of these women, explains, "As soon as we cross the Iranian border, I go to the bathroom on the airplane and put on the hijab." The experiences of our other native-born Iranian woman, Fatima, speak even more directly to the practical nuances that undergird unveiled women's tolerance for their veiled counterparts. On one hand, Fatima is highly critical of the veil, which has been the legally required dress for women in Iran during the past two decades. Referring to this fact, she impugns the veil as a "political...weapon" used by religious elites to reinforce invidious distinctions between Westerners and Middle Easterners. Yet, on the other hand, her personal experiences with hijab lead her to reject the stereotype that women who veil are "backward": "Progress has nothing to do with veiling. Countries without veiling can be very backwards...I have nothing against veiling. I feel very modern [in not veiling], but I respect those who veil." Like so many of her unveiled sisters, then, Rabeeya is critical of the veil as a religious icon but is unwilling to look down on Islamic women who wear hijab.

Conclusion and Discussion

This study has examined how a sample of Muslim women living in Austin, Texas, negotiate their gender identities in light of ongoing Islamic disputes about the propriety of veiling. Interview data with 12 veiled and 12 unveiled women reveal that many of them draw upon the pro-veiling and antiveiling discourses of Muslim elites, respectively, to justify their decisions about the veil. At the same time, the women highlight various subjective contradictions manifested in many of their accounts of veiling. Women who veil are not typically disdainful toward their unveiled Muslim sisters, and unveiled women in our sample seem similarly reluctant to impugn their veiled counterparts. Such findings were unanticipated in light of elite Muslim debates about the propriety of veiling.

What are we to make of the fact that the acrimony manifested between elite Muslim proponents and opponents of veiling is largely absent from these women's accounts of the veil? Several possible answers to this question emerge from our investigation. First, both the veiled and unveiled women in our study clearly exercise agency in crafting their gender identities. Drawing on themes of individualism and tolerance for diversity, the women are able to counterpose their own "choice" to veil or to remain unveiled on one hand with the personal inclinations of their sisters who might choose a path that diverges from their own. In this way, the respondents fashion gender identities that are malleable and inclusive enough to navigate through the controversy surrounding the veil. Second, the social context within which the women are situated seems to provide them with resources that facilitate these gender innovations. As noted above, our sample is composed of middle-class, well-educated Muslim women. We suspect that the progressive, multicultural climate of Austin and the human capital enjoyed by the women foster greater empathy between the veiled respondents and their unveiled counterparts. This degree of tolerance between veiled and unveiled Muslim women evinced in our study may be decidedly different for Islamic women living in other parts of the United States, other Western nations, or particular countries in the Middle East where the veil is a more publicly contested symbol.

Consequently, this study lends further credence to the insight that culture is not simply produced from "above" through the rhetoric of elites to be consumed untransformed by social actors who are little more than judgmental dopes. While the pro-veiling and antiveiling discourses have carved out distinctive positions for veiled Muslim women and their unveiled counterparts within the late twentieth century, the respondents in our study are unique and indispensable contributors to contemporary Islamic culture. It is these women, rather than the often combative elite voices within Islamic circles, who creatively build bridges across the contested cultural terrain of veiling; who

forge ties of tolerance with their sisters, veiled and unveiled; and who help foster the sense of community (*ummah*) that is so esteemed by Muslims around the world. Convictions about Islamic culture and community take on new meaning as they are tested in the crucible of Muslim women's everyday experiences. These findings parallel those that have emerged from other studies of politicized issues in the contemporary United States, including debates about abortion, family decision making, and women's paid labor force participation (Bartkowski 1997b, 1999; Gallagher and Smith 1999; Hunter 1994). These studies have revealed that the contemporary "culture wars" over gender are often waged by a select few—namely, elite ideologists and vanguard activists—whose views do not wholly correspond with the local standpoints of actual women at whom such rhetoric is targeted.

Several avenues for future research emerge from this study. First, observational research exploring the actual interactions between veiled and unveiled Muslim women in the United States is warranted. While our study suggests a level of ideological tolerance among veiled and unveiled Muslim women for "sisters who choose otherwise," the question remains: Does this ideological tolerance lead to practical collaboration among veiled and unveiled Muslim women, particularly if they are frequenting the same mosque? Because our study focuses on *perceptions* of veiling and *cognitive meanings* attributed to the veil, we are unable to answer such vexing questions about the actual *practice* of gender. One recent ethnographic study highlights how Muslim women with divergent views of the veil can, under some circumstances, forge meaningful community ties with one another (Walbridge 1997). Nevertheless, additional research is needed to clarify the specific circumstances under which such collaboration between veiled and unveiled women may be facilitated and those contexts under which such connections might be inhibited.

Second, our study pays short shrift to the patriarchal institutional structure that remains prevalent within so many mosques and Muslim communities located in the United States. By drawing on interview data with Muslim women rather than ethnographic observations from Austin mosques, our study is unable to assess the prospects for structural changes in gender relations within these religious institutions. We have emphasized the agency of Muslim women in recrafting Islamic culture and suggest that power is not monopolized by the all-male Muslim religious leaders charged with leading the Islamic laity. Nevertheless, we would be remiss if we failed to acknowledge the structural advantage enjoyed by all-male Muslim clerics for potential agenda setting within mosques and other Muslim religious institutions (cf. Kandiyoti 1988). Will the critiques of leading Islamic feminists—and the egalitarian sensibilities of some Muslim American women—present an effective challenge to the long-standing institutionalization of male authority within these religious organizations? In light of the growing literature on gendered organizations (e.g., Acker 1990; Britton 1997), this question undoubtedly deserves attention from gender scholars and researchers of Muslim communities.

Finally, there are some telling points of convergence between gender relations in contemporary Islam, Orthodox Judaism, and conservative Protestantism. Given the spate of recent studies which suggest that gender is negotiated by conservative Protestants and Orthodox Jews (e.g., Bartkowski 1997b, 1999, 2000; Brasher 1998; Davidman 1993; Gallagher and Smith 1999; Griffith 1997; Manning 1999; Stacey 1990), what parallels might exist between the gendered experiences of Muslim women and their conservative Protestant or Orthodox Jewish counterparts? And, in what ways might the gender practices and the enactment of specific definitions of the religiously "devout woman" (whether Muslim, evangelical, or Orthodox Jew) diverge? No research of which we are aware has compared the processes of identity negotiation among Muslim women with those manifested in other conservative religious contexts.[3] When interpreted in light of the emerging literature on gender negotiation within conservative Protestantism and Orthodox Judaism,

our findings suggest that there is much to be gained by drawing more detailed cross-cultural comparisons between the gendered experiences of such women, as well as the culturally specific "patriarchal bargains" (Kandiyoti 1988) with which these groups of women are confronted. In the end, arriving at a richer understanding of gender negotiation in those contexts where we might least expect to find it can shed new light on the transformation of gender relations as we begin the millennium.

Acknowledgments

Earlier versions of this article were presented at the 1998 meetings of the Southern Sociological Society in Atlanta, Georgia, and the 1999 meetings of the American Sociological Association in Chicago, Illinois. Special thanks to Susan Marshall and Faegheh Shirazi-Mahajan for their guidance and comments throughout this project. This article has benefited from the insightful comments of James Fraser, Helen Regis, Debra Umberson, and Christine Williams. We wish to acknowledge the assistance of Amer Al-Saleh in securing select documentary data for this study. All interpretations presented here are our own.

Notes

1. The merits of this insider or "emic" perspective are also clearly evidenced by a growing body of research that highlights the heterogeneous and contested character of gender relations among conservative Protestants (e.g., Bartkowski 1997a, 1997b, 1998, 1999, 2000; Gallagher and Smith 1999; Griffith 1997; Stacey 1990) and Orthodox Jews (Davidman 1993), an issue to which we return in the final section of this article.

2. For stylistic convenience, we often refer to the veil as *hijab*.

3. Gerami (1996) provides one exception to this general neglect of interreligious comparisons, although her analyses are largely survey based. Comparisons between Orthodox Jewish American women and their Muslim counterparts might be particularly telling in light of these women's similar experiences as devout, largely middle-class non-Christians living in the United States.

References

AbuKhalil, As'ad. 1993. Toward the study of women and politics in the Arab world: The debate and the reality. *Feminist Issues* 13:3–23.

Abu-Lughod, Lila. 1986. *Veiled sentiments.* Berkeley: University of California Press.

Acker, Joan. 1990. Hierarchies, jobs, bodies: A theory of gendered organizations. *Gender & Society* 4:139–58.

Afshar, Haleh. 1985. The legal, social and political position of women in Iran. *International Journal of the Sociology of Law* 13:47–60.

Ahmed, Gutbi Mahdi. 1991. Muslim organizations in the United States. In *The Muslims of America*, edited by Y. Y. Haddad. Oxford, UK: Oxford University Press.

Ahmed, Leila. 1992. *Women and gender in Islam: Historical roots of a modern debate.* New Haven, CT: Yale University Press.

Al-Hibri, Azizah, ed. 1982. *Women and Islam.* Oxford, UK: Pergamon.

Al-Marayati, Laila. 1995. Voices of women unsilenced—Beijing 1995 focus on women's health and issues of concern for Muslim women. *UCLA Women's Law Journal* 6:167.

Al-Swailem, Sheikh Abdullah Ahmed. 1995. Introduction. In *A comparison between veiling and unveiling*, by Halah bint Abdullah. Riyadh, Saudi Arabia: Dar-es-Salaam.

Anees, Munawar Ahmad. 1989. Study of Muslim women and family: A bibliography. *Journal of Comparative Family Studies* 20:263–74.

An-Na'im, Abdullahi. 1987. The rights of women and international law in the Muslim context. *Whittier Law Review* 9:491.

Arat, Yesim. 1994. Women's movement of the 1980s in Turkey: Radical outcome of liberal Kemalism? In *Reconstructing gender in the Middle East: Tradition, identity, and power*, edited by F. M. Gocek and S. Balaghi. New York: Columbia University Press.

Badran, Margot. 1991. Competing agendas: Feminists, Islam and the state in 19th and 20th century Egypt. In *Women, Islam & the state*, edited by D. Kandiyoti. Philadelphia: Temple University Press.

Bartkowski, John P. 1997a. Debating patriarchy: Discursive disputes over spousal authority among evangelical family commentators. *Journal for the Scientific Study of Religion* 36:393–410.

———. 1997b. Gender reinvented, gender reproduced: The discourse and negotiation of spousal relations within contemporary Evangelicalism. Ph.D. diss., University of Texas, Austin.

———. 1998. Changing of the gods: The gender and family discourse of American Evangelicalism in historical perspective. *The History of the Family* 3:97–117.

———. 1999. One step forward, one step back: "Progressive traditionalism" and the negotiation of domestic labor within Evangelical families. *Gender Issues* 17:40–64.

———. 2000. Breaking walls, raising fences: Masculinity, intimacy, and accountability among the promise keepers. *Sociology of Religion* 61:33–53.

Bloul, Rachel A. 1997. Victims or offenders? "Other" women French sexual politics. In *Embodied practices: Feminist perspectives on the body*, edited by K. Davis. Thousand Oaks, CA: Sage.

Bozorgmehr, Mehdi, Claudia Der-Martirosian, and Georges Sabagh. 1996. Middle Easterners: A new kind of immigrant. In *Ethnic Los Angeles*, edited by R. Waldinger and M. Bozorgmehr. New York: Russell Sage Foundation.

Brasher, Brenda E. 1998. *Godly women: Fundamentalism and female power.* New Brunswick, NJ: Rutgers University Press.

Brenner, Suzanne. 1996. Reconstructing self and society: Javanese Muslim women and the veil. *American Ethnologist* 23:673–97.

Britton, Dana M. 1997. Gendered organizational logic: Policy and practice in men's and women's prisons. *Gender & Society* 11:796–818.

Currie, Dawn H. 1997. Decoding femininity: Advertisements and their teenage readers. *Gender & Society* 11:453–57.

Davidman, Lynn. 1993. *Tradition in a rootless world: Women turn to Orthodox Judaism.* Berkeley: University of California Press.

Davis, Kathy, ed. 1997. *Embodied practices: Feminist perspectives on the body.* Thousand Oaks, CA: Sage.

Dellinger, Kirsten, and Christine L. Williams. 1997. Makeup at work: Negotiating appearance rules in the workplace. *Gender & Society* 11:151–77.

Dragadze, Tamara. 1994. Islam in Azerbaijan: The position of women. In *Muslim women's choices: Religious belief and social reality*, edited by C. F. El-Solh and J. Mabro. New York: Berg.

El-Guindi, Fadwa. 1981. Veiling Infitah with Muslim ethic: Egypt's contemporary Islamic movement. *Social Problems* 28:465–85.

———. 1983. Veiled activism: Egyptian women in the contemporary Islamic movement. *Mediterranean Peoples* 22/23:79–89.

El-Solh, Camillia Fawzi, and Judy Mabro, eds. 1994. *Muslim women's choices; Religious belief and social reality.* New York: Berg.

Esposito, John L., ed. 1995. *The Oxford encyclopedia of the modern Islamic world.* New York: Oxford University Press.

———. 1998. Women in Islam and Muslim societies. In *Islam, gender, and social change*, edited by Y. Y. Haddad and J. L. Esposito. New York: Oxford University Press.

Fernea, Elizabeth W. 1993. The veiled revolution. In *Everyday life in the Muslim Middle East*, edited by D. L. Bowen and E. A. Early. Bloomington: Indiana University Press.

———. 1998. *In search of Islamic feminism: One woman's journey.* New York: Doubleday.

Fox, Greer L. 1977. "Nice girl": Social control of women through a value construct. *Signs: Journal of Women in Culture and Society* 2:805–17.

Gallagher, Sally K., and Christian Smith. 1999. Symbolic traditionalism and pragmatic egalitarianism: Contemporary Evangelicals, families, and gender. *Gender & Society* 13:211–233.

Gerami, Shahin. 1996. *Women and fundamentalism: Islam and Christianity.* New York: Garland.

Ghanea Bassiri, Kambiz. 1997. *Competing visions of Islam in the United States: A study of Los Angeles.* London: Greenwood.

Gocek, Fatma M., and Shiva Balaghi, eds. 1994. *Reconstructing gender in the Middle East: Tradition, identity, and power.* New York: Columbia University Press.

Griffith, R. Marie. 1997. *God's daughters: Evangelical women and the power of submission.* Berkeley: University of California Press.

Haddad, Yvonne Yazbeck. 1991a. American foreign policy in the Middle East and its impact on the identity of Arab Muslims in the United States. In *The Muslims of America*, edited by Y. Y. Haddad. Oxford, UK: Oxford University Press.

———. 1991b. Introduction. In *The Muslims of America*, edited by Y. Y Haddad. Oxford, UK: Oxford University Press.

Hatem, Mervat F. 1994. Egyptian discourses on gender and political liberalization: Do secularist and Islamist views really differ? *Middle East Journal* 48:661–76.

Hermansen, Marcia K. 1991. Two-way acculturation: Muslim women in America between individual choice (liminality) and community affiliation (communitas). In *The Muslims of America*, edited by Y. Y. Haddad. Oxford, UK: Oxford University Press.

Hessini, Leila. 1994. Wearing the hijab in contemporary Morocco: Choice and identity. In *Reconstructing gender in the Middle East: Tradition, identity, and power*, edited by F. M. Gocek and S. Balaghi. New York: Columbia University Press.

Hollway, Wendy. 1995. Feminist discourses and women's heterosexual desire. In *Feminism and discourse*, edited by S. Wilkinson and C. Kitzinger. London: Sage.

Hunter, James Davison. 1994. *Before the shooting begins: Searching for democracy in America's culture war.* New York: Free Press.

Johnson, Steven A. 1991. Political activity of Muslims in America. In *The Muslims of America*, edited by Y. Y. Haddad. Oxford, UK: Oxford University Press.

Kadioglu, Ayse. 1994. Women's subordination in Turkey: Is Islam really the villain? *Middle East Journal* 48:645–60.

Kandiyoti, Deniz. 1988. Bargaining with patriarchy. *Gender & Society* 2:274–90.

———, ed. 1991. *Women, Islam & the state.* Philadelphia: Temple University Press.

———. 1992. Islam and patriarchy: A comparative perspective. In *Women in Middle Eastern history: Shifting boundaries in sex and gender*, edited by N. R. Keddie and B. Baron. New Haven, CT: Yale University Press.

Mahoney, Maureen A., and Barbara Yngvesson. 1992. The construction of subjectivity and the paradox of resistance: Reintegrating feminist anthropology and psychology. *Signs: Journal of Women in Culture and Society* 18:44–73.

Mann, Susan A., and Lori R. Kelley. 1997. Standing at the crossroads of modernist thought: Collins, Smith, and the new feminist epistemologies. *Gender & Society* 11:391–408.

Manning, Cristel. 1999. *God gave us the right: Conservative Catholic, Evangelical Protestant, and*

Orthodox Jewish women grapple with feminism. New Brunswick, NJ: Rutgers University Press.

Memissi, Fatima. 1987. *Beyond the veil.* Rev. ed. Bloomington: Indiana University Press.

———. 1991. *The veil and the male elite: A feminist interpretation of women's rights in Islam.* Translated by Mary Jo Lakeland. New York: Addison-Wesley.

Mishler, Elliot G. 1986. *Research interviewing: Context and narrative.* Cambridge, MA: Harvard University Press.

Munson, Henry Jr. 1988. *Islam and revolution in the Middle East.* New Haven, CT: Yale University Press.

Odeh, Lama Abu. 1993. Post-colonial feminism and the veil: Thinking the difference. *Feminist Review* 43:26–37.

Papanek, Hanna. 1973. Purdah: Separate worlds and symbolic shelter. *Comparative Studies in Society and History* 15:289–325.

Philips, Abu Ameenah Bilal, and Jameelah Jones. 1985. *Polygamy in Islam.* Riyadh, Saudi Arabia: International Islamic Publishing House.

Schmidt, Alvin J. 1989. *Veiled and silenced: How culture shaped sexist theology.* Macon, GA: Mercer University Press.

Shaheed, Farida. 1994. Controlled or autonomous: Identity and the experience of the network, women living under Muslim laws. *Signs: Journal of Women in Culture and Society* 19:997–1019.

———. 1995. Networking for change: The role of women's groups in initiating dialogue on women's issues. In *Faith and freedom: Women's human rights in the Muslim world,* edited by M. Afkhami, New York: Syracuse University Press.

Sherif, Mostafa H. 1987. What is hijab? *The Muslim World* 77:151–63.

Shirazi-Mahajan, Faegheh. 1995. A dramaturgical approach to hijab in post-revolutionary Iran. *Journal of Critical Studies of the Middle East* 7 (fall): 35–51.

Siddiqi, Muhammad Iqbal. 1983. *Islam forbids free mixing of men and women.* Lahore, Pakistan: Kazi.

Smith, Dorothy E. 1987. *The everyday world as problematic: A feminist sociology.* Boston: Northeastern University Press.

Stacey, Judith. 1990. *Brave new families.* New York: Basic Books.

Stombler, Mindy, and Irene Padavic. 1997. Sister acts: Resisting men's domination in Black and white fraternity little sister programs. *Social Problems* 44:257–75.

Stone, Carol L. 1991. Estimate of Muslims living in America. In *The Muslims of America,* edited by Y. Y. Haddad. Oxford, UK: Oxford University Press.

Todd, Alexandra Dundas, and Sue Fisher, eds. 1988. *Gender and discourse: The power of talk.* Norwood, NJ: Ablex.

Walbridge, Linda S. 1997. *Without forgetting the imam: Lebanese Shi'ism in an American community.* Detroit, MI: Wayne State University Press.

Webster. Sheila K. 1984. Harim and hijab: Seclusive and exclusive aspects of traditional Muslim dwelling and dress. *Women's Studies International Forum* 7:251–57.

West, Candace, and Sarah Fenstermaker. 1995. Doing difference. *Gender & Society* 9:8–37.

Wodak, Ruth, ed. 1997. *Discourse and gender.* Thousand Oaks, CA: Sage.

Women Remain Oppressed

ANTHONY LAYNG

The Growing political influence of religious fundamentalism in the world has encouraged many of us to revisit the subject of woman's rights. Back in the 1960s and 1970s, feminism and liberalism in general were popular American perspectives, and there was much concern in the media and elsewhere about discrimination against women. At some point, those of us who were committed to end male chauvinism began to realize that feminism and liberalism had lost their popular appeal. Regarding the status of females some seemed to believe that "women's rights" had been achieved, and that glass ceilings and sexist humor no longer warranted protest.

Following the lead of Margaret Mead, many anthropologists had stressed the primacy of culture in determining gender roles but, in the 1980s and 1990s, scientific research began finding a good deal of evidence indicating that women and men were, by their biological nature; quite dissimilar, implying, sometimes overtly, that it was not entirely inappropriate to treat them differently. At the same time, clothing fashions, high school proms, and popular literature all seemed to take us back to a pre-feminist era.

The issue of discrimination against women resurfaced, however, when several nations in the Islamic world further restricted the activities of their female population. The Taliban in Afghanistan was perhaps the most extreme case in point, but we soon became aware that other governments, in Iran and Saudi Arabia, for instance, were treating women in a highly discriminatory fashion—there was, of course, the widely publicized 2007 case of the 19-year-old Saudi who, after being gang-raped by seven men, initially was sentenced to six months in jail and 200 lashes.

Concern for the rights of women had evolved from focusing on an American problem in the 1970s to condemning traditional Muslim culture in the 21st century. According to the Koran, women socially are interior to men and appropriately are beaten if they misbehave. Additionally, women easily are divorced from their husband and children, and can inherit only half as much as their brothers: Moreover, men are instructed to separate themselves from menstruating women.

Among those American leaders who appear most indignant about how females are treated by fundamentalist Islamic regimes, there is little expressed awareness about how Protestant fundamentalism, an expanding influence in the U.S., could affect the status of women in this country. It seems that contemporary Americans have been quick to recognize sexual discrimination when it is promoted by Islamic dogma, but far less inclined to notice such discrimination when it is based on Christian beliefs. Elizabeth Cady Stanton, one of the most quoted suffragettes, in the U.S., insists, 'The Bible and the church have been the greatest stumbling blocks in the way of woman's emancipation." Is this statement fair? After all, Mary, the mother of Jesus, is portrayed in the Bible as admirable in the extreme, so much so that she has millions of devotees throughout the world. Of course, her popularity has everything to do with the fact that she gave birth to Jesus, and it is difficult to consider her a realistic role model since she did so while retaining her virginity.

When the Bible was being written, a young woman's virginity was valued highly, As we read in Deuteronomy: "A man who is responsible for deflowering another man's daughter must compensate the father for that loss." Notice that the compensation is paid not to the devalued daughter but to her father. In biblical times, every woman was considered to be the property of her father or husband. Elsewhere in the Bible, we read that women should remain silent and learn from men (Timothy) and wives must be led by their husbands in all matters (Ephesians). Corinthians recommends that, since "the head of every man is Christ and the head of every woman is the man," so "let your women keep silent in the churches."

Guided by the Bible

If the Bible were our only guide for how we all should behave, women would be restricted to a very different role in society from that of men, requiring a dissimilar route to salvation. According to Genesis, women were created as somewhat of an afterthought, once it became evident that Adam could use a helper. After Eve demonstrated that women were disobedient and a bad influence, God said to her, "I will greatly multiply your pain in childbearing; in pain you shall bring forth children, yet your desire shall be for your husband and he shall rule over you."

Of course, God also was perturbed by Adam for following the advice of a woman, so he kicked them both out of the Garden of Eden and made them wear clothing. As further punishment, Adam was compelled to invent agriculture; As God told him, "Because you have listened to the voice of your wife...cursed is the ground because of you; in toil you shall eat of it all the days of your life; thorns and thistles it shall bring forth to you, and you shall eat of the plants of the field." Most Americans, however, do not believe that women necessarily should suffer in childbirth and blindly be obedient to their husbands—nor, in spite of God's directive to Adam, do they consider nonagrarian careers to be unsuitable for men.

Archaeologically, we know that, for most of human history, people subsisted by hunting and gathering, not farming, and those who lived in warm climates were content to be naked. This is in sharp contrast to what Genesis would have us believe. Understandably, the people who wrote the Bible had a very limited knowledge of such things and knew nothing about how cultures evolve over time. From their perspective, everything they were familiar with (clothing and sheep herding, for example) was pretty much as God had created it just a few thousand years before.

The Bible informs us that, following parturition. a woman must be secluded from others, for two weeks if the baby is a girl, but only one week if it is a boy. Additionally, we are told that menstruating women are unclean and menstrual blood is magically dangerous to others. Belief about the value of female seclusion and the harmful supernatural power of menstrual blood arc common in tribal societies; but even fundamentalist preachers, known for their condemnation of sexual equality, seldom cite these biblical passages. Do they not realize that the biblical belief about the supernatural dangers of menstrual blood further would support their conviction that men must control women? What they do understand, of course, is that such beliefs are so antithetical to modern thinking that citing Leviticus on this subject only would encourage questioning the credibility of the Bible.

All tribal societies have their traditional beliefs about the nature of women contained in mythic tales told to children and acted out in dramatic rituals. The Adam and Eve account is typical of this genre. As the circumstances of a society change, as their technology and economy progress, the telling of origin myths concerning women evolves as well, and thus stays more current with changing times. The Bible, though was written down, causing this anthology to atrophy intellectually, to remain more or less constant even as the rest of the culture changed dramatically. Consequently, it is little wonder that the Bible's theory of the nature of women quaintly is contrastive to how women are perceived by most educated Americans today. Of course, the Koran and its recorded dogma suffer from the same rigidity.

As the Bible and the Koran would have it, women, as they relate to men are inferior, less righteous, and dangerous—besides being the possessions of, and appropriately subordinate to, men. Not surprisingly, fundamentalist Christian organizations have a history of opposing women's suffrage, painkillers during childbirth, and equal rights for women. It is fortunate for women that the Bible's admonitions are not the only criteria Americans rely on when evaluating the behavior and character of females.

Yet, in the modern industrial world, Americans are quite religious, and this seems to be especially characteristic of American women. Their enthusiasm for sacred rituals is somewhat ironic since, crossculturally, religious beliefs so often imply that women are inferior to men and in need of male guidance. In the Western tradition, church weddings, usually the bride's preference, reflect traditional religious beliefs about women. Until recently, wedding vows had women promising to "obey" their husbands. It still is de rigueur for the bride to wear white, representing virginity, even though this symbolism seems rather hollow and even sexist today. After all, nothing the groom wears symbolizes anything about his sexual history—and the bride continues- to be "given away" by her father, as if the groom is receiving some sort of property. Accordingly, most brides continue to change their surname to that of their husband.

In the U.S. and elsewhere, some of the most reactionary responses to newly won women's rights have come from religious fundamentalists—Muslims, Jews, and Christians. The Iranian revolution reestablished a theocratic government and forces Muslim women to wear a hijab to conceal their hair. The Taliban in Afghanistan insist that females cannot attend school or work outside the household, and women in Saudi Arabia are banned from driving cars, or being unchaperoned in the company of an unrelated male. Ultraorthodox Jews in Israel—as well as in Brooklyn, N.Y.—diligently proscribe the social activities of women, lest they be corrupted by the dominant environing society. The Catholic Church remains steadfast in its opposition to women assuming the role of priests, and Protestant evangelists frequently bemoan feminist goals such as sexual equality in a marital relationship.

Men control all major religious organizations, and it appears that male-dominated religion has a very long history, dating back at least to our tribal origins. Following ancient traditions, tribal men conduct the most important sacred rituals, those that supposedly ensure the well-being of the entire community. Females either are excluded from these calendrical ceremonies or are limited to an ancillary role. Such restrictions are reflective and symbolic of the inferior social status of these women.

Females in such societies must content themselves with more private magical rites intended to affect the welfare of only a single individual or, at most, a household. Men and women agree that (the dramatic communal rituals, those conducted by the men of the tribe, are far more essential than are the women's personal and domestic rituals, thus reinforcing the belief that men are more important than women.

Although women are overrepresented in most U.S. congregations, even those founded by or run by women do not challenge the long-established male dominated religious institutions, nor are they in conflict with the gender hierarchical structure of our society. Evangelical congregations tend to concentrate more on spirituality and an otherworldly existence than on political or economic reforms. As such. they tend to shun or oppose modern social trends like sexual equality, stay-at-home dads, and career-seeking mothers.

New Age spirituality

Women especially seem drawn to astrology and faith healing, New Age spirituality, and occult beliefs, as well as to charlatans who, for a price, offer to predict their future, help them communicate with the dead, and. by manipulating supernatural power, promise them wealth and good fortune. These alternative religious practices are very similar to the types of fringe religious pursuits engaged in by tribal women. In numerous tribes in South America, Africa, and Australia, recounted myths tell of a chaotic ancient time when women were in charge of society and men were forced to take control to introduce order and stability. These tribal tales and the Adam and Eve story are told to children, presumably in order to make it clear that the subordination of women is necessary for the common good of the community.

A majority of religions impose taboos on the sexual behavior of women. The most common, perhaps, is based on the belief that the loss of virginity has undesirable supernatural repercussions. Of course, the virginity of men seldom is given any mystical significance. Other religious taboos seem designed to conceal the sex appeal of women, lest they corrupt good men. Muslim women who must cover their hair, wear a veil, or shroud their entire body are familiar examples. Fundamentalist preachers although they do not advocate the wearing of burkas, certainly disapprove of women who expose "too much" flesh in public. According to them, even the breastfeeding of infants must be concealed from public view. Similarly, very conservative priests, rabbis, and imam espouse beliefs about the sacredness of a woman's virginity. Whether a society uses menstrual taboos, veils, or a double standard regarding virginity, the message is the same: women's sexual nature must be controlled because everyone will suffer if women are too independent. Religious myths illustrate what happens when severe restrictions are absent, and sacred rituals dramatically reinforce the belief that it is men who must rein in women.

Additionally, menstrual taboos and others that specifically restrict the sexual behavior of women reflect and reinforce the belief that the measure of a woman's worth is her sexuality and reproductive capacity. Whatever additional roles a woman may play in the community—political or economic, for instance—her value will be judged primarily on her performance as wife and mother.

Why, in spite of these sexist tribal vestiges, do women continue to be so committed to faith in supernatural power? Perhaps, like low-status minorities who seem especially attracted to cults and small independent sects, women are looking to spiritual empowerment as compensation for their lack of instrumental power. African and Native Americans, so long dominated by whites; have sought refuge in religious rituals and other escapist forms of expressive behavior. If women, like blacks and Indians, are so committed to religious beliefs and organizations because they lack real power, their faith only serves to perpetuate their inferior status.

The Koran is no more sexist than the Bible. Fortunately for females, we do not yet have an example of a contemporary country basing its laws on fundamentalist Christian doctrine. There are many fundamentalist Jews who want to reform the Israeli legal system so that it represents their interpretation of the Old Testament. but they have yet to achieve their goal. However, several countries have adopted sharia law where madrassahs (Koranic schools) indoctrinate children to fifth-century norms. Numerous and popular Bible based schools in the U.S. have this same capacity.

Our nation has a tradition that discourages publicly disputing religious views that differ from our own. Although I long have supported this politically correct prohibition, now that legislation and education are being influenced so zealously by religious fundamentalism, the time has come to challenge biblical literalism in defense of reason and social liberalism. Most of us readily condemn the treatment of women in fundamentalist Muslim countries. but fail to recognize that further erosion of democracy and women's rights could happen here if the growing influence of religious fundamentalism remains largely unchallenged.

Gender Differences in Religion: A Test of the Structural Location Theory*

DAVID DE VAUS AND IAN MCALLISTER

One of the most consistent findings in the sociology of religion is that women tend to be more religious than men. Surprisingly, given its universality there are relatively few attempts to explain this phenomenon empirically. This article examines the extent to which gender differences in religious orientation can be attributed to the structural location of women in society. Three explanations to account for gender variations in religion are tested: (1) the child-rearing role of females, (2) lower levels of female work force participation relative to males, and (3) differing attitudes toward work and its relationship to family values. The analysis uses the nationally representative data collected in Australia in 1983 to show that the child-rearing role and differing attitudes toward work do not account for the greater religiousness of women. By contrast, the lower rate of female work force participation is an important explanatory factor. Possible reasons for this effect are discussed.

A consistent finding in studies of religion is that on a wide range of measures females tend to be more religious than males. While there is no shortage of ex post facto explanations for this phenomenon, there are virtually no attempts to test these explanations empirically. Two major explanations have been put forward. The first and the most widely canvassed explanation uses psychological theories. These have included notions that females are naturally more inclined towards religion than males and that they experience greater feelings of guilt and turn to religion to relieve this guilt (Gray 1971; Suziedelis and Potvin 1981). It has also been suggested that females identify with God as a male father figure and therefore find religion more attractive than do males (Argyle and Beit-Hallahmi 1975, p. 77).

A second explanation focuses on socialization theory. This argues that the particular childhood experiences of females predispose them towards religious values and involvements (Argyle and Beit-Hallahmi 1975. p. 77; D'Andrade 1967: Suziedelis and Potvin 1981, p. 39). More specifically, the socialization of females is said to emphasize conflict resolution, submission, gentleness, nurturance, and other expressive values that are congruent with religious emphases. By contrast, the more instrumental emphases in male socialization are said to make religion less consonant with male roles, values, and self-images (Mol 1985, p. 74).

More recently, a third explanation for the stronger religious orientation of females has emerged. This has emphasized the importance of their structural location in society. The structural location argument takes three basic forms. First, it is argued that the child-rearing role of females induces a greater commitment to religion

* The 1983 Australian Values Survey was originally collected by Roy Morgan Research Pty. Ltd. and supplied by the Social Science Data Archive at the Australian National University. Neither the original collectors of data nor the disseminating agency bears any responsibility for the analyses or interpretations presented herein.

David de Vaus and Ian McAllister, "Gender Differences in Religion: A Test of the Structural Location Theory" from *American Sociological Review*, Vol. 52., No. 4 (Aug., 1987), pp. 472–481.

and, second, that the lower rates of labor force participation among females are a cause. Third, the attitudes women have toward work and its relationship to family values are often seen as a factor.

In this paper, we apply multivariate analysis to nationally representative Australian survey data collected in 1983 to test these three structural location explanations. The results show that the lower rates of female labor force participation are the major cause of their greater religious commitment, though there remains a significant residual effect for gender which cannot be explained by the variables included in the model. Finally, various implications of these findings are discussed.

Theory and Hypotheses

The popularity of structural location theory to explain gender variations in religion stems partly from the perceived inadequacy of the prevailing psychological and socialization theories, and partly from an increasing awareness of the differing and changing role of women in society. The commonest structural location explanation concerns the role that most sets females apart from males: their child-rearing role. A variety of reasons are offered for the proposed link. Martin (1967, p. 125; see also Lazerwitz 1961, p. 308) argues that the involvement of children in church organizations such as Sunday School draws their primary caregivers (mothers) into the church. Martin (1967, p. 125) further suggests that parents feel that the church is good for their children and that mothers, as primary caregivers, go to church to encourage their children's involvement (Nelsen and Nelsen 1975).

Additional explanations for the importance of child rearing argue that since the links between church and family are strong, those most concerned with family well-being become most involved in the church (Glock, Ringer, and Babbie 1967, p. 43). Moberg (1962, p. 395) argues that the family-centered role of females encourages dependence on personal influences and that religion, which deals with the personality, is therefore more easily appreciated by females than males. Moberg (1962, p. 399) also suggests that the child-rearing

role of females leads to greater social isolation and that church involvement is one way of overcoming this. Finally, it is argued that females at home looking after children have available time and this permits church involvement while the occupational role of males inhibits it. According to this model, the differences between the religious orientation of males and females will be greatest among those with younger children (de Vaus 1982).

A competing explanation suggests that children discourage religious involvements (Glock et al. 1967, p. 59). The time-consuming task of child rearing leaves little time and energy for religion, and as child care becomes less demanding, female interest in religion is revived. This explanation argues that when the responsibilities for child care are greatest for females, the religiosity of males and females will be most similar. When there are no dependent children the gender-related differences will be greatest.

These propositions give rise to several hypotheses.

> HYPOTHESIS 1. *The child-rearing role of females suggests that, other things being equal, the differences between the religious orientation of males and females will be removed once the effect of stage in the child-rearing cycle is removed.*
>
> HYPOTHESIS 2. *The differences between the religiosity of males and females will vary at different stages of the child-rearing cycle. These differences will be greater either: (a) when there are dependent children (general view); or (b) when the respondent does not have dependent children (Glock et al. view).*

A second version of the structural location model highlights the importance of work force participation. The argument is that work force participation militates against religious commitment. Since fewer females than males are in the work force, so more females than males will be religious. This argument is a popular one (Lenski 1953, p. 535; Luckmann 1967, p. 30; Martin 1967, p. 128; Nelsen and Potvin 1981, p. 280: Moberg 1962, p. 300). Luckmann argues that "the degree of involvement in the work processes of modern industrial society correlates negatively with the degree of involvement in church-oriented religion" and has suggested that the religious commitment of working females will resemble that of males more than that of females in the home. Martin (1967, p. 126) has predicted that as females become more involved in the work force, gender differences in religion will decline.

The reasons why work force participation should lead to a decline in religious commitment are not always explicitly stated but may be inferred from the literature. Luckmann's argument about societal secularization is that industrialization and urbanization have led to institutional specialization which leads to the "shrinking relevance of the values institutionalized in church religion for the integration and legitimation of everyday life in modern society" (1967, p. 39). Equally, work force participation can provide alternative sources of identity, interests, values, legitimations, and commitments so that religion simply becomes less important. In addition, the instrumental orientation encouraged by involvement in the competitive workplace is seen by some to create conflicts with more expressive Christian values. Changes in identity due to work force participation may lead to conflicts with a religious identity.

Other explanations which focus on work force participation suggest that those who work are said to have less time to get involved in the church (Clock et al. 1967, p. 45). Social networks are often seen as important: those not working have "narrower contacts" (Yinger 1970, p. 133) and are "relatively protected" from secularization pressures (Lenski 1953, p. 535). Work is also said to provide adequate social interaction whereas those at home lack social interaction and church involvement helps alleviate this isolation (Moberg 1962, p. 399).

The hypotheses that stem from these arguments are:

HYPOTHESIS 3. *Females in the work force will be less religious than females not in the work force.*

HYPOTHESIS 4. *The religious orientation of females in the work force will be more similar to males in the work force than to females not in the work force.*

A third structural location explanation draws, in part, on the previous two. It focuses on the priority which people give their family over their work. It could be argued that females will give their family greater priority over paid work than will males. The stronger family focus of females could help account for their greater levels of religiousness for two reasons. Firstly, a family orientation may promote an interest in religion because of the perceived consonance between religious values and family values. Secondly, in our society roles tend not to be highly valued unless they produce an income. It is possible that those who focus more on family than work tend to experience some sense of deprivation and turn to religion for comfort (Argyle and Beit-Hallahmi 1975; Borque and Back 1966; Glock et al. 1967; Yinger 1970, p. 134).

The hypothesis that can be derived from this explanation is:

HYPOTHESIS 5. *Those who are focused more on family than work will be more religious than those with less of a family focus.*

Data, Measurement, Method
Data

The data are from the 1983 Australian Values Survey ($N = 1,228$), which was a national probability sample of the Australian population aged 14 and over. Because of the problems in examining child-rearing, life-cycle, and labor force patterns among the younger respondents, the analyses are restricted to the 1,127 respondents who were aged 18 or over.

Measuring Religious Commitment

The survey asked a wide range of questions covering religious affiliation, behavior, values, and beliefs. Since the survey contained so many items, these had to be refined into a parsimonious set of reliable measures reflecting the main dimensions of contemporary religious life. Various possible dimensions of religious commitment have been elaborated. Lenski (1963, pp. 17–23), for example, distinguishes between commitment to a socio-religious group and commitment to a religious orientation, while others have identified up to nine dimensions (Demerath 1965, pp. 59–69; King 1967; O'Connell 1975). The most influential analysis of religious commitment has been provided by Glock and Stark (1965, pp. 16–18), who define five dimensions ranging from belief in the basic tenets of religion, to knowledge of its consequences for secular life.

In this analysis, we identify four dimensions: church attendance, commitment, belief, and revelation. These are not intended to be exhaustive, but to measure the most common aspects of religion. In each case, except one, they are measured by multiple-item scales. The exception is *church attendance* which is a common and widely used measure of religious behaviour. Religious *commitment* is represented by two items measuring the importance of God to the individual, and the person's own religious self-definition. Religious *belief* is measured by five fundamentalist religious beliefs (see Table 2), while religious *revelation* is measured by whether or not the respondent had ever been aware of a presence, or ever felt close to the spiritual life.[1]

The multiple-item scales were constructed by coding missing data to the mean of each separate item, dividing each by its standard deviation (in order to ensure that the scoring of one particular variable did not bias the overall scale), and summing them. Since the resulting scale had no natural metric, they were rescored on a scale running from 0 to 10.[2] The variable is scaled so that the higher the score the more religious the response.

Measurement of Other Variables

The control variables were chosen to represent as wide a range as possible of the lifetime experiences of individuals; the variables, together with their scoring and means, are shown in Table 1. Ascribed characteristics are measured by the respondent's age, whether or not they were born in Australia, and by the relative urbanization of the area in which they live. Socioeconomic status is measured by education, whether or not the head of the household is a nonmanual worker, and by family income. There are obvious problems including adequate occupational controls through

head-of-household measures when one of the areas of interest is employment status: as such, the occupational and income variables used here are intended to represent the general socioeconomic status of the household.

The variable indicating stage in the child-rearing cycle was divided into four categories: single; married without any children; married with children under 18 in the home; and married with children but the children have left the home. Table 1 shows that more males than females (21 percent as against 13 percent) tend to be single, while more females than males are married with children living in the home (58 percent as against 45 percent). Some 15 percent of the respondents did not fall into these four categories (mainly because they were widowed or divorced) and they have been excluded from the analysis.[3]

Labor force participation is divided into five categories: working full-time, working part-time, unemployed, home duties, and retired. Students and those with another employment status (some 6 percent of the total sample) were excluded from the analysis.[4] Nearly half the females (48 percent) were engaged in home duties, while three-quarters of the males were in full-time employment.

The final structural location variable was constructed from four items measuring the relationship between work and family values and is intended to reflect the degree of family focus. These items asked how important it was to have a job that did not disrupt family life, did not interfere with the spouse's career, did not require having to move home, and that the family thought was worthwhile. Combining the items produced a scale running from 0 to 4: 0 meant that the respondents failed to mention any of the four items, a score of 4 that they mentioned all four. Means for the dummy variables constructed from the scale are shown in Table 1.

Method

The analysis relies on ordinary least squares regression techniques, which assume that relations among the variables are, to a reasonable approximation, linear and additive (Hanushek and Jackson 1977). The regression estimates used

Table 1. Variables, Definitions, Means

Variable	Definition	Means Male	Means Female
Ascribed characteristics			
Age	Years	41.1	38.2
Australian born	1 = yes, 0 = no	.77	.78
Lives in urban area	From a low of 0 to a high of 1	.80	.80
Socioeconomic status			
Education	Years	12.2	11.2
Head of household nonmanual worker	1 = yes, 0 = no	.44	.41
Family income	$1,000s	21.5	21.5
Life-cycle effects			
Single		.21	.13
Married, no children	1 = yes, 0 = no	.09	.09
Married, children in home		.45	.58
Married, children not in home		.25	.20
Labor force participation			
Working, full-time		.76	.23
Working, part time		.03	.22
Unemployed	1 = yes, 0 = no	.05	.04
Home duties		.00	.48
Retired		.15	.03
Family responsibilities and work			
Very important		.10	.15
Fairly important		.13	.19
Indifferent	1 = yes, 0 = no	.27	.26
Fairly unimportant		.31	.27
Very unimportant		.19	.13

Source: 1983 Australian Values Survey.
Note: Excludes respondents who were aged less than 18 years when the survey was carried out, and respondents who were not included in the four life-cycle or five labor force participation categories. With these exclusions, the total *N* is 895.

in Tables 3, 4, and 5 were made by first calculating a regression equation, including dummy variables to account for structural location, and then evaluating at the mean. In each case, the control variables are the respondents ascribed characteristics and socioeconomic status, as defined in Table 1. For example, to estimate church attendance at different stages of the life cycle in Table 3, the following equation was calculated.

$$ChAtt = a + b_1 Age + b_2 Aust + b_3 Urban$$
$$+ b_4 Educ + b_5 HHWhiteC$$
$$+ b_6 FamInc + b_7 MarrNoC$$
$$+ b_8 MarrCH + b_9 MarrCLH + e,$$

where *b* is the partial regression coefficient and the variable name the mean value. In this case, the excluded category is those who are single: evaluating the equation at the mean produces the regression estimate for church attendance among single

Table 2. Gender Variations in Religious Orientation (Mean Scores)

	Male	Female	Difference, Female-Male
Church attendance	3.2	4.0	+0.8**
Commitment			
1. Importance of God	5.7	6.6	+0.9**
2. Religious self-definition	7.5	8.1	+0.6**
(1 and 2 combined)	(6.2)	(7.1)	(+0.9)**
Belief			
1. Believe in soul	6.6	8.2	+1.4**
2. Believe in devil	3.5	5.2	+1.7**
3. Believe in hell	3.4	5.0	+1.6**
4. Believe in heaven	5.6	7.5	+1.9**
5. Believe in sin	6.6	7.4	+0.8**
(1 to 5 combined)	(5.2)	(6.6)	(+1.4)**
Revelation			
1. Aware of presence	2.2	2.8	+0.6**
2. Close to spiritual life	1.5	1.9	+ 0.4*
(1 and 2 combined)	(1.8)	(2.3)	(+0.5**)

Source: 1983 Australian Values survey.

Note: All variables are scored 0 to 10. Full questions are as follows:

Church attendance: Apart from weddings, funerals, and baptisms, about how often do you attend religious services these days?

Importance of God: How important is God in your life?

Religious self-definition: Independently of whether you go to church or not, would you say you are a religious person, not a religious person, or a convinced atheist?

Belief: Which, if any, do you believe in…?

Aware of presence: Next about being aware of, or influenced by, a presence or power, either God or something else—but different from your everyday self. Have you been aware of such a presence, or not?

Close to spiritual life: Have you ever felt as though you are very close to a powerful, spiritual life force that seemed lo lift you out of yourself?

**p < .01, *p < .05 both two tailed.

respondents. The partial regression coefficients of the other dummy variables are then either added or subtracted depending on their sign to the regression estimate for single respondents.

The decomposition in Table 6 follows the technique devised by Alwin and Hauser (1975). Gender was first regressed on the particular religious orientation under investigation, and variables were progressively entered into the equation; the resulting change in the partial regression coefficient for gender reflects the indirect effects of the blocks of variables being added. The partial regression coefficient for gender when all other variables have been added to the equation represents the direct effect of gender.

Full regression results and correlations are too extensive to report here, but are available from the authors on request.

Results

Aggregate Differences

The aggregate differences in gender variations in religious orientation are shown in Table 2; all the figures are mean scores, where each variable has been scored on a scale running from 0 to 10. On each of the indicators of religious orientation females were more religious than males and each was statistically significant at the .01 level, save one, which was significant at the .05 level. The differences were least marked for the religious revelation measures and greatest for the items measuring religious belief. For example, the average male scored 1.5 on the 0 to 10 scale for closeness to the spiritual life, compared to 1.9 for the average female. By contrast, females scored 7.5 on the scale for belief in heaven, compared to only 5.6 for males.

In general, all the respondents scored highest on commitment, and least on revelation. This probably reflects the fact that it is easier to volunteer a general commitment to religion, and more difficult to give details of that commitment, through church attendance or detailed beliefs. Among the fundamentalist religious beliefs, the existence of a soul was the belief most likely to be endorsed. The New Testament ideas of the devil and hell were least likely to be believed in.

Life Cycle

Table 3 shows the importance of different stages in the life cycle on the four measures of religious orientation. For each measure, the figures represent differences in male and female regression estimates. These control for the ascribed characteristics and socioeconomic status of the respondent. Because the regression estimates were estimated separately for males and females all possible interactions between the independent variables have been allowed for.

These results do not support the first hypothesis that gender differences in religiosity will disappear when the effect of stage in the child-rearing cycle is removed; in fact, the gender differences persist at most stages of the life cycle. It is only among those whose children have left home that the gender differences are less than for the sample as a whole (Table 3). The second hypothesis, that gender differences in religious orientation will vary at different stages of the life cycle, is supported in its general form but not in either of its two specific forms. Neither the particular predictions made by the general view (greater differences when dependent children are present) nor the predictions of Glock et al. (greater differences when no children are present) are supported.

Table 3 presents the differences between the regression estimates of males and females at each stage of the life cycle. These are compared with gender differences regardless of life-cycle stage. Differences are most marked among single people and least marked among those married but whose children have left home. Those in the "middle" stages of the life cycle generally displayed differences between these two extremes. In general, the presence or absence of children in the home does not seem to be a decisive factor influencing gender differences in religious orientation. Among those without dependent children there is considerable variation, and gender differences are greatest

Table 3. Life-cycle Variations in Religious Orientation: Differences in Regression Estimates Between Males and Females

	Mean (1)	Stage in Life Cycle			
		Single (1)	Married, No Children (3)	Married, Children in Home (4)	Married, Children Left Home (5)
Church attendance	0.8	1.5	0.6	0.7	0.1
Commitment	0.9	0.8	0.3	1.0	0.5
Belief	0.9	2.0	1.2	1.3	0.6
Revelation	0.5	0.8	0.9	0.5	−0.1
(Mean)	(0.8)	(1.3)	(0.8)	(0.9)	(0.3)

Source: 1983 Australian Values Survey.

Note: Positive values indicate a higher estimate for females than for males. Religious variables are all scored 0 to 10. The regression estimates (cols. 2 to 5) were calculated by evaluating a regression equation at the mean; see text for details.

among single respondents and least among married respondents whose children have left home, Married people without children display moderate gender differences.

These results do not consistently support the views of Glock et al. who predict that general differences will be greatest when people do not have dependent children. Although the differences are greatest among single people, their prediction that as children leave the home female interest in religion will be revived is not supported. The more general view that gender differences will be greatest when people have dependent children also was largely unsupported. The greatest gender differences are among single respondents. The only instance in which the general hypothesis is supported is with religious commitment: on this dimension gender differences are greatest among those with dependent children.

These results suggest a different formulation of the life cycle model. Rather than reflecting the presence or absence of children, as the various versions of the child-rearing model would suggest, stage in the life cycle is relevant to gender differences but it is not the child-care responsibilities that seem to be a causal factor. As people move through the various stages in the life cycle, gender differences in religious orientation tend to decline.

Labor Force Participation

Table 4 shows the effect of labor force participation on gender variations in religious orientation. In a number of different ways, the results indicate the importance of labor force participation in helping to account for gender differences in religiosity. Since no males reported home duties as their current employment status, no gender differences can be reported for column 4. Working full-time appears to be the most effective in reducing any interest in religion; the mean female-male difference for the four scales is only 0.2 (Table 4, col. 2). Being unemployed tends to produce similar levels of religious orientation to working part-time, while the largest variations—overall, eight times greater than working full-time—are found among those who are unemployed (Table 4, col. 5).

Among females a major test of the structural location theory is the religious orientation of those who are in the labor force compared to those who are not. In this case, the theory produces the predicted results. Females who work full-time are less religious than their counterparts who are full-time housewives: the mean regression estimate for the four scales is 4.4, compared to 5.2 for females engaged in home duties.

These results therefore support hypothesis 3—that females who work will be less religious than females who do not—and hypothesis 4—that the religious orientation of females in the work

Table 4. Labor Force Participation and Variations in Religious Orientation: Differences in Regression Estimates between Males and Females

| | | Labor Forte Status | | | | |
	Mean (1)	Working Full-Time (2)	Working Part-Time (3)	Home Duties (4)	Unemployed (5)	Retired (6)
Church attendance	0.8	−0.1	1.5	na	1.2	−0.1
Commitment	0.9	0.2	1.3	na	1.8	0.0
Belief	1.4	0.6	1.0	na	2.0	1.3
Revelation	0.5	0.2	−0.5	na	1.2	1.6
(Mean)	(0.9)	(0.2)	(0.8)		(1–6)	(0.7)

Source: 1983 Australian Values Survey.

Note: Positive values indicate a higher estimate for females than males. Religious variables are all scored 0 to 10. The regression estimates (cols. 2 to 6) were calculated by evaluating a regression equation at the mean: see text for details.

force is very similar to males in the work force. Indeed, hypothesis 4 is underscored by the finding that females who work full-time actually attend church *less* than comparable males—a striking and important result. There are, however, several anomalies in these results. The first is that part-time work appears to have only marginal importance in reducing gender variations. But several possible factors present themselves. First, those who work part-time may have a high commitment to their family, in the sense that they are employable but have chosen a median solution. Alternatively, they may wish to make up for their absences from the home by inculcating greater religious feeling than those who stay at home full-time.

A second anomaly is that there are such large gender variations among the unemployed. Indeed, females who are out of the labor force and unemployed are generally more religious (mean on all measures of 5.3) than those who are in it (mean of 4.4), while unemployed males are the least religious of all (mean of 3.8 on all measures).

One possibility is that for males being out of the full-time labor force is atypical (23 percent) whereas for females being out of it is typical (77 percent). It may be that level of religiousness is associated with levels of conventionality. That is, females who are conventional are more likely to

be doing what is typical of their gender and more likely to be religious.

Family Focus

The final test of the structural location theory involves examining attitudes towards family responsibilities and work and their effect on religion. The theory predicts that those who have most commitment to integrating family and work responsibilities will be the most religious; conversely, those with least commitment to this aim will be least religious. The results of the analysis, shown in Table 5, are inconclusive. Gender variations are greater at the opposite ends of the scale—those who feel a family focus is important or unimportant—and least among those who feel indifferent about the issue. There is no support, then, for the fifth hypothesis.

Overall, then, two of the three structural location explanations—life cycle and labor force participation—each appear to have some validity in explaining the gender gap in religious orientation. So far, however, the results have not addressed two central questions. First, to what extent does the explanatory power of these explanations persist when other aspects of the structural location of individuals are introduced? For example, to what extent does the influence of stage in the life cycle persist when labor force participation is controlled for? Second and relatedly,

Table 5. Family Focus and Work, and Variations in Religious Orientation: Differences in Regression Estimates Between Males and Females

		Family Focus				
	Mean (1)	Very Important (2)	Fairly Unimportant (3)	Indifferent (4)	Fairly Important (5)	Very Important (6)
Church attendance	0.8	0.8	0.9	0.6	0.8	0.4
Commitment	0.9	0.8	0.8	0.2	0.9	0.8
Belief	1.3	2.0	1.1	0.9	1.4	1.8
Revelation	0.2	0.3	0.5	0.0	0.4	0.5
(Mean)	(0.8)	(1.0)	(0.8)	(0.4)	(0.9)	(0.9)

Source: 1983 Australian Values Survey.

Note: Positive values indicate a higher estimate for females than for males. Religious variables are all scored 0 to 10. The regression estimates (cols. 2 to 6) are made by evaluating a regression equation at the mean; see text for details.

what is the exact contribution from each of the three structural location explanations in explaining the gender gap in religious orientation? To address these questions, the next section decomposes the gender gap into its various component parts.

Decomposing the Gender Gap

These calculations first involve taking the aggregate (and uncontrolled) differences in religious orientation attributable to gender, which were shown in Table 2, and estimating what proportion of the gap can be attributed to various factors. This is estimated by first calculating an ordinary least squares regression equation, predicting each of the four religious measures, and then entering the independent variables in blocks. The resulting change in the value of the partial regression coefficient for gender shows the indirect effect of the variables being entered at that particular time (Alwin and Hauser 1975).[5]

The results of this analysis are shown in Table 6. Line 1 shows the total effect: that is the same result as shown in Table 2. For example, the gender gap in church attendance is 0.8 of a point on the 0 to 10 scale: this is the total effect attributable to gender. Line 2 shows the direct effect, that is, the remaining gap after all the variables have been taken into

account. Line 3 shows the indirect effect, that is, the effect which can be attributed to the other variables; together, the direct effect (line 2) and the indirect effect (line 3) make up the total effect. For example, the total effect of 0.8 for church attendance (line 1) is made up of a direct effect of 0.3 (line 2) and an indirect effect of 0.5 (line 3) (0.3 + 0.5 = 0.8).

The actual decomposition of the indirect effects is shown in lines (a) to (e); the sum of lines (a) to (e) add up to the figure given for the indirect effect. Five separate components are tested. Ascribed characteristics are measured by age, birthplace, and place of residence, while socioeconomic status is measured by education, occupation, and income. Life cycle, labor force participation, and family focus effects are all measured by dummy variables representing the categories shown in Tables 3 to 5, respectively.

The results show one unambiguous finding: the predominant effect in explaining the greater religious orientation of women is labor force participation. While there is some limited explanatory power for stage in the life cycle, the strongest and most consistent effect is the individual's labor force participation. Once the effect of work force participation is removed, the gap between the religious orientation of men and women declines markedly.

Table 6. Decomposing the Gender Gap in Religious Orientation

	Church Attendance (1)	Commitment (2)	Belief (3)	Revelation (4)
1. Total effect (lines 2 + 3)	0.8	0.9	1.4	0.5
2. Direct effect	0.3	0.4	0.7	0.1
3. Indirect effect (lines (a) + (b) + (c) + (d) + (e))	0.5	0.5	0.7	0.4
(a) Ascribed characteristics	0.0	+0.1	0.0	0.0
(b) Socioeconomic status	+0.1	0.0	+0.1	0.0
(c) Life cycle	−0.1	−0.1	−0.1	0.0
(d) Labor force participation	−0.5	−0.5	−0.6	−0.4
(e) Family focus	0.0	0.0	−0.1	0.0

Source: 1983 Australian Values Survey.
Note: OLS decomposition showing direct and indirect effects of variables in predicting religious orientations. All religious variables are scored from 0 to 10. See text for details of the method used.

Examining the results in wider perspective, Table 6 also shows that, with the exception of one aspect of religion, structural location explains the majority of the gender gap. In church attendance, for example, the indirect effect of structural location explains 0.5 of the total 0.8 gap; structural location explains 0.4 of the 0.5 gap in revelation. The exception is belief, where exactly half of the substantial 1.4 gender gap—0.7—can be explained by structural location, leaving a similar amount unexplained.

Discussion

The importance of structural location, and in particular work force participation, suggests that the greater religiosity of women is not simply because of psychological dispositions or differential socialization. On the contrary, a person's position in society and the role they perform affects their religiosity.

The results presented here have shown that the female child-rearing role does not account for the higher level of female religiosity after other aspects of structural location are controlled for. Similarly, family focus does not have much explanatory power after these controls are introduced. By contrast there was clear evidence that work force participation is an important factor. Females in the full-time work force are less religious than those out of it and have a broadly similar religious orientation to males. Gender differences in religiosity are reduced substantially when the effect of different rates of work force participation is removed. If it were not for the lower rate of female participation in the full-time labor force, the gender differences in religious orientation would not be as marked as they are. These results highlight the importance of location in the social structure for religious orientation. Although sociologists have long emphasised this, few have used it to explain empirically gender differences in religion.

The question remains as to why work force participation affects the religious orientation of females. Two speculative answers deserve consideration. One possibility is that working provides a substitute for the sociopsychological benefits that individuals derive from religion and church involvement. Working can provide activities, alternative interests which act as competing commitments to religious involvements, and perhaps more importantly act as a source of values, identity, and the social relationships that in Luckmann's (1967) terms provide "the integration and legitimation of everyday life."

From this perspective, church involvements and religious views become less necessary if the workplace replaces many of the things the church previously provided. In a society where work force participation is highly valued and people tend to be valued according to whether they are employed, working can be an important source of identity. In this respect it is understandable that the effect of work force participation is most marked on church involvement and religious commitment. In other words, working simply makes religion less important and less relevant for some people.

Another possible explanation for the effect of labor force participation focuses on the structure of the work situation and the argument that subordinate groups often adopt the values of dominant groups. It is based on the view that female work force participation does not imply equality. Typically females occupy subordinate positions and positions of authority are occupied by males. Additionally, males often substantially outnumber females. Given that males in general are less religious than females and, one suspects, less tolerant of religiosity, it is likely that some females will modify their views towards what are perceived to be those of males or the "normal" view in their workplace.

This tendency for working females to modify their views towards those of males in their workplace may reflect conformism, the desire to win approval, a change in reference group which indicates deference to those in authority or the result of being in a minority in many work situations (Kanter 1977). The argument that subordinate and relatively powerless groups will identify with and internalize the values of dominant groups is hardly novel. It has been used in studies of assimilation of migrant groups and is consistent with findings which show those who move into the work force experience substantial religious change (de Vaus 1980, p. 143).

A further possibility is that work force participation affects the amount of time available for involvement in religious activities. This explanation is consistent with the effect that working has on church attendance, but it is less helpful in explaining the effects on beliefs, commitment, and revelation. Unless beliefs, commitment, and revelation are a function of church attendance, it is unlikely that these aspects of religiosity are affected simply because working leaves people with less flexible time. It is more likely that working has its effect because it occupies *attention* rather than *time*. If the time factor was crucial in affecting religious orientation, we might expect that stage in the child-rearing cycle would have had more effect that it does.

The results presented here provide an interesting contrast with those in the United States where work force participation does not appear to affect female religious orientation (de Vaus 1984). This may reflect the integration of religion into mainstream culture in the United States and Australia. In the United States religion is much more part of the dominant culture than it is in Australia. Religion has been co-opted into American political culture and is used explicitly in discussions of social questions (for example, the moral majority) and in justifying the ethics of the workplace where success, hard work, and prosperity are seen as religious virtues. Since religion is an important part of mainstream culture, a religious person will be more easily tolerated even by those who do not see themselves as religious. As a result, the pressure to conform to nonreligious mores in the workplace will be less.

In Australia, where religion plays a more marginal role in the culture, it will be harder to maintain a religious position in a work environment that is perceived to be nonreligious. Those who are not religious will also be less tolerant of religion if it is seen as a marginal part of the culture. The application of this idea to explaining the convergence of attitudes among males and females in the work force deserves further attention. It may well have relevance in explaining the gender gap

in voting preferences and on a whole range of social and ethical issues ranging from attitudes to nuclear issues to sexual ethics. In these areas, too, the reentry of females into the full-time work force may lead to a greater convergence in gender orientations. The interesting question will be whether in these areas, like religion, working females will become more like males in their orientations or whether the process of attitude change will be reciprocal, with males adopting some of the attitudes which tend to characterize females.

Notes

1. These groupings were justified by the zero-order correlations between the items. In addition, a factor analysis of the fundamentalist religious beliefs produced a single factor with an eigenvalue greater than one when the structure was rotated to simple solution.

2. This rescaling was carried out using the simple transformation:

    New scale = ((old scale – lowest score)/range × 10).

3. This group was excluded for two reasons. First, it is socially heterogeneous—widows tend to be old, divorcees young—and its impact on religious orientation is unclear. Second, the numbers involved were small, and their inclusion would have raised problems of statistical reliability.

4. This group was excluded on the same grounds as given in note 3.

5. Since gender is a zero-one variable, the indirect effects through gender are easy to interpret.

References

Alwin, Duane F. and Robert M. Hauser. 1975. "The Decomposition of Effects in Path Analysis." *American Sociological Review* 40:37–47.

Argyle, Michael and B. Beit-Hallahmi. 1975. *The Social Psychology of Religion*. London: Routledge and Kegan Paul.

Australian Values Survey. 1983. Social Science Data Archive, The Australian National University, Canberra, ACT 2600, Australia (SSDA Study Number 375).

Berger, Peter. 1973. *The Social Reality of Religion*. Ringwood, Vic: Penguin.

Berger, Peter and T. Luckmann. 1967. *The Social Construction of Reality*. Ringwood, Vic: Penguin.

Bourque, L.B. and K.W. Back. 1966. "Values and Transcendental Experiences." *Social Forces* 47:34–37.

D'Andrade, R.G. 1967. "Sex Differences and Cultural Institutions." Pp. 173–203 in *The Development of Sex Differences*, edited by E.E. Maccoby. London: Tavistock.

Demerath, N.J. 1965. *Social Class and American Protestantism*. Chicago: Rand McNally.

de Vaus, David A. 1980. *The Process of Religious Change in Senior Adolescents*. Ph.D. diss., La Trobe University.

———. 1982. "The Impact of Children on Sex Related Differences in Religiousness." *Sociological Analysis* 43:145–54.

———. 1984. "Workforce Participation and Sex Differences in Church Attendance." *Review of Religious Research* 25:247–58.

Glock, Charles Y., B. Ringer, and E. Babbie. 1967. *To Comfort and to Challenge*. Berkeley: University of California Press.

Glock, Charles Y. and Rodney Stark. 1965. *Religion and Society in Tension*. Chicago: Rand McNally.

Gray, J.A. 1971. "Sex Differences in Emotional Behaviour in Mammals including Man Endocrine Basis." *Acta Psychologica* 35:29–48.

Hanushek, E.A. and John A. Jackson. 1977. *Statistical Methods for Social Scientists*. New York: Academic Press.

Kanter, Rosebeth M. 1977. "Some Effects of Proportions on Group Life: Skewed Sex Ratios and Responses to Token Women." *American Journal of Sociology* 82:965–90.

King, Morton. 1967. "Measuring the Religious Variable: Nine Proposed Dimensions." *Journal for the Scientific Study of Religion* 6:173–208.

Lazerwitz. B. 1961. "Some Factors Associated with Church Attendance." *Social Forces* 39:301–9.

Lenski, G.E. 1953. "Social Correlates of Religious Interest." *American Sociological Review* 18:533–44.

———. 1963. *The Religious Factor*. New York: Anchor.

Luckmann, T. 1967. *The Invisible Religion*. New York: Macmillan.

Martin, David. 1967. *A Sociology of English Religion*. London: SCM Press.

Moberg, D.O. 1962. *The Church as a Social Institution*. Englewood Cliffs, NJ: Prentice-Hall.

Mol, Hans. 1985. *The Faith of Australians*. Sydney: George, Allen and Unwin.

Nelsen, H.M. and A.K. Nelsen. 1975. *Black Church in the Sixties*. Lexington: University Press of Kentucky.

Nelsen, H.M. and R.H. Potvin. 1981. "Gender and Regional Differences in the Religiosity of Protestant Adolescents." *Review of Religious Research* 22:288–85.

O'Connell, Brian J. 1975. "Dimensions of Religiosity Among Catholics." *Review of Religious Research* 16:198–207.

Suziedelis, A. and R.H. Potvin. 1981. "Sex Differences in Factors Affecting Religiousness Among Catholic Adolescents." *Journal for the Scientific Study of Religion* 20:38–51.

Weigert, A.J. and D.L. Thomas. 1970. "Socialization and Religiosity: A Cross-National Analysis of Catholic Adolescents." *Sociometry* 33:305–28.

Yinger, J.M. 1970. *The Scientific Study of Religion*. New York: Macmillan.

The Gendered Workplace

Perhaps the most dramatic social change in industrial countries in the twentieth century has been the entry of women into the workplace. The nineteenth-century ideology of "separate spheres"—the breadwinner husband and the homemaker wife—has slowly and steadily evaporated. While only 20 percent of women and only 4 percent of married women worked outside the home in 1900, more than three-fourths did so by 1995, including 60 percent of married women. In the first decade of the next century, 80 percent of the new entrants into the labor force will be women, minorities, and immigrants.

Despite the collapse of the doctrine of separate spheres—work and home—the workplace remains a dramatically divided world, where women and men rarely do the same jobs in the same place for the same pay. Occupational sex segregation, persistent sex discrimination, wage disparities—all these are problems faced by working women.

Even women who are seeking to get ahead by entering formerly all-male fields frequently bump into the "glass ceiling"—a limit on how high they can rise in any organization. On the other hand, as Christine Williams argues, men who do "women's work"—taking occupations such as nurse, nursery school teacher, librarian—not only avoid the glass ceiling but actually glide up a "glass escalator"—finding greater opportunities at the higher, better paying levels of their professions than women. Adia Winfield makes clear that the glass escalator is also a racialized ride—and that men of color may have a different set of experiences entirely.

And even when women are protected by a variety of laws that promise comparable worth for equal work, wage and salary parity, and no occupational sex segregation, they still face a myriad of psychological and interpersonal struggles, such as sexual harassment, the creation of a "hostile environment" that keeps them in their place. Men, Karla Erickson and Jennifer Pierce make clear, face new problems in a new global workplace—the "feminization" of various traits and expectations in service-sector jobs. By comparing two types of service workers, Erickson and Pierce suggest that gender is not only a property of the individuals who inhabit occupational positions, but gender is also a property of the criteria used to evaluate them.

Finally, Kristen Schilt and Matthew Wiswall make clear that gender becomes most visible when it changes. Among transgendered people, male-to-female transgendered people face significantly more discrimination after their transition; female to make male transgendered people face significantly less. The gender you are is more important than the gender you were. Changing gender is also changing social status.

The Glass Escalator: Hidden Advantages for Men in the "Female" Professions

CHRISTINE L. WILLIAMS

The sex segregation of the U.S. labor force is one of the most perplexing and tenacious problems in our society. Even though the proportion of men and women in the labor force is approaching parity (particularly for younger cohorts of workers), men and women are still generally confined to predominantly single-sex occupations. Forty percent of men or women would have to change major occupational categories to achieve equal representation of men and women in all jobs, but even this figure underestimates the true degree of sex segregation. It is extremely rare to find specific jobs where equal numbers of men and women are engaged in the same activities in the same industries.

Most studies of sex segregation in the work force have focused on women's experiences in male-dominated occupations. Both researchers and advocates for social change have focused on the barriers faced by women who try to integrate predominantly male fields. Few have looked at the "flip-side" of occupational sex segregation: the exclusion of men from predominantly female occupations. But the fact is that men are less likely to enter female sex-typed occupations than women are to enter male-dominated jobs. Reskin and Roos, for example, were able to identify 33 occupations in which female representation increased by more than nine percentage points between 1970 and 1980, but only three occupations in which the proportion of men increased as radically (1990).

In this paper, I examine men's underrepresentation in four predominantly female occupations—nursing, librarianship, elementary school teaching, and social work. Throughout the twentieth century, these occupations have been identified with "women's work"—even though prior to the Civil War, men were more likely to be employed in these areas. These four occupations, often called the female "semi-professions," today range from 5.5 percent male (in nursing) to 32 percent male (in social work). (See Table 1.) These percentages have not changed substantially in decades. In fact, as Table 1 indicates, two of these professions—librarianship and social work—have experienced declines in the proportions of men since 1975. Nursing is the only one of the four experiencing noticeable changes in sex composition, with the proportion of men increasing 80 percent between 1975 and 1990. Even so, men continue to be a tiny minority of all nurses.

Although there are many possible reasons for the continuing preponderance of women in these fields, the focus of this paper is discrimination. Researchers examining the integration of women into "male fields" have identified discrimination as a major barrier to women. This discrimination has taken the form of laws or institutionalized rules prohibiting the hiring or promotion of women into certain job specialties. Discrimination can also be "informal," as when women encounter sexual harassment, sabotage, or other forms of hostility from their male co-workers resulting in a

Table 1. Percent Male in Selected Occupations, Selected Years

Profession	1990	1980	1975
Nurses	5.5	3.5	3.0
Elementary teachers	14.8	16.3	14.6
Librarians	16.7	14.8	18.9
Social workers	31.8	35.0	39.2

Source: U.S. Department of Labor. Bureau of Labor Statistics. *Employment and Earnings* 38:1 (January 1991), Table 22 (Employed civilians by detailed occupation), 185; 28:1 (January 1981), Table 23 (Employed persons by detailed occupation), 180; 22:7 (January 1976), Table 2 (Employed persons by detailed occupation). 11.

poisoned work environment. Women in nontraditional occupations also report feeling stigmatized by clients when their work puts them in contact with the public. In particular, women in engineering and blue-collar occupations encounter gender-based stereotypes about their competence which undermine their work performance. Each of these forms of discrimination—legal, informal, and cultural—contributes to women's underrepresentation in predominantly male occupations.

The assumption in much of this literature is that any member of a token group in a work setting will probably experience similar discriminatory treatment. Kanter (1977), who is best known for articulating this perspective in her theory of tokenism, argues that when any group represents less than 15 percent of an organization, its members will be subject to predictable forms of discrimination. Likewise, Jacobs argues that "in some ways, men in female-dominated occupations experience the same difficulties that women in male-dominated occupations face" (1989:167), and Reskin contends that any dominant group in an occupation will use their power to maintain a privileged position (1988:62).

However, the few studies that have considered men's experience in gender atypical occupations suggest that men may not face discrimination or prejudice when they integrate predominantly female occupations. Zimmer (1988) and Martin (1988) both contend that the effects of sexism can outweigh the effects of tokenism when men enter nontraditional occupations. This study is the first to systematically explore this question

using data from four occupations. I examine the barriers to men's entry into these professions; the support men receive from their supervisors, colleagues and clients; and the reactions they encounter from the public (those outside their professions).

Methods

I conducted in-depth interviews with 76 men and 23 women in four occupations from 1985–1991. Interviews were conducted in four metropolitan areas: San Francisco/Oakland, California; Austin, Texas; Boston, Massachusetts; and Phoenix, Arizona. These four areas were selected because they show considerable variation in the proportions of men in the four professions. For example, Austin has one of the highest percentages of men in nursing (7.7 percent), whereas Phoenix's percentage is one of the lowest (2.7 percent). The sample was generated using "snow-balling" techniques. Women were included in the sample to gauge their feelings and responses to men who enter "their" professions.

Like the people employed in these professions generally, those in my sample were predominantly white (90 percent). Their ages ranged from 20 to 66 and the average age was 38. The interview questionnaire consisted of several open-ended questions on four broad topics: motivation to enter the profession; experiences in training; career progression; and general views about men's status and prospects within these occupations. I conducted all the interviews, which generally lasted between one and two hours. Interviews took place in restaurants, my home or office, or the respondent's home or office. Interviews were tape-recorded and transcribed for the analysis.

Data analysis followed the coding techniques described by Strauss (1987). Each transcript was read several times and analyzed into emergent conceptual categories. Likewise, Strauss' principle of theoretical sampling was used. Individual respondents were purposively selected to capture the array of men's experiences in these occupations. Thus, I interviewed practitioners in every specialty, oversampling those employed in the *most* gender atypical areas (e.g., male kindergarten teachers). I also selected respondents from throughout their occupational hierarchies—from students to administrators to retirees. Although the data do not permit within-group comparisons, I am reasonably certain that the sample does capture a wide range of experiences common to men in these female-dominated professions. However, like all findings based on qualitative data, it is uncertain whether the findings generalize to the larger population of men in nontraditional occupations.

In this paper, I review individuals' responses to questions about discrimination in hiring practices, on-the-job rapport with supervisors and co-workers, and prejudice from clients and others outside their profession.

Discrimination in Hiring

Contrary to the experience of many women in the male-dominated professions, many of the men and women I spoke to indicated that there is a *preference* for hiring men in these four occupations. A Texas librarian at a junior high school said that his school district "would hire a male over a female."

> I: Why do you think that is?
> R: Because there are so few, and the...ones that they do have, the library directors seem to really...think they're doing great jobs. I don't know, maybe they just feel they're being progressive or something, [but] I have had a real sense that they really appreciate having a male, particularly at the junior high.... As I said, when seven of us lost our jobs from the high schools and were redistributed, there were only four positions at junior high, and I got one of them. Three of the librarians, some who had been here longer than I had with the school district, were put down in elementary school as librarians. And I definitely think that being male made a difference in my being moved to the junior high rather than an elementary school.

Many of the men perceived their token status as males in predominantly female occupations as an *advantage* in hiring and promotions. I asked an Arizona teacher whether his specialty (elementary special education) was an unusual area for men compared to other areas within education. He said,

> Much more so. I am extremely marketable in special education. That's not why I got into the field. But I am extremely marketable because I am a man.

In several cases, the more female-dominated the specialty, the greater the apparent preference for men. For example, when asked if he encountered any problem getting a job in pediatrics, a Massachusetts nurse said,

> No, no, none....I've heard this from managers and supervisory-type people with men in pediatrics: "It's nice to have a man because it's such a female-dominated profession."

However, there were some exceptions to this preference for men in the most female-dominated specialties. In some cases, formal policies actually barred men from certain jobs. This was the case in some rural Texas school districts, which refused to hire men in the youngest grades (K–3). Some nurses also reported being excluded from positions in obstetrics and gynecology wards, a policy encountered more frequently in private Catholic hospitals.

But often the pressures keeping men out of certain specialties were more subtle than this. Some men described being "tracked" into practice areas within their professions which were considered more legitimate for men. For example, one Texas man described how he was pushed into administration and planning in social work, even though "I'm not interested in writing policy; I'm much more interested in research and clinical stuff." A nurse who is interested in pursuing graduate study in family and child health in Boston said he was dissuaded from entering the program specialty in favor of a concentration in "adult nursing." A kindergarten teacher described the difficulty of finding a job in his specialty after graduation: "I was recruited immediately to start getting into a track to become an administrator. And it was men who recruited me. It was men that ran the system at that time, especially in Los Angeles."

This tracking may bar men from the most female-identified specialties within these professions. But men are effectively being "kicked upstairs" in the process. Those specialties considered more legitimate practice areas for men also tend to be the most prestigious, better paying ones. A distinguished kindergarten teacher, who had been voted city-wide "Teacher of the Year," told me that even though people were pleased to see him in the classroom, "there's been some encouragement to think about administration, and there's been some encouragement to think about teaching at the university level or something like that, or supervisory-type position." That is, despite his aptitude and interest in staying in the classroom, he felt pushed in the direction of administration.

The effect of this "tracking" is the opposite of that experienced by women in male-dominated occupations. Researchers have reported that many women encounter a "glass ceiling" in their efforts to scale organizational and professional hierarchies. That is, they are constrained by invisible barriers to promotion in their careers, caused mainly by sexist attitudes of men in the highest positions (Freeman 1990). In contrast to the "glass ceiling," many of the men I interviewed seem to encounter a "glass escalator." Often, despite their intentions, they face invisible pressures to move up in their professions. As if on a moving escalator, they must work to stay in place.

A public librarian specializing in children's collections (a heavily female-dominated concentration) described an encounter with this "escalator" in his very first job out of library school. In his first six-months' evaluation, his supervisors commended him for his good work in storytelling and related activities, but they criticized him for "not shooting high enough."

Seriously. That's literally what they were telling me. They assumed that because I was a male— and they told me this—and that I was being hired right out of graduate school, that somehow I wasn't doing the kind of management-oriented work that they thought I should be doing. And

as a result, really they had a lot of bad marks, as it were, against me on my evaluation. And I said I couldn't believe this!

Throughout his ten-year career, he has had to struggle to remain in children's collections.

The glass escalator does not operate at all levels. In particular, men in academia reported some gender-based discrimination in the highest positions due to their universities' commitment to affirmative action. Two nursing professors reported that they felt their own chances of promotion to deanships were nil because their universities viewed the position of nursing dean as a guaranteed female appointment in an otherwise heavily male-dominated administration. One California social work professor reported his university canceled its search for a dean because no minority male or female candidates had been placed on their short list. It was rumored that other schools on campus were permitted to go forward with their searches—even though they also failed to put forward names of minority candidates— because the higher administration perceived it to be "easier" to fulfill affirmative action goals in the social work school. The interviews provide greater evidence of the "glass escalator" at work in the lower levels of these professions.

Of course, men's motivations also play a role in their advancement to higher professional positions. I do not mean to suggest that the men I talked to all resented the informal tracking they experienced. For many men, leaving the most female-identified areas of their professions helped them resolve internal conflicts involving their masculinity. One man left his job as a school social worker to work in a methadone drug treatment program not because he was encouraged to leave by his colleagues, but because "I think there was some macho shit there, to tell you the truth, because I remember feeling a little uncomfortable there…; it didn't feel right to me." Another social worker, employed in the mental health services department of a large urban area in California, reflected on his move into administration:

The more I think about it, through our discussion, I'm sure that's a large part of why I wound up in administration. It's okay for a man to do the administration. In fact, I don't know if I fully answered a question that you asked a little while ago about how did being male contribute to my advancing in the field. I was saying it wasn't because I got any special favoritism as a man, but...I think...because I'm a man, I felt a need to get into this kind of position. I may have worked harder toward it, may have competed harder for it, than most women would do, even women who think about doing administrative work.

Elsewhere I have speculated on the origins of men's tendency to define masculinity through single-sex work environments. Clearly, personal ambition does play a role in accounting for men's movement into more "male-defined" arenas within these professions. But these occupations also structure opportunities for males independent of their individual desires or motives.

The interviews suggest that men's underrepresentation in these professions cannot be attributed to discrimination in hiring or promotions. Many of the men indicated that they received preferential treatment because they were men. Although men mentioned gender discrimination in the hiring process, for the most part they were channelled into the more "masculine" specialties within these professions, which ironically meant being "tracked" into better paying and more prestigious specialties.

Supervisors and Colleagues: The Working Environment

Researchers claim that subtle forms of work place discrimination push women out of male-dominated occupations. In particular, women report feeling excluded from informal leadership and decision-making networks, and they sense hostility from their male co-workers, which makes them feel uncomfortable and unwanted. Respondents in this study were asked about their relationships with supervisors and female colleagues to ascertain whether men also experienced "poisoned" work environments when entering gender atypical occupations.

A major difference in the experience of men and women in nontraditional occupations is that men in these situations are far more likely to be supervised by a member of their own sex. In each of the four professions I studied, men are overrepresented in administrative and managerial capacities, or, as in the case of nursing, their positions in the organizational hierarchy are governed by men. Thus, unlike women who enter "male fields," the men in these professions often work under the direct supervision of other men.

Many of the men interviewed reported that they had good rapport with their male supervisors. Even in professional school, some men reported extremely close relationships with their male professors. For example, a Texas librarian described an unusually intimate association with two male professors in graduate school:

I can remember a lot of times in the classroom there would be discussions about a particular topic or issue, and the conversation would spill over into their office hours, after the class was over. And even though there were...a couple of the other women that had been in on the discussion, they weren't there. And I don't know if that was preferential or not...it certainly carried over into personal life as well. Not just at the school and that sort of thing. I mean, we would get together for dinner...

These professors explicitly encouraged him because he was male:

I: Did they ever offer you explicit words of encouragement about being in the profession by virtue of the fact that you were male?...

R: Definitely. On several occasions. Yeah. Both of these guys, for sure, including the Dean who was male also. And it's an interesting point that you bring up because it was, oftentimes, kind of in a sign, you know. It wasn't in the classroom, and it wasn't in front of the group, or if we were in the student lounge or something like that. It was...if it was just myself or maybe another one of the guys, you know, and just talking in the office. It's like...you know, kind of an opening-up and saying, "You know, you are really lucky that you're in the profession because you'll really go to the top real quick, and you'll be able to make real definite improvements and changes. And you'll have a real influence," and all this sort of thing. I mean, really, I can remem-ber several times.

Other men reported similar closeness with their professors. A Texas psychotherapist recalled his relationships with his male professors in social work school:

I made it a point to make a golfing buddy with one of the guys that was in administration. He and I played golf a lot. He was the guy who kind of ran the research training, the research part of the master's program. Then there was a sociologist who ran the other part of the research program. He and I developed a good friendship.

This close mentoring by male professors con-trasts with the reported experience of women in nontraditional occupations. Others have noted a lack of solidarity among women in nontradi-tional occupations. Writing about military acad-emies, for example, Yoder describes the failure of token women to mentor succeeding generations of female cadets. She argues that women attempt to play down their gender difference from men because it is the source of scorn and derision.

Because women felt unaccepted by their male colleagues, one of the last things they wanted to do was to emphasize their gender. Some women thought that, if they kept company with other women, this would highlight their gender and would further isolate them from male cadets. These women desperately wanted to be accepted as cadets, not as *women* cadets. Therefore, they did everything from not wearing skirts as an option with their uniforms to avoiding being a part of a group of women. (Yoder 1989:532)

Men in nontraditional occupations face a differ-ent scenario—their gender is construed as a *pos-itive* difference. Therefore, they have an incentive to bond together and emphasize their distinctive-ness from the female majority.

Close, personal ties with male supervisors were also described by men once they were established in their professional careers. It was not uncommon in education, for example, for the male principal to informally socialize with the male staff, as a Texas special education teacher describes:

Occasionally I've had a principal who would regard me as "the other man on the campus" and "it's us against them," you know? I mean, nothing really that extreme, except that some male principals feel like there's nobody there to talk to except the other man. So I've been in that position.

These personal ties can have important con-sequences for men's careers. For example, one California nurse, whose performance was judged marginal by his nursing supervisors, was trans-ferred to the emergency room staff (a prestigious promotion) due to his personal friendship with the physician in charge. A Massachusetts teacher acknowledged that his principal's personal inter-est in him landed him his current job.

I: You had mentioned that your principal had sort of spotted you at your previous job and had wanted to bring you here [to this school]. Do you think that has anything to do with the fact that you're a man, aside from your skills as a teacher?

R: Yes, I would say in that particular case, that was part of it.... We have certain things in common, certain interests that really lined up.

I: Vis-à-vis teaching?

R: Well, more extraneous things—running specifically, and music. And we just seemed to get along real well right off the bat. It is just kind of a guy thing; we just liked each other...

Interviewees did not report many instances of male supervisors discriminating against them, or refusing to accept them because they were male. Indeed, these men were much more likely to report that their male bosses discriminated against the *females* in their professions. When asked if he thought physicians treated male and female nurses differently, a Texas nurse said:

> I think yeah, some of them do. I think the women seem like they have a lot more trouble with the physicians treating them in a derogatory manner. Or, if not derogatory, then in a very paternalistic way than the men [are treated]. Usually if a physician is mad at a male nurse, he just kind of yells at him. Kind of like an employee. And if they're mad at a female nurse, rather than treat them on an equal basis, in terms of just letting their anger out at them as an employee, they're more paternalistic or there's some sexual harassment component to it.

A Texas teacher perceived a similar situation where he worked:

> I've never felt unjustly treated by a principal because I'm a male. The principals that I've seen that I felt are doing things that are kind of arbitrary or not well thought out are doing it to everybody. In fact, they're probably doing it to the females worse than they are to me.

Openly gay men may encounter less favorable treatment at the hands of their supervisors. For example, a nurse in Texas stated that one of the physicians he worked with preferred to staff the operating room with male nurses exclusively—as long as they weren't gay. Stigma associated with homosexuality leads some men to enhance, or even exaggerate their "masculine" qualities, and may be another factor pushing men into more "acceptable" specialties for men.

Not all men who work in these occupations are supervised by men. Many of the men interviewed who had female bosses also reported high levels of acceptance—although levels of intimacy with women seemed lower than with other men. In some cases, however, men reported feeling shut-out from decision making when the higher administration was constituted entirely by women. I asked an Arizona librarian whether men in the library profession were discriminated against in hiring because of their sex:

> Professionally speaking, people go to considerable lengths to keep that kind of thing out of their [hiring] deliberations. Personally, is another matter. It's pretty common around here to talk about the "old girl network." This is one of the few libraries that I've had any intimate knowledge of which is actually controlled by women.... Most of the department heads and upper level administrators are women. And there's an "old girl network" that works just like the "old boy network," except that the important conferences take place in the women's room rather than on the golf course. But the political mechanism is the same, the exclusion of the other sex from decision making is the same. The reasons are the same. It's somewhat discouraging....

Although I did not interview many supervisors, I did include 23 women in my sample to ascertain their perspectives about the presence of men in their professions. All of the women I interviewed claimed to be supportive of their male colleagues, but some conveyed ambivalence. For example, a social work professor said she would like to see more men enter the social work profession, particularly in the clinical specialty (where they are underrepresented). Indeed, she favored affirmative action hiring guidelines for men in the profession. Yet, she resented the fact that her department hired "another white male" during a recent search. I questioned her about this ambivalence:

> I: I find it very interesting that, on the one hand, you sort of perceive this preference and perhaps even sexism with regard to how men are evaluated and how they achieve higher positions within the profession, yet, on the other hand, you would be encouraging of more men to enter the field. Is that contradictory to you, or...?
>
> R: Yeah, it's contradictory.

It appears that women are generally eager to see men enter "their" occupations. Indeed, several men noted that their female colleagues had facilitated their careers in various ways (including mentorship in college). However, at the same time, women often resent the apparent ease with which men advance within these professions, sensing that men at the higher levels receive preferential treatment which closes off advancement opportunities for women.

But this ambivalence does not seem to translate into the "poisoned" work environment described by many women who work in male-dominated occupations. Among the male interviewees, there were no accounts of sexual harassment. However, women do treat their male colleagues differently on occasion. It is not uncommon in nursing, for example, for men to be called upon to help catheterize male patients, or to lift especially heavy patients. Some librarians also said that women asked them to lift and move heavy boxes of books because they were men. Teachers sometimes confront differential treatment as well, as described by this Texas teacher:

> As a man, you're teaching with all women, and that can be hard sometimes. Just because of the stereotypes, you know. I'm real into computers...and all the time people are calling me to fix their computer. Or if somebody gets a flat tire, they come and get me. I mean, there are just a lot of stereotypes. Not that I mind doing any of those things, but it's...you know, it just kind of bugs me that it is a stereotype, "A man should do that." Or if their kids have a lot of discipline problems, that kiddo's in your room. Or if there are kids that don't have a father in their home, that kid's in your room. Hell, nowadays that'd be half the school in my room (laughs). But you know, all the time I hear from the principal or from other teachers, "Well, this child really needs a man...a male role model" (laughs). So there are a lot of stereotypes that...men kind of get stuck with.

This special treatment bothered some respondents. Getting assigned all the "discipline problems" can make for difficult working conditions, for example. But many men claimed this differential treatment did not cause distress. In fact, several said they liked being appreciated for the special traits and abilities (such as strength) they could contribute to their professions.

Furthermore, women's special treatment sometimes enhanced—rather than poisoned—the men's work environments. One Texas librarian said he felt "more comfortable working with women than men" because "I think it has something to do with control. Maybe it's that women will let me take control more than men will." Several men reported that their female colleagues often cast them into leadership roles. Although not all savored this distinction, it did enhance their authority and control in the work place. In subtle (and not-too-subtle) ways, then, differential treatment contributes to the "glass escalator" men experience in nontraditional professions.

Even outside work, most of the men interviewed said they felt fully accepted by their female colleagues. They were usually included in informal socializing occasions with the women—even though this frequently meant attending baby showers or Tupperware parties. Many said that they declined offers to attend these events because they were not interested in "women's things," although several others claimed to attend everything: The minority men I interviewed seemed to feel the least comfortable in these informal contexts. One social worker in Arizona was asked about socializing with his female colleagues:

> I: So in general, for example, if all the employees were going to get together to have a party, or celebrate a bridal shower or whatever, would you be invited along with the rest of the group?
>
> R: They would invite me, I would say, somewhat reluctantly. Being a black male, working with all white females, it did cause some outside problems. So I didn't go to a lot of functions with them...
>
> I: You felt that there was some tension there on the level of your acceptance...?
>
> R: Yeah. It was OK working, but on the outside, personally, there was some tension there. It never came out, that they said, "Because of who you are we can't invite you" (laughs), and I wouldn't have done anything anyway. I would have probably respected them more for saying what was on their minds. But I never felt completely in with the group.

Some single men also said they felt uncomfortable socializing with married female colleagues because it gave the "wrong impression." But in general, the men said that they felt very comfortable around their colleagues and described their work places as very congenial for men. It appears unlikely, therefore, that men's underrepresentation in these professions is due to hostility towards men on the part of supervisors or women workers.

Discrimination from "Outsiders"

The most compelling evidence of discrimination against men in these professions is related to their dealings with the public. Men often encounter negative stereotypes when they come into contact with clients or "outsiders"—people they meet outside of work. For instance, it is popularly assumed that male nurses are gay. Librarians encounter images of themselves as "wimpy" and asexual. Male social workers describe being typecast as "feminine" and "passive." Elementary school teachers are often confronted by suspicions that they are pedophiles. One kindergarten teacher described an experience that occurred early in his career which was related to him years afterwards by his principal:

> He indicated to me that parents had come to him and indicated to him that they had a problem with the fact that I was a male....I recall almost exactly what he said. There were three specific concerns that the parents had: One parent said, "How can he love my child; he's a man." The second thing that I recall, he said the parent said, "He has a beard." And the third thing was, "Aren't you concerned about homosexuality?"

Such suspicions often cause men in all four professions to alter their work behavior to guard against sexual abuse charges, particularly in those specialties requiring intimate contact with women and children.

Men are very distressed by these negative stereotypes, which tend to undermine their self-esteem and to cause them to second-guess their motivations for entering these fields. A California teacher said,

> If I tell men that I don't know, that I'm meeting for the first time, that that's what I do, . . . sometimes there's a look on their faces that, you know, "Oh, couldn't get a real job?"

When asked if his wife, who is also an elementary school teacher, encounters the same kind of prejudice, he said,

> No, it's accepted because she's a woman....I think people would see that as a...step up, you know. "Oh, you're not a housewife, you've got a career. That's great...that you're out there working. And you have a daughter, but you're still out there working. You decided not to stay home, and you went out there and got a job." Whereas for me, it's more like I'm supposed to be out working anyway, even though I'd rather be home with [my daughter].

Unlike women who enter traditionally male professions, men's movement into these jobs is perceived by the "outside world" as a step down in status. This particular form of discrimination may be most significant in explaining why men are underrepresented in these professions. Men who otherwise might show interest in and aptitudes for such careers are probably discouraged from pursuing them because of the negative popular stereotypes associated with the men who work in them. This is a crucial difference from the experience of women in nontraditional professions: "My daughter, the physician," resonates far more favorably in most people's ears than "My son, the nurse."

Many of the men in my sample identified the stigma of working in a female-identified occupation as the major barrier to more men entering their professions. However, for the most part, they claimed that these negative stereotypes were not a factor in their own decisions to join these occupations. Most respondents didn't consider entering these fields until well into adulthood, after working in some related occupation. Several social workers and librarians even claimed they were not aware that men were a minority in their chosen professions. Either they had no well-defined image or stereotype, or their contacts and mentors were predominantly men. For example, prior to entering library school, many librarians held part-time jobs in university libraries, where there are proportionally more men than in the profession generally. Nurses and elementary school teachers were more aware that mostly women worked in these jobs, and this was often a matter of some concern to them. However, their choices were ultimately legitimized by mentors, or by encouraging friends or family members who implicitly reassured them that entering these occupations would not typecast them as feminine. In some cases, men were told by recruiters there were special advancement opportunities for men in these fields, and they entered them expecting rapid promotion to administrative positions.

> I: Did it ever concern you when you were making the decision to enter nursing school, the fact that it is a female-dominated profession?
> R: Not really. I never saw myself working on the floor. I saw myself pretty much going into administration, just getting the background and then getting a job someplace as a supervisor and then working, getting up into administration.

Because of the unique circumstances of their recruitment, many of the respondents did not view their occupational choices as inconsistent with a male gender role, and they generally avoided the negative stereotypes directed against men in these fields.

Indeed, many of the men I interviewed claimed that they did not encounter negative professional stereotypes until they had worked in these fields for several years. Popular prejudices can be damaging to self-esteem and probably push some men out of these professions altogether. Yet, ironically, they sometimes contribute to the "glass escalator" effect I have been describing. Men seem to encounter the most vituperative criticism from the public when they are in the most female-identified specialties. Public concerns sometimes result in their

being shunted into more "legitimate" positions for men. A librarian formerly in charge of a branch library's children's collection, who now works in the reference department of the city's main library, describes his experience:

> R: Some of the people [who frequented the branch library] complained that they didn't want to have a man doing the story-telling scenario. And I got transferred here to the central library in an equivalent job...I thought that I did a good job. And I had been told by my supervisor that I was doing a good job.
> I: Have you ever considered filing some sort of lawsuit to get that other job back?
> R: Well, actually, the job I've gotten now...well, it's a reference librarian; it's what I wanted in the first place. I've got a whole lot more authority here. I'm also in charge of the circulation desk. And I've recently been promoted because of my new stature, so...no, I'm not considering trying to get that other job back.

The negative stereotypes about men who do "women's work" can push men out of specific jobs. However, to the extent that they channel men into more "legitimate" practice areas, their effects can actually be positive. Instead of being a source of discrimination, these prejudices can add to the "glass escalator effect" by pressuring men to move *out* of the most female-identified areas, and *up* to those regarded more legitimate and prestigious for men.

Conclusion: Discrimination Against Men

Both men and women who work in nontraditional occupations encounter discrimination, but the forms and consequences of this discrimination are very different. The interviews suggest that unlike "nontraditional" women workers, most of the discrimination and prejudice facing men in the "female professions" emanates from outside those professions. The men and women interviewed for the most part believed that men are given fair—if not preferential—treatment in hiring and promotion decisions, are accepted by supervisors and colleagues, and are well-integrated into the work place subculture. Indeed, subtle mechanisms seem to enhance men's position in these professions—a phenomenon I refer to as the "glass escalator effect."

The data lend strong support for Zimmer's (1988) critique of "gender neutral theory" (such as Kanter's [1977] theory of tokenism) in the study of occupational segregation. Zimmer argues that women's occupational inequality is more a consequence of sexist beliefs and practices embedded in the labor force than the effect of numerical under-representation per se. This study suggests that token status itself does not diminish men's occupational success. Men take their gender privilege with them when they enter predominantly female occupations: this translates into an advantage in spite of their numerical rarity.

This study indicates that the experience of tokenism is very different for men and women. Future research should examine how the experience of tokenism varies for members of different races and classes as well. For example, it is likely that informal work place mechanisms similar to the ones identified here promote the careers of token whites in predominantly black occupations. The crucial factor is the social status of the token's group—not their numerical rarity—that determines whether the token encounters a "glass ceiling" or a "glass escalator."

However, this study also found that many men encounter negative stereotypes from persons not directly involved in their professions. Men who enter these professions are often considered "failures," or sexual deviants. These stereotypes may be a major impediment to men who otherwise might consider careers in these occupations. Indeed, they are likely to be important factors whenever a member of a relatively high status group crosses over into a lower status occupation. However, to the extent that these stereotypes contribute to the "glass escalator effect" by channeling men into more "legitimate" (and higher paying) occupations, they are not discriminatory.

Women entering traditionally "male" professions also face negative stereotypes suggesting they are not "real women." However, these stereotypes do not seem to deter women to the same degree that they deter men from pursuing nontraditional professions. There is ample historical evidence that women flock to male-identified occupations once opportunities are available. Not so with men. Examples of occupations changing from predominantly female to predominantly male are very rare in our history. The few existing cases—such as medicine—suggest that redefinition of the occupations as appropriately "masculine" is necessary before men will consider joining them.

Because different mechanisms maintain segregation in male- and female-dominated occupations, different approaches are needed to promote their integration. Policies intended to alter the sex composition of male-dominated occupations—such as affirmative action—make little sense when applied to the "female professions." For men, the major barriers to integration have little to do with their treatment once they decide to enter these fields. Rather, we need to address the social and cultural sanctions applied to men who do "women's work" which keep men from even considering these occupations.

One area where these cultural barriers are clearly evident is in the media's representation of men's occupations. Women working in traditionally male professions have achieved an unprecedented acceptance on popular television shows. Women are portrayed as doctors ("St. Elsewhere"), lawyers ("The Cosby Show," "L.A. Law"), architects ("Family Ties"), and police officers ("Cagney and Lacey"). But where are the male nurses, teachers and secretaries? Television rarely portrays men in nontraditional work roles, and when it does, that anomaly is made the central focus—and joke—of the program. A comedy series (1991–92) about a male elementary school teacher ("Drexell's Class") stars a lead character who *hates children!* Yet even this negative portrayal is exceptional. When a prime time hospital drama series ("St. Elsewhere") depicted a male orderly striving for upward mobility, the show's writers made him a "physician's assistant," not a nurse or nurse practitioner—the much more likely "real life" possibilities.

Presenting positive images of men in nontraditional careers can produce limited effects. A few social workers, for example, were first inspired to pursue their careers by George C. Scott, who played a social worker in the television drama series, "Eastside/Westside." But as a policy strategy to break down occupational segregation, changing media images of men is no panacea. The stereotypes that differentiate masculinity and femininity, and degrade that which is defined as feminine, are deeply entrenched in culture, social structure, and personality. Nothing short of a revolution in cultural definitions of masculinity will effect the broad scale social transformation needed to achieve the complete occupational integration of men and women.

Of course, there are additional factors besides societal prejudice contributing to men's underrepresentation in female-dominated professions. Most notably, those men I interviewed mentioned as a deterrent the fact that these professions are all underpaid relative to comparable "male" occupations, and several suggested that instituting a "comparable worth" policy might attract more men. However, I am not convinced that improved salaries will substantially alter the sex composition of these professions unless the cultural stigma faced by men in these occupations diminishes. Occupational sex segregation is remarkably resilient, even in the face of devastating economic hardship. During the Great Depression of the 1930s, for example, "women's jobs" failed to attract sizable numbers of men. In her study of American Telephone and Telegraph (AT&T) workers, Epstein (1989) found that some men would rather suffer unemployment than accept relatively high paying "women's jobs" because of the damage to their identities this would cause. She quotes one unemployed man who refused to apply for a female-identified telephone operator job:

> I think if they offered me $1000 a week tax free, I wouldn't take that job. When I...see those guys sitting in there [in the telephone operating room], I wonder what's wrong with them. Are they pansies or what? (Epstein 1989:577)

This is not to say that raising salaries would not affect the sex composition of these jobs. Rather,

I am suggesting that wages are not the only—or perhaps even the major—impediment to men's entry into these jobs. Further research is needed to explore the ideological significance of the "woman's wage" for maintaining occupational stratification.

At any rate, integrating men and women in the labor force requires more than dismantling barriers to women in male-dominated fields. Sex segregation is a two-way street. We must also confront and dismantle the barriers men face in predominantly female occupations. Men's experiences in these nontraditional occupations reveal just how culturally embedded the barriers are, and how far we have to travel before men and women attain true occupational and economic equality.

References

Epstein, Cynthia Fuchs. 1989. "Workplace boundaries: Conceptions and creations." *Social Research* 56: 571–590.

Freeman, Sue J. M. 1990. *Managing Lives: Corporate Women and Social Change.* Amherst, Mass.: University of Massachusetts Press.

Jacobs, Jerry. 1989. *Revolving Doors: Sex Segregation and Women's Careers.* Stanford, Calif.: Stanford University Press.

Kanter, Rosabeth Moss. 1977. *Men and Women of the Corporation.* New York: Basic Books.

Martin, Susan E. 1980. *Breaking and Entering: Police Women on Patrol.* Berkeley, Calif.: University of California Press.

———. 1988. "Think like a man, work like a dog, and act like a lady: Occupational dilemmas of police-women." In *The Worth of Women's Work: A Qualitative Synthesis*, ed. Anne Statham, Eleanor M. Miller, and Hans O. Mauksch, 205–223. Albany, N.Y.: State University of New York Press.

Reskin, Barbara. 1988. "Bringing the men back in: Sex differentiation and the devaluation of women's work." *Gender & Society* 2: 58–81.

Reskin, Barbara, and Patricia Roos. 1990. *Job Queues, Gender Queues: Explaining Women's Inroads into Male Occupations.* Philadelphia: Temple University Press.

Strauss, Anselm L. 1987. *Qualitative Analysis for Social Scientists.* Cambridge, England: Cambridge University Press.

Yoder, Janice D. 1989. "Women at West Point: Lessons for token women in male-dominated occupations." In *Women: A Feminist Perspective,* ed. Jo Freeman, 523–537. Mountain View, Calif.: Mayfield Publishing Company.

Zimmer, Lynn. 1988. "Tokenism and women in the workplace." *Social Problems* 35: 64–77.

Racializing the Glass Escalator: Reconsidering Men's Experiences with Women's Work

ADIA HARVEY WINGFIELD

[handwritten annotation: Women in more feminine jobs that involve nurturing etc.]

Sociologists who study work have long noted that jobs are sex segregated and that this segregation creates different occupational experiences for men and women (Charles and Grusky 2004). Jobs predominantly filled by women often require "feminine" traits such as nurturing, caring, and empathy, a fact that means men confront perceptions that they are unsuited for the requirements of these jobs. Rather than having an adverse effect on their occupational experiences, however, these assumptions facilitate men's entry into better paying, higher status positions, creating what Williams (1995) labels a "glass escalator" effect.

The glass escalator model has been an influential paradigm in understanding the experiences of men who do women's work. Researchers have identified this process among men nurses, social workers, paralegals, and librarians and have cited its pervasiveness as evidence of men's consistent advantage in the workplace, such that even in jobs where men are numerical minorities they are likely to enjoy higher wages and faster promotions

[handwritten annotation: why? Still get higher pay even when mostly women.]

(Floge and Merrill 1986; Heikes 1991; Pierce 1995; Williams 1989, 1995). Most of these studies implicitly assume a racial homogenization of men workers in women's professions, but this supposition is problematic for several reasons. For one, minority men are not only present but are actually overrepresented in certain areas of reproductive work that have historically been dominated by white women (Duffy 2007). Thus, research that focuses primarily on white men in women's professions ignores a key segment of men who perform this type of labor. Second, and perhaps more important, conclusions based on the experiences of white men tend to overlook the ways that intersections of race and gender create different experiences for different men. While extensive work has documented the fact that white men in women's professions encounter a glass escalator effect that aids their occupational mobility (for an exception, see Snyder and Green 2008), few studies, if any, have considered how this effect is a function not only of gendered advantage but of racial privilege as well.

[handwritten annotation: Only white men + women have been studied]

In this article, I examine the implications of race–gender intersections for minority men employed in a female-dominated, feminized occupation, specifically focusing on Black men in nursing. Their experiences doing "women's work" demonstrate that the glass escalator is a racialized as well as gendered concept.

Theoretical Framework

In her classic study *Men and Women of the Corporation,* Kanter (1977) offers a groundbreaking analysis of group interactions. Focusing on high-ranking women executives who work mostly with men, Kanter argues that those in the extreme numerical minority are tokens who are socially isolated, highly visible, and adversely stereotyped. Tokens have difficulty forming relationships with colleagues and often are excluded from social networks that provide mobility. Because of their low numbers, they are also highly visible as people who are different from the majority, even though they often feel invisible when they are ignored or overlooked in social settings. Tokens are also stereotyped by those in the majority group and frequently face pressure to behave in ways that challenge and undermine these stereotypes. Ultimately, Kanter argues that it is harder for them to blend into the organization and to work effectively and productively, and that they face serious barriers to upward mobility.

Kanter's (1977) arguments have been analyzed and retested in various settings and among many populations. Many studies, particularly of women in male-dominated corporate settings, have supported her findings. Other work has reversed these conclusions, examining the extent to which her conclusions hold when men were the tokens and women the majority group. These studies fundamentally challenged the gender neutrality of the token, finding that men in the minority fare much better than do similarly situated women. In particular, this research suggests that factors such as heightened visibility and polarization do not necessarily disadvantage men who are in the minority. While women tokens find that their visibility hinders their ability to blend in and work productively, men tokens find that their conspicuousness

can lead to greater opportunities for leadership and choice assignments (Floge and Merrill 1986; Heikes 1991). Studies in this vein are important because they emphasize organizations—and occupations—as gendered institutions that subsequently create dissimilar experiences for men and women tokens (see Acker 1990).

In her groundbreaking study of men employed in various women's professions, Williams (1995) further develops this analysis of how power relationships shape the ways men tokens experience work in women's professions. Specifically, she introduces the concept of the glass escalator to explain men's experiences as tokens in these areas. Like Floge and Merrill (1986) and Heikes (1991), Williams finds that men tokens do not experience the isolation, visibility, blocked access to social networks, and stereotypes in the same ways that women tokens do. In contrast, Williams argues that even though they are in the minority, processes are in place that actually facilitate their opportunity and advancement. Even in culturally feminized occupations, then, men's advantage is built into the very structure and everyday interactions of these jobs so that men find themselves actually struggling to remain in place. For these men, "despite their intentions, they face invisible pressures to move up in their professions. Like being on a moving escalator, they have to work to stay in place" (Williams 1995, 87).

The glass escalator term thus refers to the "subtle mechanisms in place that enhance [men's] positions in [women's] professions" (Williams 1995, 108). These mechanisms include certain behaviors, attitudes, and beliefs men bring to these professions as well as the types of interactions that often occur between these men and their colleagues, supervisors, and customers. Consequently, even in occupations composed mostly of women, gendered perceptions about men's roles, abilities, and skills privilege them and facilitate their advancement. The glass escalator serves as a conduit that channels men in women's professions into the uppermost levels of the occupational hierarchy. Ultimately, the glass escalator effect suggests that men retain consistent occupational advantages over women, even when women are numerically in the majority (Budig 2002; Williams 1995).

Though this process has now been fairly well established in the literature, there are reasons to question its generalizability to all men. In an early critique of the supposed general neutrality of the token, Zimmer (1988) notes that much research on race comes to precisely the opposite of Kanter's conclusions, finding that as the numbers of minority group members increase (e.g., as they become less likely to be "tokens"), so too do tensions between the majority and minority groups. For instance, as minorities move into predominantly white neighborhoods, increasing numbers do not create the likelihood of greater acceptance and better treatment. In contrast, whites are likely to relocate when neighborhoods become "too" integrated, citing concerns about property values and racialized ideas about declining neighborhood quality (Shapiro 2004). Reinforcing, while at the same time tempering, the findings of research on men in female-dominated occupations, Zimmer (1988, 71) argues that relationships between tokens and the majority depend on understanding the underlying power relationships between these groups and "the status and power differentials between them." Hence, just as men who are tokens fare better than women, it also follows that the experiences of Blacks and whites as tokens should differ in ways that reflect their positions in hierarchies of status and power.

Burbank

POINT

The concept of the glass escalator provides an important and useful framework for addressing men's experiences in women's occupations, but so far research in this vein has neglected to examine whether the glass escalator is experienced among all men in an identical manner. Are the processes that facilitate a ride on the glass escalator available to minority men? Or does race intersect with gender to affect the extent to which the glass escalator offers men opportunities in women's professions? In the next section, I examine whether and how the mechanisms that facilitate a ride on the glass escalator might be unavailable to Black men in nursing.[1]

Relationships with Colleagues and Supervisors

One key aspect of riding the glass escalator involves the warm, collegial welcome men workers often receive from their women colleagues. Often, this reaction is a response to the fact that professions dominated by women are frequently low in salary and status and that greater numbers of men help improve prestige and pay (Heikes 1991). Though some women workers resent the apparent ease with which men enter and advance in women's professions, the generally warm welcome men receive stands in stark contrast to the cold reception, difficulties with mentorship, and blocked access to social networks that women often encounter when they do men's work (Roth 2006; Williams 1992). In addition, unlike women in men's professions, men who do women's work frequently have supervisors of the same sex. Men workers can thus enjoy a gendered bond with their supervisor in the context of a collegial work environment. These factors often converge, facilitating men's access to higher-status positions and producing the glass escalator effect.

The congenial relationship with colleagues and gendered bonds with supervisors are crucial to riding the glass escalator. Women colleagues often take a primary role in casting these men into leadership or supervisory positions. In their study of men and women tokens in a hospital setting, Floge and Merrill (1986) cite cases where women nurses promoted men colleagues to the position of charge nurse, even when the job had already been assigned to a woman. In addition to these close ties with women colleagues, men are also able to capitalize on gendered bonds with (mostly men) supervisors in ways that engender upward mobility. Many men supervisors informally socialize with men workers in women's jobs and are thus able to trade on their personal friendships for upward mobility. Williams (1995) describes a case where a nurse with mediocre performance reviews received a promotion to a more prestigious specialty area because of his friendship with the (male) doctor in charge. According to the literature, building strong relationships with colleagues and supervisors often happens relatively easily for men in women's professions and pays off in their occupational advancement.

For Black men in nursing, however, gendered racism may limit the extent to which they establish bonds with their colleagues and supervisors. The concept of gendered racism suggests that racial stereotypes, images, and beliefs are grounded in gendered ideals (Collins 1990, 2004; Espiritu 2000; Essed 1991; Harvey Wingfield 2007). Gendered racist stereotypes of Black men in particular emphasize the dangerous, threatening attributes associated with Black men and Black masculinity, framing Black men as threats to white women, prone to criminal behavior, and especially violent. Collins (2004) argues that these stereotypes serve to legitimize Black men's treatment in the criminal justice system through methods such as racial profiling and incarceration, but they may also hinder Black men's attempts to enter and advance in various occupational fields.

For Black men nurses, gendered racist images may have particular consequences for their relationships with women colleagues, who may view Black men nurses through the lens of controlling images and gendered racist stereotypes that emphasize the danger they pose to women. This may take on a heightened significance for white women nurses, given stereotypes that suggest that Black men are especially predisposed to raping white women. Rather than experiencing the congenial bonds with colleagues that white men nurses describe, Black men nurses may find themselves facing a much cooler reception from their women coworkers.

Gendered racism may also play into the encounters Black men nurses have with supervisors. In cases where supervisors are white men, Black men nurses may still find that higher-ups treat them in ways that reflect prevailing stereotypes about threatening Black masculinity. Supervisors may feel uneasy about forming close relationships with Black men or may encourage their separation from white women nurses. In addition, broader, less gender-specific racial stereotypes could also shape the experiences Black men nurses have with white men bosses. Whites often perceive Blacks, regardless of gender, as less intelligent, hardworking, ethical, and moral than other racial groups (Feagin 2006). Black men nurses may find that in addition to being influenced by gendered racist stereotypes, supervisors

also view them as less capable and qualified for promotion, thus negating or minimizing the glass escalator effect.

Suitability for Nursing and Higher-Status Work

The perception that men are not really suited to do women's work also contributes to the glass escalator effect. In encounters with patients, doctors, and other staff, men nurses frequently confront others who do not expect to see them doing "a woman's job." Sometimes this perception means that patients mistake men nurses for doctors; ultimately, the sense that men do not really belong in nursing contributes to a push "*out* of the most feminine-identified areas and *up* to those regarded as more legitimate for men" (Williams 1995, 104). The sense that men are better suited for more masculine jobs means that men workers are often assumed to be more able and skilled than their women counterparts. As Williams writes (1995, 106), "Masculinity is often associated with competence and mastery," and this implicit definition stays with men even when they work in feminized fields. Thus, part of the perception that men do not belong in these jobs is rooted in the sense that, as men, they are more capable and accomplished than women and thus belong in jobs that reflect this. Consequently, men nurses are mistaken for doctors and are granted more authority and responsibility than their women counterparts, reflecting the idea that, as men, they are inherently more competent (Heikes 1991; Williams 1995).

Black men nurses, however, may not face the presumptions of expertise or the resulting assumption that they belong in higher-status jobs. Black professionals, both men and women, are often assumed to be less capable and less qualified than their white counterparts. In some cases, these negative stereotypes hold even when Black workers outperform white colleagues (Feagin and Sikes 1994). The belief that Blacks are inherently less competent than whites means that, despite advanced education, training, and skill, Black professionals often confront the lingering perception that they are better suited for lower-level service work (Feagin and Sikes 1994). Black men in fact often fare better than white women in blue-collar jobs such as policing and corrections work (Britton 1995), and this may be, in part, because they are viewed as more appropriately suited for these types of positions.

For Black men nurses, then, the issue of perception may play out in different ways than it does for white men nurses. While white men nurses enjoy the automatic assumption that they are qualified, capable, and suited for "better" work, the experiences of Black professionals suggest that Black men nurses may not encounter these reactions. They may, like their white counterparts, face the perception that they do not belong in nursing. Unlike their white counterparts, Black men nurses may be seen as inherently less capable and therefore better suited for low-wage labor than a professional, feminized occupation such as nursing. This perception of being less qualified means that they also may not be immediately assumed to be better suited for the higher-level, more masculinized jobs within the medical field.

As minority women address issues of both race and gender to negotiate a sense of belonging in masculine settings (Ong 2005), minority men may also face a comparable challenge in feminized fields. They may have to address the unspoken racialization implicit in the assumption that masculinity equals competence. Simultaneously, they may find that the racial stereotype that Blackness equals lower qualifications, standards, and competence clouds the sense that men are inherently more capable and adept in any field, including the feminized ones.

Establishing Distance from Femininity

An additional mechanism of the glass escalator involves establishing distance from women and the femininity associated with their occupations. Because men nurses are employed in a culturally feminized occupation, they develop strategies to disassociate themselves from the femininity associated with their work and retain some of the privilege associated with masculinity. Thus, when men nurses gravitate toward hospital emergency wards rather than obstetrics or pediatrics, or emphasize that they are only in nursing to get into hospital administration, they distance themselves from the femininity of their profession and thereby preserve their status as men despite the fact that they do "women's work." Perhaps more important, these strategies also place men in a prime position to experience the glass escalator effect, as they situate themselves to move upward into higher-status areas in the field.

Creating distance from femininity also helps these men achieve aspects of hegemonic masculinity, which Connell (1989) describes as the predominant and most valued form of masculinity at a given time. Contemporary hegemonic masculine ideals emphasize toughness, strength, aggressiveness, heterosexuality, and, perhaps most important, a clear sense of femininity as different from and subordinate to masculinity (Kimmel 2001; Williams 1995). Thus, when men distance themselves from the feminized aspects of their jobs, they uphold the idea that masculinity and femininity are distinct, separate, and mutually exclusive. When these men seek masculinity by aiming for the better paying or most technological fields, they not only position themselves to move upward into the more acceptable arenas but also reinforce the greater social value placed on masculinity. Establishing distance from femininity therefore allows men to retain the privileges and status of masculinity while simultaneously enabling them to ride the glass escalator.

For Black men, the desire to reject femininity may be compounded by racial inequality. Theorists have argued that as institutional racism blocks access to traditional markers of masculinity such as occupational status and economic stability, Black men may repudiate femininity as a way of accessing the masculinity—and its attendant status—that is denied through other routes (hooks 2004; Neal 2005). Rejecting femininity is a key strategy men use to assert masculinity, and it remains available to Black men even when other means of achieving masculinity are unattainable. Black men nurses may be more likely to distance themselves from their women colleagues and to reject the femininity associated with nursing, particularly if they feel that they experience racial discrimination that renders occupational advancement inaccessible. Yet if they encounter strained relationships with women colleagues and men supervisors because of gendered racism or racialized stereotypes, the efforts to distance themselves from femininity still may not result in the glass escalator effect.

On the other hand, some theorists suggest that minority men may challenge racism by rejecting hegemonic masculine ideals. Chen (1999) argues that Chinese American men may engage in a strategy of repudiation, where they reject hegemonic masculinity because its implicit assumptions of whiteness exclude Asian American men. As these men realize that racial stereotypes and assumptions preclude them from achieving the hegemonic masculine ideal, they reject it and dispute its racialized underpinnings. Similarly, Lamont (2000, 47) notes that working-class Black men in the United States and France develop a "caring self" in which they emphasize values such as "morality, solidarity, and generosity." As a consequence of these men's ongoing experiences with racism, they develop a caring self that highlights work on behalf of others as an important tool in fighting oppression. Although caring is associated with femininity, these men cultivate a caring self because it allows them to challenge racial inequality. The results of these studies suggest that Black men nurses may embrace the femininity associated with nursing if it offers a way to combat racism. In these cases, Black men nurses may turn to pediatrics as a way of demonstrating sensitivity and therefore combating stereotypes of Black masculinity, or they may proudly identify as nurses to challenge perceptions that Black men are unsuited for professional, white-collar positions.

Taken together, all of this research suggests that Black men may not enjoy the advantages experienced by their white men colleagues, who ride a glass escalator to success. In this article, I focus on the experiences of Black men nurses to argue that the glass escalator is a racialized as well as a gendered concept that does not offer Black men the same privileges as their white men counterparts.

Data Collection and Method

I collected data through semi structured interviews with 17 men nurses who identified as Black or African American. Nurses ranged in age from 30 to 51 and lived in the southeastern United States. Six worked in suburban hospitals adjacent to major cities, six were located in major metropolitan urban care centers, and the remaining five worked in rural hospitals or clinics. All were registered nurses or licensed practical nurses. Six identified their specialty as oncology, four were bedside nurses, two were in intensive care, one managed an acute dialysis program, one was an orthopedic nurse, one was in ambulatory care, one was in emergency, and one was in surgery. The least experienced nurse had worked in the field for five years; the most experienced had been a nurse for 26 years. I initially recruited participants by soliciting attendees at the 2007 National Black Nurses Association annual meetings and then used a snowball sample to create the remainder of the data set. All names and identifying details have been changed to ensure confidentiality (see Table 1).

I conducted interviews during the fall of 2007. They generally took place in either my campus office or a coffee shop located near the respondent's home or workplace. The average interview lasted about an hour. Interviews were tape-recorded and transcribed. Interview questions primarily focused on how race and gender shaped the men's experiences as nurses. Questions addressed respondents' work history and current experiences in the field, how race and gender shaped their experiences as nurses, and their future career goals. The men discussed their reasons for going into nursing, the reactions from others on entering this field, and the particular challenges, difficulties, and obstacles Black men nurses faced. Respondents also described their work history in nursing, their current jobs, and their future plans. Finally, they talked about stereotypes of nurses in general and of Black men nurses in particular and their thoughts about and responses to these stereotypes. I coded the data according to key themes that emerged: relationships with white patients versus minority

Table 1. Respondents

Name	Age	Specialization	Years of Experience	Years at Current Job
Chris	51	Oncology	26	16
Clayton	31	Emergency	6	6
Cyril	40	Dialysis	17	7
Dennis	30	Bedside	7	7 (months)
Evan	42	Surgery	25	20
Greg	39	Oncology	10	3
Kenny	47	Orthopedics	23	18 (months)
Leo	50	Bedside	20	18
Ray	36	Oncology	10	5
Ryan	37	Intensive care	17	11
Sean	46	Oncology	9	9
Simon	36	Oncology	5	5
Stuart	44	Bedside	6	4
Terrence	32	Bedside	10	6
Tim	39	Intensive care	20	15 (months)
Tobias	44	Oncology	25	7
Vern	50	Ambulatory care	7	7

patients, personal bonds with colleagues versus lack of bonds, opportunities for advancement versus obstacles to advancement.

The researcher's gender and race shape interviews, and the fact that I am an African American woman undoubtedly shaped my rapport and the interactions with interview respondents. Social desirability bias may compel men to phrase responses that might sound harsh in ways that will not be offensive or problematic to the woman interviewer. However, one of the benefits of the interview method is that it allows respondents to clarify comments diplomatically while still giving honest answers. In this case, some respondents may have carefully framed certain comments about working mostly with women. However, the semistructured interview format nonetheless enabled them to discuss in detail their experiences in nursing and how these experiences are shaped by race and gender. Furthermore, I expect that shared racial status also facilitated a level of comfort, particularly as respondents frequently discussed issues of racial bias and mistreatment that shaped their experiences at work.

Findings

The results of this study indicate that not all men experience the glass escalator in the same ways. For Black men nurses, intersections of race and gender create a different experience with the mechanisms that facilitate white men's advancement in women's professions. Awkward or unfriendly interactions with colleagues, poor relationships with supervisors, perceptions that they are not suited for nursing, and an unwillingness to disassociate from "feminized" aspects of nursing constitute what I term *glass barriers* to riding the glass escalator.

Reception from Colleagues and Supervisors

When women welcome men into "their" professions, they often push men into leadership roles that ease their advancement into upper-level positions. Thus, a positive reaction from colleagues is critical to riding the glass escalator. Unlike white men nurses, however, Black men do not describe encountering a warm reception from women colleagues (Heikes 1991). Instead, the men I interviewed find that they often have unpleasant interactions with women coworkers who treat them rather coldly and attempt to keep them at bay. Chris is a 51-year-old oncology nurse who describes one white nurse's attempt to isolate him from other white women nurses as he attempted to get his instructions for that day's shift:

> She turned and ushered me to the door, and said for me to wait out here, a nurse will come out and give you your report. I stared at her hand on my arm, and then at her, and said, "Why? Where do you go to get your reports?" She said, "I get them in there." I said, "Right. Unhand me." I went right back in there, sat down, and started writing down my reports.

Kenny, a 47-year-old nurse with 23 years of nursing experience, describes a similarly and particularly painful experience he had in a previous job where he was the only Black person on staff:

> [The staff] had nothing to do with me, and they didn't even want me to sit at the same area where they were charting in to take a break. They wanted me to sit somewhere else....They wouldn't even sit at a table with me! When I came and sat down, everybody got up and left.

These experiences with colleagues are starkly different from those described by white men in professions dominated by women (see Pierce 1995; Williams 1989). Though the men in these studies sometimes chose to segregate themselves, women never systematically excluded them. Though I have no way of knowing why the women nurses in Chris's and Kenny's workplaces physically segregated themselves, the pervasiveness of gendered racist images that emphasize white women's vulnerability to dangerous Black men may play an important role. For these nurses, their masculinity is not a guarantee that they will be welcomed, much less pushed into leadership roles. As Ryan,

a 37-year-old intensive care nurse says, "[Black men] have to go further to prove ourselves. This involves proving our capabilities, *proving to colleagues that you can lead,* be on the forefront" (emphasis added). The warm welcome and subsequent opportunities for leadership cannot be taken for granted. In contrast, these men describe great challenges in forming congenial relationships with coworkers who, they believe, do not truly want them there.

In addition, these men often describe tense, if not blatantly discriminatory, relationships with supervisors. While Williams (1995) suggests that men supervisors can be allies for men in women's professions by facilitating promotions and upward mobility, Black men nurses describe incidents of being overlooked by supervisors when it comes time for promotions. Ryan, who has worked at his current job for 11 years, believes that these barriers block upward mobility within the profession:

> The hardest part is dealing with people who don't understand minority nurses. People with their biases, who don't identify you as ripe for promotion. I know the policy and procedure, I'm familiar with past history. So you can't tell me I can't move forward if others did. [How did you deal with this?] By knowing the chain of command, who my supervisors were. Things were subtle. I just had to be better. I got this mostly from other nurses and supervisors. I was paid to deal with patients, so I could deal with [racism] from them. I'm not paid to deal with this from colleagues.

Kenny offers a similar example. Employed as an orthopedic nurse in a predominantly white environment, he describes great difficulty getting promoted, which he primarily attributes to racial biases:

> It's almost like you have to, um, take your ideas and give them to somebody else and then let them present them for you and you get no credit for it. I've applied for several promotions there and, you know, I didn't get them.... When you look around to the, um, the percentage of African Americans who are actually in executive leadership is almost zero percent. Because it's less than one percent of the total population of people that are in

leadership, and it's almost like they'll go outside of the system just to try to find a Caucasian to fill a position. Not that I'm not qualified, because I've been master's prepared for 12 years and I'm working on my doctorate.

According to Ryan and Kenny, supervisors' racial biases mean limited opportunities for promotion and upward mobility. This interpretation is consistent with research that suggests that even with stellar performance and solid work histories, Black workers may receive mediocre evaluations from white supervisors that limit their advancement (Feagin 2006; Feagin and Sikes 1994). For Black men nurses, their race may signal to supervisors that they are unworthy of promotion and thus create a different experience with the glass escalator.

Strong relationships with colleagues and supervisors are a key mechanism of the glass escalator effect. For Black men nurses, however, these relationships are experienced differently from those described by their white men colleagues. Black men nurses do not speak of warm and congenial relationships with women nurses or see these relationships as facilitating a move into leadership roles. Nor do they suggest that they share gendered bonds with men supervisors that serve to ease their mobility into higher-status administrative jobs. In contrast, they sense that racial bias makes it difficult to develop ties with coworkers and makes superiors unwilling to promote them. Black men nurses thus experience this aspect of the glass escalator differently from their white men colleagues. They find that relationships with colleagues and supervisors stifle, rather than facilitate, their upward mobility.

Perceptions of Suitability

Like their white counterparts, Black men nurses also experience challenges from clients who are unaccustomed to seeing men in fields typically dominated by women. As with white men nurses, Black men encounter this in surprised or quizzical reactions from patients who seem to expect to be treated by white women nurses. Ray, a 36-year-old oncology nurse with 10 years of experience, states,

Nursing, historically, has been a white female's job [so] being a Black male it's a weird position to be in.... I've, several times, gone into a room and a male patient, a white male patient has, you know, they'll say, "Where's the pretty nurse? Where's the pretty nurse? Where's the blonde nurse?"... "You don't have one. I'm the nurse."

Yet while patients rarely expect to be treated by men nurses of any race, white men encounter statements and behaviors that suggest patients expect them to be doctors, supervisors, or other higher-status, more masculine positions (Williams 1989, 1995). In part, this expectation accelerates their ride on the glass escalator, helping to push them into the positions for which they are seen as more appropriately suited.

(White) men, by virtue of their masculinity, are assumed to be more competent and capable and thus better situated in (nonfeminized) jobs that are perceived to require greater skill and proficiency. Black men, in contrast, rarely encounter patients (or colleagues and supervisors) who immediately expect that they are doctors or administrators. Instead, many respondents find that even after displaying their credentials, sharing their nursing experience, and, in one case, dispensing care, they are still mistaken for janitors or service workers. Ray's experience is typical:

> I've even given patients their medicines, explained their care to them, and then they'll say to me, "Well, can you send the nurse in?"

Chris describes a somewhat similar encounter of being misidentified by a white woman patient:

> I come [to work] in my white uniform, that's what I wear—being a Black man, I know they won't look at me the same, so I dress the part—I said good evening, my name's Chris, and I'm going to be your nurse. She says to me, "Are you from housekeeping?"...I've had other cases. I've walked in and had a lady look at me and ask if I'm the janitor.

Chris recognizes that this patient is evoking racial stereotypes that Blacks are there to perform menial service work. He attempts to circumvent this very perception through careful self-presentation, wearing the white uniform to indicate his position as a nurse. His efforts, however, are nonetheless met with a racial stereotype that as a Black man he should be there to clean up rather than to provide medical care.

Black men in nursing encounter challenges from customers that reinforce the idea that men are not suited for a "feminized" profession such as nursing. However, these assumptions are racialized as well as gendered. Unlike white men nurses who are assumed to be doctors (see Williams 1992), Black men in nursing are quickly taken for janitors or housekeeping staff. These men do not simply describe a gendered process where perceptions and stereotypes about men serve to aid their mobility into higher-status jobs. More specifically, they describe interactions that are simultaneously raced *and* gendered in ways that reproduce stereotypes of Black men as best suited for certain blue-collar, unskilled labor.

These negative stereotypes can affect Black men nurses' efforts to treat patients as well. The men I interviewed find that masculinity does not automatically endow them with an aura of competency. In fact, they often describe interactions with white women patients that suggest that their race minimizes whatever assumptions of capability might accompany being men. They describe several cases in which white women patients completely refused treatment. Ray says,

> With older white women, it's tricky sometimes because they will come right out and tell you they don't want you to treat them, or can they see someone else.

Ray frames this as an issue specifically with older white women, though other nurses in the sample described similar issues with white women of all ages. Cyril, a 40-year-old nurse with 17 years of nursing experience, describes a slightly different twist on this story:

> I had a white lady that I had to give a shot, and she was fine with it and I was fine with it. But her husband, when she told him, he said to me, I don't have any problem with you as a Black man, but I don't want you giving her a shot.

While white men nurses report some apprehension about treating women patients, in all likelihood this experience is compounded for Black men (Williams 1989). Historically, interactions between Black men and white women have been fraught with complexity and tension, as Black men have been represented in the cultural imagination as potential rapists and threats to white women's security and safety—and, implicitly, as a threat to white patriarchal stability (Davis 1981; Giddings 1984). In Cyril's case, it may be particularly significant that the Black man is charged with giving a shot and therefore literally penetrating the white wife's body, a fact that may heighten the husband's desire to shield his wife from this interaction. White men nurses may describe hesitation or awkwardness that accompanies treating women patients, but their experiences are not shaped by a pervasive racial imagery that suggests that they are potential threats to their women patients' safety.

This dynamic, described primarily among white women patients and their families, presents a picture of how Black men's interactions with clients are shaped in specifically raced and gendered ways that suggest they are less rather than more capable. These interactions do not send the message that Black men, because they are men, are too competent for nursing and really belong in higher-status jobs. Instead, these men face patients who mistake them for lower-status service workers and encounter white women patients (and their husbands) who simply refuse treatment or are visibly uncomfortable with the prospect. These interactions do not situate Black men nurses in a prime position for upward mobility. Rather, they suggest that the experience of Black men nurses with this particular mechanism of the glass escalator is the manifestation of the expectation that they should be in lower-status positions more appropriate to their race and gender.

Refusal to Reject Femininity

Finally, Black men nurses have a different experience with establishing distance from women and the feminized aspects of their work. Most research shows that as men nurses employ strategies that distance them from femininity (e.g., by emphasizing nursing as a route to higher-status, more masculine jobs), they place themselves in a position for upward mobility and the glass escalator effect (Williams 1992). For Black men nurses, however, this process looks different. Instead of distancing themselves from the femininity associated with nursing, Black men actually embrace some of the more feminized attributes linked to nursing. In particular, they emphasize how much they value and enjoy the way their jobs allow them to be caring and nurturing. Rather than conceptualizing caring as anathema or feminine (and therefore undesirable), Black men nurses speak openly of caring as something positive and enjoyable.

This is consistent with the context of nursing that defines caring as integral to the profession. As nurses, Black men in this line of work experience professional socialization that emphasizes and values caring, and this is reflected in their statements about their work. Significantly, however, rather than repudiating this feminized component of their jobs, they embrace it. Tobias, a 44-year-old oncology nurse with 25 years of experience, asserts.

> The best part about nursing is helping other people, the flexibility of work hours, and the commitment to vulnerable populations, people who are ill.

Simon, a 36-year-old oncology nurse, also talks about the joy he gets from caring for others. He contrasts his experiences to those of white men nurses he knows who prefer specialties that involve less patient care:

> They were going to work with the insurance industries, they were going to work in the ER where it's a touch and go, you're a number literally. I don't get to know your name, I don't get to know that you have four grandkids, I don't get to know that you really want to get out of the hospital by next week because the following week is your birthday, your 80th birthday and it's so important for you. I don't get to know that your cat's name is Sprinkles, and you're concerned about who's feeding the cat now, and if they remembered to turn the TV on during the day so

that the cat can watch *The Price Is Right*. They don't get into all that kind of stuff. OK, I actually need to remember the name of your cat so that tomorrow morning when I come, I can ask you about Sprinkles and that will make a world of difference. I'll see light coming to your eyes and the medicines will actually work because your perspective is different.

Like Tobias, Simon speaks with a marked lack of self-consciousness about the joys of adding a personal touch and connecting that personal care to a patient's improvement. For him, caring is important, necessary, and valued, even though others might consider it a feminine trait.

For many of these nurses, willingness to embrace caring is also shaped by issues of race and racism. In their position as nurses, concern for others is connected to fighting the effects of racial inequality. Specifically, caring motivates them to use their role as nurses to address racial health disparities, especially those that disproportionately affect Black men. Chris describes his efforts to minimize health issues among Black men:

> With Black male patients, I have their history, and if they're 50 or over I ask about the prostate exam and a colonoscopy. Prostate and colorectal death is so high that that's my personal crusade.

Ryan also speaks to the importance of using his position to address racial imbalances:

> I really take advantage of the opportunities to give back to communities, especially to change the disparities in the African American community. I'm more than just a nurse. As a faculty member at a major university, I have to do community hours, services. Doing health fairs, in-services on research, this makes an impact in some disparities in the African American community. [People in the community] may not have the opportunity to do this otherwise.

As Lamont (2000) indicates in her discussion of the "caring self," concern for others helps Chris and Ryan to use their knowledge and position as nurses to combat racial inequalities in health. Though caring is generally considered a "feminine" attribute, in this context it is connected to challenging racial health disparities. Unlike their white men colleagues, these nurses accept and even embrace certain aspects of femininity rather than rejecting them. They thus reveal yet another aspect of the glass escalator process that differs for Black men. As Black men nurses embrace this "feminine" trait and the avenues it provides for challenging racial inequalities, they may become more comfortable in nursing and embrace the opportunities it offers.

Conclusions

Existing research on the glass escalator cannot explain these men's experiences. As men who do women's work, they should be channeled into positions as charge nurses or nursing administrators and should find themselves virtually pushed into the upper ranks of the nursing profession. But without exception, this is not the experience these Black men nurses describe. Instead of benefiting from the basic mechanisms of the glass escalator, they face tense relationships with colleagues, supervisors' biases in achieving promotion, patient stereotypes that inhibit caregiving, and a sense of comfort with some of the feminized aspects of their jobs. These "glass barriers" suggest that the glass escalator is a racialized concept as well as a gendered one. The main contribution of this study is the finding that race and gender intersect to determine which men will ride the glass escalator. The proposition that men who do women's work encounter undue opportunities and advantages appears to be unequivocally true only if the men in question are white.

This raises interesting questions and a number of new directions for future research. Researchers might consider the extent to which the glass escalator is not only raced and gendered but sexualized as well. Williams (1995) notes that straight men are often treated better by supervisors than are gay men and that straight men frequently do masculinity by strongly asserting their heterosexuality to combat the belief that men who do women's work are gay. The men in this study (with the exception of one nurse I interviewed) rarely discussed sexuality except to say that they were straight and were not bothered by "the gay stereotype." This

is consistent with Williams's findings. Gay men, however, may also find that they do not experience a glass escalator effect that facilitates their upward mobility. Tim, the only man I interviewed who identified as gay, suggests that gender, race, and sexuality come together to shape the experiences of men in nursing. He notes,

> I've been called awful things—you faggot this, you faggot that. I tell people there are three *Fs* in life, and if you're not doing one of them it doesn't matter what you think of me. They say, "Three *Fs*?" and I say yes. If you aren't feeding me, financing me, or fucking me, then it's none of your business what my faggot ass is up to.

Tim's experience suggests that gay men—and specifically gay Black men— in nursing may encounter particular difficulties establishing close ties with straight men supervisors or may not automatically be viewed by their women colleagues as natural leaders. While race is, in many cases, more obviously visible than sexuality, the glass escalator effect may be a complicated amalgam of racial, gendered, and sexual expectations and stereotypes.

It is also especially interesting to consider how men describe the role of women in facilitating—or denying—access to the glass escalator. Research on white men nurses includes accounts of ways white women welcome them and facilitate their advancement by pushing them toward leadership positions (Floge and Merrill 1986; Heikes 1991; Williams 1992, 1995). In contrast, Black men nurses in this study discuss white women who do not seem eager to work with them, much less aid their upward mobility. These different responses indicate that shared racial status is important in determining who rides the glass escalator. If that is the case, then future research should consider whether Black men nurses who work in predominantly Black settings are more likely to encounter the glass escalator effect. In these settings, Black men nurses' experiences might more closely resemble those of white men nurses.

Future research should also explore other racial minority men's experiences in women's professions to determine whether and how they encounter the processes that facilitate a ride on the glass escalator. With Black men nurses, specific race or gender stereotypes impede their access to the glass escalator; however, other racial minority men are subjected to different race or gender stereotypes that could create other experiences. For instance, Asian American men may encounter racially specific gender stereotypes of themselves as computer nerds, sexless sidekicks, or model minorities and thus may encounter the processes of the glass escalator differently than do Black or white men (Espiritu 2000). More focus on the diverse experiences of racial minority men is necessary to know for certain.

Finally, it is important to consider how these men's experiences have implications for the ways the glass escalator phenomenon reproduces racial and gendered advantages. Williams (1995) argues that men's desire to differentiate themselves from women and disassociate from the femininity of their work is a key process that facilitates their ride on the glass escalator. She ultimately suggests that if men reconstruct masculinity to include traits such as caring, the distinctions between masculinity and femininity could blur and men "would not have to define masculinity as the negation of femininity" (Williams 1995, 188). This in turn could create a more equitable balance between men and women in women's professions. However, the experiences of Black men in nursing, especially their embrace of caring, suggest that accepting the feminine aspects of work is not enough to dismantle the glass escalator and produce more gender equality in women's professions. The fact that Black men nurses accept and even enjoy caring does not minimize the processes that enable *white* men to ride the glass escalator. This suggests that undoing the glass escalator requires not only blurring the lines between masculinity and femininity but also challenging the processes of racial inequality that marginalize minority men.

Acknowledgments

Special thanks to Kirsten Dellinger, Mindy Stombler, Ralph LaRossa, Cindy Whitney, Laura Logan, Dana Britton, and the anonymous reviewers for their insights and helpful feedback. Thanks also to Karyn Lacy, Andra Gillespie, and Isabel Wilkerson for their comments and support.

Note

1. I could not locate any data that indicate the percentage of Black men in nursing. According to 2006 census data, African Americans compose 11 percent of nurses, and men are 8 percent of nurses (http://www.census.gov/compendia/statab/tables/08s0598.pdf). These data do not show the breakdown of nurses by race and sex.

References

Acker, Joan. 1990. Hierarchies, jobs, bodies: A theory of gendered organizations. *Gender & Society* 4:139–58.

Britton, Dana. 1995. *At work in the iron cage.* New York: New York University Press.

Budig, Michelle. 2002. Male advantage and the gender composition of jobs: Who rides the glass escalator? *Social Forces* 49 (2): 258–77.

Charles, Maria, and David Grusky. 2004. *Occupational ghettos: The worldwide segregation of women and men.* Palo Alto, CA: Stanford University Press.

Chen, Anthony. 1999. Lives at the center of the periphery, lives at the periphery of the center: Chinese American masculinities and bargaining with hegemony. *Gender &. Society* 13:584–607.

Collins, Patricia Hill. 1990. *Black feminist thought.* New York: Routledge.

———. 2004. *Black sexual politics.* New York: Routledge.

Connell, R. W. 1989. *Gender and power.* Sydney, Australia: Allen and Unwin.

Davis, Angela. 1981. *Women, race, and class.* New York: Vintage.

Duffy, Mignon. 2007. Doing the dirty work: Gender, race, and reproductive labor in historical perspective. *Gender & Society* 21:313–36.

Espiritu, Yen Le. 2000. *Asian American women and men: Labor, laws, and love.* Walnut Creek, CA: AltaMira.

Essed, Philomena. 1991. *Understanding everyday racism.* New York: Russell Sage.

Feagin, Joe. 2006. *Systemic racism.* New York: Routledge.

Feagin, Joe, and Melvin Sikes. 1994. *Living with racism.* Boston: Beacon Hill Press.

Floge, Liliane, and Deborah M. Merrill. 1986. Tokenism reconsidered: Male nurses and female physicians in a hospital setting. *Social Forces* 64:925–47.

Giddings, Paula. 1984. *When and where I enter: The impact of Black women on race and sex in America.* New York: HarperCollins.

Harvey Wingfield, Adia. 2007. The modern mammy and the angry Black man: African American professionals' experiences with gendered racism in the workplace. *Race, Gender, and Class* 14 (2): 196–212.

Heikes, E. Joel. 1991. When men are the minority: The case of men in nursing. *Sociological Quarterly* 32:389–401.

hooks, bell. 2004. *We real cool.* New York: Routledge.

Kanter, Rosabeth Moss. 1977. *Men and women of the corporation.* New York: Basic Books.

Kimmel, Michael. 2001. Masculinity as homophobia. In *Men and masculinity,* edited by Theodore F. Cohen. Belmont, CA: Wadsworth.

Lamont, Michelle. 2000. *The dignity of working men.* New York: Russell Sage.

Neal, Mark Anthony. 2005. *New Black man.* New York: Routledge.

Ong, Maria. 2005. Body projects of young women of color in physics: Intersections of race, gender, and science. *Social Problems* 52 (4): 593–617.

Pierce, Jennifer. 1995. *Gender trials: Emotional lives in contemporary law firms.* Berkeley: University of California Press.

Roth, Louise. 2006. *Selling women short: Gender and money on Wall Street.* Princeton, NJ: Princeton University Press.

Shapiro, Thomas. 2004. *Hidden costs of being African American: How wealth perpetuates inequality.* New York: Oxford University Press.

Snyder, Karrie Ann, and Adam Isaiah Green. 2008. Revisiting the glass escalator: The case of gender segregation in a female dominated occupation. *Social Problems* 55 (2): 271–99.

Williams, Christine. 1989. *Gender differences at work: Women and men in non-traditional occupations.* Berkeley: University of California Press.

———. 1992. The glass escalator: Hidden advantages for men in the "female" professions. *Social Problems* 39 (3): 253–67.

———. 1995. *Still a man's world: Men who do women's work.* Berkeley: University of California Press.

Zimmer, Lynn. 1988. Tokenism and women in the workplace: The limits of gender neutral theory. *Social Problems* 35 (1): 64–77.

Farewell to the Organization Man: The Feminization of Loyalty in High-End and Low-End Service Jobs

KARLA ERICKSON AND JENNIFER L. PIERCE

My boss is such a good guy. It's the [law] firm that I could care less about. They get my time, but they sure as hell don't get anything else.
—*Interview with Debbie, a paralegal*

What do I like about serving? I like interacting with the people. I've known so many people for so long, it's not really like a job. I call it my little social life.
—*Interview with Jessica, a waitress*

Karla Erickson and Jennifer L. Pierce, "A Farewell to the Organization Man: The Feminization of Loyalty in High-end and Low-end Service Jobs" from *Ethnography* 6, no. 3 (2005: 283–313). Copyright © 2005 by Sage Publications, Inc. Reprinted with the permission of Sage Publications, Inc.

We are currently experiencing nostalgia for the golden age of company loyalty…Is the death of the company man something that should be lamented or celebrated?

—*Adrian Wooldridge,* New York Times Magazine, *March 2000*

The notion of the "organization man" as loyal and conformist to corporate life was a dominant cultural motif in the 1950s in the United States (Carroll and Noble, 1988; Mills, 1951; Newman, 1998; Whyte, 1957). Contained within this narrative is an implicit social contract between workers and corporations: if workers are loyal to the company and work hard, they will be rewarded in terms of promotions, raises, and job security by the employer. The meaning of this social contract is also structured by gender. In the immediate post–Second World War era, the organization man was not a generic person, but specifically a *man* who was expected to be the mainstay breadwinner of the heterosexual family. This image, in turn, was buttressed by the reemerging cult of domesticity in popular culture following the war (Breines, 1992; May, 1988; Spiegel, 1992; Welter, 1966). Thus, in the cultural currency of the day, company loyalty was conflated with masculinity, while personal loyalty to husbands and family was associated with femininity.[1]

Since the 1950s, the American economy has undergone a dramatic shift that has challenged the possibilities of this social contract and the meaning of loyalty at work. The decline of the industrial economy and the rise of the service sector have brought about changes in the labor force and the labor process, in possibilities for workers' long-term financial security, and in culture(s) of work for those working in service jobs (Herschenberg et al., 1998). First, unlike manufacturing work, service work, as we define it, involves face-to-face interactions with customers and often requires emotional labor on the part of the workers (Hochschild, 1983). Consequently, the product is typically the service interaction itself and the formerly dyadic model of worker–management relations now includes a third element—the customer (Leidner, 1993). For service workers, this triangulation of power raises the question: to whom is

one loyal? Second, women have entered work in steadily increasing numbers since the 1950s. From 1950 to 1998, the percentage of women in the paid labor force increased from 31 percent to 60 percent (Cleveland et al., 2000; Reskin and Padavic, 2002). Given this increase in numbers, how has this narrative changed? Third, unlike manufacturing jobs, the majority of service jobs tend to be either temporary or part time, rarely include benefits, are highly feminized, and have been difficult sites for attempts at worker union organization. Compared to both manufacturing and white-collar office jobs, the service sector is marked by a remarkable annual turnover in staff, due in part to the minimal rewards accrued from staying at one particular company (MacDonald and Sirianni, 1996). Recent studies of American workplaces as well as articles in the popular press suggest that a new culture of work has emerged emphasizing flexibility over predictable career paths and opportunity over job security (Bridges, 1994; Martin, 2000; Munk, 2000; Sennett, 1998; Smith, 2001). Whereas in the age of the "organization man," loyalty and hard work supposedly paid off in terms of recognition, promotion, and financial security, today's ambitious worker is encouraged instead to be flexible, mobile, and self-directed.

In jobs where service workers are treated as imminently replaceable, where the potential for exploitation originates not only from management, but from customers as well, how do women and men make sense of company loyalty? In other words, how have these changes transformed the narrative of the organization man? To answer these questions, we draw from two ethnographic case studies, one of high-end service workers in a powerful corporate law firm (paralegals) and another of low-end service workers in a small family-run restaurant (food servers), to consider the consequences that the transformation of the U.S. economy and accompanying changes in the culture(s) of work has had for the ways women and men understand the meanings of loyalty in our contemporary service society. By focusing on service jobs at each end of the spectrum, our intent is to reveal the range of narratives service workers draw upon to make sense of changes in the culture of work in two different service work regimes.

As feminist scholars, we also pay close attention to the fact that service work is highly feminized. In the United States, the predominance of women in particular jobs and occupations is associated with low pay, low status, and no ladders for mobility both historically and contemporarily (Reskin and Padavic, 2002). "Idioms of gender" also shape the meaning of occupations, rendering women as naturally more suitable for particular jobs in varied social and historical times and places (Acker, 1990; Milkman, 1987). So-called women's work and men's work can take on a variety of meanings—for instance, in one context women are deemed most suited to be clerical workers, while in another, men are preferred (Davies, 1982). As Leslie Salzinger argues, "femininity is a trope—a structure of meaning through which workers, potential or actual, are addressed, understood, and around which production itself is designed" (2003: 15). Consequently, we ask how gender structures these two service workplaces and the meanings through which paralegals and food servers make sense of loyalty.

In this article, we begin by rethinking conventional understandings of loyalty. Because our focus is on service jobs, we maintain that loyalty can take many forms—not only to an organization, but to customers, managers, co-workers, or to the practice of work itself. Further, as our multi-sited ethnography demonstrates, particular work cultures contribute to distinctive gendered meanings and practices through which loyalty is understood. The stories paralegals and food servers tell about loyalty draw rhetorical elements from informal values and practices at work as well as from larger discursive fields of femininity and masculinity to make *gendered sense* of their experiences. As we find, loyalty has not entirely disappeared in these jobs, but has taken on new forms.

Rethinking Loyalty and Gender in Service Work

The theoretical questions we pose about loyalty and gender in the new service economy draw from several overlapping areas in the broad field of the sociology and the anthropology of work. Here, we begin by critically assessing some of the conceptual problems in the literature on loyalty at work. To improve upon these weaknesses, we draw from Raymond Williams to conceptualize loyalty as a "structure of feeling" (Williams, 1966: 64) and further complicate this understanding by locating loyalty within the triangulated relations of power between managers, customers, and workers which characterize service work. Finally, we turn to feminist scholarship to emphasize the importance of gender in constructing meanings about loyalty in varied workplace cultures.

In his influential essay on bureaucracy, Max Weber (1944 [1922]), distinguished personal forms of loyalty from what he called modern or institutional loyalty. In Weber's ideal type of the modern bureaucracy, entrance into a particular position or office within an organization does not establish a personal relationship to employer, but rather an impersonal one based on modern loyalty. With the rise of western capitalism in the late 19th century and the increasing rationalization of all forms of life, Weber saw modern loyalty as a form of commitment to an organization rather than to an individual person.

In the scholarship on American workers in the 1950s, loyalty and conformity to corporate life was a finding in many studies of middle-class, white-collar men (Hughes, 1951; Mills, 1951; Whyte, 1957). Since the 1950s, other studies have shown that despite Weber's notion of modern loyalty, personal loyalty continues to function alongside institutional loyalty as an important feature of organizational life (Kanter, 1979; Pringle, 1988). Most recently, popular critics have alternately lamented or celebrated the death of company loyalty (Wooldridge, 2000), while others have argued that the model of the loyal worker is an outmoded one in the new economy where successful workers must be flexible in their individual quest to develop new skills, moving from job to job to find better opportunities (Munk, 2000).

In the midst of these more recent debates, scholars from business schools maintain that loyalty is an important issue for management, particularly in terms of the retention of their customers and investors who are a locus of profit for the firm. Workers also play a part in this equation; for in their view, loyal workers, in turn, produce loyal customers. In *The Loyalty Effect*, for example, Frederick Reichheld defines loyal business as "systems that incorporate customers, employees, and investors in a single constellation of common interests and mutual benefits" and reminds employers that loyal workers save companies money (Reichheld with Teal, 1996: 26).

While these studies are useful in distinguishing between different types of loyalty, none adequately conceptualize the term loyalty itself.[2] For instance, when Weber writes about loyalty, he describes an overarching contractual relationship between the bureaucracy and the employee. In this contract, workers exchange their commitment to the organization in return for a secure existence. But just what does commitment entail? For Reichheld and others writing from the managerial perspective, loyalty means repeat business by the customer. Loyal customers and investors keep coming back. Although he doesn't discuss the workers' point of view, given this logic, one would assume that loyal workers just keep coming back to work everyday. Hence, loyalty would be equated with long-term tenure. The problem with this conceptualization, however, is that workers stay in jobs for a variety of reasons that may have nothing to do with feeling loyal—they lack better job opportunities, they need the money, or they are not able to relocate.

Several recent studies on professional women and work find that corporations and law firms evaluate commitment[3] by looking at the overtime hours an employee puts in each month (Bailyn, 1993; Epstein et al., 1999; Fried, 1998; Hochschild, 1997; Pierce, 2002). In what Mindy Fried (1998: 37) describes in her study of a large Boston corporation as an "overtime work culture," women are seen as less committed than men because they either work fewer hours or would like to work part-time in order to better balance family and career. Here, commitment is equated with long hours in the office. As Fried and others find, women in these corporations see long hours as unnecessary, recognizing that the work can get done in less time. Further, they see themselves as highly committed professionals and resent the notion that long hours—as opposed to the quality of one's work—signify commitment.

Rather than looking at hours worked or length of tenure within a firm, we define loyalty as a "structure of feeling" produced at work. Like Raymond Williams (1977) who uses this term to describe how specific emotions are constructed in particular social and historical contexts through social consciousness, we see loyalty as produced through collective practices and narratives on the job. This structure of feeling is produced when workers say they feel a sense of investment and ownership in their jobs or take pride in doing their jobs well. In describing their work and themselves as significant, important, or special, it bears some similarity to craft pride, but differs in that it also expresses a sense of obligation to others such as customers, co-workers, or bosses. For example, narratives about loyalty may emphasize pride about doing good work as well as their obligation to others in doing it well. Consequently, this sentiment is not an individual quality, but rather is collectively practiced and produced.

What is further distinctive about our understanding of loyalty is that we conceive of it within unstable relations of power. Like Weber, we place loyalty within an institutional context where one group of workers has more status and power than another. However, because we are studying service work, we see these structural relationships as less fixed and more variable in the deployment of power than Weber's ideal type of the regimented hierarchical bureaucracy. The triad of worker, employer, and customer not only introduces a new element into worker-management models of organizations, but also complicates the dynamics of power (Fuller and Smith, 1996; Leidner, 1996). Consequently, we examine not only how workers narrate institutional and personal loyalty in this new economic, organizational, and cultural context, but how their understandings of *customer* (or client) loyalty figure into working relationships.

Finally, as the growing literature on gender, work, and sociology of emotions finds, the production of feelings on the job, or what Arlie Hochschild (1983) terms emotional labor, is shaped by gender

(*Annals of the American Academy of Political and Social Sciences*, 1999; Halle, 1990, 1993; Leidner, 1991; Pierce, 1995). While this literature considers the social construction of variety of emotions, it does not examine loyalty.[4] Nevertheless, it does provide two important insights that we draw upon and extend to further complicate our theoretical understanding of loyalty in service work. First, feminist scholars argue that gender shapes the meaning of occupations, rendering women as naturally more suitable for particular jobs in varied social and historical times and places (Acker, 1990; Milkman, 1987; Reskin and Padavic, 2002; Salzinger, 2003). For example, during the Second World War, women's war work in factories was defined as an extension of their domesticity, and then, after the war, reconstrued as men's work. As Ruth Milkman argues, the war mobilization demonstrates "how idioms of sex typing can be flexibly applied to whatever women and men happen to be doing" (1987: 50). Further, workers themselves draw upon these idioms to make sense of who they are and what they are doing at work. This research prompts us to ask how gender structures service workplaces and the meanings through which workers make sense of loyalty.

Second, we take seriously the argument from feminist anthropologists that workplaces are sites for the reproduction of culture. In her classic book, *Counter Cultures*, Susan Porter Benson was among the first to describe a work culture as "the ideology and practice with which workers stake out a relatively autonomous sphere of action on the job" (1986: 228). In this light, work cultures can be understood as the underlying rules and practices established by employees to contain the alienating potential and exploit the potential for recognition and pride of their jobs. Studies of work cultures bring us to our third and final insight from this literature: work cultures vary from site to site (Lamphere et al., 1993). Hence, we take seriously insights from feminist geographers who insist upon the importance and specificity of place in understanding practices and meaning (Rose, 1993). For example, as Salzinger finds in her comparative study of four maquiladora factories on the Mexican border, despite the prevailing trope of women as docile labor, each workplace had a different gendered regime. As she writes:

> gendered subjectivity intervenes at all levels of the process, from managerial decision making to worker consent and resistance, but it is never fixed....Docile labor cannot be bought, it is produced, or not, in the meaningful practices and rhetorics of shop-floor life. (2003: 15–16)

Building on this scholarship, we argue that loyalty must be understood as a structure of feeling that is produced at work. Because we are studying service work, we contend that loyalty can take many forms—loyalty to customers, managers, co-workers, or the practice of work itself. Finally, we argue that work cultures contribute to the gendered meanings and practices through which loyalty is understood by workers, and further, that gendered meanings and practices are not fixed, but vary within and between different workplaces.

The Selection of Cases and Method

We address these central questions through a close examination of the ways service workers narrate the meaning of loyalty in two different service sites. In the first site, we consider the experiences of paralegals in a large corporate law firm, and in the second, we focus on the work of food servers in a family-style restaurant. By focusing on service jobs at each end of the spectrum, our intent is to reveal the range of narratives service workers draw upon to make sense of changes in the culture of work in two different service regimes. Throughout, we use the term narrative purposefully to emphasize the socially constructed nature of the material from our interviews and fieldwork. As Susan Chase has argued, "narrative[s] share a fundamental interest in making sense of experience, in constructing and communicating meaning" (1995: 8). Furthermore, narratives are always constructed in particular contexts, most immediately within the fieldwork encounter, but more broadly within particular social and historical times and places. This is not to say that narratives do not contain individual biographical or idiosyncratic elements, but rather to underscore the point that they always draw from larger cultural discourses (Scott, 1991). As we will demonstrate, paralegals and food servers tell at once similar, yet distinctive stories about loyalty, stories that reflect not only their different standpoints and personal biographies, but also draw from larger cultural narratives about gender and the changing meaning of work in the new economy.

Methodologically, we utilize the extended case method in comparing these two service work occupations (Burawoy, 1991). The extended case method uses participant observation to reconstruct existing theory, relying upon intensive study of specific cases to draw out the links between micro and macro levels of analysis. By comparing these two sites, we uncover both similarities and differences in the contradictions and tensions that revolve around the meanings of loyalty, particularly as it is expressed in one's investment in the work itself within the larger landscape of the new economy. Our intent is not to generalize about all service workers, but rather to critically thematize and problematize the evidence relative to our theoretical questions about how the new service economy shapes and gives meaning to workers' investment in these jobs and to extend and reconstruct existing theory about how gender and loyalty operates within these triadic working arrangements.

Paralegal and food service jobs are both highly feminized service sector occupations that are characterized by triadic work relations and require emotional labor. Our first site, a large corporate law firm located in a luxurious high rise building in the San Francisco Bay Area's financial district, is highly sex segregated with a preponderance of men (88 percent) who work as attorneys, while the majority of women work as paralegals (86 percent). Pierce conducted fieldwork as a participant observer there for six months in the litigation department between 1988 and 1989 and interviewed legal assistants as well as lawyers and secretaries.[5] The second field site is a family-oriented neighborhood bar and grill located in a suburban strip mall. From 1999 to 2001, Erickson conducted participant observation and 30 interviews at her primary research site, a Tex-Mex restaurant called the Hungry Cowboy.[6] At any given time, the service staff is ordinarily 75 percent female, while most bartenders are male. All five of the male servers interviewed worked primarily in the bar, while 10 of the women interviewed worked solely in the restaurant. In addition to workers and managers, Erickson also interviewed and surveyed customers to include their voice in her study of the triadic power arrangements which take place within interpersonal service exchanges.

Paralegals and food servers are also both situated within triangular service relations. Although paralegals may appear to work for lawyers, their work is paid for by clients in whose interests they labor. In this particular firm, legal assistants tend to have limited direct contact with clients, but as our examples below illustrate, it is the client behind the scenes who unwittingly orchestrates the flow of work in the office. By contrast, in food service, the interaction of the three parties is inextricably linked. For the food server, both customers and managers are immediately present and contact is face-to-face. In addition, each job requires emotional labor. And, despite the fact that 10 years separate these studies, both workplaces are squarely situated within the new economy of the last 30 years and changes in cultures of work.

By contrast, in terms of physical space, organizational structure, and salaries and wages, these two workplaces differ, highlighting some of the key differences between high-end and low-end service work cultures. Visually and spatially, these sites look quite different. At the law firm, an oriental rug in the rather grand entry way and an antique Chinese vase filled with fresh-cut birds of paradise on the receptionist's desk mark the space as corporate and professional. The distribution of space coincides with the relative prestige of the job. While senior partners are located in luxuriously furnished, large corner offices with unencumbered views of the San Francisco Bay, paralegals are housed in closet-sized offices on the inside of the corridor without windows to the outside.

In contrast to this lush corporate setting, the Hungry Cowboy is decked out with silverware, ashtrays, and stained carpeting. The restaurant is designed for the convenience and enjoyment of the customers, not the employees or managers.

Servers have no personal space in the restaurant, while three to four managers share one office located between the food preparation area and the cooler. Managers do have access to a phone, a desk, and a computer, while hourly employees store their personal belongings in their car, due to the lack of any employee-dedicated space. In contrast to the front of the house, meticulously maintained by staff for the customers, the back of the house, the only place workers can go to "get away" from customers, is often in disrepair, uncomfortably hot, and overcrowded with work products.

The two workplaces also differ structurally. The law firm is a pyramid structure with a professional stratum resting on top of a non-professional or support-staff tier. The top comprises lawyers—partners and associates—most of whom are male. The bottom tier contains librarians and their assistants, personnel employees, paralegals, secretaries, receptionists, case clerks, duplicating operators—most of whom are female. The law firm, then, is stratified by occupational status and by gender.

The restaurant is cross-cut by the front-of-the-house/back-of-the-house division. For example, while cooks are just as essential to the delivery of food to the customers as food servers, their invisibility behind the scenes of the restaurant insulates them from the brunt of the service interaction but also lowers their level of control in the restaurant. Next, like most bar/restaurant establishments, working on the "bar side" versus the "restaurant side" of the establishment is twice as lucrative due to the higher volume and the higher tips associated with bartending. At the time of the study, 50 percent of the bartenders and only 10 percent of the food servers were male. Finally, within the front of the house staff, power is also influenced by proximity to the customer. While managers have access to the front of the house and the back of the house, their contact with customers is not as immediate, limiting their power and increasing servers' power. Knowing the customers' wants and needs lends power to the servers, in contrast to the paralegals who are asked to react and respond to a client who is primarily invisible to them.

In terms of pay and status, the pyramid structure in the law firm reflects pay differentials, whereas in restaurant work, multiple pay structures create multiple hierarchies within one workplace. Because paralegals do not possess law degrees, they are invariably paid less than attorneys with comparable years of experience. In 1989, the average salary for beginning paralegals was US$22,000 a year (*San Francisco Association for Legal Assistants Survey*, 1989). By contrast, the average salary for first-year associates just out of law school at this firm was US$58,500. Thus, beginning lawyers at the private firm were paid between two and three times as much as the beginning paralegal in the same office. These disparities in income widen as the two groups become more experienced. Paralegals with seven-plus years experience averaged US$35,000 a year, while partners at the same firm could earn up to US$250,000, plus earnings from profit sharing. At the Hungry Cowboy, managers are salaried, and are often scheduled to work up to 60 hours per week. While tipped incomes are difficult to track, easy to spend, and impossible to rely on due to the seasonal and even weekly variability of tips earned, at the time of the study the servers' total income of minimum wage (US$5.15) plus tips ranged between US$20,000 and US$50,000 for servers, while managers made between US$35,000 and US$80,000. Tipped employees often averaged more per hour than managers. Of all the tipped employees, bartenders routinely earned up to 50 percent more than servers in the restaurant. Subsequently, power differentials between managers and workers were not always directly correlated to income. Unlike the clear distinction between lawyers and paralegals, servers, and specifically bartenders, are not always situated below managers on the pay scale.

Benefits such as healthcare and paid vacations also differ at each site. As part of a professional and corporate work space, paralegals, like the lawyer for whom they work, receive healthcare and two weeks' vacation with increasing vacation days over years of tenure at the firm. Food servers, on the other hand, are not eligible for vacation or health insurance. Managers receive healthcare benefits and bonuses based on profits and labor efficiency. Unlike the law firm, the service workers in restaurants are offered no incentives for longevity of employment other than improved access to lucrative shifts.

The differences in these two sites reflect the range of jobs in the service sector. Many jobs, like food serving, have work arrangements with irregular hours, low pay, and no benefits, while those at the higher end include predictable work schedules, better pay, and benefits (Barker and Christiansen, 1998; Herschenberg et al., 1998; Rogers, 2000).

Gendered Narratives of Loyalty

In this section, we describe and compare service workers' gendered narratives about loyalty at each workplace while attending to the triangulation of power between worker, manager, and customer, and the cultures of work in each site. As we argue, femininity and masculinity operate as structures of meaning through which workers make gendered sense of loyalty to organizations, supervisors, and customers, but also serve as ways that service workers themselves are addressed and understood. We identify two main narrative strategies for coping with the tensions and contradictions that surround loyalty in the workplace: investment and detachment. Investment, as a narrative, entails a sense of ownership in the service process, positioning the paralegal or server as an authority or bearer of good will through their labor in the service encounter. It highlights the significance of how one does one's job, overlooking the relative prestige of the job, deferring to employers or customers and insisting that their work does have meaning. By contrast, narratives of detachment describe the job as "just a job" and minimize personal engagement with other coworkers, employers, or customers. In doing so, it presumably protects workers by limiting the significance of their work. As the narratives we share below demonstrate, although these narrative strategies emerge at each service workplace, they take different forms in each.

Loyalty in a Corporate Law Firm

At 5 o'clock one winter evening, John, a partner at the law firm, told Debbie, a paralegal, to do an urgent project for him as he was leaving the office. The client had called him at the last minute with an emergency request. Debbie didn't realize how time-consuming the project was until she started working on it and ended up staying at the office all night to finish it. The next day, she bragged to her paralegal and secretary friends that she had stayed up all night to complete the work, sleeping for only a few hours on a couch in the attorney's office. Her continual bragging served to advertise the importance of her work to others in the office. It also hinted at the closeness of her relationship with John. After all, she had spent the night on the couch in his office.

The significance of this last detail was not lost on her audience. Some immediately responded, "You slept on his couch!" Debbie invariably giggled and said, "Yes, yes, I slept all night on the couch." Despite the obvious sexual overtones, John had not even been in his office that night. Nor did he and Debbie have any romantic involvement. In fact, he and Debbie didn't even socialize together. Nevertheless, Debbie delighted in telling and retelling the story. And, when anyone commented that it was a lot to expect on such short notice, she proudly exclaimed: "But I did it [staying up all night] because I really like John." No one made her do it; she did it because she chose to do something nice for John whom she liked. Thus, she characterized her fondness for her work in terms of an interpersonal relationship with her boss.

Like Debbie, over half of the women paralegals Pierce interviewed told narratives about work and working relationships that revealed a strong sense of investment in the job, insisting that their work had meaning and that they took pleasure in doing it well. These women also expressed a sense of loyalty to their bosses, and sometimes to the firm and its clients. These investment narrative strategies took two forms. The first narrative personalized work relationships. Here, we are referring to the tendency for paralegals to redefine their working relationships with attorneys as personal friendships. In formal and informal interviews, these women often said they "liked" the attorneys for whom they worked. Although they recognized that many attorneys were difficult to work with, they often regarded their bosses as "different." In recasting their working relations as personal ones, these women sought to make themselves feel "indispensable," "important," or "special."

This strategy seemed to work when attorneys also participated in this process. It made paralegals feel important and special. However, attorneys often had different interests in pursuing this strategy than paralegals did. In his interview, John explicitly stated that he "put up with it" to get work done. And another lawyer described encouraging such relationships as a means to "lubricate the squeak in the wheel." As other scholars have observed, personalizing relationships between employer and employee can be a subtle form of psychological exploitation (Rollins, 1985). Treating workers "as if" they are friends when in fact they are not, obscures the asymmetrical nature of the relationship. Further, it becomes difficult for the paralegal to complain about mistreatment when the attorney encourages a personal relationship.

These women expressed a strong sense of personal loyalty to the lawyers for whom they worked. Expressions of loyalty to the firm and its clients, however, were not as common. Women who personalized relationships were, on the one hand, loyal to their bosses, and, on the other, openly critical of the firm and its clients. Debbie, for instance, though uncritical of her boss' last minute request, had this to say about the client:

> He [the client] always does that. He always waits until things get really bad before he calls John. John has to explain to him over and over that he shouldn't do that—but, [name of client] is so bull-headed. I can't stand him.

In her interview, Debbie had more to say about problems with the firm itself.

> John always gives me the highest rating for my performance evaluation, but that doesn't mean I get a good raise. The firm doesn't deliver raises like that to paralegals. John's gone to bat for me with the managing partner, but they wouldn't do it, because they think I get paid too much already anyway.[7]

Like other women who adopted this narrative strategy, she expressed a strong sense of personal loyalty to her boss, while denying client and institutional loyalty.

The second narrative strategy adopted by women was simply "being nice." This is similar to personalizing work relationships in that it involves creating personal relationships; however, it operates on a more general level. These women were not simply interested in creating exclusive friendships with their bosses, but in creating a pleasant and humane working environment. By taking an active role in making the office a nice place these women were organizing the workplace in ways that felt comfortable to them.

These women attempted to please attorneys and other office workers by doing "nice" things such as remembering birthdays with cards or flowers, throwing anniversary luncheons for various employees, and having baby showers. Others attempted to please attorneys by doing excessive amounts of overtime and running personal errands for them. For example, during the holiday season, Anna did enormous amounts of overtime work, spent her lunch hours helping an associate with his Christmas shopping, and baked cookies for everyone in her team [five attorneys, three secretaries, and two paralegals]. These women workers seemed to think that if they were "nice," the attorneys would eventually be nice back.

Women paralegals who employed this strategy also expressed a strong sense of loyalty to their bosses and sometimes to the firm as well. Cindi, for example, repeated several times in her interview how fortunate she was to be working for such a prestigious firm, enumerating the many benefits it provided such as health insurance, a Christmas bonus, and a two-week paid vacation. She was also impressed by the national and international stature of some of the banks and corporations the firm represented. Others were more ambivalent. Marsha, for instance, described many of the same benefits, but later when her daughter became seriously ill, requiring a long hospital stay and a longer period of recuperation at home, the firm refused to grant her an unpaid three-month leave of absence.[8]

I couldn't believe it when they told me that they couldn't promise that my job would be here when I got back. I kept saying, but I have worked so hard for you people, I've stayed late, I've worked weekends. Doesn't that count for anything?

In light of larger shifts in the economy, particularly the downsizing of large corporations, Marsha's question about whether her commitment "counts" expresses a more generalized anxiety about the obligations (or lack thereof) of the firm to its employees, one voiced by many of the legal assistants interviewed. It would appear that the contract implied in Weber's notion of modern loyalty, in other words, the "acceptance of a specific obligation" in exchange for a "secure existence," has been broken. Given this understanding, it is not surprising that the majority of paralegals neither expressed loyalty to the firm nor to its clientele. What is striking, however, is how many women continued to feel a sense of personal loyalty to their bosses and to invest in their jobs.

In contrast to narratives of investment, other paralegals told stories about work that emphasized their detachment from and sometimes disdain for lawyers and the job itself. Detachment strategies for negotiating loyalty and commitment to the job manifested themselves in several ways. The first detachment strategy entailed defining oneself as an occupational transient. "I'm planning to go to law school [or business school or graduate school] after working as a legal assistant for a few years. This is a good way to get experience." For men—and most of the legal assistants who adopted this strategy were men—being a paralegal was a means to an end—money, experience, and a letter of recommendation to graduate or professional school. They were willing to tolerate the job because it was temporary. Although almost half of the men interviewed said they planned to go to professional school, only two actually went, suggesting that even if they didn't actually go to law school, it was important to define themselves in this way.

Some of the men, however, had no interest in going to professional school. For them, rather than defining themselves as occupational transients, they described themselves in terms of their "real"

interests and accomplishments. Over half told me (Pierce) that they were artists, writers, actors or photographers—the job was "just for money." In fact, during the course of my interviews, several men insisted upon showing me their artistic work which was prominently displayed on the walls of their offices or apartments. For these men, being a paralegal was not part of their occupational identity: they were artists—not paralegals. As a consequence, they did not take the job very seriously. Jonathan, a 25-year-old paralegal, said: "I don't let all the firm politics get to me—I don't care about those people [the attorneys]. It's not my life!" Like Goffman's strategic actors in *The Presentation of Self in Everyday Life* (1959), these workers viewed social interaction with attorneys as a carefully stage-managed affair. The performance was conveyed through the proper dramatic props: a Brooks Brother look-alike suit purchased at a thrift shop, the proper demeanor, and the proper tone of voice. Such an instrumental, pragmatic approach made life at the law firm bearable—"I'm just waiting 'till 5 o'clock so that I can go home and do my 'real' work"—and their real interests and accomplishments which lay outside the office made them feel important.

For men who adopted these detachment strategies, neither personal loyalty nor institutional loyalty was exchanged within the context of their working relationships. They distanced themselves from lawyers, from co-workers (particularly from women), and from the law firm as an organization. None expressed loyalty to the firm or its clients. For example, when the firm was sponsoring a blood drive to create a private blood bank for its attorneys, one paralegal retorted: "Give my blood to the firm! Ha! They already get my sweat. They're not gonna get my blood too."[9]

In the third detachment strategy, employed primarily by women, workers did not deny their occupational identities as legal assistants, but instead distanced themselves from their bosses through an attitude of disdain or irreverence. This social psychological strategy became evident when I sat in on "gripe" sessions that paralegals held when lawyers weren't around. In these sessions, attorneys were frequently denigrated as egotistical jerks, petty tyrants, "drones," "dweebs," or workaholics with no social skills. But what came up with equal frequency was the tendency to describe an attorney as a "baby" or a child and to describe one's job as a paralegal as "babysitting." One woman paralegal was even referred to as Michael's [an attorney] "security blanket." Michael's secretary said about Debbie and Michael's working relationship: "Michael is like Linus. He needs her to go everywhere [court, settlement conferences, depositions, etc.] with him—it makes him feel more secure."

By reversing the asymmetrical relationship between attorney and paralegal, this strategy serves an interesting psychological sleight of hand. The powerful attorney becomes the powerless, helpless, ineffectual, demanding baby, whereas the paralegal becomes the all-powerful, all-knowing, competent mother. In the short run, such a characterization made legal assistants feel better about themselves and the work they did for attorneys. By making fun of their bosses, they could feel superior, knowledgeable, and competent—feelings their work rarely gave them. It also served as an ironic twist on the attorneys' implicit assumption about "mothering." Rather than refusing to take care of them altogether, Marilyn, a 34-year-old paralegal, said, "So they want me to be their mother? Fine! Then I'll treat them just like they are little kids."

These moves involved a careful balancing act on the part of paralegals. As long as the attorneys thought their comments or actions humorous or even useful, they were successful. Paralegals continued to feel superior and contemptuous and attorneys received the assistance and support they needed. However, paralegals could not push the strategy too far. Those who did were quickly reminded of their appropriate place in the law-firm hierarchy. One attorney yelled at a legal assistant who had previously worked as a first-grade teacher: "Stop talking to me like I'm a five year old." She immediately backed down, "Sorry, I used to be a school teacher. It's hard to lose that tone of voice." Nevertheless, she managed to retain her sense of dignity. As she related in a later conversation, "What he doesn't know is that I didn't even talk to my first graders that way."

Like the men who employed detachment strategies, these women expressed neither personal nor institutional loyalty on the job. And, though they were often friendly with co-workers, they distanced themselves from lawyers, clients, and from the firm itself. Many depicted the firm and its clients in negative terms, telling stories about clients' various misdeeds. In describing a controversial employment case, one paralegal said, "[Name of lawyer] actually had to explain to the client [a foreign national] that in this country, sex discrimination is illegal. Can you believe it? What idiots!"

Overall, more women paralegals told stories of investment in their work, while more men constructed tales of detachment. These findings suggest that women were more likely to understand work through personal connections and relationships, to express personal loyalty to their bosses, although not to the firm or the client. By contrast, men's attachments to work and their loyalty appeared to be more fleeting and strategic. Closer examination reveals, however, not only a difference in who tells what kind of story, but in the structures of meaning contained in the stories themselves. Investment narratives emphasize elements such as personal concern, caretaking, and "being nice." This rhetoric operates on a still larger field of practices and images of femininity—a field which clusters around women's traditional position as primary caretaker in the family (Hays, 1996; Salzinger, 2003). The logic of this structure is also heteronormative: as in the family, at work it was women (and not male) paralegals who were expected to care for men attorneys (Butler, 1990). At the same time, male lawyers also participated in this discursive field, for instance, explaining in their interviews that they preferred to have women working for them, particularly women who were attentive to their needs. Thus, gender structured the meanings through which women legal assistants were understood and addressed and the ways they, in turn, talked about this workplace and about personal loyalty.

A gendered structure of meaning also underlies the logic of narratives of detachment. While investment narratives draw from discourses of traditional femininity, detachment narratives respond to a larger field of practices and images about masculinity. Hegemonic understandings of masculinity underscore success and the achievement of identity through work, the breadwinner role, rationality, and neutrality (Connell, 1995). Given these discursive elements and the fact that the male paralegals worked in a female-dominated occupation, the logic of their detachment narratives entailed locating the sources of their identity and self-esteem somewhere outside the workplace. Their stories highlighted preparation for a career, the job as only temporary. Others said they kept the job to make money to enable them to pursue other more appropriate male occupational identities, for example, as the virtuous artist. In defining themselves as occupationally transient in a female-dominated occupation, by emphasizing other more appropriate male occupational identities, or downplaying their loyalty to the firm, male paralegals at once defended against their gender transgression and mobilized their masculinity (Yancey Martin, 2003).

At the same time, the rhetoric of preparing for the future, assuming this work as a temporary step to another job, and developing other skills and expertise—also draws from newer managerial discourses of the flexible worker who is encouraged to invest in themselves rather than in organizations, and in potential opportunities rather than predictable career paths. Attorneys, as professionals who were once in training, also participated in constructing these narratives. They encouraged male paralegals to go to professional school, wrote them letters of recommendation, and recognized their other identities and achievements as appropriately masculine. As a consequence, male paralegals were not treated in the same way that female paralegals were. They were addressed as "professionals in training," while women were addressed as caretakers and mothers.

Not all women told stories of investment and personal loyalty in the workplace—think, for instance, of the women who adopted the "babysitting strategy." Significantly, these women distanced themselves from the job through humor or irreverence, but they also drew upon the field of practices and images associated with traditional femininity to exaggerate and parody the role of mother. While the tone of their story may be contemptuous or disdainful, the rhetorical elements they utilized are gendered as traditionally feminine. Interestingly, when women tried to draw from elements of masculine narratives such as the occupational transient, they were not taken seriously. For example, when Pierce was doing her fieldwork, many of the lawyers knew she was in graduate school, but they could never remember what field she was in—"Social work, isn't it?" Nor could they seem to recall that she was pursuing a PhD—"What are you getting your master's in again?" What her transgression suggests is the power of narrative strategies in making gendered sense of workers. Women paralegals who went to professional school and pursued higher degrees were unintelligible within this context.

Loyalty in a Family Restaurant

Jessica is a 34-year-old single mother of two children who works two jobs. She is hard working, but more than anything, she is friendly and a good conversationalist. For her, serving work has always been a form of support—from the customers that she has known for years who ask about her life and progress, who ask to see pictures of her children—and also as a way of hearing about other people's lives, subsequently fulfilling her natural curiosity about other people. For her, work time is "social time."

On any given night, a dozen customers request Jessica's section. When she is on vacation or sick, customers ask where she is and express concern that they didn't get to see her. In surveys, when customers were asked what they liked best about eating at the Hungry Cowboy, over a third named Jessica as part of what makes the restaurant a special favorite of their families. Obviously her approach appeals to many customers, and encourages them to also view the exchange of cash for food as an opportunity to exchange pleasantries and perhaps even form relationships.

Like Jessica, Beth likes to come into work to "see who's there." When describing their jobs, the labor of serving disappears: they say they come in to work to hang out and drink coffee, even though they spend much of their time lifting trays, filling orders, clearing dishes, and rushing to gather supplies. They say they "really care" about what they do.

Because both Beth and Jessica have worked at the Hungry Cowboy for a decade, their approach to the work has a profound influence on the work culture as a whole. As an investment narrative, "really caring" was the most common strategy, 12 of 20 servers used it. As servers who train in many new employees, Beth and Jessica have a lot of clout with both regular customers and managers, and derive power from their knowledge of the work process and the shared history of the work site, these waitresses in particular influence what Susan Porter Benson calls the "realm of informal, customary values and rules" which are "created as workers confront the limitations and exploit the possibilities of their jobs" (Benson, 1986: 228). Performing a form of work that is often viewed as demeaning and belittling, these waitresses say they care about the people they serve, and seem to inspire reciprocity in some of their customers.

The second investment narrative, the "server as authority" strategy, involves an attitude, in contrast to popularized notions of waitresses and waiters as servile and insignificant, that food servers are in control and the most important players in the restaurant (Paules, 1991). Unlike the servers who "really care," these workers do not immediately trust the intentions of either managers or customers, instead, they invest in the importance of the work process and the centrality of their expertise. Unlike the loyalty expected of the organization man, these workers are loyal to their own mastery of the skills necessary to excel at their jobs. They see customers and managers as often getting in the way of the agenda, which is to make sure that customers are fed, servers are paid, and everyone has a good night. Patty, a 40-year-old waitress of 15 years, described a night when "everything was going well, and then one table turned my mood entirely. They just wouldn't be satisfied, no matter what I did. Why can't they just play along?" Patty explained that she preferred waiting on regular customers rather than new customers because

they "know the rules, know how it works." Patty believes that everyone (workers and customers alike) can have a good time and the evening can flow smoothly as long as customers and managers cooperate with the tone she sets and with communicating clearly what they need.

This narrative makes sense of the triadic power relationship by repositioning the food server as central. These workers discuss the "mistakes" made by customers: violations that cause servers to withdraw their concern about the customer's satisfaction. The individuals who use this strategy also describe managers as transitory and hopelessly unaware of what is happening in the workplace. They view themselves as responsible for training in new managers, so that they "know how things are done," and also for deciding which workers and managers will "make it" in the job setting. The "server as authority" narrative was employed by three of the 20 servers interviewed, two women and one man. Its logic exposes the spectrum between investment and detachment. While the servers who utilize this narrative feel loyal to co-workers and bring meaning to their work by believing that their skills are significant and can produce rewarding service experiences, their stance also sets greater limits regarding the degree of emotional labor they are willing to offer.

Servers who invested in their work narrated their commitment to their work through interpersonal loyalty to both customers and co-workers, but not to managers or to the company itself. In fact, both managers and the owners of the restaurant were positioned as the least knowledgeable regarding the proper functioning of the restaurant and the delivery of quality service. In other words, servers who invested believed that they were responsible for the success of the restaurant. Considering that servers do not receive benefits or raises, the only structural motivations for performing their work well are tips and better shifts. Given this, it is not surprising that servers feel tied to the needs of the customers. What is interesting is that the majority of servers, and particularly waitresses, chose to invest in and develop the interactions required by their work. Their sense of loyalty to customers made their jobs more enjoyable and meaningful as long as customers participated, but also made them more vulnerable to abusive or uncooperative customers.

Despite the pressure from formal training and the examples of other servers, not all servers invest. Four of the five men interviewed used what we term the "just another dead end job" detachment narrative of detachment. They highlighted aspects like fast cash, flexibility in terms of the time of day of the shift, not having to take work home, not having to dress up, wake up early, or participate in official work functions. For example, when I asked Joey what he liked about his job, he said "When the shift is over, it's over, and I have cash in my pocket to go and do the things I want to do." Waiting tables provided Joey with quick cash to go out, play tennis and golf, and party all night without the pressure of lingering concerns about his job. Joey professed to be unaffected by customer insults and mistreatment because for him, customers were equivalent to the dollars they would leave on the table. He wasn't concerned with what they thought of him, only how their payment could contribute to his lifestyle of hanging out with friends until late in the night, drinking, and playing games. Joey described a particularly difficult group of customers who became angry about not being served enough alcohol and who complained directly to Joey and later reported their displeasure to the manager. Since the tip was the only goal of his service, he said he did not care what this particular group of customers wanted since they clearly wouldn't be tipping him. Because this narrative rejects understanding the job as being part of his identity, Joey was able to withdraw emotionally from the situation.

In the "just another dead end job" strategy, workers share an outlook that jobs in general tend to involve alienating conditions. One of the waiters who employed this approach explained that while he did not like this job, he was not eager to join what he referred to the "cubicle culture" of the 9-to-5 world. These workers disengaged from difficult and demeaning moments at the Hungry Cowboy by maintaining an attitude that work is, by its nature, a task to be endured. In the logic of their narratives, food service work is selected from out of a landscape of jobs that all appear to be unrewarding and difficult. When I asked Billy, a 29-year-old whose whole family worked in a variety of restaurant jobs, what he would do if he didn't do this work, he explained that he had trained to work in the music industry but soon realized that that job was "just the same as everything else—lots of politics, you need to know somebody to get in, and there's no guarantees." Later he left serving for a while to work at "a desk job" which not only pained him because of "the clothes, the schedule, and the competition" but also because he did not maintain the same income as he had received at the Hungry Cowboy.

The "just another dead end job" narrative downplays the absence of formalized structure like job titles, seniority, and benefits as negative attributes because it allows them to remain "free." In their definition, suits and ties and regular hours are characteristics of a real job, as well as a sense of passion and ambition that they leave at the door when they come to work. The four men who used this approach implicitly referred to the image of the organization man when they were describing the sorts of empty promises they felt they were avoiding by working a "not-real" job. Billy said:

> It's kind of a funny, ironic thing, that you can be waiting on someone that's in for lunch in a suit and tie and they're making less a year than you are and they're working 30 more hours a week than you are and giving you attitude like you're some peon, and you go back and laugh at those people, they have no clue.

Trevor also compared himself to the man in the suit to justify his work.

> What society deems as normal doesn't do what we do because the hours suck and that section of society that doesn't do this perceives us as being a lower class in a way and you get looked down upon and normal people just don't do what we do, they just don't, and it's not something for everybody, but a lot of times I'm waiting on a guy in a suit and I make more than him, but he's got no idea!

The similarities in their detachment narratives illustrate that these men have developed a shared explanation for why service work fits them. The "just another dead end job" strategy downplays the importance of work in general to identity and juxtaposes their "set up" as being preferable to jobs which require more of their selves but turn out to be hollow in terms of rewards.

In the second detachment narrative, the "not my life model," servers point to how their work arrangements makes possible the lives they want to lead. Two waitresses at the Hungry Cowboy used this approach. Both women consciously resisted playing into the prevailing work culture by emphasizing the temporary and strategic nature of their participation in service work. Both of these women emphasized a sense of having "stumbled" into food service and a prevailing desire to "move on," despite the fact that they had both worked at the Hungry Cowboy for over five years. The primary difference between these women and the majority who invested was that they were currently in training for professional careers, came from upper-middle-class families who looked askance at their work in the service sector, and were single and childless. These characteristics made it possible for them to emphasize the utilitarian and temporary nature of their service work even though they did not quickly move on to their "real lives." What is most marked about their narratives is the explicit tension with how most women at the Hungry Cowboy perform their jobs. Both of these women were careful to say, "I'm not Jessica" or "I'm not like those other girls." In other words, they seemed aware of performing their work in contest with the predominant gendered narrative for women at the Hungry Cowboy.

The Feminization of Loyalty

In comparing food servers' narratives about loyalty with those of paralegals, several similarities and differences emerge. Most waitresses, like most women paralegals, told stories about investment at work, detailing their feelings of personal loyalty to customers, co-workers and to their mastery of their own skills and expertise. Here again, closer examination reveals not only a difference in who tells what kind of story, but in the structures of meaning contained within the stories themselves. At the Hungry Cowboy, like the law firm, narratives of investment contained rhetorical elements such as care, concern, and a feeling of family—elements that operate on a larger field of practices and images associated with femininity. Further, both managers and customers participated in this discursive field. Managers preferred hiring women because, as one manager reported, they are "more diplomatic, charming, better able to 'take it' without getting pissed." Customers' stated preferences for servers like Jessica highlights their gendered expectations of receiving genuine concern as part of the service interaction. And, finally, because most women themselves participated in the investment strategy, they unwittingly reinforced the fiction that women excel at nurturing and tending to others.

While investment prevailed in both service workplaces, we also find that the focus of loyalty differed in each job. At the law firm, most women legal assistants expressed personal loyalty to bosses, but not to the client or the firm, while at the restaurant, it was often to customers. Here, we argue that specific triadic arrangement of power in each work culture directs the focus of these narratives. While paralegals may appear to work only for lawyers, they also work for the client. Even if the paralegal never actually meets the client, the client is nevertheless always already there lurking somewhere behind the rhythm of daily work life. In practice, this means when the client calls needing something right away, then the lawyer needs it right away, and this "need" eventually trickles down to the paralegal. Lawyers may be able to blame demands they make as not their fault or as necessary to the satisfaction of the client. Not surprisingly, then, paralegals' work is influenced mainly by lawyers. They make sense of their job, have conflicts with and negotiate their work in reaction to lawyers much more than clients, in part due to the invisibility of the client as third party in the labor process. In fact, they too were willing to blame the client and overlook last-minute requests from attorneys, thereby maintaining personal loyalty to their bosses.

By contrast, the role of the customer in food service emerges as more salient, while the role of the managers appears less significant to the work of food servers. For the food server, both customers and managers are immediately present and contact is face-to-face. In most restaurants, servers spend more time and interact more directly with customers than with managers, but since customers also have direct access to managers, the three-way play of power can express itself differently from moment to moment. Customers may ask servers to "do them a favor" by overriding company policy and therefore forming an allegiance with the server or customers may ask to see a manager, overriding the server's authority at the table. Managers and servers may exchange complaints about difficult customers in the back of the house, while moments later the manager will collude with a customer about the incompetence of a server and promise to reprimand them. Despite the degree to which power is up for grabs, at the Hungry Cowboy women servers' narratives emphasize the role of the customers, while the role of managers, despite their official power, is downplayed. For food servers, the variations in these three-way arrangements are further exaggerated by the direct exchange of cash—in the form of a tip contingent on service—from customer to server, versus the indirect set salary wage received by paralegals. Servers and managers are interested in encouraging customers to return, but the server brings home a source of income that the manager only indirectly influences. In contrast to paralegals, food servers invest more routinely in relationships with co-workers and customers.

Despite the predominance of investment narratives in both field sites, waiters, like male paralegals, tell tales of detachment and of no loyalty to customers, co-workers, or managers. Again, gender structures the meanings contained within these stories. As we have argued, detachment narratives respond to the larger field of hegemonic masculinity. Waiting tables requires deferring to others, emotional labor, and teamwork and it has been traditionally conceived of as women's work. In addition, waiting tables does not offer the autonomy, room for ambition and opportunity for

career building that men have traditionally been encouraged to pursue (Cleveland et al., 2000). In a narrative sleight of hand, male servers repositioned the precarious employment qualities of waiting tables as an advantage for them because it gave them permission to put as little energy and attention toward work as possible. It appears they held onto these stories in defiance of the unsatisfying occupational landscape available to them as working-class men. While in the professional space of the law firm, male paralegals detached by telling narratives of a middle-class, professional masculinity, waiters justified their work in a female-dominated, low-end service job as a reaction to the lack of promise and security in more professional work settings. They mocked the "man in the suit" to legitimate the greater freedom they had by donning an apron. These differences arise in part from the particularities of each work culture. In the professional space of the law firm, it makes sense that men would appeal to dominant narratives of a middle-class, professional masculinity. By contrast, at the Hungry Cowboy, a working-class job where women co-workers predominate and set the tone, male servers detach by rejecting narratives of professional masculinity.

Among servers, we also find that a small number of women tell stories of detachment. However, their narratives differed from male servers. These two women used future plans to justify their distance from the potential enjoyment of the service encounter, even though they were clearly aware of alternative approaches to the work of waiting tables. They viewed service work as instrumental, a stepping stone to an eventual career, and defended their choice to perform service differently than the majority of workers—and specifically waitresses—at the Hungry Cowboy, by investing in a future vision of themselves. Like the male paralegals (but not like the male servers), these two women invested in their aspirations and skill sets, in keeping with popular images of the new flexible worker. At the same time, however, they seemed to anticipate that their story might not make gendered sense to others. Hence, the repeated qualification of their service to others: "I'm not like those other girls."

Despite these variations, overall, narratives of investment prevailed in both workplaces pointing to interesting historical shifts in the gendered meanings of loyalty in the workplace. While the dominant narrative of the 1950s emphasized the loyalty of men to organizations, our findings underscore the marked absence of institutional loyalty in these two service sector jobs. In light of larger shifts in the economy since the 1950s, particularly the downsizing of large corporations, it is not surprising that the majority of service workers did not express loyalty to their workplace organization. What is striking however, is how many women constructed narratives of investment to describe their jobs, while most men did not, suggesting that loyalty as a structure of feeling has not only become personal, but feminized as well.

The feminization of loyalty has a number of consequences for women workers. In many ways, women who invest say they enjoy their jobs more, are more content at work, and are able to incorporate their working roles into their larger self-concepts than men do in the same jobs. At the same time, however, there is the potential for exploitation. In the case of Debbie, the paralegal who worked overnight, her loyalty to her boss made her feel proud of herself, but also caused her to willingly overwork herself, sacrificing her personal time and life to the needs of the job—all at one-tenth the salary of her boss. In the same way, the waitresses who said they come to work to hang out, overwrite the demands of their work with the social scene, and are less able to address aspects of the workplace that are exploitative, like the lack of benefits, irregular working hours, or sexual harassment at work. As we find, women in both high-end and low-end service jobs, narratives of investment may serve to justify the meaning and dignity of their work, but this strategy also encourages them to overlook negative aspects of their work and internalize bad feelings at work in order to maintain their investment to their work culture. Finally, by participating in the feminization of loyalty, service workers, wittingly or not, reinforce the notion that women are most suited for these low-paying, dead-end jobs.

Conclusion

By conceptualizing loyalty as a structure of feeling, our multi-sited ethnography makes several theoretical and empirical contributions. First, rather than seeing loyalty as long-term tenure within an organization, hours worked, or a personal quality, we define loyalty as a structure of feeling that is collectively produced at work through narrative practices. These narratives draw not only from stories circulating within particular workplace cultures, but also from larger social and historical discourses about femininity and masculinity as well as a newer managerial ethos emphasizing flexibility and mobility. Furthermore, in drawing from the cultural repertoires available, women and men make gendered sense of loyalty. Women, who are the vast majority of workers in these two jobs, tell stories of investment in their jobs and personal loyalty to their co-workers, customers, and bosses. On the other hand, the small number of men working in these jobs mobilize their masculinity by detaching their sense of self from feminized work and alternately emphasizing themselves as occupational transients who are on their way to more male-appropriate careers or, in the case of waiters, rejecting narratives of professional masculinity in defiance of the unsatisfying occupational landscape available to them as working-class men. As we argued, these differences between men reflect the particularities of a high-end and low-end workplace cultures. In the professional space of the law firm, men appeal to dominant narratives of a middle-class, professional masculinity, while in the restaurant, working-class men reject and mock "the man in the suit." Finally, our research also makes empirical contributions to scholarship on the triangulated relations between workers, managers, and customers that characterize service interactions. As we find, to whom women service workers direct loyalty—for example, to lawyers in the law firm or to customers in the restaurant—is determined by the dynamics of particular service sites.

While our findings suggest that loyalty has not disappeared, but rather transformed in these two workplaces, there are many other jobs to consider in our expanding service sector raising a number of questions for future studies of service work. First, what does loyalty as a structure of feeling look like in other service jobs? Do narratives of investment predominate in other occupations? Are these narratives feminized? And, if so, how does it play out in the geographies of work across different types of service jobs? Second, in our focus on gender, we have not considered how race and ethnicity structure stories about loyalty. For instance, in a recent article on self-employed women and emotion work, Kiran Mirchandani (2003) finds that racial inequality influences the kind of feelings women of color are expected to produce in exchanges with white customers which suggests that race is also important to consider in studies of service work. Finally, more research needs to be done which critically assesses corporate responsibility to workers. While theorists of management such as Reichheld (Reichheld with Teal, 1996) assume that loyal employees produce loyal customers and companies, they fail to discuss the consequences of mass lay-offs for workers in the new economy. While some of these scholars may lament "the death of the company man" and its consequences for corporate profits, we ask instead why corporations do not provide more protections and benefits for women and men working in the service society.

Notes

1. Our point here is not to suggest that all men conformed to this narrative, but rather to highlight its power in shaping the stories people tell about work and loyalty. As Richard Maxwell (2001) argues, culture provides "the sum total of stories we tell about ourselves and what we want to be, individually and collectively . . . [It] works as a 'staging ground of these identity narratives and everyday narratives'" (pp. 2–3).
2. Dictionaries do not provide much more insight into what loyalty means in concrete terms. While loyalty is defined as being "faithful in one's commitments to one's friends or beliefs," faithful is defined as "loyalty." Commitment, in turn, is defined as "the state of being involved in an obligation" (*Oxford English Dictionary*, 1995: 476, 286, 159).

3. These studies use the term "commitment" rather than "loyalty."
4. Some of the emotions studied include: friendliness, caretaking, gratitude, sympathy, deference, flirting, intimidation, aggression, and rationality (Barbelet, 1998; Clark, 1997; Halle, 1993; Hochschild, 1983; Lyman, 1984; Pierce, 1995).
5. Of the 37 paralegals in the firm, the vast majority were white women with college degrees, with ages ranging from 22 to 28. The relatively youthful overall age is attributed in part to the newness of the occupation and to its high occupational drop-out rate—the average tenure in the occupation is five years. See Pierce (1995) for a complete description of all workers in this firm.
6. Names of individuals and workplaces have been changed in each field site to protect confidentiality.
7. In fact, Debbie was the highest paid paralegal in the litigation department at US$29,000. Lawyers just out of law school were making about two times her salary, and John, one of the senior partners, was making almost 10 times as much as she was.
8. This occurred before the 1993 Family and Medical Leave Act.
9. The drive was created in response to problems with blood contaminated with the AIDS virus in local blood banks during the 1980s.

References

Acker, Joan (1990) "Hierarchies, Jobs, Bodies: A Theory of Gendered Organizations," *Gender & Society* 4(2): 139–58.

Annals of the American Academy of Political and Social Sciences (1999) Special Issue on "Emotional Labor in the Service Economy." Vol. 561 (January): 127–42.

Bailyn, Lotte (1993) *Breaking the Mold: Women, Men, and Time in the New Corporate World*. New York: Free Press.

Barbelet, J. M. (1998) *Emotion, Social Theory, and Social Structure*. New York: Cambridge University Press.

Barker, Kathleen and Kathleen Christiansen (1998) *Contingent Work American Employment Relations in Transition*. Ithaca, NY: ILR Press.

Benson, Susan Porter (1986) *Counter Cultures: Saleswomen, Managers and Customers in American*

Department Stores, 1890–1940. Urbana, IL: University of Illinois Press.

Breines, Wini (1992) *Young, White, and Miserable: Growing Up Female in the Fifties*. Boston, MA: Beacon Press.

Bridges, William (1994) *Job Shift: How to Prosper in a Workplace Without Jobs*. Reading: Addison-Wesley Publishing.

Burawoy, Michael (1991) *Ethnography Unbound*. Berkeley and Los Angeles, CA: University of California Press.

Butler, Judith (1990) *Gender Trouble: Feminism and the Subversion of Identity*. New York: Routledge.

Carroll, Peter and David Noble (1988) *The Free and the Unfree*. New York: Penguin.

Chase, Susan (1995) *Ambiguous Empowerment: The Work Narratives of Women School Superintendents*. Amherst, MA: University of Massachusetts.

Clark, Candace (1997) *Sympathy and Misery*. Chicago, IL: University of Chicago Press.

Cleveland, Jeanette N., Margaret Stockdale and Kevin R. Murphy (2000) *Women and Men in Organizations: Sex and Gender Issues at Work*. Mahwah, NJ: Lawrence Erlbaum Associates.

Connell, Robert (1995) *Masculinities*. Berkeley and Los Angeles, CA: University of California Press.

Davies, Margery (1982) *Women's Place Is at the Typewriter: Office Work and Office Workers, 1870–1930*. Philadelphia, PA: Temple University Press.

Epstein, C., C. Seron, B. Oglensky and R. Saute (1999) *The Part Time Paradox*. New York: Routledge.

Erikson, Karla (2004) "To Invest or Detach? Coping Strategies and Workplace Culture in Service Work," *Symbolic Interaction* 27(4): 549–72.

Fried, Mindy (1998) *Taking Time: The Parental Leave Policy and Corporate Culture*. Philadelphia, PA: Temple University Press.

Fuller, Linda and Vicki Smith (1996) in Cameron Lynne MacDonald and Carmen Sirianni (eds) *Working in the Service Society*, pp. 74–90. Philadelphia, PA: Temple University.

Goffman, Erving (1959) *The Presentation of Self in Everyday Life*. Garden City, NY: Doubleday.

Halle, Elaine (1990) *Waiting on Tables: Gender Integration in a Service Occupation*. Hartford, CT: University of Connecticut.

—— (1993) "Waitering/Waitressing: Engendering the Work of Table Servers," *Gender and Society* 7(3): 329–46.

Hays, Sharon (1996) *The Cultural Contradictions of Motherhood*. New Haven, CT: Yale University Press.

Herschenberg, Stephen, John Alic and Howard Wial (1998) *New Rules for a New Economy Employment and Opportunity in Postindustrial America*. Ithaca, NY: ILR Press.

Hochschild, Arlie (1983) *The Managed Heart: Commercialization and Human Feeling*. Berkeley, CA: University of California Press.

—— (1997) *The Time Bind*. New York: Vintage Books.

Hughes, Everett (1951) "Work and the Self," in *The Sociological Eye: The Selected Papers of Everett Hughes*, pp. 95–124. New Brunswick, NJ: Transaction.

Kanter, Rosabeth Moss (1979) *Men and Women of the Corporation*. New York: Basic Books.

Lamphere, L., P. Zavella, F. Gonzales and P. B. Evans (1993) *Sunbelt Working Mothers: Reconciling Family and Factory*. Ithaca, NY: Cornell University Press.

Leidner, Robin (1991) "Selling Hamburgers and Selling Insurance: Gender, Work and Identity in Interactive Service Jobs," *Gender and Society* 5(2): 154–77.

—— (1993) *Fast Food, Fast Talk: Service Work and the Routinization of Everyday Life*. Berkeley, CA: University of California Press.

—— (1996) "Rethinking Questions of Control: Lessons from McDonald's," in Cameron Lynne MacDonald and Carmen Sirianni (eds) *Working in the Service Society*, pp. 81–95. Philadelphia, PA: Temple University Press.

Lyman, Peter (1984) "Be Reasonable: Anger and Technical Reason in Middle-Class Culture," paper presented at the Society for the Study of Social Problems panel on Social Control and Everyday Life, San Francisco, 4 September.

MacDonald, Cameron Lynne and Carmen Sirianni (eds) (1996) *Working in the Service Society*. Philadelphia, PA: Temple University Press.

Martin, Emily (2000) "Flexible Survivors," *Cultural Values* 4(4): 512–17.

Maxwell, Richard (2001) "Why Culture Works," in Richard Maxwell (ed) *Culture Works: The Political Economy of Culture*, pp. 1–22. Minneapolis, MN: University of Minnesota Press.

May, Elaine Tyler (1988) *Homeward Bound: American Families in the Cold War Era*. New York: Basic Books.

Milkman, Ruth (1987) *Gender at Work: The Dynamics of Job Segregation by Sex During World War II.* Urbana, IL: University of Illinois Press.

Mills, C. Wright (1951) *White Collar.* New York: Oxford University Press.

Mirchandani, Kiran (2003) "An Anti-Racist Feminist Critique of Scholarship on Emotion Work: The Case of Self-Employed Women," *Organization Studies* 24(5): 721–42.

Munk, Nina (2000) "The Price of Freedom," *The New York Times Magazine*, March, pp. 50–5.

Newman, Katherine (1998) *Falling From Grace.* Berkeley and Los Angeles, CA: University of California Press.

Oxford English Dictionary (1995) New York: Oxford University Press.

Paules, Greta (1991) *Dishing It Out.* Philadelphia, PA: Temple University Press.

Pierce, Jennifer (1995) *Gender Trials: Emotional Lives in Contemporary Law Firms.* Berkeley, CA: University of California Press.

——— (2002) " 'Not Committed?' or 'Not Qualified?': A Raced and Gendered Organizational Logic in Contemporary Law Firms," in Reza Banakar and Max Travers (eds) *An Introduction to Law and Social Theory*, pp. 155–71. London: Hart Publishing.

Pringle, Rosemary (1988) *Secretaries' Talk.* Sydney: Allen and Unwin.

Reichheld, Frederick with Thomas Teal (1996) *The Loyalty Effect.* Boston, MA: Harvard Business School Press.

Reskin, Barbara and Irene Padavic (2002) *Women and Men at Work.* 2nd edn. Thousand Oaks, CA: Pine Forge Press.

Rogers, Jackie Krasas (2000) *Temps: The Many Faces of the Changing Workplace.* Ithaca, NY: ILR Press.

Rollins, Judith (1985) *Between Women: Domestics and Their Employers.* Philadelphia, PA: Temple University Press.

Rose, Gillian (1993) *Feminism and Geography: The Limits of Geographical Knowledge.* Minneapolis, MN: University of Minnesota Press.

Salzinger, Leslie (2003) *Genders in Production: Making Workers in Mexico's Global Factories.* Berkeley and Los Angeles, CA: University of California Press.

San Francisco Association for Legal Assistants Survey (1989) San Francisco Association for Legal Assistants Newsletter, San Francisco.

Scott, Joan (1991) "The Evidence of Experience," *Critical Inquiry* 17 (Summer): 773–97.

Sennett, Richard (1998) *The Corrosion of Character and the Personal Consequences of Work in the New Capitalism.* New York: Norton.

Smith, Vicki (2001) *Crossing the Great Divide.* Ithaca, NY: Cornell University Press.

Spiegel, Lynn (1992) *Make Room for TV: Television and the Family Ideal in Postwar America.* Chicago, IL: University of Chicago Press.

Weber, Max (1944 [1922]) "Bureaucracy," in Hans Girth and C. W. Mills (Trans and eds) *From Max Weber: Essays in Sociology*, pp. 196–244. New York: Oxford University Press.

Welter, Barbara (1966) "The Cult of True Womanhood, 1820–60," *American Quarterly* XVIII: 151–74.

Whyte, William (1957) *The Organization Man.* Garden City, NY: Doubleday.

Williams, Raymond (1966) *The Long Revolution.* New York: Columbia University Press.

——— (1977) *Marxism and Literature.* Oxford: Oxford University Press.

Wooldridge, Adrian (2000) "Come Back, Company Man!" *The New York Times Magazine*, 5 March, pp. 82–3.

Yancey Martin, Patricia (2003) " 'Said and Done Versus Saying and Doing': Gendering Practices, Practicing Gender at Work," *Gender & Society* 17(3): 342–66.

Before and After: Gender Transitions, Human Capital, and Workplace Experiences

KRISTEN SCHILT AND MATTHEW WISWALL

Introduction

When economics professor Donald McCloskey announced he was becoming Deirdre, the chair of his department joked that working as a woman would mean getting a pay cut (McCloskey 1999). While the chair's comment was made in jest, it speaks to a larger and long-standing question of what role gender plays in workplace outcomes. Social scientists have long documented the relationship between an employee's gender and his or her opportunities for advancement in pay and authority. While the gender gap in earnings has narrowed for men and women in comparable occupations, men continue to outpace women in salaries, promotions, and workplace authority (Valian 1999; Padavic and Reskin 2002, Blau and Kahn 2006). Yet, as existing surveys cannot measure gender bias directly or capture all the relevant characteristics of men and women, the source of these workplace disparities remains unknown.

As McCloskey's story illustrates, the workplace experiences of transgender people—individuals who transition from one recognized gender category to another—offer an innovative way to explore the importance of gender in the workplace.[1] People who undergo gender transitions are estimated to makeup only .01% of the United States population, with equal numbers of men becoming women—a group we refer to as MTFs (male-to-female)—and women becoming men—a group we refer to as FTMs (female to male).[2] Yet, we argue that the experience of a person who works both as

a man and as a woman can illuminate the subtle ways that gender inequality is socially produced in the workplace. While transgender people have the same human capital and pre-labor market gender socialization after their gender transitions, their workplace experiences often change radically. Existing autobiographical and scholarly research demonstrates that for many MTFs, becoming women brings a loss of authority and pay, as well as workplace harassment and, in many cases, termination (Bolin 1988; Griggs 1998; McCloskey 1999; Schilt 2006a). On the other hand, for many FTMs, becoming men can bring an increase in workplace authority, reward, and respect, as well as new job opportunities and promotions (Griggs 1998; Schilt 2006b). The *before* and *after* workplace experiences of transgender people, then, can make visible the hidden processes that produce workplace gender inequality.

In this article, we use the pre- and post-gender transition workplace experiences of MTFs and FTMs to examine the persistence of gendered workplace disparities. Drawing on survey data about transgender employment experiences, we demonstrate that gender transitions bring important changes in workplace outcomes. In becoming women, MTFs experience significant losses in hourly earnings. In contrast, FTMs experience no change in earnings or small positive increases in earnings from becoming men. These findings suggest that regardless of childhood gender socialization and prior human capital accumulation,

Kristen Schilt and Matthew Wiswall, "Before and After: Gender Transitions, Human Capital, and Workplace Experiences" from *The B.E. Journal of Economic Analysis & Policy* 8, No. 1 (2008): article 9. Reprinted with permission of The Berkeley Electronic Press.

becoming women for MTFs creates a workplace penalty that FTMs do not generally encounter when they become men. And, while MTFs may benefit from being men at work before their gender change, they cannot always take this gender advantage with them into womanhood. We view these findings as evidence that the gender gap in workplace outcomes does not entirely reflect omitted variables, such as unobserved human capital. Rather, the change in post-transition MTFs' earnings suggests that the labor market is not gender neutral.

Theories of Workplace Gender Inequality

A fundamental question in the social sciences is why women continue to lag behind men in salary, promotion, and authority. Although prior research attributes much of the gender wage gap to measurable differences in education, occupations, and labor force attachment, these factors still do not entirely explain all of the gender gap in earnings (Goldin 1990; Paglin and Rufolo 1990; Fuller and Schoenberger 1991; Groshen 1991; Wood, Corcoran and Courant 1993; Brown and Corcoran 1997; Altonji and Blank 1999; Blau and Kahn 2006). Although white-collar men and women with equal qualifications can begin their careers in similar positions in the workplace, men tend to advance faster, creating a gendered promotion gap (Valian 1999; Padavic and Reskin 2002). Even in female-dominated professions, such as nursing and teaching, men outpace women in advancement to positions of authority (Williams 1995). Similar patterns exist among blue-collar professions, as women are often denied sufficient training for advancement in manual trades, passed over for promotions, or subjected to sexual harassment (Miller 1997; Yoder and Aniakudo 1997; Byrd 1999).

There are several conflicting theories to explain these remaining gendergaps.[3] "Omitted variables" theories argue that differences in the types of unobserved human capital accumulated by men and women and/or differences in preferences for certain types of occupations and work settings account for the workplace gender gap. To the extent these differences are not measured in our data, we cannot control for these factors and the currently estimated gender gaps in earnings suffer from omitted variable bias. "Discrimination theories," in contrast, posit that women and men with the same levels of human capital and who hold equivalent jobs or occupations experience different labor market outcomes due to gender discrimination on the part of employers.

Omitted Variable Theories

Omitted variable theories argue that observed differences in workplace outcomes are due to gender differences in human capital accumulation and childhood socialization. As women are more likely to take time off from work for childrearing and family obligations, they obtain less education and work experience on average than men. Men, in contrast, invest much more in their job training and education, giving them more human capital on average than women. Observed differences in labor market outcomes by gender therefore stem at least partly from these disparities in skills and experience. Men are rewarded more than women because they have more human capital.

The patterns of these gender differences in human capital accumulation can be shaped by childhood gender socialization. Children receive messages from a variety of socialization agents—parents, peers, teachers, the media—about what types of behaviors are appropriate for boys and girls (Marini 1989; Subich et al. 1989; Kimmel 2000). This pre-labor market socialization can affect human capital accumulation before men and women even enter the labor force by creating gender-specific preferences for types of occupations (Corcoran and Corcoran 1985). Women learn that feminine traits include caring and nurturing. They then are more likely to seek out jobs that reinforce these traits, explaining their predominance in the "helping" professions, such as nursing and elementary school teaching. Men, on the other hand, are socialized to seek out high paying jobs that carry a great deal of authority to reinforce their sense of masculinity (Gould 1974; Kimmel 2000). This masculine socialization accounts for the predominance of men in blue-collar occupations, as well as high-powered professional occupations.

As women are socialized to put family obligations first, women workers are more likely than men to seek out jobs that provide more flexibility for family schedules, but carry lower earnings and fewer opportunities for advancement. Women may also avoid higher paying blue-collar jobs, as these types of occupations as generally viewed as "unfeminine" (Paap 2005).

Discrimination Theories

Discrimination theories point to employer discrimination as the cause of the observed gender differences in workplace outcomes. Taste discrimination, originally formulated in the context of racial discrimination (Becker 1971), posits that employers have explicit preferences for hiring workers that have characteristics with no relation to worker productivity. Employers may engage in what has been termed "homosocial reproduction," hiring workers who reflect their own identities and characteristics (Bird 1996). As white men are more likely to be in control of the hiring process, this means a preference for other white men (Williams 1995; Bird 1996; Padavic and Reskin 2002). Another more widely cited form of discrimination, statistical discrimination, occurs when employers base hiring, promotion, and compensation on worker stereotypes because of incomplete information about worker productivity (Phelps 1972; Arrow 1973; Bowlus and Eckstein 2002; Moro and Norman 2004).

An extensive empirical literature documents that employers have preconceptions as to what types of characteristics the workers who fill specific jobs should carry (Acker 1990; Williams 1995; Moss and Tilly 2001; Padavic and Reskin 2002; Martin 2003). "Feminine" characteristics, such as caring and sympathy, are typically preferred for jobs that involve a large amount of customer service interaction (Hochschild 1983; Leidner 1993). "Masculine" characteristics, such as rationality and competitiveness, are typically preferred for managerial positions (Kanter 1977; Acker 1990), even within female-dominated professions (Williams 1995). These same general patterns of gender segregation in work tasks are also found in high paying professions, such as in the legal profession (Wood et al. 1993; Valian 1999). This attribution of gender to jobs reproduces sex segregation so that, within the same work settings, women tend to be clustered with other women in lower paying jobs, while men are clustered at the top with greater pay, authority, and autonomy (Padavic and Reskin 2002).

While these gender stereotypes have important repercussions for men and women's labor market outcomes, it is difficult to quantify their importance for several reasons. First, while men and women with similar measured education and workplace experiences can be compared in a multivariate analysis, differences in outcomes can be attributed to unmeasured characteristics of workers rather than to systematic gender bias. Second, gendered expectations about what types of jobs women and men are suited for are strengthened by existing occupational segregation. The fact that there are more women nurses and more men doctors comes to be seen as proof that women are better suited for "helping" professions and men for "rational" professions. The normalization of these disparities as inevitable differences obscures the actual operation of men's advantages and therefore makes it difficult to document them empirically. Finally, men's advantages in the workplace are not a function of one simple process but rather a complex interplay between many factors, such as human capital differences, differences in employers' expectations about skills and abilities by gender, and differences between men and women in family and childcare obligations. It may be difficult to understand the interplay of these multiple factors by merely examining existing observed workplace outcomes.

Using Gender Transitions to Study the Workplace Gender Gap

In this article we propose a unique test of the role of gender in the workplace. Consider an idealized experiment in which a random sample of adults wake up and have unexpectedly undergone a gender transition overnight. Omitted variable theories predict that there should be no change in labor market outcomes, as the skills and backgrounds of the workers remain the same. Discrimination theories, on the other hand, predict that these workers would experience a reversal in labor market outcomes. To test these theories, we designed a before and after panel study that uses the experiences of transgender workers as an approximation to this idealized experiment. With this unique panel data, we can net out the unobserved differences along with observed differences. We would predict that, even after controlling for observed and unobserved differences, women who become men (FTMs) would experience a gain in earnings in relative to men who become women (MTFs). This method is a natural extension of previous methods that use panel data to eliminate time invariant unobservable variables in earnings models. The main innovation of our article is that by focusing on gender transitions, we take a variable of interest that is typically considered invariant—gender—and make it time varying in a within-person panel.

The remainder of this article is organized as follows. The next section provides a brief overview of the existing scholarly research on the before and after workplace experiences of transgender people. Next, we outline the survey design and our original data collection. We then discuss the econometric specifications and results. We conclude with a discussion of the results that puts the quantitative findings in a fuller context by using related qualitative research.

The Gender Transition Process and Workplace Outcomes

A set of guidelines developed in 1979 by the Harry Benjamin International Gender Dysphoria Association—now known as the World Professional Association for Transgender Health (WPATH)—regulates the medicalized process of transitioning from one gender to another. The guidelines, referred to as the Standards of Care, stipulate a set path for a client seeking to change his or her gender.[4] First, this client is instructed to undergo a minimum of three months of therapy (though the time limit is at the discretion of the therapist). If the therapist agrees that medical transition is the appropriate pathway, an open letter to

medical personnel is written that recommends this client for hormone treatment—estrogen for MTFs and testosterone for FTMs. Some clients, however, choose not to take hormones for a variety of personal, cultural, and health-related reasons. Therapists also can write a second letter addressed to surgeons that recommends their client for surgical interventions. For MTFs, these interventions can include facial feminizing surgery, vaginoplasty (genital surgery), breast augmentation, and tracheal shaves. For FTMs, these interventions can include chest reconstruction surgery, phalloplasty or metadioplasty (genital surgeries), and hysterectomy (see Griggs 1998 and Green 2004 for more detail on surgeries). While a gender transition often is synonymous with "sexual reassignment surgery" or genital surgery in popular conceptions, however, there is a great deal of variation in which surgeries, if any, transgender people choose to adopt during their transitions (see Griggs 1998; Rubin 2003; Green 2004).

While there is little historical data on gender transitions and workplace outcomes, some information on occupations before and after transitions can be gleaned from the first wave of research on transgender people that emerged in the social sciences in the 1970s and 1980s. In that time period, both MTFs and FTMs tended to be in their twenties, as older clients were viewed as bad candidates for transition as they were already too established in their work and personal lives (Kando 1973; Lothstein 1983). Many pre-transition FTMs worked in male-dominated fields, such as construction, or more gender-neutral fields, such as retail (Feinbloom 1976; Sorensen 1981; Lothstein 1983). In contrast, many pre-transition MTFs worked in female-dominated fields, such as modeling, hairdressing, and secretarial work (Benjamin 1966; Hore, Nicolle, and Calnan 1975; Perkins 1983; Rakic, Starcevic, Maric, and Kelin 1996). MTFs who did work in professional jobs as men were encouraged to move into more "feminine" careers post-transition that were seen as better suited for their new gender. Executives, then, became secretaries—a change that resulted in a large pay cut (Bolin 1988). In the 1990s, however, the demographics of people seeking gender transitions shifted somewhat, as more middle-aged MTFs who were already established in professional careers began seeking access to gender transitions (Lawrence 2003). And, with the aid of the growing transgender rights movement (Frye 2000), FTMs and MTFs increasingly started to make the choice to openly transition and remain in the same job—regardless of the gender stereotyping of their occupations (Schafer 2001).

Researchers who followed up with post-transition individuals reported mixed success for MTFs in the labor market. In one of the earliest studies, Lauband Fisk (1974)—a plastic surgeon and psychiatrist who operated the Stanford Gender Clinic—rated post-operative MTFs on their "economic adjustment" using a four point grading scale. They found that 10 of 18 MTFs interviewed had improved scores following their surgery. Other researchers, however, found an increase in the numbers of MTFs who went on disability after their transition, and who had difficulty maintaining employment (Sorensen 1981a; Lindemalm, Korlin, and Uddenberg 1986). FTMs also reported mixed workplace outcomes. While many of them remained in the same jobs post-transition, there were problems with acceptance, particularly if they were not on hormones and thus did not have an undisputed masculine appearance (Sorensen 1981b). Other studies, however, described FTMs as more satisfied with their work lives post-transition than their MTF counterparts (Kuiper and Cohen-Kettenis 1988). More recent qualitative data suggests that some MTFs leave high-paying professional jobs for lower-paying retail jobs because of employment discrimination (Griggs 1998). When they do remain in "masculine" professions, some MTFs report a devaluation of their skills and abilities by co-workers and employers (Schilt and Connell 2007). Many FTMs, in contrast, report gaining authority and respect at work once they look like men, even when they remain in the same jobs (Griggs 1998; Schilt 2006). To date, however, there still is little information on how gender transitions impact the before and after salaries of transgender people.

Data Collection

Survey Design and Administration

This article draws on survey data from a sample of transgender workers collected in 2004–2005 by the authors. To allow for comparability between the data on the general population and this transgender population, survey questions were modeled after the 2002 Current Population Survey (CPS). Our transgender survey was constructed as a three period panel. The survey asked respondents to provide hours, occupation, industry, and earnings information for jobs held at three distinct points in their lives: the last job held before they underwent any procedures to change their gender, the first job held after their gender transition, and their most recent job. For the last job held before their gender transition, respondents were asked, "Please think back to the last time you worked for pay (full or part time) BEFORE you underwent any procedures to change your gender that would have been noticeable to your supervisors or co-workers."[5] For the second period of the panel, respondents were asked about their workplace experiences immediately after their transition. Specifically, we asked, "Please answer these questions thinking about the first job you held for pay (part or fulltime) in which you were hired in your current gender." For the third period, respondents answered a similar question about their current main job.

Respondents were asked to self-report a date for each of these time periods (e.g., the last day worked before their transition), and retrospectively report their employment and earnings information as of that date. For most respondents, there was little (less than 1 year) or no gap between their report for the "immediately after" and "most recent" job. Because there is less non-response for the questions corresponding to the job held immediately *after* the gender change, we use this information to contrast to the period *before* the gender change.[6]

For each period, respondents were asked to report how much they "usually earn" at their "main job." We constructed an hourly earnings variable based on reported earnings and the number of weeks and hours the respondent reported that he or she usually worked at this main job. Because earnings were reported for several different calendar periods, the hourly earnings are adjusted for inflation using the Consumer Price Index (CPI-U series). All earnings in the paper are reported in 2004 dollars.

Our survey supplemented the earnings and employment questions with a battery of questions specific to the transgender population. Respondents were asked about their decisions regarding the use of surgical and hormonal treatments to change their gender, their beliefs about how well they passed in their new gender, and how much face-to-face contact they had with co-workers and customers.

Collecting a random sample of transgender people is not possible, as the population is small, widely dispersed, and often hidden. Additionally, there is no way to gather a random sample of the population of transgender people through traditional means (mailings, telephone calls, etc.). Instead, the survey was handed out at transgender conferences—conferences organized by transgender people around transgender issues—and made available on-line through a website advertisement. As most transgender conferences charge a registration fee, our sample is skewed more toward the middle-class. However, we purposefully included one conference that was free to the public to try to obtain a broader class representation.

The survey was handed out to voluntary participants at three transgender conferences: Transunity in Los Angeles, California in June 2004, Gender Odyssey in Seattle, Washington, in September 2004, and the International Foundation for Gender Education in Austin, Texas, in April 2005. Most of the respondents completed the survey on site, but a few of them mailed the survey to the authors later. In addition, the survey was posted online at the website *transacademics.org*, and readers were asked to email or mail completed surveys to the authors.

Transgender Sample

Of the 64 returned surveys, 54 were from respondents who attended one of the three conferences. The remaining ten surveys were obtained by email or mail from non-conference attendees. Because we are concerned with changes in workplace experiences before and after gender transitions, we included only respondents who were employed and reported positive earnings before and after their gender change in the analysis. This excludes all individuals who never held a job before their gender transition and individuals who were employed before their gender transition but were now unemployed.

Including only individuals who were employed before and after limits the final sample to 43 respondents: 16 MTFs and 27 FTMs. The original MTF and FTM composition among all of the 64 returned surveys was similar (27 MTF and 37 FTM). The higher proportion of FTMs is due to the conferences we attended. The Gender Odyssey conference at which 25 surveys were completed is almost exclusively a conference for FTMs.

Descriptive Statistics

Table 1 shows descriptive statistics for our transgender sample. To provide a comparison to the general population, we also report the same descriptive statistics for a sample of the general population taken from the March 2003 Current Population Survey (CPS).[7] Examining Table 1, two important differences between the CPS sample and our pre-transition transgender sample stand out. First, while MTFs are on average about the same age as the general male population, FTMs are on average about 10 years younger than the general female population and 10 years younger on average than MTFs. As discussed below, we interpret this as evidence that MTFs attempt to preserve their male advantage at work for as long as possible, whereas FTMs may seek to shed their female gender identity more quickly. A second important difference is that both MTFs and FTMs are twice as likely to have a college degree as the general population. This difference likely reflects that our sample was collected from transgender conference attendees. Being alerted to these conferences means having internet access, as well as the means to travel—all indicators of a higher socio-economic class associated with higher levels of education.

Table 1. Descriptive Statistics Before Gender Change

	All Males	MTF	All Females	FTM
Mean Age	40.0	39.6	40.2	30.0
(std. error)	(0.072)	(2.57)	(0.074)	(2.18)
Median Age	40	39	40	29
Percent White	83.7	72.2	80.7	72.0
Percent College Degree	28.6	50.0	28.5	64.0
Percent Private Sector Job	81.2	77.8	78.9	56.0
Percent Government Job	13.1	16.7	18.7	32.0
Percent Self-Employed	5.6	5.6	2.4	12.0
Percent White Collar Occupation	47.8	61.1	72.1	64.0
Mean Hourly Earnings (Col. Deg.)	35.67	31.88	24.33	22.38
(std. error)	(1.15)	(5.09)	(0.32)	(3.82)
Mean Hourly Earnings (No Col. Deg.)	18.47	21.87	13.89	12.59
(std. error)	(0.48)	(5.09)	(0.18)	(5.09)
Observations	52,420	18	42,259	25

Notes: All Males and All Females refer to the sample of working adults from the 2003 Current Population Survey (CPS). CPS statistics are calculated using sample weights. Male-to-Female (MTF) and Female-to-Male (FTM) are transgender survey respondents who reported working. Data for transgender workers is for the period before their gender change. Age is the age at the time the respondent completed the survey. Hourly earnings are reported in 2004 dollars.

On other dimensions, the transgender sample and general population sample are more comparable. Both populations are between 70 and 80 percent white. The composition of types of employment (private, government, and self-employment) for pre-transition MTFs is similar to that of all men. Reflecting the higher level of education among the MTF sample, more MTFs are employed in white-collar occupations than the general male population. There are a higher proportion of pre-transition FTMs employed in the government sector than in the general female population.

The bottom rows of Table 1 compare mean hourly earnings for the pre-transition transgender sample with earnings for the general population, conditional on education.[8] College educated MTFs earn on average $31.88 per hour before their gender transitions, compared to $35.67 for all college educated males. College educated FTMs earn $22.38 per hour before their gender transitions, compared to $24.33 for all college educated females. Non-college educated MTFs earn on average $21.87 before their gender transitions, compared to $18.47 for all non-college educated males. For non-college educated FTMs, mean hourly wages are $12.59 before transition, compared to $13.89 for all non-college educated females.

Econometric Specification

This section describes how our transgender data can be used to examine the long-standing issue of gender differences in earnings. Below, we interpret the earnings results in more detail and examine these results in the context of other employment outcomes.

Given the structure of our data collection, we consider a two period model in which the first period, denoted t = b, is the period at which the respondent was last employed before his or her gender transition. The second period t = a is the period in which earnings are observed after the gender transition. Note that each survey respondent potentially can provide a different calendar time for the before and after periods. Wages are deflated for each of these different calendar times and we include an indicator of the number of years between the before and after periods in the regression models.

Log hourly earnings for individual i in each of the two periods (t = b,a) are assumed to take the following form:

$$\ln W_{it} = \gamma_t + \delta male_{it} + X_{it}'\beta + \alpha_i + \varepsilon_{it}, \qquad (1)$$

where γ_t is the intercept for the log earnings before and after the gender transition, $male_{it}$ is a dummy variable for whether the individual is male in gender in period t, X_{it} is a vector of time varying observable characteristics, such as age and education, α_i is an individual specific fixed effect reflecting the remaining unobserved differences across individuals, and ε_{it} represents the remaining residual error.

We take the difference in earnings between the after period (t = a) and before period (t = b) in (1) to eliminate the α_i fixed effects:

$$\Delta \ln W_i = \Delta\gamma + \delta\Delta male_i + \Delta X_i'\beta + \Delta\varepsilon_i, \qquad (2)$$

where $\Delta \ln W_i = \ln W_{ia} - \ln W_{ib}$ is the change in log earnings between the after and before periods. $\Delta\gamma = \gamma_a - \gamma_b$ is the intercept for the first difference and indicates the change in log earnings following the gender transition. As we discuss in more detail below, if there is an earnings penalty related to non-normative appearance for transgender people, then we expect $\Delta\gamma$ to be negative. $\Delta X_i = X_{ia} - X_{ib}$ is the change in the vector of time varying observable variables, such as the increase in age between the two periods.

$\Delta male_i = male_{ia} - male_{ib}$ is the difference in gender following the gender transition, where $\Delta male_i = +1$ for FTMs, and $\Delta male_i = -1$ for MTFs. We take a positive value for δ to indicate an earnings premium for male gender. The unique feature of our transgender data is that there is within person variation in gender that can be separately identified from the individual specific fixed effect. In traditional panel data, where $\Delta male_i = 0$ for all i, the effect of gender and unobservable characteristics correlated with gender represented by α_i cannot be separately identified.

Results

Table 2 reports the results from estimating (2) using OLS where the dependent variable is the difference in log hourly earnings before and after the gender transition. The first model includes only an intercept $\Delta\gamma$ and the change-to-male variable $\Delta male_i$. In this specification, the intercept $\Delta\gamma$ is estimated at −0.107 (with a p-value of 0.08), and the coefficient on the change-to-male variable is estimated at 0.206 (with a p-value of 0.001). These estimates imply that male-to-female respondents ($\Delta male_i = -1$) lose about 31 percent of their earnings after their gender transition (−0.107 − 0.206 = 0.313). Female-to-male respondents ($\Delta male_i = +1$) are estimated to gain about 10 percent in earnings following their gender transition (−0.107 + 0.206 = 0.099).

Model 2 in Table 2 adds the number of years between the self-reported before and after earnings observations. The average number of years between these two periods was 2.8 years, with a median of 2 years and a standard deviation of 4.1 years. The main effect of this variable is small and not statistically significant at the 10 percent level. Including this variable reduces the intercept and the change-to-male variables only slightly.

Model 3 in Table 2 adds three time varying covariates to the specification: i) a variable for whether a respondent reports obtaining a college degree (0 if no change, 1 if no college degree before but a college degree after), ii) a variable indicating that the respondent changed to a white collar job from a blue collar job (−1 if white collar before and blue collar after, 0 if no change, 1 if blue collar before and white collar after), and iii) a variable for whether the respondent changed to a private sector job from a public sector job (−1 if private before and public after, 0 if no change, 1 if public before and private after). This specification also includes three missing variable flags, one for each of the included additional variables.[9] Of the three additional variables included in Model 3, only the change to a private sector job is statistically significant from zero at the 10 percent level. The coefficient estimate indicates that transgender people who switched to private sector jobs lost 25.8 percent of their previous earnings. Given the selection into job types, it is unclear how to interpret this finding.

Including these additional control variables in Model 3 increases the estimated transgender wage

Table 2. Earnings Before and After Gender Change

Variables	1	2	3
Intercept	−0.107 (0.060)	−0.097 (0.073)	−0.154 (0.090)
Change-to-Male (Δmale$_i$)	0.206 (0.060)***	0.205 (0.061)**	0.169 (0.063)*
Difference in Years Before and After	—	−0.003 (0.014)	0.014 (0.030)
Gain College Degree	—	—	0.014 (0.265)
Change to White Collar Job	—	—	0.128 (0.184)
Change to Private Sector Job	—	—	−0.258 (0.153)
Observations	43	43	43
R-Squared	0.226	0.227	0.344
Adjusted R-Squared	0.207	0.189	0.235

Notes: Standard errors in parentheses. The dependent variable is the difference in log hourly earnings: log hourly earnings after the gender change minus log hourly earnings before the gender change. *Change to Male* (Δmale$_i$) equals +1 for Female-to-Male respondents and −1 for Male-to-Female. *Gain College Degree* equals 1 if the respondent earned a 4-year college degree between the before period and the after period, and 0 otherwise. *Change to White Collar Job* equals +1 for individuals who move from blue collar jobs before to white collar jobs after, 0 for those who do not change, and −1 for individuals who move from white collar to blue collar jobs. *Change to Private Sector Job* is defined similarly. Model 3 also includes missing variable flags. *$p < 0.05$; **$p < 0.01$; ***$p < 0.001$ (two-tailed tests).

penalty (Δγ) from a loss of 9.7 percent of hourly earnings in Model 2 to 15.4 percent in Model 3. This may indicate that transgender people are adapting to workplace appearance discrimination by switching to job types that are less discriminatory. Not controlling for these characteristics in Models 1 and 2 masks the larger transgender earnings penalty that is revealed in Model 3. In addition, the gain to becoming male (the coefficient on Δmale$_i$) is estimated to be 16.9 percent in Model 3. This is still large and statistically significant (p-value 0.020), but is smaller than the gain estimated in Models 1 and 2. In Model 3, becoming men for FTMs brings a small increase in overall earnings (−0.154 + 0.169 = 0.015), while becoming women for MTFs brings a large reduction in earnings of about 32 percent (−0.154 − 0.169 = − 0.323).

It is important to note that for most of the sample these multivariate regressions only capture the immediate change in earnings following a gender transition. A longitudinal study of transgender employment over a longer period may reveal more substantial changes. As we discuss in the next section, interview evidence indicates that FTMs experience more subtle changes in their labor market opportunities after becoming men as they gain increased authority and respect in the workplace. MTFs on the other hand experience a decline in these same areas, and more MTFs than FTMs report experiencing harassment and discriminatory promotion and retention decisions (Griggs 1998; Schilt 2006a; Schilt and Connell 2007). We suspect that over time these changes would affect earnings even more substantially than we are able to document here.

Discussion

Although our sample of transgender people is not a random sample from the general population, we argue that studying gender transitions leads to important insights into how gender impacts workplace outcomes. While MTFs and FTMs change their outward gender, their skills, abilities, and gender socialization remain the same.[10] The substantial loss of earnings experienced by MTFs, but not FTMs, suggests that omitted variables theories do not fully account for the role of gender in the workplace.

Endogenous Gender Transitions

An issue with interpreting the identification of the earnings gains to becoming men is that people considering gender transitions may endogenously choose whether or not to transition based on their anticipated earnings from this change. For example, MTFs who expect to experience economic losses due to working as women may be less likely to make this transition. On the other hand, FTMs who expect to gain from working as men may be more likely to make this transition. This implies that the transgender population we surveyed is not representative of the actual population of all potential transgender people, as it does not include individuals who want to change their gender but do not because the labor market penalty is too high. If gender transitions are endogenous, this would bias downward the transgender penalty (the intercept $\Delta\gamma$ estimated in (2)) and bias upward the earnings gains to becoming men (the δ parameter in (2)).

Speaking to this potential bias, we find evidence, documented below, that suggests that the age at transition is influenced by earnings considerations, as MTFs are considerably older on average at the time of their transitions than FTMs. Thus, it may be that MTFs are waiting to transition at a later age because they want to maintain "male" earnings for as long as possible. FTMs, in contrast, may be transitioning earlier because they anticipate they will earn more once they enter the workforce as men. There is some evidence to support this interpretation. Bolin (1988) and Griggs (1998) find, for example, that some MTFs live as women but continue to work as men because they do not want to move to "women's work" or experience employment discrimination. Most of them do eventually make the workplace transition, however, as their increasingly feminized appearance becomes harder to account for at work. In a follow-up study

of transgender people who have been accepted for surgery but have not yet undergone a transition, "hesitating" MTFs cite economic concerns, along with health concerns and family concerns, as a justification for their delay (Kockott and Fahrner 1987). This group, however, also is identified as the least psychologically adjusted (compared to those who do transition or to those who still plan to in the near future), suggesting this hesitation is not a tenable position over time.

The importance of living in their desired gender is underscored by the findings that on average both MTFs and FTMs who do transition sacrifice substantial earnings. In Table 2, the transgender penalty (the intercept) is estimated to be large for both MTFs and FTMs. The penalty for the gender transition is large enough that it nearly offsets the gains to becoming men for FTMs, so that for FTMs there is essentially no change in earnings on average after their transitions. This willingness to give up earnings in order to live in their desired gender is supported by qualitative data in which interviewed FTMs expect employment discrimination but decide to transition anyway (Schilt 2006a). We interpret this evidence as suggestive that, while there is a population of people who may not transition for a variety of reasons, most transgender people do eventually transition.

Timing of Transition

One of the more salient patterns evident in the transgender sample is the stark difference in the timing of the gender transition: MTFs transition on average 9.6 years after FTMs. As seen in Table 1, MTFs on average remain in their male gender until age 40, whereas FTMs on average transition at age 30. This later age at transition is consistent with the hypothesis that MTFs seek to preserve working as men as long as possible. We argue that this difference suggests that some MTFs anticipate that their pre-transition human capital will not receive the same value after they become women. As women workers, however, FTMs may feel that they have less to lose and potentially more to gain from making the transition to become men at work.

Table 3 explores whether this difference in age at transition is robust to the inclusion of control

Table 3. Age at Gender Change

Variables	1	2	3	4
Intercept	39.56***	30.68***	28.34***	28.12***
	(2.57)	(3.77)	(3.80)	(4.33)
FTM	−9.60**	−10.36***	−8.91**	−7.74*
	(3.36)	(2.94)	(2.97)	(2.94)
College Degree	—	10.62	8.03	9.76
		(3.84)	(4.04)	(3.79)
White Race	—	6.32	4.56	3.36
		(3.23)	(3.25)	(3.03)
White Collar Before Job	—	−0.66	0.09	−2.07
		(3.97)	(4.02)	(3.90)
Same Job Before and After	—	—	6.85*	2.42
			(3.15)	(3.29)
Years Worked at Before Job	—	—	—	0.67*
				(0.26)
Observations	43	43	43	43
R-Squared	0.166	0.414	0.482	0.585
Adjusted R-Squared	0.145	0.352	0.396	0.488

Notes: Standard errors in parentheses. FTM is Female-to-Male. The dependent variable is the age at which the transgender respondents reported completing their gender change. *p <0.05; **p< 0.01; ***p < 0.001 (two-tailed tests). Models 2–4 include missing variable flags.

variables. The dependent variable for the regression models in Table 3 is the age at which the respondent was last employed before beginning his or her gender transition. The regression models are estimated on the pooled FTM and MTF samples. Model 1 includes an intercept and a dummy variable for FTMs. The estimated intercept replicates the MTF average age at gender transition reported in Table 1. The estimated coefficient on the FTM dummy variable for Model 1 is −9.60, indicating that FTMs transition 9.6 years earlier than MTFs. This coefficient estimate is statistically significant at the 1 percent level.

Models 2–4 in Table 3 add various covariates to the regression model as controls for education, demographics, and pre-transition employment. Looking across the regression models in Table 3, the estimated coefficient on the FTM dummy variable remains statistically significant at the 5 percent level or higher. In Model 2, inclusion of dummy variables for college degree, white race, and white-collar employment before gender change increases the estimated difference between the age at gender

change for FTMs and MTFs to −10.36, indicating that FTMs change their gender 10.36 years earlier than MTFs. Model 3 in Table 3 adds a dummy variable (*Same Job Before and After*), which indicates whether the respondent continued to be employed in the same job following his or her gender transition. Inclusion of this variable reduces the estimated coefficient on the FTM dummy variable to −8.91, but it is still significantly different from 0 at the 1 percent level.

Interestingly, the estimated coefficient on the *Same Job Before and After* variable indicates that transgender people who keep the same job following their gender change wait nearly 7 additional years to change their gender than transgender people who get new jobs after transition. To see whether or not this finding reflects strategic behavior to delay a gender transition until stable employment is attained, Model 4 adds to the regression model the number of years respondents report holding their jobs before their gender transition (*Years Worked at Before Job*). The estimated coefficient on this variable is 0.67 and is statistically significant at the

5 percent level. This indicates that both MTFs and FTMs who have accumulated valuable workplace experience in a particular job choose to delay their gender transitions, possibly to avoid disruption to their employment. Taken together, Models 3 and 4 provide additional evidence that the age at gender change is strategically chosen to avoid workplace losses and employment discrimination anticipated to accompany gender transitions.

Other Employment Outcomes

Looking beyond earnings, MTFs in our sample seem to experience a wider range of workplace hardships in becoming women than FTMs experience in becoming men. Survey respondents were provided a blank space to write comments about their workplace experiences. Five FTMs elected to write comments. All five praised their workplaces for their tolerance and acceptance. One respondent in a blue-collar job wrote: "My transition went extremely smoothly. I was shocked at how smooth. No one even talks about it and it had no effect on my pay. If anything, I have been better accepted at work because people don't see me as a dyke like before." The two MTFs who wrote comments, in contrast, emphasized workplace dilemmas. One respondent who transitioned in a blue-collar job she had worked in for twenty years as a man wrote that the women's restroom she used was "booby trapped," and mean notes were left on her desk telling her to quit. Another MTF wrote: "I was 'laid off' from my 10 year management position for having a 'bad attitude.'" She noted that she was laid off the first week that she began coming to work dressed in women's clothing. These comments certainly are not a systematic sample. However, they suggest that MTFs cannot take their masculine workplace advantage with them into womanhood.

Further supporting our argument that a workplace gender penalty often accompanies the move from male-to-female, Schilt (2006a) finds that MTFs experience a much wider range of obstacles to openly transitioning and remaining in the same jobs than their FTM counterparts. In a content analysis of news stories and legal cases about transgender employment from 1977–2005,

Schilt shows that many MTFs experience harassment and often termination once they begin their gender transitions, even when they transition in jobs they have held for many years. Some of the most virulent harassment is experienced by MTFs in blue-collar occupations. This is an unsurprising finding, as blue-collar occupations are associated with homophobia and sexism (Welsh 1999). However, what is interesting about this blue-collar context is that in these news stories and legal cases, MTFs reported fitting into this masculine workplace culture prior to their gender transition. That pre-transition MTFs conformed to and benefited from masculine workplace gender norms in blue-collar occupations suggests that they have a great-deal to lose when they become women, even though they retain their human capital and prior male socialization. We argue that the losses which accompany becoming women accounts for why MTFs in our sample may delay transitioning, as well as why some MTFs live full-time as women outside of the workplace but continue to work as men for as long as possible (Griggs 1998).

In contrast, Schilt (2006a) found that FTMs experience fewer obstacles to open workplace transitions than their MTF counterparts. In in-depth interviews with FTMs in California, Schilt (2006b) found that many of her respondents experienced an increase in authority, reward, and respect at work once they began working as men—even when they remained in the same jobs they had as women. While FTMs were subjected to feminine gender socialization as children, and had the same skills and abilities as they had as women workers, becoming men brought positive workplace outcomes.[11] Not being male-socialized may mean that FTMs benefit less than male-born men, as male-born men may be socialized to be more aggressive about seeking workplace rewards (Padavic and Reskin 2002). However, many FTMs generally are not penalized for their gender transitions, even though they, like MTFs, are making a "discredited identity" (Goffman 1963) public. Placing our survey data in context with this previous research suggests that being a man garners more workplace rewards than being a woman, even net of all other omitted variables.

Is It Gender or Appearance?

In analyzing the before and after gender change workplace experiences of transgender people, an important question is whether their workplace outcomes are due to changes in gender or changes in appearance. Prior research suggests that the appearance and attractiveness of workers does affect their labor market outcomes (Biddle and Hamermesh 1994; Biddle and Hamermesh 1998). Since transgender people can undergo a number of changes to their physical appearance in the process of their transition, they may be adversely affected by a non-normative appearance. The effects of hormone therapy, the physical structure of male bodies, and the different level of appearance scrutiny of men and women can cause MTFs to face more difficulties passing in their new gender than their FTM counterparts. With the use of testosterone, many FTMs develop thicker facial and body hair, deeper voices, and male-pattern baldness (Rubin 2003; Green 2004). With these masculine appearance cues, they are read as men in interactions often within a few weeks of beginning hormone therapy. Estrogen has fewer feminizing effects on male bodies. MTFs may experience some breast growth, but they do not stop growing facial hair or develop higher voices (Griggs 1998). Estrogen cannot alter physical characteristics that are typically interpreted as masculine, such as height over six feet, visible Adam's apples, and big hands and feet. MTFs can use feminine appearance cues as passing aids, such as feminine clothing, but these often cannot override masculine body cues.

This difference in post-gender change appearance is clearly evident in our survey data. Fifty-six percent of FTM respondents describe themselves as "always" passing as men. In contrast, 17 percent of MTFs describe themselves as "always" passing as women. Some MTFs who had been transitioned for over ten years still described themselves as only passing "sometimes." Some of the adverse employment outcomes for MTFs which we document above may be attributable to their changed appearance rather than to their changed gender.

However, we argue that gender is still likely a leading cause of the before and after differences we document for transgender workers. Ethnographic research suggests that men express concern about their MTF colleagues' work abilities *as women*, not because of their appearance (Schilt and Connell 2007). Demonstrating this anxiety, one MTF who had co-owned a business with two other men was asked, post-transition, if she was still going to be able to run a company if she was always "thinking about nail polish" (Schilt and Connell 2007:606). Additionally, as many FTMs pass successfully as men within a short time of beginning hormone therapy, we can more confidently argue that the workplace benefits they experience are related to becoming men.

Conclusion

This study uses the pre- and post-transition experiences of transgender workers as a novel way to explore the factors that contribute to the persistence of gendered workplace disparities. As existing surveys can neither measure discrimination directly nor measure all the relevant characteristics of men and women, we use the before and after workplace outcomes for transgender people as a unique test of omitted variables theories of workplace gender inequality. The statistical analysis shows that transgender people in our sample are relatively comparable to the general population before their gender transitions in many dimensions, although, notably, transgender people are more educated. Analyzing the earnings of transgender workers before and after their gender changes, we find that MTFs experience a substantial and statistically significant decrease in earnings while FTMs experience either no change or a slight increase. These findings suggest that the male gender carries a workplace benefit that cannot be carried over in a gender transition. That MTFs cannot take male privilege with them into womanhood may account for their significantly later age at transition than their FTM counterparts.

There are a number of limitations to this study. The small size of our sample reduces the precision of our statistical findings and precludes extensive multivariate analysis. A second limitation is our inability to control for the non-normative appearance of post-transition transgender people. Because of this limitation, the outcomes we document for gender transitions may be conflated with appearance discrimination. In an ideal experiment, we could compare a group of transgender people who definitely pass as women with a group who do not to gain a deeper understanding of how appearance interacts with gender to affect workplace outcomes. A third limitation of our study is that gender transitions do not occur overnight as in the ideal experiment, but may in fact take several years.

Future research can build upon this study in several ways. First, replicating this study with a longitudinal study of transgender workers that tracks earnings and other workplace outcomes long after initial transitions could illuminate whether these gains and losses associated with gender changes plateau or expand. Second, future studies could extend the analysis of before and after workplace outcomes beyond earnings and more traditionally measured workplace outcomes. As we discuss above, many of the forms of gender inequality are subtle, but can become apparent in an in-depth, qualitative examination of the experiences of transgender workers.

The experience of Ben Barres, an FTM neurobiology professor at Stanford, underscores the importance of these subtle forms of gender inequality. As a woman who excelled in math and science, Barres recounts constantly having her intellectual abilities questioned and undermined (Begley 2006). As a man, however, audiences who do not know about his gender change tell him that his scholarly research is much better than that of "his sister." Barres' experiences show how socially constructed beliefs about men and women's natural abilities cloud perceptions and evaluations, thus producing gendered workplace disparities. Our study demonstrates that the workplace experiences of transgender people are a fruitful way to explore these long-standing debates about gender and work, as they clearly illuminate the impact of subtle assumptions about inevitable gender differences on men and women's workplace outcomes.

Notes

1. "Transgender" is an umbrella term that encompasses a wide variety of people who cross socially constructed gender boundaries in some way (Meyerowitz 2002). For instance, people who choose to undergo gender transitions via hormone therapy and genital surgery can be referred to as transgender, as can individuals who cross-dress on occasion. For the purposes of our paper, we are using the term "transgender" to refer to individuals who are working in a gender other than that which they were assigned at birth. Some of our respondents transition medically using hormones and surgical body modifications, while others do not. We discuss this further in the section on appearance discrimination and workplace outcomes.

2. The total percentage of transgender people and the gender breakdown of that percentage are widely contested. The .01% was estimated by the number of people seeking genital surgery. This estimation is flawed, however, as many FTMs and MTFs do not undergo genital surgery (Meyerowitz 2002; Green 2004). Additionally, as MTFs have sought out institutionalized services more frequently than FTMs, there long has been an assumption that there are more men becoming women than vice versa. Transgender community estimates, however, place the percentage as much higher (see Conway 2001 for a discussion of this percentage) and argue for a more equal gender breakdown (Califia 1998; Meyerowitz 2003).

3. Blau, Brinton, and Grusky (2006) provide a recent review of some of the major theories.

4. The actual text of these standards is available at http://wpath.org/Documents2/socv6.pdf.

5. Measuring the start of a gender transition is difficult. Many transgender people feel that they have been in the process of transitioning since childhood, as they might adopt appearance and behavior cues of their destination gender long before they decide to undergo any physical body modifications. The phrasing of this question was designed to create a uniform starting point for transition, i.e., the point at which transgender people seek to have their new gender recognized by their co-workers and employers. *Starting point*

6. Although recall bias for past earnings is a concern, it is not clear that this would bias the results in terms of the differences between FTMs and MTFs in any particular direction.

7. Our CPS sample includes all adults age 18 or older who report working at least 1 hour the past year

can't really measure the start of gender transition

for pay. The demographic, education, occupation, and industry questions in this survey are nearly identical to those in our transgender survey. For the CPS data, we construct as closely as possible an equivalent measure of hourly earnings using reported hours worked during the year and usual hours worked per week. Earnings for the CPS comparison sample are adjusted for inflation and expressed in 2004 dollars.

8. To address the difference in the distribution of ages in the transgender sample relative to the general population, we calculate average hourly earnings using the distribution of ages in the CPS data to weight the transgender sample to be representative of the general population. In results available on request, we find that mean hourly earnings for the transgender sample change only slightly using the age-weighted sample.

9. Sample distribution of these variables: gain degree (3 gain degree, 39 no change, 1 missing), change to white collar (4 change to white collar, 36 no change, 2 change to blue collar, 1 missing), change to private sector (2 change to private sector, 34 no change, 6 change to public sector, 1 missing).

10. In some cases, transgender people lose some of their human capital, as they cannot always take their work and education history with them into their new gender if they intend to successfully pass. However, as more transgender people are openly identifying as transgender, this has become less of an issue. Additionally, FTMs might be expected to suffer most from this, as they can more easily find jobs as "just men" because they pass more successfully in their new gender than MTFs (Griggs 1998; Schilt 2006a). Yet, as we show in this study, even if this is occurring, FTMs experience a gain in earnings relative to MTFs.

11. As some evidence on the heterogeneity of the outcomes for transgender people, Schilt (2006) shows that FTMs who were white benefited more than FTMs who were black, Latino, or Asian.

References

Acker, J. 1990. "Hierarchies, jobs, bodies: A theory of gendered organizations." *Gender & Society* 4 (2): 139–158.

Altonji, J. G. and R. M. Blank. 1999. "Race and gender in the labor market." In *Handbook of labor*

economics, vol. 3, edited by O. Ashenfelter and D. Card. New York: Elsevier Sci.

Arrow, K. 1973. "The theory of discrimination." In *Discrimination in labor markets*, edited by O. Ashenfelter and A. Rees. Princeton: Princeton University Press.

Becker, G. S. 1971. *The economics of discrimination*, 2nd Edition. Chicago: University of Chicago Press, originally published 1957.

Begley, S. 2006. "He, once she, offers own view on science spat." *The Washington Post*. July 13: BI.

Benjamin, H. 1966. *The transsexual phenomenon*. New York: Warner Books.

Biddle, J. E., and D. Hamermesh. 1994. "Beauty and the labor market." *American Economic Review* 84 (5): 1174–94.

———. 1998. "Beauty, productivity, and discrimination: Lawyers' looks and lucre." *Journal of Labor Economics* 16 (1): 172–201.

Bird, S. 1996. "Welcome to the men's club: Homosociality and the maintenance of hegemonic masculinity." *Gender & Society* 10 (2): 120–32.

Blau, F. D., and L. M. Kahn. 2006. "The gender pay gap: Going, going…but not gone." In *The declining significance of gender?*, edited by F. D. Blau, M. C. Brinton, and D. B. Grusky. New York: Russell Sage Foundation.

Bolin, A. 1988. *In search of Eve: Transsexual rites of passage*. South Hadley, MA: Bergin & Garvey.

Bowlus, A., and Z. Eckstein. 2002. "Discrimination and skill differences in an equilibrium search model." *International Economic Review* 43 (4): 1309–45.

Brown, C., and M. Corcoran. 1997. "Sex-based differences in school content and the male/female wage gap." *Journal of Labor Economics* 15 (3): 431–65.

Byrd, B. 1999. "Women in carpentry apprenticeship: A case study." *Labor Studies Journal* 24 (3): 3–22.

Califia, P. 1997. *Sex changes: The politics of transgender*. San Francisco: Clevis Press.

Conway, L. 2001. "How frequently does transsexualism occur?" Accessed online on February 9, 2008 at http://ai.eecs.umich.edu/people/conway/TS/TSprevalence.html.

Corcoran, M. E., and P. N. Courant. 1985. "Sex role socialization and labor market outcomes." *American Economic Review, Papers and Proceedings* 75 (2): 275–78.

Feinbloom, D. 1976. *Transvestites and transsexuals.* New York: Delta Books.

Fuller, R., and R. Schoenberger. 1991. "The gender salary gap: Do academic achievement, internship experience, and. college major make a difference?" *Social Science Quarterly* 72: 715–26.

Goffman, E. 1963. *Stigma.* New York: Prentice Hall.

Goldin, C. 1990. *Understanding the gender gap: An economic history of American women.* New York: Oxford University Press.

Gould, R. 1974. "Measuring masculinity by the size of a paycheck." In *Men & masculinity*, edited by J. Pleck and J. Sawyer. Englewood Cliffs, NJ: Prentice Hall.

Green, J. 2004. *Becoming a visible man.* Nashville: Vanderbilt University Press.

Griggs, C. 1998. *S/he: Changing sex and changing clothes.* New York: Berg.

Groshen, E. L. 1991. "The structure of the female/male wage differential." *Journal of Human Resources* 26: 457–72.

Hochschild, A. R. 1983. *The managed heart: Commercialization of human feeling.* Berkeley: University of California Press.

Hore, B. D., F. V. Nicolle, and J. S. Calnan. 1975. "Male transsexualism in England: Sixteen cases with surgical intervention." *Archives of Sexual Behavior* 4 (1): 81–88.

Kando, T. 1973. *Sex change: The achievement of gender identity among feminized transsexuals.* Springfield, IL: Charles C. Thomas Publisher.

Kanter, R. M. 1977. *Men and women of the corporation.* New York: Basic Books.

Kimmel, M. 2000. *The gendered society.* New York: Oxford University Press.

Kockott, G., and E. M. Fahrner. 1987. "Transsexuals who have not undergone surgery: A follow-up study." *Archives of Sexual Behavior* 16 (6): 511–23.

Kuiper, B., and P. T. Cohen-Kettenis. 1988. "Sex reassignment surgery: A study of 141 Dutch transsexuals." *Archives of Sexual Behavior* 17: 439–57.

Laub, D., and N. Fisk. 1974. "A rehabilitation program for gender dysphoria syndrome and surgical sex change." *Plastic and Reconstructive Surgery* 53: 388–403.

Lawrence, A. 2003. "Factors associated with satisfaction or regret following male-to-female sex reassignment surgery." *Archives of Sexual Behavior* 32:299–315.

Leidner, R. 1993. *Fast food, fast talk: Service work and the routinization of everyday life.* Berkeley: University of California Press.

Lindemalm, G., D. Korlin, and N. Uddenberg. 1986. "Long-term follow-up of 'sex change' in 13 male-to-female transsexuals." *Archives of Sexual Behavior* 15: 187–210.

Lothstein, L. 1983. *Female-to-male transsexualism: Historical, clinical and theoretical issues.* Boston: Routledge & Kegan Paul.

Marini, M. 1989. "Sex differences in earnings in the United States." *Annual Review of Sociology* 15: 348–80.

Martin, P. Y. 2003. "'Said and done' versus 'saying and doing': Gendering practices, practicing gender at work." *Gender & Society* 17 (3): 342–66.

McCloskey, D. 1999. *Crossing: A memoir.* Chicago: University of Chicago Press.

Meyerowitz, J. 2002. *How sex changed: A history of transsexuality in the United States.* Cambridge, MA: Harvard University Press.

Miller, L. 1997. "Not just weapons of the weak: Gender harassment as a form of protest for army men." *Social Psychology Quarterly* 60 (1): 32–51.

Moro, A., and P. Norman. 2004. "A general equilibrium model of statistical discrimination." *Journal of Economic Theory* 114: 1–30.

Moss, P., and C. Tilly, 2001. *Stories employers tell: Race, skill, and hiring in America.* New York: Russell Sage.

Paap, K. 2005. *Working construction.* New York: Cornell University Press.

Padavic, I., and B. Reskin. 2002. *Women and men at work*, 2nd ed. Thousand Oaks: Pine Forge Press.

Paglin, M., and A. M. Rufolo. 1990. "Heterogeneous human capital, occupation choice, and male-female earnings differences." *Journal of Labor Economics* 8: 123–44.

Perkins, R. 1983. *The 'drag queen' scene: Transsexuals in Kings Cross.* Sydney: George Allen & Unwin.

Phelps, E. S. 1972. "The statistical theory of racism and sexism." *American Economic Review* 62 (4): 659–61.

Rakic, Z., V. Starcevic, J. Maric, and K. Kelin. 1996. "The outcome of sex reassignment surgery in Belgrade: 32 patients of both sexes." *Archives of Sexual Behavior* 25: 515–25.

Rubin, H. 2003. *Self made men: Identity and embodiment among transsexual men.* Nashville, TN: Vanderbilt University Press.

Schafer, S. 2001. "More transgenders start new life with old jobs." *Times-Picayune* (February 4). Living: 15.

Schilt, K. 2006a. "Just one of the guys? How female-to-male transsexuals make gender inequality at work visible." Ph.D. dissertation, Department of Sociology, University of California–Los Angeles.

———. 2006b. "Just one of the guys? How transmen make gender visible at work." *Gender & Society* 20 (4): 465–490.

Schilt, K., and C. Connell. 2007. "Do workplace gender transitions make gender trouble?" *Gender, Work and Organization* 14(6): 596–618.

Sorensen, T. 1981a. "Follow-up study of operated transsexual males." *Acta Psychiatria Scandanavica* 63: 486–503.

———. 1981b. "Follow-up study of operated transsexual females." *Acta Psychiatria Scandanavica* 64: 50–64.

Subich, L., G. Barret, D. Doverspike, and R. Alexander. 1989. "The effects of sex role related factors on occupational choice and salary." In *Pay equity: Empirical inquiries*, edited by R. Michael, H. Hartmann, and B. O'Farrell. Washington, DC: National Academy Press: 45–62.

Valian, V. 1999. *Why so slow?: The advancement of women.* Cambridge, MA: MIT Press.

Welsh, S. 1999. "Gender and sexual harassment." *Annual Review of Sociology* 25: 169–90.

Williams, C. 1995. *Still a man's world: Men who do women's work.* Berkeley: University of California Press.

Wood, R. G., M. E. Corcoran, and P. N. Courant. 1993. "Pay differentials among the highly paid: The male-female earnings gap in lawyers' salaries." *Journal of Labor Economics* 11 (3): 417–41.

Yoder, J., and P. Aniakudo. 1997. "Outsider within the firehouse: Subordination and difference in the social interactions of African American women firefighters." *Gender and Society* 11 (3): 324–41.

The Gendered Media

Do the media *cause* violence, or do the media simply reflect the violence that already exists in our society? Think of how many times we have heard variations of this debate: Does gangsta rap or violent video games or violent movies or violent heavy metal music lead to increased violence? Does violent pornography lead men to commit rape? Or do these media merely remind us of how violent our society already is?

And how do the various media contribute to our understanding of gender? What role do the various media play in the maintenance of gender difference or gender inequality?

Like other social institutions, the media are a gendered institution. The media (1) reflect already existing gender differences and gender inequalities, (2) construct those very gender differences, and (3) reproduce gender inequality by making those differences seem "natural" and not socially produced in the first place. Part of its function of maintaining inequality is to first create the differences, and then to attempt to conceal its authorship so that those differences seem to flow from the nature of things.

Media reflect already existing gender differences and inequalities by targeting different groups of consumers with different messages that assume prior existing differences. In a sense, women and men don't use or consume the same media—there are women's magazines and men's magazines, chick flicks and action movies, chick lit and lad lit, pornography and romance novels, soap operas and crime procedurals, guy video games and girl video games, blogs, and 'zines—and, of course, advertising that is intricately connected to each of these different formats. As with other institutions, there are "his" and "hers" media.

Not only his and hers, but also "ours" and "theirs." Jane Brown and Carol Pardun find that girls and boys may watch different television shows, but, more significantly, blacks and whites watch different shows. When they do "cross over" it's almost entirely in one direction—one group watches the other's shows. Which way do you think it goes? Do whites watch black-themed shows, or do blacks watch white-themed shows?

The essays in this part explore the gendering of the media, and the gendering of people *through* the media. From video games (Kathy Sanford and Leanna Madill), Disney movies (Ken Gillam and Shannon Wooden), and rap music (Ronald Weitzer and Charis Kubrin), people draw gendered images and both reinforce and resist the dominant images of women and men.

Misogyny in Rap Music: A Content Analysis of Prevalence and Meanings

RONALD WEITZER AND CHARIS E. KUBRIN

That's the way the game goes, gotta keep it strictly pimpin',
> Gotta have my hustle tight, makin' change off these women.
>> You know it's hard out here for a primp,
>> When he tryin' to get this money for the rent.
>>> *"It's Hard Out Here For a Pimp"*
>>> *—Three 6 Mafia*

The 2005 Academy Award for best original song in a feature film went to Three 6 Mafia's controversial "It's Hard Out Here For a Pimp" from the film *Hustle and Flow*. The song was performed at the Oscars, and immediately provoked a storm of criticism for glorifying the exploitation of women. This is only the most recent chapter in the mounting criticism directed at rap music's presentation of women. A few years earlier, rapper Eminem won a Grammy for his 2001 album, *The Marshall Mathers LP*—an album whose lyrics contained extreme hostility and violence toward women. Women's groups promptly condemned the award. More recently, the African American women's magazine *Essence* launched a campaign in 2005 against sexism in rap music. The magazine lamented the depiction of black women in rap and solicited feedback from readers on ways to challenge it.

Much of the criticism of rap music is impressionistic and based on a handful of anecdotes, rather than a systematic analysis. Exactly how prevalent are misogynistic themes in this music, and what specific messages are conveyed to the listeners? The current study addresses this question through a content analysis of over 400 rap songs. We document five themes related to the portrayal of women in rap music and link them to the larger cultural and music industry norms and the local, neighborhood conditions that inspired this music.

Images of Women in Popular Music

Gender stereotypes are abundant in popular music, where women are often presented as inferior to men or are trivialized and marginalized (Tuchman 1978). Women are not portrayed monolithically, however (Butruille and Taylor 1987; Lay 2000; van Zoonen 1994), and lyrical depictions appear to have changed somewhat over time. It has been argued that the overall trend is one of "greater diversity, more complexity, and dramatically mixed messages about the individual female persona and women's roles in society" (Cooper 1999, 355). Despite this variegation, it remains uncommon for women to be presented as independent, intelligent, enterprising, or superior to men (Cooper 1999). Derogatory images are far more common.

A body of research documents depictions of men and women in different genres. A content analysis of rock music videos found that a majority (57 percent) presented women in a "condescending" manner (e.g., unintelligent, sex object, victim) and one-fifth placed them in a traditional sex role (e.g., subservient, nurturing, domestic roles), while 8 percent displayed male violence against women (Vincent, Davis, and Boruszkowski 1987). Only

Ronald Weitzer and Charis E. Kubrin, "Misogyny in Rap Music: A Content Analysis of Prevalence and Meanings" from *Men and Masculinities* 2009; 12: 3–29.

14 percent presented women as fully equal to men. A more recent study of rock videos found that traditional sex role stereotypes continue to predominate: 57 percent of videos in which women were present depicted them in a "conventional" manner (passive, dependent on men, "accentuating" physical appearance), while a third presented them as strong and independent (Alexander 1999).

Country music also casts women in subordinate roles. A study of 203 country music videos featuring male performers found that two-thirds devalued women (portraying them in a condescending manner or in traditional roles), while only 9 percent presented women as fully equal to men (Andsager and Roe 1999). Of the 80 videos by female artists, by contrast, half fit the fully equal category. Interestingly, country songs and videos do not feature violence against women or portray them as strippers and prostitutes, apparently because of strong industry norms against such images (Andsager and Roe 1999, 81). In fact, one study found that country music advertisers pressure radio stations to screen out misogynistic songs in order to attract desired female listeners (Ryan and Peterson 1982).

Although rap music has been a topic of heated public debate for years, systematic content analyses are rare. One analysis of rap and heavy metal songs from 1985–1990 found that rap was more sexually explicit and graphic, whereas heavy metal's allusions to sexual acts or to male domination were fairly subtle (Binder 1993), which is consistent with other studies of heavy metal songs and videos that have found that "blatant abuse of women is uncommon" in this genre (Walser 1993, 117). Binder's comparative analysis was limited to only 20 songs which she deemed "controversial," and the time period examined preceded rap's ascendancy in the music field. In a unique study of Chicano rap songs from 1999–2002, McFarland (2003) identified two main themes: a critique of racial inequality and injustice and an endorsement of male supremacy over women. Of the 263 songs that mentioned women, 37 percent depicted them "simply as objects of male desire and pleasure," while 4 percent justified violence against them. McFarland's sampling frame was based on songs he identified as popular in focus

groups and on the Brown Pride web site, rather than a more objective measure of popularity. Armstrong (2001) conducted a content analysis of 490 rap songs during 1987–1993. Lyrics featuring violence against women were found in 22 percent of the songs, and the violence perpetrated against women included assault, rape, and murder. Although his study makes a valuable contribution to the literature in its systematic focus on violence against women, it does not discuss other (nonviolent) depictions of women, provides little indication of coding procedures, and presents the lyrics in a brief and sketchy manner, decontextualized from larger song segments. Other content analyses of rap music (Kubrin 2005a, 2005b; Martinez 1997) do not examine the depiction of women or gender relations more broadly. The present essay addresses this issue.

Social Sources of Rap Lyrics

Most of the studies reviewed previously did not attempt to *explain why* lyrics portray women as they do—an admittedly difficult task. Yet artists do not work in a vacuum. We suggest that rappers whose songs portray women negatively are influenced by three major social forces: larger gender relations, the music industry, and local neighborhood conditions. The most diffuse influence is the larger gender order, which includes the cultural valorization of a certain type of masculinity. *Hegemonic masculinity* has been defined as attitudes and practices that perpetuate heterosexual male domination over women. It involves "the currently most honored way of being a man, it requires all other men to position themselves in relation to it, and it ideologically legitimates the global subordination of women to men" (Connell and Messerschmidt 2005, 832). For this type of masculinity, to be a "man" requires the acceptance of attitudes that objectify women, practices that subordinate them, and derogation of men who adopt an egalitarian orientation, equally affirmative of men and women and all sexual orientations (Connell 1987; Connell and Messerschmidt 2005; Donaldson 1993). Hegemonic masculinity exists alongside and in competition with what Connell calls "subordinated masculinities," and to remain normative, it requires ongoing reproduction via the mass media, the patriarchal family, and other socializing institutions. Media representations of men, for example, often glorify men's use of physical force, a daring demeanor, virility, and emotional distance (see Hanke 1998). Popular music is a case in point: As indicated by the studies reviewed previously, only a minority of songs, across music genres, espouse egalitarian gender relations or alternative masculinities, whereas the majority can be viewed as texts on hegemonic masculinity. We argue that rap, like the other music genres, is part of this broader culture of gender relations, even as some of the music challenges the dominant culture (Lay 2000).[1]

Some argue that popular music over the past three decades is also part of a larger cultural resistance to feminism, an attempt to block progress toward gender equality and resuscitate male domination. As Lay (2000, 239) argues, "Popular music can be read as a vehicle for heterosexual male concerns [over the advancement of women and gays] and, more importantly, for the recuperation of hegemonic masculinity." Stated differently, this music can be seen as part of a larger ideological process of persuading the population that heterosexual male supremacy is natural and normal. Rap is part of this backlash. Collins (2000, 82, 144) considers rap to be one of the contemporary "controlling images" used to subordinate black women, and Oliver (2006, 927) argues that rap's sexist lyrics "provide justifications for engaging in acts of violence against black women" (see also hooks 1994; Rhym 1997). But it may also be seen as an effort to control *all* women, since rap is consumed by youth from all racial and ethnic groups. Such images have real-world effects insofar as they contribute to gendered socialization and perpetuate gender inequality (Barongan and Hall 1995; Johnson, Adams, Ashburn, and Reed 1995; Martino et al. 2006; Wester, Crown, Quatman, and Heesacker 1997).

Rap artists are also influenced by pressures from elites in the music industry. To maximize sales, record industry moguls encourage provocative, edgy lyrics. Producers not only encourage artists to become "hardcore" but they also reject or marginalize artists who go against the grain. As a result of such practices, a directly proportional relationship has developed between rap music's explicitness and the sale of its records.

In response to corporate pressures, many rappers abandon political and social messages and focus instead on material wealth and sexual exploits (Powell 2000). In his documentary, "Hip-Hop: Beyond Beats and Rhymes," Byron Hurt (2007) asks one aspiring rapper why rap artists focus on violence and misogyny. The rapper freestyles a verse about whether he could have been a doctor, a father, or police officer. He then says, "That's nice, but nobody wanna hear that right now. They don't accept that shit." When Hurt asks, "Who is 'they'," the rapper answers, "The industry. They usually don't give us deals when we speak righteously." Indeed, Kitwana (1994, 23) finds that artists in search of securing record deals are often told their message is not hard enough, they are too clean cut, that "hardcore" is what is selling now, and that they should no longer engage in social commentary (see also Krims 2000:71). The consequence? According to Smith (1997, 346), "Many of today's rappers make the ghetto visible in order to sell and to be sold."

The pressure for artists to rap about hardcore themes is perhaps most evident in gangsta rap.[2] A statement by Carmen Ashhurst-Watson, former President of Def Jam Records, is revealing:

> The time when we switched to gangsta music was the same time that the majors [record companies] bought up all the [independent] labels. And I don't think that's a coincidence. At the time that we were able to get a bigger place in the record stores, and a bigger presence because of this major marketing capacity, the music became less and less conscious. (Ashhurst-Watson, quoted in Hurt 2007)

Her account is confirmed by recent research which documents that as rap increasingly became produced by major record labels, its content became more hardcore to encourage sales. In a longitudinal analysis of rap music production and lyrical content, Lena (2006, 488) finds that "starting in 1988 the largest record corporations charted substantially more 'hardcore' rap songs than did independent labels. In the eight years between 1988 and 1995, majors charted up to five-and-a-half times as many hardcore rap singles as all their independent competitors combined." She concludes that "major record labels produced the majority of puerile rap" during this later time period. This was in stark contrast to earlier periods of production where rap lyrics emphasized features of the local environment and hostility to corporate music production and values.

The bias fostered by record companies is recapitulated in the kind of rap music that gets the greatest airplay on radio stations. Hip-hop historian Kevin Powell points out that "in every city you go to in America... [rap stations are] playing the same 10–12 songs over and over again. So what it does is perpetuate the mindset that the only way you can be a man—a black man, a Latino man—is if you hard. To denigrate women. To denigrate homosexuals. To denigrate each other. To kill each other" (Kevin Powell, quoted in Hurt 2007). This privileging of hegemonic masculinity and negative depiction of women is driven by an interest in selling records (Rhym 1997). As long as this type of music continues to sell, "record labels will continue to put ethics and morality aside to release [violent or sexist rap]" (McAdams and Russell 1991, R-22).

Consumers play a key role in this process. Misogynistic representations of women and the more general marketing of "hood narratives" (Watkins 2001: 389) occur, in part, in response to a perceived consumer demand for stereotypical representations of the ghetto, and specifically of young black men and women. Listeners of rap, many of whom are white youth, can vicariously experience the ghetto, a place symbolizing danger and deviance (Quinn 2005, 85). As one white listener of rap music claims,

> I've never been to a ghetto. I grew up in upper middle-class, basically white suburbia....And to listen to [rap music] is a way of us to see...a completely different culture. It's something that most of us have never had the opportunity to experience....And the stuff in the music, it appeals to our sense of learning about other cultures and wanting to know more about something that we'll never probably experience. (quoted in Hurt 2007)

Such cross-cultural learning may be quite biased. As Quinn (2005, 91) argues, "with its provocative pop-cultural portrayals of the ghetto, there can be little doubt that gangsta rap helps to reinforce racial stereotypes held by many whites." Indeed, when Hurt asked the white listener quoted above whether the music reinforces stereotypes, she answered affirmatively. While explicit lyrics and misogynistic representations of women have made rap music highly marketable, they have also "reinvigorated popular beliefs about black deviance and social pathology" (Watkins 2001:389). In short, the production and lyrical content of rap music are inextricably linked; as such, music industry interests can be viewed as one important source of rap music lyrics.

Rap music also has local roots, which help shape the content of the lyrics. More so than other genres, rap is a "localized form of cultural expression" (Bennett 1999a, 77; 1999b). Hip hop and rap initially developed out of the lived experiences of youth in disadvantaged, black neighborhoods and was "incubated in the black community's house parties, public parks, housing projects, and local jams" (Powell 1991, 245; Rose 1994a). And although the music industry's influence has become increasingly apparent, even today rap continues to be marketed as a cultural reflection of life on "the streets" of America's inner-cities. In fact, the music industry sends agents into these neighborhoods for the express purpose of gathering "street intelligence" on what is popular; they do this by visiting record stores, clubs, and parties (Negus 1999, 502).

The degree to which a particular music genre, and particularly male artists within that genre, endorse male supremacy in their lyrics may be related to broader, societal opportunities for affirming hegemonic masculinity—opportunities that vary to some extent by racial and class background. Poor, marginalized black males have historically faced obstacles to asserting their masculinity, and they continue to be denied access to conventional institutional avenues through which masculinity may be established. According to Skeggs (1993), music historically served as a medium that provided black men with an alternative resource for asserting their masculinity.

This opportunity structure can be linked specifically to the conditions in disadvantaged neighborhoods. It has been argued that the content of rap music reflects, at least to some extent, gender relations among youth in many inner-city communities. Several ethnographic studies provide evidence of discord between men and women in disadvantaged, minority neighborhoods. The harsh conditions of the ghetto and barrio provide residents with few conventional sources of self-esteem (Bourgois 1995; Horowitz 1983; Liebow 1967), which can lead to unconventional means to win respect. Violence is one means of eliciting respect from others or punishing those who withhold it (Kubrin and Weitzer 2003), but men are also admired for economically and sexually exploiting women. Four decades ago, Liebow's (1967, 140–144) ethnographic study of a low-income, black neighborhood described how important it was for men to be seen as "exploiters of women," even if they did not always treat women in this way. Recent research indicates that exploitation and degradation of young women is still a feature of some inner-city communities today and continues to shape gender relations (Miller and White 2003). Anderson's (1999) study of an African American community identified several dimensions of a distinctive neighborhood culture, what he calls the "code of the street." For many young men in such neighborhoods, the street code places a high value on sexual conquest, promiscuity, and the manipulation of women:

> Because of the implications sex has for their local social status and esteem, the young men are ready to be regaled with graphic tales of one another's sexual exploits....Status goes to the winner, and sex is prized as a testament not of love but of control over another human being. The goal of the sexual conquests is to make a fool of the young woman....[The male] incurs sanctions [from his peers] for allowing a girl to "rule" him or gains positive reinforcement for keeping her in line....In many cases the more the young man seems to exploit the young woman, the higher is his regard within the peer group. (Anderson 1999, 150, 153, 154)

A similar male street culture is documented in an ethnographic study of a Puerto Rican barrio in New York City (Bourgois 1995, 1996). Rooted in conditions of socioeconomic disadvantage which strip men of traditional sources of dignity, this street culture is characterized by a high level of male promiscuity, the "celebration of the gigolo image," the value of "being an economic parasite" on one's girlfriends, and justifications for violence against women (Bourgois 1995, 276–295).

We do not argue that either neighborhood or industry forces, as just described, are necessarily direct causes of the lyrical content or images, but instead that these forces are an essential part of the *context* within which the messages contained in rap are best understood. Our study thus can be situated within the recent literature on gender relations, which recognizes the importance of multiple contexts in which gender roles and identities are reproduced (Connell and Messerschmidt 2005).

Research Methods

The current study focuses on a time period that has not been examined in previous research on this topic. All rap albums from 1992 through 2000 that attained platinum status (selling at least one million copies) were identified (N = 130). Sampling only platinum albums ensured that the music had reached a substantial segment of the population. To identify the sample, we obtained a list of all albums that went platinum between 1992 and 2000 from the Recording Industry Association of America (RIAA). The RIAA, which compiles, analyzes, and reports on the quantity and value of recorded music shipped into market channels, is considered the premier source for comprehensive market data on music trends in the United States. We went through the list and used the web site ARTISTdirect (http:///www.artistdirect.com) to identify "rap" albums. ARTISTdirect is a comprehensive online network of resources that provides, among other things, detailed information about artists/groups. We typed in the name of each artist/group and the web site classified the precise music genre.

Our analysis begins in 1992 because gangsta rap began to flourish around this time (Kelley 1996, 147; Keyes 2002, 104; Kitwana 2002, xiv; Krims 2000, 83; Smith 1997, 346; Watkins 2001, 389).[3] Our interest in this starting point is related to the fact that misogyny and related themes (i.e., violence) are popularly thought to be more prevalent in gangsta rap than in rap generally. Yet these themes are not exclusive to gangsta rap, which is why we selected all rap albums rather than just gangsta albums. As noted by Krims (2000, 87), rap albums typically mix genres and so songs that contain misogynistic lyrics would have been left out of the analysis had we only sampled gangsta rap albums.

The analysis ends in 2000 because that year marked a turning point in the industry's increasing commercialization and greater detachment from its neighborhood sources (Kitwana 1994, 23; Krims 2000, 71; Watkins 2001, 382). This time frame thus captures a period when rap music more closely reflected grass-roots values and local conditions on the street and was somewhat less commercialized then today, although the interests of record labels were important during this time period as well.

The 130 albums contained a total of 1,922 songs. Using Statistical Package for the Social Sciences (SPSS), a simple random sample of 403 songs was drawn and then analyzed.[4] Each song was listened to twice in its entirety by the authors, while simultaneously reading the lyrics. The lyrics were obtained from *The Original Hip-Hop/Rap Lyrics Archive* (www.ohhla.com/all.html). Each line was coded to identify major misogynistic themes. *Misogyny* refers to lyrics that encourage, condone, or glorify the objectification, exploitation, or victimization of women. In cases of uncertainty regarding the meaning of a particular word or phrase, we consulted *The Rap Dictionary* (www.rapdict.org), a comprehensive online dictionary of rap terms. During the coding, careful attention was paid to the context in which the lyrics were stated. This is especially important in rap, given that it is rooted in the Black oral tradition of signifying and other communicative practices (Smitherman 1997, 14). Signifying is a way of speaking that involves ritual insult (commonly referred to as "playing the dozens") and double entendre (Lee 2005, 83; see also Keyes 2002). With signifying, words have alternative meanings beyond their conventional practices and should not necessarily be taken literally. In our coding, we were careful to interpret the lyrics within their larger contexts. Finally, an independent researcher coded a random subset (16 percent of the sample songs) in order to assess inter-coder reliability. With respect to misogyny, agreement occurred in 73.4 percent of the songs, indicating fairly strong consensus.

Findings

Misogyny was present in 22 percent of the 403 songs (N = 90 songs, by 31 rappers).[5] This means that misogyny is much less pervasive in rap music than some critics believe, but is clearly a significant theme. Female rappers accounted for only 5 of the 90 misogynistic songs, as well as an additional 8 songs (out of the remaining 313) that did not have misogynistic lyrics. The scarcity of female artists shows just how male-dominated rap was during this time period, especially at the platinum level (George 1998; Troka 2002, 82). We include a separate analysis of the 8 non-misogynistic songs by female artists for purposes of comparison to the messages contained in our main sample.

Although misogynistic messages appear less frequently in rap than is commonly believed, significance is not simply a matter of frequency. Also important is the nature and intensity of the messages. Our content analysis identified five misogynistic themes that appear with some frequency: (1) derogatory naming and shaming of women, (2) sexual objectification of women, (3) distrust of women, (4) legitimation of violence against women, and (5) celebration of prostitution and pimping. Our presentation of findings identifies the frequency of each theme, substantive messages and subthemes in the lyrics, and the ways in which the lyrics reflect societal gender relations, record industry pressures, and neighborhood conditions in disadvantaged communities.

Table 1. Misogynistic Themes

Theme	Frequency in Songs (%)*
Naming and Shaming	49
Sexual Objectification	67
Can't Trust 'Em	47
Legitimating Violence	18
Prostitutes and Pimps	20

*Frequency in songs identified as misogynistic, not within the larger sample of rap songs (where 22 percent of the songs were categorized as misogynistic).

Naming-and-Shaming

A number of rap songs can be described as a full-fledged "status degradation ceremony" directed at women—a "ritual destruction of the person denounced" (Garfinkle 1956, 421). In these songs, it is typically women in general, rather than a specific person, who are shamed with derogatory names. This theme was present in half (49 percent) of the misogynistic songs.

Our analysis identified instances of naming-and-shaming but, as discussed earlier, we did not automatically assume that all conventionally "negative" labels were necessarily disparaging. For instance, in rap culture the terms "bitch" and "ho" are not necessarily intended to be derogatory, depending on the lyrical context (Keyes 2002; Kitwana 1994, 25). Ice Cube talks about a "wholesome ho," and Too $hort refers to his "finest bitches" and a "top-notch bitch." While recognizing that some listeners consider such terms offensive in all usage, we coded conservatively by including in our naming-and-shaming category only lyrics that were unambiguously derogatory. For example, Eminem's song *Kill You* talks about "vile, venomous, volatile bitches." Other rappers condemn the slut, tramp, whore, hoochie, "lying-ass bitch," "shitty hoe," "prima donna bitch," and so forth. A favorite rap term is "chickenhead," which reduces a woman to a bobbing head giving oral sex. Status degradation was the sole theme of some songs, present in every verse. Sweeping attacks are sometimes generalized, while other lyrics reveal particular rationales for degradation, such as women's failure to cooperate with men:

We couldn't get no play from the ladies
> With seven niggas in a Nav [Navigator] is you crazy?...
> So we all said "fuck you bitch" and kept rolling. (Snoop Dogg, *DP Gangsta*)

Even rappers' female relatives are not immune from such attacks. Eminem says that "all bitches is hoes, even my stinkin' ass mom" (*Under the Influence*). Eminem's unbridled hostility toward all women, including relatives, is somewhat extreme but not unique in this music genre.[6]

The flipside of this naming process is found in lyrics that praise men who treat women poorly. In these lyrics, it is a badge of honor for men to verbally and physically abuse women, and men win respect from other men when they act like "players," "pimps," and exploiters of women—financially, sexually, and emotionally. This theme is reflected throughout the data, closely mirroring the neighborhood street code described by Anderson and others. The variety of disparaging labels for women is not paralleled for men, either in rap or in the larger culture. Insofar as rappers derogate other men, they tend to use feminized terms, such as bitch or pussy—a staple of hegemonic masculinity.

It is important to point out that these lyrics essentialize women by portraying them as inherently "Other" and different from men by nature. Many of the labels refer to women's anatomy or sexuality, and the lyrics endorse the age-old notion that "biology is destiny."

Some rappers report that verbal abuse of women is encouraged and rewarded by the music industry:

> Rappers like me always disrespectin' ladies,
> Wonder why it's like that, well so do I.
> But I just turn my back and then I go get high,
> 'Cause I get paid real good to talk bad about a bitch.
> And you bought it, so don't be mad I got rich. (Too $hort, *Thangs Change*)

In an interview, Brother Marquis from 2 Live Crew echoed these sentiments: "I'm degrading [women] to try to get me some money.... And besides, you let me do that. You got pimps out here who are making you sell your body. Just let me talk about you for a little while…and make me a little money" (quoted in Collins 2000, 143–144). By this logic, because women are already exploited by pimps, there is no harm in subjecting them to lyrical shaming. The larger point is that rap industry norms, more than in other types of music, encourage artists to disparage women (Kitwana 1994, 23; Krims 2000, 71; Smith 1997, 346).

Sexual Objectification

Sexual objectification of women was evident in 67 percent of our misogynistic songs. Sexual objectification refers to the idea that women are good only for sex. These lyrics mirror the street code's exhortation that men avoid commitment, marriage, and caring for children; instead, women are to be sexually used and then quickly discarded (Anderson 1999; Bourgois 1995; Liebow 1967; Miller and White 2003). N.W.A. captures this theme with a song titled "Findum, Fuckum, and Flee." Puff Daddy offers another example: "Call me Sean if you suck, call me gone when I nut. That's the end of us, get your friend to fuck" (Sean "Puffy" Combs, on Notorious B.I.G., *Notorious B.I.G.*). Consider also the following songs:

Bitches ain't shit but hoes and tricks
    Lick on these nuts and suck the dick
    Get's the fuck out after you're done
    And I hops in my ride to make a quick run.
(Dr. Dre, *Bitches Ain't Shit*)

I'm only out to fuck a bitch, fuck tryin' to charm her.
    I treat a fine ass bitch like dirt
    No money in her purse, a fuck is all it's worth.
    'Cause Short Dawg'll never cater to you hoes
    And if you ain't fuckin,' I say "later" to you hoes. (Too $hort, *Coming up $hort*)

High value is placed on having scores of sexual partners and even sharing them, another way in which women are de-individualized:

I meet a bitch, fuck a bitch
    Next thing you know you fuckin' the bitch. (Notorious B.I.G., *Friend of Mine*)

Anderson (1999) discusses the extreme peer pressure on young men in disadvantaged neighborhoods to have casual sex with women as a way of affirming their masculinity. This norm is a hallowed one in song lyrics:

I had niggas making bets like, did he fuck her yet?
    Ask her did he touch her bra, when I say nah they say ahh
    So tomorrow I use that pressure to undress her
    But the more I caress her, more I feel like a molester. (Mase, *I Need to Be*)

By the end of this stanza, peer pressure has resulted in sexual aggression.

Some rappers make it clear that they intend to put women "in their place" by demeaning strong and independent women: Redman boasts, "I turn an independent woman back into a hoochie" (*Keep On '99*) and Notorious B.I.G. raps, "I like 'em…educated, so I can bust off on they glasses" (*Big Booty Hoes*). Some of the lyrics in this thematic category, therefore, may be seen as resistance to women's growing autonomy, education, and independence—messages that cross-cut the other themes in this music as well. As indicated earlier, this backlash against women's liberation and reassertion of traditional masculinity can be found in other popular music genres as well.

Sexual objectification of women has a flip side in the sexual empowerment of men. Male sexual bravado and hypersexuality were present in 58 percent of the misogynistic songs. A common practice is bragging about how easy it is for "players" to get women to have sex: "Witness me holla at a hoochie, see how quick the game takes" (2Pac, *All 'Bout U*).

Men win respect from other men for a high number of sexual conquests without commitment. Although present throughout the culture, it appears to be especially prized in disadvantaged neighborhoods where men often lack other sources of dignity and self-esteem. In fact, there is a striking correspondence between the street code in inner-city communities and this music theme. Just as young men earn respect from their peers if they are viewed as having casual sex with many women (Anderson

1999; Bourgois 1995, 1996; Liebow 1967; Miller and White 2003), rappers likewise frequently brag about their sexual exploits, and are rewarded for doing so. A good example is rapper 50 Cent, who in the last several years has been frequently nominated for Grammy Awards for songs with precisely these themes (e.g., *Candy Shop* and *Magic Stick*). Both in rap songs and among neighborhood peers, bragging earns respect because the "expression [of masculinity] requires performance and recognition: masculinity is not only a state that men have to achieve, they have to be seen to achieve it" (Fiske 1993, 129). Low sexual achievers and those who seek a long-term relationship with a woman are ridiculed and subordinated because they are less active practitioners of this (extremely utilitarian) version of hegemonic masculinity: "their games [are] seen as inferior, and their identities devalued" (Anderson 1999, 151).

If having multiple sex partners earns respect, men also face an ongoing threat of sexual competition from other men. In other words, "Women provide heterosexual men with sexual validation, and men compete with each other for this" (Donaldson 1993, 645). Men are thus instructed to use their sexual talents or material goods to steal other men's women:

Say dog, what kinda nigga be on top of the world?
Million dollar status got me on top of ya girl.
(Hot Boys, *Fired Up*)

Men are also rewarded for demonstrating that they are sexually superior to other men:

Get freaky, and do it wild
On the floor, doggy style.
While your bitch be crying "please don't stop"....
I fuck her like I know you won't.
If that's your bitch, homeboy you'd better keep her
'Cause she won't stay off my beeper.
You can't fuck her and I appreciate it
Even though I know you hate it. (Too $hort, *Step Daddy*)

Finally, sexual objectification is expressed in gangbanging. In these songs, several men have sex with one woman, whether consensually or not, and the woman is highly depersonalized. Some involve gangbangs with underage girls, while others describe sex with heavily intoxicated women:

All on the grass [marijuana], every bitch passed [out]
A first not last, when we all hit the ass.
Doin' tricks jacked up like a six
One pussy, and thirteen dicks. (Westside Connection, *The Gangsta, the Killa, and the Dope Deala*)

Kisha got did right yeah
Fucked the whole Cash Money clique all in one night yeah. (Lil' Wayne, *Kisha*)

There is evidence that such gangbanging takes place in some disadvantaged minority neighborhoods. One study of black youth in north St. Louis, for example, reported that 40 percent of the young men interviewed admitted they had engaged in such behavior, which helped them gain status among their peers (Miller and White 2003, 1219).

The sexual objectification of women and the hypersexuality of black men portrayed in these lyrics can be linked to larger stereotypes about black sexuality—stereotypes that date back to colonialism and slavery and that are still quite salient for consumers of rap music today (Skeggs 1993). Rappers exploit these stereotypes in their music.

Can't Trust 'Em

Suspicion of women is a significant theme in rap songs—a tension that is mirrored to some extent in the communities in which rap originated (Anderson 1999). Almost half (47 percent) of the misogynistic songs displayed deep distrust of women. There is both a diffuse sense of distrust (e.g., Dr. Dre's verse, "How could you trust a ho?", *Bitches Ain't Shit*) and several specific reasons to be suspicious of women, who are seen as prone to entrap, betray, exploit, or destroy men. First, it is claimed that teenage girls lie about their age:

See nowadays man you got to know these bitches age

'Cause they ass be real fast when they be goin'
through that phase.
    You fuck a girl that's young, and you gonna
end up in the cage (Mase, *I Need to Be*)

Second, women stand accused of making false
rape accusations in order to get a financial
settlement:

Don't take the pussy, if she fightin'
    'Cause you saw what happened to Tupac and
Mike Tyson.
    'Specially if you large [famous], some hoes is
trife [petty]
    Get you on a rape charge, have you servin'
your life. (Nas, *Dr. Knockboot*)

Third, men are warned to be wary of *the femme
fatale*—especially women who seek to set them up
for robbery, assault, or murder. Ice Cube's song,
Don't Trust 'Em, talks about a woman who lured a
man to her home where there were four men who
beat the man, stole his money, and killed him. The
song ends, "I told you the bitch was a trap. Don't
trust 'em." This scenario seems to be fairly common, judging from our data:

You know they [women] might be the one to set
me up
    Wanna get they little brother to wet [kill] me
up....
    Bitches be schemin', I kid ya not
    That's why I keep my windows locked and my
Glock cocked. (Notorious B.I.G., *Friend of Mine*)

The *femme fatale* is iconic in popular culture, as
illustrated in many films (e.g., *Double Indemnity*,
Fatal Attraction, *Basic Instinct*), all of which feature a villainous woman who uses her beauty and
sexuality to exploit or victimize innocent men.
These women are presented as thoroughly evil and
condemned for departing from their traditional
gender role. Interestingly, there is no equivalent
label for men who act this way toward women.
What is especially remarkable about rap's use of
this icon is its claim that *all* young women are
potential *femmes fatales;* the music sends a strong
signal to men to be wary of women generally.
    A fourth refrain is that women frequently lie
to men in order to get pregnant. The value many

young poor women place on having babies, as one
of the few sources of dignity in their lives, is quite
strong (Anderson 1999, 162–166; Edin and Kefalas
2005). For many young men in these neighborhoods, a woman's pregnancy is viewed quite differently, something to be feared and denied: "To
own up to a pregnancy is to go against the peer-
group street ethic of hit and run" (Anderson 1999,
156). Rappers express an identical concern. 2Pac
asks, "Why plant seeds in a dirty bitch, waitin' to
trick me? Not the life for me" (*Hell 4 a Hustler*).
Paying child support is just one of the fears. Snoop
Dog raps:

I ain't lettin' nothin' leak cause if things leak, then
I'm a get caught
    And I can't get caught cause you know how
they do it about that child support.
    Shit, bitches is cold on a nigga who ain't got
his game tight
    Getting 18.5 percent [child support pay-
ments] half your life. (Snoop Dogg, *Freestyle
Conversation*)

Too $hort describes an even worse scenario after
getting a woman pregnant:

No more player, no Shorty the Pimp
    I get paid, divert a check and get 40 percent.
    All the homies talkin' bad, hair down, walkin'
sad
    Got the broad livin' with me, baby sayin'
"Dad!"...
    I could try to mack again but the bitches won't
want me
    'Cause I'm all washed up, broke, fat, and
funky.
    I lost everything that I worked to be
    Never thought I'd be a trick, payin' hoes to
serve me. (Too $hort, *Coming Up Short*)

Young men who fall prey to such women are ridiculed by their peers (Anderson 1999). It is not
only the material costs of fathering a child that is
feared in these songs, but also fatherhood in general. This may be regarded as an extreme form of
traditional masculinity, where the father is largely
absent from his children's lives. As Donaldson
(1993, 650) states, "In hegemonic masculinity,
fathers do not have the capacity or the skill or

the need to care for children.... Nurturant and care-giving behavior is simply not manly." Our rap songs convey this message in no uncertain terms.

Even more common than the other subthemes in this category is our final one: the woman as gold digger only interested in men for their money:

> Watch the honeys check your style
> Worthless, when they worship what you purchase.
> They only see ice [diamonds], not me, under the surface
> What's the purpose? (The Lox, *I Wanna Thank You*)

> You must be used to all the finer things
> Infatuated by what money brings.
> It seems to me you hoes will never change (Scarface, *Fuck Faces*)

It is significant that the 2006 Grammy Award for Best Rap Solo Performance went to Kanye West's song, "Gold Digger," which complains about a woman who seduces a man to get his money. Such recognition can be interpreted as one way in which the music industry helps to perpetuate stereotyped images of women.

Several female rappers in our sample reinforce the idea of women as gold diggers interested solely in exploiting men (cf. Pough 2004). Missy Misdemeanor Elliott sings, "If you want me, where's my dough? Give me money, buy me clothes" (*All 'N My Grill*), and in another song:

> Hot boys
> Baby you got what I want.
> See 'cause y'all be drivin' Lexus jeeps
> And the Benz jeeps, and the Lincoln jeeps.
> Nothin' cheaper, got them Platinum Visa's (Missy Misdemeanor Elliott, *Hot Boys*)

As does Lil' Kim:

> I fuck with dudes with Member's Only jackets
> That sleep on brass beds, with money for a mattress.
> Everything I get is custom made
> Niggas wanna get laid; I gotta get paid. (Lil' Kim, *Custom Made*)

Men's fear of being exploited by women has a long history and is by no means unique to rap music. Yet, the gold digger fear is especially acute among men who are *nouveau riche* such as the newly successful rapper. They have achieved rapid upward mobility and celebrity status, and thus have precarious new wealth that can be lost. It may be less salient among poor men who have few assets to lose.

Legitimating Violence

Norms regarding appropriate conduct are ineffectual if not backed up with sanctions for those who disregard the norms. Violent punishment is one such sanction. Compared to the previous themes, condoning violence against women was less frequent but does appear in almost one-fifth (18 percent) of the misogynistic songs. Violence is portrayed in these songs, first of all, as the most appropriate response to women who act disrespectfully toward men, just as it is for men who disrespect other men (Anderson 1999; Kubrin 2005a; Kubrin and Weitzer 2003). Juvenile asks, "If she think you're jokin', is she goin' get a quick chokin'?" (*March Nigga Step*), and Dr. Dre tells us that "snobby-ass bitches get slapped out of spite" (*Ackrite*). Violence is seen as fitting for other "offenses" as well. Mase raps, "If she make my nuts itch [from an STD], I kill that slut bitch" (*I Need to Be*); N.W.A. has a song titled *To Kill a Hooker*; and Eminem tells listeners to "rape sluts" (*Who Knew*), prostitutes, and other women:

> Slut, you think I won't choke no whore
> 'Til the vocal cords don't work in her throat no more?!
> Shut up slut, you're causin' too much chaos
> Just bend over and take it like a slut, okay Ma? (Eminem, *Kill You*)

Several rappers threaten women with assault or rape if they refuse sex:

> Slap you with my paw, all across your jaw
> Break fool [act violent] on these bitches while I'm breakin' the law
> You come up in my room, look bitch you takin' it off. (Snoop Dogg, on Notorious B.I.G., *Dangerous MC's*)

These sorts of justifications for the use of violence are mirrored, to some extent, in disadvantaged communities, as borne out in some ethnographic research. For instance, Miller and White (2003, 1237) found that both girls and boys in the inner city believed that male violence was appropriate when the girl seemed to have "forgotten her place." Examples of such misconduct include girls who "run their mouth," "act a fool," dress inappropriately, or drink too much. As in rap music, violence in these communities is portrayed as situationally appropriate. By contrast, girls' violence was defined by boys as "rooted in their greater emotionality," which is another example of how gender differences are naturalized (Miller and White 2003, 1242).

A related subtheme is the positive value placed on sex that is aggressive and injurious to women. Rappers take pride in women being "drilled," "wrecked," and otherwise roughed up during intercourse. Men demonstrate their dominance over women by such representations of rough sex. This subtheme was also evident in rap during the preceding time period, as documented in Armstrong's (2001) study of songs produced in 1987–1993.

In the songs in this category, rappers (1) pride themselves on sex acts that appear to harm women, (2) justify other acts of violence, (3) warn women who challenge male domination that they will be assaulted, and (4) seem to invite male violence against women. There is a dual message here, one for women and one for men: Violence is portrayed as the most appropriate response to women who violate gendered etiquette or who don't "know their place" and men are encouraged to abide by this principle. The main purpose of such songs, therefore, appears to be the *normalization of violence against women as a means of social control.* The music both espouses a set of gendered norms and advocates sanctions for those who violate these norms.

Women as Prostitutes, Men as Pimps

Pimp chic is a recent cultural innovation. It draws on pimp imagery and the language of pimping and prostitution, but has broader meaning. As Quinn (2000, 116) observed, "The divergent articulations of the pimp as trope and type point to the versatility of this misogynist, street-heroic figure." To "pimp" something can mean to promote it or to accessorize it. MTV, for example, has a show called "Pimp My Ride," where old cars are spruced up with expensive gadgets to create the ultimate pimpmobile. The term pimp is often synonymous with "player," a man who excels at attracting women or glamorized hustlers who conspicuously display their riches. Here, "the pimp image is more central than his occupation" (Quinn 2000, 124). The celebration of both pimp imagery and real pimps is pervasive in rap culture. Ice-T, Snoop Dogg, Jay-Z, and others claim to have been real-life pimps; at least one rapper (K-Luv the Pimp) has been arrested for pimping and pandering; a 2003 film called *Lil' Pimp* starred a 9-year-old boy as the film's hero; and a year after Nelly released his 2002 song and video, "Pimp Juice," he launched a new energy drink of the same name.

Although the mainstreaming of pimp chic is a fascinating cultural trend, we do not include it in this thematic category. Instead, we use the conventional, narrow definitions—namely, men who employ prostitutes. In coding, we were careful to distinguish references to prostitution and pimping, in the strict sense, from pimp chic. Women as prostitutes / men as pimps was a theme in 20 percent of the misogynistic songs.

Prostitutes are the quintessential figures of sexual objectification and exploitation, even if many of them see themselves as exploiting customers instead (Weitzer 2005). In rap, both prostitution and pimping are defined as legitimate economic pursuits and celebrated—themes which are almost non-existent in other music genres (Quinn 2000). The notion that women are only good for sex is epitomized in male discourse regarding prostitutes, and some rappers go to great lengths to present such women in one-dimensional, impersonal terms:

> Let's me and you lay in these hoes
> And show 'em what they pussy made fo'…
> Let's leave without payin' these hoes
> And show 'em what they pussy made fo'.
> (Scarface, *Use Them Ho's*)

Here women are reduced to their sex organs, and not even worth paying for their services.

Some artists describe the hardships faced by pimps, such as Ice-T's "Somebody's Gotta Do It, Pimpin' Ain't Easy!" and Three 6 Mafia's academy award winning song, "It's Hard Out Here for a Pimp." Others revel in the multiple benefits of pimping:

> Around the world, getting money,
>> I'm pimpin' hoes on Sunday.
>> I'm the kind of nigga you'll work all night
> fo'...
>> Wanna see how much pussy these hoes can
> sell.
>> It's like hypnosis, I pimps your mother, I
> pimps yo sis'
>> Hoes be nothin' but slaves for me, ready to go
> to their graves for me. (Too Short, *Pimp Me*)

Pimping and prostitution are glorified:

> Nuthin' like pimpin'...
>> I'll make the White House a hoe house, and
> all the pimps
>> To just set up shops like they do in Vegas
>> Legalize pimpin' for all the playas.
>> Puttin' fine ass bitches in the streets and the
> hood
>> Every year a nigga trade for a new Fleetwood
> [Cadillac]. (Too Short, *Ain't Nothing Like Pimpin'*)

And rappers ask listeners to give pimps the respect they deserve:

> This ho, that ho make me rich....
>> I'm back in the game, getting' my dough
>> And fuck any motherfucker that say it ain't so.
> (Snoop Dogg, *Buck 'Em*)

Quinn (2000, 117, 135) argues that simply by drawing attention to pimps' exploitative practices and misogyny, these lyrics contain a "dissident" subtext that partially undermines such conduct even as it reinforces and condones it. This interpretation, of dual and perhaps contradictory messages, is a function of Quinn's broad definition of pimping to include both "players" and traditional pimps. In our sample of lyrics we found celebration, not critique, to be the norm with respect to the pimp–prostitute relationship.

Street prostitution is typically located in both disadvantaged and marginal/transitional neighborhoods. Residents of these areas face obstacles in finding work, and prostitution and pimping may be seen as preferable to dead-end, low-paying jobs. Insofar as rap music emerged out of conditions in these neighborhoods, we might expect the sex trade to be one theme, and indeed it is in one-fifth of our misogynistic songs. At the same time, neighborhood conditions do not exist in a vacuum but interact with external factors. Ice-T invokes legendary pimp Iceberg Slim's book, *Pimp: The Story of My Life*, as the inspiration for his lyrics: "Ghetto hustlers in my neighborhood would talk this nasty dialect rich with imagery of sex and humor. My buddies and I wanted to know where they picked it up, and they told us, 'You better get into some of the Iceberg stuff!'" (quoted in Quinn 2000, 123). Several rappers also claim to have been influenced by the romanticization of the iconic pimps featured in the blaxploitation films of the 1970s (Quinn 2000). Snoop Dogg, for instance, states, "When I started seeing those movies in the '70s, like *The Mack* and *Superfly*, that helped me to more or less pick who I wanted to be in life, how I wanted to live my life, how I wanted to represent me" (quoted in Moody 2003). Those films not only painted pimps as role models for young black men but also purported to describe life in the ghetto—well illustrated in the 1999 documentary, *American Pimp*. Coming full circle, several famous pimps have appeared in rap videos. Rap's glorification of pimping is thus linked to both neighborhood conditions and a larger, preexisting pimp culture (in films and books), which itself originated on the streets.

The Voices of Female Rappers

According to one analyst, "Rap provides a medium to mobilize feminist strategies of resistance, to give voice to the experience and concerns shared by young black women, or to explore and articulate various aspects of desire and pleasure" (Forman 1994, 54). Did the lyrics of female rappers, during this time period, contain elements of an oppositional subculture directed at misogynistic male rap? Did they call hegemonic masculinity into question and reject the negative images and messages regarding women? Or were they silent or compliant with respect to male constructions of proper gender relations?

To determine whether female rappers objected to the negative portrayal of women in rap, we analyzed lyrics by female rappers that were not included in our original sample (because they did not contain misogynistic themes). Recall that only 13 of our 403 songs were by women; 8 of these 13 did not contain misogynistic lyrics. Analysis of these 8 songs reveals very little resistance to sexism during the time period under study. Only one song, by Eve (*Love Is Blind*), directly challenges male mistreatment of women. In this song, Eve alternates between cursing a man who abused her girlfriend and questioning her girlfriend's decision to stay with this "snake motherfucker." In one stanza, she asks her friend:

> What kind of love from a nigga would black your eye?
> What kind of love from a nigga every night make you cry?
> What kind of love from a nigga make you wish he would die?
> And you stayed, what made you fall for him?
> That nigga had the power to make you crawl for him....
> Smacked you down cause he said you was too tall for him, huh? (Eve, *Love Is Blind*)

This song stands alone in its rejection of violence toward women. This is not to suggest that female rappers accepted misogynistic lyrics; instead, the fact that they offered such little resistance likely reflects industry norms at the time. During the 1990s, women were grossly underrepresented in rap generally, and gangsta rap in particular, and were channeled instead into hip-hop and R&B. For women to gain acceptance in this male-dominated industry, they had to conform to existing industry norms and required male sponsors, who often appeared on one of their songs or in their videos (Emerson 2002; George 1998, 184). For this reason, the most common theme in our sample of songs by female artists involves the entry-level claim to being a bona fide, skilled

rapper. Like many male artists at the time (Kubrin 2005a), women demanded respect for their talents as rappers and would boast about this. In nearly all cases, bragging about one's skills on the microphone was the entire point of the song.

Apart from Eve's oppositional song, there was one remaining theme associated with gender relations—competition and fighting over men. In these songs, female rappers disparaged other women who they accused of trying to steal their men:

> Get your own stacks [money]
> Why you think these niggas pussy hungry?
> Cause you actin' triflin'
> Layin' up, takin' his money. (Eve, *Let's Talk About*)

In other scenarios, female rappers claimed ownership of their man even if he had sex with other women, usually because the former was the man's wife or longtime girlfriend:

> Shit, I got the ring bitch and his last name....
> Any bitch could luck up and have a kid
> Any chick could fuck a nigga for spite
> But the nigga got to love you if he make you his wife
> Ughh, ya'll chicks is lonely, I'm ownin' that dick
> And on top of all this bullshit, I'm still his chick. (Foxy Brown, *It's Hard Being Wifee*)

Although our sample of female rappers is too small for definitive conclusions, most did not challenge the degradation of women by male artists at the time. Some female artists adopt the persona and status afforded them by men: Lil' Kim calls herself "Queen Bitch," Mia X is a "Boss Bitch" (Pough 2004), and others pride themselves on being gold diggers. But it is also important to remember that most songs by women neither accepted nor opposed such degradation. This pattern appears to have changed subsequent to the time period covered by our study. Currently female rappers more actively confront male domination and seek to empower women, although songs by female artists today still contain a contradictory mix of themes that both challenge and perpetuate misogynistic themes (Emerson 2002; Jennings 2004; Pough 2004, 85–87; Troka 2002, 83).

Conclusion

According to one review of popular music over the past century, the portrayal of women has increasingly shown "greater diversity, more complexity, and dramatically mixed messages about the individual female persona and women's roles in society" (Cooper 1999, 355). Much rap music, at least rap produced by male artists, runs counter to this larger trend. Indeed, a segment of rap music naturalizes certain alleged characteristics of men and women and, in accordance with these imputed differences, seeks to restrict, rather than broaden, women's proper roles and resuscitate male domination. The messages are thus both essentialist and normative—portraying men and women as inherently different and unequal and espousing a set of conduct norms for each gender's proper behavior toward the other and sanctions for those who violate these norms.

Some analysts describe rap music as part of a larger reaction against the feminist movement, seeking to perpetuate women's inequality and re-empower men. As bell hooks (1994, 6) argues, "Gangsta rap is part of the anti-feminist backlash that is the rage right now." The music contains a variety of "controlling images" directed at women (Collins 2000), and goes to great lengths to define strict gender roles, with women subordinate to men in several ways. In this sense rap speaks to larger gender relations by making universalistic claims and instructing all men on appropriate conduct toward women. But rap artists are not solely responsible for the content of their work. The entertainment industry plays an essential role, cultivating sexist lyrics and rewarding artists who produce them with huge sums of money, Grammy and Oscar awards, and spin-off products like Pimp Juice. In addition to this top-down dynamic, we have also pointed to a bottom-up process in which, as Negus (1999, 490) argues, neighborhood "culture produces industry" as much as "industry produces culture." In other words, rap's messages have been incubated and resonate in communities where men have few opportunities for socioeconomic success and dignity and where respect is instead often earned by mistreating young women (Anderson 1999; Bourgois 1996; Liebow 1967) as

well as other men (Kubrin and Weitzer 2003). As Connell and Messerschmidt (2005) point out, hegemonic masculinity is reinforced reciprocally at multiple levels—societal, community, and interactional.

It is important to emphasize that, like other music genres, rap is more varied in its content than is often recognized. For instance, this music has served as a consciousness-raising, politically progressive, liberating form of popular culture (Martinez 1997). Therefore, we want to emphasize that misogyny does not characterize rap music as a whole. A majority of songs in our sample do *not* degrade women, which we consider a major finding in itself. And there are rappers who actively challenge rap's misogynistic messages and endorse a more egalitarian form of masculinity. At the same time, a sizeable segment (more than one-fifth) of this genre does contain such messages, and our analysis indicates that these messages are rather extreme. While women are presented as subordinate to men in a majority of rock and country songs as noted earlier, rap stands out for the *intensity* and *graphic* nature of its lyrical objectification, exploitation, and victimization of women. Other genres, in the aggregate, make more subtle allusions to gender inequality or present more muted criticisms of women (Andsager and Roe 1999; Binder 1993; Cooper 1999; Rhym 1997; Ryan and Peterson 1982; Walser 1993). Furthermore, it is important to consider what themes are largely *absent* in rap lyrics. Rare are lyrics that describe women as independent, educated, professional, caring, and trustworthy. While the majority of songs in the original sample did not contain misogynistic lyrics, even these songs failed to present women in a favorable light. In other words, absence of misogyny does not equate with a positive representation of women.

Given its sources, we argue that changing the content of this music—specifically with respect to the portrayal of women—requires in part changing the conditions under which it is created, conditions that lie at the intersection of three important forces: socioeconomic disadvantage and associated gender relations in local communities, the material interests of the record industry, and the larger cultural objectification of women and associated norms of hegemonic masculinity.

Acknowledgments

Authors' Note: For their helpful comments on this essay, we are grateful to Ivy Ken, Michael Kimmel, Theresa Martinez, and the anonymous reviewers, and for research assistance we thank Ami Lynch.

Notes

1. It is important to recognize that rap is not monolithic. There are various themes in rap music, ranging from Afro-Centric community building to support for liberation struggles, to celebration of partying to problems of racism and drug dealing. See Kitwana (1994, 32) and Krims (2000, 55) for evidence of rap music's varied content.

2. Gangsta rap is a subgenre of rap music. It describes life in the ghetto, and has been controversial in part because it provides an insider's view of crime, violence, and social conflict in the inner city (Kitwana 1994, 19; Krims 2000, 70). More so than other rap genres, gangsta rap is noted for its violent and misogynistic lyrics, which depart from the rich political and social commentary that characterizes some other rap music (Kelley 1996, 147).

3. We recognize that a few artists, such as NWA, produced gangsta rap songs before this time period. However, gangsta rap gained ascendancy in the early 1990s.

4. Originally a random sample of one-third of the 1,922 songs was selected to be analyzed (N = 632). The findings are based on a final sample size of 403 because, during the course of coding, after song 350 we no longer encountered new themes. Nevertheless, we coded an additional 53 songs to ensure that we had reached saturation, which is standard practice in qualitative analysis (Glaser and Strauss 1967, 111).

5. At first glance, it might appear that negative portrayals of women were less frequent in rap than in the other music genres reviewed earlier, based on the percentage differences. However, each study operationalized such depictions in somewhat different ways, so study findings cannot be directly compared. Similarly, our finding on rap music cannot be compared to Armstrong's (2001) study of earlier rap songs because he focused on expressions of violence against women, whereas our measure of misogyny is more inclusive.

6. Eminem has marketed himself as a poor or working-class white youth, which gives him some "street credibility" among black rappers and record producers, and it has been argued that his misogynistic lyrics are intended to gain credibility as a rapper (Stephens 2005).

References

Alexander, Susan. 1999. The gender role paradox in youth culture: An analysis of women in music videos. *Michigan Sociological Review* 13:46–64.

Anderson, Elijah. 1999. *Code of the street: Decency, violence, and the moral life of the inner city.* New York: W.W. Norton.

Andsager, Julie, and Kimberly Roe. 1999. Country music video in country's year of the woman. *Journal of Communication* 49:69–82.

Armstrong, Gerald. 2001. Gangsta misogyny: A content analysis of the portrayals of violence against women in rap music, 1987–1993. *Journal of Criminal Justice and Popular Culture* 8:96–126.

Barongan, Christy, and Gordon Hall. 1995. The influence of misogynous rap music on sexual aggression against women. *Psychology of Women Quarterly* 19:195–207.

Bennett, Andy. 1999a. Rappin' on the Tyne: White hip-hop culture in northeast England. *Sociological Review* 47:1–24.

———. 1999b. "Hip hop am Main: The localization of rap music and hip hop culture. *Media, Culture & Society* 21:77–91.

Binder, Amy. 1993. Media depictions of harm in heavy metal and rap music. *American Sociological Review* 58:753–67.

Bourgois, Philippe. 1995. *In search of respect: Selling crack in El Barrio.* New York: Cambridge University Press.

———. 1996. In search of masculinity: Violence, respect, and sexuality among Puerto Rican crack dealers in East Harlem. *British Journal of Criminology* 36:412–27.

Butruille, Susan, and Anita Taylor. 1987. Women in American popular song. In *Communication, gender, and sex roles in diverse interactional contexts,* ed. L. Stewart and S. Ting-Toomey, 179–88. Norwood, NJ: Ablex.

Collins, Patricia Hill. 2000. *Black feminist thought.* 2nd ed. New York: Routledge.

Connell, R. W. 1987. *Gender and power.* Cambridge: Polity.

Connell, R. W., and James Messerschmidt. 2005. Hegemonic masculinity: Rethinking the concept. *Gender & Society* 19:829–59.

Cooper, B. Lee. 1999. From Lady Day to Lady Di: Images of women in contemporary recordings, 1938–1998. *International Journal of Instructional Media* 26:353–58.

Donaldson, Mike. 1993. What is hegemonic masculinity? *Theory and Society* 22:643–57.

Edin, Kathryn, and Maria Kefalas. 2005. *Promises I can keep: Why poor women put motherhood before marriage.* Berkeley: University of California Press.

Emerson, Rana. 2002. "Where my girls at?" Negotiating black womanhood in music videos. *Gender and Society* 16:115–35.

Fiske, John. 1993. *Power plays, power works.* London: Verso.

Forman Murray. 2002. *The 'hood comes first: Race, space, and place in rap and hip hop.* Hanover, NH. Wesleyan University Press.

Garfinkle, Harold. 1956. Conditions of successful degradation ceremonies. *American Journal of Sociology* 61:420–24.

George, Nelson. 1998. *Hip hop America.* New York: Penguin Books.

Glaser, Barney, and Anselm Strauss. 1967. *The discovery of grounded theory.* Chicago: Aldine.

Hanke, Robert. 1998. Theorizing masculinity within the media. *Communication Theory* 8:183–203.

hooks, bell. 1994. Misogyny, gangsta rap, and the piano. *Z Magazine*, February.

Horowitz, Ruth. 1983. *Honor and the American dream: Culture and identity in a Chicano community.* New Brunswick, NJ: Rutgers University Press.

Hurt, Byron. 2007. *Hip hop: Beyond beats and rhymes.* Independent Lens series, PBS. First broadcast February 20th.

Jennings, Tom. 2004. Dancehall dreams. *Variant 2* (Summer):9–13.

Johnson, James, Mike Adams, Leslie Ashburn, and William Reed. 1995. Differential gender effects of exposure to rap music on African American adolescents' acceptance of teen dating violence. *Sex Roles* 33:597–605.

Kelley, Robin. 1996. Kickin' reality, kickin' ballistics: Gangsta rap and postindustrial Los Angeles. In *Droppin' science: critical essays on rap music and hip hop culture*, ed. W. Perkins, 117–58. Philadelphia: Temple University Press.

Keyes, Cheryl L. 2002. *Rap music and street consciousness.* Chicago: University of Chicago Press.

Kitwana, Bakari. 1994. *The rap on gangsta rap.* Chicago: Third World Press.

———. 2002. *The hip hop generation: Young blacks and the crisis of African American culture.* New York: Basic Books.

Krims, Adam. 2000. *Rap music and the poetics of identity.* Cambridge: Cambridge University Press.

Kubrin, Charis E. 2005a. Gangstas, thugs, and hustlas: Identity and the code of the street in rap music. *Social Problems* 52:360–78.

———. 2005b. I see death around the corner: Nihilism in rap music. *Sociological Perspectives* 48:433–59.

Kubrin, Charis E., and Ronald Weitzer. 2003. Retaliatory homicide: Concentrated disadvantage and neighborhood culture. *Social Problems* 50:157–80.

Lay, Frank. 2000. "Sometimes we wonder who the real men are": Masculinity and contemporary popular music. In *Subverting masculinity: Hegemonic and alternative versions of masculinity in contemporary culture*, ed. R. West and F. Lay, 227–46. Amsterdam: Rodopi.

Lee, Carol D. 2005. Intervention research based on current views of cognition and learning. In *Black education: A transformative research and action agenda for the new century*, ed. J. King, 73–114. Washington, DC: American Educational Research Association.

Lena, Jennifer C. 2006. Social context and musical content of rap music, 1979–1995. *Social Forces* 85:479–95.

Liebow, Elliot. 1967. *Tally's corner.* Boston: Little, Brown.

Martinez, Theresa A. 1997. Popular culture as oppositional culture: Rap as resistance. *Sociological Perspectives* 40:265–86.

Martino, Steven, Rebecca Collins, Marc Elliott, Amy Strachman, David Kanouse, and Sandra Berry. 2006. Exposure to degrading versus nondegrading music lyrics and sexual behavior among youth. *Pediatrics* 118:430–41.

McAdams, Janine, and Deborah Russell. 1991. Rap breaking through to adult market. *Hollywood Reporter* Sept. 19:4.

McFarland, Pancho. 2003. Challenging the contradictions of Chicanismo in Chicano rap music and male culture. *Race, Gender, and Class* 10:92–107.

Miller, Jody, and Norman White. 2003. Gender and adolescent relationship violence. *Criminology* 41:1207–47.

Moody, Nekesa Mumbi. 2003. Pimps: The new gangstas of rap. *Associated Press,* July 21.

Negus, Keith. 1999. The music business and rap: Between the street and the executive suite. *Cultural Stages* 13:488–508.

Oliver, William. 2006. The streets: An alternative black male socialization institution. *Journal of Black Studies* 36:918–37.

Pough, Gwendolyn. 2004. *Check it while I wreck it: Black womanhood, hip-hop culture, and the public sphere.* Boston: Northeastern University Press.

Powell, Kevin. 2000. My culture at the crossroads: A rap devotee watches corporate control and apolitical times encroach on the music he has loved all his life. *Newsweek*, October 9:66.

Powell, Catherine T. 1991. Rap music: An education with a beat from the street. *Journal of Negro Education* 60:245–59.

Quinn, Eithne. 2000. "Who's the mack?" The performativity and politics of the pimp figure in gangsta rap. *Journal of American Studies* 34:115–36.

———. 2005. *Nuthin' but a "G" thang: The culture and commerce of gangsta rap.* New York: Columbia University Press.

Rhym, Darren. 1997. "Here's for the bitches": An analysis of gangsta rap and misogyny. *Womanist Theory and Research* 2:1–14.

Rose, Tricia. 1994. *Black noise: Rap music and black culture in contemporary America.* Hanover, NH: Wesleyan University Press.

Ryan, John W., and R. A. Peterson. 1982. The product image: The fate of creativity in country music songwriting. *Sage Annual Reviews of Communication Research* 10:11–32.

Skeggs, Beverley. 1993. Two minute brother: Contestation through gender, race, and sexuality. *Innovation: The European Journal of Social Sciences* 6:299–323.

Smith, Christopher H. 1997. Method in the madness: Exploring the boundaries of identity in hip hop performativity. *Social Identities* 3:345–74.

Smitherman, Geneva. 1997. "The chain remain the same": Communicative practices in the hip hop nation. *Journal of Black Studies* 28:3–25.

Stephens, Vincent. 2005. Pop goes the rapper: A close reading of Eminem's genderphobia. *Popular Music* 24:21–36.

Troka, Donna. 2002. "You heard my gun cock": Female agency and aggression in contemporary rap music. *African American Research Perspectives* 8:82–89.

Tuchman, Gaye. 1978. The symbolic annihilation of women by the mass media. In *Hearth and home: Images of women in the mass media*, ed. G. Tuchman, A. Daniels, and J. Benet, 3–38. New York: Oxford University Press.

van Zoonen, Liesbet. 1994. *Feminist media studies.* Thousand Oaks, CA: Sage.

Vincent, Richard, Dennis Davis, and Lilly Boruszkowski. 1987. Sexism on MTV: The portrayal of women in rock videos. *Journalism Quarterly* 64:750–55.

Walser, Robert. 1993. *Running with the Devil: Power, gender, and madness in heavy metal music.* Hanover, NH: Wesleyan University Press.

Watkins, S. Craig. 2001. A nation of millions: Hip hop culture and the legacy of black nationalism. *The Communication Review* 4:373–98.

Weitzer, Ronald. 2005. New directions in research on prostitution. *Crime, Law, and Social Change* 43:211–35.

Wester, Stephen, Cynthia Crown, Gerald Quatman, and Martin Heesacker. 1997. The influence of sexually violent rap music on attitudes of men with little prior exposure. *Psychology of Women Quarterly* 21:497–508.

Post-Princess Models of Gender: The New Man in Disney/Pixar

KEN GILLAM AND SHANNON R. WOODEN

Lisping over the Steve McQueen allusion in Pixar's *Cars* (2006), our two-year-old son, Oscar, inadvertently directed us to the definition(s) of masculinity that might be embedded in a children's animated film about NASCAR. The film overtly praises the "good woman" proverbially behind every successful man: the champion car, voiced by Richard Petty, tells his wife, "I wouldn't be nothin' without you, honey." But gender in this twenty-first-century bildungsroman is rather more complex, and Oscar's mispronunciation held the first clue. To him, a member of the film's target audience, the character closing in on the title long held by "'The King" is not "Lightning McQueen" but "Lightning the queen"; his chief rival, the always-a-bridesmaid runner-up "Chick" Hicks.

Does this nominal feminizing of male also-rans (and the simultaneous gendering of success) constitute a meaningful pattern? Piqued, we began examining the construction of masculinity in major feature films released by Disney's Pixar studios over the past thirteen years. Indeed, as we argue here, Pixar consistently promotes a new model of masculinity, one that matures into acceptance of its more traditionally "feminine" aspects.

Cultural critics have long been interested in Disney's cinematic products, but the gender critics examining the texts most enthusiastically gobbled up by the under-six set have so far generally focused on their retrograde representations of women. As Elizabeth Bell argues, the animated Disney features through *Beauty and the Beast* feature a "teenaged heroine at the idealized height of puberty's graceful promenade [...f]emale wickedness [...] rendered as middle-aged beauty at its peak of sexuality and authority [..., and] [f]eminine sacrifice and nurturing [...] drawn in pear-shaped, old women past menopause" (108). Some have noted the models of masculinity in the classic animated films, primarily the contrast between the ubermacho Gaston and the sensitive, misunderstood Beast in *Beauty and the Beast*,[1] but the male protagonist of the animated classics, at least through *The Little Mermaid*, remains largely uninterrogated.[2] For most of the early films, this critical omission seems generally appropriate, the various versions of Prince Charming being often too two-dimensional to do more than inadvertently shape the definition of the protagonists' femininity. But if the feminist thought that has shaped our cultural texts for three decades now has been somewhat disappointing in its ability to actually rewrite the princess trope (the spunkiest of the "princesses," Ariel, Belie, Jasmine, and, arguably, even Mulan, remain thin, beautiful, kind, obedient or punished for disobedience, and headed for the altar), it has been surprisingly effective in rewriting the type of masculine power promoted by Disney's products.[3]

Disney's new face, Pixar studios, has released nine films—*Toy Story* (1995) and *Toy Story 2* (1999); *A Bug's Life* (1998); *Finding Nemo* (2003); *Monsters, Inc.* (2001); *The Incredibles* (2004); *Cars* (2006); *Ratatouille* (2007); and now *WALL•E* (2008)—all of which feature interesting male figures in leading positions. Unlike many of the princesses, who remain relatively static even through their own adventures, these male leads are actual protagonists; their characters develop and change over the course of the film, rendering the plot. Ultimately these various developing characters—particularly Buzz and Woody from *Toy Story*, Mr. Incredible from *The Incredibles,* and Lightning McQueen from *Cars*—experience a common narrative trajectory, culminating in a common "New Man" model[4]: they all strive for an alpha-male identity; they face emasculating failures; they find themselves, in large part, through what Eve Sedgwick refers to as "homosocial desire" and a triangulation of this desire with a feminized object (and/or a set of "feminine" values); and, finally, they achieve (and teach) a kinder, gentler understanding of what it means to be a man.

Emasculation of the Alpha Male

A working definition of *alpha male* may be unnecessary; although more traditionally associated with the animal kingdom than the Magic Kingdom, it familiarly evokes ideas of dominance, leadership, and power in human social organizations as well. The phrase "alpha male" may stand for all things stereotypically patriarchal: unquestioned authority, physical power and social dominance, competitiveness for positions of status and leadership, lack of visible or shared emotion, social isolation. An alpha male, like Vann in *Cars,* does not ask for directions; like Doc Hudson in the same film, he does not talk about his feelings. The alpha male's stresses, like Buzz Lightyear's, come from his need to save the galaxy; his strength comes from faith in his ability to do so. These models have worked in Disney for decades. The worst storm at sea is no match for *The Little Mermaid's* uncomplicated Prince Eric—indeed, any charming prince need only ride in on his steed to save his respective princess. But the postfeminist world is a different place for men, and the post-princess Pixar is a different place for male protagonists.

Newsweek recently described the alpha male's new cinematic and television rival, the "beta male": "The testosterone-pumped, muscle-bound Hollywood hero is rapidly deflating .[...] Taking his place is a new kind of leading man, the kind who's just as happy following as leading, or never getting off the sofa" (Yabroff 64). Indeed, as Susan Jeffords points out, at least since *Beauty and the Beast,* Disney has resisted (even ridiculed) the machismo once de rigueur for leading men (170). Disney cinema, one of the most effective teaching tools America offers its children, is not yet converting its model male protagonist all the way into a slacker, but the New Man model is quite clearly emerging.

Cars, Toy Story, and *The Incredibles* present their protagonists as unambiguously alpha in the opening moments of the films. Although Lightning McQueen may be an as-yet incompletely realized alpha when *Cars* begins, not having yet achieved the "King" status of his most successful rival, his ambition and fierce competitiveness still clearly valorize the alpha-male model: "Speed. I am speed...I eat losers for breakfast," he chants as a prerace mantra. He heroically comes from behind to tie the championship race, distinguishing himself by his physical power and ability, characteristics that catapult him toward the exclusively male culture of sports superstars. The fantasies of his life he indulges after winning the coveted Piston Cup even include flocks of female cars forming a worshipful harem around him. But the film soon diminishes the appeal of this alpha model. Within a few moments of the race's conclusion, we see some of Lightning's less positive macho traits; his inability to name any friends, for example, reveals both his isolation and attempts at emotional stoicism. Lightning McQueen is hardly an unemotional character, as can be seen when he prematurely jumps onto the stage to accept what he assumes to be his victory. For this happy emotional outburst, however, he is immediately disciplined by a snide comment from Chick. From this point until much later in the film, the only emotions he displays are those of frustration and anger.

Toy Story's Buzz Lightyear and Sheriff Woody similarly base their worth on a masculine model of competition and power, desiring not only to be the "favorite toy" of their owner, Andy, but to possess the admiration of and authority over the other toys in the playroom. Woody is a natural leader, and his position represents both paternalistic care and patriarchal dominance. In an opening scene, he calls and conducts a "staff meeting" that highlights his unambiguously dominant position in the toy community. Encouraging the toys to pair up so that no one will be lost in the family's impending move, he commands: "A moving buddy. If you don't have one, GET ONE." Buzz's alpha identity comes from a more exalted source than social governance—namely, his belief that he is the one "space ranger" with the power and knowledge needed to save the galaxy; it seems merely natural, then, that the other toys would look up to him, admire his strength, and follow his orders. But as with Lightning McQueen, these depictions of masculine power are soon undercut. Buzz's mere presence exposes Woody's strength as fragile, artificial, even arbitrary, and his "friends," apparently having been drawn to his authority rather than his character, are fair-weather at best. Buzz's authority rings hollow from the very beginning, and his refusal to believe in his own "toyness" is at best silly and at worst dangerous. Like Lightning, Buzz's and Woody's most commonly expressed emotions are anger and frustration, not sadness (Woody's, at having been "replaced") or fear (Buzz's, at having "crash-landed on a strange planet") or even wistful fondness (Woody's, at the loss of Slink's, Bo Peep's, and Rex's loyalty). Once again, the alpha-male position is depicted as fraudulent, precarious, lonely, and devoid of emotional depth.

An old-school superhero, Mr. Incredible opens *The Incredibles* by displaying the tremendous physical strength that enables him to stop speeding trains, crash through buildings, and keep the city safe from criminals. But he too suffers from the emotional isolation of the alpha male. Stopping on the way to his own wedding to interrupt a crime in progress, he is very nearly late to the service, showing up only to say the "I dos." Like his car and toy counterparts, he communicates primarily through verbal assertions of power—angrily dismissing Buddy, his meddlesome aspiring sidekick; bantering with Elastigirl over who gets the pickpocket—and limits to anger and frustration the emotions apparently available to men.

Fraught as it may seem, the alpha position is even more fleeting: in none of these Pixar films does the male protagonist's dominance last long. After Lightning ties, rather than wins, the race and ignores the King's friendly advice to find and trust a good team with which to work, he browbeats his faithful semi, Mack, and ends up lost in "hillbilly hell," a small town off the beaten path of the interstate. His uncontrolled physical might destroys the road, and the resultant legal responsibility—community service—keeps him far from his Piston Cup goals. When Buzz appears as a gift for Andy's birthday, he easily unseats Woody both as Andy's favorite and as the toy community's leader. When Buzz becomes broken, failing to save himself from the clutches of the evil neighbor, Sid, he too must learn a hard lesson about his limited power, his diminished status, and his own relative insignificance in the universe. Mr. Incredible is perhaps most obviously disempowered: despite his superheroic feats, Mr. Incredible has been unable to keep the city safe from his own clumsy brute force. After a series of lawsuits against "the Supers," who accidentally leave various types of small-time mayhem in their wake, they are all driven underground, into a sort of witness protection program. To add insult to injury, Mr. Incredible's diminutive boss fires him from his job handling insurance claims, and his wife, the former Elastigirl, assumes the "pants" of the family.

Most of these events occur within the first few minutes of the characters' respective films. Only Buzz's downfall happens in the second half. The alpha-male model is thus not only present and challenged in the films but also is, in fact, the very structure on which the plots unfold. Each of these films is about being a man, and they begin with an outdated, two-dimensional alpha prototype to expose its failings and to ridicule its logical extensions: the devastation and humiliation of being defeated in competition, the wrath generated by power unchecked, the paralyzing alienation and fear inherent in being lonely at the top. As these characters begin the film in (or seeking) the tenuous alpha position among fellow characters, each of them is also stripped of this identity—dramatically emasculated—so that he may learn, reform, and emerge again with a different, and arguably more feminine, self-concept.

"Emasculated" is not too strong a term for what happens to these male protagonists; the decline of the alpha-male model is gender coded in all the films. For his community service punishment, Lightning is chained to the giant, snorting, tar-spitting "Bessie" and ordered to repair the damage he has wrought. His own "horsepower" (as Sally cheerfully points out) is used against him when literally put in the service of a nominally feminized figure valued for the more "feminine" orientation of service to the community. If being under the thumb of this humongous "woman" is not emasculating enough, Mater, who sees such subordination to Bessie as a potentially pleasurable thing, names the price, saying, "I'd give my left two lug nuts for something like that!"

Mr. Incredible's downfall is most clearly marked as gendered by his responses to it. As his wife's domestic power and enthusiasm grow increasingly unbearable, and his children's behavior more and more out of his control, he surreptitiously turns to the mysterious, gorgeous "Mirage," who gives him what he needs to feel like a man: superhero work. Overtly depicting her as the "other woman," the film requires Elastigirl to intercept a suggestive-sounding phone call, and to trap her husband in a lie, to be able to work toward healing his decimated masculinity.

In *Toy Story*, the emasculation of the alpha male is the most overt, and arguably the most comic. From the beginning, power is constructed in terms conspicuously gender coded, at least for adult viewers: as they watch the incoming birthday presents, the toys agonize at their sheer size, the longest and most phallic-shaped one striking true fear (and admiration?) into the hearts of the spectators. When Buzz threatens Woody, one toy explains to another that he has "laser envy." Buzz's moment of truth, after seeing himself on Sid's father's television, is the most clearly gendered of all. Realizing for the first time that Woody is right, he is a "toy," he defiantly attempts to fly anyway, landing sprawled on the floor with a broken arm.

Sid's little sister promptly finds him, dresses him in a pink apron and hat, and installs him as "Mrs. Nesbit" at her tea party. When Woody tries to wrest him from his despair. Buzz wails, "Don't you get it? I AM MRS. NESBIT. But does the hat look good? Oh, tell me the hat looks good!" Woody's "rock bottom" moment finds him trapped under an overturned milk crate, forcing him to ask Buzz for help and to admit that he "doesn't stand a chance" against Buzz in the contest for Andy's affection, which constitutes "everything that is important to me." He is not figured into a woman, like Buzz is, or subordinated to a woman, like Lightning is, or forced to seek a woman's affirmation of his macho self, like Mr. Incredible is, but he does have to acknowledge his own feminine values, from his need for communal support to his deep, abiding (and, later, maternal) love of a boy. This "feminine" stamp is characteristic of the New Man model toward which these characters narratively journey.

Homosociality, Intimacy, and Emotion

Regarding the "love of a boy," the "mistress" tempting Mr. Incredible away from his wife and family is not Mirage at all but Buddy, the boy he jilted in the opening scenes of the film (whose last name, Pine, further conveys the unrequited nature of their relationship). Privileging his alpha-male emotional isolation, but adored by his wannabe sidekick, Mr. Incredible vehemently protects his desire to "work alone." After spending the next years nursing his rejection and refining his arsenal, Buddy eventually retaliates against Mr. Incredible for rebuffing his advances. Such a model of homosocial tutelage as Buddy proposes at the beginning of the film certainly evokes an ancient (and homosexual) model of masculine identity; Mr. Incredible's rejection quickly and decisively replaces it with a heteronormative one, further supported by Elastigirl's marrying and Mirage's attracting the macho superhero.[5] But it is equally true that the recovery of Mr. Incredible's masculine identity happens primarily through his (albeit antagonistic) relationship with Buddy, suggesting that Eve Sedgwick's notion of a homosocial continuum is more appropriate to an analysis of the film's gender attitudes than speculations about its reactionary heteronormativity, even homophobia.

Same-sex (male) bonds—to temporarily avoid the more loaded term *desire*—are obviously important to each of these films. In fact, in all three, male/male relationships emerge that move the fallen alphas forward in their journeys toward a new masculinity. In each case, the male lead's first and/or primary intimacy—his most immediate transformative relationship—is with one or more male characters. Even before discovering Buddy as his nemesis, Mr. Incredible secretly pairs up with his old pal Frozone, and the two step out on their wives to continue superheroing on the sly; Buddy and Frozone are each, in their ways, more influential on Mr. Incredible's sense of self than his wife or children are. Although Lightning falls in love with Sally and her future vision of Radiator Springs, his almost accidentally having befriended the hapless, warm Mater catalyzes more foundational lessons about the responsibilities of friendship—demanding honesty, sensitivity, and care—than the smell-the-roses lesson Sally represents. He also ends up being mentored and taught a comparable lesson about caring for others by Doc Hudson, who even more explicitly encourages him lo resist the alpha path of the Piston Cup world by relating his experiences of being used and then rejected. Woody and Buzz, as rivals-cum-allies, discover the necessary truths about their masculine strength only as they discover how much they need one another. Sedgwick further describes the ways in which the homosocial bond is negotiated through a triangulation of desire; that is, the intimacy emerging "between men" is constructed through an overt and shared desire for a feminized object. Unlike homosocial relationships between women—that is, "the continuum between 'women loving women' and 'women promoting the interests of women'"—male homosocial identity is necessarily homophobic in patriarchal systems, which are structurally homophobic (3). This means the same-sex relationship demands social opportunities for a man to insist on, or prove, his heterosexuality. Citing Rene Girard's *Deceit, Desire, and the Novel*, Sedgwick argues that "in any erotic rivalry, the bond that links the two rivals is as intense and potent as the bond that links either of the rivals to the beloved" (21); women are ultimately symbolically exchangeable "for the primary purpose of cementing the bonds of men with men" (26).

This triangulation of male desire can be seen in *Cars* and *Toy Story* particularly, where the homosocial relationship rather obviously shares a desire for a feminized third. Buzz and Woody compete first, momentarily, for the affection of Bo Peep, who is surprisingly sexualized for a children's movie (purring to Woody an offer to "get someone else to watch the sheep tonight," then rapidly choosing Buzz as her "moving buddy" after his "flying" display). More importantly, they battle for the affection of Andy—a male child alternately depicted as maternal (it is his responsibility to get his baby sister out of her crib) and in need of male protection (Woody exhorts Buzz to "take care of Andy for me!").[6] *Cars* also features a sexualized romantic heroine; less coquettish than Bo Peep, Sally still fumbles over an invitation to spend the night "not with me, but…" in the motel she owns. One of Lightning and Mater's moments of "bonding" happens when Mater confronts Lightning, stating his affection for Sally and sharing a parallel story of heterosexual desire. The more principal objects of desire in *Cars*, however, are the (arguably) feminized "Piston Cup" and the Dinoco sponsorship. The sponsor itself is established in romantic terms: with Lightning stuck in Radiator Springs, his agent says Dinoco has had to "woo" Chick instead. Tia and Mia, Lightning's "biggest fans," who transfer their affection to Chick during his absence, offer viewers an even less subtly gendered goal, and Chick uses this to taunt Lightning. It is in the pursuit of these objects, and in competition with Chick and the King, that Lightning first defines himself as a man; the Piston Cup also becomes the object around which he and Doc discover their relationship to one another.

The New Man

With the strength afforded by these homosocial intimacies, the male characters triumph over their respective plots, demonstrating the desirable modifications that Pixar makes to the alpha-male model. To emerge victorious (and in one piece) over the tyrannical neighbor boy, Sid, Buzz, and Woody have to cooperate not only with each other but also with the cannibalized toys lurking in the dark places of Sid's bedroom. Incidentally learning a valuable lesson about discrimination based on physical difference (the toys are not monsters at all, despite their frightening appearance), they begin to show sympathy, rather than violence born of their fear, to the victims of Sid's experimentation. They learn how to humble themselves to ask for help from the community. Until Woody's grand plan to escape Sid unfolds, Sid could be an object lesson in the unredeemed alpha-male type: cruelly almighty over the toy community, he wins at arcade games, bullies his sister, and, with strategically placed fireworks, exerts militaristic might over any toys he can find. Woody's newfound ability to give and receive care empowers him to teach Sid a lesson of caring and sharing that might be microcosmic to the movie as a whole. Sid, of course, screams (like a girl) when confronted with the evidence of his past cruelties, and when viewers last see him, his younger sister is chasing him up the stairs with her doll.

Even with the unceremonious exit of Sid, the adventure is not quite over for Buzz and Woody. Unable to catch up to the moving van as Sid's dog chases him, Woody achieves the pinnacle of the New Man narrative: armed with a new masculine identity, one that expresses feelings and acknowledges community as a site of power, Woody is able to sacrifice the competition with Buzz for his object of desire. Letting go of the van strap, sacrificing himself (he thinks) to Sid's dog, he plainly expresses a caretaking, nurturing love, and a surrender to the good of the beloved: "Take care of Andy for me," he pleads. Buzz's own moment of truth comes from seizing his power as a toy: holding Woody, he glides into the family's car and back into Andy's care, correcting Woody by proudly repeating his earlier, critical words back to him: "This isn't flying; it's falling with style." Buzz has found the value of being a "toy," the self-fulfillment that comes from being owned and loved. "Being a toy is a lot better than being

a space ranger," Woody explains. "You're *his toy*" (emphasis in original).

Mr. Incredible likewise must embrace his own dependence, both physical and emotional. Trapped on the island of Chronos, at the mercy of Syndrome (Buddy's new super-persona), Mr. Incredible needs women—his wife's superpowers and Mirage's guilty intervention—to escape. To overpower the monster Syndrome has unleashed on the city, and to achieve the pinnacle of the New Man model, he must also admit to his emotional dependence on his wife and children. Initially confining them to the safety of a bus, he confesses to Elastigirl that his need to fight the monster alone is not a typically alpha ("I work alone") sort of need but a loving one: "I can't lose you again," he tells her. The robot/monster is defeated, along with any vestiges of the alpha model, as the combined forces of the Incredible family locate a new model of postfeminist strength in the family as a whole. This communal strength is not simply physical but marked by cooperation, selflessness, and intelligence. The children learn that their best contributions protect the others; Mr. Incredible figures out the robot/monster's vulnerability and cleverly uses this against it.

In a parallel motif to Mr. Incredible's inability to control his strength, Buddy/Syndrome finally cannot control his robot/monster; in the defeat, he becomes the newly emasculated alpha male. But like his robot, he learns quickly. His last attempt to injure Mr. Incredible, kidnapping his baby Jack-Jack, strikes at Mr. Incredible's new source of strength and value, his family. The strength of the cooperative family unit is even more clearly displayed in this final rescue: for the shared, parental goal of saving Jack-Jack, Mr. Incredible uses his physical strength and, with her consent, the shape-shifting body of his super-wife. He throws Elastigirl into the air, where she catches their baby and, flattening her body into a parachute, sails gently back to her husband and older children.

Through Lightning McQueen's many relationships with men, as well as his burgeoning romance with Sally, he also learns how to care about others, to focus on the well-being of the community, and to privilege nurture and kindness. It is Doc, not

Sally, who explicitly challenges the race car with his selfishness ("When was the last time you cared about something except yourself, hot rod?"). His reformed behavior begins with his generous contributions to the Radiator Springs community. Not only does he provide much-needed cash for the local economy, but he also listens to, praises, and values the residents for their unique offerings to Radiator Springs. He is the chosen auditor for Lizzy's reminiscing about her late husband, contrasting the comic relief typically offered by the senile and deaf Model T with poignancy, if not quite sadness. Repairing the town's neon, he creates a romantic dreamscape from the past, a setting for both courting Sally ("cruising") and, more importantly, winning her respect with his ability to share in her value system. For this role, he is even physically transformed: he hires the body shop proprietor, Ramone, to paint over his sponsors' stickers and his large race number, as if to remove himself almost completely from the Piston Cup world, even as he anticipates being released from his community service and thus being able to return to racing.

Perhaps even more than Buzz, Woody, and Mr. Incredible do, the New Man McQueen shuns the remaining trappings of the alpha role, actually refusing the Piston Cup. If the first three protagonists are ultimately qualified heroes—that is, they still retain their authority and accomplish their various tasks, but with new values and perspectives acquired along the way—Lightning completely and publicly refuses his former object of desire. Early in the final race, he seems to somewhat devalue racing; his daydreams of Sally distract him, tempting him to give up rather than to compete. The plot, however, needs him to dominate the race so his decision at the end will be entirely his own. His friends show up and encourage him to succeed. This is where the other films end: the values of caring, sharing, nurturing, and community being clearly present, the hero is at last able to achieve, improved by having embraced those values. But Lightning, seeing the wrecked King and remembering the words of Doc Hudson, screeches to a stop inches before the finish line. Reversing, he approaches the King, pushes him back on the track, and acknowledges the relative insignificance of the Piston Cup in comparison to his new and improved self. He then declines the Dinoco corporate offer in favor of remaining faithful to his loyal Rust-eze sponsors. Chick Hicks, the only unredeemed alpha male at the end, celebrates his ill-gotten victory and is publicly rejected at the end by both his fans, "the twins," and, in a sense, by the Piston Cup itself, which slides onto the stage and hits him rudely in the side.

Conclusion

The trend of the New Man seems neither insidious nor nefarious, nor is it out of step with the larger cultural movement. It is good, we believe, for our son to be aware of the many sides of human existence, regardless of traditional gender stereotypes. However, maintaining a critical consciousness of the many lessons taught by the cultural monolith of Disney remains imperative. These lessons—their pedagogical aims or results—become most immediately obvious to us as parents when we watch our son ingest and express them, when he misunderstands and makes his own sense of them, and when we can see ways in which his perception of reality is shaped by them, before our eyes. Without assuming that the values of the films are inherently evil or representative of an evil "conspiracy to undermine American youth" (Giroux 4), we are still compelled to critically examine the texts on which our son bases many of his attitudes, behaviors, and preferences.

Moreover, the impact of Disney, as Henry Giroux has effectively argued, is tremendously more widespread than our household. Citing Michael Eisner's 1995 "Planetized Entertainment," Giroux claims that 200 million people a year watch Disney videos or films, and in a week, 395 million watch a Disney TV show, 3.8 million subscribe to the Disney Channel, and 810,000 make a purchase at a Disney store (19). As Benjamin Barber argued in 1995, "[T]he true tutors of our children are not schoolteachers or university professors but filmmakers, advertising executives and pop culture purveyors" (qtd. in Giroux 63). Thus we perform our "pedagogical intervention[s]" of examining Disney's power to "shap[e] national identity, gender roles, and childhood values" (Giroux 10). It remains a necessary and ongoing task, not just for concerned parents, but for all conscientious cultural critics.

Notes

1. See Susan Jeffords, "The Curse of Masculinity: Disney's *Beauty and the Beast?*" for an excellent analysis of that plot's developing the cruel Beast into a man who can love and be loved in return: "Will he be able to overcome his beastly temper and terrorizing attitude in order to learn to love?" (168). But even in this film, she argues, the Beast's development is dependent on "other people, especially women," whose job it is to tutor him into the new model of masculinity, the "New Man" (169, 170).

2. Two articles demand that we qualify this claim. Indirectly, they support the point of this essay by demonstrating a midcentury Disney model of what we call "alpha" masculinity. David Payne's "Bambi" parallels that film's coming-of-age plot, ostensibly representing a "natural" world, with the military mindset of the 1940s against which the film was drawn. Similarly, Claudia Card, in "Pinocchio," claims that the Disneyfied version of the nineteenth-century Carlo Collodi tale replaces the original's model of bravery and honesty with "a macho exercise in heroism [...and] avoiding] humiliation" (66–67),

3. Outside the animated classics, critics have noted a trend toward a postfeminist masculinity—one characterized by emotional wellness, sensitivity to family, and a conscious rejection of the most alpha male values—in Disney-produced films of the 1980s and 1990s. Jeffords gives a sensible account of the changing male lead in films ranging from *Kindergarten Cop* to *Terminator 2.*

4. In Disney criticism, the phrase "New Man" seems to belong to Susan Jeffords's 1995 essay on *Beauty and the Beast,* but it is slowly coming into vogue for describing other postfeminist trends in masculine identity. In popular culture, see Richard Collier's "The New Man: Fact or Fad?" online in *Achilles Heel: The Radical Men's Magazine* 14 (Winter 1992/1993). http://www.achillesheel.freeuk.com/article14_9.html. For a literary-historical account, see *Writing Men: Literary Masculinities from Frankenstein to the New Man* by Berthold Schoene-Harwood (Columbia UP, 2000).

5. Critics have described the superhero within some framework of queer theory since the 1950s, when Dr. Fredric Wertham's *Seduction of the Innocent* claimed that Batman and Robin were gay (Ameron Ltd, 1954). See Rob Lendrum's "Queering Super-Manhood: Superhero Masculinity, Camp, and Public Relations as a Textual Framework" (*International Journal of Comic Art* 7.1 [2005]: 287–303) and Valerie Palmer-Mehtan and Kellie Hay's "A Superhero for Gays? Gay Masculinity and Green Lantern" (*Journal of American Culture* 28.4 [2005]: 390–404), among myriad nonscholarly pop-cultural sources.

6. Interestingly, Andy and *Toy Story* in general are apparently without (human) male role models. The only father present in the film at all is Sid's, sleeping in front of the television in the middle of the day. Andy's is absent at a dinner out, during a move, and on the following Christmas morning. Andy himself, at play, imagines splintering a nuclear family: when he makes Sheriff Woody catch One-Eyed Black Bart in a criminal act, he says, "Say goodbye to the wife and tater tots...you're going to jail."

Works Cited

Bell, Elizabeth. "Somatexts at the Disney Shop: Constructing the Pentimentos of Women's Animated Bodies." Bell, *From Mouse to Mermaid* 107–24.

Bell, Elizabeth, Lynda Haas, and Laura Sells, eds. *Front Mouse to Mermaid: the Politics of Film, Gender, and Culture.* Bloomington: Indiana UP, 1995.

Card, Claudia. "Pinocchio." Bell, *From Mouse to Mermaid* 62–71.

Cars. Dir. John Lasseter. Walt Disney Pictures/Pixar Animation Studios, 2006.

Collier, Richard. "The New Man: Fact or Fad?" *Achilles Heel: The Radical Men's Magazine* 14 (1992–93). <http://www.achillesheel.freeuk.com/article14_9.html>.

Eisner, Michael. "Planetized Entertainment." *New Perspectives Quarterly* 12.4 (1995): 8.

Giroux, Henry. *The Mouse that Roared: Disney and the End of Innocence.* Oxford, Eng.: Rowman, 1999.

The Incredibles. Dir. Brad Bird. Walt Disney Pictures/ Pixar Animation Studios, 2004.

Jeffords, Susan. "The Curse of Masculinity: Disney's *Beauty and the Beast*." Bell, *From Mouse to Mermaid* 161–72.

Lendrum, Rob. "Queering Super-Manhood: Superhero Masculinity, Camp, and Public Relations as a Textual Framework." *International Journal of Comic Art* 7.1 (2005): 287–303.

Palmer-Mehtan, Valerie, and Kellie Hay. "A Superhero for Gays? Gay Masculinity and Green Lantern." *Journal of American Culture* 28.4 (2005): 390–404.

Payne, David. "Bambi." Bell, *From Mouse to Mermaid* 137–47.

Schoene-Harwood, Berthold. *Writing Men: Literary Masculinities from Frankenstein to the New Man.* Columbia: Columbia UP, 2000.

Sedgwick, Eve Kosofsky. *Between Men: English Literature and Male Homosocial Desire.* New York: Columbia UP, 1985.

Toy Story. Dir. John Lasseter. Wall Disney Pictures/ Pixar Animation Studios, 1995.

Wertham, Fredric. *Seduction of the Innocent.* New York: Reinhart, 1954.

Yabroff, Jennie. "Betas Rule." *Newsweek* 4 June 2007: 64–65.

Little in Common: Racial and Gender Differences in Adolescents' Television Diets

JANE D. BROWN AND CAROL J. PARDUN

The world of television has changed dramatically over the past two decades as technological developments have resulted in many more channels and greater access than any previous generation has experienced. Recent studies have found that two-thirds of young people (8 to 18 years old) have a television set in their bedrooms, and many of these sets are hooked up to cable television and VCRs or DVDs (Roberts, 2000). As channel capacity and access have increased, the television industry has created networks and channels targeted to more narrowly defined audience segments— based on both basic demographic categories such as age, race, and gender, as well as interests and activities—so that now we have cable channels for everybody from sports fans to shoppers and news hounds. Whole channels and programs have been developed primarily to appeal to younger audiences segmented by race and gender. Following the lead of MTV and the Black Entertainment Network (BET), the networks WB, UPN, and Fox have created a stable of programs designed especially for adolescents, with much more programming than ever aimed specifically at different racial and gender groups.

The basic premise of segmented programming is that viewers will choose programs that feature people who are like them (and will buy the products advertised). From a marketer's point of view, it is an advantage to have a relatively narrowly defined audience so products can be pitched more precisely to the specific needs and desires of that audience. From the consumer's point of view, the programming is more relevant to their lives

© 2004 Broadcast Education Association *Journal of Broadcasting & Electronic Media* 48(2), 2004, pp. 266–278.

because it features people, situations, and dilemmas similar to their own. From a cultural point of view, however, audience segmentation could have the undesirable effect of reducing exposure to other generations, alternative viewpoints and values, and perhaps reducing what might be called the common culture. As Wilson and Gutierrez (1995) suggest, "The media, rather than trying to find commonalities among diverse groups in the mass audiences, classify the differences and ways to capitalize on those differences through content and advertising. The force in society that once acted to bring people together, now works to reinforce the differences that keep them apart" (pp. 260–261).

Thus, television may no longer be the glue that keeps the melting pot together but rather may be "a new form of segregation" (Salamon, 2002, p. E1). In this article we consider to what extent television is serving as a form of common culture or as a form of segregation for young adolescents. We look at what kinds of television worlds Black and White, male and female adolescents are living in. Is the world so fragmented and specialized that there is little in common, or is it a world in which racial and gender differences are less important than they were in the past?

Literature Review
Adolescents and the Media

Steele and Brown (1995) and Steele (1999) proposed a model of adolescents' media practice that suggests that identity formation is a key motivation in the selection of, attention to, and interpretation of media. They theorized that as adolescents take on the developmental task of creating a sense of self, they may use the media as sources of models. Building on the Media Practice Model, Brown and Witherspoon (2001) proposed a model of teens' media diets, focused on the differential selection of media among adolescents. They theorized that adolescents will select media with the goal of creating a sense of self in which they are sometimes like all other members of their age cohort, sometimes like only some of their peers, and sometimes like no one else. They predicted that some of the

variance in choice will be explained by basic social positions, such as gender and class, such that girls will choose different television shows than boys and Blacks will choose different television shows than Whites. They also predicted, however, that some shows will be watched by all teens, regardless of race or gender, and those shows could be considered the "common teen culture." That proposition has not been tested empirically since the segmentation of the television market.

Studies have shown that even young children prefer characters who are similar to themselves in gender, age, or race, and "wishful identification" with characters the viewer would like to resemble increases with age (Comstock & Scharrer, 2001; von Feilitzen & Linne, 1975). Recent work suggests that it may be useful to think of these kinds of identifications as part of the development of "social" identities. As first defined by Tajfel (1978), "social identities" derive from the individual's knowledge of membership in social groups. In one of the first studies to apply Social Identity Theory to media use, Harwood (1999) found that college students who had strong identification with being young were more likely to say they watched television because they enjoyed "watching young people like me" and were more likely to choose shows that featured young characters. The study also found some evidence of reciprocal causation—i.e., as shows were chosen because they featured young people, the viewer's identification with the age group increased. Thus, Harwood (1999) concluded, "the mere act of making a viewing choice may enhance one's sense of belonging in a group and be important to overall self-concept" (p. 129).

Interestingly, Social Identity Theory also predicts that prejudice toward outgroups is a function of identification with ingroups because part of the process of developing a social identity involves comparison with the other group. A young Black male, for example, in the process of distinguishing himself as a Black man may compare what it is to be Black and male with what the culture says it is to be a White male and/or female and may in the process accept negative stereotypes that make Whites and females less attractive. Thus, it may be that as young people identify more strongly as "Black" or "White," "male" or "female," and are reinforced in these group identifications by what they see on television, prejudices toward the other gender or race may be developing, and the idea of a "common culture" may break down as differences rather than similarities become more salient.

In this study we take a first step toward expanding on these ideas to see if young people are making television choices based on race and gender. With increased programming directed at young people segmented by race and gender, television may be serving as a way to strengthen identifications as a male or female or as a Black or White young person. It remains to be seen if this is overall a healthy or unhealthy trend for the culture.

Age and Gender Differences in Media Choices

Media research has long shown that gender is a significant predictor of media choices. Some of the first studies of children's use of television found that girls and boys choose different kinds of programming along stereotypical lines (Himmelweit, Oppenheim, & Vince, 1958; Schramm, Lyle, & Parker, 1961). Gender differences show up early. In one study of three to five year old children, twice as many girls as boys named a family cartoon (*The Flintstones*) as a favorite, while boys were three times as likely as girls to name a violent cartoon (Comstock, 1991).

Recent studies of European and American children and adolescents have found significant and consistent age and gender preferences. From a comprehensive cross-sectional study of 6- to 16-year-olds in 12 European countries, Garitaonandia, Juaristi, and Oleaga (2001) reported that both older boys and girls were less interested in cartoons than younger children. Girls between 9 and 13 years old were most interested in soap operas, but maintained a lack of interest in sports. Sports, in contrast, increased in interest for boys. In a longitudinal analysis of 9- to 12-year-olds in Belgium, Roe (1998) also found increasing gender differentiation of media preferences in 11 of 15 television genres and concluded that "it is perhaps not too much of an exaggeration

to say that, in this period of their lives, boys and girls increasingly inhabit different media worlds" (p. 23). Girls rated children's programs, music, quiz and talk shows, and soap operas more highly than boys, who preferred sports, movies and science/technology programs.

A nationally representative sample of more than 2,000 8- to 18-year-olds in the United States found similar patterns: Boys were more than three times as likely as girls to say they had watched sports programs the previous day and girls were slightly more likely than boys to say they had watched a comedy program (Roberts & Foehr, 2004).

Racial Differences in Media Choices

The proportion of Black characters on entertainment television has increased dramatically since the 1980s. In an analysis of the 1996–97 television season, Mastro and Greenberg (2000) found that Blacks occupied 16% of the main and minor roles on prime time, exceeding their proportion in the population (12%). Despite their increased prevalence, critics remain concerned that Black characters are "largely ghettoized by network, day of the week, and by show type (i.e., concentrated in sitcoms)" (Hunt, 2002, p. 3). A content analysis of 85 fictional series airing on the 6 major networks (ABC, CBS, NBC, Fox, WB, and UPN) in fall 2001 found that Black characters were concentrated on UPN, the network with the lowest total audience share, and Black characters were more likely to appear on shows airing on Monday and Friday nights, the two weekday evenings attracting the fewest viewers. Black characters also were most likely to appear in situation comedies, and no prime-time drama on any of the major networks focused on Black characters. Three of the newest networks, Fox (debuted in 1985), WB, and UPN (both begun in 1995), grew quickly because they initially featured predominantly Black shows such as *In Living Color, The Steve Harvey Show,* and the multiracial *21 Jump Street,* that drew the Black audience. But by early 2001, UPN was the only network that continued to feature prime-time shows with primarily Black casts (Freeman, 2001).

Even in the 1980s, when there were far fewer portrayals of Blacks on television, it was clear that Black audiences favored shows featuring Black characters or all Black casts (Dates, 1980; Eastman & Liss, 1980). Black adolescents also reported greater levels of identification with Black rather than White characters (Greenberg & Atkin, 1982). In a recent study of 200 Black urban adolescent girls, Edwards (2001) found strong preferences for Black television programming and preferences for characters who looked like them and had lifestyles they admired.

Since the recent studies of gender differentiation in television program preferences were conducted without simultaneously considering racial differences, and most of the research on racial differences in television viewing preferences and motivations was conducted before the proliferation of demographically segmented channels, it is valuable to now look at how the social identities of race and gender intersect to affect television programming preferences. Has the burgeoning of cable channels designed especially for young Black audiences and young White audiences and shows designed to appeal to girls and/or boys decreased the possibility of a common youth culture? Do Black and White males and females live in a segregated television world?

Method

Sample

Students from three public school districts in the southeastern United States that included urban, suburban, and rural populations, and approximately equal proportions of Black and White male and female students, were recruited to participate in a study of 7th and 8th graders' media use. Fourteen of the 16 eligible middle schools agreed to be involved. Students were recruited over an 8-week period in the Fall of 2001. Members of the research team went to each participating school and told groups of students about the study. Students who were interested in participating filled out cards with their names, addresses, and telephone numbers. A packet of materials, including the parental consent form, the media use survey, and return stamped envelopes, were sent to parents. Each packet was given a unique ID number

so that when questionnaires were returned, all other identifying information was removed. All aspects of the protocol were approved by the university's institutional review board for protection of human subjects.

Based on the average monthly attendance for students across all participating schools (5,886), the questionnaire successfully reached 85% of the currently enrolled students. Initial nonresponders were sent follow-up postcards and a second set of materials to maximize response rates. By the end of the 4-month survey administration period, 3,262 completed surveys (with parent consent forms) were returned, for a final response rate of 65%.

Participant demographics were generally representative of the entire student body, although White females were slightly overrepresented in the sample compared to the school population (26% vs. 22%), and Black males were slightly underrepresented (18% vs. 22%). The income of the sample was somewhat higher than the total student body; 28% of the sample reported receiving free or reduced price breakfast or lunch, while 34% of the total school enrollment did.

Measures

The questionnaire was a 36-page booklet that included a number of questions about adolescents' current use of 6 different kinds of media (television, music, movies, newspapers, magazines, and the Internet). We focused only on the following variables in these analyses:

Gender

Respondents self-reported whether they were a "Girl" or "Guy." If this question was left blank, earlier self-reports from the school recruitment information were used to determine gender.

Race/Ethnicity

Respondents were asked to circle one of the following categories in response to the question: "The race that best represents you is?" "White," "African-American," "Hispanic," "Asian," or "Other (write in)." If left blank, school recruitment information was used. Due to the relatively small number of Hispanic, Asian, or "other" respondents (about

7% of the sample), analyses focused on only those respondents designating themselves as "White" or "African-American."

The analyses reported here focus on the 2,942 teens who provided complete responses to the 6 pages of questions about their television use and those respondents who identified themselves as African-American or White (93% of the sample). These analyses include 761 (26%) Black females, 577 (20%) Black males, 843 (29%) White females, and 761 (26%) White males. Respondents ranged in age from 11 to 16, with a mean and median of 12.8 years old.

Time spent watching television

Respondents were asked: "How often do you watch TV Mondays through Fridays during the school year?" and circled one of the following categories: "never," "once a week or less," "two or three times a week," "almost every day," "at least once a day," or "almost all the time I'm not in school."

Television shows watched regularly

A list of 140 currently running television programs was included in alphabetical order with the instruction, "Circle all the TV shows that you watch regularly." This list was created after extensive pilot work that generated a comprehensive inventory of shows most often watched by this age group. Commercial lists typically are based only on relatively small samples of larger age ranges and thus many of the shows on our list would not achieve sufficient audience numbers to be included. We began by visiting classrooms in area schools in the spring and summer previous to survey administration, and showing students a list of all television shows that Nielsen data indicated

were watched by 12- to 17-year-olds. The students were encouraged to name other shows they watched frequently. This enlarged list was then tested in focus groups and in other classrooms. The list was then supplemented with all prime-time shows that would debut during the data collection period.

Results

There is little evidence of a common teen television culture across race and gender among adolescents in this sample. Strikingly, only 4 of the 140 television shows included on the list were watched regularly by more than one-third of each of the four race/gender groups (see Table 1). These four shows would have little in common if they had been grouped by genre as most previous studies have done, and only two of the shows were in the top 10 shows on prime-time at the time of the survey (Network prime-time averages, 2002). *Who Wants to Be a Millionaire?*, one of the hottest shows of the 2001 season, is a game show, and *The Simpsons* is a long-running prime-time cartoon, and both were watched by adults as well. *Boy Meets World* and *Malcolm in the Middle*, in contrast, are coming-of-age situation comedies, both featuring a White boy. Neither of them has ever been in the top 10 of shows overall.

Black teens, regardless of gender, showed a clear preference for shows featuring Black characters. All ten shows watched by the largest proportions of Black teens in the sample featured Black characters. As shown in Table 2, the proportion of Black teens who reported watching these shows regularly is quite remarkable, ranging from almost

Table 1. Television Shows Watched by More Than One-Third of Each Teen Audience Segment

Television Shows	% Black Females N = 761	% Black Males N = 577	% White Females N = 843	% White Males N = 761
Who Wants to Be a Millionaire?	59.9	52.3	45.9	40.9
Boy Meets World	51.1	41.1	63.8	36.1
The Simpsons	40.1	61.9	40.3	65.0
Malcolm in the Middle	33.9	44.9	35.8	40.7

Note: All row entries are significantly different, χ^2, $p < .001$.

Table 2. Top 10 Television Shows Watched by Black Teens

Television Show	% of Black Teens Who Watch N = 1,338	% of White Teens Who Watch N = 1,604
Parkers	85.0	8.3
Martin	81.4	14.3
Hughleys	78.8	12.2
Moesha	78.8	15.3
106 and Park	78.4	10.6
Wayan Brothers	71.6	15.9
Parenthood	70.6	12.5
One on One	70.3	3.2
Steve Harvey Show	69.0	5.4
Living Single	67.0	11.0

Note: All row entries are significantly different, χ^2, $p < .001$.

Table 3. Top 10 Television Shows Watched by White Teens

Television Show	% of White Teens Who Watch N = 1,604	% of Black Teens Who Watch N = 1,338
The Simpsons	51.5	49.4
Boy Meets World	50.2	46.8
Whose Line Is it Anyway?	48.5	25.5**
Friends	47.8	23.4**
Who Wants to Be a Millionaire?	43.2	56.6**
Seventh Heaven	40.2	38.1
Sabrina the Teenage Witch	39.9	48.8**
Malcolm in the Middle	37.8	38.6
Survivor	36.7	30.3**
Lizzy McGuire	35.5	33.1

Note: **$p < .001$, χ^2.

two-thirds to more than three-fourths. None of the Black teens' top 10 shows were watched by more than 16% of the White teens.

For Whites, the apparent interest in same race characters prevailed as the top 10 shows for White teens all featured White casts (see Table 3). In contrast with the Black teens' top shows, however, the highest proportion of White teens watching any one show was only about half (51.5%) for *The Simpsons*, as compared to the Black teens' number one show that 85% reported watching regularly. Interestingly, all of the top 10 shows for the White teens were also watched by sizeable proportions of Black teens, and in some cases, such as *Sabrina the Teenage Witch* and *Who Wants To Be a Millionaire?*, a higher proportion of Blacks watched than Whites.

Overall, Blacks reported many more shows they watched regularly. White teens, on average, circled 20.5 (SD = 15.12) television shows while Black teens circled 34.6 (SD = 17.83) shows, t [2,938] = −23.14, $p < .000$. The difference in the number of shows watched by Blacks and Whites is probably due to the more time the Black teens spent watching television than the Whites. In this sample, 39% of the Black teens reported watching television "almost all the time I'm not in school" as compared to 16% of the White teens, X^2 [5, N = 2,947] = 297, p < .001. These patterns are similar to those found in a national sample of U.S. teens in which Black adolescents reported watching almost two hours more per day (4:41 hrs.) than Whites (2:47 hrs.) (Roberts, 2000). There was no significant difference in time spent viewing television by gender in our sample.

In general, gender differences were less dramatic than racial differences, but still only two of the top 10 shows for boys were also in the girls' list (*Cribs*—a show about celebrities' homes—and *Who Wants to be a Millionaire?*) (see Tables 4 and 5). The other eight shows watched regularly by sizeable proportions of boys consistently featured men or boys engaged in male adolescent humor (e.g., *Jackass, Southpark*) or action and/or adventure (e.g., *WWF Smackdown* [professional wrestling]). Interestingly, sizeable proportions ranging from one-fourth to one-half of the girls watched

Table 4. Top 10 Television Shows Watched by Teen Boys

Television Show	% of Boys Who Watch N = 1,485	% of Girls Who Watch N = 1,776
The Simpsons	62.9	40.5
Who Wants to Be a Millionaire?	44.4	51.3
Rocket Power	44.3	37.6
Jackass	43.6	28.9
South Park	42.5	27.8
Dragon BallZ	42.3	10.1
Malcolm in the Middle	41.7	34.8
Cribs	41.3	47.5
Celebrity Deathmatch	40.9	25.3
WWF Smackdown	40.7	26.7

Note: All row entries are significantly different, χ^2, p < .001.

Table 5. Top 10 Television Shows Watched by Teen Girls

Television Show	% of Girls Who Watch N = 1,776	% of Boys Who Watch N = 1,485
Sabrina the Teenage Witch	59.6	24.6
Boy Meets World	57.3	37.2
Seventh Heaven	54.1	20.7
Moesha	52.5	30.2
Who Wants to Be a Millionaire?	51.3	44.4
Clueless	50.1	15.0
Cribs	47.5	41.3
Parkers	47.5	33.3
Lizzy McGuire	47.2	18.0
Braceface	46.5	14.2

Note: All row entries are significantly different, χ^2, p < .001.

the boys' top 10 shows, too. The one exception, *Dragon BallZ*, is an animated show based on a videogame. Only 10% of the girls said they watched that program regularly.

In contrast, boys were less likely to watch the girls' top 10 shows. Four shows featuring White teen girls (*Sabrina the Teenage Witch, Seventh Heaven, Clueless,* and *Braceface*) were watched regularly by about half the girls, but fewer than one-fourth of the boys. Shows that both boys and girls watched either featured Black casts (e.g., *Moesha, Parkers*) or were shows that all groups tended to watch (e.g., *Who Wants to Be a Millionaire?, Boy Meets World*).

Discussion and Conclusions

There is little evidence of a common teen television culture among adolescents in this sample. The most striking findings are that, overall, only 4 of 140 television programs were watched by more than one-third of all the teens, and that so few of the shows watched regularly by Black teens are watched by White teens. Although it appears there is more commonality in television show viewing among males and females, males are less likely to be watching girls' shows than vice versa. In general, these analyses suggest that adolescent Black and White boys and girls in the United States are living in largely different television worlds.

This pattern of findings suggests that race and gender are basic motivators for choice of television content, and that adolescents may, indeed, be seeking models with whom they can identify as they develop a sense of themselves in the larger culture. These analyses suggest, too, that race may be a primary motivator, especially among Blacks, and perhaps more salient than gender. Ten of the programs listed were watched regularly by more than two-thirds of the Black teens, both male and female. All of those shows featured Black casts. None of those shows were watched by more than 17% of the White teens. These patterns may be explained to some extent by the still smaller range of selection Black teens have in the television landscape. Although Black characters occur much more frequently than they once did on television, there still are relatively few shows that include Black characters in contrast to the vast majority that include only White characters (Hunt, 2002). Apparently, Black adolescents have found and are loyal to these few shows that feature Blacks in the overall whiteness of the television world.

Observers have noted that the media world is more male than female oriented, and that girls will attend to content created for boys, but boys will rarely cross over to "girl" content (Cassell & Jenkins, 1998). We found more evidence of this phenomenon, as girls watch shows featuring teen girls struggling with teen relationships while boys watch boys behaving badly.

Given these different television worlds in which young people are living, we should learn much more about how adolescent audiences are interpreting and applying what they see in these television portrayals to their own lives. If, indeed, they are coming to television with an interest in learning more about how others their age, gender, and race are coping with similar issues, we should know more about what they are taking away. A small body of adolescent audience interpretation studies suggests that all adolescents will not interpret or incorporate gender portrayals in the same way (Ward, 2003), and some will critique and resist potentially harmful stereotypes (Brown, White, & Nikopoulou, 1993). Some viewers may be empowered by the newer portrayals of capable adolescent girls such as on *Charmed,* and *Sabrina the Teenage Witch,* but critics have argued that such portrayals may also reinforce "dominant norms of femininity, sexuality, race, class and the disciplining of the female body, all in the interests of capital" (Durham, 2003, p. 30).

Previous studies of the effects of television portrayals of minorities have found that programs such as *The Cosby Show* that attracted both White and Black audiences increased racial understanding and enhanced Black viewers' self-esteem, but the show may also have contributed to the perpetuation of the stereotype that Black people who are not successful have only themselves to blame (Inniss & Feagin, 2002). With more programs now on the air featuring Black casts, it is important to know if stereotypes are being reinforced or broken down. Our data suggest that it is unlikely that Whites are seeing many more Black characters than they ever did since most of the Black characters are appearing on programs White teens rarely watch.

In the future, given the rapid penetration of the Internet into homes and children's bedrooms (Roberts, 2000), we might expect such trends of bifurcated media worlds to be even more pronounced. The Internet is the epitome of segmentation, designed to appeal to highly idiosyncratic tastes and interests. Surveys show that young people often go to media sites on the Internet and join chat rooms and virtual fan clubs for their favorite television shows and characters (Teenage life online, 2001).

Finally, it is important to consider what it means for young people to grow up in an increasingly segregated media world while the world in which they are living is increasingly diverse. Since the civil rights era and the feminist movement of the 1960s and 1970s, we have been concerned about the lack of minority representation and racial and gender stereotyping on television (Signorielli, 2001). The television world today, in some ways, is much different than it was then, but it is not clear that as a culture we are in any better shape if our children can now choose a television diet that features only people who look like them.

Acknowledgments

This research was funded by a grant from the National Institute of Child Health and Human Development. An earlier version of this paper was presented at the International Communication Association conference in San Diego, CA in May 2003. The authors wish to thank Kelly L'Engle, who has been integral to the project since its inception.

References

Brown, J. D., White, A. B., & Nikopoulou, L. (1993). Disinterest, intrigue, resistance: Early adolescent girls' use of sexual media content. In B. S. Greenberg, J. D. Brown, & N. L. Buerkel-Rothfuss (Eds.), *Media, sex and the adolescent* (pp. 177–195). Cresskill, NJ: Hampton Press.

Brown, J. D., & Witherspoon, E. M. (2001). The mass media and adolescents' health in the United States. In Y. R. Kamalipour & K. R. Rampal (Eds.), *Media, sex, violence, and drugs in the global village* (pp. 77–96). Boulder, CO: Rowman & Littlefield.

Cassell, I., & Jenkins, H. (Eds.) (1998). *From Barbie to Mortal Kombat, gender and computer games.* Cambridge, MA: MIT Press.

Comstock, G. (1991). *Television and the American child.* San Diego, CA: Academic Press.

Comstock, G., & Scharrer, E. (2001). The use of television and other film-related media. In D. G. Singer & J. L. Singer (Eds.), *Handbook of children and the media* (pp. 47–72). Thousand Oaks, CA: Sage.

Dates, J. (1980). Race, racial attitudes and adolescent perceptions of Black television characters. *Journal of Broadcasting, 24(4)*, 549–560.

Durham, M. G. (2003). The girling of America: Critical reflections on gender and popular communication. *Popular Communication. 1(1)*, 23–31.

Eastman, H., & Liss, M. (1980). Ethnicity and children's preferences. *Journalism Quarterly, 57*, 277–280.

Edwards, L. (2001). Black like me: Value commitment and television viewing preferences of U.S. Black teenage girls. In K, Ross & P. Playdon (Eds.), *Black marks: Minority ethnic audiences and media* (pp. 49–66). Burlington, VT: Ashgate.

Freeman, M. (2001, November 26). Black-oriented sitcoms gaining White viewers. *Electronic Media, 20*, 1A.

Garitaonandia, C., Juaristi, P., & Oleaga, J. A. (2001). Media genres and content preferences. In S. Livingstone & M. Bovill (Eds.), *Children and their changing media environment: A European comparative study* (pp. 141–157), Mahwah, NJ: Erlbaum.

Greenberg, B. S., (1974). Gratifications of television viewing and their correlates for British children. In J. G. Blumler & E. Katz (Eds.), *The uses of mass communications: Current perspectives on gratifications research* (pp. 71–92), Beverly Hills, CA: Sage.

Greenberg, B. S. & Atkin, C (1982). Learning about minorities from television: A research agenda. In G. Berry & C. Mitchell-Kernan (Eds,), *Television and the socialization of the minority child* (pp. 215–243). New York: Academic Press.

Harwood, J. (1999). Age identification, social identity gratifications, and television viewing. *Journal of Broadcasting & Electronic Media, 43*(1), 123–136.

Himmelweit, H. T., Oppenheim, A. N., & Vince, P. (1958). *Television and the child.* London: Oxford University Press.

Hunt, D. (2002, June). Prime time in Black and White: Making sense of the 2001 fall season. *The CAAS Research Report* (1, pp. 1–11). Los Angeles: UCLA Center for African American Studies.

Inniss, L.B. & Feagin, J.R. (2002). The Cosby Show: The view from the Black middle class. In R. R. M. Coleman (Ed.), *Say it loud! African-American audiences, media, and identity* (pp. 187–204). New York: Routledge.

Mastro, D. E. & Greenberg, B. S. (2000). The portrayal of racial minorities on prime time television. *Journal of Broadcasting & Electronic Media, 44*(4), 690–703.

Roberts, D. F. (2000). Media and youth: Access, exposure, and privatization, *Journal of Adolescent Health, 27*(Suppl. 2), 8–14.

Roberts, D. F., & Foehr U. G. (2004). *Kids and media in America.* New York: Cambridge University Press.

Roe, K. (1998). "Boys will be boys and girls will be girls": Changes in children's media use. *European Journal of Communication, 23*(1), 5–25.

Salamon, J. (2002, February 1). An evolving vision in Black and White. *The New York Times*, p. E1.

Schramm, W., Lyle, J., & Parker, E. B. (1961). *Television in the lives of our children.* Stanford, CA: Stanford University Press.

Signorielli, N. (2001). Television's gender role images and contribution to stereotyping: Past, present, future. In D. C. Singer & J. L. Singer (Eds.), *Handbook of children and the media* (pp. 341–358). Thousand Oaks, CA: Sage.

Steele, J.R. (1999). Teenage sexuality and media practice: Factoring in the influences of family, friends and school. *Journal of Sex Research, 36*(4), 331–341.

Steele, J. R., & Brown, J. D. (1995). Adolescent room culture: Studying media in the context of everyday life. *Journal of Youth and Adolescence, 24*(5), 551–576.

Tajfel, H. (1978). Social categorization, social identity, and social comparison. In H. Tajfel (Ed.), *Differentiation between social groups: Studies in the social psychology of intergroup relations* (pp. 61–76). London: Academic Press.

Teenage life online: The rise of the instant-message generation and the Internet's impact on friendships and family relationships. (2001, June 20). Pew Research Center for People and the Press. Retrieved Oct. 1, 2003, *http://www.pewinternet.org*

Von Feilitzen, C., & Linne, O. (1975). Identifying with television characters. *Journal of Communication, 25*(4), 51–55.

Ward, L. M. (2003). Understanding the role of entertainment media in the sexual socialization of American youth: A review of empirical research. *Developmental Review, 23,* 347–388.

Wilson, C. C. & Gutierrez, F. (1995). *Race, multiculturalism, and the media: From mass to class communication* (2nd ed.). Thousand Oaks, CA: Sage.

Resistance Through Video Game Play: It's a Boy Thing

KATHY SANFORD AND LEANNA MADILL

Youth, in particular boys, are finding many literacy activities, largely outside the realm of the school institution, that engage them and sustain long-term interest, e.g., video games (including computer and console systems). These games provide an interesting, engaging, dynamic, social space for many types of boys, both those who succeed at school literacy and those who struggle; they do not have to fit into any particular affinity group, they can engage without interference or sanction from adults, whenever they choose or when they have opportunities, and in ways that provide social capital for making connections with peers in real-time and virtual spaces. The lack of boys' success in formal schooling activities, so frequently reported in public press, can, we argue, be framed as resistance, both unconscious and conscious, against meaningless, mindless, boring schooling or workplace activities and assignments; instead, they engage in activities that provide them with active involvement and interest. Video game play also serves as a form of resistance to stereotypical views of boys as a category who, by virtue of the fact that they are boys, has been categorized as unsuccessful learners—video games are spaces where players can be successful in their endeavours.

Video Game Culture, Gender, and New and Critical Literacies

Video Game Culture

According to the Kaiser Family Foundation study *Kids, Media, and the New Millennium*, boys and girls differ in the amount of time engaged with media. Girls aged 8 to 18 spent less time per day than boys with the combination of media surveyed. Boys spent more time with TV, video games, and computers than did girls who spent more time with music media and print materials (as cited in Newkirk, 2002, p. 42). Rowan, Knobel, Bigum, and Lankshear (2002) report similar findings, claiming that "girls use the internet more than do the boys surveyed, but the girls use it more for educational purposes" (p. 131). The Canadian Teachers' Federation (2003), in *Kids' Take on Media: Summary of Findings*, report that almost 60 percent of boys in grades 3–6 play video or computer games almost every day, 38 percent for boys in grade 10. For girls, 33 percent of grade-3 girls play interactive games every day, but only 6 percent of grade-10 girls (p. iv).

Boys and male youth are far more involved in video games than are girls. By engaging in these activities that resist traditional literacy learning, video game players are keeping up with the changing technological world faster and more productively than schools are. Gee (2000) describes this changing world: "If our modern, global, high-tech, and science-driven world does anything, it certainly gives rise to new semiotic domains and transforms old ones at an even faster rate" (p. 19).

"Attempts to assess the effects of video games on young people have been extensive," report Alloway and Gilbert (1998), "and have come from a variety of research domains and methodologies" (p. 95). Although some studies (Alloway & Gilbert, 1998; Alvermann, 2002, Rowan, Khobel, Bigum, &

Lankshear, 2002) have focused on connections between gender and video game play, many have focused on these issues separately, addressing video game play and learning (Gee, 2003), identity development through video game play (Filiciak, 2003), the nature of computer games (Myers, 2003), the value of video games (Newman, 2004), and gendered marketing strategies for video games (Ray, 2004).

Although video game culture is strongly male-focused and masculinist, developing aggressive themes and situations (Alloway & Gilbert, 1998), often children and youth are represented as a homogeneous group, ignoring issues of difference connected to gender (Kline, 2004) and differing impacts on diverse populations.

Gender and Masculinity

Gender as a social construct impacts learning both in and out of school, dictating what is and can be learned and what is out of bounds. Gender, and therefore masculinity, is not fixed in advance of social interaction, but is constructed in interaction, and masculinity must be understood as an aspect of large-scale social structures and processes (Connell, 1995, p. 39). From a poststructural perspective, there are multiple ways of being a male and creating/negotiating male subjectivity. These multiple and diverse positions open up the possibility of constituting subjectivity as multiple and contradictory (Davies, 1992): every individual male accesses, performs, and transforms multiple versions of masculinity in various contexts and at various times. There are multiple ways that masculinity is performed; however hegemonic versions of masculinity are most highly valued, that is, performances of masculinity that embody "the currently accepted answer to the problem of the legitimacy of patriarchy, which guarantees (or is taken to guarantee) the dominant position of men and the subordination of women" (Connell, 1995, p. 77).

Family activities and values transfer into schooling practices where notions of masculinity (often linked to images of such things as strength, cleverness, winning, power, and status) are further developed and reinforced, creating powerful

sites for gendered messages to be reinforced by teachers and young people themselves (Browne, 1995; Sanford, 2002). Hegemonic masculinity not only naturalizes masculine behaviours, but also male discipline areas, such as science, mathematics, mechanics, and technology—those areas seen to require rational, unemotional engagement.

Males and females develop attitudes towards science and machines differently, and at a very young age. As Ray (2004) notes, the concept of the computer as a male object is reinforced in children very early in their lives. Males, given machine-type toys, including computers, are encouraged to experiment with them; they are more likely to receive training (formal and informal) in using computers. One young participant in our study commented, "You've got to know how to make what go where and stuff. I learned some of that from a game manual, mostly just clicking around…that's how I learn that kind of thing, just trial and error." Males, like this participant, are socialized to engage with computers and video games.

New and Critical Literacies

In this article, we have discussed not only how males use video games to create resistances, but also our concerns related to video game play when viewed simply as another form of "text." We have raised questions about operational, cultural, and critical dimensions of learning. Based on a sociocultural perspective in examining new or alternative literacies comprehensively, we draw on Green's (1997) three-dimensional model that considers operational, cultural, and critical dimensions of literacy and learning. Operational literacy "includes but also goes beyond competence with the tools, procedures, and techniques involved in being able to handle the written language system proficiently. It includes being able to read and write/key in a range of contexts in an appropriate and adequate manner" (Lankshear & Knobel, 2003, p. 11). Cultural literacy "involves competence with the meaning system of a social practice; knowing how to make and grasp meanings appropriately within the practice…this means knowing what it is about given contexts of practice that makes for appropriateness or inappropriateness of particular ways of reading and writing" (Lankshear & Knobel, 2003, p. 11). Critical literacy addresses "awareness that all social practices, and thus all literacies, are socially constructed and 'selective': they include some representations and classifications—values, purposes, rules, standards, and perspectives—and exclude others" (Lankshear & Knobel, 2003, p. 11). We believe that as educators embrace video games as a powerful learning tool (Gee, 2003), they must also find ways to raise critical questions relating to these texts and to disrupt unexamined hegemonic masculine attitudes related to power, status, and exclusivity.

Methodology

In this article, we examine video games as a domain that many boys and men choose to resist traditional school-based literacy, and examine how they use games to resist controlling societal forces and so-called feminized spaces such as home, daycare, and school. Given the considerable and growing involvement of boys with this alternative form of learning about literacy, technology, and the world, it is critical for both males and females that researchers and educators examine the implication of this male immersion into these new semiotic and technological domains.

In this study, we elucidate the complexity of the interplay between gender and video game play, to better understand the nature of the learning done by male youth, and to consider the impact of this learning on them and on others in society. We observed the youths (predominantly male) in this study as they engaged in the literacy practice of video game play as a discursive tool. These observations provided a context in which we examined the performance of gender subjectivities through a range of alternative literacy practices (Gee, 1992; Street, 1984).

Participants and Data Collection

The informants for this study included two groups of participants/players. The first group, six young adolescent males attending a middle school in a small Canadian community, volunteered to participate in this study. Throughout the year, we observed them at school, both in classrooms and in less regulated spaces such as the hallways, out-of-doors, and in computer labs. We interviewed each participant twice throughout the year, where the discussion focused on his use of and interest in computers generally and game playing particularly. We transcribed the interviews, and used the first interview to shape the discussion of the second interview.

Our second group of participants, five young adult males, referred to us by acquaintances and selected for their interest in video game play, were observed and videotaped in their home environments, playing video games both independently and with a friend. We interviewed them in-depth two to three times over three months, where they discussed the nature of their video game playing and reflected on the influences of video game play on their lives. As with the first group, we transcribed the interviews, using the first interview to shape the focus of subsequent interviews. Both groups of participants, from the same geographical region, were predominantly from white, middle-class backgrounds. Our gender as two white females might have initially imposed barriers; however, the participants became very willing to share their ideas and expertise about video games and helped us understand their specific references and to share their insider knowledge.

The interviews were analyzed and coded using NVivo text analysis software program. The data were coded into categories, mapped, searched, synthesized, and analyzed. We also conducted manual coding of themes to supplement the computer analysis which we shared with boys. To recognize themes of significance, we used critical discourse analysis to identify oppositions, recurrent key terms, and subjects spoken about by the participants and connected to the video games identified by the participants.

Findings

A significant theme that we identified through the analysis was the participants' perception of resistance as they engaged in video game play: resistance to institutional authority, hegemonic masculinity, and femininity. These themes often overlapped or were sometimes even contradictory as the participants talked about how and why they played. Some of the forms of resistance were consciously selected (resistance to societal rules and resistance to school) while others were not consciously selected, but seemed to us to be pushing back on some of the restrictions and taboos they faced in school and current Western society (versions of restrictive masculinity and at the same time all types of femininity).

Through discussions with the participants, we learned what games they played, the types of games available, and their operational critique of the games (Lankshear & Knobel, 2003). We observed and videotaped the young adult players as they engaged in a variety of games (e.g., NBA Live 2005; Grand Theft Auto: Vice City; Counter Strike). Surprisingly to us, the games discussed by the adolescents and the young adults were very similar. They identified a range of game types: role play games—RPG (Final Fantasy, Halo), first person shooter—FPS (Max Payne, Medal of Honour, James Bond), strategy/simulation (Sims), Real Time Strategy—RTS (Counterstrike), multigenre role play/first person shooter (Grand Theft Auto), sports games (NBA 2005; Triple Play 2001, NHL Hockey 2002), and movie games (Harry Potter, Star Wars, Punisher, Man Hunt) as being games they chose to spend hours playing, with their friends or on their own. Boys and male youth are engaging in the same types of video games as adults, even though the games are intended for mature adult players (Canadian Teachers' Federation study, 2003).

Sites of Resistance

We examined the role(s) that video games play for males in challenging existing societal norms and expectations as they sought to define their masculine subjectivities in appropriate ways. Popular culture and media have historically been used as sites of resistance, whether through music, banners, graffiti, or alternative newspapers (Guzzetti & Gamboa, 2004) and this use of popular media continues today to resist constricting forms of education that stereotype, limit learning

opportunities for segments of the population, and prevent meaningful learning for a rapidly increasingly global, technological, and digital world. Video game players demonstrate many examples of resistance through challenges to rules and structures imposed by existing societal regulation and through challenges to restrictive identity formations and stereotypes.

Three significant areas of potential conflict and resistance include: institutional authority, hegemonic masculinity, and femininity. There are many ways in which students, particularly boys, overtly resist the hegemony of adult authority, and video game play offers them a safe place to contest these power structures.

Resistance to Institutional Authority

Whether purposefully or unconsciously, youth engage in practices that serve to resist imposition of structures and rules currently prevailing in society. These rules are challenged in both private and social spaces. Even when speaking to us as researchers, the participants seemed more willing to share their expertise once it was clear that we were not negatively judging their video game play. Players shared their frustrations and (either overtly or subtly) opposed authority within their cultural groups, ignoring and reshaping the rules. As they gained skills and confidence in playing games, they felt more able to resist traditional authority, relying on their fellow gamers for support and understanding—of the risks, the meaning, and the value. "I like lots of video games," said one younger participant, "though there are some games that I had to defend that adults would think are stupid." They received immediate feedback not only from the game but also from their peers as they developed greater skill and confidence in playing the game.

The world of school, followed by the world of work, offers many routinized, dull tasks that do not offer the qualities reported by males as required for meaningful engagement, that is, personal interest, action, fun, purpose, or opportunities for success (Smith & Wilhelm, 2002; Blair & Sanford, 2004). Instead, they faced a world of ordinariness, lacking excitement or purpose. "I get bored quite a bit," one adolescent participant told us, "at school and at home. Then I usually go up and play on the computer." All the adult male participants explained that they used games to "zone out," to stop thinking or engaging with real people in their lives who have demands and remind them of their responsibilities. Video games enabled players to create fantasy worlds for themselves where they were heroic, active, and respected.

Video games also offer opportunities for players to learn information in alternate multi-modal ways through playing video games, unlike traditional school learning that is most often linear and book based. Engaging in *Medal of Honor: Pacific Assault* allows youth to gain information about a significant historic event, but goes far beyond transmission of facts because adrenaline allows the players to feel the experience through sound and vibration, newer aspects of video game play. Simulation games (Sim City, Speed Racing, Air Strike) enable players to learn about valued workplace and life skills, such as driving a car, flying a plane, or building a city. The immersion experiences that are promised, engaging players in the action, enabling them to feel the exhilaration and the fear, create a far more powerful and memorable learning experience than the reading of a textbook. One young adolescent participant reported, "I've learned tons about history, tons and tons, from *Civilization* 3. You just learn lots of stuff, and you don't really think about it." Not a far stretch, then, for students to begin to challenge the material (both content and format) being presented in school, and to resist the linear, unidimensional approach to learning that is so often used in school.

Video games provide many opportunities for players to explore alternatives to the reality of adult society and its patriarchal, imposed rules. These rules, or laws, create restrictive structures that adolescents yearn to resist. As one young adult commented, "…it's cool, you can just explore…you can fly with a jet pack, break into an airport, grab some pizza…you're not limited to what you can do." Through video game play, they can try out resistant and dangerous choices and experience the consequences, all within the safety of game play. The opportunity to adopt an alternative persona and to experience characters' perceptions and actions, which are often inappropriate or illegal actions in the real world, and usually have no consequences, was a powerful enticement. One young adult participant commented,

"You take street racing that's illegal and you take new cars and you soup them up and you make them look all flashy and crazy…and you race them on the street, swerving in and around other cars and things like that—it's slightly rebellious or whatever, but I'd like to see what that's like."

The players assume authority as the game character and thereby gives their individual consent for the actions and attitudes that they role play (Leonard, 2004). Playing games that transgress societal, family, and school rules and norms enables a freedom to experiment with and challenge existing restrictions that, while providing safety, are also limiting and dull. Trying on resistant thoughts and actions is highly appealing to our participants.

The technology of video games allows players to cheat by downloading codes or finding glitches in the game. One participant explained that players use cheats[1] because "at the moment they're so angry or frustrated with the game that they just want to go ahead, or they wonder, Wow! It would be so great if I had that." By using cheats, and engaging in a community that understands the purpose of cheats and the importance of them, players can band together to resist traditional and mainstream rules as a community, using their social connections to succeed at their game play.

Many video game story lines encourage players to resist society's expectations. From stealing cars to killing enemies or random people, the game allows players to play out scenarios that they would never actually do: "It's kinda fun to do because it's not something that you would do everyday, obviously." Video games allow players to forego the rules of the real world and engage in a new fantasy frontier where they can be mavericks, able to ignore rules that others have to abide. When players state that the reason they play video games is to escape, they suggest that they are not having to think critically about what they play: "I definitely play it to get into the role and forget about other things" and "I just go and play it and space out" are answers from our adult participants as to why they play video games. This attitude allows them the right to ignore stereotypes, prejudices, or other usually conflicting messages that they would otherwise not be allowed to (or even want to) participate with. "It's like a feeling of power, but it's sadistic," one adult participant explained, "You really enjoy it, like killing someone, blasting them in the head...maybe it's cause you can't do it, it's such a forbidden thing, but like they make it so real and powerful, like in a game you can have the ability to smoke people continuously." Another participant commented, "I don't know why I enjoy it, I imagine myself living in Vice City [Grand Theft Auto] just doing missions and you can kill people and steal cars and just do bad stuff. You do all these things that you don't necessarily want to do, but it gives you so much power...." To succeed the participants engaged in the rules of the game, even if the rules did not match socially constructed values or rules.

Resistance to Hegemonic Masculinity

Western society has responded to expanded and alternative gender positions with a rigid homophobic stance regarding masculinity. Young males today are faced with a fierce policing of traditional masculinity, and the rules of masculinity are enforced in many overt and subtle ways. Being a male who does not exhibit characteristics of physical strength, individuality, and machismo can find the world dangerous and lonely space (Connell, 1995; Frank, Kehler, & Davison, 2003; Kehler, 2004; Martino & Pallotta-Chiarolli, 2001). Video games provide players with spaces in which to experiment with identity: to safely resist traditional masculinities currently prevailing in society, or conversely, to demonstrate their heterosexual masculinity and resist connections to the feminine, and to challenge societal expectations of appropriateness regarding attitude, appearance, or behaviour. By adopting roles through which they can experiment with their identity formation, they can expand their sense of self and

understand their world from new perspectives. One adult participant negotiated his identity as he described a game, "In *Halo*, I really like that it is shoot 'em up, not that I am a killer, but you know...I just like that it is go and shoot, shoot, and kill, kill, kill."

In another interview, an adult male participant was asked what characteristics of male video game characters he admired. He responded: "I'd like to have the big body, a six-pack not an 8 pack!...I'd like to be built; I don't want to be a drug dealer, king of the city." When he was asked, "What about saving the girl?" he answered, "That would be neat...I've often had dreams about that, meeting a girl by doing something courageous, you know." Another adult participant commented on his desire to be a hockey player. "I didn't ever play hockey; I don't know the rules. But in the game I'm always trying to start a body check or start a fight...I like all the silly things like how the glass breaks when you do a body check."

Video games provide a way to resist traditional hegemonic masculinities in a safe space, to play out alternative personas, such as personas of men of colour or of females. In reality, not all males are strong and macho (and may not want to be), but they may wish to try on the persona of a rugged heroic figure who rescues the weak from dangerous situations. By using on-line forums and Internet game play, subjectivities can be disguised and trans/reformed in myriad ways. One participant talked about a friend whom he described as a "very fairy tale type of person, similar to the *Everquest* type of thing. He's kind of creative, and likes imaginary types of stuff." This friend was able to engage in the video game as a character who did not display traditional masculinity traits, yet in the context of the game it was safe for him to do so. However, his alternative masculine persona might not have been as safe to perform in reality.

As suggested earlier in this article, the media and the public have categorized boys as regularly experiencing failure in school, of underperforming, and of being less literate than girls. Video games provide spaces where boys can dominate and create an alternative sense of success. They are finding many activities that engage them and sustain long-term interest; video games provide an interesting, engaging, dynamic social space for many types of boys who do not have to fit into any particular category. Video games also allow for the creation of additional social spaces where boys from various social groups (athletes, trades, academics, rebels) can belong, resisting imposed societal roles and positions. By creating fantasy personas for themselves, heroic powerful figures able to rescue innocent girls and garner the respect of their peers, they resist the traditionally stereotypical ways they are viewed in society. Additionally, they develop skills that are valued in the workplace, giving them future social capital through which to be successful.

By connecting to communities, face-to-face or on-line, and engaging in extensive rounds of play, players gain skills in manual dexterity, ability to read multiple screens or texts simultaneously, and make quick, accurate decisions based on information provided. These operational literacies referred to earlier in this article (Lankshear & Knobel, 2003) teach the mostly male players how to use many functions of computers, to make repairs and adjustments to programs and glitches, to make accurate predictions, and to apply their knowledge to new situations—most importantly, they gain a confidence in their ability to use computers effectively, not just video games, but many aspects of computers. This confidence enables them to resist traditional school literacies, choosing instead modes of literacy that support the particular type of masculine persona they have selected for themselves, and make a commitment to that self-selected identity. As Gee (2003) comments, "Such a commitment requires that they are willing to see themselves in terms of a new identity, that is, to see themselves as the *kind of person* who can learn, use, and value the new semiotic domain" (p. 59, italics in original). And if they are successful, then they will be valued by and accepted in that affinity group.

Rejecting Femininity

One way that male game players use video games as a form of resistance is to create a clearly non-female identity, that is, muscular, big, and dangerous-looking. Although it is interesting to try on different personas, even those of females, it is personally dangerous to associate oneself with the feminine. One young adult male participant explained how sometimes a friend of his might choose to be the princess in a Mario Bros, game and they would all tease him. "We started calling him princess." This adult participant is a football player in real life and he attempted to masculinize his interest in video games; he comments,

> "I don't think many girls are too interested in playing a game of *Dead or Alive* and seeing another girl's scantily clad body bounce around like it is, that kind of stuff appeals to guys. It's on more of a primal level, just kinda like one-on-one combat. It really turns guys on for some reason."

He differentiates males from females in this sexual way, and includes himself in this masculine description; he is not sure why males are drawn to these primal interests but is not inclined to question his theory or his participation in this world.

A similar example of resistance within the role playing games is the type of avatars (game characters) that players select to become in the video games. The selected character is often the strong, independent rebel, such as in *Max Payne*, all the *Grand Theft Auto* games, *Man Hunt*, and *Counter Strike;* one adult gamer described these characters as "not really dependent on anyone else, very like 'I am going to do this my way.'" The players' desire to shape their identity as rugged, independent, and strong precludes them from making choices of characters who seem weak, dependent, and feminine. This same participant talked about Max Payne as a character he admired. "He's kind of a dark and lonely character, very dark and devious, and he talks with kind of a low deep voice and he's very masculine and he usually gets with one woman in the storyline."

Although choice of creating video game characters helps the players to experiment with diverse subjectivities, again the hegemonic masculinity model looms large in most of the games the participants report playing regularly. As they negotiate their sense of self through various video game characters, we worry that they are reinforcing the binary that relegates females to subordinate positions and does not allow any space or opportunity for a critical reading of the gender positions offered in the games.

Discussion

There is no question in our minds that video games encourage resistance to school values, parental authority, and societal expectations, and partly because of the perception of resistance are hence a major attraction for youth. Video games are fun, and this is partly because they are perceived as dangerous, entering forbidden territory. There is no doubt that video game players are developing an understanding of learning principles through playing games, as suggested by Gee (2003), in relation to text design, intertextuality, semiotics, transfer of knowledge, or probing and identifying multiple approaches. However, we are not convinced that, as Gee claims, there is significant learning about cultural models. We did not find evidence that learners were thinking consciously and reflectively about cultural models of the world, or that they were consciously reflecting on the values that make up their real or video game worlds. The resistance that we have observed in one area of the players' lives did not necessarily lead to resistance of imposed stereotypical and potentially harmful beliefs and attitudes. Resistance to hegemonic hypermasculinity in game play does not necessarily lead the players to challenge gender stereotypes, or present themselves to the world in alternative representations of masculinity. And although resistance to anything feminine enables male players to develop their own subjectivity, it does not cause them to be more aware of their privileged positions of power or to respect difference in any significant way. We are concerned that the resistances made possible by video game play serves only to reify the traditional stereotypes and cement them firmly in place.

There is, perhaps, a place to encourage resistance on a more conscious and responsive level through video game play. Is it possible that spaces for critical questioning can be identified and taken up in relation to the images, actions, attitudes, and values being presented at hyperdrive speeds throughout the duration of a video game? As we began to see in our interviews with young adult males, there is a place for them to critically examine their motivation and attitudes as they engage in games. Critical questions, such as those posed by Rowan and colleagues (2002), can help to shape resistances that change the world, rather than merely playing with the world as it exists.

- Who and what are included? What groups of people are included or excluded? How do you know?
- What do those who are included get to do? What roles are taken by men/boys, women/girls? What evidence do you have?
- Which people and roles are valued, and how is this communicated?
- Who has control? Who has access to power? Who exercises power? Who acts independently? Who initiates action?
- What are various people rewarded for and with?
- In what ways does the inclusion or exclusion reflect to your own life?
- What are the consequences of this relationship?
- What alternatives are there? (pp. 117–118)

These types of questions enable engagement with and purpose for resistance, encouraging video game players to look beyond the superficial qualities of action, speed, and excitement to a consideration of more fundamental levels of meaning and value that includes issues of power, control, and difference.

Conclusion

Popular media has historically been used as sites of resistance, through underground newspapers, graffiti, and music. And it is being used today to resist constricting forms of education that stereotype, limit learning opportunities, and prevent meaningful learning for a rapidly and increasingly global, technological, and digital world. The speed at which literacies are being challenged and reshaped defies institutional support and knowledge from maintaining the pace. Children create connections when they learn: "Our experiences in the world build patterns in our mind, and then the mind shapes our experience of the world (and the actions we take in it), which, in turn, reshapes our mind" (Gee, 2003, p. 92). Gee acknowledges that the harmful side of patterned thinking can lead to prejudices or stereotypes. If video games are a main area from which players gain knowledge about a certain type of person, setting, or event, then knowledge is heavily influenced by the limitations, biases, and values found in the video games. It is these potentially harmful effects that cause us to draw on Lankshear and Knobel's (2003) framework that includes a critical dimension of literacy and learning, and to recognize the need for further research into the effects of video game playing in the long term, both for boys and for girls.

Through an examination of the opportunities for resistance to traditional authority and identity formation through video game play, we can see the multiple types of literacy learning that are possible. Players are developing a wide range of useful operational knowledge that can be used as social capital in the workplace. As discussed previously, they are gaining a confidence in using new technologies, a belief that they can use and create programs effectively; they are becoming accomplished at making speedy decisions and reactions, developing a new level of manual dexterity, and are able to read/process multiple pieces of information (text or screen) simultaneously.

However, as Gee (2003) points out, it is the potentially harmful effects of such opportunities for subversive and localized resistance as video game play affords that also need to be interrogated. Educators and researchers need to be aware of the cultural and critical literacies that may or may not be addressed through the extensive video game play that is currently in vogue with many boys and young men. Resistance to the video game representations of gender, race, and sexual orientation are generally uni-dimensional and highly stereotypical; these can serve to reinforce societal prejudices that maintain hegemonic patriarchal power structures and understandings if the various types

of resistance available to game players are not recognized and encouraged. More thought needs to be given to considerations of appropriateness related to specific contexts, indeed appropriateness of values and respect for diverse perspectives needs to be encouraged and supported.

In our observations of video game play, we believe that the speed of decision making and action taking in video games mitigates any reflective element of the game beyond how to win—during game play there is often little opportunity to consider alternative, more complex issues and decisions. There is opportunity to learn and experience historical events in multiple modes, but space and encouragement to reflect upon which of these perspectives holds more evidence of ethical and moral truth is also important.

Clearly evident in discussion with these video game players is an element of critical literacy in relation to technical and technological qualities of video games, in relation to the realism of visual components of the games, and in relation to comparisons with other modes of interaction. The participants are highly articulate about aspects of the game that function well, glitches in the games, and visual elements of the game. However, we are concerned about a lack of demonstrated critical thought in relation to alternate worldviews and perspectives on sociocultural issues. As Lankshear and Knobel (2003) suggest,

> to participate effectively and productively in any literate practice, people must be socialized into it. But if individuals are socialized into a social practice without realizing that it is socially constructed and selective, and that it can be acted on and transformed, they cannot play an active role in changing it (p. 11).

If players are not critically engaged in the literacies of video games, they will not be able to understand the transformative and active production aspects of meaning making; rather they will be limited to existing in and engaging with literacies as they are created by others. There will be little room for players to consider the origins of the games, who creates the characters and the commercial aspects of the games, and the values that are subtly (or overtly) being perpetuated and encouraged.

Both educators and researchers need to consider whether the resistance to authority and to identity shaping enables future citizens to engage critically in the world, or whether their resistance is limited to small acts of adolescent defiance. Is the nature of their resistance limited itself to the individual or self-selected affinity group, or does their engagement in oppositional interactions engage the broader world? Do video games desensitize players from moral and ethical responsibility for the world? Do video games support concern for environmental and ecological realities that continue to consume the human and natural world or do they provide escapes from these global issues?

Further, how are schools developing the increased sophistication in operational literacies, but also creating opportunities for students to engage with cultural and critical literacies that are so necessary for the twenty-first century? How are schools understanding and addressing the knowledge capital that will be needed by our future generations for being successful in an increasingly technological and changing world? These are some of the concerns that need to be taken up by educators and researchers as they attempt to gain deeper and broader understandings of the nature of video game learning and the nature of resistance.

Note

1. Cheat is a code a player can enter into the game to make play easier.

References

Alloway, N., & Gilbert, P. (1998). Video game culture: Playing with masculinity, violence and pleasure. In S. Howard (Ed.), *Wired Up: Young people and the electronic media* (pp. 95–114). London, UK: UCL Press.

Alvermann, D. (Ed.). (2002). *Adolescents and literacies in a digital world.* New York: Peter Lang.

Blair, H. & Sanford, K. (2004). Morphing literacy: Boys reshaping their school-based literacy practices. *Language Arts*, 81(6), 452–460.

Browne, R. (1995). Schools and the construction of masculinity. In R. Browne & R. Fletcher (Eds.), *Boys in schools: Addressing the real issues* (pp. 224–233). Sydney, AU: Finch Publishing.

Canadian Teachers' Federation. (2003). *Kids/ take on media: Summary of finding.* Retrieved April 6, 2006, from www.ctf-fce.ca/en/projects/MERP/summaryfindings.pdf

Connell, R. W. (1995). *Masculinities.* Berkeley and Los Angeles, CA: University of California Press.

Davies, B. (1992). Women's subjectivity and feminist stories. In C. Ellis & M. Flaherty (Eds.), *Investigating subjectivity: Research on lived experience* (pp. 53–76). London, UK: Sage Publications.

Filiciak, M. (2003). Hyperidentities: Postmodern identity patterns in massively multiplayer online role-playing games. In M. Wolf & B. Perron (Eds.), *The videogame theory reader* (pp. 87–102). New York: Routledge.

Frank, B., Kehler, M., & Davison, K. (2003). A tangle of trouble: Boys, masculinity and schooling, future directions. *Educational Review*, 55(2), 119–133.

Gee, J. P. (1992). *The social mind: Language, ideology and social practice.* New York: Bergin & Harvey.

Gee, J. P. (2000). Teenagers in new times: A new literacy perspective. *Journal of Adolescent & Adult Literacy*, 43, 412–120.

Gee, J. P. (2003). *What video games have to teach us about learning and literacy.* New York: Palgrave MacMillan.

Green, B. (1997, May). Literacies and school learning in new times. Keynote address at the Literacies in Practice: Progress and Possibilities Conference, South Australian Department of Education and Children's Services and the Catholic Education office, Adelaide, Australia.

Guzzetti, B. J., & Gamboa, M. (2004). Zining: The unsanctioned literacy practice of adolescents. In C. Fairbanks, J. Worthy, B. Maloch, J. Hoffman & D. L. Schallert (Eds.), *53rd yearbook of the National Reading Conference* (pp. 208–217). Oak Creek, WI: National Reading Conference.

Kehler, M. (2004). "The Boys" interrupted: Images constructed, realities translated. *Education and Society*, 22(2), 83–99.

Kline, S. (2004, January). Technologies of the imaginary: Evaluating the promise of toys, television and video games for learnin.' Paper presented at the Sixth Australian and New Zealand Conference on the First Years, Tasmania.

Lankshear, C., & Knobel, M. (2003). *New literacies: Changing knowledge and classroom learning*, Buckingham, UK: Open University Press.

Leonard, D. (2003). Live in your world, play in ours: Race, video games, and consuming the other. *Studies in Media & Information Literacy Education*, 3(4). Retrieved September 25, 2005, from http://www.utpjournals.com/jour.ihtml?lp=simile/issue12/leonardX1.html

Leonard, D. (2004) Unsettling the military entertainment complex: Video games and a pedagogy of peace. *Studies in Media & Information Literacy Education*, 4(4). Retrieved September 25, 2005, from http://www.utpjournals.com/jour.ihtml?lp=simile/issue16/leonardx1.html

Martino, W., & Pallota-Chiarolli, M. (Eds). (2001). *Boys' stuff: Boys talking about what matters.* Sydney, AU: Allen & Unwin.

Myers, D. (2003). *The nature of computer games: Play as semiosis.* New York: Peter Lang.

Newkirk, T. (2002). Foreword. In M. Smith & J. Wilhelm, *Reading don't fix no Chevys: Literacy in the lives of young men* (pp. ix–xi). Portsmouth, NH: Heinemann.

Newman, J. (2004). *Videogames.* London, UK: Routledge.

Ray, S.G. (2004). *Gender inclusive game design: Expanding the market.* Hingham, MA: Charles River Media, Inc.

Rowan, L., Knobel, M., Bigum, C., Lankshear, C. (2002). *Boys, literacies and schooling.* Buckingham, UK: Open University Press.

Sanford, K. (2006). Gendered literacy experiences: The effects of expectation and opportunity for boys' and girls' learning. *Journal of Adult and Adolescent Literacy*, 49(4), pp. 302–314.

Smith, M., & Wilhelm, J. (2002). *Reading don't fix no Chevys: Literacy in the lives of young men.* Portsmouth, NH: Heinemann.

Street, B. (1984). *Literacy in theory and practice.* New York: Cambridge University Press.

The Gendered Body

Perhaps nothing is more deceptive than the "naturalness" of our bodies. We experience what happens to our bodies, what happens *in* our bodies, as utterly natural, physical phenomena.

Yet to the social scientist nothing could be further from the truth. Our bodies are themselves shaped and created, and interpreted and understood by us, in entirely gendered ways. How we look, what we feel, and what we think about how our bodies look and feel, are the products of the ways our society defines what bodies should look like and feel. Thus, for example, cultural standards of beauty, musculature, and aesthetics are constantly changing—and with them our feelings about how we look stacked up against those images.

Take, for example, women's notions of beauty. Feminist writer Naomi Wolf argued that "the beauty myth"—constantly shifting and unrealizable cultural ideals of beauty—traps women into endless cycles of diets, fashion, and consumer spending that render them defenseless. Fortunes are made by companies that purvey the beauty myth, reminding women that they do not measure up to these cultural standards and then provide products that will help them try. By such logic, women who experience eating disorders are not deviant nonconformists, but rather overconformists to unrealizable norms of femininity. Feminist philosopher Susan Bordo's essay reminds us of the ways in which cultural conceptions of women's bodies articulate with notions of femininity. And Sarah Grogan and Nicola Wainwright describe the consequences for girls who grow up in this culture of slenderness.

A parallel process engages men. While women can never be thin enough, men can never be pumped up enough. Musculature remains the most visible signifier of masculinity. Men have far lower rates of health-seeking behavior—it's more manly to ignore health problems and live with pain—and there are gender differences in rates of various illnesses. And it's entirely sexualized, as Raine Dozier explains in her analysis of how one performs both sexuality and gender through embodied practices. There is even some evidence that the "truth" of our bodies may be quite deceiving. Transgendered people, intersexed people, and people with ambiguous genitalia all throw into stark relief the ways in which our assumptions that gender adheres to a specific body may not hold in all circumstances.

The Body and the Reproduction of Femininity

SUSAN BORDO

Reconstructing Feminist Discourse on the Body

The body—what we eat, how we dress, the daily rituals through which we attend to the body—is a medium of culture. The body, as anthropologist Mary Douglas has argued, is a powerful symbolic form, a surface on which the central rules, hierarchies, and even metaphysical commitments of a culture are inscribed and thus reinforced through the concrete language of the body.[1] The body may also operate as a metaphor for culture. From quarters as diverse as Plato and Hobbes to French feminist Luce Irigaray, an imagination of body morphology has provided a blueprint for diagnosis and/or vision of social and political life.

The body is not only a *text* of culture. It is also, as anthropologist Pierre Bourdieu and philosopher Michel Foucault (among others) have argued, a *practical,* direct locus of social control. Banally, through table manners and toilet habits, through seemingly trivial routines, rules, and practices, culture is *"made* body," as Bourdieu puts it—converted into automatic, habitual activity. As such it is put "beyond the grasp of consciousness...[untouchable]. by voluntary, deliberate transformations."[2] Our conscious politics, social commitments, strivings for change may be undermined and betrayed by the life of our bodies—not the craving, instinctual body imagined by Plato, Augustine, and Freud, but what Foucault calls the "docile body," regulated by the norms of cultural life.[3]

Throughout his later "genealogical" works (*Discipline and Punish, The History of Sexuality*),

Foucault constantly reminds us of the primacy of practice over belief. Not chiefly through ideology, but through the organization and regulation of the time, space, and movements of our daily lives, our bodies are trained, shaped, and impressed with the stamp of prevailing historical forms of selfhood, desire, masculinity, femininity. Such an emphasis casts a dark and disquieting shadow across the contemporary scene. For women, as study after study shows, are spending more time on the management and discipline of our bodies than we have in a long, long time. In a decade marked by a reopening of the public arena to women, the intensification of such regimens appears diversionary and subverting. Through the pursuit of an ever-changing, homogenizing, elusive ideal of femininity—a pursuit without a terminus, requiring that women constantly attend to minute and often whimsical changes in fashion—female bodies become docile bodies—bodies whose forces and energies are habituated to external regulation, subjection, transformation, "improvement." Through the exacting and normalizing disciplines of diet, makeup, and dress—central organizing principles of time and space in the day of many women—we are rendered less socially oriented and more centripetally focused on self-modification. Through these disciplines, we continue to memorize on our bodies the feel and conviction of lack, of insufficiency, of never being good enough. At the farthest extremes, the practices of femininity may lead us to utter demoralization, debilitation, and death.

Viewed historically, the discipline and normalization of the female body—perhaps the only gender oppression that exercises itself, although to different degrees and in different forms, across age, race, class, and sexual orientation—has to be acknowledged as an amazingly durable and flexible strategy of social control. In our own era, it is difficult to avoid the recognition that the contemporary preoccupation with appearance, which still affects women far more powerfully than men, even in our narcissistic and visually oriented culture, may function as a backlash phenomenon, reasserting existing gender configurations against any attempts to shift or transform power relations.[4] Surely we are in the throes of this backlash today. In newspapers and magazines we daily encounter stories that promote traditional gender relations and prey on anxieties about change: stories about latch-key children, abuse in day-care centers, the "new woman's" troubles with men, her lack of marriageability, and so on. A dominant visual theme in teenage magazines involves women hiding in the shadows of men, seeking solace in their arms, willingly contracting the space they occupy. The last, of course, also describes our contemporary aesthetic ideal for women, an ideal whose obsessive pursuit has become the central torment of many women's lives. In such an era we desperately need an effective political discourse about the female body, a discourse adequate to an analysis of the insidious, and often paradoxical, pathways of modern social control.

Developing such a discourse requires reconstructing the feminist paradigm of the late 1960s and early 1970s, with its political categories of oppressors and oppressed, villains and victims. Here I believe that a feminist appropriation of some of Foucault's later concepts can prove useful. Following Foucault, we must first abandon the idea of power as something possessed by one group and leveled against another; we must instead think of the network of practices, institutions, and technologies that sustain positions of dominance and subordination in a particular domain.

Second, we need an analytics adequate to describe a power whose central mechanisms are not repressive, but *constitutive*: "a power bent on generating forces, making them grow, and ordering them, rather than one dedicated to impeding them, making them submit, or destroying them." Particularly in the realm of femininity, where so much depends on the seemingly willing acceptance of various norms and practices, we need an analysis of power "from below," as Foucault puts it; for example, of the mechanisms that shape and proliferate—rather than repress—desire, generate and focus our energies, construct our conceptions of normalcy and deviance.[5]

And, third, we need a discourse that will enable us to account for the subversion of potential rebellion, a discourse that, while insisting on the necessity of objective analysis of power relations, social hierarchy, political backlash, and so forth, will nonetheless allow us to confront the mechanisms by which the subject at times becomes enmeshed in collusion with forces that sustain her own oppression.

This essay will not attempt to produce a general theory along these lines. Rather, my focus will be the analysis of one particular arena where the interplay of these dynamics is striking and perhaps exemplary. It is a limited and unusual arena, that of a group of gender-related and historically localized disorders: hysteria, agoraphobia, and anorexia nervosa.[6] I recognize that these disorders have also historically been class- and race-biased, largely (although not exclusively) occurring among white middle- and upper-middle-class women. Nonetheless, anorexia, hysteria, and agoraphobia may provide a paradigm of one way in which potential resistance is not merely undercut but *utilized* in the maintenance and reproduction of existing power relations.[7]

The central mechanism I will describe involves a transformation (or, if you wish, duality) of meaning, through which conditions that are objectively (and, on one level, experientially) constraining, enslaving, and even murderous, come to be experienced as liberating, transforming, and life-giving. I offer this analysis, although limited to a specific domain, as an example of how various contemporary critical discourses may be joined to yield an understanding of the subtle and often unwitting role played by our bodies in the symbolization and reproduction of gender.

The Body as a Text of Femininity

The continuum between female disorder and "normal" feminine practice is sharply revealed through a close reading of those disorders to which women have been particularly vulnerable. These, of course, have varied historically: neurasthenia and hysteria in the second half of the nineteenth century; agoraphobia and, most dramatically, anorexia nervosa and bulimia in the second half of the twentieth century. This is not to say that anorectics did not exist in the nineteenth century—many cases were described, usually in the context of diagnoses of hysteria[8]—or that women no longer suffer from classical hysterical symptoms in the twentieth century. But the taking up of eating disorders on a mass scale is as unique to the culture of the 1980s as the epidemic of hysteria was to the Victorian era.[9]

The symptomatology of these disorders reveals itself as textuality. Loss of mobility, loss of voice, inability to leave the home, feeding others while starving oneself, taking up space, and whittling down the space one's body takes up—all have symbolic meaning, all have *political* meaning under the varying rules governing the historical construction of gender. Working within this framework, we see that whether we look at hysteria, agoraphobia, or anorexia, we find the body of the sufferer deeply inscribed with an ideological construction of femininity emblematic of the period in question. The construction, of course, is always homogenizing and normalizing, erasing racial, class, and other differences and insisting that all women aspire to a coercive, standardized ideal. Strikingly, in these disorders the construction of femininity is written in disturbingly concrete, hyperbolic terms: exaggerated, extremely literal, at times virtually caricatured presentations of the ruling feminine mystique. The bodies of disordered women in this way offer themselves as an aggressively graphic text for the interpreter—a text that insists, actually demands, that it be read as a cultural statement, a statement about gender.

Both nineteenth-century male physicians and twentieth-century feminist critics have seen, in the symptoms of neurasthenia and hysteria (syndromes that became increasingly less differentiated as the century wore on), an exaggeration of stereotypically feminine traits. The nineteenth-century "lady" was idealized in terms of delicacy and dreaminess, sexual passivity, and a charmingly labile and capricious emotionality.[10] Such notions were formalized and scientized in the work of male theorists from Acton and Krafft-Ebing to Freud, who described "normal," mature femininity in such terms.[11] In this context, the dissociations, the drifting and fogging of perception, the nervous tremors and faints, the anesthesias, and the extreme mutability of symptomatology associated with nineteenth-century female disorders can be seen to be concretizations of the feminine mystique of the period, produced according to rules that governed the prevailing construction of femininity. Doctors described what came to be known as the hysterical personality as "impressionable, suggestible, and narcissistic; highly labile, their moods changing suddenly, dramatically, and seemingly for inconsequential reasons...egocentric in the extreme...essentially asexual and not uncommonly frigid"[12]—all characteristics normative of femininity in this era. As Elaine Showalter points out, the term *hysterical* itself became almost interchangeable with the term *feminine* in the literature of the period.[13]

The hysteric's embodiment of the feminine mystique of her era, however, seems subtle and ineffable compared to the ingenious literalism of agoraphobia and anorexia. In the context of our culture this literalism makes sense. With the advent of movies and television, the rules for femininity have come to be culturally transmitted more and more through standardized visual images. As a result, femininity itself has come to be largely a matter of constructing, in the manner described by Erving Goffman, the appropriate surface presentation of the self.[14] We are no longer given verbal descriptions or exemplars of what a lady is or of what femininity consists. Rather, we learn the rules directly through bodily discourse: through images that tell us what clothes, body shape, facial expression, movements, and behavior are required.

In agoraphobia and, even more dramatically, in anorexia, the disorder presents itself as a virtual, though tragic, parody of twentieth-century constructions of femininity. The 1950s and early 1960s, when agoraphobia first began to escalate among women, was a period of reassertion of domesticity and dependency as the feminine ideal. *Career woman* became a dirty word, much more so than it had been during the war, when the economy depended on women's willingness to do "men's work." The reigning ideology of femininity, so well described by Betty Friedan and perfectly captured in the movies and television shows of the era, was childlike, nonassertive, helpless without a man, "content in a world of bedroom and kitchen, sex, babies and home."[15] The housebound agoraphobic lives this construction of femininity literally. "You want me in this home? You'll have me in this home—with a vengeance!" The point, upon which many therapists have commented, does not need belaboring. Agoraphobia, as I. G. Fodor has put it, seems "the logical—albeit extreme—extension of the cultural sex-role stereotype for women" in this era.[16]

The emaciated body of the anorectic, of course, immediately presents itself as a caricature of the contemporary ideal of hyper-slenderness for women, an ideal that, despite the game resistance of racial and ethnic difference, has become the norm for women today. But slenderness is only the tip of the iceberg, for slenderness itself requires interpretation. "C'est le sens qui fait vendre," said Barthes, speaking of clothing styles—it is meaning that makes the sale.[17] So, too, it is meaning that makes the body admirable. To the degree that anorexia may be said to be "about" slenderness, it is about slenderness as a citadel of contemporary and historical meaning, not as an empty fashion ideal. As such, the interpretation of slenderness yields multiple readings, some related to gender, some not. For the purposes of this essay I will offer an abbreviated, gender-focused reading. But I must stress that this reading illuminates only partially, and that many other currents not discussed here—economic, psychosocial, and historical, as well as ethnic and class dimensions—figure prominently.[18]

We begin with the painfully literal inscription, on the anorectic's body, of the rules governing the construction of contemporary femininity. That construction is a double bind that legislates contradictory ideals and directives. On the one hand, our culture still widely advertises domestic conceptions of femininity, the ideological moorings for a rigorously dualistic sexual division of labor that casts woman as chief emotional and physical nurturer. The rules for this construction of femininity (and I speak here in a language both symbolic and literal) require that women learn to feed others, not the self, and to construe any desires for self-nurturance and self-feeding as greedy and excessive.[19] Thus, women must develop a totally other-oriented emotional economy. In this economy, the control of female appetite for food is merely the most concrete expression of the general rule governing the construction of femininity: that female hunger—for public power, for independence, for sexual gratification—be contained, and the public space that women be allowed to take up be circumscribed, limited. Figure 10.1, which appeared in a women's magazine fashion spread, dramatically illustrates the degree to which slenderness, set off against the resurgent muscularity and bulk of the current male body-ideal, carries connotations of fragility and lack of power in the face of a decisive male occupation of social space. On the body of the anorexic woman such rules are grimly and deeply etched.

On the other hand, even as young women today continue to be taught traditionally "feminine" virtues, to the degree that the professional arena is open to them they must also learn to embody the "masculine" language and values of that arena—self-control, determination, cool, emotional discipline, mastery, and so on. Female bodies now speak symbolically of this necessity in their slender spare shape and the currently fashionable men's-wear look. (A contemporary clothing line's clever mirror-image logo, shown in Figure 10.2, offers women's fashions for the "New Man," with the model posed to suggest phallic confidence combined with female allure.) Our bodies, too, as we trudge to the gym every day and fiercely resist both our hungers and our desire to soothe ourselves, are becoming more and more practiced at the "male" virtues of control and selfmastery.

Figure 10.1.

Figure 10.3 illustrates this contemporary equation of physical discipline with becoming the "captain" of one's soul. The anorectic pursues these virtues with single-minded, unswerving dedication. "Energy, discipline, my own power will keep me going," says ex-anorectic Aimee Liu, recreating her anorexic days. "I need nothing and no one else....I will be master of my own body, if nothing else, I vow."[20]

The ideal of slenderness, then, and the diet and exercise regimens that have become inseparable from it offer the illusion of meeting, through the body, the contradictory demands of the contemporary ideology of femininity. Popular images reflect this dual demand. In a single issue of *Complete Woman* magazine, two articles appear, one on "Feminine Intuition," the other asking, "Are You the New Macho Woman?" In *Vision Quest*, the young male hero falls in love with the heroine, as he says, because "she has all the best

things I like in girls and all the best things I like in guys," that is, she's tough and cool, but warm and alluring. In the enormously popular *Aliens*, the heroine's personality has been deliberately constructed, with near-comic book explicitness, to embody traditional nurturant femininity alongside breathtaking macho prowess and control; Sigourney Weaver, the actress who portrays her, has called the character "Rambolina."

In the pursuit of slenderness and the denial of appetite the traditional construction of femininity intersects with the new requirement for women to embody the "masculine" values of the public arena. The anorectic, as I have argued, embodies this intersection, this double bind, in a particularly painful and graphic way.[21] I mean *double bind* quite literally here. "Masculinity" and "femininity," at least since the nineteenth century and arguably before, have been constructed through a process of mutual exclusion. One cannot simply

Figure 10.2.

Figure 10.3.

add the historically feminine virtues to the historically masculine ones to yield a New Woman, a New Man, a new ethics, or a new culture. Even on the screen or on television, embodied in created characters like the *Aliens* heroine, the result is a parody. Unfortunately, in this image-bedazzled culture, we find it increasingly difficult to discriminate between parodies and possibilities for the self. Explored as a possibility for the self, the "androgynous" ideal ultimately exposes its internal contradiction and becomes a war that tears the subject in two—a war explicitly thematized, by many anorectics, as a battle between male and female sides of the self.[22]

Protest and Retreat in the Same Gesture

In hysteria, agoraphobia, and anorexia, then, the woman's body may be viewed as a surface on which conventional constructions of femininity are exposed starkly to view, through their inscription in extreme or hyperliteral form. They are written, of course, in languages of horrible suffering. It is as though these bodies are speaking to us of the pathology and violence that lurks just around the corner, waiting at the horizon of "normal" femininity. It is no wonder that a steady motif in the feminist literature on female disorder is that of pathology as embodied *protest*—unconscious, inchoate, and counterproductive protest without an effective language, voice, or politics, but protest nonetheless.

American and French feminists alike have heard the hysteric speaking a language of protest, even or perhaps especially when she was mute. Dianne Hunter interprets Anna O.'s aphasia, which manifested itself in an inability to speak her native German, as a rebellion against the linguistic and cultural rules of the father and a return to the "mother-tongue": the semiotic babble of infancy, the language of the body. For Hunter, and for a number of other feminists working with Lacanian categories, the return to the semiotic level is both regressive and, as Hunter puts it, an "expressive" communication "addressed to patriarchal thought," "a self-repudiating form of feminine discourse in which the body signifies what social conditions make it impossible to state linguistically."[23] "The hysterics are accusing; they are pointing," writes Catherine Clément in *The Newly Born Woman;* they make a "mockery of culture."[24] In the same volume, Hélène Cixous speaks of "those wonderful hysterics, who subjected Freud to so many voluptuous moments too shameful to mention, bombarding his mosaic statute/law of Moses with their carnal, passionate body-words, haunting him with their inaudible thundering denunciations." For Cixous, Dora, who so frustrated Freud, is "the core example of the protesting force in women."[25]

The literature of protest includes functional as well as symbolic approaches. Robert Seidenberg and Karen DeCrow, for example, describe agoraphobia as a "strike" against "the renunciations usually demanded of women" and the expectations of housewifely functions such as shopping, driving the children to school, accompanying their husband to social events.[26] Carroll Smith-Rosenberg presents a similar analysis of hysteria, arguing that by preventing the woman from functioning in the wifely role of caretaker of others, of "ministering angel" to husband and children, hysteria "became one way in which conventional women could express—in most cases unconsciously—dissatisfaction with one or several aspects of their lives."[27] A number of feminist writers, among whom Susie Orbach is the most articulate and forceful, have interpreted anorexia as a species of unconscious feminist protest. The anorectic is engaged in a "hunger strike," as Orbach calls it, stressing that this is a political discourse, in which the action of food refusal and dramatic transformation of body size "expresses with [the] body what [the anorectic] is unable to tell us with words"—her indictment of a culture that disdains and suppresses female hunger, makes women ashamed of their appetites and needs, and demands that women constantly work on the transformation of their body.[28]

The anorectic, of course, is unaware that she is making a political statement. She may, indeed, be hostile to feminism and any other critical perspectives that she views as disputing her own autonomy and control or questioning the cultural ideals around which her life is organized. Through embodied rather than deliberate demonstration she exposes and indicts those ideals, precisely by pursuing them to the point at which their destructive potential is revealed for all to see.

The same gesture that expresses protest, moreover, can also signal retreat; this, indeed, may be part of the symptom's attraction. Kim Chernin, for example, argues that the debilitating anorexic fixation, by halting or mitigating personal development, assuages this generation's guilt and separation anxiety over the prospect of surpassing our mothers, of living less circumscribed, freer lives.[29] Agoraphobia, too, which often develops shortly after marriage, clearly functions in many cases as a way to cement dependency and attachment in the face of unacceptable stirrings of dissatisfaction and restlessness.

Although we may talk meaningfully of protest, then, I want to emphasize the counterproductive, tragically self-defeating (indeed, self-deconstructing) nature of that protest. Functionally, the symptoms of these disorders isolate, weaken, and undermine the sufferers; at the same time they turn the life of the body into an all-absorbing fetish, beside which all other objects of attention pale into unreality. On the symbolic level, too, the protest collapses into its opposite and proclaims the utter capitulation of the subject to the contracted female world. The muteness of hysterics and their return to the level of pure, primary bodily expressivity have been interpreted, as we have seen, as rejecting the symbolic order of the patriarchy and recovering a lost world of semiotic, maternal value. But *at the same time*, of course, muteness is the condition of the silent, uncomplaining woman—an ideal of patriarchal culture. Protesting the stifling of the female voice through one's own voicelessness— that is, employing the language of femininity to protest the conditions of the female world—will always involve ambiguities of this sort. Perhaps this is why symptoms crystallized from the language of femininity are so perfectly suited to express the dilemmas of middle-class and upper-middle-class women living in periods poised on the edge of gender change, women who have the social and material resources to carry the traditional

construction of femininity to symbolic excess but who also confront the anxieties of new possibilities. The late nineteenth century, the post–World War II period, and the late twentieth century are all periods in which gender becomes an issue to be discussed and in which discourse proliferates about "the Woman Question," "the New Woman," "What Women Want," "What Femininity Is."

Collusion, Resistance, and the Body

The pathologies of female protest function, paradoxically, as if in collusion with the cultural conditions that produce them, reproducing rather than transforming precisely that which is being protested. In this connection, the fact that hysteria and anorexia have peaked during historical periods of cultural backlash against attempts at reorganization and redefinition of male and female roles is significant. Female pathology reveals itself here as an extremely interesting social formation through which one source of potential for resistance and rebellion is pressed into the service of maintaining the established order.

In our attempt to explain this formation, objective accounts of power relations fail us. For whatever the objective social conditions are that create a pathology, the symptoms themselves must still be produced (however unconsciously or inadvertently) by the subject. That is, the individual must invest the body with meanings of various sorts. Only by examining this productive process on the part of the subject can we, as Mark Poster has put it, "illuminate the mechanisms of domination in the processes through which meaning is produced in everyday life"; that is, only then can we see how the desires and dreams of the subject become implicated in the matrix of power relations.[30]

Here, examining the context in which the anorexic syndrome is produced may be illuminating. Anorexia will erupt, typically, in the course of what begins as a fairly moderate diet regime, undertaken because someone, often the father, has made a casual critical remark. Anorexia *begins in*, emerges out of, what is, in our time, conventional feminine practice. In the course of that practice, for any number of individual reasons, the practice is pushed a little beyond the parameters of moderate dieting. The young woman discovers what it feels like to crave and want and need and yet, through the exercise of her own will, to triumph over that need. In the process, a new realm of meanings is discovered, a range of values and possibilities that Western culture has traditionally coded as "male" and rarely made available to women: an ethic and aesthetic of self-mastery and self-transcendence, expertise, and power over others through the example of superior will and control. The experience is intoxicating, habit-forming.

At school the anorectic discovers that her steadily shrinking body is admired, not so much as an aesthetic or sexual object, but for the strength of will and self-control it projects. At home she discovers, in the inevitable battles her parents fight to get her to eat, that her actions have enormous power over the lives of those around her. As her body begins to lose its traditional feminine curves, its breasts and hips and rounded stomach, begins to feel and look more like a spare, lanky male body, she begins to feel untouchable, out of reach of hurt, "invulnerable, clean and hard as the bones etched into my silhouette," as one student described it in her journal. She despises, in particular, all those parts of her body that continue to mark her as female. "If only I could eliminate [my breasts]," says Liu, "cut them off if need be."[31] For her, as for many anorectics, the breasts represent a bovine, unconscious, vulnerable side of the self. Liu's body symbolism is thoroughly continuous with dominant cultural associations. Brett Silverstein's studies on the "Possible Causes of the Thin Standard of Bodily Attractiveness for Women"[32] testify empirically to what is obvious from every comedy routine involving a dramatically shapely woman: namely, our cultural association of curvaceousness with incompetence. The anorectic is also quite aware, of course, of the social and sexual vulnerability involved in having a female body; many, in fact, were sexually abused as children.

Through her anorexia, by contrast, she has unexpectedly discovered an entry into the privileged male world, a way to become what is valued in our culture, a way to become safe, to rise above it all—for her, they are the same thing. She has discovered this, paradoxically, by pursuing conventional feminine behavior—in this case, the discipline of perfecting the body as an object—to excess. At this point of excess, the conventionally feminine deconstructs, we might say, into its opposite and opens onto those values our culture has coded as male. No wonder the anorexia is experienced as liberating and that she will fight family, friends, and therapists in an effort to hold onto it—fight them to the death, if need be. The anorectic's experience of power is, of course, deeply and dangerously illusory. To reshape one's body into a male body is *not* to put on male power and privilege. To *feel* autonomous and free while harnessing body and soul to an obsessive body-practice is to serve, not transform, a social order that limits female possibilities. And, of course, for the female to become male is only for her to locate herself on the other side of a disfiguring opposition. The new "power look" of female body-building, which encourages women to develop the same hulklike, triangular shape that has been the norm for male body-builders, is no less determined by a hierarchical, dualistic construction of gender than was the conventionally "feminine"norm that tyrannized female body-builders such as Bev Francis for years.

Although the specific cultural practices and meanings are different, similar mechanisms, I suspect, are at work in hysteria and agoraphobia. In these cases too, the language of femininity, when pushed to excess—when shouted and asserted, when disruptive and demanding—deconstructs into its opposite and makes available to the woman an illusory experience of power previously forbidden to her by virtue of her gender. In the case of nineteenth-century femininity, the forbidden experience may have been the bursting of fetters—particularly moral and emotional fetters. John Conolly, the asylum reformer, recommended institutionalization for women who "want that restraint over the passions without which the female character is lost."[33] Hysterics often infuriated male doctors by their lack of precisely this quality. S. Weir Mitchell described these patients as "the despair of physicians," whose "despotic selfishness wrecks the constitution of nurses and devoted relatives, and in unconscious or half-conscious self-indulgence destroys the comfort of everyone around them."[34] It must have given the Victorian patient some illicit pleasure to be viewed as capable of such disruption of the staid nineteenth-century household. A similar form of power, I believe, is part of the experience of agoraphobia.

This does not mean that the primary reality of these disorders is not one of pain and entrapment. Anorexia, too, clearly contains a dimension of physical addiction to the biochemical effects of starvation. But whatever the physiology involved, the ways in which the subject understands and thematizes her experience cannot be reduced to a mechanical process. The anorectic's ability to live with minimal food intake allows her to feel powerful and worthy of admiration in a "world," as Susie Orbach describes it, "from which at the most profound level [she] feels excluded" and unvalued.[35] The literature on both anorexia and hysteria is strewn with battles of will between the sufferer and those trying to "cure" her; the latter, as Orbach points out, very rarely understand that the psychic values she is fighting for are often more important to the woman than life itself.

Textuality, Praxis, and the Body

The "solutions" offered by anorexia, hysteria, and agoraphobia, I have suggested, develop out of the practice of femininity itself, the pursuit of which is still presented as the chief route to acceptance and success for women in our culture. Too aggressively pursued, that practice leads to its own undoing, in one sense. For if femininity is, as Susan Brownmiller has said, at its core a "tradition of imposed limitations,"[36] then an unwillingness to limit oneself, even in the pursuit of femininity, breaks the rules. But, of course, in another sense the rules remain fully in place. The sufferer becomes wedded to an obsessive practice, unable to make any effective change in her life. She remains, as Toril Moi has put it, "gagged and chained to [the] feminine role," a reproducer of the docile body of femininity.[37]

This tension between the psychological meaning of a disorder, which may enact fantasies of rebellion and embody a language of protest, and the practical life of the disordered body, which may utterly defeat rebellion and subvert protest, may be obscured by too exclusive a focus on the symbolic dimension and insufficient attention to praxis. As we have seen in the case of some Lacanian feminist readings of hysteria, the result of this can be a one-sided interpretation that romanticizes the hysteric's symbolic subversion of the phallocentric order while confined to her bed. This is not to say that confinement in bed has a transparent, univocal meaning—in powerlessness, debilitation, dependency, and so forth. The "practical" body is no brute biological or material entity. It, too, is a culturally mediated form; its activities are subject to interpretation and description. The shift to the practical dimension is not a turn to biology or nature, but to another "register," as Foucault puts it, of the cultural body, the register of the "useful body" rather than the "intelligible body."[38] The distinction can prove useful, I believe, to feminist discourse.

The intelligible body includes our scientific, philosophic, and aesthetic representations of the body—our cultural *conceptions* of the body, norms of beauty, models of health, and so forth. But the same representations may also be seen as forming a set of *practical* rules and regulations through which the living body is "trained, shaped, obeys, responds," becoming, in short, a socially adapted and "useful body."[39] Consider this particularly clear and appropriate example: the nineteenth-century hourglass figure, emphasizing breasts and hips against a wasp waist, was an intelligible *symbolic* form, representing a domestic, sexualized ideal of femininity. The sharp cultural contrast between the female and the male form, made possible by the use of corsets and bustles, reflected, in symbolic terms, the dualistic division of social and economic life into clearly defined male and female spheres. At the same time, to achieve the specified look, a particular feminine *praxis* was required—straitlacing, minimal eating, reduced mobility—rendering the female body unfit to perform activities outside its designated sphere. This, in Foucauldian terms, would be the "useful body" corresponding to the aesthetic norm.

The intelligible body and the useful body are two arenas of the same discourse; they often mirror and support each other, as in the above illustration. Another example can be found in the seventeenth-century philosophic conception of the body as a machine, mirroring an increasingly more automated productive machinery of labor. But the two bodies may also contradict and mock each other. A range of contemporary representations and images, as noted earlier, have coded the transcendence of female appetite and its public display in the slenderness ideal in terms of power, will, mastery, the possibilities of success in the professional arena. These associations are carried visually by the slender superwomen of prime-time television and popular movies and promoted explicitly in advertisements and articles appearing routinely in women's fashion magazines, diet books, and weight-training publications. Yet the thousands of slender girls and women who strive to embody these images and who in that service suffer from eating disorders, exercise compulsions, and continual self-scrutiny and self-castigation are anything *but* the "masters" of their lives.

Exposure and productive cultural analysis of such contradictory and mystifying relations between image and practice are possible only if the analysis includes attention to and interpretation of the "useful" or, as I prefer to call it, the practical body. Such attention, although often in inchoate and theoretically unsophisticated form, was central to the beginnings of the contemporary feminist movement. In the late 1960s and early 1970s the objectification of the female body was a serious political issue. All the cultural paraphernalia of femininity, of learning to please visually and sexually through the practices of the body—media imagery, beauty pageants, high heels, girdles, makeup, simulated orgasm—were seen as crucial in maintaining gender domination.

Disquietingly, for the feminists of the present decade, such focus on the politics of feminine praxis, although still maintained in the work of individual feminists, is no longer a centerpiece

of feminist cultural critique.[40] On the popular front, we find *Ms.* magazine presenting issues on fitness and "style," the rhetoric reconstructed for the 1980s to pitch "self-expression" and "power." Although feminist theory surely has the tools, it has not provided a critical discourse to dismantle and demystify this rhetoric. The work of French feminists has provided a powerful framework for understanding the inscription of phallocentric, dualistic culture on gendered bodies, but it has offered very little in the way of concrete analyses of the female body as a locus of practical cultural control. Among feminist theorists in this country, the study of cultural representations of the female body has flourished, and it has often been brilliantly illuminating and instrumental to a feminist rereading of culture.[41] But the study of cultural representations alone, divorced from consideration of their relation to the practical lives of bodies, can obscure and mislead.

Here, Helena Mitchie's significantly titled *The Flesh Made Word* offers a striking example. Examining nineteenth-century representations of women, appetite, and eating, Mitchie draws fascinating and astute metaphorical connections between female eating and female sexuality. Female hunger, she argues, and I agree, "figures unspeakable desires for sexuality and power."[42] The Victorian novel's "representational taboo" against depicting women eating (an activity, apparently, that only "happens offstage," as Mitchie puts it) thus functions as a "code" for the suppression of female sexuality, as does the general cultural requirement, exhibited in etiquette and sex manuals of the day, that the well-bred woman eat little and delicately. The same coding is drawn on, Mitchie argues, in contemporary feminist "inversions" of Victorian values, inversions that celebrate female sexuality and power through images exulting in female eating and female hunger, depicting it explicitly, lushly, and joyfully.

Despite the fact that Mitchie's analysis centers on issues concerning women's hunger, food, and eating practices, she makes no mention of the grave eating disorders that surfaced in the late nineteenth century and that are ravaging the lives of young women today. The practical arena of women dieting, fasting, straitlacing, and so forth is, to a certain extent, implicit in her examination of Victorian gender ideology. But when Mitchie turns, at the end of her study, to consider contemporary feminist literature celebrating female eating and female hunger, the absence of even a passing glance at how women are *actually* managing their hungers today leaves her analysis adrift, lacking any concrete social moorings. Mitchie's sole focus is on the inevitable failure of feminist literature to escape "phallic representational codes."⁴³ But the feminist celebration of the female body did not merely deconstruct on the written page or canvas. Largely located in the feminist counterculture of the 1970s, it has been culturally displaced by a very different contemporary reality. Its celebration of female flesh now presents itself in jarring dissonance with the fact that women, feminists included, are starving themselves to death in our culture.

This is not to deny the benefits of diet, exercise, and other forms of body management. Rather, I view our bodies as a site of struggle, where we must *work* to keep our daily practices in the service of resistance to gender domination, not in the service of docility and gender normalization. This work requires, I believe, a determinedly skeptical attitude toward the routes of seeming liberation and pleasure offered by our culture. It also demands an awareness of the often contradictory relations between image and practice, between rhetoric and reality. Popular representations, as we have seen, may forcefully employ the rhetoric and symbolism of empowerment, personal freedom, "having it all." Yet female bodies, pursuing these ideals, may find themselves as distracted, depressed, and physically ill as female bodies in the nineteenth century were made when pursuing a feminine ideal of dependency, domesticity, and delicacy. The recognition and analysis of such contradictions, and of all the other collusions, subversions, and enticements through which culture enjoins the aid of our bodies in the reproduction of gender, require that we restore a concern for female praxis to its formerly central place in feminist politics.

Acknowledgments

Early versions of this essay, under various titles, were delivered at the philosophy department of the State University of New York at Stony Brook, the University of Massachusetts conference on Histories of Sexuality, and the twenty-first annual conference for the Society of Phenomenology and Existential Philosophy. I thank all those who commented and provided encouragement on those occasions. The essay was revised and originally published in Alison Jaggar and Susan Bordo, eds., *Gender/Body/Knowledge: Feminist Reconstructions of Being and Knowing* (New Brunswick: Rutgers University Press, 1989).

Notes

1. Mary Douglas, *Natural Symbols* (New York: Pantheon, 1982), and *Purity and Danger* (London: Routledge and Kegan Paul, 1966).

2. Pierre Bourdieu, *Outline of a Theory of Practice* (Cambridge: Cambridge University Press, 1977), p. 94 (emphasis in original).

3. On docility, see Michel Foucault, *Discipline and Punish* (New York: Vintage, 1979), pp. 135–69. For a Foucauldian analysis of feminine practice, see Sandra Bartky, "Foucault, Femininity, and the Modernization of Patriarchal Power," in her *Femininity and Domination* (New York: Routledge, 1990); see also Susan Brownmiller, *Femininity* (New York: Ballantine, 1984).

4. During the late 1970s and 1980s, male concern over appearance undeniably increased. Study after study confirms, however, that there is still a large gender gap in this area. Research conducted at the University of Pennsylvania in 1985 found men to be generally satisfied with their appearance, often, in fact, "distorting their perceptions [of themselves] in a positive, self-aggrandizing way" ("Dislike of Own Bodies Found Common Among Women," *New York Times,* March 19, 1985, p. C1). Women, however, were found to exhibit extreme negative assessments and distortions of body perception. Other studies have suggested that women are judged more harshly than men when they deviate from dominant social standards of attractiveness. Thomas Cash et al., in "The Great American Shape-Up," *Psychology Today* (April 1986),

p. 34, report that although the situation for men has changed, the situation for women has more than proportionally worsened. Citing results from 30,000 responses to a 1985 survey of perceptions of body image and comparing similar responses to a 1972 questionnaire, they report that the 1985 respondents were considerably more dissatisfied with their bodies than the 1972 respondents, and they note a marked intensification of concern among men. Among the 1985 group, the group most dissatisfied of all with their appearance, however, were teenage women. Women today constitute by far the largest number of consumers of diet products, attenders of spas and diet centers, and subjects of intestinal by-pass and other fat-reduction operations.

5. Michel Foucault, *The History of Sexuality.* Vol. 1: *An Introduction* (New York: Vintage, 1980), pp. 136, 94.

6. On the gendered and historical nature of these disorders: the number of female to male hysterics has been estimated at anywhere from 2:1 to 4:1, and as many as 80 percent of all agoraphobics are female (Annette Brodsky and Rachel Hare-Mustin, *Women and Psychotherapy* [New York: Guilford Press, 1980], pp. 116, 122). Although more cases of male eating disorders have been reported in the late eighties and early nineties, it is estimated that close to 90 percent of all anorectics are female (Paul Garfinkel and David Garner, *Anorexia Nervosa: A Multidimensional Perspective* [New York: Brunner/Mazel, 1982], pp. 112–13). For a sophisticated account of female psychopathology, with particular attention to nineteenth-century disorders but, unfortunately, little mention of agoraphobia or eating disorders, see Elaine Showalter, *The Female Malady: Women, Madness and English Culture, 1830–1980* (New York: Pantheon, 1985). For a discussion of social and gender issues in agoraphobia, see Robert Seidenberg and Karen DeCrow, *Women Who Marry Houses: Panic and Protest in Agoraphobia* (New York: McGraw-Hill, 1983). On the history of anorexia nervosa, see Joan Jacobs Brumberg, *Fasting Girls: The Emergence of Anorexia Nervosa as a Modern Disease* (Cambridge: Harvard University Press, 1988).

7. In constructing such a paradigm I do not pretend to do justice to any of these disorders in its individual complexity. My aim is to chart some points of intersection, to describe some similar patterns, as they emerge through a particular reading of the phenomenon—a political reading, if you will.

8. Showalter, *The Female Malady*, pp. 128–29.

9. On the epidemic of hysteria and neurasthenia, see Showalter, *The Female Malady;* Carroll Smith-Rosenberg, "The Hysterical Woman: Sex Roles and Role Conflict in Nineteenth-Century America," in her *Disorderly Conduct: Visions of Gender in Victorian America* (Oxford: Oxford University Press, 1985).

10. Martha Vicinus, "Introduction: The Perfect Victorian Lady," in Martha Vicinus, *Suffer and Be Still: Women in the Victorian Age* (Bloomington: Indiana University Press, 1972), pp. x–xi.

11. See Carol Nadelson and Malkah Notman, *The Female Patient* (New York: Plenum, 1982), p. 5; E. M. Sigsworth and T. J. Wyke, "A Study of Victorian Prostitution and Venereal Disease," in Vicinus, *Suffer and Be Still*, p. 82. For more general discussions, see Peter Gay, *The Bourgeois Experience: Victoria to Freud.* Vol. 1: *Education of the Senses* (New York: Oxford University Press, 1984), esp. pp. 109–68; Showalter, *The Female Malady,* esp. pp. 121–44. The delicate lady, an ideal that had very strong class connotations (as does slenderness today), is not the only conception of femininity to be found in Victorian cultures. But it was arguably the single most powerful ideological representation of femininity in that era, affecting women of all classes, including those without the material means to realize the ideal fully. See Helena Mitchie, *The Flesh Made Word* (New York: Oxford, 1987), for discussions of the control of female appetite and Victorian constructions of femininity.

12. Smith-Rosenberg, *Disorderly Conduct*, p. 203.

13. Showalter, *The Female Malady*, p. 129.

14. Erving Goffman, *The Presentation of the Self in Everyday Life* (Garden City, N.Y.: Anchor Doubleday, 1959).

15. Betty Friedan, *The Feminine Mystique* (New York: Dell, 1962), p. 36. The theme song of one such show ran, in part, "I married Joan...What a girl...what a whirl...what a life! I married Joan...What a mind...love is blind...what a wife!"

16. See I. G. Fodor, "The Phobic Syndrome in Women," in V. Franks and V. Burtle, eds., *Women in Therapy* (New York: Brunner/Mazel, 1974), p. 119; see also Kathleen Brehony, "Women and Agoraphobia," in Violet Franks and Esther Rothblum, eds., *The Stereotyping of Women* (New York: Springer, 1983).

17. In Jonathan Culler, *Roland Barthes* (New York: Oxford University Press, 1983), p. 74.

18. For other interpretive perspectives on the slenderness ideal, see "Reading the Slender Body" in this volume; Kim Chernin, *The Obsession: Reflections on the Tyranny of Slenderness* (New York: Harper and Row, 1981); Susie Orbach, *Hunger Strike: The Anorectic's Struggle as a Metaphor for Our Age* (New York: W. W. Norton, 1985).

19. See "Hunger as Ideology," in this volume, for a discussion of how this construction of femininity is reproduced in contemporary commercials and advertisements concerning food, eating, and cooking.

20. Aimee Liu, *Solitaire* (New York: Harper and Row, 1979), p. 123.

21. Striking, in connection with this, is Catherine Steiner-Adair's 1984 study of high-school women, which reveals a dramatic association between problems with food and body image and emulation of the cool, professionally "together" and gorgeous superwoman. On the basis of a series of interviews, the high schoolers were classified into two groups: one expressed skepticism over the superwoman ideal, the other thoroughly aspired to it. Later administrations of diagnostic tests revealed that 94 percent of the pro-superwoman group fell into the eating-disordered range of the scale. Of the other group, 100 percent fell into the noneating-disordered range. Media images notwithstanding, young women today appear to sense, either consciously or through their bodies, the impossibility of simultaneously meeting the demands of two spheres whose values have been historically defined in utter opposition to each other.

22. See "Anorexia Nervosa" in this volume.

23. Dianne Hunter, "Hysteria, Psychoanalysis and Feminism," in Shirley Garner, Claire Kahane, and Madelon Sprenger, eds., *The (M)Other Tongue* (Ithaca: Cornell University Press, 1985), p. 114.

24. Catherine Clément and Hélène Cixous, *The Newly Born Woman,* trans. Betsy Wing (Minneapolis: University of Minnesota Press, 1986), p. 42.

25. Clément and Cixous, *The Newly Born Woman,* p. 95.

26. Seidenberg and DeCrow, *Women Who Marry Houses,* p. 31.

27. Smith-Rosenberg, *Disorderly Conduct,* p. 208.

28. Orbach, *Hunger Strike,* p. 102. When we look into the many autobiographies and case studies of hysterics, anorectics, and agoraphobics, we find that these are indeed the sorts of women one might expect to be frustrated by the constraints of a specified female role. Sigmund Freud and Joseph Breuer, in *Studies on Hysteria* (New York: Avon, 1966), and Freud, in the later *Dora: An Analysis of a Case of Hysteria* (New York: Macmillan, 1963), constantly remark on the ambitiousness, independence, intellectual ability, and creative strivings of their patients. We know, moreover, that many women who later became leading social activists and feminists of the nineteenth century were among those who fell ill with hysteria and neurasthenia. It has become a virtual cliché that the typical anorectic is a perfectionist, driven to excel in all areas of her life. Though less prominently, a similar theme runs throughout the literature on agoraphobia.

One must keep in mind that in drawing on case studies, one is relying on the perceptions of other acculturated individuals. One suspects, for example, that the popular portrait of the anorectic as a relentless over-achiever may be colored by the lingering or perhaps resurgent Victorianism of our culture's attitudes toward ambitious women. One does not escape this hermeneutic problem by turning to autobiography. But in autobiography one is at least dealing with social constructions and attitudes that animate the subject's own psychic reality. In this regard the autobiographical literature on anorexia, drawn on in a variety of places in this volume, is strikingly full of anxiety about the domestic world and other themes that suggest deep rebellion against traditional notions of femininity.

29. Kim Chernin, *The Hungry Self: Women, Eating, and Identity* (New York: Harper and Row, 1985), esp. pp. 41–93.

30. Mark Poster, *Foucault, Marxism, and History* (Cambridge: Polity Press, 1984), p. 28.

31. Liu, *Solitaire*, p. 99.

32. Brett Silverstein, "Possible Causes of the Thin Standard of Bodily Attractiveness for Women," *International Journal of Eating Disorders* 5 (1986): 907–16.

33. Showalter, *The Female Malady*, p. 48.

34. Smith-Rosenberg, *Disorderly Conduct*, p. 207.

35. Orbach, *Hunger Strike*, p. 103.

36. Brownmiller, *Femininity*, p. 14.

37. Toril Moi, "Representations of Patriarchy: Sex and Epistemology in Freud's Dora," in Charles Bernheimer and Claire Kahane, eds., *In Dora's Case: Freud—Hysteria—Feminism* (New York: Columbia University Press, 1985), p. 192.

38. Foucault, *Discipline and Punish*, p. 136.

39. Foucault, *Discipline and Punish*, p. 136.

40. A focus on the politics of sexualization and objectification remains central to the anti-pornography movement (e.g., in the work of Andrea Dworkin, Catherine MacKinnon). Feminists exploring the politics of appearance include Sandra Bartky, Susan Brownmiller, Wendy Chapkis, Kim Chernin, and Susie Orbach. And a developing feminist interest in the work of Michel Foucault has begun to produce a poststructuralist feminism oriented toward practice; see, for example, Irene Diamond and Lee Quinby, *Feminism and Foucault: Reflections on Resistance* (Boston: Northeastern University Press, 1988).

41. See, for example, Susan Suleiman, ed., *The Female Body in Western Culture* (Cambridge: Harvard University Press, 1986).

42. Mitchie, *The Flesh Made Word*, p. 13.

43. Mitchie, *The Flesh Made Word*, p. 149.

Growing Up in the Culture of Slenderness: Girls' Experiences of Body Dissatisfaction

SARAH GROGAN AND NICOLA WAINWRIGHT

Nickie Charles and Marion Kerr (1986) report the results of interviews with women where they discussed attitudes to dieting and satisfaction with their present weight. The results were fascinating and revealed the extent of women's dissatisfaction with their body shape and weight. They conclude that:

> What emerges from these comments is a strong dissatisfaction with their body image, a dissatisfaction which was not confined to women who were dieting or were trying to diet but was shared by almost all the women we spoke to. (Charles & Kerr, 1986, p. 541)

Charles and Kerr (1986) suggest that the societal goal of the abnormally thin body is not attainable by most women, except by severe restriction of food intake. The inability of most women to attain this unrealistic goal leaves them feeling guilty and dissatisfied with their body shape and weight. They argue convincingly that, in Western cultures, most women have a contradictory and problematic relationship with their body and with food, and are dissatisfied with their body shape and weight.

Body dissatisfaction in women is widely documented, mostly in the psychology literature. Susie Orbach (1993), in an extensive review of relevant literature argues that there is good evidence that women in Western society are stigmatized for not being slim, and that we internalize this stigma and become dissatisfied with our body shape and weight. She suggests that we are taught to view our bodies from the outside, as if they were commodities, which causes distortion of body image, and a disjuncture from our own bodies, which are objectified and continually monitored for faults. Orbach suggests that a smaller body size for women was being proposed at the same time that women were demanding to be taken more seriously in the workplace.

> The shrinking of the American and British woman, or rather the idea that she should shrink, coincides too uncomfortably with changes women have been demanding about their social role for one to regard it as merely coincidence. Body maintenance, body beautiful, exercise and the pursuit of thinness are offered as valued arenas for concern precisely at the moment when women are trying to break free of such imperatives. (Orbach, 1993, p. 56)

It is generally accepted that pressures on women are qualitatively and quantitatively different from pressures on men. Women are more often the subjects of "the gaze" than vice versa. Women are more likely to diet, have cosmetic surgery, and have eating disorders (Davis, 1994). It has recently become fashionable to talk about the objectification of the male body, and the possible effects of this objectification on men's body image. Frank Mort (1988) discusses the "hyper-cultivation" of the male body, encouraging men to look at themselves and each other as possible objects of consumer desire, Mishkind, Rodin, Silberstein, and Streigel-Moore (1986) argue that examination of current magazines and other media suggest that bodily concern is strong for men. However, there is still a wide gap in the presentation of the male and female body in mainstream media, and the cultural meanings of the messages associated with the portrayal of men and women. Rowena Chapman (1988) argues that there is still an inequity in cultural images of the male and the female body, showing how the myth of the "new man" who is sensitive, aware, and concerned about his body functions to disempower women by creating the appearance of equity whilst maintaining the old power differentials.

It seems likely that women will be more resistant to cultural pressures to be slim if we grow up with a reasonably positive image of our body and are able to maintain it through adolescence and into adulthood. Body image in preadolescent girls has been largely neglected in the social sciences literature. In one of the few studies in this area, Marika Tiggemann and Barbara Pennington (1990) have produced evidence that Australian girls as young as 9–10 years report body dissatisfaction. In this study, adult undergraduates, adolescents aged 15–16 years, and children aged 9–10 years were presented with sets of age-relevant silhouette drawings ranging from very thin to very heavy. Women in all three age groups rated their current figures as larger than their ideal. They suggest that body dissatisfaction is the normal experience of women from age 9 upwards, and that the imagery surrounding fatness and slimness on television and through other media is very influential in determining children's beliefs concerning correct and incorrect body size. Andy Hill, Sarah Oliver, and Peter Rogers (1992), in a recent British study, have produced similar findings from body dissatisfaction questionnaires, and body figure preferences indicated using line drawings of female figures. They conclude that girls from 9 years are dissatisfied with their body shape and size. They argue that children consume adult beliefs, values and prejudices around body shape and size and adopt them as their own.

Although there is a notable lack of research on body satisfaction in children, there has been a lot of interest in body satisfaction in adolescence. Betty Carruth and Dena Goldberg (1990) argue that adolescence is seen as a time where body image concern is at its peak due to physical changes in shape that may move girls away from their goal or ideal. Adolescence is also a time of change, self-consciousness, and identity search (Tiggemann & Pennington, 1990). Studies have reliably shown that young women between 13 and 16 years are dissatisfied with their body shape and size. Researchers working in this area have tended to infer body satisfaction from surveys of dieting and body satisfaction (Bunnell, Cooper, Hertz, & Shenker, 1992; Hill et al., 1992; Toro, Castro, Garcia, Perez, & Cuesta, 1989; Wadden, Brown, Foster, & Linowuaritz, 1991) or from judgements of self in relation to silhouette figures (Tiggemann & Pennington, 1990). It has been suggested that most adolescent girls say that they feel fat and want to lose weight. Data come from British (Hill et al., 1992), United States (Wadden et al., 1991), Australian (Maude, Wertheim, Paxton, Gibbons & Szmukler, 1993), and Spanish (Toro et al., 1989) sources. Thomas Wadden and colleagues (1991) argue that adolescent girls are at odds with their bodies, and report (on the basis of survey questionnaire data) that body concern is one of the most important worries in the lives of teenage girls.

We have been unable to find any study in the published literature where girls and adolescent women have been asked to describe their experiences of (dis)satisfaction with their body shape and size. This seems the most valid way to try to understand how girls and adolescents feel, and incorporates sufficient flexibility to allow investigation of areas of experience that adult researchers may not predict prior to talking with the participants. Our experience of talking with adult women suggests that many women remember feeling under pressure to be slim from primary school onwards. We wanted to explore the issues around body image and food with young women who could share with us their ongoing experiences, rather than investigating memories of such experiences with adult women. The study that follows reports two interviews; one with a group of 8-year-olds and one with a group of 13-year-olds. It gives some interesting insights into these young women's experiences and beliefs about their bodies, dieting, exercise, and food.

Method

Participants

The interviews were part of a larger project involving young women's body image and body (dis)satisfaction. Four 8-year-old and four 13-year-old girls were selected from one state primary and one state secondary school in Sheffield where the second author had been a pupil herself. Participants were chosen on a volunteer basis. All were of average build for their height, were White, and from working- and middle-class backgrounds.

Materials

A set of themes was produced to be used as an interview guide. These covered body image issues such as weight, appearance, and food. Pictures of food were cut out of magazines to give the children something concrete to focus on. A cassette recorder with a directional microphone was used to record the interviews.

Procedure

Children were interviewed in two groups; one for each age. Group (rather than individual) interviews were run because pilot work had suggested that girls were more likely to talk freely in a group than alone. The interviews took place in the school library and were conducted by the second author, a 21-year-old, White woman who was a university student at the time, and who was an ex-student at the school. Children were first engaged in semiformat chat to try to make them feel at ease. When they seemed relaxed, the cassette recorder was turned on and the interview started. The interview was unstructured to add flexibility and centered on ideas about body-shape, weight, and diet. Interviews lasted about 30 minutes and were closed when the conversation "dried up" naturally. Children were assured of anonymity and all gave permission for the conversation to be recorded prior to the interview taking place. Their permission was given for material to be used after the interview and the resulting data was fed back to them by the second author once analysis had taken place.

Results and Discussion

The resulting data offer an insight into the way that these young women experience their bodies, and their body shape ideals. Transcripts were analysed within a Grounded Theory framework (Strauss & Corbin, 1990). A number of interrelated themes emerged from each group which will be discussed in turn. The four participants in the 8-year-old group will be identified by the letters A–D, and the four 13-year-olds by the numbers 1–4.

The Ideal Body

The 8-year-olds agreed that they wanted to be thin; both now and when they grew up. When asked whether they worried about how they looked they said that they worried about getting fat:

> INTERVIEWER: What do you worry about then?
> A: Being fat mostly.
> B: Being fat.

When they were asked how they would like to look when they were older they were quite clear that they wanted to be thin:

> INTERVIEWER: How would you like your body to look when you are older?
> ALL: Thin.
> C: Not fat. Really thin.
> B: Not really thin. Like how thin I am now.
> D: I would like to keep thin like I am now.

This contrasted with the 13-year-olds who said that they wanted to be of average size; not too thin or too fat:

> 3: Not too fat.
> 4: Not too thin.
> 2: Normal.

They expressed a dislike for the body shape of models in magazines because they thought they were too thin:

> 1: They look horrible. They're ugly half the time.
> 2: Yeah they are.
> 1: I think they do sometimes look too thin, they look anorexic.

However, they were envious of those of their friends who were skinny (like the models) and who ate "fattening" foods such as chocolate and did not put on weight. They shared stories about skinny people they knew who could eat anything they liked and how they envied them:

> 3: Well, my friend used to come round all the time but she's a right fussy eater and she's right skinny but she eats a right lot of chocolate bars and everything.
> 2: I hate it when really skinny people say "Oh, I'm fat." They just do it to annoy you.

All 8-year-olds cited members of the entertainers "The Gladiators" as role models, although they said that they did not want to get too muscled. Interestingly, having muscle was seen as attractive to men, and thus to be avoided because it would lead to an increase in male attention. For instance, when asked whether they would like a lot of muscle like Jet (woman Gladiator):

> ALL: No.
> A: No, cos men'd be all around you.
> INTERVIEWER: Do you think men like women with muscles?
> B: Yeah.
> C: Yeah.
> A: Yeah, but I would like to be like Jet though.
> C: Yes, but I wouldn't want muscles.

Similarly, the 13-year-olds expressed a dislike for muscles, which they saw as inappropriate for women because they made women look too masculine:

> 4: I don't like women body builders cos they're right.
> 1: Fat and uhhh.
> 2: It's alright for them to have a few muscles but not like.
> 4: Be like a man.
> 2: Just looks totally.
> 1: Out of shape.

Both groups of young women presented conventional Western societal ideals of what constitutes an attractive and acceptable body shape and size. None of them wished to be fatter. The eight-year-olds expressed the desire to be thin in the present and the future. None wanted muscles because they were seen as "masculine." These findings support Hill et al.'s (1992) suggestion that girls of these ages have already internalised adult's ideals of slimness. The 13-year-olds presented some contradictory ideas. They said that skinny models were unattractive, but expressed envy for their skinny friends who could eat fattening foods without gaining weight.

Body Dis(satisfaction)

When asked about their satisfaction with their present body shape, two of the 8-year-old girls said that they felt thin (and were satisfied with their weight) and two felt fat (and were dissatisfied). Participants A and C felt fat. When asked what they would change about their bodies both girls said they would want to lose weight:

> INTERVIEWER: Is there anything you like to do to change your body shape?
> C: Lose weight.
> INTERVIEWER: Would you like to lose weight?
> C: Yeah.
> A: Lose weight.
> C: You're thin enough.
> A: I'm fat.
> C: Look at your legs.
> A: They're fat.

The 13-year-old girls were dissatisfied with their "stomachs," which were perceived to be too fat:

> 1: I'd maybe change my tummy.
> 3: Yeah, I'd like to be a bit thinner.
> 4: Yeah, just got a bit of a bulge on my tummy.

The dissatisfaction reported by these young women was similar in kind to that reported by the adult women in the Nickie Charles and Marion Kerr (1986) study. Two of the 8-year-olds felt that they were fat and needed to lose weight. Three of the 13-year-olds were dissatisfied with their "stomachs," thinking they were too fat, and none could think of any part of their body that was satisfactory.

This dissatisfaction with body shape and size is similar to that documented in adult women. Girls from age 8 showed concern with their body shape and size. These findings support quantitative research by Marika Tiggemann and Barbara Pennington (1990) on Australian girls and Andy Hill and colleagues (1992) on British girls, showing that body dissatisfaction in young women may start as young as 8 years. These results provide direct evidence that these young women were dissatisfied with their body shape and size, rather than inferring dissatisfaction from the results of comparison of silhouette figures representing self with those representing ideal, or from results of body esteem/satisfaction questionnaires (as in the Australian and British studies cited above).

Dieting and Exercise to Change Body Shape and Size

The 8-year-olds were clear about the concept of "dieting." They knew what it meant and why people did it They saw dieting as a means to losing weight; something that people did to look better rather than to be healthier:

> INTERVIEWER: Do you know what it means to be on a diet?
> C: You have to stop eating.
> A: Stop eating a lot so you don't get fat.
> INTERVIEWER: Do they go on diets to feel better then or because they want to look better?
> B: Look better.
> A: Be thinner.

However, dieting to lose weight was seen as something that adults (and not children) did. When asked about dieting, they described it as something that their parents (or other family members) did. None of them had dieted themselves. Two of the girls described the ways in which they were helping their parents to keep to their reducing diets:

> C: I put a sign on my mum's fridge and it said "Stop, don't open the fridge mummy."
> INTERVIEWER: Are you trying to help your mummy to diet then?

C: Yeah, she keeps on eating biscuits, chocolate biscuits.

B: I put a sticker on my dad's bedroom to remind him not to open the fridge because he is on a diet.

Even though two of them expressed dissatisfaction with their size, none of them had tried to change their body shape through diet. One girl said she was on a diet (for health reasons) and this was greeted with surprise by the others:

C: A little girl like you and you're on a diet!

This suggests that although these children may have internalised adult ideas of acceptable body size, they had not yet adopted the adult coping mechanism of dieting described by Charles and Kerr (1986) and Orbach (1993). They did not consider that changing their eating patterns was a viable way to change their body shape, although it was seen as a reasonable way for adults to try to change their shape. The underlying idea that wanting to change shape was a reasonable goal was accepted by all the girls, with two of them giving examples of how they were helping the adults in their lives to achieve this goal, suggesting that they had internalised the idea that slimness was "good" as suggested by Marika Tiggemann and Barbara Pennington (1990).

The 13-year-olds reported occasional avoidance of particular foods to try to lose weight but stressed that they were not "seriously" dieting and had not been able to keep to any strict regime:

INTERVIEWER: Have any of you ever tried dieting?

2: Yeah, once but...

3: Not seriously dieting.

2: Not the dieting really the cutting out foods.

1: Cutting out chocolates.

2: Like cutting out fatty foods and that. A couple of tries but it worked for about a day (laughs). Just trying to lose some.

3: Yeah.

In general, dieting was viewed negatively by these young women as representing too "serious" an attempt to change body shape.

However, although they did not identify what they were doing (avoiding fattening foods) as "dieting," their behaviour closely matches that described as dieting by Charles and Kerr's (1986) adult respondents. For instance, one of their adult respondents says, "If I find I have put on a little bit of weight I'd probably go through the next couple of weeks cutting out cakes and sweets and having fruit instead" (Charles & Kerr, 1986, p. 549). This is very similar to the quote from the 13-year-olds above, and suggests that they are exercising self-denial in relation to food in a similar way to adult women.

The 13-year-olds were keen to show that they were not "obsessive" about their eating, and wanted to distance themselves from women with problematic relationships with food. The word "anorexic" was used disparagingly to describe how models look. There was a general consensus that exercise, rather than restriction of food intake, was to be preferred as a means for controlling weight:

1: I prefer exercise rather than diet. Just want exercise so you don't get fat,

3: Yeah.

2: Yeah.

Eating sweets and chocolates was seen as an activity that led to feeling "fat" directly afterwards:

INTERVIEWER: How do you feel afterwards, does it make you feel...

1: Fat.

3: Yeah, you do. Sometimes when you've eaten a right lot it makes you feel sick and then you wish you hadn't eaten it.

4: And then you'll have a big bulge in the morning.

Again, there are similarities to Charles and Kerr's (1986) adult respondents who reported feeling fat and guilty after eating food that they thought they should deny themselves. For instance, one woman said that her partner "brought in two Mars bars the other day and I thought that one is going to be mine in a minute and sure enough it was. I felt awful after I'd eaten it. I felt a right pig" (Charles & Kerr, 1986, p. 563).

When asked about whether they noticed their weight, two of the four young women said that they were not concerned with their weight and did not bother to weigh themselves. Participants 1 and 2 did weigh themselves.

> INTERVIEWER: Do you weigh yourselves?
> 1: Yeah, I do.
> 2: Sometimes.
> 1: For the past month I've been the same weight every time. I just normally weigh myself every time I go into the bath just to see.

There was a consensus that putting on half a stone in weight would be too much and that they would then try to lose it again:

> 1: It would bother me if it was half a stone.
> 2: I'd try and get it off.

This "magic" figure of half a stone was mentioned by some of the adult women interviewed by Charles and Kerr (1986) who believed that if they were half a stone lighter they would be happy with their weight and their bodies.

The interview data presented here suggest that ideas around body shape and size may change as children become older. Although two of the 8-year-olds thought they were too fat, they had not tried to restrict their food intake to try to remedy this. They saw dieting as an activity that was appropriate for adults but not for children. They did not report actively trying to lose weight. The adolescents, three of whom expressed body dissatisfaction, said that they used exercise to stop them getting fat rather than dieting. However, they also said that they avoided fatty foods and related this directly to the effects of such foods on body shape and weight (rather than health). Eating such foods was said to result in "feeling fat." Although only two young women said that they weighed themselves, all agreed that putting on half a stone was a problem that would be rectified by trying to lose the weight again. These experiences are similar to those of the adults interviewed by Charles and Kerr (1986). What is of particular concern is that these 13-year-olds are of an age when they could be expected to put on at least half a stone when they

go through puberty. If they see this as a problem they might exercise, or they might restrict their food intake. Either strategy could lead to problems if engaged in to excess (Carruth & Goldberg, 1990).

Food as Comfort

Food played a complex role in these girls' lives. Young women in both age groups described reasons for eating that were close to adult women's experiences described in the Charles and Kerr (1986) paper. They described eating for reasons other than hunger. Unhappiness and situations where they were bored lead them to resort to food as a comfort. Eating to relieve boredom or unhappiness was described by the 8-year-olds:

> A: I eat when I'm sad.
> B: I eat when I'm bored.

The 13-year-olds described the same scenario:

> 2: I eat chocolate when I'm depressed.
> 1: I eat loads when I'm bored.
> 3: If there isn't ought on tely you eat a right load.

The 13-year-olds said that food choice (when eating because of boredom) was determined by the amount of effort required in preparation. "Healthy" food was less likely to be eaten at these times because it was thought that it took longer to prepare:

> INTERVIEWER: What sort of foods do you eat when you're bored?
> 3: Anything.
> 2: Biscuits.
> 1: You won't make anything healthy when you're bored cos its so much trouble.

Charles and Kerr (1986) have argued that food, particularly sweet food, is used to reward and comfort children and as a substitute for attention. They argue that these practices teach children to regard food as a means of comfort and to relieve boredom. Charles and Kerr (1986) and Orbach (1993) argue that the association between food and comfort that women learn in childhood directly contradicts adult women's need to deny themselves food to remain slim and therefore sexually desirable. This contradiction can lead to an almost obsessive relationship with food, and often a vicious circle where food is used to reduce stress, which leads to weight gain that causes social censure that increases stress. It is a matter for concern that the 8- and 13-year-olds interviewed here were already using food as a source of comfort.

Limitations of the Study

The young women we interviewed were all White and working- or middle-class. This was because we wanted to maximise explanation through understanding by picking girls who were as much like us as possible. We shared with these girls the experience of being White women from similar backgrounds, educated in similar schools (in the second author's case, in the same school). We found that these shared experiences helped in our interpretation of the data. However, we recognise that these findings may not be relevant to young Black women, or those in other social classes. Wardle, Bindra, Fairclough, and Westcombe (1993), in a review of relevant studies, show that fewer Black and Asian girls want to lose weight than White girls, suggesting that there are important cultural differences in body shape ideals. Further work could involve interviews with Black women to investigate this.

Implications of the Findings

These findings suggest that these young women have learned about the acceptability of the slim body in Western society (and the unacceptability of the body that does not fit the slim ideal). By the age of 8 these girls knew about dieting as a means of trying to attain this goal, although they did not use this strategy themselves. The 13-year-olds reported denying themselves "fattening" foods and felt "fat" when they did eat them, in line with accounts from adult women. What struck us most reading the transcripts was the similarity between the accounts given by these 8- and 13-years olds, and those of the adults in the Charles and Kerr (1986) study. The accounts presented here add to

the existing body of knowledge by showing that girls as young as 8 year-old report dissatisfaction with their body weight and shape and show a preference for a socially acceptably slim body. Charles and Kerr (1986) conclude that adult women have a problematic relationship with food and body image. Our findings suggest that this problematic relationship may start early in women's lives, as early as 8 years of age.

These findings have important implications for the role of body image in women's lives. Susie Orbach has argued that we (as women) are taught to view our bodies as commodities from an early age, continually monitoring them for faults, which causes an objectification of our own bodies. The young women we interviewed here presented accounts that suggested that they objectified and criticised their bodies. Their accounts provide support for suggestions that women from primary-school age onwards are sensitive to cultural pressures to conform to a limited range of acceptable body shapes. Wendy Chapkis (1986) argues that the cultural idealisation of a limited range of body shapes is a central feature of women's oppression. She shows how the global culture machine makes a Western model of beauty mandatory for women all over the world. She notes how women suffer when our bodies do not conform to the limited range of acceptable shapes and sizes. She presents a solution to oppression by the beauty system that involves resistance and a refusal to comply with the unrealistic norms propagated by the global culture machine. Her work recognises cultural pressures on women to conform to an ideal that has been imposed on us. Adult women can make an active choice to accept or reject current concepts of body image, in the knowledge that rejection of the norms will mean nonacceptance by dominant cultural groups. Refusal to accept the dominant images of feminine beauty is becoming more prevalent. Many feminists have rejected dominant images of beauty, showing that even in a context of oppression there are possibilities for action (Chapkis, 1986; Wolf, 1991). The advent of the National Association to Advance Fat Acceptance in the United States, and the "Anti-Dieting" lobby in the United Kingdom has brought the issue of antifat prejudice into the cultural mainstream. Even popular women's magazines are starting to carry stories about the attractions of women who do not conform to the cultural ideal and who are happy to be fat (*Marie Claire*, December 1995, "Why I Adore Large Women," pp. 43–46); and about thin women who are unhappy with the way they look (*New Woman*, December 1995, I'm Tall, Skinny, Blonde, and I Hate It," p. 81); although the messages in these articles are somewhat contradicted by the photographs of skinny models that surround them.

Adolescent women and girls may find it particularly difficult to challenge dominant cultural representations of femininity at a time when they are still learning about what it means to be a woman in society, and when they are experiencing changes in body shape and size as they move into womanhood. Magazines aimed at girls and young women tend to present traditional slim images of attractiveness. Eileen Guillen and Susan Barr (1994) investigated body image in *Seventeen Magazine* (the best friend of high school girls in the United States) between 1970 and 1990 and concluded that the magazine contributes to the current cultural milieu in which thinness is expected of women, be they adults or adolescents. These images have powerful effects on their readers, serving to foster and maintain a "cult of femininity," supplying definitions of what it means to be a woman (Ferguson, 1985). It is a matter of concern that the images presented in teen-magazines present such a restricted range of models for young women. If women's body image can be bolstered by alternative sources of information, they may be more resilient against influences such as teen-magazines, because young women who grow up with a positive body image are less likely to be affected by cultural messages (Orbach, 1993).

Susan Bordo (1993) is pessimistic about the possibilities of change, arguing that women are embedded in the culture that oppresses them, and cannot help but collude in it. We think that this view is overpessimistic. It devalues the efforts of the large number of women who manage to resist the system and forge their own alternative positive body images, and the potential for these women

to become positive role models for girls and adolescent women. In the public sphere, Delia Grace, Roseanne Barr, Jo Brand, Dawn French, and many others have shown how alternative images of beauty can be brought into mainstream culture to challenge and subvert the beauty system. These women present positive role models for women, presenting them with additional choices. The accounts of the young women here suggested that these role models are not so influential on girls and young women as younger conventionally slim models such as Jet the Gladiator (although even she was seen as inappropriately muscular). Media aimed at girls and adolescent women abound with thin role models but lack positive images of young women who are not conventionally attractive. Children's television presenters are uniformly thin. Television soaps such as "Neighbours," "Home and Away," "Biker Grove," "Heartbreak High," "Brookside," and "Eastenders," which are watched by large numbers of British young women, all lack positive images of young women who do not conform to the stereotypically slim ideal. The new British soap "Hollyoaks" is typical in its choice of thin, conventionally attractive actresses to play the lead roles. Increased exposure in the media of positive images of strong young women who challenge accepted notions of beauty may encourage young women to be more happy about (and less vigilant over) their bodies. Clearly, this would require a cultural shift in the social construction of beauty, A replication of this study in (say) 10 years time may then produce very different results.

References

Bordo, Susan. (1993). *Unbearable weight: Feminism, western culture, and the body*. Berkeley: University of California Press.

Bunnell, Douglas, Cooper, Peter, Hertz, Stanley, & Shenker, Ronald. (1992). Body shape concern among adolescents. *International Journal of Eating Disorders, 11*, 79–83.

Carruth, Brenda, & Goldberg. Dena. (1990). Nutritional issues of adolescents: Athletics and the body image mania. *Journal of Early Adolescence, 10*, 122–140.

Chapkis, Wendy. (1985). *Beauty secrets*. London: Women's Press.

Chapman, Rowena. (1988). The great pretender: Variations on the new man theme. In Rowena Chapman & Jonathan Rutherford (Eds.), *Male order: Unwrapping masculinity* (pp. 225–248). London: Lawrence and Wishart.

Charles, Nickie, & Kerr, Marion. (1986). Food for feminist thought. *The Sociological Review, 34,* 537–572.

Davis, Kathy. (1994). *Reshaping the female body.* London: Sage.

Ferguson, Marjorie. (1985). *Forever feminine: Women's magazines and the cult of femininity.* Aldershot: Gower.

Guillen, Eileen, & Barr, Susan. (1994). Nutrition, dieting, and fitness messages in a magazine for adolescent women, 1970–1990. *Journal of Adolescent Health, 15,* 464–472.

Hill, Andy, Oliver, Sarah, & Rogers, Peter. (1992). Eating in the adult world: The rise of dieting in childhood and adolescence. *British Journal of Clinical Psychology, 31,* 95–105.

Maude, Dana, Wertheim, Eleanor, Paxton, Susan, Gibbons, Kay, & Szmukler, George. (1993). Body dissatisfaction, weight loss behaviors, and bulimic tendencies in Australian adolescents, with an estimate of female data representativeness. *Australian Psychologist, 28,* 128–132.

Mishkind, Marc, Rodin, Judith, Silberstein, Lisa, & Striegel-Moore, Ruth. (1986). The embodiment of masculinity: cultural, psychological, and behavioural dimensions. *American Behavioural Scientist, 29,* 545–562.

Mort, Frank. (1988). Boy's own? Masculinity, style and popular culture. In Rowena Chapman & Jonathan Rutherford (Eds.), *Male order: Unwrapping masculinity* (pp. 225–248). London: Lawrence and Wishart.

Orbach, Susie. (1993). *Hunger strike: The anorectics struggle as a metaphor for our age.* Penguin: London.

Strauss, Anselm, & Corbin, J. (1990). *Basics of qualitative research: Grounded theory procedures and techniques.* Newbury Park. CA: Sage.

Tiggemann, Marika, & Pennington, Barbara (1990). The development of gender differences in body-size dissatisfaction. *Australian Psychologist, 25,* 306–313,

Toro, Josep, Castro, Josefina, Garcia, Marta, Perez, Pau, & Cuesta, Lidia. (1989). Eating attitudes, sociodemographic factors and body shape evaluation in adolescence. *British Journal of Medical Psychology, 62,*61–70.

Wadden, Thomas, Brown, Gary, Foster. Gary, & Linowuaritz, Jan. (1991). Salience of weight-related worries in adolescent males and females. *International Journal of Eating Disorders, 10,* 407–414.

Wardle, Jane, Bindra, Renu, Fairclough, Beverley, & Westcombe, Alex (1993). Culture and body image: Body perception and weight concern in young Asian and Caucasian British women. *Journal of Community and Applied Social Psychology, 3,* 173–181.

Wolf, Naomi. (1991). *The beauty myth: How images of beauty are used against women.* New York: Morrow and Co.

Beards, Breasts, and Bodies: Doing Sex in a Gendered World

RAINE DOZIER

Gender is ubiquitous and, along with race and class, orders most aspects of daily life. "Talking about gender for most people is the equivalent of fish talking about water" (Lorber 1994, 13). Because transsexuals, transgendered people, and others at the borders of gender and sex are fish out of water, they help illuminate strengths and weaknesses in common conceptions of gender. This project clarifies the relationship between sex, gender, and sexual orientation through interviews with female-to-male transsexuals and transgendered people.[1] The interviewees challenge the underlying assumption in much of gender literature that sex, gender, and sexual orientation align in highly correlated, relatively fixed, binary categories. Instead, these categories are a process of differentiation and constructed meaning that is bound in social context.

Sex, Gender, and Sexuality

In the United States, the term "gender" is increasingly used as a proxy for the term "sex" (Auerbach 1999). My own small rebellion against this tendency is to respond literally. When asked to indicate sex, I reply female; when asked for gender, I reply male. Perhaps I am doing little to change concepts of gender and sex,[2] but at least I am on mailing lists that target my diverse interests! At the same time that the public seems to be increasingly using "gender" as proxy for "sex," gender theorists are more clearly delineating the relationship between sex and gender. However, because gender and sex are seemingly inexplicably connected in most aspects of social life, theorists have

difficulty in retaining these delineations throughout their work.

Intellectuals have been creating, critiquing, and advancing concepts of gender for the past 30 years. Generally, gender is defined as the socially constructed correlate of sex. The concept of gender as socially constructed has been theorized extensively and illustrated in a variety of arenas from the playground to the boardroom (Fausto-Sterling 2000; Kanter 1977; Kessler 1990; Lorber 1994; Messner 2000; Thorne 1993; West and Zimmerman 1987). However, many definitions positing gender as an ongoing accomplishment rely on sex as the "master status" or "coat rack" on which gender is socially constructed (Nicholson 1994). Although there is a general consensus that gender is socially constructed, theorists have too often relied on sex as its initiating point.

Delphy (1993) critiqued the overreliance on sex in defining gender. She claimed that illustrating the social construction of gender by describing the cross-cultural variation in men's and women's behavior and social roles only reinforces the notion that gender originates in sex. The description of cross-cultural variation further entrenches the notion of "gender as the *content* with sex as the *container*" (Delphy 1993, 3). Both Nicholson (1994) and Delphy (1993) challenged the view that gender derives from sex and, in a sense, posited the opposite: That "gender is the knowledge that establishes meanings for bodily differences" (Scott 1988, 2). Gender, then, is the concept that creates and defines sex differences.

Typically, sex is assigned based on genital inspection at birth, but biological sex is a complex constellation of chromosomes, hormones, genitalia, and reproductive organs. The study of intersexed and sex-reassigned children illustrates that social notions of sex are employed when biological sex is ambiguous (Fausto-Sterling 2000; Kessler 1990). Because sex is an organizing principle of most societies, people are forced to be one or the other, even when "only a surgical shoehorn can put them there" (Fausto-Sterling 1993, 24). Given this, sex is both a physical attribute and socially constructed.

West and Zimmerman (1987) grappled with the social aspect of sex by adding a category to the sex, gender, and sexuality framework. They defined "sex category" as socially perceived sex and claimed that "recognition of the analytical independence of sex, sex category, and gender is essential for understanding the relationships among these elements and the interactional work involved in 'being' a gendered person in society" (West and Zimmerman 1987, 127). However, the categories of sex category, gender, and sexuality are not just analytically, but also practically, distinct. West and Zimmerman ultimately identified gender as the performance one is accountable for based on sex category's leaving little room for feminine men and masculine women. "In virtually any situation, one's sex category can be relevant, and one's performance as an incumbent of that category (i.e., gender) can be subjected to evaluation" (West and Zimmerman 1987, 145). We are left with the ironic conclusion that gender is socially constructed yet is rigidly defined by sex category—an inadequate framework for the explanation of atypical gender behavior.

Lorber (1994, 1999) attempted to uncouple masculinity and femininity from sex category by developing subcategories of gender including gender status (being taken for a man or woman), gender identity (sense of self as a man or woman), and gender display (being feminine and/or masculine). Even with this delineation, Lorber, like West and Zimmerman (1987), consistently slipped into assumptions of the "natural" link between categories. For instance, she claimed transsexuals and "transvestites" do not challenge the gender order because "their goal is to be feminine women and masculine men" (Lorber 1994, 20). As well, she described socialization as a woman or man as "produce[ing] different feelings, consciousness, relationships, skills—ways of being that we call feminine or masculine" (Lorber 1994, 14). This account fails to explain the behavior and identity of trans people for two reasons. First, it assumes the intransigence between the categories man/masculine and woman/feminine, which is not the experience of transsexuals and transgendered people. Not all men, constructed or biological, are masculine or wish to be. Second, Lorber asserted that being treated as a man or woman in social interaction creates a masculine or feminine consciousness. This assertion fails to explain how people grow up to have a gender identity contrary to that expected from their socialization. Lorber's work is important in defining gender as an institution that creates and reinforces inequality, but it also illustrates how easily sex and gender (masculinity and femininity) become elided when sex is used as the initiating point for gendering individuals.

Just like sex and gender, sexuality can also be defined as socially constructed. Sexual behaviors and the meanings assigned to them vary across time and cultures. For instance, Herdt's (1981) study of same-sex fellatio in a tribe in Papua, New Guinea, found that this behavior did not constitute homosexuality or pedophilia, although it might be defined as both in the United States. In the United States, same-sex behavior is assumed to occur only in individuals with a gay or bisexual orientation, yet the AIDS epidemic forced educators and epidemiologists to acknowledge the lack of correlation between identity and behavior (Parker and Aggleton 1999). Schippers (2000) documented a lack of correlation between sexual orientation and sexual behavior in her study of alternative hard rock culture in the United States. Seeing sexual behavior and its meaning as highly reliant on social context helps explain the changing attractions and orientation of female-to-male transsexual and transgendered people (FTMs) as they transition.

Sex, gender, and sexuality, then, are all to varying degrees socially interpreted, and all contribute to an overarching concept of gender that relies on both perceived sex and behaviors and their attribution as masculine or feminine.

A growing number of scholars are writing particularly about FTMs and female masculinities. The longest-term contributor has been Devor (1989, 1997, 1998, 2004). Adding to Devor's work in recent years have been Cromwell (1999), Halberstam (1998), Prosser (1998), and Rubin (2003). Although transsexuals are increasingly represented in academic research, concepts of gender, sex, and sexuality are rarely explored. Gender theorists have often examined transsexuality through the lens of gender (Kessler and McKenna 1978; Nicholson 1994; West and Zimmerman 1987); less often have transsexual theorists interrogated gender through the lens of transsexuality. Using transsexuality as a standpoint to complicate and critique gender has been more common in nonacademic writing (Bornstein 1995; Califia 1997; Feinberg 1998).

Most work in the social sciences regarding transsexuals has focused largely on male-to-female transsexuals (Bolin 1988; Ekins 1997; Lewins 1995). Work by social scientists is important because it can help transform individual, personal experiences into broader social patterns and illuminate the role of social interaction and institutions. The limited research on FTMs offers a unique construction to social science research regarding transsexuality. Devor (1997) documented the lives of 46 FTMs using extensive quotes, allowing FTMs to speak about their lives, their upbringing, and their experiences with transitioning. Although this work is an incredibly detailed recording of the life experiences of FTMs, Devor avoids interpreting or theorizing about the experiences of FTMs and the potential meanings they have for the field of gender studies.

Prosser (1998) took to task the loss of materiality and "the body" in postmodern work regarding transsexuals. Prosser reminded theorists that gender is not simply conceptual but real, and experienced in the body (see Devor 1999). Although Prosser's critique of postmodern thought around transsexuality is extremely important, my

interviews indicate that he may overemphasize the importance of the body in transsexual experience. Particular body characteristics are not important in themselves but become important because of social interpretation.

Cromwell (1999) eloquently summarized notions of gender and sexuality and described them as being located in either essentialist or constructed frameworks. He criticized both and claimed that exclusively constructionist explanations rely on the primacy of social interaction, implying that gender identity does not exist when individuals are alone. He claimed that trans people are important to study because, through them, it is evident that even if socially constructed, there is an underlying, unwavering gender identity. Most important though, Cromwell asserted that trans people's construction of identities, bodies, and sexualities as different rather than deviant subverts the dominant gender/sex paradigm. Rubin (2003) concurred with Cromwell's view of the paradox that gender identity is socially constructed yet at the same time embodied and "absolutely real" (Cromwell 1999, 175). Prosser (1998), Cromwell, and Rubin all challenge aspects of gender theory that do not mesh with the experiences of transsexuals and transgendered people. The body is a very real aspect of the (trans)gendered experience and expression, and even though gender identity is socially constructed, it takes on a solidity and immutability that is not dependent on social interaction.

With this emerging academic work regarding transsexuality, the need to examine how transsexuality and transgenderism complicate the gender field has arisen. Questions such as the following have become increasingly compelling:

What is the impact of changing sex on the individual's social and sexual behaviors? How does an individual's sex affect other people's interpretation of his or her behavior? As sex changes, how does social interaction change?

By investigating the changing behaviors and interactions of FTMs as they transition, this article illustrates important connections between gender and perceived sex and contributes to the social scientific understanding of transsexuality. Examining the experience of FTMs clarifies that masculinity and femininity are not inextricably linked with male and female and that perceived sex is important in interpreting behavior as masculine or feminine. This project also adds to social scientific work on transsexuality by using transsexuality as a standpoint to critique gender in a systematic, empirically based manner. As well, it supports recent academic work regarding FTMs (Cromwell 1999; Prosser 1998; Rubin 2003) by illustrating the importance of the body to gender and gender identity and helps to increase the representation of FTMs in the social scientific literature on transsexuality.

Study Design and Sample

For this project, I interviewed 18 trans-identified people, all born female, the majority residing in Seattle, Washington. I sought informants in a variety of ways. I contacted friends and acquaintances with contacts in the trans community and introduced myself to people I knew to be trans, soliciting interviews. I also attended the National Gay and Lesbian Task Force conference, Creating Change, in Oakland, California, in November 1999, recruiting two informants and attending two trans-specific workshops, one regarding families and the other regarding relationships. I relied on snowball sampling to recruit the majority of the interviewees. Although this small sample is not random, the interviewees were able to provide a great deal of information regarding the relationship between perceived sex and gendered behavior.

Respondents ranged in age from 20 to 45 and had begun living as trans between the ages of 18 and 45 (see Table 1). I say this with some hesitation because many FTMs privately identify as trans for years before transitioning or being out about their identity. In this case, I am defining "living as trans" as being referred to as "he" consistently, publicly and/or in their subcultural network. With this definition, three of the respondents were not living as trans even though they identified as transgendered.

Fourteen of the respondents were white, one was African American, two were Latino, and one was Chinese American. Only one respondent did not previously identify as lesbian or bisexual. After transitioning, defining sexual orientation becomes more complicated since sex, and sometimes sexual preference, changes. Assigning sexual orientation requires assigning people to categories based on the sex of the sexual participants. Since many FTMs report being newly attracted to men after transitioning, it appears that their orientation has changed even though, in a sense, they remain homosexual (previously a lesbian, now gay). However, if they are still primarily involved with lesbians or with feminine women, it is difficult to say their orientation has changed when only their perceived sex is different. As well, if an individual is primarily attracted to feminine people, but after transitioning dates feminine men as well as feminine women, his gendered sexual preference has not changed, so it is unclear whether this describes a change in sexual orientation. Because of these complexities, the Table records the reported sexual preference as closely as possible without relying on usual categories of sexual orientation.

Even though they were raised in a variety of locations, the great majority of respondents currently live in urban areas. The sample is probably not representative of the trans population in the United States because it is overwhelmingly urban and emphasizes FTMs who have chosen not to assimilate into mainstream, heterosexual culture. These people, it seemed, might be better positioned to comment on changes in the trans community regarding notions of sex, gender, and sexuality because they have access to greater numbers of trans people and are more often engaged with others about trans issues.

At the time of the interviews, five of the informants were nonoperative and not taking hormones. Only one seemed certain he never wanted medical intervention, and that was due to a compromised immune system. Of these five, none have seriously considered taking hormones, but four expressed a strong desire for chest surgery that involves removal of the breasts and repositioning

Table 1. Sample Characteristics

Pseudonym	Age	Race/Ethnicity	Current Sexual Preference	Time from Beginning of Physical Transition	Transition Status
Aaron	34	White	Bio women, bio men, FTMs	1 year	Hormones
Billy	30	White	Bio men, FTMs	6 years	Hormones, chest surgery
Brandon	20	African American	FTMs, male-to-female transsexuals, bio women		Nontransitioned
Dick	27	White	Bisexual	2 years	Hormones, chest surgery
Jessica	22	White	Mainly bio women, femmes		Nontransitioned
Jay	27	Chinese American	Bio women		Nontransitioned
Joe	38	Latino	Bio women, FTMs	8 years	Hormones, chest surgery
Kyle	25	White	Bio women		Nontransitioned
Luke	25	White	Mainly bio women		Nontransitioned
Max	21	White	Bio women, femmes	1 year	Hormones, chest surgery
Mick	38	White	Lesbians	2 years	Chest surgery
Mitch	36	White	Bio women, femmes	4 years	Hormones, chest surgery
Pete	34	White	Queer, bisexual	3 years	Hormones, chest surgery
Rogelio	40	Latino/Black	Bio women	6 years living as trans, 1 year taking hormones	Hormones
Sam	30	White	Bio women, bio men, FTMs	4 years	Hormones, chest surgery
Ted	29	White	Pansexual	1 year	Hormones
Terry	45	White	Unknown because of recent transition	3 months	Hormones
Trevor	35	White	Bio women, femmes	1 year	Hormones, chest surgery

Note: Bio women = biological women; bio men = biological men; FTMs = female-to-male transsexual and transgendered people.

of the nipples if necessary. Two could not have surgery for financial reasons and one for medical reasons, and one was hesitant for family and political reasons.[3]

Only 1 of the 18 interviewees had had chest surgery, was not taking hormones, and had no further plans for medical intervention. Twelve of the 13 taking hormones had had chest surgery or were planning to do so. The remaining individual was not considering chest surgery due to concerns about keloids due to his dark skin.[4] He expressed frustration at how little information was available to darker-skinned transmen about the potential effects of surgery.

I interviewed FTMs using a general set of questions regarding their experiences with the medical community, the trans community, their families, and their relationship to masculinity. I did not set out to prove a preformulated hypothesis regarding the relationship between sex, gender, and sexual orientation; nor did I predetermine the ideal number of respondents. Instead, in a manner derived from grounded theory, I interviewed respondents until I started to hear common patterns in their comments and stories. Ekins (1997, 3), utilizing grounded theory in his exploration of identity processes for female-to-male transsexuals, described grounded theory as that "which demands intimate appreciation of the arena studied, but which writes up that intimate appreciation in terms of theoretical analyses." Grounded theory expands our understanding of qualitative research; it relies not only on documentation of interviews but also on the standpoint of the researcher and her or his intimate relationship with the topic of interest. For this reason, I reveal myself as transgendered, born female, with no immediate plans to transition. By "transition," I mean to live as a man by taking hormones and acquiring whatever surgeries necessary. This position as both transgendered and not transitioned gives me a keen interest in the relationship between sex, sex category (perceived sex), and gender and perhaps a voyeuristic interest in hearing what it is like to "cross over"—the difference between internal identity as a man and social interaction when perceived as one. I believe being trans identified gave me easier access to trans people and made it easier for interviewees to confide in me not only because they felt more at ease but because I had familiarity with common cultural terms, customs, and issues.

Findings

The perceived sex of individuals, whether biological or not, influences the meaning assigned to behavior and the tenor of social and sexual interaction. FTMs illustrate the reliance on both sex and behavior in expressing and interpreting gender. Perceived sex and individual behavior are compensatory, and both are responsible for the performance of gender: When sex is ambiguous or less convincing, there is increased reliance on highly gendered behavior; when sex is obvious, then there is considerably more freedom in behavior. For this reason, sex is not the initiating point for gender. Instead, sex, whether biological or constructed, is an integral aspect of gender. "If the body itself is always seen through social

interpretation then sex is not something that is separate from gender but is, rather, that which is subsumable under it" (Nicholson 1994, 79).

As I listened to interviewees, the tension and balance between behavior and appearance, between acting masculine and appearing male, became evident. In general, interviewees confirmed Nicholson's (1994) assertion that (perceived) sex is an important aspect of the construction of gender and that perceived sex is a lens through which behavior is interpreted. However, particular sex characteristics such as a penis or breasts are not as crucial to the perception of sex as their meanings created in both social and sexual interaction.

Generally, after taking hormones, interviewees were perceived as men regardless of behavior and regardless of other conflicting sex signifiers including breasts and, in the case of one interviewee, even when nine months pregnant.[5] The physical assertion of sex is so strong through secondary sex characteristics that gender identity is validated. Interviewees find certain sex characteristics to be particularly important to their social identity as male: "I think it's all about facial hair. It's not about my fetish for facial hair, but socially, when you have facial hair, you can pass regardless of what your body looks like. I mean, I was nine months pregnant walking around and people were like, 'Ooh, that guy's fat' " (Billy).

Another interviewee also finds facial hair to be particularly important to initial gender/sex attribution. In reply to the question, "For you, what is the most important physical change since transitioning," he responds, "Probably facial hair, because nobody even questions facial hair....I've met FTMs that have these huge hips. I mean this guy, he was [shaped] like a top, and he had a full beard. Nobody questioned that he had huge hips, so that is the one key thing. And probably secondary is a receding hairline. Even with a high voice, people accept a high voiced man" (Joe).

As the interviewees became socially recognized as men, they tended to be more comfortable expressing a variety of behaviors and engaging in stereotypically feminine activities, such as sewing or wearing nail polish. The increase in male sex characteristics creates both greater internal comfort with identity and social interactions that are increasingly congruent with sex identity. As a result, some FTMs are able to relax their hypermasculine behavior.

> I went through a phase of thinking every behavior I do is going to be cued into somehow by somebody. So, I've got to be hypervigilant about how many long sentences I say, does my voice go up at the end of a sentence, how do I move my hands, am I quick to try and touch someone.... And I got to a point where I said, This is who I am.... There are feminine attributes and there are masculine attributes that I like and I am going to maintain in my life.... If that makes people think, "Oh you're a fag," well great, all my best friends are fags.... But when I was first coming out, it was all about "I've got to be perceived as male all the time, no matter what." That bone-crushing handshake and slapping people on the back and all of that silliness. I did all that. (Rogelio)

Like Rogelio, Pete finds transitioning gave him the freedom to express his feminine side: "It was very apparent how masculine a woman I was...and now it's like I've turned into this flaming queen like 90 percent of the time. And so my femininity, I had an outlet for it somehow, but it was in a kind of gay way. It wasn't in a womanly kind of way, it was just femininity. Because I don't think that female equals femininity and male equals masculinity" (Pete).

Sex category and gendered behavior, then, are compensatory; they are both responsible for the social validation of gender identity and require a particular balance. When sex is ambiguous or less convincing, there is increased reliance on highly gendered behavior. When sex category is obvious, then there is considerably more freedom in behavior, as is evident when talking to FTMs about the process of transitioning.

For two interviewees, gay men are particularly valuable role models in deconstructing traditional masculinity and learning to incorporate "feminine" behavior and expression into a male identity:

> So, those fairly feminine men that I have dated have been very undeniably male, but they haven't been a hundred percent masculine all the time, and I think I've learned from my relationships with them to sort of relax. Lighten up a little; nail polish isn't going to kill anybody. I think that I'm more able to be at peace with all of the aspects of myself.... [Now] I'm not going to go out of my way to butch it up. I'm male looking enough to get away with it, whereas when I did that kind of stuff before I transitioned people were like, "Well, you're not butch enough to be a man." (Billy)

FTMs transition for many reasons, but aligning external appearance with internal identity and changing social interaction were the chief reasons given by my interviewees. "Doing gender" (West and Zimmerman 1987) in a way that validates identity relies on both internal and external factors. Being able to look like one feels is key to the contentment of many FTMs. More than interacting with the social world as a man, comfort in one's body can be a chief motivator for FTMs, especially when seeking chest surgery. "I'd say that having a flat chest really seems right, and I really like that. I can throw a T-shirt on and feel absolutely comfortable instead of going [hunching shoulders]. And when I catch my reflection somewhere or look in the mirror, it's like, 'Oh, yeah' instead of, 'Oh, I forgot,' and that's been the most amazing thing...recognizing myself" (Trevor).

Some interviewees believed they would be content to live without any medical treatment or with chest surgery but not hormones as long as they were acknowledged as transgendered by themselves and their social circle. Even for those who were able to achieve a reasonable level of internal comfort, social interaction remained an ongoing challenge. Feeling invisible or not being treated in congruence with their gender identity motivated them to take hormones to experience broader social interaction appropriate to their gender identity. Some FTMs reported the desire to be seen as trans by other FTMs as an important factor in their decision to transition. For others, being called "ma'am" or treated as a woman in public was particularly grating. Being "she'd" was a constant reminder of the incongruence between social identity and internal gender identity.

> And the longer I knew that I was transgendered, the harder it got to live without changing my body. It's like the acknowledgment wasn't enough for me, and it got to a point where it was no longer enough for the people who knew me intimately to see my male side. It just got to be this really discordant thing between who I knew I was and who the people in my life knew I was...because I was perceived as a woman socially. I was seen as a woman and was treated differently than how I was treated by my friends and the people that I loved....So finally after a couple of years...I finally decided to take hormones. (Billy)

The potential impact on social interaction is key to the decision to transition. Although for some FTMs, gaining comfort in their body is the crucial element in decision making, for most interviewees, the change in social interaction is the motivating factor. Being treated as a man socially is important enough to risk many other things including loss of family, friends, and career. For other interviewees, though, not wanting to be treated as a man in all social situations motivated them not to transition. "In some ways, I wouldn't really want to give up my access to woman's space, and I think that would be a big reason why I wouldn't do it because I like being around women. I don't feel like I'm women identified, but I'm women centered. So in that sense, I wouldn't want to give up being able to spend a lot of time with women in different contexts that I might lose if I passed as a man" (Jay).

Some interviewees also worried that appearing as a biological man would make them no longer identifiable as trans or queer, making them invisible to their communities. As well, for some of those not transitioning, the potential loss of friends and family outweighed their desire to transition.

As expected, social interaction changed radically after transitioning, but sometimes in ways not anticipated. Whether these changes were positive or negative, expected or not, they still provided FTMs with social validation of their gender identity and the clear message that they were passing.

Changing Interaction

Many transmen found being perceived as a man enlightening. The most often noted changes to social interaction included being treated with more respect, being allowed more conversational space, being included in men's banter, and experiencing an increase in women's fear of them. Some FTMs realized that they would be threatening to women at night and acted accordingly while others were surprised to realize that women were afraid of them. "I remember one time walking up the hill; it was like nine o'clock, and this woman was walking in front of me, and she kept looking back, and I thought, 'What the hell is wrong with that girl?' And then I stopped in my tracks. When I looked at her face clearly under the light, she was afraid. So I crossed the street" (Joe).

For many FTMs, becoming an unquestioned member of the "boys' club" was an educational experience. The blatant expressions of sexism by many men when in the company of each other was surprising to these new men.

> I was on one of the school shuttles on campus and it was at a time when there weren't a lot of people on. There was a male bus driver, myself, and a young woman on the bus, and she had long blonde hair, a very pretty girl. She got off the bus, and there was just me and the bus driver, and the bus driver was reading me as a guy and totally being a sexist pig. I did not know how to deal with it or how to respond, let alone call him on his shit because I wasn't particularly, at this point, feeling like I wanted to get read or anything. So I basically just nodded my head and didn't say anything. (Ted)

One nontransitioned FTM who is usually taken for a man at work also feels pressure to conform and to ward off suspicion by either ignoring or contributing to sexist and homophobic comments when among coworkers. This is in direct contrast to Pete's experience, who became known as an outspoken advocate for women and minorities at his job after transitioning: "I feel like I'm one of the guys, which is really kind of odd. In some ways, it's really affirming, and in some ways, it's really unsettling. In Bellevue [his former job], it was a joke. 'Pete's here, so you better shut up.' Because they're sexist, they're homophobic, they're racist. And I would say, 'This is not something I think you should be talking about in the lunch room.' So I was constantly turning heads because I'm kind of an unusual guy" (Pete).

Acting like a "sensitive new age guy" did not challenge Pete's masculinity or essential maleness but simply defined him as "kind of an unusual guy." He was able to assume this role because his gender was established and supported through his unquestionably male appearance.

Interviewees found that their interactions with both men and women changed as they transitioned. After transitioning, a few FTMs, like the previously quoted interviewee, maintained strong feminist ideals and worked hard to change to appropriate behavior for a feminist man. This was an effort as behavioral expectations for men and butch lesbians differ radically, and what may be attributed to assertiveness in a masculine woman becomes intolerable in a man:

> I found that I had to really, really work to change my behavior. Because there were a lot of skills that I needed to survive as a butch woman in the world that made me a really obnoxious guy. There were things that I was doing that just were not okay. Like in school, talking over people. You know when women speak, they often speak at the same time with each other and that means something really different than when a guy speaks at the same time. And so it wasn't that I changed, it was that people's perceptions of me changed and that in order to maintain things that were important to me as a feminist, I had to really change my behavior. (Billy)

The perception that behavior had not really changed, but people's assignation of meaning to that behavior had, was common in the interviews. That is, what is masculine or feminine, what is assertive or obnoxious, is relative and dependent on social context. And the body—whether one appears male or female—is a key element of social context. These interviews suggest that whether a behavior is labeled masculine or feminine is highly dependent on the initial attribution of sex.

Besides gaining information as insiders, FTMs also felt they gained permission to take up more space as men. Many FTMs transition from the lesbian community, and most in this sample had been butch identified. As a result, they were used to having what they perceived to be a comfortable amount of social space even though they were women. As they transitioned, however, they were surprised at how much social privilege they gained, both conversationally and behaviorally. Terry, a previously high-profile lesbian known for her radical and outspoken politics, reported, "I am getting better service in stores and restaurants, and when I express an opinion, people listen. And that's really weird because I'm not a shy person, so having people sort of check themselves and make more conversational space than they did for me before is really kind of unsettling" (Terry).

As well as being allowed conversational space, many of these new men received special attention and greater respect from heterosexual women because their behavior was gender atypical yet highly valued. They were noticed and rewarded when confronting sexist remarks, understanding women's social position, and performing tasks usually dominated by women. Billy reports an experience in a women's studies class where he was the only man siding with the female students' point of view: "A woman came up to me after class and said, 'Wow, you know you're the most amazing feminist man I've ever met.' I just did not have the heart to ruin that for her. I was just like, you know, there are other guys out there who are capable of this, and it's not just because I'm a transsexual that I can be a feminist" (Billy). The ability to shop for clothes for their girlfriends was cited by two interviewees as a skill much admired. They reported excessive attention from saleswomen as a result of their competence in a usually female-dominated area:

> One other thing I have noticed about women, and in particular saleswomen in stores, is that they're always shocked that I can pick out good clothing items either for myself or for someone else, and I don't really need help with that. And I get flirted with constantly by saleswomen, I think largely because they get that I get how to shop. So, they see this guy that's masculine and secure in himself and he's not having to posture, and he can walk up with an armload of women's clothes that he's been picking out. . . . She [the saleswoman] says, "Wow, I want a boyfriend like you." So I get a lot of that. (Mitch)

These accounts underscore the relationship between behavior and appearance. When FTMs are perceived as men, their gender-atypical behavior is not sanctioned or suspect but admired and rewarded. Their perceived status as male allows their masculinity to remain intact even in the face of contradictory evidence. This contrasts with the experience of one FTM not taking hormones who is usually taken for a butch lesbian. Saleswomen at Victoria's Secret treated him rudely when he shopped for lingerie for his girlfriend until he made a greater effort to pass as a man. When passing as a man, he received markedly better service.

Not all FTMs gain social status by being perceived as men. It is a common assumption, bordering on urban legend, that transitioning brings with it improved status, treatment, and financial opportunities. However, having a paper trail including a previous female name and identity can severely compromise job prospects, especially in a professional position.

> The reality is we are on the bottom of the economic totem pole. And it does not matter what our educational background is. We could be the most brilliant people on the planet and we're still fucked when it comes to the kinds of jobs that we've gotten or the kinds of advances that we've gotten in the job market. Here I am, I've been out of law school for nearly 10 years, and I'm barely scraping by. And if I go in and apply for a job with a firm, well yeah, they may really like me, but once they start doing any investigating on my background, my old name comes up. (Mitch)

The assumption of a rise in status after sex reassignment also rests largely on the assumption of whiteness. Through my limited sample and conversations with friends, it appears that becoming a Black man is often a step down in status. Rogelio talks about the change in his experience as he becomes more consistently taken for a man:

> I am a Black male. I'm the suspect. I'm the one you have to be afraid of. I'm the one from whom you have to get away, so you have to cross the street, you have to lock your doors. You have to clutch whatever you've got a little closer to your body. . . . It's very difficult to get white FTMs to understand that. . . . [As a Black person], if I go into a store, I am followed. Now I am openly followed; before it was, "Oh, let's hide behind the rack of bread or something so that she won't see us." Now it's, "Oh, it's a guy, he's probably got a gun; he's probably got a knife. We have to know where his hands are at all times." (Rogelio)

Although it is an unpleasant experience, he reports that at least he knows he is consistently passing as a man by the rude treatment he receives from other men in social situations.

Another group of FTMs also experiences being perceived as male as a liability, not a privilege. Even though FTMs can have feminine behavior without calling their maleness into question, feminine behavior does lead to an increase in gay bashing and antigay harassment. FTMs who transitioned from being very butch to being perceived as male generally experienced a radical decline in harassment. Two of these butches were even gay bashed before transitioning because they were perceived to be gay men. With additional male sex characteristics, however, they were no longer perceived to be feminine men. For these men, the transition marked a decline in public harassment and intimidation. However, for more feminine FTMs, the harassment increased after transitioning. Appearing as small, feminine men made them vulnerable to attack. This interviewee reported a marked increase in violence and harassment after transitioning:

> I get gay bashed often. That's my biggest fear right now is male-on-male violence....Once I just got over pneumonia. I was downtown and I was on my way to choir, and some guy looked at me, and I was wondering why he was staring. I looked at him and I looked away. He called me a faggot because I was staring. He said, "Stop looking at me, faggot," and he chased me seven blocks. At first I thought he was just going to run me off, but I kept running and he was running after me as fast as he could and everybody was standing around just kind of staring. And I became really panicked that no one was ever going to help if I really needed it. People yell "faggot" at me all the time. (Dick)

One interviewee experienced about the same level of violence and harassment before and after transitioning. Unfortunately, he was attacked and harassed as a gay man as often before as after transitioning. On one occasion before transitioning, he was followed home and badly beaten by two men who forced their way into his house believing that they were assaulting a gay man: "If I'm with my partner I'm read as straight so I don't have to worry about being jumped as a gay guy, but if I am at a queer event and my partner's not around or if I'm just by myself....But I've just gotten to a point where I'm like, 'Fuck it.' At least now that I am on hormones, I have a little more strength to fight back" (Ted).

In sum then, FTMs are motivated to change their physical presentations for two reasons: First, to become more comfortable with their bodies and achieve greater congruence between identity and appearance and, second, to change social interaction so that it better validates their gender identity, both subculturally and in the wider social world. This strategy to change social interaction is very effective. All FTMs who transitioned noticed a marked change in their social interactions. Not all of these changes in interaction were positive,

however. First, the recognition that women are treated poorly compared to men was a shock. Second, being identified as a man was a liability when one was Black or appeared feminine. In other words, the assumption of an increase in privilege only consistently applied to masculine, non-Black men. Even then, the liabilities of being found out, especially on the job, remained.

Sexual Orientation and Gender Identity

Sexual behavior is another site that more clearly explicates the relationship between sex and gender. Sexual orientation is based not solely on the object of sexual and erotic attraction, but also on the sex category and gender performance created in the context of sexual interaction. The performance of gender is crucial in the sexual arena for two reasons: First, because sexuality is expressed through the body, which may or may not align with an individual's gender identity and, second, because heterosexual intercourse can symbolize the social inequalities between men and women. Altering the body alters the sexual relationships of FTMs by changing their gender/sex location in sexual interaction.

Many FTMs change sexual orientation after transitioning or, at the least, find that their object attraction expands to include both sexes. Devor (1997) found a large increase in the number of FTMs who, after transitioning, were sexually attracted to gay men. Why do many transmen change sexual orientation after transitioning? Even the earliest sexuality studies such as the Kinsey report (Kinsey, Pomeroy, and Martin 1948) provide evidence that individuals' attractions; fantasies, and behaviors do not always align with their professed sexual orientation. Currently, a diverse gay culture and the increased ease of living a gay lifestyle have created a wide variety of options for people with attractions to the same or both sexes (Seidman 2002). As well, coinciding with a rise in gay and lesbian cultures in the 1960s and 1970s was a heightened feminist consciousness. For some feminists, sexual relationships with men are problematic because of the power dynamic and broader cultural commentary enacted in heterosexual relations. Bisexual women sometimes find the dynamic untenable and choose to identify as lesbians. Aaron, a previously bisexual woman, confirms:

I do have an attraction to men; however, when I was a straight woman, I totally gave up going out with men because I was a strong female person and had a lot of problems interacting with men, even in the anarchist community, the punk community. They like tough girls, this strong riot girl persona, and yet when you're in the relationship with those same people, they still have those misogynistic, sexist beliefs about how you're supposed to interact in bed, in the relationship. I just never fit into that mold and finally said, "Fuck you guys; I'm not going there with you," and just came out as a dyke and lived happily as a dyke.... What I realize coming into the transgendered community myself was that it made so much sense to become transgendered, to become visually male, and to be able to relate to men as a man because then they would at least visually see me as part of who I am in a way that they could not see me when I was female.... That's really exciting for me.... I can still relate to femmes who are attracted to transmen. I can still relate to butches. I can still relate to straight women... but I also get back being able to relate to men, and that's definitely a gift. (Aaron)

In another example, Dick was primarily involved with men and briefly identified as a lesbian before transitioning. He found sexual orientation and gender identity to be inexplicably entangled as he struggled to clarify his identity. When he was a woman and in a long-term relationship with a man, he began to identify as queer. He assumed that his male partner was incongruent with his queer orientation. Over time, he realized that the sex of his partner was not as crucial to his queer identity as was the gender organization of the relationship. Identifying as queer was an attempt to express the desire for interaction congruent with gender identity rather than expressing the desire for a partner of a particular sex.

[Transitioning] makes a difference because it's queer then, and it's not locating me as a straight woman, which is not going to work. The way that I came out as queer, I thought it was about sexuality but it's really about gender. I was in a relationship with a man who I had been with for a couple of years... and then I started figuring out this thing about queerness, and I could not put my finger on it and I couldn't articulate it, but I knew that I couldn't be in a relationship with him.... But what I figured out a lot later was that it wasn't about not wanting to be with a guy; it was about not wanting to be the girl. (Dick)

Heterosexuality, then, is a problem for these FTMs not because of object choice but because of the gendered meaning created in intimate and sexual interaction that situates them as women. Most of the FTMs in the sample who changed sexual orientation or attractions after transitioning did not previously identify as bisexual or heterosexual. Two key changes allowed them to entertain the idea of sexual involvement with men. First, the relationship and power dynamic between two men is very different from that between a man and a woman. Second, in heterosexual interactions previous to transitioning, the sexual arena only reinforced FTMs' social and sexual position as women, thus conflicting with their gender identity. After transitioning, sexual interaction with men can validate gender identity:

So, it's okay for me to date men who were born men because I don't feel like they treat me weird. I couldn't stand this feminization of me, especially in the bedroom. Now I feel like I actually have a sex drive. Hormones didn't make me horny, the combination of me transitioning and taking hormones made me have maybe a normal sex drive. (Dick)

I've never totally dismissed men as sexual partners in general, but I knew that I'm very much dyke identified. But I think being masculine and having a male recognize your masculinity is just as sexy as a woman recognizing your masculinity, as opposed to a man relating to you as a woman. (Trevor)

I do not wish to imply that many lesbians are simply repressed bisexuals or heterosexuals using sex reassignment to cope with their sexual attraction toward men. Instead, I am arguing that the sexual interaction between FTMs and men is decidedly different from heterosexual interaction. The type of male partner generally changes as well—from straight to gay. For many FTMs, their change in sexual orientation and the degree of that change were a welcome surprise. Some appreciated the opportunity to interact with men on a sexual level that felt free of the power dynamics in heterosexual relations. Others were happy to date other FTMs or biological men as a way of maintaining their queer identity. Several interviewees who transitioned from a lesbian identity did not like appearing heterosexual and identified as queer regardless of their object choice because their body and gender status disrupted the usual sexuality paradigm. Still, they struggled with their invisibility as queer after transitioning. "Being with an FTM, we're the same, it's very queer to me....A lot of times, I'm bugged if I walk down the street with a girl and we seem straight....I think that's the worst part about transitioning is the queerness is really obliterated from you. It's taken away. I mean you're pretty queer, somebody walking down the street with a guy with a cunt is queer, but it's invisible" (Joe).

In his work with male-to-female transsexuals, Lewins (1995) discussed the relationship between gender and sexual orientation in the context of symbolic interactionism. The sexual arena is a site for creating and validating sex and gender identity because "when we desire someone and it is reciprocated, the positive nature of continuing interaction reaffirms and, possibly for some, confirms their gender identity" (Lewins 1995, 38). Sexual interaction, depending on the sexual orientation of the partner, is key to validating the male identity of FTMs. Whether that partner is a heterosexual or bisexual woman or a gay man, the interaction that involves the FTM as male confirms gender identity.

Conclusion

Trans people are in the unique position of experiencing social interaction as both women and men and illustrate the relativity of attributing behavior as masculine or feminine. Behavior labeled as assertive in a butch can be identified as oppressive in a

man. And unremarkable behavior for a woman such as shopping or caring for children can be labeled extraordinary and laudable when performed by a man. Although generally these new men found increased social privilege, those without institutional privilege did not. Becoming a Black man or a feminine man was a social liability affecting interaction and increasing risk of harassment and harm. Whether for better or worse, being perceived as a man changed social interaction and relationships and validated gender identity.

In addition to illustrating the relativity of assignation of meaning to behavior, these interviews illustrate the relativity of sexual orientation. Sexual orientation is based not exclusively on object attraction but also on the gendered meanings created in sexual and romantic interaction. Sexual orientation can be seen as fluid, depending on both the perceived sex of the individuals and the gender organization of the relationship.

This study of a small group of FTMs helps clarify the relationship between sex and gender because it does not use sex as the initiating point for gender and because most respondents have experienced social interaction as both men and women. Much sociological theory regarding gender assumes that gender is the behavioral, socially constructed correlate of sex, that gender is "written on the body." Even if there are case studies involving occasional aberrations, gender is generally characterized as initiating from sex. With this study, though, the opposite relationship is apparent. Sex is a crucial aspect of gender, and the gendered meaning assigned to behavior is based on sex attribution. People are not simply held accountable for a gender performance based on their sex (see West and Zimmerman 1987); the gendered meaning of behavior is dependent on sex attribution. Whether behavior is defined as masculine or feminine, laudable or annoying, is dependent on sex category. Doing gender, then, does not simply involve performing appropriate masculinity or femininity based on sex category. Doing gender involves a balance of both doing sex and performing masculinity and femininity. When there is no confusion or ambiguity in the sex performance, individuals are able to have more diverse expressions of masculinity and femininity. This balance between behavior and appearance in expressing gender helps explain the changing behavior of FTMs as they transition as well as the presence of men and women with a diversity of gendered behaviors and display.

Notes

1. Interviewees do not necessarily identify as female-to-male transsexual and transgendered people (FTMs). There are many terms that more closely describe individuals' personal identity and experience including "trans," "boy dyke," "trannyboy," "queer," "man," "FTM," "transsexual," and "gender bender." For simplicity and clarity, I will use "FTM" and "trans" and apologize to interviewees who feel this does not adequately express their sex/gender location.

2. See Lucal (1999) for an excellent discussion regarding interpersonal strategies for disrupting the gender order.

3. Politically, some feminist FTMs express discomfort at becoming members of the most privileged economic and social class (white men).

4. A keloid is thick, raised, fibrous scar tissue occurring in response to an injury or surgery; it occurs more often in darker-skinned individuals.

5. After taking testosterone, an individual appears male even if he or she discontinues use. The interviewee who became pregnant discontinued hormones to ovulate and continue his pregnancy, then began hormones again after childbirth.

References

Auerbach, Judith D. 1999. From the SWS president: Gender as proxy. *Gender & Society* 13: 701–703.

Bolin, Anne. 1988. *In search of Eve: Transsexual rites of passage*. South Hadley, MA: Bergin & Garvey.

Bornstein, Kate. 1995. *Gender outlaw: On men, women, and the rest of us*. New York: Vintage.

Califia, Patrick. 1997. *Sex changes: The politics of transgenderism*. San Francisco: Cleis Press.

Cromwell, Jason. 1999. *Transmen and FTMs: Identities, bodies, genders, and sexualities*. Urbana: University of Illinois Press.

Delphy, Christine. 1993. Rethinking sex and gender. *Women's Studies International Forum* 16: 1–9.

Devor, Holly [Aaron Devor]. 1989. *Gender blending: Confronting the limits of duality*. Bloomington: Indiana University Press.

———. 1997. *FTM: Female-to-male transsexuals in society*. Bloomington: Indiana University Press.

———. 1998. Sexual-orientation identities, attractions, and practices of female-to-male transsexuals. In *Current concepts in transgender identity*, edited by Dallas Denny. New York: Garland.

———. 1999. Book review of "Second skins: The body narratives of transsexuality" by Jay Prosser. *Journal of Sex Research* 36:207–208.

Devor, Aaron H. 2004. Witnessing and mirroring: A fourteen stage model of transsexual identity formation. *Journal of Gay and Lesbian Psychotherapy* 8:41–67.

Ekins, Richard. 1997. *Male femaling: A grounded theory approach to cross-dressing and sex-changing*. New York: Routledge.

Fausto-Sterling, Anne. 1993. The five sexes: Why male and female are not enough. *Sciences* 33 (2): 20–24.

———. 2000. *Sexing the body: gender politics and the construction of sexuality*. New York: Basic Books.

Feinberg, Leslie. 1998. *Trans liberation: Beyond pink or blue*. Boston: Beacon.

Halberstam, Judith. 1998. *Female masculinity*. Durham, NC: Duke University Press.

Herdt, Gilbert. 1981. *Guardians of the flutes: Idioms of masculinity*. New York: McGraw-Hill.

Kanter, Rosabeth Moss. 1977. *Men and women of the corporation*. New York: Basic Books.

Kessler, Suzanne J. 1990. The medical construction of gender: Case management of intersexed infants. *Signs: Journal of Women in Culture and Society* 16:3–27.

Kessler, Suzanne J., and Wendy McKenna. 1978. *Gender: An ethnomethodological approach*. New York: John Wiley.

Kinsey, Alfred C., Wardell B. Pomeroy, and Clyde E. Martin. 1948. *Sexual behavior in the human male*. Philadelphia: W. B. Saunders.

Lewins, Frank. 1995. *Transsexualism in society: A sociology of male-to-female transsexuals*. Melbourne: Macmillan Education Australia.

Lorber, Judith. 1994. *Paradoxes of gender*. New Haven, CT: Yale University Press.

———. 1999. Embattled terrain: Gender and sexuality. In *Revisioning gender*, edited by Myra Marx Ferree, Judith Lorber, and Beth Hess. Thousand Oaks, CA: Sage.

Lucal, Betsy. 1999. What it means to be gendered me: Life on the boundaries of a dichotomous gender system. *Gender & Society* 13:781–97.

Messner, Michael A. 2000. Barbie girls versus sea monsters: Children constructing gender. *Gender & Society* 14:765–84.

Nicholson, Linda. 1994. Interpreting gender. *Signs: Journal of Women in Culture and Society* 20:79–105.

Parker, Richard, and Peter Aggleton. 1999. *Culture, society and sexuality: A reader*. Los Angeles: UCLA Press.

Prosser, Jay. 1998. *Second skins: The body narratives of transsexuality*. New York: Columbia University Press.

Rubin, Henry. 2003. *Self-made men: Identity and embodiment among transsexual men*. Nashville, TN: Vanderbilt University Press.

Schippers, M. 2000. The social organization of sexuality and gender in alternative hard rock: An analysis of intersectionality. *Gender & Society* 14:747–64.

Scott, Joan. 1988. *Gender and the politics of history*. New York: Columbia University Press.

Gendered Intimacies

"Man's love is of man's life a thing apart," wrote the British Romantic poet, Lord Byron. "'Tis woman's whole existence." Nowhere are the differences between women and men more pronounced than in our intimate lives, our experiences of love, friendship, and sexuality. It is in our intimate relationships that it so often feels like men and women are truly from different planets.

The very definitions of emotional intimacy bear the mark of gender. As Francesca Cancian argues, the ideal of love has been "feminized" since the nineteenth century. No longer is love the arduous pining nor the sober shouldering of familial responsibility; today, love is expressed as the ability to sustain emotional commitment and connection—a "feminine" definition of love.

But there are signs of gender convergence. Women, it appears, find themselves more interested in pursuing explicitly sexual pleasures, despite their "Venutian" temperament that invariably links love and lust. As Sharon Lamb points out, sexuality and friendship are both salient features of adolescent girls' lives, and they are frequently in tension as new definitions of femininity crash into older ones. And Susan Sprecher and Maura Toro-Morn suggest in their humorously titled article that women and men have mostly similar beliefs about sex, love, and romance.

On the other hand, gender inequalities persist. In a report from the largest study of campus "hooking up" sexual culture, Paula England and her colleagues suggest that while women and men are both doing an increasing amount of hooking up, those behaviors may mean different things to college women and men. And Beth Quinn provides a sober reminder that sexual harassment is based not only on desire but on entitlement and contempt.

The Feminization of Love

FRANCESCA M. CANCIAN

A feminized and incomplete perspective on love predominates in the United States. We identify love with emotional expression and talking about feelings, aspects of love that women prefer and in which women tend to be more skilled than men. At the same time we often ignore the instrumental and physical aspects of love that men prefer, such as providing help, sharing activities, and sex. This feminized perspective leads us to believe that women are much more capable of love than men and that the way to make relationships more loving is for men to become more like women. This paper proposes an alternative, androgynous perspective on love, one based on the premise that love is both instrumental and expressive. From this perspective, the way to make relationships more loving is for women and men to reject polarized gender roles and integrate "masculine" and "feminine" styles of love.

The Two Perspectives

"Love is active, doing something for your good even if it bothers me," says a fundamentalist Christian. "Love is sharing, the real sharing of feelings," says a divorced secretary who is in love again. In ancient Greece, the ideal love was the adoration of a man for a beautiful young boy who was his lover. In the thirteenth century, the exemplar of love was the chaste devotion of a knight for another man's wife. In Puritan New England, love between husband and wife was the ideal, and in Victorian times, the asexual devotion of a mother for her child seemed the essence of love. My purpose is to focus on one kind of love: long-term heterosexual love in the contemporary United States.

What is a useful definition of enduring love between a woman and a man? One guideline for a definition comes from the prototypes of enduring love—the relations between committed lovers, husband and wife, parent and child. These relationships combine care and assistance with physical and emotional closeness. Studies of attachment between infants and their mothers emphasize the importance of being protected and fed as well as touched and held. In marriage, according to most family sociologists, both practical help and affection are part of enduring love, or "the affection we feel for those with whom our lives are deeply intertwined."[1] Our own informal observations often point in the same direction: if we consider the relationships that are the prototypes of enduring love, it seems that what we really mean by love is some combination of instrumental and expressive qualities.

Historical studies provide a second guideline for defining enduring love, specifically between a woman and a man. In precapitalist America, such love was a complex whole that included work and feelings. Then it was split into feminine and masculine fragments by the separation of home and workplace. This historical analysis implies that affection, material help, and routine cooperation all are parts of enduring love.

Consistent with these guidelines, my working definition of enduring love between adults is a relationship wherein a small number of people are affectionate and emotionally committed to each other, define their collective well-being as a major goal, and feel obliged to provide care and practical assistance for each other. People who love each other also usually share physical contact; they communicate with each other frequently and cooperate in some routine tasks of daily life. My discussion is of enduring heterosexual love only; I will for the sake of simplicity refer to it as "love."

In contrast to this broad definition of love, the narrower, feminized definition dominates both contemporary scholarship and public opinion. Most scholars who study love, intimacy, or close friendship focus on qualities that are stereotypically feminine, such as talking about feelings. For example, Abraham Maslow defines love as "a feeling of tenderness and affection with great enjoyment, happiness, satisfaction, elation and even ecstasy." Among healthy individuals, he says, "there is a growing intimacy and honesty and self-expression."[2] Zick Rubin's "Love Scale," designed to measure the degree of passionate love as opposed to liking, includes questions about confiding in each other, longing to be together, and sexual attraction as well as caring for each other. Studies of friendship usually distinguish close friends from acquaintances on the basis of how much personal information is disclosed, and many recent studies of married couples and lovers emphasize communication and self-disclosure. A recent book on marital love by Lillian Rubin focuses on intimacy, which she defines as "reciprocal expression of feeling and thought, not out of fear or dependent need, but out of a wish to know another's inner life and to be able to share one's own."[3] She argues that intimacy is distinct from nurturance or caretaking and that men are usually unable to be intimate.

Among the general public, love is also defined primarily as expressing feelings and verbal disclosure, not as instrumental help. This is especially true among the more affluent; poorer people are more likely than they to see practical help and financial assistance as a sign of love. In a study conducted in 1980, 130 adults from a wide range of social classes and ethnic backgrounds were interviewed about the qualities that make a good love relationship. The most frequent response referred to honest and open communication. Being caring and supportive and being tolerant and understanding were the other qualities most often mentioned. Similar results were reported from Ann Swidler's study of an affluent suburb: the dominant conception of love stressed communicating feelings, working on the relationship, and self-development. Finally, a contemporary dictionary defines love as "strong affection for another arising out of kinship or personal ties" and as attraction based on sexual desire, affection, and tenderness.

These contemporary definitions of love clearly focus on qualities that are seen as feminine in our culture. A study of gender roles in 1968 found that warmth, expressiveness, and talkativeness were seen as appropriate for women and not for men. In 1978 the core features of gender stereotypes were unchanged although fewer qualities were seen as appropriate for only one sex. Expressing tender feelings, being gentle, and being aware of the feelings of others were still ideal qualities for women and not for men. The desirable qualities for men and not for women included being independent, unemotional, and interested in sex. The only component perceived as masculine in popular definitions of love is interest in sex.

The two approaches to defining love—one broad, encompassing instrumental and affective qualities, one narrow, including only the affective qualities—inform the two different perspectives on love. According to the androgynous perspective, both gender roles contain elements of love. The feminine role does not include all of the major ways of loving; some aspects of love come from the masculine role, such as sex and providing material help, and some, such as cooperating in daily tasks, are associated with neither gender role. In contrast, the feminized perspective on love implies that all of the elements of love are included in the feminine role. The capacity to love is divided by gender. Women can love and men cannot.

Some Feminist Interpretations

Feminist scholars are divided on the question of love and gender. Supporters of the feminized perspective seem most influential at present. Nancy Chodorow's psychoanalytic theory has been especially influential in promoting a feminized perspective on love among social scientists studying close relationships. Chodorow's argument—in greatly simplified form—is that as infants, both boys and girls have strong identification and intimate attachments with their mothers. Since boys grow up to be men, they must repress this early identification, and in the process they repress their capacity for intimacy. Girls retain their early identification since they will grow up to be women, and throughout their lives females see themselves as connected to others. As a result of this process, Chodorow argues, "girls come to define and experience themselves as continuous with others;...boys come to define themselves as more separate and distinct."[4] This theory implies that love is feminine—women are more open to love than men—and that this gender difference will remain as long as women are the primary caretakers of infants.

Scholars have used Chodorow's theory to develop the idea that love and attachment are fundamental parts of women's personalities but not of men's. Carol Gilligan's influential book on female personality development asserts that women define their identity "by a standard of responsibility and care." The predominant female image is "a network of connection, a web of relationships that is sustained by a process of communication." In contrast, males favor a "hierarchical ordering, with its imagery of winning and losing and the potential for violence which it contains." "Although the world of the self that men describe at times includes 'people' and 'deep attachments,' no particular person or relationship is mentioned. ... Thus the male 'I' is defined in separation."[5]

A feminized conception of love can be supported by other theories as well. In past decades, for example, such a conception developed from Talcott Parsons's theory of the benefits to the nuclear family of women's specializing in expressive action and men's specializing in instrumental action. Among contemporary social scientists, the strongest support for the feminized perspective comes from such psychological theories as Chodorow's.

On the other hand, feminist historians have developed an incisive critique of the feminized perspective on love. Mary Ryan and other social historians have analyzed how the separation of home and workplace in the nineteenth century polarized gender roles and feminized love. Their argument, in simplified form, begins with the observation that in the colonial era the family household was the arena for economic production, affection, and social welfare. The integration of activities in the family produced a certain integration of expressive and instrumental traits in the personalities of men and women. Both women and men were expected to be hard working, modest, and loving toward their spouses and children, and the concept of love included instrumental cooperation as well as expression of feelings. In Ryan's words, "When early Americans spoke of love they were not withdrawing into a female byway of human experience. Domestic affection, like sex and economics, was not segregated into male and female spheres." There was a "reciprocal ideal of conjugal love" that "grew out of the day-to-day cooperation, sharing, and closeness of the diversified home economy."[6]

Economic production gradually moved out of the home and became separated from personal relationships as capitalism expanded. Husbands increasingly worked for wages in factories and shops while wives stayed at home to care for the family. This division of labor gave women more experience with close relationships and intensified women's economic dependence on men. As the daily activities of men and women grew further apart, a new worldview emerged that exaggerated the differences between the personal, loving, feminine sphere of the home and the impersonal, powerful, masculine sphere of the workplace. Work became identified with what men do for money while love became identified with women's activities at home. As a result, the conception of love shifted toward emphasizing tenderness, powerlessness, and the expression of emotion.

This partial and feminized conception of love persisted into the twentieth century as the division of labor remained stable: the workplace remained impersonal and separated from the home, and married women continued to be excluded from paid employment. According to this historical explanation, one might expect a change in the conception of love since the 1940s, as growing numbers of wives took jobs. However, women's persistent responsibility for child care and housework, and their lower wages, might explain a continued feminized conception of love.

Like the historical critiques, some psychological studies of gender also imply that our current conception of love is distorted and needs to be integrated with qualities associated with the masculine role. For example, Jean Baker Miller argues that women's ways of loving—their need to be attached to a man and to serve others—result from women's powerlessness, and that a better way of loving would integrate power with women's style of love.[7] The importance of combining activities and personality traits that have been split apart by gender is also a frequent theme in the human potential movement. These historical and psychological works emphasize the flexibility of gender roles and the inadequacy of a concept of love that includes only the feminine half of human qualities. In contrast, theories like Chodorow's emphasize the rigidity of gender differences after childhood and define love in terms of feminine qualities. The two theoretical approaches are not as inconsistent as my simplified sketches may suggest, and many scholars combine them; however, the two approaches have different implications for empirical research.

Evidence on Women's "Superiority" in Love

A large number of studies show that women are more interested and more skilled in love than men. However, most of these studies use biased measures based on feminine styles of loving, such as verbal self-disclosure, emotional expression, and willingness to report that one has close relationships. When less biased measures are used, the differences between women and men are often small.

Women have a greater number of close relationships than men. At all stages of the life cycle,

women see their relatives more often. Men and women report closer relations with their mothers than with their fathers and are generally closer to female kin. Thus an average Yale man in the 1970s talked about himself more with his mother than with his father and was more satisfied with his relationship with his mother. His most frequent grievance against his father was that his father gave too little of himself and was cold and uninvolved; his grievance against his mother was that she gave too much of herself and was alternately overprotective and punitive.

Throughout their lives, women are more likely to have a confidant—a person to whom one discloses personal experiences and feelings. Girls prefer to be with one friend or a small group, while boys usually play competitive games in large groups. Men usually get together with friends to play sports or do some other activity, while women get together explicitly to talk and to be together.

Men seem isolated given their weak ties with their families and friends. Among blue-collar couples interviewed in 1950, 64 percent of the husbands had no confidants other than their spouses, compared to 24 percent of the wives. The predominantly upper-middle-class men interviewed by Daniel Levinson in the 1970s were no less isolated. Levinson concludes that "close friendship with a man or a woman is rarely experienced by American men."[8] Apparently, most men have no loving relationships besides those with wife or lover; and given the estrangement that often occurs in marriages, many men may have no loving relationship at all.

Several psychologists have suggested that there is a natural reversal of these roles in middle age, as men become more concerned with relationships and women turn toward independence and achievement; but there seems to be no evidence showing that men's relationships become more numerous or more intimate after middle age, and some evidence to the contrary.

Women are also more skilled than men in talking about relationships. Whether working class or middle class, women value talking about feelings and relationships and disclose more than men about personal experiences. Men who deviate and talk a lot about their personal experiences are commonly defined as feminine and maladjusted. Working-class wives prefer to talk about themselves, their close relationships with family and friends, and their homes, while their husbands prefer to talk about cars, sports, work, and politics. The same gender-specific preferences are expressed by college students.

Men do talk more about one area of personal experience: their victories and achievements; but talking about success is associated with power, not intimacy. Women say more about their fears and disappointments, and it is disclosure of such weaknesses that usually is interpreted as a sign of intimacy. Women are also more accepting of the expression of intense feelings, including love, sadness, and fear, and they are more skilled in interpreting other people's emotions.

Finally, in their leisure time women are drawn to topics of love and human entanglements while men are drawn to competition among men. Women's preferences in television viewing run to daytime soap operas, or if they are more educated, the high-brow soap operas on educational channels, while most men like to watch competitive and often aggressive sports. Reading-tastes show the same pattern. Women read novels and magazine articles about love, while men's magazines feature stories about men's adventures and encounters with death.

However, this evidence on women's greater involvement and skill in love is not as strong as it appears. Part of the reason that men seem so much less loving than women is that their behavior is measured with a feminine ruler. Much of this research considers only the kinds of loving behavior that are associated with the feminine role and rarely compares women and men in terms of qualities associated with the masculine role. When less biased measures are used, the behavior of men and women is often quite similar. For example, in a careful study of kinship relations among young adults in a southern city, Bert Adams found that women were much more likely than men to say that their parents and relatives were very important to their lives (58 percent of women and 37 percent of men). In measures of actual contact

with relatives, though, there were much smaller differences: 88 percent of women and 81 percent of men whose parents lived in the same city saw their parents weekly. Adams concluded that "differences between males and females in relations with parents are discernible primarily in the subjective sphere; contact frequencies are quite similar."[9]

The differences between the sexes can be small even when biased measures are used. For example, Marjorie Lowenthal and Clayton Haven reported the finding, later widely quoted, that elderly women were more likely than elderly men to have a friend with whom they could talk about their personal troubles—clearly a measure of a traditionally feminine behavior. The figures revealed that 81 percent of the married women and 74 percent of the married men had confidants—not a sizable difference.[10] On the other hand, whatever the measure, virtually all such studies find that women are more involved in close relationships than men, even if the difference is small.

In sum, women are only moderately superior to men in love: they have more close relationships and care more about them, and they seem to be more skilled at love, especially those aspects of love that involve expressing feelings and being vulnerable. This does not mean that men are separate and unconcerned with close relationships, however. When national surveys ask people what is most important in their lives, women tend to put family bonds first while men put family bonds first or second, along with work. For both sexes, love is clearly very important.

Evidence on the Masculine Style of Love

Men tend to have a distinctive style of love that focuses on practical help, shared physical activities, spending time together, and sex. The major elements of the masculine style of love emerged in Margaret Reedy's study of 102 married couples in the late 1970s. She showed individuals statements describing aspects of love and asked them to rate how well the statements described their marriages. On the whole, husband and wife had similar views of their marriage, but several sex differences emerged. Practical help and spending time together were more important to men. The men were more likely to give high ratings to such statements as: "When she needs help I help her," and "She would rather spend her time with me than with anyone else." Men also described themselves more often as sexually attracted and endorsed such statements as: "I get physically excited and aroused just thinking about her." In addition, emotional security was less important to men than to women, and men were less likely to describe the relationship as secure, safe, and comforting.[11] Another study in the late 1970s showed a similar pattern among young, highly educated couples. The husbands gave greater emphasis to feeling responsible for the partner's well-being and putting the spouse's needs first, as well as to spending time together. The wives gave greater importance to emotional involvement and verbal self-disclosure but also were more concerned than the men about maintaining their separate activities and their independence.

The difference between men and women in their views of the significance of practical help was demonstrated in a study in which seven couples recorded their interactions for several days. They noted how pleasant their relations were and counted how often the spouse did a helpful chore, such as cooking a good meal or repairing a faucet, and how often the spouse expressed acceptance or affection. The social scientists doing the study used a feminized definition of love. They labeled practical help as "instrumental behavior" and expressions of acceptance or affection as "affectionate behavior," thereby denying the affectionate aspect of practical help. The wives seemed to be using the same scheme; they thought their marital relations were pleasant that day if their husbands had directed a lot of affectionate behavior to them, regardless of their husbands' positive instrumental behavior. The husbands' enjoyment of their marital relations, on the other hand, depended on their wives' instrumental actions, not on their expressions of affection. The men actually saw instrumental actions as affection. One husband who was told by the researchers to increase his affectionate behavior toward his wife decided to wash her car and was surprised when

neither his wife nor the researchers accepted that as an "affectionate" act.

The masculine view of instrumental help as loving behavior is clearly expressed by a husband discussing his wife's complaints about his lack of communication: "What does she want? Proof? She's got it, hasn't she? Would I be knocking myself out to get things for her—like to keep up this house—if I didn't love her? Why does a man do things like that if not because he loves his wife and kids? I swear, I can't figure what she wants." His wife, who has a feminine orientation to love, says something very different: "It is not enough that he supports us and takes care of us. I appreciate that, but I want him to share things with me. I need for him to tell me his feelings."[12] Many working-class women agree with men that a man's job is something he does out of love for his family,[13] but middle-class women and social scientists rarely recognize men's practical help as a form of love. (Indeed, among upper-middle-class men whose jobs offer a great deal of intrinsic gratification, their belief that they are "doing it for the family" may seem somewhat self-serving.)

Other differences between men's and women's styles of love involve sex. Men seem to separate sex and love while women connect them, but paradoxically, sexual intercourse seems to be the most meaningful way of giving and receiving love for many men. A twenty-nine-year-old carpenter who had been married for three years said that, after sex, "I feel so close to her and the kids. We feel like a real family then. I don't talk to her very often, I guess, but somehow I feel we have really communicated after we have made love."[14]

Because sexual intimacy is the only recognized "masculine" way of expressing love, the recent trend toward viewing sex as a way for men and women to express mutual intimacy is an important challenge to the feminization of love. However, the connection between sexuality and love is undermined both by the "sexual revolution" definition of sex as a form of casual recreation and by the view of male sexuality as a weapon—as in rape—with which men dominate and punish women.

Another paradoxical feature of men's style of love is that men have a more romantic attitude toward their partners than do women. In Reedy's study, men were more likely to select statements like "we are perfect for each other." In a survey of college students, 65 percent of the men but only 24 percent of the women said that, even if a relationship had all of the other qualities they desired, they would not marry unless they were in love. The common view of this phenomenon focuses on women. The view is that women marry for money and status and so see marriage as instrumentally, rather than emotionally, desirable. This of course is at odds with women's greater concern with self-disclosure and emotional intimacy and lesser concern with instrumental help. A better way to explain men's greater romanticism might be to focus on men. One such possible explanation is that men do not feel responsible for "working on" the emotional aspects of a relationship, and therefore see love as magically and perfectly present or absent. This is consistent with men's relative lack of concern with affective interaction and greater concern with instrumental help.

In sum, there is a masculine style of love. Except for romanticism, men's style fits the popularly conceived masculine role of being the powerful provider. From the androgynous perspective, the practical help and physical activities included in this role are as much a part of love as the expression of feelings. The feminized perspective cannot account for this masculine style of love; nor can it explain why women and men are so close in the degrees to which they are loving.

Negative Consequences of the Feminization of Love

The division of gender roles in our society that contributes to the two separate styles of love is reinforced by the feminized perspective and leads to political and moral problems that would be mitigated with a more androgynous approach to love. The feminized perspective works against some of the key values and goals of feminists and humanists by contributing to the devaluation and exploitation of women.

It is especially striking how the differences between men's and women's styles of love reinforce men's power over women. Men's style involves giving women important resources, such as money and protection that men control and women believe they need, and ignoring the resources that women control and men need. Thus men's dependency on women remains covert and repressed, while women's dependency on men is overt and exaggerated; and it is overt dependency that creates power, according to social exchange theory. The feminized perspective on love reinforces this power differential by leading to the belief that women need love more than do men, which is implied in the association of love with the feminine role. The effect of this belief is to intensify the asymmetrical dependency of women on men. In fact, however, evidence on the high death rates of unmarried men suggests that men need love at least as much as do women.

Sexual relations also can reinforce male dominance insofar as the man takes the initiative and intercourse is defined either as his "taking" pleasure or as his being skilled at "giving" pleasure, either way giving him control. The man's power advantage is further strengthened if the couple assumes that the man's sexual needs can be filled by any attractive woman while the woman's sexual needs can be filled only by the man she loves.

On the other hand, women's preferred ways of loving seem incompatible with control. They involve admitting dependency and sharing or losing control, and being emotionally intense. Further, the intimate talk about personal troubles that appeals to women requires of a couple a mutual vulnerability, a willingness to see oneself as weak and in need of support. It is true that a woman, like a man, can gain some power by providing her partner with services, such as understanding, sex, or cooking; but this power is largely unrecognized because the man's dependency on such services is not overt. The couple may even see these services as her duty or as her response to his requests (or demands).

The identification of love with expressing feelings also contributes to the lack of recognition of women's power by obscuring the instrumental, active component of women's love just as it obscures the loving aspect of men's work. In a culture that glorifies instrumental achievement, this identification devalues both women and love. In reality, a major way by which women are loving is in the clearly instrumental activities associated with caring for others, such as preparing meals, washing clothes, and providing care during illness; but because of our focus on the expressive side of love, this caring work of women is either ignored or redefined as expressing feelings. Thus, from the feminized perspective on love, child care is a subtle communication of attitudes, not work. A wife washing her husband's shirt is seen as expressing love, even though a husband washing his wife's car is seen as doing a job.

Gilligan, in her critique of theories of human development, shows the way in which devaluing love is linked to devaluing women. Basic to most psychological theories of development is the idea that a healthy person develops from a dependent child to an autonomous, independent adult. As Gilligan comments, "Development itself comes to be identified with separation, and attachments appear to be developmental impediments."[15] Thus women, who emphasize attachment, are judged to be developmentally retarded or insufficiently individuated.

The pervasiveness of this image was documented in a well-known study of mental health professionals who were asked to describe mental health, femininity, and masculinity. They associated both mental health and masculinity with independence, rationality, and dominance. Qualities concerning attachment, such as being tactful, gentle, or aware of the feelings of others, they associated with femininity but not with mental health.[16]

Another negative consequence of a feminized perspective on love is that it legitimates impersonal, exploitive relations in the workplace and the community. The ideology of separate spheres that developed in the nineteenth century contrasted the harsh, immoral marketplace with the warm and loving home and implied that this contrast is acceptable. Defining love as expressive, feminine, and divorced from productive activity maintains this ideology. If personal relationships and love are reserved for women and the home, then it is acceptable for a manager to underpay workers or for a community to ignore a needy family. Such behavior is not unloving; it is businesslike or shows a respect for privacy. The ideology of separate spheres also implies that men are properly judged by their instrumental and economic achievements and that poor or unsuccessful men are failures who may deserve a hard life. Levinson presents a conception of masculine development itself as centering on achieving an occupational dream.[17]

Finally, the feminization of love intensifies the conflicts over intimacy between women and men in close relationships. One of the most common conflicts is that the woman wants more closeness and verbal contact while the man withdraws and wants less pressure. Her need for more closeness is partly the result of the feminization of love, which encourages her to be more emotionally dependent on him. Because love is feminine, he in turn may feel controlled during intimate contact. Intimacy is her "turf," an area where she sets the rules and expectations. Talking about the relationship, as she wants, may well feel to him like taking a test that she made up and that he will fail. He is likely to react by withdrawing, causing her to intensify her efforts to get closer. The feminization of love thus can lead to a vicious cycle of conflict where neither partner feels in control or gets what she or he wants.

Conclusion

The values of improving the status of women and humanizing the public sphere are shared by many of the scholars who support a feminized conception of love; and they, too, explain the conflicts in close relationships in terms of polarized gender roles. Nancy Chodorow, Lillian Rubin, and Carol Gilligan have addressed these issues in detail and with great insight. However, by arguing that women's identity is based on attachment while men's identity is based on separation, they reinforce the distinction between feminine expressiveness and masculine instrumentality, revive the ideology of separate spheres, and legitimate the popular idea that only women know the right way to love. They also suggest that there is no way to overcome the rigidity of gender roles other than by pursuing the goal of men and women becoming equally involved in infant care. In contrast, an androgynous perspective on love challenges the identification of women and love with being expressive, powerless, and nonproductive and the identification of men with being instrumental, powerful, and productive. It rejects the ideology of separate spheres and validates masculine as well as feminine styles of love. This viewpoint suggests that progress could be made by means of a variety of social changes, including men doing child care, relations at work becoming more personal and nurturant, and cultural conceptions of love and gender becoming more androgynous. Changes that equalize power within close relationships by equalizing the economic and emotional dependency between men and women may be especially important in moving toward androgynous love.

The validity of an androgynous definition of love cannot be "proven"; the view that informs the androgynous perspective is that both the feminine style of love (characterized by emotional closeness and verbal self-disclosure) and the masculine style of love (characterized by instrumental help and sex) represent necessary parts of a good love relationship. Who is more loving: a couple who confide most of their experiences to each other but rarely cooperate or give each other practical help, or a couple who help each other through many crises and cooperate in running a household but rarely discuss their personal experiences? Both relationships are limited. Most people would probably choose a combination: a relationship that integrates feminine and masculine styles of loving, an androgynous love.

Notes

1. See John Bowlby, *Attachment and Loss* (New York: Basic Books, 1969), on mother-infant attachment. The quotation is from Elaine Walster and G. William Walster, *A New Look at Love* (Reading, Mass.: Addison-Wesley Publishing Co., 1978), 9. Conceptions of love and adjustment used by family sociologists are reviewed in Robert Lewis and Graham Spanier, "Theorizing about the Quality and Stability of Marriage." in *Contemporary Theories about the Family,* ed. W. Burr, R. Hill, F. Nye, and I. Reiss (New York: Free Press, 1979), 268–94.

2. Abraham Maslow, *Motivation and Personality,* 2d ed. (New York: Harper & Row, 1970), 182–83.

3. Zick Rubin's scale is described in his article "Measurement of Romantic Love." *Journal of Personality and Social Psychology* 16, no. 2 (1970): 265–73; Lillian Rubin's book on marriage is *Intimate Strangers* (New York: Harper & Row, 1983), quote on 90.

4. Nancy Chodorow, *The Reproduction of Mothering* (Berkeley: University of California Press, 1978), 169. Dorothy Dinnerstein presents a similar theory in *The Mermaid and the Minotaur: Sexual Arrangements and Human Malaise* (New York: Harper & Row, 1976). Freudian and biological dispositional theories about women's nurturance are surveyed in Jean Stockard and Miriam Johnson, *Sex Roles* (Englewood Cliffs, N.J.: Prentice-Hall, Inc., 1980).

5. Carol Gilligan, *In a Different Voice* (Cambridge, Mass.: Harvard University Press, 1982), 32, 159–61; see also L. Rubin, *Intimate Strangers.*

6. I have drawn most heavily on Mary Ryan, *Womanhood in America,* 2d ed. (New York: New Viewpoints, 1978), and *The Cradle of the Middle Class: The Family in Oneida County, N.Y., 1790–1865* (New York: Cambridge University Press, 1981); Barbara Ehrenreich and Deidre English, *For Her Own Good: 150 Years of Experts Advice to Women* (New York: Anchor Books, 1978); Barbara Welter, "The Cult of True Womanhood: 1820–1860," *American Quaterly* 18, no. 2 (1966): 151–174.

7. Jean Baker Miller, *Toward a New Psychology of Women* (Boston: Beacon Press, 1976). There are, of course, many exceptions to Miller's generalization, e.g., women who need to be independent or who need an attachment with a woman.

8. Daniel Levinson, *The Seasons of a Man's Life* (New York: Alfred A. Knopf, 1978), 335.

9. Bert Adams, *Kinship in an Urban Setting* (Chicago: Markham Publishing Co., 1968), 169.

10. Marjorie Lowenthal and Clayton Haven, "Interaction and Adaptation: Intimacy as a Critical Variable." *American Sociological Review* 22, no. 4 (1968): 20–30.

11. Margaret Reedy, "Age and Sex Differences in Personal Needs and the Nature of Love."

(Ph.D. diss. University of Southern California, 1977). Unlike most studies, Reedy did not find that women emphasized communication more than men. Her subjects were upper-middle-class couples who seemed to be very much in love.

12. Lillian Rubin, *Worlds of Pain* (New York: Basic Books, 1976), 147.

13. See L. Rubin, *Worlds of Pain;* also see Richard Sennett and Jonathan Cobb, *Hidden Injuries of Class* (New York: Vintage, 1973).

14. Interview by Cynthia Garlich, "Interviews of Married Couples" (University of California, Irvine, School of Social Sciences, 1982).

15. Gilligan (n. 5 above), 12–13.

16. Inge Broverman, Frank Clarkson, Paul Rosenkrantz, and Susan Vogel, "Sex-Role Stereotypes and Clinical Judgments of Mental Health," *Journal of Consulting Psychology* 34, no. 1 (1970): 1–7.

17. Levinson (n. 8 above).

Sexual Tensions in Girls' Friendships

SHARON LAMB

Girlhood sexuality is one aspect of girlhood that has been suppressed or that has developed outside our notice. Discussion of girls' sexual play and erotic feelings towards one another is almost unheard of. While scholarship on *adolescent* girls' sexuality, which explores girls as subjects rather than only as objects of desire, now abounds (Fine, 1988; Tolman, 1994, 2002; Walkerdine, 1984), this focus tends to support biologism's notion that erotic life begins at puberty even when such research broadens the exploration beyond heterosexual desire.

This article (based on research published in a trade book aimed at a parent audience) examines sexual tensions in the private play of girls between the ages of 6 and 12 (Lamb, 2002). Using snowball sampling, I and two additional interviewers conducted semi-structured interviews with 30 girls (ages 7–18) and 92 adult women (ages 19–72) beginning with general questions about childhood play

and friendships before asking specifically about a variety of types of childhood sexual play. These included:

- Did you ever play any practice kissing games?
- Did you ever play any imaginary games with other children where sex was involved?
- What was the game that was the most fun for you?
- What was the game you felt most ashamed about?

Depending on the interview, we also asked, "Did you or the other child(ren) ever experience sexual feelings in play?"

Participants came from over 25 states in the United States; 29 of the 122 identified as African-American, 21 as Puerto Rican, three as Asian American. Low-income, working-class, middle-class, and wealthy White, Puerto-Rican, and African-American girls and women were represented in the sample.

All participants, even the younger ones, were asked to "look back" on their childhood. Because sexuality in childhood is still a taboo topic, this approach was deemed necessary despite the concomitant distortions over time that such stories might reflect. No girl under 12 produced stories of her own sexual play, although some discussed "other girls" who played those sorts of games. Teenagers and adults remembered stories about sexual play as well as feelings about and during such play. Of these stories, the majority were girl-to-girl games and these were used for this analysis. The stories produced never emerged as narratives that defined a participant's sexuality (as in "coming out" stories, Weeks and Holland, 1996); instead stories were described as "play." Stories of same-sex erotic "play" were commonly produced by women who self-identified in adulthood as heterosexual and identified themselves as such to the interviewers, although no questions about adult sexual identity were asked.

These narrative retellings of experiences varied in clarity. Some only remembered a story when prompted with a question; others practiced telling stories that they "had never told anyone before" before coming to the interview; and some told stories that seemed to emerge from the developing conversation (see Chase, 1995). There are always tensions between what the girl herself experienced, and what the adult woman, looking back, having constructed a present identity as well as her memory of her childhood, believes she experienced at the time. It is unlikely, though, that these games did not exist, and the cultural heterosexual bias and the belief in girlhood innocence would likely work against remembering sexual feelings rather than towards fantasy creations. The importance of uncovering these stories as a part of suppressed girlhood history outweighs the problems of getting a narrative that closely corresponds to the details of an event.

Three tensions were uncovered in these stories:

- the tension in the friendship produced by girls' secrecy about sexual feelings with and for each other;
- the tension created in the framing of sexual play as "just pretending"; and
- the tension between male versus female subjectivity when girls perform both these roles in play.

The Secrecy of Girlhood Sexuality

Prior research shows that sexual play and games are part of many girls' worlds (Friedrich et al., 1992; Haugaard, 1996; Haugaard and Tilly, 1988; Lamb and Coakley, 1993; Larsson and Svedin, 2002). However, in this research girls often felt that what they were doing was wrong and must remain hidden. Said one participant, looking back: "If somebody saw us doing this, they would think it was very, very wrong." The reasons for this secrecy go beyond fear of parental disapproval. Memories of girls' friendships in general are culturally suppressed, and there is "immense ideological pressure to restrict interpretations of these memories" (Hey, 1997: 2). Girls implicitly understand that they live in a culture where permission for sexuality begins at puberty; when they have sexual feelings they interpret as early, or too young, or too sexual they describe themselves as different from other girls, using words like "bizarre" and "weird." Secrecy around girlhood sexual feelings may also derive from internalizing cultural anxieties about the media's "oversexualizing" of girls and objectification of women. Depending on class and race, girls may have been taught that sex is shameful and dirty, their shame encouraging them to police their sexuality (Foucault, 1979). Fear of an accusation of lesbianism in a homophobic culture (given much of their sexual play is same-sex) could also be behind the secrecy of girls' erotic games.

In my research, girls not only kept their mutual games secret from parents and other adults—they also kept their feelings of physical excitement and erotic feelings secret from each other. Some girls and women used language that suggests erotic feelings: "We did wondrous things with her (playing doctor)"; and "It was very thrilling"; and "It was titillating and fun...it was a feeling." Others explicitly revealed that they had sexual feelings in the play: "It was very, you know, intoxicating...very arousing"; and "I think I got sexually excited." Although no interviewee had talked about her sexual feelings with her girlfriend/playmate at the time, some believed their friend also experienced sexual feelings. To acknowledge such feelings to another would be tantamount to confessing a sexuality that they believed was "adult," not appropriate to a child, male, and, in some cases, lesbian.

Hence there was a double secrecy to contend with—the secrecy of doing sexual things that the culture and parents (they believed) would find unacceptable, and the secrecy of their own or their playmates "thrills" in the playing of such games. This latter secret kept girls distanced from the play and from public accusations of lesbianism, but it also, in some cases, isolated them, leaving them feeling different and too sexual. One way girls attempted to make such play and feelings more acceptable was to couch them in heterosexual romance scenarios.

Just Pretend

"You be the boy; I'll be the girl; and then we'll switch" was one common way that sexual play between girls was negotiated. Such framing of the play reflects the romance narrative that organizes female sexuality (Holland et al., 1990; Kirkman et al., 1998; McRobbie, 1982; Walkerdine, 1984, 1990) and the compulsory nature of the transition to heterosexuality (Griffin, 2000; Rich, 1993); but it also shows their strategizing to express affection as well as erotic feeling towards a girlfriend within a framework that conforms to social expectations. Heterosexual dating games of imagination, common in the "practice" kissing that occurs in girls' bedrooms and at slumber parties, reiterates heterosexual norms at the same time it subverts them by creating a space for same-sex desire and same-sex sexual play in the lives of young girls. Desire

aroused in play can be constructed as heterosexual desire and permitted expression in the guise of "practice" or play; yet the binary of heterosexual/lesbian sex is blurred because there are in fact two *girls* "practicing" heterosexual romance and sex. Even the idea of "practice" or "play" confirms adult sex as "not play" and "real," while childhood play does not "really" count as sex.

Female Versus Male Subjectivity

The idea of one girl pretending to be a boy, and the other girl pretending to be a girl creates a different kind of tension regarding subjectivity. As Marjorie Garber (1989) writes of transsexuals and cross-dressers, the male-to-female transsexual expresses female subjectivity while the cross-dresser expresses a man's version or understanding of female subjectivity. What do we make of the little girl pretending to be an adolescent boy feeling aroused when play-kissing her girlfriend? Does the girl playing the girl, ravished or courted by the girl playing the boy (as is often the scenario in imaginary games), have greater permission to experience erotic feelings? After all, she imagines herself the object of some man's or boy's overwhelming desire. One participant recalled a game in which she was to lie on the ground, in a sexy pose, scantily clothed, disheveled, playing a dead woman tied up and lying in a pool of blood (as seen on the front of her grandfather's detective magazines). The sexual thrill for her, the erotic moment, and one she felt deep shame about for 40 years after the game, was when the "detectives," played by her cousins, walked in, surrounded her, and remarked: "Isn't she beautiful!" She remembers herself "perversely" longing to perform the part of the dead woman in order to re-experience that erotic thrill.

It is easy to see the construction or performance of gender in the play of little girls and to understand that, as Butler (1991) suggests, the parodies of heterosexual romance in a non-heterosexual frame call into question the claim of realness or originality in heterosexuality. In play girls retain that quality of parody, excerpting from the culture's omnipresent romance narratives the most dramatic moments of objectification (a beauty pageant contestant) or romance (a ravishing of a girl at a teen beach party by the handsomest boy there). But within the game structure, the boundary between mimicry and realness is blurred when physical feelings or arousal accompany the play. The game is dress-ups, pretend, mimicry, a performance—but then the body responds. This phenomenological experience of arousal in the pretend play of little girls changes the experience from "just a game" of dress-ups. It invokes a sense of reality that is sometimes disturbing to the girl's sense of pretend. Physical sensations cannot be removed as easily as clothing and must be made accountable to the psyche—that is, they need to be incorporated into the child's subjectivity or the identity of the girl.

So what of the girl playing the boy? Is her subjectivity within the game a male one? Are her erotic feelings identified with being a boy or understood as male because they are not female? One girl who noticed her friend was "getting into" a kissing game more than she was, began to understand her friend as having lesbian feelings towards her. Talking about "the make-out game," Gina remembers: "So she would play the boy or I would play the boy and we would do this, but I sensed already something different…Then one time, it meant more. It wasn't just a game for her…(and I thought) 'she's a lesbian. She likes me. She *likes* me likes me.'"

Other girls claimed sexual feelings as their own but had difficulty understanding what they meant. One girl who enjoyed playing doctor claimed she "didn't deserve to be a girl" for her sexual feelings. Another who "got into the games" more than her playmates, and who frequently looked for opportunities to play these games, saw herself as more male than the other girls, different, "very bizarre." She said, "I was a girl and I shouldn't want that," referring to her interest in sex. When a girl feels something that doesn't fit within the frame of the ravished, courted, pursued girlfriend, she calls this subjectivity either "male" or "weird." Only when it is the "other" girl feeling what's presumed to be excessive do the girls label these feelings as "lesbian." Woman, to the "straight mind," borrowing a phrase from Monique Wittig, only exists in relation to male, so when a girl experiences desire acting as a male or acting as a female towards a female, then she is no longer a girl in her own mind—and thinking that way always confirms the rightness of heterosexuality (Wittig, 1993).

Conclusion

Erotic pairing within and outside of best friendships is an important area for future research. Research has shown that girls are capable of having intense friendships at a young age and over time, but it is possible that one reason research focuses on these "best friendships" (seeing them as a skill, a resource, and a natural part of girlhood) is to protect girls from an accusation of lesbianism that tinges any all-female space. Hey (1997) suggests that girls' friendships are always constituted through "the socially coercive presence of the male gaze" (pp. 64–65), where girls' intimacy gets constructed as merely and only "best friendships" while the girls themselves insert boys into their eroticized play through scenarios of heterosexual romance. Audre Lorde's (1984) reminder that the erotic is "a resource within each of us," and Adrienne Rich's idea of the "lesbian continuum" might be usefully brought to bear on the growing literature on girls' friendships. In so doing, current research can no longer ignore the sexual tensions and forbidden pleasures that are a part of the intimacy in little girls' play.

References

Butler, J. (1991) "Imitation and Gender Insubordination," in H. Abelove, M. Aina Barale, D. M. Halperin (eds.) *The Lesbian and Gay Studies Reader*. New York: Routledge.

Chase, S. (1995) "Taking Narrative Seriously: Consequences for Method and Theory in Interview Studies," in R. Josselon and A. Lieblich (eds.) *Interpreting Experience: The Narrative Study of Lives*, pp. 1–26. Thousand Oaks, CA: Sage.

Fine, M. (1988) "Sexuality, Schooling, and Adolescent Females: The Missing Discourse of Desire," *Harvard Educational Review* 58: 29–53.

Foucault, M. (1979) *Discipline and Punish: The Birth of the Prison*. New York: Vintage.

Friedrich, W. N., Grambsch, P., Damon, L., Hewitt, S. K., et al. (1992) "Child Sexual Behavior Inventory: Normative and Clinical Comparisons," *Psychological Assessment* 4: 303–11.

Garber, M. (1989) "Spare Parts: The Surgical Construction of Gender," *Differences: A Journal of Feminist Cultural Studies* 1(3): 137–59.

Griffin, C. (2000) "Absences That Matter: Constructions of Sexuality in Studies of Young Women's Friendships," *Feminism & Psychology* 10: 227–46.

Haugaard, J. (1996) "Sexual Behaviors Between Children: Professionals' Opinions and Undergraduates' Recollections," *Families in Society: The Journal of Contemporary Human Services*, February: 81–9.

Haugaard, J. J. and Tilly, C. (1988) "Characteristics Predicting Children's Reactions to Sexual Encounters with Other Children," *Child Abuse and Neglect* 12: 209–18.

Hey, V. (1997) *The Company She Keeps: An Ethnography of Girls' Friendships*. Philadelphia, PA: Open University Press.

Holland, J., Ramazanoglu, C., Scott, S. and Thompson, R. (1990) "Sex, Gender and Power: Young Women's Sexuality in the Shadow of AIDS," *Sociology of Health and Illness* 12: 336–50.

Kirkman, M., Rosenthal, D. and Smith, A. M. A. (1998) "Adolescent Sex and the Romantic Narrative: Why Some Young Heterosexuals Use Condoms to Prevent Pregnancy but Not Disease," *Psychology, Health, and Medicine* 3: 355–70.

Lamb, S. (2002) *The Secret Lives of Girls: What Good Girls Really Do—Sex Play, Aggression, and Their Guilt*. New York: Free Press.

Lamb, S. and Coakley, M. (1993) "'Normal' Childhood Play and Games: Differentiating Play from Abuse," *Child Abuse and Neglect* 17: 515–26.

Larsson, I. and Svedin, C. (2002) "Sexual Experiences in Childhood: Young Adults' Recollections," *Archives of Sexual Behavior* 31: 263–74.

Lorde, A. (1984) *Sister Outsider: Essays and Speeches by Audre Lorde*. Freedom, CA: The Crossing Press.

McRobbie, A. (1982) "*Jackie:* An Ideology of Adolescent Femininity," in B. Waites, T. Bennett and G. Martin (eds.) *Popular Culture: Past and Present*, pp. 263–83. London: Croom Helm and Open University Press.

Rich, A. (1993) "Compulsory Heterosexuality and Lesbian Existence," in H. Abelove, M. Aina Barale and D. M. Halperin (eds.) *The Lesbian and Gay Studies Reader*, pp. 227–54 (reprinted from Rich, *Blood, Bread, and Poetry*, 1986). New York: Routledge.

Tolman, D. (1994) "Dating to Desire: Culture and the Bodies of Adolescent Girls," in J. Irvine (ed.) *Sexual Cultures: Adolescents, Communities, and the Construction of Identity*, pp. 250–84. Philadelphia, PA: Temple University Press.

Tolman, D. (2002) *Dilemmas of Desire: Teenage Girls and Sexuality*. Cambridge, MA: Harvard University Press.

Walkerdine, V. (1984) "Some Day My Prince Will Come: Young Girls and the Preparation for Adolescent Sexuality," in A. McRobbie and M. Nava (eds.) *Gender and Generation*, 162–84. London: Macmillan.

———. (1990) *Schoolgirl Fictions*. London: Verso.

Weeks, J. and Holland, J., eds. (1996) *Sexual Cultures: Communities, Values and Intimacy*. London: Macmillan.

Wittig, M. (1993) "One Is Not Born Woman," in H. Abelove, M. Aina Barale and D. M. Halperin (eds.) *The Lesbian and Gay Studies Reader*, pp. 103–9 (reprinted from Wittig, *The Straight Mind*, 1992). New York: Routledge.

A Study of Men and Women from Different Sides of Earth to Determine If Men Are from Mars and Women Are from Venus in Their Beliefs About Love and Romantic Relationships[1]

SUSAN SPRECHER AND MAURA TORO-MORN

Introduction

Some popular writers have claimed that men and women are from two different planets, with different patterns of behaviors, feelings, and cognitions in close relationships (Gray, 1992; Tannen, 1990). Although research has found some reliable differences between men and women, particularly in their *attitudes* and *beliefs* about romantic relationships (e.g., Hendrick & Hendrick, 1995), the popular literature tends to exaggerate those differences. The fashionable paradigm of gender differences (i.e., men are from Mars, women are from Venus) is also problematic because it is frequently based on anecdotal evidence and tends to universalize what are mostly Western cultural patterns about men and women. Within this rather reductionist paradigm, gender alone is assumed to explain the complexities of emotions, feelings, and views that men and women hold about relationships. This body of work fails to recognize the complexity of social and cultural variables that shape love and romantic relationships across cultures.

Alternatively, in the social sciences a vast body of literature exists that seeks to compare men and women and explore the extent of gender differences in relationship beliefs and attitudes (for a review, see Winstead, Derlega, & Rose, 1997). However, one limitation of research examining gender differences in relationship beliefs is the failure to consider at the same time how other social group memberships, including culture, race/ethnicity, and social class, also influence beliefs and attitudes. There are at least two important reasons to examine gender differences (and similarities) in beliefs about love and romantic relationships in conjunction with the influence of other social group memberships. First, it allows us to examine the importance of membership in a gender group as compared to membership in other social groups in explaining variation in beliefs about love and relationships. Second, a consideration of gender in combination with other social group memberships allows us to examine whether a particular gender effect depends on or differs on the basis of membership in other social groups. For example, differences between men and women in beliefs about love may be more pronounced in one culture or subculture than those in another. Hence, we can examine the universality of gender differences. Another limitation of the prior research upon which findings about gender differences in beliefs are based is that generally only one belief or set of beliefs has been examined in any one study. As a result, it is generally unknown how the strength of the effect of gender may vary across types of beliefs.

In this study, we overcome these limitations by examining gender differences and similarities

Susan Sprecher and Maura Toro-Morn, "A Study of Men and Women from Different Sides of Earth to Determine If Men Are from Mars and Women Are from Venus in Their Beliefs About Love and Romantic Relationships" from *Sex Roles* 46, no. 5/6 (March 2002). Copyright © 2002 by Plenum Publishing Corporation. Reprinted with the permission of Springer Science and Business Media.

in several relationship beliefs and also by considering cultural differences (data were collected in North America and China), and ethnic/racial and social class differences more specifically within the North American sample. The relationship beliefs we consider are love as a basis for marriage (e.g., Kephart, 1967), romantic beliefs (Sprecher & Metts, 1989), beliefs in a romantic destiny and/or fate (Goodwin & Findlay, 1997; Knee, 1998), and love styles (e.g., Hendrick & Hendrick, 1986).

Review of the Literature

Love as a Basis for Marriage

In the United States, Canada, and other Western cultures, it is generally assumed that two people will marry each other only if there is love between them. In the 1960s, Kephart (1967) asked more than 1,000 U.S. college students the following question: "If a boy (girl) had all the other qualities you desired, would you marry this person if you were not in love with him (her)?" Kephart found that 65% of the men but only 24% of the women said they would not. However, when the same question was posed to later cohorts of students, 80–90% of both genders indicated that they would not marry without love, and no gender differences were found (Allgeier & Wiederman, 1991; Levine, Sato, Hashimoto, & Verma, 1995; Simpson, Campbell, & Berscheid, 1986; Sprecher et al., 1994).

In two of the above studies (Levine et al., 1995; Sprecher et al., 1994), the Kephart question was posed to samples from more than one country, and some cross-cultural differences were found. Levine et al. (1995) reported that the percentage of respondents indicating that they would not marry someone they did not love was highest in the United States (85.9%), and, in the 10 other countries represented, ranged from a low of 24.0% (India) to a high of 85.7% (Brazil). Although China was not included in the sample, Thailand and Japan, countries similar to China in degree of collectivism, were included. The percentages of respondents in these two countries who said they would not marry someone they did not love were 33.8 and 62.6%, respectively, which were lower than that for the United States. Levine et al. (1995)

did not find any gender differences in responses, either overall or in any of the countries. However, one limitation of Levine et al.'s study was the small sample size within each country (ns ranged from 71 to 156; Levine et al., 1995).

Sprecher et al. (1994) included a version of the Kephart question in their cross-cultural study, which included respondents from the United States ($n = 1{,}043$), Russia ($n = 401$), and Japan ($n = 223$). No significant difference was found in the proportion of Japanese and U.S. respondents who said they would insist on love in a marriage partner (81% for the Japanese sample and 89% for the U.S. sample); however, respondents from Japan and the United States were significantly more likely to expect love in a mate than were respondents in the Russian sample (64%). Sprecher et al. (1994) found no gender differences in their total cross-national sample or in their Japanese and U.S. samples, but a greater proportion of Russian men than Russian women (70% vs. 59%) said they would insist on love in marriage.

The belief that love is necessary to *maintain* a marriage seems to be pervasive as well, although perhaps not as pervasive as the belief that love is necessary for entering marriage. In their survey study of U.S. college students (collected in both 1976 and 1984), Simpson et al. (1986) included the Kephart question and two questions on the importance of love for the maintenance of marriage. Although the respondents were less likely to agree that they would leave a marriage if love had disappeared than they were to agree that they would not marry without love, a greater proportion of respondents agreed than disagreed that love would be necessary for the maintenance of marriage. The belief that love is necessary for the maintenance of marriage was held less strongly in their 1984 sample than in their 1976 sample. Simpson et al. (1986) found no gender differences in beliefs about the importance of love for the maintenance of marriage.

In their cross-cultural study, Levine et al. (1995) also included the Simpson et al. (1986) questions about the importance of love for the maintenance of marriage and found cross-cultural variation in responses. Among the countries represented, the

U.S. sample was intermediate in its endorsement that love is necessary to maintain the marriage. The Japan and Thailand samples were more likely than the U.S. sample to agree with the statement, "If love has completely disappeared from a marriage, I think it is probably best for the couple to make a clean break and start new lives." Levine et al. (1995) did not find any gender differences in beliefs about love as necessary for the maintenance of marriage, either in the overall sample or in any of the separate country samples.

In commenting on Simpson et al.'s findings on the love–marriage connection, Berscheid and Meyers (1996) observed that Kephart's question referred to "in love" whereas the two questions assessing the importance of love for the maintenance of marriage referred to "love" (Kephart, 1967). They noted that there are differences between the experience of being "in love" and the experience of "love," with the former being a more passionate type of love and the latter being a more companionate type of love (for a discussion of the distinction between passionate and companionate love, see Berscheid & Walster, 1974; Sprecher & Regan, 1998). In this study, we include not only the three questions used in prior research (e.g., Simpson et al., 1986), but also two questions that assess the importance of passionate love (or sexual attraction) for the establishment of marriage and the maintenance of marriage.

Romantic Attitudes

The belief that love should be a basis of marriage is only one of several romantic beliefs. A larger constellation of beliefs has been called the "romantic ideology" and includes such beliefs as love at first sight, there is only one true love, true love lasts forever, idealization of the partner and of the relationship, and love can overcome any obstacle (e.g., Knox & Sporakowski, 1968; Sprecher & Metts, 1989). In most studies on romantic attitudes, conducted primarily in the United States, men have been found to be more romantic than women (e.g., Knox & Sporakowski, 1968; Sprecher & Metts, 1989), although in some studies no gender differences have been found (e.g., Cunningham & Antill, 1981; Sprecher & Metts, 1999).

Sprecher et al. (1994) found that their U.S. and Russian samples scored higher on a Romantic Beliefs Scale (Sprecher & Metts, 1989) than their Japanese sample. However, they found no gender differences in romantic attitudes, either overall or in any of the three cultures. In another cross-cultural study, Simmons, Vomkolke, and Shimizu (1986) administered romanticism scales to university students in Japan, West Germany, and the United States. On some of the subscales, Japanese students scored lowest on Romanticism, whereas the West German students were most romantic. On other subscales, no cross-cultural differences were found. Overall, there were no gender differences in romantic attitudes, although Gender × Culture interactions were found for some of the individual romanticism items.

Belief in Destiny or Fate in Love

Goodwin and Findlay (1997) have explored a concept specific to love in China, which is "yuan," the belief that a relationship is either destined to be "the one" or to fail (similar to the romantic belief there is only one true love). Thus, if a relationship works, it is because of fate, and not because of individual actions. As noted by Goodwin and Findlay (1997), yuan comes from traditional Buddhist beliefs. They found that Chinese respondents scored higher on the Yuan Scale than British respondents, although they found that the British respondents also scored high on many of the Yuan Scale items. Commenting on these findings, Hendrick and Hendrick (2000) wrote, "there remains a fascinating question about whether Eastern notions of fatalism as well as duty and obligation also can be found in Western concepts of love" (p. 212).

Goodwin and Findlay (1997) found no gender differences in scores on yuan, either in the Chinese or in the British samples. Knee (1998) developed a scale to measure a similar concept to yuan—a destiny belief—which was defined as a belief that "holds that potential relationship partners are either meant for each other or not" (p. 360). To our knowledge, the Knee (1998) Destiny Scale has not been used in cross-cultural research, and no gender differences have been found in either his original study or any follow-up studies (Knee, personal communication, January 13, 2002).

Love Styles

Lee (1973) proposed a love taxonomy that included six styles of loving, also referred to as attitudes about love. Hendrick and Hendrick (1986) developed a scale to measure these six styles of love, which are Eros (romantic, passionate love), Ludus (game-playing love), Storge (friendship love), Pragma (logical, shopping-list love), Mania (possessive, dependent love), and Agape (selfless love). Across several studies, the most consistent gender difference found is that men score higher than women on Ludus. Furthermore, in several studies, women have been found to score higher than men on Storge, Pragma, and Mania (for a review of these findings, see Hendrick & Hendrick, 1992, 2000).

Sprecher et al. (1994), in their cross-cultural study, included a short version of the Hendrick and Hendrick Love scales (three items to measure each love style) and found cross-cultural differences in some of the styles. For example, they found that both the Japanese sample and the Russian sample were less erotic and storgic than the U.S. sample. They also found that gender differences varied by culture. For example, the U.S. men were more ludic than the U.S. women (a finding consistent with considerable previous research), whereas no gender differences were found on Ludus in Russia or Japan. In addition, women were more pragmatic than men in the U.S. sample, whereas no gender differences on Pragma were found in Russia or Japan. Finally, women were more manic than men in the U.S. sample, whereas in the Russian and Japanese samples, the reverse gender difference was found (men were more manic than women). Hence, their research with the love styles suggests that what have been considered to be robust and universal gender differences may, in fact, not be.

In an earlier cross-cultural study, Murstein, Merighi, and Vyse (1991) compared French students with U.S. students on love styles and found that French students had higher levels of Storge and Mania and lower levels of Agape. A comparison of men and women revealed no gender differences

in the U.S. sample and a higher score on Ludus for men than that for women in the French sample. The researchers concluded that "differences in nationality were more pronounced than gender differences within nationality" (p. 43).

Hendrick and Hendrick (1986) also compared ethnic groups within the United States. They found that Asian students, compared to students from other ethnic backgrounds, scored lower on Eros and higher on Storge and Pragma. They also found that Black respondents were less agapic as compared to other racial/ethnic groups. In a later study, Contreras, Hendrick, and Hendrick (1996) compared three groups of participants recruited from urban areas in Southwestern United States: Anglo Americans, Mexican Americans with a high level of acculturation, and Mexican Americans with a low level of acculturation. Ethnic differences were found in scores on Ludus, Pragma, and Mania. Among the three groups, Anglo (White) participants were least ludic and most manic, whereas the low-acculturation Mexican American group had the highest Pragma scores. However, to our knowledge, no other research has compared ethnic groups on the love styles or on other beliefs about love, and no analyses have been conducted to examine gender differences in relationship beliefs within different ethnic/racial groups.

Summary of the Purposes of This Investigation

Although researchers who study relationship beliefs have routinely examined gender differences, conclusions about the influence of gender on relationship beliefs are limited by the inability to compare the effect of gender across a variety of relationship beliefs (i.e., rarely are several beliefs examined in the same study), and by homogeneous samples limited to one culture and often only one subculture within the larger culture. In this study, on the other hand, we examine gender differences on *several* relationship beliefs in two very different cultures (North America and China), and also examine how gender differences (and similarities) depend on ethnic/racial and social class membership. As part of the investigation, we also examine how the American sample differs from the Chinese sample in relationship beliefs and also how relationship beliefs may depend on race/ethnicity and social class within the American sample.

Method

Participants

The (North) American sample consisted of 693 university students most of whom were from a public, midwestern university in the United States ($n = 484$). However, data also were collected from a midwestern private university ($n = 27$), a university in southwestern United States ($n = 77$), a university in eastern United States ($n = 35$), and a university in Canada ($n = 70$). Of the 693 American participants, 230 were male and 456 were female (and 7 did not specify their gender). The mean age of the American participants was 21.29 ($SD = 5.11$). To a question asking about racial/ethnic background, 74.3% chose White, 11.7% chose Black, 8.5% chose Hispanic/Latino, and the remaining (5.5%) checked either Asian, American, Indian, or Other. To a question asking about the social class of their parental family during adolescent and teenage years, 3.9% chose upper class, 26.6% chose upper-middle class, 49.1% chose middle class, 11.8% chose lower-middle class, 6.5% chose working class, and 2.0% said lower class.

The Chinese sample consisted of 735 university students, primarily from Lanzhou University ($n = 510$), which is a major university in Northwest China. Data also were collected at a Northwest National Minorities University ($n = 151$) and a Medical school also located in Northwest China ($n = 74$). Of the Chinese participants, 352 were male, 343 were female, and 40 did not respond directly to the gender question (the question on gender was located at the end of the questionnaire, and missed by some of the respondents). The mean age of the Chinese sample was 21.04 ($SD = 4.62$). Standard questions on ethnicity/race and social class were not asked of the Chinese sample.

Procedure

In the various locations in both cultures, the questionnaire was distributed in class under anonymous and voluntary conditions. For the Chinese sample, the questionnaire was translated into Chinese. This was done by a professor from the Department of Sociology and Philosophy at Lanzhou University. Several drafts of the translation were conducted to ensure accuracy of items and scales. Once the questionnaire was translated into Chinese, two Chinese graduate students who were fluent in English were asked to review and check the translation for accuracy and clarity of language. In addition, at a later date, a third Chinese graduate student, who was studying in the United States and fluent in both languages (informally), back-translated each item and concluded that overall, the translation was good and highlighted for us some of the nuances.

Measurement

Love as a Basis for Marriage

Kephart's question "If a man (woman) had all other qualities you desired, would you marry this person if you were not in love with him (her)?" was the first question that appeared on the questionnaire (Kephart, 1967). Kephart (1967) and other researchers using this item have generally included either three options (no, yes, undecided) or two options (yes, no), whereas we provided five options: *strongly no, moderately no, undecided, moderately yes,* and *strongly yes*. We also asked another version of this question, which asked specifically about the importance of passionate love for entering marriage. This question was phrased, "If a man (woman) had all the other qualities you desired and you experienced a friendship/companionate love but not a sexual attraction or passionate love for him (her), would you marry him or her?" The same five response options were provided (ranging from *strongly no* to *strongly yes*). The responses to both items were recoded so that a higher score indicated a stronger love–marriage connection.

Also included in the questionnaire were two items designed by Simpson et al. (1986) to measure the role of love in the maintenance of marriage: (1) "If love has completely disappeared from a marriage, I think it is probably best for the couple to make a clean break and start new lives." (2) "In my opinion, the disappearance of love is not a sufficient reason for ending a marriage, and should not be viewed as such." Each of the items was followed by a 5-point response scale: *strongly disagree, moderately disagree, neutral, moderately agree,* and *strongly agree.* Hence, a higher score for each of these items indicated a stronger importance of love for the maintenance of marriage. Because the items were conceptually similar and positively correlated ($r = .68, p < .001$, in the American sample; $r = .29, p < .001$, in the Chinese sample), they were combined. A third item was included that specifically assessed the importance of passionate love for maintenance of marriage: "In your opinion, if passionate love or sexual attraction has disappeared from a marriage, but the two still love each other in a companionate/friendship way, is it probably best for the couple to make a clean break and start new lives?" (the same 5-point response scale was used). Finally, participants were also asked about the importance of emotional satisfaction and physical pleasure for continuing a marriage. The two questions were (1) "How important is it to you that a marriage be emotionally satisfying in order for you to want to continue it?" (2) "How important is it to you that a marriage be physically pleasurable in order for you to want to continue it?" Five responses followed each item, ranging from *extremely important* to *not at all important.* These responses were re-coded so that higher scores indicated greater importance of emotional satisfaction and physical pleasure to marriage.

Romantic Attitudes

The Sprecher and Metts (1989) Romantic Beliefs Scale was included as a measure of romantic attitudes or beliefs. This scale contains 15 items that measure a variety of romantic beliefs: love finds a way (e.g., "If I love someone, I know I can make the relationship work, despite any obstacles"), one and only (e.g., "There will be only one real love for me"), idealization (e.g., "I'm sure that every new thing I learn about the person I choose for a long-term commitment will please me"), and

love at first sight (e.g., "When I find my 'true love' I will probably know it soon after we meet"). Participants responded to each of the 15 items on a response scale ranging from 1 (*strongly disagree*) to 7 (*strongly agree*). Thus, the higher the score, the more romantic was the respondent. For the total scale, coefficient alpha was .81 for the American sample and .76 for the Chinese sample. In our analysis, we also considered three of the four subscales identified by Sprecher and Metts (1989), which were those that had an adequate coefficient alpha (.50) in our particular samples. These were as follows: love finds a way (.75 for the American sample and .68 for the Chinese sample), one and only (.69 for the American sample and .61 for the Chinese sample), and idealization (.71 for the American sample and .52 for the Chinese sample). (We did not present analyses for the subscale, love at first sight, because of its lower reliability in both samples.)

Belief in Destiny or Fate

To measure the degree to which our respondents believed in destiny or fate, we included both the four items from Knee's belief in Destiny Scale and three items from the larger Goodwin and Findlay (1997) Yuan Scale (Knee, 1998). The items from Knee's scale were as follows: (1) "Potential relationship partners are either compatible or they are not," (2) "A successful relationship is mostly a matter of finding a compatible partner right from the start," (3) "Potential relationship partners are either destined to get along or they are not," and (4) "Relationships that do not start off well inevitably fail." The three items selected from the Goodwin and Findlay (1997) Yuan Scale were those that appeared, on the face of it, to best measure the concept of fate. These items were as follows: (1) "A relationship is something that develops outside human control," (2) "The relationship between two people has already been decided upon, even before they meet," and (3) "If a relationship fails, it is not the individuals who are at fault; it is the result of fate." Each of the seven items was followed by a response scale ranging from 1 (*strongly disagree*) to 7 (*strongly agree*).

The coefficient alpha for the combined seven items was .71 in the American sample and .60 in the Chinese sample. The coefficient alpha for the original four-item Knee (1998) Destiny Scale was .71 in the American sample and .40 in the Chinese sample. (Because the short scale had a coefficient alpha below .50 in the Chinese sample, only the combined scale will be used in analyses including the Chinese sample.)

Love Styles

To measure the six love styles, we included the Hendrick, Hendrick, and Dicke (1998) short form of the Love Attitudes Scale (e.g., Hendrick & Hendrick, 1986). In the questionnaire distributed to the American sample, the participants responded to each of the 24 items on a response scale ranging from 1 (strongly disagree) to 5 (strongly agree). However, in the questionnaire translated into Chinese, a response scale similar to that used for the romanticism scale (a 7-point response scale ranging from strongly disagree to strongly agree) was inadvertently used. To allow for direct comparisons of scores between the two samples, item scores in the Chinese sample were mathematically transformed to have the same 5-point response scale (i.e., scores were multiplied by .714). Unfortunately, the coefficient alpha was below .50 for both the Eros and Ludus scales in the Chinese sample, and thus no analyses will be conducted on these two scales with the Chinese sample. However, the coefficient alphas for these scales in the American sample were adequate—.65 and .69, respectively. The other love styles had the following coefficient alphas for the American sample and the Chinese sample, respectively: Storge (.78 and .77), Pragma (.66 and .59), Mania (.60 and .52), and Agape (.80 and .79).

Results

Gender Differences and Similarities in the North American Sample

First, we compared American men and women on the various love beliefs, through Independent t test analyses. To control for making a Type I error due to the number of comparisons made in combination with the relatively large sample, the significance level was set to $p < .01$. The results are presented in the first two columns of Table 1.

Love–Marriage Connection

In response to Kephart's question, both men and women indicated that love would be necessary for entering marriage. However, women agreed to a significantly greater degree than did men that they would need to be in love to enter marriage. Both genders also agreed that a passionate love (or sexual attraction) would be necessary to experience before entering marriage, although men and women endorsed less strongly this item than the item asking about being "in love," as indicated by paired t tests, this difference was significant ($p < .001$) for both men and women.

Both genders also tended to believe that love was important to maintain marriage, although felt less strongly about the importance of love for the maintenance of marriage than for entering marriage.[2] No gender differences were found on the two-item index of the importance of love for maintaining marriage or on the item asking about the importance of passionate love (sexual attraction) for maintaining marriage. To the latter item, men and women expressed more disagreement than agreement. That is, both men and women generally did not believe that the disappearance of passionate love or sexual attraction would be a sufficient reason for ending a marriage as long as the marriage still had companionate love.

Not surprising, both men and women judged emotional satisfaction to be more important than physical pleasure for maintaining a marriage, as indicated by paired t tests, this difference was significant ($p < .001$) for both men and women. Although there was not a gender difference in the importance of physical pleasure, women rated emotional satisfaction to be significantly more important than did men.

Romantic Attitudes and Belief in Destiny

Men and women in the American sample did not differ from each other on the total score of the Romantic Beliefs Scale. However, men endorsed the Idealization dimension of this scale more

Table 1. Gender Differences in Love Beliefs in the North American Sample and in the Chinese Sample

	North American Sample		Chinese Sample	
	Men (*n* = 230)	Women (*n* = 456)	Men (*n* = 352)	Women (*n* = 343)
Love–marriage connection				
Importance of love for entering marriage	4.22 (0.94)	4.45 (0.86)**	4.05 (1.16)	3.88 (1.16)
Importance of passionate love for entering marriage	3.92 (1.05)	4.04 (0.98)	3.81 (1.18)	3.82 (1.20)
Importance of love for maintaining marriage	3.10 (1.03)	3.09 (1.15)	3.78 (1.04)	3.70 (0.93)
Importance of passionate love for maintaining marriage	2.20 (1.00)	2.20 (1.03)	3.37 (1.43)	3.23 (1.41)
Importance of emotional satisfaction for maintaining marriage	4.23 (0.79)	4.54 (0.65)***	4.38 (0.62)	4.39 (0.62)
Importance of physical pleasure for maintaining marriage	3.72 (0.84)	3.65 (0.82)	3.57 (0.85)	3.34 (0.90)***
Romanticism				
Total Romantic Beliefs scale	4.49 (0.85)	4.36 (0.90)	4.94 (0.83)	4.74 (0.88)**
Belief in love finds a way	5.25 (0.99)	5.15 (1.03)	5.31 (1.04)	4.97 (1.03)***
Belief in one and only	3.86 (1.37)	3.90 (1.52)	4.67 (1.44)	4.71 (1.58)
Belief in idealization	4.02 (1.37)	3.62 (1.31)***	4.49 (1.29)	4.35 (1.27)
Belief in destiny and fate				
Destiny scale	4.19 (1.12)	4.03 (1.23)	—	—
Destiny + yuan items	3.74 (0.94)	3.71 (1.07)	3.53 (0.91)	3.72 (0.99)**
Love styles				
Eros	3.65 (0.80)	3.87 (0.78)***	—	—
Ludus	2.56 (0.97)	2.10 (0.89)***	—	—
Storge	3.23 (1.00)	3.34 (1.03)	3.56 (0.95)	3.30 (1.02)***
Pragma	2.29 (0.90)	2.45 (0.88)	2.68 (0.80)	2.53 (0.82)
Mania	3.08 (0.84)	3.00 (0.87)	3.37 (0.79)	3.22 (0.83)
Agape	3.58 (0.91)	3.16 (0.86)***	3.73 (0.82)	3.19 (1.01)***

Note: ANOVA indicated significant Gender × Culture interactions for importance of love for entering marriage (*p* = .001), importance of emotional satisfaction for maintaining marriage (*p* < .001), Storge (*p* = .001), and Pragma (*p* < .01). The dash (—) indicates that data were not reported because of low reliability.
** *p* ≤ .01. *** *p* ≤ .001.

strongly than did women. Hence, men were more likely than women to idealize the partner and the relationship. In general, men and women were moderately romantic overall.

In the American sample, no gender difference was found in the belief in romantic destiny. Scores on both Knee's four-item Destiny Scale and the expanded destiny scale, which also included three items from the Goodwin and Findlay (1997) Yuan Scale, did not significantly differ between the genders (Knee, 1998). Both genders only moderately endorsed beliefs of destiny or fate.

Love Styles
Of the six love styles, gender differences were found on three in the American sample. Women

scored significantly higher than men on the Eros scale, whereas men scored significantly higher than women on the Ludus and Agape scales. No gender differences were found on the Storge, Pragma, and Mania scales.

Gender Differences and Similarities in the Chinese Sample

Next, we compared Chinese men and women on the various love beliefs, also through Independent *t* test analyses, using $p < .01$ as the significance level. The results are presented in the right portion of Table 1.

Love–Marriage Connection

In China, no gender differences were found in the importance of love for either entering or maintaining marriage. The Chinese, similar to the Americans, believed that love was important for marriage. Although the Chinese also believed that passionate love was slightly less important than being "in love" for entering marriage, the difference in the responses to the two items was significant ($p < .001$) only for men. On the other hand, and similar to the findings in the American sample, passionate love (sexual attraction) was viewed as less important than "love" for maintaining marriage. Although love was considered to be more important for entering marriage than for maintaining marriage in the Chinese sample (as it was for the American sample), the difference was not large.

The Chinese, similar to the Americans, believed that emotional satisfaction was more important than physical pleasure for maintaining marriage, as indicated by paired *t* tests, the difference was significant ($p < .001$) for both men and women. A gender difference was found in the importance of physical pleasure for the maintenance of marriage: Chinese men rated physical pleasure to be more important than did Chinese women. However, no gender difference was found in the importance of emotional satisfaction for maintaining marriage.

Romantic Attitudes and Belief in Destiny

In the Chinese sample, men had a higher score than women on the Romantic Beliefs Scale. Specifically, Chinese men scored higher than Chinese women on the Love Finds a Way dimension of the romanticism scale, indicating that Chinese men were more likely to believe that love can overcome all obstacles. However, Chinese women scored higher than Chinese men on the expanded destiny scale, indicating that Chinese women were more likely to believe in destiny or fate in romantic relationships.

Love Styles

The results for only four love styles are presented for the Chinese sample (because of the low reliability for the Eros and Ludus scales). Gender differences were found for two of the four scales, with men scoring higher than women. Chinese men were more storgic and agapic in their love styles than were Chinese women.

The Combined Samples

Thus far, we have presented the results of analyses conducted with each sample separately. Next, with the combined samples, we conducted a 2 (gender) × 2 (culture) ANOVA on each relationship belief (that had adequate reliability in both samples) for the primary purpose of examining whether there were any significant Gender × Culture interactions. A significant interaction would indicate that the effect of gender on a particular relationship belief depends on culture. The Gender × Culture interaction was found to be significant (at the $p < .01$ level) for four relationship beliefs: importance of love for entering marriage, $F(1, 1372) = 11.70, p = .001$; importance of emotional satisfaction for maintaining marriage, $F(1, 1373) = 17.25, p < .001$; Storge, $F(1, 1356) = 10.96, p = .001$; and Pragma, $F(1, 1361) = 9.79, p = 002$. In each case, a gender difference was found in one sample that was not found (or was even reversed) in the other sample. The means are presented in Table 1 and were discussed earlier.

In addition, the ANOVA analyses indicated that the culture main effect was significant ($p < .01$) for several relationship beliefs. The means for each sample (for men and women combined) are reported in Table 2. As compared to the Chinese sample, the American sample expressed

Table 2. Cultural Differences and Similarities in Love Beliefs

	North American Sample (n = 693)	Chinese Sample (n = 735)	F for Main Effect of Culture
Love–marriage connection			
Importance of love for entering marriage	4.38 (0.89)	3.98 (1.16)	42.01***
Importance of passionate love for entering marriage	4.00 (1.01)	3.81 (1.18)	7.45**
Importance of love for maintaining marriage	3.10 (1.11)	3.76 (0.98)	124.29***
Importance of passionate love for maintaining marriage	2.21 (1.02)	3.31 (1.42)	255.53***
Importance of emotional satisfaction for maintaining marriage	4.43 (0.72)	4.38 (0.62)	0.01
Importance of physical pleasure for maintaining marriage	3.66 (0.84)	3.46 (0.88)	22.99***
Romanticism			
Total Romantic Beliefs scale	4.40 (0.88)	4.85 (0.86)	73.71***
Belief in love finds a way	5.18 (1.02)	5.15 (1.06)	1.18
Belief in one and only	3.88 (1.47)	4.71 (1.50)	97.23***
Belief in idealization	3.75 (1.34)	4.44 (1.28)	69.50***
Belief in destiny and fate			
Destiny scale	—	—	—
Destiny + yuan items	3.72 (1.02)	3.63 (0.97)	3.40
Love styles			
Eros	—	—	—
Ludus	—	—	—
Storge	3.30 (1.02)	3.43 (1.00)	6.63
Pragma	2.39 (0.89)	2.62 (0.84)	24.56***
Mania	3.02 (0.86)	3.30 (0.81)	29.27***
Agape	3.30 (0.90)	3.47 (0.96)	3.29

Note: The dash (—) indicates that the data were not reported because of low reliability in Chinese sample.
** $p \leq .01$. *** $p \leq .001$.

a stronger love–marriage connection in response to Kephart's question and also believed that passionate love was a more important prerequisite for entering marriage. However, the Chinese sample was more likely than the American sample to believe that love and passionate love were important for maintaining marriage (the difference between the cultures was particularly large on the item measuring the importance of passionate love for maintaining marriage). On the other hand, Americans rated physical pleasure as being more important for maintaining marriage than did the Chinese.

The Chinese sample scored higher than the American sample on the Romantic Beliefs Scale as well as on two specific dimensions of romanticism, belief in One and Only and Idealization. However, no cultural differences were found in the belief in a romantic destiny, as indicated by scores on the expanded destiny scale. On the love styles, cultural differences were found on two of the four scales for which analyses were possible.

Table 3. Gender Differences and Similarities in Love Beliefs in Both Samples Combined

	Men (n = 582)	Women (n = 799)	F for Main Effect of Gender
Love–marriage connection			
Importance of love for entering marriage	4.12 (1.08)	4.21 (1.04)	0.34
Importance of passionate love for entering marriage	3.85 (1.13)	3.94 (1.09)	0.98
Importance of love for maintaining marriage	3.51 (1.09)	3.35 (1.11)	0.62
Importance of passionate love for maintaining marriage	2.90 (1.40)	2.64 (1.31)	0.88
Importance of emotional satisfaction for maintaining marriage	4.32 (0.70)	4.47 (0.64)	19.55***
Importance of physical pleasure for maintaining marriage	3.62 (0.85)	3.52 (0.87)	10.19**
Romanticism			
Total Romantic Beliefs scale	4.76 (0.87)	4.52 (0.91)	11.41**
Belief in love finds a way	5.28 (1.02)	5.07 (1.03)	14.63***
Belief in one and only	4.35 (1.47)	4.25 (1.60)	0.25
Belief in idealization	4.30 (1.34)	3.93 (1.34)	13.87***
Belief in destiny and fate			
Destiny scale	—	—	—
Destiny + yuan items	3.61 (0.93)	3.71 (1.04)	1.96
Love styles			
Eros	—	—	—
Ludus	—	—	—
Storge	3.43 (0.98)	3.33 (1.02)	1.42
Pragma	2.53 (0.86)	2.48 (0.88)	0.00
Mania	3.25 (0.82)	3.09 (0.86)	6.36
Agape	3.67 (0.86)	3.17 (0.93)	92.03***

Note: The dash (—) indicates that the data were not reported because of low reliability in Chinese sample.
** $p \leq .01$. *** $p \leq .001$.

The Chinese sample scored higher on the Pragma and Manic scales.

The main effect of gender from these analyses was significant for importance of emotional satisfaction (higher for women), importance of physical pleasure (higher for men), Total Romantic Beliefs Scale (higher for men), belief in Love Finds a Way (higher for men), belief in Idealization (higher for men), and Agape (higher for men). Table 3 gives means for men and women from the combined samples.

We also compared the eta-square (i.e., effect size, or the proportion of variance in the dependent variable that is attributable to a particular effect) for the gender main effect, the culture main effect, and the Gender × Culture interaction effect. The effect size for gender was greatest for Agape (.06). Otherwise, gender's effect size was either .00 or .01 (the mean eta-square for gender was .007). Eta-square was higher for culture; it ranged from .00 to .16 (importance of passionate love for marriage); the mean eta-square was .035. Finally, the proportion of variance (i.e., eta-squared) attributed to the Gender × Culture interaction was also low (mean = .003; see Table 4).

Gender and Other Subcultures Within the American Sample

As indicated earlier, gender interacted with culture for four specific relationship beliefs. With the American sample, we also examined the possibility that the effect of gender depended on (or interacted with) other subculture memberships (i.e., race/ethnicity and social class). We used the standard significance level ($p < .05$) for these analyses because the smaller size of the minority groups in the American sample reduces statistical power for detecting differences.

Table 4. Eta-Square (Effect Size) for Main Effect of Gender, Main Effect of Culture, and Gender × Culture Interaction

	Eta-Square for Gender	Eta-Square for Culture	Eta-Square for the Gender × Culture Interaction
Love–marriage connection			
Importance of love for entering marriage	.00	.03	.01
Importance of passionate love for entering marriage	.00	.01	.00
Importance of love for maintaining marriage	.00	.08	.00
Importance of passionate love for maintaining marriage	.00	.16	.00
Importance of emotional satisfaction for maintaining marriage	.01	.00	.01
Importance of physical pleasure for maintaining marriage	.01	.02	.00
Romanticism			
Total Romantic Beliefs scale	.01	.05	.00
Belief in love finds a way	.01	.00	.00
Belief in one and only	.00	.07	.00
Belief in idealization	.01	.05	.00
Belief in destiny and fate			
Destiny scale	—	—	—
Destiny + yuan items	.00	.00	.00
Love styles			
Eros	—	—	—
Ludus	—	—	—
Storge	.00	.01	.01
Pragma	.00	.02	.01
Mania	.00	.02	.01
Agape	.06	.00	.00

Note: The dash (—) indicates that the data were not reported because of low reliability in Chinese sample.
**p ≤ .01. ***p ≤ .001.

In our examination of differences based on racial/ethnic group (to be referred to as race), we compared only the races having the most members in this sample, which were Whites (*n* = 463), Blacks (*n* = 78), and Hispanic/Latinos (*n* = 56). We also had eliminated the small Canadian subsample because it consisted primarily of White respondents.

As indicated by the ANOVAs, no significant Gender × Race interactions were found for any of the relationship beliefs, indicating that the effect of gender was similar across the three races. However, a significant main effect for race was found for five relationship beliefs. The means of the relationship beliefs for each major race are reported in Table 5. First, a race main effect was found for

Table 5. Racial/Ethnic Differences in Love Beliefs (Within the U.S. Sample)

	Whites (*n* = 463)	Blacks (*n* = 78)	Hispanic/Latino (*n* = 56)	F for Main Effect of Race
Love–marriage connection				
Importance of love for entering marriage	4.42 (0.84)	4.36 (0.93)	4.34 (0.92)	1.02
Importance of passionate love for entering marriage	4.07 (0.95)	3.90 (1.04)	3.91 (1.23)	1.59
Importance of love for maintaining marriage	3.12 (1.06)	2.94 (1.28)	3.04 (1.34)	1.65
Importance of passionate love for maintaining marriage	2.19 (0.99)	2.23 (1.12)	2.09 (1.13)	0.34
Importance of emotional satisfaction for maintaining marriage	4.47 (0.70)	4.35 (0.75)	4.50 (0.74)	0.57
Importance of physical pleasure for maintaining marriage	3.69 (0.82)	3.67 (0.82)	3.55 (0.87)	0.56
Romanticism				
Total Romantic Beliefs scale	4.38 (0.86)	4.37 (0.88)	4.29 (1.04)	0.03
Belief in love finds a way	5.17 (1.02)	5.28 (0.89)	4.99 (1.30)	1.00
Belief in one and only	3.86 (1.41)	3.71 (1.53)	3.89 (1.71)	0.24
Belief in idealization	3.70 (1.29)	3.65 (1.39)	3.71 (1.55)	0.50
Belief in destiny and fate				
Destiny scale	4.10 (1.15)	3.99 (1.27)	3.69 (1.41)	2.88
Destiny + yuan	3.68 (0.97)	3.86 (1.05)	3.47 (1.28)	3.04*
Love styles				
Eros	3.85 (0.79)	3.64 (0.87)	3.73 (0.73)	1.89
Ludus	2.21 (0.93)	2.33 (0.94)	2.48 (1.06)	4.33*
Storge	3.24$_a$ (1.01)	3.56$_a$ (1.02)	3.42 (1.01)	3.08*
Pragma	2.34$_a$ (0.89)	2.64$_a$ (0.83)	2.58 (0.91)	5.77**
Mania	3.03 (0.86)	3.00 (0.86)	2.84 (0.83)	0.67
Agape	3.39$_{ab}$ (0.86)	2.99$_a$ (0.93)	2.96$_b$ (0.95)	8.40***

Note: The same subscripts within a row indicate significant differences between the two cultures on the basis of follow-up Bonferonni tests. A preliminary 3 (race) × 2 (gender) ANOVA indicated no significant Race × Gender interactions.
*$p \leq .05$. **$p \leq 0.01$. ***$p \leq .001$.

the expanded destiny belief scale. Whites had the highest score and Hispanic/Latinos had the lowest scores, although a follow-up Bonferonni test indicated no group was significantly different from another group. Second, a significant race effect was found for Ludus, and Hispanics/Latinos had the highest scores. However, a follow-up Bonferonni test indicated that no group was significantly different from another group. Third, a significant race effect was found for the Storge love style. Blacks had the highest Storge scores, whereas Whites had the lowest scores. A follow-up Bonferonni test indicated that a significant difference existed, more specifically, between Whites and Blacks. Fourth, a significant race effect was found for the Pragma love style scale. Blacks and Hispanic/Latinos scored higher than Whites on Pragma (the follow-up Bonferonni test indicated that the difference was significant between Whites and Blacks). Finally, a significant main effect for race was found for the Agape scale. The mean was highest for Whites and lowest for Blacks; a follow-up Bonferonni test indicated that the scores of White respondents scored significantly higher than both Black respondents and Hispanic/Latino respondents. The eta-square attributed to each effect (gender, race, Gender × Race), however, was quite low; that is, <.01.

For the purpose of examining the possible effect of social class on relationship beliefs, we divided our North American sample (including the Canadians) into two groups: (1) those who identified their family's social class as either upper class (3.9%), upper-middle class (26.6%), or middle class (49.1%); and (2) those who identified their family's social class as either lower-middle class (11.8%), working class (6.5%), or lower class, working poor (2.0%). As indicated by a 2 (gender) × 2 (social class) ANOVA, no significant Gender × Social Class interactions were found for any of the relationship beliefs, indicating that the effect of gender was similar in the different social classes.

However, a significant main effect for social class was found for five relationship beliefs. Those of the middle/upper classes scored higher than those of the lower classes on the item that passionate love is necessary for entering marriage, on the total romanticism scale, on the idealization component of romanticism, on the expanded destiny scale, and on Pragma. The means are presented in Table 6. The eta-square attributed to each effect (gender, social class, Gender × Class) was quite low; that is, <.01.

Discussion

This study contributes in several ways to our knowledge base about the influence of gender on relationship beliefs. Below, we first discuss general findings on the basis of our comparisons across genders, cultures, race and social class, and relationship beliefs. Second, we highlight and discuss our findings on beliefs related to the love–marriage connection. Third, we provide an interpretation of some of our findings unique to China by discussing recent changes in this country. Last, we note the limitations of the study.

Some General Findings

One issue we examined was the importance of gender relative to other cultural and subcultural memberships in influencing relationship beliefs. In comparing the effects of gender with the effects of culture (China vs. North America) on the relationship beliefs, we found that there were more differences based on culture than those based on gender. This finding suggests that the social conditions that influence relationship beliefs are likely to differ more for members of two very diverse cultures than for men and women within a culture. In our comparison of subgroups within the American sample, approximately as many ethnic/race and social class differences were found as gender differences, as indicated in the bivarate analyses. In the multiple regression analyses, in which all the social group membership variables were included as predictors, gender was least often a significant predictor. These results suggest that gender may be overrated as a social group membership variable likely to lead to differences in relationship beliefs and phenomena.

A second issue we examined was whether gender differences were similar (or different) in the two cultures as well as in the subcultures

Table 6. Social Class Differences in Love Beliefs (Within North American Sample)

	Lower/Working Classes (n = 140)	Middle/Upper Classes (n = 548)	F for Main Effect of Social Class
Marriage–love connection			
Importance of love for entering marriage	4.26 (1.00)	4.41 (0.86)	3.00
Importance of passionate love for entering marriage	3.80 (1.09)	4.05 (0.97)	6.15*
Importance of love for maintaining marriage	3.11 (1.23)	3.09 (1.08)	0.09
Importance of passionate love for maintaining marriage	2.14 (1.01)	2.22 (1.02)	0.36
Importance of emotional satisfaction for maintaining marriage	4.43 (0.74)	4.44 (0.71)	0.29
Importance of physical pleasure for maintaining marriage	3.55 (0.79)	3.70 (0.84)	2.50
Romanticism			
Total score	4.26 (0.90)	4.44 (0.87)	5.26*
Belief in love finds a way	5.09 (1.15)	5.20 (0.98)	1.21
Belief in one and only	3.70 (1.41)	3.92 (1.48)	2.94
Belief in idealization	3.48 (1.29)	3.82 (1.34)	8.71**
Belief in destiny and fate			
Destiny scale	3.93 (1.20)	4.12 (1.19)	2.40
Destiny + yuan items	3.57 (1.06)	3.76 (1.01)	4.29*
Love styles			
Eros	3.72 (0.81)	3.82 (0.79)	1.33
Ludus	2.18 (1.00)	2.27 (0.92)	1.68
Storge	3.32 (1.03)	3.30 (1.02)	0.04
Pragma	2.24 (0.83)	2.44 (0.90)	4.59*
Mania	2.97 (0.89)	3.04 (0.86)	0.47
Agape	3.26 (0.93)	3.31 (0.89)	0.29

Note: A 2 (social class) × 2 (gender) ANOVA indicated no significant Social Class × Gender interactions.
*$p \leq .05$. **$p \leq .01$.

based on race/ethnicity and social class within the American sample. In both the Chinese and the American samples, several gender differences were found in relationship beliefs, but with only one exception, the gender differences found in the American sample were not the same as the gender differences found in the Chinese sample. (The ANOVA results indicated a significant Gender × Culture interaction more specifically for four relationship beliefs.) These results, combined with other cross-cultural studies that have examined gender differences in relationship beliefs in diverse cultures (e.g., Sprecher et al., 1994), suggest that the gender differences that have consistently been found in North American and West European samples may not be found in other cultures. On the other hand, we found gender differences and similarities to be generally consistent in the different subcultures within the American sample. We found no Gender × Race or Gender × Social Class interactions, which indicate that the gender effect was the same regardless of these other subcultural memberships.

Because we included measures of several relationship beliefs in this study, a third issue we could examine is how the strength of the gender effect varied across types of relationship beliefs. It was clear that the effect of gender differed in strength across relationship beliefs, although as already noted, these differences were not the same in the Chinese sample as those in the American sample. In general, for the samples combined, the largest effect for gender (the greatest variance explained) was for Agape.

The Love–Marriage Connection

We highlight some of our findings for the beliefs about the love–marriage connection because we included new measures in this study resulting in new insights on the topic. Furthermore, we found an interesting gender difference that was the reverse of what has been found in past research.

Kephart (1967) found in the 1960s that women were more willing than men to marry without love, but Simpson et al. (1986) found no gender differences with samples from the 1970s and 1980s. Generally, other studies conducted in the 1990s that included the Kephart question on the importance of love–marriage connection also did not find a gender difference (e.g., Sprecher et al., 1994). Interestingly, in this American sample, obtained in 1999–2001, a gender difference was found, but a reverse one of that found by Kephart in the 1960s. Both men and women believed it was important to be in love with the person they married, but women felt more strongly about this than did men. The explanation provided for the gender difference found by Kephart in the 1960s was that women needed to be pragmatic about marriage choices because their husband often determined their financial security and social status. Simpson et al. (1986), in discussing why they found no gender differences in the samples they obtained from college students in 1976 and 1984, highlighted changes in society since the mid-1960s, including greater proportions of women seeking college education and entering the workforce. The cohort of young adults represented in this study not only experienced the opportunities that women in the 1960s did not have, but also were socialized by mothers who had these opportunities. Thus, it is possible that when women are unconstrained by practical considerations and are free to emphasize emotional considerations in a marriage partner, they actually emphasize love as a prerequisite for marriage to a greater degree than do men. In fact, our findings that the middle- and upper-class respondents were more likely than the lower-class respondents to have a stronger passionate love–marriage connection also suggests that financial stability contributes to the freedom to focus on love, particularly passionate love, in marriage choices.

Although the gender difference found to the Kephart question in this sample was significant, it was a small difference compared to the reverse gender difference found by Kephart in the 1960s. Hence, until this difference is replicated in future studies, we cannot assume that it is a strong and robust new gender difference. It was not found in the Chinese sample (the means were in the opposite directions, although not significantly different), which may reflect the greater traditionalism of the Chinese.

We also had included a variation of the Kephart question that asked about the willingness to marry someone who had "all other qualities you desired" and to whom a "friendship/companionate love was experienced" but "not passionate love or sexual attraction." Similar to how they responded to the Kephart question, our participants were more likely to say *no* than *yes* to this question. However, they were significantly more moderate in their no than they were to Kephart's original question, suggesting that the respondents' interpretation of the "in love" in the Kephart measure included something in addition to or other than passionate love and sexual attraction (see discussion by Berscheid & Meyers, 1996).

Although the responses to the questions asking about the importance of love for the maintenance of marriage were not compared directly with responses to the Kephart's question and our variation of Kephart's question (because of differences in response formats), nonetheless the lower means on the former items justify the conclusion that our participants believed less strongly that love is important for the maintenance of marriage than that love is important for the entrance into marriage. The participants were particularly likely to believe that passionate love is not necessary for the maintenance of marriage. No gender differences were found in the perceived importance of love or passionate love for the maintenance of marriage. Women, however, believed to a greater degree than men that emotional satisfaction was important for maintaining marriage.

Making Sense of Findings with the Chinese Sample in Light of Recent Changes in China

Our research findings with respect to the Chinese sample deserve some discussion and elaboration, given the lack of empirical research about Chinese love and romantic attitudes available to English-speaking audiences. In addition, our data offer a unique opportunity to compare and contrast two cultural traditions that have evolved along different conventions with respect to love and romantic relationships. In Western cultures, research supports the view that love is intensely individual. In Asian cultures, love is expected to develop more gradually and not to disrupt established family relations, an important feature of life in predominantly collective societies. More specifically, in China, researchers have found that the concept of yuan, the belief that a relationship is preordained by destiny, shapes beliefs about love and relationships (Goodwin & Findlay, 1997).

Although there is a rich tradition of love and romantic attitudes in China that goes back many centuries, under the influence of the Chinese Communist Party that came to power in the late 1940s, much of that history was lost and new cultural practices were introduced in keeping with communist values. For example, under Mao's totalitarian rule the individual was completely subordinated to the community. Relationships between men and women were strictly monitored and "falling in love" was considered a "bourgeois" sin punishable with years in prison. In the same vein, open expressions of love and affection were seen as signs of weaknesses. According to Xiaohe

and Whyte (1990), the communist regime erected considerable barriers that inhibited young people from developing a dating culture. Under the austere communist regime, much like the feudal system it sought to replace, marriage was a practical choice between two parties. Yet, recent economic reforms and China's integration to a global economy have brought important changes in the lives of Chinese men and women. For example, there is more freedom for young men and women to select their own partners (Xiaohe & Whyte, 1990). In addition, as Li (1998) observed, recent economic reforms have led to the adoption of Western ideals of fashion, beauty, and feminine values. Without prior research as a basis to compare we speculate that the gender differences we found in love styles speak to the changes taking place in the country with respect to relationships. In a country where marriages were arranged, and love was probably an outcome of marriage, not a precursor, it is significant to find that men were more romantic than women and more likely to view physical pleasure as important for maintaining marriage.

Yet, for all of the social and cultural changes taking place in China as the country moves from a state-controlled to a market economy, our data indicate that some cultural values tend to be more resistant to change than others. For example, their practical approach to love and romantic relationships can be grounded in the notion that a potential partner is the source of important resources such as housing, ability to move to more lucrative places, and access to schools and other resources still needed to maintain a family. Clearly, more research needs to be done to further explore gender differences across class and nationality groups within China. We are hopeful that China's opening to the world community will result in more research opportunities for Chinese scholars and for more collaborations between Western and Chinese researchers.

Limitations of the Study

Research in more than one country is important to conduct but is not without problems. One limitation of our study is that the samples for both cultures were convenience samples, each with an unknown degree of representation of its larger culture. Another limitation, also a sampling issue, is that the data were collected exclusively from university and college settings. Hence, we cannot generalize our findings to young adults who do not go to college and who are often from the lower classes. The predominantly middle-class college sample also limited our ability to compare relationship beliefs across social classes because we had few respondents representing the lowest classes. A third limitation is that we can never be sure that a cross-cultural difference (or similarity) found is not simply an artifact of a poor or an impossible translation. That is, we cannot be sure that individuals in both cultures are responding to items with equivalent meanings. A fourth limitation is that we are using measures that were developed by researchers belonging to only one of the cultures represented; hence, there may be important beliefs about love that were unique to China that were not assessed.

We anticipated all of these limitations before undertaking this study, but chose to pursue the research anyway because of our belief that imperfect research in understudied countries (e.g., China) is more desirable than no research.

Conclusions

As we conclude, we return to the question raised by the title of our paper: Are men from Mars and women from Venus? Our research suggests that this popular paradigm loses ground when held against scientifically collected data and analysis. For example, when comparing Chinese and American samples, cultural differences seemed to override differences based on gender. Equally significant is our finding that gender may be an overrated variable that does not explain much variance in relationship beliefs and other phenomena. Yet, this is no reason to completely abandon the idea that there are important differences between men and women. Instead, future researchers need to pay more attention to the effects of other social variables such as ethnicity, race, and social class and how they intersect with gender.

Acknowledgments

The authors thank Scott Christopher, Beverley Fehr, Juanita Goergen, Frank Morn, Lourdes Torres, Ann Weber, and Mingju Xu for collecting data in their classes.

Notes

1. An earlier version of this paper was presented at the International Conference on Personal Relationships, sponsored by INPR and ISSPR, Prescott, AZ, June 29 to July 3, 2001.
2. Because the format of the questions and response options for the Kephart question differed from that of the questions that asked about the importance of love for the maintenance of marriage, a paired t test was not conducted to directly compare the responses.

References

Allgeier, E. R., & Wiederman, N. W. (1991). Love and mate selection in the 1990s. *Free Inquiry, 11*, 25–27.

Berscheid, E., & Meyers, S. (1996). A social categorical approach to a question about love. *Personal Relationships, 3*, 19–43.

Berscheid, E., & Walster (Hatfield), E. (1974). A little bit about love. In T. L. Huston (Ed.), *Foundations of interpersonal attraction* (pp. 356–381). New York: Academic Press.

Contreras, R., Hendrick, S. S., & Hendrick, C. (1996). Perspectives on marital love and satisfaction in Mexican American and Anglo couples. *Journal of Counseling and Development, 74*, 408–415.

Cunningham, J. D., & Antill, J. H. (1981). Love in developing romantic relationships. In S. W. Duck & R. Gilmour (Eds.), *Personal relationships: vol. 2. Developing personal relationships* (pp. 27–51). New York: Academic Press.

Goodwin, R., & Findlay, C. (1997). "We were just fated together"…Chinese love and the concept of yuan in England and Hong Kong. *Personal Relationships, 4*, 85–92.

Gray, J. (1992). *Men are from Mars and women are from Venus: A practical guide for improving communication and getting what you want in your relationship*. New York: HarperCollins.

Hendrick, C., & Hendrick, S. S. (1986). A theory and method of love. *Journal of Personality and Social Psychology, 50*, 392–402.

Hendrick, S. S., & Hendrick, C. (1992). *Romantic love.* Newbury Park, CA: Sage.

———. (1995). Gender differences and similarities in sex and love. *Personal Relationships, 2,* 55–65.

———. (2000). Romantic love. In C. Hendrick & S. S. Hendrick (Eds.), *Close relationships: A sourcebook* (pp. 203–215). Thousand Oaks, CA: Sage.

Hendrick, C., Hendrick, S. S., & Dicke, A. (1998). The Love Attitudes Scale: Short form. *Journal of Social and Personal Relationships, 15,* 147–159.

Kephart, W. (1967). Some correlates of romantic love. *Journal of Marriage and the Family, 29,* 470–479.

Knee, C. R. (1998). Implicit theories of relationships: Assessment and prediction of romantic relationship initiation, coping, and longevity. *Journal of Personality and Social Psychology, 74,* 360–370.

Knox, D. H., & Sporakowski, J. J. (1968). Attitudes of college students toward love. *Journal of Marriage and the Family, 30,* 638–642.

Lee, J. A. (1973). *Colors of love: An exploration of the ways of loving.* Don Mills, ON: New Press. (Popular edition, 1976)

Levine, R., Sato, S., Hashimoto, T., & Verma, J. (1995). Love and marriage in eleven cultures. *Journal of Cross-Cultural Psychology, 26,* 554–571.

Li, X. (1998). Fashioning the body in post-Mao China. In A. Brydon & S. Niessen (Eds.), *Consuming fashion: Adorning the transnational body* (pp. 71–89). New York: Berg.

Murstein, B. I., Merighi, J., & Vyse, S. A. (1991). Love styles in the United States and France: A cross-cultural comparison. *Journal of Social and Clinical Psychology, 10,* 37–46.

Simmons, C. H., Vomkolke, A., & Shimizu, H. (1986). Attitudes toward romantic love among American, German, and Japanese students. *Journal of Social Psychology, 55,* 29–46.

Simpson, J. A., Campbell, B., & Berscheid, E. (1986). The association between romantic love and marriage: Kephart (1967) twice revisited. *Personality and Social Psychology Bulletin, 12,* 363–372.

Sprecher, S., Aron, A., Hatfield, E., Cortese, A., Potapova, E., & Levitskaya, A. (1994). Love: American style, Russian style, and Japanese style. *Personal Relationships, 1,* 349–369.

Sprecher, S., & Metts, S. (1989). Development of the "Romantic Beliefs Scale" and examination of the effects of gender and gender-role orientation. *Journal of Social and Personal Relationships, 6,* 387–411.

———. (1999). Romantic beliefs: Their influence on relationships and patterns of change over time. *Journal of Social and Personal Relationships, 16,* 834–851.

Sprecher, S., & Regan, P. (1998). Passionate and companionate love in courting and young married couples. *Sociological Inquiry, 68,* 163–185.

Tannen, D. (1990). *You just don't understand: Men and women in conversation.* New York: Random House.

Winstead, B. A., Derlega, V. J., & Rose, S. (1997). *Gender and close relationships.* Thousand Oaks, CA: Sage.

Xiaohe, X., & Whyte, M. K. (1990). Love matches and arranged marriages: A Chinese replication. *Journal of Marriage and the Family, 52,* 709–722.

Hooking Up and Forming Romantic Relationships on Today's College Campuses

PAULA ENGLAND, EMILY FITZGIBBONS SHAFER, AND ALISON C. K. FOGARTY

The "sexual revolution" of the 1960s and 1970s marked a sea change in public attitudes toward sexuality. Prior to this, premarital sex had been taboo. The norm was often broken, but most women who had sex before marriage did so only with the man they were going to marry. Women who had nonmarital sex were so stigmatized that the discovery of a premarital pregnancy was seen as a crisis that often led to a "shotgun" marriage. The sexual revolution rendered premarital sex acceptable, at least in a relationship. Not all groups accepted the new norm, but its mainstream acceptance can be seen by how common cohabitation before marriage became; by the early 1990s, well over half of marriages were preceded by cohabitation (Bumpass and Lu 2000).

The pre-1970s sexual norms went together with a particular gender system. Women's virginity was seen as more important than men's, men were seen as the leaders in politics and the economy, and men were supposed to be the initiators in dating, proposals of marriage, and sexuality. Women's primary adult role was that of wife and mother, and men's primary role *in* the family was accomplished precisely by his role *outside* the family as a breadwinner. Men were seen as the heads of their family.

The "gender revolution" shook some of this up, with the most important change being the increase in women's employment and career orientation. In 1960, 41% of American women between 25 and 54 years of age were in the labor force, but this figure had climbed to 74% by 2000. Today, more women than men are graduating from college, and while college majors are still substantially segregated by sex, more women than previously are entering traditionally male fields in management and the professions (England and Li 2006).

In the aftermath of these two "revolutions," what do dating, sexuality, and relationships look like on today's college campuses? We report here on a study we undertook to answer this question. As undergraduate readers of this article know, casual dating is no longer as common as "hooking up" among college students. So our first goal is simply to clarify the definition and characteristics of the new social form, the "hook up." Our second goal is to probe how meanings and behavior in hook ups or relationships are structured by gender.

Our Study

We collected quantitative and qualitative data on college students. In this report, we limit ourselves to heterosexual students because we are interested in how gender structures their romantic and sexual relations. The quantitative data come from an online survey of over 4,000 undergraduate students at several universities who answered fixed-response questions suitable for statistical analysis. Questions covered their experiences of and attitudes toward hooking up, dating, and relationships. Participating universities include University of Arizona, Indiana University,

Stanford University, University of California at Santa Barbara, and State University of New York at Stony Brook.[1] Statistics presented later in this paper are from the data from the online survey.

The second part of our study makes use of qualitative data gathered from in-depth face-to-face discussions with students at Stanford, where the authors work. We conducted focus groups in large Sociology classes in 2004 and 2006.[2] In 2004, 270 undergraduates in a class taught by the first author interviewed one fellow undergraduate student (not in the class) about experiences with relationships, hooking up, and dating. Based on what we learned from the large number of 2004 face-to-face interviews, 25 more elaborate interviews were carried out by a trained team of undergraduate and graduate student interviewers during 2006, with a random sample of Stanford seniors as the target.[3] In all the qualitative interviews, interviewers worked from an interview guide delineating the topics to cover, and were trained to add probe questions so as to encourage respondents to tell relevant stories in their own words. All quotes below are from these two sets of interviews of Stanford undergraduates.

The Hook Up: A New Social Form

The hook up has replaced the casual date on college campuses today, students told us. The term "hook up" is ambiguous in definition. But, generally, students use it to refer to a situation where two people are hanging out or run into each other at an event (often a party), and they end up doing something sexual, usually after going to one person's room. In some cases the sexual behavior is intercourse, but not in the majority of cases. (Sexual behavior that doesn't include intercourse is not seen as "having sex," as students typically use the term.) A hook up carries no expectation that either party has an interest in moving toward a relationship, although in some cases such an interest is present either before or after the hook up. By their senior year, while 24% of respondents have never hooked up, on average they have had 6.9 hook ups (the median is 5), and 28% have had 10 or more. Hook ups often happen after a good bit of drinking. The median number of drinks

men had drunk the night of their last hook up was 6, whereas women had consumed 4.[4]

We asked respondents to the online survey to tell us about their most recent hook up, thinking that asking about a specific and fairly recent event would allow more accurate recall. While the most recent event may be atypical for any one respondent, with a large sample, as we have, what is typical should emerge from the statistics. Figure 11.1 shows what sexual activity occurred during respondents' most recent hook ups. The categories are arrayed so that a hook up is categorized by the behavior the couple engaged in that entailed going "farthest," as students generally see it. (For example, if a couple had oral sex and had intercourse, they would be categorized in the "intercourse" category.[5]) As Figure 11.1 shows, 31% made out and touched but didn't have any genital contact, 16% had some hand/genital contact, 15% had oral sex, and 38% had intercourse on their most recent hook up.[6]

While a hook up implies no commitment to hook up again, we found that it was not uncommon to hook up with the same person more than once, as Figure 11.2 shows. When students reported about their most recent hook up, we asked them how many previous times they had hooked up with this same person. About half of hook ups were the first time with this person. Only 11% were second hook ups, 8% were third, 6% were fourth, and so on, until we come to the last category for those who had hooked up 10 or more times with this person. Fully 16% of these hook ups involved someone the student had hooked up with 10 or more times. When students hook up regularly with the same person outside of a romantic relationship, it is sometimes called "friends with benefits," "fuck buddies," or, simply, "a regular hook up." Although we don't show the statistics here, when couples have hooked up more times, they are more likely to have intercourse on the hook up.

The hook up is clearly a product of the increased permissiveness that came with the sexual revolution. Its mainstream adoption among college students shows a change to norms that permit some amount of sexual behavior that is casual. The sexual behavior in hook ups is not seen to have

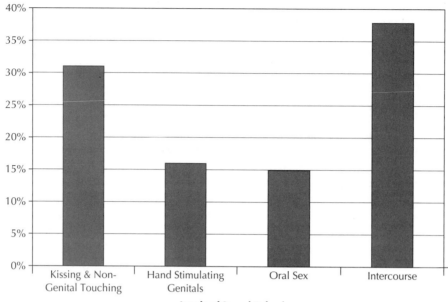

Figure 11.1. Percent of Hook Ups Involving Levels of Sexual Behavior.

Note: Categories to the right may also include behaviors in those to the left, but not vice versa. N = 2,904 undergraduates, reporting on their most recent hook up.

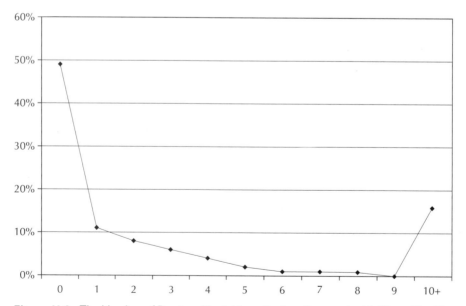

Figure 11.2. The Number of Previous Hook Ups a Student Reported with His or Her Most Recent Hook Up Partner.

Note: N = 2,510 undergraduates, reporting on their most recent hook up.

affection, an exclusive romantic relationship, or even an interest in such a relationship as a prerequisite. Although the idea that hooking up is acceptable is quite pervasive, students are divided on whether it is okay to have intercourse (which is what they mean when they talk about "having sex") on a casual hook up. Some see oral sex as the typical limit for casual hook ups, with intercourse signifying a pretty big step. As one male respondent put it, "She was very happy to hook up, but actually having sex was gonna really mean something to her." Another male said, "There are all these little lines…gradations, then there's a *big* line between oral sex and intercourse." Widespread acceptance of hooking up can coexist with a large minority of both men and women who disapprove of casual sex in part because the term "hook up," while always entailing some casual sexual behavior, is ambiguous enough that it does not necessarily entail "sex" in the sense of intercourse.

Gender and the Hook Up

Hook ups are "gendered" in three important ways. First, men initiate more of the interaction, especially the sexual action. Second, men have orgasms more frequently than women. Men's sexual pleasure seems to be prioritized. Third, a sexual double standard persists in which woman are more at risk than men of getting a bad reputation for hooking up with multiple partners.

Initiation

Most hook ups start at parties or hanging out in (often coed) dorms. To get things started, one of the two partners has to initiate talking or dancing. Our survey asked who did this: him, her, or both equally. In about half the cases, initiation of talking or dancing was deemed equal. But where one of the two was reported to have initiated talking or dancing it was more likely the man. When we asked who initiated the sexual interaction, things were much more gendered. Less than a third thought both had initiated equally, and a preponderance of cases were seen as initiated by men.[7] Hook ups were almost twice as likely to happen in the man's room as the woman's.[8] This suggests that men have initiated the move from the party

or public area of the dorm into the room in order to facilitate sexual activity.[9] These patterns of male initiation may mean that men are more eager for hook ups than women. Or they might mean that both men and women feel accountable to norms of how gender is to be displayed that dictate male, not female, initiation.[10] In the "old days," men asked women on dates and initiated most sexual behavior. One might have thought that the gender revolution would de-gender scripts of initiation on dates or in sexual behavior. But this transformation hasn't happened; initiation is nowhere near equal.

The Orgasm Gap

Since hook ups are defined by some sexual activity occurring, with no necessary implication of any future, we might expect people to judge them by the sexual pleasure they provide. Orgasm is one good barometer of sexual pleasure (although we recognize that sexual behavior can be pleasurable without orgasm). Our survey asked students whether they had an orgasm on the most recent hook up and whether they thought their partner did. Figure 11.3 shows men's and women's reports of their own orgasm on their most recent hook up, depending on what sexual behavior occurred. (Here we omit hook ups that involved no more than kissing and nongenital touching, since virtually none of them led to orgasm.) What is notable is how much more often men have orgasms on hook ups than women. When men received oral sex and did not engage in intercourse, they had an orgasm 57% of the time, but women only experienced orgasm a quarter of the time they received oral sex and did not engage in intercourse. Men who engaged in intercourse but who did not receive oral sex had an orgasm 70%; however, intercourse without receiving oral sex led to orgasm for women only 34% of the time. Even when women received oral sex *and* had intercourse, they had orgasms just under half the time on these hook ups, while men had orgasms about 85% of the time in this situation.

Of all hook ups (regardless of what sexual activity took place) 44% of men experienced an orgasm while only 19% of women did. One

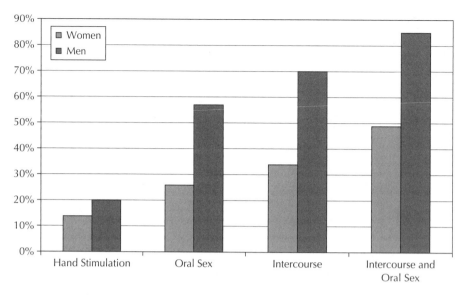

Figure 11.3. Men's and Women's Report of Whether They Had an Orgasm in Hook Ups Involving Various Sexual Behaviors.

Note: Statistics include only men's report of men's orgasm and women's report of women's orgasm. Women's orgasm for hook ups involving oral sex include only those where she received oral sex, whether he did or not. Men's orgasm for hook ups involving oral sex include only those where he received oral sex, whether she did or not. Hand stimulation (of genitals) was treated analogously. Each category excludes any case where the couple also engaged in behaviors in the categories to the right. N = 2,693 undergraduates, reporting on their most recent hook up.

factor contributing to this overall orgasm gap is that couples are more likely to engage in behavior that prioritizes male pleasure and orgasm. One key example of this is nonreciprocal oral sex. Figure 11.4 shows that in hook ups where there was some oral sex but no intercourse, the oral sex was reciprocal less than 40% of the time. In 45% of the cases, men were the only ones to receive oral sex, whereas it was only 16% of the cases where only women received it. Thus, when oral sex is not reciprocal, men are on the receiving end three times as often as women. Even when men do give women oral sex, they are either unable to or do not make it a priority to bring the woman to orgasm (refer back to Figure 11.3).

Moreover, men often believe their partner had an orgasm when she really didn't, if we believe that each sex accurately reports their own orgasm. Figure 11.5 compares women's and men's reports of the *woman's* orgasm on the most recent hook up.

It shows, for example, that when women receive cunnilingus, they report an orgasm about a quarter of the time, but men who performed cunnilingus on their partners report the woman to have had an orgasm almost 60% of the time—a huge disparity. A large disparity exists between men and women's reports of women's orgasm from intercourse as well. For example, when the couple had intercourse (but the women did not receive oral sex), women reported orgasm 34% of the time, but 58% of men reported the woman to have had an orgasm in this situation. Although the figure doesn't show these statistics, women's reports of men's orgasms lines up quite well with men's own reports. Of course, male orgasm, usually accompanied with ejaculation, is fairly easy to identify.

Why are men so misinformed about their female partner's orgasms on hook ups? Being drunk and lack of communication may contribute to misperception. Another factor is that women

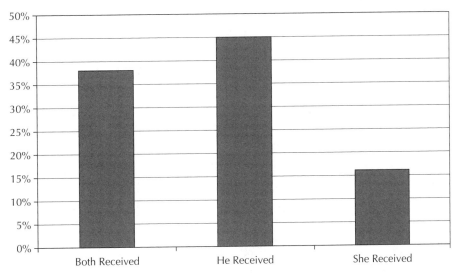

Figure 11.4. Who Received Oral Sex in Hook Ups Where Oral Sex Occurred But Intercourse Did Not.

Note: N = 443 undergraduates, all of whom engaged in some form of oral sex (giving or receiving) in their most recent hook up but did not engage in intercourse. "He received" means that only he received oral sex; "she received" means that only she received oral sex.

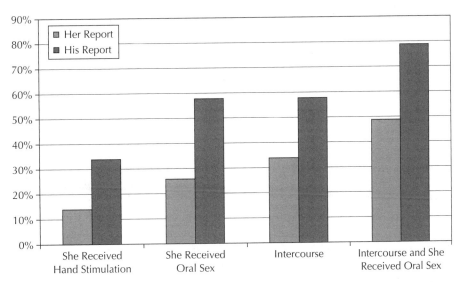

Figure 11.5. Men's and Women's Perceptions of the *Woman's* Orgasm in Hook Ups Involving Various Sexual Behaviors.

Note: All categories to the right of "She Received Hand Stimulation" may also include her receiving hand stimulation. Oral sex and intercourse, however, occur only in each category as labeled. Statistics for hook ups involving oral sex or hand stimulation for her (she received) include such cases whether or not these occurrences entailed oral sex or hand stimulation for him. N = 2,630 undergraduates, reporting on their most recent hook up.

sometimes fake orgasms. One woman reported doing this "to make that person feel good, to make them feel like they've done their job." She also said that sometimes it was "just really to end it," continuing, "a lot of people say they've faked it just because they're like bored with it."

Despite the orgasm gap, if we ask students how much they enjoyed the hook up overall, and how much they enjoyed the sexual part of it, men and women give very similar and largely positive responses. Women's lesser rate of orgasm doesn't translate into lower reported satisfaction on average. Perhaps women are evaluating hook ups on a standard of what seems possible to them in their social world. Social psychologists often find that groups that recurrently have lower rewards (for example, pay from jobs) focus on within-group rather than between-group comparisons, which leads them to develop a lesser sense of entitlement. Expecting less, they tend not to be disappointed when they get less (Major 1987).

But not all women accept nonreciprocal oral sex and the orgasm gap as "natural." Some try to assert their wants and are critical of men's lack of concern for their orgasm. One woman said, "When I...meet somebody and I'm gonna have a random hook up...from what I have seen, they're not even trying to, you know, make a mutual thing." She went on to say that in cases like this, she doesn't even bother to fake orgasm. Referring to nonreciprocal oral sex, another complained, "He did that thing where...they put their hand on the top of your head...and I hate that!...Especially 'cause there was no effort made to, like, return that favor." One woman who is assertive about her sexual wants said, "(I)n my first relationship...it was very one way... and that just didn't do much for me in terms of making me feel good about myself... so... I hate it when a guy is like take your head and try and push it down, because I then just switch it around to make them go down first usually. And some guys say no and then I just say no if they say no."

Some men conceded that if they see a hook up as a one time thing, they aren't concerned about women's orgasm. One said, "I mean like if you're just like hooking up with someone, I guess it's

more of a selfish thing...." Another said, "If it's just a random hook up.... Say, they meet a girl at a party and it's a one night thing, I don't think it's gonna matter to them as much." Other men said they tried but were often unsure what worked and whether the woman had had an orgasm.

The Sexual Double Standard

Decades ago, the double standard took the form of an expectation of virginity before marriage for women but not men. One might have thought that the emphasis on equal opportunity of the gender revolution would have killed the double standard. While the expectation that women be virgins before marriage is now a thing of the past in most social groups,[11] women are still held to a stricter standard than men when it comes to sex. But today, the difference is in how men versus women who hook up a lot are viewed. In focus groups, students told us that women who hook up with too many people, or have casual sex readily, are called "sluts" by both men and women. While some men who hook up a lot are called "man whores," such men also encounter accolades from other men for "scoring" more. Women are held to a stricter standard, but it is fairly vague exactly what that standard is.

As an illustration of the double standard, Figure 11.6 shows that when students in our online survey were asked if they had ever respected someone less because that person hooked up with the respondent, 34% of men but only 22% of women answered yes. When asked if they ever hooked up with someone who they think respected them less because of the hook up, 55% of women but only 21% of men said yes. Thus, men disrespect their partners for hooking up with them more than women do, and women seem to know this (and even exaggerate it).[12]

One male respondent illustrates the double standard when he says "I definitely see some girls out there just wanting to hook up.... Sometimes they're called 'slutty'...I guess it's...less stigmatic for a guy to go out and be, like, 'I'm gonna go get some ass' than for a girl..." He dissociates himself from the double standard but attributes it to his friends when he says, "I mean not myself—... women are sexual creatures too; they can do what they want.

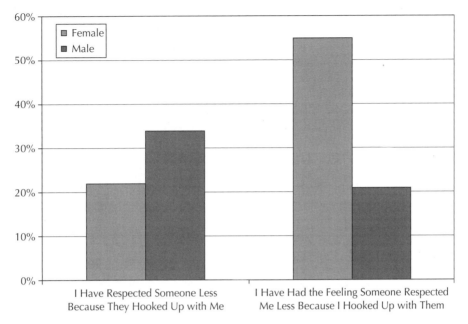

Figure 11.6. Percentage of Students Who, After a Hook Up, Have Ever Respected Someone Less or Felt a Partner Respected Them Less, by Gender.

Note: N = 2,931 and 2,928 undergraduates, respectively.

But…they…see this girl and go… there's no way I can date her, but… she's hot for a hook up." Indeed, in focus groups students said that men would sometimes decide that a woman was relationship material because she wouldn't hook up with them the first time they were together. This presents women who want relationships with a real dilemma: the main path into relationships today is through hook ups, but through hooking up they also risk men's thinking that they aren't relationship material.

Gender, Dating, and Exclusive Relationships

By their senior year, 71% of students report that they've been in a relationship that lasted at least six months while in college. Hook ups have not replaced relationships, but they have altered the pathway into relationships and may have largely replaced casual dating. One woman bemoaned this, saying, "(S)ometimes I wish that this environment here were…more conducive to just like

casual dating, because…it's difficult to go on actual dates without…already being in a relationship…." A male student said, "So there's no such thing as causally going out to…gauge the other person….I mean you can hang out….But we're only dating once we've decided we like each other…and want to be in a relationship."

Thirty to forty years ago a common college pattern involved casually dating a number of people. Dating did not necessarily imply an interest in a relationship with the person. But sometimes a succession of dates led to a relationship simultaneous with a progression of sexual activity.[13] Today, college students generally use the term "dating" to refer to a couple who has already decided they are in an exclusive relationship. (This is also called "going out," or being "official" or "exclusive.") "Dating" is different than going on a "date." Dates may be between people who are not already in a relationship. While less common than decades back, dates are sometimes present in the sequence leading to relationships.

Indeed, because casual dating has become less common, dates may be more indicative of relational intent today than decades ago. Among respondents in our online survey, by their senior year, students had been on an average of 4.4 dates (the median is 3).[14] This is less than the number of times seniors had hooked up (a mean of 6.9 and median of 5), but shows that dates are not completely dead. What has changed is the typical sequence. Dates often come after a hook up, and thus after some sexual behavior. They often have the function of expressing an interest in a possible relationship. When reporting on those with just the person with whom they had their most recent relationship of at least six months, 4% had at least one hook up but no dates, 26% had at least one date but no hook ups, while the majority, 67%, had at least one of each before it became a relationship. In cases where there were both dates and hook ups, our qualitative data suggest that the hook ups usually came first.

Many hook ups never lead to either another hook up or a relationship, and some lead only to more hook ups with the same person. But, as we've just seen, some lead to a relationship ("dating") via the pathway of one or more dates. Who initiates these dates? The gender revolution seems to have changed attitudes but not behavior in this area. When asked about their attitudes, students approve heartily of women asking men on dates (well over 90% of both men and women agreed that it is okay). Yet it rarely happens; as Figure 11.7 shows, asked about their most recent date with someone with whom they weren't already in a relationship, 87% claimed that the man had asked the woman out on this date. Focus groups suggested that asking a woman on a date is a way that men signal their interest in a possible relationship.

Who pays on these dates? Asked about their most recent date with someone with whom they were not already in a relationship, two-thirds said the man paid, and less than 5% said the woman did. The remainder was evenly split between reporting that no money was spent and that they split the cost. Indeed, in qualitative interviews, when women report some event that might have been considered a date or not, they sometimes use

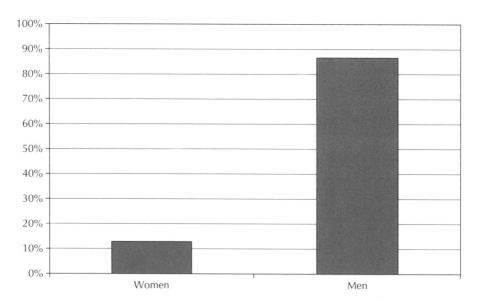

Figure 11.7. Who Asked Whom Out on Student's Most Recent Date.

Note: N = 2,870 undergraduates, reporting on their most recent date with someone with whom they were not already in an exclusive relationship.

the fact that he paid as evidence that it was a real date. One woman described such a situation this way: "It also kind of threw me that he like insisted on paying because I didn't really think of it as like a date.... I thought we were just hanging out.... I think I sort of knew that maybe he was thinking it was a date, but I definitely offered to pay for my meal... And he was like, 'No, no, no.' "

Relationships are often made "official" or exclusive via "the talk"—where one of the two people seek to define the relationship more clearly. This may happen after a few hook ups followed by hanging out or some dates. Some students call this a "DTR" or "define the relationship" talk. Others just call it "the talk." In the old days, it would be the man who would ask a woman to "go steady" or "be pinned" or who would propose marriage. We sought to ascertain who initiates the talk to define things as a relationship on today's campuses. In focus groups and in-depth interviews, the consensus was that these talks are more often initiated by the woman who wants to know where she stands with the guy after several hook ups. As one female interviewee said, "I feel like it's... the stereotypical girl thing to do, like... the guy feels like the girl is boxing him into a relationship." To confirm this statistically, we asked students in the survey how it became "clear that this person was your boy/girlfriend." About half of men and women say that the man initiated it, while about a fifth say that the woman did. Most of the rest say they "just knew." Thus, at least in the cases where a relationship ensued, it was typically not the woman initiating the talk. Of course, this is not inconsistent with the possibility that women initiate more talks overall, but get shut down by men who don't want relationships. To find out about those DTRs that didn't lead to relationships, we also asked how many times the student ever initiated a talk to try to define a relationship as exclusive but had the partner respond that s/he didn't want a relationship. The distribution of male and female responses was very similar, with "never" the most frequent category. This suggests that, counter to the stereotype students themselves seem to have, women do *not* initiate such talks more than men. At this point in our research, we aren't sure what to make of this

discrepancy between the generalizations students make in focus groups, and what they report about their own experiences in the survey.

Whether or not women initiate more talks to define relationships, the larger question is whether women are more interested in relationships than men. Our attitudinal data suggest that they are, while men express a more recreational view of sex, although the two sexes overlap substantially. As Figure 11.8 shows, asked if they had been interested in a relationship with the person they hooked up with *before* the hook up, 47% of women but only 35% of men said they had at least some interest. Asked about their feelings of interest in a relationship right after the hook up, almost half the women but only 36% of the men had at least some interest in a relationship with this person. We think this indicates more interest in relationships among women. But there are other possible interpretations. It is possible that women's responses are different than men's because social pressures lead the two genders in the opposite direction of reporting bias. That is, women may feel they are supposed to limit hook ups to those in whom they have a relational interest, while men feel they are supposed to be ready for sex all the time. Alternatively, women may want relationships not because they like them more, but because they believe more strongly that sex should be relational, or because they know they will be judged more harshly than men for nonrelational sex. Indeed, given the statement, "I would not have sex with someone unless I was in love with them," 49% of women agreed but only 34% of men.[15]

One advantage of relationships for women is that most women have a better chance of orgasm when having sex with a regular partner. In our survey, we asked those in a relationship about the last time they did something sexual with their partner, so we could compare what happens in those situations to what happens on first-time hook ups. Figure 11.9 shows that women are much more likely to orgasm with a regular relationship partner than when hooking up with someone for the first time. ("For the first time" here refers to the first time with this partner.) First-time hook ups in which women received oral sex but did not

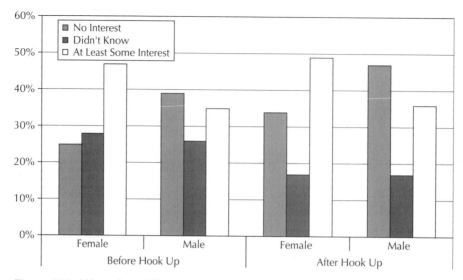

Figure 11.8. Women's and Men's Interest in a Relationship with This Partner Before and After Their Most Recent Hook Up.

Note: N = 2,144 and 2,903 undergraduates, respectively, reporting on their interest before and after their most recent hook up.

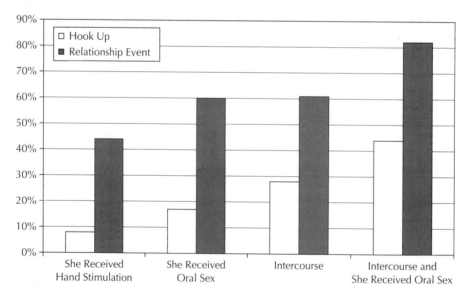

Figure 11.9. Women's Report of Own Orgasm in Last Hook Up That Was a First Hook Up with a Particular Partner and Last Relationship Sexual Event.

Note: N = 1,865 and N = 1,276 female undergraduates, respectively, reporting (white bar) on their sexual behavior and orgasm on their most recent hook up (only includes those that were first-time hook ups with that partner) and reporting (gray bar) on their sexual behavior and orgasm the last time they did anything sexual with a person with whom they had been in a relationship for at least six months.

have intercourse led to orgasm for women only 17% of the time, but, within a relationship, oral sex without intercourse led to orgasm 60% of the time. When couples had intercourse, women had orgasm about 28% of the time in first-time hook ups but over 60% of the time in relationships. Although we don't show these statistics in the figure, the analogous percents for men are 52% and 89%; so relationships are also better for men than first-time hook ups with a given partner, although the gain is not quite as great as for women.

If the higher rates of orgasm in a relationship come mainly from communication and "practice" with this particular partner, then we might expect this advantage to be present in "friends with benefits" or "regular hook up" situations as well, even where there is not a professed romantic relationship. We don't show statistics on this in the figure, but there is evidence of this. Where couples had intercourse, women's orgasm rates were 28% in first-time hook ups and 60% in a relationship as shown in Figure 11.9; in hook ups where they had previously hooked up at least ten times with this person, women's rate was 54%, not quite as good as the 60% in relationships but much better than in first-time hook ups. Perhaps the genuine caring in relationships explains their added advantage for orgasms.[16] Of course, relationships may have disadvantages as well as advantages. Both men and women lose autonomy while gaining intimacy, and women may be expected to redefine themselves more than men.[17]

Talking about why she has orgasm more easily in a relationship, one woman said, "I'm more comfortable with the person." The same male student we quoted above about men not caring about the woman's orgasm in one-time hook ups said this: "If you're with somebody for . . . more than just that one night, I think . . . it is important for guys. . . . And I think if you're in a long-term relationship, like I know I feel personally responsible."

Two Partial Revolutions and Today's College Scene

What is happening on college campuses today reflects the two large-scale social changes that some have dubbed revolutions: the sexual revolution and the gender revolution. But it simultaneously reveals many aspects of the gender system left relatively untouched by these revolutions. The sexual revolution was pushed along by the availability of the birth control pill starting in the 1960s, and by the legalization of abortion with a Supreme Court decision in 1973. Both made it more possible to have sex without fear of having an unwanted birth. Unquestionably, norms about premarital sex have become more permissive, and the new social form of the hook up is one result. We have shown that hooking up is now quite mainstream among college students, however vague the norms surrounding it are.

The gender revolution also contributed to sexual permissiveness. As more women decided to train for careers, this pushed up age at marriage, which made sex before marriage more likely. More directly, the feminist idea that women should be free to pursue careers—even in traditionally male fields—may have spilled over into the idea that women as well as men had a right to sexual freedom. Clearly women have won the right to be nonvirgins at marriage in most social groups. But beyond this gain, what is striking to us is how little gender revolution we see in sexual and romantic affairs. The double standard has not changed to a single "equal opportunity" standard for men and women. Rather, the standard, vague though it is, has shifted to a less restrictive line for each sex but remained dual; women who hook up a lot or have sex too easily are more at risk of a bad reputation than are men. One might have thought that the gender revolution would lead to women asking men out on dates. Instead, the casual date not preceded by a hook up has almost died. In both hook ups and the dates that sometimes come after them, men are initiating much of the action. The gender initiating the action seems to be getting more of the sexual rewards, particularly in hook ups, where women give men oral sex more than vice versa, and even when women receive oral sex or have intercourse, they have orgasms much less often than men. Equal opportunity for women appears to have gone farther in the educational and career world than in the college sexual scene.

Notes

1. In almost all cases, respondents were recruited through classes. The numbers of respondents at the universities were: U. Arizona 309, Indiana U. 1,616, Stanford U. 925, U. California Santa Barbara 745, and SUNY-Stony Brook 628. We also collected a small number of responses from students at the Evergreen State College in Olympia, Washington (27) and Ithaca College (69). These are included in the results reported here. Overall, we had 2,779 women and 1,550 men, a total of 4,329 respondents. Our sample is not a probability sample from any of the participating colleges, so cannot be said to be strictly representative of college students at these institutions.

2. What we learned in the focus groups informs our discussion. We took notes in these groups, but did not record them. Therefore, we use no direct quotes from these sessions.

3. We started from a random sample of 118 seniors provided by the Registrar. Data collection is ongoing, but this preliminary analysis uses the 25 interviews that have been conducted and transcribed to date. Given the low response rate so far, and the fact that the other larger group of 270 interviews conducted in 2004 obtained respondents through a convenience sample (students chose an acquaintance to interview), the qualitative data should not be considered representative. The data should, however, reveal most of the range of behaviors and meanings present in the undergraduate culture.

4. The mean number of drinks on the most recent hook up was 6.7 for men and 3.9 for women. Extreme outliers affect means more than medians.

5. Classifying hand stimulation of genitals as "going less far" than oral sex is somewhat arbitrary, but we did so because we believe students see oral sex as "going farther," and also because the data show that, as practiced by college students, hand stimulation of genitals leads to orgasm less often than oral sex. Our rankings imply no value judgment about which practices are better; we are trying to rank order practices as students see them in terms of which are seen as "going farther."

6. There were a few cases where the couple had anal sex but not vaginal intercourse; we classified these as intercourse. While about a quarter of women say they have ever had anal sex, a very small percent engage in this on any one occasion, which is why we did not include the practice in our classification.

7. While both men and women are more apt to report male than female initiation, the disparity is actually much greater in women's reports. This suggests that some events that women see as male initiation are seen by men as female initiation, or that women are more reluctant to report initiating because it is more stigmatized for them.

8. Twenty-four percent of men reported hooking up in the woman's room, while 44% said it was in their own room. Similarly, 25% of women said it was in their own room, while 42% said it was in the guy's room. The remainder of cases were in some other room.

9. Students also told us that male roommates are more accepting of hook ups occurring in the room, and even feel under pressure to help their roommates "score" by allowing them to use the room. In all-male focus group discussions, men were candid about the challenge of coming up with a pretext for getting the young woman to his room. Sometimes suggesting that they watch a movie on a DVD serves this function.

10. For a discussion of the theoretical perspective called "doing gender" that posits such gender display, see West and Fenstermaker 1993. The idea is that people are accountable to norms and conform their behavior to them even if they have not deeply internalized the belief that this is how it should be.

11. This standard is still emphasized among Mexican immigrants to the U.S., according to Gonzáléz-López (2005). Although most of the women she interviewed were not virgins when they married, the norm was that women should be, while men were expected to have their first sexual experience with a sex worker. Since the 1980s, fundamentalist Christian groups have encouraged youth to take a pledge to remain virgins till marriage, as discussed by Bearman and Brückner (2001). While endorsing many other forms of gender differentiation and male leadership, fundamentalist Christians generally encourage a single standard of virginity before marriage for both men and women.

12. Responses to another question showed a fascinating pattern in which each sex appears to have a double standard favoring their own sex, but men having a much harsher double standard against women than women have against men. Our survey asked students if they agree or disagree with

the statement: "If women hook up or have sex with lots of people, I respect them less." They were given the same item about men. While 58% of female respondents agreed that they respected women less if they hook up or have sex with lots of people, they agreed by a somewhat wider margin (69%) that they respect men less who do this. Among men, however, only 41% agreed when asked about men but 67% agreed concerning women. Despite women's answer on the survey suggesting that they hold men a more exacting standard than women, focus groups said that women talk a lot amongst themselves about whether other women are "slutty."

13. For a history of courtship and dating in America, see Bailey 1988.

14. This excludes fraternity or sorority events, which some students don't view as "real dates." Including those, the mean number of dates is 6 and the median is 4.

15. This is consistent with national survey data on adults that shows a higher percent of men than women to have a "recreational" (as opposed to "relational") orientation to sex (Michael et al. 1995).

16. Where couples had intercourse (but he didn't receive oral sex), male orgasm rates were also higher in hook ups with partners with whom they had hooked up at least ten times than in first-time hook ups with this partner (83% versus 52%), but even higher in relationships (89%).

17. Writing about the late 1980s, Holland and Eisenhart (1990) argue that the culture elevating "romance" seduces college women into relationships that pull them away from solidarity with other women, seriousness about their education, and career plans. Hamilton and Armstrong's (2007) more recent interviews of college women at a large state university show that many of them give up time with friends when they are in relationships. They also find working class women particularly likely to drop out of the university because of boyfriends back home. Other authors, such as Glenn and Marquardt (2001), argue that the college hook up culture is bad for women because it discourages relationships and the movement toward marriage, things that many of their female respondents said they wanted.

References

Bailey, Beth. 1988. *From Front Porch to Back Seat: Courtship in Twentieth-Century America.* Baltimore: Johns Hopkins University Press.

Bearman, Peter S. and Hannah Brückner. 2001. "Promising the Future: Virginity Pledges and First Intercourse." *American Journal of Sociology* 106(4): 859–912.

Bumpass, Larry and Hsien-Hen Lu. 2000. "Trends in Cohabitation and Implications for Children's Family Contexts in the United States." *Population Studies* 54:2941.

England, Paula and Su Li. 2006. "Desegregation Stalled: The Changing Gender Composition of College Majors, 1971–2002." *Gender & Society* 20:657–677.

Glenn, Norval and Elizabeth Marquardt. 2001. *Hooking Up, Hanging Out, and Hoping for Mr. Right: College Women on Dating and Mating Today.* New York: Institute for American Values.

Gonzáléz-López, Gloria. 2005. *Erotic Journeys: Mexican Immigrants and Their Sex Lives.* Berkeley: University of California Press.

Hamilton, Laura and Elizabeth A. Armstrong. 2007. "Public Conformity, Private Rebellion: How Young Women Navigate Contemporary Sexual Dilemmas." Unpublished paper, Department of Sociology, Indiana University.

Holland, Dorothy C. and Margaret A. Eisenhart. 1990. *Educated in Romance: Women, Achievement, and College Culture.* Chicago: University of Chicago Press.

Major, Brenda. 1987. "Gender, Justice, and the Psychology of Entitlement." *Review of Personality and Social Psychology* 7:124–148, ed. P. Shaver and C. Hendricks. Newbury Park, CA: Sage.

Michael, Robert T., John H. Gagnon, Edward O. Laumann, and Gina Kolata. 1995. *Sex in America: A Definitive Survey.* New York: Little, Brown.

West, Candace and Sarah Fenstermaker. 1993. "Power, Inequality, and the Accomplishment of Gender: An Ethnomethodological View." Pp. 151–174 in *Theory on Gender/Feminism on Theory*, ed. Paula England. New York: Aldine de Gruyter.

Sexual Harassment and Masculinity: The Power and Meaning of "Girl Watching"

BETH A. QUINN

Confronted with complaints about sexual harassment or accounts in the media, some men claim that women are too sensitive or that they too often misinterpret men's intentions (Bernstein 1994; Buckwald 1993). In contrast, some women note with frustration that men just "don't get it" and lament the seeming inadequacy of sexual harassment policies (Conley 1991; Guccione 1992). Indeed, this ambiguity in defining acts of sexual harassment might be, as Cleveland and Kerst (1993) suggested, the most robust finding in sexual harassment research.

Using in-depth interviews with 43 employed men and women, this article examines a particular social practice—"girl watching"—as a means to understanding one way that these gender differences are produced. This analysis does not address the size or prevalence of these differences, nor does it present a direct comparison of men and women; this information is essential but well covered in the literature.[1] Instead, I follow Cleveland and Kerst's (1993) and Wood's (1998) suggestion that the question may best be unraveled by exploring how the "subject(ivities) of perpetrators, victims, and resistors of sexual harassment" are "discursively produced, reproduced, and altered" (Wood 1998, 28).

This article focuses on the subjectivities of the perpetrators of a disputable form of sexual harassment, "girl watching." The term refers to the act of men's sexually evaluating women, often in the company of other men. It may take the form of a verbal or gestural message of "check it out," boasts of sexual prowess, or explicit comments about a woman's body or imagined sexual acts. The target may be an individual woman or group of women or simply a photograph or other representation. The woman may be a stranger, coworker, supervisor, employee, or client. For the present analysis, girl watching within the workplace is centered.

The analysis is grounded in the work of masculinity scholars such as Connell (1987, 1995) in that it attempts to explain the subject positions of the interviewed men—not the abstract and genderless subjects of patriarchy but the gendered and privileged subjects embedded in this system. Since I am attempting to delineate the gendered worldviews of the interviewed men, I employ the term "girl watching," a phrase that reflects their language ("they watch girls").

I have chosen to center the analysis on girl watching within the workplace for two reasons. First, it appears to be fairly prevalent. For example, a survey of federal civil employees (U.S. Merit Systems Protection Board 1988) found that in the previous 24 months, 28 percent of the women surveyed had experienced "unwanted sexual looks or gestures," and 35 percent had experienced "unwanted sexual teasing, jokes, remarks, or questions." Second, girl watching is still often normalized and trivialized as only play, or "boys will be boys." A man watching girls—even in his workplace—is frequently accepted as a natural and commonplace activity, especially if he is in the presence of other men.[2]

Beth A. Quinn, "Sexual Harassment and Masculinity: The Power and Meaning of 'Girl Watching'" from *Gender & Society* 16, no. 3 (June 2002): 386–402. Copyright © 2002 by Sociologists for Women in Society. Reprinted with the permission of Sage Publications, Inc.

Indeed, it may be required (Hearn 1985). Thus, girl watching sits on the blurry edge between fun and harm, joking and harassment. An understanding of the process of identifying behavior as sexual harassment, or of rejecting this label, may be built on this ambiguity.

Girl watching has various forms and functions, depending on the context and the men involved. For example, it may be used by men as a directed act of power against a particular woman or women. In this, girl watching—at least in the workplace—is most clearly identified as harassing by both men and women. I am most interested, however, in the form where it is characterized as only play. This type is more obliquely motivated and, as I will argue, functions as a game men play to build shared masculine identities and social relations.

Multiple and contradictory subject positions are also evidenced in girl watching, most notably that between the gazing man and the woman he watches. Drawing on Michael Schwalbe's (1992) analysis of empathy and the formation of masculine identities, I argue that girl watching is premised on the obfuscation of this multiplicity through the objectification of the woman watched and a suppression of empathy for her. In conclusion, the ways these elements operate to produce gender differences in interpreting sexual harassment and the implications for developing effective policies are discussed.

Previous Research

The question of how behavior is or is not labeled as sexual harassment has been studied primarily through experimental vignettes and surveys.[3] In both methods, participants evaluate either hypothetical scenarios or lists of behaviors, considering whether, for example, the behavior constitutes sexual harassment, which party is most at fault, and what consequences the act might engender. Researchers manipulate factors such as the level of "welcomeness" the target exhibits and the relationship of the actors (supervisor-employee, coworker-coworker).

Both methods consistently show that women are willing to define more acts as sexual harassment (Gutek, Morasch, and Cohen 1983; Padgitt and Padgitt 1986; Powell 1986; York 1989; but see Stockdale and Vaux 1993) and are more likely to see situations as coercive (Garcia, Milano, and Quijano 1989). When asked who is more to blame in a particular scenario, men are more likely to blame, and less likely to empathize with, the victim (Jensen and Gutek 1982; Kenig and Ryan 1986). In terms of actual behaviors like girl watching, the U.S. Merit Systems Protection Board (1988) survey found that 81 percent of the women surveyed considered "uninvited sexually suggestive looks or gestures" from a supervisor to be sexual harassment. While the majority of men (68 percent) also defined it as such, significantly more men were willing to dismiss such behavior. Similarly, while 40 percent of the men would not consider the same behavior from a coworker to be harassing, more than three-quarters of the women would.

The most common explanation offered for these differences is gender role socialization. This conclusion is supported by the consistent finding that the more men and women adhere to traditional gender roles, the more likely they are to deny the harm in sexual harassment and to consider the behavior acceptable or at least normal (Gutek and Koss 1993; Malovich and Stake 1990; Murrell and Dietz-Uhler 1993; Popovich et al. 1992; Pryor 1987; Tagri and Hayes 1997). Men who hold predatory ideas about sexuality, who are more likely to believe rape myths, and who are more likely to self-report that they would rape under certain circumstances are less likely to see behaviors as harassing (Murrell and Dietz-Uhler 1993; Pryor 1987; Reilly et al. 1992).

These findings do not, however, adequately address the between-group differences. The more one is socialized into traditional notions of sex roles, the more likely it is for both men and women to view the behaviors as acceptable or at least unchangeable. The processes by which gender roles operate to produce these differences remain underexamined.

Some theorists argue that men are more likely to discount the harassing aspects of their behavior because of a culturally conditioned tendency to misperceive women's intentions. For example,

Stockdale (1993, 96) argued that "patriarchal norms create a sexually aggressive belief system in some people more than others, and this belief system can lead to the propensity to misperceive." Gender differences in interpreting sexual harassment, then, may be the outcome of the acceptance of normative ideas about women's inscrutability and indirectness and men's role as sexual aggressors. Men see harmless flirtation or sexual interest rather than harassment because they misperceive women's intent and responses.

Stockdale's (1993) theory is promising but limited. First, while it may apply to actions such as repeatedly asking for dates and quid pro quo harassment,[4] it does not effectively explain motivations for more indirect actions, such as displaying pornography and girl watching. Second, it does not explain why some men are more likely to operate from these discourses of sexual aggression contributing to a propensity to misperceive.

Theoretical explanations that take into account the complexity and diversity of sexual harassing behaviors and their potentially multifaceted social etiologies are needed. An account of the processes by which these behaviors are produced and the active construction of their social meanings is necessary to unravel both between- and within-gender variations in behavior and interpretation. A fruitful framework from which to begin is an examination of masculine identities and the role of sexually harassing behaviors as a means to their production.

Method

I conducted 43 semistructured interviews with currently employed men and women between June 1994 and March 1995. Demographic characteristics of the participants are reported in Table 1. The interviews ranged in length from one to three hours. With one exception, interviews were audiotaped and transcribed in full.

Participants were contacted in two primary ways. Twenty-five participants were recruited from "Acme Electronics," a Southern California electronic design and manufacturing company. An additional 18 individuals were recruited from

an evening class at a community college and a university summer school class, both in Southern California. These participants referred 3 more individuals. In addition to the interviews, I conducted participant observation for approximately one month while on site at Acme. This involved observations of the public and common spaces of the company.

At Acme, a human resources administrator drew four independent samples (salaried and hourly women and men) from the company's approximately 300 employees. Letters of invitation were sent to 40 individuals, and from this group, 13 women and 12 men agreed to be interviewed.[5]

The strength of organizationally grounded sampling is that it allows us to provide context for individual accounts. However, in smaller organizations and where participants occupy unique positions, this method can compromise participant anonymity when published versions of the research are accessed by participants. Since this is the case with Acme, and since organizational context is not particularly salient for this analysis, the identity of the participant's organization is sometimes intentionally obscured.

The strength of the second method of recruitment is that it provides access to individuals employed in diverse organizations (from self-employment to multinational corporations) and in a range of occupations (e.g., nanny, house painter, accounting manager). Not surprisingly, drawing from college courses resulted in a group with similar educational backgrounds; all participants from this sample had some college, with 22 percent holding college degrees. Student samples and snowball sampling are not particularly robust in terms of generalizability. They are, nonetheless, regularly employed in qualitative studies (Chen 1999; Connell 1995) when the goal is theory development—as is the case here—rather than theory testing.

The interviews began with general questions about friendships and work relationships and progressed to specific questions about gender relations, sexual harassment, and the policies that seek to address it.[6] Since the main aim of the project was to explore how workplace events

Table 1. Participant Demographic Measures

Variable	Men		Women		Total	
	n	%	n	%	n	%
Student participants and referrals	6	33	12	67	18	42
Racial/ethnic minority	2	33	2	17	4	22
Mean age	27.2		35		32.5	
Married	3	50	3	25	6	33
Nontraditional job	1	17	4	33	5	28
Supervisor	0	0	6	50	6	33
Some college	6	100	12	100	18	100
Acme participants	12	48	13	52	25	58
Racial/ethnic minority	2	17	3	23	5	20
Mean age	42.3		34.6		38.6	
Married	9	75	7	54	16	64
Nontraditional job	0	0	4	31	4	16
Supervisor	3	25	2	15	5	20
Some college	9	75	9	69	18	72
All participants	18	42	25	58	43	100
Racial/ethnic minority	4	22	5	20	9	21
Mean age	37.8		34.9		36.2	
Married	12	67	10	40	22	51
Nontraditional job	1	6	8	32	9	21
Supervisor	3	17	8	32	11	26
Some college	15	83	21	84	36	84

are framed as sexual harassment (and as legally bounded or not), the term "sexual harassment" was not introduced by the interviewer until late in the interview.

While the question of the relationship between masculinity and sexual harassment was central, I did not come to the research looking expressly for girl watching. Rather, it surfaced as a theme across several men's interviews in the context of a gender reversal question:

> It's the end of an average day. You get ready for bed and fall to sleep. In what seems only a moment, the alarm goes off. As you awake, you find your body to be oddly out of sorts.... To your surprise, you find that you have been transformed into the "opposite sex." Even stranger, no one in your life seems to remember that you were ever any different.

Participants were asked to consider what it would be like to conduct their everyday work life in this transformed state. I was particularly interested in their estimation of the impact it would have on their interactions with coworkers and supervisors. Imagining themselves as the opposite sex, participants were forced to make explicit the operation of gender in their workplace, something they did not do in their initial discussions of a typical workday.

Interestingly, no man discussed girl watching in initial accounts of his workplace. I suspect that they did not consider it to be relevant to a discussion of their average *work* day, even though it became apparent that it was an integral daily activity for some groups of men. It emerged only when men were forced to consider themselves as explicitly gendered workers through the hypothetical question, something they were able initially to elide.[7]

Taking guidance from Glaser and Strauss's (1967) grounded theory and the methodological insights of Dorothy Smith (1990), transcripts were analyzed iteratively and inductively, with the goal of identifying the ideological tropes the speaker used to understand his or her identities, behaviors, and relationships. Theoretical concepts drawn from previous work on the etiology of sexual harassment (Bowman 1993; Cleveland and Kerst 1993), the construction of masculine identities (Connell 1995, 1987), and sociolegal theories of disputing and legal consciousness (Bumiller 1988; Conley and O'Barr 1998) guided the analysis.

Several related themes emerged and are discussed in the subsequent analysis. First, girl watching appears to function as a form of gendered play among men. This play is productive of masculine identities and premised on a studied lack of empathy with the feminine other. Second, men understand the targeted woman to be an object rather than a player in the game, and she is most often not the intended audience. This obfuscation of a woman's subjectivity, and men's refusal to consider the effects of their behavior, means men are likely to be confused when a woman complains. Thus, the production of masculinity through girl watching, and its compulsory disempathy, may be one factor in gender differences in the labeling of harassment.

Findings: Girl Watching as "Hommo-Sexuality"

[They] had a button on the computer that you pushed if there was a girl who came to the front counter....It was a code and it said "BAFC"—Babe at Front Counter....If the guy in the back looked up and saw a cute girl come in the station, he would hit this button for the other dispatcher to [come] see the cute girl.

—*Paula, police officer*

In its most serious form, girl watching operates as a targeted tactic of power. The men seem to want everyone—the targeted woman as well as coworkers, clients, and superiors—to know they

are looking. The gaze demonstrates their right, as men, to sexually evaluate women. Through the gaze, the targeted woman is reduced to a sexual object, contradicting her other identities, such as that of competent worker or leader. This employment of the discourse of asymmetrical heterosexuality (i.e., the double standard) may trump a woman's formal organizational power, claims to professionalism, and organizational discourses of rationality (Collinson and Collinson 1989; Gardner 1995; Yount 1991).[8] As research on rape has demonstrated (Estrich 1987), calling attention to a woman's gendered sexuality can function to exclude recognition of her competence, rationality, trustworthiness, and even humanity. In contrast, the overt recognition of a man's (hetero)sexuality is normally compatible with other aspects of his identity; indeed, it is often required (Connell 1995; Hearn 1985). Thus, the power of sexuality is asymmetrical, in part, because being seen as sexual has different consequences for women and men.

But when they ogle, gawk, whistle and point, are men always so directly motivated to disempower their women colleagues? Is the target of the gaze also the intended audience? Consider, for example, this account told by Ed, a white, 29-year-old instrument technician.

When a group of guys goes to a bar or a nightclub and they try to be manly....A few of us always found [it] funny [when] a woman would walk by and a guy would be like, "I can have her." [pause] "Yeah, OK, we want to see it!" [laugh]

In his account—a fairly common one in men's discussions—the passing woman is simply a visual cue for their play. It seems clear that it is a game played by men for men; the woman's participation and awareness of her role seem fairly unimportant.

As Thorne (1993) reminded us, we should not be too quick to dismiss games as "only play." In her study of gender relations in elementary schools, Thorne found play to be a powerful form of gendered social action. One of its "clusters of meaning" most relevant here is that of "dramatic performance." In this, play functions as both a source of fun and a mechanism by which gendered identities, group boundaries, and power relations are (re)produced.

The metaphor of play was strong in Karl's comments. Karl, a white man in his early thirties who worked in a technical support role in the Acme engineering department, hoped to earn a degree in engineering. His frustration with his slow progress—which he attributed to the burdens of marriage and fatherhood—was evident throughout the interview. Karl saw himself as an undeserved outsider in his department and he seemed to delight in telling on the engineers.

Girl watching came up as Karl considered the gender reversal question. Like many of the men I interviewed, his first reaction was to muse about premenstrual syndrome and clothes. When I inquired about the potential social effects of the transformation (by asking him, Would it "be easier dealing with the engineers or would it be harder?") he haltingly introduced the engineers' "game."

> KARL: Some of the engineers here are very [pause] they're not very, how shall we say? [pause] What's the way I want to put this? They're not very, uh [pause] what's the word? Um. It escapes me.
> RESEARCHER: Give me a hint?
> KARL: They watch women but they're not very careful about getting caught.
> RESEARCHER: Oh! Like they ogle?
> KARL: Ogle or gaze or [pause] stare even, or [pause] generate a commotion of an unusual nature.

His initial discomfort in discussing the issue (with me, I presume) is evident in his excruciatingly formal and hesitant language. The aspect of play, however, came through clearly when I pushed him to describe what generating a commotion looked like: "'Oh! There goes so-and-so. Come and take a look! She's wearing this great outfit today!' Just like a schoolboy. They'll rush out of their offices and [cranes his neck] and check things out." That this is as a form of play was evident in Karl's boisterous tone and in his reference to schoolboys. This is not a case of an aggressive sexual appraising of a woman coworker but a commotion created for the benefit of other men.

At Acme, several spatial factors facilitated this form of girl watching. First, the engineering department is designed as an open-plan office with partitions at shoulder height, offering a maze-like geography that encourages group play. As Karl explained, the partitions offer both the opportunity for sight and cover from being seen. Although its significance escaped me at the time, I was directly introduced to the spatial aspects of the engineers' game of girl watching during my first day on site at Acme. That day, John, the current human resources director, gave me a tour of the facilities, walking me through the departments and offering informal introductions. As we entered the design engineering section, a rhythm of heads emerged from its landscape of partitions, and movement started in our direction. I was definitely aware of being on display as several men gave me obvious once-overs.

Second, Acme's building features a grand stairway that connects the second floor—where the engineering department is located—with the lobby. The stairway is enclosed by glass walls, offering a bird's eye view to the main lobby and the movements of visitors and the receptionists (all women). Robert, a senior design engineer, specifically noted the importance of the glass walls in his discussion of the engineers' girl watching.

> There's glass walls around the upstairs right here by the lobby. So when there's an attractive young female…someone will see the girl in the area and they will go back and inform all the men in the area. "Go check it out." [laugh] So we'll walk over to the glass window, you know, and we'll see who's down there.

One day near the end of my stay at Acme, I was reminded of his story as I ventured into the first-floor reception area. Looking up, I saw Robert and another man standing at the top of the stairs watching and commenting on the women gathered around the receptionist's desk. When he saw me, Robert gave me a sheepish grin and disappeared from sight.

Producing Masculinity

I suggest that girl watching in this form functions simultaneously as a form of play and as a potentially powerful site of gendered social action. Its social significance lies in its power to form identities and relationships based on these common practices for, as Cockburn (1983, 123) has noted, "patriarchy is as much about relations between man and man as it is about relations between men and women." Girl watching works similarly to the sexual joking that Johnson (1988) suggested is a common way for heterosexual men to establish intimacy among themselves.

In particular, girl watching works as a dramatic performance played to other men, a means by which a certain type of masculinity is produced and heterosexual desire displayed. It is a means by which men assert a masculine identity to other men, in an ironic "hommo-sexual" practice of heterosexuality (Butler 1990).[9] As Connell (1995) and others (Butler 1990; West and Zimmerman 1987) have aptly noted, masculinity is not a static identity but rather one that must constantly be reclaimed. The content of any performance—and there are multiple forms—is influenced by a hegemonic notion of masculinity. When asked what "being a man" entailed, many of the men and women I interviewed triangulated toward notions of strength (if not in muscle, then in character and job performance), dominance, and a marked sexuality, overflowing and uncontrollable to some degree and natural to the male "species." Heterosexuality is required, for just as the label "girl" questions a man's claim to masculine power, so does the label "fag" (Hopkins 1992; Pronger 1992). I asked Karl, for example, if he would consider his sons "good men" if they were gay. His response was laced with ambivalence; he noted only that the question was "a tough one."

The practice of girl watching is just that—a practice—one rehearsed and performed in everyday settings. This aspect of rehearsal was evident in my interview with Mike, a self-employed house painter who used to work construction. In locating himself as a born-again Christian, Mike recounted the girl watching of his fellow construction workers with contempt. Mike was particularly disturbed by a man who brought his young son to the job site one day. The boy was explicitly taught to catcall, a practice that included identifying the proper targets: women and effeminate men.

Girl watching, however, can be somewhat tenuous as a masculine practice. In their acknowledgment (to other men) of their supposed desire lies the possibility that in being too interested in women the players will be seen as mere schoolboys giggling in the playground. Taken too far, the practice undermines rather than supports a masculine performance. In Karl's discussion of girl watching, for example, he continually came back to the problem of men's not being careful about getting caught. He referred to a particular group of men who, though "their wives are [pause] very attractive—very much so," still "gawk like schoolboys." Likewise, Stephan explained that men who are obvious, who "undress [women] with their eyes" probably do so "because they don't get enough women in their lives. Supposedly." A man must be interested in women, but not too interested; they must show their (hetero)sexual interest, but not overly so, for this would be to admit that women have power over them.

The Role of Objectification and (Dis)Empathy

As a performance of heterosexuality among men, the targeted woman is primarily an object onto which men's homosocial sexuality is projected. The presence of a woman in any form—embodied, pictorial, or as an image conjured from words—is required, but her subjectivity and active participation are not. To be sure, given the ways the discourse of asymmetrical sexuality works, men's actions may result in similarly negative effects on the targeted woman as that of a more direct form of sexualization. The crucial difference is that the men's understanding of their actions differs. This difference is one key to understanding the ambiguity around interpreting harassing behavior.

When asked about the engineers' practice of neck craning, Robert grinned, saying nothing at first. After some initial discussion, I started to ask him if he thought women were aware of their game ("Do you think that the women who are walking by...?"). He interrupted, misreading my question.

What resulted was a telling description of the core of the game:

> It depends. No. I don't know if they enjoy it. When I do it, if I do it, I'm not saying that I do. [big laugh]...If they do enjoy it, they don't say it. If they don't enjoy it—wait a minute, that didn't come out right. I don't know if they enjoy it or not [pause]; that's not the purpose of us popping our heads out.

Robert did not want to admit that women might not enjoy it ("that didn't come out right") but acknowledged that their feelings were irrelevant. Only subjects, not objects, take pleasure or are annoyed. If a woman did complain, Robert thought "the guys wouldn't know what to say." In her analysis of street harassment, Gardner (1995, 187) found a similar absence, in that "men's interpretations seldom mentioned a woman's reaction, either guessed at or observed."

The centrality of objectification was also apparent in comments made by José, a Hispanic man in his late 40s who worked in manufacturing. For José, the issue came up when he considered the topic of compliments. He initially claimed that women enjoy compliments more than men do. In reconsidering, he remembered girl watching and the importance of intent.

> There is [pause] a point where [pause] a woman can be admired by [pause] a pair of eyes, but we're talking about "that look." Where, you know, you're admiring her because she's dressed nice, she's got a nice figure, she's got nice legs. But then you also have the other side. You have an animal who just seems to undress you with his eyes and he's just [pause], there's those kind of people out there too.

What is most interesting about this statement is that in making the distinction between merely admiring and an animal look that ravages, José switched subject position. He spoke in the second person when describing both forms of looking, but his consistency in grammar belies a switch in subjectivity: you (as a man) admire, and you (as a woman) are undressed with his eyes. When considering an appropriate, complimentary gaze, José

described it from a man's point of view; the subject who experiences the inappropriate, violating look, however, is a woman. Thus, as in Robert's account, José acknowledged that there are potentially different meanings in the act for men and women. In particular, to be admired in a certain way is potentially demeaning for a woman through its objectification.

The switch in subject position was also evident in Karl's remarks. Karl mentioned girl watching while imagining himself as a woman in the gender reversal question. As he took the subject position of the woman watched rather than the man watching, his understanding of the act as a harmless game was destabilized. Rather than taking pleasure in being the object of such attention, Karl would take pains to avoid it.

> So with these guys [if I were a woman], I would probably have to be very concerned about my attire in the lab. Because in a lot of cases, I'm working at a bench and I'm hunched over, in which case your shirt, for example, would open at the neckline, and I would just have to be concerned about that.

Thus, because the engineers girl watch, Karl feels that he would have to regulate his appearance if he were a woman, keeping the men from using him in their game of girl watching. When he considered the act from the point of view of a man, girl watching was simply a harmless antic and an act of appreciation. When he was forced to consider the subject position of a woman, however, girl watching was something to be avoided or at least carefully managed.

When asked to envision himself as a woman in his workplace, like many of the individuals I interviewed, Karl believed that he did not "know how to be a woman." Nonetheless, he produced an account that mirrored the stories of some of the women I interviewed. He knew the experience of girl watching could be quite different—in fact, threatening and potentially disempowering—for the woman who is its object. As such, the game was something to be avoided. In imagining themselves as women, the men remembered the practice of girl watching. None, however, were able to comfortably describe the game of girl watching from the perspective of a woman and maintain its (masculine) meaning as play.

In attempting to take up the subject position of a woman, these men are necessarily drawing on knowledge they already hold. If men simply "don't get it"—truly failing to see the harm in girl watching or other more serious acts of sexual harassment—then they should not be able to see this harm when envisioning themselves as women. What the interviews reveal is that many men—most of whom failed to see the harm of many acts that would constitute the hostile work environment form of sexual harassment—did in fact understand the harm of these acts when forced to consider the position of the targeted woman.

I suggest that the gender reversal scenario produced, in some men at least, a moment of empathy. Empathy, Schwalbe (1992) argued, requires two things. First, one must have some knowledge of the other's situation and feelings. Second, one must be motivated to take the position of the other. What the present research suggests is that gender differences in interpreting sexual harassment stem not so much from men's not getting it (a failure of the first element) but from a studied, often compulsory, lack of motivation to identify with women's experiences.

In his analysis of masculinity and empathy, Schwalbe (1992) argued that the requirements of masculinity necessitate a "narrowing of the moral self." Men learn that to effectively perform masculinity and to protect a masculine identity, they must, in many instances, ignore a woman's pain and obscure her viewpoint. Men fail to exhibit empathy with women because masculinity precludes them from taking the position of the feminine other, and men's moral stance vis-à-vis women is attenuated by this lack of empathy.

As a case study, Schwalbe (1992) considered the Thomas-Hill hearings, concluding that the examining senators maintained a masculinist stance that precluded them from giving serious consideration to Professor Hill's claims. A consequence of this masculine moral narrowing is that "charges of sexual harassment...are often seen as exaggerated or as fabricated out of misunderstanding or

spite" (Schwalbe 1992, 46). Thus, gender differences in interpreting sexually harassing behaviors may stem more from acts of ignoring than states of ignorance.

The Problem with Getting Caught

But are women really the untroubled objects that girl watching—viewed through the eyes of men—suggests? Obviously not; the game may be premised on a denial of a woman's subjectivity, but an actual erasure is beyond men's power! It is in this multiplicity of subjectivities, as Butler (1990, ix) noted, where "trouble" lurks, provoked by "the unanticipated agency of a female 'object' who inexplicably returns the glance, reverses the gaze, and contests the place and authority of the masculine position." To face a returned gaze is to get caught, an act that has the power to undermine the logic of girl watching as simply a game among men. Karl, for example, noted that when caught, men are often flustered, a reaction suggesting that the boundaries of usual play have been disturbed.[10]

When a woman looks back, when she asks, "What are you looking at?" she speaks as a subject, and her status as mere object is disturbed. When the game is played as a form of hommosexuality, the confronted man may be baffled by her response. When she catches them looking, when she complains, the targeted woman speaks as a subject. The men, however, understand her primarily as an object, and objects do not object.

The radical potential of sexual harassment law is that it centers women's subjectivity, an aspect prompting Catharine MacKinnon's (1979) unusual hope for the law's potential as a remedy. For men engaged in girl watching, however, this subjectivity may be inconceivable. From their viewpoint, acts such as girl watching are simply games played with objects: women's bodies. Similar to Schwalbe's (1992) insight into the senators' reaction to Professor Hill, the harm of sexual harassment may seem more the result of a woman's complaint (and law's "illegitimate" encroachment into the everyday work world) than men's acts of objectification. For example, in reflecting on the impact of sexual harassment policies in the workplace, José lamented that "back in the '70s, [it was] all peace and love then. Now as things turn around, men can't get away with as much as what they used to." Just whose peace and love are we talking about?

Reactions to Anti-Sexual Harassment Training Programs

The role that objectification and disempathy play in men's girl watching has important implications for sexual harassment training. Consider the following account of a sexual harassment training session given in Cindy's workplace. Cindy, an Italian American woman in her early 20s, worked as a recruiter for a small telemarketing company in Southern California.

> [The trainer] just really laid down the ground rules, um, she had some scenarios. Saying, "OK, would you consider this sexual harassment?" "Would you…" this, this, this? "What level?" Da-da-da. So, um, they just gave us some real numbers as to lawsuits and cases. Just that "you guys better be careful" type of a thing.

From Cindy's description, this training is fairly typical in that it focuses on teaching participants definitions of sexual harassment and the legal ramifications of accusations. The trainer used the common strategy of presenting videos of potentially harassing situations and asking the participants how they would judge them. Cindy's description of the men's responses to these videos reveals the limitation of this approach.

> We were watching [the TV] and it was [like] a studio audience. And [men] were getting up in the studio audience making comments like "Oh well, look at her! I wouldn't want to do that to her either!" "Well, you're darn straight, look at her!"

Interestingly, the men successfully used the training session videos as an opportunity for girl watching through their public sexual evaluations of the women depicted. In this, the intent of the training session was doubly subverted. The men interpreted scenarios that Cindy found plainly harassing into mere instances of girl watching and sexual (dis)interest. The antiharassment video

was ironically transformed into a forum for girl watching, effecting male bonding and the assertion of masculine identities to the exclusion of women coworkers. Also, by judging the complaining women to be inferior as women, the men sent the message that women who complain are those who fail at femininity.

Cindy conceded that relations between men and women in her workplace were considerably strained after the training ("That day, you definitely saw the men bond, you definitely saw the women bond, and there was a definite separation"). The effect of the training session, rather than curtailing the rampant sexual harassment in Cindy's workplace, operated as a site of masculine performance, evoking manly camaraderie and reestablishing gender boundaries.

To be effective, sexual harassment training programs must be grounded in a complex understanding of the ways acts such as girl watching operate in the workplace and the seeming necessity of a culled empathy to some forms of masculinity. Sexually harassing behaviors are produced from more than a lack of knowledge, simple sexist attitudes, or misplaced sexual desire. Some forms of sexually harassing behaviors—such as girl watching—are mechanisms through which gendered boundaries are patrolled and evoked and by which deeply held identities are established. This complexity requires complex interventions and leads to difficult questions about the possible efficacy of any workplace training program mandated in part by legal requirements.

Conclusion

In this analysis, I have sought to unravel the social logic of girl watching and its relationship to the question of gender differences in the interpretation of sexual harassment. In the form analyzed here, girl watching functions simultaneously as only play and as a potent site where power is played. Through the objectification on which it is premised and in the nonempathetic masculinity it supports, this form of girl watching simultaneously produces both the harassment and the barriers to men's acknowledgment of its potential harm.

The implications these findings have for anti-sexual harassment training are profound. If we understand harassment to be the result of a simple lack of knowledge (of ignorance), then straightforward informational sexual harassment training may be effective. The present analysis suggests, however, that the etiology of some harassment lies elsewhere. While they might have quarreled with it, most of the men I interviewed had fairly good abstract understandings of the behaviors their companies' sexual harassment policies prohibited. At the same time, in relating stories of social relations in their workplaces, most failed to identify specific behaviors as sexual harassment when they matched the abstract definition. As I have argued, the source of this contradiction lies not so much in ignorance but in acts of ignoring. Traditional sexual harassment training programs address the former rather than the later. As such, their effectiveness against sexually harassing behaviors born out of social practices of masculinity like girl watching is questionable.

Ultimately, the project of challenging sexual harassment will be frustrated and our understanding distorted unless we interrogate hegemonic, patriarchal forms of masculinity and the practices by which they are (re)produced. We must continue to research the processes by which sexual harassment is produced and the gendered identities and subjectivities on which it poaches (Wood 1998). My study provides a first step toward a more process-oriented understanding of sexual harassment, the ways the social meanings of harassment are constructed, and ultimately, the potential success of antiharassment training programs.

Notes

1. See Welsh (1999) for a review of this literature.
2. For example, Maria, an administrative assistant I interviewed, simultaneously echoed and critiqued this understanding when she complained about her boss's girl watching in her presence: "If he wants to do that in front of other men…you know, that's what men do."
3. Recently, more researchers have turned to qualitative studies as a means to understand the process of labeling behavior as harassment. Of note are Collinson and Collinson (1996), Giuffre and Williams (1994), Quinn (2000), and Rogers and Henson (1997).
4. Quid pro quo ("this for that") sexual harassment occurs when a person with organizational power attempts to coerce an individual into sexual behavior by threatening adverse job actions.
5. This sample was not fully representative of the company's employees; male managers (mostly white) and minority manufacturing employees were underrepresented. Thus, the data presented here best represent the attitudes and workplace tactics of white men working in white-collar, technical positions and white and minority men in blue-collar jobs.
6. Acme employees were interviewed at work in an office off the main lobby. Students and referred participants were interviewed at sites convenient to them (e.g., an office, the library).
7. Not all the interviewed men discussed girl watching. When asked directly, they tended to grin knowingly, refusing to elaborate. This silence in the face of direct questioning—by a female researcher—is also perhaps an instance of getting caught.
8. I prefer the term "asymmetrical heterosexuality" over "double standard" because it directly references the dominance of heterosexuality and more accurately reflects the interconnected but different forms of acceptable sexuality for men and women. As Estrich (1987) argued, it is not simply that we hold men and women to different standards of sexuality but that these standards are (re)productive of women's disempowerment.
9. "Hommo" is a play on the French word for man, *homme*.
10. Men are not always concerned with getting caught, as the behavior of catcalling construction workers amply illustrates; that a woman hears is part of the thrill (Gardner 1995). The difference between the workplace and the street is the level of anonymity the men have vis-à-vis the woman and the complexity of social rules and the diversity of power sources an individual has at his or her disposal.

References

Bernstein, R. 1994. Guilty if charged. *New York Review of Books*, 13 January.

Bowman, C. G. 1993. Street harassment and the informal ghettoization of women. *Harvard Law Review* 106:517–80.

Buckwald, A. 1993. Compliment a woman, go to court. *Los Angeles Times*, 28 October.

Bumiller, K. 1988. *The civil rights society: The social construction of victims*. Baltimore: Johns Hopkins University Press.

Butler, J. 1990. *Gender trouble: Feminism and the subversion of identity*. New York: Routledge.

Chen, A. S. 1999. Lives at the center of the periphery, lives at the periphery of the center: Chinese American masculinities and bargaining with hegemony. *Gender & Society* 13:584–607.

Cleveland, J. N., and M. E. Kerst. 1993. Sexual harassment and perceptions of power: An under-articulated relationship. *Journal of Vocational Behavior* 42 (1): 49–67.

Cockburn, C. 1983. *Brothers: Male dominance and technological change*. London: Pluto Press.

Collinson, D. L., and M. Collinson. 1989. Sexuality in the workplace: The domination of men's sexuality. In *The sexuality of organizations*, edited by J. Hearn and D. L. Sheppard. Newbury Park, CA: Sage.

———. 1996. "It's only Dick": The sexual harassment of women managers in insurance sales. *Work, Employment & Society* 10 (1): 29–56.

Conley, F. K. 1991. Why I'm leaving Stanford: I wanted my dignity back. *Los Angeles Times*, 9 June.

Conley, J., and W. O'Barr. 1998. *Just words*. Chicago: University of Chicago Press.

Connell, R. W. 1987. *Gender and power*. Stanford, CA: Stanford University Press.

———. 1995. *Masculinities*. Berkeley: University of California Press.

Estrich, S. 1987. *Real rape*. Cambridge, MA: Harvard University Press.

Garcia, L., L. Milano, and A. Quijano. 1989. Perceptions of coercive sexual behavior by males and females. *Sex Roles* 21 (9/10): 569–77.

Gardner, C. B. 1995. *Passing by: Gender and public harassment*. Berkeley: University of California Press.

Giuffre, P., and C. Williams. 1994. Boundary lines: Labeling sexual harassment in restaurants. *Gender & Society* 8:378–401.

Glaser, B., and A. L. Strauss. 1967. *The discovery of grounded theory: Strategies for qualitative research*. Chicago: Aldine.

Guccione, J. 1992. Women judges still fighting harassment. *Daily Journal*, 13 October, 1.

Gutek, B. A., and M. P. Koss. 1993. Changed women and changed organizations: Consequences of and coping with sexual harassment. *Journal of Vocational Behavior* 42 (1): 28–48.

Gutek, B. A., B. Morasch, and A. G. Cohen. 1983. Interpreting social-sexual behavior in a work setting. *Journal of Vocational Behavior* 22 (1): 30–48.

Hearn, J. 1985. Men's sexuality at work. In *The sexuality of men*, edited by A. Metcalf and M. Humphries. London: Pluto Press.

Hopkins, P. 1992. Gender treachery: Homophobia, masculinity, and threatened identities. In *Rethinking masculinity: Philosophical explorations in light of feminism*, edited by L. May and R. Strikwerda. Lanham, MD: Littlefield, Adams.

Jensen, I. W., and B. A. Gutek. 1982. Attributions and assignment of responsibility in sexual harassment. *Journal of Social Issues* 38 (4): 121–36.

Johnson, M. 1988. *Strong mothers, weak wives*. Berkeley: University of California Press.

Kenig, S., and J. Ryan. 1986. Sex differences in levels of tolerance and attribution of blame for sexual harassment on a university campus. *Sex Roles* 15 (9/10): 535–49.

MacKinnon, C. A. 1979. *The sexual harassment of working women*. New Haven, CT: Yale University Press.

Malovich, N. J., and J. E. Stake. 1990. Sexual harassment on campus: Individual differences in attitudes and beliefs. *Psychology of Women Quarterly* 14 (1): 63–81.

Murrell, A. J., and B. L. Dietz-Uhler. 1993. Gender identity and adversarial sexual beliefs as predictors of attitudes toward sexual harassment. *Psychology of Women Quarterly* 17 (2): 169–75.

Padgitt, S. C., and J. S. Padgitt. 1986. Cognitive structure of sexual harassment: Implications for university policy. *Journal of College Student Personnel* 27:34–39.

Popovich, P. M., D. N. Gehlauf, J. A. Jolton, J. M. Somers, and R. M. Godinho. 1992. Perceptions of sexual harassment as a function of sex of rater and incident form and consequent. *Sex Roles* 27 (11/12): 609–25.

Powell, G. N. 1986. Effects of sex-role identity and sex on definitions of sexual harassment. *Sex Roles* 14: 9–19.

Pronger, B. 1992. Gay jocks: A phenomenology of gay men in athletics. In *Rethinking masculinity: Philosophical explorations in light of feminism*, edited by L. May and R. Strikwerda. Lanham, MD: Littlefield Adams.

Pryor, J. B. 1987. Sexual harassment proclivities in men. *Sex Roles* 17 (5/6): 269–90.

Quinn, B. A. 2000. The paradox of complaining: Law, humor, and harassment in the everyday work world. *Law and Social Inquiry* 25 (4): 1151–83.

Reilly, M. E., B. Lott, D. Caldwell, and L. DeLuca. 1992. Tolerance for sexual harassment related to self-reported sexual victimization. *Gender & Society* 6:122–38.

Rogers, J. K., and K. D. Henson. 1997. "Hey, why don't you wear a shorter skirt?" Structural vulnerability and the organization of sexual harassment in temporary clerical employment. *Gender & Society* 11:215–38.

Schwalbe, M. 1992. Male supremacy and the narrowing of the moral self. *Berkeley Journal of Sociology* 37:29–54.

Smith, D. 1990. *The conceptual practices of power: A feminist sociology of knowledge*. Boston: Northeastern University Press.

Stockdale, M. S. 1993. The role of sexual misperceptions of women's friendliness in an emerging theory of sexual harassment. *Journal of Vocational Behavior* 42 (1): 84–101.

Stockdale, M. S., and A. Vaux. 1993. What sexual harassment experiences lead respondents to acknowledge being sexually harassed? A secondary analysis of a university survey. *Journal of Vocational Behavior* 43 (2): 221–34.

Tagri, S., and S. M. Hayes. 1997. Theories of sexual harassment. In *Sexual harassment: Theory, research and treatment*, edited by W. O'Donohue. New York: Allyn & Bacon.

Thorne, B. 1993. *Gender play: Girls and boys in school*. Buckingham, UK: Open University Press.

U.S. Merit Systems Protection Board. 1988. *Sexual harassment in the federal government: An update*. Washington, DC: Government Printing Office.

Welsh, S. 1999. Gender and sexual harassment. *Annual Review of Sociology* 1999:169–90.

West, C., and D. H. Zimmerman. 1987. Doing gender. *Gender & Society* 1: 125–51.

Wood, J. T. 1998. Saying makes it so: The discursive construction of sexual harassment. In *Conceptualizing sexual harassment as discursive practice*, edited by S. G. Bingham. Westport, CT: Praeger.

York, K. M. 1989. Defining sexual harassment in workplaces: A policy-capturing approach. *Academy of Management Journal* 32:830–50.

Yount, K. R. 1991. Ladies, flirts, tomboys: Strategies for managing sexual harassment in an underground coal mine. *Journal of Contemporary Ethnography* 19:396–422.

The Gender of Violence

As a nation, we fret about "teen violence," complain about "inner city crime" or fear "urban gangs." We express shock at the violence in our nation's public schools, where metal detectors crowd the doorways, and knives and guns commingle with pencils and erasers in students' backpacks. Those public school shootings leave us speechless and sick at heart. Yet when we think about these wrenching events, do we ever consider that, whether white or black, inner city or suburban, these bands of marauding "youths" or these troubled teenagers are virtually all young men?

Men constitute 99 percent of all persons arrested for rape; 88 percent of those arrested for murder; 92 percent of those arrested for robbery; 87 percent for aggravated assault; 85 percent of other assaults; 83 percent of all family violence; 82 percent of disorderly conduct. Men are overwhelmingly more violent than women. Nearly 90 percent of all murder victims are murdered by men, according to the United States Department of Justice (Uniform Crime Reports 1991, 17).

From early childhood to old age, violence is perhaps the most obdurate, intractable gender difference we have observed. The National Academy of Sciences (cited in Gottfredson and Hirschi; 1990) puts the case most starkly: "The most consistent pattern with respect to gender is the extent to which male criminal participation in serious crimes at any age greatly exceeds that of females, regardless of source of data, crime type, level of involvement, or measure of participation." "Men are always and everywhere more likely than women to commit criminal acts," write the criminologists Michael Gottfredson and Travis Hirschi (1990, 145). Yet how do we understand this obvious association between masculinity and violence? Is it a biological fact of nature, caused by something inherent in male anatomy? Is it culturally universal? And in the United States, what has been the association between gender and violence? Has that association become stronger or weaker over time? What can we, as a culture, do to prevent or at least ameliorate the problem of male violence?

My concern throughout this book has been to observe the construction of gender difference and gender inequality at both the individual level of identity and the institutional level. The readings here reflect these concerns. Carol Cohn's insightful essay penetrates the gendered language of masculine "war-talk," in which the human tragedy of nuclear war preparation is masked behind discussions of kill ratios, body counts, and megaton delivery.

And Russell and R. Emerson Dobash and their colleagues use a gendered power analysis to explain why it is that men batter women they say they love in far greater numbers than women hit men. They bring a sensible sobriety to current discussions that suggest that women are just as likely to commit acts of violence against their husbands as men are against their wives.

Of course, to argue that men are more prone to violence than women are does not resolve the political question of what to do about it. It would be foolish to resignedly throw up our hands in despair that "boys will be boys." Whether you believe this gender difference in violence derives from different biological predispositions (which I regard as dubious because these biological impulses do not seem to be culturally universal) or because male violence is socially sanctioned and legitimated as an expression of masculine control and domination (a far more convincing explanation), the policy question remains open. Do we organize society so as to maximize this male propensity toward violence, or do we organize society so as to minimize and constrain it? The answers to this question, like the answer to the questions about alleviating gender inequality in the family, in our educational institutions, and in the workplace, are more likely to come from the voting booth than from the laboratories of scientists. As a society, we decide how much weight to give what few gender differences there are, and how best to alleviate the pain of those who are the victims of gendered violence.

Anthropologist Peggy Reeves Sanday explores the ways in which gender inequality is also a predictor for the likelihood that a culture will have either high or low rape rates. By locating the origins of rape in male domination—dramatic separation of spheres, gender inequality, low levels of male participation in child care—Sanday effectively lays to rest the facile biological argument that rape is the evolutionary sexual strategy of male "failures" in reproductive competition. What's more, she makes clear a central argument of this book: that alleviating gender inequality will reduce violence.

References

U. S. Department of Justice, Uniform Crime Reports, 1991. Washington, DC: Dept of Justice.

Michael Gottfredson and Travis Hirschi, *A General Theory of Crime* (Stanford: Stanford University Press, 1990).

Wars, Wimps, and Women: Talking Gender and Thinking War

CAROL COHN

I start with a true story, told to me by a white male physicist:

> Several colleagues and I were working on modeling counterforce attacks, trying to get realistic estimates of the number of immediate fatalities that would result from different deployments. At one point, we remodeled a particular attack, using slightly different assumptions, and found that instead of there being thirty-six million immediate fatalities, there would only be thirty million. And everybody was sitting around nodding, saying, "Oh yeah, that's great, only thirty million," when all of a sudden, I heard what we were saying. And I blurted out, "Wait, I've just heard how we're talking—Only thirty million! Only thirty million human beings killed instantly?" Silence fell upon the room. Nobody said a word. They didn't even look at me. It was awful. I felt like a woman.

The physicist added that henceforth he was careful to never blurt out anything like that again.

During the early years of the Reagan presidency, in the era of the Evil Empire, the cold war, and loose talk in Washington about the possibility of fighting and "prevailing" in a nuclear war, I went off to do participant observation in a community of North American nuclear defense intellectuals and security affairs analysts—a community virtually entirely composed of white men. They work in universities, think tanks, and as advisers to government. They theorize about nuclear deterrence and arms control, and nuclear and conventional war fighting, about how to best translate military might into political power; in short, they create the discourse that underwrites American national security policy. The exact relation of their theories to American political and military practice is a complex and thorny one; the argument can be made, for example, that their ideas do not so much shape policy decisions as legitimate them after the fact. But one thing that is clear is that the body of language and thinking they have generated filters out to the military, politicians, and the public, and increasingly shapes how we talk and think about war. This was amply evident during the Gulf War: Gulf War "news," as generated by the military briefers, reported by newscasters, and analyzed by the television networks' resident security experts, was marked by its use of the professional language of defense analysis, nearly to the exclusion of other ways of speaking.

My goal has been to understand something about how defense intellectuals think, and why they think that way. Despite the parsimonious appeal of ascribing the nuclear arms race to "missile envy," I felt certain that masculinity was not a sufficient explanation of why men think about war in the ways that they do. Indeed, I found many ways to understand what these men were doing that had little or nothing to do with gender. But ultimately, the physicist's story and others like it made confronting the role of gender unavoidable. Thus, in this paper I will explore gender discourse and its role in shaping nuclear and national security discourse.

I want to stress, this is not a paper about men and women, and what they are or are not like. I will not be claiming that men are aggressive and women peace loving. I will not even address the question of how men's and women's relations to war may differ, nor the different propensities they may have to committing acts of violence. Neither will I pay more than passing attention to the question which so often crops up in discussions of war and gender, that is, would it be a more peaceful world if our national leaders were women? These questions are valid and important, and recent feminist discussion of them has been complex, interesting, and contentious. But my focus is elsewhere. I wish to direct attention away from gendered individuals and toward gendered discourses. My question is about the way that civilian defense analysts think about war, and the ways in which that thinking is shaped not by their maleness (or, in extremely rare instances, femaleness), but by the ways in which gender discourse intertwines with and permeates that thinking.

Let me be more specific about my terms. I use the term *gender* to refer to the constellation of meanings that a given culture assigns to biological sex differences. But more than that, I use gender to refer to a symbolic system, a central organizing discourse of culture, one that not only shapes how we experience and understand ourselves as men and women, but that also interweaves with other discourses and shapes *them*—and therefore shapes other aspects of our world—such as how nuclear weapons are thought about and deployed.

So when I talk about "gender discourse," I am talking not only about words or language but about a system of meanings, of ways of thinking, images and words that first shape how we experience, understand, and represent ourselves as men and women, but that also do more than that; they shape many other aspects of our lives and culture. In this symbolic system, human characteristics are dichotomized, divided into pairs of polar opposites that are supposedly mutually exclusive: mind is opposed to body; culture to nature; thought to feeling; logic to intuition; objectivity to subjectivity; aggression to passivity; confrontation to accommodation; abstraction to particularity; public to private; political to personal, ad nauseam. In each case, the first term of the "opposites" is associated with male, the second with female. And in each case, our society values the first over the second.

I break it into steps like this—analytically separating the *existence* of these groupings of binary oppositions, from the association of each group with a gender, from the valuing of one over the other, the so-called male over the so-called female, for two reasons: first, to try to make visible the fact that this system of dichotomies is encoding many meanings that may be quite unrelated to male and female bodies. Yet once that first step is made—the association of each side of those lists with a gender—gender now becomes tied to many other kinds of cultural representations. If a human activity, such as engineering, fits some of the characteristics, it becomes gendered.

My second reason for breaking it into those steps is to try to help make it clear that the meanings can flow in different directions; that is, in gender discourse, men and women are supposed to exemplify the characteristics on the lists. It also works in reverse, however; to evidence any of these characteristics—to be abstract, logical or dispassionate, for example—is not simply to be those things, but also to be manly. And to be manly is not simply to be manly, but also to be in the more highly valued position in the discourse. In other words, to exhibit a trait on that list is not neutral—it is not simply displaying some basic human characteristic. It also positions you in a discourse of gender. It associates you with a particular gender, and also with a higher or lower valuation.

In stressing that this is a *symbolic* system, I want first to emphasize that while real women and men do not really fit these gender "ideals," the existence of this system of meaning affects all of us, nonetheless. Whether we want to or not, we see ourselves and others against its templates, we interpret our own and others' actions against it. A man who cries easily cannot avoid in some way confronting that he is likely to be seen as less than fully manly. A woman who is very aggressive and incisive may enjoy that quality in herself, but the fact of her aggressiveness does not exist by itself; she cannot avoid having her own and others' perceptions of that quality of hers, the meaning it has for people, being in some way mediated by the discourse of gender. Or, a different kind of example: Why does it mean one thing when George Bush gets teary-eyed in public, and something entirely different when Patricia Shroeder does? The same act is viewed through the lens of gender and is seen to mean two very different things.

Second, as gender discourse assigns gender to human characteristics, we can think of the discourse as something we are positioned *by*. If I say, for example, that a corporation should stop dumping toxic waste because it is damaging the creations of mother earth, (i.e., articulating a valuing and sentimental vision of nature), I am speaking in a manner associated with women, and our cultural discourse of gender positions me as female. As such I am then associated with the whole constellation of traits—irrational, emotional, subjective, and so forth—and I am in the devalued position. If, on the other hand, I say the corporation should stop dumping toxic wastes because I have calculated that it is causing $8.215 billion of damage to eight nonrenewable resources, which should be seen as equivalent to lowering the GDP by 0.15 percent per annum, (i.e., using a rational, calculative mode of thought), the discourse positions me as masculine—rational, objective, logical, and so forth—the dominant, valued position.

But if we are positioned *by* discourses, we can also take different positions *within* them. Although I am female, and this would "naturally" fall into the devalued term, I can choose to "speak like a man"—to be hard-nosed, realistic, unsentimental, dispassionate. Jeanne Kirkpatrick is a formidable example. While we can choose a position in a discourse, however, it means something different for a woman to "speak like a man" than for a man to do so. It is heard differently.

One other note about my use of the term *gender discourse:* I am using it in the general sense to refer to the phenomenon of symbolically organizing the world in these gender-associated opposites. I do not mean to suggest that there is a single discourse defining a single set of gender ideals. In fact, there

are many specific discourses of gender, which vary by race, class, ethnicity, locale, sexuality, nationality, and other factors. The masculinity idealized in the gender discourse of new Haitian immigrants is in some ways different from that of sixth-generation white Anglo-Saxon Protestant business executives, and both differ somewhat from that of white-male defense intellectuals and security analysts. One version of masculinity is mobilized and enforced in the armed forces in order to enable men to fight wars, while a somewhat different version of masculinity is drawn upon and expressed by abstract theoreticians of war.

Let us now return to the physicist who felt like a woman: what happened when he "blurted out" his sudden awareness of the "only thirty million" dead people? First, he was transgressing a code of professional conduct. In the civilian defense intellectuals' world, when you are in professional settings you do not discuss the bloody reality behind the calculations. It is not required that you be completely unaware of them in your outside life, or that you have no feelings about them, but it is required that you do not bring them to the foreground in the context of professional activities. There is a general awareness that you *could not* do your work if you did; in addition, most defense intellectuals believe that emotion and description of human reality distort the process required to think well about nuclear weapons and warfare.

So the physicist violated a behavioral norm, in and of itself a difficult thing to do because it threatens your relationships to and your standing with your colleagues.

But even worse than that, he demonstrated some of the characteristics on the "female" side of the dichotomies—in his "blurting" he was impulsive, uncontrolled, emotional, concrete, and attentive to human bodies, at the very least. Thus, he marked himself not only as unprofessional but as feminine, and this, in turn, was doubly threatening. It was not only a threat to his own sense of self as masculine, his gender identity, it also identified him with a devalued status—of a woman—or put him in the devalued or subordinate position in the discourse.

Thus, both his statement, "I felt like a woman," and his subsequent silence in that and other settings are completely understandable. To have the strength of character and courage to transgress the strictures of both professional and gender codes *and* to associate yourself with a lower status is very difficult.

This story is not simply about one individual, his feelings and actions; it is about the role of gender discourse. The impact of gender discourse in that room (and countless others like it) is that some things get left out. Certain ideas, concerns, interests, information, feelings, and meanings are marked in national security discourse as feminine, and are devalued. They are therefore, first, very difficult to *speak,* as exemplified by the physicist who felt like a woman. And second, they are very difficult to *hear,* to take in and work with seriously, even if they *are* said. For the others in the room, the way in which the physicist's comments were marked as female and devalued served to delegitimate them. It is almost as though they had become an accidental excrescence in the middle of the room. Embarrassed politeness demanded that they be ignored.

I must stress that this is not simply the product of the idiosyncratic personal composition of that particular room. In other professional settings, I have experienced the feeling that something terribly important is being left out and must be spoken; and yet, it has felt almost physically impossible to utter the words, almost as though they could not be pushed out into the smooth, cool, opaque air of the room.

What is it that cannot be spoken? First, any words that express an emotional awareness of the desperate human reality behind the sanitized abstractions of death and destruction—as in the physicist's sudden vision of thirty million rotting corpses. Similarly, weapons' effects may be spoken of only in the most clinical and abstract terms, leaving no room to imagine a seven-year-old boy with his flesh melting away from his bones or a toddler with her skin hanging down in strips. Voicing concern about the number of casualties in the enemy's armed forces, imagining the suffering of the killed and wounded young men, is

out of bounds. (Within the military itself, it is permissible, even desirable, to attempt to minimize immediate civilian casualties if it is possible to do so without compromising military objectives, but as we learned in the Persian Gulf War, this is only an extremely limited enterprise; the planning and precision of military targeting does not admit of consideration of the cost in human lives of such actions as destroying power systems, or water and sewer systems, or highways and food distribution systems.) Psychological effects—on the soldiers fighting the war or on the citizens injured, or fearing for their own safety, or living through tremendous deprivation, or helplessly watching their babies die from diarrhea due to the lack of clean water—all of these are not to be talked about.

But it is not only particular subjects that are out of bounds. It is also tone of voice that counts. A speaking style that is identified as cool, dispassionate, and distanced is required. One that vibrates with the intensity of emotion almost always disqualifies the speaker, who is heard to sound like "a hysterical housewife."

What gets left out, then, is the emotional, the concrete, the particular, the human bodies and their vulnerability, human lives and their subjectivity—all of which are marked as feminine in the binary dichotomies of gender discourse. In other words, gender discourse informs and shapes nuclear and national security discourse, and in so doing creates silences and absences. It keeps things out of the room, unsaid, and keeps them ignored if they manage to get in. As such, it degrades our ability to think *well* and *fully* about nuclear weapons and national security, and shapes and limits the possible outcomes of our deliberations.

What becomes clear, then, is that defense intellectuals' standards of what constitutes "good thinking" about weapons and security have not simply evolved out of trial and error; it is not that the history of nuclear discourse has been filled with exploration of other ideas, concerns, interests, information, questions, feelings, meanings and stances which were then found to create distorted or poor thought. It is that these options have been *preempted* by gender discourse, and by the feelings evoked by living up to or transgressing gender codes.

To borrow a term from defense intellectuals, you might say that gender discourse becomes a "preemptive deterrent" to certain kinds of thought.

Let me give you another example of what I mean—another story, this one my own experience:

One Saturday morning I, two other women, and about fifty-five men gathered to play a war game designed by the RAND Corporation. Our "controllers" (the people running the game) first divided us up into three sets of teams; there would be three simultaneous games being played, each pitting a Red Team against a Blue Team (I leave the reader to figure out which color represents which country). All three women were put onto the same team, a Red Team.

The teams were then placed in different rooms so that we had no way of communicating with each other, except through our military actions (or lack of them) or by sending demands and responses to those demands via the controllers. There was no way to negotiate or to take actions other than military ones. (This was supposed to simulate reality.) The controllers then presented us with maps and pages covered with numbers representing each side's forces. We were also given a "scenario," a situation of escalating tensions and military conflicts, starting in the Middle East and spreading to Central Europe. We were to decide what to do, the controllers would go back and forth between the two teams to relate the other team's actions, and periodically the controllers themselves would add something that would ratchet up the conflict—an announcement of an "intercepted intelligence report" from the other side, the authenticity of which we had no way of judging.

Our Red Team was heavily into strategizing, attacking ground forces, and generally playing war. We also, at one point, decided that we were going to pull our troops out of Afghanistan, reasoning it was bad for us to have them there and that the Afghanis had the right to self-determination. At another point we removed some troops from Eastern Europe. I must add that later on my team was accused of being wildly "unrealistic,"

that this group of experts found the idea that the Soviet Union might voluntarily choose to pull troops out of Afghanistan and Eastern Europe so utterly absurd. (It was about six months before Gorbachev actually did the same thing.)

Gradually our game escalated to nuclear war. The Blue Team used tactical nuclear weapons against our troops, but our Red Team decided, initially at least, against nuclear retaliation. When the game ended (at the end of the allotted time) our Red Team had "lost the war" (meaning that we had political control over less territory than we had started with, although our homeland had remained completely unviolated and our civilian population safe).

In the debriefing afterwards, all six teams returned to one room and reported on their games. Since we had had absolutely no way to know why the other team had taken any of its actions, we now had the opportunity to find out what they had been thinking. A member of the team that had played against us said, "Well, when he took his troops out of Afghanistan, I knew he was weak and I could push him around. And then, when we nuked him and he didn't nuke us back, I knew he was just such a wimp, I could take him for everything he's got and I nuked him again. He just wimped out."

There are many different possible comments to make at this point. I will restrict myself to a couple. First, when the man from the Blue Team called me a wimp (which is what it felt like for each of us on the Red Team—a personal accusation), I felt silenced. My reality, the careful reasoning that had gone into my strategic and tactical choices, the intelligence, the politics, the morality—all of it just disappeared, completely invalidated. I could not explain the reasons for my actions, could not protest, "Wait, you idiot, I didn't do it because I was weak, I did it because it made sense to do it that way, given my understandings of strategy and tactics, history and politics, my goals and my values." The protestation would be met with knowing sneers. In this discourse, the coding of an act as wimpish is hegemonic. Its emotional heat and resonance is like a bath of sulfuric acid: it erases everything else.

"Acting like a wimp" is an *interpretation* of a person's acts (or, in national security discourse, a country's acts, an important distinction I will return to later). As with any other interpretation, it is a selection of one among many possible different ways to understand something—once the selection is made, the other possibilities recede into invisibility. In national security discourse, "acting like a wimp," being insufficiently masculine, is one of the most readily available interpretive codes. (You do not need to do participant observation in a community of defense intellectuals to know this—just look at the "geopolitical analyses" in the media and on Capitol Hill of the way in which George Bush's military intervention in Panama and the Persian Gulf War finally allowed him to beat the "wimp factor.") You learn that someone is being a wimp if he perceives an international crisis as very dangerous and urges caution; if he thinks it might not be important to have just as many weapons that are just as big as the other guy's; if he suggests that an attack should not necessarily be answered by an even more destructive counterattack; or, until recently, if he suggested that making unilateral arms reductions might be useful for our own security. All of these are "wimping out."

The prevalence of this particular interpretive code is another example of how gender discourse affects the quality of thinking within the national security community, first, because, as in the case of the physicist who "felt like a woman," it is internalized to become a self-censor; there are things professionals simply will not *say* in groups, options they simply will not argue nor write about, because they know that to do so is to brand themselves as wimps. Thus, a whole range of inputs is left out, a whole series of options is foreclosed from their deliberations.

Equally, if not more damagingly, is the way in which this interpretive coding not only limits what is *said*, but even limits what is *thought*. "He's a wimp" is a phrase that *stops* thought. When we were playing the game, once my opponent on the Blue Team "recognized the fact that I was a wimp," that is, once he interpreted my team's actions through the lens of this common interpretive code

in national security discourse, he *stopped thinking*; he stopped looking for ways to understand what we were doing. He did not ask, "Why on earth would the Red Team do that? What does it tell me about them, about their motives and purposes and goals and capabilities? What does it tell me about their possible understandings of *my* actions, or of the situation they're in?" or any other of the many questions that might have enabled him to revise his own conception of the situation or perhaps achieve his goals at a far lower level of violence and destruction. Here, again, gender discourse acts as a preemptive deterrent to thought.

"Wimp" is, of course, not the only gendered pejorative used in the national security community; "pussy" is another popular epithet, conjoining the imagery of harmless domesticated (read demasculinized) pets with contemptuous reference to women's genitals. In an informal setting, an analyst worrying about the other side's casualties, for example, might be asked, "What kind of pussy are you, anyway?" It need not happen more than once or twice before everyone gets the message; they quickly learn not to raise the issue in their discussions. Attention to and care for the living, suffering, and dying of human beings (in this case, soldiers and their families and friends) is again banished from the discourse through the expedient means of gender-bashing.

Other words are also used to impugn someone's masculinity and, in the process, to delegitimate his position and avoid thinking seriously about it. "Those Krauts are a bunch of limp-dicked wimps" was the way one U.S. defense intellectual dismissed the West German politicians who were concerned about popular opposition to Euromissile deployments. I have heard our NATO allies referred to as "the Euro-fags" when they disagreed with American policy on such issues as the Contra War or the bombing of Libya. Labeling them "fags" is an effective strategy; it immediately dismisses and trivializes their opposition to U.S. policy by coding it as due to inadequate masculinity. In other words, the American analyst need not seriously confront the Europeans' arguments, since the Europeans' doubts about U.S. policy obviously stem not from their reasoning but from the "fact" that they "just don't have the stones for war." Here, again, gender discourse deters thought.

"Fag" imagery is not, of course, confined to the professional community of security analysts; it also appears in popular "political" discourse. The Gulf War was replete with examples. American derision of Saddam Hussein included bumper stickers that read "Saddam, Bend Over." American soldiers reported that the "U.S.A." stenciled on their uniforms stood for "Up Saddam's Ass." A widely reprinted cartoon, surely one of the most multiply offensive that came out of the war, depicted Saddam bowing down in the Islamic posture of prayer, with a huge U.S. missile, approximately five times the size of the prostrate figure, about to penetrate his upraised bottom. Over and over, defeat for the Iraqis was portrayed as humiliating anal penetration by the more powerful and manly United States.

Within the defense community discourse, manliness is equated not only with the ability to win a war (or to "prevail," as some like to say when talking about nuclear war); it is also equated with the willingness (which they would call courage) to threaten and use force. During the Carter administration, for example, a well-known academic security affairs specialist was quoted as saying that "under Jimmy Carter the United States is spreading its legs for the Soviet Union." Once this image is evoked, how does rational discourse about the value of U.S. policy proceed?

In 1989 and 1990, as Gorbachev presided over the withdrawal of Soviet forces from Eastern Europe, I heard some defense analysts sneeringly say things like, "They're a bunch of pussies for pulling out of Eastern Europe." This is extraordinary. Here they were, men who for years railed against Soviet domination of Eastern Europe. You would assume that if they were politically and ideologically consistent, if they were rational, they would be applauding the Soviet actions. Yet in their informal conversations, it was not their rational analyses that dominated their response, but the fact that for them, the decision for war, the willingness to use force, is cast as a question of masculinity—not prudence, thoughtfulness, efficacy, "rational" cost-benefit calculation, or morality, but masculinity.

In the face of this equation, genuine political discourse disappears. One more example: After Iraq invaded Kuwait and President Bush hastily sent U.S. forces to Saudi Arabia, there was a period in which the Bush administration struggled to find a convincing political justification for U.S. military involvement and the security affairs community debated the political merit of U.S. intervention. Then Bush set the deadline, January 16, high noon at the OK Corral, and as the day approached conversations changed. More of these centered on the question compellingly articulated by one defense intellectual as "Does George Bush have the stones for war?" This, too, is utterly extraordinary. This was a time when crucial political questions abounded: Can the sanctions work if given more time? Just what vital interests does the United States actually have at stake? What would be the goals of military intervention? Could they be accomplished by other means? Is the difference between what sanctions might accomplish and what military violence might accomplish worth the greater cost in human suffering, human lives, even dollars? What will the long-term effects on the people of the region be? On the ecology? Given the apparent successes of Gorbachev's last-minute diplomacy and Hussein's series of nearly daily small concessions, can and should Bush put off the deadline? Does he have the strength to let another leader play a major role in solving the problem? Does he have the political flexibility to not fight, or is he hellbent on war at all costs? And so on, ad infinitum. All of these disappear in the sulfuric acid test of the size of Mr. Bush's private parts.

I want to return to the RAND war simulation story to make one other observation. First, it requires a true confession: *I was stung by being called a wimp.* Yes, I thought the remark was deeply inane, and it infuriated me. But even so, I was also stung. Let me hasten to add, this was not because my identity is very wrapped up with not being wimpish—it actually is not a term that normally figures very heavily in my self-image one way or the other. But it was impossible to be in that room, hear his comment and the snickering laughter with which it was met, and not to feel stung, and humiliated.

Why? There I was, a woman and a feminist, not only contemptuous of the mentality that measures human beings by their degree of so-called wimpishness, but also someone for whom the term *wimp* does not have a deeply resonant personal meaning. How could it have affected me so much?

The answer lies in the role of the context within which I was experiencing myself—the discursive framework. For in that room I was not "simply me," but I was a participant in a discourse, a shared set of words, concepts, symbols that constituted not only the linguistic possibilities available to us but also constituted *me* in that situation. This is not entirely true, of course. How I experienced myself was at least partly shaped by other experiences and other discursive frameworks—certainly those of feminist politics and antimilitarist politics; in fact, I would say my reactions were predominantly shaped by those frameworks. But that is quite different from saying "I am a feminist, and that individual, psychological self simply moves encapsulated through the world being itself"—and therefore assuming that I am unaffected. No matter who else I was at that moment, I was unavoidably a participant in a discourse in which being a wimp has a meaning, and a deeply pejorative one at that. By calling me a wimp, my accuser on the Blue Team *positioned* me in that discourse, and I could not but feel the sting.

In other words, I am suggesting that national security discourse can be seen as having different positions within it—ones that are starkly gender coded; indeed, the enormous strength of their evocative power comes from gender. Thus, when you participate in conversation in that community, you do not simply choose what to say and how to say it; you advertently or inadvertently choose a position in the discourse. As a woman, I can choose the "masculine" (thoughtful, rational, logical) position. If I do, I am seen as legitimate, but I limit what I can say. Or, I can say things that place me in the "feminine" position—in which case no one will listen to me.

Finally, I would like to briefly explore a phenomenon I call the "unitary masculine actor problem" in national security discourse. During the Persian Gulf War, many feminists probably noticed that both the military briefers and George Bush himself frequently used the singular masculine pronoun "he" when referring to Iraq and Iraq's army. Someone not listening carefully could simply assume that "he" referred to Saddam Hussein. Sometimes it did; much of the time it simply reflected the defense community's characteristic habit of calling opponents "he" or "the other guy." A battalion commander, for example, was quoted as saying "Saddam knows where we are and we know where he is. We will move a lot now to keep him off guard."[1] In these sentences, "he" and "him" appear to refer to Saddam Hussein. But, of course, the American forces had *no idea* where Saddam Hussein himself was; the singular masculine pronouns are actually being used to refer to the Iraqi military.

This linguistic move, frequently heard in discussions within the security affairs and defense communities, turns a complex state and set of forces into a singular male opponent. In fact, discussions that purport to be serious explorations of the strategy and tactics of war can have a tone which sounds more like the story of a sporting match, a fistfight, or a personal vendetta.

> I would want to suck him out into the desert as far as I could, and then pound him to death.[2]
>
> Once we had taken out his eyes, we did what could be best described as the "Hail Mary play" in football.[3]
>
> [I]f the adversary decides to embark on a very high roll, because he's frightened that something even worse is in the works, does grabbing him by the scruff of the neck and slapping him up the side of the head, does that make him behave better or is it plausible that it makes him behave even worse?[4]

Most defense intellectuals would claim that using "he" is just a convenient shorthand, without significant import or effects. I believe, however, that the effects of this usage are many and the implications far-reaching. Here I will sketch just a few, starting first with the usage throughout defense discourse generally, and then coming back to the Gulf War in particular.

The use of "he" distorts the analyst's understanding of the opposing state and the conflict in which they are engaged. When the analyst refers to the opposing state as "he" or "the other guy," the image evoked is that of a person, a unitary actor; yet states are not people. Nor are they unitary and unified. They comprise complex, multifaceted governmental and military apparatuses, each with opposing forces within it, each, in turn, with its own internal institutional dynamics, its own varied needs in relation to domestic politics, and so on. In other words, if the state is referred to and pictured as a unitary actor, what becomes unavailable to the analyst and policy-maker is a series of much more complex truths that might enable him to imagine many more policy options, many more ways to interact with that state.

If one kind of distortion of the state results from the image of the state as a person, a unitary actor, another can be seen to stem from the image of the state as a specifically *male* actor. Although states are almost uniformly run by men, states are not men; they are complex social institutions, and they act and react as such. Yet, when "he" and "the other guy" are used to refer to states, the words do not simply function as shorthand codes; instead, they have their own entailments, including assumptions about how men act, which just might be different from how states act, but which invisibly become assumed to be isomorphic with how states act.

It also entails emotional responses on the part of the speaker. The reference to the opposing state as "he" evokes male competitive identity issues, as in, "I'm not going to let him push me around," or, "I'm not going to let him get the best of me." While these responses may or may not be adaptive for a barroom brawl, it is probably safe to say that they are less functional when trying to determine the best way for one state to respond to another state. Defense analysts and foreign policy experts can usually agree upon the supreme desirability of dispassionate, logical analysis and its ensuing rationally calculated action. Yet the emotions evoked by the portrayal of global conflict in the personalized terms of male competition must, at the very least, exert a strong pull in exactly the opposite direction.

A third problem is that even while the use of "he" acts to personalize the conflict, it simultaneously abstracts both the opponent and the war itself. That is, the use of "he" functions in very much the same way that discussions about "Red" and "Blue" do. It facilitates treating war within a kind of game-playing model, A against B, Red against Blue, he against me. For even while "he" is evocative of male identity issues, it is also just an abstract piece to be moved around on a game board, or, more appropriately, a computer screen.

That tension between personalization and abstraction was striking in Gulf War discourse. In the Gulf War, not only was "he" frequently used to refer to the Iraqi military, but so was "Saddam," as in "Saddam really took a pounding today," or "Our goal remains the same: to liberate Kuwait by forcing Saddam Hussein out."[5] The personalization is obvious: in this locution, the U.S. armed forces are not destroying a nation, killing people; instead, they (or George) are giving Saddam a good pounding, or bodily removing him from where he does not belong. Our emotional response is to get fired up about a bully getting his comeuppance.

Yet this personalization, this conflation of Iraq and Iraqi forces with Saddam himself, also abstracts: it functions to substitute in the mind's eye the abstraction of an implacably, impeccably evil enemy for the particular human beings, the men, women, and children being pounded, burned, torn, and eviscerated. A cartoon image of Saddam being ejected from Kuwait preempts the image of the blackened, charred, decomposing bodies of nineteen-year-old boys tossed in ditches by the side of the road, and the other concrete images of the acts of violence that constitute "forcing Hussein [*sic*] out of Kuwait."[6] Paradoxical as it may seem, in personalizing the Iraqi army as Saddam, the individual human beings in Iraq were abstracted out of existence.

In summary, I have been exploring the way in which defense intellectuals talk to each other—the comments they make to each other, the particular usages that appear in their informal conversations or their lectures. In addition, I have occasionally left the professional community to draw upon public talk about the Gulf War. My analysis does *not* lead me to conclude that "national security thinking is masculine"—that is, a separate, and different, discussion. Instead, I have tried to show that national security discourse is gendered, and that it matters. Gender discourse is interwoven through national security discourse. It sets fixed boundaries, and in so doing, it skews what is discussed and how it is thought about. It shapes expectations of other nations' actions, and in so doing it affects both our interpretations of international events and conceptions of how the United States should respond.

In a world where professionals pride themselves on their ability to engage in cool, rational, objective calculation while others around them are letting their thinking be sullied by emotion, the unacknowledged interweaving of gender discourse in security discourse allows men to not acknowledge that their pristine rational thought is in fact riddled with emotional response. In an "objective" "universal" discourse that valorizes the "masculine" and deauthorizes the "feminine," it is only the "feminine" emotions that are noticed and labeled as emotions, and thus in need of banning from the analytic process. "Masculine" emotions—such as feelings of aggression, competition, macho pride and swagger, or the sense of identity resting on carefully defended borders—are not so easily noticed and identified as emotions, and are instead invisibly folded into "self-evident," so-called realist paradigms and analyses. It is both the interweaving of gender discourse in national security thinking *and* the blindness to its presence and impact that have deleterious effects. Finally, the impact is to distort, degrade, and deter roundly rational, fully complex thought within the community of defense intellectuals and national security elites and, by extension, to cripple democratic deliberation about crucial matters of war and peace.

Notes

1. Chris Hedges, "War Is Vivid in the Gun Sights of the Sniper," *New York Times,* February 3, 1991, A1.

2. General Norman Schwarzkopf, National Public Radio broadcast, February 8, 1991.

3. General Norman Schwarzkopf, CENTCOM News Briefing, Riyadh, Saudi Arabia, February 27, 1991, p. 2.

4. Transcript of a strategic studies specialist's lecture on NATO and the Warsaw Pact (summer institute on Regional Conflict and Global Security: The Nuclear Dimension, Madison, Wisconsin, June 29, 1987).

5. Defense Secretary Dick Cheney, "Excerpts from Briefing at Pentagon by Cheney and Powell," *New York Times,* January 24, 1991, A 11.

6. Scarry explains that when an army is described as a single "embodied combatant," injury, (as in Saddam's "pounding"), may be referred to but is "no longer recognizable or interpretable." It is not only that Americans might be happy to imagine Saddam being pounded; we also on some level know that it is not really happening, and thus need not feel the pain of the wounded. We "respond to the injury...as an imaginary wound to an imaginary body, despite the fact that that imaginary body is itself made up of thousands of real human bodies" (Elaine Scarry, *Body in Pain: The Making and Unmaking of the World* [New York: Oxford, 1984], p. 72).

The Myth of Sexual Symmetry in Marital Violence

RUSSELL P. DOBASH, R. EMERSON DOBASH, MARGO WILSON, AND MARTIN DALY

Long denied, legitimized, and made light of, wife-beating is at last the object of widespread public concern and condemnation. Extensive survey research and intensive interpretive investigations tell a common story. Violence against wives (by which term we encompass *de facto* as well as registered unions) is often persistent and severe, occurs in the context of continuous intimidation and coercion, and is inextricably linked to attempts to domininate and control women. Historical and contemporary investigations further reveal that this violence has been explicitly decriminalized, ignored, or treated in an ineffectual manner by criminal justice systems, by medical and social service institutions, and by communities. Increased attention to these failures has inspired increased efforts to redress them, and in many places legislative amendments have mandated arrest and made assault a crime whether the offender is married to the victim or not.

A number of researchers and commentators have suggested that assaults upon men by their wives constitute a social problem comparable in nature and magnitude to that of wife-beating. Two main bodies of evidence have been offered in support of these authors' claims that husbands and wives are similarly victimized: (1) self-reports of violent acts perpetrated and suffered by survey respondents, especially those in two U.S. national probability samples; and (2) U.S. homicide data. Unlike the case of violence against wives, however, the victimization of husbands allegedly continues to be denied and trivialized. "Violence by wives has not been an object of public concern," note Straus and Gelles (1986:472). "There has been no publicity, and no funds have been invested in ameliorating this problem because it has not been defined as a problem."

We shall argue that claims of sexual symmetry in marital violence are exaggerated, and that wives' and husbands' uses of violence differ greatly, both quantitatively and qualitatively. We shall further argue that there is no reason to expect the sexes to be alike in this domain, and that efforts to avoid sexism by lumping male and female data and by the use of gender-neutral terms such as "spouse-beating" are misguided. If violence is gendered, as it assuredly is, explicit characterization of gender's relevance to violence is essential. The alleged similarity of women and men in their use of violence in intimate relationships stands in marked contrast to men's virtual monopoly on the use of violence in other social contexts, and we challenge the proponents of the sexual symmetry thesis to develop coherent theoretical models that would account for a sexual monomorphism of violence in one social context and not in others.

A final thesis of this paper is that resolution of controversies about the "facts" of family violence requires critical examination of theories, methods, and data, with explicit attention to the development of coherent conceptual frameworks, valid and meaningful forms of measurement, and appropriate inferential procedures. Such problems are not peculiar to this research domain, but analysis of the claims regarding violence against husbands provides an excellent example of how a particular approach to construct formation and measurement has led to misrepresentation of the phenomena under investigation.

The Claim of Sexually Symmetrical Marital Violence

Authoritative claims about the prevalence and sexual symmetry of spousal violence in America began with a 1975 U.S. national survey in which 2,143 married or cohabiting persons were interviewed in person about their actions in the preceding year. Straus (1977/78) announced that the survey results showed that the "marriage license is a hitting license," and moreover that the rates of perpetrating spousal violence, including severe violence, were higher for wives than for husbands. He concluded:

> Violence between husband and wife is far from a one way street. The old cartoons of the wife chasing the husband with a rolling pin or throwing pots and pans are closer to reality than most (and especially those with feminist sympathies) realize (Straus 1977/78:447–448).

In 1985, the survey was repeated by telephone with a new national probability sample including 3,520 husband-wife households, and with similar results. In each survey, the researchers interviewed either the wife or the husband (but not both) in each contacted household about how the couple settled their differences when they had a disagreement. The individual who was interviewed was presented with a list of eighteen "acts" ranging from "discussed an issue calmly" and "cried" to "threw something at him/her/you" and "beat him/her/you up," with the addition of "choked him/her/you" in 1985 (Straus 1990a:33). These acts constituted the Conflict Tactics Scales (CTS) and were intended to measure three constructs: "Reasoning," "Verbal Aggression," and "Physical Aggression" or "Violence," which was further subdivided into "Minor Violence" and "Severe Violence" according to a presumed potential for injury (Straus 1979, Straus and Gelles 1990a). Respondents were asked

how frequently they had perpetrated each act in the course of "conflicts or disagreements" with their spouses (and with one randomly selected child) within the past year, and how frequently they had been on the receiving end. Each respondent's self-reports of victimization and perpetration contributed to estimates of rates of violence by both husbands and wives.

According to both surveys, rates of violence by husbands and wives were strikingly similar. The authors estimated that in the year prior to the 1975 survey 11.6 percent of U.S. husbands were victims of physical violence perpetrated by their wives, while 12.1 percent of wives were victims of their husbands' violence. In 1985, these percentages had scarcely changed, but husbands seemed more vulnerable: 12.1 percent of husbands and 11.3 percent of wives were victims. In both surveys, husbands were more likely to be victims of acts of "severe violence": in 1975, 4.6 percent of husbands were such victims versus 3.8 percent of wives, and in 1985, 4.4 percent of husbands versus 3.0 percent of wives were victims. In reporting their results, the surveys' authors stressed the surprising assaultiveness of wives:

> The repeated finding that the rate of assault by women is similar to the rate by their male partners is an important and distressing aspect of violence in American families. It contrasts markedly to the behavior of women outside the family. It shows that within the family or in dating and cohabiting relationships, women are about as violent as men (Straus and Gelles 1990b:104).

Others have endorsed and publicized these conclusions. For example, a recent review of marital violence concludes, with heavy reliance on Straus and Gelles's survey results, that "(a) women are more prone than men to engage in severely violent acts; (b) each year more men than women are victimized by their intimates" (McNeely and Mann 1990:130). One of Straus and Gelles's collaborators in the 1975 survey, Steinmetz (1977/78), used the same survey evidence to proclaim the existence of "battered husbands" and a "battered husband syndrome." She has remained one of the leading defenders of the claim that violence between men and women in the family is symmetrical. Steinmetz and her collaborators maintain that the problem is not wife-beating perpetrated by violent men, but "violent couples" and "violent people". Men may be stronger on average, argues Steinmetz, but weaponry equalizes matters, as is allegedly shown by the nearly equivalent numbers of U.S. husbands and wives who are killed by their partners. The reason why battered husbands are inconspicuous and seemingly rare is supposedly that shame prevents them from seeking help.

Straus and his collaborators have sometimes qualified their claims that their surveys demonstrate sexual symmetry in marital violence, noting, for example, that men are usually larger and stronger than women and thus able to inflict more damage and that women are more likely to use violence in self-defense or retaliation. However, the survey results indicate a symmetry not just in the perpetration of violence but in its initiation as well, and from this further symmetry, Stets and Straus (1990:154–155) conclude that the equal assaultiveness of husbands and wives cannot be attributed to the wives acting in self-defense, after all.

Other surveys using the CTS in the United States and in other countries have replicated the finding that wives are about as violent as husbands. The CTS has also been used to study violence in dating relationships, with the same sexually symmetrical results.

Some authors maintain not only that wives initiate violence at rates comparable to husbands, but that they rival them in the damage they inflict as well. McNeely and Robinson-Simpson (1987), for example, argue that research shows that the "truth about domestic violence" is that "women are as violent, if not more violent than men," in their inclinations, in their actions, and in the damage they inflict. The most dramatic evidence invoked in this context is again the fact that wives kill: spousal homicides—for which detection should be minimally or not at all biased because homicides are nearly always discovered and recorded—produce much more nearly equivalent numbers of male and female victims in the United States than do sublethal assault data, which are subject to sampling biases when obtained from police, shelters

and hospitals. According to McNeely and Mann (1990:130), "the average man's size and strength are neutralized by guns and knives, boiling water, bricks, fireplace pokers, and baseball bats."

A corollary of the notion that the sexes are alike in their use of violence is that satisfactory causal accounts of violence will be gender-blind. Discussion thus focuses, for example, on the role of one's prior experiences with violence as a child, social stresses, frustration, inability to control anger, impoverished social skills, and so forth, without reference to gender. This presumption that the sexes are alike not merely in action but in the reasons for that action is occasionally explicit, such as when Shupe et al. (1987:56) write: "Everything we have found points to parallel processes that lead women and men to become violent.… Women may be more likely than men to use kitchen utensils or sewing scissors when they commit assault, but their frustrations, motives and lack of control over these feelings predictably resemble men's."

In sum, the existence of an invisibles legion of assaulted husbands is an inference which strikes many family violence researchers as reasonable. Two lines of evidence—homicide data and the CTS survey results—suggest to those supporting the sexual-symmetry-of-violence thesis that large numbers of men are trapped in violent relationships. These men are allegedly being denied medical, social welfare, and criminal justice services because of an unwillingness to accept the evidence from homicide statistics and the CTS surveys.

Violence Against Wives

Any argument that marital violence is sexually symmetrical must either dismiss or ignore a large body of contradictory evidence indicating that wives greatly outnumber husbands as victims. While CTS researchers were discovering and publicizing the mutual violence of wives and husbands, other researchers—using evidence from courts, police, and women's shelters—were finding that wives were much more likely than husbands to be victims. After an extensive review of extant research, Lystad (1975) expressed the consensus: "The occurrence of adult violence in the home usually involves males as aggressors towards females." This conclusion was subsequently supported by numerous further studies of divorce records, emergency room patients treated for non-accidental injuries, police assault records, and spouses seeking assistance and refuge. Analyses of police and court records in North America and Europe have persistently indicated that women constitute ninety to ninety-five percent of the victims of those assaults in the home reported to the criminal justice system.

Defenders of the sexual-symmetry-of-violence thesis do not deny these results, but they question their representativeness: these studies could be biased because samples of victims were self-selected. However, criminal victimization surveys using national probability samples similarly indicate that wives are much more often victimized than husbands. Such surveys in the United States, Canada and Great Britain have been replicated in various years, with essentially the same results. Beginning in 1972 and using a panel survey method involving up to seven consecutive interviews at six-month intervals, the U.S. National Crime Survey has generated nearly a million interviews. Gaquin's (1977/78) analysis of U.S. National Crime Survey data for 1973–1975 led her to conclude that men "have almost no risk of being assaulted by their wives" (634–635); only 3 percent of the violence reported from these surveys involved attacks on men by their female partners. Another analysis of the National Crime Survey data from 1973 to 1980 found that 6 percent of spousal assault incidents were directed at men (McLeod 1984). Schwartz (1987) re-analyzed the same victimization surveys with the addition of the 1981 and 1982 data, and found 102 men who claimed to have been victims of assaults by their wives (4 percent of domestic assault incidents) in contrast to 1,641 women who said they were assaulted by husbands. The 1981 Canadian Urban Victimization Survey and the 1987 General Social Survey produced analogous findings, from which Johnson (1989) concluded that "women account for 80–90 percent of victims in assaults or sexual assaults between spouses or former spouses. In fact, the number of domestic assaults involving

males was too low in both surveys to provide reliable estimates" (1–2). The 1982 and 1984 British Crime Surveys found that women accounted for all the victims of marital assaults. Self-reports of criminal victimization based on national probability surveys, while not without methodological weaknesses, are not subject to the same reporting biases as divorce, police and hospital records.

The national crime surveys also indicate that women are much more likely than men to suffer injury as a result of assaults in the home. After analyzing the results of the U.S. National Crime Surveys, Schwartz (1987:67) concludes, "there are still more than 13 times as many women seeking medical care from a private physician for injuries received in a spousal assault." This result again replicates the typical findings of studies of police or hospital records. For example, women constituted 94 percent of the injury victims in an analysis of the spousal assault cases among 262 domestic disturbance calls to police in Santa Barbara County, California; moreover, the women's injuries were more serious than the men's. Berk et al. (1983:207) conclude that "when injuries are used as the outcome of interest, a marriage license is a hitting license but for men only." Brush (1990) reports that a U.S. national probability sample survey of over 13,000 respondents in 1987–1988 replicated the evident symmetry of marital violence when CTS-like questions about acts were posed, but also revealed that women were much more often injured than men (and that men down-played women's injuries).

In response, defenders of the sexual-symmetry-of-violence thesis contend that data from police, courts, hospitals, and social service agencies are suspect because men are reluctant to report physical violence by their wives. For example, Steinmetz (1977/78) asserts that husband-beating is a camouflaged social problem because men must overcome extraordinary stigma in order to report that their wives have beaten them. Similarly, Shupe et al. (1987) maintain that men are unwilling to report their wives because "it would be unmanly or unchivalrous to go to the police for protection from a woman" (52). However, the limited available evidence does not support these authors' presumption that men are less likely to report assaults by their spouses than are women. Schwartz's (1987) analysis of the 1973–1982 U.S. National Crime Survey data found that 67.2 percent of men and 56.8 percent of women called the police after being assaulted by their spouses. One may protest that these high percentages imply that only a tiny proportion of the most severe spousal assaults were acknowledged as assaults by respondents to these crime surveys, but the results are nonetheless contrary to the notion that assaulted men are especially reticent. Moreover, Rouse et al. (1988), using "act" definitions of assaults which inspired much higher proportions to acknowledge victimization, similarly report that men were likelier than women to call the police after assaults by intimate partners, both among married couples and among those dating. In addition, a sample of 337 cases of domestic violence drawn from family court cases in Ontario showed that men were more likely than women to press charges against their spouses: there were 17 times as many female victims as male victims, but only 22 percent of women laid charges in contrast to 40 percent of the men, and men were less likely to drop the charges, too. What those who argue that men are reluctant or ashamed to report their wives' assaults overlook is that women have their own reasons to be reticent, fearing both the loss of a jailed or alienated husband's economic support and his vengeance. Whereas the claim that husbands underreport because of shame or chivalry is largely speculative, there is considerable evidence that women report very little of the violence perpetrated by their male partners.

The CTS survey data indicating equivalent violence by wives and husbands thus stand in contradiction to injury data, to police incident reports, to help-seeking statistics, and even to other, larger, national probability sample surveys of self-reported victimization. The CTS researchers insist that their results alone are accurate because husbands' victimizations are unlikely to be detected or reported by any other method. It is therefore important to consider in detail the CTS and the data it generates.

Do CTS Data Reflect the Reality of Marital Violence?

The CTS instrument has been much used and much criticized. Critics have complained that its exclusive focus on "acts" ignores the actors' interpretations, motivations, and intentions; that physical violence is arbitrarily delimited, excluding, for example, sexual assault and rape; that retrospective reports of the past year's events are unlikely to be accurate; that researchers' attributions of "violence" (with resultant claims about its statistical prevalence) are based on respondents' admitting to acts described in such an impoverished manner as to conflate severe assaults with trivial gestures; that the formulaic distinction between "minor" and "severe violence" (whereby, for example, "tried to hit with something" is definitionally "severe" and "slapped" is definitionally "minor") constitutes a poor operationalization of severity; that the responses of aggressors and victims have been given identical evidentiary status in deriving incidence estimates, while their inconsistencies have been ignored; that the CTS omits the contexts of violence, the events precipitating it, and the sequences of events by which it progresses; and that it fails to connect outcomes, especially injury, with the acts producing them.

Straus (1990b) has defended the CTS against its critics, maintaining that the CTS addresses context with its "verbal aggression" scale (although the assessment of "verbal aggression" is not incident-linked with the assessment of "violence"); that the minor-severe categorization "is roughly parallel to the legal distinction between 'simple assault' and 'aggravated assault'" (58); that other measurement instruments have problems, too; and that you cannot measure everything. Above all, the defense rests on the widespread use of the instrument, on its reliability, and on its validity. That the CTS is widely used cannot be gainsaid, but whether it is reliable or valid is questionable.

Problems with the Reliability and Validity of CTS Responses

Straus (1990b:64) claims that six studies have assessed "the internal consistency reliability" of the CTS. One of the six (Barling and Rosenbaum 1986) contains no such assessment, a second is unreferenced, and a third unpublished. However, a moderate degree of "internal consistency reliability" of the CTS can probably be conceded. For example, those who admit to having "beat up" their spouses are also likely to admit to having "hit" them.

The crucial matter of interobserver reliability is much more problematic. The degree of concordance in couples' responses is an assay of "interspousal reliability" (Jouriles and O'Leary 1985), and such reliability must be high if CTS scores are to be taken at face value. For example, incidence estimates of husband-to-wife and wife-to-husband violence have been generated from national surveys in which the CTS was administered to only one adult per family, with claims of victimization and perpetration by male and female respondents all granted equal evidentiary status and summated. The validity of these widely cited incidence estimates is predicated upon interspousal reliability.

Straus (1990b:66) considers the assessment of spousal concordance to constitute an assay of "concurrent validity" rather than "interspousal reliability," in effect treating each partner's report as the violence criterion that validates the other. But spousal concordance is analogous to interobserver reliability: it is a necessary but by no means sufficient condition for concluding that the self-reports accurately reflect reality. If couples generally produce consistent reports—Mr. and Mrs. Jones both indicate that he struck her, while Mr. and Mrs. Smith both indicate that neither has struck the other—then it is possible though by no means certain that their CTS self-reports constitute valid (veridical) information about the blows actually struck. However, if couples routinely provide discrepant CTS responses, data derived from the CTS simply cannot be valid.

In this light, studies of husband/wife concordance in CTS responses should be devastating to those who imagine that the CTS provides a valid account of the respondents' acts. In what Straus correctly calls "the most detailed and thorough analysis of agreement between spouses in

response to the CTS," Szinovacz (1983) found that 103 couples' accounts of the violence in their interactions matched to a degree little greater than chance. On several CTS items, mainly the most severe ones, agreement was actually below chance. On the item "beat up," concordance was nil: although there were respondents of both sexes who claimed to have administered beatings and respondents of both sexes who claimed to have been on the receiving end, there was not a single couple in which one party claimed to have administered and the other to have received such a beating. In a similar study, Jouriles and O'Leary (1985) administered the CTS to 65 couples attending a marital therapy clinic, and 37 control couples from the local community. For many of the acts, the frequency and percentage data reported are impossible to reconcile; for others, Jouriles and O'Leary reported a concordance statistic (Cohen's Kappa) as equalling zero when the correct values were negative. Straus (1990b) cites this study as conferring validity on the CTS, but in fact, its results replicated Szinovacz's (1983): husband/wife agreement scarcely exceeded chance expectation and actually fell below chance on some items.

Straus (1990b) acknowledges that these and the other studies he reviews "found large discrepancies between the reports of violence given by husbands and by wives" (69). He concludes, however, that "validity measures of agreement between family members are within the range of validity coefficients typically reported" (71), and that "the weakest aspect of the CTS are [sic] the scales that have received the least criticism: Reasoning and Verbal aggression" (71), by which he implies that the assessment of violence is relatively strong.

Ultimately, Straus's defense of the CTS is that the proof of the pudding is in the eating: "The strongest evidence concerns the construct validity of the CTS. It has been used in a large number of studies producing findings that tend to be consistent with previous research (when available), consistent regardless of gender of respondent, and theoretically meaningful." And indeed, with respect to marital violence, the CTS is capable of making certain gross discriminations. Various studies have found CTS responses to vary as a function of age, race, poverty, duration of relationship, and registered versus de facto marital unions, and these effects have generally been directionally similar to those found with less problematic measures of violence such as homicides. However, the CTS has also failed to detect certain massive differences, and we do not refer only to sex differences.

Consider the case of child abuse by stepparents versus birth parents. In various countries, including the United States, a stepparent is more likely to fatally assault a small child than is a birth parent, by a factor on the order of 100-fold; sublethal violence also exhibits huge differences in the same direction. Using the CTS, however, Gelles and Harrop (1991) were unable to detect any difference in self-reports of violence by step- versus birth parents. Users of the CTS have sometimes conceded that the results of their self-report surveys cannot provide an accurate picture of the prevalence of violence, but they have made this concession only to infer that the estimates must be gross underestimates of the true prevalence. However, the CTS's failure to differentiate the behavior of step- versus birth parents indicates that CTS-based estimates are not just underestimates but may misrepresent between-group differences in systematically biased ways. One must be concerned, then, whether this sort of bias also arises in CTS-based comparisons between husbands and wives.

Problems with the Interpretation of CTS Responses

With the specific intention of circumventing imprecision and subjectivity in asking about such abstractions as "violence," the CTS is confined to questions about "acts": Respondents are asked whether they have "pushed" their partners, have "slapped" them, and so forth, rather than whether they have "assaulted" them or behaved "violently." This focus on "acts" is intended to reduce problems of self-serving and biased definitional criteria on the part of the respondents. However, any gain in objectivity has been undermined by the way that CTS survey data have then been analyzed and interpreted. Any respondent who acknowledges a single instance of having "pushed," "grabbed,"

"shoved," "slapped" or "hit or tried to hit" another person is deemed a perpetrator of "violence" by the researchers, regardless of the act's context, consequences, or meaning to the parties involved. Similarly, a single instance of having "kicked," "bit," "hit or tried to hit with an object," "beat up," "choked," "threatened with a knife or gun," or "used a knife or fired a gun" makes one a perpetrator of "severe violence."

Affirmation of any one of the "violence" items provides the basis for estimates such as Straus and Gelles's (1990b:97) claim that 6.8 million U.S. husbands and 6.25 million U.S. wives were spousal assault victims in 1985. Similarly, estimates of large numbers of "beaten" or "battered" wives and husbands have been based on affirmation of any one of the "severe violence" items. For example, Steinmetz (1986:734) and Straus and Gelles (1987:638) claim on this basis that 1.8 million U.S. women are "beaten" by their husbands annually. But note that any man who once threw an "object" at his wife, regardless of its nature and regardless of whether the throw missed, qualifies as having "beaten" her; some unknown proportion of the women and men who are alleged to have been "beaten," on the basis of their survey responses, never claimed to have been struck at all. Thus, the "objective" scoring of the CTS not only fails to explore the meanings and intentions associated with the acts but has in practice entailed interpretive transformations that guarantee exaggeration, misinterpretation, and ultimately trivialization of the genuine problems of violence.

Consider a "slap." The word encompasses anything from a slap on the hand chastizing a dinner companion for reaching for a bite of one's dessert to a tooth-loosening assault intended to punish, humiliate, and terrorize. These are not trivial distinctions; indeed, they constitute the essence of definitional issues concerning violence. Almost all definitions of violence and violent acts refer to intentions. Malevolent intent is crucial, for example, to legal definitions of "assault" (to which supporters of the CTS have often mistakenly claimed that their "acts" correspond; e.g., Straus 1990b:58). However, no one has systematically investigated how respondents vary in their subjective definitions of the "acts" listed on the CTS. If, for example, some respondents interpret phrases such as "tried to hit with an object" literally, then a good deal of relatively harmless behavior surely taints the estimates of "severe violence." Although this problem has not been investigated systematically, one author has shown that it is potentially serious. In a study of 103 couples, Margolin (1987) found that wives surpassed husbands in their use of "severe violence" according to the CTS, but unlike others who have obtained this result, Margolin troubled to check its meaningfulness with more intensive interviews. She concluded:

> While CTS items appear behaviorally specific, their meanings still are open to interpretation. In one couple who endorsed the item "kicking," for example, we discovered that the kicking took place in bed in a more kidding, than serious, fashion. Although this behavior meets the criterion for severe abuse on the CTS, neither spouse viewed it as aggressive, let alone violent. In another couple, the wife scored on severe physical aggression while the husband scored on low-level aggression only. The inquiry revealed that, after years of passively accepting the husband's repeated abuse, this wife finally decided, on one occasion, to retaliate by hitting him over the head with a wine decanter (1987:82).

By the criteria of Steinmetz (1977/78:501), this incident would qualify as a "battered husband" case. But however dangerous this retaliatory blow may have been and however reprehensible or justified one may consider it, it is not "battering," whose most basic definitional criterion is its repetitiveness. A failure to consider intentions, interpretations, and the history of the individuals' relationship is a significant shortcoming of CTS research. Only through a consideration of behaviors, intentions and intersubjective understandings associated with specific violent events will we come to a fuller understanding of violence between men and women. Studies employing more intensive interviews and detailed case reports addressing the contexts and motivations of marital violence help unravel the assertions of those who claim the widespread existence of

beaten and battered husbands. Research focusing on specific violent events shows that women almost always employ violence in defense of self and children in response to cues of imminent assault in the past and in retaliation for previous physical abuse. Proponents of the sexual-symmetry-of-violence thesis have made much of the fact that CTS surveys indicate that women "initiate" the violence about as often as men, but a case in which a woman struck the first blow is unlikely to be the mirror image of one in which her husband "initiated." A noteworthy feature of the literature proclaiming the existence of battered husbands and battering wives is how little the meager case descriptions resemble those of battered wives and battering husbands. Especially lacking in the alleged male victim cases is any indication of the sort of chronic intimidation characteristic of prototypical woman battering cases.

Any self-report method must constitute an imperfect reflection of behavior, and the CTS is no exception. That in itself is hardly a fatal flaw. But for such an instrument to retain utility for the investigation of a particular domain such as family violence, an essential point is that its inaccuracies and misrepresentations must not be systematically related to the distinctions under investigation. The CTS's inability to detect the immense differences in violence between stepparents and birth parents, as noted above, provides strong reason to suspect that the test's shortcomings produce not just noise but systematic bias. In the case of marital violence, the other sorts of evidence reviewed in this paper indicate that there are massive differences in the use of confrontational violence against spouses by husbands versus wives, and yet the CTS has consistently failed to detect them. CTS users have taken this failure as evidence for the null hypothesis, apparently assuming that their questionnaire data have a validity that battered women's injuries and deaths lack.

Homicides

The second line of evidence that has been invoked in support of the claim that marital violence is more or less sexually symmetrical is the number of lethal outcomes:

> Data on homicide between spouses suggest that an almost equal number of wives kill their husbands as husbands kill their wives (Wolfgang 1958). Thus it appears that men and women might have equal potential for violent marital interaction; initiate similar acts of violence; and when differences of physical strength are equalized by weapons, commit similar amounts of spousal homicide (Steinmetz and Lucca 1988:241).

McNeely and Robinson-Simpson (1987:485) elevated the latter hypothesis about the relevance of weapons to the status of a fact: "Steinmetz observed that when weapons neutralize differences in physical strength, about as many men as women are victims of homicide."

Steinmetz and Lucca's citation of Wolfgang refers to his finding that 53 Philadelphia men killed their wives between 1948 and 1952, while, 47 women killed their husbands. This is a slender basis for such generalization, but fuller information does indeed bear Steinmetz out as regards the near equivalence of body counts in the United States: Maxfield (1989) reported that there were 10,529 wives and 7,888 husbands killed by their mates in the entire country between 1976 and 1985, a 1.3:1 ratio of female to male victims.

Husbands are indeed almost as often slain as are wives in the United States, then. However, there remain several problems with Steinmetz and Lucca's (as well as McNeely and Robinson-Simpson's) interpretation of this fact. Studies of actual cases lend no support to the facile claim that homicidal husbands and wives "initiate similar acts of violence." Men often kill wives after lengthy periods of prolonged physical violence accompanied by other forms of abuse and coercion; the roles in such cases are seldom if ever reversed. Men perpetrate familicidal massacres, killing spouse and children together; women do not. Men commonly hunt down and kill wives who have left them; women hardly ever behave similarly. Men kill wives as part of planned murder-suicides; analogous acts by women are almost unheard of. Men kill in response to revelations of

wifely infidelity; women almost never respond similarly, though their mates are more often adulterous. The evidence is overwhelming that a large proportion of the spouse-killings perpetrated by wives, but almost none of those perpetrated by husbands, are acts of self-defense. Unlike men, women kill male partners after years of suffering physical violence, after they have exhausted all available sources of assistance, when they feel trapped, and because they fear for their own lives.

A further problem with the invocation of spousal homicide data as evidence against sex differences in marital violence is that this numerical equivalence is peculiar to the United States. Whereas the ratio of wives to husbands as homicide victims in the United States was 1.3:1, corresponding ratios from other countries are much higher: 3.3:1 for a 10-year period in Canada, for example, 4.3:1 for Great Britain, and 6:1 for Denmark. The reason why this is problematic is that U.S. homicide data and CTS data from several countries have been invoked as complementary pieces of evidence for women's and men's equivalent uses of violence. One cannot have it both ways. If the lack of sex differences in CTS results is considered proof of sexually symmetrical violence, then homicide data must somehow be dismissed as irrelevant, since homicides generally fail to exhibit this supposedly more basic symmetry. Conversely, if U.S. homicide counts constitute relevant evidence, the large sex differences found elsewhere surely indicate that violence is peculiarly symmetrical only in the United States, and the fact that the CTS fails to detect sex differences in other countries must then be taken to mean that the CTS is insensitive to genuine differences.

A possible way out of this dilemma is hinted at in Steinmetz and Lucca's (1988) allusion to the effect of weapons: perhaps it is the availability of guns that has neutralized men's advantage in lethal marital conflict in the United States. Gun use is indeed relatively prevalent in the U.S., accounting for 51 percent of a sample of 1706 spousal homicides in Chicago, for example, as compared to 40 percent of 1060 Canadian cases, 42 percent of 395 Australian cases, and just 8 percent of 1204 cases in England and Wales (Wilson and Daly forth-coming). Nevertheless, the plausible hypothesis that gun use can account for the different sex ratios among victims fails. When shootings and other spousal homicides are analyzed separately, national differences in the sex ratios of spousal homicide remain dramatic. For example, the ratio of wives to husbands as gunshot homicide victims in Chicago was 1.2:1, compared to 4:1 in Canada and 3.5:1 in Britain; the ratio of wives to husbands as victims of non-gun homicides was 0.8:1 in Chicago, compared to 2.9:1 in Canada and 4.5:1 in Britain (Wilson and Daly forthcoming). Moreover, the near equivalence of husband and wife victims in the U.S. antedates the contemporary prevalence of gun killings. In Wolfgang's (1958) classic study, only 34 of the 100 spousal homicide victims were shot (15 husbands and 19 wives), while 30 husbands were stabbed and 31 wives were beaten or stabbed. Whatever may explain the exceptionally similar death rates of U.S. husbands and wives, it is not simply that guns "equalize."

Nor is the unusual U.S. pattern to be explained in terms of a peculiar convergence in the United States of the sexes in their violent inclinations or capabilities across all domains and relationships. Although U.S. data depart radically from other industrialized countries in the sex ratio of spousal homicide victimization, they do not depart similarly in the sex ratios of other sorts of homicides (Wilson and Daly forthcoming). For example, in the United States as elsewhere men kill unrelated men about 40 times as often as women kill unrelated women.

Even among lethal acts, it is essential to discriminate among different victim-killer relationships, because motives, risk factors, and conflict typologies are relationship-specific. Steinmetz (1977/78, Steinmetz and Lucca 1998) has invoked the occurrence of maternally perpetrated infanticides as evidence of women's violence, imagining that the fact that some women commit infanticide somehow bolsters the claim that they batter their husbands, too. But maternal infanticides are more often motivated by desperation than by hostile aggression and are often effected by acts of neglect or abandonment rather than by assault. To conflate such acts with aggressive attacks is to misunderstand their utterly distinct motives, forms, and perpetrator profiles, and the distinct social and material circumstances in which they occur.

How to Gain a Valid Account of Marital Violence?

How ought researchers to conceive of "violence"? People differ in their views about whether a particular act was a violent one and about who was responsible. Assessments of intention and justifiability are no less relevant to the labelling of an event as "violent" than are more directly observable considerations like the force exerted or the damage inflicted. Presumably, it is this problem of subjectivity that has inspired efforts to objectify the study of family violence by the counting of "acts," as in the Conflict Tactics Scales.

Unfortunately, the presumed gain in objectivity achieved by asking research subjects to report only "acts," while refraining from elaborating upon their meanings and consequences, is illusory. As noted above, couples exhibit little agreement in reporting the occurrence of acts in which both were allegedly involved, and self-reported acts sometimes fail to differentiate the behavior of groups known to exhibit huge differences in the perpetration of violence. The implication must be that concerns about the validity of self-report data cannot be allayed merely by confining self-reports to a checklist of named acts. We have no more reason to suppose that people will consensually and objectively label events as instances of someone having "grabbed" or "hit or tried to hit" or "used a knife" (items from the CTS) than to suppose that people will consensually and objectively label events as instances of "violence."

If these "acts" were scored by trained observers examining the entire event, there might be grounds for such behavioristic austerity in measurement: whatever the virtues and limitations of behavioristic methodology, a case can at least be made that observational data are more objective than the actors' accounts. However, when researchers have access only to self-reports, the cognitions of the actors are neither more nor less accessible to research than their actions. Failures of candor and memory threaten the validity of both sorts of self-report data, and researchers' chances of detecting such failures can only be improved by the collection of richer detail about the violent event. The behavioristic rigor of observational research cannot be simulated by leaving data collection to the subjects, nor by active inattention to "subjective" matters like people's perceptions of their own and others' intentions, attributions of loss of control, perceived provocations and justifications, intimidatory consequences, and so forth. Moreover, even a purely behavioristic account could be enriched by attending to sequences of events and subsequent behavior rather than merely counting acts.

Enormous differences in meaning and consequence exist between a woman pummelling her laughing husband in an attempt to convey strong feelings and a man pummelling his weeping wife in an attempt to punish her for coming home late. It is not enough to acknowledge such contrasts (as CTS researchers have sometimes done), if such acknowledgments neither inform further research nor alter such conclusions as "within the family or in dating and cohabiting relationships, women are about as violent as men" (Straus and Gelles 1990b:104). What is needed are forms of analysis that will lead to a comprehensive description of the violence itself as well as an explanation of it. In order to do this, it is, at the very least, necessary to analyze the violent event in a holistic manner, with attention to the entire sequences of distinct acts as well as associated motives, intentions, and consequences, all of which must in turn be situated within the wider context of the relationship.

The Need for Theory

If the arguments and evidence that we have presented are correct, then currently fashionable claims about the symmetry of marital violence are unfounded. How is it that so many experts have been persuaded of a notion that is at once counterintuitive and counterfactual? Part of the answer, we believe, is that researchers too often operate without sound (or indeed any) theoretical visions of marital relationships, of interpersonal conflicts, or of violence.

Straus (1990a:30), for example, introduces the task of investigating family violence by characterizing families as instances of "social groups" and by noting that conflicts of interest are endemic to groups of individuals, "each seeking to live out their lives in accordance with personal agendas that inevitably differ." This is a good start, but the analysis proceeds no further. The characteristic features of families as distinct from other groups are not explored, and the particular domains within which the "agendas" of wives and husbands conflict are not elucidated. Instead, Straus illustrates family conflicts with the hypothetical example of "Which TV show will be watched at eight?" and discusses negotiated and coerced resolutions in terms that would be equally applicable to a conflict among male acquaintances in a bar. Such analysis obscures all that is distinctive about violence against wives which occurs in a particular context of perceived entitlement and institutionalized power asymmetry. Moreover, marital violence occurs around recurring themes, especially male sexual jealousy and proprietariness, expectations of obedience and domestic service, and women's attempts to leave the marital relationship. In the self-consciously gender-blind literature on "violent couples," these themes are invisible.

Those who claim that wives and husbands are equally violent have offered no conceptual framework for understanding why women and men should think and act alike. Indeed, the claim that violence is gender-neutral cannot easily be reconciled with other coincident claims. For example, many family violence researchers who propose sexual symmetry in violence attribute the inculcation and legitimation of violence to socializing processes and cultural institutions, but then overlook the fact that these processes and institutions define and treat females and males differently. If sexually differentiated socialization and entitlements play a causal role in violence, how can we understand the alleged equivalence of women's and men's violent inclinations and actions?

Another theoretical problem confronting anyone who claims that violent inclinations are sexually monomorphic concerns the oft-noted fact that men are larger than women and likelier to inflict damage by similar acts. Human passions have their own "rationality," and it would be curious if women and men were identically motivated to initiate assaults in contexts where the expectable results were far more damaging for women. Insofar as both parties to a potentially violent transaction are aware of such differences, it is inappropriate to treat a slap (or other "act") by one party as equivalent to a slap by the other, not only because there is an asymmetry in the damage the two slaps might inflict, but because the parties differ in the responses available to them and hence in their control over the dénouement. Women's motives may be expected to differ systematically from those of men wherever the predictable consequences of their actions differ systematically. Those who contend that women and men are equally inclined to violence need to articulate why this should be so, given the sex differences in physical traits, such as size and muscularity, affecting the probable consequences of violence.

In fact, there is a great deal of evidence that men's and women's psychologies are not at all alike in this domain. Men's violent reactions to challenges to their authority, honor, and self-esteem are well-known; comparable behavior by a woman is a curiosity. A variety of convergent evidence supports the conclusion that men (especially young men) are more specialized for and more motivated to engage in dangerous risk-taking, confrontational competition, and interpersonal violence than are women. When comparisons are confined to interactions with members of one's own sex so that size and power asymmetries are largely irrelevant, the differences between men and women in these behavioral domains are universally large.

We cannot hope to understand violence in marital, cohabiting, and dating relationships without explicit attention to the qualities that make them different from other relationships. It is a cross-culturally and historically ubiquitous aspect of human affairs that women and men form individualized unions, recognized by themselves and by others as conferring certain obligations and entitlements, such that the partners' productive and reproductive careers become intertwined.

Family violence research might usefully begin by examining the consonant and discordant desires, expectations, grievances, perceived entitlements, and preoccupations of husbands and wives, and by investigating theoretically derived hypotheses about circumstantial, ecological, contextual, and demographic correlates of such conflict. Having described the conflict of interest that characterize marital relationships with explicit reference to the distinct agendas of women and men, violence researchers must proceed to an analysis that acknowledges and accounts for those gender differences. It is crucial to establish differences in the patterns of male and female violence, to thoroughly describe and explain the overall process of violent events within their immediate and wider contexts, and to analyze the reasons why conflict results in differentially violent action by women and men.

References

Barling, Julian, and Alan Rosenbaum. 1986. "Work stressors and wife abuse." Journal of Applied Psychology 71:346–348.

Berk, Richard A., Sarah F. Berk, Donileen R. Loseke, and D. Rauma. 1983. "Mutual combat and other family violence myths." In The Dark Side of Families, ed. David Finkelhor, Richard J. Gelles, Gerald T. Hotaling, and Murray A. Straus, 197–212. Beverly Hills, Calif.: Sage.

Brush, Lisa D. 1990. "Violent acts and injurious outcomes in married couples: Methodological issues in the National Survey of Families and Households." Gender and Society 4:56–67.

Gaquin, Deirdre A. 1977/78. "Spouse abuse: Data from the National Crime Survey." Victimology 2:632–643.

Gelles, Richard J., and John W. Harrop. 1991. "The risk of abusive violence among children with nongenetic caretakers." Family Relations 40:78–83.

Johnson, Holly. 1989. "Wife assault in Canada." Paper presented at the Annual Meeting of the American Society of Criminology, November, Reno, Nevada.

Jouriles, Ernest N., and K. Daniel O'Leary. 1985. "Interspousal reliability of reports of marital violence." Journal of Consulting and Clinical Psychology 53:419–421.

Lystad, Mary H. 1975. "Violence at home: A review of literature." American Journal of Orthopsychiatry 45:328–345.

Margolin, Gayla. 1987. "The multiple forms of aggressiveness between marital partners: How do we identify them?" Journal of Marital and Family Therapy 13:77–84.

Maxfield, Michael G. 1989. "Circumstances in Supplementary Homicide Reports: Variety and validity." Criminology 27:671–695.

McLeod, Maureen. 1984. "Women against men: An examination of domestic violence based on an analysis of official data and national victimization data." Justice Quarterly 1:171–193.

McNeely, R.L., and CoraMae Richey Mann. 1990. "Domestic violence is a human issue." Journal of Interpersonal Violence 5:129–132.

McNeely, R.L., and Gloria Robinson-Simpson. 1987. "The truth about domestic violence: A falsely framed issue." Social Work 32:485–490.

Rouse, Linda P., Richard Ereen, and Marilyn Howell. 1988. "Abuse in intimate relationships. A comparison of married and dating college students." Journal of Interpersonal Violence 3:414–429.

Schwartz, Martin D. 1987. "Gender and injury in spousal assault." Sociological Focus 20:61–75.

Shupe, Anson, William A. Stacey, and Lonnie R. Hazelwood. 1987. Violent Men, Violent Couples: The Dynamics of Domestic Violence. Lexington Mass.: Lexington Books.

Steinmetz, Suzanne K. 1977/78. "The battered husband syndrome." Victimology 2:499–509.

———. 1986. "Family violence. Past, present, and future." In Handbook of Marriage and the Family, ed. Marvin B. Sussman and Suzanne K. Steinmetz, 725–765. New York: Plenum.

Steinmetz, Suzanne K., and Joseph S. Lucca. 1988. "Husband battering." In Handbook of Family Violence ed. Vincent B. Van Hasselt, R.L. Morrison, A.S. Bellack and M. Hersen, 233–246. New York: Plenum Press.

Stets, Jan E., and Murray A. Straus 1990. "Gender differences in reporting marital violence and its medical and psychological consequences." In Physical Violence in American Families, ed. Murray A. Straus and Richard J. Gelles, 151–165. New Brunswick, N.J.: Transaction Publishers.

Straus, Murray A. 1977/78. "Wife-beating: How common, and why?" Victimology 2:443–458.

———. 1990a. "Measuring intrafamily conflict and violence: The Conflict Tactics (CT) Scales." In Physical Violence in American Families, ed. Murray A. Straus and Richard J. Gelles, 29–47. New Brunswick, N.J.: Transaction Publishers.

———. 1990b. "The Conflict Tactics Scales and its critics: An evaluation and new data on validity and reliability." In Physical Violence in American Families, ed. Murray A. Straus and Richard J. Gelles, 49–73. New Brunswick, N.J.: Transaction Publishers.

Straus, Murray A., and Richard J. Gelles, eds. 1990a. Physical Violence in American Families. New Brunswick, N.J.: Transaction Publishers.

Straus, Murray A., and Richard J. Gelles. 1986. "Societal change and change in family violence from 1975 to 1985 as revealed by two national surveys." Journal of Marriage and the Family 48:465–480.

———. 1987. "The costs of family violence." Public Health Reports 102:638–641.

———. 1990b. "How violent are American families? Estimates from the National Family Violence Resurvey and other studies." In Physical Violence in American Families ed. Murray A. Straus and Richard J. Gelles, 95–112. New Brunswick, N.J.: Transaction Publishers.

Szinovacz, Maximiliane E. 1983. "Using couple data as a methodological tool: The case of marital violence." Journal of Marriage and the Family 45:633–644.

Wilson, Margo, and Martin Daly. Forthcoming. "Who kills whom in spouse-killings? On the exceptional sex ratio of spousal homicides in the United States." Criminology.

Wolfgang, Marvin E. 1958. Patterns in Criminal Homicide. Philadelphia: University of Pennsylvania Press.

Rape-Prone Versus Rape-Free Campus Cultures

PEGGY REEVES SANDAY

In *Fraternity Gang Rape* (Sanday 1990) I describe the discourse, rituals, sexual ideology, and practices that make some fraternity environments rape prone. The reaction of fraternity brothers to the book was decidedly mixed. Individuals in some chapters were motivated to rethink their initiation ritual and party behavior. In sarcastic opinion pieces written for campus newspapers others dismissed the book on the grounds that I was "out to get" fraternities. As recently as December 1995, a young man wrote a letter to the editor of *The Washington Post* criticizing me for allegedly connecting hate speech and sexual crimes on college campuses with "single-sex organizations." Having set me up as the avenging witch, this young man then blames me for perpetuating the problem. My "[a]cross-the-board generalizations," he claims "only make it more difficult for supportive men to become involved and stay active in the fight against these attacks."

It is one of the tragedies of today's ideological warfare that this writer finds such an easy excuse to exempt himself from participating in the struggle to end violence against women. To make matters worse, his rationalization for opting out is based on a trumped-up charge. In the Introduction to my book, I carefully note that I am dealing with only "a few of the many fraternities at U. and on several other campuses." I state the case very clearly:

> The sexual aggression evident in these particular cases does not mean that sexual aggression is restricted to fraternities or that all fraternities

indulge in sexual aggression. Sexist attitudes and the phallo-centric mentality associated with "pulling train" have a long history in Western society. For example, venting homoerotic desire in the gang rape of women who are treated as male property is the subject of several biblical stories. Susan Brownmiller describes instances of gang rape by men in war and in street gangs. Male bonding that rejects women and commodifies sex is evident in many other social contexts outside of universities. Thus, it would be wrong to place blame solely on fraternities. However, it is a fact also that most of the reported incidents of "pulling train" on campus have been associated with fraternities (Sanday 1990:19).

As an anthropologist interested in the particulars of sexual ideologies cross-culturally, I am very wary of generalizations of any sort. In 1975 I was very disturbed to read Susan Brownmiller's claim in the opening chapter of *Against Our Will* (1975:15) that rape is "a conscious process of intimidation by which all men keep all women in a state of fear." This statement was inconsistent with the compelling argument she presents in subsequent chapters that rape is culturally constructed and my own subsequent research on the sociocultural context of rape cross-culturally, which provided evidence of rape-free as well as rape-prone societies.

In the following, I will briefly summarize what we know about rape-prone fraternity cultures and contrast this information with what a rape-free context might look like. Since the available data are sparse my goal here is mostly programmatic, namely to encourage studies of intra- campus and cross-campus variation in the rates and correlates of sexual assault.

Rape-Prone Campus Environments

The concept of rape-free versus rape-prone comes from my study of 95 band and tribal societies in which I concluded that 47% were rape free and 18% were rape prone (Sanday 1981). For this study I defined a rape-prone society as one in which the incidence of rape is reported by observers to be high, or rape is excused as a ceremonial expression of masculinity, or rape is an act by which men are allowed to punish or threaten women. I defined a rape-free society as one in which the act of rape is either infrequent or does not occur. I used the term "rape free" not to suggest that rape was entirely absent in a given society but as a label to indicate that sexual aggression is socially disapproved and punished severely. Thus, while there may be some men in all societies who might be potential rapists, there is abundant evidence from many societies that sexual aggression is rarely expressed.

Rape in tribal societies is part of a cultural configuration that includes interpersonal violence, male dominance, and sexual separation. Peallocentrism is a dominant psycho-sexual symbol in these societies and men "use the penis to dominate their women" as Yolanda and Robert Murphy say about the Mundurucu (Sanday 1981:25). Rape-prone behavior is associated with environmental insecurity and females are turned into objects to be controlled as men struggle to retain or to gain control of their environment. Behaviors and attitudes prevail that separate the sexes and force men into a posture of proving their manhood. Sexual violence is one of the ways in which men remind themselves that they are superior. As such, rape is part of a broader struggle for control in the face of difficult circumstances. Where men are in harmony with their environment, rape is usually absent.

In *Fraternity Gang Rape* I suggest that rape-prone attitudes and behavior on American campuses are adopted by insecure young men who bond through homophobia and "getting sex." The homoeroticism of their bonding leads them to display their masculinity through heterosexist displays of sexual performance. The phallus becomes the dominant symbol of discourse. A fraternity brother described to me the way in which he felt accepted by the brothers while he was a pledge.

> We...liked to share ridiculously exaggerated sexual boasting, such as our mythical "Sixteen Kilometer Flesh-Weapon"....By including me in this perpetual, hysterical banter and sharing laughter with me, they showed their affection for me. I felt happy, confident, and loved. This really helped my feelings of loneliness and my fear of being sexually unappealing. We managed to give ourselves a satisfying substitute for sexual relations. We acted out all of the sexual tensions between us as brothers on a verbal level. Women, women everywhere, feminists, homosexuality, etc., all provided the material for the jokes (Sanday 1990: 140–41).

Getting their information about women and sex from pornography, some brothers don't see anything wrong with forcing a woman, especially if she's drunk. After the 1983 case of alleged gang rape I describe in the book one of the participants, a virgin at the time, told a news reporter:

> We have this Select TV in the house, and there's soft porn on every midnight. All the guys watch it and talk about it and stuff, and [gang banging] didn't seem that odd because it's something that you see and hear about all the time. I've heard stories from other fraternities about group sex and trains and stuff like that. It was just like, you know, so this is what I've heard about, this is what it's like.... (Sanday 1990:34).

Watching their buddies have sex is another favorite activity in rape-prone campus environments. A woman is targeted at a party and brothers are informed who hide out on the roof outside the window, or secret themselves in a closet, or look through holes in the wall. Since the goal is to supply a live pornography show for their buddies, the perpetrators in these cases may easily overlook a woman's ability to consent. They certainly don't seek her consent to being watched. It is assumed that if she came to the house to party she is prepared for anything that might happen, especially if she gets drunk. On some campuses I have been told that this practice is called "beaching" or "whaling."

Taking advantage of a drunk woman is widely accepted. As a group of brothers said in a taped conversation in which they discussed the young woman in the 1983 case:

> "She was drugged."
> "She drugged herself."
> "Yeah, she was responsible for her condition, and that just leaves her wide open...so to speak." [laughter] (Sanday 1990:119)

In a 1990 talk show on which I appeared with the victim of gang rape a young man from a local university called up and admitted that the goal of all parties at his fraternity was "To get em drunk and go for it." In 1991, I read an article entitled, "Men, Alcohol, and Manipulation," in a campus newspaper from still another university. The author reported hearing several members of a fraternity talking with the bartender about an upcoming social event as follows:

> *Brother 1:* Hey, don't forget—make the women's drinks really strong.
> *Bartender:* Yeah, I won't forget. Just like usual.
> *Brother 2:* We need to get them good and drunk.
> *Bartender:* Don't worry, we'll take care of it.
> *Brother 3:* That'll loosen up some of those inhibitions.

This is the kind of discourse I would classify as rape prone.

Getting a woman drunk to have sex in a show staged for one's buddies is tragically evident in the testimony heard in the St. Johns' sex case tried in Queens, New York, in 1991–92. This case involved six members of the St. Johns University lacrosse team who were indicted for acts ranging from unlawful imprisonment and sexual abuse to sodomy. A seventh defendant pleaded guilty and agreed to testify for immunity (see Sanday 1996 for a description of the case and the subsequent trial). From the testimony in the case and interviews with the complainant and members of the prosecution team, I reconstructed the following scenario.

A young, naive woman student, whom I call Angela (pseudonym), accepted a ride home from school from a male friend, Michael. On the way, he stopped at the house he shares with members of the St. Johns lacrosse team to get gas money and invited her inside. At first she refused to go in but upon his insistence accepted the invitation. Inside she met his roommates. Left alone in the third floor bedroom, she accepted a drink from Michael.

The drink tasted terrible. It was bitter and stung her throat. When she asked what was in it, Michael said he put a little vodka in it. When she explained that she never drank, because drinking made her sick, Michael didn't listen. Then she tried to tell him that she hadn't eaten anything since lunch, But, this did not move him. "Vodka is a before dinner drink," he explained, insisting that she drink it.

Finally, she gave into his pressure and downed the contents of the first cup in a few gulps because of the bitter taste. When she finished, Michael went over to the refrigerator and brought back a large container, which he said was orange soda with vodka. He placed the container on the floor beside her feet. When Michael poured another cup, she told him, "But Michael, I couldn't finish the first one. I don't think I will be able to finish another." Michael said again: "It's only vodka. It can't do anything to you, Angela." He also said, "You know, Angela, in college everyone does something, something wild they can look back on."

"Something wild?" Angela asked quizzically.

"Something wild," Michael said again. "Something you can look back on and talk about later in life." With the beer can that he was holding in his hand but never drank from, he hit her cup and said, "Here's to college life."

Later, Angela blamed herself for accepting the drinks from Michael. She was caught between wanting to please the host and wanting to assert her own needs. She had tried to please him by finishing the first drink. Now, she drank the second.

Then, he poured a third drink. When she balked at drinking this one, he started getting upset and annoyed. He told her it was a special drink, made just for her. He accused her of making him waste it. He started pushing the drink up to her mouth. He put his hands over the cup and pushed it to her lips. He said, "Oh Angela, don't make me waste it. It's only vodka. A little vodka can't do anything to you."

By now, Angela felt dizzy and her hands were shaking. She felt lost, unable to move. She had spent a life time doing what she was told to avoid being punished. Here was Michael upset with her because she didn't want the drink he had made for her. She thought to herself, "If he wants me to drink it, I'll drink it for him." After she drank most of the third cup, Michael went to put the container back. Her head was spinning and she began to feel really sick, like she was going to vomit. She tried to tell Michael that she was sick, but he didn't seem interested in how she was feeling.

Michael sat next to her and massaged her shoulder. She would never forget his pseudo-seductive voice. She hardly knew him, and here he was talking to her like he really cared for her. It was so obviously a put on, she was shocked by the insincerity. He kept telling her, "You need to relax. You are too tense. If you relax, you will feel better." She tried to get up but she was too weak and she fell back down (Sanday 1996:11–12).

Testimony in the case revealed that after Angela passed out from Michael's drinks, three house members stood on the landing and watched as Michael engaged in oral sodomy. After Michael left the house, these three took their turns while visitors invited over from another lacrosse team house watched. At the trial these visitors testified that they left the room when Angela woke up and started screaming. One of the lead prosecutors speculated that they left because they realized only then that she was not consenting. They did not understand that the law applies to using drugs and alcohol as it does to using force.

Cross-Campus Variation in Rape and Sexual Coercion

In his paper, Boeringer reports that 55.7% of the males in his study at a large southeastern university obtained sex by verbal harassment (i.e., "threatening to end a relationship unless the victim consents to sex, falsely professing love, or telling the victim lies to render her more sexually receptive," the variable labelled Coercion). One-quarter of the males in Boeringer's study reported using drugs or alcohol to obtain sex (Drugs/Alcohol) and 8.6% of the sample reported at least one use of force or threatened force to obtain sex (Rape).

Schwartz and Nogrady found a much lower incidence of sexual coercion and assault at their research site, a large midwestern university. These authors (private communication) reported that 18.1% of the 116 males in their sample reported some form of unwanted sex: sex by pressure (6.9%); forced sex play/attempted rape (5.2%); or completed rape (6.0%). Of the 177 women interviewed 58.6% reported some form of unwanted sex; sex by pressure (24.1%); forced sex play/attempted rape (14.4%); and completed rape (20.1%).

The effect of fraternities is quite different on the two campuses. Boeringer found that fraternity men reported a higher overall use of coercion short of physical force to obtain sex. According to Boeringer, "fraternity members engage in significantly greater levels of sexual assault through drugging or intoxicating women to render them incapable of consent or refusal" (p. 9). Fraternity members are also more likely than independents to use "nonassaultative sexual coercion," or verbal pressure. "While not criminal in nature," Boeringer points out, "these verbally coercive tactics are nonetheless disturbing in that they suggest a more adversarial view of sexuality in which one should use deceit and guile to 'win favors' from a woman" (p. 10). From his study, Boeringer concludes that "fraternity members are disproportionately involved in some forms of campus sexual aggression." Like the prosecutor in the St. John's case mentioned above, he suggests that in all likelihood the process of "working a yes out" which I describe (Sanday 1990:113) is viewed by fraternity members as a "safer path to gaining sexual access to a reluctant, non-consenting woman than use of physical force" (p. 12).

Schwartz and Nogrady find no effect of fraternity membership. The most important predictor of sexual victimization in their study involves alcohol. It is not drinking per se that they found important, but whether or not a male perceives that his friends approve of getting a woman drunk for the purpose of having sex (the APPROVE variable). Also important is whether a male reports that he has friends that actually engage in this behavior (the GETDRUNK variable). The drinking variable that is the most influential in predicting a man's reported sexual assault is the intensity of his drinking, that is the number of drinks he consumes when he goes out drinking (DRINKS). Thus, the authors conclude that "the level of the perceived male peer support system for exploiting women through alcohol, plus the amount of alcohol actually consumed by men when they drink, are the primary predictors of whether they will report themselves as sexual victimizers of women."

The differences reported by Boeringer and Schwartz and Nogrady suggest not only that fraternities vary with respect to rape-prone behaviors but also that campuses vary with respect to overall rates of sexual assault. The latter result suggests that we need to look at cross-campus variation as well as at intra-campus variation. There are several problems that need to be addressed before either intra- or cross-campus variation can be established. First, in studying intra-campus variation we must be careful in reaching conclusions about the effect of such factors as drinking intensity or fraternity membership because the dependent variable is frequently lifetime prevalence rates rather than incidence in the past year.

Regarding cross-campus variation, there is the problem of comparability of studies. Boeringer (private communication), for example, measures prevalence rates in his study, while Schwartz and Nogrady (private communication) measure incidence. Since incidence rates are always lower, we cannot conclude that the campuses studied by these authors are that much different. Additionally, as noted by Schwartz and Nogrady as well as by Koss (1993), victimization rates from one study to another may not be comparable because of different methodologies, definitions, questions, and sampling procedures.

Nevertheless, some trends can be noticed. The available evidence against variation is seen in the fact that Koss's 15% completed rape prevalence rate in the national study of 32 campuses is replicated by other studies of college students on particular campuses. Koss and Cook (1993:109) note, for example, that estimates of completed rape frequency in the 12% range have been reported for two campuses and estimates "as high or higher than 12% for unwanted intercourse have been reported in more than 10 additional studies lacking representative sampling methods." According to these authors "there are no studies that have reported substantially lower or higher rates of rape among college students."

Evidence for variation comes from Koss's analysis of the relationship of prevalence rates to the institutional parameters used to design the sample (Koss 1988:11–12). She found that rates varied by region and by governance of the institution. Rates were twice as high at private colleges and major universities (14% and 17% respectively) than they were at religiously affiliated institutions (7%).

Ethnicity of the respondent (but, interestingly not the respondent's family income) was also associated with prevalence rates. More white women (16%) reported victimization than did Hispanic (12%), Black (10%), or Asian women (7%). These figures were almost reversed for men. Rape was reported by 4% of white men, 10% of black men, 7% of Hispanic men, and 2% of Asian men. Prevalence rates reported by men also differed by region of the country. More men in the Southeast region (6%) admitted to raping compared with men in the Plains states (3%) and those in the West (2%) (Koss 1988:12).

Intriguing evidence for cross-campus variation in rape rates and related variables comes from Koss's national study of 32 campuses. Using Koss's data I looked at prevalence and incidence rates for each of 30 campuses in her study (2 campuses were excluded because of the amount of missing information.) The results show a wide discrepancy when campuses are compared. For example the campus percentages of males admitting that they have used alcohol or force to obtain sex (Koss's 1988:11 rape variable) range from 0% to 10%. Campus percentages of males who admit to perpetrating unwanted sex in the past year (as opposed to since the age of 14) range from 6% to 22%. The latter percentages are higher because I computed them using all the sexual experience questions (excluding the two authority questions). Since the latter percentages are based on a question that measures incidence ("How many times in the past school year?") the results provide a measure of an dependent variable that can be compared with drinking intensity.

The Koss survey includes two questions that might be taken as measures of drinking intensity. Both questions are asked in such a fashion as to measure drinking intensity in the past year. One asks "How often do you drink to the point of intoxication or drunkenness"; the other asks "On a typical drinking occasion, how much do you usually drink?" The campus percentages of males checking the most extreme categories of the first question (1–2 or more times a week) ranges from 1% to 24%. The campus percentages of males checking the most extreme categories of the second question (more than 5 or 6 cans of beer or other alcoholic beverages) ranges from 6% to 71%. Since all studies—Schwartz, Boeringer, Koss and Gaines (1993)—are unanimous on the effect of drinking this information, perhaps more than any other, is suggestive of variation in the rape-prone nature of campus environments.

The Concept of a Rape-Free Society

Assuming that we could identify campuses on which both males and females reported a low incidence of rape and/or unwanted sex, the next question would be whether there is a significant difference in the sexual culture on these campuses compared to the more rape-prone campuses. My cross-cultural research which demonstrated differences in the character of heterosexual interaction in rape-free as opposed to rape-prone societies would suggest that the answer to this question is yes. The outstanding feature of rape-free societies is the ceremonial importance of women and the respect accorded the contribution women make to social continuity, a respect which places men and women in relatively balanced power spheres.

Rape-free societies are characterized by sexual equality and the notion that the sexes are complementary. Although the sexes may not perform the same duties or have the same rights or privileges, each is indispensable to the activities of the other.

Since 1981 when this research was published, I spent approximately twenty-four months (extended over a period of fourteen years) doing ethnographic research among the Minangkabau, a rape-free Indonesian society. I chose the Minangkabau because of social factors that conformed with my profile of rape-free societies. The Minangkabau are the largest and most modern matrilineal society in the world today. Women play an undisputed role in Minangkabau symbol system and daily life, especially in the villages. Among the most populous of the ethnic groups of Indonesia, the Minangkabau are not an isolated tribal society in some far off corner of the world. Banks, universities, modern governmental buildings are found in two of the major cities of West Sumatra, the traditional homeland of the Minangkabau people. At the major universities, it is not uncommon to find Minangkabau Ph.D's trained in the U.S. People own cars and travel by bus throughout the province. Most children go to local schools, and many increasingly attend college.

The challenge facing me when I went to West Sumatra was first to find out whether the incidence of rape was low and if so to crack the cultural code that made it so. In the early years there was ample evidence from police reports and from interviews conducted all over the province that this was a rape-free society. Ethnographic research conducted in several villages provided confirmation. This research demonstrated that women are the mainstays of village life. The all-important family rice fields are inherited through the female line. Husbands live in their wives' houses. It is believed that this is the way it should be, because otherwise in the event of a divorce women and children would be left destitute. The main reason given for the matrilineal inheritance of property is that since women bear the infant and raise the child it is in keeping with the laws of nature to give women control of the ancestral property so that they will have the wherewithal to house and nurture the young.

Missing from the Minangkabau conception of sexuality is any show of interest in sex for the sake of sex alone. Sex is neither a commodity nor a notch in the male belt in this society. A man's sense of himself is not predicated by his sexual functioning. Although aggression is present, it is not linked to sex nor is it deemed a manly trait. The Minangkabau have yet to discover sex as a commodity or turn it into a fetish.

There is a cultural category for rape, which is defined as "forced sex" and is punishable by law. Rape is conceived as something that happens in the wild which places men who rape beyond the pale of society. In answer to my questions regarding the relative absence of rape among them compared to the United States, Minangkabau informants replied that rape was impossible in their society because custom, law, and religion forbade it and punished it severely. In the years that I worked in West Sumatra, I heard of only two cases of rape in the village where I lived. One case involved a group of males who ganged up on a young, retarded woman. In this case the leader of the group hanged himself the next day out of fear of avenging villagers. The rest of the assailants went to jail. The second case involved a local woman and a Japanese soldier during the Japanese occupation of the second world war and after. To this day people remember the case and talk about the horror of the Japanese occupation.

In the past few years, Indonesia's entrance into the global economy has been accompanied by an amazing shift in the eroticization of popular culture seen on TV. In 1995 the signs that this culture was filtering into Minangkabau villages were very evident. To the extent that commodification and eroticization breaks down the cultural supports for its matrilineal social system, the Minangkabau sexual culture will also change. Indeed, today in the provincial capital some argue that the Minangkabau are not rape free.

During my last field trip in 1995, I heard of many more reports of rape in the provincial capital. In the early 1990's, for example, there was a widely publicized acquaintance gang rape of a young woman by a group of boys. Interviewing court officers in the capital, I was told that this was the only case of its kind. Compared with similar cases in the U.S., such as the St. Johns case, the outcome was still very different. While the St. Johns defendants were either acquitted or got probation after pleading guilty, all the defendants in the Sumatran case were convicted and sent to jail. But, one may well ask whether the criminal justice system will continue to convict defendants as tolerance for sexual coercion begins to permeate popular beliefs.

Rape-Free Campus Cultures

A rape-free campus is relatively easy to imagine, but hard to find. Based on anecdotal information one candidate comes to mind. On this campus everyone, administrators, faculty, and students are on a first-name basis, which makes the atmosphere more egalitarian than most campuses. Decision making is by consensus and interpersonal interaction is guided by an ethic of respect for the individual. Those who are disrespectful of others are ostracized as campus life is motivated by a strong sense of community and the common good. No one group (such as fraternities, males, or athletes) dominates the social scene. Sexual assault is a serious offense treated with suspension or expulsion. Homophobic, racist, and sexist attitudes are virtually nonexistent. Individuals bond together in groups not to turn against others but because they are drawn together by mutual interests. Interviews suggest that the incidence of unwanted sex on this campus is low, however this must be corroborated by a campus-wide survey.

For information on a rape-free fraternity culture I turn to a description offered by a student who wrote a mini-ethnography on his fraternity for a class project. Corroboration of his description was offered by another brother in the same fraternity who read the ethnography and added additional information. In the following, the fraternity is referred to by the pseudonym QRS. With their permission, the fraternity brothers are identified by name.

Noel Morrison and Josh Marcus recognize that fraternities on their campus (called U.) "propagate sexist attitudes and provide a breeding ground for insecure acts of sexism, racism, and homophobia." According to Noel, U.'s fraternities "tend to be self-segregating entities which seek to maintain the inferior social position of women and minority students through exclusion" and social intolerance. QRS, however, consciously fights against this norm.

QRS is one of the oldest fraternities at U., going back at least 100 years. It was like all other fraternities at U. until 1977 when it was almost forced to disband due to insufficient numbers. At that time, a group of nine first year males pledged as a group knowing that their numbers would give them control of house decisions. They exercised this control by rewriting the house constitution and initiation rituals. Today the brothers are proud to say that they are "not a real fraternity." Interestingly, although both Joel and Noel treasure their lives in QRS (because of the fun, companionship of respected friends, and community the house offers), both feel that fraternities should be abolished.

Partly as a defense mechanism and partly to underscore their difference, QRS brothers stigmatize members of other fraternities as "jarheads." The word "jarhead" is used to refer to the "loud, obnoxious, sexist, racist, homophobic" members of U.'s fraternities. Most of the brothers in QRS do not participate in the campus inter-fraternity council and prefer to see themselves as "a group of friends," rather than as a fraternity, and their house as "a place to have concerts." Parties are always open to anyone and are either free to everyone or everyone pays, contrary to parties at other houses in which men pay and women are admitted for free.

At QRS heavy drinking is not a requisite for membership and is not a part of initiation. There are no drinking games and binge drinking does not occur. While some brothers drink to get drunk more than once a week, most don't. At parties there are always brothers who watch out for women or house members who have had too much to drink. Josh stressed that "it is clearly not acceptable for someone to take advantage of a drunk woman, because that's rape." There is no talk in the house

about getting a girl drunk to have sex, he says. Members are very aware that where there is heavy drinking someone can be taken advantage of. If a female passes out or is very drunk she is watched or escorted home. Both Josh and Noel remember an incident during a party in the fraternity next door, in which several members of QRS came to the aid of a young woman whose shirt was above her waist and who had passed out on their porch, left there perhaps by friends from the party who had deserted her. Their intervention may have saved her life. When they were unable to get her to talk, they took her to the emergency room of a nearby hospital only to learn that she was in a coma and her heart had stopped. Fortunately, they were in time and she responded to treatment.

Women are not seen as sex objects in the house, but as friends. Unlike other fraternities at U., there is no distinction drawn between "girlfriends" and friends and there are no "party girls." Noel says that when he was rushing he would often hear women referred to as "sluts" in other fraternities. However, at QRS this is unheard of. According to Josh, a brother who acted "inappropriately" with a woman would be severely reprimanded, perhaps even expelled from the fraternity. The brothers are not afraid of strong women. There are women's studies students who are regulars at the house, along with outspoken feminists and activists. Noel quotes one of them:

> I guess there's a few brothers who make sexist jokes, but I don't know how seriously people take them. I remember last year in the middle of midterms I was studying late at night and was feeling sick and tired, and in a span of about five minutes, four people offered their beds to me, not as a sexual thing at all, but just because they cared.

One QRS brother started the Men's Association for Change and Openness (MAChO) and is an active participant in U's student peer-counseling group for sexual health. One brother displays a "Refuse and Resist" sticker on his door, proclaiming, "Date rape: cut it out or cut it off." In a 1993 pamphlet advertising QRS as the site of the National Anarchist gathering, the brothers wrote "Although QRS is a frat, it is generally a friendly place, along with being a safe haven for women."

Most interesting about QRS is its acceptance of homosexuality, and bisexuality. Homophobia does not become the basis for males to prove their virility to one another. Because of its openness about sex and acceptance of homosexuality, QRS has earned the reputation on campus of being "the gay frat" or "faggot house." Josh comments on this reputation and what it means to him:

> QRS's attitudes about homosexuality are complex, but fundamentally tolerant and respectful. Some brothers revel in rumors that we are the "gay frat." It is rumored that a few years ago a few of the brothers were involved sexually, and one of our most involved alumni is homosexual.

Although most fraternities have had or have a few homosexual brothers, this honest acceptance of homosexuality is unusual. QRS brothers are proud of being called the "gay frat." Evidence of this is the humorous statement in the letters given prospective pledges offering bids, which ends with the phrase "we are all gay."

Conclusion

The first step in the struggle against "hidden rape," which began in the late sixties with consciousness raising groups (see Sanday 1996, Chapter 8), was to recognize the problem and speak out against it. The next step was to change outmoded rape laws and assess the causes and frequency of sexual violence against women. Mary Koss's national survey of 1985 demonstrated that one in four women will experience rape or attempted rape in her lifetime. Since the eighties many other surveys have replicated her findings. The search for causes has been the subject of numerous studies, including those represented in this volume.

The next step is to go beyond the causes and study solutions. One approach would be to find naturally occurring rape-free environments on today's college campuses. QRS is one example. No rape-free campuses have been identified by research, yet I have heard descriptions from

students that lead me to believe that such campuses exist. Identifying such campuses and seeking out environments like QRS is the next step for research. In this paper I have identified the kinds of problems such research must address. First, it is necessary to obtain incidence as well as prevalence data. Secondly, we need more subtle measures of the kinds of sociocultural correlates that have been discussed in this paper: drinking intensity; using pornography to learn about sex rather than talking with one's partner; bragging about sexual conquests; setting women up to display one's masculinity to other men; heterosexism; homophobia; and using pornography as a guide to female sexuality. Finally, we need to develop a consensus on the criteria for labelling a campus either rape free or rape prone. If at least one in five women on a given campus say they have experienced unwanted sex in the last year, I would label the campus rape prone. However, others may want to propose different criteria. Once a consensus is reached, the movement to make our campuses safe for women might include identifying rape-free and rape-prone campuses.

Acknowledgment

This article has benefited from the comments of Mary P. Koss. I am also grateful to Koss for supplying me with the data on her 1986 study of 32 campuses. Martin D. Schwartz and Scot B. Boeringer graciously supplied me with additional data from their studies and answered my many questions. Noel Morrison played an important role by giving me permission to summarize his description of his fraternity. John Marcus, a brother in the same fraternity, was also helpful in corroborating Noel's observations and supplying a few of his own.

References

Boeringer, S. (1996). "Influences of fraternity membership, athletics, and male living arrangements on sexual aggression." *Violence Against Women*, 2, no. 2, 134–137.

Brownmiller, S. (1975). *Against Our Will: Men, Women, and Rape*. New York: Simon and Schuster.

Koss, M. P. (1988). "Hidden rape: Sexual aggression and victimization in a national sample of students in higher education." In A.W. Burgess (ed.), *Rape and Sexual Assault II* (3–25). New York: Garland.

———. (1993). "Rape: Scope, impact, interventions, and public policy responses." *American Psychologist.* October 1062–1069.

Koss, M. P., & S. L. Cook. (1993). "Facing the facts: Date and acquaintance rape are significant problems for women." In R.J. Gelles and D.R. Loseke (eds.), *Current Controversies on Family Violence* (104–119). Newbury Park, CA: Sage.

Koss, M. P., & Gaines, J. A. (1993). "The prediction of sexual aggression by alcohol use, athletic participation, and fraternity affiliation." *Journal of Interpersonal Violence* 8, 94–108.

Sanday, P. R. (1981). "The socio-cultural context of rape: a cross-cultural study." *Journal of Social Issues,* 37, 5–27.

———. (1990). *Fraternity Gang Rape: Sex, Brotherhood and Privilege on Campus.* New York: New York University Press.

———. (1996). *A Woman Scorned: Acquaintance Rape on Trial.* New York: Doubleday.